Magill's Cinema Annual 1997

Magill's Cinema Annual 1997

16th Edition
A Survey of the Films of 1996

Beth A. Fhaner, Editor

Devra M. Sladics, Christopher P. Scanlon, and Terri Schell,
Contributing Editors

Christine Tomassini, Michelle Banks, and Jeff Hermann, Associate Editors

A VideoHound® Reference

GALE

DETROIT • NEW YORK • TORONTO • LONDON

Beth A. Fhaner, *Editor*
Devra M. Sladics, Christopher P. Scanlon, and Terri Schell, *Contributing Editors*
Christine Tomassini, Michelle Banks, and Jeff Hermann, *Associate Editors*
Mary Beth Trimper, *Production Director*
Shanna Heilveil, *Production Assistant*
Cynthia Baldwin, *Product Design Manager*
Michelle S. DiMercurio, *Art Director*
Sherrell Hobbs, *Macintosh Artist*
Randy Bassett, *Image Database Supervisor*
Robert Duncan and Mikal Angari, *Imaging Specialists*
Pamela A. Hayes, *Photography Coordinator*
Jeffrey Muhr, *Editorial Technical Services Specialist*

ISBN 0-7876-1155-7
ISSN 0739-2141

Printed in the United States of America

Table of Contents

Preface

Magill's Cinema Annual 1997 continues the fine film reference tradition that defines the VideoHound series of entertainment industry products published by Gale Research. The sixteenth annual volume in a series that developed from the 21-volume core set, *Magill's Survey of Cinema*, the *Annual* was formerly published by Salem Press. Gale's third volume, as with the previous Salem volumes, contains essay-reviews of significant domestic and foreign films released in the United States during the preceding year.

The *Magill's* editorial staff at Gale, comprising the VideoHound team and a host of *Magill's* contributors, continues to provide the enhancements that were added to the *Annual* when Gale acquired the line. These features include:

- More essay-length reviews of significant films released during the year
- Photographs which accompany the reviews and illustrate the obituaries and Life Achievement Award sections
- Trivia and "fun facts" about the reviewed movies, their stars, the crew and production
- Quotes and dialogue "soundbites" from reviewed movies, or from stars and crew about the film
- More complete awards and nominations listings, including the American Academy Awards, Golden Globe, New York Critics Awards, Los Angeles Film Critics Awards, and others (see the User's Guide for more information on awards coverage)
- Box office grosses, including year-end and other significant totals
- Critics' and publicity taglines featured in film reviews and advertisements

In addition to these elements, the *Magill's Cinema Annual 1997* still features:

- An interview with filmmaker Kenneth Branagh
- An essay reviewing the career and accomplishments of the recipient of the American Film Institute's Life Achievement Award presented each year to Hollywood luminaries. Director Martin Scorsese is the 1996 award recipient profiled in this volume.
- An obituaries section profiling major contributors to the film industry who died in 1996
- An annotated list of selected film books published in 1996
- Nine indexes: Director, Screenwriter, Cinematographer, Editor, Art Director, Music, Performer, Subject, and Title (now cumulative)

Compilation Methods

The *Magill's* editorial staff reviews a variety of entertainment industry publications, including trade magazines and newspapers, as well as online sources, on a daily and weekly basis to select significant films for review in *Magill's Cinema Annual. Magill's* staff and other contributing reviewers, including film scholars and university faculty, write the reviews included in the *Annual.*

Magill's Cinema Annual: *A VideoHound Reference*

The *Magill's Survey of Cinema* series, now supplemented by the *Annual*, is the recipient of the Reference Book of the Year Award in Fine Arts by the American Library Association.

Gale Research, an award-winning publisher of reference products, is proud to offer *Magill's Cinema Annual* as part of its popular VideoHound product line, which includes *VideoHound's Golden Movie Retriever, The Video Sourcebook, VideoHound's Family Video Guide, The VideoHound & All-Movie Guide StarGazer, VideoHound's Complete Guide to Cult Flicks and Trash Pics, VideoHound's Sci-Fi Experience, VideoHound's Video Premieres, VideoHound's Vampires on Video* and many more. Other Gale film-related products include the *St. James Dictionary of Films and Filmmakers* and the *Contemporary Theatre, Film, and Television* series.

Electronic Format Available

Data from the *Magill's* series is also available through Knight Ridder (formerly Dialog), which provides online access to nearly 4,300 entries from the *Magill's* core series as well as the *Annual*, plus brief reviews not contained in the print series. These brief reviews offer credits information and a capsule description.

Acknowledgments

Thank you to Judy Hartman, GGS Information Services, for her typesetting expertise, and Jeff Muhr, Gale Research, for his technical assistance. A special thank you to Jim Olenski of Thomas Video (Clawson, MI) for making preview copies of videos available to our staff. The *VideoHound* staff is thanked for its contributions to this project, especially Michelle Banks, Christine Tomassini, Jeff Hermann, Devra Sladics, and Christopher Scanlon for their hard work and goodwill, as well as Marty Connors, Terri Schell, and Julia Furtaw for their guidance and direction.

We most appreciate Bob Cosenza, the Kobal Collection, for his assistance in obtaining photographs.

Introduction

Independent films, William Shakespeare, big Hollywood blockbusters, and the reissue of some classic films combined to make 1996 an impressive year in cinema, not only in terms of boxoffice revenue, but in the uncommonly rich selection of films presented on the big screen. With boxoffice grosses at an all-time high of $5.9 billion and movie attendance in the U.S. at its highest level since 1959, our passion for filmgoing has prompted a record number of movies in production, plus a demand for quality projects that not only entertain, but challenge, move, and inspire as well. The 1996 movie year provided all of these experiences and more.

Independent films triumphed in 1996 not only because of their dominance of most critics' 10-best lists, but because of their appeal to mainstream moviegoers. Films financed outside the studio system scored a record 54 out of a possible 65 Academy Award nominations. Anthony Minghella's stunningly beautiful film, *The English Patient*, lead the way with 12 Academy Award nominations. Based on the Michael Ondaatje novel, this romantic epic garnered nine Oscars, including wins for Best Picture, Best Direction, and Best Supporting Actress (Juliette Binoche). *The English Patient* was not the only indie film to bring home the golden statuette. Both the Best Actor and Best Actress Oscars went to performers in independent films—Geoffrey Rush for his brilliant depiction of a troubled pianist in *Shine* and Frances McDormand for her pregnant police chief Marge in the Coen brothers' dark comedy *Fargo*. Billy Bob Thornton, the sentimental dark horse who epitomized the spirit of independent filmmaking as director/writer/actor/producer of the low-budget surprise *Sling Blade*, copped Best Adapted Screenplay honors.

Other independents collecting critics' awards throughout the year included Mike Leigh's *Secret & Lies*, a compassionate tale of rapprochement between an interracial mother and daughter, and Lars von Trier's *Breaking the Waves*, a transfixing saga of love, madness, and spiritual anguish. Winning audience approval among the small films with non-commercial subjects were Stanley Tucci's *Big Night*, an arthouse favorite about two immigrant brothers struggling to make good with their Italian restaurant; John Sayles' *Lone Star*, a western murder mystery involving Texas lawmen past and present; and the amoral Scottish comedy *Trainspotting*, which dealt with drug addiction and inspired headlines about heroin chic.

Some other noteworthy gems stood out amongst the indie crowd this past year—namely the hip and hilarious *Swingers*, a comedy about Hollywood wannabes set against the backdrop of L.A.'s lounge scene, and Todd Solondz's brutally funny tale of junior high geekdom, *Welcome to the Dollhouse*. Even Woody Allen's latest film, the magical old-fashioned musical *Everyone Says I Love You*, was a pure cinematic delight. Indeed, low-budget, personal, non-mainstream fare made 1996 a memorable year at the movies.

Back in Hollywood, the huge summer blockbuster *Independence Day* smashed boxoffice records by bringing in a record $100 million in its first week alone. Other "event" movies coming out of Hollywood included the special effects extravaganza *Twister*, Tom Cruise as special agent Ethan Hunt in *Mission: Impossible*, and the Sean Connery/Nicolas Cage thriller *The Rock*. Top grossers such as *The Birdcage*, *Phenomenon*, *The Nutty Professor*, and *A Time to Kill* also scored in the $100 million-plus range.

The smart romantic comedy/drama *Jerry Maguire* redeemed the Hollywood studios in 1996 as the only non-indie Academy Award nominee for Best Picture. In this touching and witty film, Tom Cruise stars as Jerry Maguire, a sports agent who develops a conscience and promptly loses his job. Cuba Gooding, Jr., brought home Oscar gold as the only remaining ("Show me the money!") football-player client, and newcomer Renee Zellweger generated a buzz as Cruise's sole employee and love interest. In crafting this heartwarming comedy, writer-director Cameron Crowe proved to audiences that Hollywood could still make endearing and satisfying films.

Just as 1995 was the year of Jane Austen, 1996 brought a mini renaissance for film adaptations of the work of William Shakespeare. Four productions of the Bard's plays appeared on-screen in 1996, including new Hollywood versions of *Romeo and Juliet*, *Twelfth Night*, and *Hamlet*, as well as the docu-drama *Looking for Richard*.

In *William Shakespeare's Romeo and Juliet*, the most radically updated version of Shakespeare's work, director Baz Luhrmann MTV-ized the famous story, setting it in fictional Verona Beach in the midst of warring Capulet/Montague gangs. With young actors Leonardo DiCaprio and Claire Danes playing the star-crossed lovers, Luhrmann's film is possibly the hippest version of Shakespeare ever to appear on celluloid. On the other end of the spectrum, actor/director Kenneth Branagh took on *Hamlet*, one of the Bard's best-known tragedies. Branagh, whose 1989 film version of *Henry V* introduced contemporary audiences to Shakespeare, remains faithful to the original play in his lavish four-hour opus, the screen's first complete *Hamlet*. Director Trevor Nunn also served up Shakespeare with his version of *Twelfth Night*, the comedy of mistaken identities, and Academy Award-winning actor Al Pacino was a triple threat as director, producer and star of the superb docu-drama *Looking for Richard*, which chronicled an acting troupe making a movie of *Richard the III*. The Bard's plays proved once again to be timeless, resulting in a banner year for Shakespeare on the big screen.

In another significant movie trend, dozens of actors switched hats in 1996 in order to make their directorial debuts. Consider these actors whose novice efforts appeared in 1996: Tom Hanks with *That Thing You Do!*, Steve Buscemi with *Trees Lounge*, Stanley Tucci and Campbell Scott with *Big Night*, Matthew Broderick with *Infinity*, and Nick Cassavetes with *Unhook the Stars*, among others. Many actors are turning to directing not only for the love of their art, but to gain greater creative control, with focus not on big vanity-driven productions, but rather small, low-budget, personal films. Although boxoffice success for this new wave of first-time directors has been hard to come by (many efforts were well received critically but not financially), this trend seems very likely to continue. In fact, audiences can look forward to the directorial debuts of Kevin Spacey, Vondie Curtis-Hall, Griffin Dunne, Gary Oldman, Timothy Hutton, Johnny Depp, and Alan Rickman in 1997.

The restoration and rerelease of some classic films, notably Hitchcock's 1958 masterpiece *Vertigo* and George Stevens' great American epic *Giant*, proved to be another promising highlight of 1996. The reissue of such classics allows new generations of filmgoers to not only experience these incredible films on the big screen, most likely for the first time, but to also discover the rich heritage of American film. Director/producer Martin Scorsese, the recipient of the American Film Institute's twenty-fifth annual Life Achievement Award, has been instrumental in the fight to preserve and restore films of the past. This cause is extremely important, as film survival rates demonstrate: of the more than 21,000 feature films made in the U.S. before 1951, only half exist today. Thousands of films have been lost, destroyed or deteriorated beyond repair. In fact, in 1996 the AFI discovered and preserved the oldest surviving American feature film: the 1912 silent film version of Shakespeare's *Richard III*. As this effort demonstrates, the preservation and restoration of these early films is essential in order to honor the classics and preserve the cinematic past.

As far as new talent making the scene in 1996, the arrival of actor Matthew McConaughey sent the media hype into overdrive. Presented as the heir apparent to Paul Newman, the hot new star succeeded with critics in the $100-million hit *A Time to Kill*, then immediately landed a Warner Bros. production deal. McConaughey could also be seen this past year in *Lone Star* and *Larger Than Life*. Another breakout star of the summer was Gwyneth Paltrow, who emerged as a leading lady with her winning turn in Jane Austen's *Emma*. And Will Smith proved that he could successfully move from TV to film with his smash hit *Independence Day*. Other new faces that arrived in 1996: Courtney Love, Edward Norton, Emily Watson, and Liv Tyler, each of which brought a compelling freshness and energy to the film scene.

Sadly, the film industry also lost some beloved stars in 1996: the exotic Dorothy Lamour, Bob Hope and Bing Crosby's sarong-clad sidekick in the *Road* movies; popular actor and comedian George Burns; Claudette Colbert, the leading lady of screwball comedy; African American actor Howard Rollins; acclaimed Polish director Krzysztof Kieslowski; Gene Kelly, the actor, dancer, choreographer, and director famous for his athletic-style dancing; Academy Award-winning actress Greer Garson; prominent French film director Rene Clement; and Italian actor and international star Marcello Mastroianni. See the Obituaries section in the back of this book for profiles of these and other major contributors to the film industry who died in 1996.

As the silver screen fades out upon another year of moviemaking, the *Magill's* staff looks forward to preparing the 1998 *Annual*, for which additional changes and enhancements are planned. We invite your comments. Please direct all questions and suggestions to:

Beth Fhaner
Editor, *Magill's Cinema Annual*
Gale Research
835 Penobscot Bldg.
Detroit, MI 48226-4094
Phone: (313)961-2242
Toll-free: 800-347-GALE
Fax: (313)961-6812

Contributing Reviewers

Michael Adams
Graduate School, City University of New York
Vivek Adarkar
Long Island University
Michael Betzold
Freelance Reviewer
David L. Boxerbaum
Freelance Reviewer
Beverley Bare Buehrer
Freelance Reviewer
Reni Celeste
University of Rochester
Robert F. Chicatelli
Freelance Reviewer
J.M. Clark
99Xpress Magazine (Atlanta) Film Editor
Paul B. Cohen
Freelance Reviewer
Bill Delaney
Freelance Reviewer
Roberta F. Green
Virginia Polytechnic Institute and State University
Diane Hatch-Avis
Freelance Reviewer
Debbi Hoffman
Freelance Reviewer
Glenn Hopp
Howard Payne University
Eleah Horwitz
Freelance Reviewer
David King
Freelance Reviewer
Jim Kline
Freelance Reviewer
Patricia Kowal
Freelance Reviewer/Script Consultant
Leon Lewis
Appalachian State University
Nancy Matson
Freelance Reviewer
Karl Michalak
Freelance Reviewer
Robert Mitchell
University of Arizona
Paul Mittelbach
KNX-AM (Los Angeles) Entertainment Reporter
Lisa Paddock
Freelance Reviewer
Carl Rollyson
Baruch College, City University of New York
Kirby Tepper
Freelance Reviewer
Terry Theodore
University of North Carolina at Wilmington
Hilary Weber
Freelance Reviewer
James M. Welsh
Salisbury State University

User's Guide

Alphabetization

Film titles and reviews are arranged on a word-by-word basis, including articles and prepositions. English leading articles (A, An, The) are ignored, as are foreign leading articles (El, Il, La, Las, Le, Les, Los). Other considerations:

- Acronyms appear alphabetically as if regular words.
- Common abbreviations in titles file as if they are spelled out, so *Mr. Wrong* will be found as if it was spelled "*Mister Wrong*."
- Proper names in titles are alphabetized beginning with the individual's first name, for instance, *Jerry Maguire* will be found under "J."
- Titles with numbers, for instance, *2 Days in the Valley*, are alphabetized as if the number was spelled out, in this case, "Two." When numeric titles gather in close proximity to each other, the titles will be arranged in a low-to-high numeric sequence.

Special Sections

List of Awards. An annual list of awards bestowed upon the year's films by ten international associations: Academy of Motion Picture Arts and Sciences, Directors Guild of America Award, Golden Globe Awards, Golden Palm Awards (Cannes International Film Festival), Los Angeles Film Critics Awards, National Board of Review Awards, National Society of Film Critics Awards, New York Film Critics Awards, and the Writer's Guild Awards.

Life Achievement Award. An essay reviewing the career and accomplishments of the recipient of the American Film Institute's Life Achievement Award presented each year to Hollywood luminaries. Director Martin Scorsese is the 1996 award recipient profiled in this volume.

Obituaries. Profiles major contributors to the film industry who died in 1996.

Selected Film Books of 1996. An annotated list of selected film books published in 1996.

Indexes

Film titles and artists are arranged into nine indexes, allowing the reader to effectively approach a film from any one of several directions, including not only its credits but its subject matter.

Director, Screenwriter, Cinematographer, Editor, Music, Art Director and *Performer Indexes* are arranged according to artists appearing in this volume, followed by a list of the films on which they worked.

Subject Index. Films may be categorized under several of the subject terms arranged alphabetically in this section.

Title Index. A cumulative alphabetical list of nearly 4,870 films covered in the sixteen volumes of the *Magill's Cinema Annual,* including over 300 films covered in this volume. Films reviewed in past volumes are cited with the year in which the film was originally released; films reviewed in this volume are cited with the film title in bold with a bolded Arabic numeral indicating the page number on which the review begins. Original and alternate titles are cross-referenced to the American release title in the Title Index. Titles of retrospective films are followed by the year, in brackets, of their original release.

Sample Review

Each *Magill's* review contains up to sixteen items of information. A fictionalized composite sample review containing all the elements of information that may be included in a full-length review follows the outline below. The circled number preceding each element in the sample review on page XV designates an item of information that is explained in the outline on the next page.

(1) **Title:** Film title as it was released in the United States.

(2) **Foreign or alternate title(s):** The film's original title or titles as released outside the United States, or alternate film title or titles. Foreign and alternate titles also appear in the Title Index to facilitate user access.

(3) **Taglines:** Up to ten publicity or critical taglines for the film from advertisements or reviews.

(4) **Box office information:** Year-end or other box office domestic revenues for the film.

(5) **Film review or abstract:** A one-paragraph abstract or 750-1500-word signed review of the film, including brief plot summary, and for full-length reviews, an analytic overview of the film and its critical reception.

(6) **Principal characters:** Up to 25 listings of the film's principal characters and the names of the actors who play them in the film. The names of actors who play themselves are cited twice (as character and actor).

(7) **Country of origin:** The film's country or countries of origin if other than the United States.

(8) **Release date:** The year of the film's first general release.

(9) **Production information:** This section typically includes the name(s) of the film's producer(s), production company, and distributor, director(s), screenwriter(s), author(s) or creator(s) and the novel, play, short story, television show, motion picture, or other work, or character(s), that the film was based upon; cinematographer(s) (if the film is animated, this will be replaced with Animation or Animation Direction); editor(s); art director(s), production designer(s), set decorator(s) or set designer(s); music composer(s); and other credits such as visual effects, sound, casting, costume design, and song(s) and songwriter(s).

(10) **MPAA rating:** The film's rating by the Motion Picture Association of America. If there is no rating given, the line will read, "no listing."

(11) **Running time:** The film's running time in minutes.

(12) **Reviewer byline:** The name of the reviewer who wrote the full-length review. A complete list of this volume's contributors appears in the "Contributing Reviewers" section which follows the Introduction.

(13) **Reviews:** A list of up to 25 brief citations of major newspaper and journal reviews of the film, including publication title, date of review, and page number.

(14) **Awards information:** Awards won by the film, followed by category and name of winning cast or crew member. Listings of the film's nominations follow the wins on a separate line for each award. Awards are arranged alphabetically. Information is listed for films which won or were nominated for the following awards: American Academy Awards, Australian Film Institute, British Academy of Film and Television Arts, Canadian Genie, Cannes Film Festival, Directors Guild of America, French Cesar, Golden Globe, Independent Spirit, Los Angeles Film Critics Association Awards, Montreal Film Festival, MTV Movie Awards, National Board of Review Awards, National Society of Film Critics Awards, New York Critics Awards, Sundance Film Festival, Toronto-City Awards, Writers Guild of America, and others.

(15) **Film quotes:** Memorable dialogue directly from the film, attributed to the character who spoke it, or comment from cast or crew members or reviewers about the film.

(16) **Film trivia:** Interesting tidbits about the film, its cast, or production crew.

2

1 The Gump Diaries (Los Diarios del Gump)

3 "Love means never having to say you're stupid."
—Movie tagline

"This was a really good movie. I liked it." —Joe Critic, *Daily News*

4 

Box Office Gross: $10 million (December 15, 1994)

5 In writer/director Robert Zemeckis' *Back to the Future* trilogy (1985, 1989, 1990), Marty McFly (Michael J. Fox) and his scientist sidekick Doc Brown (Christopher Lloyd) journey backward and forward in time, attempting to smooth over some rough spots in their personal histories in order to remain true to their individual destinies. Throughout their time-travel adventures, Doc Brown insists that neither he nor Marty influence any major historical events, believing that to do so would result in catastrophic changes in humankind's ultimate destiny. By the end of the trilogy, however, Doc Brown has revised his thinking and tells Marty that, "Your future hasn't been written yet. No one's has. Your future is whatever you make it. So make it a good one."

In *Forrest Gump*, Zemeckis once again explores the theme of personal destiny and how an individual's life affects and is affected by his historical time period. This time, however, Zemeckis and screenwriter Eric Roth chronicle the life of a character who does nothing but meddle in the historical events of his time without even trying to do so. By the film's conclusion, however, it has become apparent that Zemeckis' main concern is something more than merely having fun with four decades of American history. In the process of re-creating significant moments in time, he has captured on celluloid something eternal and timeless—the soul of humanity personified by a nondescript simpleton from the deep South.

15 "The state of existence may be likened unto a receptacle containing cocoa-based confections, in that one may never predict that which one may receive." —Forrest Gump, from *The Gump Diaries*

The film begins following the flight of a seemingly insignificant feather as it floats down from the sky and brushes against various objects and people before finally coming to rest at the feet of Forrest Gump (Tom Hanks). Forrest, who is sitting on a bus-stop bench, reaches down and picks up the feather, smooths it out, then opens his traveling case and carefully places the feather between the pages of his favorite book, *Curious George*.

In this simple but hauntingly beautiful opening scene, the filmmakers illustrate the film's principal concern: Is life a series of random events over which a person has no control, or is there an underlying order to things that leads to the fulfillment of an individual's destiny? The rest of the film is a humorous and moving attempt to prove that, underlying the random, chaotic events that make up a person's life, there exists a benign and simple order.

Forrest sits on the bench throughout most of the film, talking about various events of his life to others who happen to sit down next to him. It does not take long, however, for the audience to realize that Forrest's seemingly random chatter to a parade of strangers has a perfect chronological order to it. He tells his first story after looking down at the feet of his first bench partner and observing, "Mama always said that you can tell a lot about a person by the shoes they wear." Then, in a voice-over narration, Forrest begins the story of his life, first by telling about the first pair of shoes he can remember wearing.

16 Hanks was the first actor since Spencer Tracy to win back-to-back Oscars for Best Actor. Hanks received the award in 1993 for his performance in *Philadelphia*. Tracy won Oscars in 1937 for *Captains Courageous* and in 1938 for *Boys Town*.

The action shifts to the mid-1950's with Forrest as a young boy (Michael Humphreys) being fitted with leg braces to correct a curvature in his spine. Despite this traumatic handicap, Forrest remains unaffected, thanks to his mother (Sally Field) who reminds him on more than one occasion that he is no different from anyone else. Although this and most of Mrs. Gump's other words of advice are in the form of hackneyed cliches, Forrest whose intelligence quotient is below normal, sincerely believes every one of them, namely because he instinctively knows they are sincere expressions of his mother's love and fierce devotion.

The action shifts to the mid-1950's with Forrest as a young boy (Michael Humphreys) being fitted with leg braces to correct a curvature in his spine. The action shifts to the mid-1950's to a in his spine. When the first U.S. Ping-Pong team to This of movie magic has not accomplished by special effects or computer-altered images, by something much more impressive and harder to achieve.

12 —*John Byline*

AWARDS AND NOMINATIONS

14 **Academy Awards 1994:** Best Film, Best Actor (Hanks), Best Special Effects, Best Cinematography
Nominations: Best Actress (Fields), Best Screenplay, Best Director (Zameckis)
Golden Globe Awards 1994: Best Film,
Nominations: Best Actor (Hanks), Best Supporting Actress (Wright), Best Music, Best Special Effects

CREDITS

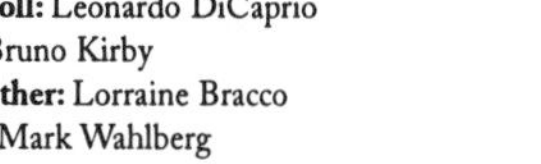

6 **Jim Carroll:** Leonardo DiCaprio
Swifty: Bruno Kirby
Jim's Mother: Lorraine Bracco
Mickey: Mark Wahlberg

7 **Origin:** United Kingdom
8 **Released:** 1993
Production: Liz Heller, John Bard Manulis for New Line
9 Cinema; released by Island Pictures
Direction: Scott Kalvert
Author: Bryan Goluboff; based on the novel by Jim Carroll
Cinematographer: David Phillips
Editing: Dana Congdon
Production design: Christopher Nowak
Set decoration: Harriet Zucker
Sound: William Sarokin
Costume design: David C. Robinson
Music: Graeme Revell
10 **MPAA rating:** R
11 **Running time:** 102 minutes

REVIEWS

13 Entertainment Weekly. July 15, 1994, p. 42.
The Hollywood Reporter. June 29, 1994, p. 7.
Los Angeles Times. July 6, 1994, p. F1.

Interview with Kenneth Branagh

Irish-born Kenneth Branagh made his cinematic debut in 1987 with the Masterpiece Theater production *Fortunes of War*. It was the first of several projects where he would share the spotlight with actress Emma Thompson, whom he eventually married and has since divorced. In 1989, still relatively unknown at the time, Branagh wrote, directed and played the title role in Shakespeare's *Henry V*, for which he received acting and directing Oscar nominations. Not bad notice for his directorial debut. With his stellar performance and subsequent accolades, Branagh was labelled the new Laurence Olivier. High praise indeed, but a moniker that carries with it a great deal of expectations to deliver.

Since *Henry V*, Branagh has intertwined other Shakespearean works with mainstream films and is now widely regarded as the premier authority on all things Shakespearean, at least in the world of film. 1996 saw the release of *Hamlet*, his most ambitious project to date. Clocking in just two minutes shy of four hours, it contains each and every word of Shakespeare's longest play. Luckily for Branagh, and anyone who sees the film, there isn't one iota of unnecessary footage or superfluous filler. He has crafted the definitive *Hamlet*. *Magill's* contributor J.M. Clark spoke with him on his promotional tour in Atlanta in late December.

Do you have any interest in making a biographical film about Shakespeare?

There are several scripts out there right now and I have been approached about it. Problem is, there's so little known about him, it would be difficult to get it right. There was a British TV version a while back starring Tim Curry that was quite good. But there are also several conspirators who say that there never was a Shakespeare at all; that he was merely an amalgamation of a group of starving actors, a theory I don't subscribe to. It's a close call. It would really have to be a good script.

Is there ever any temptation to modernize the dialogue, make it "audience friendly" or easier to understand?

Not on my part. I think Shakespeare works on several different levels. The language is so artistic. It has a rhythm and an almost lyrical sound. The beauty of the words is what makes it so special. Changing it all would destroy it. I liken it to colorizing black and white films. It is how it is and it's very good as it is, so bloody leave it alone. As far as understanding it is concerned, keep in mind, no one understands all of it; I don't even understand all of it. I think Al [Pacino] did everyone a great service by saying what he did in his movie (*Looking for Richard* in which Branagh appeared). You don't have to get all of it to get the point.

What other Shakespearean works do you want to adapt?

It's hard to say. I never like to think too far ahead. I have to look at a play that I like and imagine a central or anchor scene to base a script on. I knew a while ago that *Hamlet* would be the next one, because I'm getting too old to play the part. If I had to pick one right now, I'd have to say *MacBeth*.

Are there any plays you would absolutely avoid?

That's easy. *Measure for Measure*.

For what reason?

I don't understand a bloody word of it. [laughs]

Do you think that the Olivier and Zeffirelli versions (of *Hamlet*) were lacking in any way?

Absolutely not. They're both fantastic pictures. Olivier painted a dark, Gothic version; closer to the original text and it was good enough to win several Oscars. I think a lot of the apprehension people have about Shakespeare stems from the perception people have about everything being gloomy and morose. There's nothing at all wrong with gloomy, I like gloomy; but sometimes you need to be upbeat. Franco had a great idea by setting his version in Scotland; I've heard that's where Mel [Gibson] started mapping out his initial plans for *Braveheart*. These versions are more faithful to the original spirit than mine is, but neither of them include all of the text. Ian's [McKellen] *Richard III* did quite well last year because he set it in a time frame (the 1930s) that people were more familiar with.

Is that why you set your *Hamlet* in the 19th century?

Partly. My paramount concern was to make it brighter. More opulent. Something that was much more pleasant to look at. The palaces, the well-appointed decor, the regal costuming and so forth. It also allowed us to use some props that weren't around in the 17th century—locomotives, electricity, that sort of thing. Hamlet himself is basically a happy, well-adjusted guy. He is distressed by the death of his father and misses him dearly. The fact that his mother doesn't wait very long before she marries his uncle doesn't even bother him as much as you might think. That is, of course, until he finds out who's behind the crime and the cover-up. Even then, he battles his growing depression with a lot of humor. The story is a tragedy, you never want to lose sight of that. I wanted to give our production a more vivid, aesthetic appearance.

Did Castle Rock (the studio that produced the film) have any problems with the length?

No. They knew going in what to do and they backed me 100%. Doing the play in its entirety was part of the deal. I'll give you an example of just how committed they really were to the project. We had originally planned to show the full version in only the top ten markets because of some complaints from a few of the national theater chains. I'm glad to say that the full length version will be the only one shown (theatrically) in this country. The edited (two hours, 25 minutes) version will be distributed in some foreign markets; because some of them just flat refuse to show the long one. Most of the commercial airlines will also get the edited version.

What did you think of Baz Luhrmann's *Romeo and Juliet*?

I absolutely loved it! After seeing *Strictly Ballroom*, I knew he'd come up with something special. He took a great many chances with that project. Again, he didn't change the language at all and pointed out just how universal these stories are. The angst and the anger, the confusion about love and adolescence are still the same now as they were back then. Swords in the 17th century, automatic pistols in the 20th! Really great movie. Made pretty good money too, as I recall.

A few of the detractors of your *Hamlet* found fault with some of the casting decisions you made regarding Robin Williams, Billy Crystal and Jack Lemmon. The same thing happened a few years back with *Much Ado About Nothing* and your casting of Keanu Reeves. How do you respond?

Shakespeare's plays have been performed the world over for hundreds of years in dozens of languages with interpretations that run the gamut. Yet, there is still a perception that only classically trained British stage actors can perform the material. As the director, I'm looking for people who can bring something interesting to the role. Someone recently suggested that I include Jack and Billy and Robin for their marquee value, which is understandable. But if I can entice someone into the theater who wants to see a performer whose work they're familiar with, that's fine by me. The folks who have accused me of selling out don't hear the complaints of the purists. They think I'm taking too much of a chance by allowing "those Americans" to appear in my movie. It's a no-win situation and there's not a whole lot I can do about it. I put a great deal of thought and consideration into these choices and I firmly stick by my decisions.

What does your next project *Shakespeare's Sister* deal with?

Well, first off, it has nothing to do with Shakespeare. William Hurt and Madeleine Stowe play a couple who are having a hard time conceiving a child. They go about trying to find surrogate parents and open up several cans of worms in the process. I play a priest whom they confide in and I eventually get sucked into the embroglio. It all gets very entangled as good mysteries often do, I think people will like it a great deal.

To what do you attribute the recent trend of actors directing?

I don't know. I think it has a lot to do with the fact that actors have a higher profile than most directors, so they make a bigger splash. It was different for me. I'd acted in three very small films before I made *Henry V*. People didn't really know who I was, so I wasn't labelled as a full time actor. I remember a conversation I had a few years back with Bill Murray. He'd just finished making *Quick Change*, which he also directed. He said he'd found it a draining and very unsatisfying experience. He said putting in 300% more effort to only see 3% more return just wasn't worth it. Personally, I'd advise any actor who's toying with the idea of directing to think about it long and hard before they decide to get behind the camera. It's not something you want to take lightly.

Is it hard to give direction to actors who also direct?

No, if anything, it's easier. They understand the requirements of the job better than anyone.

With *Hamlet*, you're wearing all the hats: lead actor, director, producer, writer. Does taking on all those chores at once dilute the effort as a whole?

Not at all. It actually makes you more leery about putting too much effort into one area or another. A very effective check and balance system.

Why the big Shakespeare resurgence, particularly in 1996?

There seems to be something cyclical about Shakespeare; the productions enjoy a great amount of prosperity and then seem to fade away for awhile. I'm not sure if there's a lack of other good material around or whether the audience is becoming more discerning. Finance is definitely a consideration; they wouldn't make the films if there wasn't an audience. So they must be making money. That's a very good sign.

One last question about the past and one for the future: you made what is widely regarded as the most authentic, faithful version of *Frankenstein* to date. Were you surprised that it received largely negative reviews?

No, not really. We knew going in that we were going to make a film that went against the grain of the audience's perceived notions of the monster. We adhered to the text, as it was written. We didn't present the monster as everyone had seen it before; the square forehead, bolts in the neck, indecipherable speech. I'm very proud of the work we did and I'm especially happy that the film has garnered such a very strong cult following.

It was rumored that you were slated to play the young Obi-Wan Kenobi in the upcoming *Star Wars* prequels. Any truth to that?

I'll tell you how the rumor started. Long after the film came out, one of the *Star Wars* fanzines, I think it was in Australia, put out a set of trading cards that came up with a "what-if" scenario regarding the prequels. There were suggestions as to who might play the characters and my name was the one most mentioned as the young Obi-Wan, which is an incredible compliment. I've long admired Sir Alec [Guinness]. The [George] Lucas camp was questioned about it and immediately denied the projects in general or that I was being considered. I made sure I let them know that I didn't start the rumor. We had some conversations and discussed the possibility, but nothing has ever come of it.

Would you take the role if it was offered to you?

Absolutely. I quite enjoy playing fictional legends, whether they be in the faraway past or the distant future.

Magill's Cinema Annual
1997

The Adventures of Pinocchio

A new angle on the classic tale . . . and that's no lie!—Movie tagline

"A magical spin on a family classic."—Jim Wilson, *Fox-TV*

"Pure magic!"—Jim Ferguson, *The Prevue Channel*

"Wonder-filled film."—Patrick Stoner, *PBS Flicks*

"The best family film of the summer!"—Jeffrey Lyons, *Sneak Previews*

Box Office: $15,094,530

The Adventures of Pinocchio is a live-action film that also uses animatronics and computer graphics to tell the familiar story of the puppet who becomes a boy. The multi-national film unit that made the motion picture under the direction of Steve Barron based their version on the original source material, the 1881 serial of thirty-five installments by Carlo Collodi called *The Tale of a Puppet.*

In its time the Collodi story differed from other works for children in its realism. Collodi peopled his tale with the commoners and have-nots rather than kings and queens. Though this screen version of Collodi's classic is more realistic than the familiar Disney cartoon, its everydayness does not lessen the life-affirming moral of the hard-won but worthwhile qualities of growing up.

"Miracles are made in the heart."—Pepe the Cricket

As a young man, the woodcarver Geppetto (Martin Landau) cut his initials and those of his beloved Leona (Genevieve Bujold) in the trunk of a tree that was struck that same night by lightning. Years later Geppetto, now a lonely bachelor with only his puppets to keep him company, brings the wood of this same tree back to his workshop and carves from it a puppet he names Pinocchio (voice of Jonathan Taylor Thomas). Pinocchio comes to life and shocks Geppetto into thinking he has lost his mind to see a puppet walking about on his own.

Like most boys, Pinocchio has a talent for finding trouble. He strays from home by following a bird across the rooftop. At school, he learns the hard way that when he lies, his nose lengthens embarrassingly. Hungering for sweets, he creates havoc in a pastry shop. When the baker and his wife sue for damages, Geppetto must finally give in to Lorenzini (Udo Kier), the sinister owner of a puppet theater who has been trying to buy Pinocchio. In order to stay out of debtors' prison, Geppetto reluctantly sells the puppet he has come to think of as his son.

Pinocchio is befriended by Pepe (voice of David Doyle), a sprightly cricket who offers the puppet wise counsel. Pinocchio's first lesson is to learn the difference between applause and love. At Lorenzini's ornate and impressive puppet theater, Pinocchio's no-strings mobility makes him the big star, and

Geppetto (Martin Landau) holds his wooden marionette, which comes to life in the form of Jonathan Taylor Thomas in the film version of Carlo Collodi's classic, *The Adventures of Pinocchio.*

he needs Pepe to remind him that Geppetto loves him for himself while Lorenzini is only using him to bring in customers. Pinocchio escapes from Lorenzini in the confusion from a fire Lorenzini himself started to add more spectacle to his show. Pinocchio next "returns to his roots" in the forest while Geppetto and Leona search for him in vain.

After two of Lorenzini's oafish underlings, Felinet (Bebe Neuwirth) and Volpe (Rob Schneider), con Pinocchio out of the five gold coins he had earned at the theater, the puppet learns from Pepe that "miracles do not grow on trees; miracles are made in the heart." Another wrong judgment leads Pinocchio to suppose that he should join a passing coach full of rowdy boys. Once at Terra Magica, a retreat Lorenzini had built for the boys, Pinocchio sees that the fun has turned to chaos. Lorenzini knows he can corrupt the children by removing all rules and restraints and by bringing out the anarchy within them. He also intends to use the magical waters at Terra Magica to turn the boys into donkeys, the animals that at present reflect the boys' unruly, headstrong nature. As the boys ride through a waterfall, Pinocchio notices that they are growing donkey ears. After he saves the boys from Lorenzini, Pinocchio watches Lorenzini splash into the magical waters and transform into a sea monster.

Returning home, Pinocchio hears from Leona that Geppetto went to sea looking for him after finding his cap on the shore. Pinocchio immediately senses the danger for Geppetto and begins to learn that love carries responsibilities. Now Pinocchio himself rows out to sea to find the man he thinks of as his father. The sea monster Lorenzini, looming beneath his tiny boat, swallows him. Inside the monster Pinocchio finds both Pepe and Geppetto. The only escape is for Pinocchio to lie so that his nose grows longer and forces open the sea monster's throat so that Geppetto can climb out. Pinocchio tells the four worst lies he can think of: "I hate you, Papa. I never, ever missed you. I don't want to be your son. I wish I'd never found you." With each lie his nose grows and opens more of the monster's mouth. Onshore Pinocchio and Geppetto weep over their safe reunion. Their tears fall on Pinocchio's heart, carved from the same wood struck years ago by lightning, and the water of their tears brings about the final transformation by turning the puppet into what he has grown to be: the real boy that Geppetto has always wanted.

As it tells its familiar story, the film offers a number of pleasing visual touches. The outdoor locations in Cesky Krumlov, part of the Czech Republic, suggest convincingly the cramped byways of a nineteenth-century Italian village. The indoor sets are all beautifully crafted and atmospheric. Geppetto's workshop evokes the creative solitude of the woodcarver. The puppet theater of Lorenzini and the Terra Magica retreat also add to the mood of the film. The first is gaudily baroque

CREDITS

Geppetto: Martin Landau
Pinocchio: Jonathan Taylor Thomas (voice)
Leona: Genevieve Bujold
Lorenzini: Udo Kier
Felinet: Bebe Neuwirth
Volpe: Rob Schneider

Origin: USA
Released: 1996
Production: Raju Patel and Jeffrey Sneller for a Kushner-Locke, Pangaea Holdings and Twin Continental Films production; released by New Line Cinema
Direction: Steve Barron
Screenplay: Sherry Mills, Steve Barron, Tom Benedek and Barry Berman; based on the novel by Carlo Collodi
Cinematography: Juan Ruiz Anchia
Editing: Sean Barton
Music: Rachel Portman
Production design: Allan Cameron
Costume design: Maurizio Millenotti
Pinocchio and animatronic creatures: Jim Henson's Creature Shop
Visual effects supervision: Angus Bicketron
Sound: Jean-Philippe Le Roux
Casting: Annette Benson, Irene Lamb
MPAA rating: G
Running Time: 96 minutes

and brings to mind the heavy-handed opulence of Lorenzini the showman while the second is rough-hewn and realistic as befits an amusement park that really serves as more of a prison.

Other elements of style appeal as well. Director Steve Barron uses low angles at times to suggest a Pinocchio-like view of the world; in the trial scene Barron's oblique angles disorient the viewer in a way suggestive of Geppetto's helpless confusion. In perhaps the most beautifully rendered shot in the film, Barron photographs from a distant, very high angle Geppetto rowing out to sea to find Pinocchio as Leona stands on the shore and tries to dissuade him. The camera pulls back as the woodcarver's little skiff gets farther out to sea, the wide lens keeping both actors in the shot as Geppetto finally shouts out to Leona, whom he may never see again, that he does love her.

Jim Henson's Creature Shop supplied the animatronic Pinocchio.

The work of the artists in the Jim Henson Creature Shop and the excellent computer graphics in the film augment these visuals nicely. Five puppeteers worked the motors inside the title character while another used a video monitor to guide his controls of the motors operating Pinocchio's facial expressions. The animatronics team used twelve different Pinocchios during the making of the film, all made from fiberglass and painted to look like wood. When Pinocchio breaks his strings and walks about on his own, the effect is completely convincing. Computer graphics technology accounts for the equally effective scenes with Pepe and the sea monster.

The performances in the film also contribute to its merits. Though Bebe Neuwirth and Rob Schneider are required to do little more than play lively caricatures as the villains, Martin Landau succeeds well at conveying the humanity of Geppetto. A live-action version of a mythic story requires that the actors play their characters believably but not too broadly, and Landau finds the needed balance that makes Geppetto touchingly human. His concern for his missing boy-puppet, his helpless amazement at the ruined pastry shop, his despair in facing debtors' prison, his resolve to find Pinocchio regardless of danger—all of these emotions are made real by Landau's fine work. This charming film does justice to Carlo Collodi's classic tale.

—*Glenn Hopp*

REVIEWS

Boxoffice Magazine Online. August 5, 1996.
Detroit News. July 26, 1996, p. 3D.
Entertainment Weekly. August 2, 1996, p. 46.
Los Angeles Times. July 26, 1996, p. F1.
New York Times. October 29, 1995, section 2, pp. 17-18.
New York Times. July 26, 1996, p. C18.
New York Times. August 4, 1996, section 2, p. H31.
The Hollywood Reporter. July 22, 1996, p. 8.
USA Today. July 26, 1996, p. 4D.
Variety. July 22, 1996.

Alaska

A missing father. A desperate search. An unforgettable adventure.—Movie tagline

"The summer's coolest action-adventure."—Susan Granger, *American Movie Classics*

"*Cliffhanger* for kids!"—Christine Spines, *Premiere*

"A stunning adventure for the whole family."—Paul Wunder, *WBAI-FM/New York*

Box Office: $11,500,000

It's not easy to make an epic family film, but *Alaska* gets an "A" for effort. Its story is simple and predictable, but the majesty of its frontier setting and the appeal of its central performances combine with dramatic adventure and rescue sequences to help it overcome the limitations of a pedestrian plot.

Alaska's ingredients are an overly familiar family stew. Its central characters are a troubled teenage boy, Sean Barnes (Vincent Kartheiser) and his resourceful younger sister Jessie (Thora Birch), who are struggling to overcome the recent death of their mother. (For some reason, a parent is always dead or divorced in modern family films.) Their father, Jake (Dirk Benedict), has abandoned his career as an airline pilot and moved the family from Chicago to a fishing village in Alaska to start over; now he's a Piper Cub pilot with a charter service. Jessie, who has struck up a friendship with a local boy, has adapted well; she loves kayaking, the wilderness and serving as a radio base for her father's flights. But Sean, who misses Wrigley Field, MTV and his favorite video games, is miserable being "stuck in the boonies," carries a chip on his shoulder, and blames his father.

For unexplained reasons, Jake takes off one evening on an emergency run even though a storm is brewing. It doesn't seem like something a trained pilot would do, but logic has little place in the plot of *Alaska*. Naturally, Dad goes down on a remote rocky peak; searchers can't find him, and the kids take off in improbable pursuit. Sean remembers his father's motto: "Never give up."

"These young people were brought up on MTV and video games. They know nothing of nature."—Perry

The pair's against-all-odds odyssey provides various physical and spiritual tests. In a refreshing reversal of gender stereotypes, the girl has the common sense, experience and leadership qualities that keep the two alive for the first part of their journey, while the boy is driven mainly by emotion. Realistically, their dialogue is spiked with sarcastic comments and put-downs, and the two young actors make the prickly-but-affectionate relationship entirely believable.

Kartheiser, who had a smaller part in *The Indian in the Cupboard* (1995) and *Little Big League* (1994), rises to the challenge of a leading role with a heartfelt, credible coming-of-age transformation. Birch, who was in *Monkey Trouble* (1994) and *Now and Then* (1995), gets top billing in the film, and deservedly so: She's a star in the making. She's sassy but likeable, cute but not cloying, and always in command. Her performance isn't at all overbearing but she somehow seems to fill the screen in nearly every scene. Films often tend to make young take-charge girls into unappealing tomboys; Birch doesn't fall into that trap. She's rock-solid, and even when the script requires her to be weepy or tired as Sean becomes more brave, we never see Jessie as a weakling. In the film's climactic cliff-hanger rescue scene, she's the one whose strength gives the rest of the family a chance to survive.

Three other elements, one unexpected, keep *Alaska* moving. They are the scenery, a cuddly but spiritually enlightened polar bear cub (this is a family film, after all), and, surprisingly, a slimmed-down, nearly unrecognizable Charlton Heston. The venerable actor has a grand, scenery-chewing role as Perry, an unspeakably nasty villain, a ruthless poacher who is trying to capture the bear cub alive. Heston plays Perry as a mannered, lying, malevolent skunk who bosses around his hired sidekick, the sniveling Koontz (Duncan Fraser). They're a delightfully despicable couple of rapscallions, and Heston is wonderfully evil.

The vile pair, who use a helicopter and a motorized rubber boat as their conveyances, keep the plot churning a little as they play cat-and-mouse games with the kids, the bear and various search parties. Heston's performance is his best in quite awhile.

Significantly for a film that is about a father-son reconciliation, *Alaska* is directed by Fraser Heston, the actor's son. The younger Heston deftly overcomes the story's lack of twists and turns by the use of unexpected transitions. Occasionally the directing falls flat, but more often it is imaginative. And at the least, *Alaska* can be remembered as the answer to a trivia question: What film was directed by a man whose name combines the last names of the actors playing the film's villains?

The bear, whom the kids unimaginatively name Cubby, becomes their unlikely guide after they rescue him from the poachers' camp. According to a wise Native American elder (another obligatory component of the family-film adventure genre), the cub is the children's spirit guide on their coming-of-age journey. He is certainly playful, cute and resourceful enough to capture the affection of the 8-and-under crowd. And, of course, he comes through when all else fails.

The children's ordeals include kayaking among narrow ocean passages, canoeing over rapids and down a waterfall, plenty of harrowing rock-climbing and endless hiking over glacial terrain. The perils, and the film itself, tend to drag on a bit too long, but they are certainly gripping; in fact, some may be too intense for tykes.

CREDITS

Jessie Barnes: Thora Birch
Sean Barnes: Vincent Kartheiser
Jake Barnes: Dirk Benedict
Perry: Charlton Heston
Ben: Gordon Tootoosis

Origin: USA
Released: 1996
Production: Carol Fuchs and Andy Burg for a Castle Rock Entertainment production; released by Sony Pictures Entertainment
Direction: Fraser C. Heston
Screenplay: Andy Burg and Scott Myers
Cinematography: Tony Westman
Editing: Rob Kobrin
Music: Reg Powell
Production design: Douglas Higgins
Art direction: Rex Raglan
Costume design: Monique Prudhomme
Sound: Eric Batut
Animal training: Mark Wiener-Dumas
Casting: Mary Gail Artz, Barbara Cohen
MPAA rating: PG
Running Time: 110 minutes

The grandeur of the landscapes is both an asset and a problem for the film. Actually filmed both in British Columbia and Alaska, the settings are gorgeous, but photographer Tony Westman tends to gorge himself on them. There are far too many shots of the kids on the journey taken from a circling plane. It is as if the filmmakers are determined to justify the rather grandiose title of *Alaska*; a little more judicious editing would have made this feel less like a travelogue and more like a fast-paced family adventure.

Director Fraser C. Heston is the son of legendary actor Charlton Heston.

Even more excessive is the musical score by Reg Powell. In fact, the score might be the most overbearing of any film in recent decades. It starts at a crescendo and never comes down. Its majestic flourishes and heavenly choruses soon become tiring. At times the music becomes almost comical: Do we really need a stirring musical backdrop for even the most routine of scenes?

A little more restraint in the music, directing and camera work, and a little more imagination in the plot, would have made *Alaska* wonderful. As it is, it's a film that strains too hard to be epic and ends up merely being more than adequate. In memory it might become hard to distinguish from other family wilderness adventure films, but *Alaska* is most likely to be remembered as the coming-of-age of Thora Birch, who shows plenty of spunk, poise and promise.

—*Michael Betzold*

Boxoffice Magazine Online. August 19, 1996.
Chicago Tribune. August 14, 1996, p. 1.
Los Angeles Times. August 14, 1996, p. F1.
New York Times. August 14, 1996, p. C16.
People. August 19, 1996, p. 20.
Variety. August 9, 1996.

All Dogs Go to Heaven 2

"Plenty of adventure and emotion."—*Philadelphia Daily News*

Box Office: $8,400,000

It is not necessarily new to pit dog people against cat people in a film or to have dogs battling cats, especially in a children's or animated film. For instance, in *101 Dalmatians*, the dalmatians are wrongly accused of household destruction, when the true troublemakers are the Siamese cats, who evilly sing, "We are Siamese if you please; we are Siamese if you don't please." More recently, in *Babe* (1994), the cat rules the house, while the dogs make do in the barn. This sinister and otherworldly reputation of cats is also showcased in *All Dogs Go to Heaven 2*, an animated film from MGM Family Entertainment.

Charlie (Charlie Sheen) loves life in the city and feels at home with the mess, the exhaust fumes and the graffiti. Indeed, it is Heaven that makes Charlie uncomfortable: too clean, no fleas, no schemes. He can do the crime but not the time. As Charlie sings, "It's too heavenly here." When Charlie's "wiener dog" friend Itchy (Dom Deluise) joins Charlie in Heaven, the place improves somewhat, but only momentarily. While Itchy loves flying everywhere he goes (because in life he had had the shortest legs and was always trying to keep up), Charlie is not so easily placated. As luck would have it, however, a malcontent dog, recruited by Satan's lot (all cats), steals Gabriel's horn, to which the Pearly Gates respond, opening to admit more dogs. God's official delegate Anabelle (Bebe Neuwirth) sends Charlie and Itchy back to life to regain the horn, and a world of trouble ensues.

While not a Disney production, *All Dogs Go to Heaven 2* follows the Disney "formula." Just as in *Lady and the Tramp* (1955), a rough and tumble mutt, here Charlie, falls for an attractive female dog, Sasha LeFleur (Sheena Easton), who is out of his league. Whereas in *Lady and the Tramp*, Lady's class would seem to separate her from her beau's affections, in *All Dogs Go to Heaven 2*, it is Sasha's strength and independence that may prove an impediment. Also, just as Cruella De Vil in *101 Dalmatians* is remarkably villainous in her production plans for puppy pelts, so too are Satan's minions horrible to look at and more than slightly demonic. For instance, when the malcontent dog Carface Carruthers (Ernest Borgnine) ends up losing his soul, two hissing, glowing, electrified felines arrive to retrieve it. The scene sizzles with their misdirected power. And like in *Lady and the Tramp* and *101 Dalmatians,* happiness in *All Dogs Go to Heaven 2* is a home with a family that loves and feeds its pets.

Portions of the film are intended for adults, it would appear. For instance, upon their return to life, Charlie and Itchy seek out and attend a speakeasy at which Sasha is performing (in return for a meal, we subsequently learn). At one point during her production number, Sasha crosses a subway vent. She pauses and strikes a pose as her fur rises and clearly the animators have created Marilyn Monroe's famous pose from *Seven Year Itch* (1955), a reference few adults will miss and few children will catch. Further, in the process of rescuing the horn, Charlie and Itchy need access to the police department. When masquerading as seeing-eye dogs fails, they implement "Plan B"—a staged donut delivery. An armada of pear-shaped officers storms in. While some children may understand the reference to police officers taking breaks at donut shops, the devilish humor of it will tickle parents most of all.

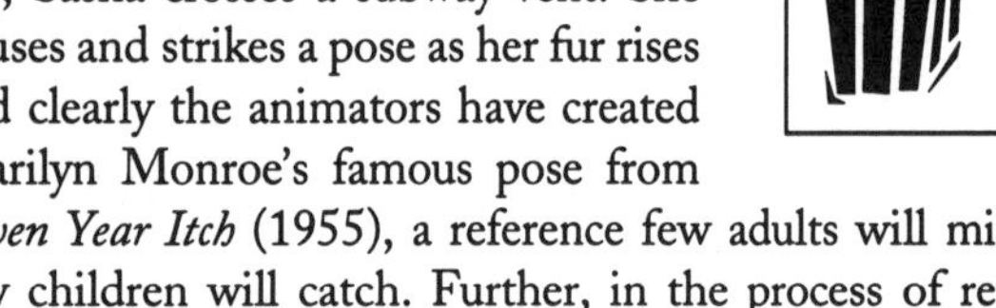
"Life is too quiet and too mellow. All your brain cells turn to Jell-O."—Charlie's complaints in the song, "It's Too Heavenly Here."

The characterization of female characters in recent animated film is an interesting and difficult issue. Consider characters such as Jessica Rabbit, in *Who Framed Roger Rabbit* (1988), who is drawn with a seductive body and brought to life through Kathleen Turner's breathy, smoky voice. She is a bombshell, a femme fatale, an "it" girl. Also, in *Cool World* (1992) an ex-con doodles and creates a femme fatale, Holli (Kim Basinger), with whom he has sex. While Disney's recent animations have starred less overtly sexual women characters, the lead women are voluptuous, exotic and interested in romance, such as Jasmine in *Aladdin* (1994). In *All Dogs Go to Heaven 2,* Sasha "tarts it up" (for example, she drops her front paws and waves her posterior in the air) during her show in order to earn her supper (not unlike Demi Moore's character in *Striptease,* or Julie Andrew's character in *Victor/Victoria* [1982]). While she disabuses the audience members and the bartender of their seduction plans, and recites a litany of qualities her dream man will have, including virtues such as humility and empathy, she, not unlike Jessica Rabbit and Holli, is a difficult—perhaps negative—role model for young audience members. Presumably the writers were working to produce what they see as a 1990s "woman": strong, independent, resourcefully seductive. All in all, it is worrisome, especially as the one human woman featured in the film, the mother of the runaway, David (Adam Wylie), is more than a little lumpy and disheveled.

Clearly *All Dogs Go to Heaven 2* offers entertainment for the whole family. What problems it has (like frightening scenes of demons and demonic power) may prove points for family discussion after the film. Full of song and action including many prank falls, *All Dogs Go to Heaven 2* may be a good film for a rainy Sunday afternoon.

—*Roberta F. Green*

CREDITS

Charlie Barkin: Charlie Sheen (voice)
Sasha La Fleur: Sheena Easton (voice)
Itchy Itchiford: Dom DeLuise (voice)
Carface: Ernest Borgnine (voice)
Red: George Hearn (voice)
Anabelle: Bebe Neuwirth (voice)
David: Adam Wyle (voice)
Chihuahua: Hamilton Camp (voice)
Labradour MC: Wallace Shawn (voice)
Thom: Bobby DiCicco (voice)

Origin: USA
Released: 1996
Production: Paul Sabella, Jonathan Dern, Kelly Ward, and Mark Young for an MGM Family Entertainment and Metro-Goldwyn-Mayer Animation production; released by MGM/UA
Direction: Paul Sabella, Larry Leker
Screenplay: Arne Olsen, Kelly Ward, Mark Young
Editing: Tony Garber
Animation direction: Todd Waterman
Art direction: Deane Taylor
Voice direction: Kelly Ward
Casting: Maria Estrada
Song: Mark Watters (music), Barry Mann, Cynthia Weil (lyrics) "It Feels So Good to Be Bad"
MPAA rating: G
Running Time: 82 minutes

REVIEWS

Detroit Free Press. March 31, 1996, p. 7F.
Los Angeles Times. April 1, 1996, p. F3.
The New York Times. March 30, 1996, p. 20.
Variety. April 1, 1996, p. 58.

American Buffalo

They had a plan. It wasn't worth a nickel.—Movie tagline

"Ground breaking forerunner to the genre that reached its pinnacle with *Pulp Fiction.*"—Stephen Holden, *New York Times*

"It would be a crime to miss it!"—Desmond Ryan, *Philadelphia Inquirer*

"Thumbs up! Hoffman, Franz and Nelson are superb!"—Gene Siskel, *Siskel & Ebert*

Box Office: $650,744

For the 1996 release *American Buffalo,* playwright David Mamet adapted his now twenty-year-old play of the same name for the screen. But the adaptation in fact involved very few changes. The recent feature film differs little from Mamet's play, first produced in Chicago in 1975. The set has been opened up very little, with the bulk of the action taking place inside the dingy, ramshackle junk shop owned by one of the play's three characters, Donny (Dennis Franz). Moviegoers do see a few scenes filmed outside the shop, but the streets of the nameless urban environment are empty. And with the exception of some unidentified figures whose profiles and hands are briefly glimpsed in the film's opening scenes, the dramatis personae in the filmed version of *American Buffalo,* as in the play, consists of three persons: in addition to Donny, we are introduced only to Teach (Dustin Hoffman), Donny's friend, and to the junk store owner's protégé, Bobby (Sean Nelson).

"There is no law. There is no right and wrong. The world is lies."—Teach

Some viewers of the movie have complained that director Michael Corrente's reverence for Mamet's text results in an experience that feels cramped and airless, while others have found that the movie replicates the exhilaration that accompanies a viewing of a stage production of the play. By changing little about Mamet's conception of the action and its dramatization, however, Corrente clearly preserves the strength of this and every other Mamet drama: its language. Mamet's chosen dialect is contemporary American vernacular, which he uses like no one else. Employing seemingly everyday diction, so banal as to appear meaningless, he nonetheless manages to endow it—and the superficially inchoate characters who speak it—with a nearly poetic resonance. Like the principals in a Samuel Beckett play, Mamet's characters convey much by saying little.

In fact, the plot of *American Buffalo* in many respects resembles Beckett's landmark drama, *Waiting for Godot* (1955), in which the action consists of a trio of characters waiting for someone who never appears. In Mamet's play, this absent center is a small-time thief whom Donny wants to help him and Bobby stage a burglary. Some time earlier, a customer had purchased a collectible American buffalo nickel from Donny, who at the time was ignorant of the coin's true value. Feeling he has been taken and seeing an opportunity for easy enrichment, Don hatches a scheme not only to take back his nickel, but to steal what he assumes to be a valuable coin collection. He includes his teenaged dogsbody, Bobby, in his plan, which he proposes to execute with the additional assistance of Fletch, who never shows up. While they wait for Fletch, Donny and Bobby must contend with Teach, who has learned of their plan and apparently determined that he should be its mastermind. Although we are treated to a scene of the unkempt Teach shaving in advance of his would-be adventure, he remains greasy-haired and unprepared to instruct this or any other group of students. Fletch, it seems, is the only one who can bring the caper off, the only one who can lend these aimless lives a purpose. In his absence, Teach attempts to fill the void with random meditations on the human condition and an unfocused malevolence.

Teach is a person who lives in the moment, one who, lacking a reason for being, finds himself obliged to search

CREDITS

Teach: Dustin Hoffman
Don: Dennis Franz
Bobby: Sean Nelson

Origin: USA
Released: 1996
Production: Gregory Mosher for a Punch Productions and Capitol Films production; released by Samuel Goldwyn Co.
Direction: Michael Corrente
Screenplay: David Mamet; based on his play
Cinematography: Richard Crudo
Editing: Kate Sanford
Music: Thomas Newman
Production design: Daniel Talpers
Costume design: Deborah Newhall
Sound: Ronald Judkins, Robert Jackson
Casting: Billy Hopkins, Suzanne Smith, Kerry Barden
MPAA rating: R
Running Time: 88 minutes

for meaning by insinuating himself into the lives of those around him. Initially, it appears that he seems bent on destroying, if not Bobby himself, then certainly the trusting relationship between the young man and his older mentor, Donny. Gradually, however, we realize that Bobby is more than a mere victim, that in fact he and Teach are both struggling, each in his own way, for Donny's soul. At the climactic moment, Teach unleashes his fury, trashing Donny's world, his store full of trash; it almost seems that Teach has won. But if this is victory, surely it is a pyrrhic one: Donny's shop, and his shop assistant, Bobby, may be injured, but both can be repaired. The status quo remains unchanged.

In stage performances, the role of Bobby has customarily been played by a young man. Here Bobby is still a boy, and the struggle between him and Teach therefore appears to be less than a fair fight. The fact that in the end their equilibrium remains essentially unchanged—despite the overwhelming display of Teach's frustration—only underscores Teach's ineffectualness and the essentially static quality of the lives of the three principals. The quest to better their lives—or at least to add some color to them—has clearly been a foolish one. These three are surely the most bumbling would-be burglars who have ever lived: bent on retrieving a coin whose value they do not even know, and stymied by a lack of organization and their failure of will, the three turn on one another, tearing down the castle in the air their dialogue has constructed. Clearly something vital is lacking—not just Fletch, but a sense of being, a faith in their own existence.

Although it is Donny who has the power and responsibility to say whether or not the heist proceeds, Teach is the key to the story. "Teach" is only a nickname—and an ironic one at that—for Walter Cole. Although Teach and Don Dubrow have apparently known one another for many years, Teach is a sorry soul who lacks any real human connection. Donny, although he seems to have no home other than his pawn shop and no real family, has at least managed to form an emotional bond with Bobby. And it is this bond, rather than the buffalo nickel, that Teach really wants to steal. If his alliance with Donny is nothing more than habit, if Donny does not even want to include him in plans for the robbery, then his life is without any meaning at all. His foul language sums up the thoroughgoing sourness of his outlook. Even the bacon he orders Bobby to retrieve from the diner across the street fails to please.

Teach has been played on stage by a number of powerful actors, including Robert Duvall and Al Pacino. The latter, in fact, was the director's first choice to play Teach on-screen, but Pacino declined Corrente's offer—as did Hoffman, initially. Hoffman's doubts, like those of many others connected with the project, seemed to arise from Corrente's status as a relatively untried director (the thirty-six-year-old had previously directed only one other film, *Federal Hill,* which was released in 1995). But Hoffman, like Mamet himself, was won over by Corrente's enthusiasm for the play, which previously Corrente had directed twice on stage, both times also playing the part of Teach.

Corrente was wise to settle on Hoffman, who does an excellent job of conveying the peculiar blend of edginess and world-weariness with which Mamet has etched Teach. Several commentators have noted the obvious similarities between Hoffman's portrayal of Teach and his memorable performance as Ratso Rizzo in *Midnight Cowboy* (1969) nearly three decades earlier. Both characters are certified losers, but both contain a certain poignancy beneath their sad veneer. Teach's dialogue manages to suggest an inner power residing within his superficial inarticulateness, and we are not surprised when he later explodes into violence.

As Donny, Dennis Franz also does a fine job of communicating the inner life of an undistinguished man. Mamet clearly has endowed Donny with a sense of integrity, which is manifested in part by Donny's stewardship of Bobby. And Franz, with his bulky worriedness and darting eyes, proves a superior foil to Hoffman's conscienceless Teach. In the end, it is Donny who manages to hold together the small world he shares with the other two characters. The sensitivity which Franz's Donny displays towards the others makes us care about him and makes his ability to reconcile with them after Teach's attack on Bobby believable. It is not every actor who could make such a lowlife empathetic without making him ridiculous; instead of incongruity, Franz delivers a performance as subtly shaded as Mamet's language. Like it, he suggests something greater than himself, something larger than his meager realm. Dennis Franz has made a name for himself on the award winning television show, "NYPD Blue." Clearly now, he is ready to break out into larger productions. A relative newcomer to film, Franz does a fine job of representing something like the essential humanity Donny displays but Teach lacks. He also serves as a kind of stand-in for the viewer, who, like the boy, at first only partially comprehends the meaning behind the words that swirl around him. Bobby is clearly attracted to Donny's tutelage, but it takes awhile before he realizes that he has apprenticed himself to a man who—no matter how welcoming—is a fence, if not a thief, who wants him to act as his accomplice.

American Buffalo is a classic piece of modern theater which has been admirably translated into that most American of art forms, the motion picture. The metamorphosis seems thoroughly appropriate: now a new generation has been given ready access to Mamet's glorious manipulation of the national idiom.

—*Lisa Paddock*

REVIEWS

Chicago Tribune. September 13, 1996, p. 5.
Entertainment Weekly. September 27, 1996, p. 58.
Los Angeles Times. September 13, 1996, p. F4.
New York Times. September 13, 1996, p. C1.
New Yorker. September 16, 1996, p. 100.
Sight and Sound. December, 1996, p. 36.
USA Today. September 13, 1996, p. 4D.
Variety Online. September 3, 1996.

Angels and Insects

"Startling and penetrating. Genuine eroticism."—Shlomo Schwartzberg, *Boxoffice*

"Clever and twisted."—Juan Morales, *Detour*

"Utterly riveting!"—Stephen Farber, *Movieline*

"Seething with sexuality. Tantalizing . . . hypnotic and hot-blooded."—Bruce Williamson, *Playboy*

"A savage portrait of the pent-up Victorian psyche."—Richard David Story, *Vogue*

Box Office: $3,300,000

Angels and Insects may be the most intellectual—or at least intellectually pretentious—film ever about sex. Set at an English country estate during the late 1850's and early 1860's, this highly original film examines the close relationships between the behavior of people and insects with the latter seeming more logical and organized than their human equivalents. Adultery and incest may occur in the natural world, but people, especially aristocratic Victorians, are supposed to be above such beastliness. That they do not is the essence of the film the husband-wife team of Philip and Belinda Haas have adapted from A. S. Byatt's 1992 novella *Morpho Eugenia.*

After years in the Amazon, entomologist and explorer William Adamson (Mark Rylance) loses most of his research specimens in a shipwreck on the way home to England and finds himself cataloging the natural history collection of the wealthy Sir Harald Alabaster (Jeremy Kemp). The Alabaster country estate is presided over by the obese, indolent Lady Alabaster (Annette Badland), who never moves from her resting place, and populated by her pale, blond offspring. William falls immediately in love with the eldest daughter, Eugenia (Patsy Kensit), who shares her name with Morpho Eugenia, one of the two species of exotic butterfly the naturalist presents her father. Eugenia is seemingly perfect, flawed only by the mysterious death of her fiancé.

Following a brief courtship, William and Eugenia are married, despite the strong opposition of her brother, Edgar (Douglas Henshall), who considers the scientist's humble Scot origins unworthy of such a prize as his beautiful sister. The Adamsons then alternate between passionate bouts of sex and periods of pregnancy during which Eugenia lounges about as bloated as her mother. During these times, William instructs his wife's younger sisters in natural history along with their tutor, Miss Mead (Anna Massey), and Matty Crompton (Kristin Scott Thomas), a poor relation of the Alabasters.

Matty is as drab as Eugenia is shiny, but William is strangely drawn to her, attaining as much sexual excitement at gazing at her wrist while she sketches as at his wife's naked body, and she clearly feels he is wasted on the Alabasters. After Matty causes William to discover Eugenia's incestuous relationship with Edgar and Eugenia admits her fiancé killed himself because of it, Matty and William run off to South America together.

Byatt contrasts modern and Victorian values, attitudes, and mores in *Possession*, her best-known novel, and she clearly intends, in *Morpho Eugenia,* for her readers to consider these characters' behavior in light of all the sexual, social, and scientific changes the intervening century has wrought. William is a Darwinian whose belief that human activities have their parallels in the animal world and whose open discussion of the mating habits of insects make Sir Harald squirm. The Alabaster incest violates Darwin's principle of natural selection and shows how the English aristocracy declined not just through inbreeding but because of narcissism and self-indulgence.

CREDITS

William Adamson: Mark Rylance
Matty Crompton: Kristin Scott Thomas
Eugenia Alabaster: Patsy Kensit
Sir Harald Alabaster: Jeremy Kemp
Lady Alabaster: Annette Badland
Edgar Alabaster: Douglas Henshall
Rowena Alabaster: Saskia Wickham
Robin Swinnerton: Chris Larkin
Miss Mead: Anna Massey
Amy: Clare Redman
Production: Joyce Herlihy and Belinda Haas for Playhouse International Pictures; released by the Samuel Goldwyn Company
Direction: Philip Haas
Screenplay: Belinda Haas and Philip Haas; based on the novella *Morpho Eugenia* by A. S. Byatt
Cinematography: Bernard Zitzermann
Editing: Belinda Haas
Production design: Jennifer Kernke
Art direction: Alison Riva
Costume design: Paul Brown
Sound: Simon Hinkly
Music: Alex Balanescu
Casting: Celestia Fox
Entomologist: Chris O'Toole
MPAA rating: Unrated
Running Time: 116 minutes

Byatt has said that she conceived her novella as a highly filmable property and gave it strong visual elements. Lady Alabaster, always dressed in white, is the queen of this colony in the manner of a queen bee or ant or termite. All her whims are to be indulged. When she dies, Eugenia becomes the new queen with a new set of whims. The blond Alabaster daughters dress either in white or in bright blues, reds, oranges, or yellows. Eugenia wears one yellow dress with black bars, making her resemble a giant bee or wasp. That the dress suggests she may be dangerous is one of the film's many heavily ironic moments. Another occurs when a glass of red wine is spilled onto the lap of Eugenia's white dress. At the time, the incident seems to suggest a threat to her virginity. After later revelations, it suggests the falsity of her virginity, her complicity in her fiancé's death, and, again, her dangerousness.

"It's not done me any good to look pretty and be admired."—Eugenia's final words to William

William's discovery of the incest makes everything that has transpired take on new, ironic dimensions. Edgar's hostility and his harangues about the low breeding of his brother-in-law are only the most obvious. Eugenia's wonder at William's having lived among naked savages is only one of numerous other ironies. As a result, *Angels and Insects* requires a second viewing to pick up on more of its verbal and visual wit.

Philip Haas, director and co-writer, and Belinda Haas, editor, co-writer, and co-producer, previously made another intellectually demanding literary adaptation, *The Music of Chance* (1993), from the novel by Paul Auster. That effort, while interesting, is hampered by a cold, dispassionate tone, a sluggish visual style, and dull casting. Philip Haas formerly made documentaries about art, and while the detached attitude of the documentarian carries over into his feature films, *Angels and Insects* has more passion and humor than *The Music of Chance* and is more smoothly paced. Among the many memorable moments in the film are the way Sir Harald impatiently and seemingly uncontrollably flutters one hands while William expounds upon Darwin and the way William, after learning his wife's secret, averts his eyes when Matty lets down her hair—a particularly apt means of demonstrating his perverse innocence.

The elaborate women's costumes by Paul Brown mimic the look of exotic butterflies and other insects.

The Haases' collaborators aid greatly in the success of the film. Paul Brown's costumes are truly the stars of *Angels and Insects*. There have been more beautiful and more original costumes in numerous films, but none have served their thematic purpose so well. Not only do the Alabaster daughters wear bright colors, but they are also occasionally adorned in elaborate headpieces of intertwined flowers, leaves, and twigs, making clear their kinship to the natural world. Matty's blacks, browns, and grays contrast strongly with the apparel of her supposed betters, making her often fade into the background.

Entomologist Chris O'Toole does an astounding job of helping incorporate insects into the drama, particularly when Eugenia is frightened as dozens of butterflies alight on her in a conservatory. Alex Balanescu's nervous, repetitive score emphasizes the chaos of this strange environment. The music recalls Michael Nyman's great score for a similar, though superior, film, Peter Greenaway's *The Draughtsman's Contract* (1982). In fact, Balanescu is the violinist on that and other Nyman soundtracks.

Angels and Insects is finally, like *The Music of Chance*, less than it could be because of uninspired casting—with one notable exception. Patsy Kensit not only seems too modern for Eugenia, but she has a suntan no Victorian lady would have thought proper. Kensit, though a limited performer, is capable of occasional bursts of creativity, as when Eugenia explains her relationship with Edgar to her husband. Kensit ably conveys Eugenia's mixture of embarrassment, regret, despair, and defiance.

Mark Rylance has been acclaimed for his stage work in England, with his Hamlet being hailed as one of the best ever by Sir Ian McKellen, but on film, he has little presence. Rylance has blandly ordinary looks and speaks with a flat, uninflected style that makes his character seem barely awake at times. The audience is meant to identify with William's innocence and confusion, but Rylance merely inhabits the role with little heat.

The one exception to the weak cast is Kristin Scott Thomas' wonderful creation of Matty. Scott Thomas has excelled before at portraying unfulfilled beautiful women, as in *Handful of Dust* (1988) and *Four Weddings and a Funeral* (1994), and her Matty is a plain variation on this type. Matty is far superior intellectually and morally to those around her, and Scott Thomas beautifully captures the ideas, creativity, and sexuality bubbling beneath this placid surface. Matty's passion and Scott Thomas' strong presence make all the other characters and actors mere appendages to her story.

—*Michael Adams*

AWARDS AND NOMINATIONS

Academy Awards 1996 Nominations: Best Costume Design

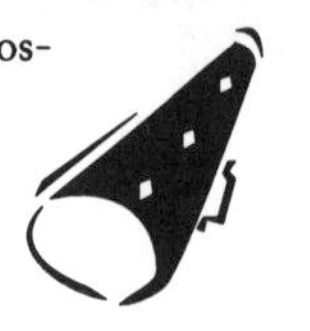

REVIEWS

Entertainment Weekly. February 2, 1996, p. 42.
Interview. February, 1996, p. 60.
Maclean's. February 12, 1996, p. 92.
The New Republic. February 19, 1996, p. 28.
New Statesman and Society. VIII, December 8, 1995, p. 25.
New York. February 5, 1996, p. 50.
The New York Times. January 26, 1996, p. C6.
The New Yorker. January 29, 1996, p. 91.
Sight and Sound. December, 1995, p. 38.
USA Today. February 19, 1996, p. 4D.
Variety. May 22, 1995, p. 95.
The Wall Street Journal. January 26, 1996, p. A9.

Anne Frank Remembered

She is perhaps Hitler's best known victim, but what was Anne Frank really like?—Movie tagline

"Fresh and moving."—Stephen Saban, *Details*

"This film deepens our connections with the story through the power of film itself."—Stanley Kauffmann, *The New Republic*

"Poignant and exhilarating!"—Marion D.S. Dreyfus, *The New York Jewish Post*

"Brings home its reality with shattering force."—Stephen Holden, *The New York Times*

"A rare piece of history that virtually comes alive, taking your breath away with its immediacy."—John Engstrom, *Seattle Post-Intelligencer*

"Inspiring! A fresh perspective. It alerts us that villainy is the rank soil in which heroism can flower."—Richard Corliss, *Time*

Box Office: $1,035,165

Anne Frank Remembered is a moving documentary of the life and death of an adolescent Jewish girl and budding writer. Few people who know anything about the Holocaust have not heard about her story or read her diary. In addition to a stage play and movie based on her diary, there have been countless discussions of her writing. She has been a symbol of history for more than two generations. It might seem that there is little more to be said, and that another movie is not needed to honor her legacy and probe her fate.

But the poignancy of Anne Frank's own words, and the fact that her whole diary has only just been published, ensure that she will remain a fascinating and haunting figure. In a sense, she has been rediscovered, with the previously censored portions of her diary revealing her growing awareness of her sexuality and her fierce individuality. She seems a less sheltered and innocent figure, and a more complex human being.

Some years ago Philip Roth published a novel, *The Ghost Writer,* imagining what Anne Frank's life would have been like had she survived the concentration camps. She is a compelling subject for writers because she wanted to be a writer and saw her diary as a literary contribution to an understanding of her time. She has become, in other words, not only a Holocaust figure, emblematic of the Jews who perished, but also a type of the struggling, articulate soul, of the individual who craves recognition and even fame. Anne

AWARDS AND NOMINATIONS

Academy Awards 1995: Best Feature Documentary

CREDITS

Kenneth Branagh: Kenneth Branagh (voice)
Glenn Close: Glenn Close (voice)
Miep Gies: Miep Gies
Anne Frank: Anne Frank

Origin: USA
Released: 1995
Production: Jon Blair for a BBC production; released by Sony Classics
Direction: Jon Blair
Screenplay: Jon Blair
Cinematography: Barry Ackroyd
Editing: Karin Steininger
Music: Carl Davis
Sound: Robert Edwards
MPAA rating: PG
Running Time: 122 minutes

Frank was unique because she wanted much more than her family's or her friends' or her community's acknowledgement. In the uncompromising way of youth she wanted the world to pay attention. Part of the grief she evokes is for the annihilated artist.

Anne Frank Remembered tells her story through the words and visual expressions of those who knew her and through her family photographs. What emerges is a much less sentimental story than the filmed and stage versions of her life. Anne was the spoiled daughter, doted on by her father and ineffectually disciplined by her mother. Anne could be a show-off and a know-it-all. As one of her friends' mother said, "God knew everything, but Anne knew it better." Anne seemed born with the writer's cruel streak, a self-absorbed and self-regarding sensibility that led her to treat others contemptuously—especially if they seemed lacking in imagination.

Includes the only known film footage of Anne, as she leans out her apartment window to watch a wedding reception pass in 1941.

Anne was also ebullient and great fun to be with. The witnesses to her life, especially men, were charmed by her insouciance. She was a precocious adolescent full of wonder about her developing body—and a little frustrated that she had no one who could really talk to her about it. She found her comfortable, middle-class home rather stuffy, and no one—not even her adoring father—ever knew just how much of her life was a kind of secret that needed the vessel of writing for its expression.

Had it not been for the Holocaust, Anne's story would not have been remarkable: a rebellious teenager, intolerant of the adult world, yearning to be a writer. But her quest to be free fused with world historical events that at first overwhelmed her family ultimately became the story of her tragedy and her triumph. As a writer she was handed material by fate, and she did not for a moment hesitate to capitalize on her terrible yet magnificent opportunity.

The Franks were a Jewish family—not particularly religious—that had moved from Germany to Holland when the Nazis seized control in 1933. Otto Frank had served in the German army in World War I, and it pained him to leave a country he had loyally served and loved. Because Holland had escaped the ravages of World War I, Frank was certain he had brought his family to a secure refuge. Only at the last minute, realizing the Nazis would invade all of the low countries, did he manage to sequester his family on the upper floors of a building where they were supposed to wait out the war until the Allies liberated them.

"Anne was, you would say in American, spicy. She was a spicy girl."—Anne's friend Hanneli Goslar

At first Anne responded exuberantly to her incarceration. She was intensely lonely, but her diary (a birthday gift) provided an outlet. Indeed, she realized she could speak to the diary as her friend in a way that she could never actually confide in a real-life girlfriend. In other words, Anne Frank discovered her literary vocation, inventing a friend and even answering that invented friend's letters. The diary became Anne's epistolary novel and the vehicle for her faith in the future—that somehow her words would make it out of her attic and into the world. Indeed, she became the very legend of the writer creating a life's work in a garret.

Cooped up and having to share her bedroom with an older man, a dentist whom Otto Frank's friends had asked Otto to hide, Anne lashed out. She found the dentist a dolt, her mother devoid of imaginative sensitivity, and even the adolescent boy to whom she at first confided in almost like a lover to be a dullard. The temperamental Anne vented her feelings in her diary, gradually seeing it, however, not merely as an exercise of her ego but as a work of literature that she began to rewrite as if for publication.

The story of Anne's growing self-consciousness and sense of isolation in *Anne Frank Remembered* is corroborated by her girlfriends and the family's supporters both before and during the war. Both the authenticity of the diary and the validity of many of Anne's judgments are secured in this testimony. At the same time, the profundity of Anne's character eluded them, for it was only fully expressed in the diary. Otto Frank would say many years later that he thought he had known his daughter quite well but that the diary revealed a person he had not really known at all. The poignancy of his statement makes Anne an even greater symbol of the mystery of individuality and of how precious and unique one life can be.

Although *Anne Frank Remembered* does full justice to the period of the Frank family's confinement in the attic, it deviates from the stage and film version of her life by spending nearly as much time on what happened to Anne and her family after they were betrayed to the Nazis. Interviews with camp survivors who befriended Otto Frank and his daughters (Anne's older sister Margo receives the least attention of all family members) make it possible to piece together those harrowing last days. Indeed, interview after interview recreates the feeling of a tragic story slowly revealing itself.

Ripped from their hiding place, packed into cattle cars, and dumped into the concentration camp, the Franks solidified. Several witnesses report that the tensions between Anne and her mother dissolved. They were as one in their suffering. Otto Frank remained in the camp what he had been all his life: a stalwart patriarch devising ways of surviving and triumphing over vicissitude. He counseled one camp inmate, Sal de Liema, to avoid a group of men obsessing about food. In their weakened condition these starving men would surely succumb if they remained fixated on their hunger. Instead, Otto advised his friend to think about music and the great composers, or about the museums he had visited—or anything that would take his mind off the camp and his present condition. In a revealing moment, Otto asked de Liema to call him Papa Frank. De Liema replied that he had a father whom he knew to be safely hidden from the Nazis. De Liema supposed that Otto was trying to bolster him. But Otto replied that it was for his own benefit that he asked Sal to call him papa. Otto Frank's identity was as a father, and he could not live without it. To the end of Otto's life, Sal continued to address him as Papa Frank.

Anne's story in the camps is unbearable, but it is told simply and with great dignity by the camp survivors. One of her friends, Hanneli Goslar, discovered that Anne was living on the other side of a barbed wire fence at Bergen-Belsen, and the two friends shouted to each other at night. Anne told Hanneli that Margo was dying. Anne's mother had already died of starvation and exhaustion, and Anne was ill—first with scabies and then most likely with typhoid. Because of illness she had missed a transport that would have taken her to a labor camp, where she probably would have survived the war. She died only a month before Bergen-Belsen was liberated.

After the war Otto Frank searched for his daughters for seven years before finally learning of their horrible fate. It was only then that his great friend, Miep Gies, who had worked for Otto and visited the family every day in their hiding place (a great act of heroism, but only one of several this courageous woman performed), told him of Anne's diary. It had been dumped out of Otto's briefcase by a Nazi officer who found the briefcase of more value than the diary, and Miep had recovered the diary the next day from the apartment's floor. Miep did not tell Otto of the diary's survival until Otto was certain of Anne's death. Why? She does not explain. But she does say that she did not read the diary—apparently safeguarding Anne's privacy as she had tried to protect her life. This is a great story of human integrity and the power of the word.

—*Carl Rollyson*

REVIEWS

Detroit News. March 29, 1996, p. 3D.
Los Angeles Times. February 23, 1996, p. F8.
New York Times. February 23, 1996, p.C5.
Variety. September 25, 1995, p. 95.
Village Voice. February 27, 1996, p. 66.

Antonia's Line

A motion picture that celebrates everything you love about life.—Movie tagline

"Wonderfully earthy, funny and sexy!"—Ken Tucker, *Entertainment Weekly*

"Beautiful, magical film! What a fairy tale!"—Kevin Thomas, *Los Angeles Times*

"Amazing! Compelling! Whimsical, magical & joyous."—Jack Mathews, *Newsday*

"Two thumbs up! A very special film!"—*Siskel & Ebert*

Box Office: $4,100,000

Director Marleen Gorris, whose prior films *A Question of Silence* (1983) and *Broken Mirrors* (1985) were characterized by angry feminism, softens her tone but not her themes with *Antonia's Line,* winner of the 1995 Best Foreign Language Film Academy Award. The Dutch-language film is perhaps one of the most enchanting stories in recent years, focusing on several generations of women in a rural village in the Netherlands. Marketed as a "women's film," *Antonia's Line* found success first at the Cannes and Toronto film festivals, and later with audiences everywhere. With the richly hued cinematography of Willy Stassen, the lush and haunting music by Ilona Sekacz, the outstanding screenplay and direction of Marleen Gorris, and the earthy, captivating central performances, this is not just a "women's film." Men who do not see it are missing a wonderful treat.

Antonia's Line is the tale of Antonia (Willeke van Ammelrooy) and her descendants. At the beginning of the film, Antonia is 90 years old, and knows that she will die today. She looks back over her life, and her story is told in flashback, beginning 50 years earlier, at the end of World War II. Antonia, widowed and accompanied by her young daughter, Danielle (Els Dottermans), returns to her hometown farming village to live the rest of her life. First, she reacquaints herself with the town's colorful residents. They include Loony Lips (Jan Steen), a simple worker who looks like Ichabod Crane; mentally retarded Deedee (a wonderfully touching Marina De Graaf); a kindly hermit (Mils Seghers) who teaches Danielle and her daughter and grandchild everything about life; Mad Madonna (Catherine ten Bruggencate), a crazy Protestant woman who howls at the moon; and Farmer Bas (Jan Decleir), who asks Antonia to marry him, but settles for a sexual arrangement when she tells him no. The story follows several generations of Antonia, as Danielle gives birth and Danielle's daughter gives birth. It is about women and their independence; about how men and women can co-exist if they treat each other with respect; about the importance of living with a healthy mixture of spirituality and individuality; and about the beauty of life and death.

"Mom, I want a child. But no husband to go with it."—Danielle

Gorris tells her tale with a sort of magic realism, similar to the mixture of reality and whimsy found in *Like Water for Chocolate* (1993). Gorris' magic is to make mundane people and situations seem mysterious and enchanted. She makes it appear as if her main characters have an unspoken, mystical connection to nature, underscoring how little we need to know about life's mysteries in order to be an integral part of the cycle of birth and death. One character quotes the bible: "she looketh well to her household and eateth not from the bread of idleness." Antonia lives simply, and like Voltaire's *Candide,* she makes her literal and metaphorical garden grow in wondrous ways.

Hardly a simpleminded, one-sided feminist treatise, Gorris makes the men in her film quite varied. Some are kind, some are not. Some are stupid, some are not. What the men all are, however, is not in control of Antonia's world, even though they are an integral part of it. When Farmer Bas asks Antonia to marry him because his five sons "need a mother," she replies, kindly, "but I don't need them." Gorris has included a villain in the form of a town rapist, who meets his comeuppance at the hands of Danielle and Antonia. Antonia's vengeance on him for the rape of her granddaughter is to curse him, and it is one of the most powerful moments in the film. Van Ammelrooy is frightening in her intensity as she, with astonishing control, tells him that "my curse will haunt you to death." Gorris' speech and Van Ammelrooy's delivery make this punishment far worse for the rapist than any revenge or violence. And sure enough, later in the film, nature obliges by destroying the young man and his wicked family.

Van Ammelrooy is a towering presence as Antonia: beautiful, earthy, wise, and independent. The actress does not overplay the strength of her character, however. For example, when she is delivering her harrowing speech to the rapist, gun in hand, Van Ammelrooy manages to convey a mother's fears underneath the immense pool of rage. The other actors are all exemplary, especially the bizarre cast of characters surrounding Antonia's family.

As the story progresses, Antonia's family takes on new members, all of whom eat at a huge table on the grounds of the farm she shares with them. By the time this wondrous film is through, you wish you were sitting there with them, surrounded by the luxurious Dutch landscape and living in the abundance created by the mixture of magic and realism of director Gorris' formidable talent.

—*Kirby Tepper*

CREDITS

Antonia: Wileke van Ammelrooy
Danielle: Els Dotermans
Sebastian: Jan DeClair
Crooked Finger: Mils Seghers
Deedee: Marina De Graaf
Therese: Veerle Van Overloop

Origin: Netherlands
Released: 1995
Production: Hans de Weers; released by First Look Pictures
Direction: Marleen Gorris
Screenplay: Marleen Gorris
Cinematography: Willy Stassen
Editing: Michel Reichwein, Wim Louwrier
Art direction: Harry Ammerlaan
Costumes: Jany Temme
Casting: Hans Kemna
Sound: Dirk Bombey
Music: Ilona Sekacz
MPAA rating: Unrated
Running Time: 105 minutes

REVIEWS

Boxoffice. November, 1995, p. 104.
Chicago Tribune. February 14, 1996, p. 1.
Los Angeles Times. February 2, 1996, p. F8.
New York Times. February 2, 1996, p. C18.
Village Voice. February 6, 1996, p. 48.
Washington Post. February 14, 1996, p. B2.

The Arrival

The greatest danger facing our world has been the planet's best kept secret . . . until now.—
Movie tagline

"It's out of this world!"—Jeanne Wolf, *Jeanne Wolf's Hollywood*

"A science fiction thriller that will keep you on the edge of your seat."—*Los Angeles Times*

"Two thumbs up!"—*Siskel & Ebert*

"Visually stunning and highly entertaining."—
Paul Wunder, *WBAI Radio*

Box Office: $14,063,331

The Arrival offers familiar science-fiction themes in an attractive new package. Zane Ziminski (Charlie Sheen), a nattily bearded radio astronomer, has an on-again-off-again relationship with the beautiful yuppie Char (Lindsay Crouse). She is a successful stockbroker but, like many contemporary career women, feels a pull towards matrimony and motherhood. Although she loves Zane, she is trying to break the spell because she feels he is too obsessed with his work to make a good husband and father.

Zane is so obsessed with his work that he often forgets Char exists. He spends most waking hours in his laboratory, hoping to pick up signals that have crossed space to disseminate advanced scientific knowledge or perhaps to signal distress on a dying planet.

Zane and his partner Calvin (Richard Schiff) are working in the wee morning hours when they pick up something dramatically different from the usual space static. There can be no doubt that these signals—whatever they mean—are coming from the stars. The two radio astronomers record them as proof of the existence of intelligent extraterrestrial life. When the ecstatic Zane communicates the discovery to his superior Gordian (Ron Silver), what follows is a scenario similar to that of the paranoia-classic *Three Days of the Condor* (1975). Far from being interested in disseminating Zane's discovery, Gordian destroys the cassette and orders the extermination of everyone who knows about the signals.

Zane is fired from the National Aeronautics and Space Administration on the pretext of cutbacks in government funding. (Critics have noted that the theme of downsizing gives the film a touch of social significance, as does the gradually unfolding theme of environmental pollution.) Calvin is murdered. Zane only escapes by luck. Without access to high-tech equipment, Zane has to improvise by pirating the private satellite dishes of his neighbors. He hooks them up so that, when the whole neighborhood is asleep, he can direct them toward the spot from which the space signals were emanating. When an inquisitive African-American neighbor lad named Kiki (Tony T. Johnson) begins snooping, Zane enlists him as an assistant. This allows the scriptwriter to dramatize his material by having Zane explain to his partner what he is trying to prove and how he hopes to prove it.

Too much explanation slows the pace of this sporadically exciting film—and yet the explanations fail to satisfy. The viewer leaves the theater still wondering why the talented aliens could not find a planet to colonize closer to home than fourteen-and-a-half light years and how they can flout Mr. Einstein's laws of physics so outrageously. (These are the two questions that still exercise the imaginations of diehards who believe flying saucers are "real.") If the earth had an exceptionally agreeable (i.e. totally poisonous) environment, that might partially answer the first question. It appears, however, that the earth has to be remade entirely before the space pilgrims begin to migrate in substantial numbers.

The answer to the question of why the aliens could not find a terraformable planet closer to home apparently has something to do with their bizarre morality. Gordian, who

CREDITS

Zane Ziminski: Charlie Sheen
Gordian: Ron Silver
Ilana Green: Lindsay Crouse
Char: Teri Polo
Calvin: Richard Schiff
Kiki: Tony T. Johnson

Origin: USA
Released: 1996
Production: Thomas G. Smith and Jim Steel for a Steelwork Films and Live Entertainment production; released by Orion
Direction: David Twohy
Screenplay: David Twohy
Cinematography: Hiro Narita
Editing: Martin Hunter
Music: Arthur Kempel
Production design: Michael Novotny
Art direction: Anthony Stabley, Hector Romero
Set decoration: Enrique Estevez, Hermilindo Hinojosa
Costume design: Mayes C. Rubeo
Sound: David Farmer
Visual effects: Charles L. Finance
MPAA rating: PG-13
Running Time: 109 minutes

is exposed as the alien mastermind in human disguise, explains that earthlings' rampant deforestation and atmospheric pollution are annihilating native life forms anyway; the invaders are only expediting the process. "If you don't tend to your own planet," he tells Zane, "maybe you don't deserve to live here." Extraterrestrials, like humans, have grown more complicated since the days of H. G. Wells's *War of the Worlds.* The Martians invaded the earth in Wells' novel for undisguised imperialistic motives. Nowadays, however, colonization is more insidious and apparently needs some moral justification.

Directorial debut of screenwriter David Twohy.

In the meantime, a climatologist named Ilana Green (Lindsay Crouse) has discovered that certain spots in Central and South America are producing unusually large quantities of noxious gases. She calculates that at the rate these gases are increasing they could destroy all life within a decade by raising the global temperature to intolerable levels. The ice caps at both poles would melt, producing a situation like that dramatized in *Waterworld* (1995). Ilana goes to Mexico to investigate one of the hot spots and encounters Zane, who is there because he has discovered that intergalactic signals are not only directed to that location but are being sent back on the same frequency.

Both scientists quickly find themselves in deep trouble. They have unwittingly discovered one of the secret underground bases of the alien invaders. Ilana is murdered by a weird medicine man who plants enormous black scorpions on the ceiling fan to be sprayed all over her hotel room when she flicks the switch. Zane is framed for her murder and barely manages to elude the Mexican police. In the interim he has boldly breached the security system of the phony "power generating plant" and has seen with his own eyes, and to his horror, exactly what is going on deep within the bowels of the earth.

The scenes inside the alien stronghold are by far the most exciting in the film. The special effects are impressive. The viewer is so caught up in Zane's emotions that he forgets his skepticism and stops asking, "How are they simulating all this?" Undoubtedly the camera is shooting the interior of a intricate model from close range, but the effect is like being inside a high-tech installation that would make the Pentagon look like a log cabin.

"If you can't tend to your own planet, maybe you don't deserve to live here."—alien invader

Evidently the extraterrestrials have developed a method of transmitting wireless signals immeasurably faster than the speed of light. They are in nightly contact with their home planet some eighty-five trillion miles away, give or take a few trillion. Furthermore, the mother planet is sending down translucent pods reminiscent of those in the classic science-fiction film *Invasion of the Body Snatchers* (1956). These pods contain more alien invaders in an embryonic state. Although it would take humans hundreds of lifetimes to travel that distance, the pods keep arriving by overnight delivery. The cold-blooded scheme is to use advanced technology to disguise the new arrivals in human forms and send them out to mingle with the unsuspecting earthlings. There is no way of telling how many of these moles have, like Gordian himself, already obtained sensitive jobs. Anybody could be an intergalactic invader—even the President of the United States.

Those aliens who stay underground to operate the invasion base do not need to take on human forms. They are like ants that never leave the nest or bees that never leave the hive. Humanity's conception of extraterrestrials has become standardized after years of reported flying-saucer sightings and alien abductions. The undisguised aliens in *The Arrival* resemble those described in Whitney Strieber's book *Communion,* made into a film of the same title in 1989. They seem more dispassionate than wicked. They have opaque, almond-shaped eyes. They are hairless, asexual, anoretic, hyper-cerebral, and not very talkative. When they do converse they emit clicks and clacks which sound a little like Donald Duck and threaten to break the tension with unintended comedy. Their legs resemble the hind legs of antelopes. Presumably because of earth's lower gravity, they are capable of spectacular leaps, even after adopting human forms.

Zane's problem, after he manages to escape from this den of horrors, is to communicate his discovery to the unsuspecting world. Like the hero of *Invasion of the Body Snatchers,* he has such a wild story to tell, and such a wild look in his eyes to go with it, that nobody will believe him. The aliens come from a planet where the natural atmosphere is what humans would consider poisonous and intolerably hot. The invaders plan to terraform the earth (or de-terraform it) by duplicating the noxious, torrid atmosphere they enjoy at home. This will kill off all indigenous life but make the earth an ideal place for the invaders to colonize.

Zane has become so paranoid that he suspects his own girlfriend Char of being an alien in disguise. She, in turn, suspects him of being totally insane. Working at cross-purposes, they play right into the hands of Gordian and his myrmidons, who corner the couple at an isolated radio astronomy facility. Zane is trying desperately to broadcast a taped conversation in which Gordian confesses his true identity and reveals the motive and strategy behind the invasion.

In addition to being chased by Gordian, Zane is also being hunted by the police as a fugitive from Mexican justice. He believes the only person he can trust is the cute, sassy little Kiki, who has stayed loyal in spite of all risks. At the crucial moment, however, Zane finds that there is such a thing as not being paranoid enough.

In the final spectacular scene, Zane and Char, out in the middle of nowhere, are trapped on a huge, dazzlingly white listening dish which is collapsing beneath their feet. Zane and Char have been bonded by their shared danger and will presumably be married if they should somehow manage to survive their present predicament. It is only by a last-minute inspiration that Zane copes with his assailants and manages to broadcast a widely televised message that humanity might still have a chance to save itself from extermination.

—*Bill Delaney*

REVIEWS

Boxoffice Magazine. July, 1996, p. 90.
Detroit Free Press. June 2, 1996, p. 9F.
Entertainment Weekly. June 7, 1996, p. 39.
The Hollywood Reporter. June 4, 1996, p. 8.
Los Angeles Times. May 31, 1996, pp. F2, F20.
The New York Times. May 31, 1996, p. C10.
Sight and Sound. March, 1997, p. 40.
Variety. June 3, 1996, p. 50.

The Associate

Behind every great man is a woman . . . Wishing he'd get the hell out of her way.—Movie tagline

"Dazzling! A must-see!"—Ron Brewington, *American Urban Radio Networks*

"Hilarious!"—Bryon Allen, *Entertainers*

"Outrageously funny! A winner!"—Paul Wunder, *WBAI Radio*

"Whoopi Goldberg delivers a hysterical performance!"—Kathryn Kinley, *WPIX-TV*

Box Office: $12,700,000

Whoopi Goldberg is not Hollywood's best actress, but she keeps working while more talented, more fussy actresses wait for the phone to ring. Whoopi's secret, as her zany name seems to suggest, is that she is willing to try anything. Stephen Holden, who reviewed *The Associate* for the *New York Times,* calls her ". . . a living, breathing smile button with dreadlocks and smart, dancing eyes." Although she often seems miscast and hopelessly mired in goofy situations, her indefatigable drive at least gets her through to the closing credits. In *The Associate* she disguises herself as a seventy-year-old white male. Impossible? Absolutely. But she does it just the same.

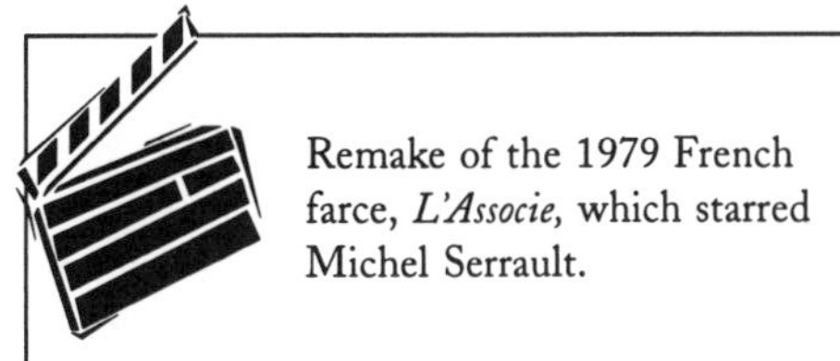

Remake of the 1979 French farce, *L'Associe,* which starred Michel Serrault.

Whoopi, as Laurel Ayres, an unappreciated financial genius, gets tired of having her smarmy male co-worker steal the credit for her moneymaking ideas. She realizes that as a woman—and a black woman at that—she has two strikes against her in any Wall Street firm, so she sets up an investment advisory service in her Brooklyn Heights apartment. She owns the building and has to mortgage it to raise the capital to get her enterprise off the ground. But she still gets no respect. She is in danger of going bankrupt until she hits on the idea of inventing a white male partner whom she names Robert S. Cutty, after the Scotch whiskey. She has to hack her way into various computer networks to create a fictitious biography, including a Harvard degree, for her nonexistent partner.

All of the sudden Laurel is receiving six-figure certified checks from grateful clients who are all clamoring to meet the eccentric, elusive male mastermind to whom Laurel is attributing all the credit. The film jump-cuts Laurel from her cramped quarters into a prestigious Manhattan high-rise. She hires her former secretary Sally (Dianne Wiest), an unrecognized genius in her own right, to manage all business affairs. Everything is going beautifully—except that Laurel's clients and the media keep insisting on meeting Cutty in person. They still consider Laurel, the real genius, little more than a glorified secretary.

Her former colleague and present arch-rival Frank (Tim Daly) creates a crisis when he informs the Securities Exchange Commission that Cutty may be guilty of white-collar crimes, including the felonious offense of insider trading. Laurel must produce Cutty—or else! Instead of thinking of the obvious ploy of hiring a stooge, Laurel decides to impersonate Cutty herself. A transvestite friend, who is a genius with makeup, shrieks with dismay at the magnitude of the miracle he is expected to perform. Finally the audience gets to see the ghastly-white Robert S. Cutty—who looks worse than the reclusive billionaire genius Howard Hughes was reputed to look shortly before he died.

Most of the laughs develop when Whoopi makes her appearance as Cutty. This inevitable event is delayed until the last possible moment. The filmmakers obviously realized that the situation could only be milked for an half-hour at most. Unfortunately, the climax is not as funny as the long build-up promises. The problem is that the star is so heavily disguised that no one can recognize her as Whoopi Goldberg. Only Cutty's incongruous yard-long ponytail suggests that there might be a woman hidden under that elaborate facade.

When Lucille Ball concocted a disguise in one of her television skits, the audience could easily see through it even if her ingenuous husband could not. When Robin Williams disguises himself as a woman in *Mrs. Doubtfire* (1993), the audience is always aware that Mrs. Doubtfire is really Robin Williams with a stuffed bosom. The same principle applied to Dustin Hoffman in *Tootsie* (1982) and Julie Andrews impersonating a man impersonating a woman in *Victor/Victoria* (1982). When Whoopi appears as an elderly white male, however, the audience is nonplussed, suspecting that Laurel Ayres has hired a weird-looking actor to impersonate her fictitious partner.

By this point Cutty has gotten so much media hype that, very much like Peter Sellers in *Being There* (1979), the eccentric financial wizard does not really have to do anything. Every hoarse word Cutty utters is received with gratitude by his greedy, fawning admirers. The disguised Laurel soon finds herself being awarded the coveted Man-of-the-Year award by an exclusive men's club whose rules prohibit women from penetrating beyond the front lobby. The point of the story is made when Laurel, holding her trophy at the glitzy black-tie banquet, reveals her identity to prove that a woman—and/or an African-American—can be every bit as capable as a white male if given a level playing field.

This is the sort of comedy that was often hilarious when Lucille Ball did it on "I Love Lucy." But her perennially popular television sitcoms last for only about twenty-five minutes (subtracting for commercials), whereas *The Associate* runs for nearly two hours. This sporadically funny film about gender discrimination in the world of big business does not have enough substance to beguile anyone but the most avid Whoopi Goldberg fan for such a long stretch.

—*Bill Delaney*

Brilliant financial broker Laurel Ayres (Whoopi Goldberg) won't let her gender stand in the way of success in *The Associate.*

CREDITS

Laurel Ayres: Whoopi Goldberg
Sally: Dianne Wiest
Frank: Tim Daly
Fallon: Eli Wallach
Camille: Bebe Neuwirth
Cindy Mason: Lainie Mason

Origin: USA
Released: 1996
Production: Frederic Golchan, Patrick Markey, Adam Leipzig for a Interscope Communications and Polygram Filmed Entertainment production; released by Hollywood Pictures
Direction: Donald Petrie
Screenplay: Nick Thiel; based on the motion picture *L'Associe* and the novel *El Socio* by Jenaro Prieto
Cinematography: Alex Nepomniaschy
Editing: Bonnie Koehler
Music: Christopher Tyng
Production design: Andrew Jackness
Art direction: Phil Messina
Costume design: April Ferry
Sound: Rosa Howell-Thornhill
Casting: Mary Colquhoun
MPAA rating: PG-13
Running Time: 113 minutes

REVIEWS

Boxoffice Online. October 25, 1996.
Detroit Free Press. October 25, 1996.
Detroit News. October 25, 1996, p. D1.
Entertainment Weekly. November 1, 1996, p. 41.
Los Angeles Times. October 25, 1996, p. F6.
New York Times. October 25, 1996, p. C14.
People. November 4, 1996, p. 29.
USA Today. October 25, 1996, p. 5D.
Variety. October 21, 1996, p. 83.
Village Voice. November 5, 1996, p. 78.

August

You can live a whole lifetime in a single week-end.—Movie tagline

"Anthony Hopkins makes an auspicious directorial debut. A story of romance, emotion and sexual tension."—Susan Granger, *CRN International*

"Hopkins proves he's as fine a director as he is an Oscar-winning actor."—Bonnie Churchill, *National News Syndicate*

"Hopkins plays his character with genius!"—Anita Peltonen, *Time Out New York*

"Hopkins is marvelous! This show is all his own."—Leslie Camhi, *Village Voice*

Box Office: $69,081

When Emma Thompson accepted the Academy Award for her screen adaptation Jane Austen's *Sense and Sensibility* (1995), she cited visiting the original author's tomb in order to "pay my respects and tell her about the grosses." Someone ought to do the same for Anton Chekhov, whose play *Uncle Vanya,* written just prior to the turn of the twentieth century, has been reincarnated twice in the last two years and now again with Anthony Hopkins' version entitled *August.*

"Scribble, scribble, scribble. Makes you feel sorry for the paper, doesn't it?"—Ieuen about his brother-in-law's habits

Michael Blakemore's *Country Life* (1995) set the events in Australia, whereas Louis Malle took Chekhov not just to New York City, but backstage of the production itself in *Uncle Vanya on 42nd Street* (1994). Hopkins transports Chekhov's Vanya to Wales and changes his name to the more local Ieuan (pronounced YAH-Yin). Here, even the dim horrors of the Welsh coal mines pale in comparison to the melancholy personalities of the community's most prosperous family.

Uncle Ieuan, for years has managed the estate of his brother-in-law, retired professor Alexander Blathwaite (Leslie Phillips). As the widow of his beloved sister and the father of his niece and co-worker in the family business, Blathwaite has been revered by Ieuan as the shining star of the family—the one that got out of Wales and made a name for himself in academia. Unasked, Ieuan sacrificed his own dreams to serve the ever increasing needs of the family estate and of the professor. When Blathwaite suddenly returns to the country with a beautiful, young second wife and plans to sell the home Ieuan has toiled all these years to maintain, Ieuan finally realizes that his brother-in-law is something of a fraud. He has received his life gifts too easily and will fritter them away thoughtlessly, unless Ieuan can do something about it.

His plan, however, is a marvel of self delusion. Ieuan attempts to woo Blathwaite's bored, taken for granted and needlessly surly wife Helen (Kate Burton), ignoring the signs that she perceives him as laughable. Furthermore, if Helen was going to cheat on her husband, she would do so with the more exciting village physician, Dr. Lloyd (Gawn Grainger), despite her step-daughter Sian's (Rhian Morgan) unrequited attachment to him. When Blathwaite casually and callously announces his plan to sell the estate, Ieuan attempts to reason for mere seconds before grabbing his rifle in an unsuccessful attempt to shoot his brother-in-law. Later, suicide seems perfectly reasonable. Failing even that, Ieuan reconciles himself to his lot and, amid heavy sighs, continues with the drudgery that will keep him and his relatives in room, board and comparative luxury, as well as gloom, doom and despair.

Original playwright, Anton Chekhov spent most of his short

CREDITS

Ieuan Davies: Anthony Hopkins
Helen Blathwaite: Kate Burton
Professor Alexander Blathwaite: Leslie Phillips
Dr. Michael Lloyd: Gwen Grainger
Sian Blathwaite: Rhian Morgan
Mair Davies: Rhoda Lewis

Origin: Great Britain
Released: 1996
Production: June Wyndham Davies, Pippa Cross for a Majestic Films/Newcomm and Granada production; released by Samuel Goldwyn Company
Direction: Anthony Hopkins
Screenplay: Julian Mitchell; based on the play *Uncle Vanya* by Anton Chekov
Cinematography: Robin Vidgeon
Editing: Edward Mansell
Music: Anthony Hopkins
Production design: Eileen Diss
Costume design: Dany Everett
Sound: Rudy Buckle
Casting: Carolyn Bartlett, Cheryl Nance, Wally Byatt
MPAA rating: PG
Running Time: 93 minutes

life battling tuberculosis, of which he died at age 44. Via Julian Mitchell's screenplay, Chekhov taps exceptionally well into the frustration of age, despite having written the play while in his mid-thirties. Anthony Hopkins enriches the premise with his appearance of genuine aging and exhaustion of body and spirit. Less sympathetic in this plight is actress Kate Burton, whose Helen seems neither old enough nor tired enough to do all the complaining she does. Bringing full circle what may have been an overwhelming psychological disparity between the playwright's youth and ill health, is Sian, the professor's daughter by his first wife and Ieuan's niece. Though fresh, young and passionate, Sian is dismissed by her family as "plain" and therefore unmarriageable and useless for anything other than labor in the family business. Resigned to their beliefs and trapped by her circumstances, Sian's life is over before it has begun, which is perhaps how Chekhov might have felt knowing his own days were numbered.

Not only does Academy Award-winning actor Anthony Hopkins act the lead in *August,* but he also debuts as its director and composer. But even with the usually exuberant and always brilliant Hopkins guiding cast, crew and screenwriter Julian Mitchell, this British adaptation of Anton Chekhov's play, *Uncle Vanya,* cannot be anything other than a relentlessly depressing story.

—*Eleah Horwitz*

Anthony Hopkins makes his directorial debut and composed the film's score.

REVIEWS

Boxoffice. July, 1996, p. 96.
The Los Angeles Times. April 19, 1996. p. F16.
The New York Times. April 19, 1996, p. C3.
Variety. April 15, 1996, p. 179.
Village Voice. April 23, 1996, p. 80.

Bad Moon

Half man. Half wolf. Total terror.—Movie tagline

Box Office: $1,055,525

The first scene of *Bad Moon* is also its most sensationalistic: in a pre-credit sequence set in the Amazon and obviously designed to hook the audience, photojournalist Ted Harrison (Michael Pare) and his girlfriend have set their camp for the night. They are enjoying an energetic bout of lovemaking when an enormous werewolf rips apart their tent, kills the woman, and bites into Ted before he manages to fire off shots to kill it. This combination of sex and violence seems to promise a lightweight, action-filled horror film, but *Bad Moon* soon turns into something unexpected.

After the credits, a helicopter shot singles out a suburban house in the Pacific northwest. Also selecting the house is a con artist, who soon finds he has chosen the wrong family to cheat. He pretends that Thor, a likable German shepherd, has attacked him, but Janet (Mariel Hemingway), a single mother, happens to be a lawyer who knows about this particular scam. She restrains both her dog and her ten-year-old son Brett (Mason Gamble) while sending away the small-time crook with the threat of legal action. It develops that Janet is Ted Harrison's sister, and she and Brett soon drive off to visit Uncle Ted at a wooded lake. Ted makes cryptic remarks about "me and my shadow," and Brett, taking a tour of Ted's Airstream trailer, finds vials of blood samples and a book on werewolves. When Janet tries to invite him to visit, Ted balks, but the next day, after the police discover a ripped body in the woods, he calls her and accepts.

The filmmaker's emphasis in these early scenes falls more on the single-parent family of Janet, Brett, and Thor than on Ted and his nocturnal prowls as a werewolf. This unexpected viewpoint produces some scenes that fail to lead anywhere. For example, after Ted has settled his trailer behind Janet's house, she notices a pair of strong handcuffs in his backpack but oddly fails to satisfy her curiosity by asking for an explanation. Later, Janet noses among her brothers' possessions and finds Ted's journal and the photographs of a bloodied body. In the journal she reads that her brother has been experiencing blackouts and waking covered with blood that is not his own. She also reads that he hopes a visit to the people who love him the most will put his "disease into remission." His journal refers to this visit as his last chance. Implausibly, none of these dire signs prompts Janet to question Ted.

Each night after Ted's arrival, Thor barks furiously, requiring Janet to release him from the house. Running toward the woods, the dog comes upon a giant werewolf handcuffed to a tree behind the trailer. The next morning the local news carries reports of dead hikers. The most interesting and subtle scene in the film occurs next, as Ted and Brett watch a classic movie, *Werewolf of London* (1935) on television. Ted scoffs at werewolf lore involving silver bullets and full moons, and Brett, sensing perhaps that his uncle speaks with firsthand knowledge, listens with widening eyes.

"We're two of a kind, pal."—Ted (the werewolf) to Thor the German shepherd

The film telegraphs the identity of Ted's next victim when the con artist from the opening scene, Jerry Mills (Hrothgar Mathews), improbably turns up in the woods. The shadow of the enormous werewolf looms behind him, and his murder sets off a new plotline in which the local sheriff (Ken Pogue) suspects Thor of the string of recent killings. Because Ted senses that Thor knows about his lycanthropy, he cooperates with this unknowing frame-up by provoking the dog into an attack with merely a well-timed wink. The animal control experts convince Janet that Thor must be taken off to the pound. The best-designed shot of the film occurs after Thor has been led away, as Janet looks doubtfully out her kitchen window, the reflection of Ted's giant Airstream trailer ominously covering her worried face.

Part of the overall disappointment of the film owes to the confusion between the marketing strategy on the one hand and the source material and its adaptation on the other. The film is based on the novel *Thor* by Wayne Smith, a book that develops as primarily a tale about a boy and his dog. After the pre-credit sequence which shows Ted being bitten, the film seems to adhere rather faithfully to the novel, even to a last-minute escape and rescue that Thor brings off. The marketing campaign for the film, however, clearly showcased the motion picture as a horror film, and the film was released in 825 theaters the weekend after Halloween. The marketing slogan for the film was "half man, half wolf, total terror." Both the title and the poster art—a moon behind sinister dark clouds—suggest a werewolf drama. For an audience expecting a special-effects-driven horror film, the first scene after the credits, in which Janet outsmarts the con artist, can only seem to be a distraction. The development of the film then makes Ted more peripheral to the action while Janet, Brett, and Thor assume center stage. When the big special-effects transformation scene occurs toward the end, few in the audience will not have had their patience tried by the way the film has more tamely reinvented itself. The decision of Warner Brothers to release *Bad Moon* with no advance screenings for reviewers may have resulted from a recognition of the oddly hybrid nature of the film.

What is worse is the way the film teases the audience with hints of returning to the werewolf story more fully, only to remain focused on the plotline of Brett and Thor. Some of these teases occur in scenes between Ted and Thor, mostly when Ted leaves the trailer and Thor blocks his way. Director Eric Red cuts back and forth between a closeup of Ted's look of uncertainty and a closeup of the dog, who emits a low growl. Ted descends a few steps, and Thor tenses suddenly, his growl growing louder. This signals another round of matching closeups between Ted and Thor as they try to outguess the other. One such scene occurs at sunset, when Ted is anxious to handcuff himself to a tree, but the cutaways to the horizon and the setting sun fail to inject the needed suspense. The point of Ted and Thor sharing a canine-wolfman telepathy has been made earlier in the film, and these matching shots needlessly belabor a redundant scene.

The same teasing applies to the scenes in which Ted chains himself to the large tree. The audience is never shown his transformation into the werewolf until fairly late in the film, and the efforts to create suspense in a number of scenes become nothing more than morning-after closeups of Ted's tattered jogging sweats, his ripped Reeboks, his bloodied

CREDITS

Janet: Mariel Hemingway
Ted: Michael Pare
Brett: Mason Gamble
Jerry Mills: Hrothgar Mathews
Sheriff Jenson: Ken Pogue
Thor: Primo

Origin: USA
Released: 1996
Production: James G. Robinson and Jacobus Rose for Morgan Creek Productions; released by Warner Bros.
Direction: Eric Red
Screenplay: Eric Red; based on the novel *Thor* by Wayne Smith III
Cinematography: Jan Kiesser
Editing: Carroll Timothy O'Meara
Production design: Linda Del Rosario, Richard Paris
Loek Dikker: Daniel Licht
Costume design: Tracey Boulton, Rita Riggs
Sound: David Husby
Special makeup effects supervisor: Steve Johnson
MPAA rating: R
Running Time: 79 minutes

sweatshirt. Intercut with some of these scenes is the talking head of a local newscaster, who dully informs the audience about the savage work of what is still thought to be a grizzly bear. The filmmakers' attempts to generate suspense in such transparent ways miscarry badly.

The climax of the film occurs when Brett sneaks out of the house at night and pedals off on his bike to let Thor out of the pound. This rescue coincides with Ted's growing malevolence and Janet's mounting fear. She takes a gun to the woods and witnesses her brother's transformation into a werewolf. Much of the drama of this long-awaited special effect is lost in Ted's banal last words to Janet, which make up the most wincingly bad line in the film: "You should have listened to the dog." Brett helps Thor out of the pound, and as they return home, the film crosscuts between the running dog and the menacing werewolf, who has by now followed Janet into the house. The final fight has the savor of an old-time movie serial, as Thor comes to the rescue and Ted limps off into the darkness. The next day Thor finds him scratched and bloodied, and with another of Ted's telepathic looks, Thor pounces on the willing Ted and finally kills him. The last scene reunites the family of mother, son, and dog.

Things can change under a full moon, and *Bad Moon* pulls a transformation itself from its exploitative opening scene to its oddly old-fashioned and slow-paced story of a boy and his dog.

—Glenn Hopp

REVIEWS

Detroit Free Press. November 3, 1996, p. 4G.
The Hollywood Reporter. November 4, 1996, p. 9.
Los Angeles Times. November 2, 1996, p. F4.
New York Times. November 2, 1996, p. 16N.
Variety. November 11, 1996, p. 59.

Barb Wire

No laws. No limits. No turning back.—Movie tagline

Box Office: $3,800,000

Pamela Anderson Lee has advanced her career a great deal in a relatively short period of time. The Vancouver native was perhaps the only person in television history to be the cast member of the number one show in America ("Home Improvement") and the number one show in the world ("Baywatch") at the same time. She is also the constituent of a very minute, distinct group of people who have (despite that lack of any noticeable acting talent) been given a lead role in their first major studio film. She's also gone through a great deal of cosmetic surgery, begun a very scandalous marriage to a notorious rock star and assumed the lofty throne as world's highest profile twinkie. Who ever cast her in *Barb Wire* knew exactly what they were doing.

Barb Wire is yet another entry in the comic book cum feature length action adventure film. Typically, films of this nature are desperately thin on a cohesive plot and rely almost exclusively on exaggerated visuals. Of all the recent comic book adaptations, only Warren Beatty's *Dick Tracy* (1990) gets close to having an interesting, original story to accompany its luscious scenery. *Barb Wire* does have something of an interesting story. It's just not original. In fact, one might be tempted to say that the story plagiarizes, almost to the letter, one of the most recognizable, successful movies of all time. More on that later.

To be fair, the movie isn't as bad as it could have been, but it's close. It is set in the year 2017 during the second American Civil War in a fictional town called Steel Harbor, the country's only "free city." Barb (Lee) owns the Hammerhead Bar and Grille, a dark, gloomy, speed metal/leather establishment in the grungy downtown area of Steel Harbor. When she's not running the bar, she's an expert gun for hire. Lee reportedly suggested to director David Hogan that the best way to introduce her multi-faceted character into the story was to hang upside down from a swinging trapeze in a rubber dress that shrinks when it's hosed down. With Lee's curves threatening to explode from her outfit, the proper tone is set: Soakin' Wet Bitchin' Biker Babes (a portion of the *Barb Wire* press kit actually features advertisements for Triumph motorcycles).

Three or four times throughout the movie, various characters [mistakenly] try to grab Barb's attention by addressing her as "Babe." This is where Lee strikes her best badass pose. In what could be her attempt at becoming the 90's version of [a female] Dirty Harry, Lee retorts, with clenched teeth and deadpan monotone, "Don't call me babe," and violently disposes of them. It's kind of hard not to call her "babe," considering her provocative wardrobe, augmented body parts and bad dye job. The essential ingredients in all celluloid forms of famous comic books are a lack of pretentiousness, a little tongue-in-cheek humor and a whole lot of camp. *Barb Wire* is completely devoid of all three. It takes itself way too seriously.

One thing it is not lacking in is gumption. With nary a detail out of place, *Barb Wire*'s story line is a carbon copy of *Casablanca* (1942). While serving the dregs and vagabonds of Steel Harbor, former freedom fighter Barbara Kopetski (Wire) comes face-to-face with her long lost flame, Axel (Temura Morrison). Axel, who has just blown into town with his new wife, a renegade scientist named Cora D (Victoria Rowell), is seeking safe passage to Canada. Lee takes on the role of Humphrey Bogart's Rick—a lonely, sullen, slightly bitter nightclub owner. Morrison assumes Ingrid Bergman's Ilsa, who was torn between two loves. Paul Henreid's part, the (mostly) thankless role as Ilsa's husband Victor Laszlo, an upstanding moralist leader with a cause, but very little else, is given to Rowell.

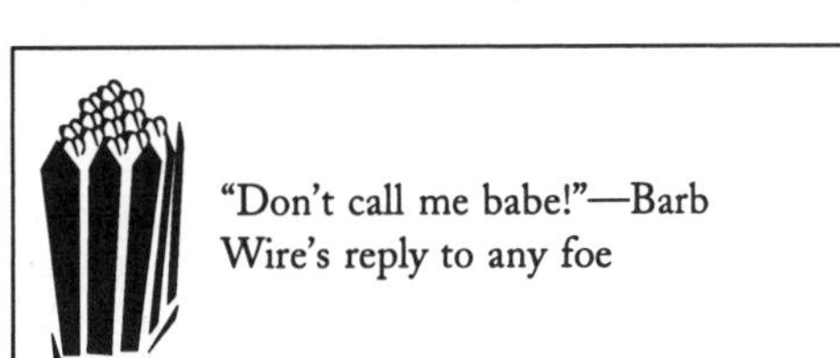

CREDITS

Barb Wire: Pamela Anderson Lee
Axel: Temuera Morrison
Cora D: Victoria Rowell
Charlie: Jack Noseworthy
Alexander Willis: Xander Berkely
Curly: Udo Kier
Col. Pryzer: Steve Railsback
Schmitz: Clint Howard

Origin: USA
Released: 1996
Production: Mike Richardson, Todd Moyer, Brad Wyman for a Propaganda/Dark Horse Entertainment and Polygram Filmed Entertainment production; released by Gramercy Pictures
Direction: David Hogan
Screenplay: Chuck Pfarrer, Ilene Chaiken; based on the Dark Horse comic book
Cinematography: Rick Bota
Editing: Peter Schink
Music: Michel Colombier
Production design: Jean-Philippe Carp
Art direction: Dins Danielson
Set design: Patricia Klawonn
Costume design: Rosanna Norton
Sound: Vince Garcia
Casting: Rick Montgomery, Dan Parada
MPAA rating: R
Running Time: 99 minutes

Next on the scene is Schmitz, a greasy sleazeball bail-bondsman, portrayed by a severely miscast Clint Howard, taking on the short-lived but indelible role turned in by Peter Lorre. Howard's sniveling attempts at being menacing fall desperately short of the classic wide-eyed, weasel-trapped-in-the-corner paranoia of Lorre's Ugarte. Mercifully, Howard's character fades away almost as quickly as it appears.

The most interesting character in *Barb Wire* is Alexander Willis (Xander Berkeley). He mirrors the is-he-a-good-guy-or-is-he-a-bad-guy role of Captain Louis Renault (immortalized by Claude Rains) in *Casablanca.* Alexander and Barb exist in something of a forced, uncomfortable alliance that Louis and Rick endured. Berkeley has had small roles in a great many successful projects (*A Few Good Men* [1992], *Leaving Las Vegas* [1995], and *Heat* [1995]) and truly deserves a role that will take advantage of his everyman appeal. Berkeley's Alexander has the ability to get Barb into and out of more than a few sticky situations and she handles him with kid gloves. Like Louis, Alexander is something of a weasel who will do the right thing, if he can see some kind of strategic or monetary profit as a result. Credit must be given to Berkeley; as was the case with Rains' Louis, you don't know which way he'll go until the final reel. The artistic pinching goes overboard as Alexander plays mediator between Barb and a band of gestapo-like police dressed completely in Nazi garb. The foreboding, futuristic SS men is a bit much to swallow.

The key to Victor and Ilsa's successful escape from *Casablanca* were the proper travelling papers, "signed by General Charles DeGaulle himself." With Ugarte out of the picture, Rick and Louis attempt to bargain with Ferrari (Sydney Greenstreet). Unlike Louis, Ferrari was a completely contemptible man who prostitutes his products and services ad infinitum. In what could be the least flattering film homage of all time, the producers cast Andre Rosey Brown as "Big Fatso," the man who possesses the almighty contact lenses. Fatso resides in a junkyard and must be "driven" to his meetings in the mouth of a front-loading, Caterpillar earth-moving machine. Despite his girth, Greenstreet was marginally fashionable. Chomping on junk food while wearing mascara that would embarrass Alice Cooper, Brown takes the parody beyond humor, beyond homage, beyond the resemblance of anything close to good taste.

Dooley Wilson, who played the always accommodating lounge singer at Rick's Place and regularly provided Rick with advice in matters of the heart is given his treatment in *Barb Wire* by the longtime B-movie stalwart, Udo Kier. As the club's maitre d', Kier's Curly is Barb's chief assistant, simultaneously keeping a watchful eye on the club's liquor cabinet and Barb's various wardrobe selections.

The movie's final scene takes place on, where else, a rainy, windswept airport runway. Reports of numerous rewrites of the final pages of the *Casablanca* script threatened to squash the finished product. The essence and spirit of the final print is found in that famous last scene: a tragedy that is uplifting. The ending of *Barb Wire* is rather academic, considering everything that precedes it.

If imitation is indeed the sincerest form of flattery, *Barb Wire* deserves high marks for its sheer chutzpah and unflinching audacity. Ditto to Pamela Anderson Lee, who obviously is aware of her limitations, but is clawing her way to the top of the junk heap anyway, artistic standards be damned. With her unrelenting drive and shameless self promotion, she would be better served to pool her talents with a writer-director team who could best utilize her more obvious charms. Joe Eszterhas and Paul Verhoeven, are you listening?

—J.M. Clark

REVIEWS

Entertainment Weekly. May 10, 1996, p. 51.
Los Angeles Times. May 3, 1996, p. F4.
New York Times. May 3, 1996, p. C18.
Sight and Sound. June, 1996, p. 34.
Variety. May 6, 1996, p. 81.

Basquiat

In 1981, a nineteen-year-old unknown graffiti writer took the New York art world by storm. The rest is art history.—Movie tagline

"Two thumbs way up!"—*Siskel & Ebert*

"Don't miss it!"—*WBAI Radio*

Box Office: $3,011,195

Basquiat tells of the rise of 1980s street artist Jean Michel Basquiat. Written and directed by Julian Schnabel, himself big in the pop art culture of the '80s, his feature film debut is unsympathetic and confusing. Jean Michel Basquiat was a pop icon, yet he lived life as a drug addict on the streets of New York. The film shows us Jean Michel's ascent from graffiti artist to Andy Warhol contemporary. A heavy drug user, Basquiat died in 1988 at the age of 27 from a heroin overdose.

The wig worn by David Bowie, who portrays Andy Warhol, was one of Warhol's actual wigs.

AWARDS AND NOMINATIONS

Independent Spirit Awards 1997: Supporting Actor (Del Toro)
Nominations: Debut Performance (Wright)

Schnabel never fleshes out the character of Basquiat (Jeffrey Wright) or analyzes his life. The film does not explore the inner man or the demons that must be plaguing him. The film briefly touches on his institutionalized mother, but does not expound on her influence in his life. There is the unanswered question of why Jean Michel, who bought caviar by the pound, still chose to live as a street rogue. The film poses two possible scenarios for the ill-fated artist: that Basquiat was either a victim of his own self-destruction, or a pawn of his exploitive surroundings, someone on whom to make money.

What Schnabel loses in film content and context, he makes up for in brilliant performances. *Basquiat* stars Jeffrey Wright (a Tony-award winner for "Angels in America") as the unassuming Jean Michel Basquiat; Benicio Del Toro as Benny Dalmau, Basquiat's best friend; David Bowie as a superbly convincing Andy Warhol; Dennis Hopper, in a refreshing change of character, as Andy Warhol's confused and nervous agent, Bruno Bischofberger; Parker Posey as Mary Boone, a snob of the art world who cares only about cashing in on the new, young artist; Gary Oldman as the self-absorbed Albert Milo, a form of director/artist Schnabel; and Michael Wincott, as poet-critic, Rene Ricard. It is Ricard who coins the film's manifesto, "nobody wants to be part of a generation that ignores another Van Gogh." Tatum O'Neal and Chuck Pfeifer have cameos as art patron wanna-bes, who have the witless attitude that if they're told it's art, then it must be art.

As Jean Michel creates a following, Wright handles his Basquiat smartly with the obtuse people into whose world he is now forced. One of the lighter scenes of the film has an uncomfortable Jean Michel as the subject of an interview. The interviewer (Christopher Walken) asks, "Do you consider yourself a painter or a black painter?" To this, Jean Michel intelligently answers, "I use other colors, not just black."

"No one wants to be part of a generation that ignores another Van Gogh."—Critic Rene Ricard

The film is loaded with banal imagery that seems only to exist for the sake of including imagery. The opening scene with a young Jean Michel wearing a crown of glowing gold while observing a Picasso seems to signify that he is next in line to inherit the kingdom. However, it is arguable that Basquiat is the next Picasso. Other images of a surfer riding waves in the sky, then plunging into the surf might signify Basquiat's own wave of fortune, yet not being able to hold on. The images, though, are awkward and do not add much to the film.

There are disturbing scenes of Jean Michel in a drug-induced hallucinogenic state that are difficult to watch. The director seems to be telling the audience to glorify a man who got many of his images from a drug-induced stupor. Perhaps this is a reflection of the underground art world of the 1980s to which the general public was not privy.

As in every film about a man who is down on his luck, there is the girlfriend who, despite knowing his dark side, sees the good in him and stands by him even through the ugliest times. Here, she is warmly portrayed by Claire Forlani, the waitress he meets at a diner. Yet, it is unclear how she can fall in love with this man so quickly, especially when he is merely a street urchin when they meet. Perhaps it is the old cliche of seeing the good in someone and knowing one day he will amount to something. Although, at this point, it is a very far-fetched idea.

If Jean Michel Basquiat was an important artist of an important decade in the art world, *Basquiat* falls short of creating a tribute to someone who made such an impact. The film does not delve deep enough into the man who most of the general public has never heard of.

—Debbi Hoffman

CREDITS

Jean Michel Basquiat: Jeffery Wright
Rene Ricard: Michael Wincott
Benny Dalmau: Benicio Del Toro
Gina Cardinale: Claire Forlani
Andy Warhol: David Bowie
Bruno Bischofberger: Dennis Hopper

Origin: USA
Released: 1996
Production: Jon Kilik, Randy Ostrow and Joni Sighvatsson for a Peter Brant/Joseph Allen production; released by Miramax
Direction: Julian Schnabel
Screenplay: Julian Schnabel; based on a story by Lech Majewski
Cinematography: Ron Fortunato
Editing: Michael Berenbaum
Music: John Cale
Production design: Dan Leigh
Art direction: C.J. Simpson
Set decoration: Susan Bode
Costume design: John Dunn
Sound: Allan Byer
Casting: Sheila Jaffe, Georgianne Walken
MPAA rating: R
Running Time: 108 minutes

REVIEWS

Entertainment Weekly. August 16, 1996, p. 46.
Hollywood Reporter. August 6, 1996, p. 6.
Los Angeles Times. August 9, 1996, p. F6.
New York Times. August 9, 1996, p. C5.
New Yorker. August 19, 1996, p. 78.
Newsweek. August 12, 1996, p. 64.
People. August 19, 1996, p. 19.
Rolling Stone. August 22, 1996, p. 105.
Variety. August 5, 1996, p. 48.

Beautiful Girls

. . . good times never seemed so good—Movie tagline

"*Beautiful Girls* treasures the good feelings!"—Roger Ebert, *Chicago Sun-Times*

"One of the year's early surprises!"—Marshall Fine, *Gannett Newspapers*

"One of the year's best casts, including Mira Sorvino, Michael Rapaport and Rosie O'Donnell!"—David Elliott, *San Diego Union-Tribune*

"Provocatively funny!"—Desson Howe, *The Washington Post*

Box Office: $10,600,000

Beautiful Girls is a high school reunion story set in New England and stocked with working class characters. The film follows Willie Conway (Timothy Hutton) on his return to his hometown, dreading the obligatory stay with his widower father and feckless younger brother. Dad does not have much to say and younger brother lacks the social graces that his mother presumably could have instilled in him. Willie seems distant but wryly tolerant of his shrunken home. Timothy Hutton plays Willie as a guy approaching his thirties without a clue about what to do with his life. His passion is the piano, but what is his ambition? His New York City bar gig hardly feeds his needs. He seems glad to see his high school buddies, who give him a rousing welcome and who want to romanticize his Big Apple life, but Willie is very low-key—almost clandestine about his emotions, drinking too much and hanging out at bars, fishing holes, and the like.

"You guys, as a gender, have got to get a grip."—Gina (Rosie O'-Donnell)

Willie's pals don't seem to notice his anomie. They want to know about his girlfriend. How long has he been living with her? How good is her face, her figure, her personality? One crude interlocutor even asks for a rating on a numbered scale, and Willie haltingly offers a triple seven for her body parts and temperament. His friends are too wrapped up in their own women troubles to appreciate Willie's frustrations. Paul (Michael Rapaport) is fussing over his girl who has dropped him after his refusal to make good on their long engagement. Paul takes time out from snowplowing to dump loads of snow in front of her garage and to philosophize about how all women are sisters engaged in a conspiracy to thwart men. He meets his match in Gina (Rosie O'Donnell), a hilarious feminist oracle who gives men the what for. Then there is that high school heartthrob Tommy "Birdman" Rowland (Matt Dillon), whose life after high school has been a bust. He ploughs snow and carries on an affair with his high school sweetheart Darian (Lauren Holly), now married to a college man, while Tommy's long-suffering girlfriend Sharon (Mira Sorvino) waits for him to make up his mind about her.

Not much happens in this movie—other than a fight scene when Darian's husband and his frat brothers beat up Tommy. Rather, it is a movie of moods and character studies, of people watching each other and yearning for fulfillment. What kind of fulfillment? They are not sure. But somehow life after high school has been a letdown, a crash into reality. When Andera (Uma Thurman), a glamorous stranger shows up, all the males have a go at her. She is bemused by their behavior, but she does not buy it. Her presence only underscores their emptiness, and she leaves abruptly like the fantasy she represents to these luckless men.

Willie is the focus of the film because he is the most self-conscious and introspective of this

CREDITS

Tommy (Birdman) Rowland: Matt Dillon
Michael (Mo) Morris: Noah Emmerich
Tracy Stover: Annabeth Gish
Darian Smalls: Lauren Holly
Willie Conway: Timothy Hutton
Gina Barrisano: Rosie O'Donnell
Marty: Natalie Portman

Origin: USA
Released: 1996
Production: Cary Woods for a Woods Entertainment production; released by Miramax
Direction: Ted Demme
Screenplay: Scott Rosenberg
Cinematography: Adam Kimmel
Editing: Jeffery Wolf
Production design: Dan Davis
Art direction: Peter Rogness
Costume design: Lucy W. Corrigan
Sound: James Thornton
Music: David A. Stewart
Casting: Margery Simkin
MPAA rating: R
Running Time: 110 minutes

male bunch. As the reunion approaches, he waits for his girlfriend, a beautiful attorney, to join him. Why does Tracy (Annabeth Gish) love him, and why is she so tolerant of his pathetic family and friends? They have their amusement value, to be sure, but why should she care? Because she is nice? That she is, but it is a poor excuse for a motivation. Perhaps Willie's artistic temperament attracts her, but if so neither she nor the film makes that clear. She just seems to be there for Willie. Should he commit to her? Should he give up his piano playing and take a sales job? Will he be grown-up then—like Mo (Michael Morris) who has a stable marriage and respectable job? The script is no help here, and Hutton is left to play his winsome self. Tracy loves Willie because he is Timothy Hutton is about what it amounts to.

> Although the setting of the film is Massachusetts, the movie was actually filmed in Minnesota.

The one area where the character of Willie is genuinely appealing is his receptiveness. He spots a thirteen-year-old girl, Marty (Natalie Portman), who has moved next door. Portman's doe-like face is arresting. She captivates Willie by asking pointed questions with such spunky wit and precocity that he is smitten. And so is she—because he listens, because he is older and she craves his knowing gaze. Portman is a stupendous actress, and it is hard not to see her entrancing any man past the first blush of youth and yearning for the renewal that her freshness promises. The way she gives him sidelong looks and keeps her distance—at a pond skating to and then quickly away from him—is mesmerizing. She embodies that desire of fulfillment that all of the film's characters search for. Portman is the best thing about the movie. That is because she personifies what the whole film, faults and all, is all about.

—*Carl Rollyson*

REVIEWS

Boxoffice Magazine. March, 1996, p. R-26.
Chicago Tribune. February 9, 1996, p. 5.
Entertainment Weekly. February 16, 1996, p. 45.
Los Angeles Times. February 9, 1996, p. F6.
New York Times. February 9, 1996, p. C6.
Rolling Stone. March 7, 1996, p. 53.
USA Today. February 9, 1996, p. 4D.
Variety. February 5, 1996, p. 59.
Village Voice. February 20, 1996, p. 68.
Washington Post. February 9, 1996, p. F1.

Beautiful Thing

An urban fairytale.—Movie tagline

"One of the most beautiful gay love stories yet recorded on film! You should see it now, so you can anticipate seeing it again!"—Stephen Brophy, *Bay Windows*

"One of the top films of the year! That rare masterpiece, a piece of celluloid you'll want to scoop up and treasure for a long, long time."—Brandon Judell, *Detour Magazine*

"Very fresh and exciting! One of the most exciting film finds of the year! *Beautiful Thing* abounds with attitude, energy, frankness and humor!"—Daphne Davis, *Movies and Videos*

"An irresistible comic fable of working class realities, pop myths and teenage gay romance!"—Bob Satuloff, *NY Native*

"Deftly combining comedy with ardent drama, *Beautiful Thing* has a script that sings, an irresistible soundtrack that really sings, and an accomplished ensemble cast worth singing about. Full of characters that you really care about, this is a tender, touching and charming movie!"—Barbara Siegel, *Siegel Entertainment Syndicate*

"Heartfelt, convincing and hard to resist."—James Ireland Baker, *Time Out New York*

"A warm and funny love story. Refreshing, spunky and unsentimental!"—Michael Musto, *Village Voice*

Box Office: **$1,472,194**

Hettie Macdonald's *Beautiful Thing* is a small gem of a movie. It is a coming-of-age story verging on a storybook romance, in which boy meets boy, but it is set against the backdrop of daily life of a particularly downtrodden segment of the British working class. Not since Stephen Frears' *My Beautiful Launderette* (1986) has a film managed to tackle simultaneously the issues of race, class and sexual preference with so much success.

"This is a play in which somebody can be working-class and still have their sexuality accepted. That was my agenda. It's not about what you get up to after lights out, it's about falling in love."—writer Jonathan Harvey

The film is based on Jonathan Harvey's play of the same name, which was a popular success in London in the 1993-94 season. (Harvey also wrote the screen adaptation.) The story unfolds in a typically overcrowded and dreary London tower block. It is the sort of place where one cannot help but know everyone else's business, as the walls are paper-thin and living space is severely limited. As a result, the air is always rife with gossip about other people's activities. All of the characters suffer greatly from living in such claustrophobic conditions. They barely have room to move, let alone think creatively or devise plans for a better future. And sexual intimacies of any kind are next to impossible.

These limitations are deeply felt by Jamie (Glen Berry), a restless 16-year-old, and his mother, Sandra (Linda Henry). Their relationship is one long intermittent argument, of the usual parent-adolescent sort, but intensified by their dismal surroundings. Jamie is bright and bookish, hates school and is staunchly uninterested in sports. Linda Henry is excellent as Sandra, Jamie's harried, hard-working single mother. She is employed as a barmaid and is shrewdly pursuing the possibility of becoming a governess of a pub of her own. For her, such a move would represent a significant step upward on the social ladder. As the story begins, she is engaged in a pleasant but unchallenging relationship with Tony (Ben Daniels), a kind but unambitious working-class lug who is a few years younger than she. He loves her dearly but has little to offer her otherwise.

Next door, Ste (Scott Neal), Jamie's schoolmate, endures beatings from his drunken father and his aimless, rage-filled brother, all of whom live in equally close quarters. Ste is adept enough at football (soccer) to meet the local standards of masculinity, but he is secretly plagued with self-doubt in regard to sexual matters. Slowly but surely, the two teenage misfits form an alliance.

When the beatings at home become too severe, Ste takes refuge in Jamie's apartment. Sandra makes this arrangement after she finds Ste wandering around the neighborhood, cast out of his home for the umpteenth time. Perhaps without intending to, she assumes the role of substitute mother to Ste, who has no one else to turn to.

Jamie is lucky enough to have a room of his own, a rare thing in the benighted neighborhood of the Thamesmead Estates. When Sandra brings Ste home, she offhandedly tells him he can "bunk in" with Jamie. The resulting physical closeness is both thrilling and terrifying for both boys. At first, Ste shares a bed with Jamie, but keeps himself at a safe distance by putting his pillow at the foot of the bed. When he relents and begins sleeping in the more usual way, it's a timid but unmistakable admission of his true feelings.

Initially, the two boys appear to have nothing in common, but their shared curiosity about sex gives them something to talk about, and both are in dire need of affection. Ste often shows up bearing bruises from his latest beating, and Jamie tends to his various wounds. The boys are also at that perilous stage where adolescents begin to wonder what they will do with their adult lives, and their prospects do not appear rosy.

A neighbor girl, Leah (Tameka Empson), the daughter of West Indian immigrants, is forced to share a similarly cramped flat, and life, with her mother. She adjusts to her predicament by running away from home for days at a time. Leah reacts to her degraded position in the local pecking order by developing a comical, but rather bizarre, infatuation with Mama Cass Elliott, a singer whom she "imitates" on a regular basis. Leah has also developed a drug habit which escalates as the film winds along. (It is significant that Leah, a very alienated black girl who is stuck on the bottom

CREDITS

Jamie Gangel: Glen Berry
Sandra Gangel: Linda Henry
Ste Pearce: Scott Neal
Leah: Tameka Empson

Origin: Great Britain
Released: 1996
Production: Tony Garnett and Bill Shapter; released by Sony Pictures Classics.
Direction: Hettie Macdonald
Screenplay: Jonathan Harvey; based on his play of the same name.
Cinematography: Chris Seager
Editing: Don Fairservice
Art direction: Alison Wratten, Chrysoula Sofitsi
Production Design: Mark Stevenson
Costumes: Pam Tait
Casting: Gail Stevens, Andy Pryor
MPAA rating: R
Running Time: 90 minutes

rung of the British class structure, has chosen a role model who is white, and distinctly American.)

The on-again, off-again friendship of Leah and the boys is an illustration of the peculiar social hierarchy of the oppressed. Leah is widely reviled by her neighbors and dismissed as a "slag" (a British working-class term for "slut" or "whore"), but she is not above engaging in games of social one-upmanship with Jamie and Ste in order to improve her relative position. Leah also has a bit of a crush on Ste, so she is hurt by the boys' constant togetherness. She is the first to suspect that Jamie and Ste have become more than friends, and she knows perfectly well that she could use their secret to her own advantage. After a ferocious tongue-lashing from Sandra, who is wise to all of her moves, Leah relents and becomes the boys' confidante, but her initial stance toward them reveals much about the harshly competitive and judgmental atmosphere in which they live.

Teenagers Glen Berry (Jamie) and Scott Neal (Ste) are both pupils at the Anna Scher Theatre School and have acted together before. Their established friendship, both admitted, made the film's romantic scenes easier to do.

The musical score, composed of well-known pop songs of the Sixties and Seventies, is extremely effective. Mama Cass Elliott, who died in 1974, would probably be pleased that her songs have been used to illustrate a movie which is all about "different ways of being different." The choice of Mama Cass as an unseen role model is especially inspired: She became a success (first in the Sixties, as a member of The Mamas and the Papas, then later as a solo performer) even though she was often dismissed as being too fat, and therefore unattractive. She had to fight very hard for the right to be seen and heard. Some of her best-known songs are used to great effect here, most notably "Dream A Little Dream of Me," and especially, "Make Your Own Kind of Music." The latter song contains a dire warning about the future ("You're gonna be nowhere/The loneliest kind of lonely") but also points to a solution. By the film's end, the song becomes an anthem for struggling teenagers everywhere, gay and straight alike.

Sandra learns of her son's emerging sexuality in time-honored fashion: She "just happens" to find an issue of London's *Gay Times* while "cleaning" his room one day. (She also discovers a notebook in which other students have left a variety of homophobic scrawls.) Initially, she is bothered less by her son's being gay than by his apparent refusal to confide in her. She is so consumed with maternal concern that she follows Jamie on his clandestine trip to a well-known gay pub in another part of town. Later, she confronts him with her discovery. "Why the Gloucester?" she moans, referring to the place which Jamie has been frequenting. "Because there is nowhere else," retorts Jamie.

It is a simple, perfect reply, one which illuminates the particular difficulties faced by young gay men and lesbians, who are given no respectable role models and have no place where they can simply relax and be themselves.

Sandra tries to be tolerant of her son's emerging sexual identity, but she does not understand the gay sensibility nearly as well as she thinks she does. ("There's a place for people like you," she tells her son, trying to be supportive. "It's an island in the Mediterranean. It's called Lesbian.") It is significant, and indicative of these perilous times, that Sandra's reservations about her son's sexuality revolve mostly around the issue of AIDS, rather than the prospect of societal scorn and humiliation. Although not much is said directly about the AIDS issue, it is obvious that Jamie is keenly aware of the specter of sexually-transmitted disease, and that this awareness inhibits his ability to make a positive adjustment to his sexuality.

The teenagers in *Beautiful Thing* respond to their oppression in a variety of ways, some of which are delusional and self-destructive. In the final reel, Jamie and Ste do indeed become a couple. It is not clear what the future will hold for them, but they derive strength from one another at a crucial stage in their lives, and they are militant enough in their way to withstand the malicious gossip of their neighbors. After a dangerous scrape with a drug overdose, Leah gains some insight into her self-destructive behavior and shows signs of improvement. And Sandra lands a better job which affords her more living space. (She ultimately parts company with Tony: Her departure is prompted less by rancor than by a mounting sense of inertia on his part. She has moved a step upward on the social ladder, and Tony is not ambitious enough to follow.)

The title is derived from the idea that every character, in one way or another, is forced to make something "beautiful" out of a set of hideously oppressive circumstances. The film ends with a surreal dance sequence, set in the middle of the concrete tower block, in which everyone pairs off with whomever they choose. Jamie and Ste lead the way, and are followed by improvised "couples" of every conceivable variety. The scene is clearly meant as sheer fantasy, but the conceit is appropriate for Jamie and Ste. They have come to realize that they are madly in love, and are beginning to like themselves enough to let it show.

Beautiful Thing works on many levels at once. To the great credit of its director and screenwriter, the film is about much more than the issue of sexual preference. *Beautiful Thing* comes into view at a time when teenagers are being bombarded as never before with messages about "safe sex" and morality, but are given very little useful information about sex itself. All of the characters suffer from a stifling kind of class anxiety which is perhaps better understood in Britain than it is here. Much of America remains enthralled by the myth of unlimited class mobility; Jamie and Ste and their contemporaries have no such illusions. The ending implies that the characters are by no means through struggling to find a place for themselves, but it indicates that struggle is possible, and that it is worthwhile. The happy ending enjoyed by Jamie and Ste is hard-won, and it is the film's greatest reward. It is a pleasure to encounter, at long last, a gay-themed film which ends with an embrace rather than a bullet.

—*Karl Michalak*

REVIEWS

Cinema Papers. October, 1996, p. 46.
Detroit Free Press. October 31, 1996.
Entertainment Weekly. November 15, 1996, p. 52.
Los Angeles Times. November 1, 1996, p. F4.
The New York Post. October 9, 1996, p. 36
The New York Times. October 9, 1996, p. C17.
San Francisco Examiner. October 18, 1996, p. C3.
Sight and Sound. June, 1996, p. 35.
Variety. March 4, 1996, p. 77.

Beavis and Butt-head Do America

Coming to a screen bigger than your TV.—Movie tagline

"Beavis and Butt-head have an essentially innocent obliviousness that makes you root for them . . . "—Kevin Thomas, *Los Angeles Times*

"A '90's version of Mark Twain's Tom and Huck. Quite funny."—Dave Kehr, *New York Daily News*

"Two thumbs up!"—*Siskel & Ebert*

Box Office: $44,547,878

Audiences came to *Beavis and Butt-head Do America* in a holiday mood and already prepared to laugh. The two nerds, who are featured in the most popular show on MTV, were like old friends or relatives to youthful television viewers. Heretofore the abrasive cartoon characters have been portrayed spending most of their time in front of their own television set commenting on what they were viewing. This convention justified the practice of strict economy through the use of very limited animation. Further economy could be practiced by reusing old footage with new dialogue. The characters' lips move so little anyway that dubbing was no problem, and producer Mike Judge provided the voices for both his heroes. The MTV format made it easy to fill up time by inserting the music-videos to which the boys are addicted. Making a full-length, 100% animated feature was a great leap forward. When Beavis and Butt-head get up from their supine positions and go outside to "do America," the effect is something like the Frankenstein monster breaking loose and climbing off the table.

What brings the two couch potatoes to their feet is the disappearance of their television set. Burglars have ripped it off. Without television Beavis and Butt-head are frantic. They might have to try reading—or even thinking. They decide to "borrow" the television set from their high school but are thwarted by a teacher and the ogre-like principal as they are wheeling the big, expensive machine down the hall. The caricatures of adults are among the best elements in this film. The painfully hip teacher, with his long hair and beard, is trying to seem more like a pal than an authority figure. He plays a guitar and sings a folk song titled "Lesbian Seagull." Like so many real-life teachers, he has become a mere entertainer and impotent custodian.

After demolishing the school's television equipment, Beavis and Butt-head try breaking into motel rooms because a sign on the roof advertises "Free TV." Muddy, a drunken goon, mistakes them for hit men he hired sight-unseen to kill his wife. When he offers them ten thousand dollars to "do her," the sex-starved morons fail to realize he means "do her in." They accept airline tickets to Las Vegas and nearly wreck the plane before it lands. The audience realizes that the boys are about to "do" America in the same way they are hoping to "do" their boss's sexy wife.

Muddy and his wife want to peddle a stolen military weapon to the highest-bidding foreign agent or terrorist. The small explosive device can discharge a virus capable of killing entire populations. The unscrupulous Muddy is furious because his even more unscrupulous wife is trying to cut him out. Agent Fleming (voice of Robert Stack) of the Bureau of Alcohol, Tobacco and Firearms (ATF) has traced the voluptuous moll to Vegas and arrives with his army of enforcers just when Beavis and Butt-head are expecting to "score" with a woman for the first time in their lives. Beavis has already taken off his short pants, which gives the foxy lady the idea of sewing the secret weapon in the lining so that the feds will find nothing incriminating on her person. She sends the boys off on a tour bus, promising to meet them in Washington, D.C. where she will fulfill their wildest fantasies.

The two skinny illiterates are soon objects of the biggest manhunt in American history. The filmmakers have evidently chosen to satirize the ATF because of the ineptitude that agency displayed in the Branch Davidian debacle at Waco, Texas and elsewhere. Agent Fleming shows imperious disregard for the rights of civilians, ordering "full cavity searches" of any male or female suspect, witness or innocent bystander.

Like Chance, the Peter Sellers character in *Being There* (1980), Beavis and Butt-head only know what they have seen on television. Although they must have been exposed to American history in high school, they never learned where Washington, D.C. is situated. After accidentally destroying Hoover Dam, they find themselves dying of exposure and dehydration while trying to walk across the desert. They have seen on some televised western that people can eat cactus to get life-saving liquid—but the only kind of cactus they can find is peyote.

"This sucks more than anything has sucked before!"—Butt-head, after their TV has been stolen

Here the film departs from stilted limited animation to indulge in an orgiastic sequence representing their drug-induced hallucinations. For a few minutes the MTV artists unleash their creative powers in a riot of colors and surrealistic imagery which is the best part of this film. The all-too-brief segment makes the viewer appreciate the abundant artistic talent bound and gagged by the monetary constraints responsible for the unimaginative artwork seen in most animated cartoons made for television.

Whiskey-swilling Muddy, who has discovered that the boys were not the killers he mistook them for, catches up with them. This human vulture temporarily saves them from the real vultures already pecking at their shirts. He plans to use his captives to get at his wife. But they manage to escape by breaking open the trunk-lid and leaping out while the car is doing seventy miles an hour on the Interstate. Trucks jackknife, cars collide like bowling pins, fires break out, police cars and ambulances arrive—but nobody notices the two fugitives as they stroll away from the scene of mass destruction saying, "Gee, that was cool!"

MTV stars Beavis and Butt-head take their adolescent humor on the road in their first feature film, *Beavis and Butt-head Do America.*

By sheer stupidity they manage to elude Fleming's forces all the way across America. The filmmakers tread on some very thin ice by using a group of touring nuns as objects of sexual innuendo ("We're on a bus with chicks!") and having their heroes mistake confessionals in a Catholic church for portable toilets. At this point, the audience's conspiratorial laughter takes on a noticeably different timbre, suggesting that modern young moviegoers may not yet have lost every vestige of respect for culture and tradition. Inside one of the confessionals, when a tearful penitent confesses that he had sexual intercourse with a woman, the hidden Beavis (or Butt-head), posing as a priest, asks, "Did she have big boobs? Heh-heh-heh!"

Eventually they make it to the nation's capital and create pandemonium in the White House. They intrude into young Chelsea Clinton's bedroom and finally into President Clinton's Oval Office. All the other visiting tourists are being herded out of the building and many subjected to "full cavity searches," but Beavis and Butt-head are overlooked. There is something so unreal about these two characters, with their expressionless faces and their robotic gaits, that nobody seems to notice them. They may be mistaken for wallpaper designs or mounted trophies or fire hydrants or poster illustrations, but they are rarely recognized as human

CREDITS

Beavis/Butt-head: Mike Judge (voice)
Agent Fleming: Robert Stack (voice)
Old Woman: Cloris Leachman (voice)

Origin: USA
Released: 1996
Production: Abby Terkuhle for a MTV and Geffen Pictures production; released by Paramount
Direction: Mike Judge
Screenplay: Mike Judge and Joe Stillman; based on MTV's Beavis and Butt-head characters by Mike Judge
Cinematography: Yvette Kaplan
Editing: Terry Kelley, Gunter Glinka and Neil Lawrence
Music: John Frizell
Sound: John Benson, John Lynn
Line producer: Winnie Chaffee
MPAA rating: PG-13
Running Time: 80 minutes

beings—one of whom is unknowingly wearing the doomsday MacGuffin inside his pants.

It is doubtful whether these cartoon characters have enough appeal to merit a sequel to *Beavis and Butt-head Do America.* They have a long way to go before they become icons like Mickey Mouse and Donald Duck. It is even hard to remember which is which. Beavis is blond and has a pointed nose. He has a fiendish look in his eyes, whereas the other only looks stupefied. They embody many of the worst faults of teenage boys, including foul language, personal uncleanliness, dirty minds, slothfulness, sadism, and that irritating jackass laughter. Both look like a couple of pot-heads—if not heroin addicts—though for obvious reasons the makers of this PG-13-rated film do not portray their creations smoking marijuana or drinking any kind of alcoholic beverage.

A comparison between *Beavis and Butt-head Do America* and one of the Walt Disney classics like *Bambi* (1942) or *Cinderella* (1950) would show what a long way we have come downhill in the past half-century. Young audiences today seem cynical, sadistic, and nihilistic. It is hard to tell whether they are laughing at the moronic heroes or laughing with them. Nothing delights these young viewers more than death and destruction. In contrast to Disney's cloying cuteness, everything in *Beavis and Butt-head Do America* is ugly. Even the brief psychedelic sequence in the desert is a rhapsody of ugliness.

What saves the film from being a total turnoff to the thoughtful critic is that it has "redeeming social value:" it suggests certain painful truths. Beavis and Butt-head did not create society; society created them. Looking at their vacuous faces, the mature viewer might be reminded of such lines in Edwin Markham's admonitory poem "The Man with the Hoe" as: "Who loosened and let down this brutal jaw?/ Whose was the hand that slanted back this brow?/Whose breath blew out the light within this brain?. . . . what to him/ Are Plato and the swing of Pleiades?" Or algebra or geometry?

Adults often do seem stupid, insensitive, repulsive, greedy and uncaring. Teenagers are justified in feeling that modern society "sucks." Without money in a money-mad society they find themselves in a world of locked doors. There is little to do but kick back and watch television, do drugs, or else be incarcerated in classrooms listening to information which may be important to the preservation of the status quo but is often meaningless to them. This is why young audiences identify with their two antiestablishment antiheroes. They are passive revolutionaries; they will prevail by doing nothing.

—Bill Delaney

REVIEWS

Entertainment Weekly. December 20, 1996, p. 54.
Los Angeles Times. December 20, 1996, p. F7.
New York Times. December 20, 1996, p. C18.
Variety. December 16, 1996, p. 79.
Village Voice. December 31, 1996, p. 74.

Bed of Roses

He gave her flowers. She gave him a chance.—Movie tagline

"You'll be touched by *Bed of Roses.*"—Howard Kissel, *New York Daily News*

"*Bed of Roses* is a feel good love story you don't want to miss."—Jim Ferguson, *Prevue Channel*

"*Bed of Roses* is a pure delight!"—Roy Leonard, *WGN Radio/TV*

Box Office: $19,030,691

A sentimental but dry romance, *Bed of Roses* is a sweet love story drenched in the colors of every flower imaginable. It follows the fairy-tale meeting of two lost souls. Though this tearjerker lacks a suspenseful plot, it makes up for it with a winning cast and beautiful cinematography.

Lisa (Mary Stuart Masterson) is a workaholic; a high-powered vice-president in an incredibly busy office with a gorgeous picture window and a lot of important things to do. She talks about "cost-benefits analyses," and other highfalutin' catchphrases familiar to workaholics the world over. As the film opens, the audience is given a glimpse into the shattering loss which precipitates her workaholism: the loss of an important man in her life. Crying in the bay window of her Manhattan apartment, Lisa is the picture of the woman whose exterior seems perfectly together, but whose loneliness is causing her no end of internal grief. She has one friend, a goofy but wise schoolteacher named Kim (Pamela Segall).

One day, however, Lisa receives a dazzling bouquet of flowers, with an unsigned note. Certain that it isn't her unthinking boyfriend (Josh Brolin), who wouldn't know FTD from CNN or NFL, Lisa wonders just who the mysterious admirer could be. At Kim's urging, she traces the flowers to the flower shop from whence they came. It is there that she finally encounters Slater, who plays the unassuming Lewis, a man so charming and sweet that he delivers flowers simply because it is "the best job in the world, you know? Everyone's always happy to see you."

> Lewis points out that delivering flowers " . . . has to be the best job in the world, you know? Everyone's always happy to see you."

The best part of all is that Lewis actually owns the flower shop, and is a recovering workaholic himself (who once worked at Goldman, Sachs, no less.) Not only does he have great taste in flowers, but he has great taste in women, too. It turns out that the introspective Lewis likes to take walks around Manhattan at night, and one night he spotted the lovely Lisa crying in her living room window. Immediately taken by her pain and her beauty, he sent her a bunch of flowers, hoping that she would feel better. This character is such a wonderful guy that he made no effort to let her know who he was; not to mention the fact that when she comes to his shop, he still doesn't tell her that he is the man responsible for the flowers.

But eventually he does tell her, of course, and she discovers how wonderful he is, and they fall in love. A couple of musical montages later, in which the young lovers cavort all over Manhattan, not to mention a few nearby beaches, their first problems occur when he decides to ask her to marry him. She has a hidden past, which she must overcome before they can get back together.

The fact that everything turns out okay should not be surprising to anyone. Usually, a film like this doesn't try to hide its inevitable happy ending; it simply tries to make it as interesting a journey as possible for its audience. The success of *When Harry Met Sally* (1989) or *Sleepless in Seattle* (1993), for example, was that both films (besides having Meg Ryan in the lead role), were darn funny. Other

CREDITS

Lewis: Christian Slater
Lisa: Mary Stuart Masterson
Kim: Pamela Segall
Danny: Josh Brolin
Wendy: Ally Walker
Mrs. Farrell: Debra Monk

Origin: USA
Released: 1996
Production: Allan Mindel and Denise Shaw; released by New Line Cinema
Direction: Michael Goldenberg
Screenplay: Michael Goldenberg
Cinematography: Adam Kimmel
Editing: Jane Durson
Music: Michael Convertino
Production design: Stephen McCabe
Art direction: Jefferson Sage
Costume design: Cynthia Flynt
Sound: Danny Michael
Casting: Meg Simon
MPAA rating: PG
Running Time: 87 minutes

romances, such as *An Affair to Remember* (1957), on which *Sleepless in Seattle* was based, had the star power of Cary Grant and Deborah Kerr, and a lot of good melodrama. *Bed of Roses* is, unfortunately, neither funny enough nor melodramatic enough to make the journey to the inevitable ending worthwhile.

This doesn't mean that *Bed of Roses* is a waste of time, however. Slater turns in a winning performance as the gentle, near-perfect Lewis. Having played Jack Nicholson-esque bad boys in the early part of his career, in such films as *Heathers* (1989), *Pump Up the Volume* (1990), and *Mobsters* (1991), Slater has recently added romance to his on-screen persona with this film and the more successful *Untamed Heart* (1994). Slater makes a thoroughly believable and likable love interest, which is no small feat considering the cliche-ridden character provided him by writer/director Michael Goldenberg. Besides taking long walks at night, Lewis regularly goes to a local library to hear stories read to schoolchildren; he has an extraordinarily neat and tidy apartment with an amazing rooftop garden; he is a fantastic cook, a great lover, is highly empathetic and understanding, and has a well-adjusted and happy family.

Lewis's rooftop garden was created by the filmmakers atop the Chelsea Hotel.

In all fairness to writer/director Goldenberg, he does infuse Lewis with a need to push Lisa to fall in love with him. Slater does an excellent job finding Lewis' few faults as well, particularly in the scene in which he asks her to marry him in front of his family on Christmas Eve. Both Goldenberg and Slater hit the mark beautifully here, making Lewis just a bit too pushy without making him bizarre.

Masterson, who made her mark in the wonderful *Fried Green Tomatoes* (1991), has a less interesting role. She does a credible job making Lisa seem like a workaholic, but has trouble making up for Goldenberg's odd choice to make Lisa a woman with literally only one friend. It seems to stretch the audience's willingness to suspend disbelief that someone this connected to her work (not to mention this intelligent, articulate, and attractive) would not have anyone else in her life besides her one friend.

Of course, that is entirely the point of the film: Lisa needs to learn to open herself up to life and love, and Lewis is just the man to teach her. Virtually immediately, she takes time off of work (forced on her by her boss), to help Lewis deliver flowers, and Masterson is quite believable as a woman who has no idea how to enjoy herself. Masterson excels in the scenes which require her to show the desperate pain underneath Lisa's careful exterior, particularly when she tells Lewis that she cannot marry him, and then again when she realizes she does need him after all.

Her one friend is played to the hilt by Pamela Segall. Some people will love Segall's adorable face and mannered delivery; some will feel that she is too self-conscious for her own good. When she smiles and tells Lewis, "if you hurt her, I'll kill you," she does so with a moderately cloying delivery which makes her seem like she is auditioning for "Saturday Night Live." Segall knows that Kim is the comic relief, and since there is little other comedy (or little other relief) in this film, she works hard to be cute, and sometimes it is a bit much.

Goldenberg seems to be aware that his story is as flimsy as a bed of rose petals; in the 87 minutes, there is more than one musical montage. One of the musical montages is basically a music video which appears to try and sell the film's main song, "Insensitive." The song has become an oft-played song on pop radio, and it seems more than obvious that either Goldenberg or the producers decided they may have an Oscar nominee on their hands, so they'd better make sure audiences hear the song. The rather pedestrian song only underscores the insubstantial nature of this film.

To sum it up, this is a boy meets girl, boy loses girl, boy gets girl film which telegraphs its ending early. It has a heartfelt pair of lead performances, but has a hard time overcoming such cliches as "my wife died, so I realized I had to smell the roses" (to paraphrase Slater's character), and "I was unloved as a child, so your love frightens me," (to paraphrase Masterson's character.)

On the plus side, there is some fine cinematography by Adam Kimmel, beautifully capturing the romance of Manhattan and the beauty of flowers in bloom; and there are some wonderful settings by production designer Stephen McCabe, particularly that spectacular rooftop garden. Goldenberg elicits likable performances not only from Masterson and Slater, but from Debra Monk as Slater's warm and thoughtful mother, and from Josh Brolin as a complete lout.

With the support of a strong cast and beautiful scenery, as a feel good love story, *Bed of Roses* does the job.

—Kirby Tepper

REVIEWS

Boxoffice. March, 1996, p. R-27.
Detroit News. January 26, 1996, p. D1.
Los Angeles Times. January 26, 1996, p. F10.
New York Times. January 26, 1996, p. C6.
Sight and Sound. March, 1996, p. 38.
USA Today. January 26, 1996, p. 7D.
Variety. January 29, 1996, p. 61.

Before and After

A murder. A suspect. A shadow of a doubt.—Movie tagline

"Compelling, powerful! Terrific performances by Streep and Neeson."—Bill Diehl, *ABC Radio Network*

"Spellbinding and challenging!"—Susan Granger, *American Movie Classics*

"Riveting! Don't miss it!"—Paul Wunder, *WBAI Radio*

Box Office: $8,700,000

It's an idyllic and picturesque New England town which Ben (Liam Neeson) and Carolyn Ryan (Meryl Streep) have chosen to live their lives and raise their family. Ben is a relatively famous artist, welding massive sculptures in his garage/studio, while Carolyn is a friendly and popular pediatrician. Their two children, 16-year-old Jacob (Edward Furlong) and his younger sister Judith (Julia Weldon) seem well-adjusted and normal. In short, Norman Rockwell would have gladly painted them.

However, as Judith tells us in a voice-over, "Your whole life can change in a moment, and you never know it's coming." What suddenly intrudes into the Ryan's ideal existence is that one evening Jacob doesn't show up for dinner, but the local sheriff does. It seems that a young girl has been found murdered, and she was last seen with Jacob who, the family discovers, is missing.

Immediately Ben and Carolyn begin handling the situation differently. While both cannot believe Jacob is responsible for the girl's death, Carolyn is worried that whoever killed the girl may have also killed Jacob while Ben becomes angry at any insinuation that Jacob may be at fault and promptly sends the sheriff packing to get a search warrant for their property.

While the sheriff is gone, Ben checks out the car Jacob had been driving and finds a bloodied tire iron and jack in the trunk. Now Ben is pushed even further into his father-protector role as he cleans out the trunk and hides all evidence he finds that might implicate his son.

Days pass and Jacob is still nowhere to be found. As the Ryans pass out flyers with their missing son's photo on it, the town they have lived in slowly begins to turn on them. Carolyn loses her patients, a large wooden statue of Ben's is set on fire in their front yard, someone writes "murderer" over a poster. The Ryans are becoming more and more isolated within their community which causes them to focus more and more on each other.

Then, five weeks later, Jacob is finally found. But he's not talking. His family visits him in jail but all he can do is to sit there looking decidedly sullen and more than a little shifty. (Is he acting guilty because he is or because the filmmakers are manipulating us?) The Ryans, however, still stand by their son and hire the best trial lawyer they can find, Panos Demeris (Alfred Molina).

Demeris is the expert the family needs, but at virtually every turn, the Ryans sabotage his best efforts, ignore his advice, and undermine his defense through stunningly imprudent spur-of-the-moment antics, all in the name of protecting their son.

This is not the first film by director Barbet Schroeder which examines the inner psychology of family members set against the backdrop of the judicial system. It is also not his first to delve into the idea that the borders between guilt and innocence (or good and evil) are often shady at best. The first was his mesmerizing telling of the Claus Von Bu-

CREDITS

Carolyn Ryan: Meryl Streep
Ben Ryan: Liam Neeson
Jacob Ryan: Edward Furlong
Judith Ryan: Julia Weldon
Panos Demeris: Alfred Molina
Fran Conklin: Daniel Von Bargen
Wendell Bye: John Heard
Terry Taverner: Ann Magnuson
Martha Taverner: Alison Folland
Marian Raynor, Prosecutor: Kaiulani Lee
Dr. Tom McAnally: Larry Pine
Panos' Assistant: Ellen Lancaster
Judge Grady: Wesley Addy
T.J.: Oliver Graney
T.J.'s Mom: Bernadette Quigley

Origin: USA
Released: 1996
Production: Barbet Schroeder and Susan Hoffman for Hollywood Pictures; released by Buena Vista Pictures
Direction: Barbet Schroeder
Screenplay: Ted Tally; based on the book by Rosellen Brown
Cinematography: Luciano Tovoli
Editing: Lee Percy
Production design: Stuart Wurtzel
Art direction: Steve Saklad
Set decoration: Gretchen Rau
Costume design: Ann Roth
Music: Howard Shore
MPAA rating: PG-13
Running Time: 108 minutes

low attempted murder case in *Reversal of Fortune* (1990). However, that's about as far as the comparison can go. *Reversal of Fortune* captivated audiences and won Schroeder a Golden Globe award as well as an Academy Award nomination as best director. This first film had a compelling story that was filled with complexities, teasingly indefinite in its conclusion and reveling in its black humor. Some of this may have been due to the amazingly wry and witty (and Oscar winning) performance of Jeremy Irons as Von Bulow.

"All I'm proposing is that we save your life first. Later we can worry about your soul."—Ben Ryan to son Jacob

Schroeder's second film, *Before and After,* however, has none of this going for it. Our "criminal" this time is a brooding teenager about whom we care very little. His defenders are either coldly logical or emotionally hyper, and because of this extremism, we are unable to identify with either of them. Neeson and Streep are two extremely competent actors, but about all they are given to do here is to react emotionally or debate the ethics of their situation. In short, the story is uninvolving and flat.

Before and After is based on the 1992 best-selling book by Rosellen Brown. (Except that for some reason Hollywood saw fit to change Brown's Jewish Reiser family to a more all-American Ryan clan. Another attempt to avoid social censure and conflict by politically correcting a story before filming it?) One might have expected more suspense or drama from screenwriter Ted Tally who won an Academy Award for his intense script for *Silence of the Lambs,* but it is entirely missing from this film. Instead the story is so even paced that there is virtually no tension and no emotional payoff. Consequently there is also no emotional commitment to the characters or the film on the part of the viewer. Tally concentrates not on the mystery of the young girl's death and Jacob's part in it, nor does he concentrate on the stress and tension of the courtroom drama. Instead he focuses on the Ryans, both their individual actions and characters and their interactions with each other as a family. Unfortunately, the Ryans are not characters capable of carrying the weight of an entire film. (Irons' Von Bulow may have been enigmatically unlikable, but he was never dull.) The result is that instead of finding ourselves caring about the Ryans, we find ourselves coldly detached from them. Instead of finding an absorbing mystery, we find a minimal curiosity which is satisfied at the half-way point and it's downhill from there.

—Beverley Bare Buehrer

REVIEWS

Chicago Tribune. February 23, 1996, Section Friday, p. B, C.
Detroit News. February 23, 1996, p. 1D.
Entertainment Weekly. March 1, 1996.
Los Angeles Times. February 23, 1996, p. F1.
New York Times. February 23, 1996, p. C10.
Rolling Stone. March 21, 1996, p. 106.
USA Today. February 23, 1996, p. 4D.
Variety. February 26, 1996, p. 64.
Village Voice. March 5, 1996, p. 44.

The Best Revenge

To seek revenge is to dig two graves.—Movie tagline

The Best Revenge is a refreshingly new take on the age-old scenario of righteous vengeance. Carlos is a man on a quest. He is tracking down the U.S. military advisor who murdered his wife and tortured him, leaving him for dead during the civil war in El Salvador. After seven years of searching, he finally hears from a friend that his wife's killer is living in Los Angeles, and he goes there to confront him.

Independent filmmaker James Becket, who wrote, directed, and co-produced the film, knows about torture and the scars it leaves on the victims. Becket has a background as a human rights lawyer and journalist, and wrote the first Amnesty International Report on Torture. For that report, Becket interviewed torture victims in Greece during the junta, and in a recent interview he recalled this story: "I remember one woman in particular who, after her release, saw in the street the police officer who tortured and raped her. To her surprise, she told me revenge was not in her heart, she felt a kind of loathsome pity for the man. When Greece returned to democracy, this man was shot and killed in the street by someone who did believe in revenge. I couldn't help wondering what would I do if I went through the hell of torture and one day, years later, found the man who tortured me?" Becket explores that question in *The Best Revenge* and has his character, Carlos, exact an unusual retribution on his tormentor.

It is 1985. Carlos (Carlos Riccelli), a journalist in El Salvador, and his fiancee Nelli (Bruna Lombardi) are arrested and taken from their home in the middle of the night at the height of the civil war in their country. Carlos watches as his fiancee is first drugged, then dragged away into another room, where he hears three shots, never seeing Nelli again. He is bound and tortured by a U.S. military advisor and left for dead. Since that time, he has been searching for the man he holds responsible for Nelli's death—a man who calls himself "Mr. Smith."

As the film opens, it is seven years later. Carlos has gotten a tip from a friend that Mr. Smith is in California, so he illegally slips into the country only to find that his friend has since died. He contacts Ellen Maguire (Pat Destro), an activist working with a human rights organization that has also been trying to find Mr. Smith because of his activities during the El Salvadorian civil war. They think they have located him, so Ellen takes Carlos to where the alleged "Smith" works, to see if they can get a positive identification. Carlos isn't quite certain that this is the same man who stood in the shadows while he was being tortured, but when Ellen leaves, he breaks into the man's car and gets his name and address from his mail.

That night after the man's wife leaves, Carlos breaks into his Beverly Hills home and confronts him. He is David Miller, who claims he is an investment banker and denies ever having been in El Salvador. Carlos doesn't believe him, and he ties him up, trying to force a confession from him by attaching electric wires to his genitals as he himself had been tortured. At the last moment, Carlos realizes that he is becoming just like the man who tortured him and he can't bring himself to flip the switch.

Miller gets lose and calls the police, but it is April 1992, and Los Angeles is in the grip of the violence that swept the city after the Rodney King trial verdict. Fires burn out of control, police are trying to stop the massive looting, and Miller's 911 call is left on hold. He runs out into the street and stops a car for help, but instead of good Samaritans, he finds a couple of gangbangers out on a looting spree. They untie Miller and take Carlos' gun away from him, and after they feel they have leveled the playing field, they leave them, driving off to collect their share of the city's booty.

Free now, Miller tries to fight Carlos, but he pulls another gun out of his waistband and returns his hostage to the house, tying him up once more.

On a hunch, Ellen comes to Miller's house. She was convinced that Carlos would do something crazy and, when she sees the bound and gagged Miller, her worst fears are

CREDITS

Carlos: Carlos Riccelli
David Miller: Robert Pine
Ellen Maguire: Pat Destro
Jennifer: Sarah Bibb
Nelli: Bruna Lombardi
John: John Toles-Bey
Ricky: Christian Svensson

Origin: USA
Released: 1995
Production: James Becket and Michael French for an IQ Entertainment, Inc. and Wild Films production
Direction: James Becket
Screenplay: James Becket
Cinematography: Denis Maloney
Editing: Michael Mayhew
Music: Parmer Fuller
Costume design: Elizabeth Jett
Art direction: Robert Schulenberg
Sound: Mark Allen
MPAA rating: Unrated
Running Time: 89 minutes

realized. She begs Carlos to find some proof that this really is Mr. Smith, before he makes the mistake of hurting an innocent man. Together they search through his papers to see where Miller was seven years ago. Finally Ellen finds an old passport and tells Carlos that Miller was in South Africa at the time of Nelli's murder. Horror-struck that he has been terrorizing an innocent man, he and Ellen quickly leave the house, abandoning Miller tied in his chair.

Carlos drives away, planning to leave the city before Miller is found and the police come after him, but something prevents him from leaving. Finally, he comes back to Miller's house and apologizes to him for treating him as he himself had been treated. When Carlos frees him, Miller grabs his gun and, bragging that indeed he is Mr. Smith, he admits to torturing Carlos. When Miller goes to shoot him, he finds that the gun isn't loaded. Carlos overcomes him and he's back in the chair once more, but now Carlos is certain that this is the man who killed his wife. He has laid a trap for Miller and has taped his confession. He pins the tape onto Miller's chest and, as he turns to shoot him, Miller's wife walks in. It is Nelli.

The final scene reveals what really occurred the night of Carlos' arrest and the true reason behind it, and although the ending is surprising, it is also totally believable. After unmasking Miller for the monster he really is, Carlos wreaks a revenge on him that will scar his entire life.

Although at first glance, the plot may remind one of Polanski's *Death and the Maiden* (1994), the mood of this film is much lighter. Becket tints his scenes with humor throughout the film. Whether he is distracting the obsessed Carlos with a street person spouting fire and brimstone, or a goofy prostitute dressed for a little "sadomachoism," or even the madness of a couple of gangbangers discussing the Bill of Rights, Becket has a talent for incorporating the absurd into a serious tale of deceit, revenge, and enduring love.

Brazilian born Carlos Riccelli, in his first English-speaking role, is passionately intense as the driven, yet torn, Carlos, who wants his revenge, but doesn't want to become a "Mr. Smith" in the process. Riccelli is well known in Brazil for his work in the theater, television, and film, and played the lead in *They Don't Wear Black Tie,* which won the Golden Lion at the Venice Film Festival in 1981.

Robert Pine, who plays David Miller, is known to audiences as Sgt. Joe Gatraer, from the TV show "CHIPS." In *The Best Revenge,* Pine successfully personifies the innocent man who is cruelly being tortured in his own home, and just when we are finally convinced of his innocence, he reveals his true nature. His transformation from a gentle banker into a self-serving despot is fascinating to watch.

Director of photography Denis Maloney's cinematography is excellent, along with all of the technical aspects of *The Best Revenge,* and the entire film is of first-rate professional quality.

When the film first opens, its subject matter appears to be primarily political, but Becket wisely allows the political aspects of the film to become backdrop to a moving flesh and blood drama. According to Becket, "The best political films for me are human stories where neither the filmmaker nor the characters step onto a soapbox. I tend to be drawn to 'political' subjects, but I've come to understand that movies are about telling a story and communicating emotion, not complex ideas, which are better suited for books."

In order to do this, Becket has made *The Best Revenge* a little less factual than it is emotional, especially when describing CIA involvement in El Salvador, and the deus ex machina of the Los Angeles riots is a bit too convenient. But despite these minor flaws, Becket manages to give us a feel-good ending for a tragic story that is, as he puts it, "as old as King David in the Bible."

—Diane Hatch-Avis

Big Bully

A comedy for the kid in all of us.—Movie tagline
"High energy and good fun."—Susan Stark, *Detroit News*
"Moranis and Arnold are first rate."—Kevin Thomas, *Los Angeles Times*

Box Office: $2,042,530

Certainly no one is surprised to see children's unkindness to other children. Indeed, bullying, beating, teasing, and terrorizing are just a few of the earmarks of playground scuffles and elementary-school and adolescent heartbreak. Such stories have been told on film in a variety of genres: horror (*Carrie,* 1976), weepie/sentimental (*Stand By Me,* 1986), comedy (*National Lampoon's Class Reunion,* 1982), and combinations of the above (*A Christmas Story,* 1983). *Big Bully* takes the typical story a bit further, pushing the edge of black comedy.

Young David Leary (Justin John Ross) spends his days trying to avoid and, where impossible to avoid, endure the bullying of Rosco "Fang" Bigger (Michael Zwiener). Repeatedly Roscoe pounds on David, until, year after year, David's family collects school pictures in which David looks like a tough: black eyes, cut lips, swollen jaws. Luckily for David, his family moves, and he is able to escape Rosco. Before he leaves, however, small David Leary, brunt of Roscoe Biggers' endless jokes and jabs, seeks revenge on his tormentor and thereby has a huge impact on Rosco Bigger's life, an impact which can be undone only by David Leary's return to town.

As unsavory as much of *Big Bully* is, in an odd way it encapsulates many of the woes of the baby boomer generation. For instance, the grown-up, divorced, disillusioned, displaced David Leary (Rick Moranis) is unable to outgrow his weaknesses. His son Ben (Blake Bashoff) may be more grown up than his father, especially once David returns to the town of his childhood. For instance, it gives little away to say that the grown Roscoe Bigger (Tom Arnold) learns to enjoy picking on the grown David as much as he did the child David. Their relationship, it would seem, is permanently fixed, and at points it appears as if for eternity they are destined to spin around each other with the same degree of animosity. This relationship is not the anomaly, however, as all of David's childhood friends have remained permanently affixed in adolescence. For instance, the pyromaniac is a fireman who sets fires for entertainment and the friend who can contort to insert his fist in his mouth continues to do so as a grown man at the local pub. And all of the "adolescent" men continue to be dazzled by Victoria (Julianne Phillips), who (as luck would have it) teaches sex education at the old school. Baby boomers have failed to grow up, it is true, but a film chronicling their numbskullery is little more than sickeningly mesmerizing.

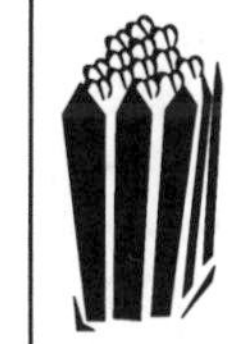

"Welcome to hell! I'll be your tour guide!"—Fang to David

Also, black humor is a troubling entertainment generally. For instance, *Neighbors* (1981), the story of how a milquetoast's life in the suburbs is overrun by the bizarre and destructive people next door, missed at the box office perhaps because cause and effect no longer motivated the characters, and the resulting film had the entertainment value of pulling cuticles. Another black comedy, *Heathers* (1989), entertained its few counterculture fans by taking the typical adolescent daydreams to life: Hate the most popular girl? Feed her Draino. Hardly run-of-the mill or family entertainment for the most hard-boiled. Likewise, *Big Bully* teaches us little about ourselves and our world but may succeed in entertaining audience members who can withstand its torturous tickling.

Even in its best reviews, *Big Bully* was labeled little more than a "corny dum-dum com-

CREDITS

David Leary: Rick Moranis
Rosco Bigger (Fang): Tom Arnold
Victoria: Julianne Phillips
Faith: Carol Kane
Art: Jeffrey Tambor
Principal Kokelar: Don Knotts

Origin: USA
Released: 1996
Production: Lee Rich, Gary Foster for a Morgan Creek production; released by Warner Bros.
Direction: Steve Miner
Screenplay: Mark Steven Johnson
Cinematography: Daryn Okada
Editing: Marshall Harvey
Art direction: Douglasann Menchions
Costume design: Monique Prudhomme
Sound: Michael Hilkene
Production design: Ian Thomas
Set decoration: Lesley Beale
MPAA rating: PG
Running Time: 93 minutes

edy ostensibly appealing to young boys but actually appealing to their 35-year-old movie-exec dads nostalgic for their childhoods" (*Entertainment Weekly*). It is a narrow category of viewers who will enjoy *Big Bully* on its own terms—and those viewers know who they are. Others may watch with a sick fascination that provides little pleasure at the time or in the long run. Most viewers will no doubt want to pass on this poisonous bonbon.

—*Roberta F. Green*

REVIEWS

Chicago Tribune. January 29, 1996, p. 2.
Detroit Free Press. January 28, 1996, p. 3P.
Detroit News. January 27, 1996, p. C1.
Entertainment Weekly. February 9, 1996, p. 38.
Los Angeles Times. January 29, 1996, p. F8.
Variety. January 29, 1996, p. 61.

Big Night

In love and life, one big night can change everything.—Movie tagline

"One of the very best films of 1996!"—David Kehr, *New York Daily News*

"Delicious! An appetite rousing delight!"—David Ansen, *Newsweek*

"Oh, let's just say it - a completely delicious movie!"—Richard Schickel, *Time*

Box Office: $7,600,000

Big Night concerns two immigrant brothers trying to make a success of their humble Italian restaurant, the Paradise. Primo (Tony Shalhoub) and Secundo Pilaggi (Stanley Tucci) settled near the New Jersey shore in the 1950s and struggle to keep the bank from foreclosing. They disagree about how much they should cater to the unrefined tastes of the neighborhood. Complicating the issue is a thriving Italian bistro down the street run by Pascal (Ian Holm), who happily compromises the quality of his cuisine to reach as many customers as possible.

Made for four million dollars and shot in thirty-five days, *Big Night* is a great example of quality independent filmmaking. Stanley Tucci was frustrated with the roles he was offered as an actor, so he worked on writing the script for *Big Night* intermittently for years before taking it to his cousin Joseph Tropiano, who provided shape and structure. Tucci also co-directed the film with his lifelong friend Campbell Scott. Tucci and Tropiano won the Waldo Salt Screenwriting Award when *Big Night* premiered at the 1996 Sundance Film Festival. Since then, *Time* magazine named *Big Night* the second-best film of the year (after *The English Patient*), and many other critics placed it on their ten-best lists. The strengths of the film lie in its ideas of art vs. money and of self-awareness, in its understanding of its characters, and in its fine ensemble acting.

The opening scenes leisurely introduce Primo and Secundo. The only couple dining at the Paradise wants a side order of spaghetti and meatballs to go with Primo's seafood risotto. Primo, the genius in the kitchen, fumes at the thought of adding starch to his perfect entree. Secundo, trying to keep the patrons happy, urges him to please them. The brothers later discuss whether the excessive preparation time and cost of the risotto can be justified by their meager income. Primo, however, favors maintaining this symbol of their quality: "If you give people time, they learn." Secundo wonders.

Secundo's awkward position as the man in the middle intensifies when he sees his girlfriend Phyllis (Minnie Driver). She asks him, "Do you want to marry me?" Secundo stammers out a reply ("Probably. Someday. Yes. In the future."), and Phyllis sums him up pretty well: "I don't think you know what you want." In hopes of getting a loan for the struggling restaurant, Secundo visits Pascal, whose business philosophy recasts the words of Primo: "You give people what they want, then later you can give them what you want." Pascal offers to invite bandleader Louis Prima to the Paradise. The attention such a star would bring the restaurant would help to build a customer base. Pascal tells Secundo that he will be his lighthouse.

The middle scenes in the film prepare for the big night of the celebrity's arrival. Primo despises Pascal's shameless profiteering ("The man should be in prison for the food he serves"), so Secundo tells his brother that Louis Prima is coming but not that it was Pascal's idea. Other secrets also unify the middle scenes. Secundo carries on a secret affair with Pascal's mistress Gabriella (Isabella Rossellini), whom he sneaks off to see on the afternoon of the big night. Primo harbors an unspoken affection for Ann (Allison Janney), the woman who runs the neighborhood flower shop. As the day wears on, Primo makes a secret phone call to an uncle in Italy to obtain a promise of a job offer if the brothers are willing to return home.

The film offers many understated, charming moments, a number of which involve Primo and Ann. When Primo goes to the flower shop to order flowers for the big night, he becomes too tongue-tied to invite Ann to the banquet that evening. His nervousness leads him to walk right into the refrigerator of flowers, causing Ann to smile at his self-consciousness. That night Ann arrives, having been invited by Secundo, and Primo brings her into his kitchen, where he becomes more eloquent on the topic of food: "To eat good food is to be close to God." When Ann sees the care and passion Primo lavishes on his food, she sees the real Primo.

The Paradise fills with family and friends on the night Louis Prima is expected, and the filmmakers make this extended moment their most lyrical scene. Primo has prepared course after course of delicious food for Ann, Phyllis, Gabriella, Pascal, Secundo, and others from the neighborhood, including a newspaper reporter there to cover the event. Title cards precede each course, and a montage of shots of the long table of satisfied guests reveal everyone's pleasure. All agree it is the greatest meal they have ever had. At one point Pascal interrupts the experience in a shout that makes Secundo wonder if he has learned about his affair with Gabriella, but Pascal simply wants to embrace the brothers and congratulate them on the best meal ever.

The oblique build up to this scene is intentional. Scriptwriters Tucci and Tropiano sought to minimize background and exposition, but they also admit that the resulting development may obscure a few points. Tropiano said that "even during the editing process, the editor [Suzy Elmiger] would say, 'Oh, so that's what that scene is about.'" And Tucci added, "Everything's so elliptical. But that's the way it is in life much of the time." Consequently, cause and effect pleasantly blur at times in the film, and the audience must be alert to intuit some of the connections. When Primo converses briefly, for example, with a customer about a painting, and this art later appears on the wall of the restaurant, the suggestion seems to be that the customer used his own painting to pay for his meal and that Primo, the artist with food, understands and supports his need to find an audience. In another example, the only conversation between Phyllis and Gabriella contains a hint about Phyllis's future plans after

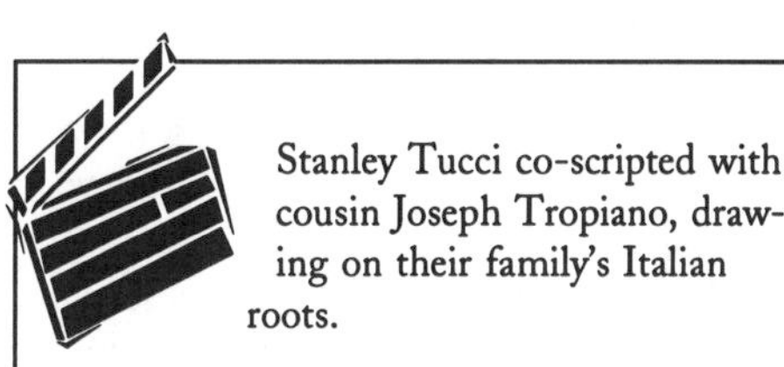

Stanley Tucci co-scripted with cousin Joseph Tropiano, drawing on their family's Italian roots.

Actor turned director Stanley Tucci serves up an Italian feast for the eyes and appetite in the Sundance favorite, *Big Night*.

CREDITS

Secundo: Stanley Tucci
Primo: Tony Shalhoub
Pascal: Ian Holm
Gabriella: Isabella Rossellini
Phyllis: Minnie Driver
Ann: Allison Janney
Cristiano: Marc Anthony

Origin: USA
Released: 1996
Production: Jonathan Filley, Elizabeth W. Alexander, and Peter Liguori for Timpano and Rysher Entertainment; released by the Samuel Goldwyn Company
Direction: Stanley Tucci and Campbell Scott
Screenplay: Stanley Tucci and Joseph Tropiano
Cinematography: Ken Kelsch
Editing: Suzy Elmiger
Art direction: Jeffrey D. McDonald, David Stein
Set decorator: Susan Raney
Production design: Andrew Jackness
Music: Gary DeMichele
Costumes: Juliet A. Polcsa
MPAA rating: R
Running Time: 90 minutes

her final breakup with Secundo. Pascal's promise to Secundo about being his lighthouse resonates more when the audience recalls that the opening shot of the film pictured a lighthouse on the New Jersey shoreline.

Another departure is the film's intentional emphasis on wide-angle shots long in duration. In an early scene this tack emphasizes the many empty tables at the Paradise, a visual way of establishing the brothers' need for business. In a kitchen scene after Primo has learned that Pascal suggested the visit by Louis Prima, such a use of proxemics conveys his anger as the brothers keep their distance from each other as they pointlessly recheck the stove. In Pascal's office the wide establishing and re-establishing shots take in the cluster of celebrity photographs on the wall, one of his proud signs of success. Stanley Tucci explained what such a style adds to the film: "I wanted to write and direct a piece that brought physicality back into film and made use of the master shot. That's a dying thing, unfortunately. I think actors are often underused. So many movies have all these close-ups. It's all coverage. . . . Whereas, the other way forces you. The script has to be tight. The blocking has to be right. The actors' intentions have to be clear. . . . Every aspect of the film has to be complete: the design, the lighting, the acting, the writing, and the direction." Some of the longer master shots in *Big Night,* like the noteworthy final shot of the film, resemble little one-act plays and recall in their subtlety and de-emphasis of editing the work of the great director William Wyler.

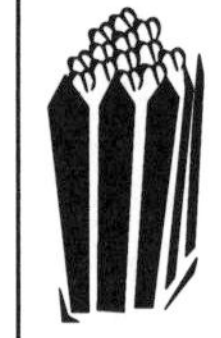

"The rape of cuisine occurs there night after night!"—Primo about a popular, rival Italian restaurant

Although most reviewers pointed out that the film explores the compromises and conflicts between art and commerce, the concluding scenes of *Big Night* suggest that self-awareness is also an important theme. The great banquet ends at three in the morning; Louis Prima never arrives. Secundo takes the plates reserved for the celebrity and drops them one by one in the kitchen trash. While the rest of the guests begin a game, he sadly tells Gabriella that he is left with nothing. She kisses him—partly out of sympathy—but Phyllis sees them together and leaves in anger. Secundo rushes after her and Gabriella, hurt by his departure, announces to Primo that Pascal had never invited Louis Prima.

A series of key confrontations concludes the film. The remaining guests and Primo rush after Secundo, who has found Phyllis wading in the ocean and has talked her back onto the shore. She again storms off, and Primo now tells his distraught brother about their uncle's job offer in Rome. "This place is eating us alive," says Primo. The brothers' ongoing argument over compromise, which now leads to a scuffle in the sand, casts Primo, perhaps for the first time, as the one who understands himself and his own needs. "If I sacrifice my work, it dies," he tells Secundo. "Better if I die." The brother who had seemed too idealistic and unwilling to adapt now appears self-aware and mature. By holding off this point until the climax when Primo's emotions emerge most fully during the brothers' fight, the film sharpens the impact of the idea: some things are above compromise; living with a purpose, the film implies, even though it is a passion for a beautifully prepared meal, is still better than merely existing. "You have rotted," Primo reproaches his brother. "I've tried to teach you, but you've learned nothing."

Another confrontation for Secundo waits in the Paradise when he approaches Pascal, who explains that the deception about Louis Prima was conceived in order to save Secundo. Pascal sought to hasten the failure of the Paradise to get Primo as his own chef: "What I did, I did out of respect," he says. Secundo's reply shows that Primo's earlier words have registered: "You will never have my brother. He lives in a world above you." The film suggests, however, that even opportunistic Pascal, has attained a measure of self-acceptance and self-awareness: "I am a businessman. I am anything I need to be at any time. Tell me, what exactly are you?" His question is the last line of the film.

The subsequent, final shot illustrates beautifully the film's many strengths of acting, simplicity, ellipsis, and understatement. In a wordless, unbroken shot the next morning in the kitchen of the Paradise, Secundo tiredly prepares an omelet for himself and Christiano (Marc Anthony), the kitchen assistant. The placement of the camera to shoot the scene in a single wide shot of five minutes allows the audience to watch both the progress of the meal and the haggard looks of the characters the morning after the brothers' argument. After Secundo serves the omelet to Christiano and they begin eating, Primo enters and slowly takes a chair next to his brother, the tension from their fight still present. Secundo prepares for Primo a serving of the omelet, and while they tiredly eat their breakfast, the brothers gradually slip their arms around each other's shoulder as the film ends.

Tucci comments tellingly on this beautifully subtle conclusion: "People love that shot. I think we did seven takes. For me, it was the most truthful way to tell that story. When we come back there at the end, that kitchen has a totally different meaning to us. So much has happened

AWARDS AND NOMINATIONS

Independent Spirit Awards 1997: First Screenplay (Tucci/Tropiano)
Nominations: First Feature (Scott/Tucci), Actor (Shalhoub), Actor (Tucci)
National Society of Film Critics 1996: Supporting Actor (Shalhoub)
New York Film Critics Circle 1996: Best First Film

in there. By letting the camera sit and take in all the elements, it, hopefully, has much more depth and meaning for the audience than it did an hour-and-a-half-before. We should be able to turn that camera on and watch them for a few minutes. Because now they're people we know. Now they're like our family, and you can watch people you know forever."

—*Glenn Hopp*

REVIEWS

Cosmopolitan. October, 1996, p. 120.
Detroit News. September 21, 1996, p. 1D.
Entertainment Weekly. September 9, 1996, p. 49.
Esquire. October, 1996, p. 36.
National Review. December 9, 1996, p. 65.
Newsweek. February 12, 1996, p. 81.
New York. October 28, 1996, p. 124.
New York Times. March 29, 1996, p. C8.
New Yorker. September 23, 1996, p. 100.
Newsweek. February 12, 1996, p. 81.
People Weekly. December 4, 1996, p. 103.
Rolling Stone. October 3, 1996, p. 78.
Time. December 23, 1996, p. 72.
USA Today. September 25, 1996, p. 9D.
Variety. February 5, 1996, p. 60.
Village Voice. September 24, 1996, p. 68.
Vogue. October, 1996, p. 212.
Washington Post. September 27, 1996, p. 42.

The Big Squeeze

A comedy about life, love . . . and loot.—Movie tagline

"Funny and provocative!"—Ron Brewington, *American Urban Radio*

"Irrepressibly hopeful . . . contagious sense of fun."—Michael Tunison, *Entertainment Weekly*

"Sharp, sassy and sexy - and surprisingly original!"—William Arnold, *Seattle Post-Intelligencer*

Box Office: $35,595

In *The Big Squeeze,* veteran cable director Marcus DeLeon tries to turn a traditional noir triangle—frustrated wife, sexually unresponsive and sadistic husband, new-in-town con artist—into a wistful comedy with mediocre results. *The Big Squeeze* ends up being an intermittently charming but mostly lame caper film that is neither suspenseful noir nor successful comedy.

Particularly unbelievable is the film's big scam, or "squeeze," which is so transparently phony, but portrayed with such sincere Frank Capra-esque corniness, that much of the film's credibility is lost.

The Big Squeeze's saving grace is an erotically charged performance by Lara Flynn Boyle, who brings subtlety and style to a woefully underwritten role. When the film works, it is mainly as a showcase for Boyle.

Benny O'Malley (Peter Dobson), a scam artist, is pushed off a freight train in Highland Park, a predominantly Latino section of Los Angeles, his poker hand of five kings thrown after him. Benny's first mark is Jesse (Danny Nucci), a sweet, hardworking gardener and painter tending roses in a public park. Ben compliments Jesse on the roses, then proceeds to tell him how to garden.

Meanwhile, Henry (Luca Bercovici), an habitual walker in the park, limps back to his run-down apartment in the middle of the day. Henry, a former major-league baseball player, has been living off disability for several years since being sidelined by a game-related injury. Henry harbors delusions of returning to the majors, which only frustrates his wife, Tanya (Boyle), to whom he offers roses picked from Jesse's garden. In a traditional noir set-up, the affection-starved Tanya tells Henry she wants money, wants a car, wants to go places.

After they make mid-day love, Henry, a fanatically devout Catholic, goes to his local parish to ask forgiveness for using his wife for carnal purposes. Unbeknownst to Henry, the parish's two priests, the older Father Sanchez (Sam Vlahos) and the younger Father Arias (Valente Rodriguez), receive notice from L.A. city building inspectors that the church must be retrofitted for earthquake safety or shut down. Benny, now hanging around the neighborhood looking for a mark, overhears the priests' dilemma.

In the bar where Tanya works the evening shift behind the counter, the shy Jesse is hassled by other, older Latino men. Tanya is attracted to his unshowy, sensitive way of handling himself and flirts with him. Benny, however, intervenes and re-introduces himself to Jesse. Jesse is suspicious, but Benny slickly tells the barflies about Jesse's talent for gardening. Cece (Teresa Dispina), Tanya's co-worker, likes both Jesse and Benny, but correctly predicts to Tanya that Benny has no money.

When Benny hears that Tanya has left the bar and is walking home, he catches up to her, and Tanya is not unwilling to entertain a flirtation with him, too. But at her apartment door, she pointedly tells him that they wouldn't want to wake her husband. Benny offers her a necklace, which she refuses, and kisses her anyway.

Back at the bar, Benny finds Cece. Benny goes home with her, and De Leon intercuts the two of them having wild sex with both Tanya unhappily lying awake next to her snoozing husband and Jesse alone in his apartment.

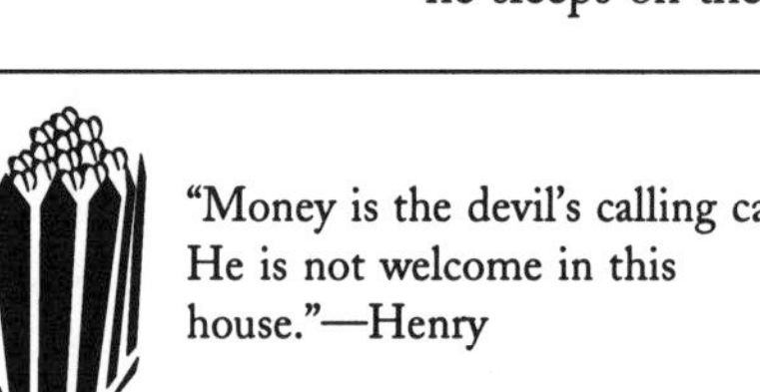

"Money is the devil's calling card. He is not welcome in this house."—Henry

The next morning, the priests price the retrofitting job at $130,000—far too much for the parish to afford. Coincidentally, at Henry and Tanya's, Tanya opens a letter from Henry's bank thanking him for opening an account for roughly the same amount. When Henry arrives home, Tanya asks him if they have ever received the insurance settlement for his baseball accident. Henry replies no, and Tanya confronts him with the letter. Henry flies into a rage, says they had an agreement never to open each other's mail, and tells Tanya it is the "devil's" money. When Tanya tells him his baseball-playing days are over, he slaps her. Tanya packs her bags, wondering how she can get her hands on the $130,000.

Knowing that Cece has slept with Benny, Tanya proposes to the grifter a strict business arrangement in which they will ferret the money out of Henry's account and split it, with two-thirds going to Tanya. Tanya also asks a jealous, smitten Jesse if she can stay with him while she gets on her feet. Jesse, ever the gentleman, offers her his bed while he sleeps on the couch.

Benny continues to stay with Cece, while the increasingly erratic Henry stays up nights smelling Tanya's clothes.

Tanya tells Benny that Henry makes a large cash donation to the beleaguered Catholic church on the 28th of every month, and Benny begins to hatch his plan. Benny hires Jesse to garden the grounds of the parish church, and offers Jesse's gardening services to the priests free for a one-week trial. Benny then has one of the priests bless a seed, which they plant methodically. Each subsequent night under cover of darkness, Benny replants a new, each time slightly bigger, tree in the parish garden, and begins convincing the priests—and Henry, who prays every day at the church—that the rapid growth of the tree is a miracle. Benny then uses Henry's own warped, religious logic to convince Henry to make a major donation to the church in order to win Tanya back.

Meanwhile, the relationship between Jesse and Tanya is growing as well. Jesse confesses his affection for her, and they engage in playful daytime lovemaking. (The "big squeeze," in addition to meaning a scam or scheme, also refers to the lemon Tanya and Jesse squeeze on each other's bodies.) Benny, however, tells Tanya that for the plan to work, she will have to return to Henry. Jesse, enraged at what he thinks is an affair between Tanya and Benny, rips his own paintings off the walls of his apartment and destroys them. When Jesse tries to tell the older priest that the growing tree is a hoax, the priest replies that Benny may be God's agent.

The tree now appears to be growing at a fantastic rate, and the "miracle" begins to attract crowds, photographers, and media coverage. Benny convinces both Henry and the priests that God's hand is at work, and tells Tanya that the "squeeze" must begin.

When Henry arrives home, he finds Tanya waiting for him, and is persuaded that it is a miracle. Benny convinces Henry to donate all his money to the church, in cash as he usually does. The only remaining obstacle is how Benny will persuade Henry to hand over the cash to him instead of directly to the priests.

Tanya, wanting Jesse back, confesses the scam to Jesse, and explains that it is the only reason she has returned to Henry. Benny, not knowing that Tanya has told Jesse about the scam and worried that Jesse needs to be bought off, cuts Jesse in on the deal as well. He tells Jesse and Tanya to meet him at Union Station the next day at five to divvy up the money. In fact, Benny tells Tanya that the real plan is that

CREDITS

Tanya: Lara Flynn Boyle
Benny: Peter Dobson
Henry: Luca Bercovici
Jesse: Danny Nucci
Cece: Teresa Dispina
Father Sanchez: Sam Vlahos

Origin: USA
Released: 1996
Production: Zane W. Levitt, Mark Yellen and Liz McDermott for a Zeta Entertainment production; released by First Look Pictures
Direction: Marcus De Leon
Screenplay: Marcus De Leon
Cinematography: Jacques Haitkin
Editing: Sonny Baskin
Music: Mark Mothersbaugh
Production design: J. Rae Fox
Set decoration: Traci Kirshbaum
Costumes: Charmian Schreiner
Sound: Don Gooch, Paul Rataczak
Casting: Laura Schiff
MPAA rating: R
Running Time: 100 minutes

they are going to ditch Jesse and hop a freight train, just the two of them. Jesse, overhearing Benny's plan of deception, tells Tanya she, not the money, matters to him, and he wishes her luck.

As Benny tries to make the final transaction with Henry, however, the plan goes awry. Henry realizes that Benny is trying to swindle him and gives chase. As Henry is about to beat Benny to death with his cane, Benny reminds Henry that he is running—and tells him that Tanya is with Jesse.

Henry tracks Jesse down, and chases him through Highland Park and Chavez Ravine, above Dodger Stadium, but in so doing loses the cash. Suddenly, in sight of the ballpark, Henry miraculously shags a fly from a children's game of softball and realizes he can return to the big leagues. Tanya gets ahold of the cash and gives it to the priests, saving the church. Tanya and Jesse speed off into the sunset, poor but happy.

The film ends with a bloodied and chastened Benny walking amid the crowds attracted by the "miracle" he has produced.

The Big Squeeze is overly contrived, often preposterous, and sometimes embarrassingly corny. Each character has his own over-schematic "arc:" Benny, the grifter, is chastened by his own miraculous powers of persuasion; Tanya, driven by unhappiness to scheming, finds that the life of a con artist is not for her; Jesse learns to assert himself; Henry finds his salvation in losing Tanya. The central conceits—that thousands of people would be duped by a patently fake "miracle" and that Henry would turn over $130,000 in a paper bag to Benny—are ridiculous, and the film fails dismally to convince the audience that they are anything but. And De Leon's tastes run to the sentimental: Tanya and Jesse's lovemaking montage plays like a television commercial, and the scenes of the crowds oohing and aahing the miracle tree play like a bad imitation of a Frank Capra film.

Well-intentioned but never believable, *The Big Squeeze* is mostly an opportunity to show off the unmined talents of Lara Flynn Boyle. Boyle, best known for her work in David Lynch's "Twin Peaks" (1990-1991), brings a torchy physicality to a sketchily conceived role. De Leon tries to make Tanya a hybrid of the traditional scheming noir female and the modern woman waking up to the poor choices she has made. But Tanya's motivation for staying for so long with Henry, who is not only poor and abusive, but a religious fanatic, remains vague. Boyle manages to fill in some of the gaps in the character's conception with sheer charm and screen presence. The film often plays as a kind of visual Valentine to Boyle.

Other performances range from adequate to sub-par. The film's corny plot is not helped any by an unremittingly cheesy musical score.

—Paul Mittelbach

REVIEWS

Boxoffice. August, 1996, p. 60.
Chicago Tribune. September 6, 1996, p. 5.
Los Angeles Times. September 6, 1996, p. F6.
New York Times. September 6, 1996, p. C8.
Variety. June 17, 1996, p. 52.

Bio-Dome

The fate of our planet is in their hands.—Movie tagline

Box Office: $13,427,615

The most appalling part of *Bio-Dome*, the latest Pauly Shore movie, is that Shore and his band of writers, producers, and investors might actually think this film is funny. Inane jokes, scatological humor, lame plot devices, and some old-fashioned male chauvinism and homophobia are the order of the day here. It is probably the weakest in Shore's oeuvre, which is quite an accomplishment when one considers such past Shore classics as *In the Army Now* (1994), *Jury Duty* (1995), and *Encino Man* (1992).

"Are you tired? You've been running through my mind all day."—Bud trying to flatter a female scientist

Pauly Shore is the boy-man comic who symbolizes the witless, "slacker" quality of some members of the twentysomething generation. Beginning his career as a stand-up comic (his mother is Mitzi Shore, the owner of the famed "Comedy Store" club in L.A.), he moved on to his own program on MTV, and then brought his selfish, lazy, stupid-guy character to films with the successful *Encino Man*. All this success understandably fooled Shore into thinking that audiences were actually laughing with him instead of at him, and he has continued to make films ever since. To be fair, there is an audience for Shore's brand of humor. Studio executives are not completely out of their minds in spending time and resources on these films, since many people (especially young men) find Shore to be the cleverest thing since Jim Carrey.

Bio-Dome is the story of Bud (Shore) and Doyle (Stephen Baldwin, who should know better), two complete losers who spend most of their time hitting each other on the head and sucking each other's toes—yes, they actually show this on camera. When their girlfriends (Joey Adams and Teresa Hill) dump them because the boys do not share their interest in the environment, Bud and Doyle go chasing around the Tucson, Arizona countryside in pursuit of their beloveds. But fate intervenes when Doyle insists on finding a restroom. Given their insistence on expressing their bodily functions at every given opportunity regardless of the place, it seems odd that they don't pull off the road and let Doyle relieve himself alongside the deserted highway, but that would foil the plot. You see, just as Doyle is insisting they find a restroom, they drive by the Bio-Dome, a wholly contained ecosphere in which five scientists are about to lock themselves in for one year.

Thinking the Bio-Dome to be a shopping mall, they slip past the security guards and get locked in with the scientists. Bud and Doyle nearly destroy the Bio-Dome by playing golf in the rain forest, poisoning the water supply, tipping the homeostatic balance by trapping all the insects on giant fly-paper, and trying to get into the beds of two gorgeous female scientists. Then, rather early in the film, the boys are banished to the desert portion of the Bio-Dome, where they discover a door that leads outside. After that, much of the action centers around their attempts to get back into the Bio-Dome to have a big party that will impress their skeptical but non-Einsteinesque girlfriends. It seems that the scriptwriters evade dealing with the consequences of Bud and Doyle's behavior inside the Bio-Dome at the expense of showing the big party scene, where the Bio-Dome is invaded by kids from the outside world.

The Bio-Dome scientists, "The Bio-Dome Five" as they refer to themselves, are led by the intense Dr. Noah Faulkner

CREDITS

Bud Macintosh: Pauly Shore
Doyle Johnson: Stephen Baldwin
Dr. Noah Faulkner: William Atherton
Monique: Joey Adams
Jen: Teresa Hill
William Leaky: Henry Gibson

Origin: USA
Released: 1996
Production: Brad Krevoy, Steve Stabler and Brad Jenkel for a Metro-Goldwyn-Mayer, Motion Picture Corp. of America/Weasel Prods./3 Arts Entertainment production; released by MGM/UA
Direction: Jason Bloom
Screenplay: Kip Koenig and Scott Marcano
Cinematography: Phedon Papamichael
Editing: Christopher Greenbury
Production design: Michael Johnston
Art direction: Don Diers, Carol Stensel
Sound: William M. Fiege
Casting: Rick Montgomery, Dan Parada
Music: Andrew Gross
MPAA rating: PG-13
Running Time: 94 minutes

(William Atherton), a man with a bad attitude and an even worse wig. At first he and the project's director (Henry Gibson) try to embrace the unwanted presence of Bud and Doyle so as not to alarm the media into thinking the Bio-Dome experiment has failed. "This pre-planned addition is intended to simulate the 'chaos' theory," says Gibson. As the film progresses, Faulkner becomes increasingly demented, particularly after his beloved Bio-Dome experiment has apparently failed.

After some scolding from their girlfriends, Bud and Doyle realize that they are responsible for the near destruction of the Bio-Dome, and they embark on a ridiculous and inexplicably successful campaign to save the Bio-Dome's ecosphere. Shore seems to enjoy portraying his dimwitted character as a person who saves the world. *In the Army Now* and *Jury Duty* both shared the same formula: A destructive and inane character wreaks havoc on a structured institution, only to change his course midway through the film and save the day.

Directorial debut for Jason Bloom.

The script, like other Shore vehicles, is credited to several people. This must be one of the great paradoxes in modern cinema. It took one person to write, direct, produce, and star in *Citizen Kane* (1941). But it took five writers to come up with such bon mots as "I have a wicked itch on my 'nads" in *Bio-Dome.* Not to mention several producers to approve the line and one star to have the artistic vision to say it. One good comment that can be said about this script is that a satire on the famed Biosphere project in Arizona is a unique idea.

Among the films other pluses: William Atherton's attempts at extracting some dignity out of his one-dimensional character; a recurring joke about "the great chipmunk fire of '79"; funnyman Henry Gibson's cameo; and Stephen Baldwin's adroit physical comedy. Baldwin would be perfectly fine if not required to clown around with Shore, but when he does, Baldwin at least brings a sort of zaniness that is reminiscent of "The Three Stooges." He is a good actor who should avoid films like this one.

Shore, on the other hand, is especially unlikable. Perhaps many audience members do enjoy him—so, admittedly, this might be a minority opinion—but from his constant stream of weird ad-lib sounds to his bad Carmen Miranda outfit to his chronic reliance on "potty" humor and childish sexual innuendo, it is mind-boggling that anyone over 10 years old would find him to be anything but awful.

First-time director Jason Bloom keeps things moving at an acceptable pace, and with his production team makes the Bio-Dome an interesting backdrop for the action. The party scene is appropriately huge in scale, with vast numbers of bikini clad babes and frat guys swilling mai-tais, and people in varying stages of inebriation performing comic-book versions of college party antics. From golfing in the rain forest to the giant flypâper to the computer which parodies "Hal" in *2001: A Space Odyssey* (1968), director Bloom does find a few moments of fun. But then he quickly allows the action to deteriorate to nothing more than crude jokes, and he loses a little credibility.

It must be emphasized that the "dumbing" of American films in recent years might be seen as a legitimate response to social problems and/or to the rise in number of moviegoing children of baby boomers. Not everyone sees this trend as alarming. Some see this trend as having no meaning at all. In fact, some people like this kind of humor. And, all kidding aside, they should be free to indulge themselves. But for those people who enjoy humor that goes beyond flatulence, genital size, masturbation, homophobic epithets, and tasteless objectification of women, this film signals the end of civilization as we know it. The success of Jim Carrey's *Dumb and Dumber* (1995) and *Ace Ventura, Pet Detective* (1994), and the continued financing of Pauly Shore's cinematic excesses are inexplicable to the majority of the moviegoing public.

REVIEWS

Boxoffice Magazine. March, 1996, p. R-28.
Detroit Free Press. January 12, 1996, p. 8D.
Los Angeles Times. January 12, 1996, p. F10.
New York Times. January 12, 1996, p. C12.
USA Today. January 12, 1996, p. 4D.
Variety. January 15, 1996, p. 126.
Washington Post. January 12, 1996, p. D7.

The Birdcage

What could possibly come between a match made in heaven? The parents. Dinner. And a nightclub called . . . —Movie tagline

"A totally hilarious treat from beginning to end!"—David Sheehan, *KCBS-TV*

"Dizzyingly farcical!"—Janet Maslin, *The New York Times*

"A very funny film! Lane and Williams are two of the world's most gifted comics."—Richard Corliss, *Time*

"*The Birdcage* is the falling-down funniest comedy you'll see this year!"—Gene Shalit, *The Today Show*

Box Office: $124,060,553

Armand Goldman (Robin Williams) is a solid member of his community. He is a hardworking businessman, running "The Birdcage," a nightclub in the trendy South Beach section of Miami, a loving spouse, and a doting father. When his college-age son, Val (Dan Futterman), informs him that he is getting married, his major reservation is that Val is too young. However, devoted father that he is, he knows he will do anything to make his son happy.

Unfortunately, the young woman whom Val has chosen to wed is Barbara Keeley (Calista Flockhart), daughter of Senator Kevin (Gene Hackman) and Louise (Dianne Wiest) Keeley. But this is no ordinary Senator. Keeley is an ultra right-wing conservative and co-founder of the Coalition for Moral Order. Val can only imagine how the Senator will respond to the news that the nightclub his father runs is a drag club and that his adoring "mother" of 20 years is a man named Albert (Nathan Lane) who, as Starina, is also the star of Armand's stage show.

Then, to the Senator's surprise, his coalition co-founder is discovered dead in the bed of a black, underage prostitute. What a field day for the press, and what a headache for the Keeleys. Very quickly their house is surrounded by reporters and cameras, their every move watched, scrutinized and flashed around the country via television. How will they ever save their reputations? Well, how about an old-fashioned wedding? Let the media focus on the glorious tradition of Barbara and Val taking the vows. It's an option pounced upon by the Senator, but Barbara has failed to tell him about Val's "mother's" high testosterone level and has even passed Armand off as the cultural attache to Greece. So, armed only with illusions, the Keeley's sneak away from their home and drive all the way to South Beach to meet their future son-in-law's family and to plan the career-saving wedding.

Now Val and Armand are faced with several difficult tasks. First of all, they have to transform their home, which is a festival of twenty years of the gay lifestyle in tropical Florida, into something more acceptable to the Senator's sensibilities. As a result out goes anything pink and risque and in comes everything dark and gothic. Out go anatomically correct statues and in come austere seats that look as if they were purloined from a monastery. In effect, out go the Goldmans (Armand's last name), and in come the Colemans (what Barbara has told her probably ethnically-distrusting father is Val's last name).

The second major problem is what to do with Albert who tearfully turns the pages of Val's childhood scrapbook after he is told that their "baby" is getting married. Obviously, Val's chances of getting the Senator's permission to

CREDITS

Armand Goldman: Robin Williams
Senator Keeley: Gene Hackman
Albert: Nathan Lane
Louise Keeley: Dianne Wiest
Val Goldman: Dan Futterman
Barbara Keeley: Calista Flockhart
Agador: Hank Azaria
Katharine: Christine Baranski
Harry Radman: Tom McGowan
Photographer: Grant Heslov
Chauffeur: Kirby Mitchell

Origin: USA
Released: 1996
Production: Mike Nichols; released by United Artists
Direction: Mike Nichols
Screenplay: Elaine May; based on the stage play *La Cage aux Folles* by Jean Poiret and the film script by Francis Veber, Edouard Molinaro, Marcello Danon and Jean Poiret
Cinematography: Emmanuel Lubezki
Editing: Arthur Schmidt
Production design: Bo Welch
Art direction: Tom Duffield
Set decoration: Cheryl Carasik
Costume design: Ann Roth
Music: Jonathan Tunick
Live Music: Steven Goldstein
MPAA rating: R
Running Time: 118 minutes

marry Barbara will be very slim if he meets the colorful Albert, so their first plan is to get him to leave town on a short vacation which is more easily envisioned than enacted.

Their next plan is for Armand to teach Albert to, in his words, "act like a man," and to pass him off as an eccentric uncle. Since Albert would do virtually anything for his baby, he tries, but it's a lost cause. Albert tries turning his stage talents to the task, but in Albert's hands, even a John Wayne walk turns swishy and the pink socks peeking out from beneath his pants are a dead giveaway.

But even this plan depends upon having a real woman around to act as a decoy. Consequently Armand visits Val's biological birth mother, Katharine Archer (Christine Baranski), who agrees that this is the least she can do since she hasn't seen Val since he was born.

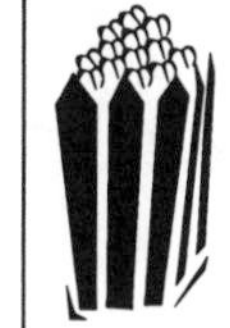

"They don't make women like that anymore."—Senator Keeley about Albert (who's dressed in dowager drag).

When the Keeleys arrive, Katharine doesn't. She's stuck in traffic. But Val and Armand suddenly find themselves with a substitute mother. Instead of acting like a man, Albert has decided to act like a woman . . . but not the glitzy prima donna Starina. Instead she's a more matronly, pearl-clad Barbara Bush. As Val's mother, Albert charms and enchants the Senator who takes to her very quickly. It would seem as if the trio has pulled off the deception but then little cracks begin to appear in the evening's facade. Their houseboy Agador (Hank Azaria) has made an unequivocally inedible meal and serves it in china decorated with naked boys playing leap frog. Albert starts to get tipsy on the wine and soon her wig begins to migrate. And when the press shows up, all hell breaks loose.

The Birdcage, which is an updated version of the French film farce *La Cage aux Folles* (1978) is one of those rare remakes that actually shines as brightly as the original. *The Birdcage* marks an artistic reunion that has been worth waiting for since it was directed by Mike Nichols who here reteams with his old 1960's comedy partner Elaine May who wrote the screenplay. They have always found their most poignant and funniest humor in the realms of politics and society, and the story of *La Cage aux Folles* is a perfect fit for them.

Based on the 1978 French film *La Cage aux Folles.*

Nichols, who is coming off several less than successful films such as *Wolf* (1994) and *Regarding Henry* (1991), with this film, again finds himself with a hit on his hands. Writer May has changed very little from the original film, the plot is virtually identical as are the jokes which echo the earlier film punchline for punchline, but she has done a terrific job of making the story seem more '90s than '70s and more American than French.

The Birdcage is a parable for our times. The very loving and tender relationship that exists between Armand and Albert is one everyone can envy. The fact that they are homosexuals seems totally irrelevant. They have raised a loving son and embody virtually all the characteristics that Senator Keeley would claim are "traditional family values." There is nothing openly sexual about *The Birdcage* (which is what will make it acceptable to mainstream American audiences). There's no hint of seduction as there was in the other recent homosexual comedy *To Wong Foo Thanks for Everything Julie Newmar* (1995), and nothing hard-hitting as in the powerful and gripping *Philadelphia* (1993). The homosexuality here is decidedly old-fashioned. No mention of AIDS, no hint of gay bashing, no suggestion of bathhouses or leather bars.

Instead, the nightclub Armand owns is a tourist spot. Attended by both gays and straights. Hey, even the Kennedys are in the audience. And the main characters are warm, loving, loyal, and sympathetic. The fact that they are gay seems important only as a comic premise. However, this is not to say audiences are laughing at the gay lifestyle. Instead they are laughing at preposterous situations. If anyone is the butt of jokes, it is the hypocritical, uptight Senator.

Besides just being a very funny (and even heartwarming) story, *The Birdcage* is also helped greatly by a cast that is packed with talent. Robin Williams, whom the studio and Nichols initially wanted to play the colorful Albert, instead preferred to play the more restrained role of Armand. Having just played a man in drag in *Mrs. Doubtfire* (1993), Williams was hesitant to do it again. It was a wise move for Williams. Audiences are used to his manic humor and his dazzling character improvisations, but here he shows he can act. As the more "manly" of the two men, Williams must be virtually the opposite of Albert. Albert is flighty and emotional, while Armand must be more composed and logical while still showing just a hint of his character. Like fathers everywhere, Armand must be all things to all the people he touches. He must be the placating partner, the serious and competent boss, the doting father, and the impeccable host. It is much harder being funny when you're the straight man (pun intended) in a comic duo, but Williams is devilishly funny in the role. His character's humor isn't over-the-top obvious, as we are used to seeing in Williams, but instead it is subversively amusing.

On the other hand, Nathan Lane as the flamboyant and campy Albert is uproariously lovable. We are as charmed by him as is the Senator. Yes, his portrayal of a literal "screaming queen" may strike some as politically incorrect, however, Albert is not just gay, she's a star! She's used to being the center of attention, and if being on the verge of a nervous breakdown or an attack of the hysterics does the job, then that's the theatrical pose she will take.

Equally important to the acceptability of the film is how the Senator is portrayed. In the capable hands of Gene Hackman, he becomes a close-minded arch conservative who spouts party lines without ever examining their underlying premises or lack of wisdom. But Hackman finds the humor in this by playing it with sincere earnestness. Who can help but smile at a man who believes the Pope is too controversial and Billy Graham is too liberal?

In a much smaller role but with just as much heart and humor is Hank Azaria as Agador. Here is one of May's major contributions to the original story where the houseboy was merely a narrative convenience. In *The Birdcage,* his part has been beefed up and, as played by Azaria, it is hilariously funny.

As *The Birdcage* racks up the boxoffice dollars, it is obvious that the film's theme is one that transcends conservative politics and alternative lifestyles. While it may adeptly deflate conservative hypocrisy, at its heart, *The Birdcage* is about loving relationships and humanity. The family in which Val was raised may have been eccentric, but it was obviously filled with respect, kindness, decency and, yes, morality. The result is a story anyone with even the slightest bit of compassion will find gentle and funny, and with all that talent, it's just made even better. If nothing else, it is worth the price of admission just to see Gene Hackman in drag.

—Beverley Bare Buehrer

AWARDS AND NOMINATIONS

Academy Awards 1996 Nominations: Best Art Direction
Golden Globe Award 1997 Nominations: Best Film-Musical/Comedy, Best Actor-Musical/Comedy (Lane)
Screen Actors Guild 1996: Cast
Nominations: Supporting Actor (Azaria), Supporting Actor (Lane)
Writers Guild of America 1996 Nominations: Adapted Screenplay (May)

REVIEWS

Boxoffice. May, 1996, p. 74.
Chicago Tribune. March 8, 1996.
Entertainment Weekly. March 15, 1996, p. 44.
Los Angeles Times. March 8, 1996, p. F1.
New York Times. March 8, 1996, p. C3.
The New Yorker. March 18, 1996, p. 109.
Premiere. January, 1996, p. 37.
Time. March 11, 1996, p. 66+.
USA Today. March 8, 1996, p. 1D.
Variety. March 4, 1996, p. 72.

Black Sheep

There's one in every family.—Movie tagline

"Farley and Spade are the comedy team of the '90's!"—Leo Quinones, *KIIS-FM*

"The best comedy I've seen this year! I couldn't stop laughing."—Brad Nimmons, *NBC-TV*

Box Office: **$32,417,164**

The idea for *Black Sheep* was evidently suggested by real-life characters who have embarrassed certain big-time politicians with unconventional behavior and controversial quotes. Such characters could include Martha Mitchell, Ronald Reagan's children, Roger Clinton, and Newt Gingrich's sister. The black sheep in this film most strongly resembles Billy Carter, the six-pack-drinking brother of President Jimmy Carter, which suggests that the script may have circulated around the movie studios for a long time before the right opportunity seemed to present itself to produce it.

Chris Farley, of television's "Saturday Night Live," must have seemed to be the right opportunity incarnate. As Mike Donnelly, kid brother of the candidate for governor of the state of Washington, Farley is well cast as a slob who could wreck any politician's career. Farley needs to be toned down if he is going to follow such comics as Dan Aykroyd, Chevy Chase, and Eddie Murphy and graduate permanently from television to feature films. He is like Lou Costello without Bud Abbott or Oliver Hardy without Stan Laurel. His co-star David Spade provides contrast but not exactly balance. Farley is like an enormous hot-air balloon that threatens to break loose and carry the whole cast up into the sky dangling from his mooring lines. He almost never seems to be off-camera. He makes adults queasy. Only small children with insatiable appetites for crude comedy could tolerate so much of him, just as they can consume incredible amounts of candy, popcorn, and other junk food while watching the screen. *Black Sheep* is junk food for the eyes, suggesting that perhaps there should be a film rating like "CG" signifying: "Unsuitable for adults unless accompanied by children."

Mike nearly wipes out the voters at one of his brother's political rallies when he shows up in a truck equipped with loudspeakers over which he has been hectoring the populace to vote for Al Donnelly (Tim Matheson). One of Farley's specialties is losing control of moving vehicles. When he gets behind the wheel the poor machine does not stand a chance. He drives on the wrong side of the highway and out into open fields. Cops can never catch him because they have too much respect for their own lives. Farley's driving mirrors his whole bull-in-a-china-shop personality. He is too stupid to do two things at the same time. If an idea occurs to him it causes him to lose control of the wheel. When the sound truck finally comes to a halt under a theater marquee with a hundred shattered light-bulbs, Al's slick campaign adviser says emphatically, "We've got to keep this bozo under wraps until the election is over."

Al loves his brother and appreciates his sincere but woefully misguided efforts to help him win the election. In desperation he hires Steve Dodds (David Spade) to keep Mike out of the public eye. His opponent's henchmen, on the other hand, intend to do everything they can to keep brother Mike in the public eye as much as they can.

"We have got to keep this bozo under wraps until the election is over."—Donnelly's campaign advisor about his brother Mike

Social psychiatrist Eric Berne, author of the best-selling book *Games People Play* (1964), would have diagnosed Farley—or at least the character he has portrayed in his two feature films—as a "schlemiel." His victim (in this case both brother Al Don-

CREDITS

Mike Donnelly: Chris Farley
Steve Dodds: David Spade
Al Donnelly: Tim Matheson
Governor Tracy: Christine Ebersole
Drake Sabitch: Gary Busey
Robbie Meighem: Grant Heslov

Origin: USA
Released: 1996
Production: Lorne Michaels; released by Paramount Pictures
Direction: Penelope Spheeris
Screenplay: Fred Wolf
Cinematography: Daryn Okada
Editing: Ross Albert
Production design: Peter Jamison
Art direction: Chris Cornwell
Costume design: Jill Ohanneson
Sound: Willie Burton
Stunt coordination: Shane Dixon
Music: William Ross
MPAA rating: PG-13
Running Time: 87 minutes

nelly and custodian Steve Dodds) is called the "schlemazl." The purpose of the game of Schlemiel, according to Dr. Berne, is to obtain love in the form of forgiveness while at the same time indulging in the infantile pleasure of making messes. The "schlemazl" goes along with the game because he gets the satisfaction of being seen as a loving, forgiving, and understanding person.

It is hard to guess which of the gubernatorial candidates is the Republican and which is the Democrat—assuming those are the two parties represented. The movie is only superficially political—and that is one of the things that it wrong with it: it does not take its own premise seriously. *New York Times* reviewer Janet Maslin complained that *Black Sheep* is "a feature film inflated from a skit's worth of material." Both Al Donnelly and Governor Tracy, it would seem, are running purely on their personalities rather than on any recognizable platforms. The fact that the story is set in the Pacific Northwest seems purely coincidental; it could have been set in Iowa or Maine or Florida. The opportunity to deal with such a controversial topic as environmental protectionism versus the needs of private enterprise is totally ignored in favor of seemingly endless somersaults, pratfalls, car chases and demolition. In one scene the seemingly indestructible Farley gets dragged behind a speeding car with sparks flying from the friction between his belt buckle and the pavement. As in animated cartoons such as "Tom and Jerry" and "Roadrunner," the sight gags are all based on physical pain.

Even though Mike and Steve spend some time in a cabin up in the serene, tree-covered mountains, the film takes little advantage of the scenery. Their destructive antics in the cabin vaguely recall Charlie Chaplin's classic *The Gold Rush* (1925)—but the comparison only highlights the modern film's lack of genuine inspiration. In one scene, for example, Farley who is sleeping in the top bunk predictably falls through and lands on top of Spade. In another they destroy the cabin trying to get rid of an intruding bat. The pair go off into the mountains only to return to the city on some flimsy pretext. The film never seems to know where it is going—and neither does the viewer.

Among their many misadventures, the heroes fall afoul of a psychotic Vietnam veteran named Drake Sabitch (Gary Busey), who lives out in the woods in a trailer protected by land mines and booby traps. The explosives are hardly necessary with Farley's self-destructive propensities. When Sabitch catches Farley and Spade on his property he threatens to kill them, but eventually he becomes their ally and contributes to bringing about the downfall of incumbent Governor Tracy (Christine Ebersole) in the final fracas.

Al Donnelly's opponent is running a campaign of dirty tricks that will remind older viewers of President Richard Nixon and company (another indication the script had been around for awhile). The tough lady has her henchmen set fire to the recreation center where good-natured, well-meaning, but terribly stupid Mike was employed until he was fired for incompetence. A photographer is posted in the dark to catch pictures of Mike apparently starting the blaze whereas he is trying desperately to put it out. Knowing that Mike represents her opponent's Achilles' heel, Governor Tracy is determined to make the most of her golden opportunity. Ebersole delivers a convincing performance of an unscrupulous politician who will stop at nothing to retain power.

The band Mudhoney make a cameo appearance at a "Rock the Vote" rally.

One of the most interesting things about this production is the fact that it was able to hit the top of *Variety*'s Box Office Chart in the first week after its release. The fact that it appeared in what promises to be one of the most critical and bitterly contested election years in American history might have helped it. It only held first place for one week but had a respectable domestic gross of nearly $31-million by the end of the sixth week.

Chris Farley and David Spade have been compared to Abbott and Costello because of some personality and physical similarities. Whether the two "Saturday Night Live" graduates can succeed as a comedy team remains a moot question. Spade has plenty of talent and personality in his own right and could eventually go off on his own. If so, Farley could conceivably team up with another straight man. He seems to need that sort of ballast because a little of him goes a long way.

Reviewers have noted that *Black Sheep* is a reprise of *Tommy Boy* (1995), in which Farley was teamed with the unflappable David Spade in a similar plot. *Variety* suggested that *Black Sheep* might have been called *Tommy Boy 2.* The earlier film was funnier and more coherent than its successor. *Tommy Boy* was also helped by the charisma of two mature and very recognizable supporting actors, Dan Aykroyd and Brian Dennehy, who both seemed more effective than Spade in holding Farley in some kind of orbit. (Barrel-chested, no-neck Dennehy actually made Farley look small.)

Although the two stories are similar there are also important differences. In *Tommy Boy,* the oafish hero has a specific objective, with his father's entire company—executives and workers—rooting for him like a Greek chorus, reminding the audience of what is at stake and how they should be feeling. In *Black Sheep,* nobody wants Farley's interference; to the contrary, everybody, including his own partner, wants him as far out of the way as possible, preferably in a cabin on a mountain-top in the middle of nowhere. It is not until the very end, when Farley miraculously uses his feeble I.Q. to figure out that Governor Tracy is feloniously stuffing ballot boxes, that he has a specific objective and a chance to be a hero. Before that discovery his actions have no direction, which is what makes him look like an intoxicated retard lost in a hall of mirrors.

—*Bill Delaney*

REVIEWS

Boxoffice. April, 1996, p. 118.
Entertainment Weekly. February 23, 1996, p. 103.
Los Angeles Times. February 2, 1996, p. F6.
New York Times. February 2, 1996, p. C19.
Variety. February 5, 1996, p. 59.

Bogus

If you believe in one thing, believe in Bogus.—Movie tagline

"A fantasy of infinite charm for all ages."—Kevin Thomas, *Los Angeles Times*

"Completely enchanting. A great spirit-lifter."—Pat Collins, *WWOR-TV*

Box Office: $4,357,406

With its unusual premise, unlikely stars, and unfortunate title, *Bogus* initially invites dismissal. At first glance, its characters seem either overdone or absurd: a mop-topped orphan with a penchant for magic, a hardened businesswoman who becomes his reluctant if not inept guardian, and a clownish Frenchman who appears as the boy's imaginary friend. Despite its shortcomings, to lump *Bogus* with other fuzzy and trite family fare is a mistake. Buoyed by strong performances and a refreshingly credible child actor, *Bogus* treads into dark territory, the psychological vulnerability of children, without getting too sappy or overwrought.

Seven year-old Albert (Osmet) has an idyllic life in Las Vegas with his single showgirl mom Lorraine (Travis) and their friends, a troupe of eccentric performers in a magic revue. Ken Adams' dreamy, circus-like opening sequence establishes whimsy and magic, both literal and figurative, as constants in Albert's life, from the skilled performers he admires and the sleight-of-hand tricks he works diligently to master to his loving relationship with his mother. When this way of life abruptly ends and Albert is sent cross-country to live with a stranger, the lonely, confused child turns to his imagination for comfort; the result is Bogus (Depardieu), a fictional friend in the form of a rumpled Frenchman.

The flip side of Vegas glitz and glamour is gritty Newark, New Jersey, where spiky Harriet Franklin (Goldberg), Lorraine's long lost childhood friend and foster sister, runs her restaurant supply business. That she's been named the boy's guardian is quite a bombshell for Harriet. She's hardly maternal, and it's only with much convincing that she agrees to take the child. The greys and browns of Harriet's wardrobe and apartment decor reflect her disposition: earthy, edgy, and most certainly no-nonsense. Even Harriet's interaction with Albert is disturbingly cold. Guarded in her expressions of affection, sympathy, or even humor, she treats him like a house guest or a business associate, not a little boy, giving the film an uncomfortable

CREDITS

Harriet Franklin: Whoopi Goldberg
Bogus: Gerard Depardieu
Albert Franklin: Haley Joel Osment
M. Antonie: Denis Mercier
Penny: Andrea Martin
Lorraine Franklin: Nancy Travis

Origin: USA
Released: 1996
Production: Norman Jewison, Arnon Milchan and Jeff Rothberg for a Regency Enterprises production; released by Warner Brothers
Direction: Norman Jewison
Screenplay: Alvin Sargent
Cinematography: David Watkin
Editing: Stephen Rivkin
Music: Marc Shaiman
Production design: Ken Adam
Art direction: Alicia Keywan
Costume design: Ruth Meyers
Sound: Bruce Cawardine
Magic consultation: Whit Haydn
Visual effects: Alan Munro
MPAA rating: PG
Running Time: 110 minutes

tension that borders on implausible. When invisible Bogus implores Harriet to "pick [Albert] up and give him a big, big kiss on his face," he echoes the audience's frustration. Her eventual admission that she wouldn't clap to save Tinkerbell during *Peter Pan* speaks volumes as the film unfolds and we learn that as a childhood of changeable foster homes has left her reluctant to demonstrate faith, trust, or love.

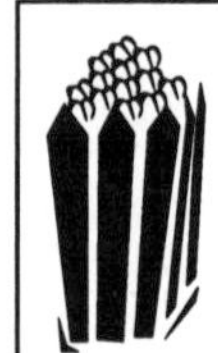

"I don't have a motherly bone in my body. I'm not a mother. And I don't want to be a mother."—Harriet Franklin

Between the two is Bogus. When Albert is frightened or lonely, Bogus appears, serving as playmate, confidant, and conscience, and it is in this relationship that the film gains its charm. The pairing of burly Depardieu and tiny Osmet makes for great visual fun as they bound and play in a pretend sword fight, or huddle tenderly when Albert is sad; Depardieu's rollicking accent and exaggerated features only add to his appeal as the ultimate pretend buddy. Like Harvey, James Stewart's inviable rabbit companion in the 1950 film of the same name, or Clarence, Stewart's angel guide in *It's a Wonderful Life* (1946), Bogus himself represents a bridge between reality and fantasy, between despair and hope. Without Bogus, Albert would surely act out or shut down completely, just as Clarence saved George Bailey from suicide, or Harvey saved Elwood Dowd from repression and boredom. Credit goes to Osmet (who previously played the young Forrest Gump Jr.) for keeping pace with the accomplished Depardieu, and to director Norman Jewison for allowing Osmet to skillfully demonstrate a range of emotions without relying on welled-up eyes or phony pouts. Overall, their relationship is a delight.

Predictably, it's only a matter of time until Bogus is able to infiltrate Harriet's consciousness and bring the new family together, beginning with a gloriously shot but strained quasi-fantasy a la Rogers and Astaire. The inevitable union, however, is decidedly flat, perhaps at the expense of avoiding schmaltz, but more likely as a result of Goldberg's restraint; although Harriet has discovered a new side of herself, all is not happily-ever-after. We're left with two scarred but hopeful souls agreeing to face the future together.

With *Bogus*, it's best to ignore the plot sags (such as the likelihood of a doting mother leaving her child in the care of someone with whom she hasn't had contact in ten years, or of an adult stranger buying a bus ticket to Atlantic City for a little boy) and appreciate the film's true pleasures: fresh performances by two of Hollywood's more distinctive personalities and a truly likable child actor, the delicacy with which Jewison handles his uneasy theme, and the ethereal beauty of the fantasy sequences. Although the sometimes frightening imagery, heavy themes, and general lack of action may be too much for small children, *Bogus* is otherwise a touching, likable family film.

—Terri Schell

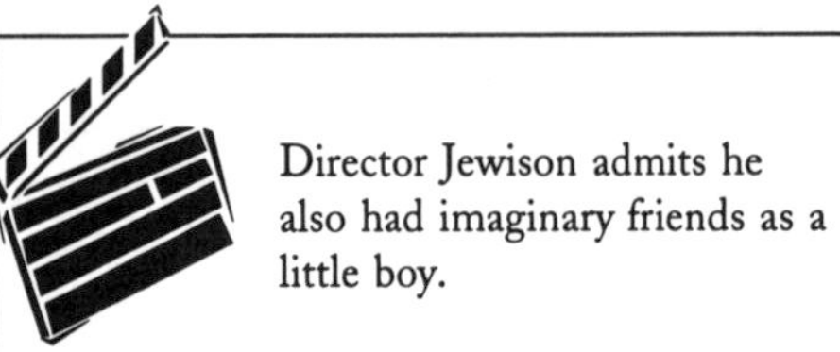

Director Jewison admits he also had imaginary friends as a little boy.

REVIEWS

Chicago Tribune. September 6, 1996, p. 4.
Detroit News. September 6, 1996, p. 1D.
Los Angeles Times. September 6, 1996, p. F8.
New York Times. September 6, 1996, p. C8.
USA Today. September 6, 1996, p. 3D.
Variety. August 21, 1996.

Born to Be Wild

What do you do when your best friend's a 400-pound gorilla? Anything she likes.—Movie tagline

"It touches your heart as well as your funny bone."—Lydia Marcus, *Interview Factory Entertainment Network*

Box Office: $3,730,409

Born to Be Wild is one of those movies born out of what is loosely termed by Hollywood insiders as a "concept." The concept here was that there was money to be made in re-hashing some elements of *Free Willy* (1993), using a different animal. It is not quite enough of a concept, however. *Born to Be Wild* is a film that is best left to the children (admittedly its intended audience), the least discerning of which will find pleasure in its slapstick humor and its heavy-handed sweetness.

Film was inspired by the real-life story of Koko, the sign-language-speaking gorilla.

Based on a real-life gorilla who was taught sign language, *Born to Be Wild* is the story of 14-year-old Rick Heller (Will Horneff) and his friendship with a gorilla named Katie. The concept: through their relationship, Katie teaches Rick a thing or two about sign language and about life as well, proving that humans are capable of anything if they are taught by experts.

Katie is the subject of a behavioral science project led by Rick's scientist mom, Margaret (Helen Shaver). Margaret, who is studying Katie for language aptitude, forces Rick (a juvenile with an aptitude for delinquency) to clean Katie's cage as a way of punishment for having driven her van without a license. It seems that Rick's father has abandoned the family, and Rick blames his mother. In what is surely an enormous shock to anyone reading this review or seeing this film, surly Rick and clever Katie become.... friends! The other novel plot twist is that Katie's safety becomes endangered when her legal owner, Gus Charnley (Peter Boyle), decides that he wants Katie to stop being used as a science project and instead become a novelty act. Everybody knows that cinematic youngsters hate having their non-human friends taken away from them. So, Rick saves Katie from Gus, hitting the road in his Mom's van and heading for the Canadian border (the film takes place in northern California, a place where most of the country fully expects to see gorillas who sign traveling in a van with 14-year-old fugitives from justice.)

The bulk of the film becomes a sort of a mixture of *Thelma and Louise* (1991) and *Every Which Way But Loose* (1978), which starred Clint Eastwood and some orangutans. Following a sort of episodic format in which the two fugitives try to make their way toward the border with no one stopping them, there is plenty of opportunity for hijinks: Katie in a bubble bath; Katie and Rick fighting for sleeping space in the back of the van; Katie swallowing red-hot candy and soap-bubble liquid. The film has serious moments, such as when Katie falls off a cliff into the ocean (although the seriousness is undercut by the fact that Rick, several hundred pounds smaller in weight, saves Katie from drowning.) The defining moment of the film comes when Katie testifies in court about the difference between right and wrong. She testifies in sign language, of course. This moment was called "a nadir of shamelessness" by one newspaper critic. But *E.T.* was shameless, too. The difference? *E.T.* was a better film. Audiences don't seem to mind being manipulated, as long as it is done with some style.

Director John Gray and writers John Bunzel and Paul

CREDITS

Rick Heller: Will Horneff
Margaret Heller: Helen Shaver
Gus Charnley: Peter Boyle
Lacey Carr: Jean Marie Barnwell
Max Carr: John McGinley
Bob: Marvin J. McIntyre

Origin: USA
Released: 1995
Production: Robert Newmyer, Jeffrey Silver for a Fuji Entertainment and Outlaw production; released by Warner Bros.
Direction: John Gray
Screenplay: John Bunzel, Paul Young
Cinematography: Donald M. Morgan
Editing: Maryann Brandon
Music: Mark Snow
Production design: Roy Forge Smith
Art direction: Gilbert Wong
Costume design: Ingrid Ferrin
Sound: John Patrick Pritchett
Makeup: Katharina Hirsch-Smith
Casting: Debi Manwiller
MPAA rating: PG
Running Time: 100 minutes

Young (who based the screenplay on a story by Young) have not fully found a way to manipulate the heartstrings of their audience without appearing obvious. The adults are all insensitive. The cops are incompetent. Rick talks about how the two of them will be "free." The musical score (by Mark Snow) sometimes telegraphs what the audience should be feeling, instead of enhancing the action. Director Gray might have been advised to find ways to make these elements play against the inherent sweetness of the story.

Some of the technical credits are fine, however. Katie is an audioanimatronic, synthetic creation—a puppet, basically. Her facial expressions are radio-controlled, and she is quite lifelike. There are also some fine visual moments, such as when the van is seen speeding along the highway, accompanied by the song "Born to be Wild." Wil Horneff does a believable job as a surly young man who learns something about himself, and Helen Shaver and Peter Boyle do credible jobs with their material.

Born to Be Wild is for the kids. Very young children will probably respond to its simplistic message, its silly humor, and its sentimentality. Everybody else should rent *Every Which Way But Loose, Children of a Lesser God* (1986), *E.T.*, and *Thelma and Louise* and watch them simultaneously.

—Kirby Tepper

REVIEWS

Detroit News. April 3, 1995, p. 4C.
Hollywood Reporter. March 28, 1995.
New York Times. April 1, 1995.

Bottle Rocket

They're not really criminals, but everybody's got to have a dream.—Movie tagline

"*Bottle Rocket* will shoot to the top of your favorite film list! Rife with goofy comedy, goose-bumpy romance, and giddy action."—Stephen Saban, *Details*

"Bright, original, and funny."—Leonard Maltin, *Entertainment Tonight*

"Wow! What a debut!"—Leah Rozen, *People Magazine*

"Sharply funny and touching. The cast sends this caper film into an exuberant comic spin."—Peter Travers, *Rolling Stone*

Box Office: $560,069

Bottle Rocket, the first feature-length film created by twenty-six-year-old writer-director Wes Anderson and twenty-seven-year-old writer-actor Owen C. Wilson, is a charmingly comic look at three men in their twenties who resort to rather pathetic attempts at crime because they are too restless or bored to abide what passes for normal American life at the end of the twentieth century. Or at least they think they are.

The film opens with Anthony Adams (Luke Wilson) pretending to escape from a voluntary mental facility in Arizona by climbing down a rope of sheets. When his psychiatrist (Ned Dowd) catches him about to descend, Anthony explains that he's appeasing the friend who has arrived to take him away from all this. This friend, Dignan (Owen C. Wilson), has an intense romantic-adventurous streak and is clearly more unstable than the depressed Anthony.

Arriving back in their hometown, they quickly break into a house and steal a coin collection and other valuables. Only afterward is it revealed to have been Anthony's home and that the two are using this "heist" as practice for more daring crimes. Anthony is upset, however, to learn that Dignan has stolen earrings he gave his mother as a birthday gift. This lack of complete satisfaction with their crime sets the pattern for their future capers.

The friends are soon joined by a third, Bob Mapplethorpe (Robert Musgrave), a rich kid who tries to strike out at his always absent parents by growing marijuana on their property. His biggest problem is his violent bully of an older brother, known as Future Man (Andrew Wilson). Bob becomes the getaway driver because he is the only one of the friends with a car.

After robbing a bookstore, the three take refuge at a motel in the middle of the nowhere. (Though the film was made in Texas, mostly suburban Dallas, its location is never specified.) Anthony quickly falls in love with Inez (Lumi Cavazos), a chambermaid from Paraguay. When Bob learns that Future Man has been arrested for growing marijuana, he heads home, leaving the others stranded until Dignan steals a car. When the car breaks down and Anthony reveals he has given all their money to Inez, Dignan explodes, striking his best friend.

Dignan's dream has been to pull off a major caper with the help of Abe Henry (James Caan). When the buddies finally reunite, Bob tells Anthony that the mysterious Henry owns a landscaping company called Lawn Wranglers for which Dignan worked until he was fired. They nevertheless become involved with the older man, and Dignan convinces Henry to let him plan and execute the robbery of a cold-storage warehouse. Needless to say, the caper results in comic chaos.

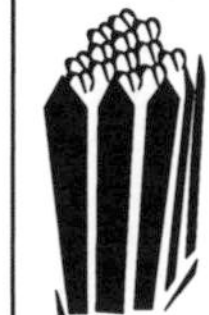

"Excuse me, are the explosives really necessary?"—Anthony thinks Dignan's gone overboard planning their heist.

The story of how *Bottle Rocket* came to be made, as reported by Jeff Silverman in *The New York Times,* is almost as interesting as the film itself. Anderson and Owen Wilson met in a playwriting class at the University of Texas at Dallas and were sharing an apartment when they decided to make a feature-length, sixteen-millimeter film in black and white. Initially, they hoped to create something gritty like Francis Ford Coppola's *Godfather* films or the work of Martin Scorsese, but they soon realized they did not have the background to make tough-guy films and settled for something more comic. After spending $10,000, they had thirteen minutes of film and no money, so they submitted what they had as a short film to the Sundance Film Festival, where it was shown in 1993.

Their short was liked at Sundance, but no one offered to provide the money for making it into a feature. Then screenwriter L. M. "Kit" Carson, who wrote the 1983 remake of *Breathless* and is a friend of the Wilson family, sent the short film and its script to producer Barbara Boyle. She sent the material on to Polly Platt, the veteran production designer, screenwriter, and producer whose credits include *The Last Picture Show* (1971) and *The War of the Roses* (1989). Platt enlisted the support of screenwriter-director-producer James L. Brooks, who made *Terms of Endearment* (1983) and *Broadcast News* (1987), to get the film financed by Columbia Pictures. Columbia's only stipulation was having a name actor play Abe Henry. Under the tutelage of Platt and Brooks, Anderson and Wilson spent eighteen months refining their screenplay before making their $5 million film.

The result of all this labor resembles the innocent, sweet-natured world of Ed Burns' *The Brothers McMullen* (1995) transposed to the Southwest and filtered through the sensibility of someone who admires the films of such directors as Michael Mann and Quentin Tarantino. Dignan, Anthony, and Bob would absolutely adore such films as Mann's *Heat* (1995) and Bryan Singer's *The Usual Suspects* (1995) and, like the characters in Tarantino's *Reservoir Dogs* (1991), would also like Lee Marvin films. *Bottle Rocket,* however, is not one of those too-common films created by people who

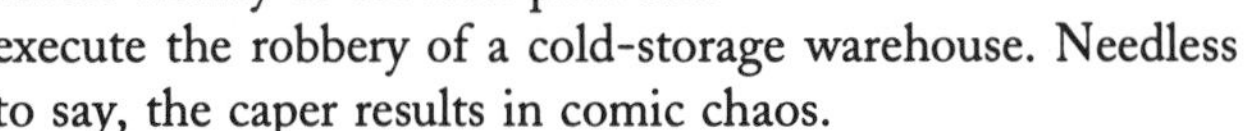

CREDITS

Dignan: Owen C. Wilson
Anthony Adams: Luke Wilson
Bob Mapplethorpe: Robert Musgrave
Inez: Lumi Cavazos
Abe Henry: James Caan
Future Man: Andrew Wilson
Gracie: Shea Fowler
Rocky: Donny Caicedo
Applejack: Jim Ponds
Dr. Nichols: Ned Dowd

Production: Polly Platt and Cynthia Hargrave for Gracie Films/Boyle-Taylor Productions; released by Columbia Pictures
Direction: Wes Anderson
Screenplay: Wes Anderson and Owen C. Wilson
Cinematography: Robert Yeoman
Editing: David Moritz
Production design: David Wasco
Art direction: Jerry N. Fleming
Set decoration: Sandy Reynolds-Wasco
Costume design: Karen Patch
Sound: Stacy Brownrigg
Music: Mark Mothersbaugh
Casting: Liz Keigley
MPAA rating: R
Running Time: 95 minutes

Friends Bob (Robert Musgrave), Anthony (Luke Wilson), and Dignan (Owen C. Wilson) learn that crime not only pays but doesn't come easy in the comedy of errors, *Bottle Rocket.*

have seen lots of films and experienced little else. Except for a target practice scene that may be an homage to Arthur Penn's *Bonnie and Clyde* (1967), also made in Texas, *Bottle Rocket* is an original on its own terms with no need to be constantly quoting the work of others.

The film is full of delightful little touches: Anthony's saying goodbye to his fellow mental patients while making his "escape;" the notebook in which Dignan has carefully outlined his and Anthony's life for the next fifty years; Future Man beating up Bob in the background while Anthony carries on a banal poolside conversation with an acquaintance in the foreground, all oblivious to the unseen violence, a device repeated when Anthony courts Inez while Dignan is being assaulted behind them; the decision to rob a bookstore—of all places; the bookstore having no bags large enough to carry the money; Anthony pausing mid-robbery to look at a book about finding government jobs; the yellow jumpsuit Dignan insists upon wearing; Henry's humiliating Future Man at a country club; and an elderly safecracker calmly sitting on a sofa when he finds he cannot crack the safe. That Dignan has a commando complex, insisting that everything about the big robbery be planned down to the smallest detail, makes their failure all the funnier.

Feature film directorial debut for Wes Anderson, who co-scripted with University of Texas classmate, Owen C. Wilson. Wilson and his younger brother Luke star in the film; their

Like *The Brothers McMullen, Bottle Rocket* is almost a celebration of the immaturity of the American male. These young men resort to crime primarily because of the excitement it offers, although Anthony and Bob do so more out of friendship to Dignan. These characters are incapable of having real jobs for any length of time because they lack discipline, concentration, and motivation. Even Gracie (Shea Fowler), Anthony's grade-school sister, is more mature and realistic than he. They deal with their maladjustment by retreating in self-absorption, as with Anthony, or fantasy, as with Dignan.

One of the many virtues of *Bottle Rocket* is that its serious themes are handled subtly. Except for dragging slightly during the motel stay, the film is fast paced and consistently amusing. Even the Anthony-Inez romance, the sort of subplot that can bring a comedy to a halt, is well handled. Inez is as amused by Anthony's immaturity as Gracie is bewildered, and their relationship has comic overtones because her limited English requires her to use a translator, leading Dignan to think the translator, a short, stocky young man named Rocky (Donny Caicedo), is in love with Anthony.

Anderson's direction is equal to the screenplay, creating comic rhythms unusually adept for a beginner. Anderson does nothing to try to display a showy visual style, and in fact, he may be too conservative, resorting to too many tight closeups. The film's production values are also far beyond those associated with low-budget beginners, particularly the expert cinematography of Robert Yeoman, editing of David Mortiz, music of Mark Mothersbaugh, and production design of David Wasco, who designed Tarantino's *Reservoir Dogs* and *Pulp Fiction* (1994).

The performances are equal to the rest of the film's quality. Cavazos, the star of *Like Water for Chocolate* (1993), is delightful as the chambermaid who cannot decide if she can love Anthony despite his lack of seriousness. Caan, who played a young thief with an older mentor in Michael Mann's *Thief* (1981), portrays both the likability that makes Dignan admire Henry and the character's essential sleaziness. Luke Wilson adeptly conveys Anthony's confusion over his relations to those around him. Best of all is Owen Wilson. He resembles Dennis Hopper, seems to be imitating Hopper, and says "man" a lot, but he also gives Dignan considerable comic energy without making him too manic. His expert comic timing balances well the comparatively laid-back styles of the other performers.

The title of *Bottle Rocket* comes from the cheap fireworks that flare for a few feet before making a tiny pop. The metaphor is appropriate for the limited horizons for these sparkling but puny characters. The film's creators seem certain to make much more noise.

—*Michael Adams*

REVIEWS

Esquire. February, 1996, p. 33.
The New York Times. February 21, 1996, p. B3.
Newsweek. March 11, 1996, p. 63.
People. February 12, 1996, p. 21.
Variety. February 5, 1996, p. 58.
The Wall Street Journal. February 23, 1996, p. A11.

Bound

Two women just made laundry day a very big deal.—Movie tagline

"Takes you to the brink and piles twist upon twist with a plot involving murder, triple-crosses, close calls, and steamy sex. Fun, smart, and very well done."—Roger Ebert, *Chicago Sun-Times*

"A taut thriller. A hold your breath climax."—Bruce Williamson, *Playboy*

"Sexy, elegant, suspenseful and exciting."—Jeff Craig, *Sixty Second Preview*

Box Office: $3,802,260

Bound is a fine film, derivative of much of what came before it, from *The Postman Always Rings Twice* (1946) to *Pulp Fiction* (1994), while still maintaining a freshness in its characters and script that are thoroughly engaging.

Ever since *Pulp Fiction,* young directors have been trying to emulate the fast and grotesque style of Quentin Tarantino, who himself was emulating a whole host of his filmmaking ancestors. This is fine, because, after all, even Shakespeare's story's were derivative. Though sometimes it would be nice if those directors would emulate Tarantino's ebullience and discard his penchant for repulsive violence.

Let's face it, films were violent long before *Pulp Fiction* and Tarantino's other bloodfests (for which he supplied scripts), such as *Natural Born Killers* (1995). But since he came on the scene, directors imitating him seem to enjoy using violence in a semi-humorous context, and the effects range from irritating to disturbing. Jerking the audience from laughter one moment to revulsion the next is de rigueur in the '90s, and it is not pretty.

Be that as it may, and admitting that not everyone is grossed out by seeing a man's face bashed into a toilet and cut up with a knife, *Bound* is a lot of fun, in a kind of horrific way.

Let's focus on the fun part. Corky (Gina Gershon) is an ex-con who is given a job renovating an apartment in present-day Chicago. Her next-door neighbors are Violet (Jennifer Tilly), a femme fatale who, for the past five years, has lived with the sleazy (but well-to-do) Caesar (Joe Pantoliano). Corky becomes the instant object of affection for the love-starved Violet, who seduces Corky with sultry ferociousness. Manipulating Corky to come over and retrieve an earring caught in her sink, Tilly is hilarious with her wonderful double-entendres about pipes that need opening. (The plumbing metaphor is hardly new, though: see the lesbian plumber in *French Twist* [1996] played by Josiane Balasko.) Next thing you know, Corky is panting over a tiny tattoo on Violet's breast, and from then on, well, you know you're not in Kansas anymore. From there, the director/writers Andy and Larry Wachowski provide a roller coaster of a plot involving $2 million, a suitcase, a lot of mobsters, and the intriguing love triangle, all filmed in a film noir style with '90s sensibilities.

You gotta love a film that has a sexual technical consultant. *Bound* boasts the articulate author Susie Bright as a technical consultant because of the lesbian content of the film. (Bright is the author of *Herotica* and other tomes on women's and lesbian sexuality.) And as insipid as the title of "technical consultant" may sound to some, Bright's con-

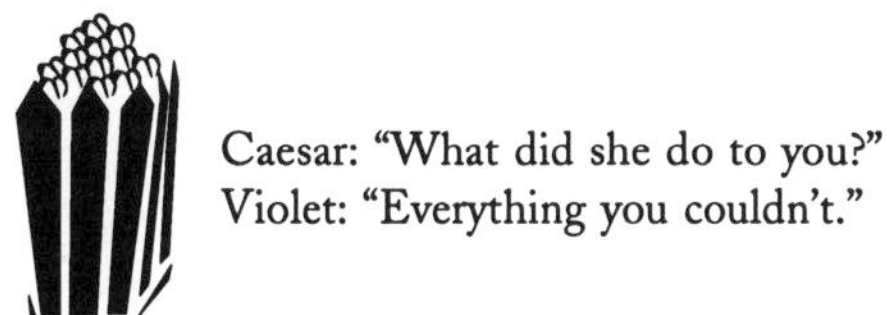

Caesar: "What did she do to you?"
Violet: "Everything you couldn't."

CREDITS

Violet: Jennifer Tilly
Corky: Gina Gershon
Caesar: Joe Pantoliano
Shelly: Barry Kivel
Johnnie Marconi: Christopher Meloni
Mickey Malnato: John P. Ryan

Origin: USA
Released: 1996
Production: Andrew Lazar, Stuart Boros for a Spelling Productions and Dino De Laurentiis production; released by Gramercy
Direction: Andy Wachowski, Larry Wachowski
Screenplay: Andy Wachowski, Larry Wachowski
Cinematography: Bill Pope
Editing: Zach Staenberg
Music: Don Davis
Production design: Eve Cauley
Art direction: Robert Goldstein
Set design: Harry E. Otto
Costume design: Lizzy Gardiner
Sound: Felipe Borrero
Casting: Nancy Foy
MPAA rating: R
Running Time: 107 minutes

tribution is welcome. The directors Wachowski and the two actresses carry off the lesbian relationship in a way that is both matter-of-fact and highly erotic. It doesn't feel as if the filmmakers are trying to be politically correct or exploitative by having lesbians as protagonists, it is merely part of the plot.

Directorial debut for screenwriting brothers, Larry and Andy Wachowski.

The actresses are wonderful. Gina Gershon, last seen in *Showgirls* (1995), clearly models her character after James Dean. Appearing in a white tank t-shirt, black leather jacket, jeans and black boots, she makes an incredibly sexy heroine who happens to occupy a role that in an old film noir might have been played by a man. Gershon is the essence of understatement, a perfect match for the over-the-top characterization by Jennifer Tilly.

"Over-the-top" may sound like a pejorative, but in this film it is a compliment. Tilly exaggerates every move, playing a similar gun-moll character to the one for which she was Oscar-nominated in Woody Allen's *Bullets Over Broadway* (1994). When she slithers over to Corky's apartment, two cups of coffee in hand, shamelessly cruising Corky's body and saying, "I'll bet your car is in perfect condition," she is somehow deadly and hilarious all at the same time.

Joe Pantoliano, known for countless roles, from *The Fugitive* (1993) to *Midnight Run* (1988), is as wonderful as ever. Pantoliano plays a sleazy mobster who is up to his ears in trouble with a combination of horror and farce that is exquisite.

Andy and Larry Wachowski, who wrote the 1994 bomb *Assassins,* starring Sylvester Stallone, maintain an artful and interesting look and pace, and their script is witty and wise. They are particularly adept at maintaining a balance between comedy and horror. Their thoroughly interesting reinvention of film noir has won them wide praise, and deservedly so. But enough already with the violence.

—Kirby Tepper

AWARDS AND NOMINATIONS

Independent Spirit Awards 1997 Nomination:
Cinematography (Pope)

REVIEWS

Boxoffice. April, 1996, p. 118.
Entertainment Weekly. October 11, 1996, p. 72.
Los Angeles Times. October 4, 1996, p. F14.
New York Times. October 4, 1996, p. C22.
People. October 21, 1996, p. 22.
Sight and Sound. March, 1997, p. 42.
Time Magazine. October 7, 1996.
USA Today. October 4, 1996, p. 4D.
Variety. January 29, 1996, p. 64.

Boys

No one stays innocent forever.—Movie tagline
"Sweet and hopeful!"—*New Yorker*
"Hip!"—*Village Voice*

Box Office: $516,349

Shortly after arriving in Hollywood, young actress Winona Ryder soon began receiving nothing short of unanimous accolades praising her work. Some even went as far as dubbing her "the best actress of her generation." She has played the vacuous, eccentric, Gen X hippiechick in *Reality Bites* (1994). She's done thoughtful and shy in *Mermaids* (1990), *Heathers* (1989) and *Beetlejuice* (1988). She's been eloquent and graceful beyond her years in *How to Make an American Quilt* (1995), *The Age of Innocence* (1993), *Bram Stoker's Dracula* (1992), and *The House of the Spirits* (1993). Never before in her brief, distinguished career has she played stupid. Until now.

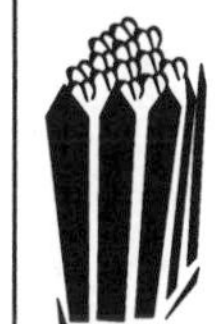

"I feel like I woke up with the dial on the wrong channel or something."—John trying to figure out his feelings for Patty

It looks like Ryder lost a bet or owed someone a favor. There can be no other logical explanation as to why she took the lead role in *Boys*. In easily the worst film of the spring and quite possibly the entire year, Ryder plays Patty Vare, a Maryland woman who has apparently just been involved in a violent car crash. The morning after, she receives a visit from a state trooper who questions her and attempts to figure out her level of involvement in the crime. Evidently, the accident took place in a stolen car and Patty can't seem to remember anything that happened to her.

The scene immediately and inexplicably shifts to Patty as the equestrian romping around the scenic Maryland countryside. Patty isn't as agile on the horse as she'd like to be, she takes a nasty tumble and loses consciousness. Two young students from the local all-male Sherwood School discover her and don't quite know what to do with her. They bolt back to school and retrieve senior class member John Baker, Jr. (Lukas Haas) who shares their confusion: a beautiful, unconscious, perhaps dying older woman (the first time Ryder has ever played The Older Woman) lying in a field. Do they call an ambulance? The police? With their imaginations limited to adolescent dreams, they do what any normal, rational, hormone-enraged high school boys would do: put her in the station wagon, haul her back to the dorm and stash her in a spare room. After what seems like hours, Patty finally comes to and gazes around at her new surroundings. For the second time in as many days, she is completely unaware of what's happened to her.

Ryder has starred opposite quite a formidable list of leading men in her career: Daniel Day-Lewis, Gary Oldman, Christian Slater, Ethan Hawke, Johnny Depp and Robert Downey, Jr. among them. Casting Lukas Haas as her romantic counterpart defies all logic. Haas made his debut in *Witness* (1985) as a gawky, quiet, confused Amish boy. Eleven years has done little to his appearance except make his gangly, angular features more pronounced. He's had some small insignificant supporting roles in even smaller insignificant films (*Lady in White* [1988], *Leap of Faith* [1992], *Music Box* [1989]) and unfortunately seems destined to be lumped into the incredibly undesirable category of has-been child actor. It might seem unfair to pick on Haas because of his unusual appearance, but his average looks are matched by his stammering, lifeless, shallow delivery and complete lack of presence.

CREDITS

Patty Vare: Winona Ryder
John Baker Jr.: Lukas Haas
Bud Valentine: Skeet Ulrich
Officer Kellogg Curry: John C. Reilly
Officer Bill Malone: Bill Sage
John Phillips: Wiley Wiggins

Origin: USA
Released: 1996
Production: Peter Frankfurt, Paul Feldsher and Erica Huggins for an Interscope Communications/Polygram Filmed Entertainment production; released by Touchstone Pictures and Buena Vista
Direction: Stacy Cochran
Screenplay: Stacy Cochran; based on the short story "Twenty Minutes" by James Salter
Cinematography: Robert Elswit
Editing: Camilla Toniolo
Music: Stewart Copeland
Production design: Dan Bishop
Art direction: Gary Kosko
Set decoration: Dianna Freas
Costume design: Lucy W. Corrigan
Sound: David Kelson
Casting: Todd Thaler
MPAA rating: PG-13
Running Time: 89 minutes

While Patty is running away from God knows what, John seems to be rebelling against his overbearing, authoritarian father who's main fault seems to be insisting that his son not do drugs and get an adequate education before handing him the keys to the (very lucrative) family business. Now there's an original story line.

After John and Patty are shown frolicking in the green rolling hills and getting drunk at a circus midway, the story shifts back to the original scenario: the car accident. Patty gets picked up at a local bar by a visiting major league pitcher from Pittsburgh, whose oafish demeanor is as uninspired as the rest of the cast. He drinks heavily, gets hammered and decides he'll impress Patty by stealing a car and assaulting her while he speeds down the road. He ends up losing control of the vehicle as it plunges into the deadly waters of a nearby creek. The film ends in a confrontation between Patty, John and his parents that descends into the truly absurd. The two lovers flee the scene and take off, heading into a Maryland sunset.

Writer/director Stacy Cochran must take complete responsibility for this unprofessional, erratic effort. Her only other project, the acclaimed satire *My New Gun* (1992), won raves from many critics after debuting at the Cannes Film Festival. Instead of developing her talent, the director has turned in what looks like the first effort of a very confused, unfocused film student that might have been improved if it had been played as satire or dark comedy. As a serious, coming-of-age film, it fails miserably. What's even harder to grasp is the normally reliable Touchstone Pictures giving it a green light and releasing it. *Boys* can now assume its rightful place amongst the worst major studio releases of all time.

—*J.M. Clark*

REVIEWS

Chicago Tribune. May 10, 1996, p. 5.
Detroit Free Press. May 12, 1996, p. 8F.
Entertainment Weekly. May 24, 1996, p. 72.
Los Angeles Times. May 10, 1996, p. F10.
New Yorker. May 27, 1996, p. 133.
USA Today. May 10, 1996, p. 4D.
Variety Online. May 10, 1996.

Breaking the Waves

Love is a mighty power.—Movie tagline

"*Breaking the Waves* is spiritual and emotionally devastating!"—Roger Ebert, *Chicago Sun-Times*

"The #1 movie of the year!"—Owen Gleiberman, *Entertainment Weekly*

"Emily Watson gives a radiant and unnerving performance!"—Kenneth Turan, *Los Angeles Times*

"An extraordinarily moving love story! In Emily Watson a star is born!"—Dave Kehr, *New York Daily News*

"A powerfully carnal love story!"—Janet Maslin, *New York Times*

"Two enthusiastic thumbs up! One of the year's best and most powerful films!"—Roger Ebert, *Siskel & Ebert*

Box Office: **$1,831,609**

Writer/director Lars Von Trier's latest effort, *Breaking the Waves,* like that urtext for Romantic poetry, Wordsworth and Coleridge's *Lyrical Ballads,* opens with an invitation to the audience to suspend disbelief. *Breaking the Waves* is the story of Bess McNeill, a simple—perhaps simpleminded—young woman who inhabits the bleak world of a coastal Scottish village which is dominated by a Calvinist cult so grim it refuses to indulge even in church bells. As the film opens, Bess is being interrogated by church elders (all of them male) about the advisability of her proposed marriage to an outsider, an offshore oil rig worker who also happens to be Scandinavian. Asked if she can possibly love such a man in the way God intended her to, Bess responds unequivocally that she knows she can. Then she steps outside, and against the naturalistic background of the windswept shore, Bess—or is it only Emily Watson, the novice film actress who plays her—turns to the camera, giving it an enigmatic smile that amounts almost to a wink and a nod.

So, from the outset of *Breaking the Waves,* viewers are put on notice that they are entering into an ambiguous enterprise. Which, for purposes of the movie, are we to accept as our reality: the archetypal world of faith, or the seemingly more concrete world that provides the backdrop for most of Bess's adventures? The answer, unquestionably, is both. And although *Breaking the Waves* is far from flawless, it is an ambitious, moving—even shattering—attempt to demonstrate how the sacred and the profane coexist in and mutually inform human existence.

The film's success rests in Emily Watson, a veteran of the British stage, here making her feature film debut as a last minute replacement for Helena Bonham Carter. Although Bonham Carter is an accomplished actress, it is hard to see how anyone could give as naked and uninhibited a performance as Watson does here. From the first frames of *Breaking the Waves,* we are aware of Watson's utter embodiment of Bess, the holy fool, and of her mastery of the film's contradictory impulses. When the helicopter ferrying the delayed Jan (the Swedish actor Stellan Skarsgard) from the oil rig to his wedding finally arrives, Bess greets her groom with blows and embraces—delivered almost simultaneously. Tricked out in full bridal regalia, Bess almost sees her dream destroyed against a backdrop of scouring winds and whirling helicopter blades. And after the nuptials have been performed, Bess—still in her white bridal gown—insists on consummating the sacrament of her marriage against the backdrop of the red flocked wallpaper in the ladies' room of a hired hall, while the wedding festivities continue downstairs.

"God gives everyone something to be good at. I've always been stupid, but I'm good at this."—Bess to Dodo about her sexual exploits

Bess is a virgin on her wedding day, but her wide-eyed wonder over the sensations of sexual intercourse and her husband's body soon give way to consuming passion. It is so consuming that when the honeymoon is over and Jan has to return to his oil rig, Bess loses all control. Her grief over his departure knows no bounds, and Watson makes it real. She also manages to make us accept the reality—or at least her character's belief in the reality—of Bess's consolation. Returning to the church that has sustained and smothered her, Bess holds conversations with God—in which she speaks both parts, playing God in a lower register. This is an outrageous conceit, but Von Trier and Watson bring it off. It helps, perhaps, that by this point we have been made aware that Bess has a history of mental instability as well as religious devotion.

Bess, fervently believing that she cannot live without Jan, prays that he will come home as soon as possible, and her prayers are answered—literally. In the aftermath of his rescue of a coworker, Jan suffers a debilitating head injury on the oil rig and returns to Bess a bedfast paraplegic. After surviving surgery and an abortive suicide attempt, Jan begins to succumb to despair. It seems he has lost his will to live. He convinces Bess that only she can save him and that he can only be saved if she agrees to have sex with other men and then relate these experiences to him. This is the turning point of the story, and not surprisingly, it is hard to determine precisely what is going on here. Is Jan making a valiant attempt to give Bess her life back, employing a simple argument to convince a simple girl? Has Jan's head injury or the medication he takes to treat it made him deranged? Or is it true that such a demonstration of faith on Bess's part will save Jan's life by recreating the physical passion that formed the sacred heart of their union?

The director, of course, leaves us to wonder. But Bess, convinced that she is responsible for Jan's accident as well as

CREDITS

Bess McNeill: Emily Watson
Jan: Stellan Skarsgard
Dodo McNeill: Katrin Cartlidge
Terry: Jean-Marc Barr
Dr. Richardson: Adrian Rawlins
Mother: Sandra Voe

Origin: Denmark, France
Released: 1996
Production: Vibeke Windelov, Peter Aalbaek Jensen for a Zentropa Entertainments and La Sept Cinema production; released by October Films
Direction: Lars Von Trier
Screenplay: Lars Von Trier
Cinematography: Robby Muller
Editing: Anders Refn
Music: Joachim Holbek
Production design: Karl Juliusson
Costumes: Manon Rasmussen
Sound: Per Streit
Casting: Joyce Nettles
MPAA rating: Unrated
Running Time: 159 minutes

A bleak Scottish village sets the stage for an unconventional marriage between Bess (Emily Watson) and Jan (Stellan Skarsgard) in Lars Von Trier's *Breaking the Waves.*

his salvation, eventually takes Jan at his word, and her actions do seem to coincide with the return of her husband's vitality. What seems to matter is not so much what she does or how she does it—tarted up in red vinyl hot pants, Bess looks like a parody of a prostitute—but that she demonstrate her faith. After Bess's initial attempt to seduce a sympathetic doctor fails, she pretends that it did not, but her account fails to convince Jan or to revive him. Other encounters, no matter how perfunctory, succeed. The important thing, it seems, is that Bess believe enough in Jan and the sacredness of their marriage to perform her sacrifice. Ultimately, she comes to believe that she need not even tell Jan about her exploits: her ritualistic acts of contrition are sufficient of themselves.

Bess's outrageous behavior finally alienates her fellows and her family; like some famous Biblical sinners, she is stoned in the streets. Only her sympathetic sister-in-law, the nurse Dodo McNeill, played with great conviction by Katrin Cartlidge, takes pity on Bess. Unlike the church elders, who condemn Bess for her prostitution, Dodo seeks to have Bess committed once again to a mental institution. For Bess, however, such confinement amounts to the same thing: being locked up and deterred from her pursuit of Jan's salvation is the equivalent of consignment to eternal damnation. Just before she is captured and carted off, Bess had extricated herself from a potentially dangerous sexual encounter with some sadistic sailors whom other hookers have learned to avoid. She returns home only to find that Jan has lapsed into a coma and, of course, she connects her failure of will with her husband's collapse. Bess knows what she must do: she escapes from the van taking her to the asylum and determinedly heads back to the ship.

Like the fates of all saints, Bess's final martyrdom seems foreordained. And, although she does not live to see it, so does Jan's miraculous recovery after Bess's death. Such eventualities are difficult for a modern audience to accept and can perhaps only be understood as religious mysteries. The conclusion of *Breaking the Waves,* which confirms Bess's sanctity in a very literal fashion, is especially hard to swallow. But in the context of Christian faith and tradition, events must always be viewed allegorically—that is, they are at once what they seem to be and something totally other and therefore nearly incomprehensible. Von Trier, who converted to Roman Catholicism only five years before the release of *Breaking the Waves,* has stated unequivocally that his latest film is about faith. But he has also been quoted as saying that he intended *Breaking the Waves* to be his most accessible film thus far.

This last statement seems to have mystified any number of filmgoers and film critics who, taking the director at his word, view the film as a trite if overblown melodrama. One consequence of this attitude has been the dismissal out of hand of those elements of the film—especially its conclusion—that defy explanation.

But while refusing to explain or to simplify such things, Von Trier has indeed made a film that invites skeptics to engage themselves with his film. In the first place, there is that knowing look Bess gives the camera as the narrative opens. Then there is the film's structure, which is divided into "chapters," each of which is given a title and introduced by trite '70s rock music played over computer enhanced countryside scenes so lush as to rival picture-postcards. The idyllic visions presented by these chapter headings are, however, immediately undercut by the postmodern techniques used to film the movie's action. Cinematographer Robby Muller, deploying a hand-held camera, achieves a cinema verite look though an almost excessive mobility. But he also distances the audience from the action, giving the film a washed-out appearance achieved by the novel means of transferring the footage to video and then back to film. We are, through such means, reminded that what we are seeing is an artifact, a man-made attempt to comprehend the ineffable. The overall effect is similar to that of an illuminated manuscript, where the chapter headings invite with their beauty but also prove to be—at least superficially—discordant with the texts that follow.

In the end, explicating *Breaking the Waves* is nearly impossible. The impact of this thoroughly original film is, however, undeniable. Blessed with superior acting, innovative techniques, and a thoroughgoing vision, it is a powerful creation.

—Lisa Paddock

AWARDS AND NOMINATIONS

Academy Award 1996 Nominations: Best Actress (Watson)
Cannes Film Festival 1996: Grand Prix
Cesar Awards 1997: Best Foreign Film
Golden Globe Award 1997 Nominations: Best Picture-Drama, Best Actress-Drama (Watson)
Independent Spirit Awards 1997 Nominations: Foreign Film
National Society of Film Critics 1996: Picture, Director (Von Trier), Actress (Watson), Cinematography (Muller)
New York Film Critics Circle 1996: Best Actress (Watson), Best Director (Von Trier), Best Cinematography (Muller)

REVIEWS

Chicago Tribune. November 29, 1996, p. 4.
Entertainment Weekly. December 6, 1996, p. 46.
Los Angeles Times. November 20, 1996, p. F5.
The Nation. December 2, 1996, p. 35.
New Republic. December 9, 1996, p. 26.
New York Observer. November 19, 1996, p. 37.
New York Times. October 4, 1996, p. C1.
New Yorker. November 18, 1996, p. 123.
Newsweek. December 9, 1996, p. 82.
Rolling Stone. November 28, 1996, p. 143.
Sight and Sound. October, 1996, p. 36.
Time Online. November 26, 1996.
Variety. May 20, 1996, p. 29.
Village Voice. November 19, 1996, p. 19.

Breathing Room

A comedy for the romantically hopeless.—Movie tagline

"A joy to watch . . . Susan Floyd and Dan Futterman are excellent!"—Edward Lewine, *Swing Magazine*

"Clever, inventive . . . extremely funny!"—Paul Wunder, *WBAI Radio*

Box Office: $14,299

Breathing Room is a claustrophobic romantic comedy that manages to combine a smart, quirky script with an almost unnervingly realistic view of relationship angst among twenty-somethings in New York. The plot is lame and predictable and the characters not sufficiently fleshed out for the film to work as more than a likeable date movie. Its low-budget feel and its lack of any recognizable stars are handicaps only partially overcome by flashes of wit and a rangy performance by its promising, engaging female lead, Susan Floyd.

David (Dan Futterman) and Kathy (Floyd) may be approaching 30, but they are certainly not Generation-X flag-wavers. They and their friends are clean-cut types with nary a pierced body part, and they look and act more like refugees from the 1970s. David and Kathy are wedged tightly into that well-populated chasm between romance and commitment. Their plight has been mined repeatedly by Hollywood scriptwriters, but rarely with this much appreciation for how untenable a situation it is.

David and Kathy can't live with or without each other. Their two-year relationship veers between sweet romance, nasty break-ups and lusty make-ups. In a rather stereotypical gender-role manner, Kathy wants to settle down and get married, while David wants to roam the planet and retain some freedom.

In a sweet but clumsy device that pinpoints the crux of the problem, David whispers to Kathy across a "whispering arch" in Grand Central Station: "Je t'aime." In fact, being a teacher of English to immigrants, he can say "I love you" in 15 languages, but refuses when Kathy asks him to do so in English. It feels like an artificial impediment: It's hard to believe that a pledge becomes authentic only in one's native tongue. Why Kathy insists on it and why David refuses are supposed to be symbolic of deeper issues.

Unfortunately the script depends heavily on such artifices, because there are few plot developments except the most predictable. The major plot device is a seemingly arbitrary decision, pushed by Kathy and accepted by David, to have a four-week separation that is supposed to last through Christmas. Because it has so little to reveal about the characters' lives and motives, the script has to hinge on this manufactured "event."

While laying on some standard romantic touches a bit too obviously, first-time director Jon Sherman and his co-writer Tom Hughes don't shy away from awkward moments. In fact, they seem to specialize in them. Early on, there's a nasty string of them at a Thanksgiving dinner party David and Kathy are throwing for two other couples. First everyone inexplicably insults one another, and then David's roommate spills the news that David has applied for a teaching job in Vietnam. "When were you planning on telling me?" Kathy asks in a tone that stops both the dinner conversation and the movie.

The idea of David taking an overseas job doesn't make sense to Kathy, and it never makes much sense to the audience either. David, who grew up in a wealthy family, has disappointed his parents by languishing in a low-level job. He seems to like to teach but can't explain why. He expects Kathy to chuck her job and follow him to the ends of the earth as both pursue their wildest dreams.

Kathy has a good job drawing animation for TV commercials. She's not willing to give it up, even though she lacks self-confidence in her work and must endure a nerdy co-worker, Larry (Stryker Hardwicke), a comic-book superhero junkie with bottle-thick glasses, knit cap and a surly attitude. But she's also not willing to give up David.

CREDITS

Kathy: Susan Floyd
David: Dan Futterman
Brian: David Thornton
Tony: Saverio Guerra
Claire: Nadia Dajani
Larry: Stryker Hardwicke

Origin: USA
Released: 1996
Production: Tim Perell for Eureka Pictures; released by Arrow Releasing
Direction: Jon Sherman
Screenplay: Jon Sherman and Tom Hughes
Cinematography: Jim Denault
Editing: Sabine Hoffman
Production design: Sharon Lomofsky
Music: Pat Irwin
Art direction: Gabriela Chistik
MPAA rating: Unrated
Running Time: 90 minutes

One of the major problems with *Breathing Room* is that it's hard to understand why an attractive, smart and well-meaning woman like Kathy is hooked on a jerk like David. David can't seem to give her a straight answer to any question; he seems full of himself and incapable of much warmth. As it turns out, it's gradually revealed that underneath his asinine exterior, David really is a vulnerable guy searching for true love. As an old flame puts it: "You try to be such an asshole, but you're really such a nice guy."

Unfortunately, Futterman is much more believable acting like a pain than he is playing the sweet romancer. He makes David annoying and whiny, veering between smug self-satisfaction and equally off-putting self-pity. Futterman plays him as a guy with a huge chip on his shoulder, griping about the injustices of life when things don't go his way. When he turns charming, it's like turning a switch on and off. It seems phony.

Floyd, on the other hand, is resplendent. Her facial features and personality are as open, inviting and warm as Futterman's are tight, angular and rocky. Her character must traverse a lot of emotional ground. Sometimes she's self-confident and take-charge, sometimes doubting and helpless, and sometimes she veers back and forth within a single conversation. She's easily unnerved, and David makes her ditzy. Floyd manages to cover this territory believably while displaying an astonishing emotional range. Watching *Breathing Room,* it's hard to believe she's not already a major star: Sandra Bullock has nothing over her in looks, personality or guts.

Floyd's Kathy is a raven-haired beauty with girl-next-door warmth, the sort of woman who can stand on her own feet but still be swept off them by the right guy. Who knows why David is that right guy; one of the major, old-fashioned themes of *Breathing Room* is that love is mysterious and irrational. But the pairing of the two is so inapt that it ruins the film.

It's not the reaction that the writers and directors are aiming at, but when David bursts in at a party to apologize to Kathy and finds her smooching with her boss, Brian (David Thornton), you wish Kathy would choose the new guy over David. Though Brian is so thinly scripted that he's almost a cipher, Thornton makes him seem like a decent, caring hunk, even if a little dull.

David would be more attractive in contrast if he were truly wild and free, but instead he just talks it. Nobody's really going anywhere; this film insists that New York City is the perfect universe, especially for lovers. As in most movies with this viewpoint, what the natives find essential outsiders might see as suffocating. All that's there is talk. *Breathing Room* could use some airing out, but it's stuck in gabby Manhattan. Everybody's talking, going in circles, trying to figure themselves out.

This is the sort of thing Woody Allen could mine, but Sherman and Hughes fall short. The dialogue's wit is sporadic, with many comic hits and misses. David tells "knock-knock" jokes to teach his immigrants; their incomprehension is funny. It's not funny when David explains to Kathy why he flubbed the turkey dinner: "Thanksgiving is not my specialty—Flag Day, Arbor Day, those I can do." Larry and his cloned comic-book-nerd friends at a party are funny, pouring Wild Turkey into Yoo-Hoo for a mixed drink. David's ex, an artist who says detonating her sculptures gets her horny, is not. And David's friend Tony's quest to get the phone numbers of a thousand girls in a year is simply stupid.

The romantic tally contains mostly clunkers. David and Kathy fight, he retreats to his apartment, he hears a knock at the door, opens it, and Kathy leaps in, executing a flying tackle. Clearly Sherman wants to suggest that lust is a major part of the glue attracting these opposites, but there are no scenes between Floyd and Futterman that are hot, and most are lukewarm at best. Their love scenes suggest desperation rather than chemistry.

Fortunately, *Breathing Room* has some quirky, intriguing and risky touches that suggest promise for Sherman. His willingness to make his characters so achingly, almost repulsively, flawed in their personalities is a pleasant switch from the standard romantic twaddle. And he's also willing to make dramatic departures from formula: He shoots a pivotal conversation in which a last attempt at reconciliation fails by putting the characters in the far corner of a screen dominated by a blank hallway, making them seem little and forlorn. It's one of several flashes of brilliance in a relatively airless film that needs as much space and ingenuity as a director can muster.

For the most part, however, *Breathing Room* doesn't exploit its low-budget possibilities, but tries and fails, on technical terms, to imitate big-name romantic comedies. We are left to imagine what the thoroughly likeable Floyd might achieve with a better script, a fuller character, and a charismatic leading man.

—Michael Betzold

REVIEWS

New York Times. November 8, 1996, p. C19.
Variety. November 4, 1996, p. 84.

Broken Arrow

Prepare to go ballistic.—Movie tagline

"In this crazily over-the-top action blowout, Mr. Woo orchestrates his daring stunts on a newly spectacular level. Travolta is an irresistible bad guy . . . stays lovable playing a terrorist audiences will love to hate."—Janet Maslin, *The New York Times*

"It will blow you away!"—Peter Travers, *Rolling Stone*

"A thrilling non-stop blast of entertainment that only a master like John Woo could create. Don't miss it!"—Paul Wunder, *WBAI Radio*

"A breathless non-stop joyride."—Dennis Cunningham, *WCBS-TV*

Box Office: $70,770,147

Subtlety is not a word in Hong Kong director John Woo's vocabulary. Incredible action, however, is. Woo is known for his elaborately choreographed action scenes with their sensational stunts, exaggerated maneuvers and elaborate dance with the camera. He has a trademark visual style in which scenes are filmed from angles that provide the maximum visible payoffs while never losing the adrenalin of the action. And while the action on screen is undoubtedly captivating, upon any kind of intelligent scrutiny, however, one realizes that the movie itself is really little more than a live cartoon. The question is, can one just sit back and let the huge plot holes, the continuity gaffes, and the leaps of logic go unnoticed in a film that is just trying to have some fun? Will audiences allow it to go over the top without demanding that it be held to the laws of probability or even common sense? If they get caught up in the momentum Woo is so good at creating, the answer is yes.

A "broken arrow" is a lost nuclear weapon. And just for the record, they have actually happened. In 1989 a nuclear submarine with two warheads aboard sank 300 miles off coast of Norway. It's still there. When a B-1 bomber crashed in the Mediterranean, its nuclear missiles were also left unretrieved.

As one government operative in this film says, "I don't know what's scarier, the fact that there are missing nuclear weapons, or that it happens so often that there's actually a term for it!" So, at least that part of Woo and screenwriter Graham Yost's plot is plausible. (Yost, by the way, made his feature film debut with *Speed.*) The rest of the story, however, is a bit of a stretch.

On a routine mission involving tests for low-level gamma and X-ray emissions, Major Vic Deakins (John Travolta) and his co-pilot Captain Riley Hale (Christian Slater) fly two nuclear warheads over the Utah desert in their top-secret B-3 Stealth bomber. What Riley doesn't know, however, is that Deakins is a disgruntled pilot and has made arrangements to steal the warheads so he and his pals can blackmail the U.S. government for $250 million.

Deakins' plans go awry, however, when Riley survives his forced low-level ejection and teams up with a resourceful and spunky park ranger, Terry Carmichael (Samantha Mathis). Together, the two set out to recover the warheads, foil Deakins, and save the West.

Broken Arrow, Woo's second American film (following Jean-Claude Van Damme's *Hard Target*), encompasses the director's favorite themes: betrayed friendship, abandoned honor, and lost loyalty. These are always good themes in an action film, but when given the Woo treatment they are writ large on the screen in language no one can misunderstand. In essence, Woo is to action films as the Marx Brothers were to comedy. Damn the logic, full speed ahead.

CREDITS

Vic Deakins: John Travolta
Riley Hale: Christian Slater
Terry Carmichael: Samantha Mathis
Colonel Max Wilkins: Delroy Lindo
Pritchett: Bob Gunton
Giles Prentice: Frank Whaley
Kelly: Howie Long
Lt. Colonel Sam Rhodes: Vondie Curtis-Hall
Chairman, Joint Chief of Staff: Jack Thompson
Johnson: Vyto Ruginis
Lt. Thomas: Ousaun Elam

Origin: USA
Released: 1996
Production: Mark Gordon and Bill Badalato for WCG Entertainment; released by Twentieth Century Fox
Direction: John Woo
Screenplay: Graham Yost
Cinematography: Peter Levy
Editing: John Wright, Steve Mirkovich, Joe Hutshing
Production design: John Wright
Art direction: William O'Brien
Set decoration: Richard Goddard
Costume design: Mary Malin
Music: Hans Zimmer
MPAA rating: R
Running Time: 108 minutes

A major part of the success of this over-the-top adventure is due to John Travolta, who manages to play a truly villainous character with his nostril's flaring and lip curling. "You love having the power of God at your fingertips. You get off on it," Hale says to Deakins, and we know he's right. After crashing his plane, Deakins comes walking out of the desert like Clint Eastwood's Man-With-No-Name in a Sergio Leone spaghetti western. He is the personification of all the great villain traits: vanity, arrogance, and malevolence. (Travolta was initially offered Slater's hero role, but he turned it down, probably realizing how much meatier the bad guy's part is.)

> "I don't know what's scarier, the fact that there are missing nuclear weapons, or that it happens so often that there's actually a term for it!"—Giles Prentice

Further enhancing the Sergio Leone feel may be the film's score, written by Hans Zimmer who early on shifts from backing the action with *Top Gun*-type music to the gonging bells and lone guitars that are a direct homage to Leone's composer Ennio Morricone.

Unfortunately, on the heroic side of the film, Christian Slater's Hale seems oddly flat in the face of Travolta's colorful Deakins. After all, if the bad guy is exaggerated, shouldn't the good guy be as well? When Deakins tells Hale, "You don't have the will to win. You could have shut me down, but you blinked," the audience, too, begins to wonder if this is the best guy for the job. Fortunately, there's another hero in the story, Samantha Mathis' park ranger. We're never told anything about her other than she's single and owns a dog, but boy can she stand up for herself. One has to wonder if self-defense is a part of the park system's training program. But then, we know little about any of the characters in this film. This is not a thinking man's film. In fact, thinking will destroy the action Woo creates.

Film debut of football player Howie Long.

Consequently, if anything carries *Broken Arrow*, it will be the stunts. They are spectacular and unbelievable. The script may be funny at times, but it doesn't make much sense. But sometimes not having to think too hard can have great audience appeal—although that type of film is usually released in the summer. Since *Broken Arrow* grossed more than $15.5 million in its opening weekend and remaining in first place for the next few weeks, it would seem that even in late winter it can be appealing. But then again, there was little box-office competition.

—Beverley Bare Buehrer

REVIEWS

Boxoffice Magazine. April, 1996, p. 116.
Chicago Tribune. February 9, 1996.
Entertainment Weekly. February 9, 1996, p. 41.
The Hollywood Reporter. February 6, 1996, p. 8.
Los Angeles Times. February 9, 1996, p. F1.
New York Times. February 9, 1996, p. C3.
The New Yorker. February 19, 1996, p. 97.
Rolling Stone. March 7, 1996, p. 54.
USA Today. February 9, 1996, p. D1.
Variety. February 9, 1996.
Village Voice. February 20, 1996, p. 59.

Brother of Sleep; Schlafes Bruder

"Sensational! An etude on creative impulses as much as a grand opera on impassioned, unrealizable love. A must see movie experience!"—Brandon Judell, *Detour Magazine*

"A stunning achievement!"—Oren Moverman, *Interview Magazine*

"Bizarre and wonderful - It's like Philip Glass on acid!"—Dennis Dermody, *Paper Magazine*

"A rare and beautiful example of truly artistic cinema. A provocative and mystical treat for the eyes, ears and mind. Haunting, highly entertaining and visually stunning!"—Paul Wunder, *WBAI Radio*

Box Office: $96,559

B*rother of Sleep* is an extraordinary film. As others have noted, this tale of an early 19th-century musical genius has some superficial similarity with *Amadeus,* Peter Schaeffer's 1981 play, later made into a movie, about the life of Wolfgang Amadeus Mozart. In fact, *Brother of Sleep* more closely resembles *Immortal Beloved,* the 1995 film biography of Ludwig van Beethoven. In *Immortal Beloved,* the deaf and aging Beethoven, recollecting a time in his childhood when he was one with the universe, is inspired to write the *Ode of Joy,* and the film portrays this episode gorgeously, showing the naked boy becoming absorbed by the stars to the strains of the composer's hauntingly beautiful music. But whereas *Immortal Beloved* has one such transporting scene, *Brother of Sleep* is filled with them.

Elias Alder (played in youth and maturity by Andre Eisermann), the musical genius in director Joseph Vilsmaier's version of *Brother of Sleep,* comes into the world stillborn, perhaps the product of an adulterous relationship. As the harried and incompetent midwife (Regine Fritsch) begins to sing the "Te Deum" over the seemingly dead baby, however, he squirms into life, smiling contentedly in response to even this strangulated version of holy sounds. His miraculous birth sets the stage for Elias's preternatural existence. Even as a child, Elias begins to exhibit signs of unearthly endowments: perfect pitch, a strong, beautiful singing voice, and the ability to wrest complex melodies out of a decrepit church organ he has never been trained to play.

Elias has been born into an extraordinarily tiny community that is so isolated and insular that generations of inbreeding have produced a disproportionate number of mentally retarded children—as well as a genius. But whereas the Down's Syndrome children have clearly been integrated into this rude Alpine society, Elias is shunned. The villagers may initially steer clear of him because of the rumors of his illegitimacy, but ultimately they keep their distance simply because he is so alien. One of the only exceptions is his cousin, Peter (Ben Becker), who from childhood loves Elias intensely.

For his part, Elias appreciates Peter's companionship—even endeavoring, at one point, to initiate the other boy into the mysteries of his unearthly sensitivity to creation—while at the same time being blind to the depth of Peter's devotion. For Elias loves Peter's sister, Elspeth (Dana Vavrova), whose heart, he says, beats with the same rhythm as his own. Elspeth returns Elias's love, but the two are kept apart—both by Peter's machinations, and by Elias's music. The unworldly Elias, it seems, is incapable of expressing himself except through his music, and he finds himself struck dumb in the face of Elspeth's professions of love.

Ironically, of course, it is Elias's musical gift that attracts Elspeth. And the other villagers, too, recognize on some level the wondrousness of Elias's abilities. The one somewhat educated man in town, the church organist, like the composer Antonio Salieri in *Amadeus,* is driven mad by the divine joke that has been played on him. As the one best equipped to appreciate Elias's endowments, he is overwhelmed by his jealousy and the consciousness of his own inferiority and ultimately commits suicide.

CREDITS

Elias: Andre Eisermann
Elsbeth: Dana Vavrova
Peter: Ben Becker

Origin: Germany
Released: 1995
Production: Perathon Film und Femsehproduktions GmbH, B.A. Filmproduktion, Iduna Film GmbH, Produktionsgesellschaft & Co., Kuchen- reuther Filmproduktion GmbH, and DOR Film Produktionsgesellschaft mbH production; released by Sony Pictures Classics
Direction: Joseph Vilsmaier
Screenplay: Robert Schneider; based on his novel *Schlafes Bruder*
Cinematography: Joseph Vilsmaier
Production design: Rolf Zehetbauer
Costume design: Ute Hofinger
Music: Hubert von Goisem, Norbert J. Schneider
MPAA rating: R
Running Time: 131 minutes

Another madman, a holy fool who lives on the outskirts of the village, acts as Elias's John the Baptist, constantly haranguing the villagers about their sinfulness and warning them to prepare to meet their maker. When Peter burns the village down in a desperate attempt to keep Elias and Elspeth apart, the citizenry turns on the most convenient scapegoat, burning the seer alive. Such could have been Elias's fate; instead, he is doomed to live out his days among a population that fails to appreciate his message and an atmosphere that does not afford him appropriate avenues of expression.

Elias is afforded one tantalizing opportunity to display his gift to the larger world. After a church official passes through the village while taking a survey (this seems not to have happened for decades, for the village priest is yet another madman) and hears Elias playing the organ, the natural genius is placed in an organ competition in the nearest large town. Arbitrarily assigned a passage from a classical piece for the organ, "Brother of Sleep," Elias, who does not know the canon, instead extemporizes. As the music inside his head fills the cathedral, those listening are at first repulsed by its uniqueness. By the time Elias concludes his feverish playing, however, the crowd is his. The adoring throng encompasses fainting women, as well as—unbeknownst to Elias—his beloved Elspeth, who has married another and fled her home. The two never meet, and Elias is immediately returned to his obscurity.

Like Christ, Elias is granted but a brief time upon this earth. He is still a young man when, like his namesake the prophet Elijah, another herald of the Messiah, he departs this earth, leaving behind no traces of his existence. After Elias climbs up into the mountains, telling Peter that he wants to go "home," he is never seen again, and the enormous rock shaped like "God's footprint" which he used as a staging ground for communion with the eternal, also disappears. Vilsmaier does not work through the Biblical parallels, and we are grateful that he does not—but they are nonetheless there. The import of *Brother of Sleep* is that genius is the product neither of evolution nor civilization, but rather a gift from God. It has no relationship to the superstitious faith espoused by the villagers, and it can be withdrawn as arbitrarily as it is manifested. Like all truly religious matters, it is ultimately a mystery.

Austrian writer Robert Schneider adapted his own 1992 novel, *Schlafes Bruder,* for *Brother of Sleep.* The novel, which has been translated into twenty-four languages and also made into a ballet and an opera, clearly has universal appeal. And Joseph Vilsmaier, who also acted as cinematographer, has done a superlative job of translating the story's ineffable qualities into pictorial images. Without belaboring the point, he manages to make *Brother of Sleep* into an allegory worthy of comparison to Ingmar Bergman's *The Seventh Seal* (1956). But Vilsmaier exhibits a lighter touch than the Swedish filmmaker ever did: his Alpine village, even with its mud-covered, dim inhabitants—perhaps because of these very elements—is wonderful to look at. And when his protagonist transcends this quotidian realm, either when Elias is playing music or when he more consciously surrenders himself to his hidden worlds, Vilsmaier manages to convey the combination of pleasure and pain that Elias experiences. Cinematography and scoring conspire to provide the audience with a truly transporting experience. *Brother of Sleep,* in the end, is an idealized form of cinematic opera, where the actors speak their lines instead of singing them, and where the audience can almost glimpse other worlds. The alpine landscape that provides the backdrop for Elias's existence is so ethereal that we are willing to believe that heaven and earth do indeed meet here.

Robert Schneider's 1992 novel has been translated into 24 languages and adapted as a ballet and an opera.

Andre Eisermann, who played the enigmatic titular figure in the 1994 film, *Kaspar Hauser,* does a great job of embodying the ethereal Elias. Small and fine-boned, he seems to be unequipped to handle the rough life demanded of his fellow villagers; in his one love scene with Elspeth he seems more a fey sprite than a man. Yet when his (or his body double's) hands and bare feet fly over the keys and pedals of an organ, Eisermann conveys the power of possession. And his otherworldliness is enhanced at times by contact lenses that turn his eyes flame yellow. After his bout with the great cathedral organ, during which he pours out his creative vitality, he seems a mere husk, his physical being consumed by the passion in his soul. All that is left for him is death, the brother of sleep.

Dana Vavrova, in contrast, is a beautiful, full-bodied young woman whose every word and gesture convey her physicality. Frustrated in her desire to consummate her love for Elias, she turns to the substantial villager to whom she is betrothed, thus sealing her fate. A child is born of their coupling, and Elspeth leaves the village with her new family. Only one more time is she granted a vision of what she has sacrificed, when she begs her way into the cathedral to hear Elias's last concert. It is as close as she has ever come to communing with the man she has always viewed as her soulmate, and Vavrova splendidly communicates the conflicting agony and ecstasy of the experience for Elspeth. In the end, though, her loss is clearly that of the whole world, which failed, as she did, to recognize the nature of Elias's psyche until it was too late.

Brother of Sleep is a brooding, thoughtful picture, and it is punctuated by a disturbing, but moving score. As in all good allegories, the surface of the film seems simple enough, but much is left unexplained. Bridging the gap between

Elias's superficial naivety and his inchoate sensibility is his stunning and utterly original music, which encompasses the mystery of existence.

—*Lisa Paddock*

REVIEWS

Boxoffice. August, 1996, p. 57.
Los Angeles Times. September 13, 1996, p. F10.
New York Times. September 13, 1996, p. C25.
Village Voice. September 17, 1996, p. 80.
Washington Post. September 27, 1996, p. D4.

Buckminster Fuller: Thinking Out Loud

Buckminster Fuller: Thinking Out Loud is an inspiring documentary that chronicles the life and contributions of R. Buckminster Fuller, a man most known for his invention of the geodesic dome. But his true contribution was not his various inventions, but rather his perspective. Fuller saw the planet as an entity, much like the human body, with all the resources to feed and house all of its inhabitants. He compared political barriers to coronary blockages that prevent the movement of resources to where they are needed. It was his faith in man's ability to overcome these obstacles and to save Spaceship Earth that permeates all his work.

Fuller's altruism and indefatigable enthusiasm were born out of a great sorrow. When he was 27, he lost his three-year-old daughter. Her death sent Fuller spiraling into an abysmal depression that finally led him to consider suicide, but when he was about to take his own life, he had an epiphany that was to shape his entire career. He realized that his life didn't belong to him but that the meaning of his existence was to work for the good of the world, and in that moment Fuller found his mission.

Fuller's contributions include the three-wheeled auto, the Dymaxion house, the geodesic dome, and a philosophy that we can help the earth function as a complete organism.

Thinking Out Loud is narrated by Morley Safer, with excerpts from Fuller's own writings read by Spalding Gray, and interviews from Fuller's wide acquaintanceship, which include artists, architects, intellectuals, friends, and family members. Interspersed with old newsreels, photos from the Fuller Archive, and outtakes from his lectures, *Thinking Out Loud* chronicles Fuller's life from childhood to the grave.

His childhood friends paint a picture of a boy, cross-eyed, badly behaved, and unpopular, who had high grades in math and science, but asked far too many questions, and always got into disputes with his teachers. He is easily distinguished in early family photos—-he is the one squinting upwards, oblivious of the photographer.

His first invention was a movable circular house that hung on a central mast and rotated with the sun. In 1928, he presented a paper model of the structure to the Architectural League, but his design was never taken seriously by the architects and engineers of the day.

His next invention, in 1933, was the three-wheeled car, called the Dymaxion auto. This car, made of airplane materials, could travel at speeds up to 100 miles per hour, could seat eleven passengers, and turned on a dime. While on a test drive with potential investors, the Dymaxion auto was involved in an unfortunate accident that killed one of the passengers, and the investment scheme was scrapped.

Inspired by the housing shortages of post World War II, Fuller made his comeback with the Dymaxion house in 1945. Again, using the central mast idea, he made a round aluminum dwelling with a revolving roof. Orders came flowing in, but when the investors pushed to go into production before Fuller felt that the house had been thoroughly tested, Fuller pulled the plug on the whole project and they went bankrupt.

This was a low point in Fuller's career, and it lasted until 1950 when Black Mountain College in North Carolina hired him to teach architecture. There he built the first geodesic dome. The military placed the first orders, Ford took up their manufacture, and at 58, Fuller finally realized his first financial success.

But Buckminster Fuller was not one to rest on his laurels. He traveled everywhere, mesmerizing his audiences with his energy and his absolute faith in man's ability to save

CREDITS

Origin: USA
Released: 1996
Production: Karen Goodman and Kirk Simon
Direction: Karen Goodman and Kirk Simon
Screenplay: Kirk Simon, Jan Hartman, Karen Goodman
Cinematography: Buddy Squires
Editing: Sara Fishko
Music: Brian Keane
MPAA rating: Unrated
Running Time: 90 minutes

the planet, and by the '60s Fuller had become a cult figure. To the anti-war generation, Fuller's simple concept that war happens when "there isn't enough to go around" hit home. This was something the new generation could do something about, and Fuller was more than ready to show them how.

Fuller died of a heart attack on July 1, 1983, while sitting at his dying wife's bedside. In a quote from the film, Fuller summed up his life in his typical style: "I did not set out to design a house on a pole, a three-wheeled car, or geodesic structures. My objective has been humanity's comprehensive welfare in the universe. I could have ended up with a pair of flying slippers."

The film is a long overdue tribute to one of the greatest minds of the 20th century, but it does have its flaws. Many of the interviews in the film tend toward redundancy, making the film excessively talky and a little long. PBS has already aired *Thinking Out Loud* and television is the appropriate stage for this film, especially since the sound quality of Fuller's lectures is so exasperatingly poor that at times he is totally unintelligible. Yet the tenor of Bucky's message shines through with a power that can shatter even our '90s cynicism, leaving the viewer with a belief in the possibility of a glorious future, and perhaps more important, a realization of man's responsibility to make that future possible.

—Diane Hatch-Avis

REVIEWS

L.A. Weekly. March 8, 1996.
Los Angeles View. March 8, 1996.
The Reader. March 8, 1996.
Variety. March 12, 1996, p. 10.

Bulletproof

Tough cop. Hostile witness.—Movie tagline

"Wayans and Sandler make a great action-comedy team."—Ron Brewington, *American Urban Radio Network*

"The freshest, funniest action-buddy movie since *48 Hours*. Wayans and Sandler are perfectly matched."—Joe Leydon, *KPRC*

"Hilarious! Loads of laughs."—Jim Ferguson, *Prevue Channel*

"Clever, fresh and entertaining."—Bill Carlson, *WCCO*

"Action-loaded. A rapid fire riot that gets big laughs."—Kyle Osborne, *WDCA*

Box Office: $21,312,641

Casting Adam Sandler in an action-comedy buddy film makes little sense. Sandler, a one-note comic from TV's "Saturday Night Live" stable, fit the rather paltry requirements of *Billy Madison* (1995) and *Happy Gilmore* (1996). But an actor with so little range and talent as Sandler has no business playing opposite Damon Wayans in *Bulletproof*. But then very little about *Bulletproof* makes sense.

For a buddy movie to work, the two male leads must have a finely tuned macho chemistry. Rapid-fire repartee, arch sarcasm, sharp personalities and clever ideas are as important to the genre as fast fists, big guns and womanizing savoir faire. *Bulletproof* has precious little of any of that.

Wayans and Sandler appear to be on two different planets. Wayans is trying hard to do a credible job of playing a dutiful, vulnerable cop with a hard veneer, and mostly he succeeds. He is a serious actor. Sandler is playing himself, as he always does—a puppy-dog adolescent with a potty mouth. The two don't feed off each other, they merely coexist. For all the chemistry they give off, their lines could have been shot separately and edited together.

The casting of *Bulletproof* is odd enough, but the script is even odder. At the start, Sandler's Archie Moses and Wayans's Rock Keats are small-time hoodlums, car thieves and best buddies. Why they're so close is never explained. But Keats is really an undercover cop, and Moses is really a bag man for Frank Colton (James Caan), a drug lord who passes himself off as a used-car dealer in patriotic-sounding TV commercials. When Keats uses Moses to try to reel in Colton, the cops mount a sting operation. Keats tries to shield his buddy, but in the mayhem Moses puts a bullet in Keats's skull.

Keats recovers, but carries a metal plate in his head and a grudge against Moses. When Moses is captured while passed out drunk in a stolen car along a desert roadside, Keats convinces his bosses to let him bring Moses back to Los Angeles. It's an implausible development, since the Arizona cops could easily ship him back themselves, but *Bulletproof* is not long on logic.

The last hour of the film has Keats and Moses trying to elude Colton's hired guns, who are out to kill Moses to prevent him from turning state's evidence, while also trying to figure out which cops are in Colton's bag. The arrangement allows for plenty of ambushes and gun battles, in which Colton's men fire off enough ammo to kill a small army but even at close range never are able to nick Keats and Moses. For an action movie, the plot is serviceable, if strained.

"Where do you draw the line between friendship and doing your job? That's what interested me so much about the film."—Damon Wayans

What's strange is that the surface plot is just a cover for a love story. The homoerotic overtones in *Bulletproof* are downright deafening. Moses and Keats have a mutual attraction that defies explanation and strains the boundaries of the genre.

When Keats wants to make sure Moses isn't killed in the sting against Colton, Keats's boss charges "You're sweet on him ... he's a low-life scumbag." Keats replies: "He's my low-life scumbag." Moses' love seemingly has no bounds. He tells Keats: "I'd take a bullet for you." He tells Colton: "I trust that guy with my life."

The desert sequences were filmed around Ridgecrest, California, and include the Trona Pinnacles and Red Rock Canyon.

Rather than treating Keats's betrayal as cold hard business, as most buddy films would, *Bulletproof* is obsessed with each man's feelings of betrayal and needs for apology, forgiveness and reconciliation. Their antipathy is expressed in highly emotional ways, thinly covered by a comic veneer. Moses pretends his dog is Keats and plays at shooting him dead. Keats, who now reveals his real name is Jack Carter, demands stern retribution.

With Moses as Keats's prisoner, the film becomes overloaded with eroticized scenes of dominance and submission. Keats tell his underlings to chain Moses, adding: "I want his asshole cuffed to his nuts." He tells Moses: "I'm your god." Moses retaliates by threatening to urinate on Keats while Keats is sleeping. Clearly playing the femme role, Moses constantly seeks an apology and insists his shooting of Keats was an accident. In one of the most ridiculous scenes, Moses refuses to use his pilot experience to pull their plane out of a nosedive, demanding: "I'm not gonna fly till you apologize to me."

The film's strange mix of violence, Sandler's trademark masturbatory humor and the homoerotic subtext goes unpleasantly over the top zenith when Keats and Moses arrive at the Hunting Gap Lodge, run by an almost-lisping proprietor who brags about his collection of porno films. Keats and Moses stay in the honeymoon suite. While Keats sprawls on a heart-shaped bed, Moses lathers up in the shower and croons the love theme from *The Bodyguard* (1992) in a falsetto. He later tells Keats: "You'll always be my bodyguard." When Moses tries to escape while showering, he ends up hanging naked halfway out a window and Keats shoves a gun into his anus. To the proprietor, out for a walk, it appears they are having sex. This is the epitome of the film's humor.

Keats punishes Moses by gagging him and tying him up on all fours, his head hanging over a toilet in which Keats has defecated. When Colton's men come calling, the gun battle rages while voices on the TV's porno film moan in ecstacy. None of this is very funny, but it is rather intriguing. What's going on here? Has Adam Sandler's lame polymorphous perversity taken over completely?

Just as in any love story about betrayal and reconciliation, the men gradually regain each other's trust. Along the way, there are almost tearful scenes. Both men recall that they have confided in the other things they've never told anyone else. In a strip bar, Moses confesses to Keats/Carter: "I'm falling in love with you all over again." Finally, when the script calls for Keats/Carter to be betrayed once again, by a woman, the message rings loud and clear: The love of another man is more reliable than that of any woman.

It's hard to know what first-time director Ernest Dickerson and scriptwriters Joe Gayton and Lewis Colick are

CREDITS

Keats/Jack Carter: Damon Wayans
Archie Moses: Adam Sandler
Frank Colton: James Caan
Traci Flynn: Kristen Wilson
Capt. Will Jensen: James Farentino
Finch: Bill Nunn

Origin: USA
Released: 1996
Production: Robert Simonds for a Bernie Brillstein-Brad Grey-Gold-Miller production; released by Universal Pictures
Direction: Ernest Dickerson
Screenplay: Joe Gayton and Lewis Colick
Cinematography: Steve Bernstein
Editing: George Folsey, Jr.
Music: Elmer Bernstein
Art direction: Perry Andelin Blake, William F. Matthews
Costume design: Marie France
Sound: Jim Stuebe
Special effects coordination: T. Brooklyn Bellissimo
MPAA rating: R
Running Time: 86 minutes

aiming at here. In many ways, *Bulletproof* is simply making more obvious the underlying suggestions in the subtext of most buddy films about the supposedly superior strength and depth of male-male affection. But it's impossible to take anything about *Bulletproof* seriously, thanks to Sandler and his tiresome shtick. How can you have a love story when the two lead actors can't even connect credibly for a minute on screen? It's also difficult to consider *Bulletproof* as a spoof of the genre; it's not clever enough for that. Instead, what results is a film that veers wildly in tone from shoot-'em-up to gross-'em-out.

Undoubtedly there's a market for this. With its rap soundtrack, *Bulletproof* combines the appeal of the urban youth guns-and-drugs subculture with a sort of cynical-laughable MTV/Comedy Channel mix. Given all its spurts of blood and leaky testosterone, unsophisticated adolescent boys should eat this up. The rest of us might be left to wonder how good a movie *Bulletproof* might have been if Halle Berry or Linda Fiorentino or even Tom Cruise had been cast in Adam Sandler's role.

—Michael Betzold

REVIEWS

Chicago Tribune. September 11, 1996, p. 2.
The Detroit News. September 6, 1996, p. 3D.
Entertainment Weekly. September 20, 1996, p. 50.
Los Angeles Times. September 6, 1996, p. F12.
New York Times. September 6, 1996, p. C21.
People. September 9, 1996, p. 18.
Time. September 16, 1996.
USA Today September 6, 1996, p. 3D.

The Cable Guy

There's no such thing as free cable. Once you're hooked . . . you're his.—Movie tagline

"Hysterically funny! Jim Carrey delivers laugh-filled, out-of-control comedy with some surprising twists that reveal a new side of his amazing talent."—Jeanne Wolf, *Jeanne Wolf's Hollywood*

"Once Carrey gets plugged in, there's no stopping him—he's brilliant."—Sara Edwards, *NBC Newschannel*

"Jim Carrey's funniest movie yet. Broderick and Carey are a hilarious odd couple."—Neil Rosen, *NYI*

Box Office: $60,240,295

Fans of the wild and wooly adventures of Ace Ventura should expect a much different film from Jim Carrey's *The Cable Guy*. Unlike the fast-paced, manic craziness of Carrey's earlier projects like *The Mask* (1994) and *Dumb and Dumber* (1994), *The Cable Guy* departs from the moneymaking scheme of these other films and takes a much darker look into the human psyche.

Jim Carrey has traded in his fun-loving, mischievous characters of the past and went over the edge in *The Cable Guy* with the maniacal, malicious, and even scary character of Chip Douglas, product of the television media. Douglas is the cable installer who enters the life of unsuspecting customer Steven Kovacs (Matthew Broderick). Steven, newly broken up with his girlfriend Robin (Leslie Mann) and now on his own, takes the advice of a friend to bribe the cable man to receive free premium channels. Unknowingly, he has given an invitation of friendship to the lonely repairman, who develops a dangerous attachment to the bachelor. Audiences may actually expect to find a rabbit boiling on Steven's stove. There's no rabbit, but Chip invades Steven's life in many strange and deranged ways.

Take, for instance, the endless messages left on Steven's answering machine and unannounced visits to his doorstep.

Steven Kovacs (Matthew Broderick) is desperate to get his cable TV but gets more than he bargained for in a twisted friendship with Jim Carrey in *The Cable Guy*.

This guy even invades his amateur basketball game one night and takes the game a little too seriously, cracking skulls with the opponents. Steven, partly acting on pity and partly to try and appease the cable installer, agrees to "hang out" with him, accompanying him to the satellite dish where he likes to relax and meditate.

"This concludes our broadcast day. Click."—Chip

The intruder forces himself even further into Steven's life, using pity to lure him to his favorite restaurant, Medieval Times, where Chip has arranged for them to battle in medieval combat. Again, Chip takes the imaginary scene, like he does TV, too seriously, and almost slaughters Steven in the process. Chip buys Steven a complete entertainment center, then invites his preferred customers (a motley crew themselves) over for a karaoke night, arranging for Steven to meet a new girl to take his mind off Robin. Unbeknownst to Steven, the girl is a prostitute paid to seduce him, and he becomes infuriated that he was tricked.

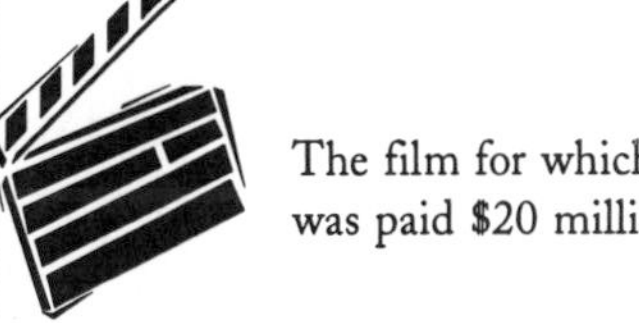

The film for which Jim Carrey was paid $20 million.

When Steven figures out how crazy Chip really is, he tries to break off the friendship, but to no avail. Chip will not go away that easily and begins to threaten Steven's attempts to reconcile with Robin, his job, and his own mental health. In fact, he comes on stronger than ever and begins to pursue Robin himself. He even shows up at Steven's parents house for a family gathering, introducing them to Porno Password, which for some reason Steven's family finds amusing. For some strange reason, Robin takes a liking to Chip and begins to see him, not knowing that earlier he trailed her on a date (as a favor to Steven) and beat the crap out of her dinner partner.

Chip takes control of Steven's life, taking his girlfriend, ruining his career, and landing him in jail. Steven finally finds out the truth about his loony cable installer: he is not named Chip Douglas and he is not a cable installer; he is a very disturbed man plagued by being raised by the television.

The climax takes the audience back to the cable guy's beloved satellite dish, where he is left dangling precariously from the monstrous cable tower, crying out literally and figuratively for human contact—something that television and uncaring parents have deprived him of.

Though the film lacks some of the wackiness and tasteless flatulence jokes of Carrey's previous efforts, it does capture his knack for physical humor and his ability to contort his personality into something unexpected and bizarre. Carrey does most of his own stunts and creates a very interesting psychedelic mood during the karaoke sequence during which he warbles "(Don't You Want) Somebody to Love?," adding a whole new and haunting slant to Grace Slick's rendition. His character is just downright spooky, swinging from friendly pal to something resembling a crazed, jilted lover.

Carrey's over-the-edge acting is a good fit for this character (almost too good of a fit), but still the film just doesn't strike the same chord as his past efforts. Maybe Carrey has been so typecast that his ability to do something different blinds the moviegoing audience. Mostly, though, the audience is stuck wondering how to feel about this cable guy—revulsion or sympathy? It's hard to laugh at a comedy about a stalker.

Broderick, on the other hand, is very convincing as the befuddled target of the cable guy's attention. His mild-mannered persona is very appropriate. He is sometimes sympathetic to the guy's plight and at others panic-stricken at the intensity with which the guy pursues their friendship, especially when the cable guy invades his family and personal life and turns it upside down. Carrey and Broderick play excellent opposites—one manic and one subdued. However, the disconnected plot takes away from the strong pairing.

CREDITS

Chip Douglas: Jim Carrey
Steven Kovacs: Matthew Broderick
Robin Harris: Leslie Mann
Rick: Jack Black
Earl Kovacs: George Segal
Mrs. Kovacs: Diane Baker
Sam Sweet: Ben Stiller

Origin: USA
Released: 1996
Production: Andrew Licht, Jeffrey A. Mueller, Judd Apatow for a Sony Pictures Entertainment production; released by Columbia Pictures
Direction: Ben Stiller
Screenplay: Lou Holtz, Jr.
Cinematography: Robert Brinkman
Editing: Steven Weisberg
Music: John Ottman
Production design: Sharon Seymour
Art direction: Jeff Knipp
Costume design: Erica Edell Phillips
Sound: Nelson Stoll
Casting: Juel Bestrop
MPAA rating: PG-13
Running Time: 95 minutes

The Cable Guy is the first completed screenplay of L.A. lawyer Lou Holtz Jr., and maybe it should be his last (although it was heavily rewritten). Unfortunately, the story does not push you to root for either character, nor does it have a real message or flow to it. The plot is disjointed and manic, and simply goes nowhere. Even director Ben Stiller, who successfully directed the critically acclaimed *Reality Bites* (1994), cannot glue together the pieces of this mismatched puzzle. He even throws in a gag about a TV trial involving a sitcom child actor murdering his own twin, which is then turned into a TV movie on the case. This bit is supposed to explore how TV reflects society and vice versa, but it's not that funny, bearing in mind the recent media circuses the public has endured concerning cases like the O.J. Simpson trials.

Overall, *The Cable Guy* is just a creepy story about a creepy repairman who enters the otherwise boring life of an otherwise boring guy. If the makers of *The Cable Guy* were trying to convey how society has become warped by media influences, it missed its mark, because this movie falls prey to the same disease, leaving it in no position to attack the media which spawned it.

—*Devra Sladics*

REVIEWS

Detroit News. June 14, 1996, p. 1D.
Entertainment Weekly. June 21, 1996, p. 46.
New York Times. June 14, 1996, p. C1.
Newsweek. June 17, 1996, p. 85.
Variety. June 10, 1996, p. 40.
Village Voice. June 25, 1996, p. 65.

Captives

How far will you go for love?—Movie tagline

"A hypnotic, riveting thriller! Tim Roth is brilliant . . . Julia Ormond is as gifted as she is beautiful."—Hariette Surovel, *Cover Magazine*

"A cauldron of intense sensuality! Tim Roth's controlled passion creates moments of sizzling heat."—*Siegel Entertainment Syndicate*

Box Office: $54,880

A love affair between a convicted murderer and a prison dentist is a decidedly offbeat plot, but *Captives,* as written by Frank Deasy and directed by Angela Pope, settles merely for having an unusual story. While always watchable, thanks mostly to the work of the cast, the film does not aim high enough. *Captives,* according to its opening credits, is based on a true story, and its makers settle for the most obvious way to tell the tale.

"You could take someone's eye out with that."—Towler about one of Rachael's dental instruments.

Rachael Clifford (Julia Ormond) has recently separated from her unfaithful husband, Simon (Peter Capaldi), also her partner in their dentistry practice. She tries to rebuild her life by taking two new jobs, one in a teaching hospital, the other in a men's prison. She seems not at all perturbed by Sexton (Richard Hawley), the helpful but flirtatious guard; Harold (Jeff Nuttall), her flighty convict assistant; Dr. Hockley (Kenneth Cope), the bedraggled, dazed prison physician; or the psychopathic prisoners, who include Lenny (Keith Allen), an Elvis Presley worshipper who sometimes thinks he is the king of rock and roll and also thinks Rachel is stealing his gold fillings.

In contrast, the scar-faced convict Philip Chaney (Tim Roth) seems normal and pleasant. Rachael bumps into her patient unexpectedly at a supermarket and learns he is released to attend college courses in computer science. Back in prison, he slips her a note saying he has not had a visitor in five years. Assuming a more casual appearance (including letting her hair down), she visits him that weekend, and a romance begins tentatively and soon escalates into a passionate encounter in the ladies' room of a bar.

Unfortunately, they are seen leaving the rest room by Kenny (Mark Strong), friend of Towler (Colin Salmon), who runs the prison's drug traffic. Towler and Lenny threaten to harm Philip, Rachael, and the young daughter of Sue (Siobhan Redmond), Rachael's best friend, unless the dentist sneaks drugs into the prison. After Philip convinces her that it is too dangerous not to acquiesce, she discovers that the package given her by one of Lenny's cohorts actually contains a gun. The already volatile situation escalates from there.

Captives could easily be considered a feminist tale of a woman rudely jolted from a conventional existence by her husband's infidelity but who has the strength to take chances to change her life. It could almost as well be seen as the story of a spoiled bourgeois taken advantage of by a wife killer. Deasy and Pope do not seem to have a clear idea of why they want to tell this mixture of love story, social commentary, and action adventure. *Captives* alternates between the points of view of Rachael and Philip (with a few shots of others responding to them), but the filmmakers are clearly primarily interested in how the dentist is affected by these events since she is changed much more than is Philip. Presenting everything from Rachael's perspective would have clarified their intentions.

Feature film debut for director Angela Pope.

Captives does convey a realistic sense of prison life without resorting much to melodrama. Philip stands out in this world because he is smarter than the other prisoners and tries to be more civilized than the sociopaths surrounding him—even if he has to beat someone to achieve it. The guards are completely indifferent to the possibility of humanity among the prisoners, referring to doctors as "vets" since they are there to treat the animals. (The prisoners also call them "vets.") Rachael can appear in the prison on visitors' day without placing her job in jeopardy because no one ever pays any attention to the girlfriends, boyfriends, wives, and other relatives of the convicts.

Cinematographer Remi Adefarasin, who shot *Truly, Madly, Deeply* (1991), another offbeat romance, and production designer Stuart Walker, whose excellent work includes *A Private Function* (1985) and *The Summer House* (1993), create a modern, spotlessly clean, but nevertheless oppressive prison by depicting it as an endless, difficult-to-navigate series of small spaces. (The film was made inside Wandsworth Prison.) This setting is fitting for protagonists who compartmentalize their lives and can be seen as prisoners of their emotions. Pope, Adefarasin, and Walker make the world outside the prison gloomy and threatening. When Rachael appears at Philip's college to break off their relationship, the confrontation takes place in a locker room with the camera revealing all the crud on top of the lockers, suggesting the dust that had settled on the characters' emotional lives before they began their affair.

Pope's credits include the 1987 television film "Sweet As You Are," in which a married professor contracts AIDS from one of his students. Like that film, *Captives* is competently made but burdened by underdeveloped characters. Deasy's screenplay gives little depth to Rachael and Philip, but Pope, who elicited remarkable performances from Miranda Richardson and Liam Neeson in "Sweet As You Are," gives her performers free rein to inject life into these stick figures.

Ormond made *Captives* before she became Hollywood's flavor of the month because of *Legends of the Fall* (1994) and before she was impaled by reviewers for not being even remotely reminiscent of Audrey Hepburn in the 1995 remake of *Sabrina.* Unlike Hepburn's cool, confident elegance, Ormond's acting style is based on tentativeness and vulnerability. It is appropriate that her character in her first major film is a suicide.

Her Rachael is both numb from the recent disruption in her life and blind to how pent-up she is psychologically. Ormond makes Rachael shy and awkward in her burgeoning relationship with Philip. Not only is the dentist new to the prison environment, but the class barrier makes her uncertain about this enigmatic patient. Ormond is equally adept at conveying the passion lurking within Rachael, especially when she drives by her former home, sees an at-

CREDITS

Rachael Clifford: Julia Ormond
Philip Chaney: Tim Roth
Lenny: Keith Allen
Towler: Colin Salmon
Sexton: Richard Hawley
Simon: Peter Capaldi
Sue: Siobhan Redmond
Harold: Jeff Nuttall
Dr. Hockley: Kenneth Cope
Kenny: Mark Strong
Maggie: Annette Badland
Estate agent: Shaheen Khan

Origin: Great Britain
Released: 1994
Production: David M. Thompson for Distant Horizon and BBC Films; released by Miramax
Direction: Angela Pope
Screenplay: Frank Deasy
Cinematography: Remi Adefarasin
Editing: Dave King
Production design: Stuart Walker
Art direction: Diane Dancklefsen
Costume design: Odile Dicks-Mireaux
Music: Colin Towns
Sound: Stuart Moser, Richard Manton
Casting: Gail Stevens
MPAA rating: R
Running Time: 99 minutes

tractive woman enter, and charges into the house swearing and throwing things only to learn that the suspected adulterer is the estate agent (Shaheen Khan) tidying the place to show it to prospective buyers.

The most notable of Ormond's achievements is holding her own with Roth, who may be the most charismatic nondescript-looking actor in films. Deasy gives Philip some edge by making him so unsure of Rachael's motives that the inmate accuses her of taking the prison position just to be attracted to dangerous men, but the character is mostly a creation of the actor as Roth uses his intensity to fill in the nuances of the thinly sketched convict. Pope gives Roth considerable leeway, allowing the camera to stare at him for long moments while the actor conveys a wide range of emotions with his eyes. *Captives* ranks with *Vincent and Theo* (1990), *Reservoir Dogs* (1991), and *Pulp Fiction* (1994) as one of Roth's best performances. Ormond and Roth are so different physically and have such different acting styles that they could easily be accused of seeming not to connect, of not being in the same film; however, their disparity underscores the social and emotional obstacles their characters must overcome.

Several of the supporting performances are also notable. Hawley, best known as Richard Haskons, Detective Chief Inspector Jane Tennison's most reliable assistant in the "Prime Suspects" series, makes his warder believable as both a help and a threat to Rachael. Annette Badland, who usually plays sluggish, stupid women, as with the divan-bound mother in *Angels and Insects* (1996), gives an uncharacteristically lively performance as a prison visitor who befriends Rachael. Allen, who has made a career of portraying sleazy creeps, most notably the treacherous Jonas Chuzzlewit in the 1995 television adaptation of Charles Dickens' "Martin Chuzzlewit," offers needed comic relief by going well over the top with Lenny's Elvis obsession. The best supporting performance is Salmon's hypnotic portrait of the evil Towler. Salmon, the police detective who has an affair with the protagonist in the second "Prime Suspect," scurries around the prison dressed only in shorts like a long-legged spider ready to pounce in for the kill.

Pope inveighs *Captives* with a good balance of the excessive, as with Lenny and Towler, and the subtle, most of the time. Rachael's sticking her bare finger into Philip's mouth and his licking it is the erotic highpoint of the film, much sexier than the later crude sex-in-the-toilet scene. While the latter scene may not work as the director intended, she could have taken more such chances to enliven an essentially good but often too remote film.

—Michael Adams

REVIEWS

Entertainment Weekly. May 17, 1996, p. 43.
The Los Angeles Times. May 3, 1996, p. F12.
The New York Times. May 3, 1996, p. C10.
Sight and Sound. May, 1995, p. 41.
Village Voice. May 7, 1996, p. 52.

Carpool

A dad in a hurry. A man on the run. And five kids with an attitude.—Movie tagline

"Fun and funny."—Don Stotter, *Entertainment Time-Out*

"Funny and entertaining. A movie the entire family will enjoy."—Maria Salas, *Telenoticias*

"Lots of fun from beginning to end."—Dr. Doug Moore, *WDAF-TV*

Box Office: $3,325,651

Tom Arnold (*The Stupids* [1996]) is cast, once again, as the high-strung, bungling fool, this time in Arthur Hiller's preposterous motion picture, *Carpool.* The film also stars David Paymer (*Quiz Show* [1994], *The American President* [1995]) as the overworked advertising executive father who never has time for his family, or to even take the kids to the Seahawks game; Rhea Perlman as a commando meter maid; Kim Coates as an overzealous detective; and Rod Steiger as a pompous gourmet food store owner. The film is predictable, with the only source of humor residing in some of the dialogue. Such characters as Martha (Perlman) the meter maid are overexaggerated, unbelievable, and don't lend anything to the plot; while such scenes as the car chase through the mall, prove to be ridiculous and just plain not funny. The film contains everything from a gun-toting geriatric to cop car crashes to the ever-predictable, inconceivable ending where the overworked businessman sees the error of his ways and is reformed by the bad guy.

Franklin Laszlo (Arnold) is a down-on-his-luck carnival owner with a mother reminiscent of Anne Ramsey's

Momma, in *Throw Momma From the Train* (1987). On this day, Franklin plans a bank heist to get the necessary money to keep his carnival alive. However, he becomes entangled in another heist at a gourmet food market before the bank opens. When he bungles the crooks' hold-up, he is the one who ends up on the run with the money. Whereas Laszlo was the one who stopped the crime at the market, he is the one left "holding the bag," taking the money and running. Although Detective Erdman (Coates) appears on the scene and pursues Laszlo, one wonders why the store clerk didn't just straighten up the confusion to begin with.

Vancouver, British Columbia, substitutes for Seattle, Washington.

Daniel Miller (Paymer) has a big presentation this day (all ad executives in motion pictures have big presentations on fateful days), and is distressed that his ill wife is asking him to drive the carpool to school. Reluctantly, he complies. The carpool is complete with Miller's young son Andrew (Mikey Kovar), teenage son Bucky (Micah Gardener), slow-moving girl Chelsea (Colleen Rennison) and her teenage sister (Rachael Leigh Cook), an obvious set-up for the teenage boy, and an obnoxious boy (Blake Warkol) who appears to be from another world, although, Miller has been assured, he has been tested.

"All you have to do is drive them to school. Fifteen, 20 minutes, tops. I'm not asking you to raise them as your own."—Mrs. Miller to her reluctant carpool husband.

CREDITS

Franklin Laszlo: Tom Arnold
Daniel Miller: David Paymer
Martha: Rhea Perlman
Mr. Hammerman: Rod Steiger
Detective Erdman: Leigh Cook

Origin: USA
Released: 1996
Production: Arnold Milchan, Michael Nathanson for a Regency Enterprises production; released by Warner Bros.
Direction: Arthur Hiller
Screenplay: Don Rhymer
Cinematography: David M. Walsh
Editing: William Reynolds, L. James Langlois
Music: John Debney
Production design: James D. Vance
Art direction: Sandy Cochrane
Set design: Gary Myers
Costume design: Trish Keating
Sound: Larry Sutton
Casting: Lynn Stalmaster
MPAA rating: PG
Running Time: 90 minutes

On the run, Laszlo hijacks Miller's car, complete with five kids and Miller in tow. Throughout the film, Miller's only concern is to get to his meeting for his big presentation. The presentation, incidentally, happens to be to the president of the gourmet food market that was just held up.

Their journey on the lam takes them through a beauty parlor, a shopping mall, to a warehouse where the carnival rides are stored (where the kids have free reign to ride the rides), and to Miller's meeting with the ad executives and Hammerman (Steiger), the gourmet market owner. Although the chase seems to have taken all day, it's a wonder how Miller even made it to a meeting in which he was already an hour and a half late in the beginning of the chase and they were only giving him fifteen more minutes to show up. Miraculously, they were still waiting to hear his ideas. And, not surprisingly, it is the kids and Laszlo who convince Hammerman to change marketing strategies. Naturally, Hammerman likes the idea and Miller passes on a partnership with the agency so he can spend more time with his family. Eventually, Hammerman and Miller do the most inane thing and become partners in Laszlo's carnival. Throughout the film, the real crooks try to retrieve their money in bungled attempts reminiscent of the crooks from *Home Alone* (1990).

Although Tom Arnold is quite good at creating characters such as Franklin Laszlo, that seems to be the only type of character he has been creating lately, and it seems to be what the audience is coming to expect from a Tom Arnold-starring film. Unfortunately, the character cannot have too much more of a shelf life, and the break-out potential that was there in *True Lies* (1994) seems to have been forgotten.

Carpool is not entirely a bad film. In fact, Paymer does a good job of playing the straight man to Arnold's comedian. But the film sinks to predictability, has unbelievable characters, leaves loose ends and ties things up ridiculously like a half-hour television situation comedy.

—Debbi Hoffman

REVIEWS

The Los Angeles Times. August 26, 1996, p. F6.
The New York Times. August 24, 1996, p. 20.
Variety. August 26, 1996, p. 60.

Carried Away

A story of first loves and last chances.—Movie tagline

"Intensely provocative and fiercely passionate."—Ron Brewington, *American Urban Radio Networks*

"Amy Irving steals the movie with her lovely performance."—Graham Fuller, *Interview Magazine*

"A wonderfully moving exploration of the meaning of love."—Jeanne Wolf, *Jeanne Wolf's Hollywood*

"Dennis Hopper gives a go-for-broke, soul-baring performance . . . it's great work from a great actor."—Rene Rodriguez, *The Miami Herald*

Box Office: $156,075

Carried Away has all of the elements of a Hollywood melodrama/soap opera, a Peyton Place stew of sex and violence. Yet the movie refuses to play by Hollywood's rules and offers, instead, an enchanting, meditative, mood piece, inspired by Dennis Hopper's best performance in years and Amy Irving's equally superb acting. Even better, supporting roles by Julie Harris and Hal Holbrook make *Carried Away* a fine ensemble effort, worthy of the Jim Harrison novel, *Farmer,* on which the film is based.

Forty-seven-year old Joseph Svenden (Dennis Hopper) has been teaching in a two-room school for nearly his entire adult life. He has no college degree, but he knows he has done a competent, if not outstanding job. At first, he seems a rather sad man, with a bad limp caused by a childhood tractor accident. His dead brother, a war hero, was supposed to marry Joseph's fellow teacher, Rosealee Henson (Amy Irving). Instead, Joseph has courted and bedded her for years while also taking care of his mother (Julie Harris), who is slowly dying.

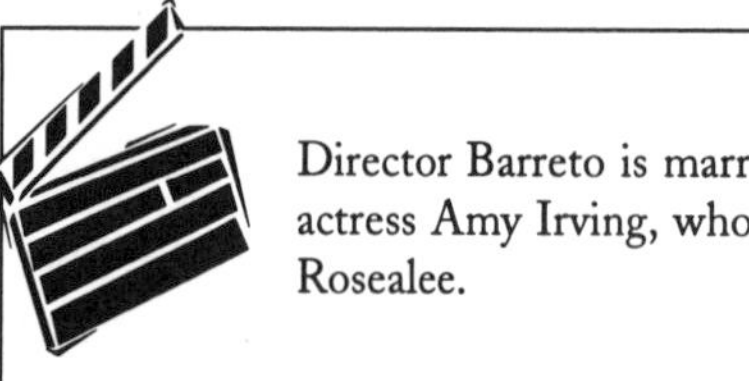

Director Barreto is married to actress Amy Irving, who plays Rosealee.

Rosealee wants to get married, but Joseph balks. He has always loved Rosealee but it bothers him that he is her second choice. They make love but without the abandon and passion that Joseph presumes Rosealee experienced with his brother. But his options are limited, especially when the school board vote goes against him, and Joseph realizes he will lose his students, who will be bused to a larger, modern school with a better qualified teaching staff. The apparently quiet, even morose Joseph comes to life, cursing the school board members and departing with his dignity intact.

In this rebellious mood, Joseph is vulnerable. He wants something more out of life, and he gets it in the figure of Catherine Wheeler (Amy Locane), a stunningly beautiful student with a body she loves to show off. When Joseph finds her naked in his barn, he runs away—only to return for a passionate lovemaking scene. Hopper at fifty-nine still has a trim, intact body, and he makes a credible lover for a young woman less than half his age. The film also plays fair—a rarity in Hollywood films—by showing the male star in the nude. (Some reviewers are so unused to this equal time given to an aging male star's body that they seem revolted by it—even though most fifty-nine-year olds would surely envy Hopper's physical condition and energy.)

Although Joseph is worried about the scandal this love affair with a student could cause, he is not embarrassed or apologetic when his mother's doctor, Hal Holbrook, discovers him in the bar with Catherine. Dr. Evans gives Joseph sensible advice. He is not moralistic, and he concedes how tempting Catherine is, and Joseph admits that he is enjoying himself too much to quit. But he has hardly given up his love for Rosealee. Indeed, he appears before her one night and demands that they make love in the light. No more huddling timidly in the dark, he tells her. At first Rosealee is aghast and acts as if Joseph is depriving her of her dignity, but given a moment to consider what he says about their tepid lovemaking she slowly and wondrously undresses, coming to Joseph with an excited, sexual shiver. This is one of the great moments in cinema, when this older couple discovers each other again, and yet for the first time.

The film has other surprises. Gary Busey (Major Wheeler) plays Catherine's father as a bluff, retired army man, who is good with guns and goes out hunting with Joseph. When Joseph realizes that Major Wheeler has learned about his affair with his daughter and is coming to see him, Joseph gets out his rifle and positions himself in the barn loft to get a good angle for what he presumes will be a shoot-out. But there is no violence, and Major Wheeler looks at Joseph incredulously. It is another fine moment, when the film denies itself the cliche of the outraged father bent on revenge. On the contrary, Major Wheeler is frustrated. He has taken his daughter to the country to get her away from an urban atmosphere where his precocious daughter had been promiscuous. And now he wants to find out what Joseph's intentions are. Joseph answers honestly that he cannot marry Catherine. This visit makes him more determined to sort things out with Rosealee.

Joseph's strength of character is surely derived from his mother. Julie Harris plays her beautifully in a scene in which she tells her son he better stop fooling with that adolescent girl. A surprised Joseph does not apologize but he acknowledges her point, which is made without a trace of moral superiority or condemnation. His mother is simply telling him that he is behaving foolishly and irresponsibly and will hurt others.

Rosealee finds out about Joseph's affair when she reads Catherine's card of condolence at Joseph's mother's funeral. She is angry and humiliated and rejects Joseph's efforts to explain that he simply got "carried away." And Joseph realizes that he must once and for all sever his ties to Catherine. It is not easy, for she parades before him naked on a horse like Lady Godiva. She is needy, and Joseph feels tender toward her. But her father's visit has reinforced how improbable it would be for Joseph to marry such a girl. He is weathered like the autumnal landscape his family has farmed, and she needs more than a teacher.

"What can I say. I'm a bad man. But sometimes it's fun to be bad."—Joseph

It is a tribute to Hopper's and Irving's acting that they can play, respectively, characters who are ten years younger and ten years older than themselves. They use their own bodies in ways that popular, mainstream actors rarely allow. Irving permits herself to be shot plain faced, without much makeup, in the nude, and with ordinary clothes. How many times has it been otherwise—when films show their stars waking up in the morning, their hair somehow in place and makeup on? In *Carried Away* the landscape of these actors bodies becomes an authentic parallel to the prairie lives they live. They have become flattened out by time and lack of drama, but both yearn to be carried away and to transcend their mundane careers.

When Rosealee is ready to reconcile with Joseph, she does so simply and sincerely. He comes back to apologize, although not really to excuse what he has done, except to express sorrow for the hurt he has caused her. What it amounts to, he explains to her, is that he wants more out of life, more out of Rosealee. Catherine was never really the issue. Standing in his way has been the memory of his brother, who has always come between him and Rosealee. In an earlier scene, his brother's son, who has always resented Joseph and his courtship of his mother, finally asks Joseph what his father was like. And Joseph's love for his brother pours out. Joseph has never resented his brother's privileged place in nearly everyone's memory. Rather, he has devalued himself for not matching his brother's spirit. Now, asking for a second chance with Rosealee, Joseph seems to have purged himself of comparisons. He has established his own terms for his love of Rosealee. And Rosealee reciprocates, admitting that all she has ever really wanted is to be "carried away."

The words resonate because they speak to a human yearning that is so rarely satisfied. Joseph often feels like the lone wolf that appears a few times in the film, an endangered species that should not appear in this habitat. The urge to do something wild, to be wild, is natural; it is also adolescent. How to foster spontaneity within the boundaries of marriage, family, and community, within the routines on which education and civilization depend, is the dilemma each individual confronts. The movie solves nothing, of course, but it presents a fresh and candid version of the human paradox.

Director Bruno Barreto (Irving's husband) and Ed Jones, who adapted Harrison's novel for the screen, render a low-key slice of American Midwestern life. But as in a Faulkner story, the intensification of the local and the regional lead to an appreciation of the universal. As Major Wheeler learns, he cannot rectify his city problems by coming to the country. He has to bring along an alcoholic wife and his Lolita-ish daughter. Being carried way is, in itself, not a solution, but it can prompt a clearer understanding of what people are running away from.

—Carl Rollyson

CREDITS

Joseph Svenden: Dennis Hopper
Rosealee Henson: Amy Irving
Catherine Wheeler: Amy Locane
Joseph's Mother: Julie Harris
Maj. Nathan Wheeler: Gary Busey
Dr. Evans: Hal Holbrook
Robert Henson: Christopher Pettiet
Lily Henson: Priscilla Pointer

Origin: USA
Released: 1996
Production: Lisa Hansen, Paul Herzberg for a CineTel production; released by Fine Line Features
Direction: Bruno Barreto
Screenplay: Ed Jones; based on the novel *Farmer* by Jim Harrison
Cinematography: Declan Quinn
Editing: Bruce Cannon
Music: Bruce Broughton
Production design: Peter Paul Raubertas
Costume design: Grania Preston
Sound: David O. Daniel
MPAA rating: R
Running Time: 107 minutes

REVIEWS

Boxoffice. May, 1996, p. 71.
Entertainment Weekly. April 19, 1996, p. 58.
Los Angeles Times. March 29, 1996, p. F12.
New York Times. March 29, 1996, p. C5.
Variety. January 29, 1996, p.62.
Village Voice. April 2, 1996, p. 66.

Caught

"A convincing portrait of obsessive sex and a poignant story of love and dreams."—Roger Ebert, *Chicago Sun-Times*

"Steamy sex scenes abound! Emphasis on the real needs that may drive decent people to infidelity, envy, cruelty and murder. *Caught* is value-collar drama with the sting of home truth and authenticity."—Bruce Williamson, *Playboy*

"A thoroughly engrossing drama!"—Amy Taubin, *Village Voice*

Box Office: $335,858

In recent years, independent filmmakers seem to have invented a new sub-genre, which might be called "The New Jersey Movie." There is indeed something strange and oddly fascinating about New Jersey. It's a place of extremes, a state in which fantastic beauty often reigns alongside the most appalling forms of urban ugliness. Filmmakers often go there in order to take advantage of its unchanging, working-class atmosphere and cheaper production costs.

The northern end of the state is renowned for its toxic waste dumps, junkyards and traffic jams. But there are also long stretches of sandy beaches, extending southward from the "Bruce Springsteen territory" of Asbury Park to the playful decadence of Atlantic City, the site of the Boardwalk and the Miss America Pageant (as well as Donald Trump's opulent casinos—the golden crown on an otherwise rotten tooth). Facades of glitz and glamour often conceal small towns quagmired in grinding poverty. And New York City is always close at hand, offering the vague promise of fame, big money and fabulous success.

American film debut for Irish actor Arie Verveen.

Robert M. Young's *Caught* adds to this rather curious cinematic tradition. The story (based on a 23-year-old novel by Edward Pomerantz, who also wrote the screenplay) is told from the point of view of Nick (Arie Verveen), a recent Irish immigrant who drifts into Jersey City, unexpectedly finds a home there, and decides to stay. The consequences of his migration are initially happy, sometimes steamily erotic, and finally, irreversibly tragic.

The film's initial set-up requires the audience to suspend a great deal of disbelief. Transformed from drifter into fugitive by a botched drug deal, Nick takes refuge in a Jersey City fish store. Within minutes, the sympathetic Betty (Maria Conchita Alonso) has convinced her stolid workhorse of a husband, Joe (Edward James Olmos) to give Nick a job helping out in the store. Shortly after that, Betty and Joe cajole the rootless Nick into moving in with them. (He even takes over their son's old room.) Nick quickly learns the finer points of the fish-boning trade and becomes the hardworking, well-adjusted son Joe and Betty never had. Once you accept this rather incredible turn of events, *Caught* becomes rather interesting, and sometimes genuinely captivating.

Caught remains ingratiating even though its plot devices quickly become rather obvious. It's the sort of movie you keep watching long after you've figured out the ending, just because the characters themselves are so interesting. The film's first image is of a school of fish maneuvering around an underwater net. Over this murky, aquatic scene, we hear Nick's narration of the story, rendered in a spooky *Sunset Boulevard* (1950) style. Some fish adroitly avoid the net, while others inadvertently veer into it, sealing their doom. From this we are meant to surmise that the random forces of nature are constantly at work, and that human beings are only victims, never the masters of their own fate. *Caught* is full of rather obvious symbolic references like these.

A shot of the New York skyline, as seen from the Jersey side, occurs early in the film: The view represents everything Joe wants—an air of sophistication, the promise of fabulous material wealth—but it is also fearsome and terrifying. The big city, with all of its perceived charms and enticements, lies just across the Hudson River, but psychologically, it's a world away, remote and inaccessible. For Joe and the other benighted residents of Jersey City, it's as far away as the moon.

Jersey City itself is a character in the film. Social life (to the extent there is any) seems to revolve around Journal Square, which is little more than a glorified taxi stand. This is a city where the Colgate clock—a local monument to toothpaste—is considered a major cultural landmark: It's aimless and sprawling, a mass of residences in search of a distinct center. As such, it's the perfect place for Nick, who has no clearly-defined goals or ambitions: He's the sort of person to whom life "just happens." As played by Arie Verveen, Nick is amiable, hardworking, and fundamentally passive: He's the blank slate upon which all the other characters scrawl their messy existential problems.

The job at Joe's fish store offers Nick an identity as well as some semblance of stability. He struggles to find his place in Joe and Betty's cramped apartment. Nick soon finds himself living in perilously close quarters with Betty, who has become his surrogate mother. This is tolerable until she begins to disclose her unsatisfied sexual longings. Nick is captivated by Betty, and they become sexually involved. In this rigid, working-class morality tale, their transgression spells doom for all concerned.

The sexual tensions mount. They are made even more unbearable by the fact that everyone involved in this unknowing menage-a-trois feels compelled to lie, to themselves as well as one another, about their true wants and needs. Like *Henry and June* (1990), a movie which approaches the matters of monogamy and fidelity from a more adventurous point of view, *Caught* is a depiction of exactly how not to engage in an "open relationship."

"Fish are his life."—Betty about husband Joe

Apart from a number of annoying adolescent jokes about "boning" and the smell of fish, the story takes itself seriously. Most of the junior-high-school humor is supplied by Danny (Steven Schub), Joe and Betty's somewhat estranged (and indeed, very strange) son. Danny assumes a role in the drama long before we ever see him in person. Nick settles into Danny's old room, which is festooned with mementos of Danny's previous attempts at rock 'n' roll stardom and comic success. The decor alone suggests that there is something seriously wrong with Danny: It is the room of an adolescent, or rather, an adult who has refused to grow up.

We are told at an early stage that Danny has been in California, pursuing a show business career. He communicates with his parents via a series of videotapes in which he is seen trying out his mostly unfunny, even rather ghoulish comedy routines. Betty is the only one who is amused by these ghastly attempts at stand-up comedy.

Danny soon shows up, live and in person, on Joe and Betty's doorstep. He has a wife and child in tow. It becomes apparent that his comedy career has stalled and that he has developed a serious addiction to cocaine. (The drug has made him paranoid and prone to fits of violence, but it's also implied that Danny was never quite right in the head in the first place.) A disturbed adolescent in an adult body, he is openly hostile to Nick, whom he instantly perceives as a rival for his parents' attention. Danny becomes the film's wild card: He slithers through the movie like a snake, eager to destroy everyone else's happiness.

The stakes are soon raised by an unexpected stroke of good fortune: Joe suddenly receives an offer to buy his store. The resulting windfall would enable him to fulfill his long-held dream of moving to Florida, owning his own fishing boat, and living in style. The prospect of success puts him in such a state of euphoria that he remains oblivious to his wife's infidelities.

Oedipal references fly in all directions. Danny's twisted intuition tells him that Nick and Betty are sexually involved. Nick and Betty live in terror of being found out, but they are unable to restrain their passion. Joe is blinded by a sudden onrush of wealth. And Danny is eager to be rid of Nick, the pseudo-brother who has usurped his position.

There are several implausible notions at work here. Joe is so involved with his work at the fish store that it takes him an incredibly long time to figure out that Nick's dealings with Betty have become much more than platonic. It's also difficult to understand why Joe would accept at face value the mad ramblings of his psychotic son, Danny, who is never presented as anything other than a coked-up ne'er-do-well.

The film is very effective in its depiction of wife-battering. This subject is handled via a subplot concerning Amy

CREDITS

Joe: Edward James Olmos
Betty: Maria Conchita Alonso
Nick: Arie Verveen
Danny: Steven Schub
Amy: Bitty Schram

Origin: USA
Released: 1996
Production: Richard Brick, Irwin Young for a Cinehaus/DuArt/Circle Films production; released by Sony Pictures Classics
Direction: Robert M. Young
Screenplay: Edward Pomerantz; based on his novel *Into It*
Cinematography: Michael Barrow
Editing: Norman Buckley
Music: Chris Botti
Production design: Hilary Rosenfeld
Costume design: Hilary Rosenfeld
Art direction: Lisa Albin
Sound: Jan McLaughlin
Casting: Kimberly Davis
MPAA rating: R
Running Time: 116 minutes

AWARDS AND NOMINATIONS

Independent Spirit Awards 1997 Nominations: Director (Young), Actress (Alonzo), Debut Performance (Verveen)

(Bitty Schram), Danny's abused wife. Amy discloses her secret to Nick, who immediately feels moved to help her. He uses part of Joe's "fish money" (a hefty cash advance derived from the impending sale of the store) to finance Amy's escape from Jersey City. Ultimately, Nick pays very dearly for doing this very decent, reasonable thing. The viewer is made to wonder why is it so impossible for Nick to admit that he has used part of the "fish money" for a noble purpose—that is, to secure Amy's escape from her dangerously psychotic husband. *Caught* never provides a sensible answer to this question.

It is a shame that the film has gotten such an indifferent reception, because there are some remarkable moments in it. This is especially true of Maria Conchita Alonso's performance as Betty, Joe's hardworking but secretly dissatisfied wife. Alonso does outstanding work here, portraying a type of character which Hollywood almost always gets wrong—the working-class female. She scores an achievement which is rare among actors, which is that she remains fascinating without having to say anything. She manages to appear glamorous even when she is cleaning fish.

Several scenes show Betty in front of her mirror, silently tending to her appearance. They're the most fascinating moments in the film. It's not that she's in love with her own image: It is clear that by keeping herself from looking like a drudge, she is bolstering her self-esteem. It is also understood that these moments of intense self-regard are the only privacy she enjoys. (In this respect, she is reminiscent of the Susan Sarandon character in Louis Malle's *Atlantic City* (1981), another film which centers upon the petty degradations of working-class characters who are stranded in New Jersey.)

Headed by Alonso, the principal actors are fine: It isn't their fault that the film is riddled with working-class cliches, rather obvious nods to Greek tragedy, and the clumsy overuse of object symbolism. (There is a lot of sexual innuendo revolving around references to fish, and once Joe's trusty fish-scaling knife comes into view, any viewer who is not asleep will surmise that it will ultimately be used for murderous purposes.)

As written, Joe is inclined toward histrionics and spouts a number of predictable, working-class homilies. Edward James Olmos, the erstwhile star of *Zoot Suit* on Broadway and an Oscar nominee for *Stand and Deliver* (1988), does what he can with a character who is saddled with a considerable number of salt-of-the-earth cliches. Steven Schub does a splendid job of portraying Danny, but the character seems to belong in another, very different kind of movie. Schub's performance recalls Brad Pitt's menacing psycho role in *Twelve Monkeys* (1995): It's well done, but it clashes enormously with the film's previously-established tone, which is one of quiet, working-class desperation.

Caught represents yet another strange turn in the wildly uneven career of Robert M. Young. His previous films include such diverse works as *Dominick and Eugene* (1988), *Triumph of the Spirit* (1989) and *The Ballad of Gregorio Cortez* (1982). He is at his best when dealing with socially isolated characters who are trapped by their own delusions. *Caught* is another offering of this type: It has a few sublime moments, but it's a hit-and-miss movie, presented by a director who seems to be experimenting with various film genres and struggling to develop a recognizable style.

Caught is not a flawless piece of work, but it is marked by a genuine sympathy for the concerns of its working-class characters. There are enough compelling performances in it to make one hope that its director, as well as its principal actors, will become more visible in the future. At the very least, *Caught* should cause some audience members to reconsider their deeply-ingrained infatuation with the traditional nuclear family, which in this film is the true source of everyone's problems, rather than the solution to them.

—Karl Michalak

REVIEWS

Boxoffice. September, 1996, p. 116.
Los Angeles Times. September 27, 1996, p. F6.
The New York Daily News. September 22, 1996, p. 40
The New York Times. September 25, 1996, p. C11.
People. September 30, 1996, p. 17.
USA Today. September 25, 1996, p. 9D.
Variety. February 5, 1996, p. 62.
Village Voice. October 1, 1996, p. 66.

Celestial Clockwork; Mecaniques Celestes

"A lyrical & jaunty midsummer frolic. Ariadna Gil is Spain's answer to Winona Ryder!"—Elizabeth Pincus, *Bazaar*

"Exuberant! A cheerful French Cinderella story!"—Lisa Henricksson, *GQ Magazine*

"Effervescent! A giddy comedy!"—Kevin Thomas, *Los Angeles Times*

"Irresistible! Giddy entertainment, silly, happy and whimsical!"—William Arnolds, *Seattle Post-Intelligencer*

"Totally engaging! Bright & fresh as a summer's day!"—Jeffrey Lyons, *Sneak Previews*

"Outlandish! Outrageous! Even zanier and more colorful than Almodovar."—Katherine Pew, *Time Out New York*

Box Office: $500,488

Venezuelan-born filmmaker Fina Torres's ultra-light fantasy, *Mecaniques Celestes* (*The Celestial Clockwork*), is an at times charming, but more often silly, contemporary re-working of the Cinderella tale against the backdrop of the Parisian opera and performance-art world. Torres combines the sunny camera work and colorful, busy decor of Pedro Almodovar's recent films, the intentional corniness of Baz Luhrmann's *Strictly Ballroom* (1993), and the magical plot twists of Woody Allen's *Alice* (1990) to create what is intended to be a frothy, effortless mix of Latin jazz, Parisian opera, fantasy fulfillment, and sexual reversal, all set against the backdrop of the Cinderella legend. But *The Celestial Clockwork*'s colorless protagonist and motiveless, cartoonish villainess are so artificially contrived, and the Cinderella storyline followed so slavishly, that there seems little doubt everything will work out in the end for the protagonist. As a result, the film's plot has little tension, and the film's essential corniness little emotional charge.

"No! No Italians allowed. Music is a serious business."—Music teacher Grigorief to Ana who wants to sing Rossini

Within the film's first five minutes, Ana (Ariadna Gil) leaves her husband-to-be at the altar in Caracas, and, with the soaring sounds of opera ringing in her ears, runs off to Paris, where she hopes to fulfill her dream of becoming an opera diva.

Penniless, Ana alights at the apartment of her friend Alma, who shares the place with another Venezuelan girl, Lucila, and pretentious video-performance-artist Celeste (Arielle Dombasle), a blonde vixen who will become Ana's sworn enemy. On her first night in Paris, Ana stands on the roof of the building in an electrical storm and sings one of her favorite arias as she fantasizes about Gene Kelly. Celeste, awoken, scowls at the new competition.

Ana finds a voice coach, the intimidating Maitre Grigorieff (Michel Debrane), who hates Italian opera and requires only that she put emotion into everything she sings. To pay for her lessons, Ana finds work as a domestic.

Meanwhile, the evil, social-climbing Celeste omits Ana from her guest list for the party celebrating the premiere of Celeste's bizarre performance-art music video (an amusing parody of music videos by French pop singer Mylene Farmer), in which she eats spiders to punk music and weird graphics. Why she chooses to victimize Ana so early on is unexplained, other than as an element of the Cinderella story.

Ana, however, is busy creating a network of fairy godfriends who will eventually support her in her battle against the nasty Celeste: Grigorieff; Armand (Frederic Longbois), a gay barkeep who also loves opera; and Alcanie (Evelyne Didi), a batty psychoanalyst in Grigorieff's building who conducts her therapy sessions via video, and who offers Ana less cramped lodging. In her new room in Alcanie's apartment, Ana hears on the radio that the famous movie director, Italo Medici, is looking for an unknown diva to play Cinderella in his next filmed opera. Ana vows to find Medici, and Armand, an astrology buff, predicts a brilliant future for her.

Invited to Celeste's party anyway by Alma and Lucila, Ana arrives accompanied by Alcanie, who quickly befriends Tonton (Lluis Homar), a Brazilian santero given to whipping up glowing magic potions. Italo is at the party, but the evil Celeste prevents Ana from meeting him, and tells her that Italo is only looking for a blonde for the role.

Crestfallen, Ana leaves the party drunk with the girls, and their erratic driving attracts the attention of the police, who discover that Ana's visa has expired. Ana must now appear at the prefecture within 24 hours to face presumable expulsion from the country.

Armand, convinced that the stars are on Ana's side, persuades Ana to stay, and Ana herself persuades a reluctant Grigorieff to help her study Rossini for a cattle-call audition for Italo. The girls, however, tell Ana that she has broken the law, and must either leave the country or get married.

As time runs out, the Machiavellian Celeste worms her way into shooting screen tests for Italo. Even though Italo thinks Celeste is completely wrong for the role, his producers are breathing down his neck to find a lead for the film, and they find the gorgeous Celeste preferable to no one at all. Desperate, Italo sends his production assistant to find Ana, whose voice he has heard on a tape mysteriously submitted to him.

Alcanie, trying to protect Ana, successfully fends off the police, but also sends away the PA, who tells Italo Ana cannot be found. Meeting with Tonton, Alcanie confesses her attraction to Ana, and Tonton gives her a love potion which will bring them together.

Armand volunteers to marry Ana so she can stay in the country, and because it would make his parents happy, and Ana accepts. At home, under the influence of the love potion, Ana jumps Alcanie and takes another step toward finding her true self.

But Celeste is not to be deterred. On the verge of clinching the Cinderella role, Celeste calls the authorities on Ana, and the police close in on Ana as she prepares for her and Armand's wedding. Celeste also seduces Tonton into providing her with a potion which will send the devoted Alcanie to New York on business, depriving Ana of much-needed support.

Italo, sick of Celeste's machinations, tells his staff to beware of an obnoxious blonde from Venezuela as auditions continue—but Ana, hoping to snare the role of Cinderella by any means, shows up for auditions in a blonde wig. Although she is able to sing enough for Italo to realize he has found his Cinderella, Italo's staff chases Ana out of the audition hall.

As the police tighten the net on Ana, Italo goes to Tonton and asks him to locate Ana by means of his psychic powers. In the final scene, as Ana and Armand get married in a church, Alcanie returns, the police and Celeste are foiled by the wedding vows, and Italo finds his Cinderella.

CREDITS

Ana: Ariadna Gil
Celeste: Arielle Dombasle
Italo Medici: Lluis Homar
Alcanie: Evelyne Didi

Origin: France; Spain
Released: 1994
Production: Fina Torres, Naoyuki Kibe, Oscar Benedetti, and Eddy Cherki; released by October Films
Direction: Fina Torres
Screenplay: Fina Torres
Cinematography: Ricardo Aronovich
Editing: Christiane Lack, Catherine Trouillet
Music: Alma Rosa Castellanos, Francois Farrugia, Michael Musseau
MPAA rating: Unrated
Running Time: 85 minutes

Co-written with five other screenwriters, including France's best-known writer of offbeat thrillers, Delacorta, *The Celestial Clockwork* wears its artifice on its sleeve, much as does the similarly plotted *Strictly Ballroom,* also about a musical competition. Unlike *Strictly Ballroom,* however, *The Celestial Clockwork* does not take the time to build sympathy for its protagonist, or motivation for its villain alongside its campy storyline. The writers' decision simply to re-work the Cinderella story makes the film tediously predictable, in spite of its zesty surface appeal. Even the film's title, *Mecaniques Celestes,* is a reflection of the script's problems, a kind of lame play on words on the machinations of the character Celeste, whose motiveless hatred of Ana drives the film.

Torres is no slouch as a director. Her opening of the film, which cuts in just a few minutes from a whirling blue globe to a church in Caracas to an Almodovar-style taxicab to a plane to the landmarks of Paris, establishes the film's premise with grace, speed, and humor. And the film's humorous touches are a pleasure to watch, especially Celeste's pretentious music videos and Didi's dithering Alcanie. Unfortunately, the thinness of the script undercuts Torres's obvious directorial talents. The film's sunny color-scheme and deliriously daffy plotting come to seem like second-rate Almodovar, without the underlying perversity that drives Almodovar's characters. Every character in *The Celestial Clockwork* besides Ana and Celeste is a fairy godmother of one sort or another, and the film ultimately becomes too cute and cloying for its own good.

Gil, best-known for her role as the smoldering, cross-dressing daughter in *Belle Epoque* (1994), here plays Ana with a bewilderingly flat blend of yearning and befuddled innocence. When Ana discovers her new sexual orientation, it seems more of an afterthought than a passionate life-force. Dombasle, the bombshell of Eric Rohmer's *Pauline at the Beach* (1982), remains a transfixingly beautiful screen presence, and brings off her amusingly pretentious villainess with panache. But Celeste has so little motivation to be mean to Ana, especially before their competition for the role of Cinderella, that Dombasle is stuck playing a cartoon she-devil. Didi and Longbois give the film's most enjoyable performances, Longbois's Armand evoking Nathan Lane.

In the end, in spite of its humor, its appealing look, and its light touch, *The Celestial Clockwork* defeats itself with its own frothiness and self-satisfied hipness. Torres's film is *Strictly Ballroom*-lite, and that is very light indeed.

—Paul Mittelbach

REVIEWS

Boxoffice Online. July 22, 1996.
The Hollywood Reporter. July 19-21, 1996, p. 12.
The Los Angeles Times. July 26, 1996, p. F6.
The New York Times. July 19, 1996, p. C8.
Washington Post. August 9, 1996, p. B7.

The Celluloid Closet

"Thoroughly enjoyable, funny and informative, a colorful overview with the popular appeal of *That's Entertainment.* Sheer fun."—Janet Maslin, *New York Times*

"A spectacular movie."—Bruce Williamson, *Playboy*

"Two thumbs up! Terrific!"—*Siskel & Ebert*

" Fascinating. A beautifully and thoughtfully made film that touches on many areas of human sexuality and human expression beyond the obvious."—Tom Shales, *Washington Post*

Box Office: $1,400,591

In 1981, author Vito Russo published a landmark book which serves as the basis for a splendid documentary. The book and the film are both called *The Celluloid Closet.* Russo, who died of complications from AIDS in 1991, could have been very proud of the outstanding film made from his thorough examination of the history of the depictions of gays and lesbians throughout American cinematic history. Rob Epstein and Jeffrey Friedman, who made two other superb films, *Common Threads: Stories from the Quilt* (1989), and the Oscar-winning *The Times of Harvey Milk* (1983), have made this film both a celebration of gay and lesbian life and an indictment of Hollywood's shameful treatment of homosexuals. *The Celluloid Closet* is entertaining and informative, touching and funny, inspiring and infuriating.

"Movies are where we learn about life," says Tony Curtis, one of the numerous famous faces whose interviews are intercut with clips from a century of filmmaking. The premise that films are a mirror for a culture is the foundation for *The Celluloid Closet*: Russo, Epstein, and Friedman describe how Hollywood's depiction of gays and lesbians mirrored cultural changes. Several successful filmmakers, such as Ron Nyswaner, who wrote *Philadelphia* (1993), and Armistead Maupin, whose *Tales from the City* books were adapted for television, describe what it was like to grow up as homosexuals whose only role models were in films. Nyswaner, referring to the ugly violence of William Friedkin's *Cruising* (1980), says that if you saw the film "you knew what you deserved." For Maupin, the homosexual blackmail victim played by Don Murray in *Advise and Consent* (1952) was a warning that "the life down the road for me" probably would end in suicide. Describing how the absolute dearth of homosexual characters affected a young lesbian starved for role models, filmmaker Susie Bright, regarding Joan Crawford's character in *Johnny Guitar* (1954), says that even though the character was not overtly lesbian, her clothing suggested otherwise. For a young woman hungry for film characters with whom she could identify, a woman in a cowboy shirt who might have been a lesbian was better than nothing. "If you are gay and accustomed to crumbs," says Bright, "you'll sit through a whole movie [just to see] an outfit."

The film is divided into loose segments which describe a type of characterization which mirrored the country's version of homosexuality. For example, the "sissy" seemed to be prevalent during the early years of film, showing homosexuality as something to laugh at, as exemplified by a silent film where an effeminate character named "Clarence the Clerk" is described as "one of nature's mistakes." During the years of the infamous Hays Code, which set about to restore "decency" to American film, gays became villains to make the characters acceptable to censors. Examples in-

CREDITS

Lily Tomlin (narrator)
Tom Hanks
Gore Vidal
Susan Sarandon
Susie Bright
Armistead Maupin

Origin: USA
Released: 1996
Production: Rob Epstein, Jeffrey Friedman for a Home Box Office and Telling Pictures production; released by Sony Pictures Classics
Direction: Rob Epstein, Jeffrey Friedman
Screenplay: Armistead Maupin; based on the book *The Celluloid Closet: Homosexuality in the Movies* by Vito Russo
Cinematography: Nancy Schreiber
Editing: Jeffrey Friedman, Arnold Glassman
Music: Carter Burwell
Art direction: Scott Chambliss
Sound: Pat Jackson
MPAA rating: R
Running Time: 102 minutes

AWARDS AND NOMINATIONS

Berlin Film Festival 1996: Teddy Bear Award
Sundance Film Festival 1996: Freedom of Expression

cluding the character of Mrs. Danvers from *Rebecca* (1940), Peter Lorre in *The Maltese Falcon* (1941), and *Dracula's Daughter* (1936) made it clear that homosexuals were not to be trusted. Ironically, one of the oldest film clips is of two men dancing together in one of Thomas Edison's demonstrations of the film medium in the 1890's.

"Hollywood taught straight people what to think about gay people and gay people what to think about themselves. No one escaped its influence."—narrator Lily Tomlin

The Celluloid Closet is not at all overly serious. It has a lot of hilarious moments, from Jane Russell singing to a bunch of bodybuilders who don't notice her in *Gentlemen Prefer Blondes* (1953) to John Ireland and Montgomery Clift in *Red River* (1948) admiring each others' pistols. The funniest moments are of Gore Vidal's recounting of how he, actor Stephen Boyd, and director William Wyler included homosexual subtext in *Ben-Hur* (1959) without telling Charlton Heston and thereby bypassing the "towering dullness and stupidity" of the status quo.

The Celluloid Closet makes the case that, mirroring society's grudging acceptance of gays and lesbians, things have somewhat improved since the 1980's, especially with the arrival of the groundbreaking (though uninspired) *Making Love* (1982). Tom Hanks and Susan Sarandon discuss their involvement in projects with positive models for gays and lesbians, most notably Hanks' Oscar-wining role in *Philadelphia* (1993). Sarandon, whose character in *Thelma and Louise* (1991) kisses her partner in crime on the lips before driving off a cliff, wonders aloud what would have happened if Butch Cassidy and the Sundance Kid would have done the same thing. Her humor masks the still difficult truth that in *Thelma and Louise* the characters were not clearly portrayed as lesbian, and their last act after kissing each other is to kill themselves. Combine that with the fact that only one famous actor (Harvey Fierstein) interviewed in *The Celluloid Closet* is an "out of the closet" gay or lesbian person, and perhaps mainstream film has not come that far after all.

—Kirby Tepper

REVIEWS

Boxoffice. November, 1995, p. 108.
Entertainment Weekly. March 22, 1996, p. 51.
Los Angeles Times. March 15, 1996, p. F10.
New York Times. October 13, 1995, p. C32.
Premiere. April, 1996, p. 27.
Sight and Sound. July, 1996, p. 40.
USA Today. January 30, 1996, p. 3D.
Variety. September 11, 1996, p. 106.

Celtic Pride

If you can't beat 'em . . . steal him!—Movie tagline

"What a picture!! It's wild!"—Ron Brewington, *American Urban Radio Network*

"This spring's ultimate comedy!"—Don Stotter, *Entertainment Time-Out Syndication*

"It's fun for everyone!"—Steve Oldfield, *KSTU-TV*

Box Office: $9,255,027

With the rule of professional basketball in the world of sports entertainment, film audiences apparently are doomed to an endless parade of basketball movies. In 1996 alone, there was *Eddie* (featuring Whoopi Goldberg as a Knicks fan who becomes their coach), *Sunset Park* (featuring Rhea Perlman as a gym teacher who becomes coach of an inner-city boys' team), *Space Jam* (Bugs Bunny meets Michael Jordan) and *Celtic Pride,* featuring Daniel Stern and Dan Aykroyd as overzealous fans who become inept kidnappers.

Whatever has made basketball popular on television doesn't translate onto film. Whatever its virtues, the game is definitely not drawn to large scale. Big men playing a quick game on a tiny court may make for excitement on a small screen, but the action doesn't fill up even a cineplex's scaled-down model of the big screen. No wonder the only successful entry in the '96 round-ball sweepstakes starred cartoon characters.

Celtic Pride has cartoon characters too, except they are flesh and blood. Stern plays Mike O'Hara, a bug-eyed high-school gym teacher so obsessed with the Boston Celtics that he would sacrifice his wife, son and career for them. Aykroyd plays his buddy Jimmy Flaherty, equally obsessed with the Celtics but possessing absolutely no life to sacrifice.

The film betrays its own title. There is nothing in the movie to explain why legions of fans are proud of the storied Celtics tradition (just as there is little in *Eddie* that explains why anyone might be infatuated with the storied

Knicks tradition). *Celtic Pride* insults Celtics fans. O'Hara and Flaherty are brainless goofballs, and so are the other regular fans who surround them (they are ridiculously superstitious and otherwise apparently unknowledgeable). The buddies kneel and kiss the wood of the Boston Garden when they enter, but the film doesn't bother to explain why.

Cameos include former Celtic stars Larry Bird, Bill Walton, and Bob Cousy.

There's the clumsy suggestion that O'Hara is a frustrated jock trying to vicariously relive his glory days of high-school ball, presented as if that is a deep revelation. Flaherty is just a stupid sports junkie. It's sufficient explanation, in the view of writer Judd Apatow and director Tom De Cerchio, that the characters are male, white, Irish and residents of Boston. "I love the Celtics!" screams Stern in the film's first two minutes. "Who cares?" the viewer already is tempted to shout back.

"At one time, in this country, sports were glorious. That's when things were in proportion. By the way, your mom and I are getting a divorce. See ya!"—Mike to his son

In fact, O'Hara and Flaherty are not merely Celtics fans, they are generic sports fans. There are occasional references to football and to baseball as inspiring similar devotion. In many ways, this is the ultimate downsizing of the modern film protagonist. The stars are two guys whose lives have no meaning apart from watching sports. This focus produces odd moments of multi-layered vicariousness, like the scenes where we watch Aykroyd at a live game watching the game on a hand-held mini-screen television. Never, even in cartoon fantasies, has an audience been so far removed from the real world.

Presumably, the advantage in scripting two sports junkies as the leads in a Hollywood movie is lots of instant audience identification. But *Celtic Pride* squanders that advantage by making its lead characters into objects of ridicule.

At first, the film is merely dumb. "Jazz music sucks!" shouts O'Hara as the Celtic prepare to battle the Utah Jazz for the NBA championship. "Go back to Utah and get a few more wives . . . Join the Mormon Tabernacle Choir." That's the script's idea of clever lines.

Soon, a lightbulb goes off in the movie's dim brain. O'Hara and Flaherty, at a bar where Jazz shooting star Lewis Scott (Damon Wayans) is dancing, plot to get him drunk. Not only is this the script's idea of a masterful ploy, but the camera lingers as the two airheads hatch and debate the idea, as if they were laying a criminal plot of intricate detail.

Immediately, the movie graduates from dumb to preposterous. Scott, the basketball film genre's stereotypical egotistic, money-grubbing black superstar, is overjoyed to have two dumb white guys professing to be Jazz fans as his drinking buddies. Sure. When O'Hara and Flaherty get him drunk and he passes out on their couch, they stumble into a plan to kidnap him to keep him from playing in the final game of the playoffs. When Scott suggests that any Celtics' win obtained through this manner would be tarnished, O'Hara, the "brains" behind the operation, speaks up for the importance of victory by any means necessary. So much for Celtic pride.

Wayans, a good comic actor trapped in a film opposite two over-the-hill comic actors, provides the film's only sizzle, using his character's superior wits to dribble circles around his opponents. When he comments on Flaherty's trophy collection—"All these pictures of other people's achievements . . . it's pathetic"—it's a solid, concise indictment of sports fandom in general. Through these words it becomes clear that the filmmakers disdain not only their subject matter, but their own protagonists. That disdain finishes off any potential audience for the film.

As comedy, *Celtic Pride* is very thin soup. Stern hits new lows on the annoyance scale and is given few opportunities to use his talent for physical comedy. Aykroyd is a flabby, listless shell of his former comic self. The two characters suffer constantly from their own incompetence, and at the

CREDITS

Lewis Scott: Damon Wayans
Mike O'Hara: Daniel Stern
Jimmy Flaherty: Dan Aykroyd
Carol: Gail O'Grady
Tommy: Adam Hendershott
Kevin O'Grady: Paul Guilfoyle
Coach Kimball: Christopher McDonald

Origin: USA
Released: 1996
Production: Roger Birnbaum for a Caravan Pictures and Hollywood Pictures production; released by Buena Vista
Direction: Tom DeCerchio
Screenplay: Judd Apatow
Cinematography: Oliver Wood
Editing: Hubert De La Bouillerie
Music: Basil Poledouris
Production design: Stephen Marsh
Art direction: Dina Lipton
Set design: Al Manzer
Costume design: Mary Claire Hannan
Sound: Clark Fisk
Casting: Ferne Cassel
MPAA rating: PG-13
Running Time: 90 minutes

movie's end are forced to suffer the humiliation of wearing Jazz uniforms to the big game and rooting for Scott. If they don't, he'll turn them in and they'll go to jail. This is not a funny plot. It's pathetic. And so are some of the crude, raunchy exchanges that pass for jokes. It makes for plenty of wincing but very little chuckling.

Basketball fans may find something to enjoy in *Celtic Pride,* but it's hard to imagine what. There's not much basketball action, and it all seems contrived. Many of the game-action scenes are shot from far off, better to minimize the appearance of ineptness by the stand-ins for NBA players. In a carbon copy of a plot device used in *Eddie,* a key game role is reserved for a towering Eastern European dolt (here a Croatian, in *Eddie* a Russian). There's also another caricature of an ineffectual, self-aggrandizing NBA coach (played here by Christopher McDonald). And, in a somewhat racist conceit that plays off another basketball stereotype, O'Hara helps the Jazz win by suggesting Scott pass the ball rather than shoot it. Why this advice, which Scott presumably has heard a million times before, suddenly sinks in is one of *Celtic Pride*'s many mysteries.

The biggest puzzle is why Buena Vista Pictures thought there would be an audience for a film based on the premise that sports fans are morally bankrupt morons. Such a film would only work if the filmmakers had the courage of their convictions and went way over the top. Instead, they are content with being contemptuous of the "pride" they pretend to be illustrating. Basketball fans won't like being insulted. And the rest of us simply won't care.

—*Michael Betzold*

REVIEWS

Chicago Tribune. April 19, 1996, p. 5.
Entertainment Weekly. May 3, 1996, p. 63.
Los Angeles Times. April 19, 1996, p. F6.
New York Times. April 19, 1996, p. C14.
People Weekly. May 6, 1996, p. 20.
USA Today. April 19, 1996, p. 4D.
Variety. April 22, 1996, p. 89.
Village Voice. April 30, 1996, p. 64.

Cemetery Man

"Frightfully funny."—Amy Dawes, *Los Angeles Daily News*

"Tantalizing! Deliriously original! A movie full of surprises."—Kevin Thomas, *Los Angeles Times*

"Wacky black comedy."—V.A. Musetto, *New York Post*

"A visual feast of ghoulishness."—Jack Mathews, *Newsday*

"Visually stunning! A delirious crack-pot film!"—Dennis Dermody, *Paper*

"A comically erotic horror show!"—Bruce Williamson, *Playboy*

Box Office: $253,986

Cemetery Man, Director Michele Soavi's first feature film release in the United States, is a deadpan rendition of stock horror genre cliches. The dead arise from their graves, usually after less than a week's residence in the ground, and caretaker Francesco Dellamorte (Brit Everett) matter-of-factly shoots these slimy, levitated corpses in the head. They are such a bother and will take a bite out of a living person's flesh if their skulls are not cleft with a bullet or some sharp instrument. A few of the corpses can talk and one even can scuttle around even though her head has been severed from her body.

In *Cemetery Man,* in other words, the fantastic is made to seem normal. There is even a bureaucratic form that can be filled out that details the cemetery's problems with the walking dead, although such inconvenient events ought to be ignored implies one Italian government official who would rather not deal with the fuss. Dellamorte is a handsome caretaker, but rather a moonstruck dunderhead. He admits to having read only two books—and one of those is the telephone directory! He falls in love with a beautiful widow and makes love to her on her husband's grave only to be attacked by his corpse, scratching his way out of his coffin.

There are some funny moments in the movie. Especially good is the tough-talking detective, played by Mickey Knox, a veteran of Italian low-budget quickies. Knox sounds like what he is, a Brooklyn denizen. How his accent is explainable in this Italian picture is beyond the normal capacities of a film reviewer. Knox is a parody of the trench-coated movie dick, doggedly on the case, but in *Cemetery Man* he is always wrong and does not know it. When Dellamorte takes to killing living people and Knox meets the murderer gun-in-hand, he congratulates Dellamorte for carrying a weapon because, he confides to Dellamorte, there is a maniac on the loose shooting people.

Dellamorte has his hands full when a whole busload of boy scouts is involved in a fatal accident. Soon the cemetery is aswarm with corpses convulsed into life, staggering about like so many extras from someone else's horror movie. With the unconventional becoming the conventional, Dellamorte loses his bearings completely. He has visions of demons who tell him to murder people.

Based on the Italian *Dylan Dog* comic book series created by Tiziano Sclavi, who reportedly asked his illustrators to model his lead character on Everett's appearance.

It is just possible that this movie is a satire on the exhaustion of Italian life, with the country as a cemetery full of people who do not realize they are in decline and well on the way to death, and with a bureaucracy that would find it a burden to admit the country's demise. Life has become so decadent that people are blase about everything. They don't bother to get things right, and they insist on their own terms no matter how inappropriate. Thus one constant cemetery visitor calls Dellamorte an engineer, although he has no degree and is nothing more than a caretaker.

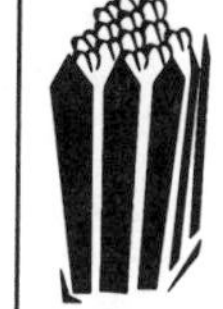

"At a certain point in your life you realize you know more dead people than living."—Francesco Dellamorte

Brit Everett plays his part without any camping. He seems genuinely perplexed by the rot that surrounds him. He does not try to put a good face on things, except when he lies to his widow/lover, telling her that he has a biology degree but is temporarily without work in his field. But unable to keep up pretense, he levels with her and admits that he has almost no education at all.

Whatever political allegories and satires on horror films *Cemetery Man* is attempting, it is curiously stocked with several bizarre love stories. There is the mayor's maladroit daughter who loves Dellamorte's drooling, mentally deficient assistant, and a girl from the town who cannot live without her dead boyfriend and throws herself on his grave until he rises, complete with motorcycle, to take her on a ghoulish night ride. Love does indeed conquer all. Dellamorte's widow/lover waxes eloquently over her dead husband's tenderness and prowess as lover—although his photograph on the gravestone shows an elderly, bald-headed man no one would take for an erotic ideal. If *Cemetery Man* means to confound our sense of conventional reality and of what people will find meaning in, it succeeds admirably. Moment by moment it seems pointless and perverse just to be perverse, and some viewers—even those finding a pattern in the perversity—may find that the film strains to hard to be original and to jazz up the tired cliches of low-budget films.

—*Carl Rollyson*

CREDITS

Francesco Dellamorte: Rupert Everett
Gnaghi: Francois Hadji-Lazaro
She: Anna Falchi

Origin: France, Italy
Released: 1996
Production: Tilde Corsi, Gianni Romoli, Michele Soavi; released by October Films
Direction: Michele Soavi
Screenplay: Gianni Romoli; based on the novel *Dellamorte, Dellamore* by Tiziano Sclavi
Cinematography: Mauro Marchetti
Editing: Franco Fraticelli
Music: Manuel De Sica
MPAA rating: R
Running Time: 100 minutes

REVIEWS

Boxoffice. April, 1996, p. 116.
Los Angeles Times. April 26, 1996, p. F12.
New York Times. April 26, 1996, p. C21.
Village Voice. April 30, 1996, p. 56.

La Ceremonie; A Judgment in Stone

"Beautifully and wickedly made! An instant suspense classic that is Claude Chabrol's best thriller in years!"—Janet Maslin, *New York Times*

"Terrific! A Gallic *Thelma and Louise*."—John Anderson, *Newsday*

"Supremely intelligent . . . filled with dark humor as well as intimations of Bunel and Hitchcock."—J. Hoberman, *Village Voice*

Box Office: $358,099

La Ceremonie has been called a French *Thelma and Louise* (1991). The comparison is apt, except that in director Claude Chabrol's film the two women, Sophie (Sandrine Bonnaire) and Jeanne (Isabelle Huppert) are united not against their male oppressors but the insufferably complacent bourgeois class, represented by the Lelievre family.

The Lelievres are not especially odious. Georges (Jean-Pierre Cassel) is a little smug and high-handed, but he is also sensitive and compassionate. His wife Catherine (Jacqueline Bisset) is breezy and superficial, but she is also courteous and thoughtful. Their children are likeable—down to earth and companionable. But what the family has in common is an inability to fathom what it must be like for the less comfortable—not to mention the poor. It is not that they cannot feel compassion; rather they lack the language, the rapport with a kind of suffering and anxiety that the less fortunate must encounter on a daily basis. The family, like their handsome furniture and country house, are cushioned from life's blows.

The Lelievres hire Sophie to be their maid. She is very quiet and efficient. Her sole entertainment is to watch television, which mesmerizes her and takes her mind off her anxieties. The family treats her civilly, but there is no real communication. What is there to say? Sophie is there to pick up after them, and she is uncomfortable when any of the Lelievres tries to strike up a conversation. Sophie does not articulate her feelings, but her blankness is surely understandable. How can she open up to people for whom she is not much more than an intelligent vacuum cleaner. Her job, as Catherine cheerfully instructs her, is to keep things neat. Director Chabrol makes no heavy-handed comment on the situation, yet somehow it appears obvious that there is something distasteful about hiring someone just to keep order in a family's life. Seldom has a movie made such a searing comment on the divisions of labor in modern life without the slightest grasping after propaganda points. It is all so very civilized, so French, so *charmante,* and yet so disgusting—this idea of hiring someone to smooth down the corners of life.

French title refers to the execution for a capital crime, which was known as "the ceremony."

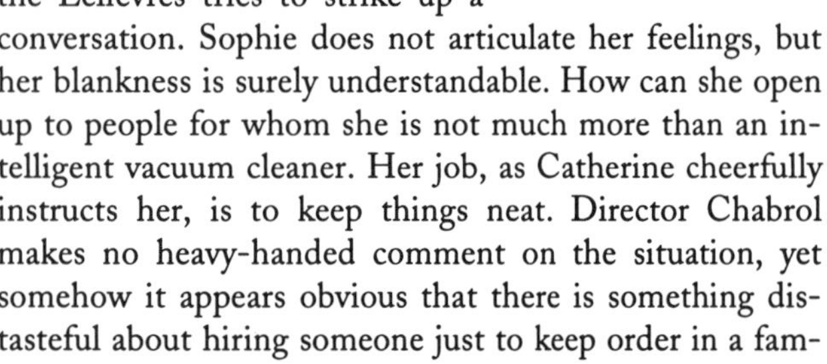

Jeanne, the local postal clerk, despises the Lelievres because they are so oblivious to how hard people like her have it. They worry, Jeanne surmises, about the next car they are going to buy. She sees in Sophie a kindred spirit. She has read about Sophie in a newspaper. Her father has died in mysterious circumstances, and there is an implication that Sophie might be implicated. Similarly, Jeanne was held on suspicion of killing her child. She later tells Sophie that her child's death was a horrible accident, but the police immediately suspected her. An outraged Jeanne points out that she could have gotten rid of her child at any time. Why wait until she was four?

In both cases, the women were released for lack of evidence. When they get to know each other, they giggle together like two conspirators. It is not that they are guilty, but rather that they regard themselves as easy targets, suspects who have narrowly escaped a society that holds no justice for them.

The extrovert Jeanne stimulates Sophie's pent up resentments. Sophie does not like being patronized; she does not like being ordered around, however nicely. Most of all, she does not being viewed as a victim of society—which is what happens when the Lelievres discover that she is illiterate. She is told that there is help for people like her. The phrase stings because it types her, dehumanizes what for her is a personal humiliation. The Lelievres do grasp how embarrassed Sophie is, but they have no vocabulary that does not sound condescending when they talk to her about it.

An aggrieved Sophie opens up to Jeanne and invites her to watch television in her room at the Lelievres. When the family learns that Jeanne is a regular visitor, Georges forbids Sophie to invite Jeanne to the house. He says she can see Jeanne anywhere else. He does not want to control her life, he assures her. Of course, he is within his rights. Yet his edict deprives Sophie of one of her few pleasures and of one of the few things she can offer Jeanne, who is always taking Sophie places and showing her a good time.

Georges has now made enemies of both women. He has even appeared at the post office, accusing Jeanne of opening up his letters and packages and then resealing them for delivery. She insults him, and he leaves in a rage. It is not clear whether she has violated his privacy; she is clearly capable of it—and does so after Sophie is fired.

The women return to the house to get Sophie's things. She is going to live with Jeanne until she finds new work. But when the two women arrive, Jeanne begins trashing the place and playing with the guns Georges uses for hunting. The two women go upstairs and Jeanne opens closets and rips clothes, pours coffee on the Lelievres bed, and smashes their bedside framed photographs.

The Lelievres are downstairs watching Mozart on television. They are the picture of bourgeois contentment. Georges goes to investigate the noises and finds Jeanne and Sophie waving guns around in the kitchen. When he commands them to get out and threatens to call the police, Sophie shoots him. As he collapses, she shoots him again. Then they proceed to murder the rest of the family.

Told in such bald fashion, the film may seem schematic—a labored throwback to Cold War Marxism. Director Claude Chabrol does have such a theme in mind. He has stated that he dislikes the smugness of capitalists who believe the class war is over. His film is a warning that the resentments Marxism addressed are still very much alive even if the ideology is dead. *La Ceremonie* is a blow against French complacency—indeed against Western society that thinks its internal tensions no longer exist. On the contrary, the violence of individuals increases because they have no political program that might harness their grievances. Jeanne and Sophie are quite happy to revenge themselves with guns.

CREDITS

Jeanne: Isabelle Huppert
Sophie: Sandrine Bonnaire
Catherine Lelievre: Jacqueline Bisset
Georges: Jean-Pierre Cassel
Melinda: Virginie Ledoyen
Gilles: Valentin Merlet

Origin: France; Germany
Released: 1995
Production: Marin Karmitz for a MK2 Productions, France 3 Cinema, Prokino Filmproduktion, Olga Film, and ZDF production; released by New Yorker Films
Direction: Claude Chabrol
Screenplay: Claude Chabrol, Caroline Eliacheff; based on the novel by Ruth Rendell
Cinematography: Bernard Zitzermann
Editing: Monique Fardoulis
Music: Matthieu Chabrol
Art direction: Daniel Mercier
Costume design: Corrine Jorry
Sound: Jean-Bernard Thomasson, Claude Villand
MPAA rating: Unrated
Running Time: 109 minutes

Words have not gotten the fast-talking, articulate Jeanne anywhere. And for lack of words Sophie has become a slave.

This message is embedded in a superbly written and acted script. Isabelle Huppert is magnificent as a woman for whom society has no ambitious role. She is aggressive and rude, but that is her form of defense against pompous male authority figures like Georges and their fawning, collaborating women, like Catherine. Jeanne's spontaneous, giving personality makes Sophie blossom. Heretofore she has had the hooded skittish look of a puppy abused by its master. The implication is that her father has hurt her, although she divulges remarkably little about her background. Huppert plays her reckless character to the hilt, earning the 1995 Venice film festival award as best actress and the Cesar, the French equivalent of an Oscar.

The class warfare of the film is all the more credible because the characters have winning traits and yet cannot escape the privileges and the rancor of their class positions. The Lelievres can only glimpse Sophie's humanity, and when they pity her or restrict her freedom, she lashes out. Jeanne, on the other hand, has lost the ability to see the Lelievres as human. To her they represent only a class symbol. Her great mistake is to think that by killing them and stealing the boom box the Lelievre daughter has received as a birthday present, she can recover what these people have stolen from her simply by virtue of their living as comfortable bourgeois.

The ending of *La Ceremonie* is quite different from *Thelma and Louise.* In the latter film, the women go out in a blaze of triumph, even though it means their deaths. They elude capture and preserve their outlaw status. They are martyrs to the cause of the underdog, the oppressed, and the scapegoat. *La Ceremonie* is far more complex and ironic. After the murders, Sophie agrees to clean up, erasing their fingerprints. Jeanne suggests she pretend to arrive home and then tell the police the gruesome event occurred while she was out. As Sophie goes about her chores, Jeanne returns to her old wreck of a car. It has battery problems—fixed once by the Lelievre daughter, who ironically is better at fixing cars than the working class Jeanne. This time the battery conks out just as Jeanne is backing out into the road. She is hit from the rear and killed by a car driven by a priest who earlier had smugly told her that her rough, unorthodox methods of collecting clothing for the church were not

AWARDS AND NOMINATIONS

Cesar Awards 1996: Best Actress (Huppert)
Nominations: Best Film, Best Director (Chabrol), Best Actress (Bonnaire), Best Supporting Actress (Bisset), Best Supporting Actor (Cassel), Best Script
Los Angeles Film Critics Association 1996: Foreign-language Film
National Society of Film Critics 1996: Foreign-language Film

needed. As Sophie leaves the house, preparing to walk away and then return, she passes the scene of the accident. The police have taken out of Jeanne's car the boombox which has been used to record the Mozart opera. As the police replay the tape, they hear the voice of Jeanne and have in hand the evidence that will condemn Sophie.

There is no escaping a reckoning with humanity. Neither the comforts of middle-class life nor nursing grudges from below it make for a whole or healthy society. Irony builds on irony. The Lelievres want to give Sophie driving lessons and to teach her how to read, but they do not know how to treat her as a human being. Jeanne dies in her flimsy tin car, fixed once by a bourgeois, yet destined to crumple completely on impact. At the scene of the accident it is said that she never had a chance. Precisely so, the movie concludes.

—Carl Rollyson

REVIEWS

Boxoffice. November, 1995, p. 106.
Entertainment Weekly. January 24, 1997, p. 39.
Los Angeles Times. December 20, 1996, p. F7.
New Yorker. January 20, 1997, p. 98.
Sight and Sound. March, 1996, p. 43.

Chain Reaction

"Keanu Reeves delivers again with his own kind of action-man charisma!"—David Sheehan, *CBS-TV*

"All the thrills of *The Fugitive* and *Speed* from the guys who gave you both. A sensational action thriller."—Don Stotter, *Entertainment Time-Out*

" . . . taut, intelligent thriller . . . "—Amy Davies, *L.A. Daily News*

"Explosive! It's a blast."—Bob Healy, *Satellite News Network*

Box Office: $20,655,819

Cheap, clean, abundant energy. Who wouldn't want it? Well, somebody doesn't, but the who and the why are very vague in the latest movie from director Andrew Davis.

The premise of *Chain Reaction* involves a team of University of Chicago researchers which includes their idealist leader Dr. Barkley (Nicholas Rudall), physicist Dr. Lily Sinclair (Rachel Weisz), machinist Eddie Kasalivich (Keanu Reeves) and an assortment of politically correct blacks, orientals, women, and old white men who have discovered how to harness the hydrogen available in water as a source of energy. After working out a few bugs, and just as they are about to put the notes to their successful experiment on the Internet for the whole world to enjoy the fruits of their labor, someone blows up the lab and eight blocks of Chicago's south side.

We know this is no accident because Eddie returned to the lab just before it blew and saw Dr. Barkley dead, tied up and with a plastic bag over his head. Eddie just manages to escape the explosion himself only to discover that he and Lily are being set up for the sabotage by parties unknown. Now Eddie and Lily are being sought by the FBI (Fred

CREDITS

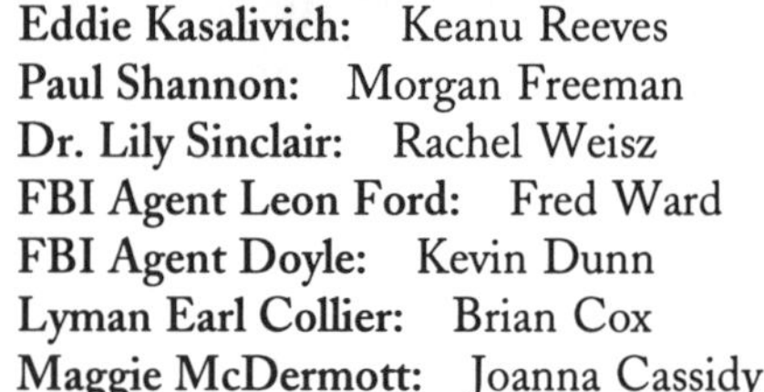

Eddie Kasalivich: Keanu Reeves
Paul Shannon: Morgan Freeman
Dr. Lily Sinclair: Rachel Weisz
FBI Agent Leon Ford: Fred Ward
FBI Agent Doyle: Kevin Dunn
Lyman Earl Collier: Brian Cox
Maggie McDermott: Joanna Cassidy

Origin: USA
Released: 1996
Production: Arne L. Schmidt, Andrew Davis for a Zanuck Co./ Chicago Pacific Entertainment production; released by 20th Century Fox
Direction: Andrew Davis
Screenplay: J.F. Lawton, Michael Bortman
Cinematography: Frank Tidy
Editing: Donald Brochu, Dov Hoenig, Arthur Schmidt
Music: Jerry Goldsmith
Production design: Maher Ahmad
Art direction: David J. Bomba
Sound: Robert R. Anderson, Jr.
Visual effects supervisor: Nick Davis
Casting: Amanda Mackey, Kathy Sandrich
MPAA rating: PG-13
Running Time: 106 minutes

Ward and Kevin Dunn), but they are also being chased by people in cahoots with those who arranged for the explosion. Unfortunately, Eddie and Lily can't tell the good guys from bad guys. The only person they think they can trust is Paul Shannon (Morgan Freeman), the man behind the project's financing. But can they really trust him? Consequently, Eddie and Lily run from everyone.

"I wish you wouldn't threaten to kill my scientists right to their faces!"—Shannon to Collier

They run to the Yerkes Observatory in Wisconsin, they run over frozen Lake Geneva, they run down Michigan Avenue and up an open drawbridge, they run through and over museum exhibits, they run over roofs and through air conditioning ducts, and eventually they run to Washington D.C. and from another explosion.

Director Davis' last action feature, also shot in Chicago, was 1993's blockbuster *The Fugitive.*

It should come as no surprise if *Chain Reaction* seems just a tad familiar. Director Davis has done this before, only the last time, in *The Fugitive* (1993), he came up with a better product. He seems to have found a generic plot—unjustly accused hero goes on the run to save his life and prove his innocence—and Davis handles the chases, stunts, and effects well, but at some point it all wears thin. That point is reached in *Chain Reaction* where the plot is unfocused and fuzzy and the hero less than compelling.

Keanu Reeves is obviously trying to capitalize on his newfound status as the action hero from *Speed* (1995), but unfortunately at his best here he is blank, at his worst he is just on another Bill and Ted adventure. Similarly forgettable is the relatively unknown Rachel Weisz (*Stealing Beauty* [1996]) as Lily who may be a brilliant physicist, but can't create any chemistry with Eddie.

Even Morgan Freeman's Shannon is problematic. Freeman, as usual, turns in a solid, multifaceted performance, but it may be too cryptic. Even at the end we don't know if he should be considered friend or foe. And just try to figure out the motivation for (or even the logic of) the actions of Brian Cox's Lyman Collier.

Chain Reaction has its moments: Good bits of dialogue, some energetic scenes, and Chicago looks great, but they are severely overshadowed by the sheer confusion of the film's story. And, what doesn't confuse us looks all too familiar. Furthermore, in these days of militias and bombings, do we really need another movie that feeds our paranoia about the government?

—Beverley Bare Buehrer

REVIEWS

Boxoffice Magazine Online. August 5, 1996.
Chicago Tribune. August 2, 1996, p. 4.
Entertainment Weekly. August 9, 1996, p. 42.
Los Angeles Times. August 2, 1996, p. F8.
New York Times. August 2, 1996, p. C3.
People. August 12, 1996, p.19.
USA Today. August 8, 1996, p. 4D.
Variety. July 29, 1996.
Village Voice. August 13, 1996, p. 62.

The Chamber

Time is running out.—Movie tagline

"An explosive, gripping drama!"—Bobbie Wygant, *KXAS*

"The best John Grisham adaptation yet."—Jeff Craig, *Sixty Second Preview*

"Riveting. An emotionally-charged film that will leave you spellbound."—Sam Hallenbeck, *WTVT*

Box Office: $14,300,075

The image of any human being walking down a long corridor to be executed is an excruciating and devastating experience. Capital punishment is never an easy issue and is always painfully controversial. Susan Hayward's Academy Award performance in *I Want to Live,* directed by Robert Wise in 1958 was based on the sensational murder trial of vice girl, Barbara Graham. The final segment dealing with her execution in the gas chamber haunted moviegoers for years to come, and was a powerful indictment of capital punishment. Lately, films such as *Dead Man Walking,* starring Susan Sarandon and Sean Penn, and *The Last Dance* with Sharon Stone, also deal with this disturbing subject. The latest entry in this crop of films, covering the "death row" experience is *The Chamber,* based on John Grisham's best-seller of the same name. A Universal release of an Imagine Entertainment presentation of a Brian Grazer-Davis Entertainment, the film stars Chris O'Donnell, Gene Hackman and Fay Dunaway. Let it be noted, however, that Grisham was quoted in *USA Today* as having said, "I have not been involved with the project and I will not, under any circumstances, waste my time visiting the set."

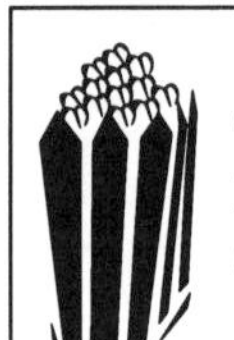

"Of all the things I've hated in my life, the one I've hated most is me."—Sam Cayhall

Grisham's earlier films, *The Firm* (1993), starring Tom Cruise and *A Time to Kill,* starring newcomer Matthew McConaughey, both met with critical as well as commercial success. *A Time to Kill,* along with *The Chamber,* both examine the agonizing ramifications of a racially motivated crime. The consequences of such actions reverberate through the fabric of society. Recently, the reaction to the Rodney King beating in Southern California, attests to this fact. Although the author has disassociated himself from the project, *The Chamber* does a commendable job of raising some important issues without proselytizing. It may not have been the film that the author had envisioned, but it successfully explores the intricate concepts of guilt and responsibility. As is true of most complex questions, there are never any easy answers. Ultimately, the members of the filmgoing audience must decide for themselves.

Adapted for the screen by William Goldman and Chris Reese, the film's story opens on a typical morning in April of 1964. Marvin B. Kramer, a Jewish civil-rights lawyer, is about to take his two young sons with him to his law office. Moments after they enter the building, it erupts into a thunderous explosion. Kramer loses his legs and the two boys lose their lives. Across from the burning building stands an impervious statue of a Confederate soldier. Suddenly, it is 1996 in Chicago, where it is revealed that former KKK Klansman, Sam Cayhall (Gene Hackman) has finally been convicted of this brutal hate crime. He is now only 28 days away from being gassed by the state of Mississippi. The clock is ticking, which establishes an extreme sense of urgency to the events that are about to unfold.

Enter Adam Hall (Chris O'Donnell), a young, wet-behind-the-ears lawyer, who takes on Cayhall's case for an appeal of the death sentence. He just happens to be the convict's grandson, who not only wishes to save Cayhall from the gas chamber, but to exorcise some of his own personal demons, as well. Adam's father (Cayhall's son) committed suicide due to the personal pain and public humiliation of being the son of such an infamous, racist terrorist. Adam found his father's body when he was just a boy, and the memory still haunts him. In a fervent search to find some answers to his tragic and complex family history, he visits his alcoholic aunt, Lee (Faye Dunaway), his father's sister. It is at this point in the narrative that he attempts to pry open some of the secrets of the past that might, possibly explain or at least justify, his father's suicide. Lee is adamant about leaving the door locked on the family's past for fear of creating another scandal. Although confused and frightened, Adam goes to prison to meet with his notorious grandfather. Unprepared for what he may find, his first encounter with Cayhall is disturbing and alarming. The depth of the prisoner's hatred and bigotry is ferocious! He lashes out at Adam's law firm—"The Jew bastards send in a greenhorn to defend me." His racist comments pour forth from his mouth like venom. The young attorney realizes that he is up against a powerful adversary and tries to convince Cayhall, as well as himself, that his life is worth saving. While Adam feverishly tries to beat the clock, he uncovers some revealing facts about Cayhall's involvement with other Klansmen at the time of the explosion. He learns of some haunting stories of his own father's childhood, as well as some political maneuvering by Mississippi's ambitious young governor (David Marshall Grant). The pieces of the puzzle begin to unfold through Adam's persistence and commitment at finding the truth.

Coinciding with the issues of guilt and responsibility, *The Chamber,* in many ways, is about love, healing and forgiveness within a family unit. The pursuit of justice is also aimed at some kind of reconciliation for the long-suffering Cayhalls. It is necessary for Adam to understand his grandfather, in order for him to have some kind of closure concerning his father's suicide. This is no easy task, since Cayhall appears to be impenetrable. Richard Corliss of *Time Magazine* wrote, "*The Chamber* is really a tale of love and forgiveness, a suturing of wounds across the generations." It is unclear as to the reason why Grisham was unhappy with the film version of his novel. Scriptors William Goldman and Chris Reese did succeed in constructing an intelligent script of complexity and urgency. It also appears that director James Foley (*Glengarry Glen Ross* [1992], *Fear* [1996], *At Close Range* [1986]) worked earnestly to bring honesty and integrity to the piece.

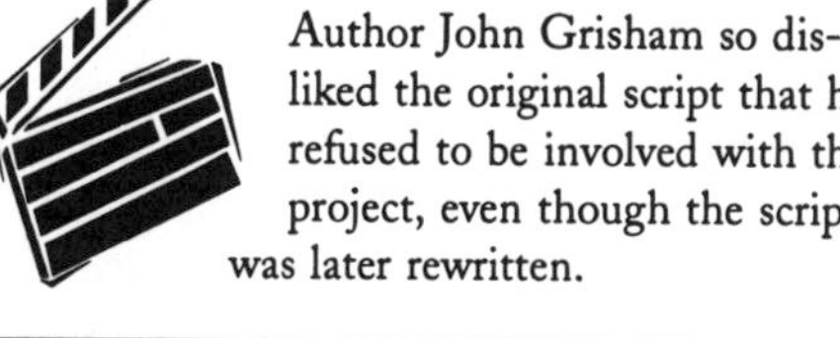

Author John Grisham so disliked the original script that he refused to be involved with the project, even though the script was later rewritten.

CREDITS

Adam Hall: Chris O'Donnell
Sam Cayhall: Gene Hackman
Lee Bowen: Faye Dunaway
Nora Stark: Lela Rochon
E. Garner Goodman: Robert Prosky
Gov. McCallister: David Marshall Grant

Origin: USA
Released: 1996
Production: John Davis, Brain Grazer, Ron Howard for an Imagine Entertainment production; released by Universal
Direction: James Foley
Screenplay: William Goldman, Chris Reese; based on the novel by John Grisham
Cinematography: Ian Baker
Editing: Mark Warner
Music: Carter Burwell
Production design: David Brisbin
Art direction: Mark Worthington
Costume design: Tracy Tynan
Sound: Jose Antonio Garcia
Special effects coordinator: Burt Dalton
Visual effects supervisor: Peter Montgomery
MPAA rating: R
Running Time: 111 minutes

No one can deny that the prolific body of work created by Gene Hackman is quite remarkable. Hackman made a powerful impact on the American public when he appeared in Warren Beatty's *Bonnie and Clyde* in 1967. (Incidentally, this same film established Faye Dunaway as a major star.) His exciting portrayal of Popeye Doyle in the 1947 cop thriller *The French Connection,* directed by William Friedkin, succeeded in making Hackman a powerful screen presence. His performance in his current project, *The Chamber,* could possibly be his best work since Clint Eastwood's, *The Unforgiven* (1992), for which he won an Oscar. He is riveting in every scene in which he appears. Sam Cayhall is a man whose entire life has been about hatred and violence. Since his childhood, he was raised with bigotry and revenge—raised to be a monster. Now, after all these years, he has to face the consequences of his actions. Not only to the legal system, but also, the impact it has had on his entire family. It is the day of reckoning. Every nuance of his painful soul-searching and ultimate regret is brought vividly to the screen by Hackman's towering, fiery performance. In one scene, where he is viewing a sunrise for the first time in fifteen years, the camera slowly moves from a long shot of a magnificent sunrise, to a close-up of the actor's face. He does not utter a sound, but the sadness and heartbreak of the last fifteen years are all registered on the man's tortured face. Hackman's ability to move an audience, in such a deeply touching manner, is unique and exceptional. To put it simply, he is brilliant.

The casting of Faye Dunaway as Lee, Sam Cayhall's estranged daughter, required Hackman to wear heavy age makeup. Even Dunaway herself admitted that they had to stretch it. According to Susan Stark of the *Detroit News,* in her review of *The Chamber,* "Faye Dunaway has her best role in ages." This well-known "method" actress has certainly played a wide range of characters in her illustrious career. Since her breakthrough role in *Bonnie and Clyde,* she has appeared in such films as *Chinatown* (1974) with Jack Nicholson, *The Thomas Crown Affair* (1968) with Robert Redford, *The Eyes of Laura Mars* (1978) with Tommy Lee Jones, and her Academy Award performance in Paddy Chayevsky's brilliant film, *Network* (1976). It is quite an exceptional body of work. The gifted actress continues to surprise audiences as she did with her gritty portrayal of a tortured alcoholic in *Barfly* (1987), with Mickey Rourke—not to mention her regrettable turn as Joan Crawford in *Mommie Dearest* (1981). Once again in *The Chamber,* she plays a tortured, long-suffering alcoholic. Although in the very beginning of the film, she overdoes the Southern belle bit (Scarlett O'Hara at 50), she creates an extremely sympathetic character with her carefully modulated, three-dimensional performance. As the history behind Sam Cayhall begins to unravel, so does her character. Her hidden wounds are deep. Her re-telling of a murder that she witnessed as a child reveals a complex, guilt-ridden past. Dunaway's richly textured characterization is poignant and heartbreaking. Her scenes with Hackman remind audiences of the power and impact of exceptional talent. It is a pleasure to watch.

Since making *The Scent of a Woman* (1992) with Al Pacino, Chris O'Donnell has been working a great deal. Fresh from his success as Robin in the third installment of *Batman,* he has been given the opportunity in *The Chamber* to determine if he is capable of carrying an entire film. It has been reported that Brad Pitt was first offered the role of Adam, but turned it down. It may be true that O'Donnell possesses a fresh-face appeal, but since he has so much resting on his young shoulders in this feature, where's the passion? Susan Stark, again from the *Detroit News,* comments, "O'Donnell is reserved to the point of seeming stiff and uncommunicative in the film's pivotal role." When Adam is making an impassioned speech before the court to save his grandfather's life, O'Donnell's delivery seems juvenile instead of dynamic. It comes across like a valedictorian address at a college graduation—not a plea to save a man's life. There is an element of detachment to his performance that renders it bland and uninteresting.

The supporting players all gave solid performances that added considerable substance to the piece. Raymond Barry (Rollie Wedge), David Marshall Grant (Governor McCallister), Robert Prosky (E. Garner Goodman) and Lela Rochon (Nora Stark) made for an impressive ensemble cast. There was a lovely portrayal by Millie Perkins of the widow of the slain civil-rights lawyer that was particularly touching and memorable. The tech credits also were fine, with a gripping musical score by Carter Burnwell that elicited the appropriate amount of urgency.

The Chamber is the fifth adaptation of John Grisham's work in three years. Grisham's thrillers are usually quite compelling and riveting stories. There is always an intelligent and purposeful use of structure to propel the action forward. There is a sense of riding on a roller coaster or speeding along on a train to an unknown destination. *The Chamber* tends to focus more on characterization than action. Also, since many of the scenes are shot in a prison, there is an added sense of claustrophobia to the setting. Many Grisham fans may be unaccustomed to the darker mood and slower-paced action in this film. Also, there undoubtedly will be the criticism that the film does not compare to the book. Taking this all into consideration, *The Chamber* is an enlightening, informative, and compelling film experience. Although it tends to stereotype everyone in the South as being maniacal, murdering Klansmen, it does fairly address some of the issues of racism. It examines the root cause of this complex issue as a result of early conditioning, rather than a genetic defect. This version of Grisham's work certainly provides a worthwhile, thought-provoking drama that invites audiences into the mind and vision of the author.

Since film is a different medium than a novel, *The Chamber* may not appeal to some of John Grisham's readers. However, it does deliver a high-calibered, well-conceived form of entertainment to film audiences. It is by far more enlightening than going to see movies based on comic books.

—Rob Chicatelli

REVIEWS

Chicago Tribune. October 11, 1996, p. 5.
Entertainment Weekly. October 18, 1996, p. 53.
Los Angeles Times. October 11, 1996, p. F1.
New York Times. October 11, 1996, p. C26.
People. October 21, 1996, p. 22.
Rolling Stone. November 14, 1996, p. 124.
Time Online. October 14, 1996.
USA Today. October 11, 1996, p. 1D.
Variety Online. October 3, 1996.
Village Voice. October 22, 1996, p. 88.

Chungking Express; Chongqing Senlin

If my memory of her has an expiration date, let it be 10,000 years . . . —Movie tagline

"A knockout! Terrifically stylish! Hong Kong is the perfect setting for a film with style to burn."—Kevin Thomas, *Los Angeles Times*

"A delicious romance!"—Richard Corliss, *Time*

Box Office: $416,660

The best way to review *Chungking Express* is to acknowledge right up front that a lot of critics liked it. That way, any unkind words that the reader comes across can be mitigated by the reality that many critics actually praised this film. Kevin Thomas of the *Los Angeles Times* stated, "Shot fast and sometimes furiously on crowded Hong Kong streets, it speaks in its own highly personal shorthand, expressed through the most fluid of cameras and punctuated with bold whooshes of color and potent bursts of American pop music."

That having been said, here's another look at *Chungking Express*: It is an unrelentingly dull, self-consciously hip modern tale of romance (or something like that) and of life in Hong Kong. Wong Kar-Wai's direction fits all of the following adjectives: stylish, fast-paced, edgy, raw. Other less flattering adjectives come to mind: overblown, overwrought, and overshot. His storyline is downright irritating.

First film released to video under Quentin Tarantino's Rolling Thunder Pictures label.

Perky waitress Faye Wang finds love in strange places in the quirky Hong Kong romance, *Chungking Express.*

It is the story of some denizens of an urban setting in present-day Hong Kong. The action revolves loosely around a fast-food joint and two different women who work there. The only theme decipherable is that Wong Kar-Wai seems to want to examine how the atmosphere at a fast-food restaurant affects the romantic inclinations of the women that work there. Surely, Wong would be insulted to have his story reduced to such a satirical explanation, but with all due respect to him, it is difficult to understand what other meaning he might have intended. The storyline borders on incomprehensible. A "Woman Wearing a Blond Wig" (Brigitte Lin) is involved in some sort of drug-smuggling operation, and then she seems to become the romantic obsession of a "Man Wearing Badge No. 223" (Takeshi Kaneshiro). He eats thirty cans of Dole pineapple because yet another woman named May has dumped him. (Don't ask me; I didn't write it.) Soon after, a new woman enters the scene at the fast-food joint where

CREDITS

The Drug Dealer: Brigitte Lin
He Qiwu, Cop #223: Takeshi Kaneshiro
Cop #663: Tony Leung
Faye: Faye Wong
Air Hostess: Valerie Chow
Manager of "Midnight Express": "Piggy" Chan

Origin: Hong Kong
Released: 1996
Production: Chan Yi-Kan for a Jet Tone production and ICA Projects; released by Miramax
Direction: Wong Kar-Wai
Screenplay: Wong Kar-Wai
Cinematography: Christopher Doyle, Lau Waikeung and Chen Guanghong
Editing: William Chang, Hai Kit-Wai, Kwong Chi-leung and Kuang Zhiliang
Production design: William Chang
Art direction: Qui Weiming
Visual effects: Cheng Xiaolong
Special effects: Ding Yunda, Deng Weijue
Costume design: Yao Huiming
Make-up: Guan Lina
Music: Frankie Chan, Roel A. Garcia
MPAA rating: Unrated
Running Time: 97 minutes

the man wearing the badge and the woman wearing the wig met. This new woman, named Faye (Faye Wang) becomes obsessed by another man called "Badge No. 663" (Tony Leung), and she breaks into his house while he is at work in order to clean up his mess. He, in turn, is lonely because he is being treated badly by a stewardess.

All kidding aside, there is probably much to say about the loneliness of urban life. Especially with Wong's deft, quick camera work, the symbolism is quite obvious that he wishes to remind us of the fleeting nature of romance and of the pathetic loneliness that engulfs many young people in today's fast-paced world. But like many young auteurs, Wong is deft with camera moves but shows his youth by inserting too many artsy shots. With leaden symbolism like the pineapple-eating man who looks at the expiration dates on the cans and says, "everything comes with an expiration date," or then the same man jogging in the rain saying, "to celebrate, I jog," Wong virtually insures the disdain of many filmgoers. Few shots last more than a few seconds, either to maintain the tension of his urban setting, or merely to irritate his audience. He succeeds on both counts.

The performers are not much more than set pieces, succeeding in looking odd or cool as the situation warrants. Faye Wang fares the best, probably because her quirky role seems to be more fleshed-out than the rest. She breaks into the home of the object of her desire, then obsessively cleans it without his being aware. She takes a magnifying glass to his bed, discovering the long hairs of his stewardess-lover. She lies to her boss that she is stuck in the rain, but is actually calling her boss from her beloved's shower. Wang's strange, doe-like expression somehow makes her character believable: she is simply a unique woman, and her strangeness explains the behavior to a certain extent.

Overall there is, however, little to recommend this self-consciously artsy film. The only way this film found a U.S. release is that Quentin Tarantino's production company distributed it. If you share the same lost sense of reality and distorted sense of black humor as Tarantino, then you will probably enjoy this film. More power to you. If you see Tarantino as the archetype of inflated cinematic artistry and hilariously overindulgent vacuity, then take a cinematic ride on anything other than the *Chungking Express.*

—*Kirby Tepper*

AWARDS AND NOMINATIONS

Independent Spirit Awards 1997 Nominations:
Foreign Film

REVIEWS

American Cinematographer. December, 1995, p. 22.
Boxoffice. February, 1996, p. R-12.
Chicago Tribune. March 15, 1996, p. 5.
Los Angeles Times. March 8, 1996, p. F10.
New York Times. March 8, 1996, p. C14.
Rolling Stone. March 7, 1996, p. 53.
Sight and Sound. September, 1995, p. 47.
Village Voice. March 12, 1996, p. 46.

Citizen Ruth

Life, liberty, money and the pursuit of happiness. She's gotta have it.—Movie tagline

"A gutsy and hilarious film! *Citizen Ruth* is a brilliant social comedy in the tradition of Preston Sturges."—Dave Kehr, *New York Daily News*

"Cleverly satirical! Laura Dern is a deadpan delight."—Janet Maslin, *New York Times*

"An often hilarious, sure-to-be-controversial crowd-pleaser! *Citizen Ruth* is a delight. Laura Dern's character is an original."—John Anderson, *Newsday*

"Irreverent and hysterically funny! Laura Dern has never been better. The cast is a dream. *Citizen Ruth* is bound to launch the career of its gifted young director, Alexander Payne."—Edward Guthmann, *San Francisco Chronicle*

Box Office: $199,096

In many ways, Alexander Payne's *Citizen Ruth* is the most daring film of the year. It is hard to imagine how anyone could derive a successful comedy from the explosive issue of abortion, but *Citizen Ruth* manages to do just that. It is most effective as a wry send-up of the crazed behavior of activists on both sides of the abortion issue, but it also examines with great sympathy the travails of one very ordinary, deeply flawed woman who unwittingly stumbles into the center of a moral and political tug-of-war she doesn't understand.

In *Citizen Ruth,* first-time director Alexander Payne and screenwriter Jim Taylor conjure many laughs from a subject which would probably cause other, more cautious filmmakers to run screaming into the Hollywood Hills. Payne displays a fine sense for the idiotic hyperbole which is often employed by both pro- and anti-abortion forces in order to capture the public's attention. He also lampoons the ridiculous tactics to which each side resorts as they struggle to gain followers and score ideological points.

The film's farcical premise revolves around one Ruth Stoops (Laura Dern), a white female indigent in an undistinguished Midwestern town. Ruth lives from moment to moment, never giving much thought to the consequences of her actions. She has a significant arrest record, has been an unwed mother several times over, and is well-known among local cops as a connoisseur of inhalants.

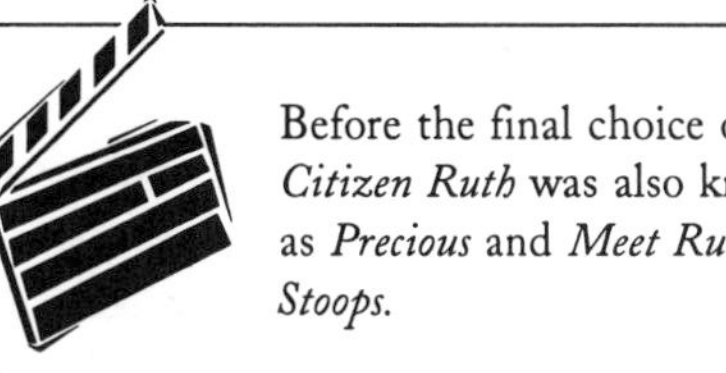

Before the final choice of title, *Citizen Ruth* was also known as *Precious* and *Meet Ruth Stoops.*

The first few scenes give the viewer a very clear idea of Ruth's priorities. Having no home of her own, she is not above using sex as a bargaining tool to secure a bed for the night. The film's first shot, comically offset by Frank Sinatra's hoary old rendition of "All the Way," depicts the decidedly unromantic tryst (set on a grimy mattress in an abandoned warehouse) which results in Ruth's latest pregnancy.

After cadging some money from her exasperated relatives, Ruth goes on a spending spree. Much like a drugged-out distant cousin to Audrey Hepburn's Holly Golightly in *Breakfast at Tiffany's* (1961), Ruth lives only to shop: She heads straight to the local hardware store, where she picks over cans of varnish and spray paint as if she were a high-society matron trying out brands of perfume at Macy's cosmetics counter.

Ruth is usually unable to think beyond her next glue-sniffing binge. This destructive habit has damaged her thought processes to such a degree that she is often several beats behind in any given conversation, even when other people are discussing crucial aspects of her future.

Inevitably, Ruth gets nailed by the police for inhaling spray paint fumes. In the course of her arrest, she is given a routine physical examination and discovers that she is pregnant. At her court appearance, Ruth is so burned out by the effects of inhalants and befuddled by the intricacies of the law that she cannot remember the pertinent details of her own arrest record, nor can she recall how many children she actually has, or the identities of their fathers. An exasperated local judge charges Ruth with endangering the life of her fetus, and virtually commands her to undergo an abortion or face the prospect of a serious prison term.

Ruth becomes isolated and desperate, so much so that she calls on God to rescue her from her plight. Much to her surprise, her prayers are answered immediately. Trapped in a dingy holding cell, she encounters a set of "pro-life" activists who have just been arrested for staging a provocation at a local abortion clinic. The comically overzealous "Baby Savers" know a public relations bonanza when they see one, and they are eager to befriend Ruth and make political hay out of her predicament.

For a time, Ruth is virtually adopted by Norm (Kurtwood Smith) and Gail Stoney (Mary Kay Place), who do not hesitate to bail her out of jail. They are friendly and care-giving but generally condescending toward Ruth, whom they view as a fallen woman in dire need of salvation. The Stoneys are the sort of born-again Christians who ask the Lord for assistance when searching for a space in a supermarket parking lot. They pray at the drop of a hat, but their displays of virtue, as well as their deeply conservative views concerning the matter of abortion, are mostly wasted on Ruth, who only wants to avoid doing jail time at all costs.

It is instantly clear that Ruth as an individual means nothing to the ardent pro-lifers. Initially, she is happy to accept the refuge which the Stoneys miraculously provide, but she soon begins to realize that she is being used: She becomes little more than a human stage prop, to be trotted into public view whenever television cameras are close at hand. Gail arranges a visit to a decidedly "pro-life" clinic where Ruth is bombarded with sweet-sounding lectures about the joys of motherhood as well as some extremely grisly videotapes concerning the abortion process, but this fundamentalist dog-and-pony show does nothing to alter Ruth's understanding of her situation.

Material concerns come first for Ruth, who has all the social graces of a junkyard dog. She is vulgar and ill-mannered and shockingly foulmouthed, but she is also essentially guileless: She is the only character in the film who persistently tells the truth (never mind that it is almost always at the wrong time, and usually laced with a steady stream of expletives).

Morally, Ruth is a blank slate: She knows only that she needs money, and lots of it, in order to escape the cycle of poverty and self-abuse to which she has become accustomed. She remains stubbornly immune to the Stoneys' dopey religiosity, but she is also unimpressed by the feverishly combative view of the world which is foisted upon her by her would-be feminist "liberators."

CREDITS

Ruth Stoops: Laura Dern
Diane: Swoosie Kurtz
Norm: Kurtwood Smith
Gail: Mary Kay Place
Rachel: Kelly Preston
Dr. Charlie: Kenneth Mars
Harlan: M.C. Gainey

Origin: USA
Released: 1996
Production: Cary Woods and Cathy Konrad for an Independent Pictures production; released by Miramax Films
Direction: Alexander Payne
Screenplay: Alexander Payne and Jim Taylor
Cinematography: James Glennon
Editing: Kevin Trent
Music: Rolfe Kent
Production design: Jane Ann Stewart
Costume design: Tom McKinley
Sound: Jay Patterson
Casting: Lisa Beach
MPAA rating: R
Running Time: 104 minutes

To Dern's great credit, Ruth remains a sympathetic figure even when she is engaged in remarkably stupid, self-damaging behavior. Ruth displays all the skills which befit her degraded position in life: She is always on the lookout for her next fix, and as we learn during one particularly funny scene which unfolds at the Stoney house, Ruth can spot a can of spray paint or a tube of airplane glue from a distance of fifty yards. Dern is marvelously adept at depicting the moment-to-moment behavioral quirks—the sudden lapses of concentration, the conversational non-sequiturs—which are common to "huffers," or hard-core abusers of inhalants.

Ruth is somewhat beguiled by a few days' exposure to the picture-perfect comfort and relative stability of the Stoney family, but despite their cloying spirituality, the Stoneys are never quite as normal as they seem. For one thing, they have a wild child of their own—a daughter, Cheryl (Alicia Witt), who smokes, drinks and freely engages in premarital sex. Despite her religious upbringing, or perhaps precisely because of it, Cheryl delights in life in the fast lane, and she finds an instant soul mate in Ruth, who gladly accompanies her on a late-night drug-and-alcohol binge.

After several incidents of this kind, the Stoneys lose their patience with Ruth and hand her over to Diane Sieglar (Swoosie Kurtz), another deeply committed member of the anti-abortion forces who regularly takes part in demonstrations at local clinics. The Stoneys have no idea that Diane is actually a pro-choice, radical feminist whose mission is to rescue Ruth from her fundamental caretakers and turn her into an exemplar of a woman's right to choose.

Money becomes the key factor in Ruth's decision whether or not to have an abortion. The "Baby Savers" understand this, and quickly offer her fifteen thousand dollars if she will agree to keep her baby. Ruth reacts to this offer with unbridled glee, as if he has just won the lottery. Aware that they have been outmaneuvered, Diane and her pro-choice cohorts are appalled by the idea of securing Ruth's loyalty with money: They want Ruth to consent to an abortion of her own free will, as evidence of her developing feminist consciousness. But they are forced to recognize that their conservative opponents have unlimited financial resources, and are equally determined to win Ruth's allegiance. The pro-choice feminists appear to be at a loss until Ruth collides with Harlan (M.C. Gainey), a disabled Vietnam veteran who has come into a small fortune as the result of an "Agent Orange" settlement. Harlan blithely offers her twenty-seven thousand dollars if she will consent to an abortion.

Ruth is at first bewildered and then overjoyed by this endless round of bargaining for her heart and mind, not to mention her unborn baby. Like a contestant in a very absurd game show, she is thrilled by the prospect of having a sizeable sum of money for the first time in her life. She is initially dumbfounded by other people's rapidly escalating interest in her, but she quickly learns to play one side of the abortion debate against the other. Her general belligerence, and her inability to dissimulate in order to please others, throw several wrenches into the elaborate plans which pro- and anti-abortion forces attempt to make for her.

Citizen Ruth is painstakingly evenhanded in its satirization of zealots on both sides of the abortion issue. For the insipid Stoney family, as well as Diane and Rachel (Kelly Preston), their equally calculating, lesbian "pro-choice" counterparts, Ruth is never much more than a symbol or an elaborate stage prop to be trotted into view whenever television cameras are close at hand.

The secondary characters in *Citizen Ruth* are startlingly funny, especially when they are engaged in fumbling attempts to seize the moral high ground. Kurtwood Smith, who was memorable as the demonic father-villain in *The Dead Poets Society* (1989), makes a fine comedic impression as Norm Stoney, Ruth's Bible-thumping but secretly lecherous benefactor. He is well-matched by Mary Kay Place, who has made a career out of playing very funny bit parts in other actors' star vehicles (most notably *The Big Chill* [1983]). She is hilarious as Gail Stoney, the deeply religious housewife whose capacity for human kindness turns on a dime.

Despite her displays of benevolence toward Ruth, Gail is also shamelessly manipulative, and when she takes part in yet another protest march at a local abortion clinic, her venomous, unforgiving side shows through. All forced smiles and barely-contained malice, Gail Stoney is a cinematic cousin to Loretta Haggers, the Scripture-quoting, wheelchair-bound chanteuse whom Place once played in the outrageous Seventies-era television sitcom "Mary Hartman, Mary Hartman."

An erstwhile songwriter, Place provides *Citizen Ruth* with several bizarre musical ditties which show both sides of the abortion debate at their most ridiculous extremes. These include "Don't Give Up On Baby Tanya" (sung to the tune of "The Battle Hymn of the Republic"), a ponderous ode to Ruth's unborn baby which is sung by the film's pro-life forces in the course of a circus-like prayer vigil. Place is also credited with a plaintive hymn to the moon which is sung by Diane and Rachel, the "lesbian warrior" activists.

Swoosie Kurtz is excellent as Diane, the moon-worshipping lesbian "spy" who infiltrates the pro-life ranks and virtually kidnaps Ruth out from under the Stoneys' watchful gaze. Kurtz, who is best known for her stage and television roles, is extremely effective as the fire-breathing radical feminist for whom Ruth is only "a symbol of women's oppression," never quite a real person.

Hollywood veterans Burt Reynolds and Tippi Hedren appear in secondary, humorous roles. Hedren is lovely as Jessica Weiss, a jet-setting celebrity feminist, but not much is made of her character. Reynolds is more formidable and genuinely funny as Blaine Gibbons, the well-heeled kingpin of the "Baby Savers" organization. He is clearly intended as the comic equivalent of Randall Terry, the real-life head of Operation Rescue. Gibbons is unabashedly sleazy and calculating, and has no compunction about using pots of money to advance his cause.

Citizen Ruth represents another stage in Laura Dern's gradual transformation into a low-key feminist icon. Here she plays yet another role which centers around the question of what a woman may or may not do with her body. This theme runs through much of her work to date, especially such films as *Smooth Talk* (1986) and *Rambling Rose* (1991), for which she received an Oscar nomination.

In the final reel, *Citizen Ruth* adroitly dodges the moral issues surrounding the question of abortion. The filmmakers choose instead to emphasize the practical dilemma with which Ruth is faced. Despite the high-minded moral arguments which are flung at her from all sides, there is only one thing Ruth truly understands, which is that without money there is no freedom of choice, no freedom of action, and ultimately, no real happiness. Discussions of morality are presented as little more than entertainments for the comfortable and the privileged. Confronted by a much harsher set of realities than those of her supposed benefactors, Ruth has no time for prolonged soul-searching: She has only one option, which is to take the money and run.

The ending of *Citizen Ruth* may not be entirely satisfying to activists on either side of the abortion issue, but it does underline one salient point, which is that philosophical disputes about the evils of abortion mean less than nothing to women like Ruth Stoops—women in dire financial straits who are often forced to cast their lot with whomever will offer them the best deal. As director Alexander Payne skillfully indicates, moral arguments such as those which are posed in *Citizen Ruth* are basically a luxury for those who enjoy freedom from want, and as Ruth knows very well from the beginning, there is no freedom without money.

—Karl Michalak

AWARDS AND NOMINATIONS

Montreal Film Festival 1996: Best Actress (Dern)

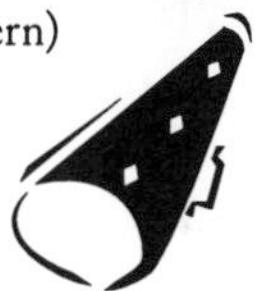

REVIEWS

Boxoffice. November, 1996, p. 136.
Entertainment Weekly. January 10, 1997, p. 42.
New York. January 27, 1997, p. 47.
The New York Daily News. December 13, 1996.
The New York Times. December 13, 1996, p. C16.
Time. December 8, 1996.
USA Today. December 13, 1996, p. 4D.
Variety. February 5, 1996, p. 61.
Village Voice. December 17, 1996, p. 80.

City Hall

A Mayor . . . A Deputy Mayor . . . A city about to explode.—Movie tagline

"One hell of a story . . . crackles with energy and intrigue."—Bill Diehl, *ABC Radio Network*

"Big city politics as real as today's headlines."—Jeanne Wolf, *Jeanne Wolf's Hollywood*

"The movie will win you over in a New York minute."—Barbara and Scott Siegel, *Siegel Entertainment Syndicate*

"A resonant, intelligent thriller."—Bruce Williamson, *Playboy*

Box Office: $20,340,204

City Hall is an ambitious, urban remake of Robert Penn Warren's novel, *All the King's Men.* Filmed twice, the novel's parable of corrupt Governor Willie Stark and his idealistic assistant, Jack Burden, seems to be the model a movie must take if it is to show both what is wrong and right about American politics. In *City Hall,* Willie becomes John Pappas (Al Pacino), New York's mayor, and Jack Burden becomes Kevin Calhoun (John Cusack). In case anyone needs reminding of the movie's debt to Warren, Calhoun (the name of a great South Carolina senator) is given a Louisiana upbringing and a penchant for quoting that state's governor, Huey Long, a.k.a. the Kingfish, whose demagoguery featured the phrase "Every Man a King" and who was contemplating a run for the White House before he was assassinated in 1935.

City Hall's strengths and weaknesses stem from this web of allusions to fictional and historical events and figures. Mayor Pappas also has presidential aspirations. Like Huey/Willie, he can sway a crowd and ham it up—although on-screen Pacino is constantly crossing the line between bravura performance and pure and simple overacting. Perhaps that is what great politicians are like. This movie has the feel of the same story told one too many times but also the aura and epic quality of Ecclesiastes' injunction that there is nothing new under the sun.

Warren's novel often soars on its eloquent prose and its lament for a politician who might have been great, and who began with the honest impulse to make life better for his people. But there is also a secondhand, shopworn quality about *All the King's Men,* precisely because the real goods—Huey Long—is masked by the semi-invention of Willie Stark. Similarly, John Pappas is only half-real. Where does he fit next to Ed Koch or Fiorella LaGuardia?—to mention two mayors the movie obviously has in mind. Pappas sits at LaGuardia's desk, and Koch is seen briefly in a television commentary. Koch's last years were rocked with scandal—as are Pappas's. LaGuardia brokered deals to improve people's lives and give them security, and it is just such deal-making that brings Pappas down.

For those who do not know Warren's work or the movies based on it, perhaps *City Hall* will seem less of a rehash. There are good performances—especially one by Danny Aiello playing Frank Anselmo, a corrupt Brooklyn political boss. His big scene with Pacino is a masterpiece, a moment when the movie really seems alive with the culture of political talk between two cronies relying on but also trying to get the best of each other. Such scenes no doubt rely on the inside knowledge of Ken Lipper, one of the film's four screenwriters and a deputy mayor under Koch. All the politicos in this picture, in fact, seem authentic—their dialogue cleansed of the usual cliches and profanity. Indeed, these characters cuss less than might be expected, but that is all to the good in keeping the film moving toward Calhoun's inexorable confrontation with his boss, mentor, and, of course, father figure. Yes, Pappas is

CREDITS

Mayor John Pappas: Al Pacino
Kevin Calhoun: John Cusack
Marybeth Cogan: Bridget Fonda
Frank Anselmo: Danny Aiello
Judge Walter Stern: Martin Landau
Abe Goodman: David Paymer

Origin: USA
Released: 1996
Production: Edward Pressman, Charles Mulvehill and Ken Lipper for a Columbia Pictures and Castle Rock Entertainment production; released by Sony Pictures Entertainment
Direction: Harold Becker
Screenplay: Ken Lipper, Paul Schrader, Nicholas Pileggi and Bo Goldman
Cinematography: Michael Seresin
Editing: Robert C. Jones, David Bretherton
Production design: Jane Musky
Art direction: Robert Guerra
Set decoration: Robert J. Franco
Costume design: Richard Hornung
Sound: Tod A. Maitland
Casting: John Lyons
Music: Jerry Goldsmith
MPAA rating: R
Running Time: 111 minutes

papa, and Calhoun, who should know better, has to go to extreme efforts to realize the king is corrupt.

Less satisfying, even for those not attuned to the political/literary derivations of the film, is the role of Bridget Fonda as a crusading attorney who helps Calhoun confront the truth. Fonda has her tough talking, tight-lipped persona in tow, but she is made into a ridiculous figure in her blonde hair turned into a flip. *City Hall* does spare viewers one cliche: Fonda and Cusack do not have a romance. But the idea of the Mayor's deputy and a lawyer representing his adversaries going off on an adventure to find out what is rotten in Denmark sinks the movie's credibility.

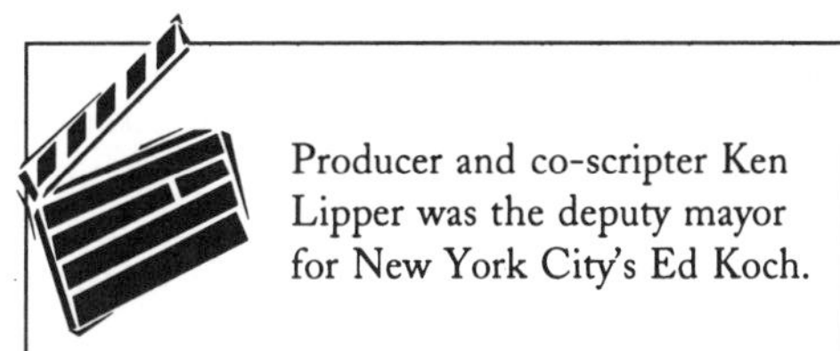

Producer and co-scripter Ken Lipper was the deputy mayor for New York City's Ed Koch.

"The scale of humanity runs from Charles Manson to Mother Teresa, and the rest of us are somewhere in between."—Mayor Pappas

The key scene of *City Hall* takes place in a black church. A six-year-old boy has been shot in a confrontation between a cop and a criminal. Why the criminal was on the street, and how the mayor and a prominent judge conspired to get him probation, is the crux of the film. How the mayor handles himself before these grieving people will reveal what kind of man and politician he is. Pappas is told that his audience and the crowd outside the church will be hostile. He speaks to them nevertheless, concocting a speech that is part opera and part revival service testimony. Perhaps some viewers will be as moved as the mayor's audience seems to be, but surely others will find the speech embarrassing and factitious and as forced as the movie's other efforts to imitate its predecessors.

—*Carl Rollyson*

REVIEWS

Chicago Tribune. February 16, 1996, p. 4.
Entertainment Weekly. February 23, 1996, p. 101.
Los Angeles Times. February 16, 1996, p. F1.
Newsweek. February 19, 1996, p. 68.
Rolling Stone. March 7, 1996, p. 52.
USA Today. February 16, 1996, p. 4D.
Variety. February 12, 1996, p. 78.
Village Voice. February 20, 1996, p. 62.

The City of Lost Children; La Cite des Enfants Perdus

Some people follow their dreams. Others steal them.—Movie tagline

"Daring! Exhilarating! The film succeeds."—Patrick Z. Gavin, *Chicago Tribune*

"Dazzling visuals, ingenious gadgets and state-of-the-art special effects. *Lost Children* is more than just a technological wonder: It's an involving adventure that puts a psychedelic spin on the theme of good versus evil!"—Stephen Saban, *Details*

"A new French fairy tale flick offers a wickedly welcome antidote to saccharine family-value films . . . Breathtaking! . . . a brilliant flashy study in terror."—Graham Fuller, *Interview*

"*The City of Lost Children* is the perfect tribute to the movie medium, full of perfectly executed special effects and bold camera wizardry . . . the brilliant Jules Verne-ish fantasy."—Howard Feinstein, *New York Post*

"Astonishing! Jam-packed with surreal imagery . . . A fantasy grab bag that encompasses everything from Grimm's fairy tales to *Star Wars* . . . Fantastically picturesque!"—Stephen Holden, *New York Times*

"*The City of Lost Children* has more ideas in any given minute than *Waterworld* has in its entire length. Jeunet and Caro may not yet be household names, but to see them in *City* is to hear DreamWorks calling . . . It doesn't disappoint!"—J. Hoberman, *Vanity Fair*

Box Office: $1,718,365

At a time when glitzy high-tech has converted the space of movie screens into arenas, today's special effects gladiators spare no cost in their bid to surprise. Lamentably, their departures from the order of the physical universe do not extend to overthrowing forms of the institutional power that surround us. Howsoever liberating the visuals, the moral stance of their narratives invariably reduces the endeavor to the "there's-no-place-like-home" brand of preachiness. Behind such 'children's classics' as *The Wizard of Oz* (1939), or *Star Wars* (1977), or even *Hook* (1991), we can now sense the effort of adult minds driven by the avowed purpose of making us behave.

We could speculate that had those narratives been truer to the thinking of children, they might not have been so preoccupied with setting things right, or finding some transcendental ideal to make existence tolerable. Instead, they might have mischievously reveled in a world gone awry, even conjured up grotesqueries-as-heroes to carry the disorder to its extreme.

Jean-Paul Jeunet and Marc Caro's *The City of Lost Children* clearly intends to make up for this loss. In the midst of its frenetically paced phantasmagoria, we become what we were never allowed to be: "lost" children.

What results then, is a narrative thread discernible not so much as a series of events propelled by the actions of human characters, as much as an invisible matrix of nodal points emitting transmissions of power that set up their own causal axis.

That such a narrative scheme should feel so bracing could be because the universe peculiar to the film is also a peculiarly filmic universe, its form actualized through the wonder of digital technology. Thus, the physical space of the world which accommodates the film's outlandish narrative content can be seen as a correlative of the digital space of the film's technological form, concomitant with its boundless possibilities.

For instance, all sunlight seems to have been banished from the nameless gloomy harbor town that provides the film with its principal setting. The decrepit buildings, the narrow pebbled streets, the squalid canals with their mesh of overhanging walkways, all bespeak an uncaring industrialized decay. In this world of a child's nightmare, a gang of grotesques with mechanical eyes are allowed to kidnap children for the purposes of the sinister Krank (Daniel Emilfork), a wizard who runs a secret laboratory aboard a labyrinthine offshore rig.

When the orphan Denree (Joseph Lucien) is abducted, the sideshow strongman named One (Ron Perlman), who has only just adopted the little boy, goes in search, soon to be aided by the feisty Miette (Judith Vittet). The narrative backbone provided by One's quest allows the film to introduce an assortment of bizarre sidekicks, using them to weave a maze of subplots that would befuddle the most attentive viewer.

Krank is assisted by a midget, Mademoiselle Bismuth (Mireille Mosse), and six identical-looking Clones (Dominique Pinon) who, unbeknownst to them, owe their appearance to Stocle, an ex-partner of Krank's, now banished to the depths of the sea, but who continues to survive as a diver in his underwater retreat, nursing his amnesia. Also under Krank's power, it would seem, is Irvin, a colleague reduced to being kept alive within a tank in the form of a disembodied brain, and who can function only as a voice (the voice of Jean-Louis Trintignant).

We soon learn that for all his technological expertise, Krank has been cursed with an existence shorn of dreams. Hence, his need for the kidnapped children. Using his psychocybernetic apparatus, Krank hopes to 'steal' their dreams. When his experiments fail, Irvin's Voice reminds him that it is the evil inside him that is transforming the children's dreams into nightmares.

Then, as if to get even, Irvin's Voice secretly directs one of the Clones to detach the receptacle containing little Denree's dream, and throw it overboard so that, "like a note in a bottle," it might guide the forces of good towards the rig.

Onshore, Miette, while helping One, has to ward off the clutches of The Octopus, the name given to a pair of ugly twin sisters, joined at the hip (Genevieve Brunet and Odile Mallet), who have been employing Miette and her gang to steal for them, and who now have to resort to preternatural wiles so as to teach the urchins a lesson. The Octopus first enlist the help of Marcello, the Flea Tamer (Jean-Claude Dreyfus), an old freak show acquaintance, who in turn drugs a flea to do his bidding. When that plan fails, The Octopus hypnotize One so that he turns against Miette, and starts slapping her violently.

We can only watch in childlike wonder as the above network of villainy, extending from shore to rig, is countered by a force that could only originate in a parallel universe.

CREDITS

One: Ron Perlman
Krank: Daniel Emilfork
Milette: Judith Vittet
Clones: Dominique Pinon
Denree: Joseph Lucien
Irvin: Jean-Louis Trintignant (voice)

Origin: France
Released: 1995
Production: Claude Ossard for a Consellation, Lumiere, Le Studio Canal, and France 3 Cinema production; released by Sony Pictures Classics
Direction: Pierre Jeunet, Marc Caro
Screenplay: Pierre Jeunet, Marc Caro, Gilles Adrien
Cinematography: Darius Khondji
Editing: Herve Schneid
Costumes: Jean-Paul Gaultier
Music: Angelo Badalamenti
Set design: Jean Rabasse
MPAA rating: R
Running Time: 114 minutes

Miette's tear, as she is being assaulted by One, elongates itself so that it sets into motion a chain of events involving a spider's web, a parakeet, a barking dog, a drunk, and eventually a seagull, who relieves itself over the windshield of a speeding car causing it to collide against a fire hydrant, which lets loose a flood which nearly electrocutes an electrical worker atop a pole, resulting in a blackout. In the pitch darkness, a steamer coming into port collides against the wharf, upon which The Octopus have been grinding the organ whose melody has put One under its spell. As the music stops, One comes to his senses, and Miette is saved from his attack.

Similarly, after the diver Stocle finds the tumbler containing Denree's dream, a stray crab is responsible for setting the dream free. In the form of a green mist, the dream first enters Stocle's nostrils, helping him to regain his memory, then winds its way across to the town until it finds the sleeping Miette and enters her nostrils, allowing her to dream of the rig where Denree is being held captive.

Before One and Miette can approach the rig however, they have to find a way to avoid the mines surrounding it. True to the vision in Miette's dream, they find a map which has been inscribed on the bald head of an Oriental tattooer. As One and Miette close in on Krank's rig, Stocle sets about on his own plan to destroy the works. It is during the climactic rescue scene, the staple of every childhood adventure, that the film executes an astounding coup de grace.

Within the rig, as One overcomes the Clones, Miette stumbles into the sanctum of Krank's lab. She is about to free the sleeping Denree when she is stopped by Irvin's Voice. Denree, it seems, is lost within a dream world, where Krank, also asleep, is making one last attempt to 'steal' the little boy's dream. Miette will therefore have to go to sleep, plugging herself into the apparatus, so she can rescue Denree from the grip of evil.

The film now comes full circle to the setting of Denree's dream-turned-nightmare with which it opened: a room festively decorated, abounding with Christmas toys. As little Miette penetrates into Denree's dream, she finds herself battling Krank in a most unexpected manner. In the space of seconds, through the wonder of digital morphing, we see Miette growing to full womanhood, and even attaining the maturity of a crone, as Krank progresses inversely, back to his infancy, only to die in his sleep.

As One, Miette and Denree make their getaway, helping the Clones and Irvin-as-Brain to escape with them, the film reasserts its ideological thrust: that it is the forces of nature that man cannot control, rather than the technology which he thinks he can, that will have the final say.

Stocle, who has bound himself to the girders of the rig in the manner of a suicide bomber, suddenly changes his mind when a scrap of paper, on which is scrawled a magic formula which he recognizes, flutters his way. He screams to be rescued, but it is too late. A stray seagull alighting on the fuse of a detonator is all it takes to set off the giant explosion.

Most critics, while acknowledging the film's visual inventiveness, have seen it as amounting to nothing more than a comic book for adults. "As fantastically picturesque as it may be," writes Stephen Holden in the *New York Times*, "*The City of Lost Children* carries little allegorical resonance. While its story seems to warn about the loss of imagination in an overly technologized world, it is too disjointed to carry much weight."

"As a 'dark fairy tale for all ages,' the movie is a non-starter," writes Tony Rayns in *Sight and Sound*, "compared with films like *Gremlins* and the first *Nightmare on Elm Street*." Rayns sees nothing original in what he calls the film's "MTV aesthetic: all surface dazzle, no space for depth or resonance."

Kristine McKenna's interview with Jeunet and Caro in the *Los Angeles Times* should prove insightful for anyone wishing to approach the film with an open mind. "In France kids have no problem with the film," they claim, "because of playing video games, (the children) have a high degree of visual sophistication." The filmmakers are thus understandably troubled by their film being rated R over here. To them, it makes no sense to protect children from the film's "bizarre images, considering that every time you turn on the TV you're bombarded with images of violence."

Jean-Pierre Jeunet and Marc Caro achieved prominence in this country with their debut feature, *Delicatessen* in 1991. *The City of Lost Children*, their second feature, was chosen to open the Cannes Film Festival of 1995.

In keeping with the times, a computer game extending the film's plot over a multitude of options is due for release by Sony on CD-ROM.

—*Vivek Adarkar*

AWARDS AND NOMINATIONS

Cesar Awards 1995 Nominations: Best Cinematography (Khondji), Best Sets, Best Costumes, Best Music (Badalamenti)

REVIEWS

The Los Angeles Times. December 22, 1995, p. F8.
The New York Times. December 15, 1995.
Sight and Sound. September, 1995, p. 48.
The Village Voice. December 26, 1995.

Cold Fever

"Bizarre, funny and curiously moving, this film has a cinematic confidence that's spellbinding."—*London Evening Standard*

"Haunting, funny, and beautiful."—Steven Rea, *Philadelphia Inquirer*

Box Office: $372,844

Mondo bizarro. A successful Japanese businessman (Masatoshi Nagase) gets sidetracked from his upcoming golfing vacation in Hawaii and succumbs to a heavy guilt trip laid on him by his grandfather. He's told he must make a trek to the arctic tundra of Iceland in the dead of winter to perform an ancient eastern burial ritual that will allow his dead parents' souls to rest. Why his parents were vacationing in Iceland is never explained. Why his grandfather waited seven years after their deaths doesn't make much sense either. But it does jibe with the rest of the movie: it doesn't make any sense at all. To its credit, *Cold Fever* never hides the fact that it is blatantly and patently obtuse. It never tries to be coherent and seems to be proud of that fact.

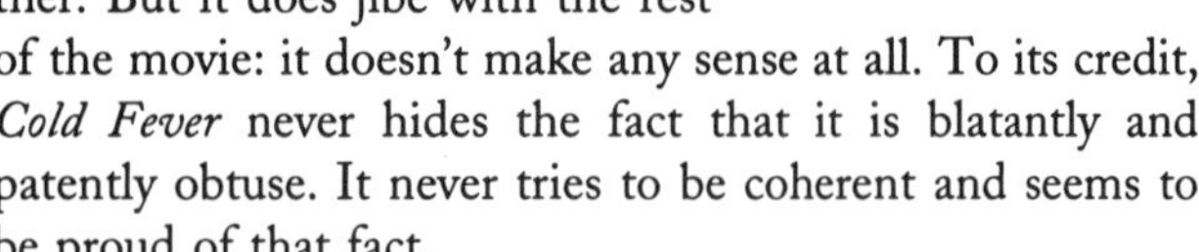

Film is shot in standard 1.66 ratio during the Japanese scenes and changes to widescreen 2.35 ratio for the shift to Iceland.

Director Fridrik Thor Fridriksson is the Scandinavian equivalent to David Lynch. Their shared art-for-arts-sake mentality definitely has a secured (albeit minuscule) audience. The line between arthouse film and fringe-oriented major studio product is appearing less clear than it used to be. This is a textbook example of the lofty, self-indulgent, complicated arthouse film that turns off mainstream patrons. It takes a very simple message (personal and spiritual closure) and complicates it with extraneous filler that ultimately annoys, bewilders and wears down the audience.

Technically, this is a road picture. But only in the loosest sense of the phrase. It's more like a stylistic, surrealistic travelogue that finds Atsushi (Nagase) making what seems like a coast to coast sojourn across the frozen white wasteland to the isolated river where his parents disappeared. Here he performs an ancient oriental chanting ritual that puts his parents' souls to rest.

Possessing the patience of Job, Atsushi's first stop during his journey puts him in contact with a woman who travels the countryside taking snapshots of grieving families at funerals. The two share some pleasant small talk, but nothing more. Fridriksson misses a great opportunity here. He could have had Atsushi bring the woman along, not only as a traveling partner, but also as someone who could have chronicled his trip. Atsushi then enlists the services of a cab driver to take him cross-country to his desired location. Shortly after the ride starts, the driver inexplicably asks Atsushi to wait in the car while he makes a quick stop. After an inordinately long wait, Atsushi goes into the building where the driver went only to discover a group of like-minded individuals chanting and singing, eating boiled sheep's heads and steamed sheep testicles, and drinking a high-octane Scandinavian liquor called "Black Death." No further explanation is given.

Abandoning the taxi driver, Atsushi buys a used car that has been frozen in its tracks for quite a long time. Miraculously, it starts and he's on his way. As the sunlight begins to disappear, he gets lost, decides to call it a night, and seeks shelter with a couple living in a nearby house. They open up hearth and home to him, however, the language barrier prohibits them from exchanging any substantial dialogue. The next day, Atsushi stops in an area landscaped with lakes and icebergs and suddenly witnesses two teenage sirens who begin a kind of screeching, operatic wail; still, nothing of note happens.

CREDITS

Atsushi Hirata: Masatoshi Magase
Jill: Lili Taylor
Jack: Fisher Stevens
Siggi: Gisli Halldorsson
Laura: Laura Hughes
Grandfather: Seijun Suzuki

Origin: Iceland
Released: 1995
Production: Jim Stark for an Icicle Films Inc. production; released by Artistic Liscense Films
Direction: Fridrik Thor Fridriksson
Screenplay: Fridrik Thor Fridriksson, Jim Stark
Cinematography: Fridrik Thor Fridriksson
Editing: Steingrimur Karlsson
Music: Hilmar Orn Hilmarsson
Production design: Arni Poll Johansson
Sound: Kjartan Kjartansson
Costume design: Maria Olafsdottir
MPAA rating: Unrated
Running Time: 86 minutes

The most striking, mainstream scene of the film follows shortly, when Atsushi picks up a pair of American hitchhikers (Lili Taylor and Fisher Stevens) who initially provide him with some much needed companionship. The two begin quarreling with each other, leaving Atsushi awkwardly embarrassed and dumbfounded. The two soon direct their hostility at him and end up stealing his car, tossing him out in the middle of nowhere. This scene, like all others that have preceded it, are just time-wasting vignettes that add nothing substantial to the plot. A charitable way of looking at Fridriksson's vision is interpreting Atsushi's travails as small bumps and bruises that serve to educate him as he plods on to his final destination. The final few minutes of the movie that focus on the burial ritual are touching and unique, and end the film on an positive, upbeat note. If Fridriksson had edited this project down to a 20 or 30 minute short, he might have had a classic. As it stands now, he has crafted a dreamy, attractive, two-hour waste of time.

—J.M. Clark

REVIEWS

Boxoffice. April, 1996, p. 108.
Hollywood Reporter. April 9, 1996, p. 6.
Los Angeles Times. May 23, 1996, p. F6.
New York Times. April 5, 1996, p. C3.
Variety. October 2, 1995, p. 42.

Courage Under Fire

A medal for honor. A search for justice. A battle for truth.—Movie tagline

"The first Hollywood movie this year that one needs to take seriously."—Jay Carr, *The Boston Globe*

"Powerful and highly entertaining."—Gene Siskel, *Chicago Tribune*

"This film is a masterpiece. The first true-blue Oscar contender of the year."—Rod Lurie, *KMPC Radio*

"One of the best films of the year."—Peter Travers, *Rolling Stone*

"The first serious Oscar contender of 1996."—Jeff Craig, *Sixty Second Preview*

"Thoughtful. Intelligent. Moving. Provocative. Yes, it's safe for adults to go back to the movies."—Susan Wloszcyna, *USA Today*

Box Office: $59,031,057

Lt. Col. Nathaniel Serling (Denzel Washington), a man of honor and valor, is fighting a personal demon. While leading an armored tank battalion in a night battle at Al Kufan during the Gulf War he suddenly finds himself being fired upon from unknown quarters. In the confusion and the dark, he fires back only to hit his best friend's tank. But the army is reluctant to admit the real cause of the death's Serling's actions have caused, even though Serling himself wants to face the truth head-on.

Now back in the States after the war, Serling is given a Pentagon desk job by his protector, friend, and superior officer Gen. Hershberg (Michael Moriarty). While haunted by his own error, he now must investigate a potential Medal of Honor recipient, Capt. Karen Walden (Meg Ryan), a Medevac helicopter pilot, who may be the first woman so honored, even though it will be awarded posthumously. Both the White House and the Pentagon are eager for Walden to receive the award—primarily because it would be great public relations and America can never have too many heroes—but Serling is determined to follow the rules and investigate her candidacy thoroughly, even though Hershberg is pressuring him to submit his report ASAP.

What is taking Serling so long is that there seem to be several discrepancies in the report of the fight in which she was killed, contradictions which are heightened as he talks to each of her crew. Ilario (Matt Damon), the ship's Medic, is very uncomfortable upon being interviewed but insists Walden was in control and acted heroically after their helicopter went down and had to fight off waves of Iraqi soldiers. The ship's gunner, Monfriez (Lou Diamond Phillips), however, has a completely different take on Walden. This macho soldier insists that Walden acted against the interests of her crew and was an outright coward who fell apart (like a typical woman) during an emergency. The one person who may be able to solve the inconsistency is crew chief Altameyer (Seth Gilliam), but he is so ill with abdominal cancer that he can barely communicate from all the drugs he takes to quell his pain. Someone is lying, but who, and why?

Throughout all these different viewpoints and disagreeing facts, Serling continues to fight his own conscience. This battle causes him to become withdrawn from his family and to begin drinking to excess. At the same time, dogging his every step is a persistent reporter from the *Washington Post,* Tony Gartner (Scott Glenn). Gartner knows about Serling's act of friendly fire, but needs proof that the army is covering it up. At first Serling avoids Gartner, but he is a man of principles and he desperately needs someone to tell the truth to.

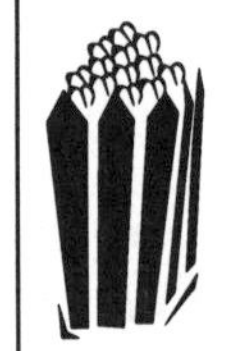

"Just do everything my way and we'll get along fine."—Presidential functionary Bruno to Serling

Serling's personal battle and his quest for the accuracy becomes more than just an episode in trying to sort out the facts of an officer's death. It is also an examination of such abstract concepts as heroism, truth, bravery, loyalty, giving one's life for another, and doing one's duty. This scrutiny is what elevates what could have been just another war movie into something more.

Matt Damon, who plays Ilario, lost 40 pounds to delineate his pre-battle character from his post-battle heroin addict.

Director Edward Zwick who took Washington to an Oscar in *Glory* (1989) (and who may do so again with this film) and who lent lyricism to the western in *Legends of the Fall* (1994), here takes the conventional war film and inspects its underpinnings and myths. His battle scenes are gripping (due in no small part to the impressive cinematography of Roger Deakins), but Zwick never loses sight of the humans behind the story.

The success of the story is due to writer Patrick Sheane Duncan (*Mr. Holland's Opus* [1996], and the much too unknown Vietnam film *84 Charlie Mopic* [1989]), who as a Vietnam combat veteran himself developed an interest in Medal of Honor recipients after doing a documentary on the topic for cable. Like Zwick, Duncan takes the old story and makes it new, infusing it with questions, intelligence, and the human factor.

The device of telling the same event through several different viewpoints is not unknown to moviegoers. Duncan, however, freely admits his debt to Japanese director Akira Kurosawa's 1950 masterpiece *Rashomon* which is based on Ryunosuke Akutagawa's period short story "In the Grove." In that tale a woman is raped (or is she?) and her husband killed, but no one can agree on the exact circumstances of the events. Even the dead man can tell his story through a medium. Thankfully, that is a contrivance that Duncan does not allow Karen Walden's character.

While Zwick and Duncan do a riveting job of presenting the big story of the battles and the people who fight them, the audience primarily feels the human level through the masterful acting of a first-rate cast. Denzel Washington is proving to be one of Hollywood's most accomplished dramatic actors. Here he takes what might have been a relatively one-note role and infuses it with dignity, depth, and sensitivity. He is a commanding presence on the screen—in a uniform or in jeans and a t-shirt.

Meg Ryan, who is probably most well-known for her romantic-comedy roles in films like *When Harry Met Sally* (1989) or *Sleepless in Seattle* (1993) has still in the past shown a more dramatic side (*When a Man Loves a Woman* (1994), *Flesh and Bone* (1993). Here she is not only unexpectedly "macha" as one character describes Walden, but also believable. But more than that, because each of the characters tells her story in flashback, Ryan must convincingly act out the subtle nuances which separate the hero from the coward—and all during different versions of the exact same scene.

The other actors in the film also have the opportunity to play the same scene from several different emotional angles. While there is not time to make complete characters out of them all, each does a solid job of conveying the necessary attitudes to make the mystery work. Lou Diamond Phillips is especially noteworthy as the super-macho Monfriez. We know he's a sexist who probably won't take orders from a woman, but there's

CREDITS

Lt. Col. Nathaniel Serling: Denzel Washington
Capt. Karen Walden: Meg Ryan
Monfriez: Lou Diamond Phillips
Gen. Hershberg: Michael Moriarty
Ilario: Matt Damon
Bruno: Bronson Pinchot
Altameyer: Seth Gilliam
Tony Gartner: Scott Glenn

Origin: USA
Released: 1996
Production: John Davis, Joseph M. Singer, David T. Friendly for a Davis Entertainment production; released by 20th Century Fox
Direction: Edward Zwick
Screenplay: Patrick Sheane Duncan; based on his novel
Cinematography: Roger Deakins
Editing: Steven Rosenblum
Music: James Horner
Production design: John Graysmark
Art direction: Steve Cooper
Costume design: Francine Jamison, Tanchuk
Sound: Willie D. Burton
Casting: Mary Colquhoun
MPAA rating: R
Running Time: 115 minutes

something more going on under his helmet and we want to know what it is. Matt Damon is also engrossing as Ilario whose nervous admiration of Walden hides its own secrets.

If there are any problems with *Courage Under Fire,* it could be that the connection between the Walden and Serling characters —both of whom may or may not have acted in a less than desirable manner under the pressure of battle—seems a bit contrived, and that one very pertinent piece of information about Serling's friendly-fire incident is purposely withheld from us until the end which makes us feel a bit cheated.

However, these are small quibbles when set against tense combat scenes, great acting, an intriguing mystery, and characters we care about. It dares to take on our glorified (and Pentagon- and Hollywood-controlled) ideas about warfare both indirectly (before the battle Serling leads his men in prayer then says "Now let's kill 'em all!") and directly. Instead it shows that admitting the truth can be as terrifying and as heroic as doing one's duty in battle.

Courage Under Fire is engrossing and thoughtful. This is not your typical summer film, but it's great to have a respite from all those special effects.

—*Beverley Bare Buehrer*

REVIEWS

Chicago Tribune. July 12, 1996, p. 4.
Detroit News. February 12, 1996, p. F1.
Entertainment Weekly. July 26, 1996, p. 32.
New York Times. July 12, 1996, p. C1.
Newsweek. July 15, 1996, p. 59.
People. July 15, 1996, p. 23.
Rolling Stone. August 8, 1996, p. 68.
Sight and Sound. October, 1996, p. 38.
Time. July 22, 1996, p. 94.
USA Today. February 12, 1996, p. D1.
Variety. June 24, 1996.
Village Voice. July 16, 1996, p. 57.

The Craft

Welcome to the witching hour.—Movie tagline

"*The Craft* is well-made with a hard-driving pace. It places heavy demands on its four lead actresses, who come through in impressive fashion."—Kevin Thomas, *Los Angeles Times*

"A tidy little thriller."—Dave Kehr, *New York Daily News*

"*The Craft* is slick, shrewd, touching, funny and most appropriately downright mean. The special effects summoned to convey the supernatural goings-on are creepy, frequently stunning and refreshingly subdued."—Arthur Salm, *San Diego Union Tribune*

"*The Craft* is the smartest, most satisfying horror thriller to come out in a while. The young actresses are superb."—Mick LaSalle, *San Francisco Chronicle*

Box Office: $24,881,501

Female adolescence once again becomes the site for mysterious bewitching in *The Craft,* as four high school girls join forces to pursue their dreams and avenge their wounds with witchcraft. One interesting aspect of this film is that it manages to sustain suspense without ever achieving any explicitly gory or even frightening scenes. Director of photography Alexander Gruszynski makes the film stylishly unique and visually contemporary by using flashes of slow motion and subtly mimicking the visuals of music television and advertising. Director Andrew Fleming co-wrote the script with Peter Filandi, whose credits include *Flatliners* (1990), but the screenplay is ultimately the weakest element in the film. Though at times this is a stylish and entertaining teen drama which benefits from the engaging cinematography, the script settles into cliches and simple dichotomies of good girls versus bad girls and ultimately falls back on regressive conclusions and solutions.

Sarah (Robin Tunney) is an emotionally troubled but ultimately good middle-class girl who moves from San Francisco to Los Angeles with her father and enrolls in a Catholic high school. On her first day of school Sarah approaches three menacing outcasts, referred to by others as the "bitches of Eastwick," but is driven away by their silent, cold stares. Later the school heartthrob, Chris Long (Skeet Ulrich), warns her that the three girls are witches and sluts. When Bonnie (Neve Campbell), one of the three, witnesses Sarah in class balancing a pencil on her desk and making it revolve, she convinces the others that Sarah just may be the coveted fourth corner needed to complete their circle of power, and soon the girls are actively pursuing Sarah's friendship. While Sarah is at first reluctant and spooked by the hobbies of her new friends, the girls soon discover that when the four unite their wills they possess the ability to control the world around them.

Despite the warnings of her new friends, Sarah begins to date Chris Long. When she refuses to sleep with him he spreads lies throughout the school and ruins her reputation. This betrayal drives her further into her friendships and experimentations with witchcraft. Intoxicated by their growing powers, the girls set out to cast spells, each focusing on one thing they would like to change. Sarah chooses to avenge herself on Chris by making him fall madly in love with her; Bonnie, who suffers from burn marks all over her body, wants to be beautiful; Rochelle (Rachel True) who is black and suffers the racism of a blond named Laura (Christine Taylor), wishes that Laura's hair would fall out; and Nancy (Fairuza Balk), the leader of the pack, an erotic bad girl with dyed black hair, black lipstick, and crucifix earrings, wants to rid her white trash family of her abusive stepfather and their depressing poverty. One by one their spells succeed. Sarah suddenly cannot rid herself of Chris and is forced to deal with his incessant longing and pathetic humiliation; Bonnie's scars disappear and she becomes increasingly narcissistic; Rochelle watches in horror as Laura's hair slowly falls out; and Nancy's stepfather suffers a heart attack and leaves her mother a great sum of money which they spend on a penthouse apartment equipped with groovy furniture and a jukebox that plays only Connie Francis songs.

The production employed a witch consultant, High Priestess Pat Devin from the Covenant of the Goddess, the largest Wiccan-based organization in America.

The girls continue to cultivate and experiment with their powers. Sarah teaches everyone how to create a visible illusion called "the glamour effect," and she momentarily morphs into a glamorous blond as an example. The antics of the four girls remain more or less harmless until one day Nancy buys a book in the occult shop that contains the secret of how to invoke the Spirit, despite a warning by the shopkeeper, Lirio (Asumpta Serna). The film gradually declines as bad witch Nancy gains excessive powers and begins to abuse them, and good witch Sarah must take her on. One evening Chris tries to rape Sarah, and Nancy storms off into the night to avenge her friend. Finding Chris at a local party, Nancy lures him into a secluded bedroom. At first he refuses her sexual advances, but when she morphs into an image of Sarah he succumbs. When the real Sarah enters the room the glamour effect is broken and Chris recedes in fear. Despite Sarah's protests, Nancy gives Chris a few words of her rage for his abuses against girls and then causes him to fall out the window to his death.

Fearful that Nancy is getting out of hand, Sarah tries but fails to bind Nancy's powers with a spell. Sarah finds that she is no match for Nancy, who can now occupy both her dreams and her personal thoughts. Sarah flees to Lirio at the occult shop and begs for help. There she learns that her mother, who died giving birth to her, was also a good witch, and that if she will only invoke the Spirit her powers will far exceed those of Nancy. But Sarah hesitates and when her friends show up at her home, she is so overcome with fear and weakness that they easily humiliate and torture her. Nancy uses the glamour effect to convince Sarah that her family died in a plane crash. She then slashes Sarah's wrists and fabricates a suicide letter in Sarah's handwriting claiming responsibility for Chris' death. Sarah retreats to her bedroom, and as she lay alone dying she notices the romantic photograph of her gentle mother on the dresser coming to life. Sarah invokes the Spirit, rises and wreaks havoc on her friends. Nancy ends up in an insane asylum fighting feverishly against a straitjacket, and the other two lose their powers and become ordinary girls. Sarah returns to her normal life and keeps her powers quietly in check.

This narrative closely emulates the traditional teen horror film—an alienated figure or group represents the weaknesses, fears, and humiliations of adolescence, but is redeemed with the aid of unexpected powers. Males often become mass murderers, like Michael Myers in *Halloween*

CREDITS

Sarah: Robin Tunney
Nancy: Fairuza Balk
Bonnie: Neve Campbell
Rochelle: Rachel True
Chris: Skeet Ulrich
Laura Lizzie: Christine Taylor
Mr. Bailey: Cliff DeYoung
Lirio: Assumpta Serna
Grace: Helen Shaver

Origin: USA
Released: 1996
Production: Douglas Wick; released by Columbia Pictures
Direction: Andrew Fleming
Screenplay: Peter Filardi, Andrew Fleming
Cinematography: Alexander Gruszynski
Editing: Jeff Freeman
Production design: Marek Dobrowolski
Costume design: Deborah Everton
Set design: Natalie Richards
Music: Graeme Revell
Visual effects supervisor: Kelley R. Ray
MPAA rating: R
Running Time: 100 minutes

(1978), who rely on their own strength and social transgression to "get even," while girls become witches imbibed with supernatural powers, like *Carrie* (1976), or get the help of a boyfriend as in *Heathers* (1989). There is one scene in this film where the girls watch the opening graphics from the 1970's television show "Bewitched," and smile approvingly at each other. This is after all their historical model for behavior. Like the magical women of "I Dream of Jeannie" and "Bewitched," they are expected to enjoy their secret feminine powers within the home and use them in support of a man active in the world, being cunning but never truly overpowering. But these contemporary girls overstep their boundaries and must be put in their place by the good witch Sarah, guided by the historical mother who came before her.

The problem with this interpretation of young female experience is that it takes a moral stand and advocates restraint and repression of female anger and power. Nancy is the only character in this film who expresses her anger at men openly and aggressively. She kills her stepfather while he is in the throes of beating her mother, and she kills Chris after first condemning him for treating women like whores, when he himself is the whore. It is disappointing and revealing that Nancy's character develops into a caricature of unbridled evil and power and that she ends in a mental institution stripped of all freedom, power, and credibility. In this sense the film is more about the anxieties and desires of males than of females, revealing attitudes and fears just South of Salem.

—Reni Celeste

REVIEWS

Boxoffice Magazine. July, 1996, p. 92.
The Chicago Tribune. May 3, 1996.
Entertainment Weekly. May 10, 1996, p. 54.
The New York Times. May 3, 1996, p. C10.
Variety. May 6, 1996, p. 82.

The Crow: City of Angels

Believe in the power of another.—Movie tagline

In a world where the forces of darkness rule, justice is about to take flight.—Movie tagline

"Classic mythology, gothic themes and a touching love story!"—*Buzz Magazine*

"The hot action picture of the summer!"—*Hits Magazine*

"This is something to crow about! Vincent Perez cuts an imposing figure!"—*Washington Post*

Box Office: $17,917,287

This has not been a good year for Los Angeles in the way the "City of Angels" has been represented on the screen. First came *John Carpenter's Escape From L.A.,* a futuristic nightmare that speculated what the city might become if separated from the mainland by an earthquake and turned into a holding pen for transported criminals and undesirables by a evangelical dictator in a nation turned fascist. Then, in *The Crow: City of Angels* the violent streets of this corrupt futurist city are ruled by brutal drug lords, punks, gangs, and kinky hedonists. Anarchy prevails here and humanity is at peril.

"They call this the city of angels, but all I see are victims. It's the city of drugs. The city of death."—Sarah

City of Angels is the first *Crow* sequel, based upon the popular James O'Barr comic books and deriving from the 1994 film that starred Brandon Lee. The film is narrated by a woman named Sarah (Mia Kirshner), who first encountered the Crow as a child in Detroit and is still bonded by a supernatural connection. The Crow sends her visions of a double murder when a young father named Ashe (Vincent Perez) and his younger son Danny (Eric Acosta) were executed after the boy had witnessed the murderous consequences of a drug deal gone wrong. "See no evil," a thug named Curve (Iggy Pop) advises, while a Vietnamese moll (Thuy Trang) gets orders from black Judah (Richard Brooks) to kill both father and son. She questions the need for killing the boy, but Judah offers no mercy.

A year later Sarah is summoned by the Crow to a pier so that she may help Ashe after he has been resurrected by the mysterious powers of the Crow. At first Ashe is confused about his identity and his mission, but he soon stalks and kills one of the gang, a thug named

Spider Monkey (Vincent Castellanos). Before completing his revenge task, however, Ashe retrieves his son's body from the river and buries it. As a consequence, he delays going after Curve, whose chest Sarah, who works in a tattoo parlor, has marked with the gestalt of a crow. Judah soon gets the message, and here the plot gets a little incoherent.

Judah is served by a blind woman seer. He somehow knows that Ashe may again become human and mortal by devices that are never quite explained. Ashe pursues Curve in a motorcycle chase and executes him at the river's edge. But Judah is a more formidable foe. He captures the symbolic Crow, pins its wings with daggers, then kills it. As a consequence, Ashe somehow becomes mortal, but just as Judah is about to kill Ashe and Sarah, a "murder" (flock) of crows gathers in the sky above him and attacks him, doing him in. Thereafter, Ashe's soul is released.

British music-video director Tim Pope makes his feature film debut.

This film is informed and driven by a particular gothic cult mythology that is never really explained for the benefit of general viewers. Narrative coherence is also a problem. Viewers who remember the first *Crow* will know that Canadian Mia Kirshner is the adult Sarah who was played as a girl by Rochelle Davis in the original story. Miramax was obviously gearing this feature to a cult punk-gothic audience and did not even bother to screen it in preview for reviewers unlikely to be impressed or to approve of its grotesquerie. To the uninitiated, it may seem merely repulsive, confusing and banal. The initiated would more likely be drawn into its metaphysical and spiritual frame of reference. That context needs to be explained.

The gothic subculture focuses upon the knowledge and acceptance of mortality and of physical decay. Death is romanticized, leaving no fear in their minds, only an embracing of the beauty of darkness and the poetic wish for eternal love after the pain and loss of this human existence. This wish appears to communicate itself through Christian beliefs and imagery, seen as immortality for those who worship the afterlife as peaceful, final destination.

However, these expressions and symbols of religious belief have been adopted by the gothic world not for their guarantee of salvation, but for their elevation of the soul above human evil and corruption. The architecture, music, and fashion chosen by this subculture symbolize life for the gothic mind rather than a worship of a single power or a higher reward. A return to the more superstitious past, as well as a respect for the almost futile attempt to find love and peace, allow gothic cultists to see the immortality of humans as they revel in the celebration of death and the spirit that transcends its power.

Both *Crow* films are gothic expressions of this power of the spirit to overcome the madness of evil and human transgression in order to experience the highest form of human emotion, eternal love beyond the grave. This wish becomes a gothic fantasy that for some replaces the ideal of a traditional Christian heaven. Thus the first film has become a gothic monument to the memory of the late Brandon Lee. By depicting the full cycle of death/rebirth/reunion-in-death, the message that "love is stronger than death" becomes a hoped-for reality. Each scene with Lee is intensified by his death, for he is eternally captured on film as "The Crow," a character who returns to avenge his lover's (and his own) murder, realizing that his own pain becomes more of a weapon than the supernatural force which he uses to destroy those who took his life from him. Seeing Lee return as The Crow to his lover at the end of the film allows the audience to worship and to celebrate death as the realization of immortality, the force which reunites lovers and which triumphs over a world of impotent evil and human control. Cultists cannot separate Lee from The Crow; for them Lee has become the character.

"I believe there's a place where the restless souls wander, attempting to set wrong things right," Sarah says in voice-over as she is seen on screen befriending a frightened, miserable waif. "Sometimes the Crow shows them the way." In the noir gothic atmosphere one notices a neon "JESUS

CREDITS

Ashe: Vincent Perez
Sarah: Mia Kirshner
Judah: Richard Brooks
Curve: Iggy Pop
Kali: Thuy Trang
Noah: Ian Dury

Origin: USA
Released: 1996
Production: Edward R. Pressman, Jeff Most; released by Miramax/Dimension Films
Direction: Tim Pope
Screenplay: David S. Goyer; based on the comic book series and comic strip by James O'Barr
Cinematography: Jean Yves Escoffier
Editing: Michael N. Knue, Anthony Redman
Music: Graeme Revell
Production design: Alex McDowell
Art direction: Gary Diamond, Charles Breen
Set design: Kristen Pratt
Costume design: Kristen Everberg
Visual effects supervisor: Robert Roger Dorney
Sound: Joseph Geisinger
MPAA rating: R
Running Time: 84 minutes

SAVES" sign with some letters darkened so that it reads "US SAVE" (i.e., "save us"). Elsewhere, the film is dominated by images of the Latino Day of Death rituals, with the continuing refrain, "Flores por los muertos" ("Flowers for the Dead"). Sarah's opening monologue wraps around the story. Later Sarah explains "Life is just a dream on the way to death," and at the end Sarah's voice proclaims "Sometimes love shows them the way because sometimes love is stronger than death."

The sequel follows the pattern of the 1994 feature directed by Australian Alex Proyas and starring Brandon Lee as working-class rocker Eric Draven in the way it mixes stylized action with gothic horror and a film noir visual style and also in its plot design. In the original, Eric and his fiancee were murdered by a gang of thugs who work for crime lord Top Dollar. One year later Eric, like Ashe, was resurrected by a supernatural power, endowed with preternatural strength and vision, and a spirit guide in the form of a hypnotic Crow in order to exact his revenge on his executioners.

City of Angels can only be compared to *The Crow* because of its basic plot similarities and its inherent purpose as a gothic film. The film hypnotizes viewers from the beginning as they approach the city through the avatar of the crow. Viewers are thrown into a confusing and menacing city, then are further disoriented by the confused dreams and memories of Sarah. This desperate city must become the City of Angels, which needs to be "saved" by the interjection of a powerful new force. Ashe becomes the angelic prophet. His character is more of this world than Lee's Crow, at first disbelieving that he is even dead. He struggles more with his state and needs more human instruction from Sarah in order to understand his mission. Vincent Perez's Crow is more of a gothic figure than Lee's interpretation, for he embodies the desire to embrace life and death at the same moment. The sequel rips into his struggle to unite these two worlds, rather than becoming a poetic testament to loss and rebirth.

The sequel also develops the character of Sarah as gothic outsider more clearly than the first *Crow.* As a child in the first film, she merely symbolized the friendship Eric left behind and the world that he could not rejoin. Now, her character falls in love with Ashe, experienced with a particular intensity. By loving Ashe and showing him mercy, she kills his power and takes it from him before Judah can crucify the bird. Sarah and Ashe face mortal death together, reborn as lovers who sacrificed their lives and power for each other. Under her influence for one moment Ashe becomes mortal again, using his sorrow and the pain of other mortals to destroy the violent power that once belonged to him.

In *City of Angels* gothic despair is laced with sadomasochistic behavior, leaving love as the only hope for salvation. Ashe mutters God's name as Sarah dies, but there is no way of knowing if anyone or any superior power hears him. These deaths celebrate Ashe's victory as a seemingly powerless man. The forces that brought him back and that took Judah away remain balancing energies that are distant, creative, yet also destructive. The film establishes no traditional faith in God or Heaven; instead, we are left with a humanistic message, mourning our need to murder, fornicate, and destroy, impulses that reside in all of us, including The Crow, and rejoicing in the eternal yet very mortal power of love to reunite souls. We all live in the City of Angels, and the film is an allegorical depiction of our internal feelings and desires.

The sequel was directed by Tim Pope, who documented the punk and ska music scenes in London during the 1970s, directing and producing music videos for such artists as David Bowie, Neil Young, and Paul McCartney, but has little apparent skill in working with film narrative. He also directed Iggy Pop's "Kiss My Blood" concert video, which helps to explain the casting of Iggy Pop. Such reviews as could be found were universally terrible, aside from treatments in *Cinefantastique,* which featured *The Crow: City of Angels* as the cover story for its August 1996 issue. Owen Gleiberman of *Entertainment Weekly* dismissed this "black-mass revenge thriller" as an "occult junkyard," and Joe Leydon of *Variety* described it as a "stunningly awful sequel." Even the fan reviewers at *Cinefantastique* admitted that the sequel "smacks of tacky commercialism." Even so, *City of Angels* reinvents the myth in a sequel-friendly way. This film is Grand Guignol cinema, probably too gruesome and violent for a general audience; nonetheless, there is a kind of energy here that may recommend it for the venturesome and for gothic punksters, but not all youngsters.

—*James M. Welsh* and *Liz Mulford*

REVIEWS

Boxoffice Online. September 13, 1996.
Cinefantastique. August, 1996, p. 16.
Entertainment Weekly. September 13, 1996, p. 112.
The Hollywood Reporter. September 3, 1996, p. 6.
Los Angeles Times. September 2, 1996, p. F12.
New York Times. August 31, 1996, p. 15.
Variety. September 2, 1996, p. 66.

The Crucible

Arthur Miller's timeless tale of truth on trial.—Movie tagline

"Electrifying! Startling . . . Pulsates with dramatic energy. *The Crucible* casts a more powerful spell than ever."—Owen Gleiberman, *Entertainment Weekly*

"A powerful film of great artistry and passion."—Rex Reed, *The New York Observer*

"Impassioned and vigorous . . . The film moves with the dangerous momentum of a runaway train."—Janet Maslin, *New York Times*

"Passionate and moving! *The Crucible* gets your blood boiling."—David Ansen, *Newsweek*

"Passionate, engrossing and invigoratingly intelligent."—Ralph Novak, *People*

"*The Crucible* achieves hurricane force. It's masterful, vibrant and compelling."—Bruce Williamson, *Playboy*

Box Office: $6,616,962

Arthur Miller's *The Crucible* makes an ultimate dramatic statement about witch hunts in the way it dramatizes the mischief caused by Abigail Williams (Winona Ryder), an oversexed teenaged girl who lusts after John Proctor (Daniel Day-Lewis), a married man. Abigail worked for Proctor and his wife (Joan Allen) but was dismissed after Mrs. Proctor found out Abigail had seduced her husband. The strong-minded Abigail leads a group of weak-minded girls into the forest one night and attempts to concoct love spells. Unfortunately, they are discovered by the Reverend Mr. Parris (Bruce Davison), who soon concludes that they were in league with the Devil. Experts are called for, the Rev. Mr. Hale (Rob Campbell) and Judge Danforth (Paul Scofield), who terrorize and interrogate the children and ask them to name other local Puritans they saw keeping company with the Devil. Those who were named had to confess; those who refused to confess were hanged.

AWARDS AND NOMINATIONS

Academy Award 1996 Nominations: Best Supporting Actress (Allen), Best Adapted Screenplay (Miller)
Golden Globe Award 1997 Nominations: Best Supporting Actress (Allen), Best Supporting Actor (Scofield)

The adaptation is uncommonly good since the original playwright was commissioned to reshape his play for the screen. The acting is as consistently good as could be found in any Hollywood film this decade. Paul Scofield is absolutely chilling as the hypocritically pious Judge who will do anything to protect the process of witchhunting he has designed and will not admit to having made mistakes. He becomes a sort of Bible-thumping Creon. Daniel Day-Lewis makes a very strong and ruggedly handsome John Proctor, and Joan Allen matches his performance as his righteous and wronged, but still understanding wife. Winona Ryder gives further evidence that she may be the most gifted actress of her generation. She is equally as good here as she had been in Martin Scorsese's *The Age of Innocence* (1993), when she also played opposite Daniel Day-Lewis. She has come a long way since *Beetlejuice* (1988).

There are two points to be made about the source of this film: 1) it was a political play intended to comment on the outrageous and shameful way too many people responded hysterically to the pressures of McCarthyism, informing out

CREDITS

John Proctor: Daniel Day-Lewis
Abigail Williams: Winona Ryder
Judge Danforth: Paul Scofield
Elizabeth Proctor: Joan Allen
Rev. Parris: Bruce Davison
Rev. Hale: Rob Campbell
Thomas Putnam: Jeffrey Jones
Tituba: Charlayne Woodard

Origin: USA
Released: 1996
Production: Robert A. Miller and David V. Picker; released by 20th Century Fox
Direction: Nicholas Hytner
Screenplay: Arthur Miller; based on his play
Cinematography: Andrew Dunn
Editing: Tariq Anwar
Production design: Lilly Kilvert
Art direction: John Warnke
Sound: Michael Barosky
Set design: Alan S. Kaye, Louis Montejano, Nick Navarro
Music: George Fenton
Costumes: Bob Crowley
Casting: Donna Isaacson, Daniel Swee
MPAA rating: PG-13
Running Time: 123 minutes

Illicit love between teenaged Abigail Williams (Winona Ryder) and married John Proctor (Daniel Day-Lewis) becomes the catalyst for a town's relentless witch-hunts in Arthur Miller's screen adaptation of his play *The Crucible.*

of fear on their friends, colleagues, and neighbors and telling outright lies, and 2) it is Arthur Miller's most-produced play and also, arguably, his most powerful play. Miller wrote this political allegory in 1953. It was answered in 1954 by Elia Kazan's *On the Waterfront,* which was intended to put an heroic spin on informers, a film that won eight Academy Awards. Although Nicholas Hytner's film version of *The Crucible* is wonderfully cast and very intelligently adapted by Arthur Miller himself, and although it is probable to get Academy Award nominations, it could not be expected to sweep the Awards for 1996 in the way *On the Waterfront* did in 1954 against weaker competition.

"I am but God's finger."—Abigail

The play's concept is based on the Salem [Massachusetts] witch trials of 1692. In commenting on the work's historical accuracy, Miller conceded that his play takes certain liberties. Although historically "there were several judges of almost equal authority," Miller wrote, "I have symbolized them all in [Judge] Hawthorne and [Deputy Governor] Danforth." The age of the spiteful and jealous Abigail Williams was "raised" (she would only have been eleven years old in 1692, while John Proctor would have been pushing 60), and "the number of girls involved in the 'crying out,'" when innocent people were accursed of consorting with the Devil, was reduced. Even so, Miller explains that the "fate of each character is exactly that of his historical model, and there is no one in the drama who did not play a similar—and in some cases exactly the same—role in history."

17th-century Salem was recreated on Hog Island, a wildlife refuge offshore of Essex Bay, Massachusetts.

Terrence Rafferty questioned the allegorical framework of the play in *The New Yorker,* asserting that "the connection between the events in Salem and the fearful atmosphere of the McCarthy era is slight." When the play was still new, critic Robert Warshow argued that "the Salem trials were not political," that the "witches" were not really "persecuted" in the way "the Puritans did persecute Quakers," and concluded, as Rafferty recalled, that the "Salem 'witches' suffered something that may be worse than persecution: they were hanged because of metaphysical error." The agenda of Miller's screen adaptation, as Rafferty understood it, was "fear of women and hatred of youth." For him, "the popularity of Miller's melodramas actually based on a universal fear of teen-age female sexuality." But this is a minority interpretation of the play, and one would be hard-pressed to deny that the play is centrally about dictatorial intimidation and the psychology that makes people inform on their friends and neighbors.

For the record, Miller himself refused to name names during the Hollywood "witchhunts" of 1956. His son Robert remarked to *The Washington Post* that Arthur Miller "was subpoenaed by HUAC [the House Un-American Activities Committee] and asked to identify writers he had seen attending Communist gatherings in living rooms years earlier," but Miller declined and as a result was held in contempt of Congress, "but the U.S. Court of Appeals overturned his conviction in 1958" and he was never sent to jail. "Until that point, no one had gotten away with it," his son recalled. They had all "folded or left the country or gone to prison."

During this "scoundrel time" Miller was deprived of his passport but managed to hold on to his integrity, like John Proctor in the play. While Senator McCarthy was powerful, no one would have dared to film this play; after McCarthy had been disgraced for his dishonest tactics, interest in the play faded, but, as Miller told *Entertainment Weekly,* "This particular play of mine is probably the only one that really cries out for a movie." Along with *The English Patient* and *Joseph Conrad's the Secret Agent,* it was the best literary adaptation of the year and certainly the best dramatic one, even if Hollywood executives tended to see it as a Puritan *Fatal Attraction* (1987), as was rumored. In the past Hollywood producers would have worried about selling a film with such a downbeat ending, one that sends its protagonist to the gallows, so, silly as it may seem, its superficial resemblance to *Fatal Attraction* probably helped to sell the project commercially. "For once," Nicholas Hytner told *The Times* of London, "Hollywood wanted to treat a great literary icon with some kind of respect while at the same time making an exciting movie; they didn't want to adulterate it." Hytner concluded that "hiding behind every bush" in Hollywood "is an intelligent, cultivated, sensitive, educated executive who can't really admit it." If so, the time was surely right to make *The Crucible.*

Thankfully, the era of the bullying Senator Joseph McCarthy feeding the fires of the Red Menace is now history, as is Communism itself, but there is no need to conclude that Miller's play about community hysteria is somehow dated. Victor Navasky, the publisher and editor of *The Nation* and a friend of Arthur Miller claimed the opposite in a *New York Times* essay "The Demons of Salem [are] With Us Still." Consider, for example, the "nationwide rash of child molestation trials in which children have charged day-care center workers with unspeakable crimes." Miller told Navasky the play would be applicable "to almost any time, the reason being it's dealing with a paranoid situation," but not one that depends on "any particular political or sociological development." The universal meanings of this play are impressive: "community hysteria, fear of the unknown, the psychology of betrayal, the cast of mind that insists on absolute truth and resorts to fear and violence to assert it," and "the fortitude it takes to resist unjust authority." In other words, the film still speaks intelligently to our times and partly for that reason it is one of the very best films of 1996. Very few films of such allegorical integrity and moral authority have come out of Hollywood.

—James M. Welsh

REVIEWS

The Baltimore Sun. December 20, 1996, p. 1.
Boxoffice Online. November 22, 1996.
Chicago Tribune. December 20, 1996, p. 5.
Entertainment Weekly. November 29, 1996, p. 68.
Entertainment Weekly. December 6, 1996, p. 18.
Hollywood Reporter. November 4, 1996, p. 5.
House Beautiful. January, 1997, p. 42.
Los Angeles Times. December 13, 1996, p. F12.
Movieline. December, 1996, p. 40.
The New York Times. November 27, 1996, p. C9.
The New Yorker. December 2, 1996, p. 119.
Newsweek. December 2, 1996, p. 80.
People. December 2, 1996, p. 20.
Rolling Stone. December 12, 1996, p. 89.
Sight and Sound. March, 1997, p. 44.
Time. December 2, 1996, p. 81.
The Times (London). January 21, 1997, p. 34.
Variety. November 4-10, 1996, p. 81.
Village Voice. December 6, 1996, p. 61.
The Washington Post. December 15, 1996, p. G1.
Washington Post Weekend. December 20, 1996, p. 45.
Washington Times Metropolitan Times. December 20, 1996, p. C16.

Curdled

After the killer kills . . . After the living are dead . . . Somebody has to clean up the mess. And you thought your job sucked.—Movie tagline

"A stylishly auspicious debut! One of the year's most uniquely unsettling finales!"—Marshall Fine, *Gannett News Service*

"Such awfully great fun!"—Gary Dauphin, *Village Voice*

Box Office: $49,620

Curdled comes billed as a comedy drenched in blood, and the description is apt. Its director, Reb Braddock, has attempted to duplicate the same blend of violence and dark humor that his executive producer, Quentin Tarantino, used to great effect in his own *Reservoir Dogs* (1992) and *Pulp Fiction* (1994). Those films managed to transcend the trashy movies that inspired them by means of rich characterization and attention to detail, even while reveling in the excesses of the disreputable genres that spawned them. Unfortunately, *Curdled* only manages to reproduce the excesses.

The film stars Angela Jones, the cabdriver from *Pulp Fiction,* as Gabriela, who has been fascinated by all things grisly ever since witnessing a murder outside her childhood home in Columbia. That was in 1977. Now, she lives in Miami, where 50,000 violent crimes take place each year: swell conditions for a girl whose hobbies include clipping out newspaper articles on bloody homicides and ducking under the police tape at crime scenes to try and get a closer look.

So, of course, Gabriela is ecstatic when she lands a job at the Post-Forensic Cleaning Service, a company specializing in tidying up murder sites. There, her enthusiastic manner while scouring the red stuff from carpets has her co-workers doing double takes. While she scrubs, she chatters away to her workmate, Elena (Mel Gorham), asking her innocently-worded questions about how and why and with what instrument she thinks each assailant might have used to assault their victims.

This much of the plot had already been detailed in a short film Braddock made a few years ago, also called *Curdled* and also starring Angela Jones. Legend has it that Tarantino caught the comic short at a film festival, liked the concept and ended up using the material as the basis for the Mr. Clean-Up character that Harvey Keitel plays in *Pulp Fiction*—and he liked Jones so much he gave her the part of the cabdriver in that film. To pay Braddock back for all his plundering, Tarantino helped him secure financing for a feature-length version of *Curdled.*

It might seem inevitable that this wisp of an idea proves just too thin a thread to hang a full-bodied plot on, but that notion apparently never occurred to the filmmakers. Braddock and his co-screenwriter, John Maass, try to flesh out the basic scenario by adding an extra character, Paul Guell (William Baldwin), aka the Blue Blood Killer, a serial murderer who concentrates his efforts on beautiful rich women, though it's obvious this character exists for the sole purpose of drawing the movie out to its current length.

Gabriela first becomes enamored of the Blue Blood Killer while watching the hit TV show "Miami DOA," but figures she can only fantasize about the Killer's bloody antics. Then one day while mopping a kitchen floor, she wipes away the blood and finds that the Killer's real name has been scrawled across the linoleum, presumably by a victim on the verge of dying. Little does she know that in the wine cellar right behind her is the actual Blue Blood Killer, who had been surprised by Gabriela while attempting to fix his mistake. A confrontation ensues, and then a friendship develops out of the respect each has for the passions of the other.

From there, the story degenerates into a series of pointless episodes where Gabriela and the Killer demonstrate to each other how theirs might potentially be a symbiotic relationship, or something. It's not clear what Braddock was even trying for in these scenes, but what he achieves is a mishmash of potential set pieces that start well enough but don't quite pay off (the exception being a nicely realized scene in which Gabriela re-creates the final throes of a victim by dancing them out).

Jones, in a difficult part, tries hard to carry the project. She does a good job of making Gabriela seem truly curious, not merely naive, and it's a fine attempt, but her effort ultimately gets buried under the gallons of gooey fake blood the filmmakers keep dumping on her. *Curdled* is indulgent like that, which would be an ok thing if its characters weren't allowed to get so lost in the mayhem. There's also Baldwin, looking uncommitted to his role, even spacey; he doesn't give Jones the support she needs, and finally the lack of chemistry between them sinks the whole bloody affair.

—David King

CREDITS

Paul Guell: William Baldwin
Gabriela: Angela Jones
Eduardo: Bruce Ramsay
Elena: Mel Gorham
Katrina Brandt: Lois Chiles
Clara: Daisy Fuentes
Lodger: Barry Corbin
Lourdes: Carmen Lopez

Origin: USA
Released: 1996
Production: John Maass, Raul Puig for a Tinderbox Films and A Band Apart production; released by Miramax Films
Direction: Reb Braddock
Screenplay: Reb Braddock, John Maass
Cinematography: Steven Bernstein
Editing: Mallory Gottlieb
Music: Joseph Julian Gonzalez
Production design: Sherman Wiliams
Costume design: Beverly Nelson Safier
Sound: Peter J. Devlin
Casting: Yvonne Casas
MPAA rating: R
Running Time: 88 minutes

REVIEWS

Boxoffice. November, 1996, p. 141.
Entertainment Weekly. October 11, 1996, p. 74.
Film Threat. January, 1997, p. 48.
Hollywood Reporter. September 10, 1996, p. 10.
Los Angeles Times. September 27, 1996, p. F18.
New York Times. September 27, 1996, p. C5.
Variety. September 23, 1996, p. 128.
Village Voice. October 1, 1996, p. 68.

Cyclo; Xich Lo

"Dazzling! Another superb picture from Hung, a world-class filmmaker if ever there was one."—Kevin Thomas, *Los Angeles Times*

"Unforgettable! Hands down one of the year's absolute best!"—Chuck Stephens, *San Francisco Bay Guardian*

Box Office: $226,206

Vietnamese filmmaker Tran Anh Hung's *Cyclo* is an unsparing account of the brutal life of some working-class residents of Ho Chi Minh City. Traversing the landscape of pain experienced by a luckless 18-year-old bicycle-taxi driver and his struggling family, *Cyclo* at its best moments achieves a breathtaking universality in its depiction of human oppression, resilience and despair.

Never doctrinaire or preachy, Hung unflinchingly trains his cameras like a documentarian on the sordid, revealing little indignities that constitute existence in the urban underclass of Vietnam. The film owes much of its stylistic touches to Italian neo-realism. But in its ability to make the hardships of a Third World culture palpable to a global audience, it is reminiscent of Indian filmmaker's Satyajit Ray's Apu trilogy.

Cyclo is a demanding film. Its deliberate pace will test audience patience, and its merciless juxtapositions of blood and beauty will test viewer tolerance for jarring, brutal scenes. The director spares his audience nothing. With equal dexterity, Hung employs delicate, painterly touches and explosive, sledgehammer-like psychic blows. The attentive viewer will be rewarded with new insights into the depths of depravity and love and the limitless capacity for human adaptability and endurance.

Perhaps to underline the universality and the elemental powerlessness of his characters, Hung gives none of them names. The 18-year-old protagonist, played by Le Van Loc, is simply "Cyclo." Having no other marketable skills, he is doomed to follow in his father's footsteps as a bicycle taxi driver who hauls people and goods around Ho Chi Minh City. It's a torturous job, stressing the feet and back and tolerance for insult.

Cyclo's father died in a traffic accident on the job, his mother during childbirth. Cyclo lives with his older sister (Tran Nu Yen Khe), who delivers water for money; his younger sister (Pham Ngoc Lieu), perhaps 8 or 9-years-old, who shines shoes, and his grandfather, who repairs bicycle tires. They crowd into a one-room hovel behind a beauty parlor.

Cyclo works for Boss Lady (Nguyen Nhu Quynh), who presides over a group of taxi drivers and divides up their turf. She seems gentle and kind, soothing her mentally impaired son with soft lullabies. Yet Cyclo soon learns she's the apparently heartless matriarch of a ruthless gang. After his bicycle is stolen by rivals, Cyclo is recruited against his will into the Boss Lady's gang activities.

He's shut up in an apartment across the street from the Poet (Tony Leung), the gang's apparent mastermind, and allowed out only to execute the Poet's nefarious commands. One of the many frustrations of *Cyclo* is that the purpose of these criminal actions are unclear, and the extent and nature of the gang opaque. What's clear is only that Cyclo is serving an apprenticeship into the gang. He graduates from ransacking warehouses to firebombing rival bike-taxi shops to instruction in the use of knives and guns.

Cyclo makes the transformation from honest work to mayhem reluctantly. He has little choice but to cooperate, since he's being kept as a virtual prisoner and is slapped around whenever he protests. Eventually the macho pleasures of gang violence and the cash payoffs win him over, and he becomes an enthusiastic conscript.

It's a matter-of-fact, frightening portrayal of a descent into hell. Cyclo at first appears hardworking, honest and dedicated to his family. As a gang recruit, he becomes cold-blooded and crazy. Le Van Loc makes the transformation utterly believable and profoundly human, even when his character becomes repulsive.

There is no romanticism in Hung's view of his characters. Cyclo reacts to the brutality of his life by becoming brutalized (and brutal himself) and emotionally distorted.

CREDITS

Cyclo: Le Van Loc
The Poet: Tony Leung
The Sister: Tran Nu Yen Khe
Boss Lady: Nguyen Nhu Quynh
The Little Sister: Pham Ngoc Lieu

Origin: France; Vietnam
Released: 1995
Production: Christophe Rossignon for a Les Productions Lazennec; released by CFP Distribution
Direction: Tran Anh Hung
Screenplay: Tran Anh Hung, Nguyan Trung Bing
Cinematography: Benoit Delhomme
Editing: Nicole Dedieu, Claude Ronzeau
Production design: Benoit Barouh
Music: Ton That Tiet
MPAA rating: Unrated
Running Time: 120 minutes

He is capable of picking the legs off a lizard and eating a live goldfish. But he never loses his humanity, thanks to Loc's performance.

One of the most fascinating aspects of *Cyclo* is that its characters experience not just social degradation, but profound psychic battering as well. Hung is most interested in what happens to the minds and feelings of his characters. *Cyclo* suggests that even the most hardened victims of a chaotic, unjust society are constantly vulnerable emotionally, suffering from the gap between what life promises and what life delivers. As if to drive home the point, Hung occasionally intersperses scenes of school children singing and playing instruments. These are the most heavy-handed moments in the film, but they are indispensable.

Tran Nu Yen Khe, who plays The Sister, is also the director's wife.

The most mentally anguished character is the Poet, a constantly brooding, chain-smoking young pimp. He recites voice-over poems but rarely speaks to other characters. His brothel soon expands to include Cyclo's sister. She is a virgin, reluctant to engage in sex, yet inexplicably mesmerized by the Poet. He is also fond of her, and employs her to service fetishistic clients who don't want outright sex: one watches her urinate, another bathes her feet and paints her toenails. When one of his client's fetishes gets out of hand, the results are disastrous.

The Poet's story soon eclipses Cyclo's, at least in terms of screen time. He is a pet of his mother, but his father brutally whips him when he and Cyclo's sister come calling. He is carrying around a huge psychic wound which is symbolized by frequent nosebleeds.

Like Cyclo, the Poet and the Sister are multiply shackled. They're trapped by economic necessity, habit and the limitations that subjugation has imposed on their feelings and actions. Their affection for each other is yet another trap. They cannot even express it openly; they are capable of feeling love, but not expressing it. Their love meets a highly stylized, tragic end, part of a sweeping, slowly building climax that has an epic feel and cooks all the characters' stories together into a simmering, inconsolable stew.

All the characters in the film seem doomed to acting out their highly circumscribed roles in a drama whose directors are never seen. They behave as marionettes controlled by a multitude of invisible strings. Given the subtlety and complexity of director Hung's vision, a semi-happy ending which suggests that American imperialism is a source of the problem is too obviously pat and clearly a concession to the Communist regime's censors. Hung doesn't need to affix blame for the straits his characters are in; it's simply the modern human condition writ especially large on a Third World canvas.

The acting, cinematography, editing and directing all are superb. Still, the film is a bitter pill. It makes no concessions to the commercial need to be entertaining, uplifting or ingratiating. Like *Once Were Warriors* (1995), it is a stunning indictment of what happens to families when Western-style modernity collides with proud, longstanding non-Western cultures. Its cinematic reach may exceed its grasp, but just barely so, and *Cyclo* reveals Tran Anh Hung (who previously directed *The Scent of the Green Papaya*) as a director with unlimited promise.

—Michael Betzold

REVIEWS

New York Times. October 12, 1995, p. C20.
Sight and Sound. April, 1996, p. 42.
Variety. September 11, 1995, p. 108.

D3: The Mighty Ducks

"*Ducks 3* scores with family fun!"—Joan Bunke, *Des Moines Register*

"Far and away the best *Ducks* yet!"—Jim Svejda, *KNX Radio*

"The quack attack is back!"—Andy Seller, *USA Today*

Box Office: $21,995,225

Several films ago, the *Mighty Duck* saga began when Gordon Bombay (Emilio Estevez), a pretentious yuppie lawyer, was arrested on drunk-driving charges and sentenced to community service: coaching a pee-wee (and correctly diverse) hockey team. Then, not unlike the Bad News Bears (in the film of the same name), the Mighty Ducks learn to respect themselves and learn to win. In the process, Gordon Bombay succeeds, learning humility and the importance of others beside himself. Now, three movies later, the Mighty Ducks must learn to succeed on their own.

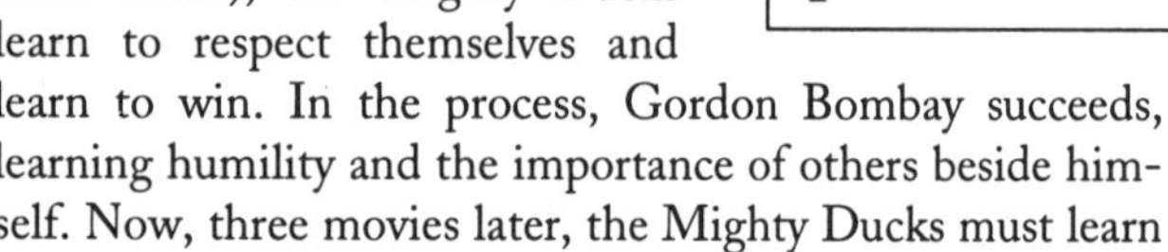

"Quack! Quack! Quack!"—the Ducks' team cry

As *D3: The Mighty Ducks* begins, the viewers learn that the Ducks have won scholarships to the prestigious prep school Eden Hall, the school their mentor Gordon Bombay attended many years before. En masse, the Ducks are now the Junior Varsity hockey team, a coup that has angered the other non-Duck players and their kin who were pushed aside and lost the chance to play. While Coach Bombay had taught the Ducks all they needed to know about offensive tactical maneuvers and about being a team, now the Ducks must learn defensive moves and must learn how to adapt to change and get along with their non-Duck classmates and very demanding new coach.

Much is made of the cultural differences between the Ducks and the other students at Eden Hall. For instance, the appearance of the other students at Eden Hall is prototypically all-American, the old-school, preppie, Ralph Lauren advertisement: tall, slim, well dressed, with clear complexions. The Ducks, on the other hand, are variously plump, poorly dressed, often ethnic and angry rubes. Charlie (Joshua Jackson) is the prototypical angry young man, angry at Coach Bombay for leaving the team to coach the Goodwill Games, angry at Coach Orion for changing the team's hot-shot style of playing, angry at a school that imports the team for its talents yet strips them of their moniker, changing the "Ducks" to the "Warriors." Audiences may find it painful to watch Charlie rail against everyone and everything around him, to watch Charlie leave the school only to sit and grumble in alleyways. And, indeed, the Ducks are reaching puberty, complete with the hormones that drive them to courtship and complaining.

Generally filmgoers enjoy a series in which the characters catch their fancy, regardless of whether the viewers are young or more mature. If James Bond films intrigue adults regardless of the films' repeated plots and gimmicks, for instance, then it is little surprise that Mickey Rooney was able to entertain audiences over two decades, appearing in more than a dozen Andy Hardy films from 1938 (*Judge Hardy's Children*) through 1958 (*Andy Hardy Comes Home*), by maintaining his good humor even while he encounters what seem to be insurmountable social problems and then luckily resolving them. In the same mold, from 1959 through 1972, Gidget (originally played by Sandra Dee) took audiences through Hawaii and Rome, and on to marriage in a continuing series of misadventures involving the same goofy "girl talk" and mooning over Moondoggie

CREDITS

Gordon Bombay: Emilio Estevez
Charlie: Joshua Jackson
Coach Ted Orion: Jeffrey Nordling
Dean Buckley: David Selby
Hans: Joss Ackland
Goldberg: Shaun Weiss

Origin: USA
Released: 1996
Production: Jordan Kerner, Jon Avnet, for a Walt Disney production; released by Buena Vista
Direction: Robert Lieberman
Screenplay: Steven Brill, Jim Burnstein, based on characters created by Brill
Cinematography: David Hennings
Editing: Patrick Lussier, Colleen Halsey
Art direction: Harry Darrow
Costume design: Kimberly A. Tillman
Music: J.A.C. Redford
Production design: Stephen Storer
Sound: Tim Cooney
Casting: Judy Taylor
MPAA rating: PG
Running Time: 104 minutes

(originally played by James Darren). And in the mid-1970s, the Bad News Bears, another adolescent sports team, took audiences from Hollywood to Japan and on to Houston.

While the games varied little (with the team trailing in the early innings and squeaking out a win in the last seconds), audiences remained loyal. By the 1980s, karate, while an individual sport, required dedication of its hormone-driven teen hero, played by Ralph Macchio. With the *Karate Kid,* the wise older guide resurfaced, playing a role not unlike that played by Andy Hardy's father, Judge Hardy. Indeed, as Judge Hardy provided a rudder for Andy Hardy's adventures, as *Star Wars*'s (1979) Luke Skywalker (Mark Hamill) studied The Force with Yoda and as the karate kid gained strength and discipline by landscaping and renovating Mr. Miyagi's (Pat Morita) garden, so too the *Ducks'* Charlie develops character from his interactions—his skate-side chats—with Hans (Joss Ackland), who, like the other mentors listed here, gave his charge perspective beyond the teen's all-consuming personal woes.

New Ducks coach Ted Orion is named for former Red Wings player Ted Lindsay.

Suffice it to say, *D3* is hardly original, yet for the audience for which it is intended, it works its formulaic charm in a comfortably predictable way. Do audience members ever doubt that James Bond will survive unscathed? Win the girl? Save the world from evil geniuses and destruction? Do they ever wish for a change in the pattern? Never, the knowledge of the pattern, the problem presented/problem resolved structure, fails to spoil the tale. So audience members will never doubt that the Ducks can and will prevail, that despite their ill humor, odd appearance and innumerable setbacks, they will pull together as a team and win as Ducks. In sum, neither originality nor surprise is acceptable, let alone sought, in this genre. The formula is all, and the film that follows it, succeeds. For these reasons, *D3: The Mighty Ducks* will flourish with its intended audience.

—Roberta F. Green

REVIEWS

Boxoffice Online. October 8, 1996.
Chicago Tribune. October 4, 1996, p. 5.
Daily Variety. October 4, 1996, p. 1.
Los Angeles Times. October 4, 1996, p. F20.
New York Times. October 4, 1996, p. C21.
People. October 14, 1996, p. 27.
USA Today Online. October 4, 1996.

Dadetown

Box Office: $27,552

Dadetown is the debut film of director Russ Hexter. It is a tragedy for American film that he died of an aortic aneurysm on April 29, 1996. Only twenty-seven years old, his work has been hailed at film festivals and given major treatment by film critics. Diane Keaton was negotiating with him about future productions. He brought to filmmaking an originality and daring reminiscent of Orson Welles.

"Alien Persons Invade?"—local woman guessing what the new corporation's API initials might mean

Dadetown is a film drenched in the history of cinema. It is cunning feature masquerading as a documentary. So well schooled is Hexter in the conventions of the nonfiction film that a few critics who did not watch the closing credits did not realize that Dadetown was the director's invention. Indeed, one audience member at a special screening denounced the director, saying he would do well in Hollywood because he enjoyed deceiving people.

Actually that irate comment is a tribute to the film's art and honesty. All films, like all art, are a construction. Audiences have become so used to the conventions of the documentary that even a fictional film faithful to those conventions will be taken for fact. Welles did something similar in *Citizen Kane* (1941), using elements like newsreels and interviews to suggest journalism rather than art. An artist who inquires into his own medium's manipulativeness is surely anything but deceitful.

Hexter spent eighteen months in a central New York town, using it to construct his fictional Dadetown. He hired local people and amateur actors, who often had gone through experiences similar to the characters in his script. Moreover, the script was used only as a basis for the film. Actors were welcome to improvise and to choose words that seemed comfortable to them. They were given a vision of small town life and then asked to shape it to their own backgrounds.

The result is stunning. In ninety minutes, Hexter portrays a setting and characters that have the resonance of a novel. There are no slack spots, yet the film has the feel of a longer work. Clearly the director and his actors have lived this material. In fact, Hexter insisted that the initial screening take place in Hammonsport, a small town in central New York where *Dadetown* was filmed. Hexter became the town's adopted son, and nearly everyone came to a showing of the film.

Director/writer Russ Hexter died of an aortic aneurysm April 29, 1996 at the age of 27.

Dadetown tells the story of a community that believes it is representative of the American dream. During World War II, the town's factory, Gorman, produced airplane fuselages. Now in a changing economy it makes paper clips—far less heroic, the townspeople concede, but work at the plant provides steady paychecks and a comfortable, if not wealthy, way of life.

The townspeople are uneasy, nevertheless, because a new company has arrived. API (American Peripheral Imaging) is bringing a workforce from New York City and other urban areas. New and rather grand houses are being built. There is a new playground and plans for other civic improvements. The town council is happy with this new industry, but the citizens are wary. Who are these people? They don't mingle well in town. They keep to themselves, even though they say they are community-oriented. And what do they do? What is peripheral imaging? What does API really stand for? Alien People Invade is the wry retort of one Dadetown native. Suffice it to say that API is a software company. It represents the future, just as Gorman embodies the past.

Dadetown splits apart when Gorman lays off more than a hundred workers. Somehow the people at API are to blame. The new company has been given tax breaks. There are rumors that API has paid off at least one town councilwoman. Another prominent local booster of API has gotten the contract for all the concrete work at the new API homes. Laid off Gorman employees angrily attack API employees—in one case dumping a dead deer on an API employee's doorstep. A town councilman tries to reason with the laid off workers and their families. How, he asks them, can API be to blame for Gorman's troubles? But in the atmosphere of paranoia, people are listening only to the rabble rousers calling for a strike against Gorman. It feels good to picket the plant and to yell at scabs, but Gorman is closing. It simply cannot compete with foreign firms that turn out paper clips and similar items so cheaply that even if the Gorman workers accepted no salary at all, the plant could not be kept open.

In *Dadetown*, there are no villains. Hexter's film is about a community in transition. The API employees do sound like big city people with few roots in the community, but they also care about Dadetown. One API wife who opens up her own store relates a story about a laid-off worker who comes into her new shop to admire her merchandise. He says he would like to buy something, but even if he could afford it, his wife would give him hell for buying from one of the new people in town. The shop owner is shaken by her memory of this incident. She has felt what it is like for the town natives to see her arrive with such a promising future.

API is really being blamed for reminding the town that their vision of small town America cannot survive. Yet it is more complicated than that because API is in Dadetown precisely because it is a small town. The new company realizes that its presence will change the town, yet it is also looking for ways to preserve the town's identity, conceding that it will grow into a small city but perhaps with many of the features associated with a small town.

What makes *Dadetown* cohere is the myth of the small town. The irony is that so many people want to live there that it is hard to see how it will remain small. Yet refusing to grow will surely mean that Dadetown will die. Some of the most moving scenes in the film are with Dadetown's councilman, the Homer of small-town life, played with con-

CREDITS

Bill Parsons: Bill Garrison
Tony Pitino: David Phelps
Tom Nickenback: Jim Pryor
Bill Bowers: Jonathan Shafer
Dan Barlitz: Stephen Beals
Joanna Barlitz: Valerie Gilbert
Susan Chambers: Frankie Earle

Origin: USA
Released: 1995
Production: Jim Carden; released by Castle Hill Productions
Direction: Russ Hexler
Screenplay: Russ Hexler, John Housley
Cinematography: W.J. Gorman
Editing: David Kirkman
Production design: J. Edward Vigeant
Music: Tom Carden
Art direction: Dan Blanchard
Sound: Alicia Quigley
MPAA rating: Unrated
Running Time: 93 minutes

summate poise by Bill Garrison, a 74-year-old former town supervisor. He is not merely a booster of his town; he realizes that Dadetown stands for a mythic vision of America that people have fought to preserve.

Garrison's character is at the center of the film because he is aware that the small town myth will have to adapt to changing times. In the film, Garrison's character dies of a sudden heart attack. A bereaved community counts on the well regarded and much younger local grocer to step into the vacant council seat. The neophyte councilman is touched by his community's faith in him. But he is almost immediately plunged into the Gorman crisis. As he shuttles between the townspeople and Gorman management—with stops at API to see if they can hire some of the laid-off workers—he realizes that he represents an isolated point of view. The strikers want a victory, and they want to feel good about the work they have spent their lives on. They do not want to hear that API is not their problem. They want a scapegoat.

At a tension-filled community meeting, the novice councilman tells the stunned crowd that the plans to shut down Gorman were initiated by his predecessor—in other words, by the very embodiment of their small town ethos. It is as if the Dadetown natives are deaf; they simply will not hear that their beloved spokesman realized that Gorman could not sustain itself. Instead they heap blame on his replacement. The irony is lost on them. Dadetown itself—not some alien company, not some duped councilman, not some paid-off councilwoman—is responsible for the changes that have led to Gorman's demise.

Hexter's film has been compared to Michael Moore's celebrated documentary, *Roger & Me.* Like Moore, Hexter is shrewd on the subject of corporate America. Like Moore, he can skewer the public relations men and women who put a happy face on downsizing and plant closings. But Hexter is the superior filmmaker. He has none of Moore's sentimental leftism, which seeks most of the time to merely bash corporations and to make people feel helpless. Hexter tells a deeper and more complex truth: everyone is implicated in the changes that are occurring today, and it is time that everyone takes responsibility for dealing with them.

—Carl Rollyson

REVIEWS

Entertainment Weekly. October 11, 1996, p. 72.
New York Times. September 18, 1996, p. C13.
Variety. September 25, 1995, p. 98.

Daylight

No Air. No Escape. No Time.—Movie tagline

"Mind-boggling, blow-you-out-of-your-seat climax."—Michael Wilmington, *Chicago Tribune*

"A great ride . . . Stallone at his best!"—Jim Ferguson, *Prevue Channel*

"A first rate thriller with superb special effects. Stallone gives one of his most effective performances."—Jeffrey Lyons, *WNBC*

Box Office: $26,070,220

It's a banner year for Sylvester Stallone, twenty years since *Rocky* (1976) was released, the film that launched his stardom. If Stallone is still looking for the right role in his post-Rocky, post-Rambo years, this time he might have found one in *Daylight,* which offers one of the most appealing Stallone heroes in recent memory, oddly named Kit Latura, well educated, compassionate, and decent enough to risk his life to save survivors from a terrible tunnel disaster, trapped under the Hudson River. The screenplay by Leslie Bohem intelligently sets the stage for the coming disaster by establishing the people who will later be seen in the tunnel as they go about their quiet lives in New York City.

In fact, however, some of these lives are more quiet than others. Roy Nord (Viggo Mortensen) is a take-charge sportswear entrepreneur who has made a bundle selling athletic shoes and is not to be daunted by a collapsing tunnel. Seeing him in the boardroom, the viewer knows he is a risk-taker, but he later overreaches himself with reckless abandon, and pays the consequences. Then there is the struggling playwright Madelyne Thompson (Amy Brenneman of "NYPD Blue"), who has had to deal with rather too many rejections from publishers and cockroaches in her flat and decides to go back to Laporte, Indiana, at exactly the wrong time. There is a devoted elderly couple (Claire Bloom and Colin Fox) and their Labrador Retriever, named Cooper. There is also the disturbed, argumentative Creighton family (Jay O. Sanders plays the whining, philandering father, Karen Young his wife, and Danielle Harris as daughter Ashley), and a truckload of convicts being transported to prison, one of whom is played by Sage Stallone, the star's son. *Rocky* veteran Stan Shaw plays George Tyrell, a likable Transit Authority cop who is also trapped while Grace, his lady love (Vanessa Bell Calloway), watches his progress in horror from a video monitor in the control booth. That's the core microcosm group for this disaster picture.

A group of thug punksters jump a diamond dealer in the City as he is unlocking his car. They steal his car and a briefcase full of diamonds and are headed for New Jersey, with the police in hot pursuit. The car swerves recklessly into tunnel traffic, threads its way in and out of traffic, then collides with a truck carrying explosive toxic waste, creating a fireball that sweeps the tunnel, sealing both ends.

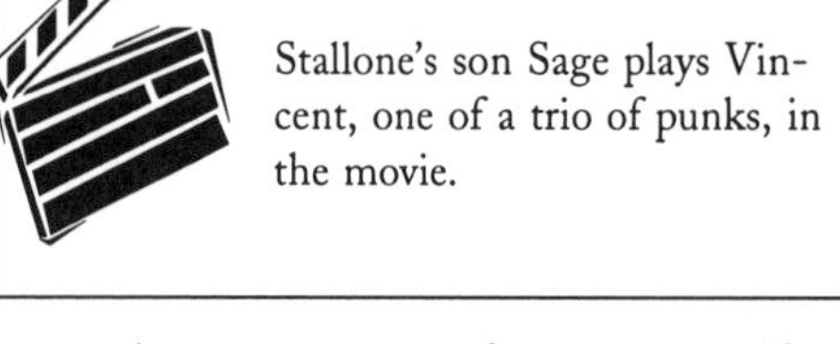

Stallone's son Sage plays Vincent, one of a trio of punks, in the movie.

Kit Latura (Stallone) is first seen as a limo driver taking a doctor and his wife to Newark International Airport, but the accident occurs just as his limo approaches the tunnel. The backstory on Latura is that he was the former head of New York's Rescue Service who somehow disgraced himself because of a bad decision (never fully explained) that caused some loss of life. Or maybe he just took the blame and was framed as the fall guy. At any rate, his lifesaving instincts kick in and Kit immediately helps to care for the wounded at the entrance of what seems to be the Holland Tunnel.

Kit then volunteers to go in after the survivors, but his offer is refused by the current Head of Rescue Services, who just wants Kit to go away. Very soon thereafter the Head is crushed as he attempts to tunnel in, and Kit is the only person available who has the courage to attempt a rescue. To get to the survivors, Kit has to lower himself down a ventilator shaft and get past four huge exhaust fans that can only be slowed down for a few seconds, but not stopped. This is the film's best heart-stopping stunt. Unfortunately, once Kit is in, he is unable to take the same route out. It's a blender up there.

Stallone's Rescue Kit is no superhero, however, so the best he can do is to improvise. Meanwhile, the tunnel is filling with toxic fumes and dank water, and the walls are in danger of collapsing. Kit leads the survivors to a tunnel branch that leads to a room where the "sand hogs" who built the tunnel rested between shifts as the tunnel was being built during the 1920s. They all have to swim underwater to get to that room, a feat that would only be feasible, as one reviewer noted, for "Navy SEALs in peak condition." Even so, nearly all of them get to the room, which is then invaded by hundreds of rats. (This film touches all phobias.) But the rats know the way out and lead them to another room from which they may escape. But as this room begins to fill up with water, sentimental Kit goes back to rescue Cooper, the dog. The pooch is rescued, but Kit and Madelyne the playwright are trapped. Can there be a final solution for them? If not, this plucky pair will die trying.

The film reaches its peak in the first hour. Everything that follows after the explosion and Kit's descent into hell tends to be contrived and anticlimactic. The theme of redemption would seem to be a prime motive for the Stallone hero, but the film is mainly about a cataclysmic car chase, an explosive fireball, and a collapsing tunnel. The action is well directed by Rob Cohen, however, and very well edited by Peter Amundson. Even so, *Daylight* looks like a summer action spectacle that somehow got off course and was mixed in with the December releases by mistake. Stallone was smart enough to delay the release so *Daylight* would not be competing head-to-head with *Ransom,* another misplaced summer film.

Stallone's recent efforts have ranged from the penny-dreadful to the Judge Dreddful, but *Daylight* is far better

AWARDS AND NOMINATIONS

Academy Awards 1996 Nominations: Best Sound Effects Editing

CREDITS

Kit Latura: Sylvester Stallone
Madelyne Thompson: Amy Brenneman
Roy Nord: Viggo Mortensen
Frank Kraft: Dan Hedaya
Steve Crighton: Jay O. Sanders
Sarah Crighton: Karen Young

Origin: USA
Released: 1996
Production: John Davis, Joseph M. Singer and David T. Friendly for a Davis Entertainment-Joseph M. Singer production; released by Universal
Direction: Rob Cohen
Screenplay: Leslie Bohem
Cinematography: David Eggby
Editing: Peter Amundson
Music: Randy Edelman
Production design: Benjamin Fernandez
Set decoration: Alberto Tosto
Costume design: Thomas Casterline, Isis Mussenden
Sound: Reinhard Stergar
Special effects: Kit West
Visual effects: Scott Farrar
MPAA rating: PG-13
Running Time: 115 minutes

than other recent outings such as *The Specialist* (1994). And though *Daylight* is mainly about splashy special-effects, the developing relationship between Kit and Madelyne is well acted and well-done. Amy Brenneman's would-be playwright Madelyne is one of the few characters in this picture who is taken beyond mere stereotyping. She risks her life by wrestling with a high-power voltage line so as to enable the convicts to escape from their wrecked van, and this demonstration of courage endears her to Kit. Her endurance matches his own. The actress has been twice nominated for Emmy Awards for her television work on "NYPD Blue," and she turns in an agreeable performance here.

At its far-fetched worst, the plot engineers a way out for Kit and Madelyne by having Kit plant an explosive charge in the tunnel roof. Blowing a hole in the roof causes everything and everyone in the tunnel to geyser up through the Hudson, saving the two of them. But Kit is knocked unconscious when he surfaces, and Madelyne saves him by swimming to his aid.

In other words, then, this is a different kind of Stallone hero and a more fallible one—strong and courageous, of course, but also sensitive and clearheaded. That's an improvement over the usual Stallone role, even if this picture has more to do with special-effects and stunting than with acting. Stallone has still managed to hold on to his superstar status even as his films fall short of superstar vehicles. There have been no sequels to *Demolition Man* or *Cliffhanger,* both made in 1993, nor will there be a sequel to *Daylight,* but Stallone has not been forced to share top billing. He is still strong enough to carry his own weight. Twenty years after *Rocky* he still commands $20 million per picture.

Having turned fifty, Stallone is entering a new mode. In *Daylight* Stallone seems to be outmachoed by Roy Nord, the sportswear executive who attempts to take charge of the situation without understanding anything about the tunnel system. Nord's reckless presumption leads only to his death, while Stallone's more moderate Kit is left to save the day. Rita Kempley of *The Washington Post* criticized the star, however, by pointing out that unlike Bruce Willis and Arnold Schwarzenegger, Stallone "can't help taking these ridiculous tales seriously." Consider, for example, as Janet Maslin did in *The New York Times,* Stallone's goofy speech that attempts to find "a lesson about heroism from the first person who ever ate an oyster." That's a truly odd paradigm. As Maslin also notes, Stallone has always fared better without dialogue.

Reviews of *Daylight* tended to be tepid. Several reviewers placed the film with the disaster genre without seeming to recognize that this was a better made disaster picture than the likes of *The Poseidon Adventure* (1972) or *The Towering Inferno* (1974). Stephen Hunter of the *Baltimore Sun* unfairly cracked jokes at the star's expense, while noting that Stallone had moved from the Rambo prototype to "a muscle-bound New Man, an Alan Alda in a Neanderthal's body." Desson Howe of *The Washington Post* described the film as "Die Hard in a Tunnel." Mike Clark made fun of Claire Bloom in *USA Today* for being in the film by raising an impertinent question: "Has anyone besides *Daylight/Limelight* co-star Bloom worked with both Stallone and Charles Chaplin?" Reviewers, in short, tended to dismiss *Daylight* as merely a latter-day variation of a tired old genre that had peaked during the 1970s, but as an action-adventure vehicle, the film in fact is not inferior to most of what comes along. What it attempts to do it does very well.

—James M. Welsh

REVIEWS

The Baltimore Sun. December 6, 1996, p. El.
Chicago Tribune. December 6, 1996, p. 4.
Entertainment Weekly. December 6, 1996, p. 43.
The New York Times. December 6, 1996, p. C23.
People. December 9, 1996, p. 25.
USA Today. December 6, 1996, p. D7.
Variety. December 2, 1996, p.67.
The Washington Post. December 6, 1996, p. Dl.
Washington Post Weekend. December 6, 1996, p. 50.
Washington Times Metropolitan Times. December 6, 1996, p. C17.

Dead Man

"One of the most exciting pictures of the year for moviegoers who like a touch of the unexpected."—David Sterritt, *Christian Science Monitor*

"Jim Jarmusch's most ambitious picture to date. Like no western the screen has seen before."—Kevin Lally, *Film Journal*

"Mysterious! Daring!"—David Ansen, *Newsweek*

Box Office: $1,037,847

Jim Jarmusch experiments with a genre new to him in *Dead Man*, a moody western that takes the viewer on a slow, no, a crawling journey, through an apocalyptic Old West setting. Jarmusch puts his completely unique touch on the western—a touch that will entrance some while bore others to tears. For those already initiated in the Jarmusch school of filmmaking, *Dead Man* will probably make more sense and, more importantly, hold one's interest. For the uninitiated, be prepared for bizarre characters spewing equally bizarre dialogue and very heavy allegory. Some viewers will applaud Jarmusch's approach of showing more than telling, however, others may find themselves annoyed by symbolism so overt, it leaves nothing for interpretation.

Dead Man is the story of a young man's transformation, one that is forced upon him by his environment. It is a classic tale of a stranger in a strange land, and the stranger is William Blake (Johnny Depp). The film opens with Blake on a train heading from Cleveland to the western frontier for a job which he has been promised. Blake clearly looks out of place in his checkered suit, floppy bow tie, and small, round eyeglasses among the hide-covered, grimy outlaw types and the spooked, desperate-looking families. During the first few minutes of the film, Jarmusch uses frequent fade-out shots of Blake and fellow passengers, eerie Neil Young guitar resonance, and no dialogue whatsoever to establish an uncomfortable mood. With every fade-out, the passengers are different and the landscape shifts from natural beauty to man-made decay. At one point, scraggly nomads randomly shoot buffalo from the train as Blake jumps and writhes in his seat. Jarmusch seems to be illustrating that regardless of what kind of white man comes West, they all bring senseless violence, destruction and decay.

Crispin Glover appears next as the train's soot-covered coalman who sits across from Blake, and in his best "way out there" stare offers a chilling prophecy of what awaits Blake. When Blake states that he's headed to Machine for a job, Glover analogizes all too obviously that the town is "the end of the line," and that he wouldn't trust a piece of paper promising a job. Upon arriving in Machine, Blake sees that it truly is the hell that Glover described, piles of bones and skulls sharing the streets with seedy gunmen and gaunt townsfolk. The town seems to subsist on Dickinson Metalworks, the company where Blake is to work as an accountant. As he makes his way through the town and then the factory, Blake makes eye contact with the wrong people and bumps into everyone else. Again, it is obvious that he doesn't belong. He finally reaches the office where his progress is once more halted by a sneering office manager (John Hurt). He bluntly tells Blake that his position has been filled and offers no explanation or option. Blake insists on speaking with the owner,

AWARDS AND NOMINATIONS

Independent Spirit Awards 1997 Nominations: Feature Film, Supporting Actor, (Farmer), Screenplay (Jarmusch), Cinematography (Muller)

National Society of Film Critics 1996: Cinematography (Muller)

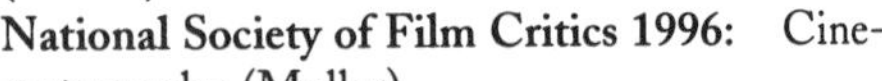

New York Film Critics Circle 1996: Best Cinematography (Muller)

CREDITS

William Blake: Johnny Depp
Nobody: Gary Farmer
Cole Wilson: Lance Henriksen
Conway Twill: Michael Wincott
Thel Russell: Mili Avital
The Fireman: Crispin Glover
Salvatore Jenko: Iggy Pop
Big George Drakoulious: Billy Bob Thornton
Benmont Tench: Jared Harris
Charlie Dickinson: Gabriel Byrne
John Scholfield: John Hurt
John Dickinson: Robert Mitchum
Johnny Pickett: Eugene Byrd

Origin: USA
Released: 1995
Production: Demetra J. MacBride for a 12 Gauge production; released by Miramax Films
Direction: Jim Jarmusch
Screenplay: Jim Jarmusch
Cinematography: Robby Muller
Editing: Jay Rabinowitz
Music: Neil Young
Costumes: Marit Allen
Production design: Bob Ziembicki
Casting: Ellen Lewis, Laura Rosenthal
MPAA rating: R
Running Time: 121 minutes

John Dickinson (Robert Mitchum in a bad wig), who orders Blake out of his office at gunpoint.

As if calling the town 'Machine' wasn't obvious enough, the fact that it's dominated by a grimy, steam-spewing "metalworks" further attests to the lack of subtlety with which Jarmusch pummels the viewer. The "industrialization is bad" and "white man is evil" messages come through loud and clear.

"That weapon will replace your tongue. Your poetry will be written in blood."—Nobody about Blake's gun

Stranded with just a few coins in his pocket, Blake shuffles into a bar where he is again stared at, and spends his last dime on a pint of whiskey. An attractive young woman (Mili Avital) trying to sell flowers is thrown out of the bar into the mud as Blake numbly watches. Remembering himself, and possibly seeing someone with whom he can relate, he goes over to help her. She takes him back to her modest rented room which is strewn with paper flowers she has made. Before long they're looking deeply into each other's eyes, and then end up in bed. Credit goes to Jarmusch for sparing us the gratuitous groping and skin shots of standard Hollywood fare. While lying in bed, the woman's distraught former boyfriend, Charlie Dickinson, (a waste of Gabriel Byrne in this brief scene) son of John Dickinson, barges in. Seeing her in bed with this stranger, he pulls out his revolver and kills the woman as the bullet passes through her and into Blake's chest. Blake fires at Charlie, missing him twice from no more than 12 feet, before finally killing him. Blake climbs out the window and rides off on Charlie's horse, leaving the two dead bodies behind. Just as it seems he has found solace, trouble again finds poor William, and due to circumstances beyond his control, his life takes another turn for the worse.

Next we see a rotund Indian (Gary Farmer) hovering over Blake who is lying on the ground with a bloody chest wound. As the Indian tries to dig out the bullet he comments that Blake has caught some of white man's metal and then disgustedly grunts, "stupid f—-ing white man." With the introduction of the Indian the film takes on a different tone. It becomes introspective as it focuses more on Blake's personal transformation as a result of being hunted instead of the transformation of the West in general. However, Blake's metamorphosis is still very representative of that of the western frontier.

The Indian dresses Blake's wound and guides him westward. As they travel and talk, the Indian asks Blake his name. When Blake tells him, the Indian mistakenly believes that he is the poet William Blake. The wounded Blake doesn't even know who the Indian is talking about, but eventually goes along with the misconception. The Indian in turn tells Blake his story, and it turns out that he too was once a stranger in a strange land. His parents were from different tribes and as a result, he was not accepted and exiled. He was captured by white men and was paraded around from city to city as a savage in a cage. Eventually he learned the ways of the white man and was educated in schools where he became familiar with the poetry of William Blake. After many years, he returned to his native land but his stories of travel proved too fantastic for his native brothers and he was again cast off. This is the reason behind the name he has given himself—Nobody.

Nobody becomes Blake's guide in this hostile land. Not only is Nobody guiding Blake through the forests and mountains, he is also leading Blake on a journey to the spirit world. Through their travels, they encounter an assortment of bizarre characters, including Iggy Pop, Billy Bob Thornton and Jared Harris as wayward frontiersmen. Meanwhile, Dickinson has hired three killers and put out a bounty on Blake. With every encounter, Blake spills more blood and continues his transformation into a cold-blooded killer. He stumbles onto two Marshals who were pursuing him and before killing them asks if they've heard of his poetry. Blake sees himself becoming something different but is trapped in a kill or be killed world. At a trading post near a river, Blake and Nobody try to swap for a canoe, but the missionary trader recognizes Blake and is gunned down. As Blake sits on the canoe near the river's edge he is shot from behind. He manages to kill his assailant but as Nobody puts it, has found more of white man's metal. Nobody takes a semi-conscious Blake downstream to an Indian village where he is to prepare for the final leg of his journey. A local woodworker makes a special canoe for Blake, one that will take him to the spirit world. Nobody prepares the canoe and pushes Blake off from the shore into the ocean. Barely conscious, Blake lifts his head just enough to see the last remaining hired gun (Lance Henrikson) shoot Nobody who returns a mortal shot as he drops. Blake drifts off into the ocean against a brightly shining sun, his journey at its end.

In a literal sense, Jarmusch has taken us on a slow albeit beautiful trip through the western frontier. It's no secret that the West was a harsh place and Jarmusch has chosen to focus on its brutality. But was the West a more peaceful, self-sufficient place before the white man arrived? Did the white man's industrialization ruin the natural beauty of the frontier and the balance of life between its native peoples and creatures? Jarmusch, as many others have and rightly so, seems to be saying 'yes.' And always the nonconformist, Jarmusch has chosen to use *a* white man to illustrate what *the* white men did to the West. Blake was transformed into a brutal killer by the violent world in which he entered, a world that the white man created. This is a wonderful story that delivers a powerful message. The only question is: did Jarmusch rely more on style than substance?

—*Christopher Scanlon*

REVIEWS

Entertainment Weekly. May 17, 1996, p. 42.
New York Times. May 10, 1996, p. C3.
Newsweek. June 3, 1996, p. 75.

Dear God

Many people write to God. Somebody is answering.—Movie tagline

"A funny, feel-good 10! A heart-warming family comedy that's heaven sent for the holiday season."—Susan Granger, *CRN International*

"Fresh and funny and marvelously performed!"—Jane Horowitz, *The Washington Post*

Box Office: $7,114,089

Con man and gambler Tom Turner (Greg Kinnear) is no more inclined to work a nine-to-five job than this movie, *Dear God,* is to have a competent ending. In this first entry into the holiday film rush, director Garry Marshall offers us plenty of feel-good characters and even some Christmas decorations, but the result is a bit of fluff with a flat conclusion.

At the start of the film, Tom Turner finds himself faced with a $1,000 gambling debt and threats of bodily harm if he doesn't pay up. So he turns to the only means of earning a living he seems to know, conning people. He pretends to be a burn victim to get cab fare, he invents a sick son to get money from a nun's collection pot, and even tries to sell bogus airline tickets to a pair of foreign visitors. Unfortunately for Tom, those foreign visitors are really undercover cops. Now Tom must use his honey-tongue and quick wits to con the judge (Larry Miller) out of putting him in jail. And it works. But the judge passes down what may be an even more severe punishment . . . Tom must get a job and hold it for a year.

Tom now calls on a relative who is a police officer at the Los Angeles Post Office for help. As a result, Tom is given a temporary holiday job in the Dead Letter Office. There Tom finds himself working alongside an eclectic group of oddballs and eccentrics: Rebecca Frazen (Laurie Metcalf) is a workaholic ex-lawyer whose facial tics belie a few personality disorders, Herman Dooley (Tim Conway) used to deliver the mail until he bit a dog, Claudio "Handsome" Gomez spends his shift watching soap operas, Lucille Barnett (Anna Maria Horsford) seems to do nothing but knit afghans, and Idris Abraham (Roscoe Lee Browne) is a frustrated musician who's just trying to stay out of trouble for the two months before he retires. In the DLO, Tom and his new cohorts are supposed to find homes for letters and packages that seem undeliverable, but the most common homes are bins of no return with labels like "Santa," "Elvis," "Easter Bunny," "Tooth Fairy," "Superman," and even "God."

At the same time that Tom's life takes this sober turn, he also meets an eligible divorcee, Gloria McKinney (Maria Pitillo), who works at a local bookstore/cafe where she comes up with imaginative menus like "Pride and Pot Roast" and "For Whom the Cinnamon Rolls." He is attracted to her, but she has a son who keeps waiting for his father to return, and she is aware of Tom's disreputable history.

Then one day Tom accidentally reads one of the letters sent to God. In it a woman named Marguerite (Ellen Cleghorne) writes of her run-down apartment and the tenants' rent strike. Not long afterward two events transpire to allow "God" to answer her letter. First Tom gets a paycheck, and then he discovers unclaimed packages whose contents—

CREDITS

Tom Turner: Greg Kinnear
Rebecca Frazen: Laurie Metcalf
Gloria McKinney: Maris Pitillo
Herman Dooly: Tim Conway
Vladek Vidov: Hector Elizondo
Idris Abraham: Roscoe Lee Browne
Handsome: Jon Seda
Lucille Barnett: Anna Maria Horsford
Whispering Wendy: Kathleen Marshall
Webster: Donal Logue
Judge Kits Van Heynigan: Nancy Marchand
State Judge: Larry Miller
Mom Turner: Rue McClanahan
Minister: Toby Huss
Jemi: Jack Klugman
Preston Sweney: Garry Marshall
Cousin Guy: Timothy Stack
Marguerite: Ellen Cleghorne

Origin: USA
Released: 1996
Production: Steve Tisch for a Rysher Entertainment production; released by Paramount Pictures
Direction: Garry Marshall
Screenplay: Warren Leight and Ed Kaplan
Cinematography: Charles Minsky
Editing: Debra Neil-Fisher
Production design: Albert Brenner
Art direction: Gregory Bolton
Set decoration: Garrett Lewis
Costume design: Deborah Hopper
Music: Jeremy Lubbock and James Patrick Dunne
MPAA rating: PG
Running Time: 112 minutes

such as jewelry—he hopes to pawn. When he is approached by his supervisor, Vladek Vidov (Hector Elizondo), Tom hastily addresses a large envelope to Marguerite and stuffs into it the jewelry he's trying to hide . . . along with his own paycheck.

Tom desperately tries to get his paycheck back, but when he shows up at Marguerite's apartment, his glibness and wit fail him, and he can't quite bring himself to reclaim it. But wouldn't ya' know it, helping the tenants with their rent strike is Rebecca who is doing pro bono work. She mistakes Tom's reluctance as an act of benevolence. Now she wants to help him in what she feels is his intentional quest to answer God's mail.

"I care about myself. Everything else is an act."—Tom

Tom tries to put Rebecca off, so she attempts to do good deeds on her own. But for her first attempt—to give a terminally ill girl her fondest dream of riding a horse—she ends up paying instead for a seedy donkey. Luckily Tom is passing by, and with his gambling connections at the local racetrack, he manages to realize the girl's wish.

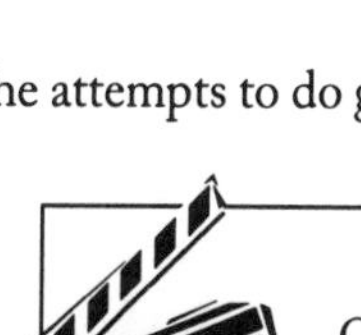

O.J. prosecutor Christopher Darden has a cameo as a TV commentator.

It doesn't take long before more post office employees begin answering God's mail, and Tom is swept along with them. They babysit for a mother with twins who really needs a night to herself, they clean the house of a hotel maid who's too burned out to clean her own home, and they save the life of Jimmy (Jack Klugman) who is bent on suicide and even manage to match him up with Tom's blind mother (Rue McClanahan).

Typical of a feel-good movie, it doesn't take long before there are more acts of goodness being performed in LA than the postal God Squad could possibly be performing. It appears that kindness and generosity are contagious. But we need conflict, so it is determined that opening mail, even if it is addressed to God, is a felony. Now Tom is back before a judge, and facing stiffer penalties than ever.

It is no overstatement to say that the best part of *Dear God* is its actors. Kinnear easily pulls off a kind of innocent smarminess at the start which makes it easy to see the expected heart of gold underneath. He is charming and likeable and we root for him to overcome his "evil" side and even to win the heart of the divorcee we know will help him to go straight.

The supporting cast is also a plus for the film. From Conway to Elizondo, they all know how to take what are essentially bit parts and turn them into effectively eccentric and endearing cameos.

But despite the casts' best efforts, they can't save the film. Director Garry Marshall too often goes for the too sweet situation, the easy sightgag, the unimaginative and predictable storyline, and most of all, an ending that defies logic and law just to make everyone happy.

What's left is a charming and easygoing leading man, a whimsically amusing supporting cast, a few smiles, a good heart, and a lousy ending in which the writers fell asleep at the wheel, drove the script through a courtroom and crashed into an empty finale.

—Beverley Bare Buehrer

REVIEWS

Boxoffice Online. November 1, 1996.
Chicago Sun Times. November 1, 1996.
Chicago Tribune. November 1, 1996, p. 5.
Detroit News. November 1, 1996, p. 3E.
Entertainment Weekly. November 15, 1996, p. 51.
Los Angeles Times. November 1, 1996, P. F8.
New York Times. November 1, 1996, p. C20.
USA Today. November 1, 1996, p. 4D.
Variety. October 28, 1996, p. 65.

Denise Calls Up

"The first true comedy about call waiting!"—Rene Rodriguez, *Miami Herald*

"Delectable! Fine, funny . . . an entire comedy around close encounters of the electronic kind! Delightful ingenuity!"—Janet Maslin, *New York Times*

"A solidly entertaining movie!"—Jack Mathews, *Newsday*

"A smart, funny, original film! Marvelous!"—Dennis Dermody, *Paper Magazine*

"Wildly funny! Inspired comic originality!"—Barbara and Scott Siegel, *Siegel Entertainment Syndicate*

Box Office: $148,121

In *Denise Calls Up,* two erstwhile lovers Frank (Tim Daly) and Gale (Dana Wheeler Nicholson) team up to arrange a blind date between their two romance-averse friends, Jerry (Liev Schrieber) and Barbara (Caroleen Feeney. Meanwhile, a pregnant Denise (Alanna Ubach) tracks down Martin (Dan Gunther) who supplied her sperm bank donation. The catch is that all this "action" takes place on the phone. These Generation-X hopefuls never seem to step out of their apartments. They are wired to their phones and computers, chary of real human contact, complaining they have no time but actually scared to death of flesh-to-flesh encounters. Instead, they inhabit the world of virtual reality—one couple actually consummating their "affair" on the phone. It is not so much phone sex as the erotics of electronic media.

Writer/director Hal Salwen does a creditable job of filming these talking figures—in bed with their computers and phones, walking around and taking to speakerphones, wearing the latest headgear that makes one of them look like a telephone operator. In fact, they all look like telephone "operators," talking about getting a life rather than actually having one. It is an amusing conceit that is wisely limited to 79 minutes running time. The constant switching from one apartment to another—occasional outside shots, and the tragic/ludicrous death of one of the phonemates, keeps the film moving in soap opera fashion.

But these characters are so afraid of commitment that it is difficult not to have contempt for them. They live in risk-free environments, in which the worse thing to contemplate is whether or not a caller has purposely hung up or has been the victim of a disconnection. With their only connection via phone lines, no wonder a disconnect is taken as a terrible blow. "Call waiting" is not an option or a convenience, but rather the way they manage their lives. When they say hold on, they are really holding on for their lives. Life is a complex of conversations, put on hold, resumed, transferred, and even turned into a conference call as Denise is wheeled, phone-to-face, into the operating room to have her baby.

The most active character is Denise. She is constantly on the phone, but she is also in motion—calling from almost exclusively outside locations. She may have had a baby via the sperm bank, but now she hankers after a real-life father for her baby. Martin is scared at the prospect of meeting Denise, but her constant calls suck him into her life, and he gets on the phone with all his friends to get them involved as well. Martin is also terribly excited about becoming a father and wants to know how to respond. This is pathetic, of course. A grown man has to call his friends to figure out how he should respond to becoming a father? But then the whole point of his sperm bank donation is that he could count on not being involved.

Debut for writer/director Hal Salwen, who shot the film in New York City in 23 days.

CREDITS

Frank: Tim Daly
Gale: Dana Wheeler Nicholson
Barbara: Caroleen Feeney
Jerry: Liev Schreiber
Martin: Dan Gunther
Linda: Aida Turturro

Origin: USA
Released: 1995
Production: J. Todd Harris for a Davis Entertainment, Skyline Entertainment Partners and Dark Matter productions; released by Sony Classic Pictures
Direction: Hal Salwen
Screenplay: Hal Salwen
Cinematography: Mike Mayers
Editing: Gary Sharfin
Production design: Susan Bolles
Costume design: Edi Giguere
Casting: Sheila Jaffe, Georgianne Walken
Music: Lynn Geller
MPAA rating: Unrated
Running Time: 80 minutes

Quite fittingly in a film about characters who live and die by the phone, Barbara dies in a car accident while talking on the phone. Why should it be Barbara of all the characters who dies? Well, she is so busy getting other people together that she becomes a fixture in their lives, and her death neatly integrates their diverse personalities as they come to terms with her sudden and shocking departure.

All these phone addicts promise to attend parties and to meet each other, but they never seem to make it out the door. It's dangerous out there—as Barbara's death confirms. But at least she has died, phone in hand, the sounds of her fatal accident echoing in her friend's phone.

In this first-ever phone-farce, Salwen shows a knack for catching the current cant, even though his characters are really caricatures. As one reviewer puts it, *Denise Calls Up* is a one-joke movie, but a pretty good one at that, redeemed by shrewd editing and an overall technical virtuosity remarkable in a low-budget production. And Denise herself performs a service, for the denouement of the film shows that her phoning Martin has indeed proved to be his wake-up call. For at least one couple, there will be a life not solely attached to a phoneline.

—Carl Rollyson

REVIEWS

The Hollywood Reporter. March 7, 1995, p. 10.
Los Angeles Times. April 12, 1996, p. F10.
The New Republic. May 6, 1996, p. 25.
New York Times. March 27, 1996, p. C15.
Variety. March 13, 1995, p. 52.

Diabolique

Two women. One man. The combination can be murder.—Movie tagline

"A stunning, tantalizing, triumphant thriller."—Jules Peimer, *KNX Radio*

"A suspense thriller with a wonderful touch of humor."—Jim Ferguson, *Prevue Channel*

"Thoroughly entertaining."—Jeff Craig, *Sixty Second Preview*

"Unpredictable, chilling."—Bill Klein, *WHEC-TV*

Box Office: $17,100,266

Diabolique is a remake of a 1955 film starring Simone Signoret. The plot remains the same: the mistress of a schoolmaster and his wife contrive an elaborate plan to murder him. Director Jeremiah Chechnik (*Benny and Joon*) has not been able to better the scary original, directed with extraordinary panache by Henri-George Clouzot, but he does evoke the ambiguities of contemporary sexuality in the tortured triangle of husband/wife/mistress. Just who is in love with who remains part of the mystery—as does who are the real partners in crime. It is difficult to describe the plot without giving away its ending.

Mia: "Am I alive?"
Nicole: "No, you are dead, this is heaven, and I am the Virgin Mary."

Chazz Palminteri plays Dr. Baran, the school's authoritarian headmaster. He is cruel and confidant of his ability to dominate his pupils in this all male school and his wife and mistress. No one is allowed to leave the dining room until they eat the slop (it literally looks like a glutinous mess)—and that includes his neurasthenic wife, played by the fey Isabelle Adjani. The school is actually hers, but through marriage Baran has assumed ownership. She is sexually enthralled even as she yearns to separate from him. A former nun, her attraction to this dark man is almost a form of devil worship. When she seems to die at the beginning of the film, having passed out on the floor—a victim of her heart condition—he simply stands over her, observing, as if waiting for her to die. Her "heart failure" is, in other words, symbolic of her inability to deal with her conflicting feelings, which literally threaten to murder her.

Baran sneers at his wife because she wants him so badly and does not have the strength to resist him. His staff and students are cowed, and like the dictator of a small country, Baran has a film crew shooting a promotional feature for the school, creating a story that is merely the projection of his domineering personality.

The heavy-handed, Gothic, atmospherics of Baran's fiefdom are necessary in order to make credible the Byzantine plans of his wife and mistress, who go out of the way to find a complicated way of murdering him. The film's star is tough talking Sharon Stone. She teaches at the school and likes her sex with Baran, but she realizes that he is a brute, and she hates him for the way he dominates everyone. All her life, it seems, she has been up against such tyrants, and the only way to get rid of them, she assures Baran's wife, is to kill him. Baran won't give up the school, and he knows his two women will not renounce him so long as he is there to control them.

But of course Baran's tyranny is precisely what unites the women against him. And it is what also motivates the police detective, Shirley Vogel (Kathy Bates), who shows up after the crime to investigate. She knows all about cruel men and seems to divine what the women have done without saying so. She is the plain, wider-framed version of Sharon Stone. The women are remarkably alike for all their physical differences. Both have the sharpness and wit of Barbara Stanwyck, which inevitably leads to comparisons with the Billy Wilder classic, *Double Indemnity,* in which Stanwyck and Fred MacMurray plot to murder her husband for the insurance money. The difference here, in the 1990s, is that a film can be about the attraction of two women for each other—as well as for a man. This is not a film about two lesbians, but it is bisexual in its implications. If Bates presents herself as a woman who has personally suffered the abuse of men, she is also a detective using the typical methods of male cops.

The most memorable performance, however, belongs to Stone. As reviewer David Denby remarks, she is the "wickedest, most beautiful witch in the movies." Indeed, her icy blonde features are reminiscent of Stone's breakthrough film, *Basic Instinct,* in which she was perfectly cast as a beautiful, bisexual murder suspect. Stone is now in Stanwyck's league. She is unforgettable—facing the hard-nosed Bates, who has just tried to discompose her by revealing that she knows Stone has been having an affair with Baran. What little boy or teacher revealed that bit of news to Bates? Stone asks sarcastically. Or did the detective learn about the affair in the school brochure?

—Carl Rollyson

CREDITS

Nicole Horner: Sharon Stone
Mia Baran: Isabelle Adjani
Guy Baran: Chazz Palminteri
Shirley Vogel: Kathy Bates
Simon Veatch: Spalding Gray
Edie Pretzer: Adam Hann-Byrd

Origin: USA
Released: 1996
Production: Marvin Worth and James G. Robinson for a Morgan Creek and ABC production; released by Warner Brothers
Direction: Jeremiah Chechik
Screenplay: Don Roos; based on the novel *Celle Qui N'Etait Plus* by Pierre Boileau and Thomas Narcejac and the film *Diabolique* (1955) by Henri-Georges Clouzet
Cinematography: Peter James
Editing: Carol Littleton
Production design/second-unit director: Leslie Dilley
Art direction: Dennis Bridges
Set decoration: Michael Seirton
Sound: Dennis Maitland
Assistant director: K.C. Colwell
Music: Randy Edelman
MPAA rating: R
Running Time: 107 minutes

REVIEWS

Boxoffice. February, 1996, p. 20.
Chicago Tribune. March 22, 1996, p. 4.
Detroit News. March 22, 1996, p. D1.
Entertainment Weekly. March 29, 1996, p. 44.
Los Angeles Times. March 22, 1996, p. F1.
Newsweek. April 1, 1996, p. 70.
USA Today. March 22, 1996, p. 4D.
Variety. March 18, 1996, p. 46.

Don't Be a Menace to South Central While Drinking Your Juice in the Hood

Finally, the movie that proves that Justice isn't always Poetic, Jungle Fever isn't always pretty and Higher Learning can be a waste of time.—Movie tagline

"Funny! A lot of big laughs."—Bruce Fretts, *Entertainment Weekly*

Box Office: $20,109,115

Giving your contemporaries a good-natured ribbing has never been a problem with the filmmaking community. Letting your associates know that they might be taking themselves a little too seriously, is not only fun to do, but from time to time, very necessary. Self-deprecating humor keeps moviemakers (relatively) humble, honest and on an even keel. But as easy at it may look, satire is extremely hard to pull off successfully.

"Sorry, baby. You know there are no positive female role models in movies like these."—Ashtray's mom to her son after he's asked if he'll see her again

The producer of the lengthy titled *Don't Be a Menace to South Central While Drinking Your Juice in the Hood* is Keenen Ivory Wayans. He was also the originator, producer, writer and virtual full-time director of the controversial and groundbreaking Fox television series "In Living Color." It resembled a predecessor, the similar "Saturday Night Live" in presentation, delivery and attitude. SNL producer Lorne Michaels and many of his not-ready-for-prime-time-players, which featured fellow "National Lampoon" alumni John Belushi and Chevy Chase, made those first few seasons liberating and truly unforgettable. Shortly after it started, the show began losing its cutting edge, but still plods onward, a mere shadow of its former self.

Wayans led a similar group, which included current wunderkind Jim Carrey through five plus seasons of uproarious, ill-mannered, in-your-face satire that took no prisoners. With the help of the (self-proclaimed) "token Caucasian" Carrey, they did what no predominantly white cast would dare do: mock-up, send-up and make fun of black issues almost exclusively. Wayans led a group that stayed relatively intact for the duration of the program that also highlighted many of his siblings. Sister Kim and brother Damon were standouts with the latter going on to his own big screen success. The two youngest children of the Wayans family (ten in all), brothers Marlon and Shawn, joined the program towards the end of its reign.

Marlon and Shawn wrote the script and took the two leads in *Menace.* Shawn plays Ashtray (a take on the overused name Tre) and Marlon is Loc Dog (a not so subtle attack on Snoop Doggy Dog). Writing and starring in their first motion picture was a huge project to take on and the boys were wise to enlist the help of their big brother. Keenen wrote, produced and directed the 1988 effort, *I'm Gonna Git You, Sucka,* a dead-on mimicking of the "blaxploitation" action films from the '60's and '70's. Many stars of those films (Jim Brown, Bernie Casey and Isaac Hayes) resurface in Wayans' film.

They were also smart to seek out director Paris Barclay, whose background started with a B.A. in English and American Literature from Harvard. In 1991, he received the MTV award for Best Director in the Black/Rap category. Directing video in its short form, is at the top of the list of reasons why *Menace,* his first feature, works so

CREDITS

Ashtray: Shawn Wayans
Loc Dog: Marlon Wayans
Dashiki: Tracey Cherelle Jones
Preach: Chris Spencer
Crazy Legs: Suli McCullough
Toothpick: Darrell Heath

Origin: USA
Released: 1996
Production: Keenen Ivory Wayans and Eric L. Gold for an Ivory Way and Island Pictures production; released by Miramax
Direction: Paris Barclay
Screenplay: Shawn Wayans, Marlon Wayans and Phil Beauman
Cinematography: Russ Brandt
Editing: William Young and Marshall Harvey
Production design: Aaron Osborne
Art direction: Reiko Kobayashi
Costume: Valari Adams
Sound: Dave Eichhorn
Casting: Robi Reed-Humes, Tony Lee, Andrea Reed
Music: John Barnes
MPAA rating: R
Running Time: 88 minutes

well. Parodies from the *Airplane!* series to *Naked Gun* and *Hot Shots!* all rely a great deal on well-linked short scenes. Keeping the film moving at a quick snap is essential. Losing momentum is certain death and well executed timing gives these, and others films like it, their believability. Looking like the real article they're imitating is one thing. Duplicating the rhythm is more toilsome.

Marlon and Shawn Wayans both wrote and star in the film while older brother Keenen Ivory has a cameo role and served as producer.

The story begins with Ashtray visiting his long lost father, played by Lahmard Tate, whose brother Larenz took the lead in two Hughes Brothers films, *Menace II Society* and *Dead Presidents.* Getting too much of an earful from his father (who is played up as being younger than his own son), he looks up his old friend, Loc Dog, who keeps his face contorted with a twisted sneer throughout the length of the film. Marlon is Lewis to Shawn's Martin. His first obvious swipe is at hairstyles. Large braids held together with pacifiers and car antennas and other assorted fasteners that are switched and augmented from scene to scene. Instead of picking out a pair from his voluminous selection of athletic shoes, he opts for a warm, fuzzy pair of rabbit slippers. No less than a half dozen beepers round out Loc Dog's haphazard fashion statement.

While attending a party for Toothpick, a recently released convict, Ashtray falls for Dashiki (Tracey Cherelle Jones), the mother of a veritable United Nations of ethnically diverse children. Warned by everyone to stay away, Ashtray overlooks her tainted history and appears willing to be not only a husband but also a father to her brood.

The dialogue is mercifully short on four letter words and the stereotypical black references. However, there's still enough here to offend. Simultaneously laughing at and scowling with disapproval of what you see and hear is entirely possible, which is almost assuredly the Wayans' point. Several other ghetto cliches (malt liquor, automatic weapons, sexual practices) are handled with the same get-over-yourself frankness, which show that no one involved is showing any favoritism. Even while lampooning these many 'hood films, it's obvious the Wayans family is still moved by their original intent. So much so that Keenen's cameo role of a local mailman, is given just one word of dialogue, repeated a handful of times: "Message." Strategically placed to accentuate a particular point, the makers of the movie want to make sure that you learn something along the way.

—J.M. Clark

REVIEWS

Boxoffice Magazine. March, 1996, p. R-28.
Detroit Free Press. January 14, 1996, p. 2F.
Entertainment Weekly. January 26, 1996, p. 40.
The Hollywood Reporter. January 16, 1996, p. 11.
Los Angeles Times. January 13, 1996, p. F2.
New York Times. January 13, 1996, p. 21.
USA Today. January 15, 1996, p. 4D.
Variety. January 15, 1996, p. 126.

Down Periscope

A rusty sub. A rebel commander. A renegade crew. When destiny called, they should have hung up.—Movie tagline

"Good-natured, amusing . . . heart-warming."—Ralph Novak, *People*

"A hilarious ride with Kelsey and his crew of misfits."—Jim Ferguson, *Prevue Channel*

Box Office: $25,809,652

Let's see, where have we seen this story before? A group of misfits have been assigned to a leader whose career someone wants to sabotage. However, instead of failing, the outcasts rise to the occasion, pull together, and by approaching their challenges with unorthodox methods, save their leader and themselves. Could this be the army tale *Stripes* (1981)? The baseball comedy *Major League* (1989)? Or maybe that homage to the patrolman, *Police Academy* (1984)? No, it's a tribute to our naval forces, *Down Periscope.* The fact that it was written by Hugh Wilson, who wrote *Police Academy* and directed by David Ward, who also directed *Major League* (both I and II), I suppose, is nothing more than coincidence.

So, it would seem that *Down Periscope* is nothing more than a typical entry in a particular comedy style we have come to know and (maybe) love. However, that doesn't mean it can't be good at what it's supposed to be. The question becomes, how well does the film hit the mark? And, in this literal and figurative comedy "sub" genre, *Down Periscope*'s torpedoes are on target.

We're not talking sophisticated comedy here. We're not even talking about hilarious comedy. *Down Periscope* is more of a sweet comedy. It never tries to be more than it is: good-natured, inoffensive, and silly.

The premise here is that Tom Dodge (Kelsey Grammer) is up for promotion for the third time. If he is not given a command his twenty-year career in the navy is over. Dodge is undeniably capable, third in his class in sub school and even receiving a citation for tactical excellence in a NATO exercise, however, Dodge is a bit of a maverick. In fact, the first time we see him, he is golfing from the deck of a submarine onto an onshore greens. One of those who seems determined to sink Tom's career is Admiral Graham (Bruce Dern) who bristles at even the mention of his name. However, another Admiral, Admiral Winslow (Rip Torn), has a special command and a special mission in mind for Tom and offers him a command of his own.

With the Cold War over, the US Navy is concerned that the old Soviet Union, in an attempt to raise much-needed money, is selling its old diesel-powered submarines to renegade countries. With our navy being geared to fight other high-tech subs, what damage might these lower-tech fighting machines do in the hands of our enemies? That is the mission given to Tom Dodge, to somehow slip through our defensive lines, especially past his old ship the Orlando, and sneak into Charleston harbor.

To perform this task, Dodge is given command of the USS Stingray, a recommissioned diesel sub which he immediately renames "the wonderful world of corrosion," and of which his second in command, Marty Pascal (Rob Schneider) later says, "the only thing holding it together is bird droppings." But the rusty wreck is only the beginning of Dodge's disadvantages during the proposed war game. Determined to

CREDITS

Tom Dodge: Kelsey Grammer
Emily: Lauren Holly
Marty Pascal: Rob Schneider
Howard: Harry Dean Stanton
Admiral Graham: Bruce Dern
Captain Knox: William H. Macy
Buckman: Ken Hudson Campbell
Nitro: Toby Huss
Jackson: Duane Martin
Spots: Jonathan Penner
Stepanak: Bradford Tatum
Sonar: Harland Williams
Admiral Winslow: Rip Torn

Origin: USA
Released: 1996
Production: Robert Lawrence; released by Twentieth Century Fox
Direction: David S. Ward
Screenplay: Hugh Wilson, Andrew Kurtzman, Eliot Wald
Cinematography: Victor Hammer
Editing: William Anderson, Armen Minasian
Production design: Michael Corenblith
Art direction: Dan Webster
Set decoration: Mickey S. Michaels
Costume design: Luke Reichle
Music: Randy Edelman
MPAA rating: PG-13
Running Time: 100 minutes

cause him to fail, Graham has assigned Dodge the most unlikely group of misfits ever to board a boat. Executive Officer Pascal is so hyper, by-the-book and even mean-spirited that the crew will eventually dress up as pirates and make him walk the plank; radar man "Sonar" Lovacelli (Harland Williams) can tell to the exact coin what change has been dropped on the floor of the ship he is listening to; the unappetizing, overweight cook, Seaman Buckman (Ken Hudson Campbell) thinks nothing of dropping cigar ashes, bandages and fingernails into the chow; radio-man Nitro (Toby Huss) often uses his own body as a connecting wire for the ship's communications systems; and engineer Howard (Harry Dean Stanton), who's old enough to have served on the Stingray during World War II, also knows the ship's machinery well enough to understand that whiskey thins down the diesel mix to give her another 50 RPMs. Rounding out the crew is dive officer Emily Lake (Lauren Holly) who, according to Graham, is part of a trial program to see how well women do in confined sub conditions.

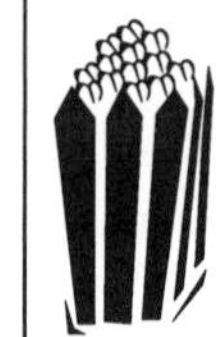

"Let's go with the bizarre and trashy. It's worked for us so far."—Spots

Standing in for the USS Stingray was the Pampanito, a 1943 diesel electric submarine used by the San Francisco-based National Maritime Museum Association as a tourist attraction docked at the Embarcadero.

So with the decks rusting and stacked against him, Dodge must now somehow get his crew into shipshape and prove himself worthy of command. Luckily, Dodge is not only as eccentric as his crew, he is also competent. He never comes down hard on them for their ineptitude, but rather forces them to use their own idiosyncrasies to rise to the challenge. When it seems as if they might have been detected by the Orlando, Dodge has a crewman climb to the top of the periscope, attach a light to it, and then raises it even though they are on the surface. By having the crew now make as much noise as possible (by singing "Louie, Louie") the Orlando sees the lit outline of a ship and believes it is listening in on the drunken crew of a fishing trawler. At another point when the Orlando's sonar may have picked them up, Dodge has Sonar make whale noises so that they think the Stingray is one of the submerged mammals.

Grammer, who plays Tom Dodge, is best known as an alumni of the television show *Cheers* who, when he gave up his stool at the bar, matriculated on to a show of his own where he plays the pretentious radio psychiatrist Frasier on the show of the same name. Here, Grammer makes his transition to the big screen using the best of his Frasier character to give Dodge a competent almost unflappable air, but then tempers it with a much more laid-back and low-key sense of foolishness. Frasier may take himself too seriously, but Tom Dodge has "welcome aboard" tattooed on his penis. Grammer manages to imbue Dodge with both standing and sedition. He is both leader and rebel, and these are just the qualities his "crew from hell" will respond to.

Despite Grammer's performance (which shows he has leading man potential on the big screen — but then, so too did Tom Selleck, and what happened to him?) and the solid comic bits from the backup players, *Down Periscope* is not great comedy. The only depth in this parody is that reached by the Stingray when it hides out on the bottom of the ocean to avoid Orlando sonar. *Down Periscope* also never reaches the lofty heights of humor required to set even silly films like *Airplane* (1980) apart in their genre. However, it is still dependable entertainment of the shallow and mindless kind. (Which is usually the kind many audiences are looking for, especially in the summer—*Down Periscope* was just released a bit too early in the season.) However, it is also one of the few films that can keep audiences in their seats during the closing credits. Who'd want to miss the disco-era Village People singing "In the Navy" while the cast lip-syncs along?

—Beverley Bare Buehrer

REVIEWS

Chicago Tribune. March 1, 1996, p. 5.
Entertainment Weekly. March 8, 1996.
Los Angeles Times. March 1, 1996, p. F6.
New York Times. March 1, 1996, p. C5.
USA Today. March 1, 1996, p. 6D.
Variety. March 3, 1996, p. 73.

Dragonheart

You will believe.—Movie tagline

"Awesome and inspiring."—Mike Katryez, *CFTO News*

"An epic filled with non-stop action and adventure. The special effects are a constellation of fun and magic. Don't miss it!"—Joanne Levenglick, *The Kids News Network*

"I loved the dragon! I loved the special effects! I loved the movie!"—Bob Healy, *KBIG, Satellite News*

Box Office: $51,385,101

Popular culture has a misconception about early English history, especially about King Arthur and the knights of the round table. The problem is, there never could have been "knights" in England before 1066 because it was a French "invention" that William the Conqueror brought with him to govern England after he subdued it. Consequently, there could have been no feudalism and no knights in shining armor in England before 1066. The Arthurian legend predates that year, and so does the pseudo-Arthurian story *Dragonheart* which takes place in 984 (and twelve years later (996). And while historians will be glad that at least the film's costumers didn't make the anachronistic mistake of dressing the characters in shining armor, its writers still insisted on calling them knights and giving them a code of chivalry which didn't exist at the time.

"When there are no more dragons to slay, how will you make a living, knight?"—Draco to Bowen

A disillusioned knight (Dennis Quaid) forms an unlikely friendship with dragon Draco to save the kingdom from an evil king in *Dragonheart*.

That historical error aside, however, this amusing adventure full of immoral villains, valiant heroes, charismatic dragons, honorable messages, and a good heart can still provide pleasant family entertainment in theaters where it is in short supply. Like many classic fairy tales which the politically correct feel are too violent, *Dragonheart,* too, has its share of blood and brutality. But for older children (who probably see worse on Saturday morning cartoon shows), *Dragonheart* at least has honorable intentions and tries to deliver an inspiring theme.

The story revolves around a knight named Bowen (Dennis Quaid) who is training the young prince Einon (Lee Oakes) in the techniques of sword fighting and the ethics of the Old Code ("A knight is sworn to valor. His heart knows only virtue. His blade defends the helpless. His word speaks only truth. His wrath undoes the wicked"). The problem is, the prince has a heart as black as his evil father King Freyne (Peter Hric) who rules his downtrodden peasants with a heavy hand. One day while terrorizing his subjects, the king is killed and the young prince mortally wounded. His mother Aislinn (Julie Christie) takes her injured son to the lair of a dragon who saves his life by sharing his own heart with him. From this point on, their lives will be intertwined.

As it turns out, dragons are very knowledgeable and ethical and in exchange for rescuing the young lad, he makes Einon promise to rule with mercy and tells Bowen to always remind him of his vow. Well, since Bowen is sure he has well taught his young charge to live by the Old Code, then there is nothing to worry about.

Years later, however, Bowen has been proved wrong. The grown Einon (David Thewlis) is even more malevolent than his father. We know he was always this way, but Bowen believes that it was the Dragon who changed him. Consequently, Bowen now spends his time tracking down and killing all dragons.

Eventually he is led to the lair of the last dragon where a Mexican standoff is resolved only by the dragon's logical

AWARDS AND NOMINATIONS

Academy Awards 1996 Nominations: Best Visual Effects

argument: "When there are no more dragons to slay, how will you make a living, knight?" And since the dragon has no desire to fight an unending stream of dragon fighters after Bowen, the two take the decidedly unusual step of teaming up. The dragon, whom Bowen eventually names after the constellation Draco, will "terrorize" a town, Bowen will ride in, the unsuspecting villagers will pay him to slay the dragon, Draco will feign his own death (the best scenes in the film), and the two will move on to the next hamlet. (Lumberjacks and sawmill owners should work out a similar deal with the trees of our old-growth forests!)

> Bowen's sword, with its dragon claw, was made by a blacksmith in Bratislava, Slovakia, where the movie was filmed, and modeled after that of Richard the Lionheart.

Soon the two find themselves back in Einon's territory where appeals by the young girl Kara (Dina Meyer), whose father was killed by Einon, revives Bowen's basic decency. With Draco's help he now organizes the peasants' rebellion against Einon's oppressive tyranny. The cost of doing so, however, will be higher than Bowen ever would have imagined.

Any actor who took on the role of Bowen has a difficult job. He has to play his part straight while still seeing the fancifulness of it all. And not only that, for many scenes in the film, he is playing opposite empty space since Draco was added later. Thankfully Dennis Quaid manages to provide a good mix of amusement and intensity and delivers a solid performance.

Other actors in the film also bring superior skills to their roles. Only Tim Roth (*Rob Roy* [1995]) can sneer better than David Thewlis, and it's a pleasure to see Julie Christie (*Dr. Zhivago* [1965]) back on the screen after a much-too-long nine-year absence—even if her part virtually disappears in the middle of the film. Also disappearing far too often is one of the film's most interesting characters, Pete Postlethwaite's (*In the Name of the Father* [1993]) travelling monk, Gilbert. He describes himself as not only a monk, but also a scholar, historian and, to our amusement, a poet. He would be Bowen's humorous sidekick, but he vanishes far too often . . . and he is missed. How much more interesting *Dragonheart* might have been if Aislinn and Gilbert had stuck around.

By far, however, the character who must carry and consequently steals the picture is Draco. This is not some dragon who acts menacingly and breaths fire every now and then. No, Draco has to be powerful, noble, intelligent, sensitive, and often drolly amusing. To buy the film, audiences have to buy Draco. To the filmmakers' credit, Draco, as realized on the screen through the remarkable technological creativity of computer graphics (CGI), has an amazingly intricate range of expressions and a life-like presence that make this easily accomplished.

Right from the start, Draco was planned around the actor most well known as James Bond, Sean Connery. To aid the special effects artists, director Rob Cohen (*Dragon: The Bruce Lee Story* [1993]) created a reference library of Connery's films which show him with various expressions and moods. From them, the experts at Industrial Light and Magic made Draco a walking, talking, living image of Connery with scales and wings. There is very little exaggeration in the filmmakers description of Draco: "he speaks, he emotes, he has feelings, a soul, and humor. He's Sean Connery, essentially, as an 18' high and 43' long dragon."

This feat was the work of ILM's Scott Squires, who won an Oscar for *Mask* (1985), and Dragon designer Phil Tippett, who won an Academy Award for Best Visual Effects for *Return of the Jedi* (1983), was nominated for *Dragonslayer* (1981) and *Willow* (1988) and won an Emmy for CBS documentary *Dinosaur!* With every film, computer graphics become more and more capable of making the unbelievable believable, or making fantasy reality. Building on the success of *Jurassic Park* (1993), *Dragonheart* is another step in what ap-

CREDITS

Bowen: Dennis Quaid
Einon: David Thewlis
Gilbert: Pete Postlethwaite
Draco: Sean Connery (voice)
Kara: Dina Meyer
Felton: Jason Isaacs
Brok: Brian Thompson
Young Einon: Lee Oakes
Hewe: Wolf Christian
Redbeard: Terry O'Neill
Aislinn: Julie Christie

Origin: USA
Released: 1996
Production: Raffaella De Laurentiis; released by Universal Pictures
Direction: Rob Cohen
Screenplay: Charles Edward Pogue
Cinematography: David Eggby
Editing: Peter Amundson
Production design: Benjamin Fernandez
Art direction: Jano Svoboda
Set decoration: Giorgio Desideri
Costume design: Thomas Casterline and Anna Sheppard
Music: Randy Edelman
Special Effects Supervisor: Kit West
Dragon Designs: Phil Tippett
Visual Effects Supervision: Scott Squires
MPAA rating: PG-13
Running Time: 108 minutes

pears to be quantum leaps of realization. For example, as a comparison, the Tyrannosaurs Rex in *Jurassic Park* had between 7,000-8,000 control vertices (screen-plotted movements), Draco has about 280,000 which enables an even more complex presentation. The result is delightfully realistic.

This is still not to say *Dragonheart* doesn't have a few problems. The worst probably rests with some of the dialogue. Sometimes it is banter that is too hokey, sometimes it becomes stilted and artificial. There is also some disorientation caused by the fact that more sophisticated viewers may not know if they should appreciate the film as campy entertainment or as an epic fantasy. The story would need more humor to be the first, or a sharper story to be the latter.

However, like the historical quibbles stated earlier, these are minor issues. The film's great special effects, the personable likability of Draco, and the touching—even metaphysical—ending will allow us to forgive the film its silliness and transgressions. If one watches *Dragonheart* with the open spirit of a child, one will find a movie that's not great, but is innocently charming.

—Beverley Bare Buehrer

REVIEWS

Boxoffice. July, 1996, p. 90.
Chicago Tribune. May 31, 1996.
Entertainment Weekly. June 7, 1996, p. 37.
The Hollywood Reporter. May 28, 1996, p. 11.
New York Times. May 31, 1996, p. C10.
Newsweek. June 10, 1996, p. 91.
Rolling Stone. June 27, 1996, p. 62.
USA Today. May 31, 1996, p. 9D.
Variety. May 27, 1996, p. 65.

Dunston Checks In

The world is his jungle.—Movie tagline
"Laugh out loud funny!"—Michael Medved, *Sneak Previews*

Box Office: $9,200,000

Dunston is the name of the orangutan who goes ape in the ultra-posh, ultra-refined Majestic Hotel, where widower Robert Grant (Jason Alexander) is not only responsible for keeping all the guests happy but raising two precocious boys capable of causing almost as much trouble as a loose orangutan. When ten-year-old Kyle (Eric Lloyd) and his adolescent brother Brian (Graham Sack) get together with Dunston, their workaholic father's troubles are increased exponentially.

"I have two words to say to you—medical experiments."—Dunston's owner Rutledge to the misbehaving orangutan.

Dunston happens to check in—or to be checked in—at just the time when Robert's no-nonsense employer Mrs. Dubrow (Faye Dunaway) has descended on the establishment with a warning that everything had better be better than first class because the historic hotel, which has sheltered royalty, presidents and robber barons, is being considered for a six-star rating in the prestigious (and fictitious) El Monte guide. Fans of Miss Dunaway will perhaps feel sorry to see her taking on a one-dimensional role of this sort after winning an Academy Award for Best Actress in *Network* (1977) and having been nominated for Best Actress Academy Awards for *Bonnie and Clyde* (1967) and *Chinatown* (1974). She enters into the zany spirit of *Dunston Checks In* with a spoof of Leona Helmsley and contributes to the good overall quality of this PG production.

Dunston's owner is the loathsome, sadistic Lord Rutledge (Rupert Everett), an international jewel thief who has trained his intelligent orangutan to be a cat burglar. Knowing that the management would balk at taking in an ape, Rutledge smuggles him into the hotel inside a trunk. The audience immediately feels a great deal of sympathy for Dunston and corresponding antipathy for his owner when they realize that the dark, narrow trunk is where the poor animal spends most of his time.

The theme of the film has to do with abuse and neglect. Dunston is getting hard to handle because of constant mistreatment. Grant's two sons are rambunctious, not because of abuse, but because their dad's preoccupation with running a big Manhattan hotel has caused him to forget their need for love and attention. Driven by ambition and fear of the terrible Mrs. Dubrow, Grant, a victim of continuous verbal abuse himself, is becoming more and more like his employer. It is Dunston, the not-so-dumb animal, who is largely responsible for teaching Grant how to be human.

Grant's two boys have the run of the hotel. They know all the desk clerks, maids, waiters, cooks, bellhops, and everyone else on the staff. Although they have a loving father, they are still a lot like neglected latchkey kids because Grant has so many things on his mind. The theme of neglect and abuse runs like a thread throughout the story. Both kids and the orangutan get into trouble when they are not receiving affection. At the end of the film, when all the disorder has been set to rights, the boys' father realizes that the push-pull effect of greed and fear has caused him to forget how much more important his children are than anything else he could ever acquire. He quits his job and takes on a less stressful position which gives him time to spend with his sons. He intends to keep his often broken promises to take them camping and fishing.

Five-year-old orangutan Sam makes his film debut.

The movie was scripted by John Hopkins and Bruce Graham, who had sense and experience enough to give it the kind of contemporary significance a wacky picture like this needs. Like *Home Alone* (1990) and *Kindergarten Cop* (1990), it deals with a serious issue in a funny way. *Dunston Checks In* is strictly family entertainment and will undoubtedly receive more profits from videocassette sales and rentals than from ticket sales. In spite of some very favorable reviews (e.g., the *Los Angeles Times* wrote that it "Rates Five-Star Fun," and *Variety* called it "a first-class, stylish farce with a brisk pace and cool wit"), the production faded quickly at the box office. After its seventh week in release it was pushed off *Variety*'s Box Office Chart while rapidly disappearing from multiplexes around the country.

After Lord Rutledge checks into his room and releases Dunston from his miserable home in the dark trunk, the viewer is treated to an example of the phony nobleman's "modus operandi." He uses a whip to enforce his commands as well as his ultimate weapon, the threat to sell the unhappy animal for "medical experiments." He orders Dunston to climb up the side of the tall building, with the lights of Manhattan winking in the background and the heavy traffic reduced to crawling pinpoints of light in the street far below. Like Edgar Allan Poe's orangutan in "The Murders in the Rue Morgue," Dunston uses a shutter to swing into the suite of a dowager who owns almost as many jewels as Queen Elizabeth. More of this Raffles-type behavior would have made the story more interesting as well as more coherent. However, the plot never focuses on "Who's been breaking into the guests' rooms and stealing jewels?" Instead it focuses on "What's a monkey doing in the Majestic Hotel?"

There can be no doubt that the star of the film is the young orangutan, a leading actor who is not interested in multi-million-dollar salaries but works for banana yogurt, sweets, licorice, and chewing gum. In time he will grow to possess six times the strength of an average man and will weigh over 200 pounds. Right now he is still a fairly cuddly armful, small enough to get into the hotel's network of ventilation ducts and create havoc. All reviewers agreed that he steals the show. He has a marvelously expressive face. He has been compared to Cheeta, the chimpanzee who appeared in *Tarzan, The Ape Man* (1932) and its many sequels starring Johnny Weissmuller and Maureen O'Sullivan. Orangutans seem to make better actors than chimps, however, perhaps because orangutans are more like method actors and do not rely on shrieking and acrobatics to convey their emotions. Dunston has a whole spectrum of facial expressions. He is moody and philosophical, witty, vindictive, eccentric, coy, curious, playful, apprehensive and affectionate—but never vicious or dangerous. He really seems to be acting as well as relating to his young friends who are trying to protect him the way the boys tried to protect the stranded alien in *E.T.: The Extraterrestrial* (1982).

It is a long time before anyone but the children and Dunston's ungrateful owner believe in his existence. How on earth could an orangutan get inside the Majestic Hotel? Eventually, however, Grant is horrified to find out the terrible truth. This is hardly the time to have an ape running

CREDITS

Robert Grant: Jason Alexander
Mrs. Dubrow: Faye Dunaway
Kyle Grant: Eric Lloyd
Lord Rutledge: Rupert Everett
Brian Grant: Graham Sack
Buck La Farge: Paul Reubens

Origin: USA
Released: 1996
Production: Todd Black, Joe Wizan; released by 20th Century Fox
Direction: Ken Kwapis
Screenplay: John Hopkins, Bruce Graham
Cinematography: Peter Collister
Editing: Jon Poll
Music: Miles Goodman
Production design: Rusty Smith
Art direction: Keith Neely
Costumes: Alina Panova
Sound: Clark D. King
Casting: Linda Lowry, John Brace
MPAA rating: PG
Running Time: 88 minutes

amok in his five-star establishment. He sends for a quasi-official animal control officer named La Farge (played by Paul Reubens, formerly known as Pee Wee Herman), who proves to be more of a liability than an asset. La Farge hunts unwanted animals the way Bill Murray and Dan Aykroyd hunted unwanted spooks in *Ghostbusters* (1984), without regard to the negative effects on the environment. When La Farge finally corners Dunston in the wilds of the hotel's arboretum, the unstable hunter fantasizes he is back in the jungle and begins terrorizing the guests with a gun big enough to bag elephants.

Adults who accompany their small offspring to the film may be surprised to find themselves actually laughing heartily at this old-fashioned farce. It relies almost entirely on sight-gags, some of which are original while others are old favorites with new twists. The contrast between the stuffy hotel guests and the outrageous behavior of the kids and their simian friend resembles the pretention-puncturing comedy that used to convulse audiences in the Marx Brothers films of the 1920s and 1930s. Dunston, of course, most closely resembles the silent Harpo. In fact, *Dunston Checks In* often seems like a spinoff of the Marx Brothers' *The Cocoanuts* (1929) and *Room Service* (1938).

The hotel is preparing for a big charity ball which will be attended by a representative of the El Monte guide visiting incognito. The grand finale was staged with two hundred extras in gowns and tuxedos and took nine days to film. Although the Majestic Hotel is supposedly located in Manhattan, everything was shot inside the old Bullocks Wilshire department store in Los Angeles, which has been taken over by the Southwest University School of Law on condition that it be preserved intact as an Art Deco historic monument.

An enormous cake has been created by the hotel's world-class culinary staff. It is covered with pink and white frosting. The adults in the audience—if not the children—have a pretty good idea of what is going to happen to that cake when the chase inevitably leads into the grand ballroom and Dunston begins swinging from ornate chandeliers attached to the twenty-foot ceiling. And they are right. Good trouper Faye Dunaway falls over backward and is nearly smothered in cake and frosting. Lord Rutledge is exposed as the crook who masterminded the theft of the dowager's diamonds. Dunston and the boys are heroes. Grant is exonerated and offered a raise and a promotion by Mrs. Dubrow's long-suffering husband. Grant refuses, however, having realized that his responsibilities as a father are more important than his career. The sugar-frosted Mrs. Dubrow is a good example of what happens to people who take themselves too seriously—at least in the movies.

—Bill Delaney

REVIEWS

Boxoffice. March, 1996, p. R-27.
Chicago Tribune. January 12, 1996, p. 5.
Detroit Free Press. January 12, 1996, p. D1.
Detroit News. January 12, 1996, p. 3D.
Los Angeles Times. January 12, 1996, p. F12.
New York Times. January 12, 1996, p. C6.
Variety. January 15, 1996, p. 125.
Washington Post. January 12, 1996, p. 32.

Ed

Minor league. Major friendship.—Movie tagline

"Wild! Wacky! Home run!"—Ron Brewington, *American Urban Radio Networks*

"A treat for the whole family."—Howard Benjamin, *The Interview Factory*

"Hilarious! Family fun!"—Joanna Levenglick, *The Kids News Network*

It is common knowledge in Hollywood that television stars have a difficult time making the transition from the small screen to the big screen. Armed with the statistics, it would certainly behoove any TV actor to select his or her first big screen outing with great care and consideration. Keeping this in mind, it is somewhat bewildering that Matt LeBlanc, one of the current stars of the NBC hit series, "Friends," would choose MCA Universal's *Ed* as his first bid for movie stardom. This unfunny, somewhat tasteless, baseball comedy could not have been a worse choice. Equally surprising is the fact that the director, respected, socially conscious documaker, Bill Couturie (best known for *Common Threads: Stories from the Quilt, Earth and the American Dream,* and *Dear America: Letters Home from Vietnam*) would make the same disastrous mistake.

Feature film debut of actor Matt LeBlanc.

Fresh off the farm, baseball "whiz" Jack Cooper (played by a heavily made-up Matt LeBlanc) lands a job pitching for a minor league baseball team, the Santa Rosa Rockets. While he was great on the farm, Cooper finds that it's a different ball game playing in front of a large crowd of people. To everyone's surprise, he immediately "chokes" on the mound. In layman's terms, he's in a big slump. Meanwhile, the team manager, Chubb (Jack Warden), just happens to acquire a chimpanzee named Ed, as the team mascot. Why this happens is never clearly explained, except that Ed once had belonged to the late Mickey Mantle. Just as puzzling, Chubb decides that Ed will somehow help Jack out of his slump and decides that they should be roommates.

Enter Ed, whose full name is Ed Sullivan (yet another baffling point) into Jack's life. Incidentally, Ed is not a real chimp. He is an animatronic puppet manned by two different actors (Jay Caputo and Denise Cheshire) and looks like a cross between Alf and the late George Burns. Once Jack gets home, he discovers that Ed is more human than most chimpanzees. For instance, Ed prefers to use Jack's toilet rather than go outside, much to Jack's chagrin. Jack laments, "How can you poop where I go to the bathroom?" Gratefully moving on to the baseball field, it seems that Ed is a superlative athlete as well as being a funny, lovable little mascot. Everyone is amazed! After much debate and quarreling, Ed is put on the team to play third base—a first in the history of baseball. Not only does he impress the fans in Santa Rosa but the entire country as well. So much so that he lands on the covers of such respected magazines as *Sports Illustrated, Muscle and Fitness,* and last, but not least, *Teen Beat* (a sex symbol, no less). The entire team shapes up due to Ed's stellar performance, not to mention his gift for motivating and inspiring everyone. The plot thickens when the owner's needy son, Kirby (Patrick Kerr) trades Ed to some shady characters who, for some reason, enjoy torturing poor Ed while he's dressed in a clown costume. All of this seems inexplicable, except to give Cooper a chance to bleat out, "He's not an animal, he's a ballplayer." Through a series of gimmicky events, Ed is hospitalized after being rescued from a chilly death inside a frozen banana truck. Just in the nick of time, Cooper gets back to play in the championship game. Miraculously, Ed recovers,

CREDITS

Jack Cooper: Matt LeBlanc
Lydia: Jayne Brook
Tipton: Bill Cobbs
Chubb: Jack Warden
Ed Sullivan: Jay Caputo
Liz: Doren Fein

Origin: USA
Released: 1996
Production: Rosalie Swedlin for a Longview Entertainment production; released by Universal
Direction: Bill Couturie
Screenplay: David Mickey Evans
Cinematography: Alan Caso
Editing: Robert K. Lambert
Production design: Curtis A. Schnell
Art direction: Michael L. Fox
Costume design: Robin Lewis
Sound: Jacob Goldstein
"Ed" special makeup: Dave Nelson
Casting: Shari Rhodes, Joseph Middleton
Music: Stephen D. Endelman
MPAA rating: PG
Running Time: 94 minutes

rips out the life support, and manages to give Cooper some winning coaching tips from the bleachers. Oh, while all of these silly shenanigans are going on, there's a tepid little romance between Cooper and his single mom neighbor Lydia ("Chicago Hope's" Jayne Brook).

To say this film was disappointing is a massive understatement. Obviously, it was targeted for young children, possibly seven years of age and younger. The filmmaker seems to have forgotten that young children have been exposed to some quality, magical films of late, such as *Beauty and the Beast* (1991), *Aladdin* (1992), *The Lion King* (1994), and *Babe* (1995), to name but a few. Although most of the aforementioned films are animated, they possess an ingredient that was sorely lacking in *Ed*—quality. Critic Marshall Fine said, "This is the kind of movie that ends careers." One can only hope. Not only is there little story or conflict but idiotic dialogue as well. It is difficult to ascertain what screenwriter David Mickey Evans had in mind—humor was certainly not one of them.

Matt LeBlanc's lifeless performance in this film will certainly not generate any excitement in the Hollywood community. After *Ed,* he should be thankful for the success of "Friends." Jack Warden does his standard, generic Jack Warden performance and the rest of the cast is sufficient. The only believable moments come from Doren Fein, who plays Liz, the little girl next door. She is the only element of charm in the entire film.

During a period of filmmaking when features aimed for young audiences are increasingly striving for excellence, why expose them to such a crassly foolish film like *Ed*? There must be better material than chimp flatulence and bathroom habits to entertain children. The discerning youngsters of today deserve better than that, not to mention the poor parents who have to take them.

—Rob Chicatelli

REVIEWS

The Detroit News. March 15, 1996, p. 5D.
Entertainment Weekly. March 29, 1996, p. 45.
Los Angeles Times. March 15, 1996, p. F12.
New York Times. March 15, 1996, p. 4C.
USA Today. March 15, 1996, p. 5D.
Variety. March 18, 1996, p. 48.

Eddie

The newest coach in the NBA has got the Knicks right where she wants them.—Move tagline

"A sure three pointer! Whoopi is hilarious."—Dr. Joy Browne, *WWOR-TV*

Box Office: $31,388,164

The stall was outlawed in professional basketball years ago. Too bad it hasn't been banned in movies. Watching *Eddie,* a saga of what happens to the National Basketball Association's New York Knicks when a fan becomes coach, is like seeing one of those 1950s basketball games where both teams are stalling and the score ends up 17-11. Not even Whoopi Goldberg in a starring role can bring this dud to life.

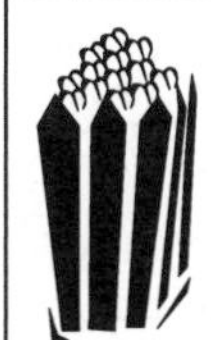

"Worse than your pants: that's how bad the call was!"—Eddie arguing with a referee

Basketball has become popular because it is so full of action. Action is what *Eddie* lacks. Except for a few uninspiring minutes of a game at the film's end, there is precious little on-court activity. And, with a script that contains virtually no plot, nothing much happens off-court either.

The film starts and ends with a tried-but-true idea: What would happen if a disgruntled fan took the reins of an underachieving team? *Eddie* has a reliable box-office star, Goldberg, in the title role. And it has a villain, though a rather lackluster one, in a new carpetbagging owner who threatens to defy the Knicks' hallowed sports traditions. It has 49 NBA players in small roles. But that's all it has. The rest is simply filler.

Viewers who live and die with the fate of the Knicks might find *Eddie* interesting. But for the 99 percent of viewers who don't identify with New York's basketball team, there is no way to make an emotional connection to the story. Shots of cabbies listening to Knicks games on the radio don't do it. And we never learn why Goldberg's title character is such a big Knicks booster until much too late in the film, and even then, the explanation is rather lame.

In fact, the script gives us little background on Eddie. It just plucks her out of the stands, where she's been badmouthing the Knicks' coach (Dennis Farina) from the cheap seats, and puts her in charge of the team. Making Eddie the coach is a publicity stunt by the new owner, Wild Bill Burgess (Frank Langella), a cowboy-showman who has so little respect for the Knicks' past that he torches Walt Frazier's jersey during a pre-game fireworks show.

Dennis Rodman, John Salley, Mark Jackson, Malik Sealy, Rock Fox, and Dwayne Schintzius are among the 49 NBA players featured in the film.

That's about as wild as Wild Bill and the film get. The miscast Langella plays the spoiled, rich, manipulative owner in a soft-spoken, understated fashion—too understated to make the character work as the film's villain.

The script's appalled tone at Burgess's showmanship and lack of respect for tradition makes little sense in the setting of modern-day pro basketball, an enterprise which is as much show business as sport. A film that expects viewers to be shocked that an NBA owner would use scantily clad cheerleaders or threaten to move the team to another city is a film that is woefully out of touch with the current world of sports.

Other than keeping her almost constantly on camera, director Steve Rash has little idea how to make good use of Goldberg, who is just about *Eddie*'s only asset. Goldberg makes a game attempt to milk some humor out of a lifeless script which gives her too few gag lines and too many uninspiring speeches. Neither Goldberg nor the film ever gets frantic or clever. In fact, Eddie seems so slow on the uptake that it's hard not to agree with Burgess' assessment that she is little more than a buffoon.

Ardent sports fans often think that, given the chance, they could do a better job of coaching their favorite team than the person being paid six or seven figures to do so. Eddie certainly appears to believe that. Before being installed as head coach, she constantly lectures the coach and his players on game strategy. You expect she'll do the same once she takes over the reins. But unfortunately the script requires her first to have a long, overwrought crisis of confidence.

Abandoning the caustic attitude which gave her character some initial pizazz, Goldberg's Eddie turns into a cloying hero worshipper, addressing the players as "Mister" and being so awed by her new responsibilities that she can hardly speak, much less bark orders during a game. It takes her way too long to realize the players are spoiled brats—something every viewer can see from the start. By the time she delivers the obligatory speech scolding the superstars for not being the heroes they're paid to be, it's way too late and way too lame.

It gets worse. Eddie next has to learn that the players really are human beings with problems like everyone else. A Russian center who can't play defense suffers from a language barrier, so Eddie learns Russian and coaches him in his native tongue. Another player is being threatened with divorce, so Eddie becomes marriage counselor. A selfish superstar, Stacy Patton, has forgotten his roots, so Eddie must arrange to get him back on the streets and learn a lesson in humility. This stuff is humorless sop.

While all this is going on, viewers are left longing for some hoops action, some plot tension, some jokes—anything to break the monotony of Eddie's apprenticeship in the human relations aspects of coaching. How many people come to a movie about Whoopi Goldberg taking over an NBA team hoping to see the comic genius practicing pop-psychology lessons? Not many, I'd wager.

When Eddie finally turns the team around, it's not due to any shrewd strategy. She merely benches the Russian and Stacy Patton, who never passes the ball to his teammates. Unrealistically, the film makes it seem as if Patton has played every minute of every game until his benching, while in fact every NBA player, even the greatest, sits a few minutes every game. The only other plot lines involving the players and the

CREDITS

Eddie: Whoopi Goldberg
Wild Bill Burgess: Frank Langella
Coach Bailey: Dennis Farina
Asst. Coach Zimmer: Richard Jenkins
Claudine: Lisa Ann Walter
Joe Nader: John Benjamin Hickey

Origin: USA
Released: 1996
Production: David Permut and Mark Burg for a Hollywood Pictures, Polygram Filmed Entertainment and Island production; released by Buena Vista
Direction: Steve Rash
Screenplay: Jon Connolly, Dacid Loucka, Eric Champnella, Keith Mitchell, Steve Zacharias and Jeff Buhai
Cinematography: Victor Kemper
Editing: Richard Halsey
Music: Stanley Clark
Production design: Dan Davis
Art direction: Robert K. Shaw Jr.
Set decoration: Roberta J. Holinko
Costume design: Molly Maginnis
Sound: James E. Webb
Basketball consultant: Glenn (Doc) Rivers
MPAA rating: PG-13
Running Time: 100 minutes

game are about an aging star's bad knees and about teaching the Russian to plant his feet and take a charge. Those don't exactly make for rousing on-court action.

When Wild Bill puts on his villain's hat and threatens to take the team out of town, it's a showdown that comes out of nowhere and carries little weight for viewers who don't bleed for the Knicks. That's the vast majority of the audience, for the film gives no reasons to embrace the Knicks legacy it holds up as sacred. It's taken for granted we know about the team's history, because nothing of it is ever shown or mentioned. This is New York provincialism at its worst—no film ever shot in Indianapolis or Cleveland would make the same assumptions about its viewers' knowledge.

Instead of explaining Eddie's background or why she or anyone else would care so much about the Knicks, director Rash kills time, resorting to meaningless, humorless man-on-the-street interviews and Donald Trump cameos as filler. About the only good gags in the film are slight and peripheral, for instance, a banner at the Knicks game, while they are still losing regularly, that reads: FOR THIS I'M MISSING BAYWATCH?

The scant game action in *Eddie* looks pretty obviously contrived, as if the players were walking through their key plays in slow-motion. The use of NBA players does lend a little authenticity, but not enough.

Eddie doesn't succeed as a sports film because it contains absolutely no insights into basketball. As a comedy, it's a lightweight, because there aren't enough jokes. And as some sort of dramatic study of a fan's transformation into a coach, it's misconceived.

Like the spoiled, smug superstars Eddie coaches, Goldberg seems all too content to be a big fish in this small pond of a film. It's a paycheck, but the role certainly doesn't stretch her talents in any way. Watching Goldberg in *Eddie* is like watching Michael Jordan shoot free throws. It's not what you paid admission to see.

—*Michael Betzold*

REVIEWS

Boxoffice Online. June 4, 1996.
Los Angeles Times. May 31, 1996, p. F16.
New York Times. May 31, 1996, p. C3.
USA Today. May 31, 1966, p. 9D.
Variety. June 3, 1996, p. 50.

Ed's Next Move

It's the hardest move a guy has to make.—Movie tagline

"Ed's fish-out-of-water misadventures and romantic fumblings will make your Saturday night a winner . . . even if you hate your date."—Juliann Garey and Bari Nan Cohen, *Glamour*

"Two thumbs up!"—*Siskel & Ebert*

Box Office: $105,941

"I've never been with a guy like you," the girl of his dreams tells the klutzy, white-bread protagonist of *Ed's Next Move*. "Have you ever considered seeing a therapist?"

"No," replies Eddie.

"That's what I mean," says the girl, Lee. "You're so—so—normal."

Despite his normality, or more likely because of it, the jaded New York City gal has a yen for Eddie, a bland Wisconsin transplant. And just because of its gently offbeat view of normal people in strange circumstances, it's easy to like *Ed's Next Move*. It's a small, low-budget, no-big-names, innocuous romantic comedy that eschews high drama and finds wry laughs in life's ordinary moments. There's no blood or guts, no raw sex, no gangsters or vampires, no grandstanding stars—just authentic, reasonably likeable people trying to find a little solace in the big city. It's so—so—normal.

Eddie Brosky (Matt Ross) is a mid-20s genetics engineer treading water in small-town Wisconsin. His girlfriend dumps him, scolding him for being obsessive and not spontaneous enough. Eddie schedules, lists and plans everything. He even asks his girlfriend for a list of all his faults; she obliges. Needing a change, he hops a train for New York City to take a job doing genetic research: breeding new drought-resistant strains of rice for Asian countries.

Eddie considers his new job exciting, important and useful. Every New Yorker he meets considers it and him impossibly square. His Wisconsin origins provide a constant running gag in the film. New Yorkers he meet confuse it with Wyoming. A liquor store owner questions him closely on the difference between white and yellow cheese. At a party, another guy confesses he's never even seen a picture of Wyoming and asks what's there. Eddie replies: "Cows. Grass. Cheese. Space." When Eddie walks away, the guy asks Eddie's roommate Ray: "Is he a poet or something?"

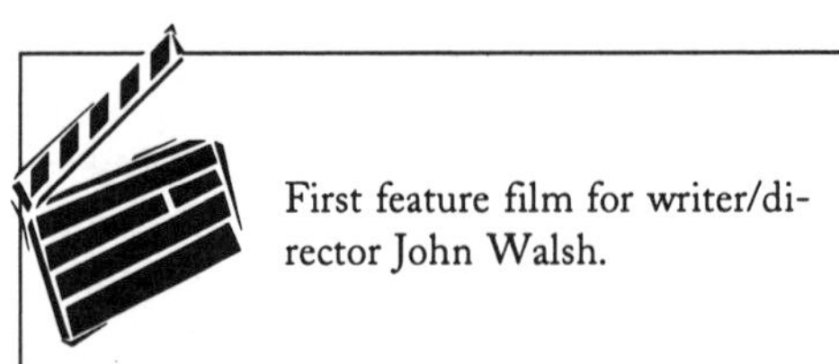

First feature film for writer/director John Walsh.

First-time writer-director John Walsh gets a lot of mileage out of the culture clash, making fun both of Eddie's naivety and New Yorkers' strained sophistication. Eddie is a clueless rube. His mouth gapes as a taxi meter runs; he is dead meat in jostling derbies on subway steps. The women Eddie meets at a party prattle on about Americans' obsession with numbers or their performance art. When Eddie naively asks, "What do you do in your performances?" the woman scolds him for asking the wrong question, telling him her art is not about "what," but about "how."

"Let's just say first dates go better when nothing dies."—Ed to roommate Ray

Ed's Next Move delights in puncturing the New York bubble. But it's done with a deft, good grace, not ill will. Walsh doesn't overdo the stranger-in-a-strange-land motif. What makes his film so likeable is that he doesn't overdo anything. The script sticks mostly to unearthing precious ironies in mundane moments, with occasional forays into the surreal. In a sequence reminiscent of Luis Bunuel, Eddie throws an annoying alarm clock out his apartment window, a rat nudges it and it resumes ringing until a woman in a house dress emerges to gun it down.

Two other hilarious fantasy sequences are more akin to Woody Allen's style. After Eddie is rebuffed in his initial attempt to hit on Lee (Callie Thorne) and a deli counter woman explains that New York women have a right to be wary, Eddie imagines a "Nice Guy ID" infomercial. When Eddie tells Ray his old girlfriend said he made her "claustrophobic," Ray boozily remarks that a guy needs a translator in such spots, and Eddie imagines his breakup conversation replayed with actual translators. It's a skit that's a real keeper.

Eddie's main pursuit is to find a woman. It's a quest for which he is ill-suited, especially in New York. His roommate Ray (Kevin Carroll) is a seemingly sophisticated ladies' man who gradually reveals he's tired of one-night stands and is pining for true love. His heart gradually opens to Eddie's sincerity. When Ray incredulously asks of Eddie: "You've never done a woman on the first date?" Eddie replies: "I do laundry. I do dishes. I don't do women." It's a line sure to win the hearts of the female audience.

Despite all his bumbling and fumbling, Eddie gradually gets the heart of Lee to open to him too. She's a singer/violinist in a bizarre, obtuse folk-rock band who is tired of living with a temperamental artist boyfriend. To Eddie, she is a goddess. At first Eddie looks to her like a buffoon.

It's a simple story, redeemed by believable characters and down-to-earth situations. No Hollywood romantic flourishes mar Walsh's view of human foibles. Eddie is far from a smooth operator. When Lee finally comes for dinner, he sidles next to her on a couch, like a pubescent boy, and lunges at her lips. Their embrace is interrupted by the meowing of Ray's cat, who's found live mice in a trap under the kitchen sink. When Eddie bonks the mice with a skillet, it totally ruins the evening.

The message of *Ed's Next Move* is simple too: When you stop trying to orchestrate life, something good might sneak up on you. The way Eddie and Lee keep bumping into each other illustrates that splendid serendipity, while providing the film's few moments that aren't totally believable. Lee keeps popping up as if Eddie were still back in his small town, not the big city. But this is, after all, a romantic fable, and Walsh keeps most of the phony magical moments at bay.

For a neophyte writer-director working with a cast of unknowns, Walsh makes all the right moves. He never suc-

CREDITS

Eddie Brodsky: Matt Ross
Lee Nicol: Callie Thorne
Ray Obregon: Kevin Carroll
Dr. Banarjee: Ramsey Faragallah
Elenka: Nina Shevaleva
Raphael: Jimmy Cummings

Origin: USA
Released: 1996
Production: Sally Roy; released by Orion Classics
Direction: John Walsh
Screenplay: John Walsh
Cinematography: Peter Nelson
Editing: Pamela Martin
Music: Benny Golson
Costumes: Maura Sircus
Production design: Kristin Vallow
Casting: Susan Shopmaker
Sound: Wim Tzouris
MPAA rating: R
Running Time: 88 minutes

cumbs to excess while providing just enough wackiness to keep the film's low-key pace from dragging too much. Walsh is a master of small moments and keen, slightly skewed observations on what passes for normal life. He doesn't overreach. *Ed's Next Move* is a precious, small gem which never dazzles but brings consistent pleasure.

Much credit goes to a uniformly excellent cast. The unknown Ross, as Eddie, brings a certain degree of slovenly sweetness but doesn't overplay the part of loveable loser. He's wonderful at portraying a guy who doesn't expect to wow anyone over but keeps fighting at overcoming his personality deficiencies with sheer effort and sincerity. His Eddie never hits a false note.

Neither do Thorne and Carroll. Thorne conveys a world-weariness that hasn't snuffed out her belief in life and love. She is a dark beauty with a solid strength. Carroll, in the role of the roommate who finds Eddie's naivete baffling, is a wonderfully understated comic presence. Practicing tai-chi in front of a mirror or primping for a date, Carroll's Ray is the face of practiced manhood that is always one notch short of grasping the ring. He and Ross play well off each other, a sort of post-modern Odd Couple.

What's most appealing about *Ed's Next Move* is its unpretentiousness. Like its protagonists, this film doesn't expect to bowl over anyone. It's content to entertain, and it does that quite well. As a writer and director, Walsh is full of promise. It will be fun to anticipate his next move.

—Michael Betzold

REVIEWS

Boxoffice. October 1996, p. 46.
Chicago Tribune. October 11, 1996, p. 7.
Entertainment Weekly. October 26, 1996, p. 96.
Film Threat. January, 1997, p. 56.
The Hollywood Reporter. September 24, 1996, p. 10.
Los Angeles Times. September 27, 1996, p. F2.
New York Times. October 18, 1996, p. C18.
Variety. Jan. 29, 1996, p. 62.

Emma

This summer cupid is armed and dangerous.—Movie tagline

"It may turn out to be not only the finest but the funniest film of 1996!"—Michael Medved, *The New York Post*

"A broadly amusing film with a show-stopping young star!"—Janet Maslin, *New York Times*

"Two thumbs up!"—*Siskel & Ebert*

"In a summer of pseudo-spectaculars, here, finally, is a movie to embrace and cherish!"—Joe Morgenstern, *Wall Street Journal*

Box Office: $22,231,658

Gwyneth Paltrow plays the naive matchmaker in Jane Austen's classic *Emma.*

Jane Austen (1775-1817) had an extremely hot year on the big screen in 1995 with the release of two highly regarded films, *Persuasion* and *Sense and Sensibility,* based on her novels as well as the popular contemporary comedy *Clueless,* loosely inspired by Austen's *Emma.* The Austen craze continued into 1996 with the American premiere of a sparkling adaptation of "Pride and Prejudice," her most famous novel, on the Arts and Entertainment cable network. To have expected Douglas McGrath's film version of *Emma* to be as good as its predecessors would be asking too much, especially considering that he is an American directing his first film, but *Emma* is, despite some sniping from a few critics, a delightful achievement because of a charming performance in the title role and the surety of McGrath's direction.

Austen's 1816 novel recounts the efforts of Emma Woodhouse (Gwyneth Paltrow) to organize the lives of her friends. The film opens with the marriage of Emma's former governess (Greta Scacchi) to Mr. Weston (James Cosmo), a well-to-do neighbor in Highbury, Surrey, a union Emma thinks she arranged. Missing the companionship of Anne Weston, Emma decides to devote her energies to finding the right mate for the unworldly Harriet Smith (Toni Collette), preventing her from accepting the proposal of Robert Martin (Edward Woodall), an awkward young farmer Emma considers unworthy of her friend. Emma encourages Harriet to have expectations for Mr. Elton (Alan Cumming), the local vicar, only to find, after a series of misunderstandings, that Elton never was entertaining hopes of winning her hand.

Phyllida Law and Sophie Thompson (mother and daughter in real life) played the same roles on-screen as Mrs. and Miss Bates.

All this maneuvering is observed with considerable annoyance by Mr. Knightley (Jeremy Northam), a wealthy neighbor whose brother (Brian Capron) is married to Emma's sister, Isabella (Karen Westwood). Knightley thinks Emma misjudges people and interferes where she should not, trying to mold Harriet into someone more like herself. Matters become even more confused with the arrival of Mr. Weston's relatively flamboyant son, Frank Churchill (Ewan McGregor). Emma hopes Harriet will attract Churchill's attention even though she gradually becomes drawn to him as well. Emma is shocked to discover Churchill secretly betrothed to the mysterious Jane Fairfax (Polly Walker), whom he has made fun of previously. Harriet then thinks she may be in love with Knightley, to whom Emma has finally become attracted. All ends well, of course, with Harriet marrying Martin and Emma Knightley. Elton is punished for misleading Harriet by acquiring a domineering wife (Juliet Stevenson).

Some reviewers faulted *Emma* for being too slight, especially in comparison with the other 1995-1996 adaptations of Austen's work. It does lack the gritty texture of the deliberately unglamorous *Persuasion,* the large-scale glamour of *Sense and Sensibility,* and the jokey liveliness of *Clueless,* but it seems a remarkably faithful interpretation of Austen's novel. While some critics complained that McGrath's version omits the novelist's ironies—ironies which these reviewers usually failed to delineate—the film is highly ironic. The most obvious irony is Emma's inflated view of her sophistication, her thinking herself a person of superior taste who can manipulate her friends into finding their destinies when, in reality, she misjudges almost everyone, Churchill in particular, and blinds herself to what should be obvious—that some people are clearly made for each other despite what might be seen as barriers. *Emma* is the story of the protagonist's moral growth as she becomes more accepting of others' faults. The key scene is Knightley's upbraiding Emma for ungenerosity after she ridicules the loquacious Miss Bates (Sophie Thompson). She realizes instantly that she has held others to a higher standard than she has held herself.

> "Vanity working on a weak mind produces every kind of mischief."—Mr. Knightley

Emma is much more comic than *Persuasion* and *Sense and Sensibility* because McGrath shows, for the most part, how the story's serious and humorous elements overlap, how the solemn is never too far from the ridiculous. When Jane Fairfax gives a concert and Churchill interjects himself to sing a duet with her, Knightley is outraged at the visitor's audacity, and Emma notices, drawing all sorts of wrong conclusions. This scene is not only masterfully directed and acted, but Lesley Walker's editing, cutting back and forth between the performers and the audience's varying responses, underscores the comic rhythms of the situation.

McGrath is an unlikely filmmaker to be making his directorial debut with an Austen novel. A former writer for "Saturday Night Live," and a former humor columnist for *The Nation* and *The New Republic,* McGrath's first screenplay was the disastrous 1993 remake of *Born Yesterday,* but he rebounded by cowriting *Bullets Over Broadway* (1994) with Woody Allen. (McGrath's wife was once an assistant to Allen.) As the director has mentioned in interviews, *Emma* is a Woody Allen comedy transplanted to the early nineteenth-century English countryside. As with such Allen films as *Annie Hall* (1977), *Manhattan* (1979), and *Hannah and Her Sisters* (1986), *Emma* deals with a small circle of privileged, reasonably well-to-do, mostly articulate characters who comically mismanage their love lives. Like Allen's best efforts, McGrath's film is extremely well paced, never going too long without the requisite humorous touches, never becoming too frivolous.

The often darkly atmospheric cinematography of Ian Wilson, who shot *The Crying Game* (1992), helps keep matters at an ironic distance, never allowing the film to become too frothy. Wilson uses his lighting sometimes to imply a dark border around the seemingly sunny goings-on. McGrath, Wilson, and production designer Michael Howells create several striking images, as with an arbor resembling an outdoor parlor, a setting in which Emma, Knightley, and Anne Weston discuss apparently mundane affairs surrounded by goldfish bowls mounted atop thin columns, sug-

CREDITS

Emma Woodhouse: Gwyneth Paltrow
Mr. Knightley: Jeremy Northam
Harriet Smith: Toni Collette
Rev. Elton: Alan Cumming
Mrs. Weston: Greta Scacchi
Mrs. Elton: Juliet Stevenson
Frank Churchill: Ewan McGregor
Jane Fairfax: Polly Walker
Miss Bates: Sophie Thompson
Mrs. Bates: Phyllida Law

Origin: USA
Released: 1996
Production: Patrick Cassavetti and Steven Haft for a Haft Entertainment, Matchmaker Films production; released by Miramax
Direction: Douglas McGrath
Screenplay: Douglas McGrath; based on the novel by Jane Austen
Cinematography: Ian Wilson
Editing: Lesley Walker
Music: Rachel Portman
Production design: Michael Howells
Art direction: Sam Riley, Joshua Meath-Baker
Costume design: Ruth Myers
Sound: Chris Munro
Casting: Mary Selway, Sarah Trevis
MPAA rating: PG
Running Time: 111 minutes

AWARDS AND NOMINATIONS

Academy Awards 1996: Best Original Score (Portman)
Nominations: Best Costume Design
Writers Guild of America 1996 Nominations:
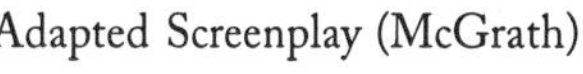
Adapted Screenplay (McGrath)

gestive of the superficial glitter of this confined, gossipy world. A cat glimpsed briefly in the background encroaching on some unseen prey hints at the danger of the unexpected always threatening to invade this ordered, mannered society. This wonderful tableau encompasses the film's themes and visual style.

McGrath's comic goals are aided immensely by his cast. As she has shown particularly in *Four Weddings and a Funeral* (1994), Thompson is wonderful at farce, and except for the humiliation scene, which McGrath lets run too long, she makes the dim, talkative Miss Bates a Dickensian delight. (Thompson plays a similar role in *Persuasion,* her sister Emma adapted and stars in *Sense and Sensibility,* and her mother, Phyllida Law, is amusingly stoic as her silent mother in *Emma.*) Cumming is an engaging young comic actor with a gift for caricature reminiscent of Peter Sellers and Alec Guinness. Best known for the Uriah Heep-like shop assistant in *Circle of Friends* (1995), he makes Elton despicably supercilious without becoming silly. The comic revelation of *Emma* is Stevenson's sublimely egocentric Mrs. Elton who can easily out-talk even Miss Bates. Normally confined to too-serious roles in films and television, Stevenson dominates each of her few scenes as much as Mrs. Elton does her husband. Elton's feeble attempts to get in a word when his wife is around are among the comic highlights of the film and display the perfect timing of Cumming and Stevenson.

The unifying performance in *Emma,* of course, is that of Paltrow. She has previously played mostly thankless roles in forgettable films, with the notable exception of Steve Kloves' interesting failure *Flesh and Bone* (1993), which she steals as the con artist who cries her way into funeral homes to take jewelry from the deceased. Her Emma is a seductive blend of innocence, cunning, insight, and self-delusion. Paltrow effortlessly gives an old-fashioned movie-star performance, leaving the audience helpless but to root for the character's happiness. Paltrow's assurance and distinctive sexuality have earned her work here comparisons with Katharine Hepburn, Audrey Hepburn, Grace Kelly, and Meryl Streep, among others. She most closely resembles, in both appearance and acting style, the Irene Dunne of *Theodora Goes Wild* (1936) and *The Awful Truth* (1937). Her quite credible English accent sounds like a tribute to Emma Thompson's patented upper-crust whine.

As Knightley, Northam's subtly masculine grace effectively complements Paltrow's flashier endeavors. The rest of the large cast is uniformly good, though Walker and Scacchi have too little to do, and Collette's Harriet is a tad bland. McGregor is unrecognizable from his distinctly contemporary roles in *Shallow Grave* (1995) and *Trainspotting* (1996). The modern swagger he brings to Churchill is appropriate for this cocky cad.

—*Michael Adams*

REVIEWS

Boxoffice Magazine Online. August 5, 1996.
Chicago Tribune. August 9, 1996, p. C7.
Christian Science Monitor. August 2, 1996, p. 11.
Detroit News. August 9, 1996, p. D3.
Entertainment Weekly. August 9, 1996, p. 43.
The Los Angeles Times. August 2, 1996, p. F6.
The New York Times. August 2, 1996, p. C1.
The New Yorker. August 5, 1996, p. 76.
Newsweek. July 29, 1996, p. 67.
People. August 5, 1996, p. 17.
Premiere. September, 1996, p. 38.
Rolling Stone. August 22, 1996, p. 103.
Sight and Sound. September, 1996, p. 40.
USA Today. August 2, 1996, p. D1.
Variety. June 17, 1996, p. 52.
The Wall Street Journal. August 2, 1996, p. A12.
The Washington Post. August 9, 1996, p. B1.

The English Patient

In memory, love lives forever.—Movie tagline

"*The English Patient* is one for the ages! Of some 6,000 film I've seen over my 28 years as a professional viewer, *The English Patient* is the best of all."—Susan Stark, *Detroit News*

"It captivates as only the greatest and most consuming passions can. *The English Patient* is the best film of the year."—Kenneth Turan, *Los Angeles Times*

"A mesmerizing tour de force . . . A stunning feat . . . A cinematic triumph."—Janet Maslin, *New York Times*

"A brilliant movie with the soul of a poet. A stunning achievement."—Jack Mathews, *Newsday*

"Extravagantly romantic. It's replete with spies, battles, and ravishing vistas. It's full of wit, sophistication and passion. *The English Patient* succeeds stunningly. It never loses its grip on your emotions."—David Ansen, *Newsweek*

"Passionate and intelligent. An event for the eyes, ears, heart and mind."—Peter Stack, *San Francisco Chronicle*

"Two big thumbs up. A fascinating puzzle of a story."—*Siskel & Ebert*

"This, you realize with a gasp of joy, is what movies can do. *The English Patient* is beyond gorgeous."—Richard Corliss, *Time*

"Completely intoxicating. As all great films must, *The English Patient* transports us to another time and place."—Rita Kempley, *Washington Post*

"Awash in heart-rending emotions and gorgeous images, this is a movie to lose yourself in."—Desson Howe, *Washington Post Weekend*

Box Office: $34,118,472

No, it's not the book, but most fans of Michael Ondaatje's dense, poetic novel, which was awarded the prestigious Booker Prize in 1992, won't be dismayed by what director/screenwriter Anthony Minghella has put on-screen as *The English Patient.* The novel, with its series of flashbacks, dwells with the shell-shocked Canadian nurse, Hana, as she struggles to regain an emotional balance in the waning days of World War II and rediscovers life and love, aided by Kip, an Indian bomb disposal expert in the British Army, as well as maimed thief, Caravaggio, an old family friend of Hana's. Hana's "English patient" is almost a male Scheherazade, spinning out a mysterious dying man's tale of obsessive love, betrayal, and tragedy to Hana and the others.

The film is stripped in plot, though complicated in execution as Minghella works seamlessly with his numerous flashbacks. It's the English patient's story, and as is quickly apparent in the film, he's not English at all but a Hungarian—erudite loner Count Laszlo de Almasy (Ralph Fiennes), a member of the International Sand Club, a group of cartographers making maps of the North African desert shortly before the outbreak of war.

Their exploration team is joined by British aristocrat Geoffrey Clifton (Colin Firth) and his wife Katharine (Kristin Scott Thomas). Geoffrey seems to be a hale-fellow-well-met type, gregarious, educated, a literal high-flyer as he and his wife make their dramatic desert landing in a gaudy yellow biplane. And the blonde, monied Katharine, who's "read everything," is another type—a cool British beauty, ready for a little adventure, her self-possession enabling her to relax in this decidedly masculine group. But as Katharine points out to Almasy, Geoffrey is not a buffoon (he's in fact an English spy), and while Katharine may appear—even wish—to be conventional, the passion she feels for Almasy (and his for her) overwhelms them both.

World War II is the backdrop for the epic and sweeping romance *The English Patient*, as Ralph Fiennes plays a dying man whose identity is unknown.

In one of the early flashbacks, Almasy is shown with an elderly Arab who's describing a particular land feature as possessing the curves of a woman's back as Almasy sketches. It's a scene that's echoed later as Almasy traces the curves of his lover Katharine's naked back as they lie in bed and he looks to claim a part of her (finally settling on the hollow at the base of her throat).

Meanwhile, in the present, an emotionally-spent Hana (Juliette Binoche), having lost her lover, her best friend, and countless patients to the ravages of war, is eager to hide away, persuading her Red Cross superiors to allow her to care for her severely burned and dying patient in an abandoned monastery in Tuscany as the rest of the convoy moves towards Florence. Hana's eager for a peaceful silence, willing to listen to her patient's reminiscences, willing to read from the one possession that's travelled with Almasy, a book of Herodotus, which is filled with the scraps of his life.

"Maddox knows, I think. He keeps talking about Anna Karenina. It's his idea of a man-to-man chat."—Almasy to Katharine about their affair

Their solitude is soon broken by the appearance of David Carravagio (Willem Dafoe), who's learned of Hana's whereabouts from one of her fellow nurses. Caravaggio tries to ingratiate himself with Hana by bringing her some fresh eggs, and by telling her they're from the same Montreal neighborhood. An admitted thief, Caravaggio is working as a translator for the Allies, trying to get the local Italian partisans to lay down their weapons, but he also has his own agenda. He'd been captured as a spy and tortured by the Germans while in North Africa, and his thumbs have been cut off. Carravaggio wants revenge on the man he believes betrayed him, and he believes that that man is Hana's patient, who's supposedly lost his name and memory. Caravaggio is also a morphine addict and why Hana would allow such a shady, perhaps unbalanced, character to remain anywhere near her is something of a mystery. Although, it's true, Caravaggio's hardly the type to take "no" for an answer.

No sooner does Hana become somewhat accustomed to having Caravaggio around than two bomb disposal experts, Kip (Naveen Andrews) and his Sergeant (Kevin Whatley), are billeted to the monastery. (They've been shown earlier working—and rescuing a grief-stricken, oblivious Hana—from a bomb in the nearby road). Hana seems fascinated by Kip's exoticness, his quiet strength, and the sure touch his profession demands. Although Binoche always seems to radiate with an inner glow, her Hana brightens more around Kip, running towards him with longing.

And longing's everywhere in *The English Patient*—longing for knowledge, for peace, for death, for passion—for love. Almasy objects to Katharine's presence on the expedition, wondering how she'll manage in the rough terrain and less-than-luxurious conditions, but his objections have a hollow ring. They're clearly fascinated with each other.

They have what appears to be a chance meeting in a Cairo bazaar, with Katharine teasing Almasy that he's been following her (he actually has). During a desert expedition, Almasy discovers a cave, the interior walls covered in paintings of swimmers, which Katharine sketches (her sketching is shown in the first scenes of the film, when it's hard to tell what the beautiful designs are—they look like ink brushes of exotic Arabic writing). She tries to give the sketches to Almasy, to place

AWARDS AND NOMINATIONS

Academy Awards 1996: Best Picture, Best Director (Minghella), Best Supporting Actress (Binoche), Best Art Direction, Best Costume Design, Best Sound, Best Film Editing, Best Original Dramatic Score (Yared), Best Cinematography (Seale)
Nominations: Best Actor (Fiennes), Best Actress (Scott Thomas), Best Adapted Screenplay (Minghella), Best Sound Effects Editing
Directors Guild of America 1996: Best Director (Minghella)
Golden Globe Awards 1997: Best Film-Drama, Best Original Score (Yared)
Nominations: Best Actress-Drama (Scott Thomas), Best Actor-Drama (Fiennes), Best Supporting Actress (Binoche), Best Director (Minghella), Best Screenplay (Minghella)
Los Angeles Film Critics Association 1996: Cinematography (Seale)
National Board of Review 1996: Best Supporting Actress (Binoche), Best Supporting Actress (Scott Thomas)
Screen Actors Guild 1996 Nominations: Actor (Fiennes), Actress (Scott Thomas), Supporting Actress (Binoche), Cast
Writers Guild of America 1996 Nominations: Adapted Screenplay (Minghella)

CREDITS

Almasy: Ralph Fiennes
Katharine Clifton: Kristin Scott Thomas
Hana: Juliette Binoche
Caravaggio: Willem Dafoe
Kip: Naveen Andrews
Geoffrey Clifton: Colin Firth

Origin: USA
Released: 1996
Production: Saul Zaentz; released by Miramax Films
Direction: Anthony Minghella
Screenplay: Anthony Minghella; based on the novel by Michael Ondaatje
Cinematography: John Seale
Editing: Walter Murch
Music: Gabiel Yared
Costumes: Ann Roth
Production design: Stuart Craig
Casting: Michelle Guish, David Rubin
MPAA rating: R
Running Time: 160 minutes

in his book of Herodotus, but he first refuses, claiming they're too good to be hidden away with him. Later, when the duo are caught in their truck in a horrendous sandstorm, Almasy speaks beautifully about the names of the various desert winds, while stroking Katharine's disheveled hair almost unconsciously.

When they first make love in Almasy's room, Katharine, in a cool white dress, reaches to brush sand from Almasy's hair—their passion ignited as Almasy literally tears her dress off. They later lie in a bath together as Katharine washes his hair and Almasy coldly warns her about the perils of possession, while stating that he hates ownership. Her face goes blank at his dismissal but he's deceiving no one but himself.

Venice, Italy substituted as a location for pre-war Cairo, Egypt.

Almasy later makes a fool of himself at a dinner party, drunk and jealous of the attention Katharine pays to others. But they can't stay apart and it's only a matter of time until Geoffrey learns what others suspect. He wants to surprise Katharine on their anniversary and leaves work early, only to see Katharine departing their hotel for a rendezvous with Almasy, thus precipitating a final tragedy.

Almasy, now alone on another mapping trip, waits to be picked up by plane when suddenly he sees Geoffrey's biplane coming straight at him—Almasy narrowly avoids being killed when it crashes, but Geoffrey is not so lucky. Then Almasy realizes Katharine was his passenger and is now badly injured. Almasy carries her to the "Cave of Swimmers," leaving her with a light, some food and water, and his book for her to write in, as he must walk for help. He promises to return. Half-crazed with fear, Almasy finally reaches civilization only to run up against two officious British soldiers.

The war's broken out, and the obviously foreign Almasy is suspected of being a spy. He can't make the fools listen to him; indeed they lock him up and transport him with other prisoners on a train, travelling ever-farther away from Katharine. Almasy manages to escape and begins his torturous journey back. He knows the whereabouts of another plane, belonging to his friend Maddox, but when he reaches it, the Germans are waiting.

Caravaggio knows the Germans have obtained the British maps detailing the desert terrain, they have photographs showing him working with the British. Caravaggio, who tells Almasy that Maddox has killed himself over Almasy's betrayal, has wanted to know how Almasy could have done it, and now he knows. Almasy betrayed not for country, not for friendship, but for love. Katharine's only chance was for Almasy to get the plane and return. And Almasy's own recourse, after being betrayed by the British, is to deal with the Germans.

Katharine has perished by the time Almasy returns to the cave—we've seen the lamplight and Katherine herself literally fade before our eyes. She's written a goodbye in his book and he tenderly carries her body, wrapped in white parachute silk (a striking visual image against the red/gold desert rock) back to the plane. In midair, the plane is struck by German guns and crashes, blazing, into the desert sands. The badly burned Almasy is found by a group of Bedouins, who care for him until, at some point, he's transported into Hana's care and to Italy. Caravaggio cannot bring himself to kill Almasy, after all.

The war is finally over. A celebratory village party has resulted in the death of Kip's sergeant, precipitating a crisis for Kip and Hana. Later, Kip's reassigned but Hana is quietly able to cope with his departure, having regained through his care, at least some of her equilibrium. Caravaggio is leaving too, and only Hana and Almasy linger—but not for long. Almasy's only remaining desire is to die, and Hana, with tears streaming down her face, fixes an overdose of morphine for her patient.

Highly praised by critics everywhere, *The English Patient* is a stunning film on every level—exquisitely shot and edited, beautifully written and directed, and featuring extraordinary performances from Fiennes, Scott Thomas, and Binoche.

With only two previous films to his credit, (*Truly, Madly, Deeply* [1991], *Mr. Wonderful* [1993]) writer/director Minghella struck gold with his third outing. Earning 12 Academy Award nominations, *The English Patient* took home nine Oscars, including Best Picture, Best Director and Best Supporting Actress for Binoche. The success of *The English Patient* was especially rewarding for Minghella and producer Saul Zaentz, who shared the passion and the vision of bringing the complex novel to the screen. As the most poetic and intelligent film of the year, this haunting love story lingers long after the credits have rolled.

—*Christine Tomassini* and *Beth Fhaner*

REVIEWS

American Cinematographer. January, 1997, p. 30-37.
Boxoffice Online. November 18, 1996.
Chicago Tribune. November 22, 1996, p. 5.
Detroit Free Press. November 22, 1996.
Detroit News. November 16, 1996, p. 1C, 3C.
Detroit News. November 22, 1996, p. 1E, 3E.
Entertainment Weekly. November 22, 1996, p. 107.
The Hollywood Reporter. November 6, 1996, p. 5.
Los Angeles Times. November 15, 1996, p. F1, F14.
New York Times. November 15, 1996, p. C1, C4.
New York Times. December 3, 1995, p. 24.
The New Yorker. November 25, 1996, p. 118.
Newsweek. November 11, 1996, p. 72-74.
People. November 18, 1996, p. 22.
Rolling Stone. November 28, 1996, p. 142.
San Francisco Chronicle. November 22, 1996, p. C1.
San Francisco Examiner. November 22, 1996, p. C1.
Sight and Sound. March, 1997, p. 45.
Time. November 11, 1996.
USA Today. November 15, 1996.
Variety. November 11, 1996, p. 57.
Washington Post. November 22, 1996, p. D1, D7.

Eraser

He will erase your past to protect your future.—Movie tagline

"Arnold's back and better than ever."—David Sheehan, *CBS-TV*

"The summer's wildest and scariest ride."—Jim Svejda, *KNX/CBS Radio*

Box Office: $101,295,562

As a summer high-budget, high-tech, low-sense blockbuster, *Eraser* should have rubbed out the competition, even if it could not exactly make *The Rock* disappear. Making people disappear is the speciality of its action-hero, U.S. Federal Marshal John Kruger (Arnold Schwarzenegger), the "eraser" of the title who takes the concept of witness protection very seriously. He is assigned Lee Cullen (Vanessa Williams), a problem witness because of what she knows about a scheme devised by defense experts to sell top secret, assault weapons to the Russian mafia. Taking care of her is a real challenge.

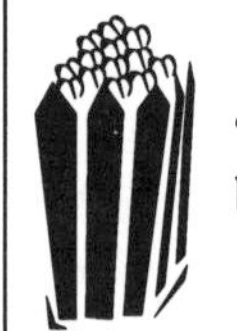

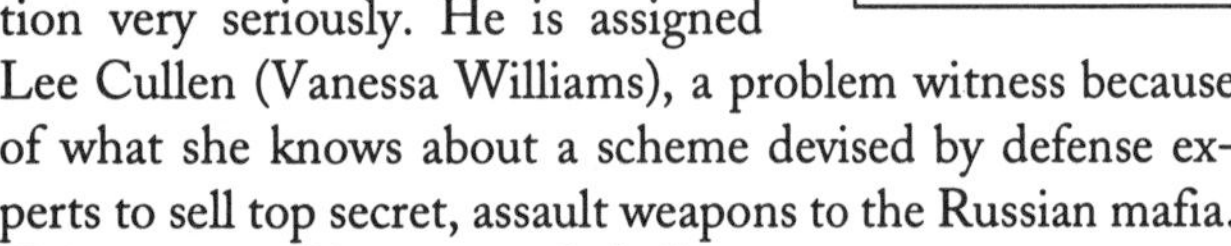

"You're luggage."—"Eraser" John blowing away some hungry gators

Lee Cullen, the whistle-blower Kruger is assigned to protect, has security clearance for the high-tech weapons corporation where she works, and discovers that her bosses plan to sell newly-developed "rail guns," hyper-velocity weapons that fire aluminum rounds at just below the speed of light. The screenplay adds an X-ray scope-sighting system that enables the shooter to see through walls. Lee realizes that this is treasonous and reports the company to the FBI, which sends her on a mission that is more dangerous than she realizes to copy a high-security computer disk that will result in high-level convictions.

Lee manages to copy the disk, making a back-up copy for her own protection, but television surveillance alerts the Vice-President of the corporation, who orders a security agent to bring her to his office. He confronts her, then commits suicide. In the confusion that follows, Lee manages to escape from the building and is picked up by an FBI van. At that point she is turned over to Kruger, the "eraser" responsible for her protection, who "erases" her past and gives her a new name, Debra Elliot.

Lee's purloined disk, submitted as evidence, ends up on the desk of Undersecretary of Defense Daniel Harper, who is masterminding the illegal weapons sale for his own profit; but he soon discovers that Lee also has a back-up disk. Harper puts Robert Deguerin (James Caan), a crooked Federal Marshal, on her trail. The disk, her insurance policy, so to speak, cannot be easily accessed, so she and Kruger need to break into the defense plant to read it through the computer of the dead Vice President, whose office is on the twenty-fifth floor. Protecting Lee in this hostile environment proves to be a real challenge for Kruger, who has already saved her from Deguerin and his henchmen at her home and, later, at the New York Zoo.

For the break-in Kruger needs help and enlists the aid of Johnny C (Robert Pastorelli, Eldin on television's "Murphy Brown"), a mafia witness Kruger saves and then "erases" during the film's opening action-packed sequence. Under a new identity Johnny now works as a bartender in a gay Village bar, a place where no "wise guy" would go, he says. The irony is that Kruger, who can trust no one in the Department of Justice, can only trust this mafia informant whose life he saved. Johnny gets to the front desk of the weapons corporation pretending to be a pizza delivery boy; when security gives him a hard time, he pretends to have a heart attack. Kruger and

CREDITS

John Kruger: Arnold Schwarzenegger
Lee Cullen: Vanessa Williams
Robert Deguerin: James Caan
Beller: James Coburn
Johnny C: Robert Pastorelli
Donahue: James Cromwell

Origin: USA
Released: 1996
Production: Arnold Kopelson and Anne Kopelson; released by Warner Bros.
Direction: Charles Russell
Screenplay: Tony Puryear and Walon Green
Cinematography: Adam Greenberg
Editing: Michael Tronick
Music: Alan Silvestri
Production design: Bill Kenney
Art direction: Bill Skinner
Costume design: Richard Bruno
Sound: Robert Eber
Stunt coordinator: Joel Kramer
Casting: Bonnie Timmermann
MPAA rating: R
Running Time: 115 minutes

Lee are ready with an ambulance to come to his rescue in the company's infirmary, which gets them past security. Breaking into the computer system they discover that the weapons are to be shipped off the Baltimore docks.

Johnny knows Kruger is headed for the Baltimore docks and offers to go along. Though Kruger prefers to work alone, he takes Johnny because Johnny's mafia cousin, Tony Two-Toes, controls the union at the docks and can help them get to the ship. When they see crates of weapons being loaded on a Russian ship, Tony curses the gunrunners as "damned Communists." Tony's nephew, Little Mike (a 300-pounder) corrects him: "They're a Federation of Independent Liberated States now," he says. Tony answers "Shut up Little Mike, before I hurt you."

The point is these mafia types are patriotic, trustworthy, and helpful, unlike the Russian mafia, led by a thug named Serge Petrovsky, who behaves like an evil, stereotyped Commie, so, our mafia are better than their mafia. Moreover, purely evil types are running the government and controlling the Department of Justice. That the FBI are idiots is a given, here, thanks to Ruby Ridge and the tarnished reputation of J. Edgar Hoover.

The production is rumored to have gone three months over the original shooting schedule and some $30 million over-budget.

The top villain, Daniel Harper, is Under secretary of Defense. "The disk, the girl, the guns—by dawn they don't exist. Are we clear on that?" Undersecretary Harper says to Robert Deguerin, his main mole in the Justice Department. When they learn that Lee Cullen has made a back-up disk for a journalist named Isaacs, Deguerin takes care of her and reports to Harper that she was "peeled like an onion." These are dangerous, wicked people.

The action is nonstop. Kruger is supposed to meet his witness at the Central Park Zoo. We have seen him leap from a jet plane without a parachute, catch up with it in midair, strap it on, get tangled in the silk, cut himself loose, use an auxiliary chute, land in a junkyard, steal a truck, and drive like a maniac into New York City. All the while Lee is being chased by assassins, but Kruger arrives just in time to save her. When she asks why he was so late, he simply says "Traffic." The dialogue is wonderfully understated, and Arnold's deadpan delivery is constantly amusing.

When Kruger rescues Lee at the Zoo, he shoots out a containment window that floods the reptile house with alligators, one of which comes after him, while the others conveniently maul the bad guys. Calmly, Arnold shoots the critter then says, "You're luggage." That's as good as the comic dialogue gets. There are no zingers here to compete with Clint Eastwood's "Go ahead, make my day" or Arnold's "Hasta la vista, baby."

According to the credits Tony Puryear and Walon Green wrote the screenplay from a story concept created by Puryear, Green, and Michael Chernuchin, but according to Judy Brennan of *Entertainment Weekly,* a larger committee of script consultants and script doctors were involved. Puryear invented the Eraser character that got Schwarzenegger interested in the project, an operative assigned to protect witnesses from the mafia. Schwarzenegger wanted Green to replot the story, Green being a veteran writer once involved with *The Wild Bunch* (1969) and, more recently, the television series "Law & Order." Green brought along Chernuchin, who added the Zoo sequence and the high-tech weapons.

Uncredited revisions were done by director Chuck Russell, screenwriter Frank Darabont (*The Shawshank Redemption,* 1994) and the dialogue doctor William Wisher, who gave Schwarzenegger some of his best signature-lines in earlier pictures, most notably "Hasta la vista, baby" and "I'll be back," among other enduring Arnoldisms. Co-producer Arnold Kopelson brought in Christine Roum from "Law & Order" for dialogue assistance, so at least six writers were involved on this $100 million blockbuster.

Director Charles Russell's greatest hit was *The Mask* (1994), which made a star of Jim Carrey. He graduated to the blockbuster level after initial mentoring from Roger Corman, whose progeny have taken over Hollywood, it sometimes seems. In 1987 Russell directed *A Nightmare on Elm Street 3: Dream Warriors,* considered to be the best of that horror series. At the time of its release, it was the highest-grossing independent film ever made, earning more than its two predecessors combined. His direction of *Eraser* is effective.

In keeping with the times, when many Americans are distrustful of big government, Kruger has to deal with a number of corrupt U.S. Federal Marshals. The FBI cannot be trusted, nor can the National Security Administration. Arnold's Kruger is a loner who trusts no one, a survivor. This was also the case in *Mission Impossible,* but in *Eraser* James Caan plays a better and more thoroughly corrupt villain than Jon Voight played in *Mission Impossible.* The one advantage *Mission Impossible* had was that it played head games with the audience. The plot of *Eraser* is more predictable, but also more comic.

In fact, what makes *Eraser* a better film than *Mission Impossible,* which it resembles in its "MacGuffin" (its motivating gimmick, in other words), a computer disk with sensitive evidence that will incriminate highly-placed government officials, is its sense of humor, and Schwarzenegger's newly enhanced comic skills. The dialogue is punchy and well-timed. *Mission Impossible* takes itself too seriously, but *Eraser* seldom does, and, as a consequence, rises above its loony cartoon plot.

Like *The Rock, Eraser* takes high-tech action-adventure formula filmmaking to the highest level of perfection.

Schwarzenegger and Caan are equally at ease with their roles as Connery and Cage in *The Rock.* Connery's delivery is hard to match, but Arnold comes close to doing just that with his stylized dialogue. *Eraser* has even more action and a greater variety of adventure than *The Rock.* It is nothing more than escapist entertainment, but it is brilliantly executed on its $100 million budget. In short, *Eraser* deserved to rub out the competition.

—*James M. Welsh*

REVIEWS

Baltimore Sun. June 21, 1996, p. E1.
Entertainment Weekly. June 21, 1996, p. 6.
The New York Times. June 21, 1996, p. C16.
Philadelphia Inquirer Weekend. June 21, 1996, p. 3.
USA Today. June 21, 1996, p. 1.
Variety. June 17, 1996, p.51.
Washington Post. June 21, 1996, p. C16.
Washington Post Weekend. June 21, 1996, p. 41.
Washington Times Metropolitan Times. June 21, 1996, p. C17.

Escape From L.A.

Snake is back.—Movie tagline

"Filled with fast-paced fun, it's your new best bet for action-adventure." Susan Granger, *American Movie Classics*

"A go-for-broke action extravaganza!"—Roger Ebert, *Chicago Sun-Times*

"A provocative high-octane action thriller."—Kevin Thomas, *Los Angeles Times*

Box Office: $25,473,642

"Call me Snake," says Kurt Russell as apocalyptic cowboy Snake Plissken, consciously echoing Alan Ladd's "call me Shane" in the classic George Stevens' western. "Snake is back!" proclaims the movie poster. But will viewers remember or care about this character created sixteen years ago by Kurt Russell in *Escape From New York* (1981), a science-fiction adventure yarn set in 1997?

Escape From L.A. shamelessly imitates a galaxy of good "bad" movies. It's like *Waterworld* (1995) with a dime-store budget, which in turn imitated the Road Warrior series. *Mad Max* (1979), the first of the apocalyptic Road Warrior epics, and *The Road Warrior* (1981) were driven by the crazy inventiveness of Australian George Miller, who had the young Mel Gibson as his cowboy hero. John Carpenter's *Escape From New York* was released the same year as *The Road Warrior.* Carpenter knows a trend when he sees one coming, but making a sequel nearly a generation later is pretty risky.

The film seems oddly dated. Of course Russell's Snake is a second-rate imitation of Gibson and a third-rate imitation of Clint Eastwood's Man With No Name. Snake has a whole lot of attitude but very little human interest. His former exploits in Cleveland and New York are frequently mentioned in the movie but never explained. He is suppos-

CREDITS

Snake Plissken: Kurt Russell
Malloy: Stacy Keach
Cuervo Jones: George Corraface
Map to the Stars Eddie: Steve Buscemi
Hershe: Pam Grier
Utopia: A.J. Langer
Taslima: Valeria Golino
President: Cliff Robertson
Pipeline: Peter Fonda

Origin: USA
Released: 1996
Production: Debra Hill, Kurt Russell for a Rysher Entertainment production; released by Paramount Pictures
Direction: John Carpenter
Screenplay: John Carpenter, Debra Hill and Kurt Russell
Cinematography: Gary B. Kibbe
Editing: Edward A. Warschilka
Music: Shirley Walker, John Carpenter
Production design: Lawrence H. Paull
Art direction: Bruce Crone
Costume design: Robin Michel Bush
Sound: Thomas Causey
Visual effects supervisor: Michael Lessa
Special makeup effects: Rick Baker
Stunt coordinator: Jeff Imada
MPAA rating: R
Running Time: 101 minutes

edly a "legend," but to understand why, viewers will have to race to the video store, if any would be so inclined after seeing this ghoulish spectacle ornamented with comic book action and adolescent satire. This is not a movie for mature adults.

"We're what America is going to be like. We're multicultural, we try our best to get along the best we can, and we're poised over the edge of the apocalypse."—John Carpenter on Los Angeles

John Carpenter's *Escape From L.A.* is set sixteen years later than *Escape From New York* to give the aging Mr. Russell some credibility, and the world has not fared very well since the original in fantasyland. Carpenter brings us up-to-date on world events by presenting a crazy chronology at the top of the film.

In 1998 an Evangelical Nazi was elected President of the United States, then, in 2000, the Big One hit the West Coast, turning Los Angeles into an island dung heap of crime and corruption. All the nation's undesirables and criminals have been transported there from the politically-correct right-wing dictatorship that America has become, including a Muslim woman from South Dakota whose only "crime" is her belief in Islam. She is played all too briefly by the astonishingly beautiful and soulful Valeria Golino. The action of the film begins in the year 2013.

Escape From L.A. is the fifth film Kurt Russell and John Carpenter have worked on together.

Legendary Snake Plissken (Russell) is called upon to infiltrate the cesspool Los Angeles has become to "rescue" the President's daughter, Utopia (A.J. Langer), who somehow managed to steal her father's Doomsday Machine and deliver it to Peruvian revolutionary Cuervo Jones (George Carraface), the really bad dude who rules L.A. and clearly resembles Che Guevara, if anyone who sees the film remembers his revolutionary exploits. Snake has been infected with a terrible virus that will destroy him in ten hours time if he fails to accomplish his impossible mission.

In fact, the President orders Snake to kill Utopia (allegory is working overtime here, but how's that for tough love?) because she has been a bad girl though he mainly wants his Doomsday Machine back so he can rule the world. Ten hours, and the digital clock is "ticking."

Snake's fame goes before him and everyone in L.A. seems to know who he is. He is betrayed by a turncoat named "Map to the Stars Eddie," played by the weasely Steve Buscemi, the smarter of the two hit-men in *Fargo* (1996). Why would anyone trust Eddie? Don't ask, but the character is a potentially amusing parody of a typically sleazy Hollywood agent trying to survive in a bad world by his native talent.

Originally Snake is coerced into his mission by the cowardly President and his tough-as-nails factotum Malloy (Stacy Keach, who has seen better days and better roles). Snake gets some help from a friendly surfer named Pipeline, played by Peter Fonda, Jane's less talented brother, forgotten by everyone but John Carpenter. He also gets help from a transsexual creature named Hershe, played by the all-but-forgotten Pam Grier, famous during the 1970s as Foxy Brown and Sheba Baby. *Baltimore Sun* critic Stephen Hunter described the movie as a series of "run-ins with bad actors in bad make-up," but, as the Coen brothers demonstrated in *Fargo,* Steve Buscemi is not such a bad actor, really. He is merely trapped in a cheesy role in a bad movie here.

Nonetheless, *Escape From L.A.* wears its tackiness with pride and has cult exploitation written all over it. It does have a sense of humor. Every time someone recognizes Snake, the joke response is "I thought you would be taller." The plot offers a single dilemma and a deadline time frame, little else, but, then, little more is needed if this hyperactive, outrageous little movie is going to work.

In a distinctively wacky way, *Escape From L.A.*, released to coincide with the Republican National Convention of 1996, anticipated the power struggle on the convention floor where Ralph Reed's Christian Coalition controlled almost 60 percent of the delegates. In the *New York Times* (August 9, A27) Anthony Lewis editorialized about "Jefferson's Nightmare," a "Major party driven by religion." Thomas Jefferson understood "the dangers of having a single religious view tied to politics," Lewis wrote, and Jefferson's most passionate effort "was to disestablish the Anglican Church in Virginia and assume religious liberty for all." John Carpenter gives us a President intolerantly driven by religion who becomes an absolute dictator, ruling the country no longer from Washington, D.C. (potentially the site for yet another *Escape From* movie because of its crime record and urban problems), but from Lynchburg, Virginia. As political allegory, the film offers an interesting interpretation of Jefferson's nightmare. But that hardly redeems it.

If writer-director John Carpenter is important enough to have his name above the title, it is because of his reputation as the horror schlockmeister who created the lucrative *Halloween* series. He wrote the screenplay for *Escape From L.A.* in collaboration with producer Debra Hill and star Kurt Russell, based on characters originally created by Carpenter and Nick Castle. The sequel mentality prevails here as the plot bumps along from one absurd crisis to the next. It constantly falls between the stools of heroic action-adventure and self-conscious parody. A strange satirical send-up of the Los Angeles fascination with plastic surgery takes place when Plissken ends up in a Beverly Hills hospital run by "surgical failures." Now, that is something to "escape" from. Fall into their clutches and one becomes an automatic organ donor. The mad doctors are interested in Snake's only remaining good eye, but he outsmarts them.

The reviews were as scrambled and mixed as the film itself. In a *Washington Post* review snidely headlined "Doom and Dumber," Esther Iverem was appalled by the film's message that "real" Americans "are squeezed between a corrupt and crazy federal government and a criminal, immoral and usually dark population of city dwellers." She considered the film "an anthem for the militia movement," a call to arms for white men determined to survive against an evil government. Convicts headed for Los Angeles are given a kind of choice: "You now have the option to repent for your sins and be electrocuted on the premises." That's about as hopeful as this movie gets. Desmond Ryan was rather more positive, contending that the film's "cool humor" set it apart "from the dourness of the other action films of the summer." Ryan was amused by the way the film "is littered with as many inside movie-industry jokes as dead bodies." Those tolerant of this trash-epic allegory tended to be impressed by Carpenter's "great" special effects and the inventive use of holograms, which are as transparent as the plot.

The strength of this movie is that it doesn't take itself too seriously, but that's also a drawback, since no intelligent viewer will take it seriously, either. The eye patch is a nice touch, but Kurt Russell hardly measures up to a Schwarzenegger, or an Eastwood, or a Banderas, for that matter, though he rides a cool motorcycle at one point. Peter Fonda who also once rode a cool motorcycle now rides a monster surfboard in this idiotic movie and catches a tsunami up Wilshire Boulevard.

—*James M. Welsh*

REVIEWS

The Baltimore Sun. August 9, 1996, E1, E6.
Boxoffice Magazine Online. August 12, 1996.
Chicago Tribune. August 9, 1996, p.5.
Entertainment Weekly. August 28, 1996, p. 102.
Los Angeles Times. August 9, 1996, p. F1.
The New York Times. August 9, 1996, p. C5.
Philadelphia Inquirer Weekend. August 9, 1996, p. 5, p. 12.
Rolling Stone. September 5, 1996, p. 68.
Sight and Sound. October, 1996, p. 44.
USA Today. August 9, 1996, D3.
Variety. August 9, 1996.
The Washington Post. August 9, 1996, B7.
Washington Post Weekend. August 9, 1996, pp. 29-30

The Evening Star

A story about friends, family and other natural disasters.—Movie tagline

"A shining success of a sequel."—Jay Carr, *The Boston Globe*

"A brilliant and charming cast."—Michael Wilmington, *The Chicago Tribune*

"The large, gifted cast creates a gallery of memorable characters. First-time director Robert Harling has an admirable way with his actors."—Michael Medved, *New York Post*

"A worthy, heartwarming successor to a film classic."—Pat Collins, *WWOR-TV*

Box Office: $12,385,239

The Evening Star is very much like viewing a month's worth of "Days of Our Lives" episodes packed into two-and-a-half hours. This film which was billed as a continuation of *Terms of Endearment* (1983) should have been called "The Never Ending Saga of Aurora Greenway." There isn't much that doesn't happen to this Texas matriarch in the Paramount release of Larry McMurtry's 1992 novel. The sentimental melodrama was written and directed for the screen by Robert Harling who also wrote *Steel Magnolias* (1989) and the recent hit *First Wives Club* (reviewed in this volume).

Shirley MacLaine reprises the Academy Award-winning role as the difficult but loveable Aurora Greenway. Ms. MacLaine was reportedly wary of returning and was quoted in *The Hollywood Reporter* as saying, "I'd have to be brain-dead not to have been concerned [about reprising the role]. I've never made clever, calculated career moves. I did *Cannonball Run II* as my follow-up picture to my Oscar." Perhaps, Shirley should have followed her well-publicized psy-

AWARDS AND NOMINATIONS

Golden Globe Award 1997 Nominations: Best Supporting Actress (Ross)

chic instincts and passed on the role. The veteran actress is an accomplished and experienced performer. Nevertheless, she could not rise above the material—a mixed bag of new and old ideas that simply didn't work. It was a meandering script that had multitudinous subplots plus some scenes that seemed to be stolen right out of TV's "Dynasty." Where is Joan Collins when you need her?

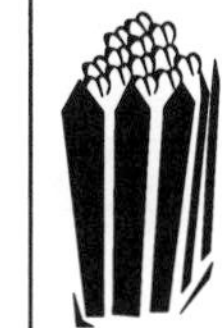

"Do you mind aging?" "No, because I've done it so well."—Aurora asks ex-lover Garrett

This time around, Aurora is fifteen years older, but still dresses in flouncy frocks and scarves. She has managed to raise the three children that her daughter (dear, departed Emma) left behind after her premature death. One is in jail, another has an illegitimate child and the third, Melanie (Juliette Lewis) is a cross between Lolita and the Bad Seed. For some reason, Aurora can't see how this happened to her. She laments "I'm surrounded by the most taxing collection of lunatics." Besides the three grandchildren, there is Hector (Donald Moffat), her former lover; Rosie (Marion Ross), the housekeeper; Jerry (Bill Paxton), the horny psychologist; Patsy (Miranda Richardson), the wealthy widow; and last but certainly not least, Garrett Breedlove (Jack Nicholson), who thinks he's playing the devil in *Damn Yankees.* Plucky as ever, Aurora dauntlessly deals with all of these "colorful characters" with the charm of a locomotive. Age hasn't slowed her down a bit, nor has it bestowed much wisdom upon her. She's as obstinate and self-willed as ever. She relentlessly goes to see grandson Tommy (George Newbern) in prison, bearing gifts of homemade cookies, bravely combats her arch rival, Patsy, patiently tolerates good old Hector and regularly confides in Rosie (her loyal and trusted servant). In between all this, she manages to have a "hot" affair with her hunky, younger counselor. Aurora is busy, busy, busy! There is so much going on in *Evening Star* that they could have made another sequel and called it a trilogy.

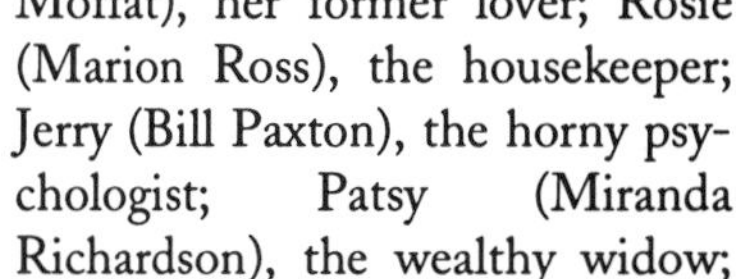

Last film role for Ben Johnson.

The problem with this epic approach to the heroine's life is that there is no coherent meaning to any of it. All the audience gets to see is this "wild and crazy" character flounce her way through a maze of contrived and incredulous events. Apparently, there was a lot of concern with the creators of *Evening Star* to match the success of *Terms* and to show the growth of this flamboyant personality. To be called a "continuation" of the original tearjerker (*Terms of Endearment*), it is essential for the audience to see Aurora's maturity as she goes through life to demonstrate change. Unfortunately, in *Evening Star*, Aurora hasn't changed, only her circumstances have, the externals. Instead of Emma, she now fights with Melanie and Patsy. In place of her love interest, Jerry, the analyst, takes over for Garrett, the astronaut. She now visits Rosie, as she lays dying in the hospital, instead of Emma. Aurora is still as wacky and unpredictable as ever. One evening, in her nightgown, she drives over to Jerry's house to seduce him. Why, she even climbs through his window instead of using the front door. When he is about to slug her over the head with a baseball bat (thinking that she's a burglar), she exclaims, "How rude!" She even takes one more ride on the beach with Jack Nicholson. What's the point? This isn't a continuation of the original, it's a copy. This has already been shown in *Terms*—there is nothing new.

The one bright spot in this film is Miranda Richardson. Whether she is playing an IRA revolutionary, as she did in Neil Jordan's, *The Crying Game* (1992) or a broken-

CREDITS

Aurora Greenway: Shirley MacLaine
Jerry Bruckner: Bill Paxton
Melanie Horton: Juliette Lewis
Patsy Carpenter: Miranda Richardson
Rosie Dunlop: Marion Ross
Garrett Breedlove: Jack Nicholson
Arthur Cotton: Ben Johnson
Tommy Horton: George Newbern
Teddy Horton: Mackenzie Astin
Bruce: Scott Wolf
Hector Scott: Donald Moffat

Origin: USA
Released: 1996
Production: David Kirkpatrick, Polly Platt, Keith Samples for a Rysher Entertainment production; released by Paramount Pictures
Direction: Robert Harling
Screenplay: Robert Harling; based on the novel by Larry McMurtry
Cinematography: Don Burgess
Editing: Priscilla Nedd-Friendly, David Moritz
Production design: Bruno Rubeo
Costume design: Renee Ehrlich Kalfus
Music: William Ross
Art direction: Richard L. Johnson
Sound: Douglas Axtell
Casting: Jennifer Shull
MPAA rating: PG-13
Running Time: 127 Minutes

hearted mother in Louis Malle's *Damage* (1992), to a Texas bitch in *Evening Star*, she is totally believable in every role. She always manages to capture the truth of the character and as Patsy, she is extremely funny and enjoyable to watch.

Evening Star may be entertaining to audience members who enjoy soap operas or love melodramas that have little to do with real life. However, even for the avid fans of both Shirley MacLaine and *Terms of Endearment*, the film fails to deliver. It was called "Terms of Endurement" by Kenneth Turan of *The Los Angeles Times*. This sequel/continuation goes on and on and on and nothing new or important is revealed. It screams for what Hollywood calls a "script doctor" to come in to rewrite and edit—to make some sense out of it all. It needs some structure and coherency. Possibly with these revisions, everyone would have been sad that Aurora died at the end. As it stands now, there is a sigh of relief—finally!!

—Rob Chicatelli

REVIEWS

Boxoffice. February, 1997, p. 62.
Chicago Tribune. December 26, 1996, p. 1.
Entertainment Weekly. January 10, 1997, p. 38.
Hollywood Reporter. December 17, 1996, p. 10.
Los Angeles Times. December 25, 1996, p. F1.
New York Times. December 25, 1996, p. C22.
People. January 13, 1997, p. 19.
USA Today. December 24, 1996, p. 3D.
Variety. December 23, 1996, p. 40.

Everyone Says I Love You

"Champagne for the eyes and ears!"—Jay Carr, *Boston Globe*

"A movie for which the word magical was invented! It has a freshness and charm that never ends . . . Absolutely wonderful."—Roger Ebert, *Chicago Sun-Times*

"This reminds us what we go to the movies for! Terrific!"—Michael Wilmington, *Chicago Tribune*

"Delightful and witty . . . festive and full of surprises."—Janet Maslin, *New York Times*

"Sublime entertainment! A burst of exhilaration!"—Peter Travers, *Rolling Stone*

"Deliriously original and very funny. Woody Allen has made something fresh and beguiling . . . terrific."—Richard Schickel, *Time*

Box Office: $2,200,552

In the ten films he has written and directed since *Hannah and Her Sisters* (1986), his most recent masterpiece, Woody Allen has gotten mixed results ranging from the stilted, *Another Woman* (1988), to the pretentious, *Shadows and Fog* (1992), to entertaining fluff, *Manhattan Murder Mystery* (1993). *Everyone Says I Love You* combines the lighthearted approach of the latter with the nostalgia seen in such films as *Radio Days* (1987) and *Bullets Over Broadway* (1994). While it has some ragged edges, *Everyone Says I Love You* is in many ways Allen's most charming film.

Joe Berlin (Woody Allen), an American writer living in Paris, is distraught because his latest girlfriend has left him for reasons he cannot grasp. In New York, Joe complains about his loveless state to his best friends, Steffi (Goldie Hawn), his ex-wife, and Bob (Alan Alda), Steffi's husband, a lawyer. Both Steffi and Bob are aware that Joe is still in love with her.

Steffi and Bob preside over a Park Avenue household crammed with their assorted offspring. Skylar (Drew Barrymore) is engaged to Holden (Edward Norton), a young lawyer in his father's firm. Bob despairs that his son, Scott (Lukas Haas), has abandoned the family's principles to become a hardened conservative Republican. The youngest daughters, Laura (Natalie Portman) and Lane (Gaby Hoffmann), are giggling teenagers. The liveliest of the young people is DJ (Natasha Lyonne), the forever-falling-in-love daughter of Steffi and Joe.

DJ joins Joe for vacation in Venice where he spots the married art historian Von (Julia Roberts) and falls in love.

AWARDS AND NOMINATIONS

Golden Globe Award 1997 Nominations: Best Film-Musical/Comedy
Los Angeles Film Critics Association 1996: Supporting Actor (Norton)
National Board of Review 1996: Best Supporting Actor (Norton)

DJ can help her father in his pursuit since she is a friend of the daughter of Von's psychiatrist (Waltrudis Buck) and has spied on Von's sessions. After DJ fills him in on Von's likes and dislikes, he woos her away from Greg (Robert Knepper), her husband, by posing as her ideal man—well, as ideal as a short, balding man twice her age can be.

"You know, I'm going to kill myself. I should go to Paris and jump off the Eiffel Tower. I'd be dead. In fact, if I got the Concorde, I could be dead three hours earlier."—Joe

Meanwhile back in New York, matters become complicated because Steffi, devoted to fashionably liberal causes, has campaigned for the release of a criminal, Charles Ferry (Tim Roth). When Ferry is released, Steffi invites him over, and Skylar becomes infatuated with someone so unlike her straitlaced fiance. Skylar eventually discovers Ferry is a bit too dangerous and goes back to Holden, while Von pronounces Joe a tad too perfect and returns to Greg.

All this is relatively minor Allen material. As in most of his recent films, some of the situations offer interesting twists, but most go nowhere. Some of the dialogue and punch lines are terrific, but too many of the lines simply serve to get from one plot point to the next. What distinguishes *Everyone Says I Love You* is that every few minutes someone breaks into a romantic song from the 1930's or 1940's. Dennis Potter uses this device for ironic counterpoint in his television miniseries "Pennies from Heaven" (1978) and "The Singing Detective" (1986). Allen uses the music to accentuate the romantic longing within the characters.

While Potter's characters lip-synch to period recordings, Allen's actors do their own singing with their limitations as song stylists adding a degree of poignancy as well as a slight degree of realism to the fantasy world Allen has imagined. Hawn and Alda have some background in musical theater and sing pleasantly, especially Hawn. Roth, a performer seemingly capable of anything, also sings reasonably well. Norton has limited singing ability but has a pleasant boy-next-door musical-comedy quality that helps him enormously, as when he deliberately dances awkwardly in one scene. Roberts has a surprisingly weak voice, and even more surprising is Allen's awful singing. All this was his idea, after all, but he sings in a terrified little whisper like he is being forced to perform at gunpoint. Only Barrymore was allowed off the hook. Since she refused to play along, her singing has been dubbed by someone of appropriately limited ability.

The musical numbers are staged in a variety of styles. While Allen's films always open with austere white credits on a black background—as if to announce that a serious artist is at work—*Everyone Says I Love You* begins with Holden singing "Just You, Just Me" in bright sunshine on Fifth Avenue. This opening song establishes that the audience is not to expect the usual Allen approach to the neurotic side of romance. The otherworldly quality is heightened by having everyone on the street, even a panhandler, take part in the singing. These additional singers are not exactly joining Holden since they and the young couple do not appear in the same shots. Allen implies that when people are in love, all the world sings. The number might have been even more charming, however, if Allen had made it consist of passersby becoming caught up in Holden's enthusiasm.

CREDITS

Joe Berlin: Woody Allen
Steffi: Goldie Hawn
Von: Julia Roberts
Bob: Alan Alda
Skylar: Drew Barrymore
Holden: Edward Norton
Charles Ferry: Tim Roth
DJ: Natasha Lyonne
Scott: Lukas Haas
Laura: Natalie Portman
Lane: Gaby Hoffmann
Holden's father: David Ogden Stiers
Holden's mother: Scotty Bloch
Grandpa: Patrick Cranshaw
Frieda: Trude Klein
Greg: Robert Knepper
Ken: Billy Crudup
Harry Winston salesman: Edward Hibbert
Jeffrey Vandermost: John Griffin
Psychiatrist: Waltrudis Buck
Cab driver: Robert Khakh

Origin: USA
Released: 1996
Production: Robert Greenhut for Sweetland Films and Jean Doumanian Productions; released by Miramax Films
Direction: Woody Allen
Screenplay: Woody Allen
Cinematography: Carlo DiPalma
Editing: Susan E. Morse
Production design: Santo Loquasto
Art direction: Tom Warren
Set design: Elaine O'Donnell
Costume design: Jeffrey Kurland
Sound: Gary Alper
Choreography: Graciela Daniele
Casting: Juliet Taylor
Special effects: Connie Brink
MPAA rating: R
Running Time: 97

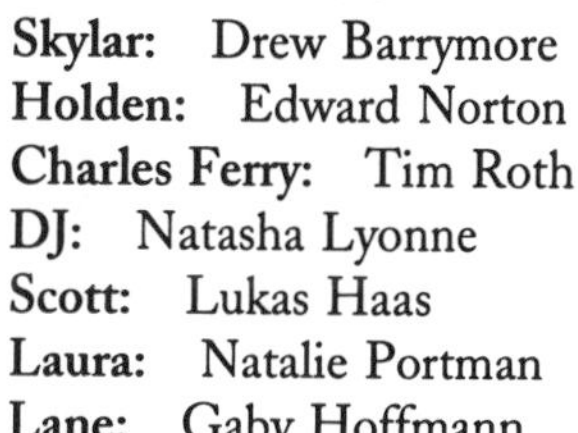

Choreographer Graciela Daniele does her best work when Holden takes Skylar to Harry Winston's expensive premises to buy her the best engagement ring he can afford and sings "My Baby Just Cares for Me." As Holden begins dancing on top of every surface, he is joined by the salesman (Edward Hibbert) and soon by all the other customers and salespeople, one of whom uses an enormous diamond necklace as a jump rope. Especially because of the tall, elegantly dressed models among the dancers, the staging seems patterned after the "Think Pink" number in Stanley Donen's *Funny Face* (1957). One difference, however, is that Allen seems to have the camera in too tight, perhaps because he shot the scene in a limited space and could not pull the camera any farther away from the performers. This slightly claustrophobic quality only deters a little from what is the most effective number in the film because of the energy of the dancers and the charming contrast with Norton's equally energetic but clumsy dancing.

Drew Barrymore is the only actor whose singing is dubbed—at her insistence.

The same lack of space limits the "Making Whoopee" number staged in a hospital's hallways. A crowd dressed as Groucho Marx singing "Hooray for Captain Spalding" in French at a party in Paris is mildly amusing though a bit long. The most charming musical moment occurs after this party at the end of the film as Steffi and Joe contemplate what should have been in their relationship, reliving their youth on the banks of the Seine. (Allen and Peter Sellers debate romantic despair in this same setting in 1965's *What's New, Pussycat,* the first film written by Allen.) Dancing in formal clothes, they evoke Fred Astaire and Ginger Rogers as Hawn floats effortlessly through the air.

Such delightfully comic touches occur in a few other numbers. When DJ is serenaded in a cab by a stranger (Billy Crudup) she has just fallen for, the driver (Robert Khakh) continues "Cuddle Up a Little Closer" in Hindi. Norton's opening number is concluded at a fashionable soiree with a violin version by Itzhak Perlman. As several characters take turns with the lament "I'm Through with Love," the song ends with a profane version by rappers (Robert Walker, Devalle Hayes, Damon McCloud). Such moments are Allen's way of indicating he is not taking his musical experiment all that seriously.

Hawn continues, after *The First Wives Club* (1996), her entirely unexpected comeback with a delightful comic performance. Alda, who does by far his best work in Allen's films, is amusing as the easily flustered father. As in *Michael Collins* (1996), Roberts carries an underwritten role with her considerable star charisma. Compared with her usual punk roles, Barrymore is a revelation as a WASP dream of youthful perfection like something out of the 1950's, a combination of Tuesday Weld sexiness and Sandra Dee innocence. Norton, playing a junior version of Allen's usual nebbish, is extremely likable, a James Stewart-like everyman. Lyonne, who actually looks and acts like a child Allen and Hawn might conceive, shows much potential as a comic performer.

Many reviewers have complained that Allen is getting too old—he turned sixty-one the week the film opened—to play his usual clumsy neurotic who strangely attracts beautiful younger women. The most self-analytical of auteurs this side of Ingmar Bergman, Allen perhaps acknowledges this fact through Joe's having to resort to subterfuge to attract Von and his losing her because of his dishonesty. While there is little chemistry between Allen and Roberts, he and Hawn perfectly complement each other.

A major complaint against Allen's films is that they are too elitist, too insular, too New Yorkish. *Everyone Says I Love You* is Allen's most obvious ode to New York since *Manhattan* (1979) as he again shows how lovely Manhattan can be, especially with the shots of Central Park reflecting the changing seasons. Allen consciously answers the elitism charge by attempting for the first time to show his city's ethnic diversity: Many of the singers and dancers are African-American, Hispanic, or Asian.

As for the charge of insularity, unfortunately, Allen's privileged upper-East Side world is more annoyingly precious than ever. Having DJ, as the film's narrator, casually announce that Lane and Laura have summer jobs at the Metropolitan Museum of Art is particularly grating. Allen is clearly evoking the fantasy worlds of wealth seen in the films of the 1930's, and in interviews he has identified *My Man Godfrey* (1936) as a partial inspiration. But such intentions must be seen in the context of his other films which fail even to contemplate the possibility that these characters might not deserve their comforts.

The arrival of the earthily vulgar Ferry in this too-ordered environment is therefore jarringly apt. Allen shoots this scene with Ferry exactly in the center of this setting so alien to his experience, and the vibrant Roth, recalling the energy of James Cagney and the cool of Humphrey Bogart, is arresting as Ferry easily takes control of the situation, even to groping Holden's staid mother (Scotty Bloch). That he clearly is a threat to the security of this world and is quickly dispensed with implies that the universes of the haves and the have-nots must be separate, even in a fantastical musical comedy.

—Michael Adams

REVIEWS

Chicago Tribune. January 17, 1997, p. 5.
Entertainment Weekly. December 13, 1996, p. 58.
Film Threat. February, 1997, p. 58.
The New Republic. November 11, 1996, p. 40.
The New York Times. December 6, 1996, p. C1.
Newsweek. December 9, 1996, p. 84.
People. January 20, 1997, p. 20.
USA Today. December 6, 1996, p. D7.
The Village Voice. December 10, 1996, p. 75.

Evita

"Madonna was born to play Eva Peron!"—Owen Gleiberman, *Entertainment Weekly*

"It's gorgeous! It's epic! It's spectacular!"—David Ansen, *Newsweek*

"Two thumbs up!"—*Siskel & Ebert*

"Overwhelming and unforgettable!"—Jeffrey Lyons, *WNBC-TV*

Box Office: $23,072,988

Originally, Oliver Stone wanted to direct the film version of Andrew Lloyd Webber's *Evita*, with lyrics by Tim Rice. The musical was a sensation in London's West End during the Faulkland's crisis, when things got tense between Argentina and the United Kingdom. Other candidates to direct were Ken Russell, Herb Ross, Alan Pakula, Hector Babenco, Francis Coppola, Franco Zeffirelli, and Richard Attenborough, among others. But Alan Parker, who ended up with the assignment, was probably the best man to direct this film in such a way that it would recall the stage production while at the same time opening it up to the cinema. Parker was willing to take chances and to embellish the film with his own highly idiosyncratic style. This film adaptation is at once bold, innovative and unique. It recalls no other musical ever filmed. It is theatrical and at the same time cinematic. It is beautifully photographed by Darius Khondji and artistically edited by Gerry Hambling. It was enough of a critical success to capture Golden Globe attention as best picture, though in the diminished category of best musical, and for Madonna as best actress. "When you act," according to the starstruck Juan Perón, "you take us away from the squalor of the real world." So does Parker's film, which substitutes a world of theatrical artifice.

"It is my sad duty to inform you that Eva Peron, spiritual leader of the nation, entered immortality this evening."—Cinema manager announcing Eva's death

Some Argentines were outraged by the casting of Madonna, whose reputation and antics they felt tarnished the image of their national icon, Maria Eva Duarte de Perón, whose standing in Argentina is perhaps best summarized by the title of the book *Santa Evita,* published in 1996 and in bookstores by the time the film was released. The film was widely criticized in Argentina long before its premiere in Buenos Aires on February 20, 1997. A locally produced film entitled *Eva Peron,* starring Esther Goris as Evita was rushed into release October 24 to pre-empt Parker's blockbuster $60 million musical treatment. The Argentine version was successful domestically and became Argentina's entry for best foreign-language film in the Oscar competition. A conventional film would have a better chance of presenting Evita as a person rather than a gaudy icon, which also describes the image of Madonna. The musical *Evita* is about celebrity and star charisma, qualities Madonna has come to embody. It is not about authenticity, or truth, for that matter, other than mythic truth.

According to the *New York Times*, Perónist President Carlos Saul Menem described Parker's musical as "a libelous interpretation of Evita's life," while members of the Argentine Congress who considered the Material Girl inappropriate to play Evita petitioned to have both Parker and Madonna named persona non grata. Madonna wrote in a diary entry published in *Vanity Fair* that Argentina was an "uncivilized" country. Radical Perónistas

AWARDS AND NOMINATIONS

Academy Awards 1996: Best Song ("You Must Love Me")
Nominations: Best Cinematography (Khondji), Best Art Direction, Best Sound, Best Film Editing
Golden Globe Awards 1997: Best Film-Musical/Comedy, Best Actress-Musical/Comedy (Madonna), Best Original Song ("You Must Love Me")
Nominations: Best Actor-Musical/Comedy (Banderas), Best Director (Parker)

The legendary life of Argentina's first lady is re-created in the dazzling Alan Parker musical *Evita*, starring Madonna in the title role.

protested with slogans proclaiming "Viva Evita (Evita Lives)!" and "Fuera Madonna (Madonna go home)!" Meryl Streep, who was Oliver Stone's candidate to play Evita, would have been less controversial, but controversy was used to generate interest and expectation in the film. Even so, Parker got permission to use the Casa Rosada balcony made famous by the historic Evita for the filming of the showstopping number "Don't Cry for Me, Argentina," lending some historical authenticity to the film's defining moment.

The film begins in 1952 when an announcement is made concerning Evita's death at the age of thirty-three on July 26 in a movie house in Argentina watching "the sort of cheesy melodrama in which Eva Duarte appeared during her career as actress," according to *Variety* reviewer Todd McCarthy, who thought this established a "crucial connection between Evita and the masses, the working-class from which she came and where she always found her greatest support." By this ploy Parker defines Evita and what she represents immediately and effectively. At the same time Parker intercuts scenes of Evita as an illegitimate child who was forbidden to attend the funeral of her father in the countryside village of Chivilcoy. Parker visited Los Toldos, where Evita was born and the town of Junín, where she grew up.

Eight people died and 2,100 were injured in the crush around the real Eva's publicly displayed coffin.

The parallel montage between flashback and flash-forward then gives way to the story of Eva as a fifteen-year-old dance-hall performer in 1936, who has an affair with tango singer AgustÌn Magaldi (Jimmy Nail), who takes her away from the countryside to the big city, where she makes her fortune, first as a bar girl and prostitute who becomes an actress and finally mistress to political leaders, as she sleeps her way to the top, discarding lovers ruthlessly as her career develops. Finally she meets General Juan Domingo Perón (Jonathan Pryce) in 1944, the right-winger destined to become Argentina's populist strongman. When Perón is imprisoned on Martín García Island, Evita campaigns on the radio on his behalf. Perón is released from prison, marries Eva Duarte, and becomes Argentina's 29th President. But was this a marriage made in heaven? The film later shows the two of them sleeping in separate bedrooms. Evita's calculation is astonishing and tends to distance the audience, Todd McCarthy rightly suggested, by means of "a constant push-pull dynamic between fascination and revulsion."

The film is not at all realistic but theatrical and stylized. The approach follows the musical and is operatic. The lines are sung or delivered through recitative. This sort of performance suits Madonna's talents exactly. Her acting is adequate, but her singing is masterful, worthy of a Golden Globe or even an Oscar nomination. Her talents are nicely matched by those of Antonio Banderas, whose film career began with the Spanish director Pedro Almodovar, who discovered him. In an interview with the *Washington Times* Banderas credited Andrew Lloyd Webber as "being responsible for me being an actor. When I saw *Jesus Christ Superstar,*" he explained, "it was a particular time in Spain. We were under a dictatorship, and it was very difficult to see that kind of movie, criticizing or having a critical point of view on the figure of Jesus Christ." The play was a revelation for him.

In *Evita* Banderas plays Ché Guevara, serving as an Everyman chorus to the action, which goes beyond the function of the Greek chorus, which is merely to point out the obvious. The Ché chorus serves as guide and mediator, leading the response of the audience from a political perspective, a left-wing commentator interpreting the career of a right-wing dictator and his more charismatic spouse who helps to define his popularity. At first the Ché narrator is cynical: "Things have reached a pretty pass," he remarks, "When someone pretty lower class,/Graceless and vulgar, uninspired,/Can be accepted and admired." But by the end he is in queue with everyone else, waiting his turn to kiss the casket.

Although the *Variety* reviewer was impressed by *Evita*, certainly not all of the reviews were favorable. "To say that

CREDITS

Eva Peron: Madonna
Che: Antonio Banderas
Juan Peron: Jonathan Pryce
Augustin Magaldi: Jimmy Nail
Dona Juana: Victoria Sus
Brother Juan: Julian Littman

Origin: USA
Released: 1996
Production: Robert Stigwood, Alan Parker and Andrew G. Vajna for a Cinergi and Dirty Hands production; released by Hollywood Pictures
Direction: Alan Parker
Screenplay: Alan Parker and Oliver Stone; based on the musical by Andrew Lloyd Webber and Tim Rice
Cinematography: Darius Khondji
Editing: Gerry Hambling
Music: Andrew Lloyd Webber
Lyrics: Tim Rice
Production design: Brian Morris
Art direction: Jean-Michel Hugon, Richard Earl
Costume design: Penny Rose
Sound: Ken Weston
Choreography: Vincent Paterson
MPAA rating: PG
Running Time: 134 minutes

Evita, the movie, is a stunning film is not to say that it is actually good," Megan Rosenfeld wrote in *The Washington Post.* "It stuns the way an avalanche would, or an elephant sitting on your lap." She felt the film "bludgeons" viewers into submission. Alan Parker's fidelity to the stage version she felt was a handicap because he underestimates "what is lost in the transfer from stage to screen." The musical is not an appropriate form for portraying politics or history, "rendered ridiculous when adapted to song," and the stylization makes the film look "stiff and synthetic." Owen Gleiberman nailed down the "real challenge," which is not that the musical is composed entirely of songs, but that the songs themselves "contain very little dramatic action." The action is not only "naggingly abstract" but utterly artificial and unconvincing. The trick is to turn the theatrical artifice into something more plausible and concrete if it is to be transformed into cinema.

On stage it was possible to trick the audience into thinking the action was somehow authentic. In fact, the largest problem is to infuse the film with the kind of excitement a live performance might have. As Peter Travers wrote for *Rolling Stone,* "Norman Jewison couldn't pull it off with the film of Webber and Rice's *Jesus Christ Superstar,* in 1973; Ken Russell failed with the Who's *Tommy,* in 1975; and Parker himself struck out with *Pink Floyd—The Wall,* in 1982." Travers dismissed the film as "a $60 million karaoke session." In *The New Yorker* Anthony Lane dismissed *Evita* as "the biggest, loudest, most expensive music video ever made."

If Parker's film errors, it is in the way it attempts to pump up the political commentary, which is easily overwhelmed by the music. But it is surely for the music, not for the history lesson, that the film earned its Golden Globe nominations. In a time when movie musicals are no longer made, *Evita* astonishes by reviving an all but forgotten genre. Surely this is the best made screen musical seen in years, daring enough to take chances in its theatrical stylization and daring to risk absurdity.

—James M. Welsh

REVIEWS

Boxoffice. February, 1997, p. 61.
Chicago Tribune. January 1, 1997, p. 1.
Entertainment Weekly. December 20, 1996, p. 49.
Hollywood Reporter. December 10, 1996, p. 12.
Los Angeles Times. December 25, 1996, p. F1.
Newsweek. December 16, 1996, p. 60.
The New York Times. January 26, 1997, p. 26.
The New Yorker. January 6, 1997, p. 74.
People. December 23, 1996, p. 17.
Rolling Stone. January 23, 1997, p. 71.
Sight and Sound. January, 1997, p. 14.
Time. December 30, 1996, p. 134.
Variety. December 16-22, 1996, p. 78.
Village Voice. December 31, 1996, p. 59.
Vogue. October, 1996, p. 300.
The Washington Post. January 1, 1997, p. Dl.
The Washington Times Metropolitan Times. January 24, 1997, p. C15.

Executive Decision

Five miles above the earth, an elite team of six men must make an air to air transfer, in order to save 400 lives on board a 747 . . . and 40 million below.—Movie tagline

"A high-tech, high tension, first-class roller-coaster of thrills. Feverish fast-paced suspense and excitement."—Susan Granger, *American Movie Classics*

"High-wattage. High-energy. Hair-raising."—Janet Maslin, *The New York Times*

"Two thumbs up."—*Siskel & Ebert*

"A nail biting spectacle."—Desson Howe, *Washington Post*

Box Office: $56,679,192

It appears that filmmakers have ambivalent feelings about today's audiences. They think that they are either morons or techno-crazed eggheads. For instance, in this summer's release of Arnold Schwarzenegger's *Eraser,* they felt that summer spectators would accept that Arnold could single-handedly take on an airplane while floating through the clouds on a parachute. On the other side of the coin is *Executive Decision,* Warner Bros. introduction to 1996's summer action season. It contains so much gadgetry, wiring, circuitry, drilling, ad infinitum, that it should create a whole new rating system—for electrical engineers only! As Owen Gleiberman of *Entertainment Weekly* wrote, "The movie's numbing barrage of logistical detail suggests that America, in its fixation on the hidden mechanics of thrills, has become a nation of vicarious techno-tinkers." Except, of course, for the millions who went to see *Eraser.*

In the first ten minutes after the opening credits, (underscored by music sounding very much like the theme from *Star Wars* [1977]), the intricate plot begins to unfold. A group of U.S. Army Special Forces, headed by Lieutenant Colonel Austin Travis (Steven Seagal), massacres a group of Chechian Mafia, in search of a lethal Soviet nerve gas, DZ-5. They discover, to their dismay, that the deadly toxin is nowhere to be found amidst the carnage. Suddenly it's three months later and Dr. David Grant (Kurt Russell) is shown taking flying lessons. He ponders the point and says, "God, why am I doing this?" Is he talking about the lessons or appearing in this film? Later on that evening, while the debonair Dr. Grant is socializing at a cocktail party, a group of Islamic militants hijack an Athens-Washington, D.C. flight. They are demanding 50 million dollars and the release of their leader Jaffa (Andreas Katsulas), who was kidnapped by the United States at his daughter's wedding. How the hijackers got past the metal detectors at the airport with an arsenal of guns and ammunition is never fully explained. Dressed to the nines in a tuxedo, Grant is whisked away to an emergency meeting with the U.S. War Council. It is here that it is divulged that the Islamic squad aboard the jet is also in possession of the deadly nerve gas DZ-5. Intervention is the only hope and a team of commandos, led by a perpetually scowling Seagal, devises an ingenious, yet risky plan. Under the supervision of crack weapons designer (Dennis Cahill), played by a fidgety Oliver Platt, they choose a Stealth prototype, the Remora, to attempt a midair maneuver to get onboard. It is agreed that Dr. Grant should go along to supervise the mission. However, there is no time to change clothes. As he is about to board the aircraft, Rat (John Leguizamo) wryly asks, "Who's this, 007?"

Once onboard the Remora, the ethnically balanced hit team plans to sneak onto the hijacked plane through a tunnel-like suction appendage. This giant vacuum cleaner hose attaches to the underbelly of the jetliner, allowing them to

CREDITS

Dr. David Grant: Kurt Russell
Jean: Halle Berry
Rat: John Leguizamo
Lt. Col. Austin Travis: Steven Seagal
Dennis Cahill: Oliver Pratt
Cappy: Joe Morton
Naji Hassan: David Suchet
Louie: B.D. Wong

Origin: USA
Released: 1996
Production: Joel Silver for a Silver Pictures production; released by Warner Brothers
Direction: Stuart Baird
Screenplay: Jim Thomas and John Thomas
Cinematography: Alex Thomson and Don Burgess
Editing: Dallas Pruitt, Frank J. Urisote and Stuart Baird
Production design: Terence Marsh
Art direction: William M. Cruse
Costume design: Louise Frogley
Sound: Clark David King
Visual effects: Peter Donen
Stunt coordinator: Dick Ziker
Music: Jerry Goldsmith
Casting: Amanda Mackey Johnson and Cathy Sandrich
MPAA rating: R
Running Time: 132 minutes

board through a small portal. All of the commandos make it, except one—Lt. Colonel Austin Travis, who gets blown into the atmosphere. This is very surprising, since Travis is played by Seagal, and it occurs within the first twenty minutes. This certainly belies the trailer, which makes it appear that Seagal and Russell are battling each other throughout the entire film. Now that the head honcho is history, Russell reluctantly becomes the man in charge.

Kurt Russell began his acting career at the age of 12, and has starred in a string of popular films including *Tequila Sunrise* (1988), *Swing Shift* (1984), *Silkwood* (1983), the successful sci-fi film, *Stargate* (1994), and the cult classic, *Escape from New York* (1981). The actor does have a virile presence and likeable charm on-screen. He gives a solid, reliable performance in all of his film roles. However, he is always Kurt Russell, whether he's playing Wyatt Earp in *Tombstone* (1993) or "Snake" in the currently released *Escape from L.A.* Perhaps this is the one quality that makes him a bankable star. Nevertheless, it would be nice to see him stretch as a performer and go beyond the popular image. He actually showed glimpses of this in *Executive Decision.* He was not just another stereotypical action-hero and was willing to expose the character's vulnerable and insecure sides. It would be exciting for him as an actor to trust these instincts and take it even further.

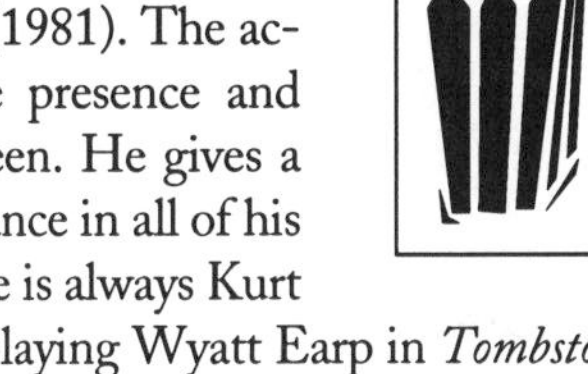

"Remember how much good press Jesse Jackson got for freeing the hostages?"—Aide to Senator Mavros

The other cast members are good, if not remarkable. John Leguizamo displays the appropriate intensity to "Rat," but, at times, he appears to be doing a Latino version of James Cagney. Halle Berry plays Jean, an airline stewardess, with an appropriate mixture of fear and pluckiness. Her sidekick, played by Marla Maples Trump, looks frightened and weepy throughout the entire ordeal. It's hard to imagine her inspiring any confidence in the other passengers—she just doesn't seem to hold up well under pressure. Joe Morton (Cappy), B.D. Wong (Louie), and Whip Hubley (Baker) all perform adequately.

Once onboard the 747, the dirty half-dozen spend much of their time trying to be quiet and tinkering away with a vast array of hardware. The first item on their agenda is to drill a hole through the cabin's floor, so as to be able to spy on the terrorists through tiny worm-like cameras. They almost drill a hole through a terrorist's foot, but, fortunately for him, he walks away just in the nick of time. This is the first in a string of many predictable "close calls." Led by a maniacal Nagi Hassan (David Suchet), these terrorists are definitely on a mission. On the surface, they seem to just want the money and their leader (in that order). Or so it seems. It is hinted that Nagi has even more devious plans. He has also managed to smuggle onboard one of the world's most sophisticated megabombs.

Once the rescue team discovers the bomb is onboard, it becomes apparent that their job is going to be more complicated than they had originally planned. They also find out that there is "enough nerve gas to wipe out the entire Eastern seaboard." At one point, while viewing the bomb, an immobilized Cappy remarks "Computer trigger, microprocessor, dedicated drive, perfect monitor, a dozen sensors—this ain't no pipe bomb and a 6-volt battery." At this point, it would be wise for the audience to take notes.

Throughout all this "gadgetry garble," there is a semblance of a story going on in the cabin above. It seems that there is an ambitious U.S. Senator (J.T. Walsh) onboard, whose aide thinks that this calamity might be an incredible opportunity. The earnest young man whispers, "Remember the mileage that Jesse Jackson got when he negotiated the release of those hostages." A close-up of the Senator's face reveals him contemplating the impact that his dilemma will have on his constituents. Meanwhile, the boys below are still hooking things up (hopefully, to code) and trying to figure out what to do. Back in Washington, the Secretary of Defense, played by a concerned-looking Len Cariou, is also trying to solve the problem. After all, no one wants Armageddon (except, perhaps, the audience members who have trouble programming their VCRs).

Recently, there has been an increasing amount of protests from the Arab community to the way in which they are depicted on film. There was a great deal of anger and dissatisfaction with *Executive Decision,* as well as *True Lies* (1994) and even *Aladdin* (1992). Janet Maslin of *The New York Times* said that the terrorists (in *Executive Decision*) were "unexplained Arab fanatics who draw on every known ethnic cliche. The Arab groups that protested unflattering stereotypes in *True Lies* have a stronger complaint about this." It is certainly true that towards the end of the film, Suchet's character, Nagi, did become more like the anti-Christ than a political fanatic. However, terrorists do exist and it is necessary to depict these characters with some basis in reality. What seems to be lacking by filmmakers is a willingness to make films that depict all aspects of any ethnic culture—the good as well as the bad. The balance seems to be lopsided. Taking all of this into consideration, however, there is also an old adage that says, "you can't please all the people all the time."

Executive Decision was helmed by first-time director, Stuart Baird. Mr. Baird is a two-time Oscar-nominated editor, admired for his action-oriented work in *Lethal Weapon* (1987) and *Die Hard 2* (1990). In this film, however, he demonstrated a considerable lack of understanding regarding structure and pacing. His meticulous attention to detail bogged down the film with too much hardware and technology. This script, written by Jim and John Thomas (who wrote the *Predator* movies) had a sufficient number of twists and turns contained in it to make it suspenseful. The unimaginative direction prevented it from ever gaining momentum.

Considering the production was shot by cinematographer Alex Thompson (*Excalibur* [1981], *Cliffhanger* [1993]) and designed by Terence Marsh (*Doctor Zhivago* [1965], *Oliver* [1968]), Baird certainly had the ingredients necessary to construct a much more vivid and compelling story. Instead, he decided to bore the audience throughout most of the film and save the exciting special effects sequences until the last ten minutes. The experience was similar to attending a dinner party where the host doesn't serve the food until after midnight. After snacking for hours—who cares?

—*Rob Chicatelli*

REVIEWS

Boxoffice. May, 1996, p. 73.
Chicago Tribune. March 15, 1996, p. 4.
Entertainment Weekly. March 22, 1996, p. 50.
Los Angeles Times. March 15, 1996, p. F1.
New York Times. March 15, 1996, p. C3.
USA Today. March 15, 1996, p. 5D.
Variety. March 11, 1996, p. 44.

Extreme Measures

Not all surgery is intended to cure.—Movie tagline

"The best thriller of the year!"—Ron Brewington, *American Urban Radio Networks*

"Ferociously suspenseful! Top-notch and mind-boggling. Grabs you and doesn't let go."—Susan Granger, *CRN International*

"A smashingly successful thriller!"—Joe Leydon, *KPRC-TV*

"Powerful! A spine-tingling thriller that grips you from the start!"—Neil Rosen, *NY 1 News*

"Riveting! An edge-of-your-seat thriller."—Jeffrey Lyons, *Sneak Previews*

Box Office: $17,380,126

As we approach the 21st century, it seems as if many of the ethical problems facing our society fall not into the laps of philosophers or even theologians, but physicians. Questions such as should an alcoholic be given a liver transplant? Is total, and often very expensive, health care a social right that should be available to everyone or a privilege available only to those who can afford it? Should tobacco companies be forced to pay for the medical care of those with illness that can be directly or indirectly related to their product such as lung cancer? And what of the polarizing issue of abortion?

> "Good doctors do the correct thing. Great doctors do the courageous thing."—Myrick

These are the kinds of questions posed in *Extreme Measures,* but this is not some dry intellectual exercise. All this food for thought is framed in a film that is interesting, exciting and suspenseful.

The ethical questions start early in *Extreme Measures.* Emergency room physician Dr. Guy Luthan (Hugh Grant) is faced with two injured patients and only one operating room. One patient is a police officer suffering from serious gunshot wounds, the other is the more critically injured dope addict who shot him. Which man should get the operating room? Faced with the police officer's friends and wife, Guy goes with the good guy. But acting as his conscience is nurse Jodie Trammel (Sarah Jessica Parker) who tells him, "You made a moral choice, not a medical one." It won't be the only moral dilemma he'll face. Furthermore, Guy has seen the impact that making the "wrong" moral choice can have: his father had his physician's license revoked because he helped "put a friend out of his misery."

Then, into Gramercy Hospital's emergency room comes a homeless man, Claude Minkins (Shaun Austin-Olsen), who is naked except for a plastic sheet and another unknown hospital's wrist ID. Claude initially seems to be suffering from a bad drug trip, but as he continues to suffer from a complete system meltdown, Guy knows there's something more mysterious going on. Just before he dies, Claude grabs Guy and gives him a solitary clue; Teddy Dolson told him to go to "the room." Neither the name nor the location mean anything to Guy.

So, as Claude's body is taken off for autopsy, the rest of the emergency room gets on with their day, but Guy can't seem to forget. It's a puzzle he just won't let go of. And when the coroner calls and says Claude died of a pulmonary embolism, which totally contradicts the lab reports, it's just too incredible for Guy to believe. Consequently, he goes to the morgue and questions the coroner, who denies he even received Claude's body. "Your hospital's known for losing patients, both living and dead," Guy is told.

Now Guy checks Claude's name against the hospital computers and finds that he was previously a patient there . . . and so was Teddy Dolson. But their files, like Claude's body, are missing. Now Guy has to dig into areas where he is not allowed and suddenly finds himself facing censure from his boss. "Let me put it to you this way. I'm your boss and I'm telling you, Drop this thing!" Is Guy facing a conspiracy and a cover up? But if so, what is being covered up, and by whom? Who can Guy trust?

First film from the Simian Films production company run by actors Hugh Grant and Elizabeth Hurley.

Despite the ominous warnings, Guy continues to dig, and this upsets someone, because the next thing he knows he's being framed for cocaine possession and losing his job at the hospital. Now the mystery has gone from just being a puzzle to be solved to being one whose solution just might salvage his career. So Guy now faces another moral dilemma. The only person he knows who might be able to help him is Bobby (John Toles-Bey), a homeless man who has pestered Guy at the hospital for prescriptions he doesn't deserve. Bobby will trade Guy information on "the room" in return for phony prescriptions. The result is a trip into the bowels of Grand Central Station where the "moles" (homeless people) live.

As Guy explores the mystery and the "room," he is also being spied upon by two menacing men, Frank Hare (David Morse) and Burke (Bill Nunn) who claim to be from the FBI and the NYPD, but who were also the ones who planted the cocaine in Guy's apartment and who are now shooting at him below Grand Central Station. Eventually Guy's investigation leads him to the door of the renowned neurologist, Dr. Lawrence Myrick (Gene Hackman) whose work in spinal regeneration is award-winning.

But Guy soon discovers that like several doctors before him, (Drs. Frankenstein and Moreau most easily come to mind), perhaps Myrick's scientific goals are being undermined by some pretty unethical practices. Or are they unethical? "If you could cure cancer by killing one person, wouldn't you have to do that?" Myrick asks coldly, logically. It's a chilling question. What if it took two people? A dozen? Two dozen? What if it were your family affected by cancer? What if it were your family that was expected to sacrifice someone?

The fact that these questions linger long after the ending credits roll indicates what a fine job screenwriter Tony Gilroy (*Dolores Claiborne* [1994]) has done of adapting, and some say improving, the 1991 bestselling novel by Michael Palmer. This is not your ordinary thriller. This is one where the dialogue is consistently thoughtful and clever, where the characters are believable and human, and where the action is tight. Gilroy puts his characters into situations where even the most God-fearing and decent can fall for the siren's song of unscrupulous behavior for the sake of their families. But wouldn't we all? An interesting question.

But this is not a dry philosophy class, this is a suspense film and Gilroy has no problem keeping us guessing—even if we already know the basics of the story going in. He constantly keeps us a bit off balance, even to the point of putting humor into the story. Guy's nemeses are named Burke and Hare, so, too, were two famous graverobbers. When Guy is asked why a woman is screaming in the hospital, he answers, "I don't know. She probably just got a bill or something."

Part of the success of that caustic remark belongs to Hugh Grant. Whoever thought that the self-deprecating, stuttering Grant who is best known for his comic turns (and

CREDITS

Dr. Guy Luthan: Hugh Grant
Dr. Lawrence Myrick: Gene Hackman
Jodie Trammel: Sarah Jessica Parker
Frank Hare: David Morse
Burke: Bill Nunn
Bobby: John Toles-Bey
Dr. Jeffery Manko: Paul Guilfoyle
Dr. Judith Grusznski: Debra Monk
Claude Minkins: Shaun Austin-Olsen
Teddy Dolson: Andre' De Shields

Origin: USA
Released: 1996
Production: Elizabeth Hurley for Simian Films; released by Castle Rock Entertainment
Direction: Michael Apted
Screenplay: Tony Gilroy; based on the book by Michael Palmer
Cinematography: John Bailey
Editing: Rick Shaine
Production design: Doug Kraner
Art direction: Paul Denham Austerberry
Set decoration: Gordon Sim
Costume design: Susan Lyall
Music: Danny Elfman
MPAA rating: R
Running Time: 117 minutes

his antics with prostitutes on Sunset Boulevard) could be an action hero? And, at first it is a bit odd watching him take control of the emergency room, yelling out orders, making life-and-death decisions. One keeps waiting for those annoying mannerisms of his, but they're nowhere to be found. However, Grant does bring intelligence and innocence as well as self-confidence and his trademark boyish charm and British humor to his role which makes him a much more interesting hero than Schwarzenegger or Stallone. He's more like everyman shoved into the unexpected and threatening, and who foils the villains with wits, not guns or muscles. Grant is proving to be a more versatile actor than many would have expected.

Besides the quality of the script, perhaps a part of Grant's successful transformation from light comedy to suspense is due to the skills of director Michael Apted (*Gorillas in the Mist* [1988], *Nell* [1994]). Capable of making fascinating fictional films as well as entertaining documentaries, Apted seems to be able to bring the best from both genres to create exceptional films. He's also not above casting fellow director David Cronenberg (*Dead Ringers* [1988]) in the cameo role of the hospital's lawyer.

Other casting, like Gene Hackman as Dr. Myrick is also solid. Hackman easily handles this portrait of a successful scientist who relishes his accomplishments, likes winning, and may go to any length to do so. He flashes us a winning smile one minute, gives a tender speech to paralyzed people the next, and can believably and easily turn around and order the murder of a fellow doctor who might get in the way of his experiments.

If there is one off note in the film, it is that of Sarah Jessica Parker's Jodie. She can moralize to Guy at the start of the film, but may be as unethical as Myrick by the end. It also doesn't help that her make-up makes her look hard, it reminds one more of her role as a witch in *Hocus Pocus* (1993) and is quite distracting. But it is a minor flaw and should not get in the way of a film that is entertaining and thoughtful.

Extreme Measures is well-made, stylish, tense, surprising, thought-provoking, and even at times humorous. It also doesn't try to solve incredibly complex ethical questions with overly simplistic answers. It forces us to think for ourselves long after we've been entertained. And that's a film worth seeing.

—*Beverley Bare Buehrer*

REVIEWS

Chicago Tribune. September 27, 1996, p. 5.
Detroit Free Press. September 27, 1996.
Detroit News. September 27, 1996, p. D1.
Entertainment Weekly. September 27, 1996, p. 42.
Los Angeles Times. September 27, 1996, p. F1.
New York Times. September 27, 1996, p. C3.
People. September 30, 1996, p. 17.
Rolling Stone. October 17, 1996, p. 144.
Time. October 7, 1996.
USA Today. September 27, 1996, p. 4D.
Variety. September 13, 1996.
Village Voice. October 1, 1996, p. 68.

Eye for an Eye

What do you do when justice fails?—Movie tagline

"An explosive thrill ride that is absolutely sizzling! A superior thriller, unbelievably powerful!"—Ron Brewington, *American Urban Radio Network*

"A first-rate thriller. Provocative."—Kerry O'Reilly, *NBC-TV*

"A very powerful movie. Fine performances."—Jeffrey Lyons, *Sneak Previews*

"It really grips you. Sally Field is outstanding."—Michael Medved, *Sneak Previews*

Box Office: $26,877,589

If one were to replace the commanding acting talents of Sally Field, Ed Harris and Joe Mantegna with the likes of Victoria Principal and a few male soap opera refugees, and replace the powerful directing talents of John Schlesinger with those of some recent UCLA graduate, the result would be a Monday night made-for-TV women's film. Unfortunately, even with these mighty talents, *Eye for an Eye* is still more appropriate fare for the small screen than the large.

One day Karen McCann's (Sally Field) life is normal. She has a beautiful home in the suburbs, a loving husband (Ed Harris), two adorable daughters (Olivia Burnette and Alexandra Kyle), and a rewarding job in the public relations department of a media research library. What are the odds that this idyllic situation will last?

On the day of her youngest daughter's 6th birthday, her older daughter has cut soccer practice to come home and help decorate for the party. Is this a great kid or what? Of course she's great, she's the victim. While on the phone to her mother, Julie answers the front door only to find a rapist and murderer on the other side. As Karen listens on her cellular phone, frantically running from car to car in a traffic jam looking for someone with another phone to call the police, she hears Julie's every plea for help and cry of pain. For Karen and her family, one minute everything is under control, and just a minute later, everything has changed forever.

In the wake of this senseless tragedy, the McCann's must try to regain any shred of control they can over their lives. They install a security system, Karen takes a self defense class and learns about guns at a firing range, and they join a support group to learn to cope with their grief. At the same time, Detective Sgt. Denillo (Joe Mantegna) finally arrests the killer. Robert Doob (Kiefer Sutherland), a tattooed, sneering deliveryman for a grocery store. It would seem the McCann's will be able to soon put all this behind them and move on with their lives.

Not so. To the McCann's shock, because the Los Angeles County Prosecutors failed to share DNA evidence with the defense, Doob is set free on a legal technicality. But Karen will never set Doob free. She believes she will never get justice from the legal system, and that she must find it for herself. She begins following Doob, charting his every move. She's not sure why she's doing it, but like the self-defense class and the firing range, it gives her a feeling that she's taking control of her life again.

Then two incidents coincide. Doob "befriends" Karen's youngest daughter on her school playground, and she overhears a conversation which implies that members of the support group may be doing more than just talking about their grief. Vigilantism may be an available extracurricular activity. Suddenly, nice, normal, suburban Karen finds herself faced with an option that she never would have considered: killing her daughter's killer herself. However, as one of her vigilante advisors tells her, "desperately wanting someone dead and actually killing them yourself are two different things." Is Karen

CREDITS

Karen McCann: Sally Field
Robert Doob: Kiefer Sutherland
Mack McCann: Ed Harris
Dolly Green: Beverly D'Angelo
Detective Sergeant Joe Denillo: Joe Mantegna
Angel Kosinsky: Charlayne Woodard
Julie McCann: Olivia Burnette
Megan McCann: Alexandra Kyle
Sidney Hughes: Philip Baker Hall
Martin: Keith David

Origin: USA
Released: 1996
Production: Michael I. Levy; released by Paramount Pictures
Direction: John Schlesinger
Screenplay: Amanda Silver and Rick Jaffa; based on a novel by Erika Holzer
Cinematography: Amir M. Mokri
Editing: Peter Honess
Production design: Stephen Hendrickson
Sound mixer: Edward Tise
Costume design: Bobbie Read
Music: James Newton Howard
MPAA rating: R

willing to mete out her own justice? Is she willing to become a murderer to rid society of a murderer? Is she ready for the legal consequences to herself if she does this?

There is no doubt that *Eye for an Eye* addresses a serious social problem, the seeming inability of the justice system to deliver justice, but in reality it doesn't address the issue as much as it exploits it. Director John Schlesinger (who won an Oscar for *Midnight Cowboy* and has also done such films as *Marathon Man* and *Pacific Heights*) and writers Amanda Silver and Rick Jaffa (best known for their cooperative effort *The Hand That Rocks the Cradle*) here ignore the complexities of the problem in order to wring as much emotional tension and identification as possible for their story. For that reason, it must be simplified and details, such as the bureaucratic ineptness of the district attorney's office and Doob's overly evil character, are meant to do little more than manipulate the viewer and enhance his or her feelings of frustration and the desire for revenge.

"Poor man's truth serum: caffeine and sugar."—Sergeant DeNello

Further manipulating the viewer is the obvious attempt to create an equation between Doob and O.J. Simpson. Simpson's trial is playing on a TV in the media library where Karen works, Doob is prosecuted in L.A. County as was Simpson, and finally the presence of DNA evidence was mentioned in both trials. This won't help one understand the issues or correct the problems, all it does is take the easy way out.

As one can imagine, a story this simplistic will also take the easy way out for the ending. Is this film really going to let sweet Karen kill Doob and go to jail? Is it really going to let Doob get away with it? Of course not. Consequently this black-and-white story will result in an all-too-easy ending—one which is intellectually bankrupt.

If there is any positive side to this film it is in the performances. Sally Field's Karen is compellingly tormented. We feel her fear, her loss, her depression, and her anger. And we're all for her as she attempts to regain power and control over her life. But again, identification with highly sympathetic Field is a part of the manipulative formula of the film—and owes more to Field's talent than the material with which she is given to work.

Similarly, revulsion at Sutherland's Doob is also made very easy. He snarls and sneers and smirks his way through this film without the writers wasting a shred of understanding or sympathy on him. When, after being set free in court, he imitates Karen's stuttering dead daughter, we know he is guilty. When he pours hot coffee on a stray dog, we know he is evil. What's to like? But if we were to understand him at all, it would muddy the water of this streamlined story. Sutherland, however, is turning out to be one of the best villains in Hollywood (*Lost Boys, Stand By Me*), but is this all he wants to do with his career?

In the end, *Eye for an Eye* does pack an immediate emotional punch, but upon reflection one feels used. That's when one realizes that it's nothing more than Charles Bronson's *Death Wish* dressed up with a first-rate cast and director.

—Beverley Bare Buehrer

REVIEWS

Boxoffice Magazine. March, 1996, p. R-28.
Chicago Tribune. January 12, 1996, p. 5.
Detroit Free Press. January 12, 1996, p. 7D.
Detroit News. January 6, 1996, p. C1.
Entertainment Weekly. January 12, 1996, p. 38.
Los Angeles Times. January 12, 1996, p. F6.
New York Times. January 12, 1996, C10.
Rolling Stone. February 8, 1996, p. 47.
USA Today. January 12, 1996, p. 4D.
Variety. January 12, 1996, p. 125.
Washington Post. January 12, 1996, p. 32.

Faithful

After 20 years of marriage, she thought she was the target of her husband's affection. She was only half right.—Movie tagline

"Cher sizzles in this fine mix of wicked humor and edgy romance!"—Michael Wilmington, *Chicago Tribune*

"A wickedly funny and devilish look at marriage, sex and betrayal."—William Wolf, *William Wolf Features*

Box Office: $2,104,439

Based on his play of the same name, Chazz Palminteri's *Faithful* is the first film written by a writer other than himself that Paul Mazursky has directed in his twenty-five year career. The director of such films as *Enemies, A Love Story* (1989) and *An Unmarried Woman* (1978) admits to being drawn to character-driven pieces and observes that "Character is pretty much gone in American films . . . ours are plot-driven." That certainly would explain Mazursky's commitment to *Faithful,* a film in which little happens outside of the three main characters all reaching certain realizations about their lives and each other through the spoken word. The film has a difficult time transcending its play quality, although Mazursky does manage to open up the sets ever-so-slightly without sacrificing the necessary claustrophobia that the characters, particularly Margaret, must feel as her house and her life close in on her.

Director Paul Mazursky threatened to remove his name from the film over a dispute with the distributor about the final cut.

Westchester housewife Margaret O'Donnell (Cher) is dazed as she walks down Manhattan's Fifth Avenue. Looking deceptively downtrodden, Margaret remarks to two men lusting after the Rolls Royce parked on the street, "It won't make you happy." She accepts the twenty dollar bill one of the men presses into her hand just before she gets into the Rolls and drives off to her sprawling mansion in the suburbs. Depressed by a phone call from her husband Jack (Ryan O'Neal) who makes the usual excuses for being late on the evening of their twentieth wedding anniversary, Margaret decides to commit suicide. As she soaks in the bath, Margaret fails to notice an intruder who has made his way into the house. No mere robber, Tony (Chazz Palminteri) is ironically a hitman hired by her husband to do away with her so he can inherit the money from the construction company that Margaret's father had built.

Tony informs Margaret that he intends to rape and murder her as soon as he receives the signal, two rings on the telephone, from Jack that he has established his alibi. As they wait, the two talk and eventually have sex while waiting for Jack's signal. It is unclear whether the attraction is mutual or if Margaret seduces Tony with the hope that she can free herself and negotiate her own contract on her adulterous husband. For despite her earlier desire to commit suicide, Margaret now finds the will to live through her anger at this latest betrayal by Jack. Along the way, Tony helps Margaret rediscover her self-esteem and Margaret helps the hitman, who periodically receives calls from his troubled therapist (Paul Mazursky), to come to terms with the accidental shooting of his sister, Maria (Elisa Leonetti).

In her first screen appearance in six years, Academy Award winner Cher (*Moonstruck* [1987]) finds the complexity of emotion in Margaret by using little more than her face and eyes, since she is tied to a chair for two-thirds of the film. Few actresses could rival Cher's ability to be seductive and sexy in such a humiliating situation. Chazz Palminteri (*A Bronx Tale* [1993] and *The Usual Suspects* [1995]) claims to have written *Faithful* in an attempt to explore his feminine side, "to write about how a woman

CREDITS

Margaret O'Donnell: Cher
Tony: Chazz Palminteri
Jack O'Donnell: Ryan O'Neal
Dr. Susskind: Paul Mazursky
Debbie: Amber Smith
Maria: Elisa Leonetti
Maria's Boyfriend: Mark Nassar

Origin: USA
Released: 1996
Production: Robert De Niro and Jane Rosenthal; A Tribeca Production, presented by Price Entertainment, released by New Line Cinema
Direction: Paul Mazursky
Screenplay: Chazz Palminteri; based on his play
Cinematography: Fred Murphy
Editing: Nicholas C. Smith
Production design: Jeffrey Townsend
Art direction: Caty Maxey
Costume design: Hope Hanafin
Music: Phillip Johnston
MPAA rating: R
Running Time: 91 minutes

feels about what men sometimes do." Several critics complained that Mr. Palminteri's daunting size and strength and the fact that he threatens Cher with a gun as she is tied up combined to bring his objective into question. Yet that very setup seems to be part of Mr. Palminteri's point: men are often bigger, stronger and more threatening than women. Yet women need not automatically consider themselves the victim, for there are other ways to defend themselves. Words can often be a very powerful tool. And so can sex.

It is interesting that the filmmakers have chosen to make the seduction scene so ambiguous, adding to the uncertainty of the situation. The fact that Palminteri's Tony is so threatening and is not just a funny gangster, but rather is believable as a killer who is willing to break his own edict of never "whacking a woman" because he needs the money, heightens the suspense. Mix in some very clever observations and witty dialogue and the result is a film that is slightly off-center. Which is very much the way life tends to be.

While the film contains some very witty observations about life, not just of the wealthy, but of the wise guys on the street as well, *Faithful* has a limited audience appeal, targeting the over-forty female who can potentially relate to the boredom and betrayal of a marriage gone stale. The film enjoyed a very short stay at the box office and was not well received by the critics.

—*Patricia Kowal*

REVIEWS

Chicago Tribune. April 3, 1996, p. 2.
Entertainment Weekly. April 12, 1996, p. 50.
Los Angeles Times. April 3, 1996, p. F1.
New York Times. April 3, 1996.
USA Today. April 3, 1996, p. 7D.
Variety. March 4, 1996, p. 76.

A Family Thing

Everything's relative.—Movie tagline

Two brothers are about to discover what's been missing in their lives . . . each other.—Movie tagline

"A rare jewel of compassion and humanity . . . as profound as it is provocative. Robert Duvall has never been better!"—Bill Diehl, *ABC Radio Networks*

"*A Family Thing* is simply astonishing!"—Henry Cabot Beck, *Interview Magazine*

"Robert Duvall and James Earl Jones are two of America's greatest actors!"—Jeff Craig, *Sixty Second Preview*

"Two thumbs up!"—*Siskel & Ebert*

"Don't miss it. A perfect movie."—Paul Wunder, *WBAI Radio*

Box Office: $10,125,417

If only racism were a "a family thing"—this is the wistful wish of *A Family Thing* and countless other recent movies, implying that racism can be conquered through the intimacy of friendship and family feeling. The idea is trite, sentimental, and simple-minded—as if the values of friendship and family can somehow override economic, political, and psychological problems that are institutionalized and magnified by social forces well beyond the correction of individuals. As several reviewers have noted, *A Family Thing* comes close to the preposterous, yet it is saved by the outstanding performances of its actors who tell human truths in spite of the movie's hackneyed plot.

Earl Pilcher Jr. (Robert Duvall) is a hardworking Southern redneck and a good family man whose life is overturned when he learns from his dead mother's letter that he is not her biological son. In fact, he is the offspring of his white father's rape of the family's black servant. The letter urges him to look up his half-brother, Ray Murdoch (James Earl Jones), who is a Chicago cop. Earl is angry at his father and ashamed to discover he is the son of a "nigger," but he is also compelled to follow the letter's plea to, in a sense, reunite a family savaged by his father's wrong.

Earl's journey North is an education in every sense of the word. He is out of place in the city and does not know what to say when he finally tracks down Ray. The men face each other in incomprehension, and Ray rejects Earl's fumbling desire to make contact. Ray knows all about what

Stage actress Irma P. Hall, who plays the blind, 88-year-old Aunt T in her first major screen role, is a youthful 60.

Earl's father did to his mother. Indeed, it is a shameful fact he has done his best to forget. With a dignity and outrage that befits an actor of James Earl Jones's stature, Ray simply acknowledges Earl's effort and bids him goodbye.

A frustrated Earl makes his way out of the city, angry at the anti-climactic nature of his meeting with Ray. When a group of young blacks pull up in a car and begin to razz him, Earl talks back and even gets out of his truck to face them. It is a foolish, self-destructive gesture, saying as much about his frustrations as his stupidity, and of course he is beaten up by the blacks who steal his pickup.

Without money or a place to stay, Earl has to return to Ray, who takes him home to recover for a few days. Ray lies to his son Virgil (Michael Beach), saying Earl is an old Korean war buddy (the only conceivable explanation for bringing home a redneck). But Aunt T., a feisty, elderly black woman, played with aplomb and humor by Irma P. Hall, is not fooled. She knows the story of Ray's half-brother, and she quickly figures out that he has come for a family reunion of sorts.

The plot and acting are strong enough to carry this improbable story. In a way, both Earl and Ray must live a lie in order to cover up the deep anger and hurt they both feel and to avoid delving into issues that would tear them apart just as their society has been riven by racism. When they find themselves sharing a bedroom, with Earl given an army cot, it is almost as if they had been together in the service. Indeed, they have been in the Korean War, although only Ray saw action. As they exchange stories, Earl learns that Ray is the boy who once hit him with a rock when he was in town with his father. Ray acknowledges him and Earl accepts the pain both have experienced in such different and yet family ways.

But neither man can quite transcend his hostility. That role is given to Aunt T., the family historian who is devoid of the male pride and stubbornness that still separates the two men. Her role is pivotal in the plot and in the evolving psychology of all the characters. Without Irma P. Hall's gritty and zestful performance, the film would founder, even with the sensitive efforts of Duvall and Jones.

The location shots of Arkansas and Chicago help set the atmosphere of the film, placing both Duvall and Jones realistically in their surroundings, and revealing both as good family men, no matter how much racial issues may have scarred their psyches. If the film never quite transcends its earnest message of racial reconciliation, it does present genuine human beings struggling with issues that are more than just "a family thing."

—Carl Rollyson

CREDITS

Earl Pilcher Jr.: Robert Duvall
Ray Murdoch: James Earl Jones
Aunt T: Irma P. Hall
Virgil Murdock: Michael Beach
Sonny: David Keith
Ruby: Grace Zabriskie
Ann: Regina Taylor

Origin: USA
Released: 1996
Production: Robert Duvall, Todd Black, Randa Haines for Butchers Run Films; released by United Artists
Direction: Richard Pearce
Screenplay: Billy Bob Thornton, Tom Epperson
Cinematography: Fred Murphy
Editing: Mark Warner
Music: Charles Gross
Production design: Linda DeScenna
Art direction: Jim Nedza
Set decoration: Ric McElvin
Costume design: Joe I. Tompkins
Sound: Glenn Williams
MPAA rating: PG-13
Running Time: 109 minutes

REVIEWS

Chicago Tribune. March 29, 1996, p. 5.
Detroit News. March 29, 1996, p. D1.
Entertainment Weekly. April 5, 1996, p. 61.
Los Angeles Times. March 29, 1996, p. F8.
New York Times. March 29, 1996, p. C3.
USA Today. March 29, 1996, p. 4D.
Variety. March 25, 1996, p. 66.
Village Voice. April 2, 1996, p. 66.

The Fan

Fear strikes today.—Movie tagline
"Fantastic!"—Jim Ferguson, *Preview Channel*
"Suspenseful!"—Alan Silverman, *Voice of America*
"Chilling!"—Mike Caccippoli, *WABC Radio*
"Fascinating!"—Bill Carlson, *WCCO-TV*

Box Office: $18,626,419

The concept of the "odd couple" is a staple of dramatic literature, an unlikely pairing (like Eddie Murphy and Nick Nolte in *48 Hours* [1982] or Mel Gibson and Danny Glover in the *Leathal Weapon* series [1987; 1989; 1992]) that often begins in distrust or rivalry and then progresses toward partnership and mutual appreciation. *The Fan* employs an effective variant of this arrangement by linking two people—a man failing in everything that matters to him and a man succeeding fabulously in terms of conventional measures of achievement—through their involvement with the game of baseball but more significantly in their efforts to find some degree of personal satisfaction and inner serenity in an extremely hostile, vicious world where humane impulses are overwhelmed by a rage for self-glorification and empty acquisition.

"They love you when you're hitting but won't come near you when you're not."—Baseball player Bobby about his fans

Gil Renard (Robert De Niro) is a salesman who cares about his product (the fine knives designed by his father) working for a company that is interested solely in profit. Divorced, friendless, driven and desperate to maintain a relationship with his young son, he depends on baseball (which he calls "better than life" since the game "is fair") as a source of psychic survival. As the film opens, he has staked his precarious mental stability on a fanciful connection to Bobby Rayburn (Wesley Snipes), the newest acquisition of the San Francisco Giants, a three-time MVP who is the beneficiary of a $40 million contract as well as the preposterous expectations of the media, fans and team owners who are ready to turn on him if he does not achieve the unattainable perfection of the superstar.

De Niro's role in *The Fan* has obvious echoes of the parts he played in *Taxi Driver* (1976), *The King of Comedy* (1983) and *Cape Fear* (1991), films in which an angry, frustrated man projected his fury against his fate into an obsessive, parasitic connection to a prominent member of the community, forcing the privileged man to consider the consequences of his success in terms of De Niro's intrusion into his life. In spite of the obviously unacceptable extremes of De Niro's behavior, he suggested a kind of symbolic moral avenger grown out of the character's conscience as well as a direct physical threat. Here, although the circumstances of their lives place them at opposites of a spectrum of fame and wealth, Renard and Rayburn—their names resonating with the parallels in their lives—are both trapped by the destructive forces of a society that rewards egocentric posturing, hyper-competitive instincts and a cold disregard for other human beings.

The first part of *The Fan* does an effective job of establishing the grounds for Renard's desperation, supplying the factors which have pushed him out of the harshness of his day-by-day existence and into a self-created domain of decency he calls "Baseball." Rayburn has been able to shield himself from similar unpleasantness through the acquisition of extravagant means of comfort and the deference that his extraordinary athletic ability commands. As the film begins just prior to Opening Day of the new season when Rayburn arrives in San Francisco, two narrative paths are launched. The scene shifts in a deft example of sustained cross-cutting between Renard's attempts to get tickets to the season opener and Rayburn's efforts to adjust to the demands of a pressure-ridden situation.

The apparent gulf between their position is exemplified by the initial sequence in which De Niro recites a very sentimental, achingly sincere poem (written by William Hughes) about the nobility of "The Game" while grainy, black and white stills depict a young boy at play in a Little League game. The purity of this scene and its place in a realm of fond nostalgic recollection is emphasized by the abrupt switch to Rayburn's entrance into the city which sees him as a savior. To the heavy bass thumping of a contemporary sound-track that mingles hip-hop rhythms with songs by the Rolling Stones and Nine Inch Nails, Rayburn, in the company of his constantly scheming agent (a portrait in knowing cynicism by John Leguizamo), drives a massive Humvee that straddles the road like a God's chariot. The almost languorous pace of the glimpses of Renard's past is accelerated into the frenzy of a motion-mad modern city. The noise and flash characteristic of Tony Scott's direction in films like *Top Gun* (1986) and *Crimson Tide* (1995) is perfectly suited to the world in which Rayburn is compelled to operate—a place where there is little time for reflection and no time for a kinder, gentler approach to life. While Rayburn seems to thrive in this atmosphere, his genuine distress when he visits a boy terminally ill with cancer is a pointed comment on the other characters who seem to have shielded themselves from any interaction which could produce the kind of emotional response that might be interpreted as a sign of weakness.

Renard is caught in the relentless pace of this world as well, but he doesn't have any of Rayburn's counter strengths. He remains in an almost constant state of irritation as he is treated with contempt, amused condescension or outright disdain by his boss, various lower-level employees and his ex-wife (played with unsettling hysteria by Patti D'Arbanville-Quinn). The degree of humiliation and frustration he suffers, the pathos of his attempts to communicate with his son through various facets of baseball and the meagerness of his dreams make his actions plausible as the film develops and arouses a feeling of sympathy for him that is essentially absent in the way Rupert Pupkin (*The King of Comedy*) or Max Cady (in *Cape Fear*) were presented. Scott isn't particularly proficient at sequences that require a quieter mood, but he has been quite successful in permitting the principal players in his films (like Denzel Washington and Gene Hackman in *Crimson Tide*) to create a character with sufficient depth and dimension to hold the audience's attention even when the narrative becomes strained by a reliance on sensational effects. De Niro is able to make Renard complex enough so that his character seems logical without being entirely predictable and to make his eventual escalation from inner obsession to an outward explosion a result of pressures that become unbearable.

On the other hand, when Renard begins to display the violent behavior apparently required by the stalker subgenre, he forfeits the audience's concern that has kept him at the center of the film's focus. The convergence of the two narrative tracks which has propelled the film to this point results in a somewhat contrived but not impossible meeting between the protagonists. Rayburn is grateful when Renard, who has been lurking near Rayburn's beach home is thus able to help pull Rayburn's son from a perilous ocean. His vulnerability makes him very appealing as he treats Renard as an equal, man to man. Even when Renard makes a show of wearing Rayburn's uniform and actually, improbably, insisting on "pitching" to Rayburn on the darkened beach, Rayburn takes it in stride, his genial tolerance of a fan's dreams demonstrating that he has not forgotten entirely what it means to yearn for the glory he now takes for granted. Were *The Fan* to proceed from this moment to depict the inevitable disappointment Renard must face when his brief contact with Rayburn ends and to show him facing with some remorse the consequences of his attempts to "assist" his idol by stabbing Juan Primo (Benicio Del Toro), Rayburn's haughty rival, a feeling of almost tragic sadness might have elevated the film beyond the cascade of violence that dominates the long last sequence.

Rather that making Renard's fall into homicidal horror the understandable if deplorable descent of an ordinary man overwhelmed by an ugly society which rewards the wrong kind of behavior, *The Fan* turns Renard into a monster on a psychotic rampage who must be obliterated. What Scott and the screenwriters have missed is the traditional convention that almost requires the audience to recognize the humanity in the madman, the element of ourselves latent in every significant movie monster from Boris Karloff's *Frankenstein* (1931) to *King Kong* (1933) and on to *Godzilla* (1956). De Niro handles the menace with his usual facility but by the end of *The Fan,* repulsion has replaced any other kind of reaction to him. The ludicrous final scene in which Renard terrorizes Rayburn by threatening his son is all overblown effect, a deluge on the diamond so preposterous that Scott's previous presentation of baseball in a kind of heightened realism seems in retrospect like straight documentary reporting. The lightning and thunder, booming soundtrack, reeling camera, blood on the mound, bodies on the baseline and so forth is more suitable to a vision of the apocalypse than any of the themes Scott has covered.

As Renard rushes out of control, the film's focus shifts to Rayburn, and Snipes does a very good job of making the star athlete progressively more appealing. The emptiness of the life of a super-celebrity is nicely conveyed as Rayburn

CREDITS

Gil Renard: Robert De Niro
Bobby Rayburn: Wesley Snipes
Jewel Stern: Ellen Barkin
Manny: John Leguizamo
Ellen Renard: Patti D'Arbanville-Quinn
Tim: Chris Mulkey
Richie Renard: Andrew J. Ferchland
Coop: Charles Hallahan

Origin: USA
Released: 1996
Production: Wendy Finerman for Mandalay Entertainment; released by TriStar Pictures
Direction: Tony Scott
Screenplay: Phoef Sutton; based on the book by Peter Abrahams
Cinematography: Dariusz Wolski
Editing: Christian Wagner
Editing: Claire Simpson
Production design: Ida Random
Costume design: Rita Ryack
Casting: Ellen Lewis
Sound: Bill Kaplan
Music: Hans Zimmer
MPAA rating: R
Running Time: 117 minutes

turns from the perks of his position toward the few possibilities for genuine feeling he has, particularly his relationship with his young son, an obvious but appropriate parallel with Renard's uneasy efforts to hold his son's affection. When Rayburn and Renard meet, Snipes's warmth indicates his own need for someone to understand the trials of his life, and the "mystical junction" Renard has mentioned seems to be less bizarre than previously suggested. Snipes is especially good at mingling vulnerability with arrogance and the facade he uses as a shield at first gives way to the openness that reveals how much those who fortune has favored share the fears and insecurities most people have. This hints at the humanity behind the self-absorption of Primo, the calculation of Leguizamo's Manny and most of all, behind the hard-edged aggression of Ellen Barkin's Jewel Stein. Barkin hits just the right note as a sports broadcaster who is tough, sassy and provocative but who might rather permit some other qualities to surface at times. The initial thrust of the film, which locates the pervasive nastiness in the agitative propensity of the media, is lost as *The Fan* degenerates into a formulaic thriller, and the skill of the actors working with an uneven script cannot entirely rescue a film which has many interesting aspects but which Todd McCarthy of *Daily Variety* has accurately categorized as ultimately "repugnant." McCarthy's judgement that *The Fan* "could fill some seats on opening weekend" but then "quickly plummet to the bottom of the (box-office) standings" seems likely in terms of the pointless, even sickening feeling the conclusion produces.

—*Leon Lewis*

REVIEWS

Detroit News. August 16, 1996, p. D1; D12.
Entertainment Weekly. August 23-30, 1996, p. 100-101.
The New Republic. September 9, 1996, p. 37-38.
Newsweek. August 26, 1996, p. 62.
The New York Times. August 16, 1996, p. C3.
Rolling Stone. September 5, 1996, p. 50.
Time. August 26, 1996, p. 61.
The Village Voice. August 27, 1996, p. 50.

Fargo

A homespun murder story.—Movie tagline

A lot can happen in the middle of nowhere.—Movie tagline

"A brilliant macabre thriller! Coen fans have reason to rejoice!"—Guy Flatley, *Cosmopolitan*

"The coolest movie you'll see this year by far."—Stephen Saban, *Details*

"Cheerfully eccentric black comedy."—Susan Stark, *The Detroit News*

"A hilarious thriller! Frances McDormand is perfect as the world's unlikeliest detective."—Lisa Henricksson, *GQ*

"Brilliant! Fiendishly funny. Keeps pulling the rug from under you. You're laughing and catching your breath at every turn."—Dennis Dermody, *Paper*

"A terrifically twisted comedy! I was helpless with laughter."—Peter Travers, *Rolling Stone*

Box Office: $24,083,318

There are a handful of filmmakers whose participation in a particular movie overshadow anyone who might be in its cast. Martin Scorsese, Francis Ford Coppola, Brian DePalma, Robert Altman, Woody Allen have all been making films since the 1960's and, with few exceptions, all solely responsible for the success or failure of their films. They all leave their indelible fingerprints on whatever project they release; they are the stars of their movies. The styles they use to express their visions and the genres they work within go hand in glove with their material. Sometimes they branch out and do films that don't really fit their forte (Scorsese's *The Age of Innocence* [1993], Altman's *Popeye* [1980], Allen's *Shadows & Fog* [1992], DePalma's *The Bonfire of the Vanities* [1990], Coppola's *Bram Stoker's Dracula* [1992]). Some of these films worked, most didn't. Whether they succeeded or not, you could still tell who was calling the shots. Branching out as artists and throwing caution to the wind is sometimes necessary. Avoiding the rut of predictability coupled with the occasional humbling flop keeps the juices flowing and the creative edges from being dulled.

Pregnancy won't slow down Police Chief Marge Gunderson (Frances McDormand) as she tracks down two vicious killers in the Joel and Ethan Coen dark comedy, *Fargo*.

For the short time they've been making movies, brothers Ethan and Joel Coen have made a mark by crafting films in a manner no one else ever has. Their alleged contemporaries Tarantino and Rodriguez may have made geekdom hip, but the Coens were the pioneers. They are relatively reclusive and tend to avoid flaunting themselves in public. The blueprint to their structural artistic framework lies almost exclusively in satire. *Fargo,* their just released sixth film, finds them back on their familiar low budget, low profile turf. This is great news after the glorious disaster of *The Hudsucker Proxy* from 1993.

CREDITS

Marge Gunderson: Frances McDormand
Carl Showalter: Steve Buscemi
Jerry Lundegaard: William H. Macy
Gaear Grimsrud: Peter Stormare
Wade Gustafson: Harve Presnell
Norm Gunderson: John Carroll Lynch
Jean Lundegaard: Kristin Rudrud
Shep Proudfoot: Steven Reevis

Origin: USA
Released: 1996
Production: Joel Coen for a Working Title Films production; released by Gramercy Pictures
Direction: Ethan Coen
Screenplay: Ethan Coen and Joel Coen
Cinematography: Roger Deakins
Editing: Roderick James
Production design: Rick Heinrichs
Art direction: Thomas P. Wilkins
Set decoration: Lauri Gaffin
Costume design: Mary Zophres
Sound: Allan Byer
Music: Carter Burwell
Casting: John Lyons
MPAA rating: R

After four gems (*Blood Simple* [1985], *Raising Arizona* [1987], *Miller's Crossing* [1990], *Barton Fink* [1991]), the overtures from mainstream Hollywood appeared to be too much to resist and the brothers made an exorbitantly high priced epic that starred equally high profile stars Paul Newman, Jennifer Jason Leigh and Tim Robbins in a sped-up version of the light romantic comedies of the 1940's golden age. There was plenty of the trademark sarcasm, but it seemed muted and the usual edginess seemed stilted. The critics, who had previously showered them with praise, slammed the film. The public stayed away in droves and the film lost immense amounts of cash. The process proved to be humbling as the brothers retreated and regrouped then went about the task of making a film that achieved the artistic excellence of their first four efforts.

"There's more to life than a little money, you know."—Marge Gunderson

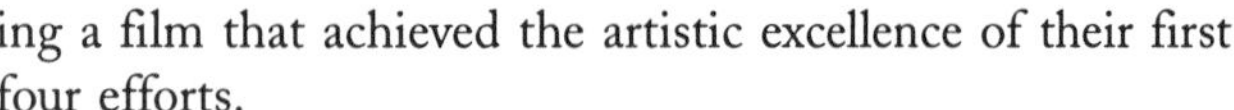

The three year wait shows that the Coens got their inspiration back and the result is one of the best films of the year. Where *The Hudsucker Proxy* was grandiose and contrived, *Fargo* is scaled down and unassuming. The glitz and grandeur of the elaborate sets and special effects has been replaced with the quiet, barren, snow covered plains of Minnesota and North Dakota.

Fargo begins with the arrival of Jerry Lundegaard (William H. Macy) a high-strung car salesman who has finally snapped and plans on getting out of his huge financial hole by hiring some low-life hoods to kidnap his wife and extort ransom money from his father-in-law. From the outset, it's painfully apparent that the men Jerry has hired are not going to pull this job off smoothly.

Relatively unknown actor Peter Stormare plays Gaear Grimsrud, one of the hired guns who prefers to communicate non-verbally. He doesn't say more than four or five lines in the whole film, but his role is pivotal. His partner, Carl Showalter is played with the trademark high-strung, wide-eyed uneasiness of Steve Buscemi. Slowly becoming the premier character actor of his generation, Buscemi has left his mark on every role he's undertaken. Besides his appearances in previous Coen ventures (*Barton Fink, Miller's Crossing, The Hudsucker Proxy*), his roles in *Desperado* [1995], *Reservoir Dogs* [1992], *Living In Oblivion* [1994] and the very under-appreciated *Things to Do in Denver When You're Dead* [1995], showcase Buscemi's unique weasel-trapped-in-the-corner look. He's perfect for the role of the paranoid, inept Carl.

Shortly after finalizing the half-baked kidnapping/extortion plan, Jerry not only finds an avenue to make the money he needs legally, he develops a deep case of the guilts, and seeks to stop the crime. He's attempting to get a deal financed through his distant, uncaring father-in-law Wade Gustafson (Harve Presnell). Wade doesn't exactly hate Jerry, but he's not enamored of him either. Presnell's clipped, agitated delivery is hilarious. Gustafson is filthy rich and Jerry is tired of having to live in his shadow. Jerry's shortcomings in life, including being a bit dim, have finally taken their toll.

The kidnapping goes down anyway and Jerry's tangled plan immediately begins to unravel. Jerry and his wife live in Brainerd, Minnesota. The town's biggest claim to fame is that it's home to the fabled literary character Paul Bunyan and his blue ox, Babe. The statue of Bunyan that lies on the town's edge says a great deal. The stoic, square-shouldered and jawed Nordic woodsman, with glaring eyes, is unaffected as it could be. The Coens were born and raised in Minnesota and their knowledge of the indigenous population is extraordinary. The rhythms of the characters speech, the cadences, nuances, tones and subtleties of their Scandinavian-Canadian heritage drive this project. The Coens have a reputation of being great authorities of spoken dialogue and *Fargo* finds them at the top of their form. It is a rarity to find a film that is practically devoid of sex and whatever violence is present is brief and mostly implied. As they did with *Blood Simple* and *Raising Arizona,* the Coens extol the glories and virtues of dialogue and language.

Top billed Frances McDormand doesn't make her appearance until close to the film's halfway point. This is McDormand's fourth appearance in a Coen film. The fact that

AWARDS AND NOMINATIONS

Academy Awards 1996: Best Actress (McDormand), Best Original Screenplay (Coen/Coen)
Nominations: Best Picture, Best Director (Coen), Best Supporting Actor (Macy), Best Cinematography (Deakins), Best Film Editing
Australian Film Institute Awards 1996: Best Foreign Film
Cannes Film Festival 1997: Best Director (Coen)
Cesar Awards 1996 Nominations: Best Foreign Film
Directors Guild of America 1996 Nomination: Best Director (Coen)
Golden Globe Award 1997 Nominations: Best Film-Musical/Comedy, Best Actress-Musical/Comedy (McDormand), Best Director (Coen), Best Screenplay (Coen, Coen)
Independent Spirit Awards 1997: Feature, Director (Coen), Actress (McDormand), Actor (Macy), Screenplay (Coen/Coen), Cinematography (Deakins)
Los Angeles Film Critics Association 1996: Best Screenplay (Coen/Coen)
National Board of Review 1996: Best Actress (McDormand), Best Director (Coen)
New York Film Critics Circle 1996: Best Film
Screen Actors Guild 1996: Actress (McDormand)
Nominations: Supporting Actor (Macy)
Writers Guild of America 1996: Original Screenplay (Coen/Coen)

she's married to Joel might have something to do with her getting the role. In recent interviews, she has joked that this might be a rare instance where an actress doesn't mind sleeping with the director in order to get a role. Nepotism aside, she is perfect for the part. McDormand plays Marge Gunderson, the chipper, almost too happy sheriff of Brainerd.

Actress Frances McDormand, who plays Marge Gunderson, is married to director, co-writer Joel Coen.

Marge is woken from an early morning slumber and arrives on the scene of what is surely Brainerd's first ever triple homicide. She has no idea that the murder and the previous day's kidnapping have anything in common. Her consistent, no-nonsense yet perky demeanor is very non-threatening and break down whatever walls of defense available witnesses might put up. Even Jerry, who talks in circles for a living, can't bullshit his way past Marge.

To further amplify the Coen's viewpoint of regular America, Marge carries on the many, sometimes dangerous aspects of her job during the third trimester of her pregnancy. She's married to Norm (John Carroll Lynch), a man who works out of the home painting pictures of ducks. His biggest worry is whether or not the postal service is going to choose his painting for use on a three cent or a 29 cent stamp. They share Arby's carry-out at her office, she brings him night crawlers and together they watch nature specials on late night television. A boring existence? Perhaps. But these are the kind of things that real people do. Real people in Minnesota, anyway.

While the Coens portray law enforcement as a mundane, almost elementary job, they also remove much of the romantic movie allure associated with organized crime. How Grimsrud and Showalter ever became partners is anyone's guess. They don't get along whatsoever. Even while on the run for murder, their biggest concerns involve their stomachs and libidos. If they would have used even the slightest bit of professionalism, they might have gotten through the ordeal unscathed and much richer than they had planned.

Fargo is the Coen's sixth film and as adored as they are with movie purists and within critics' circles, they can't seem to get arrested by regular American audiences. Their productions are all a bit self-satisfying and both brothers seem dedicated to avoiding the publicity circuit that often accompanies national release. They list a man by the name of Roderick James as their editor, which is a ruse. They do all the editing themselves. The opening credits claim that *Fargo* is based on actual events that occurred in 1987. They say that the names of the innocent have been changed, but the names of the guilty remain intact. Production notes state that "no similarity to actual persons, living or dead is intended or should be inferred." They seem to revel in the misinformation they bandy about and have gone out of their way (no doubt due in part to the debacle of *The Hudsucker Proxy*) to make a film that has very little chance of even remotely being mistaken as mainstream. Bully for them.

—*J.M. Clark.*

REVIEWS

Boxoffice Magazine. May, 1996, p. 74.
Entertainment Weekly. March 29, 1996, p. 42.
Los Angeles Times. March 8, 1996, p. F1.
New York Times. March 8, 1996, p. C1.
The New Yorker. March 25, 1996, p. 99.
Premiere. March, 1996, p. 22.
Rolling Stone. March 21, 1996, p. 104.
USA Today. March 8, 1996, p. 7D.
Variety. February 12, 1996, p. 78.
Village Voice. March 12, 1996, p. 46.

Fear

Together forever. Or else.—Movie tagline

"Unnerving. Edge-of-your-seat."—Jane Sumner, *The Dallas Morning News*

"Ripping good. James Foley has made an entertaining thriller."—David Hunter, *Los Angeles Daily News*

"Genuinely thrilling. Mark Wahlberg is utterly ruthless . . . a scary performance."—Hal Hinson, *Washington Post*

"A suspenseful, erotic thriller."—Paul Wunder, *WBAI Radio*

Box Office: $20,829,193

Like his first feature film, *At Close Range* (1986), director James Foley again showcases the strained alliance of a parent and child who have suffered through long periods of time away from each other. In the newly released *Fear,* Steven Walker (William Petersen) is a successful, workaholic architect. His daughter Nicole (Reese Witherspoon) has recently left her mother's digs in Los Angeles to set up camp in Seattle with him, his current wife Laura (Amy Brenneman) and her son Toby (Christopher Gray). Nicole and Steven seem to still be in something of an awkward breaking in period. She's 16 and beautiful and her choice and Steven's preferences in her wardrobe are world's apart. In an effort to make their new relationship cordial, he leaves the issue alone, yet worries that she might be sending out the wrong signals.

"Everybody says one thing and does another."—Nicole

Nicole's best friend Margo (Alyssa Milano) is a textbook example of what parents would call "a bad influence." Margo gets Nicole to skip school to spend some time at a local pool hall. While party girl Margo hooks up with an unwashed local, Nicole eyes perfection in the form of David McCall (Mark Wahlberg). He returns the glances, sends her a mere hint of a smile, but seems less than impressed. This, of course, drives Nicole nuts.

A few days later, Laura's planned night out with the family is cancelled and Nicole instead ventures downtown to a rave show. David just happens to be there and immediately sets about charming Nicole. With the show getting dangerously out of hand, David shelters Nicole from the chaos and whisks her away to safety. David's soft-spoken demeanor wrangles its way into Nicole's heart and she melts. David attempts to move the relationship beyond the kissing stage, and to her own insecurities, Nicole demurs. David pretends to be impressed; he says that's what he wanted to hear.

The producers of this film aren't being subtle in their approach. The byline on the promotional poster for *Fear* reads "Together forever. Or else." Wahlberg's scowl for the poster is seen a dozen or more times throughout the movie. First he ropes 'em in with some non-threatening charisma then he turns into a raging psychopath. Glenn Close (the other woman) did it in *Fatal Attraction* (1987). Rebecca DeMornay (the nanny) did it in *The Hand That Rocks the Cradle* (1992). Keith Carradine and Daryl Hannah (the parents) did so very poorly in *The Tie That Binds* (1995. The normally comic and breezy Michael Keaton (the tenant) was very convincing in *Pacific Heights* (1990). Now it's Wahlberg's turn and he's The Boyfriend From Hell.

David starts the relationship with the type of fawning attention usually reserved for members of the royal family. Nicole is now reveling in a dream existence. An older man (he's not a boy, he's 18, he's a man) picks her up from school every day in his boss' car. Nicole glances back towards her girlfriends and shoots them an "eat-your-heart-out" glance as they drive off together. Her guard stops dropping when the couple goes on a double-date to an amusement park with Margo and her talking gorilla. The Sundays' "Wild Horses" begins playing as Nicole and David climb aboard a roller coaster, Foley's clunky metaphor to their soon-to-be volatile relationship.

Nicole wants David to meet her family. His tight-lipped, rote politeness towards Steven and Laura causes both of them to doubt his sincerity. David has already implanted distrust by purposely turning Nicole's wristwatch backwards, giving her a thin excuse for missing her curfew. Steven wants to give Nicole some space, but when David pulls the same trick of turning back his clock, he sees that his worst fears might have some foundation. Laura's distrust for David is temporarily suspended, due to David's frequent compliments that she hasn't been getting from Steven.

As seems to always be the case in these movies, the people at the center of the storm are the last to notice anything strange going on around them. Nicole finally gets the message. At the precise moment she confesses her love for David to her close male friend Gary (Todd Caldecott), David pulls up to witness the two embracing, as friends might, and immediately goes ballistic. Tearing the two apart, he beats and kicks Gary within an inch of his life and in the process belts Nicole, giving her a black eye. Normally, any sane, mature woman would never give an abuser like David a second thought and Nicole ends the relationship, but only temporarily. Coupled with her teenaged naivete and David's beguiling sincerity, Nicole lets him back into her life. During their brief cooling-off period, Steven does some investigating and finds out that David's tale of homespun bliss is a crock. Repeatedly in and out of jail, he has no job and lives in a group home with a band of delinquents. When Steven informs Nicole of his findings, it gives her more resolve to stick it out with David. Teenagers will do anything to make their parents look stupid.

Wahlberg deserves considerable credit for taking on this part. Playing a lead character so loathsome is a tough choice for an actor to make. He hasn't had a starring role to this point and risks becoming typecast as a sociopath. Anthony Perkins couldn't get real work for ten years after his chilling portrayal of Norman Bates in Hitchcock's *Psycho* (1960). Anthony Hopkins, on the other hand, went from cult status to the top half of the "A" list for playing Hannibal "The Cannibal" Lecter in *The Silence of the Lambs* (1991). Wahlberg wisely resists animating and falsely energizing the character and in the process, turns in an admirable performance. A great many stalkers mask themselves well. They're often undetectable in a crowd. Wahlberg spends the bulk of his time stone-faced, but not from boredom. He seems coiled. He doesn't raise his voice very much. When he strikes, it's momentary, but brutally thorough. His vocal delivery is monotonous, but foreboding. His career as a rap singer has tinted his regional New England accent with a heavy, ominous Bronx overtone.

On Valentine's Day this year (ironically, *The Silence of the Lambs* was also released on Valentine's Day), Touchstone released *Mr. Wrong*, a sort of stalker comedy. Bill Pullman plays a character who exudes a kind of seductiveness that a David McCall might have in his mid-30's. Although it's possible to lampoon any subject, current societal fears would lead one to believe that stalking would not be one of them. Both Pullman and Wahlberg are playing individuals whose twisted, controlling behavior goes largely unnoticed and even worse, unpunished.

Michael Keaton, Keith Carradine, Glenn Close and Rebecca DeMornay and now Wahlberg have all starred in these {fill in the blank} from Hell outings that simply have too much in common. The calculating lead character nonchalantly meets the victim(s), gains their trust, and ingratiates themselves into their lives. Paranoid delusions ensue and the resulting terror suddenly becomes numbingly predictable. They all disintegrate into abhorrent stereotypes, end frantically, and leave a sour aftertaste. James Foley has used a tired formula that mainstream audiences just seem to gobble up. He even includes the requisite death of a family pet.

Hollywood would serve itself well and should seriously consider reinventing the wheel with these projects. Does all the extraneous titillation add substance to the story? The infamous stalking death of television actress Rebecca Schaffer ("My Sister Sam") is a story that needs to be told, however morbid the results. Madonna and David Letterman have had similar (though not as dire) events occur to them. Madonna pressed charges and put her stalker away. Letterman's surface devil-may-care reaction to his predicament makes for some good one-liners, but still must keep him a bit on edge. Virtually all states have passed a "stalker" law and the situation has begun to slowly improve. Perhaps Hollywood can follow suit, get rid of the formulas and do something more authentic and less contrived that cuts closer to the bone.

—J.M. Clark

CREDITS

David McCall: Mark Wahlberg
Nicole Walker: Reese Witherspoon
Steve Walker: William Petersen
Laura Walker: Amy Brenneman
Margo Masse: Alyssa Milano
Toby: Christopher Gray

Origin: USA
Released: 1996
Production: Brian Grazer, Ric Kidney for an Imagine Entertainment production; released by Universal Pictures
Direction: James Foley
Screenplay: Christopher Crowe
Cinematography: Thomas Kloss
Editing: David Brenner
Music: Carter Burwell
Production design: Alex McDowell
Art direction: Richard Hudolin
Set decoration: D. Fauquet-Lemaitre
Costume design: Kirsten Everberg
Sound: Eric J. Batut
Casting: Debra Zane
MPAA rating: R
Running Time: 96 minutes

REVIEWS

Boxoffice. July, 1996, p. 96.
Detroit News. April 12, 1996, p. 4D.
Entertainment Weekly. April 26, 1996, p. 40.
Los Angeles Times. April 12, 1996, p. F12.
New York Times. April 12, 1996, p. C20.
Sight and Sound. December, 1996, p. 44.
Variety. April 15, 1996, p. 178.

Feeling Minnesota

Just when she met the man of her dreams, her husband showed up to ruin everything.—Movie tagline

"A wonderful wild roller coaster ride."—Bill Zwecker, *NBC-TV*

"A wall-to-wall wacky movie!"—Bruce Williamson, *Playboy*

"Keanu Reeves and Cameron Diaz sizzle!"—Jim Ferguson, *Prevue Channel*

"Outrageously funny!"—Paul Wunder, *WBAI Radio*

Box Office: $3,124,440

Let's call this movie "Feeling Frustrated" or "Feeling Disgusted" instead because it's a mess. If it was indeed inspired by the Soundgarden lyric "I just looked in the mirror, things aren't looking so good, I'm looking California and feeling Minnesota" than first-time writer/director Steven Baigelman should be apologizing profusely to the band. While cinematographer Walt Lloyd comes off well by making the seedy Minnesota setting as gray and dreary as the movie warrants, he can't compensate for the bad script, bad acting, and bad direction, which reaches a particular nadir around mid-film.

"You ate my ear. You killed your wife. You framed me. And you're mad at me for lying?"—Jjaks to his brother Sam

A prologue establishes the background quickly enough. Twenty years before, eight-year-old Jjaks (the name is the result of a typo on his birth certificate) is about to be sent away by his indifferent, blowsy, divorced mother (a cameo by Tuesday Weld) to live with his father and away from his mom's favorite, witless and bullying older brother Sam.

Flash-forward to the present where Freddie (Cameron Diaz), attired in a ripped and dirty wedding dress, is being brutally chased by local crook Red (Delroy Lindo) and his men, who throw her into their car and forcibly take her to her wedding. Freddie has been accused of embezzling from Red and he's decided to punish her by marrying her off to his brutish bookkeeper, the now-grownup Sam (Vincent D'Onofrio). (It's either marriage or death.) Jjaks (Keanu Reeves), recently released from prison, also shows up at the wedding and Freddie makes a beeline for her new brother-in-law—they even have a "quickie" in the bathroom during the wedding reception. Because the brothers' mom drops dead during the reception, Jjaks is forced to hang around for the funeral and Freddie is able to persuade the dim bulb to run away with her to Las Vegas, where her big dream is to become a showgirl.

They stop overnight at a cheap motel and Freddie convinces Jjaks to return home to get the stash of cash she thinks Sam is hiding. Only when Jjaks gets there, Sam catches him, they fight, and Sam bites off part of his brother's ear before Jjaks can escape. Then revenge-minded Sam follows the oblivious Jjaks, planning to get his wife back. But when Freddie doesn't cooperate, Sam shoots her, leaving the body behind in Jjaks' motel room, and calls the cops. Jjaks thinks he's killed Freddie (he'd passed out), so he takes her body and dumps it in the woods. When the cops, led by corrupt detective Ben (Dan Aykroyd), look for the body, it's gone. Well, naturally, the movie's only about a third of the way through and Baigelman didn't see fit to kill off Diaz's bimbo character, no matter how unpleasant she might be.

Since there's no body, the cops release the brothers, who later receive a blackmail phone call from the motel owner. In order to pay him off, Sam goes to his boss Red, who's just discovered it's Sam who's the embezzler, not Freddie. In a silly gun draw, Sam kills Red and steals some ninety-eight thousand dollars in cash that Red's got in the safe and even manages to shoot himself, thanks to a ricocheting bul-

CREDITS

Jjaks: Keanu Reeves
Sam: Vincent D'Onofrio
Freddie: Cameron Diaz
Red: Delroy Lindo
Ben: Dan Aykroyd
Waitress: Courtney Love

Origin: USA
Released: 1996
Production: Danny DeVito, Michael Shamberg, Stacey Sher for a Jersey Films production; released by Fine Line
Direction: Steven Baigelman
Screenplay: Steven Baigelman
Cinematography: Walt Lloyd
Editing: Martin Walsh
Production design: Naomi Shohan
Costume design: Eugenie Bafaloukos
Casting: Francine Maisler
Music supervisor: Karyn Rachtman
MPAA rating: R
Running Time: 95 minutes

let. He returns to the motel, where Jjaks has been trying to keep the owner calm, and discovers Freddie's alive. Sam's already decided to keep the money for himself—there's another senseless shoot-em-up with Sam and Jjaks wounding each other—but Freddie's outsmarted them both by persuading corrupt cop Ben that both she and the money are his for the taking. Ben finishes off Sam and takes Jjaks in for murder. But the enterprising Freddie ultimately gets the dough, ditches Ben (who gets arrested), and heads to Vegas. Oh yeah, after a few months, Jjaks manages to hitch to Vegas and get back together with Freddie, who's realized her red sequins-and-feathers dream. They deserve each other.

Debut feature for Steven Baigelman.

There's a lot of unrelenting stupidity in this movie—apparently the local police are completely indifferent to crime since Jjaks steals a car, commits an armed robbery, steals another car (and a dog from a pet store) while Sam steals a car with a horse trailer attached (the horse is later stolen from him), and there are no repercussions. And the brothers are so unrelentingly dumb they can barely walk and talk coherently at the same time. Not that there's any snappy dialogue to bother with since all these lowlife characters barely know more than one word—and that one begins with an "f." Indeed, you wonder how Sam ever managed to get away with cooking the books since it's hard to believe he can add without using his fingers—but Red (like all the other characters) won't win any genius awards. And why is the manipulative, foul-mouthed Freddie such a catch? Even the normally attractive Diaz can't do anything with this tough, slutty character. And as for the men's roles—well, we can all wish Reeves, D'Onofrio, Lindo, and Aykroyd better luck next time.

—Kathleen Edgar and *Christine Tomassini*

REVIEWS

Boxoffice Magazine Online. September 20, 1996.
Chicago Tribune. September 13, 1996, Sec. 2, p. 5.
Detroit Free Press Online. September 13, 1996.
Detroit News. September 13, 1996, p. 3D.
Los Angeles Times. September 13, 1996, p. F16.
New York Times. September 13, 1996, p. C25.
Rolling Stone. October 3, 1996, p. 78.
USA Today. September 13, 1996, p. 4D.
Variety Online. September 13, 1996.
Village Voice. September 17, 1996, p. 78.

First Kid

He's young. He's wild. He's fun. And he's the one protecting the President's son.—Movie tagline
"A laugh-out-loud film for the whole family."—Brad Nimmons, *WFLA-TV*

Box Office: $26,154,472

The comic Sinbad is a likeable, talented guy. He has a gift for soft-spoken sarcasm and rapid-fire jive and double talk, as well as some skill at physical comedy. Think of him as a lower-key, less antic, funkier Groucho Marx in search of a good script. After *First Kid,* the search continues.

Sinbad is funnier, rangier and more appealing than Jim Carrey, Adam Sandler or most of the other stand-up comics who have wormed their way into starring film roles of late. Yet the writers of *First Kid* have no idea what to do with their promising if partially recycled premise: Sinbad as an unorthodox Secret Service agent assigned to guard Luke Davenport (Brock Pierce), the 13-year-old son of a Clintonesque president.

The film starts in fairly promising fashion with generous doses of sass and wit. Sinbad's Sam Simms is a goofy, overgrown adolescent who likes to use bluster and his badge to scare vendors out of donuts and coffee. He is a misfit who wears loud ties and chafes against the service's tight regulations. In the film's best line, delivered by Sinbad with typical aplomb, Simms defends his outrageous red bow tie against a

Screenwriter Tim Kelleher was inspired by a photo of first daughter Chelsea Clinton surrounded by Secret Service agents.

supervisor who reminds him he's attending a black-tie affair, insisting: "I've got it covered. I'm black, and I'm wearing a tie."

Davenport is clearly a match for Simms. He's a spoiled brat who's adept at getting Secret Service agents in trouble for his own misdeeds, who moons the press on a shopping trip at the mall, and who unleashes his pet snake whenever he's bored. Pierce is wonderfully annoying as this adolescent ambassador of ill will, and the script could have gone a lot further with the possibilities of Luke's antics undermining his father's re-election campaign.

Instead, writer Tim Kelleher and director David Mickey Evans (*The Sandlot* [1993]) turn Davenport's malevolence into mush. Simms lets Luke get a needed comeuppance in a schoolyard fight, Luke is grounded for a month while his parents are campaigning, and the first kid breaks down and whines about being a prisoner in a fishbowl. Simms turns into a kindly uncle who vows to risk his own job and sneak Luke out of the White House and into the world he's missed. Luke turns into a pussycat, a victim of excessive privilege who needs Simms' tutoring to ask a girl for a date, learn to dance and defend himself.

Though Simms vows to let Luke be part of a normal kids' world, inexplicably he takes him to a boxing gym where he once reigned supreme. The film veers into a sort of "Rocky" apprenticeship music video. The script runs dry and the movie almost stops in its own tracks. The tie jokes wear thin. *First Kid* has two promising, wry characters, but fumbles the comic opportunities they create.

Luke's first-kiss pursuit is merely lame (and unconsummated), but turning his cyberspace friendship into a kidnapping nightmare is a shame. What first was a snappy film, then a sappy film, becomes a totally out-of-place phony action thriller, complete with a shopping-mall gun battle featuring a wheelchair-bound minor character who comes out of nowhere, a villain who comes out of nowhere, and Simms redeeming himself as a hero. It's a horrible way to finish off an innocuous family film, sort of like sending the Terminator out to give a jolt to Cinderella.

The script of *First Kid* stalls and lurches like a jalopy in bad need of a tune-up. As a star vehicle for Sinbad, this film will have to do until a racier, more powerful model drives up. But it's a terrible waste of talent.

—Michael Betzold

CREDITS

Sam Simms: Sinbad
Luke Davenport: Brock Pierce
Dash: Blake Boyd
Woods: Timothy Busfield
Morton: Art La Fleur
Wilkes: Robert Guillaume

Origin: USA
Released: 1996
Production: Roger Birnbaum and Riley Kathryn Ellis for a Walt Disney production; released by Buena Vista
Direction: David Mickey Evans
Screenplay: Tim Kelleher
Cinematography: Anthony Richmond
Editing: Harry Keramidas
Music: Richard Gibbs
Production design: Chester Kaczenski
Art direction: Marc Dabe
Costume design: Grania Preston
Sound: Gary Cunningham
Technical advise: Bob Snow
MPAA rating: PG
Running Time: 101 minutes

REVIEWS

New York Times. August 30, 1996, p. C10.
USA Today. August 30, 1996, p. 4D.
Variety. September 2, 1996, p. 66.

The First Wives Club

Don't get mad. Get everything.—Movie tagline

"Great stars, great fun."—Joe Siegel, *Good Morning America*

"Everyone will want to join this club! The comedy hit of the year."—Rex Reed, *New York Observer*

"A comedy dream team! It's irresistible fun . . . sinfully satisfying."—Peter Travers, *Rolling Stone*

"The fun unfurls in wicked ways! A sparkling, grown-up comedy."—Gene Shalit, *Today*

Box Office: **$103,708,261**

From its retro-rock Dionne Warwick "Wives and Lovers" opening credits, *The First Wives Club* provides a strong hint that it will probably owe more to the 1960s than the 1990s. And, in fact, not only will the film's style and content be a flashback to days gone by, but so will its opening scene.

"There are only three stages for a woman in Hollywood: babe, district attorney, and *Driving Miss Daisy.*"—Elise

It is 1969, graduation day at Middlebury College. Four friends who have obviously grown close during their academic careers are now symbolically conjoined by pearl necklaces they are given by the fourth friend, Cynthia (Stockard Channing). But after graduation, the friends all drift apart. They marry, have careers and children and in general move on with their lives without each other.

Diane Keaton, Goldie Hawn and Bette Midler are ex-wives who get back at their former husbands in the comic box office hit, *The First Wives Club.*

But then one day Cynthia, a wealthy, divorced socialite whose husband has just remarried, very purposely takes a header off the balcony of her Manhattan apartment. It is her funeral that provides a reunion for the remaining three friends. There they notice that Cynthia's ex-husband, Gil (James Naughton) has arrived with his brand new trophy wife (Heather Locklear). "Can you imagine what Gil is feeling right now?" someone asks as the camera slyly pans to Gil's hands caressing his new wife.

It's too much for the three friends who decide that after almost thirty years apart, they should catch up over lunch . . . and a few drinks. To their amazement, their stories are not unlike Cynthia's.

Elise (Goldie Hawn) is an Oscar-winning actress who so frets about getting old and losing movie parts that she has resorted to everything from cosmetics to surgery, from exercise to alcohol, to help her compensate for the passage of time. Her husband, Bill (Victor Garber), is a movie producer, but only because she helped him to become one. Now in the process of a divorce, he wants not only to split their assets fifty-fifty, but he also demands that Elise pay him a monthly stipend (is this men's version of alimony?). To make it all the more insulting, Bill, too, has found a younger woman. In this case it's another actress, the bubbly and empty-headed Phoebe (Elizabeth Berkley), whose career he is now nurturing.

Brenda (Bette Midler) worked diligently beside her husband Morty (Dan Hedaya) over the years as the two built up their electronic store into a successful chain. But then Morty tired of Brenda, divorced her, and took up with one of his store clerks, Shelly (Sarah Jessica Parker), who would do anything to make it big in Manhattan society—and she's hoping Morty's money can buy that for her.

Annie (Diane Keaton), however, doesn't seem to think she quite fits in with the her pals' common stories. After all she and her husband, advertising executive Aaron (Stephen Collins), are only separated. Plus, they not only still share a bed every now and then, they also share an analyst, Dr. Leslie Rosen (Marcia Gay Harden). Eventually, however, Annie will discover that Aaron is doing more than talking to Dr. Rosen.

So these women who are all now in their 40s and who all share a common misery decide that it's payback time. The

AWARDS AND NOMINATIONS

Academy Awards 1996 Nominations: Best Original Score (Shaiman)

result is a meandering set of strategies that primarily involves getting the guys where it hurts—in their bank accounts and job identities. With the help of various friends such as Duarto (Bronson Pinchot) one of New York's ten worst interior decorators, Chris (Jennifer Dundas) Annie's lesbian daughter, Carmine (Philip Bosco) Brenda's mafioso uncle, and Gunilla Goldberg (Maggie Smith) the epitome of New York society, the three set out to take control of assets, take over businesses, and take revenge on their ex-husbands.

With three powerhouse actresses, a strong supporting cast, a bevy of amusing cameos, and a hit novel (by Olivia Goldsmith) as its source, it would seem that *The First Wives Club* has all it needs to make it big time. And indeed, it is doing well at the boxoffice (it has had the highest-grossing September opening ever with $19 million). But success here just means the film is commercial, because in reality, it is also disappointing. With all these elements going for it, it could have been so much more. Too often, the film takes the easy road, goes for the easy joke, opts for the easy answer.

Perhaps the fault lay with director Hugh Wilson (*Police Academy* [1984], *Guarding Tess* [1994]) who needed to take a sterner hand with his screenwriter Robert Harling (*Soapdish* [1991], *Steel Magnolias* [1989]), because in the end one can remember little of substance about the film. Or perhaps Harling's writing was just fine, but the editing process took its toll. In an *Entertainment Weekly* article, Harling indicates that a lot was cut from the film, including entire plotlines such as Jon Stewart's role as Hawn's boyfriend, all of Heather Locklear's dialogue, and a fight between Midler and Sarah Jessica Parker. But no matter who is to blame, the film is not all it could be.

The plot is contrived and eventually preachy and the characters are mostly cardboard, so instead one focuses on sight gags and punchlines—several of them are genuinely funny, especially the one involving Shelly attempting to purchase her way into respectability at Christies' auction house. But these few good scenes and snippets of dialogue cannot compensate for the film's weaknesses. Perhaps the worst note is struck at the film's conclusion, the opening of a women's crisis center complete with cameos by Ivana Trump and Kathy Lee. It is so moralistic that it undermines the whole tone of the film, while the fairy tale closing musical number seems to be contrived solely for the purpose of allowing the heroines a chance to sing.

This is not to say that the actresses don't do a self-assured job with their characters, it's just that they should have been able to do much more. With Hawn, Midler and Keaton promising to give us a Thanksgiving meal of great "older" actresses commanding a movie about what is essentially a woman's issue, we are instead dished out quick-fix snack food.

After all, except for the running joke about collagen injections which gives her grotesquely pouty lips, Goldie Hawn looks more like the kind of women men leave their wives for than the woman who is left. And while Bette Midler is allowed a few snappy zingers, she is basically held so much in suburban restraint that one yearns for the Divine Miss M to break out into something X-rated just to spice the story up as it begins to lag. But that would be out of character for Brenda. As for Diane Keaton, while she lends a note of compassion—at least for a while—she ends up playing some scenes so befuddled or hysterical that her character totally misrepresents what is supposed to be her trademark, strength.

The First Wives Club is a comedy about revenge, but revenge should have bite. This film only allows itself to nibble at the edges. Slapstick supersedes story; the quip displaces dialogue. It is heavy on funny "bits," but light on satire. If it weren't for the watchable trio of Hawn, Midler and Keaton, there would be little to justify plunking down the price of admission.

—*Beverley Bare Buehrer*

CREDITS

Brenda Morelli Cushman: Bette Midler
Elise Elliot Atchison: Goldie Hawn
Annie MacDuggan Paradise: Diane Keaton
Gunilla Goldberg: Maggie Smith
Shelly: Sarah Jessica Parker
Morty Cushman: Dan Hedaya
Duarto Feliz: Bronson Pinchot
Chris Paradise: Jennifer Dundas
Catherine MacDuggan: Eileen Heckart
Aaron Paradise: Stephen Collins
Bill Atchison: Victor Garber
Phoebe: Elizabeth Berkley

Origin: USA
Released: 1996
Production: Scott Rudin; released by Paramount Pictures
Direction: Hugh Wilson
Screenplay: Robert Harling; from the novel by Olivia Goldsmith
Cinematography: Donald Thorin
Editing: John Bloom
Production design: Peter Larkin
Costume design: Theoni V. Aldredge
Music: Marc Shaiman
MPAA rating: PG
Running Time: 90 minutes

REVIEWS

Chicago Tribune. September 20, 1996, p. 70.
The Detroit News. September 20, 1996, p. 1D.
Entertainment Weekly. September 20, 1996, p. 53.
The New York Times. March 24, 1996, p. H27.
The New York Times. September 20, 1996, p. C21.
Newsweek. September 23, 1996, p. 74.
Time. September 30, 1996, p. 16.
USA Today. September 20, 1996, p. 1D.
Variety. September 13, 1996.

Fled

See how they run.—Movie tagline
"Keeps the chases and bullets flying!"—Larry Worth, *New York Post*
"A beginning-to-end adrenaline rush!"—Bob Meiyamoto, *Premiere Radio*
"The hippest, hottest thrill ride of the summer!"—Bob Healy, *Satellite News Service*

Box Office: $17,201,404

The biggest problem facing the new MGM release *Fled,* will undoubtedly be the inevitable comparisons to the many previously successful "mis-matched buddy" films that it so shamelessly models itself after. The politically correct, racially balanced pairing of Laurence Fishburne and Stephen Baldwin as Georgia convicts on the run, is closely patterned after *The Defiant Ones* (1958), the Oscar winning film starring Sidney Poitier and Tony Curtis. *The Defiant Ones* used a poetic, understated approach that delved into the heated racial stereotypesrooted in the deep South. Poitier and Curtis needed to overcome their own real and imagined fears of their traveling partners to achieve their common goal of freedom.

"Didn't you see *The Fugitive?* The first thing Tommy Lee Jones did was set up road blocks at the state line!"—Piper to Dodge after their escape

The loud and boisterous *Fled* explores many of the same misconceptions between the races, but it does so with a ham-handed awkwardness. It lacks the nuances and graceful finesse of *The Defiant Ones.* With the exception of some comical pop culture verbal references by Fishburne and Baldwin to old films, it lacks anything resembling originality. In its defense, it looks good while trying.

The story starts with Piper (Fishburne) and Dodge (Baldwin) working the chain gang in a rural Georgia correctional facility. During what appears to be a staged escape attempt, a number of guards and inmates are killed. In a it-could-only-happen-in-the-movies manner, Piper and Dodge narrowly escape extinction by ducking into the nearby woods. They then begin a harrowing jaunt to Atlanta. Scriptwriter Preston A. Whitmore II immediately begins feeding the two characters threadbare and cliched vocal barbs to let you know early on that these guys despise each other.

Dodge is incarcerated as a result of some very successful computer hacking that allowed him to separate vast amounts of cash from a large, unnamed multi-national corporation. White-collar criminals are rarely handed ditchdigging chores on a chain gang and Gibson, a local Georgia lawman (Will Patton), points this out to a very inept group of FBI men investigating the breakout. It seems that Dodge has been paired with Piper for a reason.

During their cross-country jog from Covington to Atlanta, Piper and Dodge wash up on a river bank and come face-to-face with the first of several embarrassing socio-southern stereotypes. During the Atlanta press junket to promote the movie, *Fled* producer Frank Mancuso said that the story was originally set in southern California but would play better in the deep South. If that means proliferating racial tensions, Mancuso's relocation idea accomplished its goal. A large man with a big shotgun greets the duo. Piper assumes he's going to receive some of the warm, southern hospitality offered to several cast members of *Deliverance* (1972). This is also the exact point where the two lead actors begin asking each other questions that are lifted from famous old

CREDITS

Piper: Laurence Fishburne
Dodge: Stephen Baldwin
Cora: Salma Hayek
Gibson: Will Patton
Pat Schiller: Robert John Burke
Mantajano: Michael Nader
Chris Paine: David Dukes

Origin: USA
Released: 1996
Production: Frank Mancuso, Jr. for an MGM production; released by MGM/UA
Direction: Kevin Hooks
Screenplay: Preston A. Whitmore, II
Cinematography: Matthew F. Leonetti
Editing: Richard Nord, Joseph Gutowski
Music: Graeme Revell
Production design: Charles Bennett
Art direction: Charles Breen
Costume design: Jennifer Bryan
Sound: Michael Wilhoit
Stunt coordinator: John Meier
Casting: Amanda Mackey Johnson, Cathy Sandrich
MPAA rating: R
Running Time: 98 minutes

movies: "Didn't you see *Deliverance*?" The final line of the movie is one of these such quips and it allows Fishburne to poke fun at himself and his rather staid image. By making these references, Mancuso and company breathe some levity into the production, but in the process, reduce the movie (probably unintentionally) to a poor, cartoonish parody of buddy films.

Piper and Dodge blow into Atlanta and attempt to carjack the first vehicle they find. Their first choice is a car driven by Cora (Salma Hayek), a surprised but unfazed widowed housewife who subdues them with kindness and charm. During the same junket, Mexican native Hayek said she had originally turned down the role of Cora. She said she felt it was nothing more than a continuation of the sex kitten roles she'd already played in her two previous domestic releases, *Desperado* (1995) and *From Dusk Till Dawn* (reviewed in this issue). To her credit, Hayek wanted to make herself more of a "plain Jane" in order to be viewed as a "serious" actress. After a few rewrites that made Cora less adorned, she got her wish and accepted the role.

Cora rather easily gets some secretive information about Piper which fully explains his participation in the crime. Piper ends up in bed with Cora while Dodge attempts to locate the software that contains the incriminating evidence on the mob boss that so many people want.

The remainder of the movie is a vast wasteland of worn cliches. Director Kevin Hooks (*Passenger 57* [1992]) said he directed the movie with the MTV/BET crowd in mind and, on that level, he's done well. The movie seems to be nothing more than stock footage for the dozen or so hip-hop acts that perform on the soundtrack. If *Fled* was intended as a parody, it should have been funnier. If it was an homage to the buddy films of the past, it should have concentrated more on substance and less on style.

—J.M. Clark

REVIEWS

Chicago Tribune. July 19, 1996, p. 5.
Hollywood Reporter. July 15, 1996, p. 5.
Los Angeles Times. July 19, 1996, p. F10.
New York Times. July 19, 1996, p. C16.
People. August 5, 1996, p. 18.
Sight and Sound. December, 1996, p. 46.
USA Today. July 19, 1996, p.13D.
Variety Online. July 15, 1996.

Flipper

This summer it's finally safe to go back in the water.—Movie tagline

"*Flipper* is fin-tastic."—Michael Medved, *New York Post*

"A must-see for the entire family."—Jim Ferguson, *Prevue Channel*

"Flipper is a cool dude."—Richard Corliss, *Time*

Box Office: $20,080,020

Long before *Free Willy* (1993), *Andre* (1994), or *Magic In the Water* (1995), the marine mammal film franchise belonged to Flipper, the cute, squeaky dolphin who starred in two movies and a popular TV series in the 1960s. In the wake of the success of *Free Willy* (I and II) and the other recent films about whales, orcas, and seals, Flipper's return to the big screen seemed predictable. So did the characters and the plot. There would be a jaded, lonely early-teenage boy whom the finned star would befriend, a substitute parent for the boy, a teenage girl to provide a love interest, a quirky grade-schooler for younger viewers to identify with, an evil villain dumping toxic waste in the water, and a dramatic underwater rescue scene.

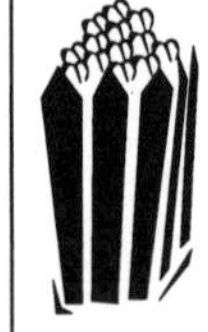

"It's good that you care. People who don't care wind up in a home drooling creamed spinach."—Uncle Porter

Flipper, in his 1996 reincarnation, has all the parts of this new formula. The film proves faithful to the stillborn genre spawned by Willy and his imitators, except for the lack of a stereotyped Native American wise elder who knows how to communicate with the marine creatures. It's a missing ingredient few will miss, and it shows that *Flipper* doesn't want to take itself too seriously. And in keeping things light, *Flipper* pulls off a surprise: It rises above the limitations of its predictable story and performs a few nice flips above the waterline of mediocrity. It's a solid if unambitious film that does unexpectedly well at holding a viewer's attention. It avoids the other films' pitfalls of an overwrought plot or an overly mystical theme. Like its dolphin protagonist, it's quite content merely with having an unspectacular good time.

Flipper's emotional target, Sandy (Elijah Wood), is, like all young heroes of 1990's Hollywood movies, the victim of divorced parents. He's been packed off for the summer to stay in Coral Key with his Uncle Porter, an aging hippie surfer who worships the Beach Boys and the sea and, inexplicably, has an Australian accent. The accent makes no sense in the film, but so what? The offbeat casting of *Crocodile Dundee* (1986) star Paul Hogan in the role of Porter is in large measure what saves *Flipper* from swimming in the doldrums.

Three trained bottle-nosed dolphins—Fatman, Jake, and MacGyver—as well as animatronic re-creations were filmed.

Far from portraying a staid avuncular type, Hogan provides plenty of prickly good humor that's a great contrast to the unabashed schmaltz of the Flipper saga. Porter's a hermit, but no misanthrope. His seaside fishing camp is the ultimate bachelor pad, and his cooking methods are suitably prehistoric: To make toast for breakfast, he hangs pieces of bread on nails on a kitchen wall and blow-torches them. His diet consists mostly of crates of canned Spaghetti-Os that he got in a wholesale barter. He keeps a beer-swilling pet pelican and washes dishes with his feet while taking a shower. Making fun of his own character keeps Hogan well-occupied for much of the film. At one point, in the midst of the film's climactic dolphin-led hunt for the toxic dump site, Porter is shown lounging on a deck chair and reading a copy of Martha Stewart's magazine. He marvels, offhand, at how the queen of decorum has made curtains out of fishnets. Because writer-director Alan Shapiro indulges himself with such offbeat moments, *Flipper* stays afloat for adults.

The dolphin star (actually a conglomeration of three live animals and a robot) is impossibly precocious and wondrously cute. Children's empathy is easily won in an early sequence when the heartless villain, who is actually named Dirk and is played with gusto by Jonathan Banks, gleefully guns down a member of Flipper's family. My six-year-old daughter automatically assumed the dead dolphin was Flipper's mother.

Animal movies depend in large measure on how lovable the animal hero is, and few cinematic pets have matched Flipper for sheer delight. As in the 1960s versions of the Flipper tales, the dolphin falls barely short of speaking English, communicating his affection for Sandy with high-pitched squeaks, fin gestures, and playful nuzzling. Shapiro appears to be gently spoofing Flipper's incredible intelligence in one sequence where Sandy is showing off his pet dolphin for Kim (Jessica Wesson), the local babe. When Kim asks what the dolphin's name is, Sandy looks puzzled and Flipper turns on his side and starts flapping his dorsal fin. "Flipper," Sandy blurts out. It looks as if the dolphin would be as good at charades as he is at retrieving pop cans and loose change, playing catch with beach balls, and taking Sandy for underwater rides.

Flipper is perfect: just realistic-looking enough to be credible, and just amazing enough to be magical. The credit goes jointly to deft underwater photography, to trainers who worked with the three real dolphins who played Flipper, and to the crew supervised by technical genius Walt Conti, who created the animatronic Robo-Dolphin who also played Flipper. (Conti also gave birth to the animatronic whale Willy.) It's nearly impossible to tell which of the film dolphins are real and which are mechanical, which is the highest compliment such an undertaking can earn. And the filmmakers also do a magnificent job with a gruesome hammerhead shark in some underwater battle sequences that harken bark to *Jaws* (1975).

Wood is credible as the disaffected kid who'd do anything for a ticket to a rock concert and would rather play with a Game Boy than go fishing. But Wood's also capable

CREDITS

Sandy: Elijah Wood
Porter: Paul Hogan
Cathy: Chelsea Field
Buck: Isaac Hayes
Dirk Morgan: Jonathan Banks
Marvin: Jason Fuchs

Origin: USA
Released: 1996
Production: James J. McNamara, Perry Katz for a Bubble Factory and American Film/Perry Katz production; released by Universal Pictures
Direction: Alan Shapiro
Screenplay: Alan Shapiro
Cinematography: Bill Butler
Editing: Peck Prior
Music: Joel McNeely
Production design: Thomas A. Walsh
Sound: Steve Aaron
Underwater photography: Pete Romano
Dolphin trainers: Scott Sharpe, Paka Nishimura
Animatronics effects supervisor: Walt Conti
Casting: Julie Ashton-Barson
MPAA rating: PG
Running Time: 96 minutes

of wide-eyed wonder when wooed by a dolphin, and he doesn't make his affection look too corny. Wesson is serviceable as Sandy's love interest. They display a certain muted chemistry, even though their teenage romance ends with only a warm hug—something else to be thankful for. Another surprise is singer Isaac Hayes, of all people, as a Coast Guard sheriff who seems too real to be in a movie. And Chelsea Field (who also appeared in *Andre*) manages to bring some life to her barely credible character as Porter's girlfriend, Cathy. We're asked to believe she's given up a career as a marine biologist and settled for selling bait so she can keep trying to beach the floundering Porter.

Flipper avoids many maudlin traps mainly because Hogan and Wood avoid sentimentality in their relationship. Shapiro seems content with letting man and boy insult each other and gradually turning their mutual suspicion into grudging admiration, then understanding, and finally a muted, barely acknowledged affection. Porter's both a crusty old salt and a self-mocking hoot, insisting he can dig the Chili Peppers: "I was grunge before they had a word for it," he points out.

Shapiro doesn't overreach. Unlike others in the marine mammal family film genre, he doesn't seek to make grand statements or embrace grandiose resolutions. Porter doesn't have to be the father Sandy never had and Sandy doesn't have to be the son Porter never had. They merely edge closer together, as do Porter and Cathy. Sandy does intone something about "family belongs together" as he lets Flipper return to his family. But that's to be expected—for all Hogan's bristling asides, this is still a mainstream family film.

Unfortunately the plot of *Flipper* is both lackluster and nonsensical. Not enough happens in the film, and what does happen often is illogical and inconsistent. There's no clear reason why Dirk is so malevolent towards dolphins and Porter, no hint of a longstanding grudge to settle. His toxic dumping is a strange weapon to employ and a trite one too. Can't anyone think of something other than polluted water on which to hinge a story line about a marine mammal? Porter's actions in turning around Sandy's quest to flee for a mainland rock concert don't ring true, and there is no explanation for how he suddenly appears on Sandy's ferry boat, which left port hours earlier. The character of Marvin, Cathy's mute, raincoat-wearing mechanical genius son, is silly. Even more ridiculous is Flipper's quest to find the ocean dump site, commanded by Cathy in a computer control center aboard Hogan's ship (where did a bait-shop owner get all this expensive high-tech stuff?).

Despite these and other shortcomings, *Flipper* is a much better time than its plodding, overwrought immediate ancestors. If you're going to make a movie about a lovable marine mammal, you'd better keep it sunny and salty. The dolphin provides the sunshine and Hogan the salt, and the result is a nice day at the beach.

—Michael Betzold

REVIEWS

Boxoffice. July, 1996, p. 91.
Detroit News. May 17, 1996, p. D1.
The Hollywood Reporter. May 6, 1996, p. 8.
Premiere. May, 1996, p. 25.
USA Today. May 17, 1996, p. 3D.
Variety. May 6, 1996.
Village Voice. May 28, 1996, p. 54.

Flirt

"Delightful! Smart, sexy, jauntily romantic."—
Stephen Holden, *New York Times*

Box Office: $262,211

If fiction films are really puppet shows in disguise, Hal Hartley's *Flirt* wants us to be aware of the hand of the puppeteer. Ambitiously setting out to tell us one story in the form of three versions, one after the other, Hartley goes on to incorporate the very process of the film's making into its overall narrative structure. Not coincidentally, the third version is set in Japan, with Hartley himself appearing not just as a pivotal character, but as the filmmaker working on the very film we are watching, much like the Bunraku puppet master under a black hood, as visible as his puppets.

What raises the film's peculiar self-reflexivity above the level of a mere filmic gimmick is the focus of its narrative: the vicissitudes of doubt that have come to plague sexual intimacy in our time. With the lack of sure knowledge about a partner's past comes the lack of moral certitude, giving rise to an all-pervasive ambiguity. We are thus justified in perceiving Hartley's characters as puppets, since we end up knowing as little about them as they do about each other. This in turn allows for a Brechtian alienation effect, whereby the film's actors seem to maintain a distance between themselves and the characters they are portraying, a distance which allows them to describe those characters, instead of becoming them as they ordinarily would. *Flirt* thus emerges as an esoteric treat for the thinking viewer prepared to unravel its filmic puzzle, a comedy of commitment, if you will, built around the motif of uncertainty.

Against the drab setting of a studio apartment in Lower Manhattan, Bill (Bill Sage), the first of the film's eponymous flirts, is presented with an ultimatum by his girlfriend Emily (Parker Posey), as she lies languorously stretched across a bed, looking up at the ceiling, with a vacuous expression that extends to the tone of her voice. She will be away in Paris for a few months, and she wants to know the answer to the all-important question that will be repeated, in those exact terms, by her counterparts in the two versions of the story to follow: "Is there a future for me and you?" As wary of commitment as the two other flirts we will come to know, Bill answers, using words that will be echoed by them, "I can't see the future." To which Emily argues: "You don't need to see the future if you know it's there." Bill's recourse then is to bide for time to decide. That time, extended to him and the two other flirts, is the ninety minutes left before their significant other's departure.

Bill runs out to ring Margaret, the married woman in his life, and asks the same question Emily has asked him, even citing Emily's argument. It proves to no avail. Neither does his confiding his predicament to total strangers in a lavatory, each of whom has only vague advice to offer. What brings Bill's plight to a head is his meeting Walter (Martin Donovan), Margaret's husband, who is sitting in a bar with a gun before him. Despondent at his marriage having fallen apart, Walter uses the gun to force Bill to ring Emily and propose to her. It is, however, too late. Then, in a strange turn of events, it is Margaret who rings to speak to Walter. As Bill later embraces Walter in an attempt to console him, we hear a gunshot, then see that Bill has been shot in the face. While being treated at the hospital, Bill realizes his love for Emily. As soon as he's released, he jumps into a cab and decides to follow her to Paris.

The second version of this story, set against the backdrop of Berlin's bohemian quarter, presents Dwight (Dwight

CREDITS

Bill: Bill Sage
Emily: Parker Posey
Walter: Martin Donovan
Dwight: Dwight Ewell
Johan: Dominik Bender
Greta: Geno Lechner
The Doctor: Peter Fitz
The Nurse: Elina Lowensohn
Miho: Miho Nikaidoh
Ozu: Toshizo Fujisawa
Yuki: Chikako Hara
Hal: Hal Hartley

Origin: USA
Released: 1995
Production: Ted Hope for a True Fiction Pictures, Pandora Films, and Nippon Film Development & Finance production; released by Cinepix Film Properties
Direction: Hal Hartley
Screenplay: Hal Hartley
Cinematography: Michael Spiller
Editing: Hal Hartley
Music: Ned Rifle, Jeffrey Taylor
Art direction: Karen Weissel, Ric Schachtebeck, Tomoyuki Mazuo
Costume design: Alexandra Weller, Ulle Gothe
Sound: Jeff Pullman, Norman Engel, Osamu Takizawa
MPAA rating: Unrated
Running Time: 84 minutes

Ewell), an expatriate black American, being put in a similar bind by Johan (Dominik Bender), his homosexual lover. The switching of genders and locales doesn't change the situation one jot. Dwight too ends up being shot by the suicidal Greta (Geno Lechner), the wife of his other male lover, Werner. Unlike Bill, however, Dwight decides to stay put in Berlin.

When the same situation is then reenacted by members of an avant-garde dance ensemble in Tokyo, the cultural jolt makes us aware of the aspect of manipulation within it. This time, it is Miho (Miho Nikaidoh) who has to choose between Hal (Hal Hartley), the filmmaker playing himself, who poses the crucial question, and Ozu (Toshizo Fujisawa), her married dance instructor. As in the ballet she is rehearsing with Yuki (Chikako Hara), Ozu's wife, Miho is drawn into events first by Ozu, then by the police, after she is implicated in Yuki's plan to kill herself upon learning of Miho's affair with her husband. Again, just like Bill before her, it is only on the operating table that Miho realizes what she must do. Silently, she snuggles up to Hal, who sits half-asleep in the hospital waiting room. At their feet, lies the film can labelled *Flirt,* the final piece of the puzzle, and perhaps its only real key.

As would be expected, critical opinion on the film has ranged from "smart, sexy . . . jauntily romantic" (Stephen Holden in *The New York Times*) to "too slight and schematic" (Amy Taubin in *The Village Voice*). Dave Kehr, in *The New York Daily News,* notes that the third version "allows a new element to creep in—something cold and eerie, as if the film were about to become a ghost story."

—*Vivek Adarkar*

REVIEWS

Los Angeles Times. August 23, 1996, p. F11.
The New York Daily News. August 7, 1996.
The New York Times. October 6, 1995, p. C21.
Sight and Sound. March, 1997, p. 47.
Variety. September 25, 1995, p. 93.
Village Voice. August 13, 1996, p. 62.

Flirting With Disaster

A comedy about sex, love, family and other accidents waiting to happen.—Movie tagline

"Uproarious! A wonderfully mad odyssey of a movie!"—Janet Maslin, *New York Times*

"Two thumbs up! Exciting and wildly original!"—*Siskel & Ebert*

"A wicked, anything-goes sex farce!"—Susan Wloszczyna, *USA Today*

"It brings back the pleasure of going to the movies!"—Joe Morgenstern, *Wall Street Journal*

Box Office: $14,702,438

Director David O. Russell didn't waste anytime making a name for himself with his first feature film, *Spanking The Monkey* (which won the 1994 Sundance Audience Award). Despite the title's comical references to solo sex, it instead focuses on the very touchy and much more serious subject of having sex with one's own mother. In *Spanking The Monkey,* newcomer Jeremy Davies must spend the better part of the summer at home taking care of his cranky, bedridden mother played by Alberta Watson. The absence of his philandering, traveling salesman father and the implementation of his gestapo-type regimen cause both mother and son to be a bit skittish around each other. What is at first an uncomfortable, close quarters alliance eventually blossoms into more of a best friend relationship. The handling of their eventual sexual union was wisely done off-screen. The son's dreams of going to college hinge on his father's approval and seem nearly impossible to attain. The mother's frustration at being immobile and knowing her husband is a cheating louse makes the situation very plausible.

Russell's second film *Flirting With Disaster* takes on a decidedly lighter tone and deals with the conundrum of one Mel Coplin (Ben Stiller). Mel is a New York entomologist who is the proud father of a baby boy. He and his wife Nancy (Patricia Arquette) are having trouble settling on a name. In his mind, Mel can't name the baby until he gets some closure in a very important area of his own life: finding his birth parents. The whole idea for the story started with Russell's own sister, who was adopted. Her trek was nowhere near as complicated and as involved as Mel's but did provide enough inspiration for Russell to explore the situation further.

Mel's adoptive parents are played with uproarious hilarity and heightened paranoia by Mary Tyler Moore and George Segal. Moore is stepping out and taking what some would call unnecessary risks in order to alter her all-American image. One scene in the film finds Moore giving Nancy unsolicited advice on the benefits of a good support bra while showing the world her own breasts in the process. Another finds television's most famous girl-next-door performing fellatio and then, of course, protecting her dental work by flossing. Moore and Segal are dumbfounded as to why Mel must seek out his birth parents. Moore smacks her forehead in disbelief and wonders aloud why Mel needs to go through this "Roots thing." They claim to have provided him with a stable upbringing. A bit of an ironic statement really, considering that they are the most neurotic characters in the film.

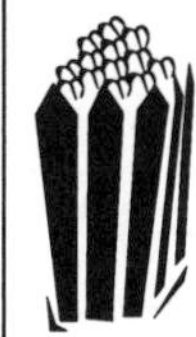

"Why does he have to do this *Roots* thing?"—Mrs. Coplin about adoptive son Mel's search for his birth parents.

Nancy is leery of Mel's compulsive need to seek out the people who abandoned him at birth but, knowing it will allow both of them to get on with their lives, is supportive of his search. After having the baby, Nancy lost interest in making love for several months. With her desire restored, she now makes "dates" with Mel just to have sex. Any married couple will speak with authority when discussing the noticeable lapse in the romance department after a child is born. In an early scene, she dresses in a flimsy teddy and decorates the bed and herself with rose petals. Mel enters the room, baby in tow, and a fumbling, ham-handed attempt at oral sex is made and just doesn't get off the ground. This is one of the most hilarious unfulfilled sex scenes ever filmed.

Mel has gotten ahold of the agency that arranged his adoption. Tina Kalb, the "specialist" in charge of reuniting him with his biological parents, is played by Tea Leoni (*Bad Boys* [1995]). Tina has a plethora of her own problems to wade through. Approaching thirty, she is in the midst of a divorce and is desperately looking for the right man, any man, to impregnate her. Leoni's angular beauty and kinetic presence lend itself well to her part. Tina's records indicate that Mel's real mother is living in San Diego. With Mel being five foot-something and dark, it's highly unlikely that the six foot plus, blond, blue-eyed Valerie Swaney (Celia Weston) is his mother. After several minutes of tearful embracing, coupled with warm and fuzzy pleasantries, the truth leaks out and it becomes painfully obvious to everyone, that they have found the wrong mother.

The next candidate, whom Tina swears is the father, is a rather boorish truck driver from rural Michigan. Fritz Boudreau (David Patrick Kelly) is very proud of the fact that he's dropped plenty of "baby batter" in his time, but he's sure he's not the proud father. But he knows who is. This is where this film, which is now something of a perverted screwball comedy, starts taking on the qualities of a well written and intricate crime thriller. Seemingly throwaway minutia suddenly changes the plot entirely. Russell's utterly original screenplay has explored areas within the comedy genre no one else has ever attempted.

Two more characters are added to the story in Michigan (it would be a crime to reveal who they are and what they do) and their involvement grows more significant with each scene. With their Michigan excursion wrapped up, the group and their two new recruits head off to the great Southwest. Their cramped travelling quarters and previous wild-goose chase cause tempers to flare and virtually everyone contemplates starting affairs right in front of their respective spouses.

Lily Tomlin and Alan Alda play Mary and Richard Schlicting (the pronunciation of their last name is a running

AWARDS AND NOMINATIONS

Independent Spirit Awards 1997 Nominations: Director (Russell), Supporting Actress (Tomlin), Supporting Actor (Jenkins), Screenplay (Russell)

CREDITS

Mel Coplin: Ben Stiller
Nancy Coplin: Patricia Arquette
Tina Kalb: Tea Leoni
Mrs. Coplin: Mary Tyler Moore
Mr. Coplin: George Segal
Richard Schlicting: Alan Alda
Mary Schlicting: Lily Tomlin
Tony: Josh Brolin
Paul: Richard Jenkins
Valerie Schlicting: Celia Weston
Fritz Boudreau: David Patrick Kelly

Origin: USA
Released: 1996
Production: Dean Silvers; released by Miramax Films
Direction: David O. Russell
Screenplay: David O. Russell
Cinematography: Eric Edwards
Editing: Christopher Tellefsen
Music: Stephen Endelman
Production design: Kevin Thompson
Art direction: Judy Rhee
Set decoration: Ford Wheeler
Costume design: Ellen Lutter
Sound: Rolf Pardula
Casting: Ellen Parks, Risa Bramon Garcia
MPAA rating: R
Running Time: 92 minutes

joke throughout the movie) during the film's final 30 minutes. They live far from the maddening crowds in a remote part of a New Mexico desert. On the surface they seem grounded in reality and their home looks safe and conservative, but the audience soon finds out that those appearances are somewhat deceiving.

The Schlictings are starving artists who must "augment" their income with another more lucrative side business (again, revealing that here would ruin another wrinkle in the plot that changes the behavior of all the characters). Mel meets his brother Lonnie (Glenn Fitzgerald) who gives the phrase "anti-social" a whole new meaning. Seeing that the grass definitely isn't greener on the other side of the country, Mel realizes that his roots aren't as important as his past. The rest of the cast find closure in situations that in any other film would stretch the bounds of believability. By now, the film has made its own rules and the final scenes make complete sense.

Russell has made a movie that is sure to offend many members of the mainstream audience. He assembled a group of actors, most of them already very successful, who had no need to do such an ungainly project. Alda and Moore have spent a lifetime building an All-American image that, while making their publicist's jobs easier, has surely left a great many producers and directors thinking they were incapable of breaking out of their archetype and taking on more meatier offers. It's got to be tempting to throw caution to the wind, get bitchy and play a malcontent every once in a while. Both have taken on darker roles before (Moore with *Ordinary People* and Alda with *Crimes & Misdemeanors*), but never with nearly this much aplomb.

It will be interesting to see Russell's next work. He's said he wants to make a film about the misunderstandings of love between the sexes somewhere on the scale of *Chinatown* or *Citizen Kane*. That's quite a lofty goal. *Spanking The Monkey*, despite its huge critical, yet mildly commercial success, was a dangerous choice for a first film. Serious drama exploring one of the most abhorrent of social taboos. Rather than becoming the newest poster child for the emotionally obsessed, Russell radically shifted gears. By doing so, he avoided the dreaded sophomore slump while showing he can masterfully direct two completely different kinds of movies. With Russell's commanding versatility, many fans anxiously await his third project.

—J.M. Clark

REVIEWS

Boxoffice Magazine. May, 1996, p. 73.
Entertainment Weekly. April 5, 1996, p. 57.
The Hollywood Reporter. March 19, 1996, p. 8.
Los Angeles Times. March 22, 1996, p. F1.
New York Times. March 22, 1996, p. C3.
Newsweek. April 8, 1996, p. 76.
USA Today. March 22, 1996, p. D1.
Variety. March 25, 1996, p. 66.
Village Voice. April 2, 1996, p. 62.

The Flower of My Secret; La Flor De Mi Secreto

"Funny and smart, but with heart! A flamenco flavored homage to Hollywood's great screwball comedies."—Jay Carr, *The Boston Globe*

"Elegant, witty, wise and deeply caring! Beautifully wrought and beautifully acted."—Kevin Thomas, *Los Angeles Times*

"Delicious! Funny! Almodovar returns to the comedy of his earlier, best work."—Caryn James, *The New York Times*

"Provocative and sophisticated."—Jeffrey Lyons, *Sneak Previews*

Box Office: $1,032,180

There are some people whom, when confronted with the suggestion of seeing a film by Pedro Almodovar, recoil at the thought of his usual cinematic stew of satire, sex, and kitsch. There are others who would just say "Who's Almodovar?." For those who have thought, especially in recent films such as *High Heels* (1991) and *Kika*, (1993) that Almodovar has taken his satire to bitter extremes, take heart. *The Flower of My Secret* represents a wiser and more restrained Almodovar, still with his characteristic satire, but minus some of the mean-spiritedness. *The Flower of My Secret* is a masterful blend of humor, pathos, and satire.

Flamenco star Joaquin Cortes is featured as the son of Leo's loyal maid.

Marisa Paredes stars as Leo, a middle-aged woman unable to see the shallowness of her marriage to the handsome Paco (Imanoel Arias). At the start of the film, she desperately misses Paco, who is a military man on assignment with NATO in Bosnia. She is also a highly successful romance novelist writing under the nom de plume of "Amanda Gris;" however, in spite of her great success, Leo hates her Barbara Cartland-esque alter ego as if Amanda Gris was a real person. Desperately needing to make a change, she takes a job at a newspaper, wishing to write serious journalism. Her editor, Angel (Juan Echanove), becomes her friend and protector, not to mention the fact that he falls in love with her. As she approaches a sort of personal and professional crossroads, Leo suffers an emotional train wreck when her best friend, Betty (Carmen Elias), steals Paco away.

As always, Almodovar has added some wonderful, colorful characters to round out the plot. The fascinating Rossy de Palma plays Leo's sister, whose bickering scenes with their mother (Chus Lampreave) are as hilarious as they are realistic. There is also an interesting subplot concerning Leo's maid (Kiti Manver), whose son (Joaquin Cortes) is coaxing her to revive her legendary flamenco dance career so that he can start a career of his own.

After Paco leaves her, Leo attempts suicide, and then accompanies her mother to La Mancha, their home village, a place where Leo witnesses a gentle matriarchal way of life which revives her enough to return to Madrid and accept the affections of the doting Angel. The plot and subplots are reflections on the life struggles faced by Leo, and are thus reflective of the theme: should a person allow themselves to sacrifice their art for the sake of personal security? Should a woman allow herself to explore her sensuality, or should she put it aside in order to serve the patriarchal ideals of home and family? This sounds like heavy stuff for a comedy, but Almodovar is so good at his storytelling that these themes are merely resonant ideas in a film that never becomes philosophical at the expense of being entertaining.

Throughout the film, Almodovar inserts his characteristic style of bright colors, offbeat camera angles, and quirky situations. For example, the opening scene throws the audience completely off-balance: two doctors are trying to convince a distraught woman

CREDITS

Leo: Marisa Paredes
Angel: Juan Echanove
Paco: Imanol Arias
Betty: Carmen Elias
Rosa: Rossy De Palma
Antonio: Joaquin Cortes

Origin: Spain
Released: 1995
Production: Esther Garcia for an El Deseo and Ciby 2000 production; released by Sony Pictures Classics
Direction: Pedro Almodovar
Screenplay: Pedro Almodovar
Cinematography: Alfonso Beato
Editing: Jose Salcedo
Music: Alberto Iglesias
Art direction: Wolfgang Burmann
Costume design: Hugo Mezcua
Sound: Bernardo Menz
MPAA rating: Unrated
Running Time: 105 minutes

that her recently dead son's organs should be donated for medicine. But after a few minutes, the camera pulls back to reveal that these are people engaged in a role-play at a seminar about organ transplantation. The seminar is led by Leo's friend Betty, who is "transplanting" Leo by becoming Paco's lover. That Betty should tell Leo early in the film is symbolized both by the role-play described above and by the fact that Leo arrives at the seminar, begging Betty's help in removing a pair of Paco's boots. The layers of symbolism continue: Betty helps "remove" (a symbol of) Paco from Leo, whose inability to see that her marriage is over is represented by the fact that she just can't seem to get out of Paco's shoes.

Marisa Paredes, who appeared in *High Heels* as the mother, is a classic Almodovar actress: She is beautiful, sensuous, and delivers a complex performance, layering naturalism with a keen sense of satire. Her scenes in which she rails against her alter ego, Amanda Gris, are wonderful. Her sense of urgency and pain about her personal and professional situations is touching—and very, very human. Each of the other actors displays a similar verisimilitude mixed with a knowing, understated satire.

Almodovar has distilled his ideas about sensuality, marriage, mid-life crises, sex, mass media, and more into a still-satirical but less bombastic film than those in the recent past. Like Woody Allen, Almodovar has taken his vast ability to be ridiculous and, in middle age, has turned it into cinematic warmth and humanity.

—*Kirby Tepper*

REVIEWS

Los Angeles Times. March 13, 1996, p. F1.
New York Times. October 13, 1995, p. C32.
Village Voice. March 12, 1996, p. 54.

Fly Away Home

A family of orphaned geese who lost their way. A 14 year old kid who will lead them home. To achieve the incredible, you have to attempt the impossible.—Movie tagline

"An instant family classic! It soars with heart-warming entertainment!"—Larry Ratliff, *KABB-TV*

"A masterpiece! It joins *The Black Stallion* and *Babe* as a great film!"—John Corcoran, *KCAL-TV*

"Thrilling and beautiful! An engaging and uplifting adventure! Anna Paquin steals your heart."—Joe Leydon, *KPRC-TV*

"One of the best films of the year. A magical movie you can't miss."—Steve Oldfield, *KSTU-TV*

"The best family film of the year!"—Sam Rubin, *KTLA-TV*

"A movie you and your family will want to see over and over again."—Bobbie Wygant, *KXAS-TV*

"Beautiful! Think of it as *Born Free* for geese!"—Jeff Craig, *Sixty Second Preview*

"Touching and moving to audiences of all ages! If I had four thumbs, they'd all be up!"—Bill Carlson, *WCCO-TV*

Box Office: $24,324,294

Ostensibly a movie about a girl, her father, some geese and a couple of planes, *Fly Away Home* turns out to be an achingly beautiful, breathtaking meditation on the challenging journeys required by love. As they did in the wondrous *Black Stallion* (1979), director Carroll Ballard and cinematographer Caleb Deschanel delicately create a beautiful, compelling film from a simple, sometimes awkward story. Studiously avoiding schmaltz but unabashedly affirming life, *Fly Away Home* has heart and courage and a prickly, unsettling honesty rarely found in a family film, yet its messages go down easily.

The very term "family film" has accumulated its own baggage and disappointments. Though this is a film anyone ought to see, the "family" label must apply because *Fly Away Home* is about the strange dance of holding, trusting and letting go that is the essence of familial love. But there's none of the cloying sentimentality and formulaic moralizing that are found in most films considered suitable for families. Ballard doesn't preach or pander. To its great credit the film makes hardly any effort to seem hip or up-to-date,

AWARDS AND NOMINATIONS

Academy Awards 1996 Nominations: Best Cinematography (Deschanel)

even though its central character is a smart, cynical, worldly adolescent. The movie has an agreeable but understated self-confidence, and you rarely get the sense that it's trying to sell itself to you or win you over.

It's clear from the start that you have to take or leave *Fly Away Home* on its own terms. Ballard doesn't ease you into the story, but begins with a riveting opening credit sequence that establishes the film's no-nonsense but heartfelt tone. A girl and her mother are smiling and talking in a car; there is a crash. The tour-de-force sequence is wordless, slow-motion and almost lyrical and wrapped in a haunting song, "10,000 Miles," performed by Mary Chapin Carpenter. The lyrics are a farewell to a lover and a promise to remain close in spirit though separated physically. The singer says: Though I am far away, I will remain.

> "You must be Amy. I gave you Silly Putty once for Christmas. You ate it."—David Alden to his estranged daughter.

The song is the movie's theme and signature; it reappears again at the climax. *Fly Away Home* is in fact a meditation on the deep mysteries suggested by the song: learning to love by learning to let go, risking trust across great gaps of distance and logic, undertaking improbable journeys of the soul.

We wake up with 13-year-old Amy (Anna Paquin), when she opens her eyes in a hospital bed to find her bedraggled father beside her. She doesn't need him to tell her that her mother has died. It is one of many awakenings for Amy in the film. New days begin for her with abrupt revelations, miracles and wonders: The first day on her father's farm, she awakens to find him flying and then crashing one of his homemade aerial contraptions.

Her father, Thomas (Jeff Daniels), is a gentle but self-absorbed latter-day hippie who bangs out metal sculptures and fantastic inventions in a dilapidated Ontario farmhouse. He hasn't seen much of Amy since she was a toddler and her mother took her away to New Zealand. His long and unexplained abandonment of her is an open wound for Amy, who is grieving and desperately lonely in her new surroundings. She carries a grudge against her father, who appears to her to be just a click away from the loony bin.

Bereft of all solace, Amy finds unexpected sustenance when she stumbles upon goose eggs in a nearby marsh; developers' bulldozers have chased away the mother. Completely absorbed in the miracles of their birth and growth, Amy becomes their surrogate mother. They imprint on her and follow her faithfully around the farm. When a local wildlife authority attempts to clip their wings, she defends them ferociously. Obviously, she understands their plight.

The untamed Thomas understands, too, and he and Amy finally find common ground in his outrageous scheme to build and fly goose-like lighter-than-air planes to lead the birds on their southerly migration. At first wary and skeptical, Amy soon sees that keeping the birds from flying would be the same as clipping their wings, and realizes that it's her responsibility to lead them through the dangers of adolescence to maturity. In so doing, of course, she undertakes her own similar spiritual journey.

The death of her mother leaves Amy (Anna Paquin) withdrawn, but she is brought out of her emotional shell by a group of goslings in the heart-warming family film *Fly Away Home*.

CREDITS

Thomas Alden: Jeff Daniels
Amy Alden: Anna Paquin
Susan Barnes: Dana Delany
David Alden: Terry Kinney
Barry Strickland: Holter Graham
Glen Seifert: Jeremy Ratchford

Origin: USA
Released: 1996
Production: John Veitch and Carol Baum for a Sandollar production; released by Sony Pictures Entertainment
Direction: Carroll Ballard
Screenplay: Robert Rodat and Vince McKewin; based on the autobiography by Bill Lishman
Cinematography: Caleb Deschanel
Editing: Nicholas C. Smith
Music: Mark Isham
Production design: Seamus Flannery
Set decoration: Dan Conley
Costume design: Marie-Sylvie Deveau
Sound: Douglas Ganton
Digital visual effects and animation: C.O.R.E. Digital Pictures
Casting: Reuben Cannon, Deirdre Bowen
MPAA rating: PG
Running Time: 107 minutes

The death of Amy's mother sets the stage for the film's theme of rebirth. That theme is evident in the birth of the geese; in Amy's assumption of maternal responsibilities; in the forging of a bond of trust between Amy and Thomas; in Amy's learning to fly, and finally, in Amy's entrance into adulthood by meeting an unexpected final challenge on her own.

Developed from Canadian artist Bill Lishman's autobiography as well as a segment shown on TV news magazine *20/20* about Lishman and his geese migrations.

Unfortunately, the script, by Robert Rodat and Vince McKewin, succumbs to a few contrivances. We get the favorite cardboard villains of 1990s filmmaking, real estate developers, pitted against virtuous environmentalists. Two confrontations between the familiar enemies serve as thin plot devices. The first, in Ontario, provides the bulldozers necessary to orphan Amy's goose eggs. The second, at the birds' destination point in North Carolina, is not only hackneyed but absurd. To save what remains of a wildlife sanctuary from becoming another piece of suburbia, Amy must get the geese there by November 1. This gives the migration a deadline and some tension. More is whipped up by a rather silly sequence in which Amy, Thomas and the geese show up as UFOs on a radar screen and put an air force base on alert.

Fortunately, *Fly Away Home* has such grace that it glides almost effortlessly past these concessions to commercialism. The photography is superb, from majestic aerial panoramas to the smallest visual details. In painting-like scenes when Amy first arrives at her father's farm, she sits, head on knees, in golden fields, alone in a vast landscape that seems unforgiving. Deschanel's camera caresses the simplest scenes with careful attention. He makes a drawer full of goose eggs into a richly hued painting. The hatching of the eggs is one of the film's most wondrous scenes, both simple and profound.

The cameras dote on the geese, but not excessively. They don't do tricks or become cartoonish the way other film animals often do. They're cute on their own terms. And in flight, they are majestic. When Amy and Thomas get lost in fog and end up flying through downtown Baltimore, startling office workers, there is a pleasing surrealism, an otherworldly feel. When Amy flies over a small town and the townspeople react, there is more simple magic.

Paquin's performance is much fuller and more remarkable than the one in *The Piano* (1993), which made her the youngest Oscar winner. Her range is breathtaking: from suspicious and cynical, cold and unforgiving, to fun-loving and tomboyish, gentle and heroic. She is perfectly poised on the cusp between childhood and adulthood. One of the film's many quietly remarkable scenes is one in which she is playing dress-up as her geese watch her, themselves preening. Paquin doesn't strike one false chord during the entire film. Hers is a complex, well-rounded and believable character. The best thing about Paquin—and what sets this performance a notch about her turn in *The Piano*—is that she never shows off.

Daniels, a hardworking actor whom stardom has eluded, also performs superbly. You get the sense from Daniels of a character struggling to learn how to rise above his limitations. Daniels is superb at conveying emotions with a slight turn of the mouth, a raising of an eyebrow, or a shrug, yet he avoids making these gestures to seem smooth or glib. You can almost see the effort he uses to suppress his natural gift for light comedy, yet that gift infuses his character with a gentle likability. When he finally apologizes to Amy for being an absent father, it's a nakedly human moment, like a window opening into Thomas's soul.

The rest of the cast is merely serviceable. In the thankless, underwritten role of Thomas' girlfriend, Dana Delany is radiant—much too radiant to be believable as the paramour of the backwoodsy Thomas. Terry Kinney, as Thomas's nerdish brother, is a Rick Moranis type who provides a few mild laughs.

Fly Away Home is a contemplation on life, love, and the urge to soar. It is a venture as delicate as the goose-plane that is the film's talisman. The plane represents an indomitable human spirit and curiosity, and the film offers a unique melding of the spirit of adventure and the warmth of maternal care, and a marriage of human technology and natural instinct.

It is refreshing to see a film that portrays the deep values that bind real families—compassion, persistent efforts to connect and understand, loyalty, and proof of love in deeds, not just words. And it does so without being rude, crude or cutesy. Also welcome is the way the film centers on how a 13-year-old gains in self-confidence—a wonderful antidote to what happens to many girls at an age where confidence is undermined.

Fly Away Home is a rare bird—simple yet profound, instructive yet not preachy, heartfelt yet not schmaltzy. It's a quirky take on the lessons of growing up and a testament to honest, unflinching filmmaking. It's one of the very best films of 1996, or any year.

—*Michael Betzold*

REVIEWS

Boxoffice. October, 1996, p. 47.
Chicago Tribune. September 13, 1996, p. 4.
The Detroit News. September 13, 1996, p. 1D.
Entertainment Weekly. September 20, 1996, p. 55.
The Hollywood Reporter. September 3, 1996, p. 6.
Los Angeles Times. September 13, 1996, p. F1.
The New York Times. September 13, 1996, p. C12.
New Yorker. September 16, 1996, p. 97.
Newsweek. September 23, 1996, p. 74.
Premiere. October, 1996, p. 38.
Variety, September 2, 1996, p. 65.
Village Voice. September 17, 1996, p. 78.

For the Moment

A moment can last a lifetime.—Movie tagline

" . . . a gorgeous-looking . . . romantic drama."—Michael Rechtshaffen, *Hollywood Reporter*

"Classic high-flying romance comes alive . . . poignant."—Stephen Holden, *New York Times*

"Beautiful and absorbing . . . often thrilling."—Jeffrey Lyons, *Sneak Previews*

"Russell Crowe gives a high-flying, romantic performance."—Barbara & Scott Siegel, *WNEW-FM*

Box Office: $15,451

The gorgeous open prairies and farmland of 1942 Manitoba provide a golden setting for a tender, if predictable, tale of wartime romance in *For the Moment.* During World War II more than 100 air bases across Canada trained some 130,000 fliers for combat duty as part of the British Commonwealth Air Training Plan, which brought together young men from numerous countries for an accelerated course, including charming and cheeky Aussie flyboy, Lachlan (Russell Crowe), and his Canadian mate, Johnny (Peter Outerbridge). This continuous stream of pilots-in-training is, as Lachlan puts it, a "continuous stream of sheep to the slaughter," since the fliers know that a combat pilot's life expectancy is a mere six weeks. Is it any wonder that Lachlan's philosophy is that life is made up of small moments and it's important to savor them while you can (which he is determined to do).

"That's the thing about life, Johnny. You never know where it's going to take you from one moment to the next. And it's always full of surprises."—Lachlan

Johnny is a local lad and his best girl, Kate (Sara McMillan), lives with her widowed father, married sister Lill (Christianne Hirt), and soon-to-leave soldier-brother Dennis (Kelly Proctor), on a farm close to the base. A young, hardworking farm wife, Lill was married only a week before her husband, also a combat pilot, was sent overseas. That was two years ago and, despite her continually reiterating the fact that she is married, it's obvious Lill (who looks to be in her very early twenties) is lonely and looking for some innocent fun.

Not-so-innocent is tart-tongued, practical Betsy (Wanda Cannon), an abandoned wife with two kids to support, who does her bit for the boys by supplying bootleg liquor and sexual favors. She does have a special friend in American flight instructor Zeek (Scott Kraft), who serves as a quasi-father figure to his group of trainees as well, telling them to "pay attention, don't be stupid, don't get too smart, and whatever you do, don't panic." Good advice that, of course, won't be followed (the movie's not that subtle about telegraphing plot points).

Lachlan is immediately drawn to Lill but tries to keep his distance when the foursome go to a local dance. But when Lachlan persuades Lill to go riding on his new motorbike, it's inevitable that the duo will get together. Neither are unaware of the consequences or the cost of their actions. During a trip to the lakeshore, Lill gently explains to Lachlan that she's not really there but is someone else playing pretend—pretending not to be married, pretending there's not a war on. But as Lachlan replies, her "pretend" self and he "pretend so well you'd swear to God it was real" and, of course, it is.

Matters between the two come to a breaking point when Lill receives a telegram from the war office. This long, silent scene between Lill, her father and sister is one of overwhelming sadness but what's not known at first is whether it is her husband or her brother who have been killed. At the farmhouse wake, Lachlan

CREDITS

Lachlan: Russell Crowe
Johnny: Peter Outerbridge
Lill: Christianne Hirt
Kate: Sara McMillan
Betsy: Wanda Cannon
Zeek: Scott Kraft
Mr. Anderson: Bruce Boa
Dennis: Kelly Proctor

Origin: Canada
Released: 1994; 1996
Production: Jack Clements, Aaron Kim Johnston for a John Aaron Features II Inc. and the National Film Board of Canada production; released by 20th Century Fox
Direction: Aaron Kim Johnston
Screenplay: Aaron Kim Johnston
Cinematography: Ian Elkin
Editing: Rita Roy
Art direction: Andrew Deskin
Music: Victor Davies
Costume design: Charlotte Penner
MPAA rating: PG-13
Running Time: 118 minutes

speaks privately with a grief-stricken Lill, who admits that the telegram had her mentally choosing between husband and brother, that if her husband was dead (he's not), she and Lachlan could be together forever. Guilty, Lill coldly breaks off with Lachlan telling him she was only looking for a "little excitement" and he could have been anyone, not that Lachlan is fooled by her protestations.

Still, when Lill's family finds out about her affair, she's able to tell her disbelieving sister that she "met the wrong man at the wrong time and it was wonderful" and the lovers reconcile enough to say their goodbyes when the pilots orders come through.

For the Moment is a leisurely-paced feature, offering a good matchup between the handsome Crowe's exuberant tenderness as Lachlan and Hirt's vulnerably serious Lill. The other characters are familiar types—Betsy's a variation on the hooker-with-the-heart-of-gold, Zeek's a bighearted-but-tragic lover—and the situations predictable (clashes between the pilots, crashes during training) but there's an appealing sweetness and decency for those who like their romances to linger.

—*Christine Tomassini*

REVIEWS

Boxoffice. July, 1996, p. 96.
Hollywood Reporter. April 23, 1996, p. 10.
Los Angeles Times. April 19, 1996, p. F18.
New York Times. April 19, 1996, p. C14.

Foxfire

It took them 17 years to learn the rules and one week to break them all.—Movie tagline

"Not since *Thelma and Louise* has a film so captured the essence of female rebellion."—Pat Kramer, *Boxoffice*

Box Office: $269,300

Instead of finding its niche as an edgy coming-of-age film about five teenage girls, *Foxfire* fell through the commercial cracks. Its presumptive target audience of high-school girls was missing during an abortive late-summer theatrical run.

Joyce Carol Oates' novel, on which the film was based, deserves a better fate. The screenplay of *Foxfire,* penned by Elizabeth White, is unfocused and poorly conceived. The film's first-time director, Annette Haywood-Carter, wastes good performances by glossing over dramatic possibilities with a pointless music-video style. *Foxfire* has attitude and moxie and some intriguing characters. But its paltry story is not dramatic enough, and as a character study it lacks depth and insight.

Oates' novel was set in the 1950s. The crucial error of the screenplay is placing the film in the 1990s. Oates' protagonist, Maddy Wirtz (Hedy Burress), is supposed to be an innocent whose world is turned upside down by the sudden appearance of a wild and worldly stranger, Legs (Angelina Jolie). The actions and ideas of Legs, a female version of James Dean, are supposed to be shocking to the sheltered Maddy, who thought she had her life together.

But the Maddy of the film is no parochial 1950s rube. She is a sophisticated and well-grounded 1990s young woman. Maddy, an aspiring photographer, is sexually active, independent, smart and artistic. At her high school in Portland, Oregon, she is surrounded by wilder, dumber, more unconventional types, and she's had the good sense not to hang with them. Her boyfriend is caring and mature and doesn't push her around, and she appears to have an incredibly egalitarian relationship with her parents (her mother's role is a tiny one played by Cathy Moriarty).

There isn't any void in Maddy's life, and when Legs appears out of nowhere to take it over, there's no credible explanation of why Maddy would find Legs so startling that she would chuck everything to follow her. The scriptwriter wants the audience to accept Maddy's infatuation, which is central to the film, as an unfathomable mystery. In Maddy's own corny words, Legs' presence is "like a charge in the air before a storm."

Legs leads Maddy and three other classmates in a battle against a biology teacher who is sexually harassing some students. It's hard to believe Legs' brand of militant feminism is new to 1990s Portland. Teenage drifters should be nothing new either. Granted, Legs does have a certain style, a bad-ass but highly moralistic attitude, but that alone is hardly enough to make her an instant icon. Teenagers of the 1990s are apt to find *Foxfire*'s situations corny despite the film's way-cool alternative-rock soundtrack.

The vengeance Legs and the others extract from the teacher lands the newly formed gang in the principal's office. They are expelled for accusing the teacher of harassment—a punishment which might have happened in the 1950s but certainly not in the 1990s. Further straining credibility, they go to an abandoned house in the woods and make it a sort of clubhouse.

Besides its two leaders, the gang consists of three out-and-out stereotypes: a slut named Violet (Sarah Rosenberg), the impossibly shy Rita (Jenny Lewis), and a drugged-out cynic, Goldie (Jenny Shimizu). The gang's activities are fairly tame and uninspiring. They include raiding the school to retrieve Maddy's art portfolio, stealing a car from a gang of boys, and spending endless hours bonding and playing house in the woods.

Feature film directorial debut of filmmaker Annette Haywood-Carter.

Director Haywood-Carter plays the gang's rather tame adventures either as loopy good times or profound spiritual awakenings. Neither mode is effective. The raid on the school turns into a played-for-laughs chase scene after Goldie's match sets off a fire that activates the school's sprinkler system. The girls scream and run through the soaking hallways while firemen pursue, and the scene plays as if Haywood-Carter is begging us to find these gutsy gals cute.

Back at the clubhouse, they celebrate with an interminable tattooing ritual that gives the filmmakers an excuse to bare a few breasts. Will teens of the 1990s find tattooing mesmerizing or mystical? It's doubtful. The awfully overdrawn sequence is like something out of a 1960s hippie film—a lot of transfixed stares around a pile of candles.

The film also doesn't know what to do with Legs' apparent lesbianism or Maddy's confusion about being attracted to her. In a scene that doesn't work, Maddy confesses to Legs that she loves her but worries that Legs will "take it the wrong way;" Legs agreeably says she's take it whatever way Maddy wants. And we're left unsure which way that is. Were the sexual aspects of their relationship played out or at least openly confronted, *Foxfire* would be more interesting. Instead it's remarkably bloodless. Rather than take risks with the material, Haywood-Carter seems content to pose and manipulate her cast of characters.

In its last half, the film goes from merely uninspired to baffling. Legs is betrayed, but by a minor character who is not a part of the gang. She is sent to jail, and the gang members brood without her, perching on street corners in a lackluster music-video montage. The plot then veers to Goldie, who has a heroin habit. When the gang forces her off drugs, she becomes violently ill. Legs returns and goes ballistic.

The story's moral requires Maddy to discover that Legs is not a goddess but a confused and impulsive loser. The events that fulfill this plot mission are outrageous and unbelievable, involving Legs' gunpoint kidnapping of Goldie's father, who until then has figured not at all in the film. Legs' dethroning is abrupt and clumsy; she turns suddenly from shaman to buffoon. Just when *Foxfire* should be coming together, it unravels.

What saves the movie are several strong performances. Jolie, the daughter of veteran actor Jon Voight, is mesmerizing as Legs. She looks like a female Mick Jagger, but rather than swaggering, Jolie agreeably underplays her role. She is effectively soft-spoken, intriguing and dangerous. Jolie does an excellent job of masking her character's vulnerability behind a macho facade without making her seem needy or fake.

Burress, of TV's "Boston Common," is weaker than Jolie in a more difficult role. When the script calls for Maddy to be an awakening innocent, Burress acts the part well, but when Maddy gets mean, sexy or wicked, Burress seems at a loss. When in doubt, Burress falls back on looking confused, an appropriate expression, since Maddy's attraction for Legs is confusing.

Among the minor characters, Lewis is quietly outstanding as Rita, the ugly duckling of the gang. She makes the most of the film's most natural role, lighting up the

CREDITS

Maddy Wirtz: Hedy Burress
Legs Sadovsky: Angelina Jolie
Rita Faldes: Jenny Lewis
Goldie Goldman: Jenny Shimizu
Violet Kahn: Sarah Rosenberg
Ethan Bixby: Peter Facinelli

Origin: USA
Released: 1996
Production: Jeffrey Lurie, John Bard Manulis and John P. Marsh for a Rysher Entertainment, Chestnut Hill and Red Mullet productions; released by Samuel Goldwyn
Direction: Annette Haywood-Carter
Screenplay: Elizabeth White; based on the novel by Joyce Carol Oates
Cinematography: Newton Thomas Sigel
Editing: Louise Innes
Music: Michel Colombier
Production design: John Myhre
Art direction: Alan Locke
Set decoration: Marthe Pineau
Costume design: Laura Goldsmith
Sound: Jim Hawkins
Casting: Emily Schweber
MPAA rating: R
Running Time: 100 minutes

screen and effortlessly stealing small scenes. In pigtails, Rosenberg looks and acts more like Shelley Duvall as Olive Oyl than a nymphomaniac; she is happy-go-lucky, a little dimwitted and underwritten. Rosenberg gives the thankless role a game try. As Goldie, boyish-looking supermodel Shimizu doesn't have to act much beyond wearing a dazed look and delivering a jaded line or two.

The intriguing aspect of *Foxfire* is that Legs inhabits a role traditionally written for a male: the dark stranger who sweeps an innocent girl off her feet and forces her to choose between a wild and a civilized life. But instead of exploiting this agreeable twist on an oft-told tale, *Foxfire* merely changes the gender of the stranger and keeps the rest of the familiar conventions intact. *Foxfire* contains much posturing at deep meaning and emotional consequence, but gives few insights into growing up female. That might explain why most adolescent girls didn't go to see it.

—*Michael Betzold*

REVIEWS

Boxoffice. August, 1996, p. 58.
Los Angeles Times. August 23, 1996, p. F8.
New York Times. August 23, 1996, p. C8.
Variety. August 5, 1996.

Freeway

"Two thumbs up."—*Siskel & Ebert*

Box Office: $257,702

Matthew Bright's debut film *Freeway* aims for cult status as a nightmarish, black-comic updating of "Little Red Riding Hood." The innocent little girl of the fairy tale is transposed into a jaded southern California white-trash teen runaway, Vanessa Lutz (Reese Witherspoon). The big bad wolf is a counselor for troubled boys turned into a freeway slasher, Bob Wolverton (Kiefer Sutherland). Grandma's house is a trailer park in Stockton.

Sutherland creates a character that is equally chilling and hilarious, achieving the delicate balance of mockery and terror that is cult pay dirt. But when Sutherland is off camera, *Freeway* fails to get that tenor right, and the result is a film that veers crazily from slapstick to melodrama to crude, cartoonish violence. Witherspoon gives a raw, all-out and often entertaining performance, but her character, central to the film, suffers from the film's scattershot ambitions.

That the film is meant to be a cartoon is made apparent from the comic-strip depiction of a wolf chasing a runaway girl that serves as backdrop for the opening credit sequence. The first live-action shot (in a high-school classroom that looks more like a slumber party) asks audiences to believe that Vanessa can barely read the word "cat."

How crudely does Bright draw the character of Vanessa? Her mother (Amanda Plummer, in a typically twisted turn) is a trashy, addled hooker; her stepfather, tattooed and bedraggled, is a drug dealer and her mother's pimp, and he also molests Vanessa. When the cops corral her guardians, Vanessa, little red basket in hand, takes to the road to escape another stint in a foster home and finds her grandmother, who has never met her.

Bright's dangerously wacky game is to create a miserably unappealing, crude, violent and uneducated Vanessa and then turn her into a white-trash heroine who is morally superior to every adult she encounters and every part of the system she fights. The project might have succeeded as a sort of nightmarish fairy-tale horror film had Bright not succumbed to the temptation to try to make the audience cheer for Vanessa. As it is, the sheer lunatic force of having Vanessa run amok is tempered and ultimately ruined by the hokey ways the script makes her into a victim begging for the audience's sympathy.

In tried and true fashion, *Freeway* presents Vanessa as the unwitting product of a failed educational system, miserable parents, greedy and cruel foster care workers and rapacious law-enforcement officials. Her mother yells at her: "You don't know a goddamn thing about nothing." Her stepfather threatens to "take a shit on your pointy little head." After the police arrest her mother and stepfather, a policewoman spurns Vanessa's bid to take her under her wing. After Vanessa kisses her boyfriend goodbye to take off on her search for grandma, he is gunned down on the street.

But Vanessa is most victimized by Wolverton, who picks her up after her car breaks down on the freeway. While manipulating her into revealing her sordid past, Wolverton at first appears to be a squeaky-clean friend. Sutherland gives a fascinating, hilarious portrayal of a sick, oily spider spinning an elegant web. Their conversations are the best part of the film, and Bright cunningly closes in on Sutherland's face as he tries to spring his trap. His game is to get Vanessa to describe her stepfather's sexual abuse in graphic detail.

When she catches on to his game, he reveals himself as the freeway killer, a psychopath seething with anger about the depraved, degraded "garbage people"—Vanessa's kind of folk—whom he wants to destroy.

But Vanessa soon gains the upper hand. After he talks her out of turning him in, convincing her the authorities would believe his word and not hers, she makes him pay for what she calls his "bad manners." Using a gun her boyfriend gave her, she shoots him repeatedly. In a masterful touch of wackiness, she gets down on her knees and prays to God: "That was so bad, but I was at a loss as to what to do. I hope you don't hate me any more than you already do." When a comet shoots across the sky, it seems as if Bright has begun to unleash a sort of twisted antidote to a Frank Capra fantasy.

Freeway turns even crazier and more horrifying when Wolverton somehow survives his multiple gunshots, stumbles to the hospital and identifies his assailant. Vanessa is arrested and grilled by two cops who have been investigating the freeway slasher. They are pressured to put away Vanessa by Wolverton's wife, a sort of grown-up Barbie doll played by Brooke Shields in a way which wonderfully mocks her own image.

To this point, Bright has assembled a promisingly offbeat story and a wonderfully motley cast of characters, including Wolfgang Bodison as the straight-arrow cop and Dan Hedaya as his slightly perverted sidekick. Sutherland, the former Boy Scout with the twisted soul, now is a grotesquely deformed invalid who speaks through a voice box. Halfway through *Freeway,* the film appears to have the makings of a cult classic. But then it all goes awry.

When Vanessa ridicules Wolverton in court, a judge decides she'll be tried as an adult. She's locked away in a women's prison, and for a long time it appears the film has skipped over the trial and she's already been convicted and sentenced. In fact, we later learn, she's only awaiting trial. By then the film has become a muddle.

The prison sequences, utterly useless, focus on Vanessa'a battles with a Donna-Reed-type warden with a malicious heart, an Hispanic inmate who is the prison's head bitch (Vanessa pummels her; they later become friends and fellow escapees), and an emotionally disturbed lesbian who wants to be Vanessa's bunkmate. These sequences add nothing to the film.

Vanessa escapes and becomes a vigilante prostitute who assaults and robs her hapless tricks. Somewhere along the way, *Freeway* has become a guerilla-feminist revenge movie, a gangster-girl-on-the-loose saga. The cops expose Wolverton, and all the major parties head to grandmother's house for a bloody happy ending.

Bright obviously takes delight in breaking all the rules, but he rarely achieves the sort of antic mayhem that would sustain even a cult film audience's interest. The sporadic efforts to cast Vanessa in the victim role are annoying; the prison sequences are grating, and the comic possibilities set up by a potential showdown between Vanessa, Wolverton and his wife are unrealized.

Shields and Sutherland are terrific, and Witherspoon tries to carry the film as the script demands she must. She looks the part of a terrorist teen and she acts like one of those inane guests on trashy TV talk shows. But it's hard to work up any sympathy for her as Bright seems to demand. The script creates an internally inconsistent character: a bitch on wheels with a heart of gold. The concept of a modern Little Red Riding Hood as an innocent betrayed by a cruel world is serviceable, but she can't also be a gun-toting, castrating, grudge-against-the-world proto-feminist. If Bright had simply kept the character cartoonish, *Freeway* would have a better ride.

As it is, *Freeway* enjoys a future only as a minor cult item, unless Bright realizes the occasional flashes of promise shown in this film and goes on to a career as an auteur. More likely, *Freeway* will be remembered as Kiefer Sutherland's finest moment and also as the movie in which Brooke Shields held up a mirror to her persona and screamed. That's not enough to make most folks want to take a ride to grandma's mobile home.

—Michael Betzold

CREDITS

Vanessa Lutz: Reese Witherspoon
Bob Wolverton: Kiefer Sutherland
Ramona Lutz: Amanda Plummer
Detective Breer: Wolfgang Bodison
Detective Wallace: Dan Hedaya
Mimi Wolverton: Brooke Shields

Origin: USA
Released: 1996
Production: Chris Hanley and Brad Wyman for Illusion Entertainment Group and Muse/Wyman Productions; released by Republic Pictures
Direction: Matthew Bright
Screenplay: Matthew Bright
Cinematography: John Thomas
Editing: Maysie Hoy
Production design: Pam Warner
Music: Danny Elfman
Costume design: Merrie Lawson
MPAA rating: R
Running Time: 102 minutes

REVIEWS

Los Angeles Times. October 11, 1996, p. F14.
Variety. January 29, 1996, p. 67.

French Twist; Gazon Maudit

A scorned wife. An outrageous affair. The perfect revenge.—Movie tagline

"A romantic comic romp!"—Barbara & Scott Siegel, *Siegel Entertainment Syndicate*

"Great fun! A cunning, robust farce! Brisk and sassy. A mature sex comedy."—Richard Corliss, *Time*

"Totally refreshing!"—Paul Wunder, *WBAI Radio*

Box Office: $1,026,646

La Cage aux Folles (1980) broke new ground in the early eighties by being a sex farce that wasn't particularly bawdy but, because of its homosexual content, raised many an eyebrow. It allowed filmgoers all over the world to see that homosexuals could get themselves mixed up in benignly romantic, messy situations with the same haplessness as heterosexuals.

In that tradition, this year a film called *French Twist* (*Gauzon Maudit*) took France by storm, and extended its reach into the U.S. and beyond. It is a romantic comedy, with emphasis on "romantic," which has at its center a love triangle between a man, his wife, and her lesbian lover, and it is a thoroughly enchanting movie that has audiences referring to it as "the next *La Cage aux Folles.*"

The story, by Josiane Balasko and Telshe Boorman, is about a beautiful and incredibly sexy housewife named Loli (Victoria Abril), who is probably the only woman around who has not lately had sex with her husband, the selfish philanderer Laurent (Alain Chabat). While he is away at work one day, Loli finds herself becoming interested in a plumber whose car has broken down near Loli and Laurent's rural home. The plumber's name is Marijo (played by writer/director Josiane Balasko), and sparks fly as the two women spend time together while Marijo gets her van fixed. Eventually sharing a stolen kiss in the courtyard, Loli and Marijo enter into a romance, which, when discovered by the hypocritical Laurent, sets the stage for a never-ending series of situations that are plausible only in romantic comedy, but are delightful nonetheless.

Marijo moves in with the two of them (and their child), and the complications get more . . . well. . . . complicated. Sharing Loli's affections (she sleeps with each of them three nights per week, saying "on the seventh day we rest") proves to be emotionally disastrous, and after much soul-searching (mostly on the part of Loli) some interesting resolutions are reached.

The film is a constant series of surprises, right up through its final frame, which make it more than just a French version of some British sex comedy filled with double entendres. Granted, this film might not be considered brilliant, but it is wise and funny. Director/actress/writer Balasko keeps a knockabout pace, throwing in everything from slapstick humor to some fairly tearful dramatic scenes, and in between manages to satisfy the arthouse film crowd's need to have a little social commentary with their fluffy romances. Without giving away the surprises of the latter part of the film, suffice it to say that Balasko finds a way to point out that no one in our society is exactly who he or she seems to be, and that traditional male and female roles are as tenuous as life itself.

Once Marijo moves into the house, the film does become a more typical domestic comedy, full of squabbles and tears, but that doesn't make it less funny than the more unusual first half. Even a lowbrow scene involving spaghetti seems fresh in the hands of the delightful and inventive lead

AWARDS AND NOMINATIONS

Cesar Awards 1996: Best Script
Nominations: Best Film, Best Director (Balasko), Best Actor (Chabat), Best Supporting Actor (Holgado)

CREDITS

Marijo: Josiane Balasko
Loli: Victoria Abril
Laurent: Alain Chabat
Antoine: Ticky Holgado
Diego: Manuel Bose

Origin: France
Released: 1995
Production: Claude Berri for a Renn Productions, TF1 Films, and Les Films Flam production; released by Miramax Films
Direction: Josiane Balasko
Screenplay: Josiane Balasko
Cinematography: Gerard De Battista
Editing: Claudine Merlin
Music: Manuel Malou
Production design: Carlos Conti
Costume design: Fabienne Katany
Sound: Pierre Lenoir, Dominique Hennequin
MPAA rating: R
Running Time: 100 minutes

actors. Victoria Abril, known as one of the regulars in the films of Pedro Almodovar (*Tie Me Up! Tie Me Down!* [1990], *High Heels* [1991], *Kika* [1994]), is perfect as the slightly lippy Loli. She is beautiful and sad and determined and confused; it is hard to imagine another actress being able to keep this role from being a one-note characterization, particularly in light of all the crying she is called upon to do.

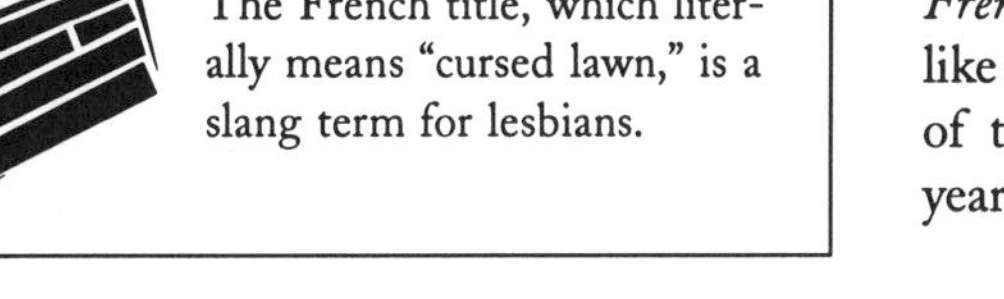

The French title, which literally means "cursed lawn," is a slang term for lesbians.

Alain Chabat is a handsome and rakish leading man on whom all the sexual rules change just when he is winning the game. Chabat remains likable even when his character is at his most dangerous and hypocritical, such as when he threatens to kill Marijo one night. Chabat plays Laurent as a man who reacts in a stereotypically male fashion to a situation which endangers his family life, his personal comfort, his career, and his reactionary understanding of what a "normal" man/woman relationship should be.

Finally, Josiane Balasko, known as Gerard Depardieu's mistress in *Too Beautiful for You* (1989), directs her script with simplicity, keeping the tempestuous characters and relationships from becoming overwhelming. As an actress, Balasko is cool and confident, portraying Marijo as a woman who may look like a stereotype, but has her own distinctive motivations and responses. *French Twist* may not be a classic like *La Cage,* but it is surely one of the most enjoyable films this year.

—*Kirby Tepper*

REVIEWS

Detroit News. March 1, 1996, p. 5D.
Entertainment Weekly. February 16, 1996, p. 48.
Los Angeles Times. January 12, 1996, p. F6.
New York Times. January 12, 1996, p. C20.
Sight and Sound. March, 1996, p. 41.
Variety. February 14, 1995, p. 14.
Village Voice. January 23, 1996, p. 63.

The Frighteners

Dead Yet?—Movie tagline
"High-tech horror!"—George Pennacchio, *KABC*
"A summer scarefest!"—Sara Edwards, *NBC Newschannel*
"A non-stop special effects rollercoaster."—John Platt, *Sci-Fi Buzz*
"It will frighten you to death."—Maria Salas, *Telenoticias*
"A perfect mixture of chills and thrills."—Kyle Osborne, *WDCA*
"It'll leave you breathless."—Sam Hallenbeck, *WTVT*

Box Office: $16,300,000

There are several stories providing the momentum for *The Frighteners.* One takes place in 1964 when an orderly at Fairwater Hospital, Johnny Bartlett (Jake Busey), inexplicably decides one day to gun down 12 innocent people. He is aided in his efforts by his paramour, the hospital administrator's 15-year-old daughter Patricia Bradley (Dee Wallace Stone). Bartlett is subsequently caught, tried, and executed, while Patricia is sentenced to life in prison. Patricia, however, is released early—five years ago, to be exact—and she now lives the life of a recluse with her domineering mother (Julianna McCarthy) on the ruins of the old hospital grounds. But the two women are not alone in their house. Spirits travel under carpets and grab Patricia through the walls. There is no rest for this wicked woman.

At the same time that Patricia was being released from prison, architect Frank Bannister (Michael J. Fox) was building his dream house. However, although he promised his wife Debra (Angela Bloomfield) a garden, he instead laid 12' of concrete and put up a basketball net. The two argue, and while driving down Halloway Road they have an accident which kills Debra. Since then, Frank's life has been plagued by guilt . . . and by the ability to see and communicate with ghosts.

Frank now no longer has the heart to finish his house and just lives in its half-done shell. He also refuses to continue his career as an architect and instead has created a new business. He's a psychic investigator. The thing is, he usually ends up "investigating" hauntings which he has created himself with the help of three ectoplasmic ghosts: Cyrus (Chi McBride) who died during the seventies and is stuck with a large Afro and disco clothes; Stuart (Jim Fyfe), a bow-tied, bespectacled bookish fellow; and The Judge (John Astin), a gun-toting leftover from the Wild West who has been around so long there's not much ectoplasm left to the old guy.

Then one day Frank accidentally drives his car through a fence and over the lawn of Ray Lynskey (Peter Dobson). Ray threatens to sue, but instead, that night he and his wife, a physician named Lucy (Trini Alvarado), find themselves in need of Frank's psychic services as the bed levitates, kitchenware goes flying, and a statue of Elvis comes to life. Lucy calls Frank who delivers the diagnosis: "Persistent residue of the departed. It's always a problem, this time of year." It will cost the Lynskey's about $450 . . . or the price of the fence, whichever they'd like. The convenient haunting is the work of Frank's spectral cronies. It's just another con.

"Frightening is a young man's game, Frank, and I ain't got no more hauntings in me. My ectoplasm is all dried up."—The Judge

But there are two surprises waiting for Frank on this job. For one thing, Lucy is very attractive and her husband is a jerk. For another, for some reason Frank can't explain, he sees the number 37 supernaturally carved onto Ray's forehead. No one else can see it, but not long afterward, Ray is dead.

Ray is just the latest victim in a plague of corpses showing up in the coastal town of Fairwater. There have been more than a dozen, and all very unusual. As Sheriff Perry (Troy Evans) describes it, "They look like heart attacks, but when they slice these people open, their arteries are clean as a whistle. The life's been squeezed out of them."

After Ray's funeral, both the ghostly Ray and very real Lucy contact Frank. They arrange for a dinner where Lucy and Ray communicate through Frank with about as much success as they had when they were both alive. Then, while in the restaurant's bathroom, Frank sees another man with a number carved on his forehead. But this time he also sees the blackest of black spirits murdering the man. Frank gives chase to the ominous apparition, but without success. And it gets worse for Frank. Not only can he not stop the homicidal demon, but because no one else can see it and Frank always seems to be around when one of the numbered people follow the tunnel of light into the next world, Frank is now the prime suspect.

Enter the weirder than weird FBI agent Milton Dammers (Jeffrey Combs) who becomes so obsessed with proving Frank guilty of the murders that he actually has him arrested. But the black-cloaked, scythe-carrying phantom continues to rack up victims, and only Frank has the ability to see, let alone stop him. Will he be able to stop him before he claims his next victim, the lovely Lucy?

It is a beguiling story, filled with interesting subplots, escalating frenzy, and fascinating special effects. But in the end, *The Frighteners* becomes just another entry in the summer of 1996 special effects olympics (*Twister, Independence Day*). At least in this film there is a more complex plot and even the special effects have personalities. In fact, it almost seems as if the ghosts have more personality than the living.

Michael J. Fox's Frank takes a while to warm up to. Here he has traded in the boyish innocence that made him so appealing in all the *Back to the Future* films for a more sullen, cynical, and disagreeable character. He has his moments of humor, but they are always couched in pessimism and world-weariness. By the time he ends up in jail, he's downright uncommunicative. But as soon as his character senses Lucy is in danger, Frank comes alive and Fox makes him much more likeable.

Alvarado's Lucy is a relatively competent character (although why she ever married Ray is a complete mystery), but both Lucy and Frank often take courses of action that if the story weren't so feverish we might be scratching our heads and wondering why on Earth would they do that?

Perhaps the most perplexing character in the film is FBI agent Dammers. Verging on being psychotic and a neo-Nazi, Jeffrey Combs (no stranger to the offbeat; he was the star of the two *Re-Animator* films) comes off more like Hitler than a idiosyncratic addition to the cast. He is definitely im-

CREDITS

Frank Bannister: Michael J. Fox
Lucy Lynskey: Trini Alvarado
Ray Lynskey: Peter Dobson
The Judge: John Astin
Milton Dammers: Jeffery Combs
Patricia Bradley: Dee Wallace Stone

Origin: USA
Released: 1996
Production: Jamie Selkirk and Peter Jackson for a Wingnut Films production; released by Universal
Direction: Peter Jackson
Screenplay: Fran Walsh and Peter Jackson
Cinematography: Alun Bollinger and John Blick
Editing: Jamie Selkirk
Music: Danny Elfman
Production design: Grant Major
Art direction: Dan Hennah
Costume design: Barbara Darragh
Sound: Hammond Peek
Digital effects: Charlie McClellan
Creature and miniature effects: Richard Taylor
MPAA rating: PG-13
Running Time: 109 minutes

possible to warm up to. In fact, repulsion is the knee-jerk reaction every time Dammers comes on-screen.

All the ghosts do a fine job keeping their end of the film up, but special kudos go to John Astin (TV's "The Addams Family") virtually unrecognizable as the Judge and R. Lee Ermey who makes Frank's visits to the cemetery to drum up business hell on Earth as he recreates his *Full Metal Jacket* drill sergeant role.

> Director Peter Jackson filmed in his homeland of New Zealand, overseeing a record-breaking 400-plus computer-enhanced visual effects at his production studios.

Dee Wallace Stone (best known as ET's "mom") is convincingly innocent and/or guilty as Johnny Bartlett's handmaiden, and Jake Busey (son of actor Gary) seems to be picking up the over-the-top and near-the-edge characters his father is often cast as.

If you stick around to read the film's end credits you'll probably be wondering why it was shot in New Zealand. Well, it's because that's where director/co-writer Peter Jackson hails from, and Jackson is a hot property. His 1994 *Heavenly Creatures* about a duo of matricidal girls (based on a true story) won a Silver Lion at Venice and an Academy Award nomination for Best Screenplay. Now Jackson and his co-author Frances Walsh have turned the murdering mayhem up several notches with *The Frighteners,* but they have also traded the insight of a little film for the big budget and special effects of a more conventional Hollywood box office contender. (If anything it harkens back to Jackson's quirky 1992 horror film *Dead Alive* about a zombie mother and son relationship.)

The result of *Dead Alive* meeting *Heavenly Creatures* is the very black comedy/horror story *The Frighteners.* We're never sure if we should cringe or giggle and the film is so fast-paced and jam-packed, that we barely have time to do one or the other before we're hurried off in another direction. We start out thinking we're watching *Topper* but end up in *The Nightmare On Elm Street.* By the time it's over, one has been entertained but also exhausted.

—Beverley Bare Buehrer

REVIEWS

Boxoffice Magazine Online. July 22, 1996.
Chicago Tribune. July 19, 1996, p. 4.
Detroit News. July 19, 1996, p. D1.
Entertainment Weekly. July 26, 1996, p. 34.
The Hollywood Reporter. July 15, 1996, p. 5.
Los Angeles Times. July 19, 1996, p. F10.
The New York Times. July 19, 1996, p. C16.
People. July 29, 1996, p. 18.
USA Today. July 19, 1996, p. 13D.
Variety Online. July 15, 1996.

From Dusk Till Dawn

A terrifying evil has been unleashed. Now, four strangers are our only hope to stop it.—Movie tagline

"A rollercoaster ride and a half! George Clooney delivers a knock-out performance!"—Bill Diehl, *ABC Radio Network*

"Dazzling, original, scary and fun! George Clooney is a sexy, charismatic new movie hero!"—Jeanne Wolf, *Jeanne Wolf's Hollywood*

"'Dusk' is a film nerd's fevered dream, a Frankenstein monster of old movie parts, deliberately mismatched styles, and deliciously implausible characters!"—Jack Mathews, *Los Angeles Times*

"Some scenes may be too intense for human beings!"—Richard Corliss, *Time*

"This is a great 70's exploitationer that took 20 years to get made. A kick-butt actioner with plenty of laughs!"—Todd McCarthy, *Variety*

Box Office: $25,836,616

The name of Quentin Tarantino associated with *From Dusk Till Dawn* guaranteed it respectful attention from critics and the movie-going public. *Pulp Fiction* (1994), directed and co-authored by Tarantino, had been the most talked about film of the year. It had received a whole list of prestigious awards and award nominations. Many felt it should have received the Academy Award for Best Picture instead of the "feel good" blockbuster *Forrest Gump* (1994). A film as violent and immoral as *Pulp Fiction,* however, had little chance of receiving many awards from the conservative, image-conscious Academy of Motion Picture Arts and Sciences. Everyone in the movie business agreed that Quentin Tarantino was the man to watch, perhaps the most talented, innovative, and daring filmmaker since Orson Welles and Alfred Hitchcock.

Unfortunately, *From Dusk Till Dawn,* based on a screenplay by Tarantino and co-starring him as a Tarantinoesque mad dog killer, was a disappointing follow-up. Although *Variety* listed it at the top of its Box Office chart and reported that the film grossed $13,198,212 during its first week of release, it took another twelve weeks for the feature to equal the first week's gross. Box office receipts plummeted after word got around that the new offering lacked the originality of the earlier Tarantino films. It was learned that Tarantino actually wrote the script in 1990 for a fee of $1500. It probably never would have been resurrected had it not been for the phenomenal success of *Pulp Fiction* and the belated attention that film brought to his earlier low-budget sleeper *Reservoir Dogs* (1992).

From Dusk Till Dawn has two of the ingredients viewers expect from a Tarantino film: plenty of bloodshed and plenty of gratuitous dialogue. As in *Pulp Fiction* and *Reservoir Dogs,* the killers in *From Dusk Till Dawn* cannot stop talking. They seem almost like Woody Allen characters in their compulsions to articulate their thoughts and feelings. No doubt the prototype that inspired Tarantino was Ernest Hemingway's famous minimalistic short story "The Killers," adapted to the screen in 1946 and again in 1964, in which the two professional killers joke and chat with each other and with their three hostages while waiting in the diner to murder Ole Andreson with a sawed-off shotgun.

In *From Dusk Till Dawn,* the two fugitives, Seth Gecko (George Clooney) and his brother Richard (Quentin Tarantino) carry on their personal arguments while holding hostages at gunpoint and even while shooting it out with a desperate clerk in a country store. They are still arguing when they walk away from the blazing building where they have left the bodies of the clerk and an unfortunate Texas Ranger who stopped in for a soda at the wrong time.

From the conversation that takes place between the store clerk and the Ranger, along with some news flashes heard on various radios, the viewers learn that the Geckos are the subjects of one of the greatest manhunts in American history. Richard had helped Seth break out of prison in a hail of bullets. They have robbed a bank, murdered a number of innocent people, taken one woman hostage, and are now on their way to the Mexican border.

"I said to keep a low profile. Don't you know the meaning of the words *low profile?!*"—Seth in response to brother Richard's carnage

The two desperados stop at a motel. When Seth comes back to the room with some take-out food, he finds that his psychopathic brother has raped and murdered their hostage. Hardly skipping a beat, the reckless brothers make hostages of three tourists who have stopped overnight at the same motel. Their victims are Jacob Fuller (Harvey Keitel), a preacher who has lost his religious faith, his teenage daughter Kate (Juliette Lewis), and his teenage adopted Chinese son Scott (Ernest Liu). The Fullers have been vacationing in a big motor home, but Jacob has insisted on stopping at a motel for the luxury of sleeping in a full-size bed. Soon five people are headed for the Mexican border, where a heavy roadblock has been set up to stop the fugitives from crossing.

It has been pointed out that Harvey Keitel seems miscast as a countrified preacher. No doubt he got the part because of his previous association with Tarantino. Keitel co-produced and starred in *Reservoir Dogs* and had a good role in the highly successful *Pulp Fiction.* The talented Juliette Lewis, who resembles a young Jodie Foster, seems perfectly cast in the role of an innocent girl who is trying to hide her fears and help her disoriented father cope with their predicament. It is Kate who hides the killers and deceives the border guards in order to forestall a shootout in which she knows she and her family would be killed. She manages to keep her cool even while the sex-crazed Richard is holding her at gunpoint and nearly drooling with desire for her vulnerable young body. Quentin Tarantino does an adequate job of portraying the psychopathic Richard Gecko, but his future in films would seem to be behind the camera.

Tarantino wrote the original script in 1990.

The most unusual thing about *From Dusk Till Dawn,* as has been pointed out by all the critics, is that it morphs outrageously from one genre into another as soon as the Fullers and Geckos cross the Mexican border and arrive at the Titty Twister ("Open from dusk till dawn"), a roadhouse patronized by bikers and truckers whose animal behavior has gotten them barred from every low dive in the U.S.A. "Rarely," writes Joe Morgenstern in his *Wall Street Journal* review, "has a movie transformed itself so completely, or with such juvenile abandon." "Juvenile" is certainly the right word. A gripping road-kill story involving desperate men and innocent hostages is suddenly transformed into yet another spinoff of *Night of the Living Dead* (1968), the low-budget horror classic which may enjoy the distinction of being the most imitated film in cinema history. Critics have also compared *From Dusk Till Dawn* to John Carpenter's *Assault On Precinct 13* (1976), which was itself an urbanized spinoff of *Night of the Living Dead.*

The judicious viewer keeps hoping this abrupt transformation is only the representation of an hallucination in the mind of one of the characters who has drunk too many boilermakers. Unfortunately, that is not the case. Once inside the Titty Twister, a place which, according to Jack Mathews' review in *The Los Angeles Times,* "looks like a Hell's Angels Fourth of July celebration in the Twilight Zone," the two brothers and their three hostages find themselves in a nightmare. The nude female dancers turn into vampires and begin biting the lewd, drunken "hairwart" patrons, who quickly turn into vampires themselves, in accordance with the well established rules of vampirism. Anybody who gets killed is sure to come back looking twice as mean and twice as ugly. Even the male and female vampires inside the bar are innocuous, however, compared to the fiends from hell who show up outside to join in this festival of horrors. The production had an $18 million budget, and much of it went into the 40 minute free-for-all between humans and assorted monsters.

Like the zombies in *Night of the Living Dead,* the vampires and demons rely more on sheer weight of numbers and their terrifying appearances than on physical strength. The humans find it easy enough to knock off heads or drive pool cues into hearts, but the odds gradually overwhelm them. First Richard Gecko is bitten and has to be killed by his own brother. Then the pacifist preacher, no longer a pacifist but a confirmed vampire hater, gets bitten and tries to kill off as many of his assailants as possible before becoming one of them. He apparently has regained his religious faith in this unlikely milieu but the exact manner of his reconversion remains somewhat ambiguous. For a Quentin Tarantino character the preacher seems strangely out of touch with his inner feelings.

CREDITS

Jacob Fuller: Harvey Keitel
Seth Gecko: George Clooney
Richard Gecko: Quentin Tarantino
Kate Fuller: Juliette Lewis
Border Guard/Chet Pussy/Carlos: Cheech Marin
Frost: Fred Williamson
Santanico Pandemonium: Salma Hayek

Origin: USA
Released: 1995
Production: Gianni Nunnari and Meir Teper for A Band Apart and Los Hooligans production; released by Dimension Films
Direction: Robert Rodriguez
Screenplay: Quentin Tarantino
Cinematography: Guillermo Navarro
Editing: Robert Rodriguez
Production design: Cecilia Montiel
Art direction: Mayne Schuyler Berke
Set design: Colin de Rouin
Set decoration: Felipe Fernandez del Paso
Costume design: Graciela Mazon
Sound: Mark Ulano
Visual effects supervision: Daniel A. Fort, Diana Dru Botsford
Music: Graeme Revell
MPAA rating: R
Running Time: 107 minutes

Finally the mild-mannered Scott Fuller (Ernest Liu) becomes a one-man vampire banquet and begs to be shot before he turns into one of those voracious creatures himself.

This leaves only Seth Gecko and the now quite militant, blood-bespattered Kate fighting against an inexhaustible horde of monsters. The experience has apparently been good for Kate, just as it was for Barbara (Patricia Tallman) in the color remake of *Night of the Living Dead* (1990). Kate has lost the persona of an inhibited, countrified, teenage virgin daughter of a fundamentalist preacher and has become a young street warrior. She would be a fitting mate for Seth Gecko. She seems to personify the thesis of the film: that you have to be tough to survive in the 90s. If circumstances had permitted, she might easily have gone off with Seth on a rampage of crime such as the one depicted in the adaptation of the Jim Thompson novel *The Getaway* (1972), starring Steve McQueen and Ali McGraw, and in the 1993 remake starring Alec Baldwin and Kim Basinger. It is too late, however.

Even though Seth and Kate manage to escape from the vampires and demons, Seth's fate is sealed. Carlos and his Mexican henchmen have arrived, as promised, to take him to that legendary hideout El Rey for well-heeled fugitives described in Thompson's *The Getaway* but left out of the film adaptation of that novel. The name El Rey is an homage to Thompson, the most hard-boiled of all the hard-boiled American novelists, including Dashiell Hammett, Raymond Chandler and James M. Cain. The connoisseur of crime fiction understands that Seth will live in luxury and security until his bank loot runs out, and then he will be reduced to the degradation and cannibalism detailed in the last gruesome pages of Thompson's book.

Kate has fallen in love with Seth and asks him to take her with him. He has somehow become softened by his recent experiences. The good side of his nature was foreshadowed in his attempts to restrain his psychopathic brother as well as in his sincere assurances that he would treat his hostages kindly if they would cooperate. Evidently his loss of his brother, along with his exposure to real fiends and his imminent dependence on El Rey's sinister hospitality, have belatedly taught him that murdering something like 20 people including four law enforcement officers in just this last outing was inappropriate behavior. He is willing to accept his fate but nobly refuses Kate's request to be taken along, explaining that even as bad a man as himself could not ask such an innocent young girl to share the life awaiting him in El Rey's sanctuary.

Todd McCarthy, reviewing the film for *Variety,* dismisses it as a trashy, vulgar, exploitation gorefest "made to order for the stimulation of teenage boys." McCarthy, however, offers an unequivocal prediction: "What demands attention by a wider audience is George Clooney's instant emergence as a full-fledged movie star." McCarthy thinks Clooney might be a new Clark Gable or a new Mel Gibson. Janet Maslin, who reviewed the film for *The New York Times,* thinks Clooney might be a new Cary Grant. The movie star whom Clooney most closely resembles, however, and seems very consciously trying to imitate, is Burt Lancaster (who, coincidentally, starred in the 1946 film version of Hemingway's *The Killers*).

Clooney has Lancaster's hungry-tiger purr in his husky voice and the same air of barely restrained power in his movements. He tilts his head the same way as the late Burt Lancaster and uses his eyes in the same brooding, introspective manner. He has the same way of dominating the camera without appearing to be doing much of anything. Like Lancaster, Clooney can be, not just a violent man, but a violent man who is also intelligent. With a duo like Richard and Seth Gecko, one might expect the bespectacled shrimp to provide the brains while the bigger brother provided the muscle. In *From Dusk Till Dawn,* however, Clooney provides both brains and brawn, which is what makes him so formidable.

No doubt Todd McCarthy is right. *From Dusk Till Dawn* is Clooney's film. He has graduated from the television series "E.R." to become one of the new young male stars of the 1990s at a time when the old dynasty, including Jack Lemmon, Robert Redford, Paul Newman, Dustin Hoffman, Warren Beatty, Jack Nicholson, and a few others are on their way to becoming vaguely familiar names on brass plaques embedded in the fickle Hollywood sidewalks.

—Bill Delaney

REVIEWS

Boxoffice. March, 1996, p. R-27.
Los Angeles Times. January 19, 1996, pp. F2, F8.
Newsweek. January 29, 1996, p. 59.
The New Yorker. February 5, 1996, pp. 76-7.
New York Times. January 19, 1996, p. B3.
USA Today. January 19, 1996, p. 4D.
Variety. January 22, 1996, pp. 98, 100.
Village Voice. January 30, 1996, p. 41.
Wall Street Journal. January 26, 1996, p. A9.

The Funeral

One family. One murder. Too many lies.—Movie tagline

"Chris Penn is knock-out brilliant!"—Shari Roman, *Detour*

"In American cinema, there's never been a gangster movie quite like this."—Kevin Thomas, *Los Angeles Times*

"*The Funeral* is the best thing Abel's done since *King of New York*."—A.J. Benza, *New York Daily News*

"The classic gangster movie, as viscerally exciting as it is intellectually captivating."—Geoff Pevere, *Toronto Globe Mail*

Box Office: $1,143,771

Dark, seamy, and brooding, *The Funeral* presents a decidedly fatalistic take on the romantic conventions that frequently give movie crime families an air of respect and dignity, however warped. For the Tempio brothers, family ties that might otherwise represent strength and pride bring only sadness and disease; religion, confusion and doubt; machismo, violence and death. Director Abel Ferrara (*King of New York* [1990], *Bad Lieutenant* [1992]) gives his trademark over-the-top treatment to frequent collaborator Nicholas St. John's subversive tale of small-time Depression-era gangsters (based on St. John's own family lore), with mixed success.

The film opens with a quick clip of Humphrey Bogart in *The Petrified Forest,* the 1936 gangster flick which is later shown to be playing at the movie house outside which Johnny Tempio (former Calvin Klein model Vincent Gallo) is slain. The Tempio clan has gathered at the home of oldest brother Ray (Christopher Walken, in a role initially claimed by Nicolas Cage), where Johnny's body is brought to lie in state. It is in this opening sequence that the temperaments and tendencies of the brothers and their wives are introduced. Cool, philosophically tormented businessman Ray suspects his brother was murdered by rival gangster Gaspare (Benicio del Toro), and he is immediately bent on avenging Johnny's death, despite his wife Jean's (Annabella Sciorra) protests. Unstable Chez, the middle brother played with conviction and pathos by Chris Penn, teeters between moments of sensitivity and temper, while his quiet Italian-born wife Clara (the luminous Isabella Rossellini) dutifully strives to keep Chez on an even keel. Also among the mourners is Johnny's beautiful, ingenuous fiancé Helen (Gretchen Mol), who was with him when was gunned down. The rest of the film focuses not so much on the obvious question of the killer's identity and motive (and that's a good thing—the resolution of these mysteries is entirely unsatisfying), but on the sordid, tortured history (revealed mostly through flashbacks) that brought these characters to this moment.

Much of the Tempios' turmoil is traced to their father, an immigrant who early on impressed his own twisted brand of justice and philosophy on his sons. A flashback shows the elder Tempio bringing the boys to a warehouse where an obviously beaten man is tied to a chair. The father explains that this man has stolen from the family, and tells adolescent Ray that he must kill the man to prevent him from repeating the offense; if Ray lets him go, the father explains, the man will undoubtedly return to kill them. With only a moment of hesitation, the obedient boy shoots the man dead, and his father rewards him with the shell casing from the bullet. "Nothing will cost you more," he tells the boy. Ray's adult struggles with

AWARDS AND NOMINATIONS

Independent Spirit Awards 1997 Nominations: Feature, Director (Ferrara), Actor (Penn), Screenplay (St. John), Cinematography (Kelsh)

CREDITS

Ray: Christopher Walken
Chez: Chris Penn
Johnny: Vincent Gallo
Gaspare: Benicio Del Toro
Jeanette: Annabella Sciorra
Clara: Isabella Rossellini

Origin: USA
Released: 1996
Production: Mary Kane for a MDP Worldwide production; released by October Films
Direction: Abel Ferrara
Screenplay: Nicholas St. John
Cinematography: Ken Kelsch
Editing: Bill Pankow and Mayin Lo
Music: Joe Delia
Production design: Charles Lagola
Costumes: Mindy Eshelman
Art direction: Beth Curtis
Sound: Rosa Howell-Thornhill
Casting: Ann Goulder, Billy Hopkins
MPAA rating: R
Running Time: 99 minutes

the concepts of justice and punishment, of free will and the grace of God, of Heaven and Hell, are traced to this moment: his need to exact revenge for Johnny's death is inherent and has rendered him morally ambiguous, and nothing—not his wife's pleas, not reason, not fear of Hell—can quell this impulse. "If this world stinks, it's His fault," he announces to Jean. "I'm working with what I've been given."

"They're criminals because they've never risen above their heartless, illiterate upbringing. And there's nothing, absolutely nothing, romantic about it."—Jeanette about the brothers

Another part of the elder Tempio's legacy—insanity—has been passed on to Chez. His swoons are perhaps the film's most compelling moments—his rage over Johnny's affair, his tender grief while standing at Johnny's coffin with his son, his showy delight performing a Cab Calloway tune at the family bar, his violent final act of despair. A flashback shows young Chez at his father's funeral, eavesdropping as mourners discuss the circumstances of his death: suicide. Although he's aware of his condition, pride keeps him from seeking treatment. Just as their father lives on in Ray's head, he lives on in Chez's blood; thus, their fate is sealed.

It is youngest son Johnny that at first seems most likely to break this trend. Of the three, he is the most idealistic, rejecting his brothers' racketeering ways in favor of Communist philosophy and relishing the escapism of movies. Although none of the brothers is comfortable with his lot in life, Johnny is the only one attempting to change his destiny instead of helplessly brooding about it. But like his brothers, he is self-indulgent and reckless, with an air of invincibility. He helps vandalize the truck of a radio manufacturer he thinks takes advantage of the working man—the same radio manufacturer his brothers agreed with Gaspare to protect. Furthermore, he undercuts his brothers' already rocky relationship with Gaspare by fooling around with his wife. Ultimately, it is this bravado and boldness that get Johnny killed.

The insight and reason of the Tempio women give the film much needed balance, and Ferrara, known for his skill directing actresses, wisely spends considerable screen time examining their suffering. Unlike conventional movie crime family wives, Jean and Clara are painfully wise to their husband's activities, and each uses her best asset—intelligence and gentleness respectively—to try to change their family's fate. Sciorra effectively plays Jean as bitter and frustrated, but never hysterical; she is coolly mesmerizing in a scene in which she sarcastically congratulates Helen on Johnny's death, since it means she won't become a part of the family after all. Her assessment that the brothers are "criminals because they've never risen above their heartless, illiterate upbringing, and there's nothing, absolutely nothing, romantic about it," is dead-on. Rossellini subtly conveys Clara's devotion and heartbreak when she suggests to Chez that they travel in secret to a Belgian town renown for its treatment of the mentally ill; although his refusal is expected, her perseverance is not.

The film's extended climax, however, is based solely on the quirks of the surviving brothers. Ray interrogates his prime suspect, who denies involvement in the murder, and brings the suspect to his home to see his brother's casket; when Johnny's wounds do not bleed, as Ray says legend dictates will happen when his killer enters the room, he sets him free, but orders him killed anyway, fearing revenge for his accusation. The real murderer is then revealed, and Ray extends his father's logic to justify his revenge. Chez, too, fulfills his father's legacy in a fit of violence that abruptly brings the family—and the film—to an end.

In many ways, *The Funeral* is traditional Ferrara fare. As in his other films that examine the underbelly of society, the characters are tortured and depraved, the violence is graphic and bloody, and the sex is kinky and frequent. Aside from the 1986 pilot for television's "Crime Story," however, this represents Ferrara's first period piece. He was initially hesitant to do the movie in part because he didn't want the audience "put off by the fact that these guys are walking around in period costume," as he told *Time Out New York* magazine. No chance. His controlled, intense direction, marked by lingering shots and extended takes, appropriately makes the characters, not the setting, the film's main focus. Coupled with Ferrara's fearlessness in showcasing his characters' intellectual struggles against visceral demons, the final product packs a definite punch. As a result, the ticks of the troubled Tempio family are undoubtedly the most compelling aspects of the film; its whodunit plot line nearly fades to an afterthought.

As its title suggests, *The Funeral* is unflinchingly grim. Its pop psychology approach to defining the Tempio family's troubles may be simplistic and heavy-handed, but strong performances and sharp dialogue (not to mention Ferrara's knack for the unexpected) keep the film interesting. Fans of epic grandiosity of the gangster genre may be put off by the film's claustrophobic focus, and characters' philosophical musings often border on the pretentious. Despite its flaws, *The Funeral* is an original, an intriguing look at the underside of the movie gangster myth.

—*Terri Schell*

REVIEWS

Boxoffice. October, 1996, p. 44.
Chicago Tribune. November 8, 1996, p. 5.
Entertainment Weekly. November 22, 1996, p. 111.
The New York Times. November 11, 1996, p. C3.
People Weekly. November 4, 1996, p. 29.
Rolling Stone. November 14, 1996, p. 126.
Time Out New York. October 24-31, 1996, p. 58.
The Village Voice. November 5, 1996, p. 71.

Get On the Bus

On October 16, 1996, the one year anniversary of the Million Man March, Spike Lee invites you to lift your head, raise your voice, and . . . get on the bus.—Movie tagline

"A powerful piece of filmmaking! Incredible uplifting, dramatically stunning and richly intense! A triumph for Spike Lee."—Ron Brewington, *American Urban Radio Network*

Box Office: $5,754,249

The historical Million Man March is the destination for a busload of African American men in Spike Lee's docu-drama, *Get On the Bus.*

Get On the Bus is Spike Lee's take on the Million Man March. This is a kind of modern pilgrimage movie. The men on the bus are not on their way to Mecca, and they do not think the march itself will be their salvation, but they do hope that the convergence of a million black men will result in a rededication of their lives. This is what Ossie Davis, playing the senior marcher on the bus, explicitly acknowledges when he begs the indulgence of his fellow travelers by offering up a prayer at the start of the journey. They are a little abashed by his overt sentiment but also touched.

Lee's pilgrims, like Chaucer's, are on the move with mixed and conflicting motivations. They are working out not just feelings about injustice, about the strengths and weaknesses of African American men, and about the failings of America, but very personal troubles. It is revealed late in the film, for example, that Ossie Davis's character feels guilty about having been an Uncle Tom. A loyal employee he took a 30% cut in pay and loss of benefits when his firm downsized. He had to literally beg for his job—and this was after a career of always being obedient, never missing a day of work, and playing the sociable, affable, colored man always amenable to white dictates. He missed Martin Luther King's March on Washington. He did not play his part in the Civil Rights crusade, and he eventually lost his job anyway—and not only his livelihood but his family as well when he turned to drink and shirked his responsibilities.

Film was independently financed by a group of African-American investors, including Danny Glover, Wesley Snipes, Johnnie L. Cochran Jr., and Spike Lee.

Thom Byrd plays a father taking his recalcitrant son to the March. The boy is literally shackled to the father's wrist for seventy-two hours. It has been ordered so by a court as the condition on which the boy (who has stolen money from a store) will be released. It gradually becomes apparent that the father is working out his own guilty feelings about having been less than an attentive parent, and the son's hostility actually grows on the trip because he believes it is too late for his father to remedy years of neglect. Father and son begin to reconcile only when the father admits he is being hard on his son because it is the only way he can be hard on himself.

Again, like Chaucer's pilgrims, each character has a story to tell. Some are on the trip just for profit—like a Memphis Lexus dealer who calls everyone nigger and is proud of his self-help Republican career. He does not acknowledge that events like marches and the civil rights movement have created the conditions in which businesses like his can thrive. When he says he is only going to Washington to make contacts and to sell cars, he is booted off the bus.

Director Lee and his fellow screenwriter, Reggie Bythewood, do an excellent job of convening this group of heterogenous African American men. But there is also more than a little earnestness and didacticism in their approach. The dialogue is too pat; the message is forced. The film is sincere but maladroit as the screenwriters try to cope with all the objections to the March. For instance, there are two scenes in which women challenge the effectiveness of a March that is reserved for men. One woman suggests the March is a kind of male fantasy in which the brothers will get together and solve things. Although *Get On the Bus* is hardly just a male fantasy, this criticism is not really examined. Or is Lee willing to let that flawed aspect of the March remain glaringly apparent? How can just men get together? Curiously no man in the movie turns the argument around by asking why women sometimes feel the need to band together in single sex organizations and groups. Instead, the men stand about, embarrassed at the women's remarks and mumbling about their need to express solidarity and to work some things out for themselves.

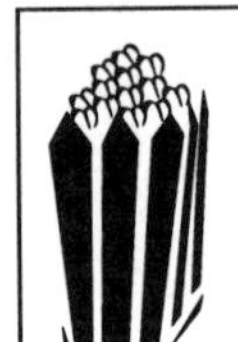

"Teenagers mess up. You know man, that's what they do best."—George

Get On the Bus is at its most forced when the bus breaks down and a new bus and replacement driver (Richard Belzer) arrives. He is white and Jewish. The men balk at boarding the bus until the bus company's black employee (Charles Dutton) cajoles them into seeing the situation as a white man chauffeuring them—a neat reversal of generations of African American subservience to white masters. Predictably, a debate ensues about African Americans and Jews. The bus driver bridles at lectures about how many Africans perished on the slave ships. Of course, he brings up the six million that died in the concentration camps. But at least Lee eschews a sentimental resolution of this conflict. The white driver refuses to carry on, asking his boss (Dutton) to "cover" for him and say he is sick. A disgusted Dutton agrees, but not before excoriating the driver for his racism. Here Lee is actually at his best. If Dutton is right about the residual racism even in rather decent white men he has worked amicably with, so is the bus driver within his rights not to drive men to a March presided over by Louis Farrakan, a notorious anti-Semite.

Farrakan, in fact, is the great missing character in this film. He is referred to several times, but the movie shows little interest in defending him. He is honored primarily for having had the idea and the wherewithal to organize the March. He is a black leader—as one of the marchers emphasizes—but not the black leader, which is a role some whites would like to pin on him in order to dismiss the aspirations of the marchers.

The bus is traveling from South Central Los Angeles and when it enters the Southern states, the movie—in a sense—holds its breath. Generations of filmgoers know all the cliches about maniacal Southern sheriffs and crude rednecks. Once again Lee does a kind of standoff, showing the good and the bad of contemporary race relations. When the black men enter a tavern, they see only white faces. Yet the whites are not so much hostile as curious. Conversations are tentative but revealing. The scene only gets embarrassing when Ossie Davis begins expatiating to an ignorant white man about black cowboys. Too often Davis, a superb actor, gets the most insufferable lines. He is too much like an urban, hip Uncle Remus. The lesson Lee so solemnly wishes to inculcate is presumably supposed to go down more easily in Davis's mellow delivery. Later the men encounter a Southern highway patrolman who looks to pin a drug case on them, but when the sniffing dog does not turn up anything, he lets the sulking men go.

Get On the Bus is rather like the proletarian fiction and movies of the 1930s. The message mongering destroys some provocative characters and scenes. Characters are made to say more than is credible. Of course, their excuse is the pilgrimage and the premise that for once in their lives they are going to level with themselves. Lee tries to strengthen the premise by making one character a budding Spike Lee. With camera in hand he exhorts stories out of the men on the bus. He is doing a film school project. But this clever ploy, like so many others, gets used up quickly.

Andre Braugher as an aspiring actor nearly saves the film from its own sentimentality. He is malevolence itself. He is anti-gay and is constantly chafing the two gay men on the bus. He is a sexist and brags about the many women he has seduced. He ridicules one of his "brothers" for being faithful to his woman, and he suggests the man is not real-

CREDITS

Jeremiah: Ossie Davis
George: Charles S. Dutton
Flip: Andre Braugher
Jamal: Gabriel Casseus
Craig: Albert Hall
Kyle: Isaiah Washington

Origin: USA
Released: 1996
Production: Reuben Cannon, Bill Borden, and Barry Rosenbush for a 40 Acres & A Mule Filmworks and 15 Black Men production; released by Columbia Pictures
Direction: Spike Lee
Screenplay: Reggie Rock Bythewood
Cinematography: Elliot Davis
Editing: Leander T. Sales
Music: Terence Blanchard
Production design: Ina Mayhew
Costume design: Sandra Hernandez
Sound: Oliver Moss
MPAA rating: R
Running Time: 122 minutes

ly black because he has a white mother. Although he riles the other men as well, they are all too noble in their efforts to defuse his provocations. Braugher finally incites one of the gay men to a fight, and he is (predictably) thrashed. The scene may appeal to an audience itching to see the actor beaten, but what is settled by the fight? Is Lee just settling for a view that sometimes the only way to deal with a villain is to knock him down?

Too many scenes like the fight seem to lack both script and director control. Where is the bus really going? What has been accomplished by the journey? Presumably these men have faced some home truths about themselves, but their struggle for understanding is constantly interrupted by movie cliches and conventions.

Get On the Bus might have benefited from a more documentary approach. Why have actors play as Marchers when so many examples of the real thing were available to Lee? Perhaps because dealing with the actual event was less tractable, less susceptible to message-shaping. Another option might have been to intercut the scripted film with witnesses to history, as Warren Beatty did in *Reds* (1981). Neither of these suggestions would necessarily have made a better film, but they are indicative of the need for a kind of tension and dialectic that is missing from *Get On the Bus.* For all the arguments and expressions of different points of view, the movie seems curiously univocal, trying too hard to prove that the Million Man March had unity and purpose. By trying so hard Lee only seems manipulative, not persuasive. And his title underlines a forcing of issues, a get with the program mentality that vitiates the power of his artistry.

REVIEWS

Boxoffice. November, 1996, p. 140.
Chicago Tribune. October 16, 1996, p. 1.
Entertainment Weekly. October 25, 1996, p. 90.
New Republic. November 4, 1996, p. 26.
New York. October 21, 1996, p. 52.
New York Times. October 16, 1996, p. C11.
Newsweek. October 28, 1996, p. 74.
People. October 28, 1996, p. 23.
Rolling Stone. October 31, 1996, p. 76.
Time. October 21, 1996.
Variety. October 8, 1996.
Village Voice. October 22, 1996, p. 73.

Getting Away With Murder

He took the law into his own hands and dropped it.—Movie tagline

Box Office: $197,322

"If you seek vengeance, dig two graves" (someone Chinese). This quote appears at the beginning of Savoy Picture's release, *Getting Away with Murder,* starring Dan Aykroyd, Lily Tomlin and Jack Lemmon. Actually, this supposed black comedy, does indeed, help dig two graves. The first one is for the now defunct Savoy Pictures and the second (hopefully) is for the concept that stories about the Holocaust and Nazi war criminals are funny.

Unfortunately, this bleak period of history provides the backdrop for this ill-conceived project, written and directed by Harvey Miller and produced by Penny Marshall and Frank Price. It seems that the "lumpy" protagonist, Jack Lambert (Dan Aykroyd) has never heard the expression "love thy neighbor." This is especially true when it is all over the television that Jack's neighbor, Max Mueller (Jack Lemmon) happens to be the infamous Nazi war criminal, Karl Luger, the dreaded "Beast of Berkau." At first, it is difficult for him to believe that this friendly, kind, old codger could possibly have committed these unspeakable horrors. Intent on finding out the truth, he begins to spy on this seemingly, good-natured gent and catches him in a revealing act of violence—beating away a harmless little squirrel. Alas, it has to be true, innocent-looking Max must be the evil Nazi, Karl Luger.

Upon making this discovery, Lambert is outraged to learn that the "Beast of Berkau" is planning to relocate to Ecuador to escape from the "unfair accusations" being made by the hounding media. According to CNN and the McLaughlin Group, 75% of the American public want Mueller/Luger dead, so Lambert must act and act quickly. He decides to take justice into his own hands and devises a scheme to poison Max by injecting arsenic into the apples growing in Max's back yard. It is difficult to ascertain how he came up with this ingenious idea—perhaps from the Biblical story about Adam and Eve. Incredibly, the plot succeeds and poor old Max goes down, as quickly as a victim from Jonestown. Feeling confident that his actions were morally commendable, Lambert goes about living his somewhat dull life, feeling revived and refreshed. However, this comes to an abrupt end when it is divulged that Max Mueller was just kindly, old Max, not the "Beast of Berkau," as was previously announced. Horrified by his premature actions, Lambert is overcome with guilt, but not enough so to confess his crime to the police. Instead, he decides to once again take measures into his own hands and punish himself for his outrageous blunder. He breaks his engagement to his one and only love, Gail (played with sweetness and charm by Bonnie Hunt), signs over all his money to Inga (Lily Tomlin), Mueller's daughter, and makes the ultimate sacrifice by marrying her. It is at this point in the already absurd story line that things become even more ludicrous and unbelievable.

When a film with such names as Lemmon, Tomlin and Aykroyd opens with no press previews, it is apparent that even the studio producing the film are none too proud. Perhaps the most glaring flaw about *Getting Away with Murder* is that it is a silly movie about an extremely serious subject. The "Springtime for Hitler" sequence of *The Producers,* directed by the mischievous Mel Brooks, succeeded mainly because of its almost surrealistic parody of these horrible events. *Getting Away with Murder* doesn't know whether it is a black comedy, a satire, or a lighthearted movie of the week. As stated by Daniel M. Kimmel of *Variety,* "the film is a mistake from start to finish."

This confused undertaking looks professional enough, as do the members of the cast. Dan Aykroyd is appropriately nerdlike and projects the proper amount of gloominess. However, he appears to be reading lines during the narration segment of the film. Jack Lemmon is also, convincing as the Nazi neighbor, but his portrayal and accent come dangerously close to becoming a caricature. As for Lily Tomlin, she is fine if she were appearing in a remake of *Judgment at Nuremberg* (1961). The portrayal of Inga was far too dark and heavy in contrast to the other players. Her body of work certainly is evidence that she can be a hilarious performer. In this project, it appeared that no one told her that she was appearing in a comedy. This mistake could either be attributed to the actress' miscalculated choices or that of the director's.

Ignoring, if in fact this is possible, the trivialization of the events that occurred in Nazi Germany, *Getting Away with Murder* does contain some funny segments. The scenes between Aykroyd and his shrink, for example, give a somewhat satirical, comic look at psychiatry in general. In an era of chemically induced personalities, it is an appropriately humorous response by Jack's doctor to respond to his patient's improved state of mental well being with "Did someone put you on Prozac?" Also, there are some bright spots in the scenes between Aykroyd and Bonnie Hunt that provide a valid and comedic look at relationships. These moments are due largely to the talent of this likeable actress.

These brief moments, however, are far too few to save the film from descending into an unfunny concoction of misconceived ideas. The film ultimately fails because of its unsuccessful attempt to combine murder and genocide with fun and frolic. If a filmmaker wishes to get laughs from an audience with these combinations, he must provide a script with razor-sharp wit and a responsible sensibility to the subject matter. *Getting Away with Murder,* unfortunately, fails on both counts.

—Rob Chicatelli

CREDITS

Jack Lambert: Dan Aykroyd
Inga Mueller: Lily Tomlin
Max Mueller/Karl Luger: Jack Lemmon
Gail Holland: Bonnie Hunt
Marty Lambert: Brian Kerwin

Origin: USA
Released: 1996
Production: Frank Price, Penny Marshall for a Parkway/Price Entertainment and Rank Film Distributors production; released by Savoy Pictures
Direction: Harvey Miller
Screenplay: Harvey Miller
Cinematography: Frank Tidy
Editing: Richard Nord
Music: John Debney
Production design: John Jay Moore
Art direction: Jeff Ginn
Costume design: Judy Gellman
Sound: Douglas Ganton, David Lee
Casting: Sheila Jaffe, Georgiane Walken
MPAA rating: R
Running Time: 92 minutes

REVIEWS

Boxoffice. July, 1996, p. 97.
Los Angeles Times. April 15, 1996, p. F8.
New York Times. April 12, 1996, p. C12.
Variety. April 15, 1996, p. 44.

The Ghost and the Darkness

Prey for the hunters.—Movie tagline

"A heart-pounding, white-knuckle adventure! A thriller of a nail-biter - leaves you breathless! Don't miss!"—Bonnie Churchill, *National News Syndicate*

"The rare Hollywood action-adventure that becomes more surprising and exotic as it moves along . . . nail-biting tension."—Janet Maslin, *The New York Times*

"A hypnotic spectacle."—Peter Travers, *Rolling Stone*

Box Office: $37,746,329

Making a movie that is based on actual events can be a dicey undertaking. Artistic interpretation will almost invariably change or alter the events to one degree or another. With *JFK* (1991), director Oliver Stone blurred the lines by mixing fact and conjecture and irritated throngs of historians with his interpretation of the events surrounding the assassination of president Kennedy. It was aesthetically breathtaking, but for many of those who weren't even alive when the event actually occurred, it has been perceived as a quasi-history lesson, with Stone's innuendo-laden celluloid serving as the text.

The stuffed remains of the two man-eating lions of Tsavo are on display at Chicago's Field Museum of Natural History.

The Ghost and the Darkness explores the bizarre events that surrounded the construction of a railroad on the plains of Africa. The film relies heavily on the book *The Man Eaters of Tsavo* written by Lt. Colonel J.H. Patterson, who is played in the movie by Val Kilmer. Patterson was an Irish engineer, commissioned by the British to construct a bridge that would connect two rail lines. According to the book, 130 or more railroad workers were killed by just two very crafty, seemingly invincible lions at the end of the 19th century. The trailers hint that these lions might have had some kind of otherworldly powers. If that's so, you certainly couldn't tell from watching the film. One scene implies that the lions could be carrying out their slaughter for another reason, but the subject is never fully explained or brought up again.

Patterson: "I'll sort this out. I will kill the lion, and I will build the bridge."
Abdullah: "Of course you will. You're white, you can do anything."

The problem with the film isn't whether or not director Stephen Hopkins has interpreted the facts correctly; he doesn't have to answer to the kind of conspiracy theorists and historians that found fault with Stone's movie. While the idea that two lions could kill that many people so easily is a bit staggering, it's not very far-fetched. The story does, after all, take place in an area inhabited by man-eating lions. Hopkins has taken material that could have been very intense and riveting and made it practically lackluster. He's made a historical action/adventure movie that lacks any noticeable punch. Watching Hopkins' previous films might explain why. His past works include *Nightmare On Elm Street 5: Dream Child* (1989), *Dangerous Game* (1990), *Predator 2* (1990), *Judgment Night* (1993), and *Blown Away* (1994). Hopkins seems almost reluctant and (even worse) incapable of ever raising the audiences' pulse. Only *Predator 2* got close to being fast-paced and it had to rely totally on an overabundance of highly graphic violent content to make up for its sophomoric script.

The casting of this film also leaves a lot to be desired. As was the case in *Blown Away,* Hopkins has American actors playing Irish characters. Jeff Bridges and Tommy Lee Jones are both very competent, highly regarded performers. While Bridges makes a feigned attempt with his accent, Jones went way over the top with his. With *The Ghost and the Darkness,* Kilmer has employed the Kevin Costner method to his interpretation: flip-flop your accents. In *Robin Hood: Prince of Thieves* (1991), Costner halfheartedly alternated between sloppy Old English and his own unspectacular American monotone, often in the same scene. It may seem inconsequential, but this small detail completely negates any suspension of disbelief. To be sure, the inclusion of the high-profile Kilmer insures a bigger box-office return. Wouldn't it simply be easier to make his character American or cast a real Irishman in the role (Liam Neeson or Stephen Rea, for example)? Vocal interpretations aside, Kilmer's meandering performance is almost a carbon copy of his equally catatonic role in *The Island of Dr. Moreau* (also reviewed in this issue).

Michael Douglas (who is also one of the film's executive producers) appears as Remington, a composite character, who doesn't make an appearance until the film's halfway point. As a freelance wild game hunter, Remington is brought in to rid the area of the lions. Douglas himself must have seen this as an excellent excuse to reprise his role of Jack Colton from the *Romancing the Stone* series. Appearing rumpled, roguish and unkempt with the trademark fedora hat and tattered

CREDITS

Charles Remington: Michael Douglas
Col. John Henry Patterson: Val Kilmer
John Beaumont: Tom Wilkinson
Samuel: John Kani
Dr. Hawthorne: Bernard Hill
Angus Starling: Brian McCardie

Origin: USA
Released: 1996
Production: Gale Anne Hurd, Paul Radin, A. Kitman Ho for a Constellation Films production; released by Paramount Pictures
Direction: Stephen Hopkins
Screenplay: William Goldman
Cinematography: Vilmos Zsigmond
Editing: Robert Brown, Steve Mirkovich
Music: Jerry Goldsmith
Production design: Stuart Wurtzel
Costume design: Ellen Mirojnick
Sound: Simon Kaye
Live-animatronic effects: Stan Wilson
Supervising animal trainer: Sled Reynolds
Casting: Mary Selway, Sarah Trevis
MPAA rating: R
Running Time: 109 minutes

vest in tow, Douglas has (probably inadvertently) parodied himself, but failed to include any of Colton's humor or snappy comebacks.

All is not lost, however. African actor/director/playwright John Kani does a good job as Samuel, who acts as the interpreter for Patterson, Remington and the British to the varied African, Muslim and Indian rail workers. Hopkins did make at least one good decision when he hired cinematographer Vilmos Zsigmond, who won an Academy Award for his work on *Close Encounters of the Third Kind* (1977). His work is of the highest quality and often lends the production a welcomed, graceful, *National Geographic* appeal.

—*J.M. Clark*

REVIEWS

Chicago Tribune. October 11, 1996, p. 4.
Entertainment Weekly. October 18, 1996, p. 55.
Los Angeles Times. October 11, 1996, p. F16.
New York Times. October 11, 1996, p. C24.
Newsweek. October 21, 1996, p. 91.
People. October 21, 1996, p. 21.
Rolling Stone. October 31, 1996, p. 78.
USA Today. October 11, 1996, p. 3D.
Variety. October 11, 1996.

Ghosts of Mississippi

In 1963 civil rights leader Medgar Evers was murdered in his own driveway. For 30 years his assassin has remained free. Is it ever too late to do the right thing?—Movie tagline

No man is above the law.—Movie tagline

"Woods is bone-chilling and Oscar-ready."—Joel Siegel, *Good Morning America*

"The year's most powerful and moving film. Woods gives a performance that deserves an Oscar."—Tom Brown, *KDNL-TV*

"Powerful and passionate! Oscar-caliber performances."—Bob Healy, *Satellite News Network*

"Brilliant and compelling! Deserves multiple Oscar nominations. A movie that every American must see!"—Pat Collins, *WWOR-TV*

Box Office: $11,775,974

Ghosts of Mississippi is based on the events leading to the conviction of Byron De La Beckwith for the murder of civil-rights leader Medgar Evers. The conviction occurred nearly thirty years after the murder. Rob Reiner's film focuses on the efforts of prosecutor Bobby DeLaughter to reopen the 1963 case that had already led to two hung juries. The film succeeds best as a courtroom drama, but it was marketed as a consciousness-raising story about race, a factor that led to some criticism for the film's shift in focus from Medgar Evers to Bobby DeLaughter.

The opening montage shows a televised address by President Kennedy on civil rights. While Kennedy's words continue on the soundtrack, Byron De La Beckwith (James Woods) hides across the street from Evers's house, ready to shoot the civil rights leader (James Pickens, Jr.) in the back with a rifle. Later Beckwith is led in handcuffs joking with police officers; during his first trial Ross Barnett, the former governor of Mississippi, walks into court to shake his hand in front of the jury. Both trials end in hung juries, but decades later the question of jury tampering raises the possibility of reopening the case. Myrlie Evers (Whoopi Goldberg), Medgar's widow, and her lawyer Morris Dees (Wayne Rogers) meet with Jackson, Mississippi, district attorney Ed Peters (Craig T. Nelson) and prosecutor Bobby DeLaughter (Alec Baldwin) about her husband's murder.

The prosecutors reasonably point out that the trail is more than cold; it has disappeared. The evidence from the original trials, including the murder weapon, is gone; city hall cannot even find a copy of the court transcript. Thinking about the case, Bobby, however, sees some similarities between himself today and Medgar Evers then: both loving fathers, both proud Mississippians, both entering the prime of promising careers. Though his wife Dixie (Virginia Madsen) and his parents warn against it, he decides to start digging. With the help of investigator Charlie Crisco (William H. Macy), Bobby eventually uncovers some evidence.

A collection of newspaper clippings leads to a former KKK member who became a paid informant for the FBI. The informant tells of hearing Beckwith appear before the Klan as an "inspirational speaker" and boast of killing Evers. Bobby also remembers that evidence in concluded trials sometimes becomes souvenirs for the officers of the court. His own father-in-law presided over Beckwith's most recent trial, and Bobby finds the murder weapon in a search of the judge's den. Though he makes weekly phone calls to Myrlie Evers to report on his progress, he withholds this news, he says, so that no leak will jeopardize his work.

The middle scenes of the film focus on the mounting pressure on Bobby at home and at work. His wife Dixie, aptly named, decides to leave Bobby and their children because of the embarrassment his work on the Beckwith case will cause her in Jackson society. Bobby's son also hears his schoolmates insult his father. At work, Ed Peters feels that Bobby is devoting too much time to the Beckwith case at the expense of his other work and tells him he wants to give the case to a different prosecutor.

The progression of these scenes indicates that Lewis Colick has written a script resulting in mostly a dialogue-driven motion picture. Many scenes show characters sharing important information as they walk to or from buildings. Other scenes take place in offices as characters sit and discuss the case. Most of Bobby's scenes with Myrlie Evers are telephone conversations. Though this talkiness produces a film that in its first half is visually dull, in the concluding trial scenes the emphasis on dialogue combines nicely with some effective depth-of-field camera shots to create some dramatic moments.

The morality-tale nature of the script may also lead to the narrow range of the actors' performances. The central characters are each depicted with one chief personality trait. Whoopi Goldberg stresses the dignity of Myrlie Evers to such an extent she may jeopardize a fuller picture of her character's humanity. Alec Baldwin's role calls for sincerity and niceness to a degree that may diminish the believability of Bobby DeLaughter. This quality emerges most clearly in the scenes with his children, including one with his daughter when he decides that she should not sing "Dixie" anymore. James Woods, playing the villain, has the most fun with his role. When the defense attorney establishes that an unfriendly witness has a history of emotional problems, the camera catches Woods in the background maliciously rolling his eyes in front of the spectators to discredit the witness further. Woods's performance as Byron De La Beckwith is entertaining in its extremes, though the role is a relatively small one.

The most honest scenes in the film depict the way this case brings home to Bobby a realization of the gulf between the races. In one scene, Bobby's father tells him that Mississippi may be legally integrated but it is still "emotionally segregated." Later, after a bomb threat has forced Bobby to move his family to a hotel for the night, he tells his new

CREDITS

Bobby DeLaughter: Alec Baldwin
Myrlie Evers: Whoopi Goldberg
Byron De La Beckwith: James Woods
Ed Peters: Craig T. Nelson
Charlie Crisco: William H. Macy
Medgar Evers: James Pickens, Jr.
Dixie DeLaughter: Virginia Madsen
Claire DeLaughter: Alexa Vega
Morris Dees: Wayne Rogers

Origin: USA
Released: 1996
Production: Rob Reiner for Castle Rock Entertainment and Columbia Pictures; released by Sony Pictures Entertainment
Direction: Rob Reiner
Screenplay: Lewis Colick
Cinematography: John Seale
Editing: Robert Leighton
Production design: Lilly Kilvert
Art direction: Christopher Burian-Mohn
Costume design: Gloria Gresham
Music: Mark Shaiman
MPAA rating: PG-13
Running Time: 123 minutes

AWARDS AND NOMINATIONS

Academy Award 1996 Nominations: Best Supporting Actor (Woods), Best Makeup
Golden Globe Award 1997 Nominations: Best Supporting Actor (Woods)

bride Claire (Alexa Vega) that his father was right. They have no black friends, they do not socialize with blacks, and they sit apart from blacks at church. He even considers dropping the case, but a drive (along Medgar Evers Boulevard) to the crime scene reminds him again of his similarities with Evers.

These brief scenes get under the surface of Bobby's motives to retry Byron De La Beckwith and reveal more of what he is like. Best of all, they touch on the sense of racial guilt felt by whites and suggest, whether intentionally or not on the part of the filmmakers, that some of Bobby's reasons for pursuing the case, in spite of his assertions about the parallels between Evers and himself, are based in conscience cleansing. At one point he walks out of a movie to place a frantic call to Myrlie Evers, begging her not to have him removed from the case. This scene registers more fully when viewed in the light of both Bobby's urge for justice and his shared sense of guilt. Walking home with Claire, he complains about Myrlie's apparent unwillingness to assist him, and Claire rightly points out that if he did not trust Myrlie enough to tell her about the discovery of the murder weapon, he should not be surprised that she is reluctant to trust him now with continuing the case. Similarly, filmmakers Reiner and Colick, thinking along traditional Hollywood lines, have not entrusted a story about injustice to blacks to a black protagonist. (At the plot level, however, the film seems to want it both ways: though she hangs up on Bobby's phone call out of a supposed sense of yet another betrayal by the system, Myrlie is sufficiently impressed by his determination to give him her copy of the trial transcript enabling his work to continue. This becomes the turning point of the film.)

Perhaps because scenes like these are so few, reviews often faulted the film for paying so little attention to the life and work of Medgar Evers. Many reviewers criticized the filmmakers for structuring the narrative around Bobby DeLaughter and his struggles rather than Medgar Evers and his. Some of their language hit hard. Writing on the editorial pages of *USA Today,* DeWayne Wickham said, "What they've done is an act of cinematic cowardice. They've taken a story about the pain and suffering of a black family and turned it into a film about the pain and suffering of a white family. . . . This movie could have helped bridge the gap of understanding between blacks and whites. Instead, it widens the rift." In *Variety,* Godfrey Chesire pointed out "When future generations turn to this era's movies for an account of the struggles for racial justice in America, they'll learn the surprising lesson that such battles were fought and won by square-jawed white guys." Roger Ebert also quoted this passage in his review of the film. Critics variously mentioned *Cry Freedom* (1987) and *Mississippi Burning* (1988) as other films guilty to a lesser extent of the same skewed focus.

These comments by reviewers may have some validity when one considers the 1995 book *Ghosts of Mississippi* by journalist Maryanne Vollers. This book more fully tells the story of the assassination of Evers in the context of his life and work. Vollers only gets to the Evers murder in the fourteenth of twenty-eight chapters; Bobby DeLaughter enters her chronicle in chapter twenty-two. The title appears to be the closest similarity between book and film. Both have looked at the same historical events, and Vollers has produced the more complete, balanced account. Her book was a finalist for the National Book Award. The filmmakers designed essentially a smoothly-made courtroom drama about the legal and emotional difficulties of resurrecting a racial murder case nearly thirty years old.

—*Glenn Hopp*

REVIEWS

Boxoffice. February, 1997, p. 63.
Entertainment Weekly. January 10, 1997, p. 41.
Los Angeles Times. December 20, 1996, p. F1.
People Weekly. January 13, 1997, p. 20.
Time. December 30, 1996, p. 140.
USA Today. December 24, 1996, p. 13A.
Variety. December 16, 1996, p. 78.
Wall St. Journal. December 20, 1996, p. A14.

Giant

Box Office: $177,909

George Stevens' classic film *Giant*, re-released in 1996 in a restored Technicolor print in honor of its 40th anniversary, remains a true American epic. Based on Edna Ferber's best-selling novel and starring Elizabeth Taylor, Rock Hudson, and James Dean, *Giant* spans three generations of the wealthy Texan family, the Benedicts, while also examining the transition of Texas from its cattle-ranching heritage to its rich oil-drilling present.

It's a long film at 202 minutes, yet it's a movie ambitious in both scale and grandeur. Everything's bigger in Texas, it's said, and in this, *Giant* does not disappoint. The audience is roped in with the late Golden Era star-power of the three leads. Hudson does the best work of his career as Texas rancher Bick Benedict, who sweeps Taylor's Eastern-born beauty Leslie right off of her feet and brings her home to Reata, his ancestral 595,000-acre spread. And, of course, there's the legendary Dean as cowhand turned oilman Jett Rink.

Both Hudson and Taylor are convincing as a married couple who love each other deeply and struggle with the challenges of the changing times. Over the decades the liberal Leslie urges her chauvinistic husband towards more humane, expansive viewpoints, and eventually gets him to develop a social conscience. Hudson, usually remembered for his appealing work in light, romantic comedies, is perfectly cast here as the handsome, rugged, fair-minded, and principled patriarch of Reata. His towering presence lends instant credibility to this position of stature and authority. This part was to remain Hudson's favorite film role of his career up until the day he died.

Taylor's Leslie is also believable as the aristocratic Virginian who takes to Texas and manages to hold her own against not only her husband, but the macho mentality of Texas as well. Upon her arrival at Reata, Leslie is confronted by Bick's domineering sister, Luz (Mercedes McCambridge), who feels that Bick betrayed her and Reata by bringing home an Eastern bride. Luz is resentful of Leslie and everything she represents. Unfortunately, as fate would have it, Luz ends up getting killed when she's thrown from a wild horse that she insisted upon riding. Luz gets revenge on Bick and Leslie when her will reveals that she left a small plot of land to cowhand Jett Rink, who soon discovers oil on his property and becomes a multimillionaire.

It has been noted that Stevens' first choice for the role of Leslie was not Taylor, but the cool blonde Grace Kelly. When she proved unavailable, he opted for the violet-eyed Taylor instead who had just given an incredible performance in Stevens' *A Place in the Sun* (1951). It was a wise choice on Stevens' behalf as Taylor's professional demeanor became a mainstay on the set. It is hard to picture Kelly in the role today, as Taylor really made it her own. Astonishingly beautiful in this film, Taylor ages so gracefully from a young bride to a grandmother that it's hard to believe she was only 23-years-old when *Giant* was made.

Most directors choose older actors and age them down for the young parts of the picture, but director Stevens chose two 23-year-olds (Taylor and Dean) and the 28-year-old Hudson and had them age upward. He also made a conscious effort in filling the key roles by using actors who had not already been typecast in westerns. Clearly, Stevens did no wrong in casting the three young, but extremely talented leads, who more than matched the material.

Giant is notable as a film that was clearly ahead of its time not only in featuring an independent female protagonist at least a decade before feminism became a movement, but in presenting the race relations theme too. Although it seems somewhat dated today, *Giant*'s handling of the discrimination of Mexican Americans was accurate for the times and Stevens laid it on pretty thick back in the conservative '50s.

In fact, one of Leslie's main causes is to ensure that the Mexican cowboys and their families who work at Reata have decent living conditions and proper medical care, much to the consternation of Bick. This all changes years later when the Benedicts' own son Jordy (Dennis Hopper) marries a Latina and produces a grandson of mixed race. Bick's change in at-

Giant, the final film of pop icon James Dean, was re-released in honor of its 40th anniversary.

titude is best illustrated in the humorous diner scene that takes place near the end of the film. When a Mexican family is refused service by the diner owner, Bick is outraged and stages a protest that turns into a brutal fight. Although he ends up losing the brawl, Bick gains greater love and respect from his family.

James Dean's character, Jett Rink, was based on the prominent oilman Glenn McCarthy.

Giant might not be remembered so much today if it weren't for the fact that it was Dean's last screen appearance. Dean's untimely death from an auto accident came just days after completing work on *Giant.* He never saw a finished print of his third and final film. The moody actor had already caused a sensation in *East of Eden* and by the time *Rebel Without a Cause* and *Giant* were released, posthumously, Dean had already become immortal.

It is near impossible to take your eyes off of Dean when he's on-screen. He's mesmerizing as Jett Rink, the poor, sympathetic ranch hand who becomes a Texas oil tycoon. One only wishes he had more screen time in this picture. As Michael Wilmington of the *Chicago Tribune* noted, "wily, graceful, impudent and dangerous, Dean compels absolute attention—whether measuring off his land in those gigantic-ecstatic steps or taking the measure of co-stars Taylor and Hudson with his sly smile."

Dean expertly conveys the vulnerability of Jett Rink as an outsider at Reata, who is at once resentful of Bick, yet hopelessly in love with Leslie. Even after he strikes oil on his little piece of land and becomes much richer than the Benedict family, Jett still doesn't fit in as he's the embodiment of nouveau riche, whereas the Benedict clan is steeped in tradition and old money. Ironically, it is Jett Rink that all of Texas is coming to honor in a huge banquet near the end, not Bick Benedict. Jett, heartbroken over his unrequited love for Leslie, gets so drunk that he passes out at the very moment thousands of people have gathered to pay tribute to him.

The antagonistic relationship between Dean and Stevens has by now almost achieved legendary proportions. Stevens' method of filming each scene from many different angles and Dean's theory of "method" acting often clashed. Although relations between star and director were tense, Stevens' did offer praise for his volatile lead actor. In "The Actor Jimmy Dean" (*Screen Stories,* November 1956), Stevens' stated the following "As an actor, Jimmy had the ability to reach people with movement. Using himself as a kind of clay, he could mold psychological impediments into his speech and into his movements . . . Instinctively, he seemed to understand all the impediments people have when they try to communicate with each other. He never gave Jett Rink one easy moment unless Jett had been drinking heavily . . . At [the time of] his death he was not yet as good an actor as he might have become, but he had already managed to achieve performances that other and more experienced performers would not hesitate to be proud of."

Although *Giant*'s reputation is closely linked with the Dean connection, Stevens must be given much of the credit. It was Stevens' first independent film after a career of working for the studios and he made all the major decisions for *Giant.* Exercising near-total artistic freedom as the film's co-producer and part-owner, Stevens was at his career peak when he directed this sincere and heartfelt film. The distinguished director started out the decade with *A Place in the Sun* (1951) and ended it with *The Diary of Anne Frank* (1959). *Giant* came right in the middle of the decade and Stevens totally immersed himself in the production. He later recalled that it was one of the hardest projects he'd ever undertaken.

After two years of intense preparation, Stevens labored diligently during the production of *Giant.* It was not an easy shoot by any means, with the fractious relations on the set and the lengthy production shoot in the tiny town of Marfa, Texas, about 200 miles southeast of El Paso. Principle photography lasted for 114 days—37 days over schedule and $5.4 million over budget. When postproduction started Stevens and the editors were left with 890,000 feet of film in the can. George Stevens Jr., who had worked with his father on script development before leaving for a stint in the Air Force, returned to help trim the footage.

CREDITS

Leslie Lynnton Benedict: Elizabeth Taylor
Bick Benedict: Rock Hudson
Jett Rink: James Dean
Luz Benedict (the older): Mercedes McCambridge
Vashti Snythe: Jane Withers
Uncle Bawley Benedict: Chill Wills
Luz Benedict (the younger): Carroll Baker
Jordan Benedict III: Dennis Hopper
Juana Benedict: Elsa Cardenas
Judy Benedict: Fran Bennett
Angel Obregon: Sal Mineo

Origin: USA
Released: 1956
Production: George Stevens and Henry Ginsberg; released by Warner Bros.
Direction: George Stevens
Screenplay: Fred Guiol and Ivan Moffat; based on the book of the same name by Edna Ferber
Cinematography: William C. Mellor
Editing: William Hornbeck, Philip W. Anderson, and Fred Bohanen
Music: Dimitri Tiomkin
Running Time: 202 minutes

One of the areas in which Stevens excels is in the way he captures the course of age and change. Stevens took great pains with detail, as illustrated by the changing decor of the Benedict mansion whose styles change from the '30s to the '50s, and the evolving of the costumes as well. The importance of details is also exemplified in the day-to-day workings of the Reata ranch and in the demanding labor of Dean's oil drilling. Besides Stevens' first-rate directing, the cinematography of William Mellor is excellent as is the musical score composed by Russian-American Dimitri Tiomkin.

When *Giant* premiered in Texas on Oct. 10, 1956, it was an immediate success. It was the third highest grossing film of the year and it won Stevens a second Oscar for Best Direction. (He won his first with *A Place in the Sun.*) Altogether *Giant* was nominated for 10 Academy Awards, including best actor nominations for both Dean and Hudson and a supporting actress nomination for McCambridge.

Under the supervision of Stevens' son, George Stevens Jr., *Giant*'s color and contrast have been painstakingly restored on the original negative via Technicolor's dye-transfer process. It's the first time in decades that this method has been used and it's resulted in a vast improvement in the picture's sharpness and grain. The restored version of *Giant* also features a revamped soundtrack that is as good as the original.

In an interview in the *Los Angeles Times/Calendar,* Stevens Jr. remarks on the importance of a film's longevity to Stevens Sr.: "He [Stevens] always had this idea for a film to be the kind of film he wanted to make, he wanted it to be something that would live."

Well, Stevens Sr. would be pleased to know that *Giant,* his career masterpiece, has not only stood the "test of time," but remains a broadly appealing film that is just as entertaining today as it was when it was released 40 years ago.

—Beth Fhaner

REVIEWS

American Cinematographer. October, 1996.
Chicago Tribune. October 4, 1996, p. 2.
Detroit Free Press. October 4, 1996, p. 8E.
Los Angeles Times. September 27, 1996, p. F10.
Los Angeles Times/Calendar. September 29, 1996.
New York Times. September 29, 1996, p. H15, 26-27.

Girl 6

When she puts love on the line, you'll always come back for more.—Movie tagline

"Cheerfully freewheeling! A high-energy party!"—Janet Maslin, *New York Times*

"Downright hilarious! One of Spike Lee's best!"—Dennis Dermody, *Paper Magazine*

"Sexy and sassy."—Dan Cox, *Time Out*

"Deliciously wicked!"—Paul Wunder, *WBAI Radio*

Box Office: $4,939,000

Spike Lee is a filmmaker who loves films and the filmmaking process. He shows this passion with his manipulation of various film stocks, use of color filters, provocative camera angles and placement of music throughout each of his films. Lee is truly a visionary artist. Sometimes his techniques are successful, as in such classics as *She's Gotta Have It* (1985) and *Do the Right Thing* (1988). But in Lee's latest, *Girl 6,* the artistry complicates and distracts what could have been a thought-provoking film.

Lee is no stranger to controversial subject matter. *Girl 6* looks at the business of phone sex through the eyes of a struggling actress looking for her voice in acting. Lee does level his taboo subjects with humor, and *Girl 6* claims to be a straight-out comedy. But with such an often seedy foray into sex and sexuality, the humor in *Girl 6* is hard to come by.

At the film's center is Girl 6 (Theresa Randle). She's a struggling New York actress who isn't having much luck finding a role that utilizes her talents. An embarrassing audition with a hotshot director named Q.T. (Quentin Tarantino), who requests that she show her breasts, sends Girl 6 her first introductory lesson on the importance of

AWARDS AND NOMINATIONS

Independent Spirit Awards 1997 Nominations:
First Screenplay (Parks)

her sexuality. Offended by the request, Girl 6 storms out of the audition, but instead of sympathy and encouragement, she is rejected by both her agent (John Turturro) and acting coach, and is simply told to grow up.

Hungry, broke, and desperate, Girl 6 turns to the fast and safe money of phone sex work with a lucrative company. She is taken in by the mother hen known as Boss #1 (Jenifer Lewis), and trained in the ways of satisfying a man sexually over the phone. With her first caller, a Texas millionaire, she successfully brings the man to ecstasy with her voice and words. Congratulated by her peers and mentor, Girl 6 begins her own personal odyssey which leads her to a blurred judgement between fantasy and reality. The fact that she has become a popular staple with the company helps propel her further. Girl 6 seems proud of her success with her new job, and doesn't hesitate to insist that what she is doing is still acting. This question comes up often with Girl 6 and her neighbor Jimmy (Spike Lee). He expresses his dislike of Girl 6's new occupation and ponders her obsession over her success. Is it acting? Most definitely, to Girl 6, and she is good at it. One of her regulars is named Bob (Peter Berg), who initially calls to talk about his relationship with his dying mother. Every week, he calls, until he suggests a meeting with Girl 6 in person at Coney Island. Bob Regular is a no-show, which, for reasons unknown, sends Girl 6 into a spiralling downfall. Lee and screenwriter Suzan-Lori Parks don't bother to explore why Bob stood her up, or why she seemed so attached to him in the first place.

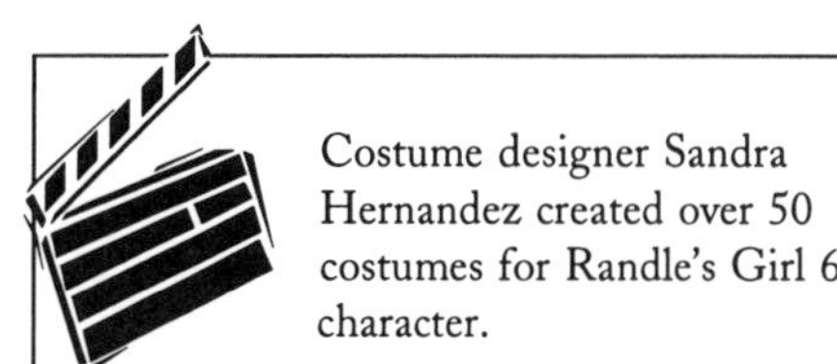
Costume designer Sandra Hernandez created over 50 costumes for Randle's Girl 6 character.

Soon, Girl 6 is creating her own phone sex fixation which begins to shut out the men in her life who really care about her; Jimmy, and an ex-husband who yearns for his suddenly sensual ex-wife. Girl 6's erotic world becomes a nightmare when a crazy, sadistic caller turns their phone conversations into a masochistic journey, and soon wants his fantasy of torture to become reality when he reveals that he knows where she lives. Terrified, Girl 6 runs to Jimmy's apartment for safety. With a snap of the finger, she decides to go to L.A. and rediscover her acting roots.

Spike Lee chose well to use the songs of Prince to accentuate the sexuality of the film and subject matter. Songs such as "Erotic City," "The Screams of Passion," and "How Come You Don't Call Me Anymore" highlight scenes which explore the many stages these women go through to perform and satisfy their customers.

Theresa Randle also was an exceptional choice for the lead character. Only having supporting roles in such films as *Sugar Hill* (1993) and *Bad Boys* (1994), Randle shines as the talented, yet misguided, struggling actress. How do we know that she's talented? Well, because Lee has her disguised as different famous African American actresses. With the proper makeup and wig, she becomes Dorothy Dandridge, Pam Grier, and the actress from the TV series "Good Times" in dream sequences that seem to celebrate the talents of these women. Just like her character, Girl 6, Theresa Randle is a sexy, gifted chameleon, and carries the entire film rather triumphantly, despite a weak plot.

There are many cameos in this film, which include Quentin and Madonna, who seem to be playing characters similar to their own celebrity personas, as well as those who make fun of their celebrity persona as supermodel Naomi Campbell does by wearing a "Models Suck" t-shirt. One of the major distractions in the film is an amateur quality to its storytelling. A subplot about a young girl falling down a well seems to pop up out of nowhere, and Girl 6 is suddenly entranced by the new story. With Lee's constant spiral shots down a cemented well, we don't need to be hit with a mallet to know that this is Lee's way of introducing symbolism to his audience. The truly manipulative spiral shots represent Girl 6's downfall into semi-madness, but it also shows how Spike Lee should learn the meaning of the word subtle.

Girl 6, with its pretty colors, high definition video shots, and sexy tunes, is nice to look at and listen to, but with a presentation similar to a film student's first experimental feature film, much is taken away from whatever message it may

CREDITS

Girl 6: Theresa Randle
Shoplifter: Isaiah Washington
Jimmy: Spike Lee
Boss #1: Jenifer Lewis
Girl 39: Debi Mazar

Origin: USA
Released: 1996
Production: Spike Lee for a 40 Acres and a Mule Filmworks production; released by Fox Searchlight
Direction: Spike Lee
Screenplay: Suzan-Lori Parks
Cinematography: Malik Hassan Syeed
Editing: Sam Pollard
Production design: Ina Mayhew
Set decoration: Paul R. Weathered
Costume design: Sandra Hernandez
Sound: Allan Byer
Casting: Aisha Coley
Music: The Artist formerly known as Prince
MPAA rating: R
Running Time: 107 minutes

have on sex, sensuality, and the means of presenting it, be it over the phone, on TV, movie screen or stage. Spike should have gone the dramatic route with *Girl 6;* maybe a much better film would have resulted, instead of this novice effort, which is a surprise from a seasoned film director such as Lee.

—*Michelle Banks*

REVIEWS

Chicago Tribune. March 22, 1996. p.5.
The Detroit News. March, 1996.
Entertainment Weekly. April 5, 1996. p.55-56.
Los Angeles Times. March 22, 1996. p. F14.
New York Times. March 22, 1996. p. C3.
Newsweek. March 25, 1995. p.72
Rolling Stone. April 18, 1996. p. 77.
USA Today. March 22, 1996. p. 4D.
Variety. March 18, 1996. p. 47.
The Village Voice. March 26, 1996. p. 47.

Girls Town

This ain't no 90210 . . . —Movie tagline

"Powerful, thought-provoking! Lili Taylor's performance is brilliant even by her standards!"—Peter Keough, *Boston Phoenix*

"The sassiest movie I've ever seen! The best, most honest movie about teenage girls."—Jane Pratt, *Sassy Magazine*

"A powerhouse! Pure exhilaration! *Girls Town* is a keeper."—Peter Travers, *Rolling Stone*

Box Office: $503,667

It is senior year in high school, and Patti (Lili Taylor), Emma (Anna Grace), Angela (Bruklin Harris), and Nikki (Aunjanue Ellis) know that their foursome is about to break up. Nikki, a sensitive black girl, has been accepted at Princeton, and Emma her closest friend and white counterpart will be going to Columbia. Exactly what feisty Angela is going to do is not certain, and Patti has never been a good student. Unmarried with a child by an abusive boyfriend, she is a great mechanic but doubts that the local carshop would hire a girl. They all feel rather tentative about their lives and are struggling to cope with the impending changes.

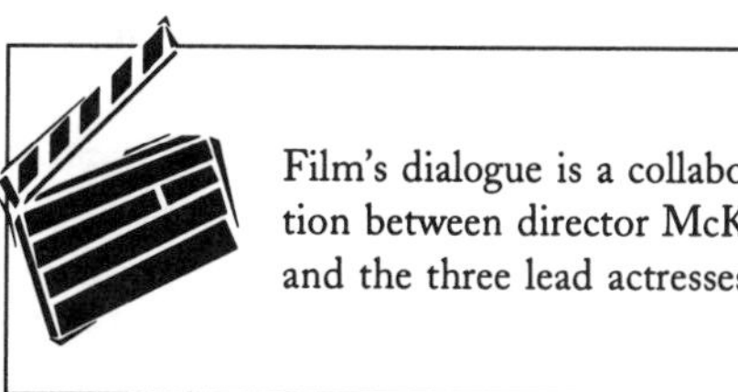

Film's dialogue is a collaboration between director McKay and the three lead actresses.

Girls Town presents its characters authentically. The film does not feel scripted. There is no forcing of plot or theme—other than the girls' hassles living in a male-dominated world. Patti cannot walk in the park without being harassed by a male park employee. Disgusted, she goes up to him and tells him off. Like her friends, she is aching to find some way to assert herself in a world that sees women mainly as objects. To make the point this way, however, suggests that the film is strident on the subject of feminism. It is not. Rather it powerfully shows how demeaning many women's lives still are, and how unthinking many men are.

The film opens with shots of Nikki walking down the street. She looks troubled and aloof. In an early scene, she is stretched out on a bed with Emma, joking about what college will be like. Emma asks her if she has sent in her housing application. Nikki says so, and a surprised Emma joshes her friend, saying they will probably find a place for Nikki in the kitchen—perhaps in a pasta pot. But Emma senses something is wrong. Nikki, an inveterate journal keeper, tries to relieve the tension by tracing Emma's hand in her diary and having her write a little message. The anxious Emma keeps repeating how much she is going to miss Nikki.

The next day the girls wait for Nikki to join them on their ritual walk to school. She does not show up. When they get to school, they learn that Nikki has committed suicide. They are stunned. Angela is angry. How could Nikki do such a thing, not only to herself, but to them? Patti is devastated because she had no idea her friend was suffering that much. Emma seems less surprised that Nikki should have hidden her feelings. As it turns out, Emma also has a secret that she will share with her friends only after they visit Nikki's mother.

The girls visit Nikki's mother to express their condolences but also because they just have to know why their friend killed herself. Nikki's mother won't say or even indicate if Nikki left any sort of explanation. As the girls awkwardly try to deal with this uncooperative parent, Emma excuses herself and goes to the bathroom. When the girls press their questions, Nikki's mother rises and shows them to the door just as Emma is coming down the stairs. She has stolen Nikki's diary.

Back at Patti's place, they discover the truth about Nikki's rape. Now Angela is really angry. This is exactly the kind of thing Nikki should have confided in her friends. Patti looks scared. If this kind of thing could happen to one of her closet friends without Patti's knowing anything about it, then how can she believe she knows anyone close to her? Emma defends Nikki. Angela attacks Emma for excusing Nikki's silence. Emma retaliates, asking how well they really know each other and if they are actually facing up to what is going on in their lives. When Patti seems to side with Angela, Emma points out Patti's vulnerability. Why does she put up with a boyfriend who beats her? It is not that bad, Patti retorts. Oh, then there is a level of abuse that is tolerable? Emma asks. Realizing, however, that her defense of Nikki has alienated her friends, Emma explains what is behind her argument. She too has been raped and said nothing. And that is the point: why do all these women put up with male abuse? Why are they silent? Even Angela, who believes she is in control of her life, tacitly accepts the notion that they have condoned male chauvinism.

So what can they do about their plight? At the very least, they can begin to speak up and refuse to play the role of victims. They are incited to action when they see the car of a male student rapist. They trash it, scratching the paint, kicking off a side view mirror, puncturing the tires, bashing in a window with a brick. Emma spray paints the word rapist on the car's hood.

There is nothing melodramatic about the scene. It is a spontaneous overflow of bottled up feelings, a rage that has been previously expressed in the school lavatory, where the girls scrawl messages about the most abusive boys. Now their aim is not just destruction but to show just how angry they are. In a more conventional film, the girls would surely be in more physical danger. Where is the obligatory scene where they get beaten up by an avenging male? The closest *Girls Town* comes to such a scene is after Patti and her friends steal her boyfriend's stereo equipment and television and pawn it, using the money for her kid. Her angry boyfriend shows up at her basement room and threatens to hit her, but she fiercely backs him down, pointing to the child sleeping in a playpen. That is where the pawnshop money went, she tells him. She is through with him, she says. He leaves in a rage. It is not the end of the story for Patti, and she knows it. Later, she sobs her heart out to Angela. Patti is right to be scared. What will happen to her in a working class neighborhood that does not like to see a woman do better at fixing cars than men? In a film distinguished by fine ensemble acting, Lili Taylor is memorable for her toughness and sensitivity. Her performance is so seamless that it does not seem like a performance.

Males are not merely villains in this film, although they are part of a problem that most of them do not even recognize. A case in point is Emma's boyfriend, Dylan (Guillermo Diaz). He is hurt because Emma is pulling away from him, not answering his calls, and leaving him wondering what to do with his weekends. He is reproachful, but he is also puzzled. The trouble is he is just too conventional. He is no male chauvinist brute, but he has no imagination. He can only respond negatively to the girls' violence. The whole school knows what they did to the car, and he seems more troubled by that than the fact that the girls were publicly exposing a rapist. Dylan reminds Emma that she is destined for Columbia. Is this the way she should behave? His inability to even begin to ask her the right questions about her feelings dooms their relationship. When he says he does not deserve to be treated so negligently, Emma agrees, as if accepting that by his standards she has behaved badly. But they are no longer her standards, and he shows no interest in discovering what her values are.

CREDITS

Patti Lucci: Lili Taylor
Emma: Anna Grace
Angela: Bruklin Harris
Nikki: Aunjanue Ellis
Dylan: Guillermo Diaz
Eddie: John Ventimiglia

Origin: USA
Released: 1996
Production: Lauren Zalaznick for a C-Hundred Film Corp and Boomer Pictures production; released by October Films
Direction: Jim McKay
Screenplay: Jim McKay, Denise Casano, Anna Grace
Bruklin Harris Lili Taylor
Cinematography: Russell Lee Fine
Editing: Jim McKay, Alex Hall
Production design: Carolyn Grifel
Sound: Charles R. Hunt, Rob Larrea, Irin Strauss, Gus Koven
Casting: Adrienne Stern
MPAA rating: R
Running Time: 90 minutes

AWARDS AND NOMINATIONS

Independent Spirit Awards 1997 Nominations:
Supporting Actress (Taylor)

Numerous shots of Patti, Emma, and Angela in the school dugout (one of their favorite meeting places) emphasize just how isolated they are—not just from males but from many of the other girls as well. *Girls Town* does not cheat; the dugout is like Patti's basement: a refuge but also a place of despair. Just because they have each other and have asserted themselves is not enough to overcome their appalling sense of humiliation. When Angela is suspended from school for getting into a fight with two girls who stick up for the rapist whose car Angela helped to trash, she confronts her angry mother who points out the self-defeating consequences of violence. How does it help Angela to be suspended from school? A sullen Angela says it felt to good to hit back. Does it feel good now? her mother asks. The film is very sympathetic to Angela, but even Angela knows that violence is hardly a solution.

Yet this remarkably unpreachy film is not through with violence. Its denouement is a confrontation between Nikki's rapist, Richard, and the avenging girls. They catch him out on the street after work, and he tries to convince them there has been a misunderstanding. But the evidence of Nikki's diary is plain and the girls attack, throwing Richard to the ground. As he grabs a leg in pain, they denounce him.

But then it is back to the dugout, listening to the sound of the train, wondering what to do next, wondering what their lives will amount to, and leaving us with a final image of the passing train that evokes their own lives, in transition.

—*Carl Rollyson*

REVIEWS

Boxoffice. April, 1996, p. 113.
The New York Times. August 21, 1996.
Variety. January 29, 1996, p. 63.
Village Voice. August 27, 1996, p. 56.

The Glimmer Man

Two good cops. One bad situation.—Movie tagline

" . . . punchy macho entertainment with Seagal in top form."—Peter Stack, *San Francisco Chronicle*

Box Office: $20,404,841

In Steven Seagal's latest action thriller, Seagal's character Jack Cole didn't start out as a cop. The mystery behind his past can be considered a mirror to Steven Seagal's own personal past, as he alleges that he worked for the CIA before pursuing an acting career. His rise as an action star was rather meteoric after his starring role in his first film, *Above the Law* (1988), and his superstar status was confirmed with the box office success of *Under Siege* (1992). After a series of vengeance films—some worked, others didn't, including his last two, *On Deadly Ground* (1994) and *Under Siege 2* (1995)—some reworking on his character image had to be done. The result is the lackluster *The Glimmer Man,* which has Seagal as a New York Cop transferred to Los Angeles to help solve a string of serial murders done by a killer nicknamed the Family Man. But unlike Seagal's other films, *The Glimmer Man* has him paired with a partner, Detective Jim Campbell (Keenen Ivory Wayans). The pairing, naturally, is like oil and vinegar, or in this case, Cole is not the ying to Campbell's yang.

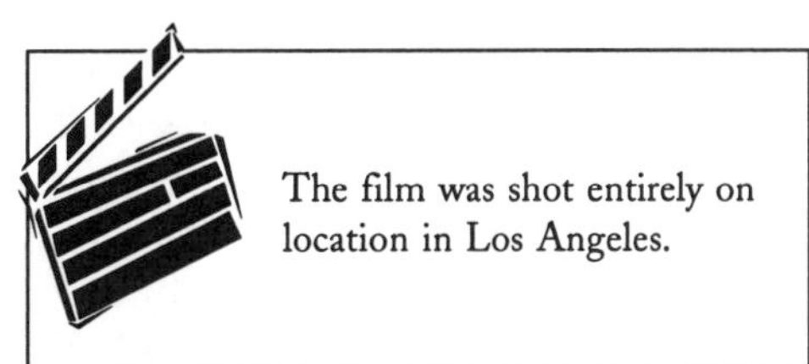

The film was shot entirely on location in Los Angeles.

The Family Man killer is given that dubious and sinister name for the way he kills families, by shooting them and crucifying them on crosses. This revelation is about all there is to the knowledge of the killer, since this film has other matters to contend with. It has to juggle the partnership of Cole and Campbell, and Cole's own mysterious past.

The film begins with Cole saving a suicidal teen from shooting up a school. It turns out that the youngster is the stepson of a powerful and wealthy participant in a half-baked scheme involving the Russian mob and the selling of chemical weapons, which leads to Campbell and the audience finding out what secrets Jack Cole has been hiding.

Even before his past is brought into light, we sense Jack Cole is not your average cop, or person for that matter. He wears a ponytail, sports an Indian Nehru jacket and prayer beads, and visits a Chinese herbalist. He oozes Zen calm in the most tense circumstances such as the confrontation with the suicidal teen in the beginning of the film, and in a face-off with a group of Russian ruffians. In this scene Seagal speaks a line that no one would ever imagine, but it's all part of that image change. He turns to partner Campbell and claims, "I can't fight." Campbell and the audience are stunned for a moment, but we know better than to believe Seagal. Sure enough, he wipes out the group with a razor blade embedded inside a credit card. Seagal elaborates, "It's not that I can't fight, it's just against my religion." The scene isn't funny because Seagal is not a comedic actor.

The film tries hard to become a suspenseful thriller, but the effort is not fruitful since it leads to implausibility. After the serial killer murders Cole's ex-wife and her husband, Cole becomes not only a suspect in the murders, but *the* suspect, as his prints are found on his ex-wife's body. Since Cole's ex-wife is not introduced into the story line until her murder, how exactly did his prints end up on her body? You don't have to be from an FBI Quantico division to figure out that Cole is not the killer, but his superiors, and even his partner, seem to think otherwise. Cole obviously is not the killer, but because of the dry delivery of such a plot twist, you don't care. When the explanation is given for this copycat murder, and when the real Family Man is apprehended, you are left with a serious deficit in your excitement and entertainment quotient.

The Glimmer Man is purely a formula film that wanted to stray from the formula, and that was a mistake. For an action picture, there was the suspicion (a.k.a. talking) built over Cole's character that confiscated time devoted toward a nominal amount of action. There is the usual scene with Seagal wrecking an Italian restaurant (it must be in his contract to demolish an eating establishment). The fight sequences are edited so fast, all you really see and hear are Seagal's hands moving, then bodies landing on the floor.

For any action movie to work, the villain has to compose a level of threat, even if the hero is as invincible as Steven Seagal. Here, you have a weak caricature of a wealthy financier, Frank Deverell (Bob Gunton), commanding one of his henchmen to take care of things while he sips brandy in his Lazyboy. He looks as if the wind alone could disable him, and his henchmen are no more diabolical than cats hissing at mice.

One highlight of the film is British actor Brian Cox, as Smith, who dons a perfect Louisiana drawl to his words and a hint of humor in his performance as the brainchild of the whole operation. He's smarmy and direct. Smith is also the former employer of Cole and knows why he is called The Glimmer Man; those who have confronted Cole in some foreign jungle and saw only a glimmer before they died. Even this myth is pretty silly since the people Cole killed can't say what they saw before they died.

There is plenty of blame to go around for this film. Director John Gray is clearly out of his element with this picture. Gray is most notable for his Hallmark Hall of Fame films and seems overwhelmed with the task of bringing an intelligent action thriller to the big screen. In an interview, Gray commented that *The Glimmer Man* was a huge departure from his character pieces on TV. It shows.

Gray also makes the mistake of labeling *The Glimmer Man* a buddy film. It is not. Steven Seagal, after years of starring roles and being the head brute in charge, does not work well with a partner, even if that partner is the reliably funny Keenen Ivory Wayans. Wayans' presence is puzzling since this is not a starring role, but a supporting role. Wayans has more than enough experience in a lead role with his satirical, *I'm Gonna Git You Sucka* (1988) and *A Low Down Dirty Shame* (1994) that he should have looked upon this role as backtracking. Or an insult, as he is reduced to being tricked into eating dried-up deer penis in a Chinese herbal shop and crying during a screening of *Casablanca.* The buddy formula is not a good vehicle for Seagal since Seagal's acting abilities are still too limited. When things get tough, Seagal squints his eyes. When things get tougher, Seagal squints his eyes harder. Also, it seems success has gone to Seagal's gut as he looks meaty in his Nehru jacket and he should have worn his prayer beads a little tighter to hide is second chin.

For Seagal to improve his image, (aside from weight loss) he should give up more control of his films. As usual, he produced this one and even did the music for the soundtrack. He may still have a solid fan base, but based on the

CREDITS

Detective Jack Cole: Steven Seagal
Detective Jim Campbell: Keenen Ivory Wayans
Frank Deverell: Bob Gunton
Smith: Brian Cox
Jessica Cole: Michelle Johnson
Donald Cunningham: John Jackson

Origin: USA
Released: 1996
Production: Steven Seagal and Julius R. Nasso; released by Warner Brothers
Direction: John Gray
Screenplay: Kevin Brodbin
Cinematography: Rick Bota
Editing: Donn Cambern
Music: Trevor Rabin
Production design: William Sandell
Art direction: Nancy Patton
Costume design: Luke Reichle
Sound: Edward Tise, Robert Allan Wald
Stunt coordination: Dick Ziker
Casting: Debi Manwiller
MPAA rating: R
Running Time: 92 minutes

box office take of *The Glimmer Man,* and the arrival of Jackie Chan, his entourage seems to be dwindling.

The Glimmer Man is a dull movie, but one thing that could have saved it and rejuvenated Seagal's image would be if he was both The Glimmer Man and The Family Man. Now that would have offered a glimmer of hope for this film.

—Michelle Banks

REVIEWS

Boxoffice. December, 1996, p. 53.
The Detroit Free Press. October 6, 1996.
Los Angeles Times. October 7, 1996. p. F6.
New York Times. October 5, 1996. p.19.
USA Today. October 7, 1996. p. 3D.
Variety (online). October 7, 1996.

Grace of My Heart

For years her songs brought fame to other people. Then she found her own voice.—Movie tagline

"Smart, hip and great fun."—Jeff Craig, *Sixty Second Preview*

"Big emotions! A great authentic-sounding score and a cast that is perfection."—Susan Wloszczyna—*USA Today*

"One of the year's best films! Allison Anders has woven a heartfelt, uplifting gem of a movie."—Mike Caccloppoll, *WABC Radio*

Box Office: $660,313

Allison Anders has devoted most of her writing-directing career so far to stories about young women who dream of an independent existence, but whose individual situations and everyday surroundings force them to be more realistic. These characters live in a society dominated by boys and men who do not respect their hopes and who seem bent on tempering their enthusiasm. The world as Anders has portrayed it in films like *Gas Food Lodging* (1992) and *Mi Vida Loca* (1994) is a harsh, oftentimes cruel place for a female to grow up in. Even so, her protagonists rarely seem despondent, maybe because in all her films, Anders takes care to provide them with some kind of shelter, a safe haven. In *Lodging,* a movie theater at the edge of town provided the escape for that film's 17 year-old heroine; in *Loca,* it was a young mother's living room which served as neutral ground for the members of rival girl gangs. And now in *Grace of My Heart,* the tiny office of a pop songwriter is the sanctuary.

Kristen Vigard supplies the singing voice for Illeana Douglas.

Grace charts the musical odyssey of Denise Waverly (Illeana Douglas), a songwriter whose talent and smarts land her a job penning top 40 hits for all-girl groups in the male-dominated world of late fifties doo-wop music, and whose subsequent three decade-long struggle to emerge a singer in her own right seems inspired by Carole King's life story.

Denise starts life as Edna Buxton, heiress to the Buxton Steel fortune in Philadelphia. The family is worth enough that she could, if she wished, be unproductive and comfortable for the rest of her life—ditto for her offspring and a dozen generations thereafter. Yet she longs for something more substantial, for a self-determined life, and it's clear why. Her mother (Christina Pickles) is the domineering sort who, when Edna announces her intentions to enter a local singing contest, stuffs her into a wedding dress and orders her to sing "You'll Never Walk Alone." When it is clear the costume and Edna's somewhat gangly figure are not a perfect match, her reaction is to insult: "The dress fits the occasion. It's you who doesn't fit."

Backstage at the singing contest, Edna meets Doris (Jennifer Leigh Warren), a blues singer whose free-spirited attitude inspires her to defy her mother. On a dare, Edna, with a gleam in her eye, swaps dresses with Doris, takes her voice down an octave and onstage launches into a particularly silky rendition of "Hey, There (You With the Stars in Your Eyes)." Before the song is over, Mrs. Buxton will have bolted her box seat for the exit, and Edna will have grabbed the first place prize: a trip to New York City for a recording contract.

As might be expected, the "contract" doesn't turn out to be much—it's not even in writing—and Edna soon finds herself out on the streets of New York, humiliated. It takes close to a year, but despair turns to hope when swanky records producer Joel Millner (John Turturro) intercepts a crude demo tape and decides he'd like her to write songs for his artists on Charny Records, although her singing is another matter. Millner, a Phil Spector type (clothes, hair and all) proceeds to "re-invent" her upper-crust background, dubbing her "Denise Waverly," from the "slums of south Philly."

He sets her to work writing ditties, stationing her in the now-legendary Brill Building, in an office so slight it might have originally been a walk-in closet for a different office. In its heyday, between 1958-1970, the Brill Building was a virtual hive of musical activity, launching hundreds of careers and spawning an astonishing number of hit records. The way the song factory worked was that each writer would sit at an upright piano in a cramped office, compose a tune, rework it until it was deemed top 40 material, then repeat the process, usually all for about $150 a week. Meanwhile, the girl groups, teen idols, and uptown soul artists and their producers made the real money.

"Maybe I put too much of myself into my songs."—Denise

Joel helps guide Denise through this divided world of behind-the-scenes laborers and above-the-line talent. When she writes a song for Doris and her backup "Luminaries" that becomes a smash, then another for a different group, Joel realizes he's got a major hitmaker on his payroll. He introduces her to another tunesmith, the better established Howard Cazsatt (Eric Stoltz), who quickly becomes a collaborator and lover, and who teaches her that a song can tackle subjects slightly weightier than teen romance (teen pregnancy, for example). Their music with a conscience raises the ire of the Bible-Belt set, which, of course, pushes sales through the roof.

Denise also learns to draw from her own experiences. When she becomes pregnant with Howard's child (in a case of life imitating art), she retreats to her office and does a little soul-searching and songwriting. When she emerges, she's made a decision: they'll just get married. The resulting scene contains the film's most wonderful dialogue, as Howard none too tactfully explains to Denise his feelings about marriage. The wording here is such that his rantings on the loose roots of the sacrament of matrimony come across less as a scathing critique of a bourgeois convention, and more as an indication of his own fear of commitment. Denise catches him in his fib. They get married. Then she catches him in bed with another woman. They split up. She writes a song about it. And it's here that the story begins to follow a pattern that will become wearisomely familiar by the end of the film, as Denise transforms each of her true-life experiences into a piece of music. Aspiring songwriters might find the movie educational, as each new scene comes with yet another lesson on how to turn a heartache into a hit single.

She is crushed, so she turns to an older man, a fan of hers named John (Bruce Davison) who is a music critic with his own radio show. John had been an early supporter, giving Denise her first on-air break, and now he reciprocates her romantic feelings towards him. They have an affair off and on, even though he is married and has a family. Then Denise starts to make unreasonable requests on his time and even appears one night below the window of his apartment, desperate. For John, this will not do. He has built up a comfortable life over the years and has a wife he loves, well, enough. This chapter culminates in a scene where the two stroll through the park at dusk. As they walk, they discuss their future, she with a naive sense of hope and he with reluctance in his voice, and as the day grows later and shad-

CREDITS

Denise Waverly/Edna Buxton: Illeana Douglas
Joel Millner: John Turturro
Jay Phillips: Matt Dillon
Howard Cazsatt: Eric Stoltz
John Murray: Bruce Davison
Cheryl Steed: Patsy Kensit
Kelly Porter: Bridget Fonda
Doris Shelly: Jennifer Leigh Warren
Matthew Lewis: Chris Isaak
Mrs. Buxton: Christina Pickles
Guru Dave: Peter Fonda (voice only)

Origin: USA
Released: 1996
Production: Ruth Charny, Daniel Hassid and Martin Scorsese; released by Gramercy Pictures
Direction: Allison Anders
Screenplay: Allison Anders
Cinematography: Jean Yves Escoffier
Editing: Thelma Schoonmaker
Editing: James Kwei
Production design: Francois Seguin
Costume design: Susan Bertram
Music: Larry Klein
Song: Burt Bacharach and Elvis Costello, "God Give Me Strength"
Song: Elvis Costello, "Unwanted Number"
Song: Carole Bayer Sager and Dave Stewart, "I Do"
Song: Gerry Goffin and Los Lobos, "In Another World"
Song: Gerry Goffin, Louise Goffin and David Baerwald "Between Two Worlds"
Song: David Baerwald, Larry Klein and Lesley Gore, "My Secret Love"
MPAA rating: R
Running Time: 116 minutes

ows start to fall across their faces, he steps behind a stone wall and continues walking, until the two come to a point where the wall has risen and now physically separates them. That the metaphor is so painfully obvious actually makes it that much more effective: its significance is not lost on these characters, but rather weighs heavily on what ends up to be their last conversation.

However, Denise has got no time to mope. Joel has teamed her with a songwriter he's imported from Britain named Cheryl Steed (Patsy Kensit) and he needs a hit pronto for a Lesley Gore-ish singer (Bridget Fonda) on loan from a different label. Denise and Cheryl are at first reluctant to work together, but soon find comfort in each other as they conspire to help the singer subvert her goody-goody image with some clever lyrics that almost, but don't quite, expose her alternative lifestyle.

As the years march on, recording artists start writing their own songs and the Brill Building era comes to a close. It is the 70's and Denise has moved to Malibu to live with her new husband, a composer named Jay Phillips (Matt Dillon), whose character has been none too subtly made in the image of the Beach Boys' Brian Wilson. Like Wilson, Jay is a musical virtuoso whose life outside of the recording studio is a drug-induced nightmare of his own making. They have children, but his increasing paranoia leads to a sad scene where he takes the kids to town and manages to forget them. Although the film up until this point has at least been a lively and engrossing look at the backstage machinery that powers the pop world, here it nearly loses whatever goodwill has been generated by neglecting Denise's story and forcing her to play nurse for her chemically impaired husband. Dillon's performance is an eerie one, and though it helps set the mood during this stretch, soon the utter blankness in his eyes only serves to underline the dreariness of this movie's final 45 minutes or so.

When, after fleeing Malibu, Denise and the children wind up in a commune, it is Joel, of course, who shows up to rescue them. Douglas and Turturro's final scene together, near the poolside of a dilapidated motel, is simple and moving. The two talk about old times and speculate on what the future might hold. Joel asks her if she would like to come back with him to write and sing her very own concept album and she accepts the offer.

Grace of My Heart ultimately ends up being about the relationship Denise has with Joel, who, she finally realizes, has been her only true supporter during three decades of trials and triumphs. In their earlier scenes together, they were so wrapped up in their work and sure of themselves that neither of them paid much attention to the other. By the time they both find themselves huddled together on the crumbling tile in the motel courtyard, though, experience has given them wisdom enough to know a soulmate when they see one.

—David King

REVIEWS

Billboard. November 9, 1996, p. 36.
Boxoffice. September, 1996, p. 118.
Entertainment Weekly. September 13, 1996, p. 111.
Los Angeles Times. September 13, 1996, p. F14.
New York Times. September 13, 1996, p. C3.
Newsweek. October 7, 1996, p. 78.
People Weekly. September 16, 1996, p. 27.
Rolling Stone. October 3, 1996, p. 79.
Sight and Sound. March, 1997, p. 48.
Time. September 16, 1996, p. 88.
USA Today. September 13, 1996, p. 4D.
Variety. September 9, 1996, p. 115.
Village Voice. September 17, 1996, p. 82.

The Grass Harp

Life's best adventures are journeys of the heart.—Movie tagline

"Rousing triumph! Piper Laurie, one of the screen's finest, is luminous."—Philip Wuntch, *Dallas Morning News*

"A subtle and powerfully spun tale about love and the limitless rewards of companionship."—Elizabeth Pincus, *Harper's Bazaar*

"A film of rare delight. One of the most lyrical and charming films I have seen in ages."—Rex Reed, *New York Observer*

"Enormously moving and funny. The superb cast does a splendid job. Don't miss it."—Paul Wunder, *WBAI*

Box Office: $512,965

The Grass Harp, published in 1951, was Truman Capote's second novel. Like his sensational literary debut, *Other Voices, Other Rooms* (1948), *The Grass Harp* drew upon his memories of growing up different in a small Southern town in the 1940s. But whereas Capote's first novel explored Gothic elements of the Southern literary tradition, *The Grass Harp* restricted its Gothicism largely to its titular metaphor. *The Grass Harp* refers to an auditory phenomenon noted by the narrator's unworldly cousin Dolly, who says that the sound of the wind in long grass is the voice of the dead.

First dramatized in 1952, when *The Grass Harp* had a brief, unsuccessful run on Broadway, Capote's autobiographical novel was also adapted for the television screen in the 1950s, a production that featured Lillian Gish in the role of Dolly. In 1995, *The Grass Harp* finally made it to the big screen, with Piper Laurie cast in this pivotal part, a love letter written to his late spinster aunt whose accepting attitudes and dreamy attentiveness to inner voices were partly responsible for Capote's upbringing and largely responsible for the formation of his imaginative life. Friends recall him weeping over his manuscript as he wrote, crying over and over, "How I loved that woman."

In the movie, as in the book, the point of view is that of a Capote surrogate, Collin Fenwick (played as a young child by Grayson Fricke, then as a boy by Edward Furlong). But whereas Capote's parents had an unstable marriage that eventually ended in divorce, Collin is orphaned at the outset of the action by an accident that takes the lives of both his parents. As a consequence, he takes up permanent residence with his father's cousins, the aging spinster sisters Dolly and Verena Talbo (Sissy Spacek). The pair live in a well-appointed Queen Anne mansion, the largest house in their small Southern community. They live amidst such splendor largely because of the efforts of Verena, a cold, driven businesswoman who owns half the town. She and Dolly are cut from entirely different cloth, and Dolly customarily dwells in the kitchen with the black cook, Catherine Creek (Nell Carter), who insists she really is of Indian extraction. The point is that neither of these women belongs to polite, front parlor society. Verena treats both of them—as well as most of the other townsfolk—like employees.

Piper Laurie and Sissy Spacek, who play the Talbo sisters, played mother and daughter in 1976's *Carrie.*

Dolly and Catherine spend much of their time gathering wild herbs which, following a secret recipe Dolly claims gypsies once gave her, they cook up into a dropsy remedy (talk about an old-fashioned malady!). For years the elixir has been distributed by mail to buyers in return for a modest fee. Eventually, however, Dolly's revenues from the undertaking grow to such a extent that they require her to pay income tax, and Verena, sensing a business opportunity, decides, without consulting her sister, to take out a patent on the formula. Dolly, who feels she has been given a sacred trust, rebels against the notion of turning her labor of love into a business enterprise, and probably for the first time in her life, she refuses to be bullied. She retreats, Collin and Catherine in tow, to a tree house in the woods, where they are surrounded by nature and can hear the sound of the grass harp.

The threesome is soon joined by two others: Judge Charlie Cool (Walter Matthau), a widower who decides to throw over convention in favor of his love for Dolly, and Riley Henderson (Sean Patrick Flanery), a local outcast who is a friend of Collin. Together they form a kind of alternative community, free of prejudice and other social ills. Much of the humor of the film arises from the attempts of the sheriff (Joe Don Baker), spurred on by Verena, to dislodge the clan of five from their pastoral homestead. A parallel plot involves the attempts of another pillar of the community, Reverend Buster (Charles Durning), to eject a free spirited evangelist, Sister Ida (Mary Steenburgen), and her brood of fifteen illegitimate children from town. Both efforts are finally successful, but the eccentrics who provide an exceptional perspective on reality are not entirely ineffectual. Although few can hear it, the grass harp is never gainsaid; it informs the lives of private people like Dolly and, through her, the more public lives of those around her. And, of course, it lives on in Collin's memory.

The Grass Harp, directed by Walter Matthau's son, Charles Matthau, is unquestionably an actor's movie. The sterling cast also includes Roddy McDowell, playing Amos Legrand, a gossipy local barber, and Jack Lemmon, who makes a brief but memorable appearance as Morris Ritz, a slick Chicago con man who first romances, then fleeces Verena. But it is Piper Laurie who holds the movie together. Softened by age and a pre-Raphaelite cloud of red hair, she plays Dolly as a warm, almost childlike individual who conveys her vaguely mystical views on life in a whispery voice not unlike the sound of the grass harp itself. She is everlastingly appealing, and we can well believe the boy Collin's voice-over confession that he fell in love with her at first sight. For the same reasons, we can buy into Judge Cool's casting off a lifelong habit of conventional behavior in favor of the possibility of late-blooming romance with Dolly. When set against the cold, unyielding image conveyed by Verena, Dolly is especially irresistible, and of course she—or more precisely, what she represents—ultimately prevails, if only in death.

The Grass Harp has its sad moments and also its maudlin moments. Unfortunately, the two come together at an especially inopportune point in the movie, when Dolly collapses after expressing her joyousness by dancing deliriously with Collin. Given the framing of the story and its central metaphor, the denouement is never in doubt, but it is nonetheless disappointing. Verena, finally seeing the error of her ways, absorbs some of Dolly's spirit. Chastened by her financial and romantic losses, she decides to follow in

Dolly's footsteps, learning how to brew, rather than mass market, the dropsy potion.

But it is Collin who is Dolly's true inheritor. Imbued with invaluable life lessons and Dolly's inner visions, Collin, like his prototype Capote, leaves for New York City, intending to become a writer. Large portions of *The Grass Harp* are narrated retrospectively in voice-over by a mature Collin, who has presumably grown into the type of artist who can pay homage to his cousin by providing her story with shape and meaning. This technique lends the production an appealing long-ago-and-faraway glow, as well as a subtle counterpoint, offsetting memory with the young Collin's maturing perspective on life—a perspective we share throughout the rest of the film. Through such means we, too, are allowed to enter the world of innocence conjured up by Dolly and, more particularly, by the artist's reconstruction of his childhood experience.

"The wind is us. It gathers and remembers all our words."—Dolly

While such structural methods are common in literature, they are prone to failure when removed from the page onto the screen, where linkages between past and present often degenerate into mere cause and effect. It is a tribute to all concerned, particularly in view of the inherently delicate, whimsical nature of the subject matter, that this dramatized version of the novel comes off so well. The story's themes—that innocence trumps social restraint, that love succeeds where acquisitiveness fails, that it is never too late to heed the message of the grass harp—are delivered with nearly as light a touch here as they were by Capote himself.

The staying power of the movie is nonetheless in question. Released late in 1995 in time to be shown at the Boston and Toronto film festivals, *The Grass Harp* was not distributed commercially until a year later. Even then it was seen only by small audiences in selected cities, where it received scant critical attention. Despite its literary pedigree and its stellar ensemble cast, the film seems not to have found an audience. There is an irony here, of course: in a year when the top grossing film was *Independence Day*, an action feature packed with special effects and no stars, the gentle nostalgia conveyed by the grass harp is barely audible. It is as if Verena Talbo triumphed after all.

—Lisa Paddock

CREDITS

Dolly Talbo: Piper Laurie
Verena Talbo: Sissy Spacek
Judge Charlie Cool: Walter Matthau
Morris Ritz: Jack Lemmon
Sister Ida: Mary Steenburgen
Collin Fenwick: Edward Furlong

Origin: USA
Released: 1996
Production: Charles Matthau, Jerry Tokofsky and John Davis; released by Fine Line Features
Direction: Charles Matthau
Screenplay: Stirling Silliphant and Kirk Ellis; based on the novel by Truman Capote
Cinematography: John A. Alonzo
Editing: Sidney Levin and Tim O'Meara
Music: Patrick Williams
Production design: Paul Sylbert
Art direction: Chris Gorak, Stan Jolley
Costumes: Albert Wolsky
Sound: Clark King
Casting: Mary Jo Slater, Shay Griffin
MPAA rating: PG
Running Time: 107 minutes

REVIEWS

Boxoffice. November, 1995, p. R-92.
Detroit News. November 1, 1996, p. 3E.
Los Angeles Times. October 11, 1996, p. F18.
New York Times. October 11, 1996, p. C5.
USA Today. October 11, 1996, p. 3D.
Variety. September 11, 1995, p. 104.

The Great White Hype

"Fast, furious, pummelingly funny . . . "—Ken Tucker, *Entertainment Weekly*

"Knockout entertainment! Smart, savvy, and very, very funny."—Joanna Langfield, *The Movie Minute*

"A happily outrageous satire."—Janet Maslin, *New York Times*

"Great fun. And that's no hype."—Leah Rozen, *People*

Box Office: $8,008,255

The Great White Hype should be a whole lot more amusing than it is, but the concept changed over the five years that passed between the initial concept (a *This Is Spinal Tap* treatment of boxing) that Ron Shelton was supposed to direct and the completed picture, directed by Reginald Hudlin, an African-American director whose biggest hit was *House Party* (1990). Tony Hendra and Ron Shelton developed the screenplay in 1990. Hendra, the founding editor of National Lampoon, had worked as an actor in *This Is Spinal Tap* (1984) and in 1993 became the editor-in-chief of Spy magazine.

The Great White Hype was originally conceived as a satire about racism and the way the "Black boxing establishment handpicks white contenders," as Hendra described the concept for *Entertainment Weekly*. The completed film seems more to reflect Hendra's cynicism than Shelton's "affection for athletes and love of sport," as Rita Kempley of *The Washington Post* described it, that was so obvious in *Bull Durhum* (1988) and *White Men Can't Jump* (1992).

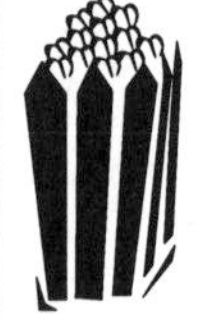

"I'm not Irish." "This is boxing—if you're white, you're Irish."—Trainer Windsor to his boxer, who's protesting his new nickname.

In the film Samuel L. Jackson plays the Reverend Fred Sultan, a flamboyant fight promoter patterned after Don King, who handles heavyweight champion James "The Grim Reaper" Roper (Damon Wayans). Another black boxer, Marvin Shabazz (Michael Jace) and his manager Hassan El Ruk'n (Jamie Foxx) want to challenge the champ in the worst way, but Sultan is worried about the gate and pay-for-view television sales, which are down. Apparently fans have tired of the black-on-black boxing scene, and something needs to be done to get the fans interested.

Ironically a groupie named Bambi (Salli Richardson) comes up with a solution the men are not clever enough to think of. As a professional "Reaper" Roper is undefeated, but she remembers that while Roper was still an amateur, he was defeated by a white boxer named Terry Conklin (Peter Berg), who has since become a punk rocker in Cleveland and the leader of a band called "Massive Head Wound." Sultan goes to Cleveland and manages to cut a deal with Conklin, who now claims to be a non-violent Buddhist devoted to a cause—helping the homeless, especially the homeless in South Dakota, he explains. After Sultan promises him $10 million for his cause, Conklin soon gets over his non-violent reservations. He gets a haircut in order to become "the clean-cut white boy" and goes into training. Meanwhile, Roper puts on twenty pounds while Conklin is in training, believing "My blackness will beat that kid."

While the fighters are (or are not) in training, a parallel plot has an investigative journalist and documentary filmmaker, Mitchell Kane (Jeff Goldblum) working to expose the Reverend Sultan. Kane has photographic evidence that shows Sultan in compromising positions with a number of women, but Sultan easily buys him off by hiring Kane to replace his public relations officer, Sol (Jon Lovitz, who is thankfully taken out of the picture early). Lovitz is a reasonably good comedian, but the role does not offer him much comic potential. He merely plays a pathetic loser. Goldblum is a much more effective con artist, but the role does not offer much opportunity for him, either.

The comedy is all situational, embellished by a few one-liners that hit the mark, as when Roper ridicules the term "white contender" as being about as meaningful as "black unity." Maybe some of the jokes fabricated by white writers are not so funny in this black-dominated sitcom that lost its focus as a satire against racism (as Tony Hendra first imagined it), but a sort of balance is achieved. As Janet Maslin noted in *The New York Times*, "racial and ethnic slurs fly everywhere" in this "scattershot comedy," but the insults are so evenly distributed that they are "cathartic rather than rude."

True to its satiric framework, all the characters tend to be played as caricatures. If Don King is the target of Samuel L. Jackson's Reverend Sultan, how can one satirize a promoter whose real life image seems to be a walking, talking caricature? The champ is mean, hungry, and black, but he is easily bilked by the fast-talking Sultan. The would-be challenger Shabazz is even more easily bilked. He is jealous because the champ has six Rolls Royces; Sultan buys him off with a "good faith" offer of a "Merlot Bro-ham" (as he mispronounces the name of the wine-colored Cadillac offered him). One gets the impression that these stupid guys are beating their brains out for fancy cars while Sulton pockets the big money, but greed and stupidity transcend color lines in this picture.

Kane turns out to be a stupidly greedy overreacher who actually comes to believe that Conklin may beat the champ and shifts his allegiance away from Sultan to become Conklin's manager; this betrayal comes just before the fight, which does not even go one round before the knockout. Conklin's trainer Johnny Windsor (John Rhys-Davies) knows what the outcome will be, but he understands boxing. His job is merely to train Conklin to look like a professional fighter.

But then Conklin himself believes he can take the champ, and there is reason for his confidence. Before the fight the overweight Roper smokes cigarettes while watching his favorite "inspirational" videotape, the perfectly awful cult blaxploitation film *Dolemite* (1975), starring comedian Rudy Ray Moore. While Roper is killing time in this way, Conklin concludes Roper is afraid to fight.

CREDITS

Rev. Fred Sultan: Samuel L. Jackson
Terry Conklin: Peter Berg
James (The Grim Reaper) Roper: Damon Wayans
Mitchell Kane: Jeff Goldblum
Sol: Jon Lovitz
Hassan El Ruk'n: Jamie Foxx
Marvin Shabazz: Michael Jace
Peter Prince: Corbin Bernsen
Julio Escobar: Cheech Marin
Johnny Windsor: John Rhys-Davies

Origin: USA
Released: 1996
Production: Fred Berner and Joshua Donen for an Atman Entertainment production; released by 20th Century Fox
Direction: Reginald Hudlin
Screenplay: Tony Hendra and Ron Shelton
Cinematography: Ron Garcia
Editing: Earl Watson
Music: Marcus Miller
Production design: Charles Rosen
Art direction: Scott Ritenhour
Costume design: Ruth Carter
Sound: David Chornow
Casting: Eileen Mack Knight
MPAA rating: R
Running Time: 90 minutes

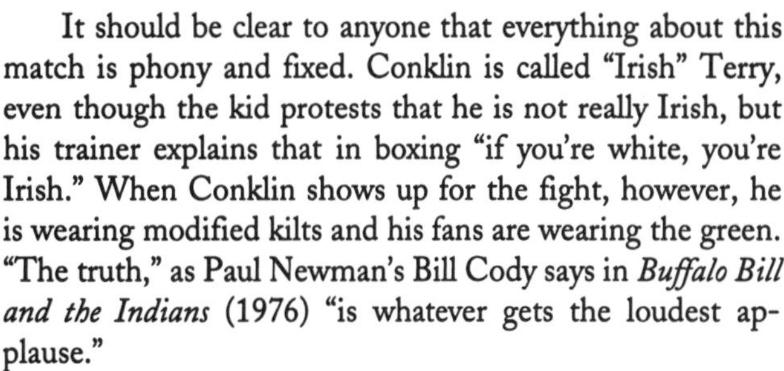

It should be clear to anyone that everything about this match is phony and fixed. Conklin is called "Irish" Terry, even though the kid protests that he is not really Irish, but his trainer explains that in boxing "if you're white, you're Irish." When Conklin shows up for the fight, however, he is wearing modified kilts and his fans are wearing the green. "The truth," as Paul Newman's Bill Cody says in *Buffalo Bill and the Indians* (1976) "is whatever gets the loudest applause."

The "hype" of the title is amusingly (if obviously) developed. At the "Fight of the Millenium" "Irish" Terry has an entourage of midgets dressed as leprechauns who accompany him into the ring with blaring bagpipes. "Reaper" Roper is robed as a hip Grim Reaper, a hooded spectre who makes his entrance accompanied by the "Reaper" Roper rappers. All of the boxers are stupid. Janet Maslin rightly described Wayans's surly Roper as "dim and suspicious." Conklin is a burned-out metalhead who wants to be idealistic about the homeless but seems to have little understanding of the cause, and his uninformed idealism also becomes a satiric target. All contender Shabazz can think about is big cars and bigger ambitions. Roper believes his "blackness" will defeat Conklin, but Shabazz is blacker than Roper. It's not about "blackness" but about angry desperation and pounding ambition. Michael Jace as Shabazz is the film's strongest emblem of an out-of-control fighter.

Reviewers hailed Damon Wayans as an up-and-coming comedian, but he is too angry and stupid to be very funny here, except as the butt of jokes and insults, as when Shabazz taunts him by saying "Isaac Hayes wants his head back." Samuel L. Jackson knows how to be flamboyant as Sultan, but, even though *Variety* judged his work as "solid," he is merely a walking caricature who speaks mainly in cliches: "I love you, man" is his favorite to defuse angry situations with his "brothers." The talents of Jon Lovitz as the Jewish stereotype and Cheech Marin as the Hispanic president of the World Boxing Association are for the most part wasted. More potential is written into Jeff Goldblum's role, but the character is far too calculating to be very funny, and too easily compromised.

The problem here is to satirize the professional boxing scene, which has been so obviously corrupted by greed and manipulation by the antics of promoters like Don King, so exaggerated as to be beyond the pale of mere satire. Surely few people take professional boxing seriously these days because of the hype generated by such flamboyant promoters. The film has its comic moments, but the reviews tended to be a cliche-ridden as the characters. "Float Like a Butterball, Hit Like a Flea" was the title of Janet Maslin's *New York Times* review. Carrie Rickey wrote in *The Philadelphia Inquirer* that the film "floats like an elephant" and "stings like a gnat," and concluded that despite its "consistently lighthearted rhythm and tone," the film was unable "to resolve in an upbeat way, the conflicts at its core." In treating an industry as corrupt as boxing "it's hard to maintain a satiric distance—not to mention a sense of humor."

Though thoroughly amused by "the hilariously dense Conklin," *Washington Post* critic Rita Kempley thought there were "more laughs in the Tyson-McNeeley bout" than in this "cynical inversion" of *Rocky* (1976). *Variety* criticized the film for its "thin, uneven scripting and unfocused direction," even though at times the satire is "dead on." In fact, there is less than meets the eye here.

—*James M. Welsh*

REVIEWS

Baltimore Sun. May 3, 1996, E3.
Chicago Tribune. May 3, 1996, p. 4.
Detroit News. May 5, 1996, p. D1.
Entertainment Weekly. May 10, 1996, p.52.
Los Angeles Times. May 3, 1996, p. F10.
New York Times. May 3, 1996, p. C3.
The Philadelphia Inquirer Weekend. May 3, 1996, p.3
USA Today. May 3, 1996, p. 10D.
The Washington Post. May 3, 1996, D6.
Washington Post Weekend. May 3, 1996, p. 48.
Washington Times Metropolitan Times. May 3, 1996, p. C16.
Variety. May 6, 1996, p. 82.

The Greenhouse; Les Jardin des Plantes

"One of the most compelling films you're likely to see this year! Deeply touching and moving."—Jeffrey Lyons, *Sneak Previews*

"A brilliant little gem of a movie that will lodge firmly in your heart and head."—Dr. Joy Browne, *WOR Radio Network*

Box Office: $10,548

The Greenhouse (*Les Jardin des Plantes*), takes its title from its setting, the Paris zoo, botanic gardens, and natural history museum complex. It is 1944, and the Nazi-occupied city is split between its majority of collaborators and small band of resistance fighters. Fernand Bronard (Claude Rich), director of the Jardin des Plantes, is quite literally cultivating his own garden—although with a bad conscience. He is particularly upset that his son Armand (Samuel Labarthe) is such a shameless collaborator. Armand says he would get his eyes slanted if the Chinese occupied Paris. He simply wants to keep working and to do his deals. He finds his father's disapproval hypocritical, since Fernand did not fight during World War I and has made up a story about his military service rather than face the facts.

"Fear is hereditary in our family. We're a family of shirkers."—Armand

Tormented by his bad conscience, Fernand argues with his son, even though it is his granddaughter's birthday. A disgusted Armand storms out of the house. It is well past the Nazi curfew, but as a practiced collaborator, Armand is sure that he can smooth his way past any problem. In short order he is shot by Nazis who are looking for Frenchman to murder in reprisal for the French underground's killing of German soldiers.

What is even more horrible, Fernand, who has been out searching for his apprehended son, actually witnesses his execution. Standing over a mass grave, he asks a grave digger to take a photograph of his son, which he later doctors to convince his granddaughter Philippine (Salomee Stevenin) that her father is still alive and on a mission for the resistance.

Why does Fernand take such elaborate steps to fool Philippine? It is, of course, hard to tell the young child that her father is dead—let alone explaining the degrading circumstances of his murder. Still, Fernand has not shown himself to be a caring grandfather. Indeed, he even suggests to his wife that he does not care that much for Philippine who, like everything else, just gets in the way of his devotion to his "garden." But Fernand feels badly because it was his quarreling with Armand that drove him out into the night. If Fernand had been less abrasive, less inclined to treat his son like a coward, Armand might still be alive. Moreover, there is Fernand's hopeless anguish as he watches his son die. Fernand has been able to do nothing for Armand.

Thus Fernand seeks to rehabilitate his son's image, portraying him as a hero for his daughter Philippine. With Philippine, Fernand has a second chance: he can instill in her the values that Armand rejected. Through Philippine, Fernand can act out his own fantasies, for he is a childlike man in many respects. He has taken no responsibility for the cause of French freedom, but in his espionage games with Philippine he can pretend to precisely the opposite. At the same time, he is genuinely taking care of the child, removing her from a rather grim Catholic school, and exposing her to the world of the imagination.

Director Philippe de Broca makes no excuses for Fernand's faults—or for France's. As other reviewers have noted, *The Greenhouse* can be interpreted as an allegory about the bad conscience the French have about their role in World War II. Many more Frenchmen pretended to heroic resistance records than the sorry story of collaboration will permit. There were all too many Armands, rationalizing their dealing with Germans as the only way to keep the country going while other Frenchmen fled. If the resistance was a formidable force, de Broca does not show it as such in this film. It has little impact on the daily life of occupied France and does little discernable damage to the Nazis. Fernand seems all too typical of the French male who talks a game of resistance but does nothing.

But to put it this way is to imply the film takes a harsh view of collaboration. Not so. It is simply a fact of life, and to some extent it is sentimentalized. Fernand's games with Philippine are presumably meant to be cute, but given the horror of the war, his playfulness seems silly and therefore hard to watch. Even Philippine tires of the charade, figuring out that her father is dead long before her doting grandfather will own up to it. If the games were initially meant for her, they ultimately serve as a salve for Fernand.

The Greenhouse tends not only to force the heartwarming story of grandfather and grandchild (Philippine's actress mother is a self-involved and absent parent) but also the plot details that are meant to make it believable. For example, there is the photograph taken of Armand in the mass grave. Supposedly Fernand doctors it to convince Philippine that her father is still alive. But the doctored photograph looks like something a sophisticated Hollywood studio might be able to bring off, not what would have to be a crude attempt at fabrication in wartime France. And why bother with doctoring a photograph at all? Surely Philippine would already have a recent photograph of her father. The pains taken over the photograph suggest how important it is to Fernand to sustain a lie, but using a contrived photograph to make this point defeats the film's verisimilitude.

CREDITS

Fernand Bronard: Claude Rich
Philippine Bornard: Salomee Stevenin
Armand: Samuel Labarthe
Micheline: Catherine Jacob
Jeanne: Rose Thiery

Origin: France
Released: 1994
Production: Harold Reichebner, Alain Clert, Yves Pasquier for an August Entertainment production; released by Castle Hill Productions
Direction: Philippe de Broca
Screenplay: Philippe de Broca, Alexandre Jardin
Cinematography: Janos Kende
Editing: Marie-Claude Lacambre
Production design: Francois de Lamothe
Costume design: Sophie Marcou
Music: Charles Court
MPAA rating: Unrated
Running Time: 93 minutes

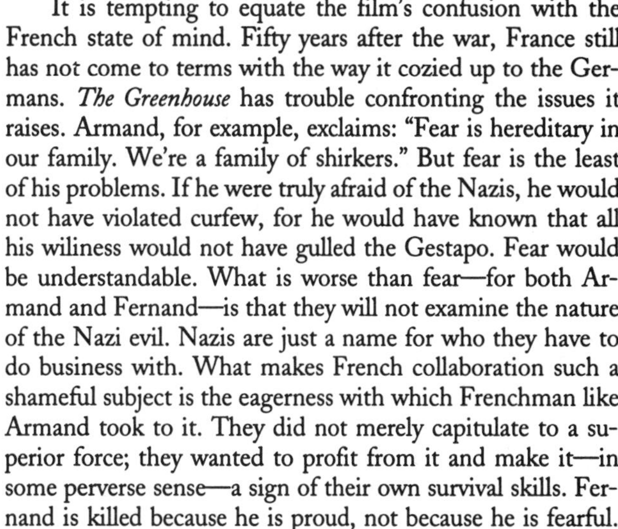

It is tempting to equate the film's confusion with the French state of mind. Fifty years after the war, France still has not come to terms with the way it cozied up to the Germans. *The Greenhouse* has trouble confronting the issues it raises. Armand, for example, exclaims: "Fear is hereditary in our family. We're a family of shirkers." But fear is the least of his problems. If he were truly afraid of the Nazis, he would not have violated curfew, for he would have known that all his wiliness would not have gulled the Gestapo. Fear would be understandable. What is worse than fear—for both Armand and Fernand—is that they will not examine the nature of the Nazi evil. Nazis are just a name for who they have to do business with. What makes French collaboration such a shameful subject is the eagerness with which Frenchman like Armand took to it. They did not merely capitulate to a superior force; they wanted to profit from it and make it—in some perverse sense—a sign of their own survival skills. Fernand is killed because he is proud, not because he is fearful.

Ignoring the logic of its own characters, *The Greenhouse* tries to make Fernand into a flawed hero—one who near the end of the film actually does carry out a mission for the French underground by convincing them that his son is a famous resistance fighter who has blown up several Nazi targets. That the resistance forces take Fernand seriously—even though they have never heard of his son—is another credulity-straining moment—worthy perhaps of a scene in the old television series "Hogan's Heroes."

It is not surprising, then, that the saving feature of the film is Philippine. Salomee Stevenin is a joy to watch, a therapeutic vision in a film that rarely confronts reality. She has the directness of an innocent and sharp perceptions that have not yet been blunted by the cant of her times. It is almost as if she indulges her grandfather in his games. Of course, she enjoys them, but they are a marking of time until her father returns. When her grandfather answers her questions with more games, she begins to realize that her father will not return. And of course she detects the fraud of the photograph, sensing that her grandfather has tried to animate a corpse.

One reviewer suggests that *The Greenhouse* is debunking the idea of war heroes, who are really the products of the kind of fantasies that Fernand perpetuates. Perhaps. But heroes seems irrelevant to this story—in the sense that they are not present. Instead we have a grimmer picture of a people, like Fernand, cultivating their own gardens and not addressing the greater evil that surrounds them. In fact, cultivating one's own garden is a myth; it cannot really be done without taking into consideration the rest of the world. Fernand is perhaps a better man for eventually accepting this truth, but so much of his struggle is viewed sentimentally that what could have been an astringent becomes an emollient.

—*Carl Rollyson*

REVIEWS

New York Times. August 30, 1996, p. C8.
Village Voice. September 3, 1996, p. 53.

Halfmoon; Paul Bowles - Halbmond

"Gorgeous Looking! Graceful, Insightful, & exotic . . . an exquisitely wrought, sophisticated diversion!"—*Los Angeles Times*

"Spellbinding! Tales of temptation, treachery and revenge."—*New York Times*

Box Office: $45,000

Narrated by expatriate writer Paul Bowles and adapted from three of his short stories, *Halfmoon* is a dreamy, exotic retelling of tales based on the theme of revenge.

CREDITS

Laheen: Samir Guesmi
Idir: Khaled Ksouri
Girl: Sondos Belhassan
Woman: Veronica Quilligan
Man: Sam Cox
Allal: Said Zakir
Old Man: Mohammed Belfquih

Origin: Germany
Released: 1995
Production: Irene von Alberti, Frieder Schlaich for a Filmgalerie 451 production; released by First Run Features
Direction: Irene von Alberti and Frieder Schlaich
Screenplay: Irene von Alberti and Frieder Schlaich; based on the writings of Paul Bowles
Cinematography: Volker Tittel
Editing: Magdolna Rokob, Margarete Rose
Music: Roman Bunka
Art direction: Harald Turzer
Costumes: Anne Schlaich
Sound: Peter Henrici, Volker Zeigermann
Special effects: Lutz Garmsen
MPAA rating: Unrated
Running Time: 90 minutes

The enigmatic, Tangiers-based author is best known for his autobiographical novel *The Sheltering Sky,* which was filmed by Bernard Bertolucci five years ago.

In *Halfmoon,* each episode runs 30 minutes and Bowles himself appears to introduce each segment with a brief explanation about how he wrote the story.

The first story, "Merkala Beach," relates the friendship of two shiftless young Morrocan men, one a drinker, the other a smoker of kef, whose friendship is tested by their involvement with a mysterious and seductive young woman. Bowles describes the story as an attempt "to show the superior effects of smoking cannabis over alcohol." However, this segment really has more to do with the male ego than drug preferences.

The second and most compelling of the three stories is "Call at Corazon," in which a pair of English newlyweds leave their luxury liner to take a crowded ship up the Amazon. The wife makes no secret of her discomfort, and her husband responds by buying a monkey and installing it in their cabin. As they head into the steamy jungle, their quarreling escalates into cruel acts of revenge and counterrevenge.

The final episode "Allal" chronicles a small orphan boy's spiritual exchange with a poisonous cobra. In a surreal and supernatural ritual, he merges identities with the beautiful green snake. The meaning of this magical transformation is ambiguous and unsettling.

Directors Frieder Schlaich and Irene von Alberti (who also produced and scripted) filmed *Halfmoon* with an acute sensitivity to the landscape and atmosphere. It's not an easy task bringing the elusive Bowles' vision of humanity to the screen, but Schlaich and von Alberti managed to successfully accomplish that, and *Halfmoon* was awarded the Critic's Prize at the 1995 Berlin Film Festival.

REVIEWS

Detroit Free Press. March 31, 1996, p. 7F.
New York Times. January 9, 1996.
San Francisco Chronicle. June 14, 1996, p. C3.
Village Voice. January 23, 1996, p. 63.

Hamlet

"Triumphant! Captivating, rare and unforgettable."—Bill Diehl, *ABC Radio Networks*

"Breathtaking! A powerhouse of a film!"—Ron Brewington, *American Urban Radio Networks*

"Stunning, memorable, monumental and visually dazzling."—Susan Granger, *CRN International*

"The best picture of the year!"—Patrick Stoner, *PBS/Flicks*

"Two very enthusiastic thumbs up! A virtuoso job of directing and acting."—*Siskel & Ebert*

"Superbly acted, directed and filmed."—Paul Wunder, *WBAI-FM*

"An electric, mesmerizing, angry, definitive *Hamlet*."—Joy Browne, *WOR Radio*

Actor and director Kenneth Branagh once again takes center stage in a film adaptation of William Shakespeare's *Hamlet*.

Box Office: $582,904

Film productions of Shakespeare almost always cut more than half of the original play. Franco Zeffirelli's 1990 production of *Hamlet* with Mel Gibson, for example, retained only thirty-seven percent of the text. Kenneth Branagh's film version of William Shakespeare's great tragedy has the distinction of performing the entire text—all 3,906 lines of it, a fullness that produces a running time of nearly four hours. More important, all four hours of the film are good. Branagh's talents as interpreter and director are at least the equal of his gifts as actor. He may not possess the strongest screen presence of those who have undertaken the part, but his performance as the Prince, like his interpretation of the play as a whole, is satisfyingly straightforward and often inspired. Branagh's superb adaptation stresses clarity, coherence, and unadorned emotions in a way that will allow general audiences to find the film accessible. He sets his film in nineteenth-century Denmark, and his version captures the climate of intrigue and the play's forceful contrast between Hamlet's search to confirm Claudius as the killer of his father and the duplicity of the Danish court in pursuing their many selfish pleasures.

The early scenes reveal one of Branagh's smartest directorial touches. During passages heavy with exposition, such as when the ghost of Hamlet's father (Brian Blessed) describes to Hamlet (Kenneth Branagh) the circumstances of his murder by his brother Claudius (Derek Jacobi), Branagh plays the spoken lines as a voice-over matched to slow-motion footage that illustrates the events being explained. This tack is also used effectively by director Al Pacino in his Shakespearean film *Looking for Richard* (1996). Like a video footnote, the images not only clarify plot-heavy scenes for audiences unfamiliar with the play, but also provide chances to slip into the film a number of famous faces in minor roles. John Gielgud, for example, appears on-screen as Priam while on the soundtrack the voice of a player visiting the royal court (Charlton Heston) recites a speech about the fall of Troy and Priam's death. Judi Dench appears as Hecuba in these same scenes. Ken Dodd, one of Britain's well-known stand-up comedians, appears as Yorick in flashback scenes running under Hamlet's graveyard reflections on finding Yorick's skull. John Mills is glimpsed briefly as Old Norway during the voice-over speech by Claudius explaining his reason for sending emissaries to Norway to curb a military incursion by Fortinbras (Rufus Sewell). In what is likely to be the most controversial of these cutaways, Branagh includes pictures of Hamlet and Ophelia (Kate Winslet) naked in bed together under the voice of Polonius (Richard Briers) belatedly instructing his daughter Ophelia on disguising her feelings for Hamlet.

The primary advantage of filming an uncut version of the play, of course, lies in rediscovering passages usually omit-

AWARDS AND NOMINATIONS

Academy Award 1996 Nominations: Best Adapted Screenplay (Branagh), Best Art Direction, Best Costume Design, Best Original Dramatic Score (Doyle)

ted from stage and film productions. When these restorations are done well, the choice to work from an uncut text seems even wiser. One such moment is the conversation between Polonius and Reynaldo (Gerard Depardieu) that opens Act Two, scene one. The scene is important in showing how pervasive dissembling and corruption are at Elsinore. Polonius asks Reynaldo to spy on his son Laertes (Michael Maloney) in France and even tells him to coarsen his son's reputation through gossip. The father assumes that such chicanery will elicit the truth of Laertes's behavior from his French companions ("Your bait of falsehood takes this carp of truth;/ And thus do we . . ./By indirections find directions out").

Branagh coarsens the scene even more by having it play in Polonius's bedchamber after his debauch with a prostitute (Melanie Ramsay). The girl lounges on the bed while Polonius, wearing a corset and adjusting his clothing, appears "completely unembarrassed by the situation," according to the screenplay. Branagh's directions in the filmscript identify Reynaldo as Polonius's pimp and ask pointedly: "What have these men done in the past? They reek of corruption." During his speech of instructions, when Polonius recounts the possible indiscretions of his son, he tilts his head toward this girl at the word "drabbing" and snaps his fingers for her to leave through a secret passage. Productions of the play too often present Polonius as merely a buffoon, and though his exchanges in the film with Claudius and Hamlet retain touches of comedy, the character nonetheless connives as a practiced hand. Richard Briers's performance captures both the father's ingratiating and his calculating sides, an interpretation the play supports.

Another advantage in reinstating the Polonius-Reynaldo plotting comes in appreciating the parallel it provides to the next scene between Claudius and his own spies, Rosencrantz and Guildenstern (Timothy Spall and Reece Dinsdale). The structure of the play invites a comparison between these two matching scenes of scheming father-figures sending out their lackeys. Claudius correctly relies on the hunger for advancement of Hamlet's old friends to outweigh their loyalty to the prince. He orders them to observe Hamlet and to seek the cause of his melancholy and distracted behavior. When Polonius and Claudius later conspire to use Ophelia as a tool to probe the cause of Hamlet's melancholy (Polonius hopes it is love for his daughter that has so distracted the Prince), the one character in the film closest to being actually what she seems now reluctantly enters the circle of the plotters. Branagh's screenplay recognizes this struggle for Ophelia, describing her lie to Hamlet about her eavesdropping father being "at home" as the "most agonizing decision of her young life." This moment of deception sunders their love.

Branagh's script also received a nomination for the motion picture Academy's best screenplay Oscar, a first for the script of a Shakespearean adaptation. Though some columnists joked that the nomination for this full-text version should have gone to Shakespeare instead of Branagh, Academy spokesman Andrew Levy explained that all material not written for the screen has to be adapted "whether the dialogue changes or not" and that adaptation covers "everything that separates a screenplay from a stage play." Branagh's full script has been published by W.W. Norton along with Russell Jackson's production diary.

As befits a play dealing so much with the contrast between seeming and being, the film features a main set that

CREDITS

Hamlet: Kenneth Branagh
Claudius: Derek Jacobi
Polonius: Richard Briers
Gertrude: Julie Christie
Ophelia: Kate Winslet
Laertes: Michael Maloney
Horatio: Nicholas Farrell
Ghost: Brian Blessed
Rosencrantz: Timothy Spall
Guildenstern: Reece Dinsdale
First Gravedigger: Billy Crystal
Second Gravedigger: Simon Russell Beale
Osric: Robin Williams
Reynaldo: Gerard Depardieu
Marcellus: Jack Lemmon
Player King: Charlton Heston
Player Queen: Rosemary Harris
Bernardo: Ian McElhinney
Francisco: Ray Fearon
Fortinbras: Rufus Sewell
English Ambassador: Richard Attenborough
Priam: John Gielgud
Old Norway: John Mills
Hecuba: Judi Dench
Yorick: Ken Dodd
Prostitute: Melanie Ramsay

Origin: USA
Released: 1996
Production: David Barron for Castle Rock Entertainment and Fishmonger Films; released by Columbia Pictures and Sony Pictures Entertainment
Direction: Kenneth Branagh
Screenplay: Kenneth Branagh, adapted from the play by William Shakespeare
Cinematography: Alex Thomson
Editing: Neil Farrell
Production design: Tim Harvey
Costumes: Alexandra Byrne
Music: Patrick Doyle
MPAA rating: PG-13
Running Time: 238 minutes

makes rich use of mirrors and secret doors. The largest sound stage at Shepperton Studios in England was splendidly dressed to represent the Danish court with a large open foyer, mirrored side doors, and labyrinthine corridors. One of the best examples of Branagh's use of mirrors to symbolize the play's double-dealing occurs when Ophelia approaches Hamlet on her father's instructions. Polonius and Claudius observe the encounter from behind a two-way mirror. At times the editing of the scene intentionally tries to disorient the audience by cutting unpredictably from Claudius's view of Hamlet behind the mirror to Hamlet's view of his own reflection on the other side. Immediately before Ophelia enters, Hamlet speaks the famous "To be or not to be" soliloquy as he stares directly into the mirror. When he mentions "the bare bodkin," he produces this dagger and points it at his reflection and, unknowingly, at Claudius, who now and in Hamlet's following conversation with Ophelia, confirms that it is not love that has brought on the prince's distraction.

Branagh has played Hamlet onstage nearly 300 times, including a production directed by Derek Jacobi (Claudius).

Shakespeare's play is, among other things, one of literature's great meditations on mortality. Hamlet's scene with the gravediggers provides an occasion for quieter moments to balance the frenzy of Hamlet's earlier confrontations with others. Billy Crystal, as the first gravedigger, also turns in one of the film's most enjoyable cameo performances. Crystal's smart delivery of the gravedigger's wordplay and verbal sparring with Hamlet nicely brings out the black comedy of the scene and serves as a thoughtful prelude to Hamlet's deeper musings on death as the great leveller. Other famous names who appear like Crystal in relatively brief speaking roles include Jack Lemmon as Marcellus, Robin Williams as the foppish courtier Osric, Rosemary Harris as the Player Queen, and Richard Attenborough, who, as the English Ambassador, speaks a total of six lines in the film's final moments.

Of the principal actors, Derek Jacobi as Claudius delivers the strongest performance. His rich voice registers the Shakespearean blank verse most sharply. His nuanced work presents Claudius as a personality pieced together from a gallery of momentary disguises: politician, king, murderer, lover, drinker, schemer. Under them all sweats the worried sinner who wants to repent of his murder but who loves too much the fruits of his sins. Jacobi also played Claudius with Branagh as Hamlet on BBC radio, and he played Hamlet in a fine 1980 BBC television production that featured Patrick Stewart as Claudius. With his other Shakespearean successes on stage (notably as Benedick in *Much Ado About Nothing*) and on the BBC, Jacobi may have now become the foremost Shakespearean actor of his generation.

Kate Winslet also excels as Ophelia. Her mad scenes are played with her straightjacketed and emerging from a padded room behind one of the court's mirrored doors, but such extremities do not overshadow the tenderness of her final scene with Laertes. Winslet gives Ophelia a passion and sincerity sometimes missing when actresses stress the character's vulnerability. (Unfortunately, some of her work is partially upstaged by Branagh's decision to use long circling shots during the conversations preceding "To be or not to be." Needlessly distracting, such fussy camerawork risks seeming a cliche; this is the one directorial touch that most obviously miscarries.) Julie Christie in her first Shakespearean role is also very good as Gertrude.

The great strength of Kenneth Branagh's film is the way it captures what almost every production of the play reaches for: the gulf between Hamlet's growing understanding of ultimate truths about life and death and the court's pursuit of such shallow concerns as their own pleasures and safety. Just before Hamlet delivers the "To be or not to be" soliloquy, Branagh addresses this point in his screenplay. As Hamlet gazes into the mirrored doors of the royal court, Branagh, who has now played Hamlet twice on stage, once on radio, and once on film, writes of this fascinating character that he keep returning to: "Here is a man faced with the prospect of murder or his own death. He faces both as absolute realities, and it is the most quiet and terrifying dread he has ever known."

—*Glenn Hopp*

REVIEWS

American Cinematographer. January, 1997, p. 58.
Boxoffice. February, 1997, p. 61.
Chicago Tribune. January 24, 1997, p. 4.
Entertainment Weekly. January 24, 1997, p. 35.
Los Angeles Times. December 25, 1996, p. F20.
New York Times. December 25, 1996, p. C7.
The New Yorker. January 13, 1997, p. 80.
People. February 3, 1997, p. 17.
Rolling Stone. January 23, 1997, p. 72.
Time Online. January 13, 1997.
USA Today. December 23, 1996, p. 3D.
USA Today. January 6, 1997, p. 1D.
Variety. December 9, 1996, p. 101.
Village Voice. December 31, 1996, p. 74.

Happy Gilmore

He doesn't play golf. He destroys it.—Movie tagline

"Sandler hits a hole-in-one!"—Elliott Francis, *Turner Entertainment Report*

"Non-stop, laugh-out-loud funny."—Alan Silverman, *Voice of America*

"Outrageously funny."—Paul Wunder, *WBAI Radio*

Box Office: $38,600,000

As a clunky vehicle for Adam Sandler, *Happy Gilmore* sputters mindlessly along, bouncing from one dumb gag to the next and spending more time in the comic rough than on the fairway. The moronic Sandler plays the title character, whose lifelong ambition is to be a pro hockey player despite his inability to skate. At least he's got the right makeup for hockey: he's brutish, bullheaded, mean and quick-tempered.

The plot is absolutely ridiculous: The IRS is dispossessing Sandler's grandmother, who forgot to pay taxes for the past 10 years. Sandler must come up with $270,000 in back taxes to save the house his grandfather built. When he discovers he can hit a golf ball a country mile, he joins the pro tour to win money to keep grandma out of a nursing home.

The idea that launched the film is transparent: the proud-to-be-crude Sandler embodies the sort of sweaty, slobbish sensibilities commonly associated with hockey fans, while golf represents the genteel sentiments he likes to offend. The film's hit-and-miss humor depends heavily on this culture clash. Gilmore wrestles with caddies, throws putters, dives into water hazards to fish out his ball, and wears hockey jerseys or rock-band T-shirts while golfing. He attracts huge, noisy crowds of bikers and guys who wear beer-dispensing hats. Trashing every golf tradition, he earns the enmity of snide pro Shooter McGavin (Christopher McDonald), who vows to destroy Gilmore.

As in all Sandler films, the jokes are mostly mean-spirited, involving mayhem, maiming and even death. He strikes people with golf balls. A woman is crushed when Gilmore tries to fix an air conditioner and it falls out a window. Chubbs (Carl Weathers), a golf legend who tries to help Sandler, lost a hand to an alligator; Happy rips off the artificial hand and it's run over by a truck. A nursing home orderly (Ben Stiller) is a brutal tyrant. Veteran TV game show host Bob Barker, paired with Gilmore in a pro-am celebrity tournament, gets into a head-butting brawl with him. It's a nice twist on Barker's image, but it's utterly ruined when Sandler intones: "The price is wrong, bitch." The script by Tim Herlihy and Sandler continually wallows in this kind of puerile take on life.

Sandler veers inexplicably between boorish and gentle, as he did in *Billy Madison* (1995). His Gilmore, not at all happy, is a violently tempered overgrown little boy with a heart of gold that seems utterly phony. He's devoted to his kindly grandmother, who raised him after his mother split to Egypt to get away from hockey and his father was killed by a hockey puck. When others in the film also die in cartoonish ways, it underlines Sandler's toddler-level view of mortality.

Thankfully, the masturbatory sexual stuff is less prevalent than in other Sandler films, but audiences still must endure scenes of Gilmore autographing the bosom of female fans, licking an intercom while trying to sweet-talk the girlfriend who's leaving him, and, worst of all, an opening collage featuring jobs in which Sandler always sticks a phallic object between his legs. There's also the obligatory leering romance, in which Sandler laughably poses as a love object for the golf tour's saucy publicist, who's played enticingly by Julie Bowen. Having Sandler and Bowen play love scenes is

CREDITS

Happy Gilmore: Adam Sandler
Shooter: Christopher McDonald
Virginia: Julie Bowen
Grandma: Frances Bay
Chubbs: Carl Weathers
Bob Barker: Bob Barker

Origin: USA
Released: 1996
Production: Robert Simonds for a Bernie Brillstein-Brad Grey production; released by Universal Pictures
Direction: Dennis Dugan
Screenplay: Tim Herlihy and Adam Sandler
Cinematography: Arthur Albert
Editing: Jeff Gourson
Music: Mark Mothersbaugh
Production design: Perry Andelin Blake, William Helsup
Art direction: Richard Harrison
Set decoration: Mark Lane
Costume design: Tish Monoghan
Sound: Rick Patton
Stunt coordination: Brent Woolsey
MPAA rating: PG-13
Running Time: 92 minutes

like serving hamburger and caviar on the same platter. Bowen, who gamely gives her character a wonderful luster that's totally out of place in such a cruddy film, deserves better.

It's telling that most of the minor characters in *Happy Gilmore* are funnier than the star. They include Stiller as the nursing-home orderly from hell; Kevin Nealon as a New Age golf pro who speaks psychobabble, and Joe Flaherty as a heckler hired by McGavin to harass Gilmore. Their shticks are more inventive than Sandler's one-note moron, but Sandler, alas, must be endured for the entire 92 minutes of a film that by all rights ought to have been confined to a TV sketch. Credit director Dennis Dugan with trying mightily to move the film along despite the albatross of Sandler hanging around his neck.

—*Michael Betzold*

REVIEWS

Entertainment Weekly. February 23, 1996, p. 103.
Los Angeles Times. February 16, 1996, p. F12.
New York Times. February 16, 1996.
People Weekly. February 26, 1996, p. 17.
Sports Illustrated. February 26, 1996, p. 33.
USA Today. February 16, 1996, p. 4D.
Variety. February 19, 1996, p. 48.

Harriet the Spy

On your case!—Movie tagline

"Delightful! A film parents and children can share."—Elayne Blythe, President, *Film Advisory Board, Inc.*

"One of the Top 10 family films of all time. Full of wit, wisdom and entertainment."—Ted Baehr, *Movie Guide*

Box Office: $26,567,568

It is impossible not to compare the movie *Harriet the Spy* to Louise Fitzhugh's classic middle-grade novel. It's impossible, anyway, for Fitzhugh's legions of fans, for whom egg cream is nothing more or less than Harriet's favorite drink, and a notebook is simply an essential tool for spying.

Harriet the Spy was not merely entertainment for those of us suffering from pre-teen angst. It taught us to be honest, and to write down everything; to always be true to ourselves; and it taught us the value of ending every school day with a piece of cake and a glass of milk.

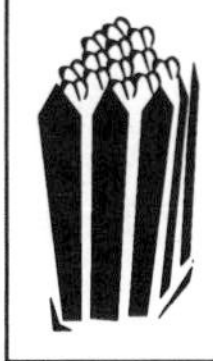

"I'll bet one day Miss Elson goes on a psycho killing spree."—one of Harriet's notebook observations

To those of us who ate tomato sandwiches or developed spy routes to be more like Harriet, the movie falls a bit short of the book's promise. Harriet, in the person of Michelle Trachtenberg, is a little too fashion conscious. And the world she inhabits walks a fine line between a slick MTV show and an afterschool special.

Everything starts out just fine for our heroine. Harriet attends the sixth grade with her best friends Sport and Janie. Janie is an aspiring scientist who conducts chemical experiments in her room. Sport balances his love of—well, sports, of course—with his responsibilities at home. It often seems as if Sport is taking care of his father, a not-very-successful writer, instead of the other way around.

Rosie O'Donnell plays Harriet's nanny, Ole Golly. She's always ready to dispense useful bits of advice, nonsense poem lyrics, or a much needed dose of reality.

Normally, Harriet spurns afterschool activities in favor of conducting her spy route. Will the man with all those cats continue to elude the health department by not answering the door to anyone wearing a hat? Will the pampered woman, who can only be seen by Harriet by using a dumbwaiter, ever get out of bed? Everything she finds out, she writes down in her trusty notebook.

One day, Harriet makes an exception and joins her classmates in the park for a game. This proves to be her undoing. Harriet loses her notebook, and before she can locate it, someone else in her class has found it. All the kids gather around to hear Harriet's often brutal observations. No one is spared, not even Sport and Janie, Harriet becomes a pariah.

In addition to losing her best friends, Harriet becomes the target of cruel pranks and the inspiration for The Spycatcher's Club. The club is formed by the entire sixth grade after the notebook is found. The club's business seems limited to deciding who gets to be president and what type of cake will be served at meetings. Sport and Janie quit in disgust. There was a reason they weren't friends with these kids before the notebook incident.

First family feature film for the Nickelodeon network.

At home things aren't much better than at school. Ole Golly has decided that Harriet's getting too old to have a nanny take care of her. After finding a new beau, Ole Golly quits, despite the protests of Harriet's parents.

This leaves Harriet's parents to deal with her. Since they have been merely peripheral players in her life until that point, this is quite an adjustment. They forbid Harriet to carry a notebook at all. She is searched at home, and, humiliatingly, at school. Any contraband notebooks are seized immediately.

Without friends, Ole Golly, or even the sanctuary of a wirebound notebook, Harriet is forced to go it alone. Her attempts to repair her friendships with Janie and Sport are thwarted. She can't even sit on a bench in the park without being harassed by members of the Spycatcher's Club.

So, Harriet goes on the offensive. She makes a list of everyone in the class and checks off names as she exacts her revenge. One girl loses a pigtail. A picture of Sport holding a mop is hung up all over school.

Ultimately, Harriet survives this crisis. She is voted editor of the school newspaper, and prints a retraction of her notebook writings. We know that she'll be okay, having learned that brutal honesty should be tempered with diplomacy.

Though *Harriet the Spy,* the movie, lacks some of the guts and quirkiness of the book, even this watered-down version of the story still has merit. It's clear the new Harriet wouldn't be caught dead in raggy old jeans and a sweatshirt, the old Harriet's trademark outfit, but at least she retains her curiosity, strength, and honesty. The power of the original story still shines through, even with all those fast cuts and hand-held shots.

—*Nancy Matson*

CREDITS

Harriet M. Welsch: Michelle Trachtenberg
Ole Golly: Rosie O'Donnell
Janie Gibbs: Vanessa Lee Chester
Sport: Gregory Smith
Mr. Welsch: Robert Joy
Mrs. Welsch: J. Smith-Cameron
Agatha K. Plummer: Eartha Kitt
Marion Hawthorn: Charlotte Sullivan
Rachel Hennessy: Teisha Kim
Sport's Dad: Gerry Quigley
Harrison Withers: Don Francks
Boy with Purple Socks: Dov Tiefenbach
Mrs. Hong Fat: Mung-Ling Tsui
Frankie Hong Fat: Byron Wong

Origin: USA
Released: 1996
Production: Marykay Powell for a Nickelodeon Movies and Rastar production; released by Paramount
Direction: Bronwen Hughes
Screenplay: Douglas Petrie, Theresa Rebeck; based on the novel by Louise Fitzhugh
Cinematography: Francis Kenny
Editing: Debra Chiate
Music: Jamshied Sharifi
Production design: Lester Cohen
Art direction: Paul Austerberry
Costume design: Donna Zakowska
Sound: Glen Gauthier
Casting: Jill Greenberg Sands
MPAA rating: PG
Running Time: 101 minutes

REVIEWS

Chicago Tribune. July 10, 1996, p. 1.
Entertainment Weekly. July 19, 1996, p. 58.
Hollywood Reporter. July 8, 1996, p. 5.
New York Times. July 10, 1996, p. C11.
People. July 15, 1996, p. 24
Sight and Sound. March, 1997, p. 49.
USA Today. July 10, 1996, p. 8D.
Variety Online. July 8, 1996.

Heaven's Prisoners

Trusting the wrong woman can be a deadly choice.—Movie tagline

"Alec Baldwin & Teri Hatcher sizzle in this steamy, sultry thriller!"—Bill Bregoli, *Westwood One Radio*

Box Office: $5,009,305

"I want a drink. I want a drink all the time," confesses Dave Robicheaux (Alec Baldwin) at the outset of *Heaven's Prisoners.* He's in a real confessional, and the priest reminds him how good a marriage and life he's had since he's quit drinking and left the police department. The priest asks Robicheaux what would happen if he began drinking again. "I would lose everything," he replies. "But knowing that, you still want to drink again?" the priest asks. "Yes," Robicheaux replies.

Heaven's Prisoners was the first of James Lee Burke's Dave Robicheaux mysteries. He's since written eight more.

This opening sequence is meant to establish Robicheaux as a restless man whose instinctual longing for danger is a constant threat to any prospects for a settled, peaceful life. And that is indeed the emotional landscape on which this sloppy, overlong, pointless film meanders. But the opening also suggests that Robicheaux has a profound spiritual core and that his addiction to alcohol is the trigger that will push him over the edge into moral quicksand. These additional motivational elements aren't fulfilled in the rest of the film, leaving the viewer unable to connect to Robicheaux's heart.

Robicheaux, also known as Streak for an inexplicable patch of gray in his dark hair, seems only slightly less craven and bloodthirsty than the endless series of picaresque hoods he stalks throughout the film. In only one sequence does he return to church, to light a votive lamp for the dead mother of the El Salvadoran refugee girl he and his wife Annie (Kelly Lynch) have rescued from a Gulf of Mexico plane crash.

Their quest to keep the girl safe from the mobsters who were mixed up in her flight to freedom is the main claim on audience empathy. But it's hard to see the Robicheauxs as paragons of virtue after they lie and cheat to circumvent the authorities and claim the girl, whom they name Alafair, as their own. They're essentially kidnappers with a heart. The filmmakers see no need for Robicheaux to confess that.

As for his drinking, Robicheaux is already well back down the road to ruin before he returns to boozing. He can't resist playing cop and tracking down gangsters he thinks might have been connected to the flight that plunked down Alafair. That's his real weakness. After he starts drinking again, he merely becomes a less effective vigilante.

Based on a book by James Lee Burke, the screenplay by Harley Peyton and Scott Frank promises much more than it delivers. So does director Phil Joanou's languorous, simmering style. George Fenton's backwater blues soundtrack and the bayou sets also suggest a murky pot of Cajun suspense. But murkiness is all you get; there's little substance in this stew. The only suspense is entirely encapsulated within each of the showdowns between Robicheaux and the various hoods he encounters. Tension doesn't build, bit by bit, it just comes and goes.

The plot is a mess of false leads and sudden, meaningless revelations. A better story would give Alafair a key secret or possession that the mobsters would need. Instead, the threat Robicheaux and his wife both fear—that someone from the shadowy underworld will return to kidnap their prize—proves illusory. In fact, it's not clear just who is after the Robicheauxs and why, and Joanou tries to milk that uncertainty for much more than it's worth. All that really happens is that Robicheaux's stirring of the pot awak-

CREDITS

Dave Robicheaux: Alec Baldwin
Robin Gaddis: Mary Stuart Masterson
Annie Robicheaux: Kelly Lynch
Claudette Rocque: Teri Hatcher
Bubba Rocque: Eric Roberts

Origin: USA
Released: 1994; 1996
Production: Albert S. Ruddy, Andre E. Morgan, Leslie Greif for a Rank Film Distributors and Peter V. Miller Corporation production; released by New Line Cinema and Savoy Pictures
Direction: Phil Joanou
Screenplay: Harley Peyton, Scott Frank; based on the novel by James Lee Burke
Cinematography: Harris Savides
Editing: William Steinkamp
Production design: John Stoddart
Music: George Fenton
MPAA rating: R
Running Time: 131 minutes

ens plenty of gangsters, and the plot turns into a revenge motif, full of pointless mayhem.

Unveiling bizarre, shady characters one at a time is not enough to sustain interest in the proceedings, but *Heaven's Prisoners* does have quite a remarkable gallery, populated by credible actors. The headliner among the villains is Eric Roberts, who proved long ago in *Star 80* (1983) that he could ooze malevolent, oily grace. Here Roberts plays Bubba Rocque, an old high-school buddy of Robicheaux who has become a big-time druglord. Rocque is so rich he lives in a mansion and for amusement boxes in a backyard ring when he's not toying with his dangerously seductive wife, Claudette (Teri Hatcher).

Hatcher makes a fine temptress, if a little too obvious, and is a long way from her role as TV's Lois Lane. Also playing against type is Mary Stuart Masterson, who tries hard to bring substance to her thankless role as Robin, a stripper with a heart of gold and a head full of drugs and booze who is in love with Dave. Among the three leading ladies, Lynch's rather washed-out-looking wife is the only one whose head is on straight. The script transforms her instantly from sexy and languid to maternal and hard-headed, and Lynch is equal to the task. She has to play scenes like the one on their front porch where she confronts her husband staring off into the bayou and intones: "Can't stop being a homicide detective, can you?"

It's that sort of script, the kind where characters spell out nearly every plot development, announcing what someone's thinking or going to do next. Little is left to the imagination. The noirish style of Joanou's direction and Harris Savides' shadowy cinematography suggest intrigues that never materialize.

Baldwin's Robicheaux does follow the noir convention of a protagonist enmeshed in a nightmare that is a product of the interaction between his feverish mind, his passion for adventure, and the real dangers that lurk in the bayou underworld. Criminals out to get him crawl out from under virtually every rock in the swampland. There's Toot (Carl McGee), a Haitian thug implied to be some sort of cannibal, who meets his demise in a trolley car chase. There's his boss, Eddie Keats (Don Stark), a heartless hood who gets treated to a bottle in the face from Robicheaux. And there's the mysterious Victor Romero (Hawthorne James), who seems to be the most threatening of all. And many more.

Robicheaux's task, made more befuddling as his quest continues, is to sort out which of these guys is working for his former pal Bubba and who isn't. It turns out, dismayingly, that they're not part of an evil web at all, but merely a lot of bugs crawling around on their own turf. It's as if the ending of *The Godfather* revealed that all the members of the Corleone family were really just freelance hoods unrelated to one another.

As a star vehicle for Baldwin, *Heaven's Prisoners* gets swamped by its own pretentious emptiness. Baldwin succeeds well as a vigilante, but he doesn't seem all that anguished about the struggle of putting his past behind him. He's seemingly clueless about the virtue and value of the settled life and shows not a hint of the compassion that would make his conflict vivid. His is a one-dimensional performance: all cop and no would-be ex-cop. It's hard to work up much interest in his fate.

For all the suggestion of an erotic web ensnaring Robicheaux, the film delivers little real sexual danger. Baldwin is standoffish with all three women, seemingly uninterested in their charms. One is left with the impression of three talented female actresses trying their hardest to awaken some spark in a corpse of a man. Encounters that ought to melt the screen end up frozen by Baldwin's icy stares.

Heaven's Prisoners is not the way to do film noir. And it is not the way to make Alec Baldwin a star. At over two hours, it's a lot of huffing and puffing, chasing and shooting to no good effect. Its script could have used a rewrite, trimming away a couple of the hoods, tightening up the plot, and suggesting a reason for all the mayhem. It's not worth taking this long trip into the bayou to come back with absolutely no revelations.

—Michael Betzold

REVIEWS

Entertainment Weekly. May 31, 1996, p. 44.
Los Angeles Times. May 17, 1996, p. F9.
New York Times. May 17, 1966, p. C5.
People Weekly. May 27, 1996, p. 19.
USA Today. May 17, 1996, p. 3D.
Variety. May 20, 1996, p. 30.
Village Voice. May 28, 1996, p. 58.
Wall Street Journal. May 17, 1996, p. A12.

Heavy

"Quietly potent. A small gem. Liv Tyler is an actress with whom the camera is in love. She's fresh, natural and lovely."—Jay Carr, *The Boston Globe*

"Outrageously enchanting. Altogether terrific."—Guy Flatley, *Cosmopolitan*

"Superb! *Heavy* is a miracle of a movie. Liv Tyler is a young actress of uncommon beauty, talent and presence."—Kevin Thomas, *Los Angeles Times*

"Quietly earthshaking . . . eloquent, purposeful. A lean, artificial drama. Liv Tyler gives a charmingly ingenuous performance."—Janet Maslin, *New York Times*

Box Office: $941,414

If the economics of the film business now allows for a low-budget venture to recoup its investment, and more, through the support of a mere coterie of film buffs across the country, then that can be seen as a healthy mandate for an innovative filmmaker to rethink the sterile tenets of filmic realism.

In Europe, similar support from state-run television and elsewhere, has led to works such as Eric Rohmer's *Claire's Knee* (1971), a narrative focussed on nothing more than the desire of a grown man to touch the knee of a plain-looking nymphette, or Chantal Ackerman's *Jeanne Dielmann* (1975) with its over three hour long depiction of the minutiae comprising a housewife's daily existence before she finally flies off the handle. Here at home, while James Mangold's bold first feature *Heavy* seems humble in comparison, it can no doubt be taken to illustrate the scope of creative freedom now open to an American filmmaker willing to work on a shoestring budget. *Heavy* grapples with that one rudiment we have come to expect of all film narratives: their ceaseless forward thrust in time, intended to take us away from the reality of a given present, and leave us on the threshold of a future of infinite possibilities. By repeatedly doubling back upon itself, the narrative thrust of *Heavy* forces us to contemplate the stasis of a closed-in world. Yet, it is in the quietly disarming lead performance of Pruitt Taylor Vince, as Victor, that this unique quality finds its clearest expression, and makes for the film's lasting impact.

Vince, who appeared as Paul Newman's sidekick in *Nobody's Fool* (1994), continues to haunt us with the minute fluctuations of mood and intent that sweep across his rotund features. His stolid reticence incorporates the spirit of the film's narrative, instead of the other way around.

We first see him in the midst of a daily chore. Inside Pete and Dolly's, a tavern beside a dense forest in upstate New York, as Dolly's son and cook-cum-janitor, Victor is morosely cleaning graffiti from the bathroom mirror. Scrawled in lipstick is the word "Slut." Victor rubs at it with a cleaning cloth, but the splotches prove stubborn.

A jowly Shelley Winters as Dolly is meanwhile interviewing a fresh-faced Liv Tyler as Callie (the film's only true class act) for the job of waitress. Strikingly pretty, Callie, a college dropout, needs the job so she can study something useful "like photography or accounting." Delores, the longtime waitress (played by a mature, but still attractive, Deborah Harry, once the lead singer of the rock group Blondie), has her own theory as to why Callie is being hired. When Leo (Joe Grifasi), a delivery man and resident barfly, suggests it could be because Dolly thinks a pretty young waitress might bring in more business, Delores snaps back, "No, I'm being punished!"

Victor spies on Callie as she's changing for her duties in the bathroom. We can see he's racked by the guilt of an urge he cannot express, either to her or to himself. Then, Callie idly rubs at the still visible signs of the lipstick on the mirror, almost repeating Victor's action, and thereby setting the tone for the doubling to follow. Victor, under the constant gaze of his doting mother, will continue to harbor a silent longing for Callie, whose sights will remain set well beyond the stale air of this claustrophobic setting. The film's opening thus prepares us for the little enigmas and petty jealousies that will lead nowhere but back to themselves. Everything that will follow will appear less a series of events than a cluster of motifs, all pointing inward to Victor's dilemma, rather than to any attempt at changing it.

For Victor, the boundaries by which the outside world functions clearly make no sense. We come to know this not only through his behavior, but through subjective flashes that at times comprise whole scenes. In turn, the film takes up Victor's ambivalence towards love and sex, towards the figure of the mother and that of the romantic love object, and most significantly, his refusal to see any difference between the past and present.

When Leo, who is allowed by Dolly to sleep off his drunken state in Victor's room, lets Victor see candid pic-

AWARDS AND NOMINATIONS

Sundance Film Festival 1995: Special Jury Prize

tures from rolls left for developing at the drugstore, Victor merely glances at them before handing them back. Leo then cuts to the chase. "You know, if you don't use it once in a while, it will fall right off." Later, when Callie shows Victor her set of photographs, mostly of her and Jeff (Evan Dando), her boyfriend, Victor quietly steals a snapshot of Callie by herself. One morning, while driving to work, Victor catches Callie and Jeff embracing on the side of a bridge above a river. Victor's response again takes an inward turn. He binges on black frosted donuts.

In one of his few articulate moments, Victor reveals how he feels about his excess weight. "I'm fat!" he moans to Dolly. "You're husky," Dolly tries to console him. "I'm fat, ma!" he retorts, as if wanting to shed her layer of protection. Though Victor does embark on a brief regimen of skim milk and diet formulas, it is Dolly's collapse that makes him revert to his old ways.

Before that event however, Victor receives a premonition of sorts. As he's walking across the bridge seen earlier, clearly for exercise, he looks down to see an unconscious Callie floating on the river. He hurries down to retrieve her limp body. As we see him trying to resuscitate her, the whirring of a biplane overhead shakes him out of this grim reverie. When he reaches home, he finds Dolly unconscious on the bathroom floor. Dolly's subsequent death in a hospital ward leads Victor to his most extreme behavior.

For a start, he refuses to clear away Dolly's untouched breakfast, much like the demonic Norman Bates in Hitchcock's *Psycho* (1960). At one point, he even flashes on Callie sitting in his mother's chair and consuming the stale food. When Delores inquires about Dolly, he replies that she is fine. It is only when Callie insists on speaking to Dolly that Victor is forced to reveal the fact of her death, and that too is done in his own private fashion.

As he is driving an unsuspecting Callie to the grave site, the ride crystallizes the basic conflict in Victor's life. As Callie sings along with the lyric on the radio, all about doing "the California thing," we can glimpse a wisp of hope cross Victor's face, as if for an instant California did hold out its customary promise. At the cemetery, Victor parks the car, then silently walks off by himself. When Callie catches up with him beside the makeshift grave, she is shaken by the truth. "When did it happen?" she asks. Victor falls silent, then replies, "Two weeks ago." "Why didn't you tell anybody?" Callie asks. "I don't know. I didn't want anything to change."

What does change, if anything, is Victor's self-assertiveness, especially towards Leo and Delores, so that for an instant we feel he might at last be ready to step into the shoes of the deceased Pete, whatever that might entail.

By himself, however, Victor can only stuff his mouth with more pizza, his self-pity turning to rage. Yet even when he smashes the glasses on the bar counter, it is more an act of frustration than rebellion. It is then that the aspect of heaviness takes on a resonance that extends beyond Victor's physique, or the pizzas he hates to make, or the motor vehicles that provide the tavern with its sustenance. We begin to see the film's title as reflecting an all-permeating malaise afflicting the other characters as well. As if to make this clear, the film executes a continuous pan from Victor, tossing Dolly's breakfast into the garbage, to a somber Leo, sitting up in Delores' bed, to a melancholy Delores, by herself at her kitchen table, to Callie, who still doesn't know what to do with her life, and back to Victor, who may possess an edge over them all, in at least being aware of what ails him.

Critics seem to have unanimously noted the film's innovative aspects, focusing on its true-to-life ethic and its bravura lead performance. Terence Rafferty in *The New Yorker* says that the film's "great surprise . . . is that it's less interested in striking attitudes toward its disappointed characters than in simply observing the texture of life in their particular nowhere." Rafferty goes on to note that the director and cameraman "are alert to the lived-in beauties of the upstate landscape, and the compositions have a restrained laconic lyricism that captures both the romantic lushness and the gray loneliness of the setting." Janet Maslin in *The New York Times* calls the film "an eloquent, purposeful first feature . . . (that) isn't always able to sustain its balance between narrative subtlety and inertia." For her, the lead performance captures the "character's darty-eyed fearfulness, but some of Victor's reactions become repetitive."

CREDITS

Victor: Pruitt Taylor Vince
Dolly: Shelley Winters
Delores: Deborah Harry
Callie: Liv Tyler
Leo: Joe Grifasi
Jeff: Evan Dando

Origin: USA
Released: 1994; 1996
Production: Richard Miller for an Available Light production; released by CFP
Direction: James Mangold
Screenplay: James Mangold
Cinematography: Michael Barrow
Editing: Meg Reticker
Production design: Michael Shaw
Music: Thurston Moore
Art direction: Daniel Goldfield
Costume design: Sara Jane Slotnick
Sound: Jan McLaughlin
Casting: Todd Thaler
MPAA rating: Unrated
Running Time: 104 minutes

She however does go on to note the overall "understated excellence" of the acting. She finds Shelley Winters "especially good" in capturing "Dolly's strength without making her an overbearing caricature" and Liv Tyler a "stunning catalyst . . . (who) gives a charmingly ingenuous performance, betraying no self-consciousness about her lush good looks." In a similar vein, Matt Zoller Seitz in *New York Press* finds "the depth of Victor's feelings has no equivalent in recent movies. He's so compelling that he connects with the audience on an almost primordial level."

Apart from proving a favorite at Cannes, London, and Toronto, *Heavy* secured for its thirty-two year old writer-director a Special Jury Prize for Best Direction at the 1995 Sundance Film Festival.

—*Vivek Adarkar*

REVIEWS

Boxoffice Online. June 6, 1996.
Detroit Free Press. September 27, 1996.
Entertainment Weekly. June 28, 1996, p. 85.
The Hollywood Reporter. January 27, 1995, p. 20.
Los Angeles Times. June 28, 1996, p. F4.
New York Press. June 5, 1996.
New York Times. June 5, 1996, p. C13, C17.
The New Yorker. June 17, 1996.
Newsday. June 5, 1996.
Sight and Sound. January, 1996, p. 41.
Variety. February 2, 1995, p. 29.

Heidi Fleiss: Hollywood Madam

Hollywood was the whore. She was just the madam.—Movie tagline

"A comedy in the footsteps of *Roger & Me*."—Georgia Brown, *Village Voice*

Box Office: $34,402

Heidi Fleiss operated a call-girl ring catering to Hollywood movie executives and to some of their stars. Convicted of pandering, as well as federal charges for conspiracy, income tax evasion, and money laundering, her lurid story made the national news, the tabloid papers and television shows. Fleiss's flamboyance and her telltale smirk suggested she was enjoying the show.

BBC documentary filmmaker, Nick Broomfield, set out to tell Heidi's story. He thought he had her cooperation, and when he arrived in Hollywood, he expected to interview her almost immediately. But he found himself plunged into the swirl of publicity surrounding her and became, in her eyes, only one more opportunist seeking to profit from her notorious case. Broomfield lost Fleiss's confidence before he ever quite had it. Consequently, he had to thread through the tangled relationships that threatened to strangle her. Like an unauthorized biographer, he had to move along the periphery of Fleiss's world, making contacts with other prostitutes and those who had only a casual or fleeting relationship with Fleiss, hoping that eventually these outlying connections would provide him with a conduit to his subject.

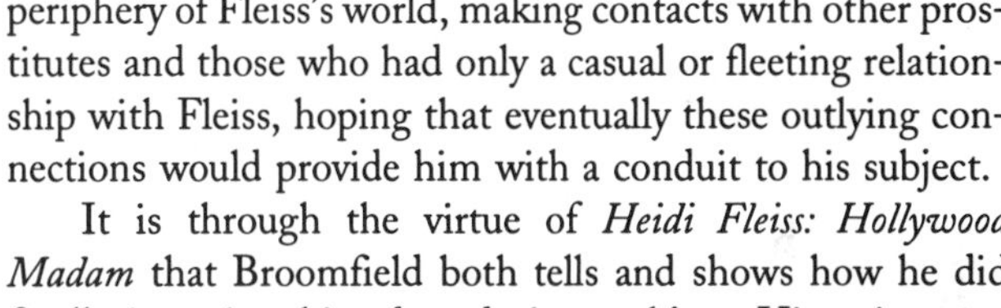
"They're doing a documentary. They want to film me right in the middle of my trial. Crazy, huh?"—Heidi Fleiss explaining Broomfield's presence to a reporter at the Channel 5 TV station.

It is through the virtue of *Heidi Fleiss: Hollywood Madam* that Broomfield both tells and shows how he did finally interview his edgy, devious subject. His voice-over narration provides background information as he drives, day and night, across the expansiveness of southern California. So many shots of him on his car phone plugging along convey the sheer doggedness of his investigation. The ominous, yet low-key soundtrack is reminiscent of film noir, but Broomfield is no Bogart. Rather than glamorizing his role as detective, Broomfield seems modest, even self-effacing, and sometimes nearly helpless—as when he pulls up beside a street walker and tries to ask her about Heidi. The likelihood of getting any real information from this source is nil. Broomfield, an experienced filmmaker, must know that, but it is an index of his frustration and of just how far he is from the center of the story. It is also, however, a signal of his persistence, no matter how much his interviewees insult him. In this case, the prostitute threatens violence.

In fact, this early scene hints at the violence lurking in Fleiss's shady life. It does not seem far-fetched to think that

Broomfield himself might be taking on a hazardous job. If he is afraid, his face never shows it. In that respect, at least, he is like the stone-faced detective, the Dana Andrews of *Laura* (1944), whose uninflected voice gives away almost no emotion. If Otto Preminger's classic film comes to mind, it is because like the Dana Andrews character, Broomfield may be in love with the mysterious woman at the center of a crime. Heidi becomes his obsession—so much so that her lover, Ivan Nagy, subjects Broomfield to a brutal verbal attack, calling him naive and a rube, someone who has been taken in by a romantic fantasy of Heidi as the young, sassy girl who has been manipulated and betrayed by Nagy, the sleazy Hungarian, director of pornographic films and CD-ROMS. Nagy's outburst at Broomfield is so ugly that it seems as if the camera is the only thing that stops him from assaulting the filmmaker. Indeed, Nagy, as a filmmaker himself, must realize that Broomfield's camera is his defense and his weapon.

Broomfield is like the investigator in *Citizen Kane* (1941), interviewing people in murky rooms. He is led to Nagy by interviews with prostitutes, who name the Hungarian as the man who introduced Fleiss via Madame Alex to the excitement and huge profitability of prostitution. These women draw a portrait of a man prone to violence, a sadist with an old world charm especially attractive to Heidi, who favors older men. Any man over forty, she will later tell Broomfield, looks good to her and seems "the right age." When Broomfield tries to get her to articulate why, she cannot or will not say. Like so much of her story, and like Broomfield's telling of the story, there is an overpowering sense of obsession that defies rational analysis.

What most troubles Broomfield, and what he tries to understand, is the love/hate between Nagy and Fleiss. They actually seem to enjoy taunting each other and then making up. Terms of endearment and abuse are virtually interchangeable—a point taken when Nagy produces a tape recording of one of his conversations with Heidi. Nagy often smiles maniacally after blaming Heidi for portraying him as a monster. Like her, he cannot hide a smirk, cannot suppress the fun he gets out of making up stories—even as he accuses others of making up stories about him.

Broomfield gets caught up in a war between two old pros—Madame Alex and Ivan Nagy. Madame Alex was the reigning madam before Heidi, and Madame Alex, old and more or less confined to her bed, tells Broomfield that Nagy groomed Heidi to steal Madam Alex's business, and then stole it himself from Heidi, setting her up for arrest by the Los Angeles Police Department. Madame Alex lays on her story very thickly. In her version, Heidi was a nothing—barely a five on a scale of ten, as Madame Alex puts it. Coming from an upper middle class family, her parents '60s types who believed in permissiveness and allowed Heidi to roam from home at the age of sixteen, Heidi apparently had no sense of restraint and took to prostitution in a greedy way that Madame Alex finds unseemly. Unlike Madame Alex, she did not play by the rules. She was supposed to be a snitch for the LAPD, but she rarely had any good information for them—as did Madame Alex, who kept her business going for thirty years because she knew how to pay off people.

Broomfield goes back and forth between Nagy and Madame Alex. Who is telling the truth? The witnesses hate each other, and eventually they turn on Broomfield. Madame Alex excoriates him for his insatiable questions and accuses him of leaking things she has told him confidentially to the press. He denies the allegation, but she cuts him off.

The truth seems to be that both Nagy and Madame Alex have seriously underestimated Broomfield. They thought they could manipulate him. His unassuming air makes him seem pliable. But his questions reveal his critical intelligence, and they react in fury when they realize he will not be content to accept their stories. They have mistaken his patient listening to their initial pitches for gullibility. When his questions reveal his skepticism—or at least his understanding that they have not satisfied his search for the truth—they are outraged and disgusted that they have spent so much time on him. He is an investment gone bad.

One of the few times that Broomfield almost loses his composure occurs when it seems that he has finally made his breakthrough to Heidi. She is working in a clothing store, trying to get away from the media frenzy, and yet not quite—for she is being interviewed by a local newswoman. As that interview is ending and Broomfield is approaching Heidi, Heidi suddenly turns to the local newswoman and asks her what she thinks of Broomfield filming her while she is going through the agony of her trial. Heidi suggests that there is something bizarre about Broomfield's project. The local newswoman treats Broomfield as an interloper, and when Heidi asks her what she should do, the woman replies that in Heidi's place she would be at home hiding from the press. This from a Channel 5 news personality fishing for a soundbite from Heidi! It is too much for Broomfield who ex-

CREDITS

Heidi Fleiss Heidi Fleiss
Ivan Nagy Ivan Nagy
Victoria Sellers Victoria Sellers
Madam Alex Madam Alex

Origin: USA
Released: 1996
Production: Nick Broomfield; released by In Pictures
Direction: Nick Broomfield
Cinematography: Paul Kloss
Editing: S.J. Bloom
Music: David Bergeaud
MPAA rating: Unrated
Running Time: 107 minutes

plodes—almost like a spurned lover—saying he has spent six months on Heidi's story. Who is this woman? he asks. What gives her the right to judge him? Is it because she has a Channel 5 on her microphone? He points to his BBC mike and sarcastically suggests that even without a number he has just as much right to film Heidi as Channel 5 does. But to the Channel 5 woman, spending six months on Heidi Fleiss is incomprehensible; it simply does not fit into her cut-and-run mentality. Heidi seems oblivious to the irony of pitting the Channel 5 woman against Broomfield. Or is Heidi being cunning, using one reporter to foil another?

The doubt arises because Heidi, once she does sit still for Broomfield, is not very communicative. Her main point is that she is her own woman. What Madame Alex, Ivan Nagy, and others who conspired against her could not abide was her independence. Throughout the interview, she cannot stop herself from smirking, from showing how much she enjoyed her million dollar lifestyle, and how much she still craves attention and recognition, and how little what she did really bothers her. Broomfield subtly undermines her sense that she was/is in control by showing how little she understands about herself. He keeps asking, why does she still have contact with Nagy? A confused Heidi keeps saying she does and she does not. She is caught in her own contradictions—a fact that Broomfield reveals in his closing credits with the bald statement that after shooting the film, Nagy testified in court against Heidi.

—*Carl Rollyson*

REVIEWS

Boxoffice. April, 1996, p. 118.
Los Angeles Times. February 9, 1996, p. F10.
New York Times. February 9, 1996, p. C15.
Newsweek. February 26, 1996, p. 66.
USA Today. February 19, 1996, p. 4D.
Village Voice. February 13, 1996, p. 68.

Hellraiser: Bloodline

"A non-stop nightmare!"—Dr. Donald Reed, *Academy of Science Fiction, Fantasy & Horror*

"The final *Hellraiser* is the most terrifying of all!"—Joseph B. Mauceri, *World of Fandom Magazine*

Box Office: $9,336,886

Hellraiser: Bloodline represents the last, dying gasp of a once-interesting idea which has finally run its course.

There used to be good reason to stay closely attuned to new developments in the *Hellraiser* series. The original *Hellraiser* (1987) had some genuinely fascinating moments. Based on a celebrated novel by Clive Barker, the film became the object of a huge cult following in science fiction/fantasy circles. Barker himself served as producer and director of the first installment, and he took the opportunity to make his wondrously maniacal presence known in nearly every aspect of the film, from the dialogue to the set design.

Director Kevin Yagher refused credit for this film and it was released under the standard director pseudonym, "Alan Smithee."

In the original *Hellraiser,* the unrelenting onslaught of blood and gore was counter-balanced by an element of raw eroticism which was sustained with great care from scene to scene. These considerations have been cynically tossed aside in *Hellraiser: Bloodline,* the fourth installment in the *Hellraiser* series. Gone are the erotic subtexts as well as the visual wizardry of the original: What we get instead is a pastiche of contrivances, a few villains (earthly and otherwise) who are not especially captivating, and an array of disposable victims who do not elicit much sympathy. The film is long on gratuitous bloodletting but painfully short on logic, as if the filmmakers had forgotten that they were actually supposed to be telling a story while serving up the expected measure of sex, violence and sadism.

The characters in *Hellraiser: Bloodline* are not helped by the feverishly convoluted plot. The first few scenes are set in the distant future, in the so-called Space Station Minos. The film's protagonist is Paul Merchant (Bruce Ramsay). Paul is described as the descendant of John Merchant (also played by Ramsay), an architect situated in present-day New York City, as well as one Philippe Marchand (Ramsay again), the original designer of the puzzle box, who resides in 18th-century France.

The plot is as thin as rice paper. For reasons which are

never entirely clear, Paul finds that he must travel into the past in order to avert a calamity which is about to unfold in the 22nd century. One section of the story centers upon John Merchant, the trendy architect who fails to realize that his elaborate designs are weirdly reminiscent of the demonic puzzle box. Another twist in the story introduces us to Philippe, who is the original maker of this device. Ramsay is given the unrewarding task of attempting a triple role in which none of the three characters is especially captivating. (Suffice it to say that Ramsay is dull, no matter which century he inhabits.)

One character transcends the passing centuries. She is Angelique (Valentina Vargas), a 500-year old vampire. (She may be viewed as a tacky distant cousin to the far more arresting and mysterious character played by Catherine Deneuve in *The Hunger* (1983), a movie which was considerably more erotic and far less bloodthirsty.) As the demonic femme fatale, Angelique travels through time and torments Paul's ancestors in the present as well as the distant past. Angelique is supposed to be a formidable figure—her "angelic" name is a perverse indication that she is really a she-demon from hell—but alas, she is played by Valentina Vargas, an actress of no discernible range.

The time-travel motif by which the origins of the puzzle box are explained seems to have been lifted from *Interview with the Vampire* (1994), and the tortuous transitions of time and place fail to disguise huge faults in the story line. The endless zigzagging through time quickly becomes tiresome in itself. The human victims come in and out of view with mind-numbing rapidity, and serve as little more than cinematic cannon fodder for the Pinhead and his diabolical companions. As usual, the unearthly villains are vastly more interesting than their quivering prey, who veer straight into trouble with idiotic consistency.

The Pinhead is a vivid and arresting character, but he requires a formidable human opponent (or at least, an earthly counterpart who is equally devious and depraved) in order to show off his best stuff. He gets neither of these in *Hellraiser: Bloodline.* Doug Bradley appears to have a ball reprising his role as the gatekeeper of hell, and the Pinhead gets all the best lines, but his devilish antics, which have now become the stuff of high camp, cannot enliven the hopelessly confusing story. "Do I look like the sort of person who cares what God thinks?," screams the perpetually irritable Pinhead. All shoulder pads and bitchy attitude, he's an extraterrestrial Joan Crawford.

Hellraiser: Bloodline has been described by its makers as the last in the *Hellraiser* series. Let's hope so: After four rounds, the Pinhead needs a rest.

—Karl Michalak

CREDITS

Phillip/John/Paul: Bruce Ramsay
Angelique: Valentina Vargas
Pinhead: Doug Bradley
Bobbi: Kim Myers
Rimmer: Christine Harnos
Genevieve: Charlotte Chatton

Origin: USA
Released: 1996
Production: Nancy Rae Stone for a Dimension Films/Trans Atlantic Entertainment production; released by Miramax
Direction: Alan Smithee
Screenplay: Peter Atkins
Cinematography: Gary Lively
Editing: Rod Dean, Randolph K. Bricker and Jim Prior
Production design: Ivo Cristante
Art direction: Ken Larson
Costume design: Eileen Kennedy
Music: Daniel Licht
Sound: Ed White
Make-up: Gary Tunnicliffe
MPAA rating: R
Running Time: 85 minutes

REVIEWS

Boxoffice. May, 1996. p. 75.
Detroit Free Press. March 10, 1996, p. 6G.
Los Angeles Times. March 11, 1996, p. F2.
The New York Daily News. March 9, 1996.
The New York Post. March 9, 1996.
The New York Times. March 9, 1996, p. 17.
Variety. March 11, 1996, p. 45.

High School High

There's a new teacha in the hood!—Movie tagline

"No holds-barred humor . . . about every funny bone is bound to be hit, some more than once."—Larry Van Gelder, *New York Times*

"Lovitz' dead-pan style is completely engaging, and at times, laugh out loud funny."—Jack Matthews, *Newsday*

"Jon Lovitz takes a flying leap into stardom, he is terrific. Director Hart Bochner displays a great deal of wit."—Michael H. Price, *Philadelphia Daily News*

Box Office: $20,951,277

Just as *Blackboard Jungle* (1955) set the tone for subsequent student/teacher melodrama, *Airplane!* (1980) remains the quintessential rapid-fire movie genre send-up. Put the two together and you get *High School High,* which aims to skewer the sanctimony of such one-teacher-can-make-a-difference films as the recent *Dangerous Minds* (1995) as well as the stereotypical issues most often identified with inner-city high schools. While the cliches found in films about the high school experience are ripe for satire, problems such as unmotivated youth, drug use, attempted rape and a crumbling educational system are hardly side-splitting fare. But political correctness isn't exactly the point here, and the result is an uneven collection of low-brow gags and guilty pleasure groaners that barely hold the film together long enough to get to the inevitable happy ending.

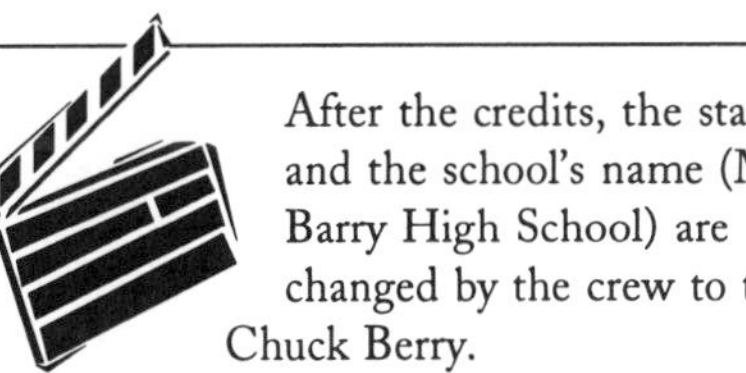

After the credits, the statue and the school's name (Marion Barry High School) are changed by the crew to that of Chuck Berry.

Amiable Jon Lovitz is Richard Clark, son of a private school headmaster who leaves his posh position at exclusive Wellington Academy (where the standard telephone greeting is, "Wellington Academy, are you white?") for Inner City's cleverly named Marion Barry High, a school so tough it has assigned parking spaces for SWAT teams. The visual and verbal gags that make up Clark's first day at the school are relatively inspired. His car radio plays only rap music. Bumper stickers identify "Proud Parents of a D Average Student." His idealistic enthusiasm for his new job soon rakes the ire of baseball bat-wielding (ala *Lean On Me* [1989]) principal Mrs. Doyle (Louise Fletcher). She's not about to tolerate Clark's do-gooder ways; after all, a photo of the last staff member who tried to control the students is now on a milk carton. Doyle's attractive assistant Victoria Chappell (a game but timing-impaired Tia Carrere), however, finds Clark's optimism charming, and the two join forces to ready his students for a college entrance exam. With the help of a former gang member (Mekhi Phifer) who is trying to go straight, they attempt to fend off a drug dealing conspiracy and transform the student body. Do they succeed? Of course.

Co-produced and co-written by *Airplane!* and *Naked Gun* alum David Zucker (or rather, as the caption under a symbol that opens the movie reads, "the producer formerly known as David Zucker,") *High School High* has a few bright spots amid the standard-issue crude and usually lame gags. Take-offs of scenes from *Rebel Without a Cause* (1955) and *The Deer Hunter* (1978) are amusingly clever, although the film's youth-oriented audience is unlikely to get the joke. Lovitz deadpans his way through his unlikely role as a sympathetic teacher with admirable success, as in a scene where he holds up a book and demonstrates, "They open like this!" Carrere (*True Lies* [1994]) and Phifer (*Clockers* [1995]) are less suited to slapstick. What begins as a mildly amusing spoof quickly becomes tedious as the skeletal plot veers a little too close to reality. At this point, *High School High* al-

CREDITS

Richard Clark: Jon Lovitz
Victoria Chappell: Tia Carrere
Evelyn Doyle: Louise Fletcher
Griff McReynolds: Mekhi Phifer
Natalie: Malinda Williams
Paco: Guillermo Diaz

Origin: USA
Released: 1996
Production: David Zucker, Robert LoCash, Gil Netter; released by TriStar Pictures
Direction: Hart Bochner
Screenplay: David Zucker, Robert LoCash, Pat Proft
Cinematography: Vernon Layton
Editing: James R. Symons
Music: Ira Newborn
Production design: Dennis Washington
Art direction: Tom Targownik
Costume design: Mona May
Sound: Hank Garfield
Casting: Elisabeth Lustig
MPAA rating: PG-13
Running Time: 86 minutes

most becomes the type of film that it intends to parody in the first place. Do we care if Clark's students pass the test? Not really—we're waiting for the next round of gags, which unfortunately, as the movie wears on, run hopelessly out of steam.

—*Terri Schell*

REVIEWS

Entertainment Weekly. November 8, 1996, p. 50.
The Detroit Free Press. October 25, 1996.
The Los Angeles Times. October 25, 1996, p. F8.
The New York Times. October 25, 1996, p. C20.
The New Yorker. November 11, 1996, p. 126.
USA Today. October 25, 1996, p. 5D.
Variety. October 28, 1996, p. 66.

Homeward Bound II—Lost in San Francisco

"Totally irresistible! A family winner!"—Ron Brewington, *American Urban Radio Networks*

"Nothing short of astounding!"—John Petrakis, *Chicago Tribune*

"It's one of those rare sequels that is better than the original. Your kids will love it and so will you."—Jim Svedja, *KNX Radio*

Box Office: $32,772,492

Pity the poor Seaver family: They never seem to learn from their mistakes. Barely recovered from the trials and travails of *Homeward Bound—The Incredible Journey* (1993), they now reappear in *Homeward Bound II—Lost in San Francisco,* a warmhearted but predictable sequel in which their beloved pets are once again exposed to an array of dangers.

In the original *Homeward Bound,* the Seavers made the dreadful mistake of leaving their precocious pets on a remote ranch while they went off to investigate a new home in the posh suburbs of San Francisco. The animals are Chance, a lovable mutt who also loves trouble; Sassy, a pampered Himalayan cat, and Shadow, an aging golden retriever who's been everywhere and seen everything. Thinking that they have been mistakenly abandoned, the pets decide to make a treacherous journey across the Sierras in order to locate their "lost" family.

"Beauty and brains. I never cease to amaze myself."—Sassy the cat

In the new film, Chance, Sassy and Shadow succeed in making their human owners seem more inept than ever. (Their voices are supplied by Michael J. Fox, Sally Field and Ralph Waite, respectively.) The Seaver family remains unfailingly kind and well-meaning, but painfully lacking in foresight. They are now happily settled into their sumptuous new home in the Mill Valley area. Initially, it appears that they may have learned a lesson from the miseries they endured in the original film: This time around, the hapless adults have the sense to bring the family pets along on their dream vacation in Canada. However, despite their best intentions, chaos quickly ensues.

The human characters stumble and blunder their way along, and as usual, it is the family pets who suffer most. The film's first extended set piece takes place in a San Francisco airport (or rather, the uninspired facsimile of one). A rather lame comedy of errors allows Chance, Shadow and Sassy to escape their carriers and turns them loose in the big, bad city. Although the film's plot is rife with situations which appear to pose a threat to the animals' safety—such as getting lost on a busy airport runway, clashing with a variety of inner-city, abandoned canines, or rescuing a child (as well as a kitten) from a burning house—it is always clear that the three principal heroes are never in any real danger. Even more so than in the original, the main question posed by the sequel is not whether the animals will find their way home, but how they will do it.

This is ultimately the film's most serious defect. *Homeward Bound II* suffers from the fact that while the possibility of catastrophe is often hinted at, no real danger is ever posed. This is to be expected in a Disney film, and may be reassuring to parents who do not wish to expose their younger children to even the slightest possibility of cinematic violence, but it also means that there is not much drama inherent in the story.

Visually, the film is an epic of laziness. Much of its credibility hinges upon the reasonably realistic depiction of San Francisco and its environs. Several scenes unfold in close proximity to easily recognizable tourist sights, such as Fisherman's Wharf and the Golden Gate Bridge, but these few paltry nods toward realism are undermined by the fact that much of the film was actually shot in Vancouver. Many discrepancies are apparent, and on the whole, the attempt at visual sleight of hand fails badly.

Ralph Waite takes over as the voice of Shadow from the late Don Ameche.

Not much effort has been spent in the evocation of authenticity. Those who attend this movie in hopes of seeing a gritty, realistic depiction of the mean streets of San Francisco are in for a rude surprise, for the sequel presents us with a fantasy San Francisco as it might be envisioned by the local board of tourism—a place remarkably free of dirt, crime and frenetic urban crowding.

The audience's attention is whipsawed back and forth between the animals' travails and the Seaver family's frantic efforts to locate them. At an early stage, Chance, Sassy and Shadow collide with a free-floating canine "gang" led by Riley, a smart-talking Doberman (whose on-screen voice is provided by Sinbad). The runaway dogs who surround Riley have all been abused or abandoned in various ways by their human owners, and are initially suspicious of their pampered suburban counterparts. Nevertheless, despite their hard knocks, they ultimately prove to be kind and benevolent.

Parents can rest assured that the film contains very little in the way of actual danger or violence. The only persistent element of menace is supplied by Ralph and Jack (Max Perlich and Michael Rispoli, respectively), the hapless dog catchers from the original film, who are at it again here. They're so ridiculously incompetent that no one could believe they would ever pose a serious threat to Chance, Sassy or Shadow or any of their clever canine pals—they're a disposable plot device, a bargain-basement equivalent of the much more outrageous thugs played by Joe Pesci and Daniel Stern in *Home Alone* (1990).

The story relies too much on coincidence, and suffers from an overabundance of cliched plot devices. Some of these seem painfully obvious, even for a film which is aimed primarily at a juvenile audience. (There is even the canine equivalent of an obligatory romantic subplot involving Chance and Delilah, the irresistible beauty—she's a Labrador retriever—from the wrong side of the San Francisco tracks.)

Homeward Bound II is clearly designed for younger children: Those older than nine are likely to be unimpressed by the film's somewhat outdated style of animation, and less tolerant of its many inconsistencies in regard to matters of setting; adult viewers run the risk of being overwhelmed by all the goo. Juvenile moviegoers who have already experienced the much more advanced feats of animation displayed by Chris Noonan's recent blockbuster, *Babe* (1995), are likely to lose patience with the predictable story and a style of animation which went out with Mister Ed and Francis the Talking Mule.

To the extent that it pretends to contain any message at all, *Homeward Bound II* seeks to remind children that not everyone is evil, and that some strangers (such as Riley and his scruffy canine pals) are indeed trustworthy. This puts the sequel very much at odds with its predecessor, in which all strangers, both human and canine, are viewed with suspicion. It also clashes with the hysterical xenophobia which most children are being taught these days.

Homeward Bound II is meant to be enjoyed rather than analyzed, much like an innocuous fairy tale. The audience is encouraged to suspend disbelief and ignore the fact that the San Francisco depicted here is about as dark and menacing as the rooftops of London in an earlier Disney success, *Mary Poppins* (1964). But even by Disney standards, this film has a peculiar, artificial feel.

As the bewildered parents, Robert Hays and Kim Griest are charming in roles which require little else of them. The children have not a hint of malice in their souls: They are al-

CREDITS

Father: Robert Hays
Mother: Kim Griest
Peter: Kevin Chevalia
Hope: Veronica Lauren
Jamie: Benj Thrall
Ralph: Max Perlich
Jack: Michael Rispoli
Chance: Michael J. Fox (voice)
Sassy: Sally Field (voice)
Shadow: Ralph Waite (voice)
Riley: Sinbad (voice)

Origin: USA
Released: 1996
Production: Barry Jossen for a Walt Disney Pictures production; released by Buena Vista
Direction: David R. Ellis
Screenplay: Chris Hanty and Julie Hickson; based on characters in *The Incredible Journey* by Sheila Burnford
Cinematography: Jack Conroy
Editing: Peter E. Berger, Michael A. Stevenson
Art direction and Set design: Michael Bolton
Costumes: Stephanie Nolin
Music: Bruce Broughton
Sound: Robert L. Sephton
Special Effects: Bill Orr
Animal Coordinator: Gary Gero
MPAA rating: G
Running Time: 89 minutes

ways well-mannered, thoughtful and kind. The adults on the scene, by contrast, are continually hapless and crisis-prone.

For those not given to rigorous analysis, *Homeward Bound II—Lost in San Francisco* is likely to be as sweet and enticing as a chocolate fudge sundae. But beware: Beneath all the spun sugar, there lies a movie with a heart of stone.

—Karl Michalak

REVIEWS

Boxoffice. May, 1996, p. 75.
Los Angeles Times. March 8, 1996, p. F14.
The New York Times. March 8, 1996, p. C12.
USA Today. March 8, 1996, p. 7D.
Variety. March 11, 1996, p. 44.

The Horseman on the Roof; Le Hussard sur le Toit

Chivalry lives. An epic adventure from the creators of *Cyrano.*—Movie tagline

"An exhilarating trip to the stunningly romantic realm of the past!"—Guy Flatley, *Cosmopolitan*

"You won't see a more romantic movie this year . . . Breathtaking!"—Jim Svejda, *CBS Radio*

"Two thumbs up!"—*Siskel & Ebert*

"Entertaining, provocative and incredibly beautiful!"—Paul Wunder, *WBAI Radio*

Box Office: **$1,320,043**

There was a lot riding on director Jean Paul Rappeneau's *The Horseman on the Roof* (*Le Hussard sur le Toit*). After the noteworthy success of his last offering, *Cyrano de Bergerac* (1990), which won the Golden Globe and National Board of Review Awards for Best Foreign Film, and an Oscar nomination in the same category, Rappeneau was in a position to realize a long-held dream: to adapt Jean Giono's 1951 novel for the screen. The book captured his imagination when he read it nearly a half century ago. Over the years, other well-know directors have been similarly inspired to film *Horseman,* including Luis Buñuel, René Clément, Roman Polanski and Constantin Costa-Gavras. Even Giono himself had the idea of directing an adaptation. Some big names were considered for the title role: Marlon Brando, Alain Delon, Anthony Perkins and Gérard Philipe. None of these projects ever got off the ground, and a film version of *Horseman* remained an illusive goal until Rappeneau thought seriously about finally trying his hand at it. "But the book frightened me as too vast, too beautiful, almost unattainable," he has said. "I was both attracted to it and scared by it." Still, Rappeneau pushed ahead, undertaking a massively expensive, elaborate production. Almost 44,000 miles of locations were scouted, over 1,000 costumes were designed by Academy Award winner Franca Squarciapino, 100 sets were constructed, and an equal number of roles were cast. Rappeneau led his cast and crew across the South of France for six broilingly-hot months until they mercifully reached the snowy Alps. In all, 176 million francs (almost $35 million) were sunk into the project, making it the most expensive cinematic effort in French history. Rappeneau's imposing project was watched with a hopeful, albeit nervously twitching, eye by the French, who, in recent years, have been increasingly unsettled by Hollywood's growing stranglehold on the imaginations and wallets of its country's filmgoing public. Remembering the triumph of Rappeneau's *Cyrano,* there was optimism that *Horseman* would come galloping to the rescue.

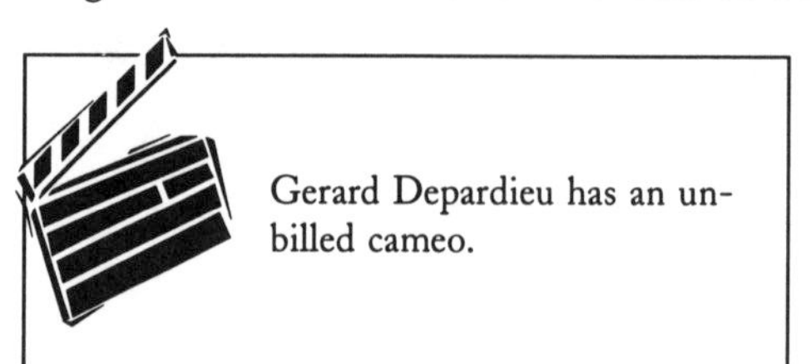

Gerard Depardieu has an unbilled cameo.

Horseman opens with an effervescent nighttime celebration in Aix-en-Provence during the summer of 1832. Noisy throngs cascade through the streets, while spectacular fireworks explode overhead. Amidst the darkness and confusion, spies from the Austrian Empire move stealthily through the town in search of members of the Carbonari, a persecuted Italian secret society which is working in exile to end Austrian domination back home. When the spies locate and murder one of the Carbonari, the pop from the gun that ends his life cannot compete with the booming fireworks for attention. The victim's distraught wife rushes to warn the gallant and dashing young Angelo Pardi (Olivier Martinez) that he may be next. As the enemy closes in around him, Angelo makes his first of many incredible (and often rather implausible), razor-thin escapes, and glides swiftly on horseback through lush forests and burgeoning farmland to warn the others. He meets up with Maggionari, a fellow Carbonari whom he has known since childhood, only to find that his longtime friend has become a traitor to the cause. Angelo makes another narrow escape, hurtling deeper into the Provençal countryside. He laments in one of his frequent letters to his mother back home that he is growing weary of constantly being on the run.

Looking for safety in the village of Manosque (the birthplace of Giono), Angelo finds it is in short supply. A cholera epidemic is raging, and mass hysteria rules the day. Hideous corpses are piling up everywhere. When Angelo stops to drink from a fountain, he is accused by the frenzied townspeople of trying to poison their water supply and is pursued through the streets. After a sword fight reminiscent of the swashbuckling films of Errol Flynn and Douglas Fairbanks, Angelo is taken to a befuddled magistrate (*Cyrano*'s Gerard Depardieu in a farcical cameo), who beats his own hasty retreat in the midst of their meeting. Angelo eventually escapes the tumult by huddling upon one of Manosque's many tiled rooftops. At night, Angelo enters the house through a window, and it appears eerily deserted. Suddenly he encounters a lovely vision in white illuminated by the glow of a candelabra. Angelo is awed by the regal beauty of Pauline de Theus (Juliette Binoche), who invites the bedraggled stranger to partake of what little food she has to offer. Even though she has a pistol hidden nearby, it is still rather odd that even a well-mannered lady would so serenely entertain an intruder (albeit a handsome one) in the midst of a plague. Pauline, a Marquise married to a man forty years her senior, explains that the house belongs to relatives of hers who left three days earlier to escape the spreading epidemic. Angelo, in turn, relates that he is transporting monies to Italy to help pay for a planned revolution. He is obviously in awe of her, and she is intrigued and amused by this sensitive, formal young gentleman. While Pauline is clearly independent and full of moxie beneath her delicately-beautiful exterior, Angelo insists that he is duty-bound to accompany her as she searches for her husband amidst the evacuees in the countryside.

After breaking through the line of soldiers who are enforcing a strict quarantine of the area, Angelo and Pauline find themselves pursued by the angry cavalrymen, as well as cholera-carrying crows which swoop down and attack a la Hitchcock's *The Birds* (1963). When they reach the home of Pauline's cherished friend, the Mayor of Mont Jay, she is chagrined to learn that her husband has gone back into the heart of the epidemic to look for her. Against the protestations of a jealous and worried Angelo, Pauline sets out alone to find him. She is immediately taken into custody by the soldiers and locked away with hordes of other people suspected of carrying the dreaded disease. Ever valiant, Angelo gets himself quarantined to be at Pauline's side. Her courage and vigor slipping away, Pauline is obviously moved, impressed and appreciative, but she also feels guilty that his unswerving devotion to her may lead him to a horrible death. "I couldn't leave you here," Angelo replies. Besides, he adds with a tone of reassurance, "Cholera avoids me like the plague." Up to this point in the film, Angelo's and Pauline's firmly-held, strict codes of conduct have kept them from acknowledging, let alone acting upon, their growing, deep feelings for each other. In addition to keeping their hands to themselves, however, they have also rather oddly and unbelievably kept their names to themselves until this late point in the film. Now more fully acquainted, the two break out of quarantine by setting the structure on fire (he) and shooting the door open (she).

When Angelo and Pauline find shelter from the rain and are enjoying wine by a fire, she presses her "guardian angel" to verbalize his feelings for her. "Am I nothing to you?" she asks. Pauline chides him for being "obstinately sensible" and "so young and so old." After she tells him more about her unfulfilling marital history, Angelo's formality re-

AWARDS AND NOMINATIONS

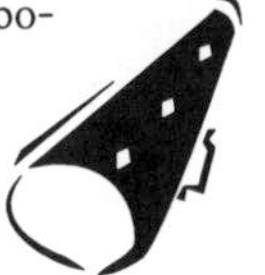

Cesar Awards 1996: Best Cinematography (Arbogast), Best Sound
Nominations: Best Film, Best Director (Rappeneau), Best Actress (Binoche), Best Sets, Best Editing, Best Costumes, Best Music

CREDITS

Angelo: Olivier Martinez
Pauline: Juliette Binoche
Governess: Isabelle Carre
Doctor: Francois Cluzet
Wayfarer: Jean Yanne
Maggionari: Claudio Amendola
Magistrate: Gerard Depardieu

Origin: France
Released: 1995; 1996
Production: Rene Cleitman for a Hachette Premiere production; released by Miramax
Direction: Jean-Paul Rappeneau
Screenplay: Jean-Paul Rappeneau, Nina Companeez, Jean-Claude Carriere; based on the novel by Jean Giono
Cinematography: Thierry Arbogast
Editing: Noelle Boisson
Music: Jean-Claude Petit
Production design: Jacques Rouxel, Christian Marti
Costume design: Franca Squarciapino
Sound: Pierre Gamet
Casting: Frederique Moidon
MPAA rating: R
Running Time: 135 minutes

laxes somewhat, and he reveals more about himself. The two briefly nuzzle before Pauline crumples upon the stairs with the sudden onset of cholera. A candelabra similar to the one she was holding when they first met falls from her hand and is ominously extinguished in a fountain below. As soon as Pauline begins vomiting (it starts to seem that almost everyone will graphically vomit at least once during the film), convulses, and turns white, one assumes that she is doomed, but Angelo rips off her clothes and rubs her with alcohol to sustain her circulation through the crisis. As he attempts to remove the proper lady's underwear, she declares, "I'd rather die." Angelo is undeterred, and, frankly, it becomes genuinely hard to tell whether she is moaning from the rubbing or the cholera. In any event, Pauline miraculously recovers due to Angelo's unceasing efforts, and he escorts her home to her husband. Though Pauline has returned, it is clear to her husband that her heart remains with Angelo. Some day soon, the Marquis will step aside and let his young wife go across the Alps to be with the man she truly loves.

The Horseman on the Rood was the top grossing film in France during its first week in release. It remained on the list of the ten top grossing films for over a month, earning $15.5 million before dropping off the list. Nearly a year later, Rappeneau's $35 million film had made just under $24 million worldwide, close to $2 million of which was earned in limited release in the United States. His *Horseman* is a film full of contrasts. On the one hand, there are the beautiful views of Provence, the pure love between Angelo and Pauline, the courageous and honorable way in which they conduct themselves, and the selfless but doomed country doctor. On the other, there is the horror of cholera, the absurdity and violence of the frightened and frightening mobs, and the treachery of Maggionari. Rappeneau, like Giono, made a conscious attempt to achieve an acceptable balance within his creation. Unfortunately, actually being able to see all the sickness and death that was described in the novel tends to emphasize it to the point that it is now the most potent force in the story, overshadowing the love story and creating a decided imbalance. Both Angelo and Pauline, as portrayed by real-life lovers Martinez and Binoche, are both so lofty and exquisite that they elicit admiration rather than a necessary empathy. Furthermore, they exhibit so much restraint that their story seems too static and muted. Still, many will probably find *Horseman* irresistibly romantic for its bridled passion.

—David L. Boxerbaum

REVIEWS

Boston Globe. May 24, 1996, p. 56.
Chicago Tribune. May 24, 1996, p. 7C.
Entertainment Weekly. June 7, 1996, p. 41.
Los Angeles Times. May 17, 1996, p. F6.
National Review. July 1, 1996, p. 58.
The New Republic. June 17, 1996, p. 24.
The New York Times. May 17, 1996, p. C3.
The New Yorker. June 10, 1996, p. 92.
Newsweek. June 3, 1996, p. 75.
People Weekly. June 10, 1996, p. 20.
Sight and Sound. January, 1996, p. 41.
USA Today. May 16, 1996, p. 6D.
Variety. September 25, 1995, p.92.
Wall Street Journal. May 17, 1996, p. A12.
Washington Post. May 24, 1996, p. D7.

House Arrest

Home is where the hostages are.—Movie tagline

"A surprising heart-warmer."—Bob Thomas, *Associated Press*

"A fun, family film that has all ages laughing."—Marilyn Beck, *Tribune Media Services*

"Funnier than *Multiplicity* and *Jack* put together."—Mike Clark, *USA Today*

Box Office: $7,032,513

House Arrest is about group therapy for married couples, an activity which lost its vogue after the 1960s because it led to more divorces than reconciliations. The interchanges "in group" often went like this: Wife: "You never talk to me." Husband: "What's there to talk about?" Wife: "You never talk about your feelings." Husband: "I feel tired."

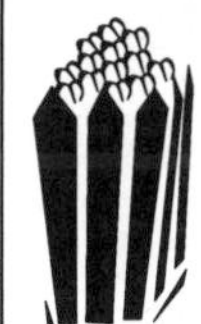

"I loved that film [*Parent Trap*] growing up and I thought it would be fun to do a *Parent Trap* for the '90s."—Screenwriter Michael Hitchcock

Precocious Grover Beindorf (Kyle Howard), a junior high school nerd, learns his parents are getting a divorce. He feels they are acting like naughty kids and should be grounded. Aided by his adoring little sister Stacy (Amy Sakasitz), Grover tricks them into going into the basement and locks the door. There is an uncanny undercurrent to this ostensible family comedy reminiscent of films like *Village of the Damned* (1960), in which super-intelligent, half-human children take control. Parents may spend the 108 minutes wondering if *House Arrest* is planting bad seeds in impressionable young minds.

Janet Beindorf (Jamie Lee Curtis) and Ned Beindorf (Kevin Pollak) run the gamut of emotion including disbelief, outrage, and panic. Their threats, pleas, and appeals to reason fall on deaf ears. Naturally they think of pretending they have actually worked everything out, thanks to their children's inspiration, and are ready to resume happy family life. Bickering has become so habitual, however, that they give themselves away even while Grover is pulling the nails out of the boarded-up door. They are told that they will have to stay put until they really work out their differences.

Other kids get in on the act. Soon the Beindorf basement is housing two more sets of parents plus the single mother of Grover's heartthrob Brooke Figler (Jennifer Love Hewitt of TV's "Party of Five"). Brooke is attracted to Grover when she realizes he is not such a nerd after all. T.J. Krupp (Russel Harper), the overgrown kid who bullied Grover at school, suddenly becomes his disciple, contributing his size and mechanical talents to keeping the parents incarcerated. T.J. jury-rigs a two-way television system for surveillance and indoctrination of the prisoners, who have to participate if they want to get fed.

Director Harry Winer has trouble with the film because it splits into two separate stories: *Home Alone* (1990) upstairs and Luis Bunuel's *The Exterminating Angel* (1962) in the basement. While the seven adults quarrel, their five children take over the house for a nonstop party. There are too many characters for all to register with the audience. The adults especially seem to be elbowing one another to get in front of the camera.

The characters who make an impression, in addition to Grover, T.J. and Grover's mom, are Vic Finley (Wallace Shawn) and T.J.'s father (Christopher McDonald). Shawn has been working regularly since he co-starred in the critically acclaimed *My Dinner with Andre* (1981), in which he spent most of his time listening, grinning and nodding because the conceited Andre was paying for the dinner. McDonald, as an attorney, only makes matters worse by threatening the kids with dire reprisals for unlawful de-

CREDITS

Janet Beindorf: Jamie Lee Curtis
Ned Beindorf: Kevin Pollak
Cindy Figler: Jennifer Tilly
Donald Krupp: Christopher McDonald
Gwenna Krupp: Sheila McCarthy
Vic Finley: Wallace Shawn

Origin: USA
Released: 1996
Production: Judith A. Polone, Harry Winer for a Rysher Entertainment production; released by MGM/UA
Direction: Harry Winer
Screenplay: Michael Hitchcock
Cinematography: Ueli Steiger
Editing: Ronald Roose
Music: Bruce Broughton
Production design: Peter Jamison
Costume design: Hope Hanafin
Art direction: Chris Cornwell
Sound: David MacMillan, David Kirshner
Casting: Wendy Kurtzman
MPAA rating: PG
Running Time: 108 minutes

tention. He is the typical grandstander who invariably surfaces in group therapy settings. His overbearing manner polarizes the others against him, including his long-suffering wife (Sheila McCarthy). The therapeutic effect of the resulting group cohesiveness exceeds Grover's fondest expectations.

Film is set in the town of Defiance, Ohio, the boyhood home of writer Michael Hitchcock, who named many of the characters after family and friends.

Jamie Lee Curtis, who played a mom in *My Girl* (1991) and *My Girl 2* (1994), stands out like the voice of reason in a lunatic asylum. Through superior acting talent, Curtis makes a ridiculous situation seem plausible as long as she is on camera. She shows wisdom in dealing with her two rebellious kids and becomes the responsible hostess even though she had not formally anybody to come over and be locked up in her basement.

Through group interaction, the three married couples develop more sensitivity and better relationships. The single mother, who has been driving Brooke crazy by trying to be a girlfriend instead of a mother, realizes she needs to relinquish her teenybopper clothes, baby talk, and Peter Pan illusions.

Joe Leydon, reviewing the film for *Variety,* thinks the underlying message of *House Arrest,* that "if kids are clever and resourceful enough, they can reunite their estranged parents. . . . will only serve to reinforce [the children's] darkest suspicions that they somehow are responsible for their parents' breakup, simply because they weren't resourceful enough to keep them together." He points out that many other comedies, including *The Parent Trap* (1961) and *All I Want for Christmas* (1991), "have peddled the same dubious bill of goods." Such comedies are like the Fred Astaire and Ginger Rogers movies of the Depression Era which made people forget their troubles until they walked back out into cold reality.

House Arrest received uniformly caustic reviews. Michael Wilmington of the *Chicago Tribune* calls it "a family comedy for people who hate families." It quickly went from ignominious double-billing with other box-office disappointments into the limbo where such films wait to be reborn as home video.

—Bill Delaney

REVIEWS

Boxoffice. July, 1996, p. 88.
Chicago Tribune. August 14, 1996, pp. 1.
Entertainment Weekly. August 16, 1996, p. 46.
Los Angeles Times. August 14, 1996, p. F6.
The New York Times. August 14, 1996, p. C16.
People. August 19, 1996, p. 19.
Variety. August 12, 1996, p. 33.

The Hunchback of Notre Dame

"A 10! This year's family hit!"—Susan George, *American Movie Classics*

"A visual feast!"—David Sheehan, *CBS-TV*

"This is a great film!"—Joel Siegel, *Good Morning America*

"One of the richest cartoon experiences of, and for, any age!"—Bob Strauss, *LA Daily News*

"Two thumbs up!"—*Siskel & Ebert*

"Magnificent! Extraordinary! Children will adore it, and adults will be flocking back to see it again!"—Gene Shalit, *Today Show*

"Enchanting! The summer's #1 family movie!"—Pat Collins, *WWOR-TV*

Box Office: $99,931,320

"One of the criteria for each new Disney animated film is to do something we've never done before," said Kirk Wise, who with Gary Trousdale directed both *Beauty and the Beast* (1991) and *The Hunchback of Notre Dame* (1996). Trousdale explained further, "[Victor] Hugo's novel is a brooding and dramatic tale, and that's the very thing that drew us to it." One of the most unlikely choices for an animated musical film, Hugo's tragic novel of the hunchback Quasimodo becomes a very effective, if somewhat grown-up, animated feature.

Tab Murphy designed a story from Hugo's 1831 novel that seems also to have borrowed from William Dieterle's 1939 film version with Charles Laughton and Maureen O'Hara. A pre-credit sequence tells in flashback how Judge Claude Frollo (voice of Tony Jay) is admonished by the Archdeacon of Notre Dame (voice of David Ogden Stiers) to care for the child of a gypsy woman trying in vain to reach the cathedral for sanctuary. Twenty years later, the deformed child has grow up to become Quasimodo (voice of Tom Hulce), the cathedral bell ringer who longs to be part of the teeming crowds below rather than live out his life in loneliness. In the adapters' most contrived touch, three gargoyles come to life in Quasimodo's imagination. This trio of comic relief is named Victor (voice of Charles Kimbrough), Hugo (voice of Jason Alexander), and Laverne (voice of Mary Wickes, additional dialogue by Jane Withers).

Their vaudeville patter urges Quasi, as they call him, to descend to the public square below and take part in the festivities of the Feast of Fools. When he does, he meets Esmeralda (voice of Demi Moore, singing voice of Heidi Mollenhauer) and her goat Djali. She has been protected from the soldiers looking for gypsies by Phoebus (voice of Kevin Kline), who later reports to Frollo as the new captain of the guard. Frollo instructs Phoebus on the need to exterminate the gypsies, and in one of the film's most memorable images he underlines his point by squashing a bug and lifting a capstone on the cathedral parapet to reveal dozens more. Frollo righteously explains that they must find the hidden lair of the gypsies, the Court of Miracles, and deal with them similarly. During the revelry in the town square, the feasters mistake Quasi's misshapen appearance for a costume and crown him the king of fools. Frollo disapproves of the hunchback leaving the cathedral, but Esmeralda rescues Quasi from the crowd's abuse. She also defies and taunts Frollo, calling him the king of fools. After Esmeralda runs from Frollo's guardsmen into the cathedral and after Phoebus prompts her helpfully, she asks for sanctuary.

Disney's animated tale of the reclusive and deformed bell ringer Quasimodo springs to life in this musical re-telling of Victor Hugo's classic, *The Hunchback of Notre Dame.*

This scene in which Esmeralda sings "God Help the Outcasts" and Quasi's earlier song "Out There" showcase well the film's most noteworthy trait: its richly textured backgrounds and amazing depth of field. "God Help the Outcasts" is the most memorable song by composer Alan Menken and lyricist Stephen Schwartz (the song was also covered by Bette Midler and included on the compact disc soundtrack for the film). The scene effectively contrasts the greed of the other supplicants, whose prayers echo with the refrain "I ask . . . I ask . . . ," with the openheartedness of Esmeralda, who asks nothing for herself and only help for the downtrodden and needy. The final image of the song lights Esmeralda in the glow of the richly textured sunlight streaming through the cathedral's massive stained glass window. Musically, visually, and dramatically, it is one of the film's most uplifting moments.

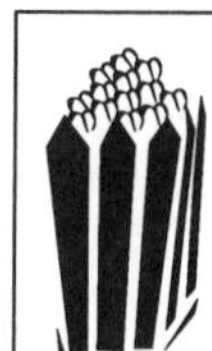

"What do they have against people who are different, anyway?"—Esmeralda

The animation team worked carefully to capture the shifting patterns of light and dark in the cathedral, partly because such a design represented the duality of the central characters. Art director David Goetz reported that the visual plan for the film was formed in part by a visit to the Bibliothèque Nationale in Paris, where the artists viewed drawings by Victor Hugo as well as the nineteenth-century illustrator Gustave Doré. "Because we wanted to honor Hugo's legacy, I remember looking at those illustrations and thinking, 'We're on the right track.' We tried to catch the feeling in the lights and darks and in the architecture, of what is going on, symbolically, in the narrative." Stephen Rebello, who wrote a book about the artwork in the film, commented that for inspiration during production the animators lined the walls of their studio with photographs of Notre Dame, pages from illuminated manuscripts from the medieval period, and reproductions of the work of old masters like Pieter Breughel and Edouard Manet. Consequently, the film rejects a picture-book ap-

AWARDS AND NOMINATIONS

Academy Awards 1996 Nominations: Best Original Score (Menken)
Golden Globe Award 1997 Nominations: Best Original Score (Menken)

proach. To co-director Kirk Wise, the look of the film is "cyberGothic, as opposed to the manicured country club look that the medieval era has in *Sleeping Beauty* [1959]."

Another distinctive feature of the film is its dramatic opposition of unhealthy religion versus Christian acceptance, the first time such a theme has been explored in a Disney animated feature. Judge Frollo embodies all that is life-denying in religion. Sneering, self-assured, harsh, and judgmental, he displays a self-righteousness that cannot tolerate the passion aroused in him by Esmeralda, and he faults her for this growing lust. His prejudice toward the gypsies and his bruised pride from Esmeralda's insult at the Feast of Fools also complicate his motives. Never has there been a Disney animated villain so psychologically and morally conflicted, nor do the filmmakers shrink from exploring Frollo's divided feelings. As co-director Gary Trousdale explained, "Every character in the book hinges on the idea of duality. The most ugly creature has the most beautiful spirit, and the most pious man has the ugliest soul."

This was the last film role for 85-year-old Mary Wickes, who died six weeks after voicing her role as gargoyle Laverne.

Frollo's song "Hellfire" renders well these contradictory traits. Cast in the form of a prayer to the Virgin Mother, Frollo's musical soliloquy contrasts Esmeralda's earlier song of Christian humility and compassion. As he fondles Esmeralda's scarf and stares into the swirling flames of his hearth, the image of Esmeralda taunts him in the fire. David Goetz, in one of the more surprising quotes from the filmmakers, said that the "Hellfire" scene would be the one place where the creative team would "very consciously retain the sexual tension around which the book seems to revolve." During the song Frollo becomes more and more heated but somehow finds a way to forgive himself: "It's not my fault/I'm not to blame/It is the gypsy girl, the witch who sent this flame/It's not my fault/If in God's plan/He made the Devil so much/Stronger than a man." The mix of self-justification and self-disgust recalls the torment of Shakespeare's Angelo in *Measure for Measure* (1601) perhaps one of Victor Hugo's inspirations in creating the character. While the film clearly endorses the tolerance of Esmeralda over the darkness of Frollo, not surprisingly, this scene is reduced to just one page in the Disney Press novelization of the film for young readers.

Esmeralda befriends Quasi when she sees the figurines and miniature village he has carved in his lonely bell tower. Reminding him of the difference between sanctuary and freedom, she lets him carry her down the outside of the cathedral to escape Frollo's men watching every entrance. Outside, she gives Quasi an amulet with the cryptic promise that it will lead him to the Court of Miracles.

The remaining scenes in the film show more changes in the source materials to bring about the expected happy ending. Frollo's intent to have or destroy Esmeralda leads to a stormtrooper-like raid of gypsy dwellings in Paris. He first intimidates then tries to bribe information about Esmeralda. At a miller's house Frollo orders Phoebus to burn the adjoining mill with the family trapped inside. Refusing, Phoebus instead saves the lives of the miller's family after Frollo has torched the building. Frollo condemns his insubordination and prepares to order Phoebus's execution when Esmeralda, observing from hiding Phoebus's brave rescue, throws a stone to startle Frollo's stallion and permit Phoebus to gallop off. As Phoebus crosses a bridge, an arrow from one of Frollo's archers catches him in the shoulder, and he plummets off his horse into the water. Esmeralda pulls him to safety in the darkness below and takes the injured Phoebus to Quasi in the cathedral bell tower.

Quasi painfully sees that Esmeralda loves Phoebus, and, after sending her away again to safety, he agrees to nurse him. Quasi conceals Phoebus under his table. Frollo has guessed that Quasi had provided Esmeralda with her escape from the cathedral, and as Paris still burns from his search, he now promises to attack all the gypsies the next morning with a thousand men. The groggy Phoebus tells Quasi that they must somehow travel to the Court of Miracles and warn

CREDITS

Quasimodo: Tom Hulce (voice)
Esmeralda: Demi Moore (voice)
Frollo: Tony Jay (voice)
Phoebus: Kevin Kline (voice)
Laverne: Mary Wickes (voice)
Hugo: Jason Alexander (voice)
Victor: Charles Kimbrough (voice)

Origin: USA
Released: 1996
Production: Don Hahn for a Walt Disney Pictures production; released by Buena Vista
Direction: Gary Trousdale and Kirk Wise
Screenplay: Tab Murphy, Irene Mecchi, Bob Tzudiker, Noni White, and Jonathan Roberts; based on the novel *Notre Dame de Paris* by Victor Hugo
Editing: Ellen Keneshea
Music: Alan Menken
Song: Stephen Schwartz (lyrics)
Art direction: David Goetz
Artistic coordination: Randy Fullmer
Casting: Ruth Lambert
MPAA rating: G
Running Time: 86 minutes

the gypsies. Quasi hesitates, having been schooled all his life by Frollo's prejudice and hatred. But he finally agrees to help and shows Phoebus the amulet Esmeralda left him. To Quasi, the design forms a map of Paris that takes them to a graveyard. They spot a headstone with a symbol matching one on the amulet, and they lift it to find an underground passage. The skeletons lining the walls of the catacomb turn out to be gypsies in disguise who arrest Quasi and Phoebus as spies. Esmeralda quickly prevents their being harmed, but Frollo and his men had followed Quasi to the Court of Miracles. He arrests the gypsies, promising a public execution the next day.

The climax of the film returns to the public square where the Feast of Fools had occurred. Now Esmeralda is tied to the stake about to be burned as a witch, and high on the cathedral above Quasi too is chained. His gargoyle friends urge him to rescue Esmeralda. In one of the film's most powerful computer-generated images, Quasi breaks his chains, loops a rope to a parapet, and swings down to save Esmeralda. Although he carries her again to sanctuary, he and Phoebus soon see that they are outnumbered by Frollo's men besieging the cathedral. Quasi scatters them by pouring down on the soldiers a vat of molten lead used to repair cracks in the cathedral bells.

The final confrontation between Quasi and Frollo begins in the chamber where Quasi has taken Esmeralda. The filmmakers find the perfect image for Frollo: he approaches Quasi speaking of duty but concealing a dagger behind his back. Their struggle leads them to the high ledges of the cathedral, where Quasi tries to hold on to Esmeralda's hand as he dangles dangerously over the square. The gargoyle supporting Frollo cracks from his weight and sends the judge falling to his death. As Esmeralda's hold on Quasi slips, he falls into the waiting arms of Phoebus reaching to catch him from a window. Now the hunchback will be greeted as a hero by the gypsies below and fulfill his dream of joining the people.

The box office returns for *The Hunchback of Notre Dame* were slightly disappointing in comparison to the large amounts brought in by previous Disney animated features. With earnings of about $100 million, the receipts fell below the marks set by both *Pocahontas* (1995; $142 million) and *The Lion King* (1994; $313 million). Many reviewers predicted that the grown-up nature of the conflict in the film might pose a problem for parents having to explain aspects of the film to their children and that the literary subject matter might also hurt the film's box office. While some reviewers noted that purists might complain that the film streamlined too much of the novel, many rightly praised the filmmakers for their willingness to take on ambitious, new challenges in a genre that Disney has made its own.

—Glenn Hopp

REVIEWS

Advertising Age. July 22, 1996, p. 1.
Boxoffice Magazine. June, 1996, p. 13.
Detroit News. June 21, 1996, p. 1D.
Entertainment Weekly. June 21, 1996, p. 28.
L.A. Magazine. July, 1996, p. 116.
Maclean's. July 1, 1996, p. 62.
New Statesman. July 12, 1996, p. 40.
Newsweek. June 24, 1996, p. 83.
The New Yorker. July 8, 1996, p. 84.
New York Times. June 23, 1996, p. H1.
People Weekly. June 24, 1996, p. 19.
Rolling Stone. July 11, 1996, p. 96.
Time. June 24, 1996, p. 73.
Variety. June 17, 1996, p. 51.
Wall Street Journal. June 21, 1996, p. A12.

I Shot Andy Warhol

You only get one shot at fame.—Movie tagline
"Funny!"—Guy Flatley, *Cosmopolitan*
"Taylor is riveting!"—Juliann Garey, *Glamour*
"The best evocation of the '60s yet captured on film."—Stephen Farber, *Movieline*
"Tantalizing, walk on the wild side black comedy."—Daphne Davis, *Movies & Videos*
"Dazzling!"—Stanley Kauffmann, *The New Republic*
"Lili Taylor gives a great, funny, furiously alive performance."—Janet Maslin, *The New York Times*
"Compelling!"—Bruce Williamson, *Playboy*

Box Office: $1,875,527

Mary Harron's first feature is a riveting account of the near-fatal shooting of pop icon Andy Warhol by one of the fringe characters of his inner-circle, radical activist Valerie Solanis. The film focuses on the assailant herself and vibrates with the restlessness and growing paranoia that led her to commit the famous crime. Indie-queen Taylor (*Mystic Pizza* [1988], *Short Cuts* [1993], *The Addiction* [1995], and *Girls Town* [1996]) slips seamlessly into the baggy, grungy clothes of Solanis, giving a deep and very believable portrayal of the disturbed fanatical feminist, playwright wanna-be, and eventually, desperate criminal. *I Shot Andy Warhol* is a well-written and visually distinct account involving the highly publicized pop artist, Andy Warhol, who happens to be enjoying a revival along with a few of his associates in the currently released *Basquiat* (in which David Bowie portrays Warhol) and *Nico Icon,* a documentary on Warhol's famous Velvet Underground singer.

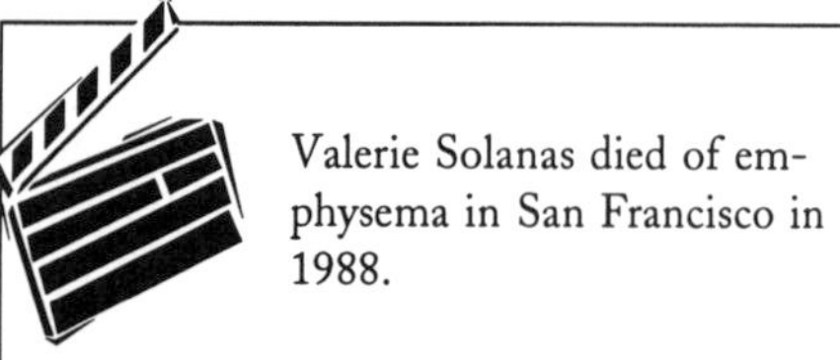

Valerie Solanas died of emphysema in San Francisco in 1988.

The film's dramatic first image is of the twitching cowboy boots of the wounded Warhol—cut to Solanis repeatedly pulling the trigger of a spent .38 automatic. Solanis immediately turns herself in and while being psychologically evaluated, the story of her life unfolds. From a childhood filled with episodes of sexual abuse by her father to a literary life in college supported by prostitution, Solanis's reasons for hating men are presented. Interspersed throughout the film is Solanis "narrating" the story directly at the camera, reading parts of the radical feminist manifesto for her one-woman society, SCUM: Society for Cutting Up Men, which denounces reproduction and touts the superiority of women by claiming the Y chromosome of the male is merely a defective and incomplete X chromosome of the female. After graduation, Solanis, a self-proclaimed "butch lesbian," begins panhandling and prostituting herself on the streets of New York to pay the bills, allowing her to "knock off for a few days and write." The streets become her domain, and she is shown, repeatedly, trying in vain to sell her manifesto and recruit members for SCUM.

Solanis's bohemian friends include drag queen Candy Darling, whom Stephen Dorff plays as a sadly eloquent individual. Candy, who frequents the trendiest nightclubs of New York, eventually leads Solanis to Warhol, who is brilliantly portrayed by Jared Harris. Warhol is outwardly the anti-Solanis and is as nonviolent, unemotional, passive, and feminine as Solanis is violent, wildly emotional, dominating, and masculine. Harron underscores the point visually by contrasting the worlds they each inhabit. Warhol's dreamy silver factory filled with his spacey and beautiful friends abuts the images of Solanis sleeping on rooftops, installed in cramped apartments, or having sex for money with sick, overweight, and abusive men. The two, however, are alike in that they each share a visionary quality and are both social misfits. Across a crowded room at a party, their eyes lock for a moment in an unspoken bond and later they are spotted amidst the revelry seated, portrait-like, at opposite ends of the couch. Solanis immediately becomes obsessed with Andy and begins harassing him with constant and urgent telephone calls after she sends him a copy of a play she wrote and thinks he ought to produce. Although Andy is a bit put off by her behavior, he is at the same time attracted to her intensity and, feeling sorry for her, he gives her a screen test and casts her in his latest movie.

Solanis's life as a literary figure seems on the upswing when she meets wealthy avant-garde Frenchman, Maurice Gerodias (Lothaire Bluteau), who claims he has published the likes of William Burroughs and Vladimir Nabokov. He urges her to write a novel and offers a generous contract for the work. When he mentions that he lives in the arty Chelsea

AWARDS AND NOMINATIONS

Independent Spirit Awards 1997 Nominations:
First Feature (Harron)

Hotel, Solanis packs her things and gets a room there also. The dichotomy found throughout the film also serves to illustrate the dichotomy of Solanis's psyche and her obsession and need of men whom she also hates by their very nature. Warhol and Gerodias seem at once to help her and be the cause of her ruin. Both supply her with money and outwardly seem generous but both also carry an underlying motive of using her for their own gain: Warhol for his movie projects and as a fresh source of amusement, and the dubious Maurice, who gives her a bad check but eventually does publish her manifesto (now regarded as a feminist classic).

"All these revolutionary girls come across very hard to me."—Candy Darling

Solanis's paranoia becomes even more obvious after she signs a contract with Maurice. She feels unnaturally bound and grows agitated and violent, repeatedly threatening him. The pivotal moment with Warhol comes when the normally verbally abusive Solanis becomes physically abusive with him as well. She feels Warhol has stolen her play (which he has merely shunted aside after his friends deem it too dirty, even for them). Despite his usual tolerance of deviant behavior, she is officially banished from Warhol's court. Now humiliated in the art and literary scene and alienated from most of her friends, Solanis becomes consumed with pushing her manifesto and her beliefs on the rest of society. Seemingly a paranoid obsessive, she begins to see conspiracy plots against her involving both men in her life. When Gerodias leaves town, her plan to seek justice against him is thwarted and she pursues her other target. Incorporating violence into her beliefs, she has no qualms with shooting Warhol in his studio along with one of his associates.

A psychological portrait of a victim of society, Solanis is portrayed realistically and sympathetically. She is seen both as an intelligent, sarcastic, streetwise freethinker and a violent conspiracy-minded, paranoid lunatic. Constantly blaming men for her own as well as all of society's problems, Solanis claims, among other things, that they are to blame for all the world's violence. Conversely, men in this film are given many of the traditional qualities of women, embodied by Darling, Warhol, and Gerodias. They are sensitive, soft-spoken, and demure while women are driven, arrogant, and sometimes violent. Solanis is an outsider begging to be let in, but is disillusioned and out of place when allowed to do so. The predominant images of Solanis are of her sleeping alone in some foreign environment. When Warhol throws a big party, Solanis is taken with the vision of a beautiful woman dancing and tries to pick her up. The woman is pleasant but clearly distressed by Solanis's intensity and is soon rescued by Warhol superstar Gerard Malanga, played by Donovan Leitch. He whisks her off to the darkroom where they make love, while Solanis is crashed out on Andy's couch alone. When she goes to her last, and probably only, friend Stevie's apartment in search of refuge, she is thrown out when Stevie tires of her rantings. A desperate Solanis heartbreakingly crys, "Don't make me go out there!" Clearly, there is no longer any place that Solanis can hide from an unaccepting world and her paranoid fears.

The famous people and landmarks of the underground New York scene are all concocted, thankfully, with great authenticity and attention to detail. Hairstyles, clothing, and boho attitudes are flawless—without a trace of stereotypical characters in sight. In a standout performance, Taylor delivers Solanis's hip dialect and bravado straight-up—swaggering, and chain-smoking her way through the film with unabashed enthusiasm.

—Hilary Weber

CREDITS

Valerie Solanas: Lili Taylor
Andy Warhol: Jared Harris
Maurice Girodias: Lothaire Bluteau
Stevie: Martha Plimpton
Candy Darling: Stephen Dorff
Iris: Anna Thompson

Origin: USA and Great Britain
Released: 1996
Production: Tom Kalin and Christine Vachon for a Playhouse Intl. Pictures, Goldwyn and BBC Arena production; released by Samuel Goldwyn Co.
Direction: Mary Harron
Screenplay: Mary Harron and Daniel Minahan
Cinematography: Ellen Kuras
Editing: Keith Reamer
Production design: Therese Deprez
Costume design: David Robinson
Sound: Rob Taz
Music: John Cale
MPAA rating: R
Running Time: 106 minutes

REVIEWS

Boxoffice. April, 1996, p. 114.
Entertainment Weekly. May 3, 1996, p. 58-59.
New York Times. April 5, 1996, C10.
Newsweek. May 6, 1996, p. 78.
Sight and Sound. December, 1996, p. 48.
USA Today. May 3, 1996, 10D.
Variety. January 29, 1996, p. 60.
Village Voice. May 7, 1996, p. 47.

If Lucy Fell

In a city with a million love stories . . . theirs was one of a kind.—Movie tagline

"Charming and sentimental. Eric Schaeffer reinvents the smart, sassy, screwball romantic comedy for twenty-somethings."—Susan Granger, *CRN International*

" . . . one of the best romantic comedies in months; outrageous, endearing and very, very funny."—Jim Svejda, *KNX Radio*

"A kinky *When Harry Met Sally* for the 90's."—Dr. Joy Browne, *WOR Radio*

Box Office: $1,300,000

Actors, directors, critics, and especially writers all say that successful and convincing comedy is the hardest thing to pull off. Action-adventure, drama, mystery all pale in comparison when faced with the daunting task of satisfying an audience by making them laugh. As fluffy and breezy as they are on the surface, the romantic comedy requires a finer touch, a dynamic and well-balanced cast and an almost perfect sense of timing. None of those qualities are found in Eric Schaeffer's *If Lucy Fell.*

If Lucy Fell is Schaeffer's first big studio effort after his low budget, independent (and far superior) *My Life's In Turnaround.* Schaeffer's first and most glaring mistake is the wearing of three different (but very important) hats at the same time. Writing, directing and taking the lead male role in a romantic comedy is just too much responsibility for a beginner to assume. Orson Wells, John Cassavetes, Woody Allen and Warren Beatty all found success doing everything, but not the first time out of the blocks. (Actually, Wells did it with *Citizen Kane,* but he was a former child prodigy whose ego dwarfed his subject matter, and that's saying a great deal). What compounds Schaeffer's dilemma is the fact that his comedy isn't funny, the direction is spotty and worst of all, he is definitely not leading man material.

Joe's artwork was created by artist Sam Messer who also aided Ben Stiller in creating his own artwork for the Bwick character.

"Sometimes I feel things, Lucy." "What you feel, I treat."—Bwick to girlfriend, and psychotherapist, Lucy.

Joining Schaeffer in other principal roles are Sarah Jessica Parker, Elle Macpherson and Ben Stiller. Joe (Schaeffer) and Lucy (Parker) have been roommates for a long while. The normally decisive Lucy can't make up her mind when it comes to choosing a male suitor. Joe has been pining for Jane (Macpherson) for well over five years. Jane occupies the apartment directly across from Joe and Lucy. He spends every available second observing her and she drives him crazy with desire.

Lucy's 30th birthday is less than a month away. Joe reminds her of a pact they made way back in the stone age, when they were teenagers. They both agreed that if neither of them was deep in love with their one and only by the time she was 30, they would both jump off the Brooklyn Bridge and plummet to their deaths. Coming up with a fresh premise for a comedy is tough. But is it comical to put a time limit on falling in love? Or to carry out a suicide pact made at a time when adulthood seemed light years in the future? These are not the workings of a sane mind or someone with any recognizable comedic talent.

With this dilapidated plot firmly intact, Joe and Lucy set about getting their act together. She promises she will stop her snide, bitchy, presumptive attitude and give one guy a real chance. He swears he will ignore his overwhelming fear of Jane and invite her to a museum exhibition of his paintings. Joe is a grade school art teacher who does more "serious" work in his free time. Strange how an artist with a museum show and a doctor (Lucy's a psychiatrist) need to share an apartment, but after all, "it is" New York. Surreptitiously placing an invitation under Jane's door, Joe is flabbergasted when she actually shows up. Joe's many phobias go into overdrive and he suffers a panic attack. His obsession with his neighbor is evident at the museum show, as every painting is a picture of Jane.

Elle Macpherson surprised many by putting on 20-odd pounds to play a bountiful nude model in John Duigan's 1994 sleeper *Sirens.* She showed a comedic timing no one expected from a supermodel. She also had a small role in Woody Allen's *Alice* (1990). You don't get a part, however small, in a Woody Allen film based solely on looks. She can currently be seen in Franco Zeffirelli's *Jane Eyre.* Again, it was small part, but effective and against type. As Jane, Macpherson plays a vacuous twinkie sleepwalking her way through her lines. She's arrogant and detached. This role was not a wise choice for Macpherson to take. In one of the most unfathomable scenes in modern film history, Jane, feeling warm and fuzzy by Joe's fawning, puppy dog loyalty, asks him to go to bed with her. He demurs. This is the same man who's been "saving" himself for her for over five years.

CREDITS

Lucy Ackerman: Sarah Jessica Parker
Joe MacGaunaughhill: Eric Schaeffer
Bwick Elias: Ben Stiller
Jane Linquist: Elle Macpherson
Simon Ackerman: James Rebhorn
Al: Dominic Luchese

Origin: USA
Released: 1996
Production: Brad Krevoy, Steve Stabler and Brad Jenkel for a TriStar and Motion Picture Corp. of America production; released by Sony Pictures Entertainment
Direction: Eric Schaeffer
Screenplay: Eric Schaeffer
Cinematography: Ron Fortunato
Editing: Sue Graef
Production design: Ginger Tougas
Costume design: Ane Crabtree
Sound: Pawel Wdowczak
Casting: Sheila Jaffe, Georganne Walken
Music: Mary Me Jane, Amanda Kravat, Charles Pettis
MPAA rating: R
Running Time: 94 minutes

At the same museum show, Lucy meets another artist named [really] Bwick (Stiller). Bwick is a monosyllabic ("You . . . me . . . eat.") abstract artist who creates his works by having two burly assistants dip him in paint and then throw him up against a wall. His Jamaican dreadlocks are hideous overkill. Stiller is a tremendously talented actor. He acted in and directed the impressive *Reality Bites* (1994), currently has the lead role in the near perfect *Flirting with Disaster* and directs Jim Carrey in *Cable Guy*. Stiller's turn here is wasted by playing the cosmic, mystical hippie to abhorrent extremes.

The movie concludes with a last minute, lifesaving happy ending dripping with an ersatz sentimentality that matches the banality exuded throughout the entire film. Schaeffer showed promise with *My Life's In Turnaround.* Hopefully, he can find a producer who didn't see *If Lucy Fell* to finance his next project. He would be wise to stick exclusively to direction, find a co-writer and quickly learn the lesson it took Quentin Tarantino years to figure out: don't act in your own movies.

—J.M. Clark

REVIEWS

Boxoffice Magazine. March, 1996, p. R-26.
Los Angeles Times. March 8, 1996, p. F8.
New York Times. March 8, 1996, p. C10.
Rolling Stone. March 26, 1996, p. 106.
USA Today. March 8, 1996, p. 7D.
Variety. February 5, 1996, p. 63.

Independence Day

We've always believed we weren't alone. On July 4th, we'll wish we were.—Movie tagline

"This movie is undeniably fun."—David Denby, *New York Magazine*

"*Independence Day* is a dazzling fireworks display. Full of noise and color and excitement."—Michael Medved, *New York Post*

"It's impossible to resist."—Janet Maslin, *New York Times*

"*ID4* delivers a full throttle blast. It gives you aliens to hiss at, humans to root for, and the kind of fireworks that get audiences cheering."—Peter Travers, *Rolling Stone*

"The grandest film of the summer. *ID4* is a sensation machine; you leave saying Wow!"—Richard Corliss, *Time Magazine*

Box Office: $306,155,579

Will Smith prepares to demolish hostile aliens just as his blockbuster film *Independence Day* demolished previous boxoffice records.

A shadow falls across our moon threatening the fragile Earth which lies in the near distance. Chest-vibrating rumblings shake its surface, wiping out man's first footsteps set in the dust and untouched since 1969. Whatever is making the theater shudder, it's huge! Is it a spacecraft filled with aliens coming to take over our planet? Or is it audiences stampeding to box offices across America to see the winner of the summer's mega-hit sweepstakes, *Independence Day*?

Opening a few days earlier than originally advertised, *Independence Day* began its summer run on Tuesday, July 2 for what 20th Century Fox said was a preview. But one showing turned into two, and three and four. All night the film ran to sell-out crowds, and by Wednesday morning it had taken in $11.1 million. By the end of the four-day holiday weekend, it was breaking all records. This was marketing savvy and manufactured audience anticipation at its highest.

Film's boxoffice broke the $100 million mark in a record six days.

And just what were people getting for their price of admission? Great entertainment.

In this self-admitted combination sci-fi thriller, disaster film and war movie, *Independence Day* offers us a story rife with menacing villains of astral proportions, horrendous scenes of destruction, an uplifting coming together of all peoples of the world, the danger and deliverance of technology, acts of heroism, and the triumph of the human race. What more could we want? It's our nostalgic Saturday afternoon matinees married to all the comic books we've ever read . . . and all done with just enough humor to not take itself too seriously.

As the aliens' giant mother ship (550 kilometers in diameter) sends out her smaller "daughters" (only about 15 miles across) to mysteriously hover above several of the Earth's major cities, the people of the world wait and wonder if these visitors have come in peace or not. Will they find the descendants of Steven Spielberg's *ET* or H.G. Well's "War of the World?"

While people marvel and puzzle over what it all implies, a technician, computer wizard, and chess player at a satellite television station, David Levinson (Jeff Goldblum) makes a spine-chilling discovery: the aliens are using our own satellites to communicate around the globe, they have placed the daughter ships strategically (like chess pieces) and are just waiting to checkmate us all. We have seven hours to save ourselves.

Luckily, David's ex-wife, Constance (Margaret Colin), works for the president, David Whitmore (Bill Pullman). However, she refuses to take his calls. Consequently, David packs up his laptop computer and his father, Julius (Judd Hirsch), and drives off from New York City to Washington D.C. to deliver his sermon of doom in person. By this time the aliens have shown their true colors—shooting down a helicopter with "Welcome Wagon" written on it—and the President knows we're all in trouble.

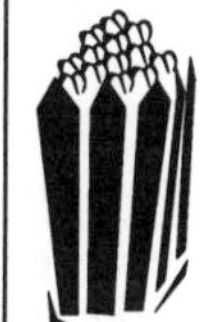

"They're like locusts, they move from planet to planet, consuming all the resources, then move on. We're next."—President Whitmore about the alien invaders.

Just as the President and his entourage escape on Air Force One, the fireworks, literally, begin. The daughter ships open up and send down a wall of flames that consume the cities over which they hover. Washington D.C., gone. Los Angeles, gone. New York City, gone. And no one has heard from Moscow.

Now it's time to get seriously angry. Mustering whatever forces are left, President Whitmore calls for a strike against the alien ships. More disaster follows. The aliens have not only surrounded their ships with a protective and totally impervious shield, they also have the same shield on the hundreds of fighter ships they discharge to take on our fighters. Our forces are wiped out . . . except for Captain Steven Hiller (Will Smith) who manages to crash and capture an alien all at the same time.

Eventually Hiller hooks up with a ragtag group in Winnebagos, one of whom is an ex-Vietnam fighter pilot and now drunken crop duster Russell Casse (Randy Quaid) who claims his life took a dive after he was abducted by aliens. Together they make their way to the legendary Area 51 in Nevada where the President, who has only just learned of its existence, is checking out what knowledge we have secretly gathered from previous alien landings. Headed by the slightly crazed Dr. Okun (Brent Spiner), Area 51 doesn't have as much information as hoped, but the alien spacecraft in their possession has, suddenly, become active and is now in working order. If we can just rally what's left of the world's resources, figure out how to fly that baby, and discover a way to penetrate their shields, then maybe the world can be saved.

These are the basics of the story. If you'll go along for the ride, it will be a hoot. If you begin to look at things logically, scientifically, then you're in trouble—and it starts early.

If the mother ship is as large as they say, and it's parked near the moon, wouldn't that effect our tides? While scientists are wondering what's going on with their radar screens, if it's that large, couldn't they have just looked out their windows and figured everything out? And with all the telescopes in the world, didn't anybody see these guys coming? And why is it that the aliens seem to function in Earthling hours and minutes? Why is it that with the huge budget the Pentagon has had the only weapons we can find to fight the aliens are fighters. (Where are all those expensive missiles and armed submarines?) And most perplexing of all, how does Capt. Hiller manage to interpret and fly the alien ship when the control panel (not to mention the ergonomics of the cockpit) are designed for aliens we don't begin to understand.

But school's out, remember? This is summer movie fare. This is science fiction. This is special effects. This is sly humor within fantastic drama. And this is entertainment, not science.

Many factors save *Independence Day* from being too closely examined. One is the cast. Like the 1960's Irwin Allen disaster films (i.e. *Airport, The Towering Inferno, Earthquake,) Independence Day* seems to have a cast of thousands, dozens of whom are leads. There are intertwining stories, characters taken from all walks of life, and we're never sure who will make it through the cataclysm, and we basically like them all.

The President, earnestly played by Bill Pullman, solidly works to keep the nation's hope alive while orchestrating all attempts at salvation. He is a onetime Gulf War fighter pilot of whom the McLaughlin Group on television says, "We elected a warrior and got a wimp." Here's his chance to prove himself.

David, the computer genius, yet another quirky intellectual in Jeff Goldblum's dossier, is the brains behind the brawn which will eventually save us. He's still in love with his wife Constance who divorced him because he'd rather use his eight years at MIT to be a "cable guy" than to really achieve something in life. Here's his chance, too.

And Captain Hiller as played by Will Smith is cocky and heroic, but is also unable to realize his dream of joining NASA. If he marries his girlfriend Jasmine (Vivica Fox) who is a stripper, he can just kiss his goal of flying in space goodbye. Or can he?

There are also many substantial secondary leads who lend interest and eccentricity to the story. Mary McDonnell, the First Lady who is caught away from her husband in Los Angeles when all hell breaks loose, unfortunately has little to do after being rescued by the resourceful Jasmine. Judd Hirsch's kvetchy Jewish father can be a bit thick, but also provides

AWARDS AND NOMINATIONS

Academy Awards 1996: Best Visual Effects
Nominations: Best Sound

much of the story's humor. And speaking of humor, the loopy Dr. Okun is an amusing change for Brent Spiner's normal emotionless Data on "Star Trek: the Next Generation." But the largest secondary role probably falls to Randy Quaid whose inebriated Russell Casse provides not only some of the film's funniest moments but also its most heroic.

There are many other subsidiary characters—homosexuals, secretive government officials, stern generals, kids, and the rest of humanity (summarized in British, Jewish and Arab pilots all flying together to save mankind)—in this film that harkens back to the 1950s, when aliens were something to be feared not welcomed and feel-good endings were preferable to today's cynicism.

CREDITS

Capt. Steven Hiller: Will Smith
President Thomas J. Whitmore: Bill Pullman
David Levinson: Jeff Goldblum
Marilyn Whitmore: Mary McDonnell
Julius Levinson: Judd Hirsch
Constance Spano: Margaret Colin
Russell Casse: Randy Quaid
Gen. William Grey: Robert Loggia

Origin: USA
Released: 1996
Production: Dean Devlin for a Centropolis Entertainment production; released by 20th Century Fox
Direction: Roland Emmerich
Screenplay: Dean Devlin, Roland Emmerich
Cinematography: Karl Walter Lindenlaub
Editing: David Brenner
Music: David Arnold
Production design: Oliver Scholl, Patrick Tatopoulos
Art direction: Jim Teegarden
Alien creature effects: Patrick Tatopoulos
Digital effects producer: Tricia Ashford
Visual effects producer: Terry Clotiaux
Stunt coordinator: Dan Bradley
MPAA rating: PG-13
Running Time: 145 minutes

If this sounds as if *Independence Day* is cliched, it's not. Sure, it borrows heavily from other genres, but that's OK. Director/writer Roland Emmerich and his partner co-writer/producer Dean Devlin (responsible for *Stargate*) have found new twists for many of the hackneyed ideas, and have woven them together in such an entertaining package that only the most critical moviegoer (the kind of person who delights in telling five-year-olds that there's no Santa Clause) will be bored or annoyed.

Another reason for this is the film's special effects. They are complex and extensive. In fact, the filmmakers used five visual-effects companies for this film. Many of the special effects were created by composites of up to 75 images as compared to the norm of such films as *Apollo 13* where five or six images were combined. Of course, the shots where the White House and other buildings and cities are blown up are eyepoppers (hint: the flames are filmed upside down), but then again, other shots like that of the air battles may be intricate, but they look like what they are, computer generated images, models, and matte shots. Sometimes less can be more—it was scarier to see the ominous alien spacecraft shadows fall across familiar terrain than to actually see the aliens.

But again, being critical is for those who just don't want to get into the spirit of this summer film. Those who just don't want to immerse themselves in a disaster/war/science fiction story because it lacks imagination, logic or total believability. Sure it's trite at points. Sure it's hokey. Sure it's bigger-than-life. Sure it's a bit short in the plausibility and logic department. But it sure is fun.

—Beverley Bare Buehrer

REVIEWS

Chicago Tribune. July 2, 1996, p. 1.
Entertainment Weekly. July 12, 1996, p. 37.
New York Times. July 2, 1996, p. C11.
Newsweek. July 8, 1996, p. 51.
People. July 8, 1996, p. 19.
Variety Online. July 1, 1996.
Village Voice. July 9, 1996, p. 41.

Infinity

He was no ordinary genius. Theirs was no ordinary love.—Movie tagline

The extraordinary true love story of a genius and the woman who knew him by heart.—Movie tagline

"Wonderful and romantic . . . an astonishing directorial debut!"—Francesca Miller, *Female FYI*

"*Infinity* is a movie worth seeing."—John Polly, *Genre*

"An intelligent, sweet-natured film . . . a touching portrait."—Stephen Holden, *The New York Times*

"Broderick and Arquette are perfect together."—Jack Mathews, *Newsday*

"An engaging and unexpected love story."—Bruce Williamson, *Playboy*

"Two thumbs up!"—*Siskel & Ebert*

Box Office: $195,170

Infinity is a slow-moving, good-looking drama that tries unsuccessfully to combine love and science (and the love of science). It covers the early life of theoretical physicist Richard Feynman, one of the scientists working on WWII's Manhattan Project, and his meeting, marriage, and the tragic early death of his first wife Arline Greenbaum.

Pic opens with a shot of the adult Feynman (Broderick) apparently stargazing and a bio crawl that briefly summarizes his importance to modern physics and his winning of a Nobel Prize in 1965. The film, based on Feynman's two volumes of memoirs, *Surely You're Joking, Mr. Feynman!* and *What Do YOU Care What People Think,* is clear in its intentions: "It has only partly to do with science. It was, in his memory, a love story."

Richard first meets, and is smitten by, Arline Greenbaum (Arquette) in 1934 (he's 16, she's presumably about the same age) and even takes art classes at the same youth center to gain her attention. (Neither Broderick nor Arquette can successfully pass for teenagers but these scenes are mercifully brief.) In 1939, with Richard a senior at MIT, the duo become lovers while in Atlantic City for the weekend, during which time Richard also tries to explain his mathematical concepts (and the difference between knowing numbers and knowing math). Arline appears interested but my eyes glazed over.

By 1941, when Feynman is in the graduate program at Princeton, the two are engaged. Arline notices a swelling in her neck, a problem with her lymph glands, and begins the first of her hospital stays. Arline's first misdiagnosed with Hodgkin's disease but further tests reveal she actually has tuberculosis—at the time contagious and incurable. Fearing for his health, Richard's family tries to persuade him to break his engagement, but he and Arline elope instead.

With the outbreak of WWII, Feynman, who's been working on a government project to separate uranium, is chosen by Robert Oppenheimer to join the Manhattan Project in Los Alamos, New Mexico and it's arranged that Arline will stay in a hospital in Albuquerque—waiting to get better or die (you're never aware of any treatment that Arline may be undergoing). Richard makes the 100 mile trip on weekends as the couple try to establish some semblance of domestic life. They have a cookout on the hospital lawn and Richard uses olives to explain neutrons, photons, and nuclei to Arline. (His continual explanations of scientific principles seem designed to remind the audience just what he's up to).

Two years pass as Arline gets more ill, even (briefly) losing her temper with her solicitous husband: "Why aren't you afraid of what you're doing? Of what's going on here?"

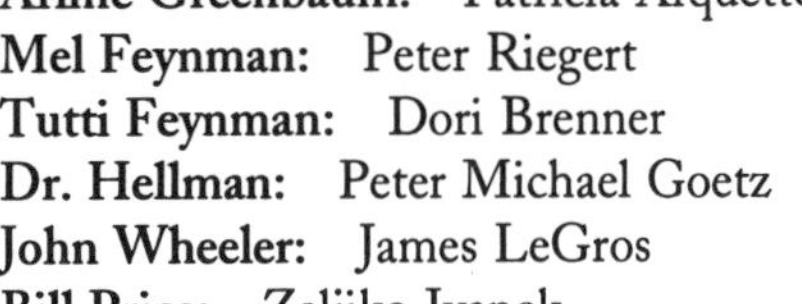

CREDITS

Richard Feynman: Matthew Broderick
Arline Greenbaum: Patricia Arquette
Mel Feynman: Peter Riegert
Tutti Feynman: Dori Brenner
Dr. Hellman: Peter Michael Goetz
John Wheeler: James LeGros
Bill Price: Zeljiko Ivanek

Origin: USA
Released: 1996
Production: Matthew Broderick, Patricia Broderick, Michael Leahy, and Joel Soisson for a Neo Motion Pictures production; released by First Look Pictures
Direction: Matthew Broderick
Screenplay: Patricia Broderick; based on the memoirs of Richard Feynman, *Surely You're Joking, Mr. Feynman!* and *What Do YOU Care What Other People Think?*
Cinematography: Toyomichi Kurita
Editing: Elena Maganini, Bill Johnson, Amy Young
Music: Bruce Broughton
Production design: Brent Capra
Art direction: Jeffrey (Tex) Schell
Costume design: Mary Jane Fort
Casting: Lisa Bankert
MPAA rating: PG
Running Time: 119 minutes

Finally on May 8, 1945 (VE Day), Richard receives a call to get to the hospital. He sits by Arline's bed as she struggles for breath and then the room is silent. The quiet is affecting as he gently touches her cheek, kisses her hair. Feynman spends the remainder of the night outside the hospital, looking at the stars, the same scene that opened the movie.

Directorial debut of Matthew Broderick, who also starred, as well as co-produced with mother Patricia Broderick.

Unfortunately, that's not the end of the film. Feynman returns to Los Alamos after Arline's funeral for the first testing of the atomic bomb, although you get no particular idea of the test's importance or the consequences of their actions (with the exception of Ivanek's Bill Price, the other scientists were a confusing blur, anyway).

"So that idea, the idea that there's no end to how big a number can be, that's called infinity."—Feynman and one of his mathematical explanations

There's a welcome lack of self-pity and tears between the characters. Arline, a seemingly smart and tough cookie, knows she's dying and so does Richard, though the two never seem to talk about what's happening. Arline's slow death doesn't have the film building to any cathartic climax—or rather it struggles to build to two—Arline's actual death and the testing of the bomb. While the final hospital scene is quietly moving, the film then lingers on too long afterwards.

Arquette has actually little to do but (mostly) lie in various hospital rooms. Her character's independent and opinionated when healthy but her illness slowly robs her of these traits, though she doesn't hesitate to tell her husband off when she thinks he's a dope.

Feynman was noted for his humor and eccentricities by his fellow scientists but these character traits must have developed later in life as they're rarely apparent in the movie. Broderick displays a steadfastness in his character's love for his wife but it's not easy to convey mathematical genius and there's no sense of urgency to the Los Alamos scenes. As a first-time director, Broderick (who also co-produced with mother Patricia Broderick, who wrote the screenplay) shows an affinity for working with actors (Riegert's Mr. Feynman is notable) but the film never manages to reconcile its humanistic qualities with the scientific.

—Christine Tomassini

REVIEWS

Boxoffice. September, 1996, p. 116.
Los Angeles Times. October 4, 1996, p. F8.
New York Times. October 4, 1996, p. C17.
New Yorker. October 7, 1996, p. 97.
People. October 14, 1996, p. 27.
Variety. September 16, 1996, p. 68.
Village Voice. October 8, 1996, p. 72.

The Island of Dr. Moreau

By turning animals into humans, he's turned heaven into hell.—Movie tagline

"Absolutely smashing!"—Ron Brewington, *American Urban Radio Network*

"Frankenheimer's back! And he's returned to top form!"—Rex Reed, *The New York Observer*

"It's campy, creepy and cool! It's a wild film!"—Jeff Craig, *Sixty Second Prevue*

Box Office: $27,682,712

One hundred years after the publication of H.G. Wells chilling novel *The Island of Dr. Moreau,* Hollywood has chosen to produce a third version of the tale. The dangers of unbridled science underpinning Wells' visionary work remain sadly pertinent to our age, whereas this new film is simply sad.

John Frankenheimer is an experienced director, but his film often feels as if it is subject to the same anarchy into which the island ultimately falls. The story opens when Englishman Edward Douglas (David Thewlis), having survived not only a plane crash but six days in a life raft with two other men who end up killing each over the last canteen of water, is rescued by a passing ship. Douglas is a United Nations representative on a peace mission. His rescuer is the inscrutable Montgomery (Val Kilmer). Montgomery administers treatment to the dehydrated Douglas and delivers him to the island until contact with the outside world can be established.

Original director Richard Stanley was fired three days into filming and actor Rob Morrow, in the Douglas role, asked to be replaced.

To Douglas's questions, Montgomery offers guarded information about the lush island, its military-style compound, and the unseen Dr. Moreau—a Nobel Prize winner for inventing velcro. Left in the main house for a while, music draws Douglas to observe a young woman dancing. This is Aissa (Fairuza Balk), and in their first conversation, it is revealed that she is Moreau's daughter. Douglas is then shown to his room, only to be locked in by Montgomery.

Our U.N. envoy turns out to be able to pick locks, and by evening, he escapes and makes his way into a laboratory in which an operation is underway. A mostly animal female, but a creature with distinctly human features, is giving birth on a table. On either side of a stupefied Douglas, animal/human fetuses are suspended in tanks. And thus a horrifying blast of the reality of the island hits Douglas in the face.

As Douglas flees from "the horror, the horror!" he is helped by Aissa. In another part of the island, they encounter the blind Sayer of the Law (Ron Perlman). He is talking to his "congregation" about morality, and what responsibilities they must uphold. For, he declares, "We are men—are we not?"

It is then that Dr. Moreau arrives on the scene and into the film. He looks rather like a Pope in a Pope-Mobile. Caked in white face paint, his lips rouged, and dressed in a tent-like white outfit, Moreau takes charge by using his console to control his flock by inflicting pain on them.

A deeply shocked Douglas is invited to dinner by Moreau, and over the table, the doctor introduces his other "children." They are all hybrids of animal and human. Perhaps most grotesque of all is Moreau's tiny cohort Majai (Nelson de la Rosa) who dresses identically to his master and apes (no pun intended) his behavior. Douglas inevitably demands explanations; Moreau contends that he could not possibly provide a thorough rationale over the dinner table, so he argues instead that his work is a search for purity and perfection in living, sentient beings.

Montgomery is served with roasted rabbit. Moreau, who claims to be against killing, is outraged, and demands to know who is the culprit. Dinner is then abandoned. The following morning, one of Moreau's creatures is to take the blame for the rabbit's slaying. The doctor apparently intends only a display of pain infliction, but one of his children takes it on himself to execute the perpetrator, and suddenly the stone of rebellion is pushed downhill as the creatures are enraged by the murder.

The following morning, Hyena (Daniel Rigney) rescues his friend's skull from a furnace and pulls out the implant with which Moreau exercises his punitive control. That night, Hyena and accomplices break into the main house and disturb Moreau, who tries to placate them by teaching them—of all things—the musical theory of Arnold Schoenberg. The response is to murder their music teacher.

The island, and unfortunately the film as well, now descends into a jumble of violence and meaninglessness. Montgomery appears to have gone mad and takes to imitating the voice and costume of his dead mentor, Moreau. This comes across less as an indication of the character's loss of sanity than a cruel parody of Marlon Brando. Douglas now learns that the beautiful Aissa is also a hybrid, and that Montgomery has destroyed the serum that enables her to appear fully human. Searching in the lab for something to help her, he discovers that his DNA was taken when he was being treated by Montgomery after his rescue at sea. Reunited with Aissa, the pair try to save themselves, but are cornered by the mob after Montgomery is murdered. Aissa is hanged.

"Has it ever occurred to you you might have totally lost your mind?"—Douglas to Dr. Moreau

In what is meant to be the climactic scene of the film, a raging Hyena tries to assert his rule over the creatures. And why not, since he has Moreau's pain-console? But as fire burns and loose-cannon creatures with guns await provocation, Hyena cannot last, and he is gunned down in a scramble for power.

The epilogue has Douglas speaking in voice-over and preparing to sail a boat back to "civilization." News footage of human violence is intercut to hammer home the idea that civilization is but a hair's breadth remove from the anarchy of Dr. Moreau's island. The wise old Sayer has taken charge, and he asks Douglas not to bring scientists back with him and bring change. The creatures must be what they are, the Sayer declares. Douglas sails off, rueful, but alive.

Manohla Douglas of *The L.A. Weekly* allowed that the final half hour of the film was "ludicrous," but found words of praise nonetheless. It called Brando "invariably fascinating" and had no problems with Thewlis or with Kilmer—"at least what's left of his transparently trimmed performance." In contrast, Susan Stark of *The Detroit News,* was scathing, and made a salient point about Douglas' voice-over. His narration calls attention "to philosophical and cautionary implications of the freak show," said Stark. "Count that 90 minutes late and the price of admission short, and you'll have it about right."

Even before its opening, *Moreau* had been reported to have been a difficult shoot. The original director was replaced; Rob Morrow dropped out of his role as Douglas, and one of the actors on set was notoriously hard to handle. Surprisingly, this was not Brando. It was Val Kilmer.

In spite of the film's sound and fury, it offers an inert experience. The screenplay by Richard Stanley and Ron Hutchinson is largely witless and lacking insight. Worse, the script artificially inserts its message about the potential for human destructiveness in a self-conscious manner through Douglas' late voice-over.

Director John Frankenheimer orchestrates the action sequences effectively, but he provides no cohesion for his cast, and certainly no perspective on the large issues at the heart of Wells' original story. As Douglas, David Thewlis is not a character one cares for enough. So effective in the films *Naked* (1993) and *Restoration* (1994), here Thewlis is awkward, and his nasally northern English accent grates. Val Kilmer sleepwalks through the film, although his character's purpose on the island is always kept vague. At least Fairuza Balk brings in a dash of emotional vulnerability—something missing from Thewlis' work.

In his role, Brando chooses to speak in a plummy English accent. More ridiculous than menacing, more camp than cunning, Brando uses buck teeth to make his top lip protrude. One cannot sense the intellect behind his character, or glimpse the evil passion that has driven Moreau to his monstrosities.

This remake of the *Island of Dr. Moreau* runs an hour and a half. It is never terminally boring, but it is shockingly uninvolving, given the talents of the cast, and the fact that we are surely not inured yet to the horrors science can produce. A whole lot of wasted effort and unfocused acting, writing and direction adds up to a highly disappointing film.

—Paul B. Cohen

CREDITS

Dr. Moreau: Marlon Brando
Montgomery: Val Kilmer
Douglas: David Thewlis
Aissa: Fairuza Balk
Sayer of the Law: Ron Perlman
M'Ling: Marco Hofschneider

Origin: USA
Released: 1996
Production: Edward R. Pressman; released by New Line Cinema
Direction: John Frankenheimer
Screenplay: Richard Stanley and Ron Hutchinson; based on the novel by H.G. Wells
Cinematography: William A. Fraker
Editing: Paul Rubell
Production design: Graham (Grace) Walker
Art direction: Ian Gracie
Set decoration: Beverley Dunn, Lesley Crawford
Costume design: Norma Moriceau
Sound: David Lee
Special creature and makeup effects: Stan Winston
Music: Gary Chang
Stunt coordination: Glenn Boswell
MPAA rating: PG-13
Running Time: 95 minutes

REVIEWS

The Detroit News. August 23, 1996, p. D1.
Entertainment Weekly. September 6, 1996, p. 52.
Los Angeles Times. August 23, 1996, p. F12.
The New York Times. August 23, 1996, p. C8.
Newsweek. September 2, 1996, p. 66.
People. September 9, 1996, p. 17.
USA Today. August 23, 1996, p. 8D.

It's My Party

A gathering of friends. A gift of love. A celebration of life.—Movie tagline

"An emotional celebration that is both heartbreaking and hilarious . . . It's the party of the season."—Stephan Saban, *Details*

"Brave, bold, beautiful, funny and heartbreaking. This is a very special film indeed."—Rex Reed, *The New York Observer*

"A celebration of life, love and friendship. *It's My Party* is right on target . . . you can't help but love this movie. Hilarious and heart-breaking . . . an eclectic and strong cast."—Bob Healy, *Satellite Network News*

Box Office: $622,503

Brandon Theis (Gregory Harrison) and Nick Stark (Eric Roberts) are obviously great friends and committed gay lovers. Brandon is a television director whose money has built the house Nick has designed and in which they both live. After being together for many years, Nick is told by his doctor (Ron Glass) that he has AIDS which he probably contracted long before he met Brandon.

Story was based on the farewell bash Hollywood decorator Harry Stein, a friend of Kleiser's, threw before his own suicide.

Two results follow from this life-shattering news. First of all, Brandon distances himself both emotionally and physically from Nick. Eventually this will cause their relationship to deteriorate and Nick is forced to move out. The second thing to occur is that Nick refuses to just wait for fate to carry out his death sentence. After his sight and memory begin to fail he is diagnosed with PML (Progressive Multifocal Leukoencephalopathy) or brain lesions. This gives him only a short time to live, but also gives him the courage to enact "Plan B," to die by his own hand while he is still himself and surrounded by his family and friends.

"When you got sick, I guess I got scared."—Brandon to ex-lover Nick, who's dying of AIDS.

To put this strategy into effect, Nick goes through his Rolodex and sends out invitations to what will become a two-day farewell party. One invitation he doesn't send out, however, is to his ex-lover Brandon. But Nick's good friend Charlene Lee (Margaret Cho) realizes that these two men need to reconcile their differences and invites Brandon anyway.

From the number of people who attend Nick's party, it is obvious that he is greatly loved. His mother Amalia (Lee Grant) and his sister Daphne (Marlee Matlin) try to protect him and support him, and showing up as a surprise guest is Nick's estranged father Paul (George Segal) who hides from life in an alcoholic stupor. Nick's friend Monty Tipton (Bronson Pinchot) tries to make him laugh, while two other friends, Rodney Bingham (Bruce Davison) and his wife Lina (Olivia Newton-John), rely on Nick to bridge the gap between themselves and their gay son Andrew (Devon Gummersall). Yet another friend, Damian Knowles (Roddy McDowall), brings a spark of intellectual interest to the story by questioning the morality of Nick's choice to commit suicide—but he is portrayed very heavy-handedly and is practically begging to be booed off the screen—but beyond this, the ethics of the situation is never discussed, it is just taken for granted.

It is a star-studded party that director-writer Randal Kleiser throws for Nick, and it is a testament to the story's sincerity that he can get so many people to "attend" his small-budget film for scale wages. But while the cast adds depth, color, and interesting background details, the story itself is too scattered when focusing on them, and too thin when focusing on Nick. There's really no narrative depth here. Once the basic premise is established, there is nothing to wonder about, no sense of expectation. We know what will inevitably happen, and that it will probably be emotional, but there's really no drama. In that respect, I suppose, *It's My Party* is trying to be more factual, more true-to-life, than it is theatrical and tense. But this matter-of-fact approach makes the movie less than memorable.

The best thing about *It's My Party,* besides its obvious commitment to and earnestness about the subject, is the presence of Eric Roberts. As a young actor in films like *King of the Gypsies* and *Star 80,* he was the critic's darling. But through his own admitted use of drugs, he self-destructed his career and is only just beginning to get his proverbial act together again. In *It's My Party,* he shows that he may be doing a successful job of doing so. While there are still hints of the older, more manic Roberts, as Nick he now gives a more controlled and sen-

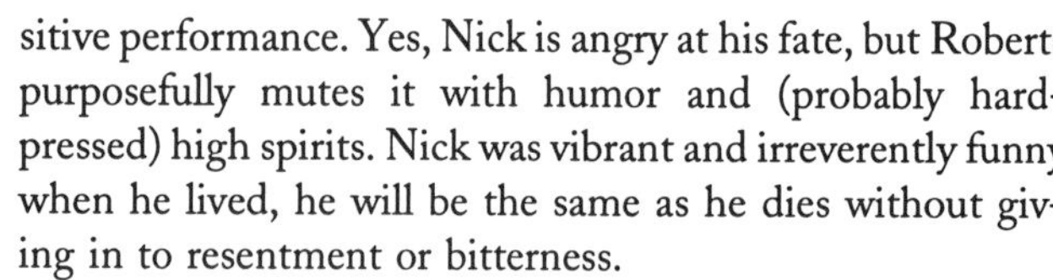

sitive performance. Yes, Nick is angry at his fate, but Roberts purposefully mutes it with humor and (probably hard-pressed) high spirits. Nick was vibrant and irreverently funny when he lived, he will be the same as he dies without giving in to resentment or bitterness.

Robert's performance, however, can't save the film. It is not as masterful or stirring as *Longtime Companion* which also covered this topic (and which also starred Bruce Davison) and it doesn't have the dramatic drive to keep our interest focused on much other than peripheral characters.

—Beverley Bare Buehrer

CREDITS

Nick Stark: Eric Roberts
Brandon Theis: Gregory Harrison
Amalia: Lee Grant
Daphne: Marlee Matlin
Tony: Paul Regina
Charlene: Margaret Cho
Monty: Bronson Pinchot
Paul Stark: George Stark

Origin: USA
Released: 1996
Production: Joel Thurm, Randal Kleiser for an Opala and United Artists Pictures production; released by MGM/UA
Direction: Randal Kleiser
Screenplay: Randal Kleiser
Cinematography: Bernd Heinl
Editing: Ila Von Hasperg
Music: Basil Poledouris
Production design: Clark Hunter
Costume design: Danielle King
Casting: Joel Thurm, Steven Fertig
MPAA rating: R
Running Time: 110 minutes

REVIEWS

Boxoffice Magazine. April, 1996, p. 116.
Chicago Tribune. March 22, 1996, p. H1.
Detroit News. May 3, 1996, p. 3D.
Entertainment Weekly. April 14, 1996.
Los Angeles Times. March 22, 1996, p. F6.
New York Times. March 22, 1996, p. C6.
Sight and Sound. April, 1996, p. 46.
Variety. January 29, 1996, p. 62.
Village Voice. March 16, 1996, p. 52.

Jack

He's a healthy 10-year-old who's growing four times faster than normal. Now he's ready for the biggest adventure of his life . . . 5th grade.—Movie tagline

"*Jack* goes for the gold and emerges a winner!"—Susan Granger, *American Movie Classics*

"The funniest and the best film you'll see."—Bonnie Churchill, *National News Syndicate*

"Robin Williams is brilliant in this extremely funny film."—Paul Wunder, *WBAI Radio*

"The summer's happiest surprise."—Mike Cidoni, *WOKR-TV*

Box Office: $58,478,604

Jack is a fable about tolerance and the poignancy of growing up too fast. Contrary to the cynicism of one Baltimore reviewer, this Jack is not a dull boy, nor is the film. How could any film starring Robin Williams and Bill Cosby directed by Francis Coppola possibly be dull? True, it gets a bit sentimental towards the end, but it's not really maudlin. This film is a mutability canto crafted by one of the true poets of the cinema, director Francis Ford Coppola. Like Jack, the picture is spectacular in its own modest way.

The film begins on a surreal note at a costume ball before Jack is born. Brian Powell (Brian Kerwin), dressed like the Tin Man from *The Wizard of Oz,* is dancing in a conga line with his pregnant wife Karen (Diane Lane), dressed like the Wicked Witch of the West, when all of a sudden, her water breaks, unexpectedly, since she is only in her first trimester. A couple dressed absurdly as a pack of cigarettes and a martini rush Brian and Karen to the hospital.

And thus Jack (Robin Williams) is born, before the credits run, over cute shots of baby Jack being calipered, weighed, and measured. This resembles the opening of Danny DeVito's *Matilda* (1996), adapted from Roald Dahl's children's story, but Jack, unlike Matilda, is blessed to have good parents. Subjective point-of-view camera shots from baby Jack's perspective effectively suggest a rapidly developing consciousness.

Jack does have his problems, however. His cells develop at four times the normal rate, so in ten weeks, he had matured to the equivalent of an infant nine months old. By his first birthday, he looked like a four-year old, and, conveniently for the casting of Robin Williams, at age 10 Jack appears to be 40 years old; but he is still mentally ten years old. To save him embarrassment, his parents have him tutored at home by kindly Mr. Woodruff (Bill Cosby), who advises the parents to send Jack to public school. The mother has doubts: "What do you think they'll do to the six-foot hairy kid?" she asks.

The film is dedicated to the memory of Gian-Carlo, the director's son, who was killed in a boating accident at age 20.

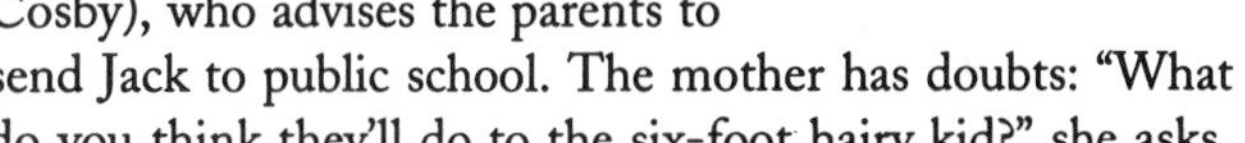

The neighborhood kids know about Jack, however. "He's like a freak or something," one says. They know a teacher comes to his house every day. "He's like a giant boy. Shaves, and stuff." But Mom eventually takes her big boy to school and introduces him to the Principal, Mr. McGee, whom a nervous Jack calls Mr. Magoo. Next he meets fifth-grade teacher Miss Marquez (Jennifer Lopez), who introduces Jack to his skeptical classmates. "Jeez, he looks just like my dad," one says. At first Jack suffers a whole lot of ridicule, until his classmates discover that he has a real advantage on the basketball court and that he can walk into a store and buy a copy of *Penthouse* magazine with no questions asked. All of a sudden, Jack gets popular.

He wins over his best friend Louis Durante (Adam Zolotin) by pretending to be the principal when Louis' mother Dolores (Fran Drescher) comes to school for a parent-teacher meeting. Dolores Durante is divorced and comes on to likable Jack, who gets through this ordeal by means of his natural, boyish charm. "He doesn't listen. Kids don't listen," she says of her son. "What were you saying?" Jack asks, as if proving her point. But Dolores is so turned on by Jack that she doesn't notice his goofy responses.

Eventually Jack comes to understand the mathematics of his predicament. If, at the age of ten, he has the body of a forty-year-old, by the time he is twenty, he will be eighty years old. Miss Marquez gives the class an assignment to write an essay on the topic "What do I want to be when I grow up?" Jack's answer is simply: "Alive!" Then Jack asks Miss Marquez to go to the school dance with him, and when she declines for professional reasons, Jack is devastated and depressed. He is so stressed that his aging body has an angina attack, and he is hospitalized.

"Ever since my husband left us, he's got such a chip on his shoulder." "Potato or corn?"—Jack's naive response when best friend Louis' mom tells Jack her troubles

Fortunately, by that time Jack has many friends who help him get over this rough patch. Mr. Woodruff constantly comes up with the right metaphors. He likens Jack to a shooting star whose course is brief but spectacular. Earlier on, when convincing Jack's parents to send him to school, Woodruff says, "Look at his eyes. They're a child's eyes." These words are voiced over shots of Jack watching with wonder and delight as a cocoon develops into a spectacularly beautiful butterfly, whose life, like Jack's, is destined to be short.

The film could be depressing, but it opts instead to be life-affirming, and in fact Jack survives high school. A coda at the end of the film shows an elderly seventeen-year-old Jack giving a commencement address as class valedictorian, and it is heartening to see Jack grow into mental as well as physical maturity.

Unfortunately, *Jack* was too good and gentle a film to please several hard-nosed reviewers. Gary Arnold of *The Washington Times* protested that *Jack* was merely "a disillusioning variation on *Big*" (1988) and dismissed it as "a dubious and indigestible blend of juvenile slapstick and mawkish sentimentality." Hal Hinson of *The Washington Post* was also critical of the film as a *Big* ripoff by screenwriters James DeMonaco and Gary Nadeau and claimed that Williams does not possess the "natural innocence" Tom Hanks brought to *Big*, but was it fair to say that the ever-adaptable Williams is unable to reveal the face of the "inner child" in this picture? After all, as Steven Rea of *The Philadelphia Inquirer* pointed out, Williams had "already played Peter Pan, the boy who won't grow up," in Steven Spielberg's *Hook* (1991) with natural and convincing exuberance. Rea was disturbed, however, by the film's "monster mood swings" from "silly to solemn to sappy."

Janet Maslin of the *New York Times*, on the other hand, found "some unexpected flashes of real emotion" in the film and praised Coppola's sensitive direction. For her Williams "mimics a child perfectly when fidgeting or horsing around" and "shows just the right comic embarrassment when trying to masquerade as a grown man," as he does on two occasions with Louis' mother. The film is "dedicated to the daughter of the director's late son," Maslin noted, and despite its cliches and predictability, it was made sincerely "from the heart."

Jack is more grown-up than *Big*. It does not avoid the issue of Jack's eventual death at an early age but celebrates the quality of his life. Coppola, who by the age of 57 had earned five Academy Awards, told the Associated Press that he regarded Jack's disease as a metaphor rather than "literally a genetic disease." Coppola, who has lived a hard though artistically successful life, summed up the message of *Jack* by saying, "All of us are kind of like Jack—our lives are whizzing by." Though this is hardly an original observation, the truth of his message is universal, and that message itself is effectively packaged. *Jack* may not have pleased some cynical reviewers, but it is a thoughtful and reflective, thoroughly decent film. Viewers should recognize that decency and ignore the hostile criticism.

What Coppola has called the "Carnival in Rio" masquerade prologue alone is worth the price of admission, and the comic complication of the Tin Man trying to pass through a metal detector at the hospital, as Jack's father desperately tries to accompany his wife to the labor room. The film opens brilliantly as surreal comedy long before it begins to turn "serious."

Very few actors would be up to the challenge of portraying Jack, but Robin Williams has specialized in odd and offbeat demanding roles, and he is perfect here. This movie has a heart as big as the Ritz and is entertaining as well as thoughtful. Along with the astonishing *Matilda,* it was one of the summer's very best family films, equally amusing for children and adults.

—James M. Welsh

CREDITS

Jack Powell: Robin Williams
Karen Powell: Diane Lane
Miss Marquez: Jennifer Lopez
Brian Powell: Brian Kerwin
Dolores Durante: Fran Drescher
Lawrence Woodruff: Bill Cosby

Origin: USA
Released: 1996
Production: Ricardo Mestres, Fred Fuchs and Francis Ford Coppola for a Hollywood Pictures production; released by Buena Vista
Direction: Francis Ford Coppola
Screenplay: James DeMonaco and Gary Nadeau
Cinematography: John Toll
Editing: Barry Malkin
Music: Michael Kamen
Production design: Dean Tavoularis
Art direction: Angelo Graham
Set design: William Beck
Set decoration: Arimin Ganz, Barbara Munch
Costume design: Aggie Guerard Rodgers
Sound: Agamemnon Andrianos
Visual effects: Gary Gutierrez
MPAA rating: PG-13
Running Time: 113 minutes

REVIEWS

The Baltimore Sun. August 9, 1996, p. E6.
Chicago Tribune. August 9, 1996, p.5.
Detroit News. August 9, 1996, p. D1.
Entertainment Weekly. August 9, 1996, p. 39.
Los Angeles Times. August 9, 1996, p. F1.
The New York Times. August 9, 1996, p. C14.
People. August 12, 1996, p. 19.
Philadelphia Inquirer Weekend. August 9, 1996, p. 3.
Sight and Sound. October, 1996, p. 42.
Time. August 12, 1996, p. 64.
USA Today. August 9, 1996, p. D3.
Variety Online. July 29, 1996.
The Washington Post. August 9, 1996, p. B7.
Washington Post Weekend. August 9, 1996, p. 29.

Jack & Sarah

He needed someone to care for his baby. He found someone to care for them both.—Movie tagline

"... a winning charm that will work its way into your heart."—Susan Granger, *American Movie Classics*

"A crowd-pleaser in the same league as *Four Weddings and a Funeral.*"—David Hunter, *The Hollywood Reporter*

"A funny and heartwarming British import."—Jeff Craig, *Sixty Second Preview*

Box Office: $218,626

First-time director Tim Sullivan both wrote and directed *Jack & Sarah,* a British comedy about Jack (Richard E. Grant), a young father whose wife has died and who must suddenly face the challenges and responsibilities of parenthood. Though the film suffers from some sudden shifts in tone and a somewhat predictable love story, *Jack & Sarah* features some first-rate ensemble acting and a well developed theme about responsibility.

The shifts in tone concern the death of Sarah (Imogen Stubbs) during childbirth. The opening scenes of the film establish Jack as a typically nervous expectant father who relies on his wife to get him through their pregnancy. In the ride to the hospital it is Jack who is strapped in the stretcher after having fallen down a flight of stairs in his excitement. Sarah looks in exasperation to the ambulance orderly and says that she hopes he will not miss the birth of their daughter.

After Jack is told that Sarah has died, he names their child after her, and the film struggles for a bit to regain its comic footing. Jack meets William (Ian McKellen), a homeless person—albeit a very dignified one—who has been living in the trash dumpster in front of Jack's flat. In the aftermath of Sarah's death, Jack hits rock bottom, and his well-meaning parents (David Swift, Judi Dench) and mother-in-law Phil (Eileen Atkins) struggle to find a way to cope with his inattentiveness toward the baby. The darkest moments of the film are two matching conversations Jack has with his father, one a harsh quarrel, the other a plea for help.

The second half of the film returns to comedy. At work as a corporate lawyer, Jack finds that the newness of taking baby Sarah (Bianca and Sophia Lee) to the office is wearing off. His boss Anna (Cherie Lunghi) tolerates these intrusions because she is attracted to Jack. Finally Jack decides to ask Amy (Samantha Mathis), an American he met on the day she got fired from her job as a waitress, to be Sarah's nanny. A number of scenes explore Jack's comic difficulties in leaving Sarah with someone new. Eventually, Amy moves in and the romance that slowly starts between Jack and Amy develops rather predictably, overcoming along the way the obstacle of the rival Anna and that of Alain (Laurent Grevill), Amy's former boyfriend.

The cast is able to maintain audience interest in this predicable aspect of the plot. As is often the case with British ensemble acting, the players work together quite smoothly and convincingly. In particular, Richard E. Grant succeeds at capturing both Jack's surface silliness and underlying warmth. In early scenes Jack collapses in sympathetic labor pains, chauffeurs little Sarah around the office in the mail cart, and chases frantically after Amy. Grant's clowning works as well as the moving, qui-

As a toddler, Sarah is played by director Tim Sullivan's daughter, Sophie.

CREDITS

Jack: Richard E. Grant
Amy: Samantha Mathis
Margaret: Judi Dench
William: Ian McKellen
Anna: Cherie Lunghi
Phil: Eileen Atkins
Sarah: Imogen Stubbs
Michael: David Swift
Alain: Laurent Grevill
Baby Sarah: Bianca Lee and Sophia Lee
Toddler Sarah: Sophie Sullivan

Origin: Great Britain
Released: 1995; 1996
Production: Pippa Cross, Simon Channing-Williams, and Janette Day for British Screen Canal Plus production; released by Gramercy Pictures
Direction: Tim Sullivan
Screenplay: Tim Sullivan
Cinematography: Jean-Yves Escoffier
Editing: Lesley Walker
Art direction: Humphrey Bangham
Music: Simon Boswell
MPAA rating: PG
Running Time: 110 minutes

eter moments when he confides his fears to his father on a snowy park bench and when he describes his grief to Amy. Eileen Atkins nicely underplays her role as the mother-in-law who has lost both a husband and a daughter and who comes to see in William the opportunity for companionship. Ian McKellen imparts a grave dignity to the role of William, the homeless alcoholic whose involvement with Jack and Sarah begins to rehabilitate him. Even Cherie Lunghi who plays what may be the most stereotyped role of Jack's predatory boss succeeds at showing her character's frailty in the scene when she overhears on an intercom Jack's dismissive comments of her as a potential wife. There is not an indifferently played role in the film.

The theme of accepting responsibility unifies the film as well. After the loss of his wife, Jack binges with William, and not until his parents and Phil leave Sarah with him while he sleeps does he finally begin to mature. William too begins to order his life when he recognizes Jack's reluctance to allow him even to take Sarah for a walk. Helping to orchestrate Jack's turnaround is Amy, whose best scene features her scolding him for ignoring Sarah upstairs while he was trying to seduce Anna downstairs. In a subplot the film suggests that caring for others also nurtures the caregiver, as Phil thinks about remarriage and the responsibilities of companionship. If the film may be faulted for its predictable love plot and sudden shifts of tone from tragic to comic, it deserves praise for depicting the many ways a baby can transform and mature others.

—*Glenn Hopp*

REVIEWS

Boxoffice. February, 1996, p. R-12.
Entertainment Weekly. March 12, 1996, p. 50.
Entertainment Weekly. July 26, 1996, p. 64.
The Hollywood Reporter. March 12, 1996, p. 10.
Los Angeles Times. March 22, 1996, pp. F4.
Maclean's. April 1, 1996, p. 75.
National Review. April 22, 1996, p. 62.
New Republic. April 15, 1996, p. 26.
New York Times. March 22, 1996, p. C17.
People Weekly. April 8, 1996, pp. 19-20.
Sight and Sound. June, 1995, pp. 45-46.

James and the Giant Peach

Adventures this big don't grow on trees. Climb aboard for the adventure of your life!—Movie tagline

"One of the most fascinating films of the season!"—Jeffrey Lyons, *ANC World News Now*

"Brilliant! Breathtaking! A creative masterpiece. A movie miracle."—Mike Reynolds, *AP Radio/Film Clips*

"An instant Disney classic!"—Leo Quinones, Jr., *The Fox Kids Countdown*

"Stunning! One of the greatest bits of animation!"—Tom Gliatto, *People*

"A thrilling, touching, thoroughly entertaining tale!"—Dr. Joy Browne, *WOR Radio*

Box Office: $28,946,127

Roald Dahl writes about kids' fears, in all their nightmare inspiring darkness. The author does not talk down to his young readers (or his mature ones, either). Perhaps that is what makes him so popular. A book of his may be the first a particular child will read that makes that child feel he or she has graduated from the baby-books to the real stuff. Sadly, this 1996 film adaptation of *James and the Giant Peach* does precisely the reverse.

Where the novel is terrifying, amazing and thrilling, the film is merely encouraging emotionally and pretty to look at. It might be said that this is the nature of animation. Then again, more sensitive children have had to be carried out of the theater, screaming, since the first feature length cartoon, Walt Disney's *Snow White and the Seven Dwarfs* (1937), throughout Disney's animation comeback *The Little Mermaid* (1989). Even producer Tim Burton's *The Nightmare Before Christmas* (1993) produced more shivers than this sugarcoated version of a real boy in real distress.

The film opens in live action with James (Paul Terry) and his parents lying on the beach, trying to make out recognizable shapes in the clouds overhead. Neither they, nor the audience have to try very hard, for the clouds look more like train engines, camels and sailboats than they do like clouds. It is one of these clouds, in the shape of a rhinoceros, that stampedes out of the sky and kills James' parents. At least in the book it was a live rhinoceros escaped from the London Zoo. So when James' suddenly finds himself sent to live with his horrible Aunt Sponge (Miriam Margolyes) and Aunt Spiker (Joanna Lumley, in vanity defying makeup and costume), his situation becomes more surreal than the escapade that will follow.

A mysterious man (Pete Postlethwaite) approaches James as he's chopping wood and offers him a bag of tiny, fluorescent, wiggling green things, that if he mixes in water with a few strands of his own hair and then drinks down in one gulp, will change his life forever. With his only promise of more chores, more beatings and more fishheads for dinner awaiting him, any change is welcome. However, on the way back to the cold, attic room, James trips, dropping the bag and spilling its magic contents into the soil. Before he can fully comprehend his loss, he hears his horrible aunts shrieking about a peach tree which, though dead for several years, has suddenly sprouted the most delicious looking peach.

Roald Dahl's first children's book is based on bedtime stories he told to his daughters, inspired by a backyard cherry tree.

Before Sponge and Spiker can scare James up the tree to pick the morsel for them, they notice it is still growing. Cut to James as the ticket taker for the roadside attraction his aunts have concocted out of their freak fruit. At the end of the day, the aunts are richer and James even poorer. Not only did he lose the unexplained magic green things that apparently made the peach grow to its present size, (roughly that of the entire hill it rests on), but he was also deprived of the opportunity to play with any of the children whose living, loving parents brought them to see the magnificent peach, despite Sponge and Spiker's exorbitant prices.

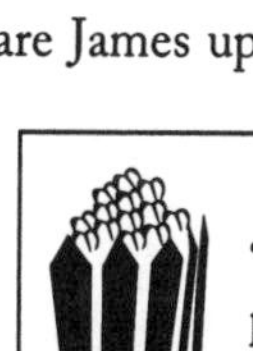

"Good heavens! He's committed pesticide!"—Grasshopper about Centipede's dive into icy waters

In the dark, assigned to pick up the carpet of litter left by the visitors, weak from hunger and feeling he has nothing left to lose, James steals a bite from the peach—a bite which happens to contain one of the still active, wiggling green things. As James eats his way into the peach, its velvet skin closes up behind him and the film just as smoothly converts from live action into animation. James tunnels to the center of the peach, where the pit is as big as a room. In fact, it is a room, now populated by friendly insects larger than James himself, and with voices provided by some performers as splendid as the peach their characters now call home.

Miss Spider (Susan Sarandon) is the Black Widow made friendly by James earlier reluctance to have her squashed by his maniacal aunts. Why she has a Russian accent is not clear. Nor is it clear how the wisecracking Mr. Centipede (Richard Dreyfuss) made it all the way to England from his native New Jersey. Among James' countrymen (or countrybugs) are the haughtily musical Grasshopper (Simon Callow), the gently maternal Ladybug (Jane Leeves), and the perpetually hysterical Earthworm (David Thewlis).

What follows is a trans-Atlantic journey to New York, via the Arctic Circle, hungry sharks, renegade seagulls, bad dreams, ghosts of sunken pirate ships, and their own foibles, fights and fears.

The trip reaches its climax when the giant peach lands in the Big Apple. James is rescued from the peach, now impaled on the Empire State Building, by friendly city officials while his insect companions waft down to the stunned but welcoming crowd on individual seagull taxis. Somehow Aunts Sponge and Spiker show up and demand that their income producing peach be returned to them. They unabashedly threaten to use axes in their determination to claim what they feel is theirs, including James. But child abuse does not go over well even in this stylized incarnation of New York. James' friends lasso the evil aunts with silk from the spider and hand them over to the discretion of the crowd. James is finally safe.

More important than the trip itself, the filmmakers, actors and first and foremost Mr. Dahl emphasize the characters' psychological and emotional journey. James and the insects find freedom from oppression. They bond and create a new family where each of them had previously been alone. They develop a sense of faith in that family and in themselves. The challenges they must work through give James and his comrades the validation that they are worthy of the love they so desire. And in the end, James winds up with a nice peach-pit house in Central Park and lots of friends to play with.

It was Burton's *The Nightmare Before Christmas* that charmed Dahl's widow into sharing the rights to this story, first published in 1961 and sought after by filmmakers for most of the three plus decades since then. Director Henry Selick then supervised several versions of the script adaptation until approval was granted by Disney, Mrs. Dahl, and the many hands invariably involved in the development and production of any motion picture. Just as too many cooks spoil the soup, it has repeatedly been demonstrated that too many writers spoil the script.

AWARDS AND NOMINATIONS

Academy Awards 1996 Nominations: Best Original Score (Newman)

The process of animation is breathtakingly time-consuming. It requires dozens of professionals a week to produce one minute's worth of film. Reasonably but still sadly, this challenge leads even the most ambitious animators to take shortcuts. The centipede who, in Roald Dahl's book not only has forty-two legs, but owns forty-two lace-up shoes which he insists on donning every morning when he wakes and removing every night before bed. For the sake of expedience, the film's Centipede has only fourteen legs and goes barefoot.

CREDITS

James: Paul Terry
Grasshopper: Simon Callow (voice)
Centipede: Richard Dreyfuss (voice)
Spider: Susan Sarandon (voice)
Ladybug: Jane Leeves (voice)
Earthworm: David Thewlis (voice)
Aunt Spiker: Joanna Lumley
Aunt Sponge/Glowworm: Miriam Margoyles
Old Man: Pete Postlethwaite

Origin: USA
Released: 1996
Production: Denise Di Novi, Tim Burton for an Allied Filmmakers and Walt Disney Pictures production; released by Buena Vista
Direction: Henry Selick
Screenplay: Karey Kirkpatrick, Jonathan Roberts, Steve Bloom; based on the book by Roald Dahl
Cinematography: Pete Kozachik, Hiro Narita
Editing: Stan Webb
Music: Randy Newman
Production design: Harley Jessup
Set decoration: Kris Boxell
Conceptual design: Lane Smith
Animation supervisor: Paul Berry
Visual effects: Pete Kozachik
Sound: Agamemnon Andrianos
MPAA rating: PG
Running Time: 80 minutes

The quest for convenience can also lead to positive changes. A new location is provided for the crew of the peach on their long overseas journey, by a picket fence the peach picked up on its long roll down the hill. But even three is a meager number of locations for these claustrophobic characters, and so the trip itself is shortened, the peach becoming the Concord of fruits, but leaving its passengers not nearly as much time to learn and grow.

While staying true to Dahl's lyrics, Randy Newman provides melodies that sound as much like each other as they do like *Oliver.* James' lonely ballad, "My Name is James" recalls the Broadway musical's "Where Is Love," (although young Paul Terry does not have the vocal skill to impart emotion to the inherently emotional words). The all cast anthem "We're Family" recalls that same musical's upbeat "Consider Yourself," and is further blessed with the better trained performances of the adult cast voices. Still, there is no one melody that stands out enough for viewers to leave the theater humming.

Most of the images created by director Henry Selick's talented team are marvelous. The animated James is the perfect cross between his former human self and his animated, insect counterparts. The widely hued and clearly fuzzy skin of the peach cries out to be touched. The Atlantic Ocean is deep Caribbean blue and dancing with waves that seem to be made of jello that possesses a sense of rhythm. But even its richly textured visuals and star-studded cast cannot save *James and the Giant Peach* from being merely a watered-down version of Roald Dahl's magnificent book. If it inspires young viewers to read the original and perhaps even other books on the shelf beside it, it will have more than done its job.

—*Eleah Horwitz*

REVIEWS

The Los Angeles Times. April 7, 1996, p. 5.
The New York Times. April 12, 1996, p. C3.
Newsweek. April 15, 1996, p. 77.
Variety. April 8, 1996, p. 58.

Jane Eyre

From the timeless classic comes this year's most beautiful love story.—Movie tagline

"Marvelous! A stunning film!"—Bill Diehl, *ABC Radio Network*

"A ravishing profound masterpiece! Flawless, detail-perfect performances by Joan Plowright and Anna Paquin."—Daphne Davis, *Movies & Videos*

"The most romantic film of the year!"—Dawn Meadows, *WEWS/ABC*

Box Office: $5,200,601

Franco Zeffirelli's remake of *Jane Eyre* marks at least the sixth time Charlotte Bronte's 1847 novel has been filmed: a forgotten 1934 version featured Virginia Bruce as Jane, the well received 1944 film starred Joan Fontaine and Orson Welles, a 1971 British television version featured Susannah York while a 1983 version (again for British TV) starred Zelah Clarke in the title role, and a still unreleased film, starring Juliette Binoche, was made as recently as 1993. Zeffirelli, who is known for his lushly romantic film adaptations of such classics as *Romeo and Juliet,* this time takes a restrained—perhaps too restrained—approach to another literary masterpiece, draining it of much of its vitality.

As part of her preparation for setting up a girls' school, Charlotte Bronte spent the better part of the years 1842 through 1844 studying languages at the Pensionnat Heger in Brussels, Belgium, where she fell deeply in love with her tutor, Monsieur Heger. M. Heger, a married man, failed to respond to the passionate letters Charlotte sent him after her return to England. This bitter experience would result, in 1853, in Bronte's novel *Villette.* Before that, however, aspects of Bronte's thwarted love affair would find their way into *The Professor,* written in 1846 but not published during her lifetime, and into her masterwork, *Jane Eyre.*

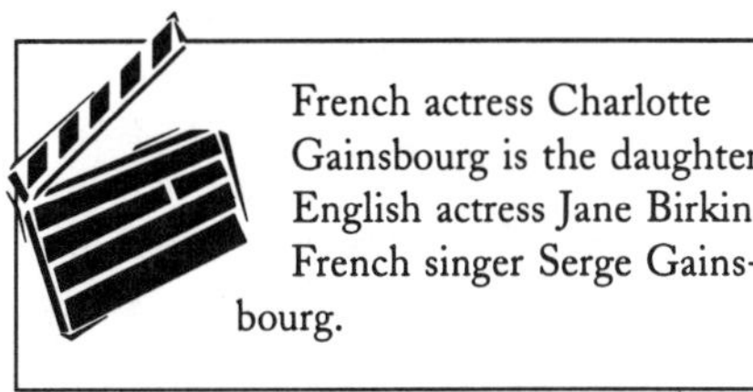

French actress Charlotte Gainsbourg is the daughter of English actress Jane Birkin and French singer Serge Gainsbourg.

Jane Eyre is fraught with autobiographical elements. Motherless from childhood, Charlotte Bronte, as well as her four sisters, were sent to board at Cowan Bridge school, a grim early Victorian institution where consumption claimed the

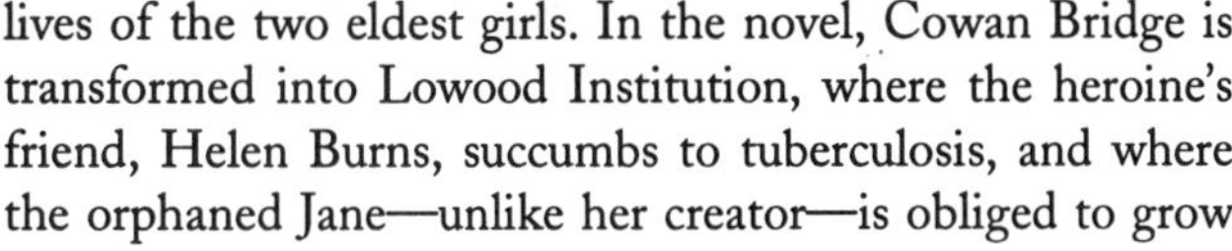

lives of the two eldest girls. In the novel, Cowan Bridge is transformed into Lowood Institution, where the heroine's friend, Helen Burns, succumbs to tuberculosis, and where the orphaned Jane—unlike her creator—is obliged to grow up. Then Jane, like Bronte, sets out into the world to work as a governess, only to lose her heart to a male authority figure whose marriage makes him out of reach.

Like Charlotte Bronte, Jane Eyre is a plain, self-contained, even headstrong girl, whose hard-won inner strength helps her survive her disappointment in love. Unlike M. Heger, however, Jane's employer, Mr. Rochester, is a Byronic figure who finds himself powerfully attracted to the young governess who shares his household. And his wife—a mad Creole woman named Bertha who is confined to the attic of Thornfield Hall—is seemingly conveniently out of the way. Rochester proposes to the unwitting Jane and, after some initial reluctance, she accepts him. But on the eve of their marriage, Bertha reasserts herself, rending her successor's wedding veil. Rochester assures Jane that this deed, like several other mysterious happenings at the Hall, is the work of a disturbed servant, Grace Poole. The ceremony goes forward the next day, only to be interrupted by the appearance of Bertha's brother, recently arrived from the West Indies.

Her eyes opened to the secret of Thornfield Hall, Jane beats a hasty retreat. Overcome during her flight across the moors, she is rescued and nursed back to health by the Reverend St. John Rivers and his sisters, who turn out to be her cousins. Jane next discovers that she, together with the Rivers', has fortuitously inherited a great sum of money from an uncle. The cousins get on very well, and eventually the Reverend Rivers proposes marriage to Jane. She is on the verge of accepting his suit when she receives a telepathic message from Mr. Rochester, sorely in need of her help.

Jane returns to Thornfield, only to find both the Hall and its master in ruins, for after Jane's departure Bertha had set fire to the building, and Rochester was maimed and blinded in a futile attempt to save his wife. But now he is at last free of his burden, and he and Jane marry. Jane uses her love and her money to help restore their home as well as Rochester's health.

Jane Eyre is, as its title connotes, the story of its protagonist, and Zeffirelli has, within the constraints of the film medium, been true to the book. The problem with the movie, it seems, rests not so much with its direction but with its casting. Charlotte Gainsbourg, a twenty-four-year-old French actress, plays Jane, and she seems just too slender a reed to bear the weight of the film. Gainsbourg, the daughter of French singer, songwriter and actor Serge Gainsbourg, and British actress Jane Birkin, is little known in this country, although she has already established herself in European cinema. Nonetheless, Gainsbourg seemingly brings little experience to her role. While she does possess the youthful gravity Bronte ascribes to her heroine, instead of conveying the depth and dimension Jane has earned in the course of her short, hard life, Gainsbourg appears merely wooden. If only Anna Paquin, who makes a highly credible, vivid young Jane, could have played the more mature Jane as well.

"Keep well and not die, sir."—Young Jane's reply to odious Mr. Brocklehurst, who's asked how she'll avoid the flames of hell for her wickedness.

Part of the problem undoubtedly arises from the foreshortening effect of the film. While viewers may be at a loss to understand what it is that Mr. Rochester sees in Jane, readers of the novel, who share Jane's point of view and who are treated to many intellectually intimate exchanges between the governess and her employer, can well conceive of the attraction. Here, there seems to be no chemistry between Gainsbourg and William Hurt, who plays Rochester, and when he finally expresses his love to her, we are as surprised as she. And one cannot help but wish that Gainsbourg were just a little bit lovely. She is truly a plain Jane, as is her fictional counterpart and as was Charlotte Bronte herself. But *Jane Eyre* is both a Gothic novel and a romance, and its heroine, an idealized version of her creator, grows on us and on Rochester (in the end she is both rich and luminous) in a way that Gainsbourg does not. For Bronte, *Jane Eyre* served on many levels as wish fulfillment. Not only was her first published novel an immediate success, it helped her to work through the hurt and resentment that lingered after her rejection by M. Heger: in her fictional version of events, the young governess, spurned because of an inconvenient wife and (Bronte probably feared) her own unattractiveness, becomes appealing even as the madwoman in the attic is dispatched.

The point is that both Jane and Rochester are emotionally scarred when they first meet. But whereas Charlotte Gainsbourg mostly comes across as prim, William Hurt does a wonderful job of conveying the grim but ironic exterior Rochester has developed as a means of dealing with the world. Despite his gruffness, his attractiveness is plain. At the outset, he is wealthy and handsome and much sought after by the local belles. And after he—quite literally—grapples with his guilty secret, he and Jane trade places.

This is a familiar and deeply gratifying romantic structure. Unfortunately—perhaps again because of the limitations of film— Rochester's transformation into a scarred, bereft shell of a man is no more convincing than Jane's metamorphosis into a wealthy object of desire. In Zeffirelli's version, after the truth about the first Mrs. Rochester is revealed—the event on which the narrative hinges—all seems anticlimactic. How is it that both Jane and Rochester come to terms with this revelation, and how does their love survive the wreckage that ensues? To be sure, Bronte leaves the answers to these questions unexpressed, but the amount of time the novel devotes to the resolution of Jane's and Rochester's story renders them deeply felt.

The film's opening section, devoted to Jane's childhood abuse at the hands of her heartless aunt and the equally unforgiving overlords at the orphanage, contain its most convincing scenes. This section, not surprisingly, is filled with wonderful performances, not just that of Ann Paquin, but those of Fiona Shaw as the odious Aunt Reed, John Wood as Mr. Brocklehurst, the ruler of the orphanage, Geraldine Chaplin as his sadistic overseer, and Amanda Root as Miss Temple, the one kindly adult encountered by the young Jane. Once the scene shifts to Thornfield Hall, the camera perforce focuses on Jane and Rochester, but we are still treated to a fair number of scenes between Jane and Mrs. Fairfax, Thornfield's welcoming housekeeper, played with wit and

CREDITS

Edward Rochester: William Hurt
Jane Eyre: Charlotte Gainsbourg
Mrs. Fairfax: Joan Plowright
Young Jane: Anna Paquin
Miss Scatcherd: Geraldine Chaplin
Blanche Ingram: Elle Macpherson
Grace Poole: Billie Whitelaw
Bertha: Maria Schneider
Mrs. Reed: Fiona Shaw
Mr. Brocklehurst: John Wood
Miss Temple: Amanda Root
Adele: Josephine Serre

Origin: USA
Released: 1996
Production: Dyson Lovell for a Rochester Films production; released by Miramax
Direction: Franco Zeffirelli
Screenplay: Hugh Whitemore, Franco Zeffirelli; based on the novel by Charlotte Bronte
Cinematography: David Watkin
Editing: Richard Marden
Music: Alessio Vlad, Claudio Capponi
Production design: Roger Hall
Art direction: Dennis Bosher, Raimonda Gaetani
Costume design: Jenny Beavan
Sound: David Stephenson
MPAA rating: PG
Running Time: 112 minutes

three dimensionality by Joan Plowright. Another wonderful actress, Billie Whitelaw, plays Grace Poole, but because of the shadowy nature of this character, Whitelaw is rather wasted.

As he has done in the past, Zeffirelli uses swelling violins to punch up the romantic scenes in the movie. Here, however, the music, composed by Alessio Vlad and Claudio Caponi, seems intrusive, perhaps because it is called upon to fill in the void that remains between Gainsbourg and Hurt. The production, art, and costumer designers (respectively, Roger Hall, Dennis Bosher and Raimonda Gaetani, and Jenny Beavan) have all done a fine job of making *Jane Eyre* look good, but the movie lacks heart, and viewers are ultimately left unsatisfied by this interpretation of what is unquestionably one of the most emotionally fulfilling stories ever told.

—Lisa Paddock

REVIEWS

Boxoffice Magazine. May, 1996, p. 72.
Chicago Tribune. April 12, 1996, p. 5.
Detroit News. April 12, 1996, p. 3D.
Entertainment Weekly. April 26, 1996, p. 38.
Los Angeles Times. April 12, 1996, p. F4.
New York Times. April 12, 1996, p. C5.
Sight and Sound. October, 1996, p. 96.
Variety. April 8, 1996, p. 58.

Jerry Maguire

Everybody loved him . . . Everybody disappeared. *Jerry Maguire*. The journey is everything.—Movie tagline

"Completely absorbing!"—David Denby, *New York Magazine*

"*Jerry Maguire* is loaded with bright, funny, tender encounters between characters who seem so winningly warm and real."—Janet Maslin, *New York Times*

"Altogether wondrous!"—Richard Schickel, *Time*

Box Office: $65,675,817

Sports agent Jerry Maguire (Tom Cruise) negotiates a big deal for his only client, football superstar Rod Tidwell (Cuba Gooding, Jr.), in *Jerry Maguire*.

Jerry Maguire (Tom Cruise) is a hotshot sports agent who unaccountably experiences a combination brainstorm and midlife crisis while only in his early thirties. He steps way out of line by distributing 150 photocopies of a "mission statement" charging that professional sports have become too commercialized and agents dehumanized by greed. They care nothing about the beauty of the games, nothing about the kids who idolize sports heroes, nothing about the athletes they represent. Agents should not handle big stables of clients but should work closely with a select few, involving themselves in their personal lives and concerning themselves about their long-term well-being.

Beau Bridges has an unbilled appearance as player Frank Cushman's (Jerry O'Connell) dad.

Jerry's employer Sports Management International (SMI) represents all kinds of professional athletes, but the emphasis throughout the film, which is reminiscent of the memorable *North Dallas Forty* (1979), is on football. These athletes have special problems because their sport is so dangerous. A single tackle can end a career. What does an injured player do with the rest of his life when he knows only football? Sports agents are guilty of helping to ruin lives by demanding such exorbitant salaries that athletes are then expected to perform at superhuman levels, playing in pain, exposing themselves to injury and burnout.

Jerry is roundly applauded by all his colleagues—and

then fired for daring to suggest that the company should be earning less rather than more. Like Laurel Ayres (Whoopi Goldberg) in *The Associate* (1996), Jerry defiantly proclaims his intention of going independent and asks who will join him in competing with monolithic SMI. Like Laurel, Jerry only enlists one humble clerical employee, while his erstwhile friends stand by the axiom that if you try to rescue a drowning man you are likely to go down with him.

"Wow, that's more than a dress. That's an Audrey Hepburn movie."—Jerry to Dorothy

Dorothy Boyd (Renee Zellweger) follows Jerry out of the office because she secretly adores him, although she believes he is too handsome and brilliant to give her a second look. She also believes in his principles. Tom Cruise, who was named Best Actor by the National Board of Review, was helped immeasurably by co-starring with lovely newcomer Zellweger. She brings out a quality lacking in most of Cruise's previous performances. She makes him seem like a human being rather than just a very handsome, virile, trendy young heartthrob.

Even *Wall Street Journal* reviewer Joe Morgenstern, who calls the film "shallow and shallower," writes: " . . . only Ms. Zellweger seems to understand the value of simplicity; not just understand it but deliver it, along with sweetness and silence and rue. . . . With her lovely full face, hooded eyes and husky voice, she's a genuine winner in a rigged game." *Jerry Maguire* may come to be remembered for introducing Zellweger to stardom. Morgenstern's negative review was an exception; most critics loved this romantic comedy. Kevin Turan of the *Los Angeles Times* called it "a triumph" and praised the entire cast, with special attention to Zellweger, whom he very accurately calls "the film's emotional center."

Like Laurel Ayres, Jerry quickly discovers that without capital and without a big company name behind him, he is not as dynamic as he thought he was. His clients all love him—but one by one they tell him they want to stick with SMI. Pro sports, after all, are about money. This is the first setback in Jerry's meteoric career. It destroys his self-confidence. He starts drinking. His ambitious, self-assertive fiancee breaks their engagement with a left and a right and a kick to the groin when she learns he has sacrificed his big income for something as unbankable as morality.

In his distress, Jerry turns to Dorothy, who is a single mom. (The film pushes many contemporary emotional hot-buttons.) She lives in a tract house with her sister, a divorcee who is thoroughly disillusioned with men. A group of divorced women meets regularly in their living room for noisy group therapy sessions. A love affair quickly blooms between lonely Dorothy and needy Jerry. (As in a pro-football game, a lot has to happen in this film in a very short time.) Dorothy's precocious little boy (winsome Jonathan Lipnicki) takes an immediate liking to his mother's new friend, partly because they are both sports enthusiasts. With characteristic impulsiveness, Jerry proposes marriage, and Dorothy—who can hardly believe her good fortune in finding a handsome lover as well as a compatible father for her son—accepts. Her sister, played by Bonnie Hunt, who resembles cynical, wise-cracking Eve Arden, predicts trouble. Dorothy is hitching her wagon to a star and is in for a wild ride before she and her son fall out of the wagon.

The only client who remains loyal is Rod Tidwell (charismatic, scene-stealing Cuba Gooding Jr.), an African-American wide receiver in the last year of his contract with the NFL's Arizona Cardinals. Tidwell, knowing that Jerry's survival is tied to his own fortunes, feels secure in demanding unlimited personal attention. The gifted black athlete likes Jerry because they are both rebels. The well-crafted script by Cameron Crowe has Jerry learning many lessons about life, including the lesson that being a rebel is not a practical full-time occupation. Ironically, he finds himself preaching conformity, diplomacy and team spirit to his renegade daredevil client.

The story helps the viewer understand the problems of professional football players. Their notorious grandstanding and showboating and hotdogging are calculated to win name recognition that will lead to better contracts and lucrative side-benefits such as product endorsements. Tidwell reminds Jerry that he needs a lot of money in a hurry because he can only hope to remain competitive for five years. His job is to go up and catch that football even when it means total exposure to a rib-crunching tackle on the way down.

Jerry would be ecstatic to get his client the ten-million-dollar contract they are holding out for. Ten percent of ten million over five years would solve Jerry's overhead problems, giving him some breathing room and allowing him time to sign a few more clients. But Jerry cannot land a big

AWARDS AND NOMINATIONS

Academy Awards 1996: Best Supporting Actor (Gooding Jr.)
Nominations: Best Picture, Best Actor (Cruise), Best Original Screenplay (Crowe), Best Film Editing
Directors Guild of America 1996 Nominations:: Best Director (Crowe)
Golden Globe Awards 1997: Best Actor-Musical/Comedy (Cruise)
Nominations: Best Film-Musical/Comedy, Best Supporting Actor (Gooding Jr.)
National Board of Review 1996: Best Actor (Cruise), Best Breakthrough Performer (Zellweger)
Screen Actors Guild Awards 1996: Supporting Actor (Gooding Jr.)
Nominations: Actor (Cruise), Supporting Actress (Zellweger)
Writers Guild of America 1996 Nominations: Original Screenplay (Crowe)

contract because Tidwell's "bad attitude" shows in every move he makes on the field.

While following Tidwell around the country, Jerry leaves Dorothy home alone with her son and her I-told-you-so sister. The crabbing divorcees' group begins to sound like the gloomily prescient chorus in a Greek tragedy. The deterioration of the marriage, instead of taking years, is subjected to a hurry-up offense because of the exigencies of the plot. Everything has to happen during one pro-football season. This is the only noticeable glitch in writer/director Crowe's otherwise admirable script.

Forced to practice what he preached, Jerry gets involved with Tidwell's entire family. In addition to learning about the very real problems of professional athletes, he witnesses exactly the kind of loving family unit he is losing. He comes to realize that the need for personal relationships he wrote about in his mission statement were really an expression of an unconscious yearning for intimacy in his personal life. No one can find complete fulfillment in work; he needs a home and someone to care about him. Tidwell is risking his neck, not for personal glory, but for his wife and kids. When Tidwell gets knocked out in a game with the Dallas Cowboys, and referees, players and trainers crowd around the fallen hero, Jerry realizes it is not only his own meal ticket that is in jeopardy but the career of a courageous man and the well-being of an entire family. Tidwell symbolizes all the talented athletes who only have a few years to grab the gold before they are trampled by hordes of hungry young college stars coming up behind them.

Tidwell gets knocked out catching the game-winning pass in the end zone on television's perennially popular "Monday Night Football." Dallas Cowboy quarterback Troy Aikman and well-known sportscaster Frank Gifford make cameo appearances, helping to lend the film the aura of a big-budget production when in fact Tom Cruise is the only star among a cast of attractive newcomers. The exposure on "Monday Night Football" is the catalyst that changes Jerry's fortunes. When Tidwell recovers consciousness he has become a household name—and he knows it. He dances and prances in the end zone, still holding the football which will soon go on the family mantlepiece. Everybody wants to interview him. Everybody wants to take his picture. Jerry can now negotiate a new five-year contract—not for just ten million but eleven-point-seven. Not only that, but Jerry's handling of his one client is sure to attract others. He will be the successful independent agent he dreamt of becoming. He can afford to give clients the solicitude they deserve because he will no longer have to hand sixty percent of his commissions over to a greedy, soulless corporate giant.

But Jerry's intense emotional experiences all crowded into one season have changed him. He barges into the circle of husband-bashing divorcees and makes the sort of schmaltzy speech that Jimmy Stewart delivered at the end of *It's a Wonderful Life* (1946). Jerry really and truly loves Dorothy and his stepson. He has learned that fame and fortune are not nearly as important as home and family. For the first time in their relationship, Dorothy realizes he really means it. All's well that ends well, and the audience walks out into the cold, cruel world feeling warm and vaguely happy.

—*Bill Delaney*

CREDITS

Jerry Maguire: Tom Cruise
Rod Tidwell: Cuba Gooding Jr.
Dorothy Boyd: Renee Zellweger
Avery Bishop: Kelly Preston
Frank Cushman: Jerry O'Connell
Marcee Tidwell: Regina King
Ray Boyd: Jonathan Lipnicki
Laurel Boyd: Bonnie Hunt
Bob Sugar: Jay Mohr

Origin: USA
Released: 1996
Production: James L. Brooks, Laurence Mark, Richard Sakai, and Cameron Crowe for a Gracie Films and TriStar Pictures production; released by Sony Pictures Entertainment
Direction: Cameron Crowe
Screenplay: Cameron Crowe
Cinematography: Janusz Kaminski
Editing: Joe Hutshing
Music: Nancy Wilson
Production design: Stephen Lineweaver
Art direction: Virginia Randolph, Clayton Hartley
Costume design: Betsy Heimann
Set decoration: Clay A. Griffith
Sound: Jeff Wexler
Casting: Gail Levin
MPAA rating: R
Running Time: 138 minutes

REVIEWS

Chicago Tribune. December 13, 1996, p. 5.
Entertainment Weekly. December 13, 1996, p. 53.
Los Angeles Times. December 13, 1996, p. F1.
New York Times. December 13, 1996, p. C1.
New Yorker. December 16, 1996, p. 118.
Newsweek. December 16, 1996, p. 68.
People. December 16, 1996, p. 25.
Rolling Stone. December 26, 1996, p. 207.
Sight and Sound. March, 1997, p. 52.
Time Online. December 16, 1996.
USA Today. December 13, 1996, p. 4D.
Variety. December 9, 1996, p. 101.
Village Voice. December 17, 1996.
Wall Street Journal. December 13, 1996, p. A12.

Jingle All the Way

Two Dads, One Toy, No Prisoners.—Movie tagline

"Side-splitting. The best holiday family film in years."—Don Stotter, *Entertainment Time-Out*

"This year's must-see holiday movie."—Tim Sherno, *FOX-TV*

"Nonstop fun. This holiday season's best movie."—Joanna Levenglick, *The Kids News Network*

"Arnold and Sinbad are hilarious . . . A comedy the entire family can enjoy."—Holly McClure, *Orange County Register*

Box Office: $54,460,867

In a world where movies can sometimes imitate real life, *Jingle All the Way* mimics the Christmas toy-buying frenzy most parents fear each holiday season. Remember the Cabbage Patch craze of the '80s and the more recent Tickle-Me-Elmo mania of Christmas 1996?

Jingle All the Way tells the story of Howard Langston (Schwarzenegger), a hardworking family man who has forgotten to buy his son Jamie (Lloyd) the hottest toy in America. No problem, except that it's Christmas Eve and the toy's been sold-out since Thanksgiving. To make matters worse, Langston's workaholic hours have kept him from family events—like attending his son's karate awards ceremony, and his wife Liz (Wilson) has had it.

Though they share no scenes in this film, Sinbad and Phil Hartman were teamed in *Houseguest*.

Howard realizes he can't screw this up, he must find a Turbo Man action figure for his son—and fast. Here begins the mad rush for the coveted doll, and as Howard waits in line outside a toy store about to open for the last-minute Christmas rush, he meets his nemesis in the form of mailman Myron Larabee (Sinbad), who also seeks the doll for his own son.

Howard must scurry from toy store to toy store, including a romp through the mega-sized Mall of America, scouring the shelves for the precious commodity, along the way being scoffed at by store clerks, battling other last-minute shoppers, and fighting tooth and nail with the crazed Myron. The audience is forced to decide if this mailman is truly crazy or just crazed by the Christmas shopping rush. You see, this man will do anything, including faking mail bomb threats, to get the coveted toy. Not a very funny prank, but then again neither are any of the racial attacks that spew from Sinbad throughout the movie.

"They use subliminal messages to suck kids' minds out."—Myron Larabee

Howard must not only battle the nutty mailman, but also a host of others, including a warehouse full of con men Santas led by Jim Belushi, who tries to sell him a defective Turbo Man look-alike. This scene ends up as an all-out brawl and a bust by the cops that seems totally idiotic—just a chance to have Schwarzenegger flex his muscles, and not exactly kiddie fare. Howard also runs into an uptight policeman, played by Robert Conrad, who shows up at the most inopportune times for the ruffled father; like when he's rushing to his kid's karate class or to the next toy store to capture the doll.

Last, but not least, while Howard combs the Twin cities for his son's gift, his near-perfect divorced neighbor Ted Maltin (Hartman) is preying on his unsuspecting wife. This guy bakes cookies, has bought his son the Turbo Man doll months in advance, and is the object of affection of all the neighborhood single mothers. And now he's weaseling in on Howard's wife in his absence.

Never fear, Howard wins the hearts of his family back in an unbelievable ending in which he "turns into" the actual Turbo Man in a mix-up during a Christmas parade. He flies through the air and battles the evil mailman, who in a last ditch effort takes on the persona of Turbo Man's nemesis to try to win the action figure which has finally been bestowed on Howard's son. There is a suspenseful cliffhanger during which Howard's son actually hangs from a building while being pursued by Myron the mailman, but Turbo Man (Howard) saves him as he flies through the air with the help of some lame special effects.

Unfortunately, this role calls for more physical humor than any of the characters can muster, especially Schwarzenegger, who is too large for these antics of falling over toys in toy shops and climbing through a jungle gym in the Mall of America. And Phil Hartman is funny for the first five minutes (the length of an average "Saturday Night Live" skit), then his annoying, neighbor character just fizzles out. His funniest line, "You can't bench-press your way out of this," directed at Howard's lack of Christmas-gift preparedness is truly ironic since indeed, Schwarzenegger cannot even bench-press his way out of this lackluster film, let alone the simple predicament his character is in.

Schwarzenegger has shown audiences a knack for very dry humor as evident in his one-liners from *The Terminator* (1984) and *The Running Man* (1987) and he's even displayed a sense of silly "big guy" humor in *Kindergarten Cop* (1990) and *Twins* (1988), but *Jingle All the Way* lacks both of these types of humor and simply falls short of what it set out to do—create a madcap holiday movie in the vein of *Home Alone* (1990), which was directed by *Jingle* producer Chris Columbus. Director Brian Levant, with family hits like *The Flintstones* (1994) and *Beethoven* (1992) under his belt, could not create a winner with this one. Instead, *Jingle All the Way* plays more like a full-length TV commercial for the number of toys displayed in the toy shops and the Christmas parade, and especially for the toy created for the film—Turbo Man.

The one shining savior of this film, as usual, is child newcomer Jake Lloyd as Jamie. His performance is priceless as the disappointed, disillusioned son. Of course, he doesn't get the screen time Schwarzenegger does. Too bad. And unfortunately for *Jingle All the Way,* playing the "cute kid card" could not save the movie. Back to the *Terminator* films for you, AH-nuld!

—*Devra Sladics*

CREDITS

Howard Langston: Arnold Schwarzenegger
Myron Larabee: Sinbad
Ted Maltin: Phil Hartman
Liz Langston: Rita Wilson
Officer Hummell: Robert Conrad
Mall Santa Claus: James Belushi
Jamie Langston: Jake Lloyd

Origin: USA
Released: 1996
Production: Chris Columbus, Mark Radcliffe and Michael Barnathan for a 1492 Picture production; released by 20th Century Fox
Direction: Brian Levant
Screenplay: Randy Kornfield
Cinematography: Victor J. Kemper
Editing: Kent Beyda, Wilton Henderson
Music: David Newman
Production design: Leslie McDonald
MPAA rating: PG
Running Time: 89 minutes

REVIEWS

Chicago Tribune. November 22, 1996, p. 5.
Detroit News. November 22, 1996, p. 1E.
Entertainment Weekly. December 6, 1996, p. 50.
Los Angeles Times. November 22, 1996, p. F6.
The New York Times. November 22, 1996, p. C10.
USA Today. November 22, 1996, p. 5D.
Variety. November 25, 1996, p. 71.

Joe's Apartment

Sex, Bugs, Rock 'n Roll—Movie tagline

"The *Citizen Kane* of cockroach movies. It should do for roaches what *Babe* did for pigs."—Larry Worth, *New York Post*

Box Office: $4,600,000

In 1992 MTV aired a short subject that combined live action and animation, *Joe's Apartment.* John Payson, the writer-director, had worked at MTV first shelving tapes and answering phones. Later he oversaw the production of MTV promotional spots. His first production experience came when he produced Henry Selick's short film *Slow Bob In the Lower Dimensions* (1991). Payson later became the supervising producer for MTV's half-hour animated series, "Liquid Television." On the strength of these credits, he has expanded the premise of his short subject about a young man's struggles with the roaches in his New York apartment into the first MTV-produced motion picture. Shortly before the release of the film, MTV featured Robert Vaughn as the host of a promotional show that had Vaughn in a tuxedo deadpanning jokes about the ordeal of working with 50,000 cockroaches. This tongue-in-cheek marketing strategy, along with the scatological humor in the film, suggests that the best way to enjoy *Joe's Apartment* is as a cult movie looking for an audience.

The computer-generated cockroaches were created and animated by Blue Sky Productions.

Payson has developed his plot from short subject to feature-length film by adding a love interest for his hero. The film opens with a singing cockroach atop the Statue of Liberty welcoming the audience to New York. Joe (Jerry O'Connell) has come from Iowa, and he is mugged right after stepping off the bus. With no job and no apartment, he nearly despairs when he sees a man unconscious on the street. He stoops to help and discovers that the supposed victim is really a performance artist pretending to be injured and recording the time it takes for someone to come to his aid. He introduces himself as Walter Shit (Jim Turner), and most of the subsequent jokes in the film follow rather predictably this unsubtle beginning.

"I never thought I'd say this, but they're actually kind of sweet."—Joe's girlfriend Lily about his cockroach pals.

Walter befriends Joe and helps him obtain a rent-controlled, seedy apartment in the only building remaining on a run-down city block in East Village. Joe tries to make himself at home, but he is observed by thousands of cockroaches. A surprise occurs when the roaches see Joe pick up his morning toast, brush a roach off it, and then eat it anyway. The roaches decide that Joe's indifference to hygiene makes him their kind of tenant. With the roaches on his side, Joe tries to find love and work in the big city.

Riding one day on a bus, Joe spots Lily (Megan Ward) tending to the flowers in an atrium she has created in what used to be a dingy alley. Lily works at a complaint bureau and aspires "to do something other than put people on hold." Joe and his bugs want to make a good impression on Lily, but his hopes are complicated when he sees her one day embracing a mysterious man. This is really Lily's Senator father (Robert Vaughn), who wants to tear down Joe's building and put up a new maximum-security prison on the site. He is helped in his efforts by Joe's crooked landlord, Mr. Bianco (Don Ho), who will make a fortune if he can evict Joe and sell the location to the government.

Joe and Lily first meet when they walk toward each other on opposite sides of a long wall for posting bills. She, wanting to beautify the city, covers her side with posters about her flowers, and he slaps up promotional flyers for Walter's band, stickers that feature Walter's last name in prominent letters. They bump into each other when they both come to the end of the wall. Payson has adapted a formula from the golden age of Hollywood by having his two lovers "meet cute" in this manner. Lily sees Joe's posters and recalls that her flowers will need some fertilizer. Their relationship commences on this earthy note.

The chance to supply his beloved with manure comes at the right time for Joe. He has already been fired as a pizza delivery boy, and another job retrieving used urinal cakes from Yankee Stadium has not been satisfying either. His roach friends offer advice on writing to Lily, give him a neck rub, and sing and dance in his garbage. A montage of shots reveals Joe gathering the droppings of horses, dogs, and elephants.

A film about roaches can probably be expected to include its share of bathroom humor. *Joe's Apartment* thrives on such jokes. One scene features the roaches doing precision swimming in Joe's dirty toilet. Their elaborately choreographed dance imitates the lavish production numbers of Busby Berkeley. Another shot shows Joe's dirty underwear twitching in the middle of the floor as a temporary roach home. When Joe courts Lily, he showers her with urinal cakes and tells her they are mulching pellets. Eventually the Featherstone Feminine Products Company closes down the urinal cake business in a hostile takeover, saying that there will be "no more trickle down economics."

In addition to the comedy of obscenity on which the film relies so heavily, it also makes use of some playful point of view shots and rapid cutting. The transitions between some scenes rely on geometric shapes and patterns that recall the style of the television program "Home Improvement." Payson also has fun creating some outlandish shots. In one, the camera seems to track toward the apartment at the level of the door jam, and another in a breakfast scene follows food as it enters Joe's mouth. The many scenes of dancing cockroaches always utilize plenty of unexpected points of view, flash cutting, and canted angles.

These roach dance numbers take up a sizeable portion of the film. After a while the plot begins to seem to be merely an excuse to showcase the computer graphics of the dancing roaches. The filmmakers introduce nearly every imaginable variation: a roach choir singing at a roach faith healing includes one crippled roach that joyfully throws away his crutches and dances on six newly healed legs, and a roach line dance brings the twang of country music to Joe's apartment. Such set pieces never let the audience forget who the real stars of the film are.

The conflict is resolved when Joe's roach friends come to his rescue by scaring off Vlad and Jesus (Shiek Mahmud-Bey and Jim Sterling), Mr. Bianco's two dimwitted nephews who are trying to evict Joe. The roaches also refurbish the run-down city block into a lush garden that convinces Lily's father to drop his plan for a prison and turn his back on Mr. Bianco. The love plot also ends happily when Lily, who was momentarily scared off by the roaches in Joe's apartment, sees the roaches spell out "Joe Loves Lily" like the marching band on a football field. The final fade-out occurs as Lily and Joe embrace in Lily's spotlessly clean apartment, which Joe's roaches slowly begin to take over. With that artistic choice, John Payson may be creating the hygienics for a sequel.

—Glenn Hopp

CREDITS

Joe: Jerry O'Connell
Lily: Megan Ward
Walter: Jim Turner
Senator Dad: Robert Vaughn
Mr. Bianco: Don Ho
Vlad: Shiek Mahmud-Bey
Jesus: Jim Sterling

Origin: USA
Released: 1996
Production: Diana Phillips and Bonni Lee for MTV and Geffen Pictures; released by Warner Bros.
Direction: John Payson
Screenplay: John Payson
Cinematography: Peter Deming
Editing: Peter Frank
Production design: Carol Spier
Music: Carter Burwell
MPAA rating: R
Running Time: 99 minutes

REVIEWS

Boxoffice Magazine Online. August 5, 1996.
Detroit Free Press. July 28, 1996, p. 9F.
Detroit News. July 26, 1996, P. 6D.
Entertainment Weekly. August 9, 1996, p. 44.
Los Angeles Times. July 29, 1996, p. F6.
New York Times. July 27, 1996, p. 17N.
People Weekly. July 15, 1996, p. 133.
USA Today. August 2, 1996, p. 4D.
Variety. July 29, 1996, p. 59.

Joseph Conrad's The Secret Agent

In Victorian London, a city of spies, one woman is about to be caught in a web of conspiracy and only one man has the power to protect her.—Movie tagline

"Riveting! Suspenseful! Bob Hoskins is masterful."—Dorothy Leeds, *WEHN Radio*

Box Office: $80,285

Francis Ford Coppola started the trend of linking adapted works with original authors with *Bram Stoker's Dracula* (1992), which was followed by *Mary Shelley's Frankenstein* (1994), and, now, *Joseph Conrad's The Secret Agent,* but, in the case of the latter film, there is a more practical reason—to keep the adaptation from being confused with Alfred Hitchcock's *Secret Agent* (1936), which had nothing to do with Joseph Conrad, even though Hitchcock's *Sabotage* (1936) was in fact an updated adaptation based on Conrad's story, starring Oscar Homolka as Verloc, Sylvia Sidney as Mrs. Verloc, and Desmond Tester as her younger brother, Stevie. During his stint as a London film reviewer, the novelist Graham Greene praised Hitchcock's treatment of Conrad's novel, published in 1906, for preserving the ruthlessness of the original, even though Hitchcock turned Verloc into a German spy and sent Stevie with the bomb that killed him to Piccadilly Circus. Hitchcock also took liberties with the conclusion and saved Winnie Verloc from the drowning Conrad imagined.

Christopher Hampton's film takes the story back to the 1880s, and, following Conrad, has Verloc involved with anarchists planning to detonate a bomb at the Royal Observatory at Greenwich. This was the only novel written by Joseph Conrad (1857-1924, born Jozef Teodor Konrad Nalecz Korzeniowski) that was set in London, probably inspired by a botched anarchist bombing in Greenwich Park.

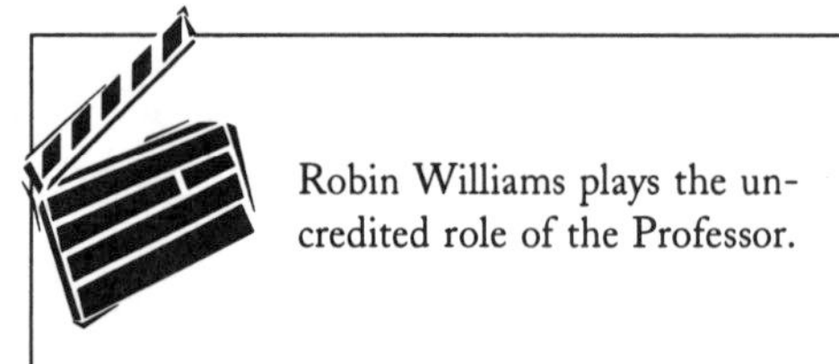

Robin Williams plays the uncredited role of the Professor.

The facts are these. On the evening of February 15, 1894, a young man, Martial Bourdin, was found "in a kneeling position, terribly mutilated" on a hill near the Royal Observatory in Greenwich Park. Bourdin had set off a bomb and died soon afterwards. His brother-in-law, H.B. Samuels, edited an anarchist newspaper and was, like Verloc, a police agent. Also like Verloc, Samuels had accompanied his brother to Greenwich Park. Conrad later described the attempt to blow up the Greenwich Observatory "a blood-stained inanity of so fatuous a kind that it was impossible to fathom its origin by any reasonable or even unreasonable process of thought." Conrad mentioned this "outrage" to a friend of his, who responded, "Oh, that fellow was half an idiot. His sister committed suicide afterwards." Conrad's imagination found a way of linking these two casual "facts."

Conrad set his novel in 1886, eight years before the "Greenwich Bomb Outrage." Verloc communes with known anarchists and spies on them. As a double-agent he is working for the Metropolitan Police and for Vladimir (British comedian Eddie Izzard in the film), the First Secretary of a foreign embassy (identified as the Russian Embassy in the film), who presses Verloc into service as an Agent Provocateur to create an incident that will make the British authorities rethink their policy of tolerance towards political malcontents and foreign dissidents. Verloc does not intend to send his mentally handicapped brother-in-law to his death, and he understandably panics after the bomb accidentally explodes.

In the Hampton film Adolph Verloc (Bob Hoskins) is involved as a double-agent with a group of anarchists from Eastern Europe. He lives above his "book" shop, where he sells "improper wares and pornographic publications," with his wife Winnie (Patricia Arquette), her mother (Elizabeth Spriggs), who moves out early in the story, and his wife's retarded brother Stevie (Christian Bale), who is referred to by one of the foreign anarchists, Ossipon (Gerard Depardieu) as a "degenerate." All of these characters are pathetic. Most of them are fatalistic and self-serving. Some of them are evil. One of them, The Professor (played by Robin Williams in an uncredited role), is a bombmaker whose goal in life is to build a perfect detonator, a goal that he seems to have achieved in the film's final freeze-frame.

Verloc is ordered by his Russian handler to take a bomb to the Royal Observatory. Verloc goes to Greenwich but sends Stevie up the hill with the bomb. The boy trips over a root and falls on the bomb, which explodes, killing him. Verloc returns home but finds Chief Inspector Heat (Jim Broadbent) there, interrogating Mrs. Verloc. The Inspector discloses that Stevie has died in a horrible way. Verloc appears to be sorry for the boy's death, but he is equally concerned about his own safety. A compulsive eater, he gnaws on thick slices of roast beef as he attempts to explain and justify his actions to his distracted wife.

When Verloc, a man of gross appetites, demands sexual consolation from his wife, she snaps and stabs him through the heart with her steak knife, telling him as he dies that she was never truly interested in him except as someone who would be kind to her brother. When Ossipon then comes to the Soho shop, he discovers that Verloc is dead and that Mrs. Verloc has a considerable sum of money Verloc drew out of the bank in panic. He buys Winnie a ticket to France via train and steamer, takes her to Waterloo Station, puts her on the train, steals her money, and jumps from the moving train as it leaves the station. Arriving at the coast, Winnie gets on the Channel steamer, deliberately removes her wedding ring, then, as Ossipon discovers reading a newspaper a day or so later, drowns herself. Only he and the viewer could understand why.

The film is artfully made and tells its story with slow deliberation. It opens with a tracking long-shot that follows Verloc through the gloomy streets of his London and into his shop and the quarters above it in one long, continuous take. The art direction manages to be convincingly atmospheric without being at all decorous. London is dark and dank. At night the Verlocs live in gaslit gloom. When Verloc walks the streets during the day, he has to avoid piles of horse dung. In no way does this film attempt to romanticize and beautify the historical setting.

CREDITS

Verloe: Bob Hoskins
Winnie: Patricia Arquette
Ossipon: Gerard Depardieu
Chief Inspector Heat: Jim Broadbent
Stevie: Christian Bale
Vladimir: Eddie Izzard

Origin: Great Britain
Released: 1996
Production: Norma Heyman for a Capitol Films production; released by Fox Searchlight
Direction: Christopher Hampton
Screenplay: Christopher Hampton; based on the novel by Joseph Conrad
Cinematography: Denis Lenoir
Editing: George Akers
Music: Philip Glass
Production design: Caroline Amies
Art direction: Frank Walsh
Costume design: Anushia Nieradzik
Sound: Peter Lindsay
Casting: Janey Fothergill
MPAA rating: R
Running Time: 95 minutes

For the most part the characters are manipulative, brutal and inhuman, with the exception of the simpleton Stevie, who cannot bear to see a coachman (Peter Vaughan) whip his horse. ("It's an 'ard world," he tells Stevie, "'ard on 'orses an' a darn sight 'arder on poor bleeders like me.") Mrs. Verloc has no feelings for her husband, whom she murders, only for her brother, whom he kills. Verloc is seen as a creature of appetites, chewing roast beef even as he speaks to Winnie about her brother's death. He is manipulated by the anarchists, by the First Secretary of the Embassy for whom he works, and by the police and the secret service. Just as Verloc betrays Winnie's trust in his ability to look after Stevie, so does Ossipon betray her later by stealing her money for the insane cause in which he believes. Hampton's film is far better in its treatment of corrupt and amoral politics than the earlier Hitchcock version.

Christopher Hampton was the playwright who successfully adapted the Choderlos de Laclos novel *Les Liaisons Dangereuses* to the London stage and then went on to write the screenplay adaptation for the film Stephen Frears directed in 1988. Hampton proved his competence as director in 1995 with *Carrington,* a film he also scripted, dealing with the relationship between the English painter Dora Carrington and the writer Lytton Strachey. That film, marking his directorial debut, won the Special Jury Prize at the Cannes Film Festival.

The film is vibrant with talent. Hampton takes a story that would seem to be tragic and plays it in the style of black comedy. Costume designer Anushia Nieradzik commented that "Stevie wears a bowler hat because Mr. Verloc has one, he has a coat because Mr. Verloc does, and they look a bit like Laurel and Hardy when they are walking along together" on their way to Greenwich Park. *Washington Times* critic Gary Arnold noticed the brilliance of the way the picture was cast against type, placing comedians in villainous and morally compromised roles: "Mr. Hampton takes a somewhat perverse pleasure in casting comic specialists against type: Mr. Hoskins as the pathetic Verloc; Mr. Izzard and Jim Broadbent as his rival mentors, the diplomat Vladimir and the methodical London police inspector Heat; and Mr. Williams and Gerard Depardieu as the Professor and Ossipon, anarchists with contrasting approaches to treachery."

The casting is certainly in keeping with the story, however. Critic J.I.M. Stewart has written that "the end of Mr. Verloc, although one of the greatest scenes in English fiction, belongs—as does the end of Stevie, if not Stevie's sister—to a world of savage comedy." The film in fact catches the sustained ironic tone of the book. Conrad was appalled by anarchist activities, the "criminal futility" of the anarchist "doctrine, action [and] mentality." Understandably Conrad turned to savage satire to expose what he called "the contemptible aspect of the half-crazy pose as of a brazen cheat, exploiting the poignant miseries and passionate credulities of a mankind always so tragically eager for self-destruction."

There can be little doubt, therefore, that Hampton's adaptation is exactly what its title proclaims: *Joseph Conrad's The Secret Agent.* This is a as satisfactory and well acted adaptation as one is likely to find in cinema these days, even if it does presume that viewers will also have read the book.

—*James M. Welsh*

REVIEWS

The Baltimore Sun. December 13, 1996, p. E9.
Boxoffice. November 1996, p. 138.
Entertainment Weekly. November 29, 1996, p. 74.
The Hollywood Reporter. September 10, 1996, p. 10.
New York Times. November 8, 1996, p. C9.
Variety. November 11-17, 1996, p. 58.
Washington Post Weekend. December 6, 1996, p. 50.
The Washington Times Metropolitan Times. December 6, 1996, p. C17.

Jude

A town without pity. A society without mercy. A love without equal.—Movie tagline

"*Jude* is handsome, fluid, intelligent and red-blooded."—Jay Carr, *The Boston Globe*

"Kate Winslet shows that last year's Oscar nominated turn in *Sense and Sensibility* was just a warm up."—Robert Hoffler, *Buzz Magazine*

"*Jude* is an extraordinary film. Kate Winslet and Christopher Eccleston are perfectly cast."—Stephen Farber, *Movieline*

"A sweeping film of power, passion and greatness. Beautifully acted, exquisitely directed. A work of art."—Rex Reed, *The New York Observer*

"One of this fall's finest feature films."—Jeff Craig, *Sixty Second Preview*

Box Office: $407,072

Jude the Obscure, the source for the film entitled merely *Jude,* directed by Michael Winterbottom, was the last novel Thomas Hardy was to write. The novel was first serialized late in 1895 by *Harper's New Monthly Magazine,* then published in book form in 1896. It is, along with *Tess of the D'Urbervilles,* Thomas Hardy's most powerful novel, but also his bleakest. The novel was never intended for mere entertainment. It is a sort of polemic of social criticism directed against the exclusiveness of English higher education, the repressiveness of British social conventions, and hypocrisy at all levels, social, religious, and academic. These are the mechanisms that grind down the character Jude Fawley.

According to Hardy scholar J.I.M. Stewart, *Jude* was "less a novel than an outcry," but certainly a "courageous and uncompromising" work. What Hardy wrote of Ibsen, Stewart contends, could also apply to Hardy's own social concerns: "To depict human beings, human emotions, and human destinies, upon a groundwork of certain of the social conditions and principles of the present day." Hardy was so surprised and hurt by the reception of his novel that he spent the rest of his life writing poetry rather than fiction—and he was to live for another thirty-three years after *Jude* was written.

The novel is hardly more endearing in its bleakness and pessimism today than it was a hundred years ago when it was written. Jude Fawley (James Daley as the boy Jude and, later, Christopher Eccleston, the young accountant in *Shallow Grave* [1995]), an orphan from Wessex (a section of England Hardy invented for his fiction), is an intelligent but disadvantaged farm boy who dreams of attending the university in the city of Christminster (Hardy was thinking of Oxford). Encouraged by Mr. Phillotson (Liam Cunningham), his friendly tutor, to embrace learning as a means of self-betterment, Jude teaches himself Latin and some Greek, but his career is diverted when he is seduced and lured into an unfortunate marriage by the vulgar Arabella (Rachel Griffiths, last seen in *Muriel's Wedding* [1995]), the daughter of a pig-farmer, who later throws him over and emigrates to Australia.

Jude then travels to Christminster to try his luck at the university and finds work as a stonemason. At Christminster he meets and falls in love with his cousin, Sue Bridehead (Kate Winslet from *Sense and Sensibility* [1995]). Sue marries the schoolmaster, Phillotson, who has gone to Oxford but is unable to help Jude get admitted. Class is obviously more important than motivation, and the university is a closed society. Phillotson treats Sue decently, but, through no fault of his, the marriage is not a happy one because Sue is neurotic and, to paraphrase one Hardy critic, "pathologically frigid." Sue eventually elopes with Jude and overcomes her frigidity long enough to bear him two children.

Hardy's "Wessex" is present-day Dorset but filming took place in Yorkshire and Durham, England, with Edinburgh, Scotland standing in for Christminster.

Their relationship is disrupted, however, when Arabella returns from Australia and leaves Jude with the wretched son she had by him, for, unbeknownst to Jude, Arabella was pregnant when she left England. This child is a neurotic malcontent identified in the novel as Little Father Time. When Jude and Sue fall upon hard times, Little Father Time, believing himself and his half-siblings to be the cause of the family's economic hardship, hangs himself and the two other children. After this tragic event Sue leaves Jude and returns to her first husband, Phillotson. Left to his own devices, Jude loses his faith and becomes an agnostic in the novel, turns to drink, and finally dies, a victim of fate and circumstance. The film adaptation does not follow the novel all the way to its fatalistic conclusion, but it goes far enough.

Hardy's grim story shows the influence of Naturalism. Heredity serves to shape and seal the fate of Jude and Sue, cousins whose ancestors were disposed to suicide (worked out by the terrible logic of Little Father Time) and unhappiness in marriage. Sue's character, moreover, was shaped partly out of Hardy's familiarity with *Hedda Gabler* and Ibsen's model for the "New Woman." Hardy's universe is passive and amoral, malevolent because of the carelessness and blindness of men capable of moral choice but inclined to make bad choices under the influence of bad luck. Hardy himself described *Jude* as a "tragedy of unfulfilled aims."

"If you want to do anything in your life, Jude, that's where you have to go."—Phillotson pointing out Christminster university

The screenplay, adapted by Hossein Amini, is reasonably faithful to the novel, though it truncates the opening and changes the focus of the conclusion. Christopher Eccleston's angular good looks are convincing enough, but the screenplay somehow fails to strike the heart of his character. Eccleston does not really come to life until his Jude gets drunk at a pub after being notified that he will not be accepted by the university. After being condescended to by arrogant and privileged university students, Jude demonstrates his knowledge of Latin by reciting the Apostle's Creed, then demands to know which of them can determine whether or not he got it right. But this scene is a long time coming, and few other scenes in the film can match its power.

In fact, the film does not hit its stride until Kate Winslet's Sue Bridehead comes into Jude's life. Winslet offers a nicely nuanced interpretation of the character, whose motives could be made more clear by the screenplay. Sue is an independent young woman, an idealist and a rebel, who will not for the sake of convention pretend that she and Jude are married, though the fact that they are living "in sin" gets them .evicted. Winslet is somehow able to make Sue seem frigid and sexy at the same time, and this is a tribute to her acting. After the death of her children she is understandably alienated from Jude, who, of course, is not exactly responsible for what happened, beyond having fathered a miserable child with an unworthy woman.

Michael Winterbottom made his feature film debut in 1995 with *Butterfly Kiss,* in which two women (Amanda Plummer and Saskia Reeves) undertook a journey of murder and self-discovery along the motorways of northwest England. His English degree from Oxford prepared him for the task of filming Thomas Hardy. Hossein Amini, who wrote the screenplay for *Jude,* also wrote the screenplay for Peter Kosminsky's *Dying of the Light,* which was nominated for a British Academy of Film and Television Award for Best Single Drama in 1995.

The film is certainly faithful to Hardy's design, broken into episodes that correspond to the divisions of the novel: "At Marygreen," for example, "At Christminster," "At Melchester," "At Shaston," and "At Aldbrickham & Elsewhere." The historical reconstruction and atmosphere are nicely captured by the cinematography of Eduardo Serra, which, during the winter scenes takes on a black-and-white bleakness in capturing the landscape of North Yorkshire. Other location filming was done in Northumberland, Durham, and Edinburgh. The atmosphere is more than merely picturesque. Thomas Hardy (1840-1928) was born the son of a master stonemason in Higher Brockhampton in Dorset. All of his novels were set in the fictional landscape he called "Wessex," which was based on Dorset and the surrounding countryside. Hardy became famous for his ability to describe the landscape so vividly that it became a sort of spiritual presence in his fiction. The bleak landscape of North Yorkshire provides an appropriate atmosphere here.

Despite the bleakness, the film does permit an isolated episode of exuberance as Jude and Sue frolic on the beach at one point, visualizing the elusive possibility of happiness before the crude Arabella returns. The utter bleakness of the conclusion of the novel is somewhat alleviated by the film, though there neither is nor can be the possibility of a happy ending. Stephen Farber, who considered the film a "brilliant, bracing success," wrote that if the adaptation "inevitably loses some of the telling details of the novel, it nevertheless affirms the potency of Hardy's tragic vision." Farber considered the ending of the film, despite the difference, "emotionally devastating in exactly the same way that the novel was." This is a film for mature grown-ups, and an intelligent attempt to adapt a classic novel to the screen. It is also a film conceived for the readers of Thomas Hardy who know the novel and will be willing and able to fill in the gaps in the screenplay.

—James M. Welsh

CREDITS

Jude Fawley: Christopher Eccleston
Sue Bridehead: Kate Winslet
Phillotson: Liam Cunningham
Arabella: Rachel Griffiths
Aunt Drusilla: June Whitfield

Origin: Great Britain
Released: 1996
Production: Andrew Eaton for a Revolution Films, BBC Films, and Polygram Filmed Entertainment production; released by Gramercy Pictures
Direction: Michael Winterbottom
Screenplay: Hossein Amini; based on the novel *Jude the Obscure* by Thomas Hardy
Cinematography: Eduardo Serra
Editing: Trevor White
Production design: Joseph Bennett
Costume design: Janty Yates
Music: Adrian Johnston
Casting: Simon Ireland, Vanessa Pereira
MPAA rating: R
Running Time: 123 minutes

REVIEWS

Boxoffice. August, 1996, p. 56.
Chicago Tribune. November 1, 1996, p. 5.
Entertainment Weekly. November 1, 1996, p. 48.
Hollywood Reporter. May 14, 1996, p. 12.
The New York Times. October 18, 1996, p. C3.
People. November 4, 1996, p. 29.
The Philadelphia Inquirer Weekend. November 1, 1996, p. 5.
Sight and Sound. October, 1996, p. 45.
Time Online. October 28, 1996.
USA Today. October 18, 1996, p. D5.
Variety Online. May 16, 1996.
Village Voice. October 22, 1996, p. 78.
Washington City Paper. November 1, 1996, p. 42.
The Washington Post. November 1, 1996, p. D7.
Washington Post Weekend. November 1, 1996, p. 44.
Washington Times Metropolitan Times. November 1, 1996, p. C16.

The Juror

There is no defense.—Movie tagline

"If a movie can be a page turner, this one is it. Moore and Baldwin are terrific . . . as in terrifying. A lot of tension, a lot of suspense."—Joel Siegel, *Good Morning America*

"Riveting! Powerful performances by Demi Moore and Alec Baldwin."—Jim Ferguson, *The Prevue Channel*

"A hypnotizing psychological thriller!"—Peter Stark, *The San Francisco Chronicle*

"The book froze your eyeballs with terror, so will the movie. The cast is terrific. Trust me on this one."—Larry King, *USA Today*

"A guilty pleasure. A thriller that leaves you with something to think about."—Alan Silverman, *Voice of America*

Box Office: $22,754,727

A high-powered creative team fails to generate any heat in *The Juror,* a muddled knock-off of a John Grisham legal thriller that in actuality is based on the novel by George Dawes Green. Penned by Oscar-winning screenwriter Ted Tally (*The Silence of the Lambs* [1991]) and directed with restraint by Brian Gibson (*What's Love Got to Do with It* [1993]), the result is a tedious and sterile psychological thriller that, like its star Demi Moore, keeps the audience at such an emotional distance that the film evokes no suspense and certainly little sympathy for our woman in jeopardy.

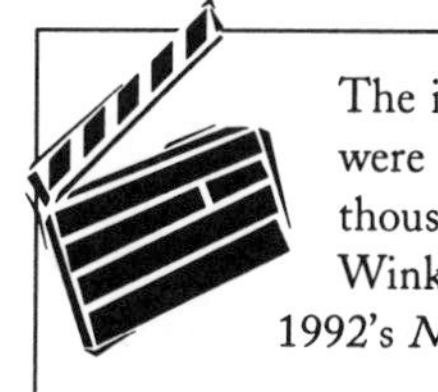

The interior courtroom scenes were shot at the Harlem Courthouse, where Cowan and Winkler had previously filmed 1992's *Night and the City.*

Moore plays Annie Laird, a sculptor and single mother who decides it is her civic duty to serve on the jury of the high profile murder trial of Mafia mob boss Louie Boffano (Tony Lo Bianco). Besides, Annie thinks it would be fun, adding a little excitement to her otherwise mundane life. Her presence on the jury also excites the mysterious mob operative known only as the Teacher (Alec Baldwin), so named because "when you see him, school's out." (Confusing, since teachers usually are present when school is in session.) The Teacher targets Annie as the prime juror to be able to pressure the others into acquitting Boffano of the murder of a mob boss and his grandson. Annie's love for her son Oliver (Joseph Gordon-Levitt) makes her vulnerable and the Teacher is intrigued by her brains and her sexiness. "Not your average mommy," he tells an associate.

"Everything we've been through's like a marriage."—The Teacher trying to soothe Annie after terrorizing her

The Teacher sets out to insinuate himself into Annie's life by purchasing some art under the guise of being a broker. And in no time, he reveals himself and his true mission. He tortures the poor girl emotionally and mentally and when he achieves his goal, when Annie succeeds in convincing the other jurors that the evidence is insufficient to convict Boffano, the Teacher, a true sociopath, still pursues her, convinced that he is in love with Annie. He is intrigued by her art, boxes on pedestals that the viewer must fondle from under the skirts. When the Teacher murders her best friend, a strung out doctor played with gusto by Anne Heche, Annie gets mad. The remainder of the film involves Annie's attempts to fight back and to protect her son, travelling to Guatemala in a ludicrous ending that only Hollywood could have dreamed up.

The Juror is simplistic in its plotting and so restrained in its direction that it lacks any degree of suspense. Story twists are telegraphed in advance and the dialogue is strained and often ludicrous, with the Teacher spewing such lines as, "It's terror that teaches me my shape" and "I bow to fear." Pity poor Alec Baldwin, an actor far too talented to have to utter such inane and pompous dialogue. While Mr. Baldwin's sadistic good looks and husky deep voice help to imbue his character with far more menace than scripted, the actor still falls short of crafting another of his patented sociopaths of the *Miami Blues* (1989) mold. Despite his oozing sex appeal—or is it the result of?—Baldwin is so much more effective as the character on the edge, the one most likely to snap if pushed too far. This brand of sex appeal arguably makes for more interesting on-screen characters, those men like Steve McQueen and Clint Eastwood who so successfully combined danger with matinee-idol good looks. While Alec Baldwin has enjoyed limited success as an action hero (*The Getaway* [1994] or *The Shadow* [1994]) or as the good guy (*The Hunt for Red October* [1990]), he has found his niche portraying the warped personality with a surprising amount of humanity. When one of Boffano's men remarks that the Teacher is "sick . . . with no friends," Baldwin's face registers the pain of the observation in a powerful, yet quiet way.

Quite possibly the biggest liability to *The Juror* is actress Demi Moore, one of the least humorous and most frigid women to appear on-screen. Her iciness rivals noir femme fatale Linda Fiorentino (*The Last Seduction* [1995]), whose similar forays outside her limited range have been met with indifference. Ms. Moore's other 1996 release, *Striptease,* was a critical and financial disaster, as well, with critics again citing the actress's lack of on-screen humor.

In the final analysis, *The Juror* is little more than a B-movie with an A-list cast and crew. Burdened with several false endings, the film takes far too long to resolve the relationship between Annie and the Teacher and shares way too much in common with 1994's *Trial By Jury.* Critics were fairly consistent in their dismissal of this unthrilling thriller.

—Patricia Kowal

CREDITS

Annie Laird: Demi Moore
The Teacher: Alec Baldwin
Oliver Laird: Joseph Gordon-Levitt
Juliet: Anne Heche
Eddie: James Gandolfini
Tallow: Lindsay Crouse
Louie Boffano: Tony Lo Bianco
Judge Weitzel: Michael Constantine
Boone: Matt Craven

Origin: USA
Released: 1996
Production: Irwin Winkler and Rob Cowan; a Columbia Pictures release
Direction: Brian Gibson
Screenplay: Ted Tally, based on the novel by George Dawes Green
Cinematography: Jamie Anderson
Editing: Robert Reitano
Production design: Jan Roelfs
Art direction: Charley Beal
Costume design: Colleen Atwood
Music: James Newton Howard
MPAA rating: R
Running Time: 120 minutes

REVIEWS

Boxoffice. April, 1996, p. 117.
Chicago Tribune. February 2, 1996, p. 4.
Detroit News. February 2, 1996, p. C1.
Entertainment Weekly. February 9, 1996, p. 36.
Los Angeles Times. February 2, 1996, p. F1.
New York. February 12, 1996, p. 52.
The New Yorker. February 12, 1996, p. 83.
New York Times. February 2, 1996, p. B1.
Rolling Stone. March 7, 1996, p. 34.
Time. February 5, 1996, p. 68.
Variety. February 5, 1996, p. 59.
Village Voice. February 13, 1996, p. 68.
Wall Street Journal. February 2, 1996, p. A8.
Washington Post. February 2, 1996, p. B7.

Justice in the Coalfields

The Appalachian region is a study in contrasts: technology and wealth versus tradition and poverty, outsiders ensconced in corporate offices versus generations of locals with their roots sunken into the hillsides and into the rich black coal beneath them. Anne Lewis's *Justice in the Coalfields* captures these contradictions by capturing each faction involved in the Pittston Coal strike of 1989.

In April 1989, 1700 members of the United Mine Workers of America (UMWA) in Virginia and in West Virginia struck Pittston Coal Company over the issue of health insurance. Citing a need to remain competitive with international suppliers of coal, Pittston officials wrote to the miners suspending health benefits. Among those affected was Gail Gentry, who is confined to a wheelchair after a rock in a Pittston mine fell on his back, crushing five vertebrae and paralyzing his legs. Through a series of interviews with miners, miners' wives, miners' children, a federal judge, a Pittston executive, a UMWA leader, State Troopers, among others, Lewis is able to convey the chasm between them. Perhaps most interestingly, Lewis avoids the temptation to find resolution in the matter, placing it instead in an historical continuum of situations that never quite work out, in an intergenerational nightmare of broken promises and forgotten dreams.

Anne Lewis's films rely heavily on people telling their own stories and on silence as well as sound, on background as well as action. For instance, in her *Fast Food Women,* Lewis chronicled the fate of women in Whitesburg, KY, whose husbands were without work and whose only options for employment were the fast-food establishments that were cropping up like cankers across coal country. Forced to work for minimal pay and no benefits, forced to spend hours over grease pits and hauling supplies, the women pause to explain to Anne Lewis's camera the need that drives them, and her camera records the fatigue in their faces, the slump in their shoulders, the coughs that shake them like trees in the wind. Wearing absurdly jaunty and childish uniforms and hats, the fast-food women do what is necessary to keep their families together.

Similarly, in *Justice in the Coalfields,* Anne Lewis interviews Redbone Stuffey who walks the picket line by day and dances to fiddle music all night to help him work through the pressure; Glen M. Williams, a senior federal judge appointed by Richard Nixon, who feels that chaos ensues when people refuse to comply with court orders and who fined the miners $52 million dollars in an effort to force compliance; high school students who skipped school to protest and who discuss politics even as they chew on Tootsie Roll Pops; scabs who feel that they took no one's job, that the miners gave up their jobs. Lewis's camera captures each person without amelioration: paunch (complete with pulling buttons), jowls, mug-like ears, snaggly teeth, poor haircuts.

Perhaps, however, the power and the lesson of *Justice in the Coalfields* comes from the land itself. Interspersed throughout the film are calm, clear panoramas of the natural beauty of the area, of blue skies and green rolling hills; of mountains and valleys without a sign of modernization or man. Contrasted with this are the bald scars left by strip mining, sawed off mountains, green peaks turned to brown, dusty shelves; the dark and incomprehensible underworld of the mines, hellish in its noise, damned in the backs it bends, the lives it takes; the poverty of the miners, their humble homes and strong pride. The true story is, once again, in the contrast.

The story is also in what the audience sees and hears beyond impassioned speech and panoramic scenery. The story is in the fiddles that create the eerily wraith-like Appalachian music. The story is in the grandfathers whose lungs are crusted with coal dust and their grandchildren who know only the poverty left by the mines. The story is in the historic footage and stills that show generation after generation of families pulled underground. The story is in the green of the State Trooper uniforms, the green of the miners' camouflage fatigues, the green of the buses that carried to jail the 1100-1500 persons arrested during the Pittston strike, the green of the spring that no one sees from inside corporate offices, inside the mines, inside the jail cells.

Documentaries and narrative films showcasing workers and their interactions with management are garnering increasing popularity and commercial recognition. For instance, Michael Moore's *Roger and Me* (1989) (auto workers), Barbara Koppel's *Harlan County, U.S.A.* (1977) (miners) and Academy Award-winning *American Dream* (1989) (meat packers), John Sayles' *Matewan* (1987) (miners), and Martin Ritt's *Norma Rae* (1979) (textile workers), perhaps the best known of the genre, are in wide distribution and have won a variety of awards and strong reviews. What each tries to convey is a sense of unity among the workers and a sense of alienation among management. As one singer in *Justice* intones, "Money has no conscience, and greed has no heart."

Anne Lewis and Appalshop have once again created a stirring documentary that shows how, once social conflict ensues, no one is the wiser or the richer for it; how only once tested can people determine how much they can bear, how much they will bear, where they will draw the line, with whom they will stand. An excellent vehicle for discussion about community, government, and corporate concepts of justice, *Justice in the Coalfields* also allows viewers to understand a bit more about the human heart and its failings.

—Roberta F. Green

CREDITS

Origin: USA
Released: 1996
Production: Anne Lewis for Appalshop
Direction: Anne Lewis
Screenplay: Anne Lewis
Cinematography: Andrew Garrison, Herb E. Smith, Joseph Gray, Tom Kaufman, and Jerry Johnson
Editing: Anne Lewis
Sound: Anne Lewis, Alex Milenic
MPAA rating: Unrated
Running Time: 56 minutes

Kansas City

1934. The mob played Kansas City like a smooth jazz riff. Until one woman started to improvise.—Movie tagline

"A down and dirty homage to Kansas City in the 30's! No movie in years has used music with such impact."—Jack Kroll, *Newsweek*

"Jazz lovers rejoice! *Kansas City* brims overs with vibrant and vital music. Belafonte is scary perfection."—Peter Travers, *Rolling Stone*

"Altman at his brilliant best! Captivating, suspenseful, and highly entertaining."—Paul Wunder, *WBAI Radio*

Box Office: **$1,356,329**

Robert Altman's *Kansas City* explores the issues of crime, race, and politics in the 1930's through the eyes of enigmatic gangster Seldom Seen (Harry Belafonte).

In Robert Altman's *Kansas City* set in 1934, there are two constants: the corruption goes on and the jazz goes on, right up to the very end, when Ray Brown's bass solo wraps up the credits. The screenplay by director Altman, who was born in Kansas City in 1925 and lived there until he enlisted in the Air Force at the age of 18, and Frank Barhydt is a little flimsy and cartoonish, but that is in keeping with Altman's style. Barhydt, like Altman, is a native of Kansas City and knows the territory. He co-wrote the screenplay for Altman's *Short Cuts* (1993), an interesting liberal adaptation of Raymond Carver's stories; on the other hand, he also co-wrote *Quintet* (1979) and *Health* (1980), two of Altman's weakest films. *Kansas City* was shot mainly in downtown Kansas City, Missouri, on a budget of $16 million.

A robbery sets the plot of *Kansas City* in motion. Johnny O'Hara (Dermot Mulroney) in blackface robs high-roller Sheepshan Red (A.C. Smith), who has come to town to play craps at the Hey Hey Club, owned by charismatic gangster Seldom Seen (Harry Belafonte), who is the black counterpart to the notorious Boss Tom Pendergast, who runs Kansas City. Black gangsters soon locate O'Hara and retrieve the stolen money belt. Seldom Seen concludes that he will have to have Johnny murdered in order to uphold his own reputation. Things look bad for Johnny.

"He's a loser and losers have to be respected. They're the backbone of my business."—Racketeer Seldom Seen about a gambler

Blondie O'Hara (Jennifer Jason Leigh) hatches a crazy plot to save her husband's life. She kidnaps Carelyn Stilton (Miranda Richardson), the wife of FDR's Presidential advisor Henry Stilton (Michael Murphy), who has just boarded a train bound for Chicago, then Washington on election day, 1934, when the Pendergast machine is attempting to fix the votes. After Blondie sends a telegram to intercept the train, Stilton returns to Kansas City to help his wife.

Blondie wants Stilton to put pressure on Pendergast so that the Kansas City machine will put pressure on Seldom Seen to spare Johnny's life. It's a long shot, and she knows it, but she is desperate. Most of the film follows Blondie and her spaced-out prisoner, who is hopelessly addicted to laudanum (an opium derivative), "her escape from the world," as Altman described it, "her way of tuning out." Blondie is a low-life psycho who considers herself a Jean Harlow look-alike. Though some reviewers complained that Leigh's performance was way over the top, in fact both Leigh and Richardson give strong performances. The problem, perhaps, is that they are too much in the limelight. On the other hand, their relationship makes thematic sense, since the film is about crossing boundaries. Just as Johnny has crossed a racial barrier by getting himself involved with black gangsters, Blondie crosses a social barrier by kidnapping the socialite.

The music also takes on thematic significance and is not simply part of the background. Jazz fans will find the film most interesting for the jam session footage at the Hey Hey Club, reconstructed at 18th and Vine for the film, with the music provided by gifted musicians representing Bill Basie, Jay McShann, Bennie Moten, Ben Webster, Jo Jones (Victor Lewis), Coleman Hawkins (Craig Handy), Lester Young (Joshua Redman), and a very young Charlie Parker

(Albert J. Burnes). "The story was constructed like a piece of jazz," Altman told Michael Henry in an interview published by the French journal *Positif* (May 1996): "I see the film as being spherical rather than linear; its structure is essentially musical. It's a slim story and the dialogue between the two girls is like jazz riffs." Many reviewers had trouble understanding what was going on between these two characters, whose relationship is the central thread or clue in the story. "You have to look at it as a song, with Jennifer and Miranda as two tenor saxophones, Belafonte as a trumpet, and everybody else coming in for a brief solo," Altman explained.

The reconstructed details are impressive and meticulous, from the period cars, to the Lucky Strike green on Blondie's cigarette pack, to the cat bank on Basie's piano. In the old days, patrons were expected to make donations—to "Feed the kitty," in other words—at Kansas City jazz clubs. At no point in the film is this explained, but the "Kitty" is there for all to see. By the age of fifteen young Robert Altman was frequenting those clubs, sitting in the balcony like the young Charlie Parker in the film, who watches the "cutting contest" between Coleman Hawkins and Lester Young, dueling with their tenor saxophones. That musical cutting contest is a parallel to the improvised dialogue elsewhere in the film, overlapping it.

But Altman makes no concessions for the ignorant. If one knows jazz, the music and the contest will be pretty exciting; if one knows Altman's work, its relationship to the film should be fairly obvious. Altman explained in his *Positif* interview that Seldom Seen was a real gangster who lived to be 98 years old, and that Charlie Parker's mother, Addie (Jeff Feringa) really worked at the Western Union office, as in the film. In fact, Altman claims all of the characters except Blondie and her husband were based on real people.

Harry Belafonte, who had not made a film in twenty years, was cast from the start: "He wrote most of his lines," Altman explains, "including the racist joke. All of his monologues were kind of comments on the times," as when he makes fun of Marcus Garvey, "the black politician who wanted to send everyone back to Africa and even started a black shipping line, the Black Star." Belafonte was voted best supporting actor of 1996 by the New York Film Critics' Circle for his portrayal of Seldom Seen. Belafonte so enjoyed working with Altman that he plans to be in Altman's next picture, *Amos and Andy*, scheduled for 1997. In an interview Altman remarked, "Without question, Harry Belafonte should be nominated for an Academy Award. The irony is that a movie that has so much jazz doesn't qualify for the Oscar music awards. It's because we play old standards instead of original tunes."

Unfortunately, *Kansas City* opened to mixed reviews in Kansas City and elsewhere. In a review entitled "The Jazz Sizzles, the Rest Fizzles" for the *Kansas City Star* (August 16), Robert W. Butler called the film "a magnificently decorated doughnut that can't hide the hollowness at its center." Butler called Jennifer Jason Leigh's portrayal her "most irritating performance to date" and found her "unrelenting dumb-blond masquerade" simply "offputting." Butler wrongly contended that Blondie had "to be taken seriously" for the film to succeed: "We almost never see the real person beneath the irritating artifice," he concluded, without seeming to realize that Blondie is a cartoon character, as her name suggests. Another, better, critic responded that Leigh "provided a beautifully realized performance that is entirely appropriate to the film." Altman himself claims that "Jennifer is one of the best actresses we have working in films today." Butler's highest praise was for Steve Buscemi as Blondie's brother-in-law, who came very near to "stealing the show" in the few scenes in which he is featured.

Robert Trussell, theater critic of the *Kansas City Star*, wrote a blistering response to Butler (August 23) entitled "The Critics Are All ... Wrong," asserting that the film was "actually an engrossing snapshot of a depraved era" back in the days when "a copy of the *Kansas City Star* cost 2 cents and votes and vices were equally affordable." In those days Kansas City was "a real city, a little Chicago that was two parts gangland and one part Wild West." Too many critics did not seem to understand what made this a typical Altman film—its "cynical overview, unsympathetic characters, meandering story, and the director's almost willful disdain of the average moviegoer's expectations." The plot incorporated "kidnappings (a growth industry in the '30s), drug addiction (as much a problem in the Depression as it is today), thuggish political tactics (he depicts the notorious, bloody municipal election of March 27, 1934), gangsterism (still with us), racism (both the benevolent and virulent strains), class warfare (the haves protecting their interests from the have-nots) and the transcendent, ennobling power of jazz." For Trussel, Altman, managed "to say more about this town's social fabric than any history book." Perhaps Altman presumed "a level of historical knowledge" that most viewers simply lacked. As Anthony Lane wrote in *The New Yorker*, "No other filmmaker wraps his movies in such a thick texture, or puts such enduring—and unfashionable—trust in the patience of his viewers."

Kansas City is remarkable as Altman's colorful, loving, atmospheric homage to his hometown and its vibrance and wide-open lawlessness in 1934. In a way it could be considered Altman's equivalent of Federico Fellini's *Amarcord* (1974), but Fellini's remembrance is far more sentimental

AWARDS AND NOMINATIONS

New York Film Critics Circle 1996: Best Supporting Actor (Belafonte)

and nostalgic, whereas Altman's is ironic and satirical. As Todd Boyd noted in *Sight and Sound*, "the film is 'trademark Altman' in that it presents a series of interconnected episodes, all linked to one central theme: The uses and abuses of power." Altman effectively weaves together "a tapestry of city life that is long gone," but in this case the multiple interconnected stories for which Altman has become famous are "curiously uninvolving." Unlike *Nashville* (1975), Boyd rightly concludes, "*Kansas City* never quite gathers its threads together," but the film is still a remarkable metaphor for the city and its preoccupations. Certainly, everyone praised the brilliantly improvised music of *Kansas City*, which Altman insisted on recording live. That music, as the legacy of Kansas City, surely lives on and can still be heard today. In a very real sense that is what Kansas City is all about. "Historically things may not be accurate," Altman noted of his film, "—but they're true." The music is both accurate and true in this underrated and undervalued film.

—James M. Welsh

CREDITS

Blondie O'Hara: Jennifer Jason Leigh
Carolyn Stilton: Miranda Richardson
Seldom Seen: Harry Belafonte
Henry Stilton: Michael Murphy
Johnny O' Hara: Dermot Mulroney
Johnny Flynn: Steve Buscemi

Origin: USA
Released: 1996
Production: Robert Altman for a Sandcastle, 5/Ciby 2000 production; released by Fine Line Features
Direction: Robert Altman
Screenplay: Robert Altman and Frank Barhydt
Cinematography: Oliver Stapleton
Editing: Geraldine Peroni
Music: Hal Willner
Production design: Stephen Altman
Art direction: Richard L. Johnson
Set design: Dawn Brown, Thomas R. Stiller
Costume design: Dona Granata
Sound: John Pritchett
Casting: Elisabeth Leustig
MPAA rating: R
Running Time: 115 minutes

REVIEWS

Boxoffice. July, 1996, p. 83.
Chicago Tribune. August 16, 1996, p. 5.
Entertainment Weekly. August 23, 1996, p. 101.
The Kansas City Star. August 16, 1996, Preview Sec., p.3.
The Kansas City Star. August 23, 1996, Preview Sec., p.3.
Los Angeles Times. August 16, 1996, p. F6.
The New York Times. August 16, 1996, p. C3.
The New Yorker. August 19, 1996, p. 78.
Newsweek. August 19, 1996, p. 66.
People. August 26, 1996, p. 17.
Rolling Stone. August 22, 1996, p. 104.
Sight and Sound December, 1996, p. 49.
USA Today. August 16, 1996, p. 4D.
Variety Online. May 14, 1996.

Kazaam

The world's most powerful genie has just met his match.—Movie tagline
"A rappin' genie with a mean dunk!"—*Newsday*

Box Office: $18,937,264

Audiences may expect Disney to deliver a genie of hysterical proportions like Robin Williams' character in *Aladdin* with the release of Touchstone Pictures' *Kazaam*, but let's hope no one's holding their breath. The only thing of hysterical proportions is the film's star, Los Angeles Laker Shaquille O'Neal. The 7-foot-1 basketball star/rapper/actor cannot breathe much life into this poor storyline, but the movie does have its moments.

"I don't do ethereal."—Kazaam

Though adults are not likely to be entertained by the story of a maladjusted, mad-at-the-world teen and his genie, kids may enjoy some of the shenanigans and special effects. Be warned though that violence makes this film unsuitable for the very small fry and the fairy-tale qualities make it nauseating for most teens.

The story begins with the hero, young Max (Francis Capra), who has been having a time of it lately—fighting off bullies at school and coping with his mother's (Ally Walker) announcement that she plans to wed her current boyfriend (John Costelloe), leaving no chance of his parents reuniting. However, this young lad makes it really hard for the viewers to care, since he is such a downright brat—screaming at his mother, getting in trouble at school, and disappearing for hours at a time with no explanation. And just why he rejects his mother's current beau, who is very well-meaning, is never quite explained.

It seems that the story will take a turn for the better when he unleashes the genie Kazaam from his magic boombox. Kazaam saves him from the bullies and insists that Max is now his master and he cannot return to his slumber until he grants Max three wishes. Max, of course, thinks this guy is just a kook and is almost proven right when Kazaam, who seems to be a little rusty, fails to grant his first wish for a Jaguar. The persistent Kazaam follows his new master, beginning to realize his teenage angst.

Most would like to have seen a lighter movie where perhaps a boy discovers friendship with a genie who helps him to battle the bullies in his life while granting a couple of whimsical wishes. No such luck! *Kazaam* turns into a confusing movie with an even more confusing subplot involving Max's no-good record producer father and some adult bullies who run a club in town and are making pirated recordings of bands that perform there. And instead of using his wishes for himself (except for the first one of "junk food to the sky"), Max chooses wishes to save his good-for-nothing father, who makes it quite clear he wants nothing to do with Max.

Another subplot involves Kazaam rappin' in the club (pure ego vehicle for O'Neal) and becoming a huge hit, much to the liking of the evil club owner (Marshall Manesh), who can't quite put his finger on what's so special about this guy. He sends his pretty assistant to befriend Kazaam and figure out his secret. Kazaam is soon smitten and yearns to be free from his eternal prison of the boom box.

The danger begins when the club owner discovers that Kazaam is a genie and wants him for his own. Young Max battles the bad guys while Kazaam

CREDITS

Kazaam: Shaquille O'Neal
Max: Francis Capra
Alice: Ally Walker
Malik: Marshall Manesh
Nick: James Acheson
Asia Moon: Fawn Reed

Origin: USA
Released: 1996
Production: Scott Kroopf, Paul M. Glaser and Bob Engelman for an Interscope Communications/Polygram Filmed Entertainment production; released by Buena Vista
Direction: Paul M. Glaser
Screenplay: Christian Ford and Roger Soffer
Cinematography: Charles Minsky
Editing: Michael E. Polokow
Music: Christopher Tyng
Production design: Donald Burt
Art direction: Mick Strawn
Set design: Kevin Cross
Set decoration: Kate Sullivan
Costume design: Hope Hanafin
Sound: Lance Brown, Victor Iorillo
Visual effects: Charles Gibson
MPAA rating: PG
Running Time: 93 minutes

is busy rappin' onstage. An accident occurs and Kazaam is forced to grant an "ethereal" wish, one that he never could before. All ends well when Max and his father are rescued and the bad guys get their due. Kazaam is free to pursue love and rappin'.

Even more hokey than the more syrupy of moviegoers can stand, and less magical than we would expect, *Kazaam* ends on the message: "Don't be a brat!" The special effects are good, but the magical moments of Kazaam flying through the air on a gold-sparkled bike, or floating in the sky of stars in Max's bedroom, cannot make-up for the lackluster script and the unconvincing psychological messages.

Audiences will get very frustrated with the snotty Max, who has a huge chip on his shoulder that even the lovable Kazaam can't knock off. He snaps at Kazaam and tells him he's not his friend, he's just a genie. And then, when Max is in trouble, which he easily seems to find, he yells for Kazaam's help. Kids and adults alike will be better off watching *Aladdin* again and enjoying the more entertaining capers of Robin Williams. Meanwhile, O'Neal should seek out more promising roles and maybe stick to that basketball gig he's got going.

—Devra Sladics

REVIEWS

Chicago Tribune. July 17, 1996, p. 1.
Los Angeles Times. July, 17, 1996, p. F7.
The New York Times. July 17, 1996, p. C10.
USA Today. July 17, 1996, p. 9D.
Variety. July 22, 1996, p. 50.

Kids in the Hall: Brain Candy

Shove this up your mind.—Movie tagline

"A sure-fire cure for depression."—Carrie Rickey, *Philadelphia Inquirer*

"Hilarious! An outrageous comedy."—Gene Siskel, *Siskel & Ebert*

Box Office: $2,654,308

Where so many other television sketches turned feature length films have gone wrong, *The Kids in the Hall: Brain Candy* gets it right. In the tradition of the classic comedy troupe Monty Python's Flying Circus, this band of young Canadian funny men, first formed in 1989, have concocted a coherent if absurd story and plunked a few dozen of their favorite characters in both the main and the supporting roles.

Another comparison can be drawn to the recent *Wayne's World* films which boasted the talents of charismatic Mike Myers and Dana Carvey in roles they created as regulars on America's longest running sketch show, "Saturday Night Live" (also produced by Lorne Michaels). One difference is that with the cast of five taking on so many roles, the story, even this relatively thin one, supersedes any one or two stars and thus rises above the status of a two hour sketch and into the realm of motion picture.

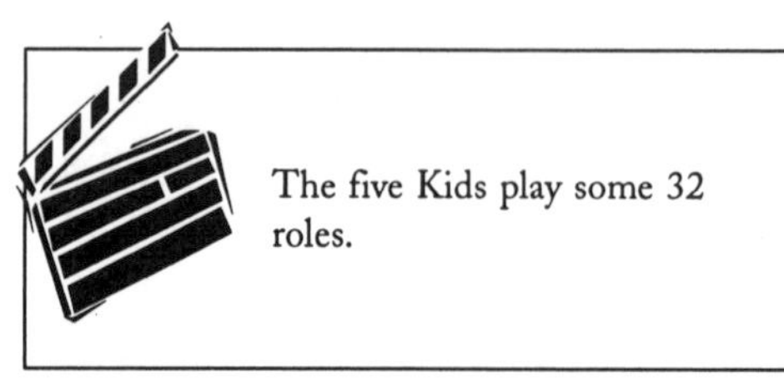
The five Kids play some 32 roles.

The simple story, in which the five members of the troupe collectively play thirty-two roles, opens with a dizzying trip through Toronto via several disparate characters well-known to viewers of "The Kids in the Hall" television series. The montage winds up in the enormous boardroom of a pharmaceutical company which has made its fortune largely from one product: an antacid which can be found in large bowls spread across the conference table and which everyone dips into ritualistically each time the name "Stummies" is mentioned. The maker of Stummies, Don Roritor (Mark McKinney), is desperate for a new product to match the last product's success and put the firm back in the black. To this end, scientists from various labs deep in the bowels of the conglomerate are hauled, willing or not, to the boardroom to report on their works in progress. One of these scientists is Dr. Chris Cooper (Kevin McDonald).

Cooper happens to be working on a new antidepressant. Roritor and his sycophantic staff leap on the idea and demand immediate production, despite Cooper's confession that the drug has not yet been fully tested. Roritor does not care, and facing the closing of his lab and the dismissal of himself and his staff, Cooper caves in to Roritor's demand.

Artists are summoned to create a pleasing color for the tablet. Advertising executives come up with the name:

"Gleemonex." The new product outperforms penicillin according to "Drug Variety," the company's stock soars, and the once reluctant Cooper becomes a media star. All the while, his staff, including Alice (Bruce McCullogh), who perpetually percolates with the unspoken crush she has on Cooper, struggle to complete the safety testing and pray that their leader's renegade decision does not wreak havoc with innocent consumers.

Havoc has never been so much fun. Gleemonex works by causing the brain to lock into each patient's happiest memory, however weird, disturbing or pathetic it may be. The side effect that does not make itself known until Gleemonex is already being marketed over the counter, is that of locking permanently into a coma version of the chosen memory, rendering the patient a living statue, albeit a happy one. Cooper must now choose between the glitzy new life that he has been bribed with, and the friends and ethics he left behind.

The Kids in the Hall: Brain Candy seems not to satirize real therapies such as Prozac, as much as it does man's desire to profit at all costs. Happiness is a good thing, greed is not.

The script was written by four of the five regulars (Dave Foley apparently was too busy with his NBC sitcom, "News Radio.") with the help of Norm Hiscock. Kelly Makin, who directed many episodes of the "Kids in the Hall" television series, makes the leap to feature film with an erratic sort of panache.

The Kids in the Hall achieve an amazing degree of believability in portraying various ages, from Kevin McDonald's corporate tycoon, Don Roritor, who is supposed to be at least somewhere in his fifties, to Bruce McCullogh's prepubescent, wheelchair bound cancer victim who finds fame as a professional whistler. Even their infamous "drag" characters possess a disturbing level of realism—they may not be women one would like to know, but they are women.

With a budget of under seven million dollars, pocket change in the feature film business, the production was small enough to necessitate the major players doing most of the work with a minimum of outside input or interference. The result is the fearlessly confrontative, gleefully tasteless brand of personal and social comedy that has made The Kids In The Hall either so loved or so hated (but rarely anything in between) translated from the small screen to the large in its purest form.

—Eleah Horwitz

CREDITS

Marv/Psychiatrist/New Guy/Raymond: David Foley
Alice/Cisco/Grivo/Worm Pill Scientist/ Cop #2/Cancer Boy/White Trash Man: Bruce McCulloch
Dr. Chris Cooper/Chris' Dad/Doreen/Lacey: Kevin McDonald
Simon/Don Roritor/Cabbie/Gunter/Cop #1/Nina Bedford/Melanie/Drill Sergeant/White Trash Woman: Mark McKinney
Baxter/Mrs. Hurdicure/Wally/Malek/The Queen/Phil/Raj/Clemptor: Scott Thompson
Woman at Party: Janeane Garofalo

Origin: USA
Released: 1996
Production: Lorne Michaels for a Lakeshore Entertainment production; released by Paramount
Direction: Kelly Makin
Screenplay: Norm Hiscock, Bruce McCulloch, Kevin McDonald, Mark McKinney, and Scott Thompson
Cinematography: David Makin
Editing: Christopher Cooper
Music: Craig Northey
Production design: Gregory P. Keen
Art direction: Paul Denham Austerberry
Sound: Bruce D. Carwardine
Casting: Ross Clydesdale
MPAA rating: R
Running Time: 88 minutes

REVIEWS

Entertainment Weekly. April 19, 1996, p. 60.
Los Angeles Times. April 7, 1996. p. 28.
New York Times. April 12, 1996, p. C23.
Newsweek. April 22, 1996. p. 73.
Variety. April 15, 1996, p. 178.

Kingpin

From the idiots what brung you *Dumb and Dumber.*—Movie tagline

"Easily the funniest movie so far this year!"—David Sheehan, *CBS-TV*

"Two thumbs up! Way up!"—*Siskel & Ebert*

Box Office: $25,020,036

Sports films have enjoyed a renaissance of sorts in the past two decades. Although virtually every sports activity—from bicycling to bobsledding, figure skating to wrestling—have been immortalized on celluloid, certain sports activities seem more suitable for dramatization: the brutal, combative game of football; the speed and grace of track and field; the fast-breaking, back-and-forth intensity of basketball; the energetic fascination of baseball. All of these sports and their agile, electrifying counterparts are infused with potential drama, heartbreak, conflict, defeat, and triumph, the crucial ingredients of any great cinematic achievement.

And then there is bowling.

The world of bowling conjures up images of dark, sweaty dens filled with the sounds of shrieking, beer-guzzling patrons, and hard, heavy balls hurled by beefy men dressed in loud, tacky matching outfits. Until recently, only one film has been made about the world of bowling, the modest, low-budget *Dreamer* (1979), made primarily to cash in on the success of *Rocky* (1976), the film that heralded the renaissance in sports movies.

Kingpin is a much more ambitious bowling film. It is not afraid to depict the sport in all of its tacky, lowbrow glory. In fact, the way *Kingpin* brings the bowling milieu to life is its main strength. It is a bawdy, affectionate, comical tribute to the sport, playing up its reputation as a game that attracts con men, hustlers and lowlifes who, in their own way, find joy and satisfaction in their love for the sport.

The film begins in nineteen sixty-nine in a small, rural town in Iowa. Calvert Munson (Danny Green) teaches his young son Roy how to bowl on a make-shift lane set up in the front yard of their ramshackle house. Calvert loves and respects the game, telling Roy that everything he needs to know to become a success in life can be learned by bowling, such things as honesty, discipline, dedication, and fair play.

Ten years pass, and Roy has matured into a dynamic bowler (Woody Harrelson). In a spectacularly gaudy scene, Roy, dressed in a spangly disco outfit, dazzles his adoring fans at the local bowling alley to the throbbing beat of disco music. Later, he tells his dad he is off to join the professional bowling league, and promises to make the name of Munson synonymous with bowling.

Roy's first professional tournament—The Odor Eater's International Championship—is a resounding success. He soundly beats the leading champion, Ernie McCracken (Bill Murray), a loud, obnoxious con man, who later offers to teach Roy how to make extra money on the bowling circuit by hustling unsuspecting locals. In awe of Ernie, the naive Roy joins the con man. Later, Roy is attacked by the enraged local bowlers when they realize they are being hustled. The despicable Ernie leaves Roy to suffer the wrath of the locals who end up mutilating Roy's bowling hand.

Ten years pass and Roy is now a paunchy, balding alcoholic, his mutilated hand replaced by a prosthetic one. He makes a meager living selling bowling supplies to alleys across the country. In one of the alleys, he spots Ishmael Boorg (Randy Quaid), an Amish man whom Roy realizes has great potential. Thinking he can make money off Ishmael's talents, Roy approaches him and offers to become his manager, a proposal that does not interest the conservative Ishmael. However, when Ishmael learns that his family is about to lose their farm to creditors, he agrees to become Roy's bowling protege.

Roy refines Ishmael's skills as they travel across the country, their destination Reno, Nevada, the location of a million-dollar bowling tournament. On the way, Roy introduces Ishmael to the bowling milieu—tawdry alleys, beer guzzling, womanizing, and hustling. Ishmael abandons his conservative, Amish ways and quickly adapts to the bowling way of life. Also along the way, they encounter Claudia (Vanessa Angel), a sexy con woman who attempts to replace Roy as Ishmael's manager when she realizes Ishmael's potential. However, when Ishmael figures out that he is being exploited by both Roy and Claudia, he runs away. Roy and Claudia track him down, finding him employed as an exotic dancer in a strip club. When they agree to mend their exploitative ways, Ishmael rejoins the two.

Finally, the trio reaches Reno and Ishmael prepares for the million-dollar tournament. One of the contestants turns out to be Ernie McCracken, who ridicules Roy as a cripple and a quitter. Ishmael attacks the flamboyantly obnoxious McCracken, but only manages to break his own hand. Realizing the only way he can win the tournament is to enter it himself, Roy begins to brush up on his bowling skills. At first, he is a laughable buffoon, his artificial, rubber hand becoming stuck in the ball as it rolls down the lane toward the pins. Gradually, his old skills return to the point where he impresses the other contestants who give him the nickname "Rubber Man Munson."

During the tournament, Roy plays spectacularly. However, he ends up losing by one point to the sleazy Mc-

Cracken. Roy, Ishmael, and Claudia all go their separate ways, Roy returning to his low-life salesman job and Ishmael returning to his farm a humiliated fool.

The film ends on an upbeat note when Claudia visits Roy who then invites her to come along with him to deliver a check for half a million dollars to Ishmael, money Roy has received as the new spokesperson for Trojan Condoms, his reputation as the "Rubber Man" having won him the lucrative contract.

The outrageousness of *Kingpin*, its ability to delight with its tawdry depiction of the bowling way of life, helps make up for some of the film's unsuccessful attempts at low-brow, gutter-ball humor. The co-directors—Peter and Bobby Farrelly—obviously wanted to use the same approach they took to their previous film, the financially successful *Dumb and Dumber* (1994), which they co-wrote. However, many of the jokes seem more suitable for the earlier film which featured two extremely naive protagonists whose stupidity made them capable of performing the most outlandish pranks and comically tasteless acts.

The principal characters in *Kingpin* are portrayed with much more integral and sly intelligence which makes the lowbrow, cartoonish jokes they perform seem out of character. For example, when Roy visits Ishmael on the Amish farm, he announces to Ishmael's family that he has just milked the cow as he drinks from a milk pail, only to be told that the family does not own a cow, only a bull. Aside from being a variation of one of the oldest jokes in existence, the scene does not fit Roy's character. True, he is portrayed as naive, but he is not completely brainless as the characters in *Dumb and Dumber.*

In fact, Roy, as well as the rest of the characters, earn the respect of the audience when they remain true to their sleazy, manipulative and tawdry selves. This type of character is best exemplified by Bill Murray's excellent, over-the-top performance as the outrageously vile and unrepentantly deplorable Ernie McCracken. Murray's character is the incarnated spirit of the bowling milieu, loud, abrasive, and garishly mesmerizing.

The film's theme of exploitation and corruption versus honesty and conservative decency is not as effective as it could have been due to the way the filmmakers handle the corruption of Ishmael by Roy, a corruption that happens far too easily and quickly. Only when the film is reveling in the bowling lifestyle does it glitter like a sequined bowling ball hurled with passion by a boozy, bowling alley regular. When the film is immersed in this realm, it is a delight. And because it does effectively capture—and exploit—bowling's reputation as a game for beefy, unsophisticated lowbrows, *Kingpin* emerges as the best bowling film ever made.

—*Jim Kline*

CREDITS

Roy Munson: Woody Harrelson
Ishmael Boorg: Randy Quaid
Claudia: Vanessa Angel
Ernie McCracken: Bill Murray
The Gambler: Chris Elliott
Mr. Boorg: William Jordan
Calvert Munson: Danny Green

Origin: USA
Released: 1996
Production: Brad Krevoy, Steve Stabler and Bradley Thomas for a Rysher Entertainment and Motion Picture Corporation of America production; released by MGM/UA
Direction: Peter Farrelly and Bobby Farrelly
Screenplay: Barry Fanaro and Mort Nathan
Cinematography: Mark Irwin
Editing: Christopher Greenbury
Music: Freedy Johnston
Production design: Sidney Jackson Bartholomew Jr.
Art direction: Bradford Johnson
Costume design: Mary Zophres
Sound: Jonathan (Earl) Stein
Casting: Rock Montgomery, Dan Parada
MPAA rating: PG-13
Running Time: 113 minutes

REVIEWS

Chicago Sun-Times. July 26, 1996, p. D3.
Chicago Tribune. July 26, 1996, p. 5.
Hollywood Reporter. July 18, 1996, p. 9.
Los Angeles Times. July 26, 1996, p. F10
New York Times. July 26, 1996, p. C18.
USA Today. July 26, 1996, p. 4D.
Variety. July 22-28, 1996, p. 49.

Lamerica

"Splendid! A magnificently resonant film. It has the kind of depth, heart and currency that make it a huge winner."—Susan Stark, *Detroit News*

"Triumphs as it echoes the heartbreak and insight of his last film, *Stolen Children*, then goes one better."—Larry Worth, *New York Post*

"A stylistic tour-de-force that recalls Bertolucci's best."—Godfrey Cheshire, *New York Press*

"Astonishing! Supremely eloquent. Profoundly startling. The triumph of the New York Film Festival."—Janet Maslin, *The New York Times*

Lamerica begins with newsreels of Mussolini's army entering Albania. It is 1939, and the confident voice of the newsreel narrator proclaims the union of Italy and Albania, the deposition of Albanian King Zog and the country's submission to Italy's king. The fascist parties of the two nations are amalgamating and various public works and welfare projects are announced. This Italian propaganda seems ludicrously antique and absurd. Could anyone ever have believed it?

Then the scene switches to Albania in 1991, just after the downfall of the Communist regime. Two Italians, Fiore (Michele Placido) and Gino (Enrico Lo Verso), are escorted by Selemi (Piro Mikani), an Albanian contact who explains the country's deplorable conditions. In their jeep they can see for themselves that the roads are crumbling, the land is dried out, masses of children beg and scavenge in the streets, young and old people stand about dazed or sit mesmerized in front of Italian television programs featuring silly game and girlie shows.

Carmelo Di Mazzarelli, who plays Spiro, makes his acting debut at the age of 80.

Fiore and Gino say they are going to build a factory and to create jobs for Albanians. In fact, they are part of a scam. They want to set up a dummy corporation, collect a grant from the Italian government, and do nothing else. Fiore has already done the same thing in Nigeria, and to him Albania will be no different. He has utter contempt for Albanians and lectures them as though they are children. He does not call himself a fascist, but he is the very type of the strutting, ridiculous fascist of the newsreel.

Gino is a little worried about this confidence game. After all, Albania is not so far away from Italy as Nigeria. But the smug Fiore dismisses his younger colleague's concerns. He leaves Albania, trusting Gino to work out the final details, which include taking care of an old man, Spiro (Carmelo Di Mazzarelli), found in an old Communist prison, who will serve as the figurehead of the bogus corporation.

The trouble starts when the old man runs away. He is scared. After fifty years of imprisonment, he cannot trust his new colleagues. Gino has made matters worse. After the frightened old man voids himself on the seat of Gino's jeep, Gino rubs his face in it. This crude and revolting moment shows just how callous Gino is and how little he cares to know about this old man's suffering. Gino acts like a fascist, although he is too young to have experienced World War II.

Gino learns that Spiro has taken a train, trying to find his way back to Italy, for Spiro is actually Italian, a deserter from Mussolini's army who thinks the war is still on and who does not realize how long he has been in prison. He thinks he still has a three-year-old son and a wife in Sicily. In a way, Spiro (his real name is Michele) is right. Everywhere he looks he sees displaced people wandering in the streets and a devastated land. Is this not a war setting? Soldiers attack Albanians desperately trying to cross a bridge into Italy. Is this not what happens in war? Michele is set upon by a gang of young children who think it is fun to torture him. Gino catches up with him in an Albanian hospital where a nurse finally convinces him that the old man is Italian. Indeed, Michele and Gino are both Sicilians, and as Gino's arrogant confidence erodes he comes to look and feel more and more like Michele.

Lamerica becomes the story of Gino's education. He is deprived of his advantages. Albanians steal the tires on his jeep. He has to ride the crammed trains and trucks with Albanian emigrants. When he finally gets to a phone (hard to find in the disintegration infrastructure of the country), he learns that he is fired. His plight draws him closer to Michele, who begins talking and grows stronger as he travels toward his beloved Sicily. But Gino reluctantly concludes that his only hope of getting out of the country is to jettison Michele. He leaves money with a man who promises to feed and to house the old man.

But when Gino makes the arduous journey to his Tirana hotel, he is arrested and thrown into prison. He yells at his jailor still assuming that as an Italian he has some authority over Albanians. He asks if this is the way Albania understands democracy. It is a ridiculous question coming from a con artist

AWARDS AND NOMINATIONS

Independent Spirit Awards 1997 Nominations:
Foreign Film

preying on this vulnerable country—as ridiculous as the scene in which Gino stands in the wasteland of an Albanian town shouting that he will not leave until the tires of his jeep are returned. Where can he go anyway? All of Albania has become a prison. Or as one of the Albanians says, the Communists are no longer in power, but the same people who were Communists are still in power. The same might be said of fascism. There is no longer a fascist government in Italy or Albania but those in power act like fascists. When the illiterate Michele sees "Enver Hoxha" etched on a mountain, he mistakes the Communist dictator's name for Mussolini's. Thus *Lamerica* implies that fascism and communism, fifty years ago and today, are not so different as might be supposed.

"The Albanians are like children. If an Italian said 'The sea is made of wine,' they'd drink it."—Fiore to his younger partner Gino

Gino is deprived of his arrogance when he faces his Albanian interrogator. Gino is entirely in his power. Capitulating, Gino asks what the man wants him to do. Confess, the official blandly remarks. And then what will happen? Gino asks. He should leave Albania, the official replies. Gino reaches for his passport, which the official withdraws. But how can he travel without papers? Gino wonders. No one in Albania has papers, the official says, smiling.

Gino's plight is, of course, reminiscent of Michele's. Michele is saved by the quirk of Fiore's and Gino's visit to the broken-down Communist prison. Michele has survived on false papers identifying him as an Albanian. Gino is saved by an official who reminisces about his father's stay in Italy and his study of Italian art. These absurdities emphasize how little has changed in history or in human mentality.

Somehow Gino does make his way onto a ship bound for Italy. Like the busses, trains, and trucks, the boat is overloaded with emigrants. A dirty, parched, and disconsolate Gino threads his way through the throngs, suddenly spotting Michele, sitting on the deck sharing his bread with children just as he had earlier shared it with Gino. Ashamed, Gino turns away. But Michele sees him and waves at him to come sit down.

Gino listens to Michele, who has become positively garrulous. He tells Gino that the ship is going to America. Michele can't wait to see New York. It is a big country, he tells Gino. Their roles are now completely reversed, with the voluble Gino having absolutely nothing to say. His degrading experiences have drained him. But Michele tells him to take heart. He will help him. Then the camera pans across and frequently stops at young and old Albanian faces, wide-eyed and weary, wondering, expectant—like Michele. They are not literally going to America, but like Michele they are going to America in their minds. America is hope itself—not just of a better life but of a way out of human suffering. America represents a triumph of the human spirit. The camera finds every face revealing; every face important. Its democratic focus is precisely the counter to the fascist newsreel, where reality is regimented and de-individualized.

The locating shooting in this film is extraordinary. It combines the best features of fiction and documentary. Scenes are scripted but settings dictate the emotional aura. A young girl vibrantly dances to rock music, showing talent akin to Michael Jackson's. She is the only show on the grim dirty floor of this institution—which has no name and serves as some combination of orphanage, transient hotel, and old age home. Someone says to Gino that he should take the girl to Italy and make her a star. These people know there is another life; they are the people on the ship; they are Gino, who like Michele, has been trapped in Albania.

The film's brilliant amalgamation of fiction and documentary is fused in the character of Michele. Carmelo di Mazzarelli is no actor. He is an eighty-year-old fisherman. Gianni Amelio, the film's director, saw him in a Sicilian harbor and learned that Mazzarelli had been in the Italian army in Albania. Mazzarelli brings to the role an overwhelming authenticity and authority. In him past and present fuse; in him Gino has to reckon with the Italian past and with his own destiny.

—*Carl Rollyson*

CREDITS

Gino: Enrico Lo Verso
Fiore: Michele Placido
Spiro: Carmelo Di Mazzarelli
Selimi: Piro Milkani

Origin: Italy
Released: 1995; 1996
Production: Mario Cecchi Gori, Vittorio Cecchi Gori; released by New Yorker Films
Direction: Gianni Amelio
Screenplay: Gianni Amelio, Andrea Porporti, Allesandro Sermoneta
Cinematography: Luca Bigazzi
Editing: Simona Paggi
Music: Franco Piersanti
Set design: Giuseppe Gaudino
MPAA rating: Unrated
Running Time: 120 minutes

REVIEWS

Chicago Tribune. December 24, 1995, p. 12.
Detroit Free Press. February 8, 1996, p. 1C.
New York Times. October 4, 1995, p. C13.
Newsweek. January 29, 1996, p. 58.
Premiere. January, 1996, p. 20.
Village Voice. December 26, 1995, p. 60.

Larger Than Life

He's got 5 days to go coast-to-coast. (There's just one BIG problem.)—Movie tagline

"Bill Murray is remarkably funny! Go see this very charming and very appealing comedy."—Dennis Cunningham, *CBS-TV*

"A family film that will amuse adults as much as it entertains the children."—Marshall Fine, *Gannett News Service*

"It's a very funny film!"—Jeffrey Lyons, *NBC-TV*

"Thumbs up!"—Gene Siskel, *Siskel & Ebert*

"A huge entertainment experience!"—Paul Wunder, *WBAI Radio*

Box Office: $8,310,694

In *Larger Than Life* Bill Murray stars as motivational speaker Jack Corcoran, whose recently deceased father, a circus clown, has bequeathed his son a rather large inheritance—in the form of Vera (Tai), the elephant partner from his act. The screenplay is written by Roy Blount Jr. Directed by Howard Franklin, the film also stars Anita Gillette as Corcoran's mother who, rather than tell her son his father is a small-time circus clown (there must not be anything worse), tells a young Jack that his father died before he was born when he saved a child from drowning; Matthew McConaughey as Tip Tucker, a maniacal truck driver whose aid and truck Corcoran connivingly enlists to get the pair across country; Janeane Garofalo, as Mo, an animal researcher who would like to include Vera in an elephant breeding project in Sri Lanka; Linda Fiorentino as Terry Bonura, a talent agent with other ideas for Vera; and Pat Hingle as Vernon, his father's close friend who knows Vera best. *Larger Than Life* tells of the unlikely bonding between an offbeat pair. It is the story of a man and his pachyderm.

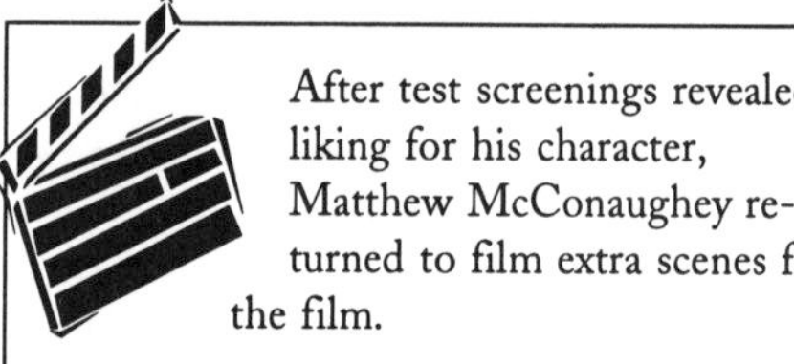

After test screenings revealed a liking for his character, Matthew McConaughey returned to film extra scenes for the film.

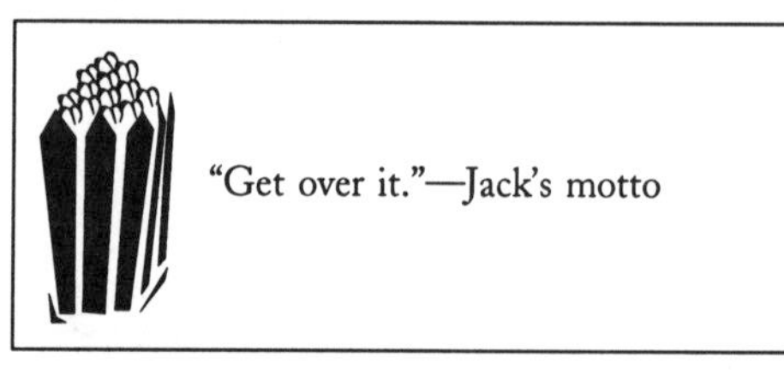

"Get over it."—Jack's motto

Jack Corcoran (Murray) is a small-time motivational speaker whose motto is "get over it." Perhaps his small-time life has more in common with his father's than his mother realized. Upon presentation of his inheritance and some other of his father's personal belongings, Corcoran is also presented with a bill for $35,000 for the damage done to the attorney's (Harve Presnell) office, with whom Vera the elephant had been staying. In order to pay his debt, he must sell Vera to either Mo (Garofalo), the humane animal researcher who wants to set her free to study her mating habits, or to Terry Bonura (Fiorentino), a Hollywood agent who has successfully evaded the Society for the Prevention of Cruelty to Animals. Of course, Bonura offers more money—and karma too irresistible for Corcoran to refuse.

On their cross-country adventure, Corcoran learns more about Vera through Vernon (Hingle), a circus oddity who understood the bond between the pachyderm and Corcoran's father. Impossible for Vernon to keep the elephant, Corcoran sets about his way west to sell Vera.

On his way, he dupes an unsuspecting trucker named Tip Tucker (McConaughey) into taking the two on their journey, by cleverly canceling the trucker's regularly scheduled load. Upon learning of the deceit, Tucker makes it his mission throughout the rest of the film to seek revenge on Corcoran; something that Jack, not surprisingly, is able to avoid.

When Jack arrives at Bonura's animal circus commercial set, he discovers behind-the-scenes cruelty that he is unwilling to have Vera endure. In the end, after a race with time through an airport (with Vera in tow the whole way), Jack does the right thing and sends Vera to Sri Lanka. The ending is hardly a surprise, although enjoyable getting there while delving through the emotions of Murray's character.

The film could take one of two directions: using the comedic and slapstick antics of comedian Bill Murray pitted against the large and sometimes immobile elephant, including pratfalls, set-ups and one-liners. But Franklin takes the film in the other direction: that of a pensive Bill Murray portraying a man who has to accept the knowledge that his father has actually been alive all these years, and now has the responsibility of deciding the fate of his father's closest companion. Pranks and pratfalls would be funny, but Murray actually makes this implausible story somewhat sentimental.

There are some humorous moments in the film, including one in which Corcoran rents a semi truck to transport Vera, and learns the worst things a truck can do when one depresses buttons when one does not know the first thing about driving a truck or the buttons a truck has. There

CREDITS

Jack Corcoran: Bill Murray
Mo: Janeane Garofalo
Tip Tucker: Matthew McConaughey
Hurst: Keith David
Vernon: Pat Hingle
Walter: Jeremy Piven
Terry Bonura: Linda Fiorentino

Origin: USA
Released: 1996
Production: Richard B. Lewis, John Watson, Pen Densham for a Trilogy Entertainment Group production; released by United Artists
Direction: Howard Franklin
Screenplay: Roy Blount, Jr.
Cinematography: Elliot Davis
Editing: Sidney Levin
Music: Miles Goodman
Production design: Marcia Hinds-Johnson
Art direction: Bo Johnson
Set design: John Berger
Costume design: Jane Robinson
Sound: Tommy Causey
Casting: Gail Levin, Tricia Tomey
MPAA rating: PG
Running Time: 93 minutes

is even some clever dialogue such as inquiring at a restaurant how much the salad bar is—the entire salad bar.

Though the film's plot is predictable and improbable, the characters keep it entertaining. Murray's Corcoran is empathetic, notably when he becomes sentimental over his father's personal effects and during a playful water scene with the elephant. McConaughey creates an exceptionally deranged trucker, whose speaking skills are as appalling as his determination to seek revenge on Corcoran.

Larger Than Life is not a wonderful motion picture. But, thanks to Murray and McConaughey, and even Tai the elephant, it is a somewhat entertaining buddy film.

—Debbi Hoffman

REVIEWS

Entertainment Weekly. November 15, 1996, p. 52.
The Los Angeles Times. November 1, 1996, p. F14.
The Nation. December 16, 1996, p. 35.
The New York Times. November 1, 1996, p. C8.
Newsweek. November 11, 1996, p. 78.
People. November 11, 1996, p. 21.
USA Today. November 1, 1996, p. 4D.
Variety. October 28, 1996, p. 66.
The Wall Street Journal. November 1, 1996, p. A11.

Last Dance

Sometimes justice is a crime.—Movie tagline
"They don't get much better than this!"—Jeanne Wolf, *Jeanne Wolf's Hollywood*
"Sharon Stone's performance is nothing short of amazing!"—Jeffrey Lyons, *Sneak Previews*
"Powerful, provocative, don't miss it!"—Paul Wunder, *WBAI Radio*

Box Office: $5,939,449

What is it that makes jailhouse dramas so appealing these days? There was the brilliant *Dead Man Walking* (1995) with Sean Penn and Susan Sarandon, *Primal Fear* (1996) starring Richard Gere, *The Chamber* (1996) with Gene Hackman and Chris O'Donnell, and now *The Last Dance*, Sharon Stone's latest attempt to prove that she's a serious actress.

There's no question that these films offer their "star thespians" the opportunity to emotionally chew up the scenery (or prison bars, as the case may be) before they are either gassed, fried or lethally injected. At this point the market has been saturated to death (no pun intended).

This latest version of *I Want to Live* (1958) finds Stone portraying yet another doomed creature named Cindy Liggett. Cindy is busy waiting for her execution on death row, learning to draw in a spanking clean prison somewhere in the South. It seems that 12 years ago she and her boyfriend brutally murdered a schoolmate and her lover. The victims happened to be home during a robbery attempt. Liggett was 19 years old at the time and was also a major crack addict. This fact could have saved her from the death penalty but was never brought out in the trial. Alas, Cindy was just served her thirty-day notice for a visit to the ultimate "Needle Park"—the death chamber.

Enter the callow, devil-may-care young lawyer Rick Hayes (Rob Morrow) who should have stopped off at the prison barber before visiting the embittered prisoner. After all, first impressions are everything on death row. Almost immediately Rick is taken with Cindy, although she snaps at him "If ah die, it's gonna be on mah own terms. It's all ah got!" in her best hillbilly twang. Nevertheless, Rick is still drawn to the cynical Cindy and sets out on a mission to save her life in spite of her own doubts and protestations.

"I don't want to die, but if I do, it's got to be on my terms. My terms, that's all I got."—Cindy

The script by Ron Koslow (*Into the Night* [1985]) focuses much of the time on the personal growth of the young lawyer rather than on the prisoner's impending reckoning with the Grim Reaper. Sad to say, none of these "breakthroughs" ever register due to the bland, disappointing performance by a dull and listless Rob Morrow. Mike Clark of *USA Today* said that "Stone's cell block encounters with Morrow, which ought to be the movie's heart, are actually tedious." Janet Maslin of the *New York Times* wrote, "Wan and lackluster. He (Morrow) simply can't hold the screen in jailhouse scenes with Ms. Stone."

Peter Gallagher plays Rick's brother John, who initially gets the "black sheep of the family" a job on the Clemency Board in a Southern state where 76% of the voters favor the death penalty. The Governor (a bombastic Jack Thompson) has little or no interest in the Liggett case. He would much rather pardon a black prisoner who just happens to have written a best-selling novel. This scholarly killer remarks to Attorney Hayes, "How are they gonna go and kill a man who's been on the *New York Times* best-seller list?"

In spite of the many obstacles, the newly dedicated attorney goes forth on his quest to save Cindy, however, the specific reasons are never made quite clear to the viewer. Certainly Ms. Stone (with minimal makeup) makes a fetching ex-drug-crazed murderer, but there is little chemistry between these two actors to indicate precisely what's going on between them. The vagueness in the script compounds the problem—it simply does not delineate the relationship clearly. In the meantime, Rick has taken up almost immediately with an old neighbor, Jill (Jayne Brooks), who he meets at a political social gathering. It appears that he is irresistible to everyone but the audience.

Traveling through a series of legal mazes, Rick happens upon the extenuating circumstances of Cindy's crack habit. He's impressed with this information, although no one else seems to be, including the Governor. It is at this point in the story where the film gets somehow bogged down with legal maneuverings to save poor Cindy's life. Most of the execution dramas seem to fall into the same trap. Meanwhile, the clock is ticking.

Bruce Beresford (*Driving Miss Daisy* [1989], *Tender Mercies* [1983], *Breaker Morant* [1979]) directs this film with respectable but passionless agility. There is a detachment to the piece that prohibits the filmgoers from getting emotionally involved (except perhaps during the last ten minutes). It's a long time to wait. Beresford's credits certainly prove that he is capable of stirring an audience. The fault lies with the script and the lack of chemistry between the stars. It diminishes the impact and stifles any involvement with the events that are unfolding.

The "legend" of Sharon Stone is now show biz history—an actress working in Hollywood without ever getting on the beloved "A-list." Then along came *Basic Instinct* (1992) directed by Paul Verhoeven with the now infamous interrogation scene. She suddenly became a household name by simply crossing her legs. After this "see-through" role, Stone has appeared in *Sliver* (1993), a remake of the 1955 classic *Diabolique* (1996), a western, *The Quick and the Dead* (1995), *The Specialist* (1994) with Sylvester Stallone, and another breakthrough role in *Casino* (1995) for which she was nominated

CREDITS

Cindy Liggett: Sharon Stone
Rick Hayes: Rob Morrow
Sam Burns: Randy Quaid
John Hayes: Peter Gallagher
The Governor: Jack Thompson
Jill: Jayne Brook
Billy: Skeet Ulrich

Origin: USA
Released: 1996
Production: Steven Haft for a Touchstone Pictures production; released by Buena Vista
Direction: Bruce Beresford
Screenplay: Ron Koslow
Cinematography: Peter James
Editing: John Bloom
Music: Mark Isham
Production design: John Stoddart
Art direction: Monroe Kelly
Set decoration: John Anderson
Costume design: Colleen Kelsall
Sound: Hank Garfield
Casting: Shari Rhodes, Joseph Middleton
MPAA rating: R
Running Time: 103 minutes

for an Academy Award. It is not surprising that Stone chose *The Last Dance* to prove once again that she is a serious actress. This choice to downplay her looks and act was only marginally effective. She still makes her entrances like a grand diva and still manages to be glamorous in her neatly pressed prison garb. There is little evidence that this woman could ever have been hooked on crack or that she was on death row for the last 12 years. She is not an embarrassment by any means, nor is she believable. Her most effective scenes are when she appears fragile and vulnerable. When she does bitter and hard-edged, it appears like she's indicating these feelings rather than experiencing them—she is acting! David Ansen in *Newsweek* (May 6, 1996) reaffirms this reaction and said that the film should have been called "I Want to Act."

Following on the heels of Tim Robbins' shattering portrait of the reality of capital punishment in *Dead Man Walking, The Last Dance* seemed even more mediocre. Audiences seemed grateful that clemency wasn't granted. At least now there can be no sequel.

—*Rob Chicatelli*

REVIEWS

Chicago Tribune. May 3, 1996, p. 5.
Entertainment Weekly. May 3, 1996, p. 61.
Los Angeles Times. May 3, 1996, p. F6.
New York Times. May 3, 1996, p. C1.
Newsweek. May 6, 1996, p. 78.
Sight and Sound. October, 1996, p. 46.
USA Today. May 3, 1996, p. 10D.
Variety. April 29, 1996, p. 132.

Last Man Standing

There are two sides to every war, and John Smith is on both of them.—Movie tagline

"The action film of the year!"—Paul Wunder, *WBAI Radio*

"An exhilarating achievement that is as stylish as it is gripping!"—Barbara & Scott Siegel, *WNEW Radio*

Box Office: $18,132,747

In 1961, renowned Japanese director Akira Kurosawa released his superior samurai with a sense-of-humor film, *Yojimbo.* Kurosawa had always been interested in the fact that most of us are too weak to stand up to evil. And when it's evil vs. evil, all we can do is stand impotently aside as they wreak havoc on our lives. But what if someone could come along and stand solidly between the battling sides and heroically stop it all. That was the starting point for *Yojimbo* which is Japanese for bodyguard.

In *Yojimbo*, it is the impressive Toshiro Mifune who plays the sword-for-hire samurai, pitting one side against the other, protecting the innocent and standing back to watch the corrupt destroy each other. The film was moral and fun, and it was so popular that it inspired a sequel, *Sanjuro* (1962). It also so impressed spaghetti western director Sergio Leone that he remade it as a *Fistful of Dollars* in 1964 and in the process made a star out of Clint Eastwood as the cigar-chomping, serape-wearing "man with no name."

Now along comes director Walter Hill to redo *Yojimbo* yet again. Only this time the setting is the West Texas town of Jericho during the heyday of prohibition. Instead of *Yojimbo*'s warring silk and sake merchant clans however, *Last Man Standing* has rival bootleggers trying to control the flow of illegal booze from Mexico. One gang is Italian and led by Fredo Strozzi (Ned Eisenberg) who must suffer his volatile cousin Giorgio Carmonte (Michael Imperioli) as his second-in-command. The other side is Irish and headed by Doyle (David Patrick Kelly) who has an infamously evil and scarred sidekick, Hickey (Christopher Walken).

Into this divided town drives John Smith (Bruce Willis) who, after watching Doyle's girlfriend Felina (Karina Lombard) cross the street in front of him, suddenly finds his Ford the subject of a beating by the Doyle gang. When he goes to report this to the local authorities, Sheriff Ed Galt (Bruce Dern) just shrugs it off. He obviously can do nothing and wants to do nothing . . . except to maybe make a few dollars where he can. With no one to help him, and a demolished car incapable of letting him leave town, Smith decides to get even on his own terms . . . and maybe make his own bit of profit on the side.

Remake of Akira Kurosawa's 1961 film *Yojimbo,* which was also the basis for Sergio Leone's 1964 spaghetti western, *A Fistful of Dollars.*

Smith starts by going into the Doyle headquarters and reducing the town's population with his two-fisted gunplay. This of course, endears him to Strozzi who immediately hires him. But it doesn't take long for Smith to realize that one gang is as bad as the other, and that they're both small-time. In the mysterious Smith's words, "I'd seen the real thing, and these guys were a long way from it."

"No matter how low you sink, there's always right and wrong, and you always end up choosing."—Smith

Now Smith gets down to business, playing one gang against the other, while at the same time befriending one of the town's few "normal" people, the owner of the Red Bird Saloon, Joe Monday (William Sanderson), and in his spare time helping a few damsels in distress.

Last Man Standing is an odd little film that may have a bit of a hard time at the box office. (However, with Willis' name, it will probably do well on video.) The film may look like it, but it's not a western. It may try to be a gangster film, but it doesn't look like it. It may aspire to relate an American myth—the loner hero—but it is hard to feel any affection for the protagonist or the plot. And to confuse us even more, the film relies heavily on a Dashiell Hammett-style narration provided by constant voice-overs. After being set up by a prostitute, we hear "crossing me was nothing personal. She was just trying to make a living in a world where big fish eat little fish." Is this film noir in sepia, or what?

As producer, writer and director, most of the film's problems fall directly in Walter Hill's lap. With titles like *The Getaway* (1993), *48 Hrs* (1982), *Geronimo: An American Legend* (1993) and his last film, the sadly poetic *Wild Bill* (1995), it's easy to see that Hill is not much of one for the tender and sentimental. Hill likes violent men, but he also portrays them as men who are forced into their brutality by a society that doesn't seem to give them much of a choice. In *Last Man Standing*, Hill has the opportunity to make one of those violent men quite moral, and he tries, but the point is virtually lost amidst the clutter of the overblown violence and a plot that becomes so predictable that it becomes monotonous.

It should also come as no surprise that Bruce Willis is no Toshiro Mifune. Constantly flashing his trademark hard-guy bemused look, Willis seems to be sneering at the audience as much as the bad guys—"doesn't anybody here get the joke but me?" he seems to be smirking. But where Mifune and Kurosawa loved to let us in on the joke, Willis and Hill seem to be unable to even find the joke. The closest they can come is a few fragments of snappy dialogue.

Instead, what they offer us is cliches. Even though totally outgunned, Smith never misses while the other guys always do. Smith is also the gun-for-hire with the heart of gold. And of course, as the most "moral" man in town, he eventually wins all the non-gang citizens over to his side.

Even the supporting cast can't help *Last Man Standing* to rise anywhere near the quality of *Yojimbo.* Christopher Walken, whose Hickey is modeled after that of the dangerous Unosuke in *Yojimbo*, plays yet another brutal psychopath (like his recent and similar role in *Nick of Time* [1995]). Bruce Dern, whose character is patterned after the petty policeman in *Yojimbo*, is basically just indifferent to everything until the end, and even then he can muster only the most meager interest. As the bosses, David Patrick Kelly and Ned Eisenberg are so operatic that one just wants to turn them down, while the women, Karina Lombard, Leslie Mann and Alexandra Powers are such cardboard cutouts that they have no life or believability in them at all.

Admittedly, *Last Man Standing* does look interesting. Its sepia tones and the powerful scene compositions of cin-

CREDITS

John Smith: Bruce Willis
Sheriff Ed Galt: Bruce Dern
Joe Monday: William Sanderson
Hickey: Christopher Walken
Doyle: David Patrick Kelly
Felina: Karina Lombard
Fredo Strozzi: Ned Eisenberg
Lucy Kolinski: Alexandra Powers
Giorgio Carmonte: Michael Imperioli
Captain Tom Pickett: Ken Jenkins
Jack McCool: R.D. Call
Deputy Bob: Ted Markland
Wanda: Leslie Mann

Origin: USA
Released: 1996
Production: Walter Hill and Arthur Sarkissian for a Lone Wolf production; released by New Line Cinema
Direction: Walter Hill
Screenplay: Walter Hill; from a screenplay by Akira Kurosawa and Ryuzo Kikushima
Cinematography: Lloyd Ahern
Editing: Freeman Davies
Production design: Gary Wissner
Art direction: Barry Chusid
Set decoration: Gary Fettis
Costume design: Dan Moore
Music: Ry Cooder
Casting: Mary Gail Artz and Barbara Cohen
MPAA rating: R
Running Time: 100 minutes

ematographer Lloyd Ahern highlight the mythical mood the film desperately tries to create, but the plot never cooperates. Occasionally the musical score by Ry Cooder does try to lend its help. The growling harmonicas of one of the themes does try to mimic the cocky theme from the original *Yojimbo,* but it comes out more sinister than insolent—which subverts any attempt to give the picture *Yojimbo*-like irony. However, what one mostly hears is Cooder's typical slide guitar blues.

So, what one is left with is an extremely violent, gloomy film in which there is no sense of anticipation and it is even hard to find enough emotion to root for the hero. When it was reviewed at the Venice Film Festival in September of 1996, *Last Man Standing* received a cool reception. Maybe the Europeans, who usually like this kind of film, realize that style and violence is not enough. In the end, all we're left with is emptiness.

—*Beverley Bare Buehrer*

REVIEWS

Chicago Sun Times. September 20, 1996.
Chicago Tribune. September 20, 1996, p. 5.
Entertainment Weekly. September 20, 1996.
Los Angeles Times. September 20, 1996, p. F10.
New York Times. September 20, 1996, p. C16.
Rolling Stone. October 17, 1996, p. 144.
Variety. September 10, 1996.

The Last Supper

"*The Last Supper* is good to the last drop of each and every dead body."—Paul Sherman, *The Boston Herald*

"An ingenious black comedy."—Bill Hoffman, *The New York Post*

"Lethally funny."—Caryn James, *The New York Times*

"This fiendishly funny political thriller skewers the right and the left with equal glee and marks Stacey Title as a talent to watch."—Peter Travers, *Rolling Stone*

Box Office: $459,749

In *The Last Supper,* a group of Iowa graduate students are sitting in a living room talking while the television drones on with a Rush Limbaugh-like pontificator, Norman Arbuthnot (Ron Perlman). No one is paying much attention, although this liberal group despises Arbuthnot's right-wing, rabble-rousing, and smugly righteous sermonizing. They feel powerless and filled with a more than a little self-loathing. What do they do, except talk, talk, talk? They seem to be unaware that their liberal opinions sound just as smug and self-assured as Arbuthnot's.

But of course these young, well fed students see Arbuthnot as exploitative while they would really want to save the world. They meet every weekend for dinner and discuss their lives and the state of the world. They usually invite a guest with something to say, which they can debate. In fact, they're waiting for one of their number to show up, Pete (Ron Eldard) so that supper can start. Pete, it turns out, has had car trouble and he brings home with him an apparently good samaritan, Zac (Bill Paxton) who has given him a lift home.

The group urges the reluctant Zac to stay and partake of dinner. They always have a guest, they inform him. In short order, they are discussing politics and Zac begins a tirade against Jews and blacks that stuns the group. They shake their heads in disbelief. They almost make a sport of Zac, drawing him out in a tolerant "liberal fashion." Sensing their contempt, Zac become abusive, taunting them with their effete lives, their dilettantish interests, and the fact that they have never really put their lives on the line for their convictions—as he has done in the Gulf War. Suddenly he grabs Pete, twisting and breaking his arm and putting a knife to his throat. Everyone is horrified as Pete screams in pain. At a loss for words, Marc (Jonathan Penner), who has been standing behind Zac, stabs him in the back.

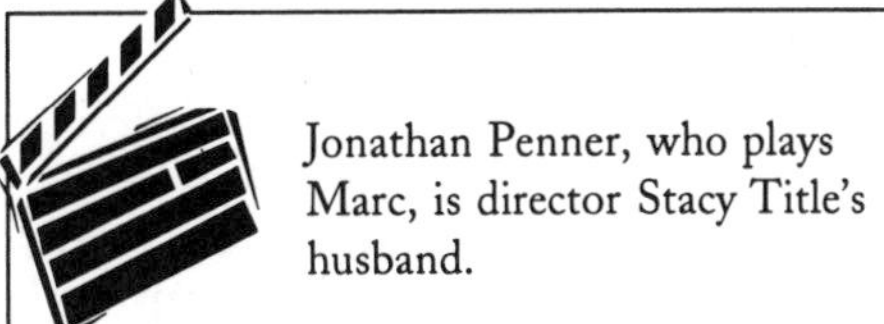

Jonathan Penner, who plays Marc, is director Stacy Title's husband.

Now what to do? Call the police? And say what? How will it look? This distrust of the cops is reminiscent of another recent film, *Loaded,* where another group of young people seek to cover up a death because they believe the politics of time will inevitably lead to their frameup—or at the very least disrupt their lives and ruin their plans.

Marc, and then some of the others, agree that Zac had it coming. And who knows what Zac would have done next? They were protecting themselves and the world is better without its Zacs.

The coolest member of the group, Luke, an African-American Ph.d student, played with finesse by Courtney B. Vance, puts the murder in a political context. Isn't Zac exactly the kind of thug who does what Arbuthnot talks about on TV? Hypothetical discussions ensue. Would they have killed Hitler if they had a chance? What if they had met him in his days as a down and out art student and knew they could prevent World War II and the Holocaust by killing Hitler before he got started?

"What if you kill somebody whose death makes the world a better place?"—Luke

The group is energized by such speculation and by the sense that they have really done something—struck a blow for their side. They decide to form a conspiracy, inviting the worst of the reactionaries to dinner, hearing them out, arguing with them, and then giving them poisoned wine if these zealots do not recant their hate speech.

The Last Supper appeals to fantasies that most people surely have. Wouldn't life be better if the hate mongers could be removed? Do they really have the right to say things that are racist, homophobic, chauvinistic, etc.? No matter how many court decisions affirm the right to free speech and claim that the surest way to tyranny is the suppression of speech, however hateful, don't people wish they could silence repugnant points of view? Isn't so-called political correctness based on the sentiment that hate speech should be suppressed?

But things go wrong very quickly, even though the group seems almost deliriously happy as the murders proceed, their backyard filling up with grave mounds and tomatoes that grow luxuriantly atop these dead right supper guests. The victims are caricatures of the self-satisfied extreme conservatives these liberals despise. A fat gourmand of a priest, played with relish by Charles Durning, spouts off about AIDS as a gay disease and God's punishment. He has absolutely no empathy for the suffering of those different from him and is just plain ignorant about the issues involved. But what is really disturbing is not that he is a bigot but that this group of graduate students does not challenge him. They ask questions that invite the man to rethink his position, but they don't even try for a vigorous give-and-take, an argument that would at least make the priest confront positions far different from his own. The truth is that these liberals have already made up their minds about him. He seems a hopeless case to them—destined for the poison they are about to minister to him, just as he, no doubt, would consider them depraved if they fully revealed their own opinions and how detestable they find his own.

So no real debate occurs at the last supper table. Guest after guest reveals his or her retrograde politics and in perverse communion with his or her adversaries drinks from the poisoned wine glass. These liberals are notching their kills, not doing anything to keep alive the spirit of debate or free inquiry. Their insular lives (graduate school becomes a good metaphor for their cloistered devotion to a demonic cause) permits them the luxury of lovingly planning their dinner guests' demises.

One of the best things about *The Last Supper* is that neither the Left nor the Right wins any points; neither side is willing to grapple with the other's ideas and experiences; neither side believes the other has a right to speak. The graduate students have simply become thugs, as sure of their cause as Zac was of his.

As the murders proliferate and the group gets bolder, they also become sloppier and even less interested in engaging their guests in any sort of genuine debate. Things come to a head when a seventeen-year-old high school girl is set up for execution. She is against distributing condoms in school and presents conservative arguments like a catechism she has memorized. An enraged but steely cold Luke cross-examines her. He exudes contempt for this ignorant white girl and essentially tells her she has not lived long enough to hold such opinions. She has not paid her dues.

CREDITS

Jade: Cameron Diaz
Pete: Ron Eldard
Paulie: Annabeth Gish
Marc: Jonathan Penner
Luke: Courtney B. Vance
Norman Arbuthnot: Ron Perlman
Sheriff Stanley: Nora Dunn
Reverend Hutchens: Charles Durning
Zack: Bill Paxton

Origin: USA
Released: 1996
Production: Matt Cooper, Larry Weinberg for a Vault production; released by Sony Pictures
Direction: Stacy Title
Screenplay: Dan Rosen
Cinematography: Paul Cameron
Editing: Luis Colina
Music: Mark Mothersbaugh
Production design: Linda Burton
Casting: Debra Zane, Bonnie Zane
MPAA rating: R
Running Time: 94 minutes

She is not entitled to her opinions. The rest of the group tries to restrain Luke, but he is livid. The girl becomes scared. Unlike the other guests, she senses she is in danger and says she is frightened. The group adjourns to another room to argue whether she deserves to die. How the group handles this moment (which will not be revealed here) determines the fate of their murder spree.

Luke has become the exact reverse of Zac, yelling at a youngster who has not earned her convictions. What had seemed black and white at the beginning of the film is black and white again, but with a twist. The black man has been just as warped by the political climate as the white. Each would silence and kill the other. The difference between the elegant African-American Ph.D. student and the crude redneck has vanished.

Of course, this neat, schematic scene shifting is what makes *The Last Supper*, starting with its title, an allegorical picture. The film is parody of the religious idea of the punishment of sin and the redemption of the world. The world cannot be saved through the murder, the film concludes. If the opposition to liberal values were actually silenced, the liberal would become intolerant and thus less liberal. Liberalism is the exercise of tolerance, not its extinction. The liberal position seems weak because it is permissive; it allows so much of what it does not approve of. But to do less, the film argues, is to ultimately lose one's own convictions.

In the film's final scenes, the group gets its ultimate catch: the TV demagogue, Norman Arbuthnot, played with superb oiliness by Ron Perlman. Arbuthnot has been waylaid at the airport and a couple members of the group persuade him to come home for a good meal. To the group's dismay, they discover that Arbuthnot is not a true believer in the conservative cause but a fascinating combination of a cynic, opportunist, and proud supporter of free speech. He joyfully concedes that on TV he exaggerates. He loves to attack, and it brings good ratings. It is how he makes a living. But whatever they think of his opinions, he tells them, they represent dissent. America has thrived on dissent, Arbuthnot opines. Dissent is what America is all about. His speech is the film's final irony, that someone so coarse and commercial understands the liberal point of view so much better than its acknowledged champions.

—Carl Rollyson

REVIEWS

Boxoffice Magazine. April, 1996, p. 108.
Detroit News. April 26, 1996, p. 3D.
Entertainment Weekly. April 26, 1996, p. 40.
Los Angeles Times. April 5, 1996, p. F6.
New York Times. April 5, 1996, p. C12.
Rolling Stone. April 18, 1996, p. 79.
USA Today. April 17, 1996, p. 7D.
Variety. October 2, 1995, p. 42.

Lawnmower Man II: Beyond Cyberspace

God made him simple, science mad him a god. Now, he wants revenge.—Movie tagline

Box Office: $2,409,225

Science fiction films have come a long way since Flash Gordon flew around in miniature spaceships suspended from wires. However, even at that time, there was a fascination with visions of what the futuristic world would look like and it continues today. The modern world is changing so quickly, due to the invention of the computer that even current filmmakers are struggling to keep up with the speed of the new technology. This "lightning rod" pace is certainly reflected in New Line Cinema's *Lawnmower Man II: Beyond Cyberspace*.

This high-tech science fiction thriller is the sequel to the surprise 1992 hit, *Lawnmower Man*, starring Pierce Brosnan. The first feature was loosely based on a short story by Stephen King, who had his name legally removed from any involvement with the project. *Lawnmower Man II* picks up where *Lawnmower Man I* ended. This fact makes the complicated plot difficult to follow for those who missed the first one. Matt Frewer (TV's Max Headroom) plays Jobe Smith, replacing the original Jeff Fahey. Jobe has been transformed into a genius by a team of electronic wizards who are working for the ominous Virtual Light Institute. This sinister organization is headed by a rather villainous businessman, Jonathan Walker (Kevin Conway). It seems that they have developed an advanced computer chip called the Chiron Chip.

This "gem of a chip" enables them to link the world's computers into one virtual reality network. This control could make them "virtually" omnipotent. Their only roadblock is a program named "Egypt," which could derail the entire project. According to Jobe, the only person who holds the key to Egypt is Dr. Benjamin Trace (Patrick Bergin), a virtual reality pioneer. Trace, in seclusion, has retired from the fierce, competitive world of virtual reality after having his patent for the Chiron Chip stolen. It appears that Jobe has not only gone from simpleton gardener to computer genius, but to mad megalomaniac, as well. There is evidence of this personality disturbance when he says to Dr. Cori Platt (Ely Pouget), "My world is in here. Out there people look at me and they see half a person. But in here (virtual reality), they see what I want them to see—how I really am." This revealing statement could apply, as well, to the millions of people living inside their computers, traveling the information highway, while excluding all other forms of socialization. It certainly is food for thought!

On the video release, the subtitle is changed from *Beyond Cyberspace* to *Jobe's War.*

Meanwhile, there is a group of techno-crazed street urchins living in an abandoned subway tunnel, underneath a futuristic Los Angeles (it seems that *Blade Runner* [1982] started a trend). Their only escape from the urban decay around them is to take refuge in cyberspace. This actually seems like a far better choice than drugs and drive-by shootings. The leader of the pack is Peter (Austin O'Brien), who happens to be an old pal of Jobe when Jobe was a simple lawnmower man. Peter runs into Jobe while on a free-spirited joy ride through virtual reality. Jobe implores Peter to find Trace, in order to save him from death (Jobe is a liar, as well). Naively, Peter sets out on a mission to locate the legendary Benjamin Trace. When Trace, in his wisdom, explains to the Dickens-like, hyperactive youths Jobe's bizarre plan, they side with Trace. The question is how to short-circuit this potential electronic Armageddon. The battle now begins between good and evil (some things never change). In the course of this heroic quest, Trace is reunited with his old flame, the somewhat sultry Dr. Cori Platt. It seems that when they weren't "on-line," they had a rather hot human romance, devoid of all gadgetry. The filmmakers obviously wanted to remind the audience that true emotion can still exist, rare though it may be.

Lawnmower Man II, according to producer Edward Sims, broke ground in filmmaking history—"What's really innovative and exciting about this movie is that at the same time we're shooting the film, we're also creating the CD-ROM game." It is debatable as to whether or not this is a good thing, but it is interesting to note, in terms of technology. Many critics felt that it would have been better to skip the film and wait for the video game. Michael Wilmington of the *Chicago Tribune* commented that the game "may not be any better (than the film), but at least you can turn it off." Terry Lawson of *The Detroit Free Press* stated "*Lawnmower II* ought to be mulched." Like it or not, the one thing for certain is that virtual reality is making its entrance into the new cinema. Where it's leading to is uncertain at this time.

In making a film whose real star is special effects, requires the actors, in many instances, to react to nothing. It could be said that this is the "blue-screen" method of acting. When this fact is taken into consideration, the ensemble of players in *Lawnmower Man II* did a commendable job. Patrick Bergin (*Sleeping with the Enemy* [1991] and *Mountains of the Moon* [1990]) provided the appropriate disillusioned intensity to the role of Dr. Trace. Unfortunately, with the long hair extensions, he did look somewhat like a poor man's version of Mel Gibson in *Braveheart* (1995). Although strapped to a chair for most of the film, Matt Frewer displayed the correct amount of genius mixed with madness, with a touch of simpleton—certainly no easy task. Kevin Conway, Austin O'Brien and Ely Pouget all gave solid supporting performances, although Conway was slightly overpowered by the "wizardry" of the computer graphics. He could have brought his "villainy" up a notch or two.

It could be easy to dismiss the screenplay in a film that is primarily focused on technology, such as *Lawnmower Man II.* However, the story, written by Farhad Mann and Michael Miner, did manage to make some valid statements about society's increasing obsession with computers. It painted a dark portrait of the real world as a somewhat hopeless and doomed

CREDITS

Dr. Benjamin Trace: Patrick Bergin
Jobe: Matt Frewer
Peter: Austin O'Brien
Cori Platt: Ely Pouget
Jonathan Walker: Kevin Conway
Jennifer: Camille Cooper

Origin: USA
Released: 1996
Production: Edward Simons and Keith Fox for an Allied Entertainment, Fuji Eight Co. Ltd. and August Entertainment, released by New Line Cinema
Direction: Farhad Mann
Screenplay: Farhad Mann
Cinematography: Ward Russell
Editing: Peter Berger and Joel Goodman
Production design: Ernest H. Roth
Art direction: Vincent Reynaud, John Michael Kelly
Costume design: Deborah Everton
Music: Robert Folk
Sound: Richard Schexnayder
Special Visual Effects: Cinesite
MPAA rating: PG-13
Running Time: 93 minutes

civilization. Therefore, it should not be surprising that people choose to escape into the "magicality" of cyberspace. Where else is there to go? This feature, in many ways, endorses the concept, while at the same time, condemns it. The danger lies in the fact that technology was originally intended to serve mankind and now, man is serving it. The roles seem to be reversing. Remember Hal in Stanley Kubrick's *2001: A Space Odyssey* (1968)? As Dr. Benjamin Trace says, "All that technology consumes us all." This may be similar to the "hazardous to your health" warning on cigarette packs.

—Rob Chicatelli

REVIEWS

Boxoffice. March, 1996, p. R-28.
Chicago Tribune. January 17, 1996, p. 7.
Detroit Free Press. January 14, 1996, p. 3F.
Hollywood Reporter. January 16, 1996, p. 11.
Los Angeles Times. January 15, 1996, p. F3.
New York Times. January 15, 1996, p. C16.
USA Today. January 15, 1996, p. 4D.
Variety. January 15, 1996, p. 127.
Washington Post. January 13, 1996, p. D3.

The Leopard Son

To earn his place in the world . . . First, he must survive.—Movie tagline

"Full of charm and wonder!"—Jim Svejda, *CBS Radio*

"Packed with beauty and wonder."—Michael Wilmington, *Chicago Tribune*

"Visually extraordinary!"—Joanne Kaufman, *Family Life Magazine*

"The most ambitious dramatic narrative about an animal in the wild since *The Bear*."—Stanley Meises, *Life Magazine*

"Spectacular!"—Jane Horowitz, *Washington Post*

Box Office: $461,937

With a distinguished, impeccable reputation behind them, The Discovery Channel cable station released their first feature film, *The Leopard Son*, in 1996 . Director Hugo Van Lawick spent the better part of two years on Africa's Serengeti Plains chronicling the maturation of a leopard. From weak and dependent cub, through mischievous adolescence, to the confusion of early adulthood and the final stage of self-sufficiency, Van Lawick parallels the life of his subject with humans, giving his project an immediate and highly approachable quality. Despite the often distanced, clinical nature of nature photography, intimacy is often (and understandably) sacrificed. Couple that with the speed, cunning and predatory nature of leopards and Van Lawick's accomplishments prove even greater.

Billed as "the real Lion King," *The Leopard Son* allows parents to show their children the more realistic side of their cute and cuddly Disney counterparts and profiles the vicious, unforgiving real world of the jungle. Although rated "G," there are violent, bloody attacks that could quite easily disturb young children, a "PG" rating would have been more appropriate. While highly entertaining and of the highest quality of its kind available, Disney's (animated) films paint a very unrealistic picture of the real world. While *The Lion King* (1994) proved to be immensely entertaining, *The Leopard Son* does the same but with real-life setbacks and victories as necessary accompaniment. Absent from the production are the trademark, Broadway-influenced song and dance numbers that proliferate all Disney productions. In their stead is an always powerful, absorbing, atmospheric soundtrack supplied by Stewart Copeland, former percussionist for The Police. Ironically, Sting, Copeland's former Police cohort, has recently supplied similar accompaniment to the IMAX feature, *The Living Sea*. It can't be overstated how important music is to nature-oriented features. *Microcosmos* [also released in 1996 and reviewed in this issue] went from being a dry, clinical observation of insects and amphibians to an emotional wellspring of a picture thanks to the wide ranging music and sound effects that were added in post-production.

Van Lawick and The Discovery Channel need to continue to produce other efforts like this one. High quality, educational family entertainment is in painfully short supply. While children's projects will always have a receptive audience, movies that simultaneously appeal to the adult and the child will not only get stronger box office but will further bond the families who see them together.

—*J.M. Clark*

CREDITS

Narrator: John Gielgud

Origin: USA
Released: 1996
Production: Hugo Van Lawick, Tim Cowling for a Nature Conservation Films production; released by Discovery Channel Pictures
Direction: Hugo Van Lawick
Screenplay: Michael Olmert
Cinematography: Hugo Van Lawick, Matthew Aeberhard
Editing: Mark Fletcher, Gerrit Netten
Music: Stewart Copeland
MPAA rating: G
Running Time: 87 minutes

REVIEWS

Boxoffice Online. October, 1996.
Detroit Free Press. September 27, 1996.
Los Angeles Times. September 27, 1996, p. F14.
New York Times. September 27, 1996, p. C12.
Washington Post. September 27, 1996, p. 43.

Little Indian, Big City; Un Indien dans la Ville

The city is a jungle. Some are just better prepared for it than others.—Movie tagline

"A pure delight!"—Ron Brewington, *American Urban Radio Networks*

Box Office: $722,182

Little Indian, Big City is a fish-out-of-water tale that is equal parts Tarzan and The Lil' Rascals. Since its French release in 1994, it has gone on to become the third largest grossing film in the history of that country. This could go far in explaining the taste of French film patrons and might help Americans understand why Parisians consider Jerry Lewis the greatest comedic actor of all time. Disney bought the American rights to the film and have repackaged it under the Touchstone label. Even before releasing it nationwide, Disney decided that they were going to remake it and send it into theaters in Spring 1997 under the title *Jungle 2 Jungle*, starring Tim Allen and Martin Short. Disney, masters of modern film marketing, have taken a stance and strategy with *Little Indian, Big City* that not only appears redundant, but self-defeating. Foreign films have never made much of dent in the American box office. Releasing a family oriented, foreign picture virtually eliminates the traditional, highbrow audiences normally associated with non-English speaking pictures. Disney considered this fact and decided to overdub the dialogue. *Little Indian, Big City* recalls the many sub-par action/adventure Japanese efforts that unintentionally made audiences giggle with its efforts to synchronize the mouths moving on the screen to the later-added English on the soundtrack. The children who watch this film probably won't notice the slipshod dubbing. To the parents accompanying said children, it will more than likely drive them up a wall. Obviously, Disney surmised that this would be a more logical choice (also offering a better bottom line in the process) than keeping the French intact and adding all those dreaded subtitles.

Disney's making an American remake, *Jungle 2 Jungle*, starring Tim Allen that's releasing in 1997.

The story centers on stockbroker Stephan Marchado (Thierry Lhermitte), a workaholic man who is preparing to get married for a second time. Realizing he must get divorced first, he tracks down wife number one who is now living in a South American jungle. Although he must travel through hell and high water to reach her, he feels he will be rewarded for his efforts. After all, this is a woman he hardly knew and hasn't seen in a dozen years. Much to his surprise, he discovers he has an adolescent son (Ludwig Briand) he's never met. The son has been raised as a jungle hunter, complete with loincloth, beads, and war paint. Children of this remote sect are permitted to choose their own names and this brazen young man calls himself Mimi-Siku. The English translation for Mimi-Siku? That would be "cat urine." Very charming. In a throwaway attempt to pacify his sons' many inquiries (and to get back to civilization as quickly as possible), Stephen halfheartedly promises Mimi-Siku that he will take him to Paris. The boy immediately accepts his offer and, much to Stephen's chagrin, the two hop aboard the canoe and head for gay Paris.

Mimi-Siku has nothing but wide-eyed enthusiasm for this new jungle; the steel, glass, and asphalt variety. But, as the saying goes, you can take the boy out of the jungle, but you can't take the jungle out of the boy. Mimi-Siku has a propensity to put an arrow or poisoned dart through any animal he sees (except, of course, his pet spider, which is roughly the size of a small import car). One of the many statue-painting French pigeons is the first of the boy's victims. Another episode finds Mimi-Siku climbing the Eiffel Tower. Although viewed as cute by the many onlookers, his

CREDITS

Stephan Marchado: Thierry Lhermitte
Mimi-Siku: Ludwig Briand
Richard: Patrick Timsit
Patricia: Miou Miou
Charlotte: Arielle Dombasle

Origin: France
Released: 1994; 1996
Production: Louis Becker for an Ice Films and TF1 Films production; released by Touchstone Pictures
Direction: Herve Palud
Screenplay: Herve Palud, Igor Aptekman, Thierry Lhermitte, and Philippe Bruneau
Cinematography: Fabio Conversi
Editing: Roland Baubeau
Production design: Ivan Maussion
Music: Manu Katche, Geoffrey Oryema, Tonton David
Costume design: Martine Rapin
Sound: Pierre Lorrain, Vincent Anardy
MPAA rating: PG
Running Time: 90 minutes

actions begin to take their toll on his exasperated father. Stephen, busy with his job and preparing for his upcoming nuptials, has had just about enough. In an attempt to keep the child occupied (and to retain his sanity), he asks his business partner Richard (Patrick Timsit) to allow Mimi-Siku to spend some quality time with his daughter. The two take quite a shine to each other and decide that the next logical step in their pre-teen dating game is to get themselves involved with the Russian mafia!

It's not strange for movies to abruptly insert implausible plot twists, but involving a scenario with the Russian mafia in the middle of a French family film defies explanation. With issues of child abuse, animal abuse, extortion, and the flippant use of deadly weapons, which are treated with a cheery, almost nonchalant sitcom-like mentality, it's very surprising Disney put its stamp of approval on this project. Perhaps the updated, Americanized version starring Allen will avoid the organized crime issue altogether and produce a film that is more in line with the audience it wishes to attract.

—J.M. Clark

REVIEWS

Boxoffice. May, 1996, p. 72.
Detroit News. March 22, 1996, p. D1.
Los Angeles Times. March 22, 1996, p. F8.
New York Times. March 22, 1996, p. C6.
USA Today. March 22, 1996, p. 4D.
Variety. January 6, 1995, p. 97.

Loaded

Seven friends are getting away for a weekend in the country. Only six are coming back.—Movie tagline

"A neo-Hitchcockian thriller . . . wildly frenetic!"—Seth Thompson, *Film Threat*

"Provocative!"—Kevin Thomas, *Los Angeles Times*

"Stylish, sexy and suspenseful!"—Bill Bregall, *Westwood One Source Network*

Box Office: $44,231

Like Pirandello's *Six Characters in Search of an Author*, *Loaded* features seven characters in search of a plot. A group of young people decides to shoot a horror movie on a deserted English estate. It is one of those low-budget, sort of make it up as you go along enterprises that allows director/screenwriter Anna Campion to explore the nexus between the actors and their roles.

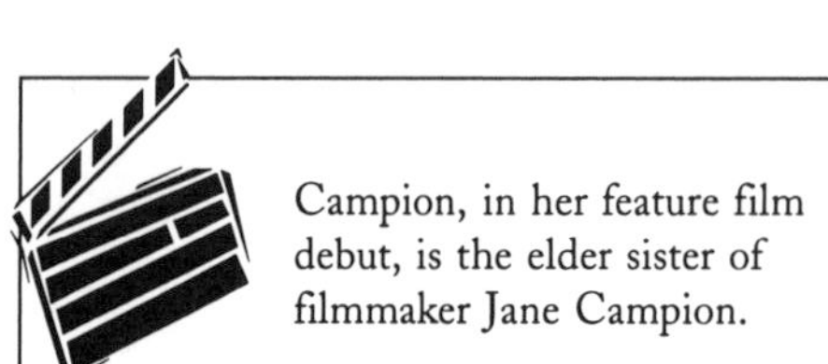

Campion, in her feature film debut, is the elder sister of filmmaker Jane Campion.

Frame by frame, the film is fascinating as each actor is both himself/herself and his or her character, thus raising questions about which is which. Rose (Catherine McCormick) suspects her role has been ripped off from her own personality—that of a young woman struggling with her virginity and wondering whether she should give herself to the sensitive and insistent Neil (Oliver Milburn). And Neil does not know what to make of it when the film's director, Lance (Danny Cunningham) says he has seen Rose kissing Lionel (Matthew Eggleton). Is Lionel making love to Rose; even the appearance of it torments Neil who imagines a scene in which he surprises the two in bed together.

Giles (Nick Patrick) is the most articulate of the filmmakers, spinning out filmic possibilities. He is discovered to have a gruesome scrapbook that details the exploits of serial killers. Offbeat Giles becomes a candidate for perpetrating some real-life horror. Everyone is a little edgy about how the film should go, as if it is their lives and not just a plot that is at stake. Adding to the ghoulish atmosphere is the fact that the estate's owner has recently committed suicide, and there is a room in which the actors are forbidden to enter.

To break through the creative jam-up Lance proposes that they take LSD. At first, the drug seems to do no more than loosen some inhibitions. Then birds start flying off the wallpaper, a table turns to water, and the world seems just as terrifyingly malleable as it is in horror movies. It would be a pity to give away the shocking climax of this LSD orgy since director Campion labors mightily to keep up the suspense. It is enough to say that one of the party is killed, and the filmmakers find themselves literally covering up the body, fearing that their explanation won't wash with the police.

Reality becomes more scary than their horror scenario, and the dead do not rise from the grave. Indeed, in a nice touch the dead body cannot be found when they decide to dig it up and turn themselves in. So glib at making up scenes, this cast does not know what to do with a real one. Life, unlike a movie plot, is truly frightening because it is open-ended and much more unpredictable. The movie, it seems, has been a kind of drug from which they are rudely awakening.

CREDITS

Neil: Oliver Milburn
Giles: Nick Patrick
Rose: Catherine McCormick
Zita: Thandie Newton
Lionel: Mathew Eggleton
Lance: Danny Cunningham
Charlotte: Biddy Hodson

Origin: Great Britain and New Zealand
Released: 1996
Production: David Hazlett, Caroline Hewitt, Bridget Ikin, and John Maynard for a New Zealand Film Commission production; released by Miramax Films
Direction: Anna Campion
Screenplay: Anna Campion
Cinematography: Alan Almond
Editing: John Gilbert
Music: Simon Fisher Turner
Production design: Alistair Kay
MPAA rating: R
Running Time: 105 minutes

That much said, it is hard to find a moral, a message, or a ruling metaphor in *Loaded.* It is all atmosphere and a little pointless after its one point has been made. Somehow these intricate characters should have more to do. The film's ending provokes the response: And? Of course, this is exactly what the actors have been asking themselves as well. They are still in search of a plot for their film and for their lives.

Although *Loaded* has been compared to Hitchcock, Campion lacks his ability to scare audiences. The terror in her film is psychological, and it is only happening to other people; it never grips and shakes the audience the way a film like *Psycho* does. *Loaded* is "daring and different," as another reviewer puts it, because it veers between the mundane and extraordinary, the ordinary and the occult.

Campion has said she was attracted to the characters because they represent a new generation: "they're facing the world smart and cynical, forced to grow up beyond their experience, left with no innocent playground." Critic Suzanne Weiss calls them "self-aware realists who can't help but see the law and other social structures breaking down around them. They have a deep underlying wariness that the world has been used up, and their generation must now make up something of the dregs." Unfortunately, the film leaves us with the dregs; not enough has been made up. Nevertheless, Anna Campion (sister of Jane Campion, director of *The Piano*), has made a provocative start with her first feature-length film.

—*Carl Rollyson*

REVIEWS

Boxoffice. March, 1996, p. R-26.
Los Angeles Times. April 12, 1996, p. F8.
New York Times. April 12, 1996, p. C23.
Sight and Sound. November, 1996, p. 55.

Lone Star

John Sayles invites you to return to the scene of the crime.—Movie tagline

" . . . elegant and richly layered, a work with the kind of reach and ambition few American films ever attempt. The cultural and generational wars tearing at America have never been more clearly or compassionately mapped."—Jay Carr, *The Boston Globe*

"This year's great American movie."—Gerard Haggerty, *Cover Magazine*

"An American masterpiece!"—Daphne Davis, *Movies & Videos*

"Ambitious and stirring . . . John Sayles' best film."—Janet Maslin, *New York Times*

"Like perfume that lingers on a scarf long after you've worn it, a great movie stays with you for days, *Lone Star* is a great movie with exactly that kind of staying power . . . done with vivid, complex characters, much humor, a corker of a story and nimble performances . . . a journey well worth taking."—Leah Rozen, *People*

"A cool classic reminiscent of *Giant* and *The Last Picture Show*."—Bruce Williamson, *Playboy*

"Two more enthusiastic thumbs up . . . a wonderful movie . . . one of the best of the year."—*Siskel & Ebert*

Box Office: $12,297,078

Slightly more than a decade ago, about the time "deconstruction" became the vogue, historians and literary critics began to speak of "revisionist history," the process of revisiting and reevaluating our culture through its historical events and icons. This new clarity of vision, or so it was touted to be, spread to individual histories as well, with people everywhere searching for their roots and constructing their family trees. Revisionist history resulted in people seeing themselves, their families, their heroes, their country, in a brighter light, and often a more harsh one. So, too, John Sayles' newest film, *Lone Star*, presents several versions of personal histories. Multilayered, the accepted versions of the stories are presented and then peeled back (through the use of clever dissolves) to expose new "truths" that will not go away nor even suffer silently.

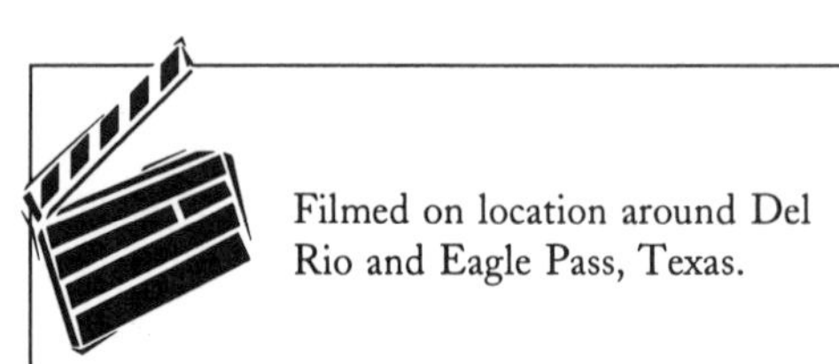

Filmed on location around Del Rio and Eagle Pass, Texas.

Sam Deeds (Chris Cooper), middle-aged, discouraged Anglo sheriff of Frontera, a Texas border town, is called in to investigate a skeleton found in the desert next to a sheriff's badge and a Masonic ring, while in town, Hispanic Pilar Cruz (Elizabeth Pena), a history teacher, discusses revising the high school curriculum with a group of angry Anglo parents. Across town, a group of good ole boys sing the praises of Buddy Deeds (Matthew McConaughey), the previous sheriff who, when a deputy in 1957, rid the town of its racist, murderous thug of a sheriff, Charlie Wade (Kris Kristofferson). Later the same day, on Frontera's outskirts, black teenager Chet Payne (Eddie Robinson) enters a roadhouse owned by Otis "Big O" Payne (Ron Canada) just as gunfire and pandemonium break out. After these initial introductions, more is gradually revealed to the audience.

Pilar is also a mother, dealing with a difficult teenaged son and with her own mother, Mercedes (Miriam Colon), from whom she feels estranged. Sam Deeds, the son of the legendary Buddy, sees himself as a failure, an anachronism, a shopworn lawman in a world of industrialized criminal justice. And Chet is the unhappy son of Col. Delmore Payne (Joe Morton), the newly appointed black commander of the local army base—and the estranged son of Big O. Through the course of the movie, each of these characters questions his or her personal past, present, and future, and that of their changing town.

In typical Sayles form (e.g., the coal mines and miners' paraphernalia in *Matewan* [1987]), *Lone Star* presents Frontera in all of its dusty, warm, musical, oppressive beauty. Specifically, behind the opening credits, Spanish music begins its throbbing tone, that, with the burnt orange and deep red of the film, creates the ruthless passion that drives it. At the Mexican restaurant owned by Mercedes, the adobe walls are warmed by the sun to the color of a corn tortilla and the customers are dressed in cool white cotton before the heat-reflecting walls. The sun, the warm light, the heat, the empty spaces become the icons of Frontera and the lives of its citizens. Cactus is included in several scenes—phenomenally large cactus, green, succulent, dangerous, with spines clearly visible. Only the modern jail has florescent light that strips the Texas sun of its orange warmth, leaving a cold, ice-white authority. The scene is set: a range of passions from ambition to carnal desire grow to uncontrollable proportions throughout the heat and heart of Frontera, while only the governmental lock-up remains cool and dispassionate. Only within its confines does anyone even bother to think he or she can determine right from wrong.

Not unlike a Tex-Mex version of a William Faulkner novel, Sayles' *Lone Star* presents generation after generation, attempting to expiate the sins of its forbearers, working to rise above and beyond that history, working to prove that that history has nothing to do with them, that they have invented themselves anew. Yet sin and secrets abound, and no matter how sons and daughters try to convince themselves that they are the future, that the troubled past has nothing to do with them, they cannot outrun the truth. Delmore Payne must face his father Otis, who deserted his family years ago, and who runs the roadhouse where so much of the past trouble occurred. In a frantic attempt to be everything his father is not, Delmore is rigid in dealing with his wife and son, demanding the same excellence and precision from them as he does from those in his command. Sayles shows Payne running precisely, sprinting quarter miles with a ramrod straight spine, running upright into the horizon, leaving his weary command team to marvel at his inflexible vision as they tread wearily back to base through the dust. With his troops, he is relentlessly interested in precision, interested in not only controlling his troops but also ensuring that they control themselves. His failure to accept his past and forgive his father drives Delmore to be ever more precise, ever more expectant, ever more rigid. In trying to escape his father, Payne drives himself to the edge and beyond.

"I'm Sheriff Deeds." "Sheriff Deeds dead, honey. You just Sheriff junior." "Story of my life."—Sam Deeds introducing himself to elderly Mrs. Bledsoe

Other children wrestle with the sins of their fathers as well. Sam may be the only person in Frontera who does not admire Buddy Deeds. Wrestling constantly with the overpowering image of his father as a legendary lawman who dealt with his predecessor's corruption, yet was privately overbearing and demanding, Sam has grown to manhood accomplishing little beyond a failed marriage and having meager credibility with the townspeople as merely a caretaker to modern law rather than an active participant in frontier justice. Through the course of the film, Sam, who knew firsthand of his father's flaws, also uncovers his father's secrets, hoping to justify his disgust and disillusionment with both his father and himself. But Sam discovers firsthand that when facing choices, we are rarely given the luxury of a full view, and hindsight is indeed 20/20.

When Sam begins his investigation he's certain the skeleton is what's left of Charlie Wade, who disappeared unmourned in 1957, and he's equally certain that the incorruptible Buddy was Wade's killer. Sam's search into the past also leads to the renewal of a romance with the widowed Pilar, their teenaged love having been cruelly cut short by both their parents for what the young lovers believed were racial reasons. The truth behind their original separation will provide yet more insight into the emotional hearts of their parents and into some unsettling decisions about the path their present lives and love will take.

While much of the historical truth in *Lone Star* is less than fixed, changing shape and color as if viewed through a kaleidoscope, some portions of it are immobile. Without a doubt, without a redeeming feature, Charlie Wade is villainous. Whether shooting people in the back, extorting money from the citizens he served, or slinging racist epithets at the powerless around him, Charlie Wade is all-around hateful. When Wade attempts to browbeat his new deputy, Buddy Deeds, into participating in his extortion plans, Deeds is uncomfortable at first, then angry, then threatening. Wade's goal was to push the envelope to the limit; his demise was in pushing someone too far. Sam's goal is to uncover his father's sins but both Big O, a victim of Wade's abuse, and Mayor Hollis Pogue (Clifton James), Buddy's fellow deputy at the time, urge Sam to let the past lie, lest he disturb more than anyone can handle. The "truth" may set no one free.

Lone Star is John Sayles' tenth film and showcases some repeat performers. Chris Cooper was also in *Matewan* [1987], Joe Morton starred as the *Brother from Another Planet* [1984], and both appeared in *City of Hope* [1991]. Also reminiscent of his other films is its slow pace—at 134 minutes the film ambles through the past and present. However, in some ways *Lone Star* is a breakthrough film for Sayles. Never known for his stylish or quirky camera work or editing, in *Lone Star* Sayles experiments with such features as match-on-action edits that add a certain zest, a self-conscious artistry, to the film. When Buddy's aging friends sit in a restaurant and recall the deputy's fiery passion, Sayles slips into the past through a matched cut from a hand reaching for a tortilla basket in the present to Charlie Wade's hand reaching for a basket of tortillas in the past, while he and Buddy argued the presumably incompatible "virtues" of honesty and wealth. Sayles also dissolves from a sensual (yet never salacious) love scene between newly re-

AWARDS AND NOMINATIONS

Academy Award 1996 Nominations: Best Original Screenplay (Sayles)
Golden Globe Award 1997 Nominations: Best Screenplay (Sayles)
Independent Spirit Awards 1997: Supporting Actress (Pena)
Nominations: Feature, Actor (Cooper), Screenplay (Sayles)
Writers Guild of America 1996 Nominations: Original Screenplay (Sayles)

CREDITS

Sam Deeds: Chris Cooper
Pilar: Elizabeth Pena
Charlie Wade: Kris Kristofferson
Buddy Deeds: Matthew McConaughey
Delmore Payne: Joe Morton
Otis Payne: Ron Canada
Hollis Pogue: Clifton James
Mercedes Cruz: Miriam Colon
Chet Payne: Eddie Robinson
Bunny: Frances McDormand

Origin: USA
Released: 1996
Production: Maggie Renzi, Paul Miller for a Rio Dulce and Castle Rock Entertainment production; released by Sony Pictures Classics
Direction: John Sayles
Screenplay: John Sayles
Cinematography: Stuart Dryburgh
Editing: John Sayles
Music: Mason Daring
Production design: Dan Bishop
Art direction: Kyler Black
Set decoration: Dianna Freas
Costume design: Shay Cunliffe
Sound: Clive Winter
Casting: Avy Kaufman
MPAA rating: R
Running Time: 134 minutes

united lovers Sam and Pilar to their bright-eyed teenaged selves.

Sayles presents a Texas that is changing, willingly or not, as the views of his characters also change. While the Anglo population of Frontera argue over the manner in which history is told, the film asks whose view of history is true and concludes that there are no absolutes—not in what is believed publicly and certainly not in what is accepted privately. *Lone Star* is quizzical and interesting enough to carry even the most restless viewer through the viewing hours. It is a manifesto on hate and forgiveness, violence and peace, love and lust. It is thoughtful and sometimes as uncomfortable and daunting to look at as the sun in a clear Texas sky. Sayles fans, and those willing to take their time, will want to experience this film.

—*Roberta F. Green* and *Christine Tomassini*

REVIEWS

Chicago Tribune. July 3, 1996, p. 1.
Detroit News. July 12, 1996, p. F3.
Entertainment Weekly. June 21, 1996, p. 47.
The Hollywood Reporter. March 19, 1996, p. 8.
Los Angeles Times. June 21, 1996, p. F12.
Newsweek. July 8, 1996, p. 64.
New York Times. June 21, 1996, p. C2.
People. July 1, 1996, p. 20.
Rolling Stone. July 11, 1996, p. 98.
Sight and Sound. October, 1996, p. 47.
Variety. March 18, 1996, p. 46.
Village Voice. June 25, 1996, p. 65.

The Long Kiss Goodnight

Eight years ago she lost her memory. Now, a detective must help her remember the past before it buries them both. What's forgotten is not always gone.—Movie tagline

"It's a high-flying hoot!"—Mike Cidoni, *ABC-TV*

"This is one great ride!"—Joel Siegel, *Good Morning America*

"This fall's best summer movie! Nonstop twists and turns!"—David Ansen, *Newsweek*

"Action-packed, smart and funny!"—Gene Siskel, *Siskel & Ebert*

Box Office: $32,836,418

Geena Davis stars as Samantha Caine, a single mother and school teacher in a picturesque small New England town. She has a beautiful young daughter, Caitlin (Yvonne Zima), and an adoring fiancE (Tom Amandes), but her idyllic world begins to unravel when a head injury jolts memories of her previous life. For the past eight years Samantha has suffered from traumatic amnesia and has no recollection of who she really is. From the moment she snaps the neck of the deer that she hit with her car on a snowy night, Samantha rediscovers some pretty handy skills: expert knife handling and sharpshooting, top-notch physical combat and a killer instinct.

When Samantha appears on the local news as the sexy Mrs. Kringle in the annual Christmas parade, she is recognized by some very seedy characters who thought she was long dead. It does not take long for Samantha's repressed alter ego to begin appearing in the mirror. For what Samantha learns is that she is really Charly Baltimore, a government contract killer. Teamed up with a down-and-out private detective, Mitch Henessey (the always impressive Samuel L. Jackson) that she had hired to help her learn her true identity, Samantha/Charly sets out to do away with the men who would prefer that she stay dead once and for all.

Shane Black received a record-setting $4 million for his script in a heated Hollywood bidding war.

Shane Black made film history when his script for *The Long Kiss Goodnight* sold for a record-setting $4 million. What earned him that hefty paycheck and what sets this project apart from the hordes of other action films, aside from Black's wicked sense of humor and perverse comic timing, is the offbeat relationship between Samantha/Charly and Mitch. These are two characters on the skids; one is a down-on-his-luck detective, the other, a woman who discovers her entire life is merely an illusion. The changes that both of these characters go through are well-crafted and expertly articulated, while the situations are campy and over-the-top.

"Easy, sport. I got myself outta Beirut. I think I can get out of New Jersey."—Charly to Mitch

Overcoming the disastrous *Cutthroat Island* (1995), director Renny Harlin stages some of the most thrilling action sequences, constantly upping the ante by having the actors do many of the stunts themselves. Computer-generated special effects were used to erase cable wires and other safety devices from the finished image, but Geena Davis (Harlin's offscreen wife) still is impressive in her commitment to realism in her portrayal of a contract killer. She proves to be a formidable opponent for her charismatic male counterpart, Timothy (Craig Bierko in his film debut), tough and resourceful, yet Ms. Davis never sacrifices her sensuality and sexuality. What is impressive about both the character that Shane Black has scripted and Ms. Davis' portrayal is that we never feel this is a woman trying to be a man. While Charly may seem to lack traditional feminine instincts, there is little doubt of her innate female power. And for Hollywood, a town fond of depicting women as little more than prostitutes or saints, that is quite a feat.

The Long Kiss Goodnight is fast, fun and funny. Geena Davis, whose appetite for action characters was whetted by her portrayal of Thelma in Ridley Scott's *Thelma & Louise* (1991), plunges headlong into the role of big-budget action star and more than holds her own against the likes of Sylvester Stallone, Arnold Schwarzenegger and Bruce Willis. She demonstrates that she can play with the Big Boys—and while she may not have been able to beat them at the box office, Ms. Davis proves that there are no limits to her physical prowess and willingness to give a project her all. Reviews for the film were decidedly mixed and box office receipts were disappointing. Apparently filmgoers were not yet ready to pay to see a female character be this tough and this competent.

—Patricia Kowal

CREDITS

Samantha Caine/Charly Baltimore: Geena Davis
Mitch Henessey: Samuel L. Jackson
Caitlin: Yvonne Zima
Timothy: Craig Bierko
Hal: Tom Amandes
Nathan: Brian Cox
Perkins: Patrick Malahide
Luke/Daedalus: David Morse

Origin: USA
Released: 1996
Production: Renny Harlin, Stephanie Austin, Shane Black; for a Forge Production; released by New Line Cinema
Direction: Renny Harlin
Screenplay: Shane Black
Cinematography: Guillermo Navarro
Editing: William C. Goldenberg
Production design: Howard Cummings
Art direction: Steve Arnold, Dennis Davenport
Costume design: Michael Kaplan
Music: Alan Silvestri
Special visual effects: Jeffrey A. Okun
Stunt Coordinator: Steve M. Davidson
MPAA rating: R
Running Time: 120 minutes

REVIEWS

Chicago Tribune. October 11, 1996, p. 5.
Entertainment Weekly. October 25, 1996, p. 93.
Los Angeles Times. October 11, 1996, p. F2.
New York Times. October 11, 1996, p. C18.
Newsweek. October 21, 1996, p. 91.
Rolling Stone. October 31, 1996, p. 76.
USA Today. October 11, 1996, p. 3D.
Variety. October 11, 1996.
Village Voice. October 22, 1996, p. 84.

Looking for Richard

A comic look at a four hundred year old work-in-progress.—Movie tagline

"A true revelation. Sharp, funny and illuminating. Mr. Pacino acts Richard's role with the crackling intensity of his great film performances."—Janet Maslin, *New York Times*

"Exuberant, spellbinding and superbly entertaining!"—Bruce Williamson, *Playboy*

"Witty and incisive . . . pays major dividends."—Peter Travers, *Rolling Stone*

Box Office: $1,339,985

Al Pacino in his much lauded directorial debut, *Looking for Richard.*

To communicate the passion and understanding of Shakespeare to others is the self-announced purpose for *Looking for Richard,* Al Pacino's effort to make *Richard III,* what he calls Shakespeare's most produced play, and its author more accessible. "He speaks to all of us about everything that's inside us," Pacino says. "That's the thing." Pacino and producer Michael Hadge spent four years shooting eighty hours of footage to create this effective potpourri of a film. At times *Looking for Richard* is a documentary, a rehearsal film, a Shakespeare celebration, a travelogue, a video lecture, and a highlight film of *Richard III.* All in all, it is a rousing exploration of Shakespeare and one of his most challenging plays.

One of the real strengths of the film comes from seeing the enthusiasm and energy of the actors as they grapple with their roles and bring meaning to scenes. Pacino has assembled a cast that permits the audience to see performers known mostly for popular films working in a demanding literary genre. Pacino is excellent as the hunchbacked villain-king, and Kevin Spacey also stands out as the Duke of Buckingham. The acted scenes illustrate the most famous set pieces from one of Shakespeare's most theatrical plays, like the brazen seduction of Lady Anne (Winona Ryder) by Richard, who has killed her husband and father. This seduction scene, Richard's famous opening soliloquy (beginning "Now is the winter of our discontent /Made glorious summer by this sun of York"), the death of Clarence, the fall of Hastings, Buckingham's fall from Richard's grace, and the climactic battle scenes are all dramatically effective. Actors also sit around a table and discuss difficult scenes, the interplay of character, and proper delivery, as when Penelope Allen speculates that Queen Margaret's lines in Act One should be delivered so as to give the greatest fury to her curse.

"So Richard figured, let me get rid of Clarence and then I'll figure out how to get rid of the kids."—Pacino explaining a plot point

Intercut at various times into the loose ongoing story of preparing scenes from the play are a number of comments by actors who have distinguished themselves in Shakespearean roles. Kenneth Branagh, for example, explains that an individual's school experiences with Shakespeare may have over formalized and revered the author and text. Kevin Kline mentions the way that Richard's opening speech has him "smirking at the audience." James Earl Jones reminisces about growing up in Michigan hearing his uncle read Shakespeare to him. Derek Jacobi comments that American actors can be made to feel inhibited with Shakespeare because they lack the literary stage tradition British actors are steeped in. F. Murray Abraham also discusses the sense of inferiority Americans bring to Shakespeare. John Gielgud traces some of this difficulty to the modern performer's inexperience with iambic pentameter. Vanessa Redgrave's insight is the most thought provoking. She politicizes Gielgud's remark about meter by saying that "in England, you've had centuries in which words have been divorced from truth and that's a problem for us." "The important thing," Redgrave insists, is to find the "iambics of the soul," and then the meter will fall into place. Her insight is an apt one since so much of Shakespeare explores the difference between seeming and being in the politics of life and of nations. Richard is Shakespeare's first great dissembler.

The early portions of the film also include comments from people on the street whom Pacino stops and questions about Shakespeare. "We're peddling Shakespeare on the street," he says exuberantly, trudging about in a floppy coat and a backward baseball cap. Some of these responses convey little more than bafflement, but a few are as discerning as anything the actors or academics come up with. One man explains how Shakespeare teaches us to feel. Another mentions rap music, which brings out the comment that tuning the ear to rap is somewhat analogous to tuning the ear to Shakespearean blank verse.

In what works as a series of video footnotes, Pacino inserts brief remarks from unidentified professors to explicate matters of the play. Some of these comments explain the history the play is based on; others interpret various scenes.

CREDITS

King Richard III: Al Pacino
King Edward IV: Harris Yulin
George, Duke of Clarence: Alec Baldwin
Duke of Buckingham: Kevin Spacey
Lord Hastings: Kevin Conway
Margaret: Estelle Parsons
Elizabeth, queen to Edward IV: Penelope Allen
Lady Anne: Winona Ryder
Henry, Earl of Richmond: Aiden Quinn
Marquis of Dorset: Gordon MacDonald
Earl Rivers: Madison Arnold
Lord Grey: Vincent Angell
Kenneth Branagh: (himself)
Kevin Kline: (himself)
James Earl Jones: (himself)
Rosemary Harris: (herself)
Derek Jacobi: (himself)
John Gielgud: (himself)
Vanessa Redgrave: (herself)
Peter Brook: (himself)

Origin: USA
Released: 1996
Production: Al Pacino and Michael Hadge for JAM; released by Fox Searchlight Pictures
Direction: Al Pacino
Screenplay: Al Pacino and Frederic Kimball (narration); based on *The Tragedy of King Richard III* by William Shakespeare
Cinematography: Robert Leacock, Nina Kedrem, John Kranhouse, Steve Confer
Editing: Pasquale Buba, William Anderson, Ned Bestille, André Betz
Art direction: Kevin Ritter
Music: Howard Shore
Costumes: Aude Bronson Howard, Deborah Scott (L.A.), Yvonne Blake (battle sequences)
MPAA rating: PG-13
Running Time: 109 minutes

The question of what academics have to contribute sparks the most volatile burst of anger from Pacino's collaborator with the spoken narration, Frederic Kimball, who opposes undue deference to such experts. During a rehearsal of the seduction of Lady Anne, Pacino calms Kimball ("A person has an opinion. It's only an opinion. It's never a question of right or wrong.") as a smiling Winona Ryder looks placidly on and waits for the rehearsal to continue. The most memorable comment from the academics is the observation that "irony is hypocrisy with style," a remark that is fittingly placed before the best example of Richard's false piety, when in public he embraces the open Bible and flanks himself with two priests. The timing and placement of the cuts of the academics highlights the beautiful editing of the film.

In the final third of the film, the ongoing interpretive comments recede in favor of additional scenes from the play. The pace of the documentary also slows as the focus shifts from a study and discussion of Shakespeare to a performance of more scenes from *Richard III.* The unifying element for this final selection of scenes is the actors' comments about their own characters. Kevin Spacey shows a solid grasp of the motivations of the Duke of Buckingham: "Everything Buckingham does in the play manages to keep the blood off his hands." Pacino supplies a telling view of the moment when Richard finally turns on Buckingham ("No one can love the king past the point of his own goodness—Buckingham has reached his point"), and he savors delivering the famous line of Richard's tragic despair: "There is no creature loves me;/And if I die, no soul will pity me." The night before the climactic battle scene on Bosworth Field Richard is visited by the ghosts of all eleven of his victims, and Pacino comments aptly: "Richard knows he has no humanity in the last scenes." Richard's heraldic symbol, the boar, also gets a good interpretation when Pacino points out that Shakespeare has subsumed all these animal images of the play to apply to Richard: "He is the boar, and all they have to do is hunt the boar."

Though the film only appeared in limited release and earned very small box-office returns, the critical reaction to

REVIEWS

Box Office. July, 1996, p. 83.
Detroit News. October 25, 1996, p. 3D.
Entertainment Weekly. November 1, 1996, p. 46.
Maclean's. November 11, 1996, p. 74.
The New Republic. October 7, 1996, p. 30.
The New Yorker. November 25, 1996, p. 65.
New York Times. October 11, 1996, p. C3.
People Weekly. November 4, 1996, p. 30.
Rolling Stone. October 31, 1996, p. 78.
Time. November 4, 1996, p. 88.
USA Today. October 11, 1996, p. 3D.
Variety. February 5, 1996, p. 58.
Vogue. October, 1996, p. 210.

the motion picture was largely favorable. A few reviewers found the improvisational nature of the film to be self-indulgent ("a high-culture version of Planet Hollywood"), but most reactions praised the film for the energy and honesty with which the participants pursued the meaning of the play. As a vehicle that explores and celebrates the genius of Shakespeare, Pacino's film is less a finished production than a four-hundred-year-old work in progress.

—*Glenn Hopp*

The Low Life

"Savvy, sad, ultimately sentimental."—Peter Keough, *Boston Phoenix*

"Touching and humorous. Delightfully off-center."—Lawrence Schubert, *Detour*

"Superlative."—*L.A. Weekly*

"Deeply felt, comical, always affecting."—Kevin Thomas, *Los Angeles Times*

"Extraordinary, timeless . . . A fine brave film."—Susan Waugh, *St. Louis Riverfront Times*

Box Office: $45,436

The Low Life is yet another saga about twenty-somethings with thwarted ambitions and stifled emotions, trying desperately to find meaning beyond their cynicism in a world filled with disillusionment. As a seriocomic portrait of post-adolescent angst, it's well-intentioned and occasionally entertaining but for the most part as limp and listless as its overworked subject matter.

John (Rory Cochrane) is a would-be writer who has recently moved to Los Angeles with a few other Yale graduate buddies. They all take jobs as temporaries, and spend their days separating carbon copies of credit card purchase slips. While John has definite ambitions, it's unclear what Chad (Ron Livingston) and Leonard (Christian Meoli) are trying to accomplish. Chad, whose father is a rich industrialist, is a cynic who specializes in mooching food and drink. Leonard is an offbeat observer of the passing social scene who would love to get rich off the Hollywood star machine, but seemingly has no talents or drive to accomplish that.

Like most of the characters in the script by John Enbom and director George Hickenlooper, Chad and Leonard are underwritten. Worse, viewers don't know enough about the protagonist, John, who is so reserved he rarely speaks. He reveals what's on his mind only in letters home to his uncle, who has advised him to avoid the "petty seductions" of life in Hollywood and concentrate on writing. But John has developed writer's block, mostly because he avoids emotional experiences that might give him something to write about.

John is jealous of his privacy. His new roommate, Andrew (Sean Astin) constantly intrudes on it. Andrew is a yokel from Modesto, a very uncool guy who paints figurines of World War II troops, hangs posters of unhip movies and dinosaur rock groups on the apartment walls, and is obsessed with trying to remember the words to his middle school anthem, a song by Journey. Like a puppy dog, Andrew longs for John's friendship but has no chance to get it. John does not suffer anyone much, and certainly not fools like Andrew.

In truth, nothing arouses John's interest. Certainly not his boring work, which gets a little more intriguing but less reputable when the temp agency assigns him to a sleazy landlord, Mike Schroeder Jr. (James LeGros) and not Suzie (Sara Melson), a cute, pigtailed barmaid who's obviously attracted to him. Not even a Hollywood mogul (Jefferson Mays) who comes on to him at a party, or a hot-to-trot woman (Shawnee Smith) who tries to seduce him at another party can pique his interest.

Cochrane has James Dean looks and a brooding Brando-type personality. But his John seems uninterested in romance until he is repeatedly teased by Bevan (Kyra Sedgwick), a Schroeder renter with a Southern drawl who is manic-depressive, self-destructive and prefers affairs with married men. For some reason John finds Bevan irresistible; maybe it's because she insults him while coming on to him. It's a match of two intelligent, attractive underachievers with low self-esteem.

The script's too-obvious challenge is for John to break through his zombie-like approach to human relationships and somehow connect with life. Obviously, he's not going to be much of a writer until he does so. The film's only surprise, a mild one at that, is that the seemingly clueless Andrew provides the means for John to emerge from his shell. But the plot insists on using tragedy to accomplish John's awakening, and it's a jarring device for a film which for 80-

plus minutes has almost reveled in the inconsequence of the non-events in its characters' lives.

Making a film about anomie and disconnection in young people's lives is a difficult undertaking, and Hickenlooper avoids anything that might jazz up the story. The directing seems as desultory as the characters, and there is nothing fresh or ingenious about his approach to a tired subject matter. The travails of Generation X already have been documented ad nauseam. It's hard to care much for John's plight when there are very few clues as to what goes on inside his head.

The characters are neither hip nor adorable. They are caught in their own hyper-awareness of the meaninglessness of their lives, and their observations on their plight often seemed forced and whiny. At work, Leonard erupts at the injustice of eating ramen noodles every night for dinner. At the bar, Chad scorns a guy across the room: "I hate these glibly cheerful idiots wearing '50s-style hats." Bevan tells John, apropos of nothing: "I'm getting so tired of not knowing the little meaningful things in life." This sort of dialogue reveals nothing.

It's hard to work up much sympathy for single people whose main complaint is that they can't find jobs with health plans and who moan that their expensive college educations haven't paid off with immediate success, especially when they seem to scorn the drive or ambition necessary to achieve that success. Yes, life in the '90s is hard and there's not enough opportunity or hope for young people. But it's not as if these characters are battling some profound injustice; they simply are intent on fulfilling their low expectations of themselves. Their lives are boring and unfulfilling, and *The Low Life* doesn't do anything to make us want to care about them.

Through its focus on John's slow awakening, the script seems to suggest that what's needed is relief of emotional constipation through acceptance of others. It's a nice but hardly original message. The minimalist ending underlines the paucity of *The Low Life*'s pantry: an hour and a half of low-energy angst just to get a man to cry? The film's few comic touches, provided mostly by M'eoli and Astin, aren't enough to overcome its long, dull stretches.

The acting is capable enough. Cochrane struggles mightily to suggest some nuances to John, despite the script's insistence on keeping him a closed book. Sedgwick tries to concoct a sort of gracelessly pathetic tragic figure out of her muddled character, but she and Cochrane fail to stir up even a spark of chemistry. Of course, Hickenlooper seems determined to avoid romance at all costs; it would ruin his characters' determinedly jaded emotional landscape.

Astin as Andrew saves the film. His is a magnificent performance as the out-of-sync, left-out guy trying desperately to ingratiate his way into the "in" crowd. Andrew can never be hip enough because he has no skill at masking his emotions. Astin's triumph is that he evokes all the annoying naivete of Andrew while maintaining the dignity the script needs to make its clumsy point: that, despite appearances to the contrary, Andrew is the character with the healthiest emotional life. It's too bad the film has to make him into a martyr to drive home its lesson, but *The Low Life* seems incapable of the subtlety to which it aspires.

Hickenlooper's film seems sincere enough, and there's a chance he eventually will find his meter as a director. At times *The Low Life* has a certain wry pungency, but far too little of it to carry audiences through its non-story. A slice of boring life might be made intriguing if a filmmaker gets inside the characters' heads, but everything in *The Low Life* is on the surface. It's like watching emotional shadowboxing.

—Michael Betzold

CREDITS

John: Rory Cochrane
Andre: Sean Astin
Suzie: Sara Melson
Bevan: Kyra Sedgwick
Mike: James Le Gros
Chad: Ron Livingston
Leonard: Christian Meoli

Origin: USA
Released: 1996
Production: Donald Zuckerman, Tobin Heminway for an Autumn Pictures production; released by Cabin Fever Entertainment and Cinepix Film Properties
Direction: George Hickenlooper
Screenplay: George Hickenlooper, John Enbom
Cinematography: Richard Crudo
Editing: Yaffa Lerea, Jim Makiej
Music: Bill Boll
Production design: Deborah Smith
Costume design: Alexandra Welker
MPAA rating: R
Running Time: 96 minutes

REVIEWS

Boxoffice. February, 1996, p. R-12.
Los Angeles Times. July 11, 1996, p. F4.
New York Times. June 28, 1996, p. C12.
Variety. April 10, 1995, p. 47.
Village Voice. July 2, 1996, p. 71.

Mad Dog Time

No laws. No meaning. No exit.—Movie tagline

"Wry, strange . . . extremely funny."—Henry Cabot Beck, *The Star Ledger*

Box Office: $105,344

Writer-director Larry Bishop tries hard to make this crime-film parody hip with familiar faces, deadpan humor, and pop-culture references, but he fails miserably in his first feature film.

The film was released to video as *Trigger Happy*.

Mad Dog Time suffers from a confusing plot that centers around crime boss Vic (Richard Dreyfuss), who is about to be released from a mental hospital, where he was judged to be a paranoid schizophrenic. Vic's chief enforcer (Gabriel Byrne) is put in charge of getting things ready, which basically means killing Vic's rivals or disloyal mob members.

Vic's assistant Mickey Holliday (Jeff Goldblum) is targeted because he's been sleeping with his boss's girlfriend, Grace Everly (Diane Lane). He's also been carrying on an affair with Grace's jealous older sister, Rita (Ellen Barkin).

The majority of the film consists of the cast spouting off nonsensically and drawing guns on each other. The characters and their actions are never fully explained. Although Bishop has created scenes that are playable, he doesn't bother to tie them in with any logic. Among the actors playing assorted mob types are Billy Idol, Kyle MacLachlan, Gregory Hines, Burt Reynolds, and the comedian Joey Bishop (who is the helmer's father).

Severely miscast as a mob kingpin, Dreyfuss actually has the best part in this unfunny crime spoof. The film is produced by Dreyfuss' company, so he wisely chose the best role. Surprisingly, the powerful, "loony" thug turns out to be the sanest character in this convoluted mess.

The pic's greatest strength lies in creating and sustaining a mood of 1950's-style Mafia—complete with the lounge music of Frank Sinatra, Dean Martin, and Sammy Davis Jr. blaring out in nightclubs filled with suave gangsters and sullen showgirls. Cinematographer Frank Byers (d.p. on David Lynch's "Twin Peaks" series) and production designer Dian Lipton contribute greatly to this area.

Mad Dog Time aspires to be a cooler-than-cool cult film along the lines of a Quentin Tarantino or Lynch flick, but all it really achieves is an air of ironic detachment. The characters don't seem to care about what's going on, so why should the audience? With all its hip pretentiousness, *Mad Dog Time* suffers the most from its ironic approach to violence—it's been done too many times before. *Mad Dog Time* was released to theaters and quickly yanked; however, Bishop's debut may find life on the vid-shelf. We can only wish him and the rest of the gang better luck next time.

CREDITS

Rita Everly: Ellen Barkin
Ben London: Gabriel Byrne
Vic: Richard Dreyfuss
Mickey Holliday: Jeff Goldblum
Grace: Diane Lane
Nick: Larry Bishop
Jules Flamingo: Gregory Hines
Jake Parker: Kyle MacLachlan
Wacky Jacky Jackson: Burt Reynolds
Sleepy Joe Carlisle: Henry Silva

Origin: USA
Released: 1996
Production: Judith Rutherford James for a Skylight Films production; released by United Artists Pictures
Direction: Larry Bishop
Screenplay: Larry Bishop
Cinematography: Frank Byers
Editing: Norman Hollyn
Music: Earl Rose
Production design: Dina Lipton
Art direction: Michael Atwell
Set decoration: Kathy Lucas
Costume design: Ileane Meltzer
Sound: Rick Waddell
Casting: Amy Lieberman
MPAA rating: R
Running Time: 93 minutes

REVIEWS

Entertainment Weekly. November 22, 1996, p. 112.
New York Times. November 8, 1996, p. C14.
Variety. November 11, 1996, p. 58.

Madagascar Skin

"The love story of the year!"—*Boston Globe*
"A delightfully original love story."—*Gay Times*
"Witty and exuberant. Bursts with happiness."—*New Statesman & Society*
"A genuine delight."—*Premiere*

Box Office: $65,000

Director Chris Newby has fashioned a sensitive and amusing gay love story in *Madagascar Skin.* Harry (John Hannah) is a tormented young man, aching to express himself sexually, yet isolated from others because he is so withdrawn. He visits a gay disco and watches lovers embrace each other. He seems unable to introduce himself to others, to catch their attention, and to make himself attractive. He is an interloper. At one point he slithers into a tight garment that encases two lovers. But they just stare at him, and he returns to his squalid flat.

In the flat, Harry disfigures his face with a razor blade, twisting the blade into a cut that accentuates a huge red facial birthmark. Apparently feeling suicidal, Harry drives himself out to the seashore, running his car up onto a stony beach where the tide comes in and swamps the car with seaweed. Inside Harry reads a book by flashlight. What is he expecting? He appears to be planning an end to his life. He takes out a suitcase and burns what looks like family photographs and a birth certificate.

The next day he hears people running about. Someone jumps on his car. When Harry emerges from his cave-like vehicle, he walks the beach and finds a bucket upside down on the sand. When he picks it up, he finds a human head underneath. Soon he realizes it is alive and attached to a body buried in the sand. Harry excavates the man and drags him into his car, which now becomes a kind of infirmary for the shaking man (Flint) suffering from exposure.

Flint (Bernard Hill) seems to take his mishap in stride. He has apparently had a falling out with a gang that has left him to perish in the tides—a fate that perhaps awaited Harry as well. Flint, as his name suggests, seems to be the opposite of Harry in every way. Flint is tough, talkative, and supremely self-confident. If Harry is wary, Flint is heedless. He accepts Harry as he is and makes his living robbing the local citizens' homes. The two men set up in an abandoned cottage, forming a marriage of convenience.

"I feel strange. I'm happy."—Harry

Harry begins to yearn for Flint, but he is afraid to express his feelings. Surely this rugged man would reject him. Flint seems oblivious. All he notices is that Harry is often depressed—but not for long because Flint is endlessly entertaining. At one point, he not only appears to eat a live mouse but to relish chewing and swallowing it. Harry cracks up at Flint's silliness. Flint will do just about anything to get a rise out of his morose mate, including smashing a light bulb and eating the pieces and calling them "electrical crisps." Flint is a show in himself, with his exotic tattoos and tales.

But Flint is not exactly what he says he is. He has told Harry that he is a scaffolder, and on that tale Harry builds a fantasy of his new friend scaling the heights and rigging the heavens with his equipment. Later Flint admits that his story is a lie. Actually he has been a window washer. He talks like a robust heterosexual, but in fact it is Flint who makes the first advance to Harry. Is Flint gay? Or has he just fallen in love with Harry? *Madagascar Skin* does not pursue that question but rather the bond that develops between these two outcasts. (At least one reviewer assumes that Flint is straight. Why? Because Flint looks and acts like a heterosexual? Because he fantasizes about a woman in a bikini? He may well be teasing Harry, whose erotic intentions are unexpressed but are surely not undetected by the observant Flint.)

The unrelenting focus on Harry and Flint makes the film seem like a Robinson Crusoe story, for the two men have to reconstruct their lives on their own. Flint, it turns out, has a real gift for interior decoration. Harry watches him and listens to his stories in wonder and longing. In any other setting, Harry would have no chance to capture Flint's attention. But in this case, he has rescued the older man who repays Harry with an ease and assurance that calms and liberates him.

Bernard Hill plays Flint like the veteran actor he is. His Flint is a man who cannot afford to be rigid and is willing to pay the price of opening himself up to the world. His tattoos are the marks the world has made on him. He wears his feelings on his skin, so to speak. He has played many roles and accepts the scripts life hands him. Although Flint never says so, Harry apparently becomes a challenge, a kind of project. Can Flint free Harry's spirit?

John Hannah's Harry is so unapproachable that only in this setting can it be imagined that he would be forced to come out of his shell. Even when he finds Flint on the beach, it takes him several moments to muster the will to excavate him from the sand. The Welsh coast setting suits his austere, bleak personality. In truth, he needs warming much more than Flint.

The most charming thing about Flint is his lack of preconceptions. He takes life as it is, including Harry with his large dark red birthmark covering the center of his face—a fitting counterpart to Flint's gaudy tattoos. Director Chris Newby could easily have played this odd couple relationship for laughs. It is amusing. But it is not a cartoon—more like an adult fantasy, with Flint acting as the ideal parent.

The curious thing about John Hannah's performance is that he does not make it easy to like Harry. There is, for example, Harry's harangue against good-looking young people: "I could see trains run over 'em until they're bacon. I just love it when planes crash." Most people would probably lose patience with Harry long before Flint does. But then Flint needs an audience as much as Harry craves a lover. And entertaining for Flint is tantamount to making love—a fact that Harry, so wrapped up in his own feelings, takes a long time to recognize. Hannah plays Harry as aggressively aloof even as he desires Flint. It is a good choice, expressing Harry's fear of rejection and his need to form a kind of armor around himself. Of course, this armor is precisely what cuts him off from experience. It prevents him from becoming sentimental, however—a good thing in a story which could easily have become cloying.

The remote seaside setting contributes to the feeling that these characters have gotten beyond the conventional boundaries of society. Relationships are not structured as straight or gay. There are no rules except for those the men agree to observe. When the nervous Harry comes upon Flint robbing a cottage, it is clear that the two men have created their own world out of the desirable parts of the world they came from. The burglary scene is a reminder of the "real world," in which the men must find a way to survive. Harry realizes that Flint's stealing will eventually lead to the discovery of their cottage and that they will have to move on. He would prefer they keep a lower profile. But Flint's career is petty crime; he expects to abandon the cottage—or at least, he is not surprised when he is forced to do so. His life has been a series of adjustments and moves that have kept him limber and resourceful.

For Flint, his adventure with Harry is just part of what it means to live in the world and to take his chances. The film's title comes from his observation that the birthmark on Harry's face reminds him of the shape of Madagascar on a map. Harry's face is an island, and it has isolated him; but it is also the world, and Flint accepts it.

The movie has a marvelous ending. The two men have had to run away from the cottage. Will they split up? Start over again? How strong is their relationship? They embrace in a cold windy landscape—once again exposed to the elements as they were at the beginning of the film. They huddle together to create as much warmth as possible. Then Harry slips under Flint's sweater—re-enacting the scene at the beginning of the film when he had tried to join the coupling males. Flint laughs and wonders where Harry picked up such a trick. That Harry has any experience to draw on startles and pleases Flint. The two men do have each other and are as close to getting under each other's skins as can be imagined.

—*Carl Rollyson*

CREDITS

Harry: John Hannah
Flint: Bernard Hill
Adonis: Mark Anthony

Origin: Great Britain
Released: 1995
Production: Julie Baines for a Dan Films production; released by International Film Circuit
Direction: Chris Newby
Screenplay: Chris Newby
Cinematography: Oliver Curtis
Editing: Chris Newby, Annabel Ware
Production design: Paul Cross
Art direction: Rachel Robertson
Costumes: Annie Symons
Sound: Mark Holding
Casting: Simone Ireland
MPAA rating: Unrated
Running Time: 96 minutes

REVIEWS

Los Angeles Times. August 24, 1996, p. F6.
New York Times. August 23, 1996, p. C16.
Sight and Sound. February, 1996, p. 48.
Village Voice. August 27, 1996, p. 56.

Magic Hunter; Buvos Vadosz

Box Office: $46,810

Hungary's Eldiko Enyedi is best-known for her debut film, *My Twentieth Century* (1990), a meditation on the 20th century's effect on women. Enyedi's latest film, *Magic Hunter*, is even more ambitious, but, in the end, maddeningly elliptical. For viewers ill-versed in the history of the spread of Christianity throughout Europe, the film's full meaning will seem tantalizingly out-of-reach.

Enyedi bases *Magic Hunter* on a European folk legend in which a hunter is given seven magic bullets by the Devil. Each is guaranteed to hit its mark, but the seventh hits the target of the Devil's choosing. In the film, Max (Gary Kemp), a modern-day police sharpshooter in Budapest who doubts his prowess, is given the magic bullets. Assigned to protect a visiting Russian chess master, however, Max finds that his Faustian bargain has compromised both his own conscience and the love of his wife, Eva (Sadie Frost).

Alexander Kaidanovsky, who plays Maxim, died of a heart attack in December, 1995 at the age of 49.

Time moves back and forth in *Magic Hunter* between this story in the present and scenes in medieval Europe at the time of the transition from pagan worship to Christianity, where Max's salvation lies. In Enyedi's script, written with Laszlo Laszlo Revesz, this past shoots a metaphorical arrow into the present, an arrow which provides the solution to modern-day Faustian conundrums like Max's. "We people living today have done all we can to put ourselves in mortal danger and only a miracle can save us," Enyedi writes in the production notes. "The problem is that we believe in everything but miracles. And the solution, the escape from the trap which we have built for ourselves, is our past, our culture, if only we could read it." Unfortunately, Enyedi's lofty goal does not find its clearest expression in *Magic Hunter.*

The film begins with Eva telling the folktale of the magic hunter to their daughter—whose knowledge of the tale ultimately saves the day. Max's life reflects the folktale. Assigned to shoot a kidnapper holding a young woman hostage, Max misses and shoots the woman, wounding her seriously.

Shaken, Max accepts the magic bullets from a colleague (Peter Vallai) so that he will pass a marksmanship test on the police shooting range. Unaware of their true power, however, Max wastes them until he has only the seventh bullet remaining.

Meanwhile, the police give Max a chance to redeem himself by assigning him to the visiting chess player, Maxim (Alexander Kaidanovsky). Max's boss tells him that Maxim has turned down protection for himself, but that, because of threats on Maxim's life, Max should tail him whenever the master appears in public.

Intercut with this story are the flashbacks to medieval Hungary, in which the pagan beliefs of simple village folk and new Christian doctrine are united in shrines which combine the villagers' worship of pagan goddesses with the new concept of the Virgin Mary.

Back in the present, Max tails Maxim to his chess matches and then to the park. In the park, Maxim strikes up a conversation with Eva, who is watching her daughter play. Eva, feeling abandoned by Max, is attracted to Maxim, and Max must watch this flirtation develop.

As the strains in Eva's and Max's marriage build, their confrontation with the consequences of Max's bargain with the Devil looms. Their daughter manages to get a hold of the seventh bullet, and this finally precipitates a crisis solved by a meeting of past and present. It is ultimately their daughter's generation, haunted by the violence of the present but illuminated by the traditions and discoveries of the past, which saves the day.

Enyedi's slow, elliptical style often employs a kind of free association among images as a means of transition be-

CREDITS

Max: Gary Kemp
Eva: Sadie Frost
Maxim: Alexander Kaidanovsky
Kaspar: Peter Vallai
Lili: Alexandra Wasscher

Origin: France, Hungary, and Switzerland
Released: 1994
Production: Andras Hamori and Wieland Schulz-Keil for a UGC Images, Vega Films, and Budapest Filmstudio production; released by Shadow Distribution
Direction: Ildiko Enyedi
Screenplay: Ildiko Enyedi, Laszlo Laszlo Reverz
Cinematography: Tibor Mathe
Editing: Maria Rigo
Production design: Attila Ferenczfy-Kovacs
Costume design: Gyorgi Szakacs
Music: Gregorio Paniagua
MPAA rating: Unrated
Running Time: 106 minutes

tween the different locations and eras. This technique is frustratingly opaque, however, just as often as it is provocative. Occasionally Enyedi's Eisensteinian metaphors work brilliantly (an acorn being planted indicates that the seed of salvation for Max has been planted in the past), but often they are simply incomprehensible to the uninitiated viewer. Enyedi's predilection for these flourishes, combined with her double-narrative structure, makes the film impenetrable at some of its key dramatic moments.

English actors Kemp and Frost, dubbed into Hungarian, and Russian stage star Kaidanovsky each give fine, nuanced performances. Kemp as a man in spiritual crisis and Kaidanovsky as a smooth, confident intellectual play well off each other, while Frost plays Eva as a woman in whom motherhood, sensuality, and intellectual and emotional needs are not incompatible.

Still, *Magic Hunter* remains a demanding, dauntingly intellectual work, in which historical forces, chance, and the wisdom and folly of the ages play with the lives and desires of modern characters. Only Enyedi's most ardent fans will find satisfaction in this highly allusive and complex film.

—*Paul Mittelbach*

REVIEWS

Los Angeles Times. July 5, 1996, p. F10.

Man of the Year

He was a centerfold who revealed everything ... but the truth.—Movie tagline

"Ruefully funny . . . Hilarious . . . A first-rate cast!"—Kevin Thomas, *Los Angeles Times*

"A rollicking, hilarious mock-documentary . . . a joy ride!"—Jeff Britton, *Update*

Box Office: $209,935

Dirk Shafer is a writer, director, actor, and model with a lot of talent, not to mention that he has (as his friend Vivian states) "a set of pecs you could hang a winter coat on." The body and the face got Dirk Shafer to be a *Playgirl* Man of the Year several years ago. His talent got him to make *Man of the Year*, a witty and wise quasi-documentary which did quite well on the film festival circuit.

This independent, low-budget film uses a tried-and-true approach: it is a mock documentary a la *This is Spinal Tap* (1984) and *Fear of a Black Hat* (1994). Dirk Shafer tells his own story—of being a gay man who becomes a sex symbol to millions of women—through simple "talking heads" interviews intercut with dramatizations of true-life events. With the exception of Shafer and his best friend Vivian Paxton, the real-life roles are played by actors. Some of the names are changed, and some of the real-life events are embellished or shifted, but Shafer remains basically true to his real story. At the time of its release, some critics complained that Shafer should have actually made a documentary instead of scripting all of the interviews, and using actors to portray people who are still alive and might have been willing to speak on camera. *Boxoffice* magazine stated that "the film leaves the viewer with no idea of what anybody actually feels about anything." That doesn't seem entirely true, though. Shafer may not be Shakespeare, but he does touch on his own feelings and the feelings of those around him as he lived a double life.

Vivian Paxton, Shafer's friend, provides much of the exposition: Dirk had moved to Los Angeles to work in films, and had jobs as a driver, a production assistant, and other low-paying, dead-end positions. Though he had become frustrated at the inactivity in his career, he had also been working out at the gym and was getting "buff." For a lark, some friends sent a picture of Shafer to *Playgirl* magazine, and before he knew it a photographer was taking his picture. The sweet-natured Shafer, claiming that "I wanted to be everything they wanted me to be,", ended up doing some nude shots which entered him in the *Playgirl* Man of the Year contest. (A rather funny explanation from the magazine's publicist played here by comedy veteran Cynthia Szegeti, describes the intricacies of nude vs. non-nude photography in the magazine.)

During the next several months, a voice mail ad in *Playgirl* touting the candidates for "Man of the Year" helped Shafer to win the title: according to Paxton and Shafer, he was so nice to the women that called his line that his responsiveness garnered him a huge following and he "inadvertently campaigned for the job."

Now, just for a moment, let us assume that Shafer truly is such a sweet guy that his sensitivity to women on the phone line, and the fact that "I just wanted to give them what they wanted" are true. There are moments when an objective audience member might sit back and say, "if this guy is so darn sweet and humble, how come he is making a film about how incredibly attractive he is?" Good point. But, just when it seems that Shafer may cross the line into egomania, he pulls the audience back with his gentle, self-deprecating humor. For example, a psychologist tells the audience that Shafer suffers from "passive-aggressive exhibitionist syndrome," which in context is a charming moment that shows Shafer can laugh at himself. Another example is when his mother (remember, all of these characters are played by actors) deadpans that when Dirk was young he bought a bunch of trophies in order to look good, and she decided that "they must be his, because he paid for them." The self-deprecation might help undercut any irritation the audience might feel for Shafer's egocentrism.

Of course, an audience can get away with being jealous by dismissing Shafer as egocentric. Is he egocentric? So what? Let's face it, the guy is better looking that almost anybody, he seems to be a talented and sensitive guy, and he pulled off the hoax of the century. (Okay, it isn't the hoax of the century, but you have to at least admit it took guts to go as far as Shafer did.) Who wouldn't be jealous?

But the plot thickens. Before he knew it, Shafer had won the Man of the Year contest, and was appearing on "The Maury Povich Show," "The Montel Williams Show," and various other programs; he started doing lots of modeling work, and was adored by millions of *Playgirl* readers, the majority of which were presumed to be women. Shafer's sense of irony is keen: He says that the *Playgirl* editors would "tell me what kind of image they wanted me to portray," and that he was trying to appeal to "today's thinking woman," but then found himself winning the "Best Buns" competition on "The Phil Donahue Show." He was probably wondering what "thinking women" were thinking about when they watched.

Shafer stayed in the closet to protect his "Man of the Year" status, and it became difficult to keep up the image. Hiding his homosexuality became even more difficult after starting a relationship with a man named Mike. "I don't know, maybe what I was doing wasn't so harmless after all," Shafer innocently states.

Events conspired to make Shafer too aware that he was a gay man posing (literally) as a straight one. One of his best friends got sick and died of AIDS. His relationship began to be affected by the deceit. "I'm sick of living in your closet," Mike tells him. "I felt like I was being rejected by everyone because I was gay, Dirk included," says Mike to the camera. In the film, Shafer can take it no longer, and tells the producer (Mindy Sterling) of a silly daytime talk show that he is gay. "I can't jeopardize the integrity of the 'Cindee' show," the producer tells him, in what must be the film's sharpest satirical comment, after all of the sleazy television talk shows to which Shafer and the audience have been subjected. Since the "Cindee" show is fictitious, it is unclear whether in real life Shafer came out to one of the real television talk show producers, or just wishes that he had. In any case, he stopped living the lie—and for the purposes of *Man of the Year*, Shafer's coming out makes for a touching climax to the film.

The story is framed around several scenes where Shafer was the "dream date" for the winner of a *Playgirl* contest. The date, played out in several black-and-white scenes, is the most charming part of the film. It is shot like a home movie, and is winsome and funny, especially when the date comes to Shafer's hotel room, and Mike has to hide in the shower. The ending, where his date proves wiser than Shafer assumed, is smart and sweet.

Shafer appears natural and comfortable as an actor, and has a lack of pretense in front of the camera that is disarming. The scenes where he is being "interviewed," while not terribly emotionally revealing, do provide some insight into his eager-to-please personality and how it both helped and hurt him. Similarly, Vivian Paxton is a natural in front of the camera, and tells her part of the story gleefully, but also with a breezy lack of pretension that sets the audience at ease.

If there is anything problematic in *Man of the Year*, it is primarily in the performances of the other actors. Several try too hard to be interesting characters, so much so that with the verisimilitude provided by real-life characters Shafer and Paxton, these actors merely look like actors. They are not bad, however, and several fare better than others. Ultimately, Shafer could have gotten more mileage from the satire if his actors had not worked so hard to let the audience know this is a satirical story.

CREDITS

Dirk Shafer: Dirk Shafer
Vivian Paxton: Vivian Paxton
Mike: Michael Ornstein
Angela: Mary Stein

Origin: USA
Released: 1995
Production: Matt Keener for an Artisan Productions; released by Seventh Art
Direction: Dirk Shafer
Screenplay: Dirk Shafer
Cinematography: Stephen Timberlake
Editing: Barry Silver, Ken Solomon
Music: Peitor Angell
Production designer: Michael Mueller
MPAA rating: Unrated
Running Time: 85 minutes

While this film is not going to bring audiences further along the continuum of understanding the vicissitudes of coming out of the closet, or of sexual objectification, or of love, family, and friendship, it sheds a modest light on all the above topics. And it does so with a dash of warmth and a healthy dose of good humor. What's wrong with a little bit of insight combined with some warmth and humor? *Man of the Year* doesn't promise more than it delivers: it is the quirky true story of a man's double life, simply told. And that seems to be just about enough for one small film.

—*Kirby Tepper*

Manny & Lo

When was the last time you saw a movie about women taking charge of their lives?—Movie tagline

"A perfectly pitched oddball comedy that reveals a wholly original sensibility."—Kenneth Turan, *Los Angeles Times*

"Odd but touching tale. A runaway success!"—Jami Bernard, *The New York Daily News*

"A warm, fabulously unsentimental comedy about two young sisters on their own. One of the finds of the year."—Caryn James, *The New York Times*

"A great tonic for the noisy stupid summer blockbusters!"—Dennis Dermody, *Paper*

Box Office: $499,048

Manny and Lo, the first feature from writer-director Lisa Krueger, falls within the gambit of many movie genres—road picture, women's movie, family film—but manages to transcend them all. When we first encounter 11-year-old Amanda ("Manny," played by Scarlett Johansson) and 16-year-old Laurel ("Lo," played by Aleksa Palladino), they are camped out on a suburban lawn. Quickly, our expectations about what this scene implies—kids camped out in their own back yard—are undermined as the two girls, and their station wagon, are chased off by the owner of the manicured lawn and the perfect suburban home it surrounds. Manny and Lo, we soon realize, are girls on the run, orphaned sisters who have escaped their respective foster homes in order to preserve some sense of family by being together. When their mother died, they hid her car, so that it could not be traced. They survive on the road now by siphoning gasoline, lifting food from convenience store shelves, and breaking into model homes, where they spend most nights. "We just stuck to Lo's number one rule," Manny informs us in voice-over narration. "Keep moving and you won't get nailed."

"The No. 1 rule is keep moving and you won't get nailed."—Lo to her sister Manny

Anyone who cared to do so could spot the sisters as outsiders: street tough Lo sports the world's worst bleach job, and the preternaturally mature Manny wears chipped blue nail polish and too much plastic jewelry. But the resourceful duo does quite well together, in fact, despite their homelessness. The poignancy of their plight is pointed up without sentimentality: Manny plainly misses her mother, but she satisfies her need by conjuring up the dead woman—a substance-abusing single mom—by spraying a borrowed bedroom with the deodorant her mother used to wear. And sometimes, because the deodorant is stolen, of course, Manny has to make do with a substitute fragrance.

Soon, however, the pair is confronted with a problem that cannot be so easily resolved: the promiscuous Lo is pregnant, and she has managed to ignore her pregnancy so long that she is now forced to deal with it. Again, Krueger skillfully forestalls potential bathos by having Lo stalk out of the abortion clinic that has rejected her, wearing only her paper examination gown. Manny, who has been in charge of the narrative, drolly commenting on her sister's actions, now takes charge of Lo. It has been clear from the outset that she is the more responsible one.

Manny and Lo opens on a blurry scene, one we share with Manny, who is gazing at the world around her through a distorting magnifying glass while asking, "Did you ever dream about someone before you saw them in life?" When she and Lo visit a baby furnishings store and she spots the white uniformed, seemingly authoritative Elaine (Mary Kay Place), Manny finds the idealized maternal figure she has been dreaming of, as well as, it appears, the answer to Lo's nascent problem. Lo agrees that someone who knows as much about babies as Elaine—a salesperson who, unbidden, dispenses her wisdom to any uncertain customer—could come in handy during childbirth. So once again the girls satisfy their needs by stealing what is required: they kidnap Elaine at gunpoint and take her to the isolated, unoccupied vacation cabin where they have taken up residence.

Although they leave Elaine's legs manacled in a locked bicycle chain, Manny and Lo remove her gag. Elaine, in high dudgeon, refuses to eat. But she cannot stop herself from talking, and her prim appeals to propriety begin to wear away the protective veneer the girls (whom Elaine calls by their given names) have acquired. Manny is converted long before her older sister. One has a sense that not only is Manny's need for someone like Elaine greater, she also has a far more mature understanding of human foibles than does Lo. Elaine's protestations to the contrary, no one seems to be looking for her very hard. Gradually it becomes clear that this middle-aged woman is as much an outcast as the sisters, her bogus nurse's uniform her bulwark against loneliness and lack of social acceptance. While such revelations seem to foster a kinship between Elaine and Manny, they only make the skeptical Lo more skeptical.

Feature debut for director/writer Lisa Krueger whose brother, Tom, is the film's cinematographer.

After a time, the girls realize that Elaine is no longer trying to escape; indeed, when the cottage's rightful owner comes to take possession of his property, Elaine takes him hostage so that he will not be able to spoil her fantasy. Plainly, she needs Manny and Lo just as much as they need her. Shuffling around the kitchen in her manacles like a geisha, she dispenses homemade hot dish along with advice to her ad hoc family. Her impersonation of a traditional mother verges on caricature, but the character flaws that make her a fraud in Lo's eyes do not, for the more credulous—or forgiving—Manny, detract from Elaine's worth as wish fulfillment. Fuming at Elaine's hypocrisy, Lo demands, "Whoever heard of a hostage taking a hostage?"—but Manny seems merely intrigued by this additional evidence of Elaine's desire to perpetuate the situation.

Elaine sets about solving the sisters' problems, thereby addressing her own. As she officiously declares, "If you two benefit in the process, well, that can't be helped." She may cut a smaller figure than she would have the rest of the world believe she does, but Elaine still comes through, not only supplying common sense prenatal guidance, but eventually helping Lo deliver a healthy baby. Elaine represents the kind of all-knowing, all-forgiving parent Manny and Lo have never known; her very disconnectedness from the mainstream makes her the perfect figure to fulfill this role in their thus far rootless, undomesticated lives. And behind the facade of this counterfeit nurse and wannabe mother is an individual both capable and loving who finds fulfillment, improbably enough, in rescuing her captors. *Manny and Lo* is a fractured fairy tale that gives a whole new meaning to female bonding.

As Elaine, Mary Kay Place is a marvel, lending dignity and poignancy to a character who might, in less expert hands, be reduced to mere parody. Place is best remembered for her portrayal, 20 years ago, of country singer Loretta Haggers in the quirky sitcom "Mary Hartman, Mary Hartman," and for her part in the ensemble cast of 1983's *The Big Chill,* in which she also played a woman, no longer so young, whose driving ambition is to have children. Both were roles, like that of Elaine, that called on Place to project warmth and genuineness onto offbeat characters.

And Place is well matched in *Manny and Lo* by two young actresses who manage to convey the sense, like Place, that their characters are more than they seem. The script plainly calls for actors who can be simultaneously wise and naive, tough and vulnerable. Johansson, who previously appeared in *If Lucy Fell* (1995), is more adept at this enactment than Palladino, for whom *Manny and Lo* was a film

AWARDS AND NOMINATIONS

Independent Spirit Awards 1997 Nominations: First Feature (Krueger), Actress (Johansson), Supporting Actress (Place), First Screenplay (Krueger)

CREDITS

Manny: Scarlett Johansson
Lo: Aleksa Palladino
Elaine: Mary Kay Place
Mr. Humphreys: Paul Guilfoyle
Joey: Glenn Fitzgerald

Origin: USA
Released: 1996
Production: Dean Silvers, Marlen Hecht for a Pope Entertainment Group production; released by Sony Pictures Classics
Direction: Lisa Krueger
Screenplay: Lisa Krueger
Cinematography: Tom Krueger
Editing: Colleen Sharp
Music: John Lurie
Production design: Sharon Lomofsky
Costumes: Jennifer Parker
Sound: Irin Straus
Casting: Ellen Parks
MPAA rating: R
Running Time: 90 minutes

debut. But then, Johansson has the advantage of supplying the film's voice-over and perspective, and viewers are thus enabled to enter more fully into her experience of the events that make up the sisters' adventures. Hers is a point of view at once funny and sad, her commentary a combination of innocence and detachment (after all, it is Lo who has the most urgent problem, the one propelling the action).

If Palladino's performance stays too long on one note—reacting to all of Elaine's blandishments with scorn—it is perhaps because it is her part to present the more "adult" reaction to Elaine, one the older woman has clearly experienced many times before. Lo has had bad experiences with maternal figures, both her own mother and the foster mothers she has known. Small wonder she holds Elaine at bay, while at the same time trying hard to avoid reckoning with her own incipient maternity. Small wonder she must accept one in order to accept the other.

Manny and Lo is a product of Robert Redford's Sundance Institute, founded to foster just such independent films as this. The sensibility Krueger displays in her maiden effort is deft, fresh, and oddly (for a fairy tale) true to life. As Manny reminds us again at the end of the film, reality can seem like a dream come true. When we want (or in Lo's case, need) something or someone badly enough, we can bring them to life through a sheer exercise of will—which in the case of *Manny and Lo* means that two juvenile girls can, on impulse, abduct an adult woman, who then turns out to be their salvation. Improbably, it works.

—Lisa Paddock

REVIEWS

Los Angeles Times. August 2, 1996, p. F1.
New York Times. July 26, 1996, p. C3.
Newsweek. August 5, 1996, p. 73.
People. July 29, 1996, p. 17.
Variety. February 5, 1996, p. 61.

Mars Attacks!

Nice planet. We'll take it.—Movie tagline
"Bizarre!"—Kenneth Turan, *Los Angeles Times*
"Demented!"—Steven Rea, *Philadelphia Inquirer*
"Warped!"—Jeff Craig, *Sixty Second Preview*
"Twisted!"—Mike Clark, *USA Today*
"This year's coolest movie by far!"—Barbara & Scott Siegel, *WNEW-FM*

Box Office: $28,075,674

"Unique" is a word that certainly applies to the films of producer/director Tim Burton. The characters which populate his films are an undeniably unusual bunch, sometimes darkly fantastic and other times just whimsically odd. This rather bizarre club includes Pee-Wee Herman (1985's *Pee-Wee's Big Adventure*), the spirited spirit in *Beetlejuice* (1988), the unusually handy *Edward Scissorhands* (1990), the various curious residents of Gotham City (1989's *Batman* and its sequels), the fanciful creatures in *The Nightmare Before Christmas* (1993) and *James and the Giant Peach* (1996), and a director who perpetrated such schlock as *Glen or Glenda? (I Changed My Sex)*, and *Plan 9 from Outer Space* (1994's *Ed Wood*). *Mars Attacks!* adds to that list an army of mischievous little galactic goons (along with some earthly ones), whose deadly antics are offset by their comical appearance and movements and the fact that they wreak havoc in this zany bit of fluff. *Mars Attacks!* is cinematic cotton candy, offering an impish "Boo!" and a wink.

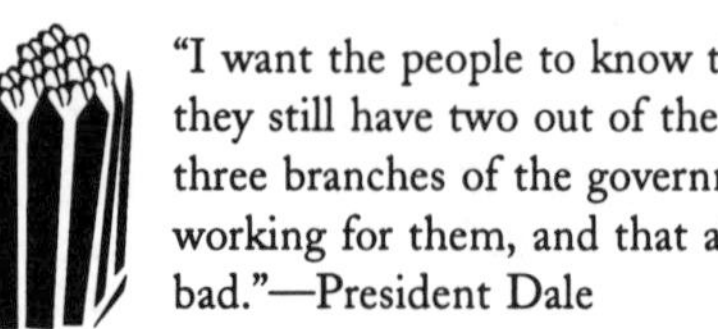
"I want the people to know that they still have two out of the three branches of the government working for them, and that ain't bad."—President Dale

Since the success of *Ed Wood*, Burton wanted to do a project which would be an amusing homage to the kind of low-budget sci-fi fare he enjoyed as a kid. All he needed was a peg to hang it on. Ideas for films have come from many different sources, but Burton's star-heavy extravaganza *Mars Attacks!* is only the second major film to spring from a most unusual one: bubble-gum trading cards. (1987's obnoxious *The Garbage Pail Kids* was also based on a set of cards put out by Topps, Inc., and featured characters such as Foul Phil and Valerie Vomit.) The film takes its title and inspiration from a set of 54 cards of the same name that Topps put out in 1962. Parents were uneasy to downright appalled by the graphic violence, gore

Martin Short thinks his date Lisa Marie is quite a looker, but will soon find out her attributes are not of this earth in *Mars Attacks!*

and scantily-clad damsels in distress, and Topps pulled the cards in short order. (The set originally sold for a nickel, but, because of its short time on the market, it is reportedly now worth over $1,000.) "I've always loved the science-fiction movies of the '50s," says Burton. "Part of what I like about the cards is they're real kids' stuff—pretty over the top." That is certainly an accurate description of his *Mars Attacks!*

The film's first scene takes place in Kansas, where citizens are not having to ride a twister to Oz in order to witness strange and unusual things. The townspeople think they smell someone barbecuing, but it turns out that they have caught a whiff of a stampeding herd of flaming cows. Clearly, something is amiss. Shortly thereafter, photographs from the Hubble telescope indicate that flying saucers from Mars are headed towards Earth. The saucers look like shiny, whirling hubcaps, a clear and evocative bow to the films Burton has such an affection for. What are their intentions? The superficial and all-too-vacuous U.S. President James Dale (Jack Nicholson) confers with a group of experts to decide how to deal with the impending crisis. Blowhard General Decker (Rod Steiger) explodes with violent enthusiasm for an all-out nuclear annihilation of the extraterrestrial tourists, while the mild-mannered General Casey (Paul Winfield) is more cautious, and the cerebral Professor Donald Kessler (Pierce Brosnan looking very much like Fred MacMurray) loftily states that the Martians are obviously advanced and therefore not barbaric. Dale sides with Kessler, which nearly gives Decker a stroke. Anxious to hit the right tone in his fireside chat announcing the martian's arrival, Dale hopes to sound both profound and homey—"Abraham Lincoln meets 'Leave it to Beaver.'" A model of self-absorption, Dale states that his momentous news ranks right up there with his marriage to the First Lady (Glenn Close) and his becoming a father. He reveals that proof has been found of intelligent life in outer space. "Glad they've got it somewhere," retorts his daughter Taffy (Natalie Portman).

During an interview that insipid, fashion-obsessed reporter Nathalie Lake (Sarah Jessica Parker) is conducting with Kessler, the Martian Ambassador interrupts their signal and appears on the screen. He frightens and confuses everyone with his bulbous green brain, pop-eyes, and exclamations of "Ack! Ack!," which sound like he either has a hairball or is, for whatever reason, in need of the Heimlich maneuver. Dale's response is a profound "Yikes!," and the First Lady states emphatically that she is not going to allow "that thing" to come into her house and use the Van Buren china. Kessler placidly reassures everyone that the Martian's large brain is a clear indication that it is an enlightened and peaceful being. Plans are made to welcome the ambassador and his entourage when they land in the Nevada desert. The country looks to the skies with uncertainty, and braces itself for the aliens' arrival. In Las Vegas, a kooky, New-Age, recently-recovered alcoholic named Barbara Land (Annette Bening) asserts to the members of her twelve-step program and her husband, Art (also played by Jack Nicholson), that the higher life forms are coming to show us the way out of our miserable problems. She punctuates her statements with bursts of hysterical giggles. (Bening and Bros-

CREDITS

President Dale/Art Land: Jack Nicholson
Marsha Dale: Glenn Close
Barbara Land: Annette Bening
Donald Kessler: Pierce Brosnan
Jerry Ross: Martin Short
Martian Girl: Lisa Marie
Nathalie Lake: Sarah Jessica Parker
Gen. Decker: Rod Steiger

Origin: USA
Released: 1996
Production: Tim Burton and Larry Franco; released by Warner Bros.
Direction: Tim Burton
Screenplay: Jonathan Gems; based on the Mars Attacks! Topps trading cards
Cinematography: Peter Suschitzky
Editing: Chris Lebenzon
Music: Danny Elfman
Production design: Wynn Thomas
Art direction: John Dexter
Set design: Richard Berger
Costume design: Colleen Atwood
Sound: Dennis Maitland Sr.
Stunt coordinator: Joe Dunne
MPAA rating: PG-13
Running Time: 110 minutes

nan are really the only consistently humorous actors in the film who are not created by the wonderful work of Industrial Light & Magic and Warner Digital Studios). Meanwhile, back in Kansas, a patriotic trailer-park family which has great affection for guns and only one of their sons, is filled with pride as that son goes off in uniform to greet the Martians.

When the spaceship arrives, Casey is there to roll out the red carpet, surrounded by the army, the media, and hordes of eager spectators. The Martians say that they have come in peace, and all goes well until they open fire and enthusiastically incinerate Casey, newsman Jason Stone (Michael J.Fox), and many of the soldiers and onlookers. Fearing political fallout, the president and his horny press secretary (Martin Short) float the idea that the incident was merely a "cultural misunderstanding." At this point, the leisurely pace of the film begins to gather a slight bit of steam. Giving the Martians a second chance, Congress agrees to hear a speech by their ambassador. Seconds into his talk (which is translated by some sort of unpredictable contraption), the congressmen are reduced to smoldering red and green skeletons. Soon after, the president's press secretary invites a creepy, Marilyn Monroe-like bombshell (memorably played by Lisa Marie) to join him for a tryst in the Kennedy room, but the rendezvous ends rather badly when this alien-in-disguise bites off his finger and beats him to death. The president is almost killed, and the First Lady is crushed underneath the Nancy Reagan chandelier. The Martians then go on a gleeful, globe-trotting killing spree of foreign officials and others, and destroy numerous treasured landmarks around the world.

Back in Las Vegas, singer Tom Jones is in the middle of his act when he turns to find some tiny, swivel-hipped Martian backup singers "Ack! Ack!"-ing behind him. They go on another rampage, and Jones and Barbara Land escape in an airplane with the help of a boxer turned casino-greeter (Jim Brown). Soon after the president is slain, the aliens attack Kansas. They are just about to kill the dotty grandmother of the aforementioned family (Sylvia Sidney, who made her first film seventy years ago) when the yodelling voice of Slim Whitman on her stereo makes the Martians' heads explode into green goop. She and the family's less-favored son (Lucas Haas) lead a force of vehicles across country, blaring Whitman's music and thereby saving the world. The film ends with Tom Jones emerging from a cave in the desert and breaking into a joyful rendition of "It's Not Unusual," accompanied by the chirping and dancing of enraptured birds and animals.

With a budget that Ed Wood could only have dreamed of, Burton has aimed for a fun, fond remembrance of the enjoyably-bad alien-invasion films of the 1950s and 1960s. Those films (and the *Mars Attacks!* trading cards) were produced during the height of the Cold War, when people were in a constant state of twitchiness about the threat of an enemy attack, fearful that shiny technology would land upon their heads with terrifyingly-destructive force. These films readily found an audience in a society growing up with that ever-present fear. When the earthlings beat the aliens in the final reel, it must have served, in a small, odd way, to boost public morale. Young people enjoyed being spooked by the films' cheesy creepiness. Today, even younger audiences are more sophisticated and expect more (especially for the price of today's admission), and many may be unfamiliar and/or unenamored with the conventions of the genre that Burton is recalling. In *Mars Attacks!*, there is never anything close to tension or terrifying menace, near-impossible things to achieve amidst the film's light, goofy atmosphere. One never fears for the safety of any of the characters, but merely watches their deaths with the same detached feeling he would have observing the deaths of characters in any other "cartoon." Burton's film is certainly impishly ludicrous, but it is never really more than modestly amusing. His attempt to make the film both homage and spoof has made it less effective and satisfying as either. Reviews were decidedly mixed, and the film made a less-than-expected $36 million in its first month and a half. Some may find *Mars Attacks!* pleasantly passable, but no one should expect anything out of this world.

—David L. Boxerbaum

REVIEWS

Boxoffice. February, 1997, p. 68.
The Chicago Tribune. December 13, 1996, p. 7A.
Entertainment Weekly. December 13, 1996, p. 58.
The Los Angeles Times. December 13, 1996, p. F14.
The New York Times. December 13, 1996, p. C5.
The New Yorker. December 16, 1996, p. 116.
Newsweek. December 23, 1996, p. 67.
People. December 23, 1996, p. 17.
Sight and Sound. March, 1997, p. 53.
USA Today. December 13, 1996, p. D4.
Variety. December 2, 1996, p. 66.
Village Voice. December 17, 1996, p. 73.
The Wall Street Journal. December 13, 1996, p. A12.
The Washington Post. December 13, 1996, p. WW50.

Marvin's Room

A story about the years that keep us apart . . . And the moments that bring us together.—Movie tagline

"A first rate experience! Rich and wonderfully funny! The acting is invigoratingly brilliant across the board."—Dennis Cunningham, *CBS-TV*

"Wonderfully life-affirming, deeply moving and funny! The cast is incredible. Leonardo DiCaprio sizzles."—Marshall Fine, *Gannett News Service*

"Sister acts simply don't get any better than Meryl Streep and Diane Keaton."—Bob Straus, *Los Angeles Daily News*

"The sublime Meryl Streep and Diane Keaton are alone worth the price of admission! This is truly the Year of the Woman in cinema. Don't miss it."—Andrew Sarris, *New York Observer*

"A film of rare magic! Funny and touching! Leonardo DiCaprio is explosively fine! Diane Keaton performs with dazzling humor and delicacy."—Peter Travers, *Rolling Stone*

"Two thumbs up!"—*Siskel & Ebert*

Box Office: $1,002,584

Based on a stage play by the late Scott McPherson, who died of complications from AIDS in 1992 at the age of thirty-three, *Marvin's Room* is a story of spiritual healing and of personal redemption. It serves as a testament to the powerful theme of the benefits of being a caretaker to the dying, or as the play calls it, "the gift of giving love"—even if that love is never reciprocated. Directed by first-timer Jerry Zaks, the film has difficulty transcending its theatrical roots and often feels more like a Hallmark Hall of Fame television production with a defiant sense of morbid humor. Still, the virtuosity of its stellar cast helps to overcome the sentimental thrust and meandering, uneven style of the film.

"He's been dying for 20 years. He's doing it real slow so I don't miss a thing."—Bessie about her father Marvin

Academy Award-winner Diane Keaton (*Annie Hall*, 1977) received another Oscar nomination for Best Actress for her portrayal of the sweet Bessie, an unmarried, selfless woman who has spent her life taking care of her eccentric Aunt Ruth (Gwen Verdon) and her bedridden father, Marvin (Hume Cronyn), in some suburban town in Florida. "He's dying real slow," Bessie says, "so I don't miss anything." But when Bessie visits the absentminded Dr. Wally (Robert De Niro in a surprisingly wacky comic turn) in search of a reason for her increasing fatigue, her bloodwork reveals that she has leukemia. Her only hope appears to be a bone marrow transplant and Bessie must call her estranged hairdresser sister, Lee (Meryl Streep), to ask for help.

Single mother Lee lives in Ohio with her two boys, the younger Charlie (Hal Scardino from *The Indian in the Cupboard*, 1996) and the troubled teenager, Hank (Leonardo DiCaprio). She is trying to get her life together with a degree in cosmetology, but first she must get Hank released from the mental institution where he has found himself after burning down the family home. The strong-willed and determined Lee has a difficult time relating to her rebellious son, perhaps because she sees too much of herself in the young man. When she visits Hank at the institution, he tells her, "They're not strapping me down anymore." Lee caustically replies, "Well, don't abuse that privilege."

Lee's reunion with her older sister is equally as strained. "Are you that old?" Bessie asks disbelievingly when she sees her sister for the first time in twenty years. Lee's stare unnerves Bessie and she quickly tries to cover up by adding, "Cause how old does that make me?" The plot thinly revolves around whether Hank will consent to the tests for bone marrow donor, but the real joy comes not from the suspense nor the outcome, but from the material's insistence on finding the humor and the love in the face of tragedy.

Ms. Streep plays the angry, cigarette-smoking Lee with a brittleness and self-determination that masks an underlying vulnerability. Her crumbling self-control is beautifully articulated in a scene where she restyles Bessie's wig that she wears to hide her baldness from the effects of chemotherapy treatment. Locked safely behind the bathroom door, Lee's composure gives way to heartache as she finally begins to cry over someone other than herself. Her fierce refusal to

AWARDS AND NOMINATIONS

Academy Award 1996 Nominations: Best Actress (Keaton)
Golden Globe Award 1997 Nominations: Best Actress-Drama (Streep)
Screen Actors Guild 1996 Nominations: Actress (Keaton), Supporting Actress (Verdon), Cast

give up the freedom that she feels she has won by leaving home so many years before slowly melts into an appreciation for the rewards of commitment that have given Bessie's life meaning. "I've had such love in my life," Bessie states simply.

Foregoing her trademark mannerisms—as well as all-star vanity—Diane Keaton imbues Bessie's virtuousness with a graceful dignity and a hauntingly delicate comic touch that echoes throughout the film. Her scenes with the talented Leonardo DiCaprio help to forge a tender bond and help the young man to move beyond his anger and resentment, but it is her interplay with Meryl Streep that resonates with honesty and with a chilling resentment. *Marvin's Room* marks the first time the two Oscar-winning actresses have worked together. According to Meryl Streep, she was originally slated to play the character of Bessie, but decided against doing another "Suffering Madonna" type of role. Her longtime friendship with producer Robert De Niro afforded her the luxury of changing parts, while at the same time being able to name the woman who would play her sister. She chose Diane Keaton.

Jerry Zaks, a veteran stage director of such things as *Guys and Dolls* and *Six Degrees of Separation*, has a great deal of difficulty juggling the varied moods of *Marvin's Room* and as a result, the film ends up being awkward and unfocused. The attempts to open up the settings, such as the joyriding on the beach scene, tend to undercut the inherent claustrophobia of the material and interrupts the intimacy of the play, while lines of dialogue sometimes state the self-evident. In addition, certain characters appear to have been inserted merely for a more varied comic relief, but they add little to the story, particularly the doddering Aunt Ruth, who spends her afternoons living the lives of her favorite soap opera characters.

Marvin's Room is a comic assault on despair and works best when it confines itself to the small, intimate moments. In the program notes to his off-Broadway play, Scott McPherson wrote: "My lover has AIDS. Our friends have AIDS. And we all take care of each other, the less sick caring for the more sick. At times, an unbelievably harsh fate is transcended by a simple act of love, by caring for one another." This is the moving legacy that the playwright has sought to leave behind with *Marvin's Room*. Reviews for the film were mixed and the box office receipts minimal.

—Patricia Kowal

CREDITS

Lee: Meryl Streep
Bessie: Diane Keaton
Hank: Leonardo DiCaprio
Dr. Wally: Robert De Niro
Marvin: Hume Cronyn
Ruth: Gwen Verdon
Bob: Dan Hedaya
Charlie: Hal Scardino

Origin: USA
Released: 1996
Production: Scott Rudin, Jane Rosenthal, Robert De Niro; A Scott Rudin/Tribecca Production, released by Miramax Films
Direction: Jerry Zaks
Screenplay: Scott McPherson, based on his play
Cinematography: Piotr Sobocinski
Editing: Jim Clark
Production design: David Gropman
Art direction: Peter Rogness
Costume design: Julie Weiss
Music: Rachel Portman
MPAA rating: PG-13
Running Time: 98 minutes

REVIEWS

Boxoffice. February, 1997, p. 66.
Chicago Tribune. January 16, 1997, p. 5.
Entertainment Weekly. December 20, 1996, p. 56.
Los Angeles Times. December 18, 1996, p. F1.
New York Times. December 18, 1996, p. C15.
New Yorker. January 20, 1997, p. 99.
Newsweek. January 13, 1997, p. 74.
People. December 23, 1996, p. 17.
Rolling Stone. December 26, 1996, p.207
Variety. December 9, 1996, p. 102.

Mary Reilly

Evil loves innocence.—Movie tagline

"A strong and memorable film."—Stephen Hunter, *The Baltimore Sun*

"An old-fashioned, romantic, horror story with a terrific cast."—Jim Ferguson, *The Prevue Channel*

"Exquisite cinematography, atmospheric direction, finely drawn performances, and a beautiful, fog-wet London mansion."—Stephen Talty, *Time-Out New York*

Box Office: $5,707,094

Director Stephen Frears (best known for *My Beautiful Laundrette* [1985], *The Grifters* [1990], and *Dangerous Liaisons* [1988]) knew from the start that it would be difficult to breathe new life into the oft-told Robert Louis Stevenson story of the mild-mannered Dr. Jekyll and his violent alter ego Mr. Hyde (John Malkovich). And I'm sure that he thought that telling the tale from the point of view of Jekyll's meek housemaid, Mary Reilly (Julia Roberts), as was done in the best-selling novel by Valerie Martin, seemed like just that spring breeze he needed. Unfortunately, it is precisely because the plot is so familiar to viewers that even this change can't prevent the film from just telling the same old story all over again.

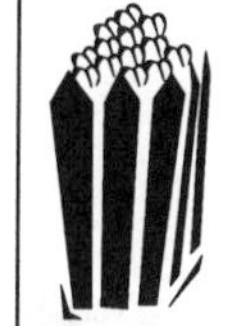

"I've never been in favor of control."—Mr. Hyde

This, however, is not to say that there aren't a few interesting things about *Mary Reilly*. For one thing the film is wonderfully atmospheric. Although filmed on a soundstage in Pinewood Studios, it successfully carries all the grayness, gloom, fog and filth of an unnamed British city in the beginnings of the industrial revolution. The unrelenting pall creates a perpetual twilight (or predawn, depending on one's psychological interpretation of the film) that makes the fact that Mary Reilly can make a garden bloom in the courtyard a positive miracle.

Many of the people behind the Academy Award-winning film *Dangerous Liaisons* also worked on *Mary Reilly*. Among them are director Frears, screenwriter Hampton, cinematographer Rousselot, production designer Craig, and producer Norma Heyman. Also repeating work in both films are Malkovich and Glenn Close in a small role.

Frears indicated that although Stevenson set his story in London, he was more interested in using the divided city of Edinburgh, Scotland as the backdrop for his film. With a high city and a low city, Edinburgh seemed a perfect symbol of Jekyll's divided soul. It's a great idea, but it only comes across in the film as there being a rich part of town and a poor part—and that could be in virtually any city. Only in this city, the gloom permeates all economic sections of the town.

Adding to the atmospherics is the gothic house created for Dr. Hyde by production designer Stuart Craig. It seems larger than life, with dark corners, cavernous corridors, and oversized staircases. And through the courtyard lies Dr. Jekyll's ominous laboratory and operating theater with its cold gray bricks and unusual hanging catwalk.

Into this oppressive atmosphere comes the young serving girl Mary Reilly who, amazingly, feels safe living there. Of course, considering Mary's background, an impoverished family where her mother worked and her abusive, alcoholic father (Michael Gambon) beat her senseless then locked her under the staircase with a ravenous rat who bites her, maybe the repressed and melancholy house of Dr. Jekyll does feel safe.

Here servants quietly go about their business, day in and day out. It is their lot in life, they have few options, they are grateful for their jobs, and they have come to expect little more than to hope for a kind employer. Mary fits in perfectly here, up at dawn, scrubbing the stoops, polishing the brass nameplates and following the butler's (George Cole) orders. She accepts and appreciates what little happiness she can find. But this intrinsic, honest innocence is what will eventually attract the attention of her employer, Dr. Jekyll. It will be she who unleashes the very proper Dr.'s repressed emotions, especially his restrained sexuality.

What Dr. Jekyll doesn't realize is that Mary may seem to be a delicate young woman, but she has a steel spine and a strong sense of loyalty to the doctor. Because of this, the shy girl is constantly spying on both Jekyll and his "new" lab assistant Mr. Hyde, following them about, even into the forbidden laboratory. Julia Roberts proves quite adept at showing both the vulnerability that would be natural for a woman in her position in 18th century Britain as well as a stoic braveness. Her downcast glances and ethereal beauty make her seem like a skittish but basically trusting colt, abused by her owners but with nowhere else to go.

The object of her loyalty, however, is not so engaging. John Malkovich's Jekyll and Hyde, the symbol of man's psychological struggle between good and evil, his id and conscience, unfortunately, provides little of the romantic tension needed to make the film rise above its slow pace. Yes, we know Dr. Jekyll is attracted to Mary. Yes, we know he is repressed, trapped by the social conventions of his day as well as his own inner psychological chains. Yes, we know Mr. Hyde will release all these shackles for him, that he will be dangerous and supposedly attractive. But Hyde is also totally resistible. So, no, we can't understand that there is any attraction between Hyde and Mary. All we see is a loyal servant trying to protect the nice man who employs her from a sinister man who has somehow wheedled his way into their lives. Love doesn't seem to enter the picture anywhere. Nor does fear for Mary's safety. The result is no tautness, no mystery, no rush of emotions to carry the viewer to the end.

The team that has put together *Mary Reilly* offered great promise. Director Frears, screenwriter Christopher Hampton and producer Norma Heyman were the acclaimed team behind the three-time Academy Award-winning *Dangerous Liaisons* which also employed the talents of *Mary Reilly*'s cinematographer Philippe Rousselot and production designer Stuart Craig. Add in the presence of the accomplished John Malkovich in both films and sprinkle in an almost uncredited (but deliciously bold) appearance by Glenn Close as the local whorehouse operator, and one would expect similarly terrific results. However, here the story may be too familiar to create the same delicious outcome. And trying to recapture past magic may explain why *Mary Reilly* had its release date postponed seven times: from summer 1995 to December, then postponed again, and again, and again.

—Beverley Bare Buehrer

CREDITS

Mary Reilly: Julia Roberts
Dr. Jekyll/Mr. Hyde: John Malkovich
Poole the butler: George Cole
Mrs. Kent, the cook: Kathy Staff
Mary Reilly's father: Michael Gambon
Mrs. Farraday: Glenn Close
Annie: Bronagh Gallagher
Bradshaw: Michael Sheen
Sir Danvers Carew: Ciaran Hinds
Haffinger: Henry Goodman

Origin: USA
Released: 1996
Production: Ned Tanen, Nancy Graham Tanen and Norma Heyman; released by Tristar Pictures
Direction: Stephen Frears
Screenplay: Christopher Hampton; based on the novel by Valerie Martin
Cinematography: Philippe Rousselot
Editing: Lesley Walker
Production design: Stuart Craig
Costume design: Consolata Boyle
Music: George Fenton
MPAA rating: R
Running Time: 118 minutes

REVIEWS

Chicago Tribune. February 23, 1996, Section Friday, page J.
Detroit News. February 23, 1996, p. 1D.
Entertainment Weekly. March 1, 1996.
Los Angeles Times. February 23, 1996, p. F1.
New York Times. February 23, 1996, p. C18.
Newsweek. February 26, 1996, p. 66.
USA Today. February 23, 1996, p. 4D.
Variety. February 26, 1996, p. 66.
Village Voice. March 5, 1996, p. 48.

Matilda

Somewhere inside all of us is the power to change the world.—Movie tagline

"Danny DeVito has made a classic!"—Sara Voorhees, *KOB-TV*

"Finally, a movie both kids and grown-ups can howl at together!"—Richard Reid, *KIRO-TV*

"A family classic for all generations! Whimsical and wonderful!"—Alan Silverman, *Voice of America*

Box Office: $33,498,222

Matilda Wormwood (Mara Wilson) was born under a dark cloud. Namely, her parents. Harry Wormwood (Danny DeVito) is an unscrupulous used car-dealer and her mother, Zinnia (Rhea Perlman) is a vulgar, self-absorbed, shop-till-you-drop bingo player. Neither one has a clue about how to raise children or any idea about what is culturally important. At worse they insult Matilda, at best they ignore her.

"No more Miss Nice Girl!"—Matilda upon discovering her powers

Matilda, however, is just the opposite of her parents. She loves to read and learn, and by the time she's four she's found her way to the local library, has read her way through the children's department and is now (at age six) reading the likes of Moby Dick and Ivanhoe. This, as one can imagine, upsets her parents. "I'm fed up with all this reading. You're a Wormwood, now start acting like one!" her father yells at her when she refuses to stop reading and watch television instead. And to further make his point he adds, "there's nothing you can get from a book that you can't get from television faster."

So self-absorbed are the Wormwoods that they don't even realize Matilda's age. She should be in school, but that would be inconvenient for Harry who needs Matilda to stay at home and sign for the illegal car parts delivered to his home. (An activity which has brought his home under the surveillance of two FBI agents [Paul Rubens and Tracey Walter].)

Co-producer Liccy Dahl is the widow of author Roald Dahl.

Then one day Harry meets the malevolent Agatha Trunchbull (Pam Ferris), the principal of Crunchem Hall. Sensing that Trunchbull could knock the love of learning out of anyone, he decides to give Matilda her most desired dream—to go to school. Trunchbull, is a behemoth of a woman prone to what have to be "roid" rages which explains her background as a competitor in the shot put, javelin and hammer throw in the 1972 Olympics. It also explains why she often uses her students as shot puts, javelins and hammers. Trunchbull's motto: "Use a rod, beat a child." Trunchbull's idea of a perfect school: "one in which there are no children at all." The motto of Crunchem Hall: "When you are having fun, you are not learning."

And so Matilda arrives at Crunchem Hall where she witnesses Trunchbull's furor and is told about the infamous "Chokey," an iron maiden closet made for punishing and isolating naughty children. As for how Trunchbull receives Matilda, well, the most affectionate thing she says to her is "Sit down, you squirming worm of vomit!"

Yes, Crunchem Hall is right out of one of Matilda's favorite author's books, Charles Dickens. Luckily, there is a silver lining to this dark cloud in Matilda's life. Her teacher, Miss Honey (Embeth Davidtz). Miss Honey immediately recognizes Matilda's special abilities, her facility to do difficult math problems in her head and read books beyond her years. In Miss Honey Matilda has found a friend, a mentor, someone who appreciates her gifts, who treats her with respect, and who maybe even loves her.

So on the one hand Miss Honey offers Matilda a safe harbor, but on the other there is still the storm of her family life and Miss Trunchbull. But Matilda soon learns that there are ways that brains can overcome brawn, malice, and stupidity . . . especially after she learns how to develop her telekinetic powers.

There should be no doubt in anyone's mind that this film skillfully adapts the spirit, tone, and personal philosophy of the writer of the original novel, Roald Dahl. Author of other stories translated onto film such as *Charlie and the Chocolate Factory* (aka *Willie Wonka and the Chocolate Factory*), and *James and the Giant Peach*, Dahl is the master of naughty and seditious, but nonetheless charming, children's stories where adults are erratic authority figures who can't be trusted but instead must be combated by children whose only weapons are their innocence and cleverness.

Luckily for Dahl, and the children who see this film, his original story has not been blunted (as it was in *Willie Wonka*), but has instead found a director who delights just as much in dark humor, Danny DeVito (*Throw Momma from the Train* and *The War of the Roses*). DeVito has been faithful to Dahl's worldview and perfectly reflects his tone of mischievous perception couched in a story which treats its ridiculous elements quite seriously, successfully capturing both the comedy and the terror that are the hallmarks of Dahl's works. DeVito finds just the right balance between over-the-top exaggeration of the terror so that children won't be upset while sneaking in enough sly humor to keep adults amused as well.

Another reason children will like *Matilda* is the performance of the totally competent Mara Wilson in the lead. Seen previously in *Mrs. Doubtfire* and the remake of *Miracle on 34th Street*, Wilson is as lovable and capable a children's heroine as one can find. We never fear for her. She may be little, but inside we know she's always got the self-possession and smarts to outwit any culturally deprived parent or physically threatening principal. Matilda will win, and we know it.

As the only adult with any degree of acceptability, Embeth Davidtz's (*Schindler's List*) Miss Honey is as radiant and fragile as the china doll she and Matilda go after, but also is just enough of a shrinking violet to ensure that Matilda (the child) and not she (the adult) will be the hero of the story.

Incredible as it may seem, while Matilda and Miss Honey carry the film, it is the other characters who steal the scenes. Obviously no one can miss Pam Ferris' remarkably menacing Miss Trunchbull. A spook house where we go to be safely scared, Ferris' Trunchbull may be one of the best children's villains since Margaret Hamilton's "Wicked Witch of the West" in the *Wizard of Oz*. Ferris seems to delight in her malevolent role, but manages to exaggerate her character enough to make it unreal so children can enjoy the mayhem.

Also walking on the edge of being villains, are Matilda's parents played with sleazy glee by DeVito and his real-life wife Rhea Perlman. Other supporting players also deserve recognition. Angel-faced Kiami Davael and Jacqueline Steiger help to make Trunchbull's wicked treatment seem even more inhuman—who could harm such children? And Paul Reubens (aka Pee Wee Herman) and Tracey Walter take their small roles as FBI agents and turn them into pure gold.

Holding the entire film together is its incredible look. From the Wormwood's boorish outfits to Trunchbull's neo-Nazi school uniform, Costume designer Jane Ruhm has easily created characters out of cloth and Ve Neill provides the perfect makeup accessories from Zinnia Wormwood's "beauty" to Trunchbull's beast. The wonderful world we visit during *Matilda* is compliments of production designer Bill Brzeski. He has created a most believable cartoon environment where libraries are churches and schools are prisons, and the whole package is imaginatively photographed by Stefan Czapsky.

In the end, *Matilda* is a great family film. Absurd and childish enough for the younger set, sly and amusing enough for adults. It mixes humor with fright and intelligent ideas with sight gags. It's twisted; it's ostentatious; it's funny. And it does something else besides entertain. It glorifies intelligence and literacy. This is *Phenomenon* for kids . . . with a sunnier ending.

—Beverley Bare Buehrer

CREDITS

Matilda Wormwood: Mara Wilson
Harry Wormwood: Danny DeVito
Zinnia Wormwood: Rhea Perlman
Miss Honey: Embeth Davidtz
Agatha Trunchbull: Pam Ferris

Origin: USA
Released: 1996
Production: Danny DeVito, Michael Shamberg, Stacey Sher, and Liccy Dahl for a TriStar Pictures and Jersey Films production; released by Sony Pictures Entertainment
Direction: Danny DeVito
Screenplay: Nicholas Kazan, Robin Swicord; based on the novel by Roald Dahl
Cinematography: Stefan Czapsky
Editing: Lynzee Klingman, Brent White
Music: David Newman
Production design: Bill Brzeski
Art direction: Philip Too Lin
Costumes: Jane Ruhm
Sound: David Kelson
Visual effects supervisor: Chris Watts
Casting: David Rubin, Renee Rousselot
MPAA rating: PG
Running Time: 100 minutes

REVIEWS

Boxoffice Magazine Online. August 12, 1996.
Chicago Sun Times. August 2, 1996.
Chicago Tribune. August 2, 1996, p. 5.
Entertainment Weekly. August 9, 1996, p. 42.
The Hollywood Reporter. July 30, 1996.
Los Angeles Times. August 2, 1996, p. F4.
New York Times. August 2, 1996, p. C3.
People. August 12, 1996, p. 19.
USA Today. August 2, 1996, p. D1.
Variety Online. July 30, 1996.

Maximum Risk

The other side of safe.—Movie tagline

"An action-packed, sexy thrill ride."—Alan Silverman, *Voice of America*

Box Office: $14,100,000

The fans of Jean-Claude Van Damme will certainly get a kick out of *Maximum Risk*, even if the plot is a bit of a retread, a trend for Van Damme in 1996. Just as *The Quest* tended to resemble *Bloodsport* (1987), so *Maximum Risk* resembles *Double Impact* (1991), as Lawrence Van Gelder noted in his *New York Times* review, describing both films as a sort of "remembrance of thunks past," as if this Proustian pun would register with the typical Van Damme fans. *Maximum Risk* is about action, not literature, however, and, taken on its own terms, it's about as good an action-thriller as was produced in 1996. Though plot logic tended to be stretched a bit, it certainly made more sense than *The Quest*, which was mainly a kickboxing spectacle and nothing more.

The film explodes into action right from the title credits, as a Russian mobster is pursued through the streets and alleys of Villefranche-sur-Mer, on the French Riviera by two renegade FBI agents intent on killing him. The Russian, Mikhail Suverov (Van Damme), is too preoccupied to talk, nor does he have anyone to talk to as he runs for his life. Unfortunately, he ends up dead. End of picture? No, it turns out that Mikhail is in the South of France attempting to locate his twin brother, Alain Moreau (also Van Damme, naturally), who is the main character of the film.

Alain is a police officer, taken by his friend and colleague Sebastien (Jean-Hughes Anglade) to see the corpse of his double. Puzzled, Alain then visits his mother (Stephane Audran), who tells him the sad story of how Alain was separated from his twin brother when they both were infants. Mikhail was sold to a Soviet diplomat and later taken to Russia, then to the United States. He eventually ended up in New York City, working for the Russian mafia in Little Odessa, New York's enclave for Russian emigres. Without having a clue about who or what Mikhail became, Alain decides to fly to New York to learn more about the dead brother he never really knew. His motive is not very coherent, as he explains it to Sebastien: "He made a sacrifice and never knew it. Hey, I gotta go." Dialogue is not exactly the high point of this movie, but at least Van Damme's accent is appropriately in character.

Arriving in New York, Alain has a single clue that takes him to a nightclub-restaurant in Brooklyn's Little Odessa. Everyone there seems to know him, especially the hostess at the Bohemia Club, Alex Minetti (Natasha Henstridge), who wants to take him home to bed as soon as possible. The only clue Alain has is a slip of paper with the words "Alex Bohemia" written on it. So why would Mikhail have to write down the name of his lover and his favorite Brooklyn nightclub? Don't ask.

Mafia boss Kirov (David Hemblen) loved Mikhail like a son and had no knowledge of his defection and death, ordered by mafia lieutenant Ivan Dzasokhov (Zach Grenier), in cahoots with two corrupt federal agents, Pellman (Paul Ben-Victor) and Loomis (Frank Senger), the renegades who pursued Mikhail to his death. Alain seems safe enough with Kirov until the power-mad Ivan murders Kirov in a steam bath, which puts Alain back on the run. Mikhail had left a list in a safe-deposit box in France that he intended to turn over to the U.S. Embassy, naming Russian mafia leaders and the renegade FBI agents.

Ivan, Pellman, and Loomis are determined to recover that evidence, but they have to contend with Alain, who is, to quote the slogan from an earlier picture, just "too Damme tough," and also looking for payback. One chase sequence after another keeps the plot in constant motion until the final showdown at the bank back in France. The plot, fabricated by screenwriter Larry Ferguson, is reasonably well constructed

CREDITS

Alain Moreau: Jean-Claude Van Damme
Alex Minetti: Natasha Henstridge
Ivan Dzasokhov: Zach Grenier
Sebastien Thirry: Jean-Hughes Anglade
Agent Pellman: Paul Ben-Victor
Agent Loomis: Frank Senger

Origin: USA
Released: 1996
Production: Moshe Diamant for a Columbia Pictures production; released by Sony Pictures Entertainment
Direction: Ringo Lam
Screenplay: Larry Ferguson
Cinematography: Alexander Gruszynski
Editing: Bill Pankow
Music: Robert Folk
Production design: Steven Spence
Set direction: Jaro Dick
Sound: Glen Gauthier
Action sequence choreographer: Charles Picerni
Casting: Deborah Brown
MPAA rating: R
Running Time: 100 minutes

for non-stop thrills. But the direction is what makes this picture tick like a bomb that could explode at any moment.

In fact, *Maximum Risk* is a Hong Kong action movie in disguise, directed by Ringo Lam, an experienced and recognized Hong Kong director making his American debut. Lam has an instinctive talent for fast-paced, high-profile action-adventure, and his talent is immediately obvious. Even so, Lam claims that in his films "drama is the most important element," and "to get drama, you must have vivid characters." Certainly the gangsters in this picture are vividly brutal and ruthless. The plot falls short of perfection, but when it falters, Lam always cuts to the chase. He knows what he is doing.

Van Damme also played twin brothers in his 1991 film *Double Impact.*

So does Larry Ferguson, the screenwriter who created and shaped the characters. Trained as an actor with the American Conservatory Theatre in San Francisco, Ferguson moved on to the Tyrone Guthrie Theatre in Minneapolis, and then to Broadway. Along the way he must have developed a sophisticated understanding of character. Though his plot resembles *Double Impact*, directed by Sheldon Lettich in 1991, the twin dilemma is better handled in *Maximum Risk.* In the earlier film Van Damme also played twins separated as infants after their parents were murdered in Hong Kong. One was raised in a Hong Kong orphanage, while the other was raised in California. Reunited as adults in Hong Kong, they sought revenge on their father's business partner who was responsible for the murders. *Maximum Risk*, on the other hand, separates the twins so that they never meet. This solution seems less awkward and more believable.

One minor character is especially well drawn in *Maximum Risk*, a manic New York cabbie named Davis Hartley (nicely portrayed by Frank Van Keeken), who hopes to write the Great American Novel and keeps close to Alain in order to research material for his first chapter. It is of course illogical that anyone would base the Great American Novel on a mysterious Frenchman who has only just arrived in America, but Hartley is borderline psychotic and gets an emotional high by living on the edge with Alain, helping him to escape from mafia killers. The film suffers a comic loss when Hartley dies before he can turn the page to Chapter Two. On the other hand, the villains are made "vivid" by the casting, such as the cartoon heavy Red Face (Stefanos Miltaskakis), who is built like a tank, and about as difficult to stop. Every Van Damme picture seems to have at least one apparently unstoppable foe.

Van Damme is in good form and in good company here. Producer Moshe Diamant has worked with the star on several pictures, including *Double Impact* (1991) and *The Quest* (1996). *Maximum Risk* is better conceived and better executed than *The Quest*, which offered little more than an absurd plot leading up to an extended "bloodsport" spectacle of kickboxing brutality. In *Maximum Risk* far more time is spent on psychology and character development, and, though Van Damme has to kick his way out of several threatening situations, *Maximum Risk* also offers several wonderfully staged chase scenes orchestrated by French stunt-master Remy Julienne.

Even so, Richard Harrington of *The Washington Post* dismissed the picture as a "crashing bore," but his crosstown colleague Judith Kreiner of *The Washington Times* "loved" the film and praised it for being "well-plotted, beautifully photographed" (by Polish cinematographer Alexander Gruszynski) and "superbly choreographed" (by Charles Picerni). Even Lawrence Van Gelder of *The New York Times* was impressed by Larry Ferguson's screenplay "that actually holds water, or in this case, blood," a screenplay that gives Van Damme an added human dimension by allowing a romance to develop amidst the murder and mayhem.

Maximum Risk has to be considered one of Jean-Claude Van Damme's very best pictures. It certainly tops *The Quest*, and is better directed, if that is not damning with faint praise, but at any rate the Damme thing works, and the star is presented in top form.

—James M. Welsh

REVIEWS

Chicago Tribune. September 13, 1996, p. 7.
Entertainment Weekly. September 27, 1996, p. 55.
Los Angeles Times. September 14, 1996, p. F15.
The New York Times. September 14, 1996, p.12.
People. September 30, 1996, p. 17.
USA Today. September 13, 1996, p. 4D.
Variety. September 16, 1996.
The Washington Post. September 13, 1996, F-6.
Washington Times Metropolitan Times. September 13, 1996, C-11.

Maybe . . . Maybe Not; The Most Desired Man; Der Bewegte Mann

The comedy that asks the question: Can a man be too desirable for his own good?—Movie tagline

"Axel's . . . a hell of a lust object!"—Lisa Henricksson, *GQ Magazine*

"One of the most exhilarating comedies of the year!"—Kevin Thomas, *Los Angeles Times*

"Riotous gender-bender! Outspoken and wickedly wild!"—Rex Reed, *New York Observer*

"An outrageous, sexy farce!"—Stephen Schaefer, *The New York Post*

Box Office: $468,930

Maybe . . . Maybe Not is a modest sex farce brought into the '90s by having the third partner in the would-be triangle be a man. Extremely attractive, selfish, and not-too-bright Axel (Til Schweiger) has his over-active libido to thank for his current crisis. His girlfriend of three years, Doro (Katja Riemann), has just caught him in flagrante delicto with another woman and thrown him out of their flat.

Axel unsuccessfully runs through the women's names on his electronic address book (the modern little black book) to find somewhere to stay but winds up at the door of a male acquaintance who happens to be hosting a men's sensitivity group ("so seventies" as one character puts it), where Axel immediately attracts the attention of the rather swish Waltraud (Rufus Beck), a gay man who's explaining the homosexual point of view to this group of clueless heteros. Hearing of Axel's dilemma, Waltraud offers him a place to stay and Axel eventually does call him, only to be invited to a party with Waltraud and his friends, Norbert (Joachim Krol) and Franzi (Nico van der Knaap), who are dressed in drag when Axel first meets them.

Axel's rather unnerved by his first gay party and depressed over the situation with Doro, so he proceeds to get very drunk—insulting Waltraud and winding up on the sofa at Norbert's instead. A kind homebody, Norbert invites Axel to stay with him as long as he likes—hoping to eventually get him into bed. Trouble as one gay puts it, since a hetero may turn to a gay for comfort but when the first woman comes along . . .

Meanwhile, the volatile Doro has discovered she's pregnant and decides she wants Axel back, only she doesn't have a clue as to where he's staying. Axel has Norbert come to Doro's to retrieve his slide projector (Axel's an amateur photographer), which just happens to be set up next to the bed and contains their vacation photos. Axel nostalgically decides to watch them and Norbert begins watching him, their close proximity on the bed putting him in a very different frame of mind. (Axel's willfully dense over the obvious crush Norbert has on him).

Thanks to the usual series of contrivances, Doro catches Axel and a now-naked Norbert in the bedroom, presumes that her ex-lover has "gone gay," and blurts out she's pregnant in the confusion of explanations. Axel decides to move back in and the wounded Norbert eventually hooks up with a crass, leather-clad butcher (who's the exact opposite of sensitive vegetarian Norbert), and whom all Norbert's friends disapprove of.

Waltraud later learns of Axel's wedding and drags an unwitting Norbert to the church, which causes angry remonstrations by the nine-months pregnant Doro, who's not happy with Axel anyway since he hasn't been eager to make love to her and she's suspicious that he's been unfaithful. Axel gets together with Norbert to tell him the problems he's caused by showing up at the wedding—a conversation that segues into Axel's sexual problems—neither topic being one

CREDITS

Axel: Til Schweiger
Doro: Katja Riemann
Norbert: Joachim Krol
Waltraud: Rufus Beck
Franzi: Nico van der Knaap
Butcher: Armin Rohde

Origin: Germany
Released: 1994; 1996
Production: Bernd Eichinger for a Neue Constantin production; released by Orion Classics
Direction: Soenke Wortmann
Screenplay: Soenke Wortmann; based on the comic books *Der Bewegte Mann* and *Pretty Baby* by Ralf Koenig
Cinematography: Gernot Roll
Editing: Ueli Christen
Music: Torsten Breuer
Production design: Monika Bauert
Costume design: Katharina von Martius
Sound: Simon Happ
MPAA rating: R
Running Time: 91 minutes

the still-smitten Norbert is eager to hear about. Later, however, Norbert is rather easily persuaded to lend his flat to Axel when the latter unexpectedly meets an old flame and needs a place for a quick romp. Since Axel's acting suspiciously, Doro calls the phone number he's left, hears Norbert's voice, and assumes that Axel's been seeing his old boyfriend all along.

Of course, everyone winds up at Norbert's flat (Axel happens to be naked and stoned) and, yes, Doro goes into labor. Norbert's forced to drive her to the hospital and even winds up in the delivery room. When a recovered Axel finally shows up the next morning, a furious Doro once again tells him to get lost. Norbert's still at the hospital and resignedly tells Axel to be patient—that Doro will probably take him back—and Axel invites Norbert out for breakfast.

Maybe . . . Maybe Not is based on two gay cult comic books *Der Bewegte Mann* and *Pretty Baby* by cartoonist Ralf Koenig. In the comics, the character of Axel is more sexually ambivalent (in German, "bewegte" is a man who "moves" back and forth between sexual preferences) but when the film's Axel makes a comment about being bi(sexual) it's never

"I think heteros should go gay. Women should go into world politics. It's the only way to save the planet."—Norbert to Axel

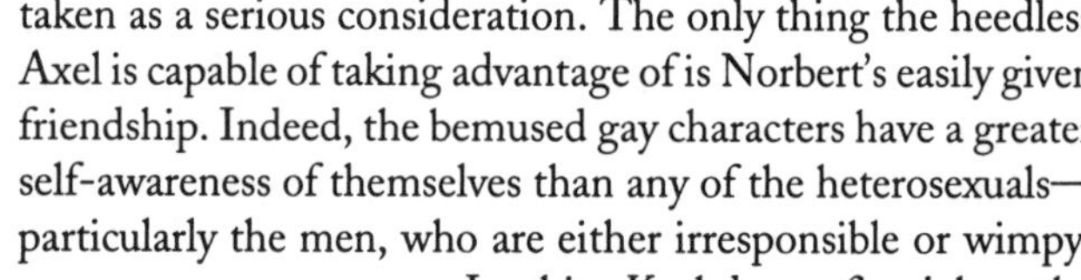

taken as a serious consideration. The only thing the heedless Axel is capable of taking advantage of is Norbert's easily given friendship. Indeed, the bemused gay characters have a greater self-awareness of themselves than any of the heterosexuals—particularly the men, who are either irresponsible or wimpy.

Joachim Krol does a fine job as the plain and polite Norbert, who realizes his infatuation may be hopeless and is also not unaware that the charming-but-immature Axel is probably not worth the effort. The film grossed a record $48 million in Germany and made a sex symbol out of the married Schweiger (whose hunky charms are on frequent display).

—*Christine Tomassini*

REVIEWS

Boxoffice. May, 1996, p. 71.
Chicago Tribune. July 19, 1996, p. 5.
New York Times. June 28, 1996, p. C12.
Sight and Sound. March, 1996, p. 46.

Michael

He's an angel . . . not a saint.—Movie tagline

"*Michael* is a heaven-sent holiday fable!"—Joel Siegel, *Good Morning America*

"*Michael* is an inspired blend of fantasy, romantic comedy and road movie."—Kevin Thomas, *Los Angeles Times*

"John Travolta's portrayal of a mischievous angel puts the film on its toes and sets it spinning!"—Stephen Holden, *New York Times*

"Travolta's a funky delight!"—David Ansen, *Newsweek*

"Two thumbs up!"—*Siskel & Ebert*

Box Office: $35,133,401

Everyone knows what angels look like. Flowing white robes, cherubic faces, wings and haloes. Right? Well, not Michael (John Travolta) . . . except for the wings, that is. However, according to Michael, "I'm not that kind of angel." He seems to be the kind that has a beer belly hanging over the waistband of his boxer shorts, a face that is unshaven and hair that's uncombed, and there isn't a halo in sight. If he is, indeed, the archangel Michael, the one who defeated Lucifer in battle, then it's no wonder that he revels in his warrior status and looks more like G.I.Joe than Gabriel. This angel takes on bulls in head-to-head combat and even smites the First Iowa Bank of Commerce in tiny Stubbs, Iowa so Pansy Milbank (Jean Stapleton) isn't pestered by financial problems.

But saving Pansy from the clutches of financiers is not Michael's only reason for an Earthly visit. When Pansy writes to Frank Quinlan (William Hurt), a reporter for the supermarket tabloid "The National Mirror," he immediately smells a story and proposes it to the paper's hyper editor, Vartan Malt (Bob Hoskins). Malt immediately seizes upon Quinlan's story, but insists that he take along fellow reporter Huey Driscoll (Robert Pastorelli) and his dog, Sparky, as well as a newly hired angel expert Dorothy Winters (Andie MacDowell).

Sparky is one of the Chicago-based paper's greatest assets, having his photo taken with popes and presidents and writing his own column has made him into a real celebrity with its readers. Unfortunately, Sparky hates Malt and loves Huey, but Malt hates Huey and wants him fired so he can exploit Sparky on his own. So here's Malt's deal to Quinlan: bring me an angel or you're both fired and he gets Sparky.

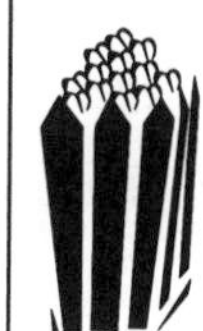

"Cookies. He smells like cookies. And the smell gets stronger when he's in heat."—Dorothy describing Michael

So the trio and pooch set off for Pansy's Milk Bottle Motel, a shell of an enterprise since they moved the highway. And to their surprise, they seem to find a real angel, wings and all. His less-than-typical physical appearance, however, initially makes them skeptical, especially when Michael starts eating his breakfast cereal with a fist-held spoon and more sugar than is harvested in Hawaii in a year. But then there's those wings . . . It's enough for the reporters to relate back to Malt that they really have found an angel, at which point Malt becomes positively orgasmic.

Michael, however, refuses to allow any photos until the four of them and Sparky reach Chicago. And he wants to take his time getting there. Why does he need time? Michael claims he wants to see some of America's best tourist attractions—the world's largest ball of twine and the world's largest non-stick fry pan—but we know it's really to accomplish his mission: to help Frank and Dorothy rediscover their hearts. And what better way to do it than in a nice long road trip that gives the two plenty of opportunities to discover each other.

It seems Quinlan lost his heart when alcohol caused him to punch out his editor and lose his job as a top investigative reporter at the *Chicago Tribune*. Dorothy, on the other hand, has been so burned by love (married at least three times) that she has resorted to the obvious hobby of country and western song writing.

So, from Iowa to Chicago, Dorothy and Frank fight and feud and eventually fall in love. While Michael attracts every woman within a two-mile radius and, warrior that he is, fights his share of barroom brawls. It turns out that Michael revels in his senses—from sugar to sex—because he thoroughly enjoys the pleasures of life (and also because this is his last trip to Earth). "Only so many visits allowed," he ruefully tells the trio. Where, exactly, this is set down in the angel rules is unsure—perhaps in the book owned by angel Denzel Washington which the Preacher pitches into the fire in this Christmas' other picture with a heavenly visitor.

Angels seem to be "in" in Hollywood, and when you think about it, what could be more fun for an actor than to play one . . . especially if, like Michael, it's not one's ordinary idea of an angel? Michael's entrance into the film—sleepily descending a flight of stairs clad only in boxers, cigarette in mouth and scratching his crotch—may be one of the best in recent film history. No one expects "this" kind of angel, and Travolta plays his role with relish (and sugar and cigarettes and sex). This angel is capricious, rebellious, bewildering, charming, and, excuse the pun, devilishly amusing. And Travolta easily slips into his character as he spreads his message that life is to be appreciated and "all you need is love."

It also helps that the film is blessed with a solid supporting cast. Hurt's Quinlan is an interesting combination of intelligence, pain and decency and Pastorelli's Huey is innocence and sentiment personified. These are no more your usual tabloid reporters than Michael is the usual angel. Andie MacDowell's Dorothy, however, is sweet but a bit insipid, and her best lines are song lyrics.

But *Michael* does have a few problems. Sometimes the supporting characters seem too thinly written, but the presence of Michael lifts them above their missing personality

CREDITS

Michael: John Travolta
Dorothy Winters: Andie MacDowell
Frank Quinlan: William Hurt
Vartan Malt: Bob Hoskins
Huey Driscoll: Robert Pastorelli
Pansy Milbank: Jean Stapleton
Judge Esther Newbert: Teri Garr
Bruce Craddock: Wallace Langham
Anita: Joey Lauren Adams
Bride: Carla Gugino
Groom: Tom Hodges
Sheriff: Calvin Trillin

Origin: USA
Released: 1996
Production: Sean Daniel, Nora Ephron and James Jacks for Alphaville Production; distributed by Turner Pictures and New Line Cinema
Direction: Nora Ephron
Screenplay: Nora Ephron, Delia Ephron, Pete Dexter and Jim Quinlan; from a story by Pete Dexter and Jim Quinlan
Cinematography: John Lindley
Editing: Geraldine Peroni
Production design: Dan Davis
Art direction: James Tocci
Set decoration: Tracey Doyle
Costume design: Elizabeth McBride
Music: Randy Newman
MPAA rating: Rated PG
Running Time: 105 minutes

parts. Director/writer/producer Nora Ephron, who initially made her name as a journalist and writer and then turned to screenplays with winners like *Sleepless in Seattle* (1993, which she also directed) and *When Harry Met Sally* (1989), again proves she has a way with the sharp and funny retort. But like her disastrous *Mixed Nuts* (1994), *Michael*, too, could have been improved with a few rewrites. (The ending is especially trite.)

Michael is a great premise, one terrific character, some memorable scenes, and a few good wisecracks. The film will inevitably leave the viewer feeling good after exiting the theater. But after awhile, just like all that sugar Michael eats, one eventually wants something more substantial to chew on. Sometimes "cute" can only carry a film just so far. For the filmmakers, however, it seems to be carrying audiences into the theaters to see "this kind" of angel for themselves.

—Beverley Bare Buehrer

REVIEWS

Chicago Sun Times. December 24, 1996.
Chicago Tribune. December 25, 1996.
Detroit News. December 25, 1996, p. G1.
Entertainment Weekly. January 10, 1997, p. 41.
The New York Times. December 24, 1996, p. C18.
Newsweek. December 23, 1996, p. 68.
Sight and Sound. March, 1997, p. 55.
Variety. December 20, 1996.

Michael Collins

Ireland 1916. His dreams inspired hope. His words ignited passion. His courage forged a nation's destiny.—Movie tagline

"Powerful, inspiring, deeply moving. If you liked *Braveheart*, you'll love *Michael Collins*. Liam Neeson is amazing."—Bill Diehl, *ABC Radio Network*

"Played with intensity and grace by Liam Neeson. Neil Jordan fills his canvas with visual swipes of valor and tenderness."—Guy Flatley, *Cosmopolitan*

"Magnificent! Liam Neeson burns up the screen with all the fiery passion that made this real-life hero a legend."—Jeanne Wolf, *Jeanne Wolf's Hollywood*

"Neil Jordan's film boasts a seductive energy and dynamic performances."—Stephen Farber, *Movieline*

"Liam Neeson gives a bold and passionate performance."—Jeff Craig, *Sixty Second Preview*

"A powerhouse of a film. One of the finest casts assembled on a film this year."—Raj Bahadur, *Westwood One*

Box Office: $10,943,262

After proving, with *The Crying Game* (1992) and *Interview with the Vampire* (1994), that he could make commercially successful films, writer-director Neil Jordan was asked by producer David Geffen what he wanted to do next. Jordan first wrote his screenplay about Irish revolutionary Michael Collins (1890-1922) in 1983 but had never been able to secure financing for an expensive project made even more risky by the lack of awareness of Collins outside Ireland. Unlike Stanley Kubrick's efforts to make a film about Napolean and Roger Corman's desire to film Robert E. Lee's life, Jordan's long-delayed wish has been realized (and Kevin Costner's plans for a Collins' film abandoned). As with Warren Beatty's dream project *Reds* (1981), dealing with similar material, the result is admirable, often exciting, but not all it might have been.

Collins (Liam Neeson) is a mere soldier fighting for the cause of Irish freedom from Great Britain during the failed Easter uprising of 1916. After a stint in an English prison, he becomes one of the leaders of the revolutionary movement, along with Eamon De Valera (Alan Rickman). Instead of carrying on the conflict in the traditional way by seizing a location and trying to keep the enemy from retaking it, Collins is credited with inventing modern guerilla warfare as he and his men conduct a hit-and-run campaign of terror against the British forces. Collins and the Irish Republican Army gradually wear down the opposition so that in 1921 David Lloyd George's government is willing to negotiate a peace.

Collins is a streetfighter and De Valera (the future Irish prime minister) a politician, yet De Valera, who has spent most of the war in the United States trying to enlist support, sends the rough-edged Collins to London. Although the two have fought for the same cause and Collins breaks De Valera out of an English prison, they are rivals. Collins suspects De Valera sends him to England so that he will be blamed if the negotiations fail. When Collins comes back having won only an Irish Free State and not a republic and with the North partitioned from the South, De Valera and his supporters initiate a civil war. When Collins leaves Dublin for his native Cork and a meeting with De Valera, he is assassinated in an ambush. Jordan offers the theory that De Valera had the hero killed. While De Valera is not seen requesting the murder, the filmmaker creates a context in which nothing else is possible.

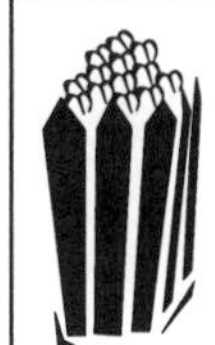

"We won't play by the rules, Harry. We'll make our own."—Collins to Harry Boland

Jordan intermingles Collins' personal life with history, showing his relations with his best friend and co-revolutionary Harry Boland (Aidan Quinn) and their both being in love with the beautiful Kitty Kiernan (Julia Roberts). Her choosing Collins contributes to Boland's later siding with De Valera against his friend. Uncharacteristically, Jordan resorts to a cinematic cliche in cutting back and forth between the assassination and Kitty's shopping for a wedding gown. Also prominent in *Michael Collins* are Joe O'Reilly (Ian Hart), Collins' most loyal aide, and Ned Broy (Stephen Rea), a high-level police officer who spies for the IRA against the British.

The film attracted as much attention from political commentators as film critics, especially in Ireland and the United Kingdom. There were fears *Michael Collins* would glamorize the Irish Republican Army and possibly incite violence. At the film's Dublin premiere, Irish Minister for Justice Nora Owen, Collins' grandniece, concluded, "It does not glorify violence." But Jordan's stance is decidedly anti-British. As British armored cars are traveling through Dublin and the residents throw garbage upon them, the soldiers open fire on the perpetrators, mostly women. Later, in retaliation for Collins' attacks, the armored cars invade a playing field and begin mowing down the innocent footballers and spectators, including children. It is no wonder that at the film's showing at the Toronto Film Festival some in the audience began expressing their anger at the British and a riot almost broke out.

The problem is that Collins is simply there as a protagonist with almost no past or any other details about his character. How he acquires his status in the revolutionary movement is never explained. More importantly, how he changes from violent guerrilla leader to the voice of reason and compromise is omitted entirely. One Michael Collins goes to London and another returns with no analysis given of this dramatic alteration. (The real-life Collins acknowledged that by signing the treaty he had signed his own death warrant.) The irony and poignancy Jordan obviously intends for Collins having to fight against the IRA men he recruited and trained is dissipated by the lack of narrative coherence. Here and elsewhere, Jordan's film shows signs of being whittled down to an acceptable length for American consumption: The released version is fifteen minutes shorter than that shown at the Venice Film Festival.

Despite all this, *Michael Collins* is entertaining with Jordan finding a good balance between politics, warfare, and romance. Jordan has clearly intended to create something with an epic, romantic sweep along the lines of David Lean's greatest films, a sort of "Collins of Hibernia," but while his hero has the potential to be a complex, contradictory figure like T. E. Lawrence, he is nothing like the enigmatic, neurotic character Lean, screenwriter Robert Bolt, and Peter

AWARDS AND NOMINATIONS

Academy Awards 1996 Nominations: Best Cinematography (Menges), Best Original Dramatic Score (Goldenthal)
Golden Globe Award 1997 Nominations: Best Actor-Drama (Neeson), Best Original Score (Goldenthal)
Los Angeles Film Critics Association 1996: Cinematography (Menges)

CREDITS

Michael Collins: Liam Neeson
Eamon De Valera: Alan Rickman
Kitty Kiernan: Julia Roberts
Harry Boland: Aidan Quinn
Ned Broy: Stephen Rea
Joe O'Reilly: Ian Hart
Soames: Charles Dance
Assassin: Jonathan Rhys Myers

Origin: USA
Released: 1996
Production: Stephen Woolley for Geffen Pictures; released by Warner Brothers
Direction: Neil Jordan
Screenplay: Neil Jordan
Cinematography: Chris Menges
Editing: J. Patrick Duffner and Tony Lawson
Production design: Anthony Pratt
Art direction: Arden Gantly, Jonathan McKinstry, Cliff Robinson
Set design: Josie MacAlvin
Costume design: Sandy Powell
Sound: Kieran Horgan
Music: Elliot Goldenthal
Casting: Susie Figgis
MPAA rating: R
Running Time: 117 minutes

O'Toole create in *Lawrence of Arabia* (1962). (Collins' complexity is limited to abhorring the violence he sets in motion.) Jordan's film is more like Lean's *Doctor Zhivago* (1965), a compilation of exciting set pieces, striking shots, and good performances yet missing some essential ingredient.

Jordan's other role model is John Ford whose films about the Irish and Irish-Americans, such as *The Quiet Man* (1952), are notable for their rambunctiousness and sentimentality, qualities on display in moderation in *Michael Collins.* (Ford gives his version of the Irish revolution in his 1936 adaptation of Sean O'Casey's *The Plough and the Stars.*) Male-bonding is also a major Ford subject as it is in Jordan's work. The homoerotic element so prominent in Jordan's previous two films is strong here with Collins seemingly loving Boland more than he does Kitty.

Jordan's film was shot in and around Dublin during a cease-fire between Catholic Republicans and Protestant Unionists in Northern Ireland. But the cease-fire was broken before the film opened, igniting even more media controversy.

Neeson is the perfect actor to play Collins. For someone of his size and presence, Neeson can be a surprisingly weak performer when called upon to play sensitive men, as in *The Good Mother* (1988) and *Husbands and Wives* (1992), when he falls into teary-eyed puppy-dog expressions. Ask him to be a man of action, as in *Shining Through* (1991) or *Under Suspicion* (1991), and he becomes more interesting. The good Neeson has larger-than-life, old-fashioned Hollywood charisma along the lines of Gary Cooper, John Wayne, and Burt Lancaster, as he especially shows in dominating Steven Spielberg's *Schindler's List* (1993). Collins is always being referred to as "the big fella," and Neeson, acting with his whole body, throws himself headlong into the part, embracing it much more energetically than he does with the title character in the similar *Rob Roy* (1995). His Collins would much rather charge into action than contemplate its consequences. Neeson, named best actor for this performance at the Venice Film Festival, embodies Collins with a credibility missing from Jordan's screenplay, which was written with him in mind.

The part of forsaken lover and disillusioned sidekick forces Quinn to bear the mantle, as he often does, of the too-sensitive-to-live. The contest for Kitty's affections between the weak Boland and the dashing Collins is no contest. Rickman, adept both at flamboyance, *Robin Hood: Prince of Thieves* (1991), and subtlety, *Sense and Sensibility* (1995), makes De Valora just stuffy and prissy enough to be untrustworthy. Rickman is at his best when an angry De Valora fights to maintain his composure only for a twitching cheek to reveal his pique and when he sneers in jealousy at Collins' nickname, vowing to show who the real "big fella" is. Early in her career, especially in *Mystic Pizza* (1988), Roberts excited many viewers not only because of her beauty and her star power but for her acting potential as well. Though Kitty is an underwritten role, Roberts, much as Neeson does, creates a character through her screen presence. She is the focus of each of her scenes—and her part is much larger than many reviews have indicated. The chameleon-like Hart, almost unrecognizable as the same actor who plays John Lennon in *Backbeat* (1994), is affecting as the loyal O'Reilly, and Jonathan Rhys Myers, who closely resembles Roberts' brother Eric, makes a strong impression as the cocky teenaged assassin.

Michael Collins was named best film at Venice but is really more like a lively history lesson than a true Neil Jordan film. Jordan is a highly eccentric filmmaker whose best work, *The Company of Wolves* (1984), *Mona Lisa* (1986), *The Miracle* (1991), *The Crying Game*, and *Interview with the Vampire*, is crammed with melodramatic excesses and baroque visuals. The more conventional *Michael Collins* lacks the style and passion that should make it the memorable film Jordan intended. The film broke the record of *Independence Day* (1996) for the biggest opening weekend in Irish filmgoing history, but it did only mediocre business in the United States, probably less because of American unfamiliarity with or indifference to its subject than as a result of its failure to be anything special.

—*Michael Adams*

REVIEWS

Entertainment Weekly. October 25, 1996, p. 89.
Maclean's. October 21, 1996, p. 78.
The New York Times. October 11, 1996, p. C4.
The New Yorker. October 14, 1996, p. 101.
People Weekly. October 21, 1996, p. 21.
Sight and Sound. November, 1996, p. 55.
USA Today. October 11, 1996, p. D3.
The Village Voice. October 22, 1996, p. 78.
Vogue. October, 1996, p. 208.

Microcosmos

15 years of research. 2 years of equipment design. 3 years of shooting. 1 great movie to restore your sense of wonder.—Movie tagline

"One of the most enjoyable movies of the year!"—Renfreu Neff, *Film Journal*

"Breathtaking and gorgeous!"—Janet Maslin, *New York Times*

"Remarkable!"—Gene Shalit, *The Today Show*

Box Office: $1,306,465

Coming up with a new way to tell a story is a difficult task indeed. The yearly glut of remakes and sequels is testimony to the fact that the film industry, Hollywood in particular, is often left scratching its head with their often half-hearted attempts to be original. More often than not, producers merely recycle the same goods in a different, albeit, more elaborate package (the recent deluge of Jane Austen adaptations and the ongoing retelling of works by William Shakespeare are a good case in point). All too often, new, innovative projects will be unleashed on the public and will likely be met with unenthusiastic yawning. By and large, people are deathly afraid of change and the unfamiliar. This is especially true for movie patrons.

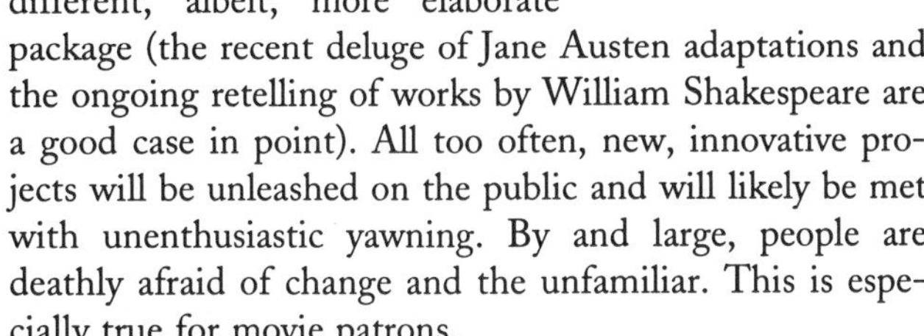

The names of the principals are included in the closing credits, i.e., "Eucera bee in love with Ophyrs orchid."

Microcosmos is a movie that shows meticulous forethought and an almost zealous commitment to the craft of filmmaking. Movies are produced for an array of different reasons. Besides the most obvious aim (commerce), film is the ultimate (modern) medium for artistic expression. If $100 million is poured into a production and it fails to recoup that investment, it is considered a failure. Artistic expression is all well and good, but if people don't get your point, it too has failed to do its job. First and foremost, a movie must entertain the viewer. If it can educate you and emotionally move you in the process, it has succeeded in its task.

AWARDS AND NOMINATIONS

Cesar Awards 1997: Best Cinematography (Nuridsany, Perennou, Ryffel, Machado), Best Editing
Nominations: Best Film

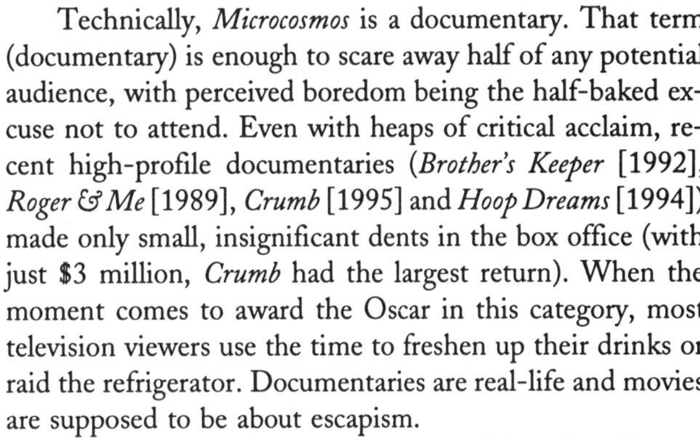

Technically, *Microcosmos* is a documentary. That term (documentary) is enough to scare away half of any potential audience, with perceived boredom being the half-baked excuse not to attend. Even with heaps of critical acclaim, recent high-profile documentaries (*Brother's Keeper* [1992], *Roger & Me* [1989], *Crumb* [1995] and *Hoop Dreams* [1994]) made only small, insignificant dents in the box office (with just $3 million, *Crumb* had the largest return). When the moment comes to award the Oscar in this category, most television viewers use the time to freshen up their drinks or raid the refrigerator. Documentaries are real-life and movies are supposed to be about escapism.

In the spring of 1996, *Microcosmos* debuted at Cannes and immediately caught fire. Viewers couldn't stop singing its praises. Attempts at relating the merits of the film to others were met with feigned indifference or contemptuous giggles. A documentary, sans narration (the U.S. version does include a brief prologue and epilogue delivered by actress Kristen Scott Thomas), concentrating on the day-to-day existence of insects, amphibians and snails? What were these people thinking?

With finance coming from a multitude of international sources, it's clear that a quick return on their investment was not the consortium's primary concern. French born co-directors Claude Nuridsany and Marie Perennou began their careers in the early '70's as biologists. Several books of photography and a 16mm short followed. It wasn't until the late '80's that the gestation for the feature began. The design and manufacturing of the cameras and lighting equipment

CREDITS

Origin: France
Released: 1996
Production: Jacques Perrin, Christophe Barratier, Yvette Mallet for a Galatee Films production; released by Miramax Films
Direction: Claude Nuridsany and Marie Perennou
Cinematography: Claude Nuridsany, Marie Perennou, Hughes Ryffel and Thierry Machado
Editing: Marie, Josephe Yoyotte and Florence Ricard
Music: Bruno Coulais
Sound: Philippe Barbeau, Bernard Leroux
MPAA rating: G
Running Time: 77 minutes

took over two years. The footage itself took three more years to shoot and six months was spent just on editing.

Roughly 90 minutes long, it is compromised of 30 or so mini-vignettes that show the world from the smallest of all possible vantage points. The sound technology seems light years beyond anything in existence. Nuridsany and Perennou took footage that is normally accompanied with dry, lifeless narration and instead chose to include sound effects that give the brief stories rich, dramatic character. The scene featuring two copulating snails coincides with the performance of a stirring, passionate Italian opera. Another scene shows a pheasant towering over an ant hill. Every time the bird sends its beak down to attack the defenseless ants, thunderous roaring drums are heard. Rather than the normal detached observers, we are experiencing the world through the senses of the insects.

Never before has art captured the life that surrounds us with such delicacy and detail. Nuridsany and Perennou have taken the raw ingredients of basic biology and delivered a finished product that includes heavy drama, whimsical humor, chilling horror, erotic couplings, birth, and barbaric fights to the death. *Microcosmos* entertains and educates. But most importantly, it moves us emotionally. It is real life escapism. Considering that nothing like it has ever been seen before, it is safe to say that it is the finest film of its kind ever produced.

—*J.M. Clark*

REVIEWS

American Cinematographer. January, 1997, p. 77.
Boxoffice. October, 1996, p. 46.
Chicago Tribune. January 10, 1997, p. 1.
Entertainment Weekly. October 25, 1996, p. 96.
Los Angeles Times. October 11, 1996, p. F15.
New York Times. October 9, 1996, p. C17.
USA Today. November 11, 1996, p. 3D.
Variety. May 20, 1996, p. 33.

A Midwinter's Tale; In the Bleak Midwinter

The drama. The passion. The intrigue . . . And the rehearsals haven't even started.—Movie tagline

"Endearing . . . Hilarious! You'll be warmed and entertained! Satire that turns into a valentine!"—Jay Carr, *Boston Globe*

"Fast and frothy . . . an amusing free-for-all spoof of the acting profession that eventually turns into a comic valentine to diehard thespian dedication."—Stephen Holden, *New York Times*

"A warmly comic tale. A sincere tribute to whatever it is that makes actors act."—Peter Travers, *Rolling Stone*

"Branagh is hugely talented! Delightfully different and altogether wonderful!"—Jeff Craig, *Sixty-Second Preview*

"Delightful, absolutely delightful! Witty, sophisticated and outrageous! Wonderful! "—Jeffrey Lyons, *Sneak Previews*

Box Office: $469,571

Kenneth Branagh's *A Midwinter's Tale* is the cinematic equivalent to a musician's rough cut demo tape. Musicians, performing composers in particular, lay down the blueprints of the songs they want to record in bare bones, skeletal arrangements to set the tone for works that they will spend hours slaving away at, in hopes of creating a pristine, polished, final product.

For better or worse (and there are many people who feel strongly in both cases), Kenneth Branagh is currently the world's most visible authority on all things Shakespearean. Although he's been involved with other projects as both a director and actor, he's most closely associated with *Henry V* (1989) and *Much Ado About Nothing* (1993), both of which he also adapted for the screen. The former, the Shakespearean war story of Herculean proportions was his rookie effort as a director and garnered him Oscar nominations for both actor and director. The latter found Branagh turning a serious drama into a lighthearted romantic romp in the sunny, English countryside. It also received severe condemnation from many Bard purists, in part due to the casting of lightweight American actors like Keanu Reeves. Both productions featured Emma Thompson, Branagh's wife at the time. He didn't direct *Othello* (1995) but his pivotal role as the evil, conniving Iago was one of the highlights of that film.

The December release of *Hamlet* (reviewed in this edition) again finds Branagh hip deep in the tragedy milieu. *A Midwinter's Tale*, the warm-up, the demo as it were, is a farcical send-up of a very dedicated, slipshod road company who is seeking to produce a provincial, Christmas time version of *Hamlet.* Comparisons (mostly unfair) find detractors comparing the project to a Woody Allen film—theory being any modern comedy filmed in black and white must be fashioned after Woody Allen. But they're not entirely wrong. Noel Coward's sarcastic "Why Must The Show Go On" opens the movie in the same fashion that Allen's short ragtime pieces open his. Branagh (who doesn't appear in the movie) facetiously preys at the insecurities and often tender, inflated egos of a group of actors who possess, at best, questionable talent, at worst, absolutely none. What they do have is a lot of heart and soul. They simply love acting and they better—the entire cast consists of six players doing 24 roles.

"The English theater is dominated by the class system and a bunch of obsolete homos."—Henry

Michael Maloney (Joe Harper/Hamlet) plays Laertes in Kenneth Branagh's 1996 *Hamlet.*

Heading the troupe is Michael Maloney as Joe Harper, (a thinly veiled Branagh) a struggling actor who bides his time waiting for that "big break" by producing *Hamlet* on a shoestring budget. He talks his agent, Margaretta D'Arcy (a perfectly cast Joan Collins) into bankrolling him. The audition process runs the gamut from the ridiculous, Nina Raymond (Julia Sawalha), who auditions for the part of Ophelia by butchering Blondie's "Heart Of Glass" to the even more ridiculous, Terry DuBois (John Sessions), a gay man who swishes his way into the role of Gertrude. And Tom Newman (Nicholas Farrell), a self-indulgent "actor's actor" who takes himself way too seriously and insists on showing off his wide array of accents and dialects for no reason whatsoever.

The cast nitpicks at each other while weathering the laborious rehearsals that take place inside of an echoing English church. The rapid-fire Queen's English bounces from one wall to another and right off the untrained American ear. The affairs, friendships, and alliances built up during the production are touching but they ultimately detract from the final finished play; only small parts are actually seen. Branagh would have served himself better to pare down the machine-gun delivery of the scenes leading up to the play. Woody Allen's *Bullets Over Broadway* (1994) showed other actors going through similar processes but the audience was given ample amounts of the play-within-the-play.

Kenneth Branagh has rubbed a lot of "serious" actors the wrong way in bringing the most famous pieces of English literature to the masses. They might be right. He nips and tucks and trims a bit here and there. Sir Ian McKellen, the world renowned heir to Olivier's thespian crown and precursor to Branagh, set his *Richard III* (1995) in 1930's Britain, casting himself as the quasi-fascist monarch. Making the most intricate, involving writer in the history of the English language palatable to the general public isn't easy. It's quite an unenviable task. Branagh missed the mark with *A Midwinter's Tale*, but only just slightly. You can be sure he hasn't lost his aim.

—J.M. Clark

CREDITS

Joe Harper: Michael Maloney
Henry Wakefield: Richard Briers
Vernon Spagreville: Mark Hadfield
Carnforth Greville: Gerard Horan
Terry DuBois: John Sessions

Origin: Great Britain
Released: 1995
Production: David Barron for a Castle Rock and a Midwinter Films production; released by TriStar
Direction: Kenneth Branagh
Screenplay: Kenneth Branagh
Cinematography: Roger Lanser
Editing: Neil Farrell
Production design: Tim Harvey
Costume design: Caroline Harris
Sound: Peter Glossop
Music: Jimmy Yuill
MPAA rating: R
Running Time: 98 minutes

REVIEWS

Boxoffice. November, 1995, p. 106.
Hollywood Reporter. September 5, 1995, p. 10.
New York Times. February 9, 1996, p. C5.
New Yorker. February 12, 1996, p. 84.
Rolling Stone. February 22, 1996, p. 70.
Sight and Sound. December, 1995, p. 47.
USA Today. February 9, 1996, p. 4D.
Variety. September 11, 1995, p. 107.

The Mirror Has Two Faces

There are two things a woman knows: what she's looking for and what she'll settle for.—Movie tagline

"A funny, joyful, romantic comedy!"—Bill Diehl, *ABC Radio Network*

"Funny and poignant! A wonderfully original love story! Filled with fun, feeling and a fresh sense of humor!"—David Sheehan, *CBS-TV*

"A pure delight! Barbra Streisand, Jeff Bridges and Lauren Bacall treat us to this year's best romantic comedy!"—Jim Ferguson, *Prevue Channel*

"Two thumbs up!"—*Siskel & Ebert*

Box Office: $40,466,068

In 1958 the French made a film starring Michele Morgan as an unattractive woman who metamorphoses into a beautiful butterfly thanks to plastic surgery. Unfortunately for her, this so muddles her relationship with her self-centered husband that he ends up killing the doctor who transformed his wife. This movie was titled *The Mirror Has Two Faces*, and while this latest film with that title, the third film from director-actor Barbra Streisand, has borrowed the French film's title, it has shrewdly replaced the original's murderous ending for one that is much happier.

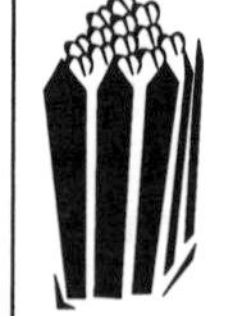

"Would telling you now that I'd like sex tonight be enough of a warning?"—Rose to hubby Greg

In the new version, Rose Morgan (Barbra Streisand) is a Columbia College professor of Romantic Literature who is talented as a teacher but a dud as a date. The romance she so expertly has researched and come to know in historical fiction seems incapable of realizing itself within her own life. Perhaps this is because Rose believes herself to be homely. Compared to her beautiful mother Hannah (Lauren Bacall) and attractive sister Claire (Mimi Rogers), Rose feels like the ugly duckling of the family. Consequently she is constantly backing out of dates she "knows" will go nowhere and sublimates by watching baseball on television, preparing scrumptious meals for her mother with whom she lives, and sneaking snacks. Romance seems destined to be nothing more than an intellectual endeavor for Rose.

Across the quad from Rose is mathematics professor Gregory Larkin (Jeff Bridges). He is having problems of his own. Unlike Rose's popular and dynamic teaching style, Gregory's technique is strictly flat and his classes boring. Also unlike Rose, Gregory seems to have no problem finding dates, he just has trouble integrating these women into his life. In fact, his latest book took 15 years to write because, in his words, "When I get involved with someone, I tend to get a little sidetracked." But that's only the half of it. When his ex-girlfriend Candy (Elle Macpherson) shows up at his first book lecture, all he can do is mumble, stumble and bumble. Pretty women seem to turn Gregory into an idiot, and he doesn't like it. If he could just get rid of romance and sex, he'd have a much more productive life.

But even Gregory knows that humans are not meant to go through life alone. So, in a desperate attempt to find companionship, he takes out a classified ad: "Columbia University professor (male) seeks woman interested in common goals and companionship. Must have Ph.D. and be over thirty-five. Physical appearance not important." Rose's sister, who has just married her third husband—the handsome Alex (Pierce Brosnan) with whom Claire is already bored and on whom Rose has a crush—sees Gregory's ad, and without her sister's knowledge, answers it for her.

So with Claire playing matchmaker, Gregory checks Rose out by sitting in on one of her classes. There he hears Rose expounding on medieval courtly love which is never consummated and it hits an immediate chord in Gregory's mind. However, he doesn't stay to the end of the class where Rose concludes that courtly love may seem nice, but we all want romance because it feels so good.

But Gregory has heard enough and asks Rose out to dinner where, to his pleasant surprise, she can actually discuss and understand his discussions about mathematical topics like prime integers. Here's a woman who not only can

AWARDS AND NOMINATIONS

Academy Award 1996 Nominations: Best Supporting Actress (Bacall), Best Song ("I've Finally Found Someone")
Golden Globe Awards 1997: Best Supporting Actress (Bacall)
Nominations: Best Actress-Musical/Comedy (Streisand), Best Original Score (Hamlisch), Best Original Song ("I've Finally Found Someone")
Screen Actors Guild 1996: Supporting Actress (Bacall)

carry on a meaningful conversation, she also intellectually understands the need for companionship . . . and the perils of romance. Believing he has found a safe and sexless harbor into which he can safely anchor his life, Gregory asks Rose to marry him. Believing that she will never get a better offer, and intrigued and attracted by the man in front of her, Rose agrees to his celibate offer.

For a while all goes well for the Larkins, but eventually Rose wants more. But when she asks if they might add sex to their marriage, Gregory is so flustered that he does the unforgivable. He tells her that he married her specifically because she was so plain that he wouldn't want to have sex with her. That night Rose moves back in with her mother. Not long afterward, Gregory goes on a European book tour.

But while Gregory's away, Rose will play. Well, actually, she exercises, and shops, and goes to the beauty parlor a lot. When Gregory gets home, he finds Rose has transformed herself into a beautiful and confident woman, and all deals are off. Boy gets girl, boy loses girl, will boy ever get girl again or will she go off with the now abandoned other boy, Alex?

As director, Barbra Streisand has done an assured job with *Mirror* and the result is an extremely watchable and intelligent romantic comedy about romance itself. As an actress, she shines on the screen and offers a most winning performance. If there is one flaw in her portrayal of Rose it is that even when she's supposed to be at her most unattractive, she is still radiant. In fact, many might find themselves preferring the earlier more unadorned and simple Rose to the glitzy and glamorous one presented at the end of the film.

This brings up the film's best and worst scenes. When Rose confronts her mother with the heart wrenching question, "How did it feel? Being beautiful?" Her mother replies, "It was wonderful." We feel Rose's sense of loss that she'll never experience that same feeling. But then, the next morning Hannah gives Rose a baby picture which Rose believes to be the pretty Claire. When her mother tells her it is her, everything changes. Rose finally hears the words she's been longing for someone to say to her: "You were such a beautiful baby," Hannah says. They are scenes for every woman who has ever felt less than pretty. They will strike a resounding chord deep in their souls.

Similarly, although it's acceptable for a woman to make the best of her physical attributes, the scenes in which Rose transforms herself into a swan feel like a slap in the face—a denial of who she really is. That even this likable and intelligent woman has to play the beauty game if she wants a man. Who she is is not enough. Barbra must become "Barbie."

While this may leave a slightly sour taste in the mind, it still shouldn't be enough to keep one from enjoying this otherwise smart film written by Richard LaGravenese (*The Fisher King* [1991]) and populated with a captivating supporting cast.

Jeff Bridges as the professor who is simultaneously a stud and a spastic is especially engaging. We are fascinated as we watch him lose himself in the cerebral world of mathematics in the classroom (much to the detriment of his students) then fall apart as he comes back to reality at the sight of a pretty co-ed flirting with him. Bridges does an outstanding job of showing how he comes to emotionally appreciate Rose's true beauty but is unwilling to compromise on the intellectual deal he has made. He captures the same combination of good-looks and vulnerability that was the hallmark of such earlier romantic comedians as Cary Grant.

Initially it would seem that Lauren Bacall was on hand just to be the elegant foil who dispenses ego-deflating zingers into Rose's life, but she, too, has her own vulnerable side which she reveals to Rose in the above mentioned poignant scene.

The Mirror Has Two Faces may find a more receptive audience with women (romantic comedies often do), but anyone who enjoys a lavishly produced, good-looking, and literate film that has laughs and warmth and an abundance of skillful supporting players should like it. Only the most

CREDITS

Rose Morgan: Barbra Streisand
Gregory Larkin: Jeff Bridges
Hannah Morgan: Lauren Bacall
Henry Fine: George Segal
Claire: Mimi Rogers
Alex: Pierce Brosnan
Doris: Brenda Vaccaro
Barry: Austin Pendleton
Candy: Elle Macpherson

Origin: USA
Released: 1996
Production: Barbra Streisand and Arnon Milchan for Phoenix Pictures; distributed by TriStar Pictures
Direction: Barbra Streisand
Screenplay: Richard LaGravenese; based on the film *Le Miroir a Deux Faces* written by Andre Cayatte and Gerard Oury
Cinematography: Dante Spinotti and Andrzej Bartkowiak
Editing: Jeff Werner
Production design: Tom John
Art direction: Teresa Carriker-Thayer
Set decoration: John Alan Hicks
Costume design: Theoni V. Aldredge
Music: Marvin Hamlisch
MPAA rating: PG-13
Running Time: 127 minutes

ardent Streisand-bashing critics will become so involved in ad hominem arguments that they fail to see the charming jewel in front of them.

—*Beverley Bare Buehrer*

REVIEWS

Boxoffice Online. November 18, 1996.
Chicago Sun Times. November 15, 1996.
Chicago Tribune. November 15, 1996, p. 5.
Detroit News. November 15, 1996, p. 4C.
Entertainment Weekly. November 22, 1996, p. 105.
Hollywood Reporter. November 11, 1996.
Los Angeles Times. November 15, 1996, p. F1.
New York Times. November 15, 1996, p. C14.
Newsweek. November 25, 1996, p. 78.
People. November 25, 1996, p. 19.
Rolling Stone. December 12, 1996, p. 90.
Time. November 25, 1996.
USA Today. November 15, 1996, p. 4D.
Variety. November 11, 1996, p. 57.
Village Voice. November 26, 1996, p. 72.

Mission: Impossible

Expect the impossible.—Movie tagline

"The wildest movie ride of the year."—Stephen Holden, *New York Times*

"Two thumbs up!"—*Siskel & Ebert*

Box Office: $180,981,866

Mission: Impossible, the television show created by Bruce Geller, ran from 1966 through 1973 and was noted for its use of a terrific ensemble cast, among them husband and wife team, Martin Landau and Barbara Bain. Each week the Impossible Missions Force, under the guidance of Team Leader, Jim Phelps (Peter Graves), would concoct elaborate sting-type operations that were designed to snare anyone who tried to get in the way of truth, justice and the American way of life. The IMF were like a well-oiled machine, each part working in synch with the others, and no one ego leading an agent to believe that they were the most important part of the operation. The IMF banded together to do battle with the Cold War enemy that lurked somewhere beyond the Iron Curtain.

Mission: Impossible, the feature film directed by Brian De Palma and starring Tom Cruise, immediately deconstructs that basic premise and instead turns the IMF against itself, rather than a good old-fashioned villain. And that is precisely what this film painfully lacks and desperately needs. Someone so nefarious, so cunning, so ruthless—someone like Hans Gruber, the Alan Rickman character in *Die Hard.* In fact, what the film needs is Alan Rickman. Someone to ground the film's paranoia and to focus its hatred. For without such a clearly defined antagonist, the film loses out on the audience's desire to root against someone in favor of the hero, in this case, Tom Cruise.

The film opens with a dynamite (no pun intended) precredit sequence that quickly encapsulates the entire story line in a rapid-fire montage. The opening is such fun that the rest of the film would, in the best of circumstances, have a difficult time living up to the energy and excitement that is generated in that brief sequence. And unfortunately, what follows is a jumbled and confusing plotline of double and triple cross that never quite congeals into a cohesive whole.

"Should you or any member of your I.M. Force be caught or killed, the secretary will disavow any knowledge of your actions."—usual warning to Jim Phelps

The story, written by high-powered hired guns David Koepp of *Jurassic Park* (1995) fame and the writer of the 1974 neo-noir *Chinatown*, Robert Towne, begins at a United States Embassy ball in Prague, where the Impossible Missions Force goes undercover with the hopes of intercepting a foreign agent before he is able to sell a stolen N.O.C. list. This list connects all C.I.A. agents with their code names and secret identities and serves as what Hitchcock would call a "MacGuffin"—something that does not necessarily make sense to the audience nor about which do they really care, but which the characters in the film desperately want or need badly enough to subject themselves to countless perilous situations in order to obtain it.

Things start to unravel quickly when all of the IMF agents end up dead, with Hunt and Phelps' wife, Claire (Emmanuelle Beart), the only survivors. Hunt is suspected of being the "mole" who is feeding top secret information to the Other Side and is "disavowed" from the Force by the

Despite all odds, Ethan Hunt (Tom Cruise) does the impossible by breaking into CIA headquarters in the film version of the popular '60s TV series, *Mission: Impossible.*

sinister U.S. governmental head, Kittridge (Henry Czerny). In an attempt to clear his name, Hunt joins forces with two other disavowed agents (Ving Rhames from 1994's *Pulp Fiction* and Jean Reno, the sensitive hit man in 1995's *The Professional*) and breaks into a computer room—in the film's most suspenseful and adrenaline-inducing scene—at C.I.A. headquarters in order to steal the N.O.C. list while literally dangling from a thread. Hunt then attempts to sell the list to the unscrupulous arms dealer, Max (the campy Vanessa Redgrave) in exchange for the true identity of the real mole, Job. Things get more than a little confusing if one tries to figure out who did what to whom. It is a challenge to piece together the connections of people and events because in part, director De Palma tends to place an equal amount of emphasis on every little detail. The end result, however, is that little makes sense and nothing has importance. As for the Big Revelation at the film's end, it comes as no surprise, since only one character is old enough to have liver spots on his hands as glimpsed from outside of the train window as the mole assembles his gun.

As in most of director Brian De Palma's films, all of the characters in *Mission: Impossible* take a backseat to the visuals. It is generally acknowledged that De Palma is fond of emulating other famous directors in his own work, such as replicating the brilliant *Odessa Steps* sequence from Soviet director Sergei Eisenstein's masterpiece, *Battleship Potemkin* (1925) in the baby carriage scene from his remake of *The Untouchables* (1987) or Alfred Hitchcock in his highly flawed 1984 thriller, *Body Double.* Few directors are as adept at the kind of visual razzle-dazzle as Brian De Palma is and *Mission: Impossible* offers up its share of exploding aquariums and struggles atop high-speed trains. But for all its visual excitement, the film is strangely humorless and dispassionate. No one aboard this freight train seems to be having much fun. Nor does anyone acknowledge the tongue-in-cheek absurdity of the whole thing; they are too busy playing it straight.

Tom Cruise, in yet another of his cocky, all-American good guys roles, plays Ethan Hunt as a bit of an egotistical loner, not unlike his role as the ace flyboy in the testosterone extended music video, *Top Gun* (1986). The actor has pumped up his biceps and is game to give all to the action sequences, but the problem here is there is no character for him to latch onto. He is indistinguishable from the hordes of other second-tier action stars, such as Steven Seagal and Jean-Claude Van Damme, whose characters all tend to blur together from one film to the next.

CREDITS

Ethan Hunt: Tom Cruise
Jim Phelps: Jon Voight
Claire Phelps: Emmanuelle Beart
Kittridge: Henry Czerny
Krieger: Jean Reno
Luther: Ving Rhames
Sarah Davies: Kristin Scott-Thomas
Max: Vanessa Redgrave
Jack: Emilio Estevez

Origin: USA
Released: 1996
Production: Tom Cruise and Paula Wagner; a Cruise/Wagner Production, released by Paramount Pictures
Direction: Brian De Palma
Screenplay: David Koepp and Robert Towne; from a story by David Koepp and Steven Zaillian; based on the television series created by Bruce Geller
Cinematography: Stephen H. Burum
Editing: Paul Hirsch
Production design: Norman Reynolds
Art direction: Frederick Hole
Costume design: Penny Rose
Sound: David Crozier
Music: Danny Elfman; "Mission: Impossible" theme by Lalo Schifrin
Special visual effects: Industrial Light & Magic
Special makeup effects: Rob Bottin
MPAA rating: PG-13
Running Time: 110 minutes

Emmanuelle Beart, previously seen in the French *Nelly and Monsieur Arnaud* (1996), is painfully miscast in the role of the younger wife of IMF leader Jim Phelps, played by the less-than-charismatic Jon Voight. The fine French actor Jean Reno is wasted in a skimpy role with limited screen time. One of the film's standout performances comes from Canadian actor Henry Czerny, who, with his work in *Clear and Present Danger* (1994) and the unnerving *The Boys of St. Vincent* (1995), seems to be making a career out of playing unscrupulous characters. As C.I.A. head, Kittridge, Czerny handles that famous "Your mission, Jim, should you decide to accept it . . . " line with an understated simplicity and grace.

First film from the Cruise/ Wagner production company.

What De Palma and his writers have done with their *Mission: Impossible* is to abscond with the basics of the television show—most notably Lalo Schiffrin's adrenaline-inducing theme song—yet they have essentially discarded its essence. Gone is the IMF team. In its place is the lone operative who is wrongly accused of being a traitor and must spend the bulk of the story trying to clear his name. This story has been told countless times—and in far more engaging ways.

Mission: Impossible holds the potential to spawn a franchise for the young Tom Cruise, much in the way *Die Hard* produced several sequels for actor Bruce Willis. The writers, however, would have to re-create the entire IMF team from scratch since all are lost, with the exception of Ethan Hunt, who is already set up in the film's end to take over the Jim Phelps' role as leader. But actor Tom Cruise does not appear to be much of a team player, if his previous films are any indication. So perhaps a wiser move might be to make Cruise the first American to play that granddaddy of all lone wolves, James Bond, Agent 007. Reviews for the film were mixed, but that did not stop its success at the box office.

—*Patricia Kowal*

REVIEWS

Box Office. July, 1996, p. 90.
Chicago Tribune. May 22, 1996.
Detroit News. May 22, 1996, p. 1B.
Entertainment Weekly. May 31, 1996, p. 39.
Los Angeles Times. May 22, 1996, p. F1.
The New Yorker. June 3, 1996, p. 85.
The New Republic. June, 1996.
New York Times. May 22, 1996, p. C13.
Newsweek. May 27, 1996, pp. 66.
Variety. May 20, 1996, pp. 29.

Mrs. Winterbourne

The story of a girl who is going from filthy to rich.—Movie tagline

"An absolute delight that's simply sensational."—Ron Brewington, *American Urban Radio Networks*

"It's Shirley MacLaine at her best and better than ever."—David Sheehan, *CBS-TV*

"Ricki Lake is a perfect Cinderella for the '90s."—Jeanne Wolf, *Jeanne Wolf's Hollywood*

"Guaranteed to add laughter, tears and a double helping of romance."—Bonnie Churchill, *National News Syndicate*

Box Office: $10,700,000

The princess in this fairy tale is Connie Doyle (Ricki Lake), a down-on-her-luck but ever plucky young woman whose lowlife boyfriend impregnates then abandons her. Soon Connie, through a highly improbable series of coincidences, finds herself mistakenly believed to be the widow of an heir to a financial and emotional fortune.

In wraparound style, the story begins with what is clearly the ending. As a self-improvement guru drones on the television inside a cheap motel room, a man lies in bed, dead of a gunshot wound. Cut to an expensive church wedding where mother of the groom, Grace Winterbourne (Shirley MacLaine), blithely confesses to having been that man's murderer. Whereupon the other Mrs. Winterbourne, the future Mrs. Winterbourne ne Connie Doyle, the Mrs. Winterbourne referred to by the title, introduces herself with a narrative promise to bring the audience up to speed.

With more optimism than an orphan and runaway such as herself, or any sentient being on earth in the nineties has any reason to possess, teenage Connie Doyle arrives in big, bad New York City to make a life for herself. She is instantly laid claim to by a lazy, swindling, beer guzzling, albeit charming-when-he-wants-to-be guy named Steve DeCunzo (Loren Dean). All he has to do is hand Connie his "business card" and she accepts that he must be a legitimate . . . whatever he is. What she becomes is more like his housekeeper than his girlfriend, and when she gleefully announces that she is pregnant with his child, he throws her out on the street and doesn't look back.

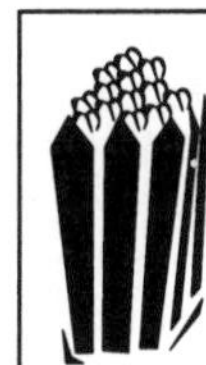

Grace: "How could I raise such a snob?" Bill: "It's a mystery, Mother. Let's ask the servants."

Previously filmed as *No Man of Her Own* (1950) and *I Married a Shadow* (1982).

In no time Connie loses her waitressing job because her uniform no longer fits over her expanding tummy, runs out of money, and overstays her welcome at the YWCA. From the sidewalk below her former home, and during a rainstorm no less, Connie pleads with the heinous DeCunzo to take her back, or at least let her sleep there until she figures out what to do next. Advising her to call someone who cares, DeCunzo tosses a quarter out of the window and, as composer Patrick Doyle's score becomes a little heavy-handed, Connie dramatically bends down to retrieve the coin because she cannot afford not to.

Near collapse from hunger and exhaustion, Connie wanders in to the giant train station where a transient approaches her with his hand out for a quarter. Connie looks at her last coin, the one that her baby's father threw at her, and actually considers giving it to the man. Instead she faints. He catches her and, seeing that she is even more pitiful than himself, gives her his last possession, a moist towlette.

The crowd pushes Connie onto a train where she meets Hugh and Patricia Winterbourne who without question rescue her from the train conductor insistent on collecting Connie's non-existent ticket, her hunger, her wet clothes and her loneliness. Just as Connie breathes a sigh of blind hope, the train crashes. When Connie awakes in a hospital several days later, not only has she had her baby, but she has been mistaken for Patricia Winterbourne who was killed in the wreck along with her husband and their unborn child.

Enter Grace Winterbourne, by telephone anyway, promising to care for her lost son's widow and her first grandchild no matter what—no matter even that Hugh's twin brother Bill is on to Connie from the start.

Based on the novel *I Married a Dead Man* by Cornell Woolrich, *Mrs. Winterbourne* was scripted by two writers from the small screen: Lisa-Marie Radano who has written sketch comedy for "The Tracey Ullman Show", and Phoef Sutton, best known for her work on the long-running hit sitcom "Cheers."

The magical quality promised by the friendly transient who helps Connie on her way then mysteriously vanishes, dips rudely into the ridiculous when Hugh's pregnant wife invites the stranger stowaway not only into their compartment and into their lives, but into her wedding ring! Bill's suspicion that his new sister-in-law is a fraud is the first logical event of the film, but when he takes longer to do anything about it than he does to fall in love with the felon, his credibility must be questioned as well. Miguel Sandoval's Paco would have been an even greater delight as the family caretaker, friend and advisor if he had not been written to endure the first half of his scenes as a merely over-talkative servant. The only character whose behavior is consistently believable is Shirley MacLaine's Grace, and that is just because her inconsistencies can

CREDITS

Grace Winterbourne: Shirley MacLaine
Connie Doyle: Ricki Lake
Bill/Hugh Winterbourne: Brendan Fraser
Paco: Miguel Sandoval
Steve DeCunzo: Loren Dean
Father Brian: Peter Gerety

Origin: USA
Released: 1996
Production: Dale Pollock, Ross Canter, Oren Koules for an A&M Films production; released by TriStar Pictures
Direction: Richard Benjamin
Screenplay: Phoef Sutton and Lisa-Maria Radano; based on the novel *I Married a Dead Man*, by Cornell Woolrich
Cinematography: Alex Nepomniaschy
Editing: Jacqueline Cambas, William Fletcher
Music: Patrick Doyle
Production design: Evelyn Sakash
Art direction: Dennis Davenport
Set decoration: Casey Hallenbeck
Costume design: Theoni V. Aldredge
Sound: Richard Lightstone
Casting: Nancy Foy
MPAA rating: PG-13
Running Time: 104 minute

be excused by her illness. But even director Richard Benjamin's erratic tone cannot stop it from being a heartwarming, smile provoking, if implausible bedtime story.

—*Eleah Horwitz*

REVIEWS

Detroit Free Press. April 19, 1996, p. D1.
Entertainment Weekly. April 26, 1996, p. 88.
The New York Times. April 19, 1996, p. C3.
Variety. April 15, 1996, p. 178.

Mr. Wrong

He loved her from afar. It wasn't far enough.—Movie tagline

"Hilarious! Painfully funny! Consistently funny!"—*L.A. Weekly*

"Extremely funny!"—Leonard Klady, *Variety*

Box Office: $12,825,141

Stand-up comedian-turned-television sitcom star Ellen DeGeneres makes her big-screen debut in a vehicle without the proverbial engine. In their attempt to ease Ms. DeGeneres into the movie theatre, the filmmakers have chosen a project that requires their star to risk little, staying safely within the confines of her small-screen persona. *Mr. Wrong* is a textbook example of how Hollywood's infatuation with all things television leads to cloudy thinking and lousy filmmaking. All that flickers on the small screen does not necessarily lead to box office gold.

"Sometimes chemistry works and sometimes it doesn't. Sometimes you get an explosion - or a really bad smell."—Martha tries to ditch her unwanted beau

Martha Alston (DeGeneres) is a thirty-something producer of a fluffy San Diego morning talk show. She seems to have it all: the career, the sweet little house, the young admirer in Walter, the show's intern (John Livingston). But as her parents are more than willing to point out as they celebrate her younger sister's marriage, there is a cavernous abyss in Martha's otherwise seemingly perfect life: a man. Compounded by the arrival of that bane of any single woman's existence, the vilest of all holidays, Valentine's Day, Martha begins to feel that tug at her heart strings, the relationship equivalent of a ticking biological clock The single existence that she once embraced now feels like a ruse. Everyone must be right, she could not possibly be content with her life the way it is.

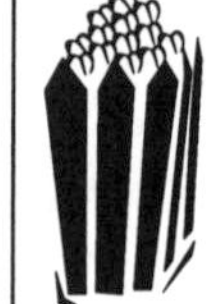

Feature film debut of comedian Ellen DeGeneres.

Martha heads down to the local lonely hearts bar and attempts to drown her sorrow over her newfound emptiness in a couple of martinis. As she scrambles around on the floor when she drops her quarter as she is about to make her selection on the jukebox, Martha suddenly hears the opening strains of her favorite song, Hank Williams' "I'm So Lonesome I Could Cry." Looking up, she sees hunky Whitman Crawford, played by the always amusing Bill Pullman. It appears to be love at first sight and although Whit has some quirks, like his extremely nauseating poetry, Martha cannot help but fall for this romantic. He sends her flowers and begins to shower her with gifts and tokens of his affection. When Martha takes Whit home to meet her family, everyone thinks he is the perfect gentleman, but Martha feels something is not quite right. Afterwards, Martha encourages Whit to just be himself and not feel that he needs to be someone he is not. Whit is relieved. It is then that things begin to get weird—although not wild enough.

Martha soon discovers that her Romeo is an obsessive psycho. Whitman trades in his tasteful silver Jaguar for a purple LeBaron ("It's more me," he tells her.) and reveals his passion for the music of Foreigner and Boston—as well as shoplifting beers from a convenience store. Martha is uncomfortable with the degree of affection displayed between Whit and his mother (Joan Plowright) and a game of charades leaves Martha feeling more like a third wheel. When she tries to break things off with Whitman, he refuses to let her go. He even breaks his little pinkie to prove his love for her. And of course, Martha's family thinks she is trying to sabotage a good thing.

The remainder of the film involves Whitman's relentless pursuit of Martha, along with Joan Cusack's over-the-top performance as his demented ex-lover in a curious subplot that moves the story to Mexico. The script reads like a gender-switched *Fatal Attraction* (1988). The film's premise is an interesting one, but not enough to sustain itself for the 92 minutes of running time. It might have made a far more engaging episode of DeGeneres' "Ellen." The sight gags become repetitive and the story predictable. Yet it is the passivity of the main character that proves the most problematic. Throughout the story, Martha remains reactive and never has any kind of character change that would allow her to become a more active participant.

DeGeneres is a talented comedian, without doubt. Her reliance on facial tics and gestures such as rolling her eyeballs in mock disgust and social disenchantment have become her comic trademark, helping to solidify her television sitcom's position on ABC's primetime line-up. But if *Mr. Wrong* is any indication, Ms. DeGeneres, sadly, is an actress of limited range. She fails to embody her character; rather, her character gives way to the comedian. No doubt the filmmakers were hoping for an easy transition from television to film for their star, but like Luke Perry of "Beverly Hills 90210", Ms. DeGeneres lacks sheer star-power—which in lieu of acting ability is an absolute must in order to make the leap.

Director Nick Castle previously helmed another comedy that misfired at the box office, *Dennis the Menace* (1993), displaying a certain knack for allowing his films to spiral out of his control. *Mr. Wrong* is sloppily directed, with several sequences rambling on with little to no build, while the photography is harsh and favors no one in the film. One of the film's few delights is actor Bill Pullman, whose work ranges from the neo-noir *The Last Seduction* (1995) to the romantic comedy *While You Were Sleeping* (1995). Here Pullman is liberated and able to do a wild comic turn as the Lover from Hell, despite the lack of chemistry with Ms. DeGeneres. "Saturday Night Live"'s Ellen Cleghorne brings a much needed energy to the part of Martha's co-worker and good friend, offering another level of comedic cynicism. "All men are horrible in their own way," she counsels, "You just have to accept it." Unfortunately, absurd plot twists undercut some witty lines of dialogue and a promising and amusing premise.

What starts out as black comedy, quickly slips into near slapstick and parody. Sadly, the film simply is not funny. Like a guest that has overstayed their welcome, *Mr. Wrong* continues on far too long, missing every clue that it is time to go. With a few exceptions, most critics were unenthusiastic in their reviews of the film with most citing the lack of chemistry between the stars and the uneven tone due to poor direction.

—Patricia Kowal

CREDITS

Martha Alston: Ellen DeGeneres
Whitman Crawford: Bill Pullman
Inga Gunther: Joan Cusack
Jack Tramonte: Dean Stockwell
Mrs. Crawford: Joan Plowright
Walter: John Livingston
Dick Braxton: Robert Goulet
Missy: Maddie Corman
Jane: Ellen Cleghorne

Origin: USA
Released: 1996
Production: Mandeville Films/Marty Katz production; released by Touchstone Pictures
Direction: Nick Castle
Screenplay: Chris Matheson, Kerry Ehrin and Craig Munson
Cinematography: John Schwartzman
Editing: Patrick Kennedy
Production design: Doug Kraner
Art direction: Nancy Patton
Costume design: Ingrid Ferrin
Music: Craig Safan
MPAA rating: PG-13
Running Time: 92 minutes

REVIEWS

Detroit Free Press. February 18, 1996, p. 3G.
Detroit News. February 17, 1996, p. C1.
Los Angeles Times. February 16, 1996, p. F8.
New York Times. February 16, 1996.
USA Today. February 19, 1996, p. 4D.
Variety. February 19, 1996, p. 47.

Moll Flanders

The remarkable story of one woman's unbreakable spirit.—Movie tagline

"What a wonderful film! You're in for a memorable experience full of romance and thrills."—Jeanne Wolf, *Jeanne Wolf's Hollywood*

"Lush and lovely. A romantic epic!"—Bob Healy, *Satellite News Network*

"Visually stunning with moving performances by Robin Wright and Morgan Freeman."—Paul Wunder, *WBAI Radio*

Box Office: $3,486,957

The oddest title among the opening credits for *Moll Flanders* reports that Pen Densham's story and screenplay are "based on characters from the novel by Daniel Defoe." That cautious acknowledgement may overstate the indebtedness of the film to its source. Densham has kept the eighteenth-century setting and the name of the main character but mostly abandoned the rest of Defoe's classic. Densham's Moll loves or hates in a grand style, but to achieve these operatic effects the film sacrifices the largest part of its subtlety and wit.

"When I close my eyes I have enough love for the world and you."—The Artist to Moll

The story of Moll (Robin Wright) is structured as an extended flashback read by a man named Hibble (Morgan Freeman) from the log of a ship's purser to Flora (Aisling Corcoran), Moll's nine-year-old daughter. Hibble tells Flora that she is to be cared for by a mysterious benefactor who has been searching for her since her mother's death. To fill the travel time en route to meet this benefactor, Hibble reads Moll's own narrative, which starts with her birth in prison to a woman whose own hanging for thievery was postponed nine months so that she could have her child. On the very night of Moll's birth, her mother is duly executed.

Except for an early scene in which Moll retaliates against a priest trying to molest her in the confessional (she plunges her knitting needles into his groping hand), Moll lacks the selfish cunning of her counterpart in the novel. She flees the cathedral into the streets and eventually is placed by a local bureau into the home of the Mazzawattis, a family of place and property. Moll undertakes charitable work in the prisons, even giving water to the hopeless cases with smallpox. The two Mazzawatti daughters (Eileen McCloskey and Nicola Techan), jealous over the approval their mother (Brenda Fricker) gives to Moll's charity, constantly tease her, and for a while the film takes on the trappings of a Cinderella story. When these pampered daughters attempt some charitable work of their own among the poor and are raped, Moll fails even to reflect in passing that her enemies have been punished. She nobly blames herself and leaves the house out of guilt.

A more-faithful version of Defoe's novel, starring Alex Kingston, was filmed for British television and was shown on PBS' "Masterpiece Theatre" in 1996.

The red light over a door beckons her to the establishment of Mrs. Allworthy (Stockard Channing), whom Moll fitly describes in the narration as having "the alluring airs of a great duchess and the survival instincts of a country cat." Here Moll makes friends with Hibble, an escaped thief that Mrs. Allworthy has taken in as her majordomo. Still a virgin, Moll gradually becomes accustomed to the life at Mrs. Allworthy's. Moll's virginity is raffled off by Mrs. Allworthy to a roomful of eager bidders; offering a hundred guineas, a wrinkled codger (Brendan Cauldwell) claims the prize. As Moll trudges off to the tortures of the bed, Mrs. Allworthy remarks: "For a hundred guineas I'd put her in bed with the devil."

Her days at Mrs. Allworthy's take their toll, and Moll escapes in drink. When a character described in the credits only as the artist (John Lynch) comes to buy a girl to model for him, Mrs. Allworthy refers to Moll as the "shame of the establishment" and sends her off for half a crown ("You'll be lucky to get your money's worth"). Living in a cold garret, the artist uses Moll as the subject for his many sketches and paintings. In the film's most predictable touch, they fall in love, and she primly insists on meeting his family before she will marry him. The artist and Moll travel to the landed estate that he has rejected to pursue his vocation in London; as his father (Jeremy Brett) heaps abuse on his son for his choice of a wife, the couple pledge their mutual love.

The audience may well foresee further melodramatic calamities. After Moll becomes pregnant, the artist contracts smallpox. Moll nurses him as best she can, but after his death she is alone to take care of her baby. When she is grabbed one day by a crowd searching for the girl who stole a jewel from a shop, Mrs. Allworthy happens by and stops the commotion. She and Hibble buy Moll's freedom and take her off in a carriage. Mrs. Allworthy, now deep in the reveries of her ever-present opium pipe, explains that she has a grant of land in the New World and plans to sail with the next tide. The melodrama intensifies as Moll sends Hibble hurriedly to bring Flora to the docks before they sail. He arrives empty-handed, reporting that a fire clogged the streets and kept him from finding the child. In tears, Moll follows Hibble and Mrs. Allworthy aboard. Predictably, the ship sinks. By the time the rough weather arrives, however, Moll has started writing her narrative in the purser's log. Hibble survives to begin his search for Flora. The present-day narrative concludes as he brings Flora to his home in the New World where she finally meets her benefactor, whom Hibble names as Mrs. Allworthy. But it is Moll who steps out to greet her daughter, having survived the tempest and having assumed the identity of one whose fortune now promises the peace she has longed for.

Throughout the film Moll's insights and interpretations, often read in voice-over narration as Hibble resumes her story, bring an oddly modern psychology to the story of a girl of the eighteenth-century streets. Moll narrates, for example, in the Mazzawatti scenes that the sisters "plan acts of war with the weapons of superior culture" but that she "has a sense of self that they don't understand or possess." Later, after Hibble loses the company of his lover Edna (Geraldine James) by enduring her sale by Mrs. Allworthy, Moll tearfully explains to him that she can stand her own woes but that his break her. In the narration, she comments: "I finally understood how caged we all are." When later hardships drive Moll to drink, she transmutes this slide into another discerning metaphor, saying she pushed herself "into a gin bottle like one of those ships a sailor makes." By presenting the title character as a woman who stoically endures repeated sufferings and devotedly loves those who are taken from her, writer-director Densham has robbed the character of much of her complexity. She has become, perhaps too obviously, a symbol of the many sufferings of the unempowered in society, and the film risks becoming more tract than drama.

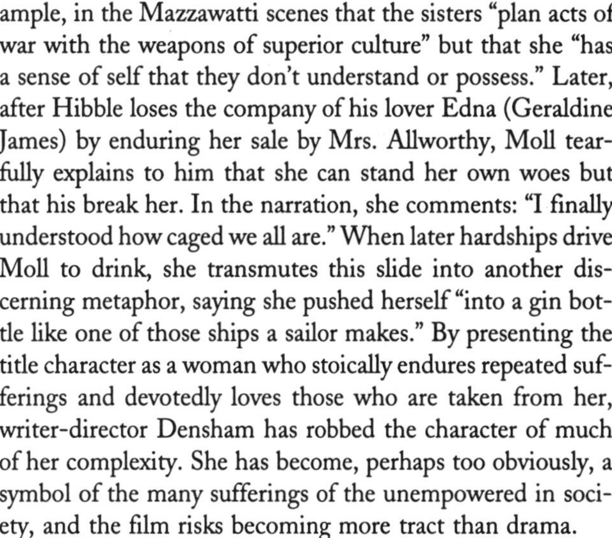

This didacticism may be seen in the moments the director chooses to linger over and those he elects to scale down. The suffering and the squalor usually receive close attention: two smallpox scenes turn up, and Moll's agonized delivery of Flora occurs in the artist's garret with no midwife or doctor since she fears her husband's family will take her child. However, the moments when wit or irony might lighten the tone—such as Moll's night with the old codger at Mrs. Allworthy's—are kept offscreen. After this incident with "Mr. 100 Guineas," as the credits refer to him, Moll strolls into the larder at Mrs. Allworthy's and announces to Hibble that she knows what she is doing in becoming one of the girls. A quick montage shows a gallery of faces while Moll's narration reports that her life became "a whirligig of men's sweating bodies." Densham, in short, rejects the irony and sexiness inherent in the story and focuses instead on the misery.

As a result of such streamlining, most of the performers are asked to play characters defined by one central personality trait. With Hibble it is his stalwart devotion, first to Moll and Edna and then to Flora. With Mrs. Allworthy it is her predatory villainy. One reviewer aptly called her an eighteenth-century Cruella de Vil, and Stockard Channing makes the most of a part seemingly written to give the performer some chances to ham it up. Hers is the most enjoyable character in the film. With Flora the dominating trait is her spoiled, sarcastic side, and Aisling Corcoran handles these challenges very well. Though its period detail is effective and its scenes of squalor are vivid, the film does not escape the solemnity that such an approach entails.

—Glenn Hopp

CREDITS

Moll Flanders: Robin Wright
Hibble: Morgan Freeman
Mrs. Allworthy: Stockard Channing
Artist: John Lynch
Mrs. Mazzawatti: Brenda Fricker
Edna: Geraldine James
Flora: Aisling Corcoran
Artist's father: Jeremy Brett
Polly: Cathy Murphy
Mr. Mazzawatti: Alan Stanford
Mazzawatti daughter one: Eileen McCloskey
Mazzawatti daughter two: Nicola Techan
Mr. 100 Guineas: Brendan Cauldwell

Origin: USA
Released: 1996
Production: John Watson, Richard B. Lewis, and Pen Densham for Spelling Films and Trilogy Entertainment; released by MGM
Direction: Pen Densham
Screenplay: Pen Densham, based on characters from the novel by Daniel Defoe
Cinematography: David Tattersall
Editing: Neil Travis, James R. Symons
Production design: Caroline Hanania
Costume designer: Consolata Boyle
Art director: Steve Simmonds
Set decorator: Fiona Daly
Music: Mark Mancina
MPAA rating: PG-13
Running Time: 123 minutes

REVIEWS

Boxoffice. July 1996, p. 89.
Detroit News. June 14, 1996, p. 3D.
USA Today. June 14, 1996, p. 4D.
Variety. May 27, 1996, p. 65.

The Monster; Il Mostre

"He *was* Down By Law . . . *In* A Night On Earth and *played* a Pink Panther. Now Roberto Benigni is . . . THE MONSTER!"—Movie tagline

"A gut-clutchingly funny and deliriously delightful comedy!"—Barbara & Scott Siegel, *Siegel Entertainment Syndicate*

"Absolutely delightful! Roberto Benigni is a comedy master."—Jeffrey Lyons, *Sneak Previews*

"One of the funniest films of the year!"—Casper Citron, *WOR-Radio*

Box Office: $615,826

Italy's most beloved comedic genius, Roberto Benigni directs, co-writes and stars in one of his most ambitious projects, the farcical social satire, *The Monster* (*Il Mostre*). But do not expect any subtle, verbally sophisticated comedy. Like his American counterpart, Jim Carrey, Benigni plunges into the waters of pure physical comedy with such gusto that the simplest gesture or glance turns into a celebration of hysterical laughter. Benigni combines the innocence of Charlie Chaplin with the physicality of Buster Keaton to build a continually misunderstood Everyman. And while Carrey's comedy tends to be more aggressively adolescent, the irresistible Benigni favors a more childlike approach, intense, yet endearing and even sexy in his silliness.

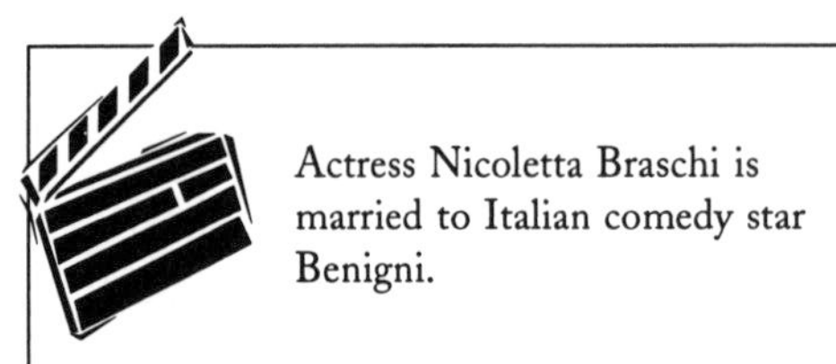

Actress Nicoletta Braschi is married to Italian comedy star Benigni.

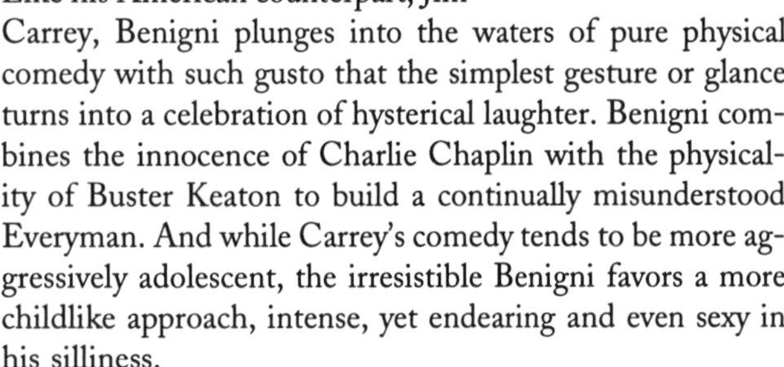

Dressed in his de rigueur baggy grey suits, Benigni plays Loris, a harmless con man who combines his brains with his dexterity in order to outwit the authorities. He is able to leave a supermarket with a trench coat stuffed with pilfered goods, only to have the honest customers trigger off the alarm with items that he has planted. He has a scheme for getting his coffee and biscuits for free and no one is better at outfoxing his landlord. But when a miscalculated come-on and an out-of-control chainsaw bring him to the attention of the local police, he suddenly becomes the prime suspect in a series of rapes and murders that are plaguing the city. But not that he notices. The insouciant Loris is too busy ogling beautiful women to notice that he is under police observation.

In one of the film's most hilarious sequences, a cigarette accidentally lands down Loris' pants and as he stops to admire a shapely brunette in tight capris, he suddenly begins flailing about, frantically trying to extinguish the fire—literally!—in his groin. To the fanatical criminal psychologist Taccone (French actor Michel Blanc of *Gross Fatigue* [1994]) this behavior clearly indicates a man with no sexual self-control. What the police need is to catch this maniac in the act, so Detective Jessica Rossetti (played by Benigni's charming wife and frequent collaborator, Nicoletta Braschi) is sent in to entice this "Mozart of vice" twenty-four hours a day with her sexual wiles until he cracks under pressure.

And crack he does. But not in the way the local Chief of Police (Laurent Spielvogel) had hoped. When Taccone searches Loris' apartment for clues to his personality, he discovers the very revealing statue of one of the Seven Dwarfs hidden away in the closet of nondescript grey suits. For despite his macho posturing, Loris turns out to be more like Bashful than "The Monster."

With such a serious set-up as a gruesome serial rapist terrorizing women, Benigni risks offending people with what might be misconstrued as sexism or even misogyny. The leering shots of women's derrieres and shapely legs are not

CREDITS

Loris: Roberto Benigni
Detective Jessica Rossetti: Nicoletta Braschi
Taccone: Michel Blanc
Chinese Teacher: Franco Mescollini
Taccone's Wife Jolanda: Dominique Lavanant
Roccarotta: Jean-Claude Brialy
Frustalupi: Laurent Spielvogel

Origin: Italy
Released: 1994; 1996
Production: Roberto Benigni and Yves Attal for a UGC Images, Melampro, and Iris Films production; released by Cinepix Film Properties
Direction: Roberto Benigni
Screenplay: Roberto Benigni, Vincenzo Cerami and Michel Blanc (written in Italian with English subtitles)
Cinematography: Carlo Di Palma
Editing: Nino Baragli
Production design: Giantito Burchiellaro
Costume design: Danilo Donati
Sound: Jean-Paul Mugel
Music: Evan Lurie
MPAA rating: Unrated
Running Time: 111 minutes

exploitative, but rather, illustrative. They show the world as Loris sees it, revealing his fixations and sexual frustrations. And these sexually provocative camera angles also help to underscore what seems to be the film's core issue of how easy it is to misinterpret a man's actions, most specifically when it comes to his appreciation of the female form, for sexist behavior. When does appreciation turn into perversity? In modern society, particularly in the United States, danger often lurks in a man's natural desire for a woman and as Benigni so aptly shows us in *The Monster*, what may appear to some as one thing is quite possibly something else in actuality. Even the clever animated opening title sequence shows how an ordinary dog can be viewed as a vicious monster—especially if you are a cat! It is in this duality and social commentary that Benigni the comedian shines. He is so gifted in his ability to build a gag, then milk it for laughs not once, but later again down the line, resulting in an even bigger comic payoff.

Benigni first came to the attention of American moviegoers with his work in Jim Jarmusch's *Down by Law* (1986) and later in a hilarious segment in *Night on Earth* (1991). His work as Inspector Jacques Clousseau's bumbling offspring in *Son of the Pink Panther* (1993) was overlooked primarily due to the film's weak story.

The Monster has become the highest grossing film in Italian history, surpassing a record held by Benigni's 1992 gangster spoof, *Johnny Stecchino*. There is little doubt that film historians will one day place this frenetic little comedian with the quizzical face right alongside the great comic masters of all time. For some of us, he is already there.

—Patricia Kowal

REVIEWS

Boxoffice. December, 1995, p. 112.
Los Angeles Times. April 19, 1996, p. F1.
New York Times. April 19, 1996, p. C8.
Village Voice. April 23, 1996, p. 69.

Mother

No one misunderstands you better.—Movie tagline

"Albert Brooks is one of the funniest comedians ever to work in American movies."—Dave Kehr, *N.Y. Daily News*

"A gem! Debbie Reynolds is superb!"—David Ansen, *Newsweek*

"Two thumbs up!"—*Siskel & Ebert*

Box Office: $5,583,290

Who says that you can't go home again? Albert Brooks does and he does with the intention of finding out why he is having such a difficult time with women. Recently divorced, he comes up with the theory that it all has to do with dear old Mom. Perhaps, by going back to live with her again, he'll discover the root cause of the dysfunction that has made him a failure with the opposite sex.

What an intriguing premise for a screenplay! Brooks, who co-wrote the script with Monica Johnson, explored this somewhat Oedipal problem in Paramount's Christmas '96 release of *Mother*. It received mostly good critical notices and re-introduced the star quality of Debbie Reynolds to today's generation of filmgoers. It is the Las Vegas trouper's first major starring role in 24 years and this is reason enough to see this psychoanalytical comedy. It was reported that Brooks originally offered the role to Nancy Reagan, who gratefully turned it down.

Going home to a mother like Beatrice Henderson (Debbie Reynolds) is no easy undertaking. She introduces son, John (Brooks) to neighbors with, "Oh, this is my son. The other one." This certainly would give anyone a complex. Brooks was quoted by Janet Maslin in the *New York Times* (12/24/96), "There are two kinds of mothers on the planet. The first kind thinks that every single thing their children do is perfect and their children are God's gift to the world. And then there's the other kind. This is about the other kind."

John is a science fiction writer who writes books with names like *The Day There Was No Earth*. Beatrice is not his biggest fan. When he tells her that it has been suggested

AWARDS AND NOMINATIONS

Golden Globe Award 1997 Nominations: Best Actress-Musical-Comedy (Reynolds)
National Society of Film Critics 1996: Screenplay (Brooks/Johnson)
New York Film Critics Circle 1996: Screenplay (Brooks/Johnson)

that he write a sequel, she responds with, "The space thing. Do you really want to bring back all those characters?" Remarks such as these reveal some of the reasons why poor John has low self-esteem. Undaunted, he insists on pressing forward with what he calls "The Experiment." It takes some effort, but he manages to reconstruct his old room, right down to the lava lamp and the *Barbarella* poster. Mother thinks that this is rather absurd, but reluctantly goes along with it. The two seem to be direct opposites in almost everything, especially their dietary habits. John is a vegetarian—Mom likes meatloaf. Beatrice buys cheap brands (a sherbet called Sweet Tooth) and John likes gourmet peanut butter. Most of their time together is spent bickering, but Beatrice remains imperturbable and John remains insistent. The conflict is exacerbated by the fact that John's brother, Jeff, (played by a surprisingly funny Rob Morrow) is a hugely successful attorney, not to mention he is also happily married. Mom likes Jeff better and he calls her every day (on a picture phone). Strangely enough, John's moving back home has had a curiously upsetting effect on his "golden boy" sibling. It seems that Jeff also has his own "momma's boy" hang-ups that seem to be surfacing.

"I wish your father was alive so HE could take some of the blame."—Beatrice to son John

All this conflict provides enough material for any director to have a field day, from Ingmar Bergman to Woody Allen. However, Albert Brooks takes the directorial helm and adds his unique wit and talent to the project. "There would be no 'Seinfeld' strain of humor on television without Mr. Brooks' pioneering approach to yuppie psycho-trivia," (Janet Maslin, *New York Times*, 12/24/96). Brooks appears to be a thirty-something alumni with a sense of humor. He has scripted (or co-scripted) and directed a series of offbeat films since his appearance in *Taxi Driver* in 1976. Films like *Real Life* (1979), *Modern Romance* (1981), *Lost in America* (1985), *Defending Your Life* (1991), and *The Scout* (1994) is a list of some of his previous work. The actor/writer/director has a distinctive brand of dry humor that at times can be hilarious. In *Mother*, the humor is based in reality, which invites audience identification, unlike, say, the black comedy *Throw Momma from the Train* (1987). This is more like "Throw Momma Onto the Shrink's Couch." Everyone, at some time or another, during a period of psychoanalyzing, decides that Mom may be the main culprit in the drama of their lives. Brooks uses this basis of identification to his advantage throughout most of the film, plus his inventiveness and his intelligence. If he had only gone the distance and continued this approach to the very end, this film would have been utterly charming and delightful. However, as it stands, he tied everything up into one big happy ending for everyone (except maybe for his brother, who just drives off). Essentially, he opted for a simplistic solution to a complex problem which left the viewer with a feeling of being ripped off. It seemed contrived and unrealistic.

Much of the film deals with the relationship between John and Beatrice, making it basically a two-character story. The advantage of this to the spectator is that they get to see a lot more of Debbie Reynolds. This performance has been unanimously praised by critics and can definitely be labeled a "come-back" vehicle for the star of yesteryear. Todd McCarthy of *Variety* said that her performance was "outstanding" and called it an "expertly judged come-back turn." Kevin Thomas of *The Los Angeles Times* wrote that in *Mother*, "Debbie Reynolds returns to the screen triumphantly, in a major role for the first time in 27 years." And Janet Maslin said that Beatrice is "played divinely by Ms. Reynolds." It is also important to mention that Albert Brooks wisely allows Ms. Reynolds to shine (after all, it is titled *Mother*). She is the perfect counterpart to his perplexed and confused John, whose undaunted persistence at finding answers is commendable, although annoying.

Lisa Kudrow of "Friends" fame makes a brief appearance as Brooks' blind date, Linda. She is quite wonderful as the airhead blonde who thinks that Charlie Chaplin was a famous author. This bright actress chose a smaller part for her film outing, which was a wise career move. Most of the other cast members of "Friends" have not seemed to fare

CREDITS

John Henderson: Albert Brooks
Beatrice: Debbie Reynolds
Jeff: Rob Morrow
Linda: Lisa Kudrow
Cheryl: Isabel Glasser
John's buddy: John C. McGinley

Origin: USA
Released: 1996
Production: Scott Rudin, and Herb Nanas; released by Paramount Pictures
Direction: Albert Brooks
Screenplay: Albert Brooks and Monica Johnson
Cinematography: Lajos Koltai
Editing: Harvey Rosenstock
Music: Marc Shaiman
Production design: Charles Rosen
Costume design: Judy L. Rustin
Sound: Kim Ornitz
MPAA rating: PG-13
Running Time: 104 minutes

well in their film debuts. Ms. Kudrow may just be the smartest dumb blonde of them all.

Fans of Albert Brooks will love *Mother*, and fans of Debbie Reynolds will be ecstatic. This film, with its unique theme, certainly will be popular with the "middle-aged" baby boomers who may not have quite figured things out, yet. The film succeeds on many levels, and the "offbeat" Brooks' humor shines through it all. The writing is sharp, funny and completely identifiable to anyone who has ever had a mother. It would be hard to imagine anyone, forty and over, not getting somewhat nostalgic about their own Moms. So, Brooks succeeded in what he set out to do. It is bothersome that it appears he ran out of ideas towards the end. However, maybe it is better to believe that life's problems can be solved easily. Why not have everything work out in one neatly tied-up little package? Shakespeare said, "It is too big a knot for me to untie." Well, Albert Brooks possibly may have done just that.

—Rob Chicatelli

REVIEWS

Boxoffice. November, 1996, p. 135.
Chicago Tribune. January 10, 1997, p. 4.
Entertainment Weekly. January 17, 1997, p. 43.
Los Angeles Times. December 25, 1996, p. F7.
New York Times. December 24, 1996, p. C9.
Newsweek. December 23, 1996, p. 67.
People. January 13, 1997, p. 19.
USA Today. December 24, 1996, p. 1D.
Variety. September 16, 1996, p. 63.

Mother Night

Howard W. Campbell is the most patriotic American in the Third Reich.—Movie tagline

"Nick Nolte gives the most thoughtful and moving performance of his career. The movie explores complex ethical issues with quick intelligence and wry humor."—David Sterritt, *Christian Science Monitor*

"Riveting. A cunning mix of comedy, tragedy, and spy thriller."—John Griffin, *Montreal Gazette*

"Compelling and provocative."—Bob Healy, *Satellite Network*

"A film with the what-happens-next tension of a page turner."—Jason Kaufman, *US Magazine*

"Unforgettable!"—Paul Wunder, *WBAI Radio*

Box Office: $390,527

Mother Night is the third film directed by Keith Gordon, who began his feature film career in front of the camera in such works as *Christine* (1984), co-starring with an evil car, and *Back to School* (1986), opposite Rodney Dangerfield, who was fairly unsettling in his own right. Since turning to directing, Gordon has dealt with battles amongst students and teachers in his admirable *The Chocolate War* (1988) and the struggles of World War II soldiers in *A Midnight Clear* (1992). In *Mother Night*, which, like the other films, is adapted from a novel, the struggle is an internal one. Based on the 1961 book by Kurt Vonnegut, it tells the story of Howard Campbell (Nick Nolte), who has chosen to surrender to U.S. authorities in 1960 and stand trial in Israel for Nazi war crimes.

"I guess the moral here is: you must be careful what you pretend to be because in the end you are who you're pretending to be."—Howard Campbell

What Campbell and only one other person knows, however, is that while the American-born playwright spent the war socializing with Nazis and delivering venomous radio addresses brimming with Hitler's hate, he was an American intelligence officer delivering encoded messages to the Allies in those very same diatribes. Campbell was told before he accepted the assignment that no one would ever be able to come forward to publicly verify his claim of being a spy, so there is no way of proving his innocence. But, Campbell broods, is he completely innocent? Totally apolitical, what seduced him into taking on the fateful task was that he was an admitted ham who looked upon the assignment as an artistic challenge, an intriguing opportunity to write a tour-de-force role and play the part himself.

Almost thirty years later, Campbell cannot shake a gnawing, haunting sense of responsibility for the corrosively negative impact of his words—his "art"—

upon the world's stage. He expresses his feeling that he whored himself and his gifts, agreeing to let it all be obliterated under layer upon layer of virulent pretense that unquestionably buoyed Nazi morale throughout the war and fed the Neo-Nazi movement thereafter. In 1960, the man beneath the creature he created has no relevance. Campbell is neither known for the plays that he wrote before the war nor for the good he did for the Allied war effort nor, indeed, for anything that he values. He utilized his talents to become a Nazi to the world, is now known solely as such, and is being judged by that world—and himself—for the choice that he made.

Author Kurt Vonnegut has a wordless cameo as a Greenwich Village pedestrian walking around Campbell.

Throughout his film, Gordon strives to be faithful to Vonnegut's tone, and the first images are characteristic of the author's deep sense of irony. A bedraggled Campbell is led to a shadowy Israeli prison cell as Bing Crosby's calm, smooth voice croons "I'm Dreaming of a White Christmas." Campbell's halting, stumbling steps act as a kind of absurd choreography to the music. He is supplied with a table, chair, typewriter, paper and ribbon and told to type his story for the Haifa Institute which collects documentation on war criminals. Some of what Campbell puts down on paper is conveyed in voice-over, while the rest is presented in the film's extensive (and sometimes distractingly flitting) use of flashbacks.

He writes about moving to Berlin from Schenectady, N.Y., when he was a boy (young Campbell is played by Brawley Nolte, Nick's son), when his father was transferred by General Electric after World War I. When the rumblings of war began anew in the 1930s, Campbell's parents returned to the U.S., but their now-grown son stayed on. He had found success in Germany: his plays, written in German, had found an audience, and he had found a dazzling German actress to marry, her father being the prestigious chief-of-police in Berlin. Campbell found the growing political strife in the world to be insanity, and he solidified his recognition and devotion to only one nation, the "nation of two" made up of himself and his beloved Helga (Sheryl Lee). He wrote plays about medieval heroism, honor and romance, and she brought tears to his eyes when she gave life to his words upon the stage.

It was the sensibility expressed in Campbell's plays that caught the eye of the U.S. War Department, which sent agent Frank Wirtanen (John Goodman) to see whether the American expatriate, now well-ensconced in German society, might be willing to use his situation to their advantage. Wirtanen felt that Campbell's plays showed him to be a man who admired "pure hearts and heroes" and would "sacrifice anything in the name of romance." Campbell first scoffed at the idea of getting involved in world affairs which did not concern or interest him in the least, but he felt that creating "the most challenging role" of his career and playing it himself would allow him to realize "the dream of every playwright."

Soon, Campbell began serving the Allies by sending out messages expressed through carefully chosen pauses, coughs and throat clearings during his weekly Sunday radio addresses which spewed Nazi propaganda to the English-speaking world. He signed off each broadcast by identifying himself as Howard W. Campbell, "the last free American," and punctuated that characterization with a convincing "Heil Hitler!" Campbell writes in prison that he was surprised listeners didn't look upon his extreme invective as a kind of burlesque caricature, not something evil that would instill fear. He was taken deadly seriously. Followers of Hitler hungrily lapped it all up and anxiously awaited the next installment. Only Campbell, Wirtanen, a general, and President Roosevelt knew what Campbell was doing for the Allies, with the President gleefully giving Campbell high marks.

In 1944, "insanity was the victor" over the "nation of two", as Helga was killed while entertaining the German troops on the Russian front. With her died everything in Campbell's life that mattered to him, leaving only the empty, rote task of coming up with new ways to rant the same old

CREDITS

Howard Campbell: Nick Nolte
Helga Noth: Sheryl Lee
George Kraft: Alan Arkin
Frank Wirtanen: John Goodman
Resi Noth: Kirsten Dunst
Abraham Epstein: Ayre Gross
Bernard B. O'Hare: David Straithairn

Origin: USA
Released: 1996
Production: Keith Gordon, Robert B. Weide for a Whyaduck production; released by Fine Line Features
Direction: Keith Gordon
Screenplay: Robert B. Weide; based on the novel by Kurt Vonnegut
Cinematography: Tom Richmond
Editing: Jay Rabinowitz
Music: Michael Convertino
Production design: Francois Seguin
Costumes: Renee April
Sound: Claude Hazanavicius
Casting: Valerie McCaffrey
MPAA rating: R
Running Time: 110 minutes

malignancy each week. He visited Helga's family, where her shell-shocked adolescent sister Resi (Kirsten Dunst) expressed love for him and her father expressed admiration for Campbell's vile speeches. Campbell was clearly shaken when his father-in-law told him that, while he sometimes wondered if Campbell might have been a spy, he figured it didn't matter since Campbell undoubtedly ended up serving the Nazis better than the United States. He stated emphatically that it was Campbell, more than anyone else, that kept Nazi Germany's hopes alive. Campbell ventured out into the countryside to "wait out the war," at which point he was captured, beaten, and almost hanged by an American soldier. Wirtanen intervened, and Campbell slipped through the bureaucratic cracks to freedom.

At this point, the film jumps to New York City in 1960, where Campbell has been living under his own name. He has not been able to write. His love for Helga has remained "the axis of his life," and he is shown talking to her picture as he sips wine by romantic candlelight. After breaking one of these glasses and cutting his hand, Campbell sought help from Dr. Epstein (Arye Gross), who lived downstairs. Epstein and his mother are survivors of Auschwitz, and she suspiciously questioned Campbell about his famous name. Shortly thereafter, an admiring Neo-Nazi organization "outed" him by revealing his whereabouts in their newsletter. As a result, Campbell was forced to deal with farcical racists who made pilgrimages to his door and angry war veterans and Holocaust survivors looking for revenge and justice. Campbell's situation worsened when his only friend, artist and neighbor George Kraft (Alan Arkin), turned out to be a Russian spy who planned to kidnap Campbell and take him to Moscow. Neo-Nazis shocked Campbell by bringing Helga to him, and his own spirit was briefly brought back to life as well until she was revealed to actually be Resi working with Kraft for the Russians.

A warning note from Wirtanen allowed Campbell to escape from the lair of these distasteful people, but not before Gordon provides us with *Mother Night*'s most memorable shot. Campbell turns to see that a younger group of racists—a whole new generation of Nazis—is learning what to believe and being stirred up by an old film of Campbell. Facing himself, both figuratively and literally, he is clearly stunned by what he sees. The film of the younger, fervent Campbell is superimposed on the face of a now older, forlorn man with tears in his eyes. The forcefulness of the earlier Campbell, along with the size of the image, drives home the fact that, due to his choice, there were two Howard Campbells, and the vile one he created has overshadowed and eclipsed the more human and humane one. Soon after is another memorable shot, showing Campbell standing frozen for hours on a busy sidewalk because he feels that there is no "reason to move in any direction." Finally, he knocked on the Epstein's door, and surrendered to them for crimes against humanity. That is how he ended up in a prison cell, having disturbing conversations through the wall with fellow inmate Adolph Eichmann. In the end, a retired Wirtanen sends Campbell a letter saying that he will break the rules and verify that Campbell was indeed a spy. "May justice be served," he says. Campbell ruminates upon Wirtanen's words and then hangs himself with the typewriter ribbon. No longer in danger of being hanged for crimes against humanity, his retribution is for crimes against himself.

"This is the only story of mine whose moral I know," wrote Vonnegut in the introduction to the 1966 edition of his novel. "We are what we pretend to be, so we must be careful what we pretend to be." Critic Richard Schickel called Vonnegut's book an "intensely charged book . . . artful, zestful," and *Life* magazine praised its "exuberant, crackling style." While such praise is appropriate for Vonnegut's work, it does not apply to Gordon's well-acted film, which received mixed reviews and was a disappointment at the box-office. Although the author makes a cameo appearance in the film, and was a cheerleader for the project, he apparently was not involved in the writing of the screen version. Perhaps this explains why the film is not quite as thought-provoking as the book, as well as how the book's vigor and glow ended up being muted in the adaptation process. While Gordon's *Mother Night* is an admirable effort, he has brought the main ingredients to the screen without much of the necessary seasoning that gives the book its rich, full-bodied flavor.

—David L. Boxerbaum

REVIEWS

Atlanta Constitution. November 15, 1996, p. P23.
Boston Globe. September 15, 1996, p. N12.
Chicago Tribune. November 15, 1996, p. C7.
Entertainment Weekly. November 15, 1996, p. 50.
Houston Chronicle. November 22, 1996, p. F4.
Los Angeles Times. November 1, 1996, p. F18.
The New York Times. November 1, 1996, p. C21.
The New Yorker. November 4, 1996, p. 119.
People. November 18, 1996, p. 20.
Sight and Sound. March, 1997, p. 56.
Time. November 11, 1996, p. 86.
USA Today. November 11, 1996, p. D3.
Variety. September 2, 1996, p. 67.
Wall Street Journal. November 1, 1996, p. A11.

Mulholland Falls

"A masterfully atmospheric film."—Roger Ebert, *Chicago Sun-Times*

"A brilliantly made film . . . one of the year's strongest casts."—Michael Wilmington, *Chicago Tribune*

"Dangerous sex, corrupt power . . . smashing and stylish."—Janet Maslin, *New York Times*

Box Office: $11,526,099

When New Zealand director Lee Tamahori splashed upon the scene with his hard-hitting story of cultural violence in *Once Were Warriors*, everyone knew he'd be offered a big-budget Hollywood film, but no one would have expected it to be a clone of Roman Polanski's 1974 labyrinthine mystery *Chinatown.*

"You can't do this. This is America." "This isn't America. This is Los Angeles."—Chicago mobster to LAPD Hat Squad

Like *Chinatown*, *Mulholland Falls* is also set in Los Angeles, but about a decade later, in the newly-atomic world of the 1950's. And like *Chinatown*, *Mulholland Falls* is also about sex and secrets, natural resources and violence, power and corruption. And also like *Chinatown*, *Mulholland Falls* has real history as its inspiration. In the first film it was the economic necessity of controlling south California's precious water supply and in the second it is the "Hat Squad;" a group of officially sanctioned rogue cops who were allowed to abuse their power on elements (i.e. gangsters) not wanted in the city. The "Hat Squad" was as well known for their sartorial splendor (they never wore guns because it ruined the drape of their suits) as for their authorized violent tactics (they preferred sleeker black jacks).

Many of the fedoras worn in the film were made by Dave Brown Hatters of Rochester, New York, the same company that made hats for the original Squad.

These qualities are easily seen in the "Hat Squad" assembled by Tamahori. At the head is a dapper but solid Max Hoover (Nick Nolte) who is married to the steamy but nonetheless domestic Katherine (Melanie Griffith). Max has three henchmen: Ellery Coolidge (Chazz Palminteri), Eddie Hall (Michael Madsen), and Arthur Relyea (Chris Penn). Like Katherine, Eddie and Arthur aren't given much to do in the film except to be a part of Max's loyal and lethal legion. Ellery, however, is lucky enough to provide the film's comic relief. Besides sublimating his violent tendencies by stuffing his face with food, it seems that Ellery is having trouble sleeping. So in a very non-fifties, non-macho way he is seeing a psychiatrist (and a female yet!) who wants him to talk about his feelings—an experience he wants to share with the guys, much to their amusement.

The film's title is also indicative of their tactics and purpose: to keep gangsters out of LA . . . by whatever means necessary. So, when Chicago gangster Jack Flynn (William Peterson) shows up in LA, he is "escorted" from dinner by Max and his pals, driven up into the hills on Mulholland Drive, then thrown off a cliff—Mulholland Falls. Peterson's appearance here, for some reason, is unbilled as are several other cameos. Rob Lowe plays a dinner companion and possible lawyer for Peterson, Bruce Dern plays the Chief of Police, and Louise Fletcher plays a police secretary. Their familiar faces lend an air of authenticity to the film similar to that of their '40s counterparts in which we saw all those great character players like Gale Sondergaard, Elisha Cook, Jr. and Mike Mazurki. Their faces are so familiar, but we aren't always able to quite place the name. Was that the objective of these uncredited performances?

With the squad's methodology established, the film now presents its main mystery. A woman's body has been found pushed into the earth at a housing construction site. Virtually every bone in her body has been crushed as if she'd been run over with a steam roller. Max and crew are sent out to investigate, only to find that the woman is known to Max. She is Allison Pond (Jennifer Connelly), a woman with whom Max had been having a torrid affair for six months.

It seems, however, that Max was not Allison's only lover as Max discovers when Allison's sleazy next door neighbor, Jimmy Fields (Andrew McCarthy), sends him a film canister which contains a hodgepodge of images, but also amorous frames of Allison and an older, bespectacled gentleman. When it is discovered that a piece of glass in Allison's foot turns out to be radioactive, Max discovers that the gentleman is none other than the chairman of the Atomic Energy Commission, General Thomas Timms (John Malkovich), who lives on the nearby Atomic Proving Grounds.

Now murder mixes with national security and in steps the overly protective Colonel Nathan Fitzgerald (Treat Williams) who does more to impede Max's investigation than to help it. But orders also are coming from higher up: FBI Agent McCafferty (Daniel Baldwin) is sent to tell the

L.A. Hoover that the Washington D.C. Hoover wants him to back off. But Max takes Allison's death very personally, and he'll do everything in his power to break the veil of secrecy that surrounds her death.

There is no doubting that one of *Mulholland Falls* strengths is its very powerful cast (although many are underused). Nick Nolte plays Max as basically sympathetic yet with a very hard edge. His brooding darkness makes us pull back from him and maybe even fear him, while at the same time, his relationship with Griffith's Katherine shows not only his road to damnation (how could he cheat on Griffith?) but also his path to redemption.

But imagine the job of the actress who has to play the woman who lures Max away from his wife . . . especially since she's dead at the start of the film. Fortunately, in Jennifer Connelly (previously seen in *Labyrinth*, *The Rocketeer*, and *Higher Learning*) the director has found an actress who can be both sexy and innocent. The beautiful Connelly is both voluptuous whore and virginal girl next door, and this anomaly gives her an elusive air of mystery. Yes, she could make a man forget Melanie Griffith . . . at least for a while.

The other interesting acting job in a roster of solid actors is that of John Malkovich who can appear to be a distracted intellectual one minute and Hitler the next. He plays one of the fathers of the atom bomb who now has such power that he doesn't think twice about sacrificing hundreds of lives in exchange for the burgeoning power of the state, while also realizing that with his power comes privileges and concessions that ordinary men can only dream of. Could murder be among them? With Malkovich's ability to be anyone from Dr. Jekyll to Mr Hyde (as he was earlier this year in *Mary Reilly*), we're never sure.

The other strongpoint for *Mulholland Falls* is the way it looks. Like *Chinatown*, it does a great job of invoking times past. Part of this success may be due to the evocative production design of Richard Sylbert who, not so coincidently, received an Oscar nomination for doing the same job in *Chinatown*. Sylbert also won an Oscar for *Dick Tracy* and, earlier in his career for *Who's Afraid of Virginia Woolf* which also won an Oscar for *Mulholland Falls'* cinematographer, Haskell Wexler. Wexler's great lensing skill is pivotal in creating the luscious look of this film. The deep earthtones of the Hat Squad's suits as the men stand above an atomic crater in the rich desert is an unforgettable scene.

Fortunately, such are the strengths of *Mulholland Falls'* stylishness and cast that they can overcome what is essentially a weak plot, especially when compared—as is inevitable—to *Chinatown*. Both stories are psychological journeys into greed and power, love and sex, but this latest film rarely surprises and virtually never offers the startling left turns that the earlier, better scripted, film does.

—Beverley Bare Buehrer

CREDITS

Max Hoover: Nick Nolte
Ellery Coolidge: Chazz Palminteri
Eddie Hall: Michael Madsen
Arthur Relyea: Chris Penn
Katherine Hoover: Melanie Griffith
Col. Fitzgerald: Treat Williams
Allison Pond: Jennifer Connelly
FBI Agent McCafferty: Daniel Baldwin
Jimmy Fields: Andrew McCarthy
Gen. Thomas Timms: John Malkovich
The Chief: Bruce Dern
Earl: Ed Lauter

Origin: USA
Released: 1996
Production: Richard D. Zanuck, Lili Fini Zanuck for a Largo Entertainment and Zanuck Co. production; released by MGM/UA
Direction: Lee Tamahori
Screenplay: Pete Dexter
Cinematography: Haskell Wexler
Editing: Sally Menke
Music: Dave Grusin
Production design: Richard Sylbert
Art direction: Gregory William Bolton
Set design: Richard Berger, Hugo Santiago
Costume design: Ellen Mirojnick
Sound: James E. Webb, Jr.
Casting: Shari Rhodes, Joseph Middleton
MPAA rating: R
Running Time: 107 minutes

REVIEWS

Boxoffice. January, 1996, p. 94.
Chicago Tribune. April 26, 1996, p. C4.
Detroit News. April 26, 1996, p. D1
Entertainment Weekly. April 26, 1996, p. 62.
New York Times. April 26, 1996, p. C16.
USA Today. April 26, 1996, p. 3D.
Variety. April 26, 1996, p. 131.

Multiplicity

Sometimes to get more out of life, you have to make more of yourself.—Movie tagline

Better living through cloning.—Movie tagline

"Wonderfully amusing! Four times Keaton equals one hilarious comedy!"—Joe Leydon, *KPRC-TV*

"Four times the laughs!"—Bobbie Wygent, *KXAS-TV*

"Hilarious! A multiplicity of laughs!"—Jim Ferguson, *Prevue Channel*

"Riotously funny, unique and entertaining!"—Paul Wunder, *WBAI Radio*

"Quadruple your fun! Keaton is contagious!"—Patrick Stoner, *WHYY-TV*

Box Office: $21,134,373

Michael Keaton explores the male psyche by playing four distinct aspects of himself in Harold Ramis' adult comedy, *Multiplicity.* While the film may have a limited target audience, Keaton's performances are the real reason to see this clever, but ultimately unsatisfying comedy about finding a way to overcome those oh-so-Nineties feelings of being overworked and overextended. Keaton manages to play four different versions of the same character, each with his own discernible personality.

Doug Kinney (Michael Keaton) is a construction company supervisor, husband and father who finds he just does not have enough time in the day to get everything he needs to do done. When his thankless boss (Richard Masur in a very humorless role) foists on even more work, but without an accompanying pay raise, the already harried Doug tries to explain it to his beautiful and loving wife, Laura (Andie MacDowell): "I think it's more of a prestige thing, hon." Laura adds on another layer of guilt and pressure by announcing that she would like to return to her real estate job, which means that Doug is now expected to pick up some of the family responsibilities as well. It does not take a genius to see that something has got to give.

When Doug snaps on the job, he is offered a possible solution to all of his time management problems by Dr. Owen Leeds (Harris Yulin), a good-natured geneticist and benevolent Dr. Frankenstein: How about a little cloning? It takes Doug no time to accept the good doctor's offer and with a little Hollywood hocus-pocus, Doug has someone with whom to share his workload. "Two"—a virtual carbon copy of our hero—is a real go-getter at work, and although he lacks the social skills of the original, he does allow Doug the time to spend at home helping with his two children. But playing *Mr. Mom* (1983) no longer suits Mr. Keaton and soon Doug is back at the geneticist's for yet another clone, nicknamed *Three.* This one is fastidious, sensitive and a whiz at wrapping up those leftovers.

Multiplicity is at its best when the clones begin to feel the pressures—and tediousness—of Doug's life. They, too, want a little excitement and fun and figure if they just had a little help . . . Yes, you guessed it. Before long, "Four" appears on the scene, but this one is a bit of a genetic mishap. "You know how sometimes you make a copy of a copy, it's not quite as sharp as the original?" Two asks Doug as he tries to explain the dim-witted Four. As things escalate, Doug seems to discover that perhaps it is not time that is the problem in his life, but rather power. For *Multiplicity* resolves the whole issue by having Doug remodel the house for his wife before starting up his own company.

CREDITS

Doug Kinney: Michael Keaton
Laura Kinney: Andie MacDowell
Del King: Richard Masur
Dr. Owen Leeds: Harris Yulin
Vic: Eugene Levy
Noreen: Ann Cusack
Ted: John DeLance
Walt: Brian Doyle-Murray
Robin: Julie Bowen
Jennifer Kinney: Katie Schlossberg
Zack Kinney: Zack Duhame

Origin: USA
Released: 1996
Production: Trevor Albert and Harold Ramis for a Columbia Pictures production; released by Sony Pictures Entertainment
Direction: Harold Ramis
Screenplay: Chris Miller, Mary Hale, Lowell Ganz, Babaloo Mandel; based on the short story by Chris Miller
Cinematography: Laszlo Kovacs
Editing: Pem Herring, Craig Herring
Production design: Jackson DeGovia
Art direction: Geoff Hubbard
Costume design: Shay Cunliffe
Visual effects supervisor: Richard Edlund
Music: George Fenton
MPAA rating: PG-13
Running Time: 117 minutes

(How many entrepreneurs do you know with time on their hands?)

One of the things missing from *Multiplicity* is the lack of conflict between the four characters. The only real comic tension comes when Doug discovers that all three of his doppelgangers have had sex with his wife—the only big carnal sin. There are moments of amusing slapstick and Keaton has some of the best comic delivery to be found, but the film plays it far too safe. As good as Keaton's work is it cannot overcome the limitations of the script, which, like the Doug Kinney clones, claims four screenwriters in its credits. Chris Miller and Mary Hales' original script was rewritten by longtime Ron Howard collaborators, Lowell Ganz and Babaloo Mandel, in an effort to add some bite to the story. Any possibility for some incisive filmmaking, however, is squashed by director Harold Ramis, who chooses instead to paint a warm and fuzzy picture for his audience. *Multiplicity* lacks an edge, a more subversive portrayal of contemporary life such as Ramis attempted in the far more daring and clever *Groundhog Day* (1993). Perhaps Ramis is merely mellowing with age. In this latest offering, the director opts for a kinder, gentler view of life, reminding his protagonist—and the audience—what Dorothy long ago learned in *The Wizard of Oz* (1939): There is no place like home.

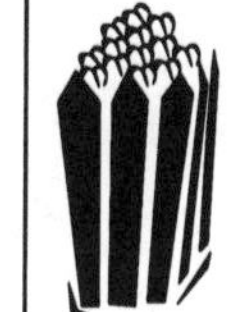

"My whole life's an emergency."—Doug

The film received a generally chilly reception from the critics and the ticket buyers alike and suffered a quick and financially painful death at the box office. Michael Keaton, however, received raves for his performance, although many critics longed for the more manic intensity that the actor displayed in his tour-de-force, *Beetlejuice.*

—Patricia Kowal

REVIEWS

Entertainment Weekly. July 19, 1996, p. 58.
Los Angeles Times. July 17, 1996, p. F1.
Los Angeles View. July 12-18, 1996, p. 17.
The New Yorker. July 29, 1996, p. 77.
New York Times. July 17, 1996, p. C9.
Rolling Stone. August 8, 1996, p. 70.
Variety. July 5, 1996.

Muppet Treasure Island

"A great family film!"—Good Morning America, *ABC-TV*

"The best Muppet movie yet!"—Paul Wunder, *WBAI Radio*

Box Office: $34,326,951

The Muppets make a hilarious and colorful return to the big screen with *Muppet Treasure Island*, a zany musical and satirical spoof of the Robert Louis Stevenson classic, *Treasure Island.* As they did with Dickens' *A Christmas Carol* in *The Muppet Christmas Carol* (1992), the goofy puppets take on a respected classic and reconstruct it for their own satirical and comic ends. Happily, their take on *Treasure Island* is clever, tuneful, and truly funny, allowing the crazy Jim Henson characters to redeem themselves after faltering a bit with Dickens. This film returns some of the smart fun that has characterized the Muppets since Kermit the Frog debuted some thirty years ago. *Muppet Treasure Island*, directed by Brian Henson, is the most worthy successor to the Muppets' first feature film, *The Muppet Movie* (1979).

Holding fast to their silly blend of sweetness and sharp wit, the Muppets make delicious mincemeat of the Stevenson classic. They are aided, as usual, by some wonderful human foils, most notably the estimable Tim Curry as Long John Silver. The role of young Jim Hawkins is played by newcomer Kevin Bishop, and he is a charming playmate for the Muppets. As usual, the Muppets have such wonderful personalities that it is hard to think of them as puppets: they are stars in their own right. To

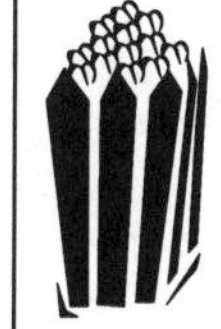

"Tim Curry is everything moi wants in a man, except he's not green."—Miss Piggy on her costar.

In *Muppet Treasure Island*, greedy pirate Long John Silver comes between the unlikely romance of Kermit the Frog and Miss Piggy.

that end, they are given credits just like the humans: "Starring Kermit the Frog as Captain Smollett," etc.

It is fun to see how the Muppets twist the old classic. The nerdy Kermit the Frog plays the dashing Captain Smollett. Miss Piggy plays Benjamina Gunn, a porcine beauty in love with Kermit (surprise), but who somehow becomes the head of a tribe of wild boars led by a character named Spa'am. (This character's name actually inspired a lawsuit for trademark infringement by the makers of Spam, a suit that was subsequently thrown out.) All of the other Muppets are here: Rizzo the Rat and Gonzo play the friends of young Jim Hawkins; Fozzie Bear plays the silly, pampered owner of the ship; even those two old codgers, Waldorf and Astoria make an appearance—attached to the bow of the ship, making nasty comments about the movie, just as they used to do about the "Muppet Show" television series.

A jaunty song called "Shiver My Timbers" sets the tone during the credits, with singing lobsters and silly lyrics, and tikis singing "a-one more time, now." This and several other wonderful songs are by famed pop writers Barry Mann and Cynthia Weil.

Director Brian Henson and writers Jerry Juhl, Kirk R. Thatcher, and James V. Hart take the Robert Louis Stevenson story hostage, and they don't give it back until some 90 happy minutes later. Jim (Kevin Bishop) is given a treasure map by a mysterious sailor name Captain Billy, played to the hilt by Billy Connolly, who dies before he can explain the map. Eager to set out for "Something Better" (an adorable song), Jim says "I feel like the world is passing me by," to which Gonzo replies, "It is." Just then an invasion by a hilarious and quite motley assortment of diminutive Muppet pirates causes Jim and friends to set out to find the treasure. They find themselves a willing shipowner (Fozzie Bear), who finances a ship whose crew includes the sinister Long John Silver (Tim Curry) and the supposedly intimidating Captain Smollett (Kermit.) After several botched tries, the crew of the ship (who are under the thumb of Long John) mutiny, just as the ship finds its way to the treasure. Along the way, Captain Smollett catches up with the lovely Benjamina Gunn (Miss Piggy), and Jim learns a thing or two about life from Long John Silver.

What is most impressive about this and other Muppet adventures is their ability to move back and forth from silly humor to genuinely touching interaction between characters. Two scenes between Long John and Jim are really quite complex in their exposition and their ability to present Long John as a man who likes young Jim even while he knows he may have to kill him in order to get his treasure map. Sitting on the bow of the ship, a beautiful moon high above them, Curry and Bishop have one of only two completely human scenes in the film. What makes the scenes all the more special is that the actors improvised their lines based on material from the writers and director Henson: the spontaneous and touching result is a wonderful way to keep the rest of the film grounded.

The silly moments are far too numerous to remember, and far too much fun to give away. However, there are some

CREDITS

Long John Silver: Tim Curry
Jim Hawkins: Kevin Bishop
Capt. Abraham Smollett (Kermit the Frog): Steve Whitmire
Benjamina Gunn (Miss Piggy): Frank Oz
Billy Bones: Billy Connolly
The Great Gonzo: Dave Goelz
Rizzo the Rat: Steve Whitmire

Origin: USA
Released: 1996
Production: Martin G. Baker and Brian Henson for a Jim Henson and Walt Disney production; released by Buena Vista Pictures
Direction: Brian Henson
Screenplay: Jerry Juhl, Kirk R. Thatcher and James V. Hart; based on the novel *Treasure Island* by Robert Louis Stevenson
Cinematography: John Fenner
Editing: Michael Jablow
Production design: Val Strazovec
Art direction: Alan Cassie
Costume design: Polly Smith
Sound: Peter Lindsay
Puppeteer coordination: Kevin Clash
Choreography: Pat Garrett
Music: Hans Zimmer
Special effects: Nick Allder
MPAA rating: G
Running Time: 99 minutes

choice moments that must be acknowledged. First is the running gag involving a bunch of mice who cavort aboard the ship as if it were a Caribbean cruise. They wear Hawaiian shirts, they dance, they drink Mai-Tais and other exotic drinks—they even have ringside tables for Miss Piggy's tribal dance on the island, as if it were a floor show provided just for them. These kinds of anomalies and anachronisms are hallmarks of the Muppets. It is the kind of humor that looks easier than it is. Many other screen comedies have tried to pull off this kind of thing, and just end up being foolish.

The film was shot over a 14 week period on seven stages at Shepperton Studios, outside London, with over 400 Muppets.

One hilarious sequence is a huge production number called "Cabin Fever," in which the occupants of the ship are supposedly going crazy from spending too long on the high seas. The production values rival Busby Berkeley's lavish sequences in *Gold Diggers of 1933* (1933), but the lyrics and the performances all have an all-knowing quality that winks at the lunacy of the lyrics, dialogue and situations.

Some of the dialogue is just plain hilarious. "Beware!" intones Captain Billy. "What?," cries Gonzo. "Beware running with scissors or any other pointy object. It's all good fun until someone gets hurt. . . . ," and then he dies. Another example, from Waldorf and Astoria, stuck on the bow of the ship: "Take a cruise, you said . . . Now we're stuck on the front of the ship." "It could be worse..we could be stuck in the audience." The consistent way the Muppets break the "fourth wall" and comment on the action makes the audience feel that nothing is to be taken seriously. It is a wonderful device that makes the poignant scenes seem all the more surprising.

Tim Curry is in splendid form as Long John Silver. Using his deep voice and his expressive eyebrows to punctuate his dialogue, Curry is wonderfully restrained in his role, as if he knows that there is no need to try and rival the Muppets for zaniness. Yet, Curry hardly walks through his role: he is energetic and full of sea-salt. Curry is particularly charming in his song (which he reminds the audience "is my only number") called "Professional Pirate." The Muppets wisely always choose actors of depth to play their foils (Michael Caine played Scrooge), which not only lends authenticity to the story, but texture to the characterizations.

Jennifer Saunders, star of the huge British television hit "Absolutely Fabulous", is absolutely fabulous in a small cameo as the owner of the inn where Jim Hawkins works. Dispatching Muppet pirates with a broom, Saunders portrays her character as a Dickensian caricature which is wonderfully appropriate to the zany style of the other actors.

There is no question about it; the Muppets are all actors. Kermit (voice of Steve Whitmire) and the rest do not settle for conventional puppet antics, which is why they have lasted so long. When Kermit is sad about the possible loss of his lady love, he is truly sad.

Brian Henson directs with a surer hand than he did *The Muppet Christmas Carol*, creating odd angles, sharp edits (with the help of editor Michael Jablow), and beautiful stage pictures (cinematography by John Fenner). The only thing approaching a misstep seems to be an overly orchestrated score, which overpowers the simple voices of the lead characters. Other than that, the jokes are on target, the sets and puppets are riotously funny and delightfully colorful, and the story moves along swiftly and with a touch of poignancy. Henson should be immensely proud that he is carrying on in the wonderful tradition started by his genius father, Jim Henson. One of the great things about the Muppets is that unlike human stars, they don't grow older, so we can look forward to many more twisted classics such as this one.

—*Kirby Tepper*

REVIEWS

Boxoffice. April, 1996, p. 117.
Chicago Tribune. February 16, 1996, p. 5.
Los Angeles Times. February 16, 1996, p. F12.
New York Times. February 16, 1996.
USA Today. February 16, 1996, p. 4D.
Variety. February 19, 1996, p. 47.

My Favorite Season; Ma Saison Preferee

France's Andre Techine has become renowned for daring to examine varieties of human relationships which most mainstream directors choose to ignore. He gained considerable critical attention for *Wild Reeds* (1995), a film which explores the complexities of the adolescent friendship as they are experienced by a young girl, the boyfriend who eagerly pursues her, and a younger boy who is attracted to both of them.

Techine's fascination for complex relationships continues with *Ma Saison Preferee*; *My Favorite Season.* The central themes of *Ma Saison Preferee* become apparent in the film's first shot, in which Emilie (Catherine Deneuve) is seen methodically shutting the windows of her mother's home. Emilie is preparing to move her ailing mother, Berthe (Marthe Villalonga), from her house in the countryside to Emilie's home on the outskirts of Toulouse. Berthe has begun to display the physical problems associated with old age, and can no longer manage the difficulties of living alone. Despite her misgivings, she has reluctantly agreed to take up residence in her daughter's house.

"Sometimes I talk to myself - it's less exhausting than talking to someone else."—Berthe

The mother is dubious about this arrangement, but Emilie is happy to take charge. She pursues her mother's *demenagement* with ruthless efficiency, as if to repel the sense of nostalgia which most people would feel on such an occasion. Her mother feels no such restraint: She wistfully looks on, clearly unhappy to be leaving her home and the memories it evokes. The strange air of detachment which Emilie displays on this occasion is an indication that she has become far too proficient at repressing her own emotions. Indeed, there is no breathing room in Emilie's tense, task-oriented existence. From the film's first moments, she devotes a furious amount of energy to maintaining a facade of normalcy, one which totters and finally collapses as the film unfolds.

Although the story is set in a proper bourgeois household where everything seems normal and happy, it is quickly apparent that the inner workings of the family members' relationships are seriously flawed. Emilie, a middle-aged lawyer, is engaged in a claustrophobic relationship with her husband, Bruno (Jean-Pierre Bouvier), with whom she shares an office as well as a comfortable home. They appear to spend every moment of the day together. This is mystifying, since it is also obvious that they no longer have anything to say to one another. Emilie's wish to sustain an illusion of domestic bliss prevents her from recognizing Bruno's mounting boredom and sense of contempt. "You're not happy unless you're organizing everything," he says.

Bruno's barbed assessment of Emilie's behavior is accurate enough. Emilie lives in a world in which bourgeois propriety is everything and messy emotional issues are to be avoided at all costs. This is reflected in the rigidity of her professional life as well as her style of housekeeping. Her house is meticulously appointed and crammed with antiques, all of which seem to be too carefully chosen. They are things which are meant to be looked upon with a detached reserve, rather than simply enjoyed.

The mother's arrival at her daughter's home in Blagnac puts a serious dent in this facade of normalcy. Emilie celebrates this occasion by arranging what she hopes will be an ideal family dinner. Despite Emilie's wish to create an air of familial *bonhomie*, the dinner is marked by polite but stilted conversation. The mother excuses herself early, dismayed and irritated by her family's inability to discuss matters of real significance, such as her declining health and the disposition of her estate.

Berthe suffers from a sense of social isolation which is common to the elderly. At an early stage in the story, Emilie discovers her mother sitting by the side of the family's ostentatious pool, which serves as a rather pointless emblem of Emilie and Bruno's class standing and income level—the beautiful pool is meticulously maintained, but is never used by anyone. The mother is quietly talking to herself.

This appears to be an established habit. Although it may be construed by others as an indication of encroaching senility, Berthe's habit of talking to herself is derived from the fact that she has no friends and cannot elicit meaningful conversation from her obliviously self-involved family. Nevertheless, the mother is quite capable of sending oblique, cutting remarks in Emilie's direction, criticizing every aspect of her behavior ("Why did you buy this house?"). Too old and too tired to restrain her true feelings, she speaks the truth, even when she is saying the wrong thing at the wrong time.

In this scene and many others, Techine displays a marvelous ability to derive meaning from the use of simple settings. This is a wise directorial choice, since so many scenes involve supercharged but fiercely repressed emotion. Scenes of great importance are often set in deceptively simple, unspectacular settings—the well-manicured backyard pool, a nondescript convenience store, a highway rest stop.

Weeks go by, and winter approaches. Suddenly, into this seemingly normal but benighted scene, comes Antoine (Daniel Auteuil), Emilie's younger brother. Emilie has invited Antoine to take part in a traditional Christmas dinner. This is presumably a conciliatory gesture, meant to undo an entrenched spell of familial bickering that has kept Emilie and Antoine apart for three years.

Antoine is a forty-year-old neurologist whose neatly ordered professional life belies the chaotic state of his emotions. Despite his fascination for the inner workings of the mind, Antoine seems to know next to nothing about himself. He lives alone in an apartment in Toulouse, and is dedicated to his career, but he appears to have no friends and no discernible personal life. His greatest pleasure is derived from watching other, younger people enjoy themselves at a local bar. Even the art of polite dinner conversation eludes him: Antoine is so unnerved by the prospect of seeing his sister that he seeks refuge in the bathroom, where he carefully rehearses his end of the dinner conversation.

The film's first extended set piece revolves around this very ill-considered Christmas dinner. Emilie makes a huge effort to make the household appear free from strife. Her hopes unravel almost immediately as she and Antoine begin to bicker over unresolved issues both trivial and profound. As in most situations where family members are unwillingly forced upon one another, the result is an unmitigated disaster.

As represented in *Ma Saison Preferee*, the younger generation also appears to be chronically befuddled and miserable. They are so out of place in Emilie's tense, well-ordered world that they sometimes seem to have walked in from another movie. Anne (Chiara Mastroianni) is fulfilling her parents' expectations by pursuing a career as a lawyer. She is studious and intelligent, but seems aimless and uninspired.

Also in attendance is Emilie and Bruno's adopted son, Lucien (Anthony Prada). He has no real intellect, is openly surly and obnoxious toward everyone, and appears to have no interests other than sexual conquest. It is only Rhadija (Carmen Chaplin), Lucien's Moroccan-born girlfriend, who displays a spark of self-knowledge and good sense: She is occasionally captivated by Lucien's relentless sexual appetite, but she is also bored by his adolescent behavior and general oafishness.

Anne also appears to be struggling with some unresolved lesbian impulses, which come to light in her anguished conversations with Rhadija. Like nearly everyone else in the story, Anne is yearning for a sense of connection which seems very much beyond her. Later that evening, Anne expresses her wish to "sleep with" Rhadija. Her intent is never entirely clear: Anne is so unfamiliar with her own wants and needs that she does not seem to know whether her interest in Rhadija is platonic, sexual, or both. It soon becomes obvious that what Anne is yearning for is not sex, but a sense of filial intimacy. Confiding in Rhadija, Anne tearfully discloses that she "wishes she had had a sister."

Daniel Auteuil and Catherine Deneuve reteamed with Andre Techine for his 1996 film *Thieves (Les Voleurs).*

After the disastrous Christmas dinner, Berthe insists upon raising the subject of her last will and testament and the disposition of her worldly goods. This sets off a familial conflagration which utterly dooms the holiday gathering and incites bad feelings on all sides. In a fit of exasperation, Berthe decides to return immediately to her house in the countryside.

Ever the dutiful son, Antoine drives his mother back to her home. When left alone with her, he is considerably more able to express his true feelings. They reminisce along the way, in a variety of mundane settings. The tone of their exchange is warm and nostalgic, rather than petty and hostile. The mother discusses the simple pleasures of everyday life—the pastimes she enjoyed with her late husband, their long marriage, and their vacations at Cap Breton.

Shortly after moving back into her own house, the mother has what appears to be a minor stroke. This causes yet another anguished round of discussion between Emilie and Antoine. Somewhat unjustly, Emilie accuses Antoine of failing to recognize their mother's mounting neurological difficulties. She also informs Antoine that she has left Bruno and is living in a hotel in Toulouse. Despite their differences in lifestyle and temperament, and their many disagreements over practical matters (such as the care of their mother), it is still quite clear that Emilie and Antoine are deeply attached to one another.

Gradually, the well-tended facade of normalcy begins to disintegrate, to the ultimate benefit of all concerned. Cajoled by her brother, Emilie later consents to stay for a while in his solitary apartment. For a brief time, while living in close quarters, the pair seem to reproduce the happy familiarity of their childhood. Antoine is more than willing to accommodate Emilie's every need, to such a degree that he allows her to make use of his bed.

This gives rise to a series of scenes which have a peculiarly incestuous subtext. Like the doomed siblings of Jean-Pierre Melville's *Les Enfants Terribles* (1949), a film which concerns similar themes but has much more tragic consequences, Emilie and Antoine seem to have eyes only for each other. They oscillate between moments of filial warmth and bitter, even nonsensical arguments over ancient injuries which seem both trivial and profound. Their dealings with each other may be described as incestuous, insofar as they are deeply intertwined with one another on the emotional level. However, what they are seeking is not physical intimacy but the recovery of a sense of connection which seems to have been lost.

In effect, Emilie and Antoine are engaged in a fitful struggle to regain the easy familiarity of their youth. Each could be described as the great love of the other's life. The film traces their efforts to rediscover this attachment. It is

Antoine who becomes the catalyst for Emilie's inner transformation. He is ultimately responsible for the thawing out of her rather cold, unapproachable exterior.

Finally, the mother moves out of her house for the last time. Emilie and Antoine transport her to a senior citizens' home, stopping along the way to reminisce at certain places which evoke fond memories for all three. Their visit to St. Loup—a calm, pastoral place which they knew well in their youth—is an especially nostalgic one, allowing us to understand even further the deep sense of attachment which once bound them together.

Once settled in at the senior citizens' home, the mother becomes even more depressed, will not eat, and occasionally appears to be somewhat delusional. Emilie and Antoine are compelled to remove their mother from the nursing home. She is taken to a clinic where Antoine subjects her to a series of neurological tests. These reveal that the mother has experienced a significant cerebral hemorrhage.

At this juncture, Techine places Emilie in a situation which gives the audience a glimmer into the life she might have had if her emotions were not so tightly restrained. While visiting the clinic, Emilie has a strange, anonymous sexual encounter with a young resident doctor. This moment of extraordinary risk-taking and spontaneity is the only one Emilie allows herself to experience in the course of the film. The incident initially seems bizarre, but hints at the inner transformation which Emilie is trying to achieve.

It is the mother, Berthe, who serves as the truth teller in this story. As we see in the film's early scenes, such as her self-directed ramblings at poolside and her insistence upon discussing the disposition of her estate, she is continually exasperated by her family's evasions and circumlocutions. Even as she lays dying, she willfully approaches subjects which everyone else is afraid to discuss. In this respect she is quite the opposite of her daughter, however, the upheaval which the mother creates has positive repercussions, as Emilie ultimately begins to realize that her overly circumscribed way of life is mostly unnecessary, does damage to her, and strikes the other members of her family as absurd.

The mother dies, but not before disclosing to Emilie and Antoine that she wishes she had had a third child—"one who would have taken care of me." This remark may be construed as a very oblique form of verbal knife-twisting on the part of a dying woman who can no longer conceal her true feelings, but it also serves to underline the fact that all of the characters in the story are yearning for something they cannot have, a sense of connection which has been lost. Emilie's recognition of this idea ("All our lives, we never know ourselves," she says) marks a kind of epiphany for her.

The mother's funeral prompts a final family gathering, during which Antoine breaks down and cries on Emilie's shoulder. The scene concludes with Emilie's recitation of a poem for Antoine, one which they knew well in their youth. The verse concerns the joys and sorrows of filial love, and serves as an indication that despite their opposing temperaments and disagreements with one another, each is eager to recapture the joyous familiarity of their youth. The final scene leaves the viewer with the impression that they will ultimately succeed.

Ma Saison Preferee is rendered in a simple, episodic fashion. This unadorned style of presentation allows the audience to focus upon the volatile emotional issues which rest at the core of the drama, whereas a more aggressive style of storytelling would almost certainly have caused the film to veer into the realm of soap opera. The ways in which Emile and Antoine, respectively, choose to voice their discontent over events of the past, as well as their dismay over the dilemmas of the present, are often totally opposite, and provide much of the film's fireworks. On one level, the film is about how petty disagreements of adolescence which remain unresolved have a way of surging to the surface in adult life, causing a new round of misery for all concerned. But it also ends on a positive note, showing how deeply-rooted filial attachments can persist despite such difficulties.

Catherine Deneuve's stock in trade has always been a kind of classical equipoise. She is best known for portraying beautiful, seemingly self-possessed women whose seemed perfection belies mounting inner turmoil. This was especially true of her performance in Roman Polanski's *Repulsion* (1965), in which she played a young girl whose dazzling beauty prevents others from noticing her increasingly psychotic behavior. Alluring women with dubious intentions also figure prominently in her films with Luis Bunuel, *Belle*

CREDITS

Emilie: Catherine Deneuve
Antoine: Daniel Auteuil
Mother (Berthe): Marthe Villalonga
Bruno: Jean-Pierre Bouvier
Anne: Chiara Mastroianni
Lucien: Anthony Prada
Rhadija: Carmen Chaplin

Origin: France
Released: 1993; 1996
Production: Alain Sarde; A Filmopolis Pictures production; a co-production of Les Films Alain Sarde, TF1 Films Production and D.A. Films.
Direction: Andre Techine
Screenplay: Andre Techine, Pascal Bonitzer
Cinematography: Thierry Arbogast
Editing: Martine Giordano
Art direction: Carlos Conti
Costumes: Claire Fraisse
Music: Philippe Sarde
MPAA rating: Unrated
Running Time: 124 minutes

de Jour (1967) and *Tristana* (1970). More recently, she has chosen to portray women in oppressive circumstances who are less able to conceal their sense of torment. This was evident in Francois Truffaut's *The Last Metro* (1983) as well as Regis Wargnier's *Indochine* (1992). The latter film won the Academy Award for Best Foreign Film, and also garnered Deneuve a Best Actress Oscar nomination.

Ma Saison Preferee marks the latest in a spate of well-regarded French films featuring Daniel Auteuil (including *Un Coeur En Hiver*, *Queen Margot*, and *The Eighth Day*). For the latter, Auteuil won the Best Actor prize at the 1996 Cannes film festival (shared with Pascal Duquenne). With *Ma Saison Preferee*, Daniel Auteuil firmly takes his place in the front ranks of European film actors, and Catherine Deneuve adds a new dimension to her already illustrious career.

But it is Andre Techine who scores the greatest triumph. He does this by examining complex relationships which other, less daring directors might consider unworthy of attention. With *Wild Reeds* and *Ma Saison Preferee* in particular, he has proved himself to be marvelously adept at charting the more unfamiliar territory of the human heart.

—*Karl Michalak*

REVIEWS

Detroit News. April 5, 1996, p. 3D.
Los Angeles Times. May 31, 1996, p. F8.
New York Daily News. April 19, 1996.
New York Post. April 19, 1996.
New York Times. April 19, 1996.
Sight and Sound. August, 1994, p. 45.
Time. May 6, 1996.
Village Voice. April 23, 1996, p. 74.

My Fellow Americans

A comedy about life, liberty and the pursuit of two ex-presidents.—Movie tagline

"Hilarious!"—Ron Brewington, *American Urban Radio Networks*

"Funny. Zany. A classic comedy."—Stephen Holden, *New York Times*

"A winning ticket. A very bright capper to the year! Two wily comic actors. Well-crafted humor."—Richard Schickel, *Time*

"Endless fun!"—Jeffrey Lyons, *WNBS-TV*

Box Office: $20,986,085

In some ways *My Fellow Americans* is a pleasant throwback to an earlier time in moviemaking. In its rapid pace, bantering dialogue, and farcical elements, the film is slightly reminiscent of Billy Wilder's classic *One, Two, Three* (1961), a political farce that features James Cagney speaking some of the fastest dialogue in film history. In *My Fellow Americans*, Jack Lemmon and James Garner team up as ex-presidents on the run from government rogue agents who seek to frame them—or worse—for a scandal. This fast-moving combination of danger and farce leads to an effective point about the diminishment of the presidency and political office.

Matt Douglas (James Garner), a liberal Democrat, and Russell Kramer (Jack Lemmon), a conservative Republican, have feuded during and after their years in office. Two recent ex-presidents, Douglas and Kramer still meet and argue occasionally at state funerals and charity golf matches. Word comes separately to each of them about a plot called Olympia, a way to "spin dry kickback money" on a defense contract. They are surprised to hear that Charley Reynolds (James Rebhorn), a government contractor they both know, plans to frame Kramer in the scandal.

When Reynolds is suddenly murdered, the current president William Haney (Dan Aykroyd) sends a helicopter to bring the two ex-chief executives to Camp David for a briefing. Once in the air, however, Douglas notices that the copter follows an unfamiliar route, and he and Kramer demand that the pilots land and let them out. Moments later the chopper explodes. Stranded in the woods, the two decide to travel to Kramer's presidential library in Ohio, where the archives should establish his innocence by showing that he never met with Charley Reynolds. They know, however, that whoever planned to kill them in the copter will probably still pursue them.

The middle scenes turn the film into a combination of a buddy film and a road picture. These scenes also feature the broadest comedy of the movie, sometimes overworking the running jokes of Kramer's stinginess and Douglas's womanizing. The two famous figures escape their pursuers momentarily by boarding a train of celebrity look-alikes. They later hitch a ride with a truck driver who turns out to be hauling illegal aliens. Hiding in a sewer with one of the refugees from the truck, Douglas exchanges his coat for a compass to guide him and Kramer to Ohio. On the road again, these retired politicians finally begin to talk about what they miss most, which is being in the spotlight. They confide their greatest thrills as president—meeting Ella Fitzgerald for Douglas, meeting Joe DiMaggio for Kramer—and agree that having millions of people vote against them constitutes a rejection of enormous magnitude.

"Let's stop talking. We're about to bond. It will make me vomit."—Douglas to Kramer

Some of the scenes and jokes throughout the film miss their targets. The role of Kramer's wife Margaret (Lauren Bacall), for example, is so limited as to be little more than a sketch. When the ex-presidents get a ride from a family on the road, the tone shifts toward the serious a bit too suddenly and awkwardly. In addition, the comic novelty of hearing two former presidents swear like sailors will wear off for most audiences.

Eventually, Kramer and Douglas reach safety, and then they must decide whether to turn their information over to trusted authorities or to continue themselves in uncovering the scandal by going in person to the White House. Their confidant Joe Hollis (Wilford Brimley), considers their fame and of course advises caution. They have done enough, he says. Douglas points out that all their lives they have "played the game" and made a career out of "just doing enough." He reminds Kramer that they have met people on the road whose existence had worsened because Kramer and Douglas spent their years in office "just doing enough." Douglas still wants to uphold his oath of office, and his patriotism inspires Kramer. For once he and Kramer agree. In a moment of Capraesque lyricism, Kramer announces to Hollis, "Mr. Kramer and Mr. Douglas are going to Washington." This fine scene gives the film an effective touch of seriousness.

The overall pacing of the film also adds energy. When Kramer storms out of a meeting with Charley Reynolds and strides into an elevator, the doors close at the same second that Douglas, on his way to see Reynolds, steps out of another elevator. The film's rapid pace ushers along the plot in the same sure manner. For example, the exposition involving the kickback scandal unfolds briskly as the film crosscuts between conversations at two parties, one between Kramer and Washington reporter Kaye Griffin (Sela Ward) and the other between Douglas and party chairman Joe Hollis. Plot points mentioned in one conversation are explained in the other; questions posed in one are answered in the other. This method not only enlivens the pace but also shows that Douglas and Kramer, in spite of party differences, are two old pros at politics and know how to distill quickly the essentials of a breaking scandal. The scene conveys its exposition in a way that also sharpens audience attention.

Another strength of the film is its carefully crafted script. One of the screenwriters, E. Jack Kaplan, worked as a speechwriter in the Carter White House, and this background provides some needed authenticity to balance the farce of the cross-country chase. Dan Aykroyd commented on both aspects of the screenplay: "The script reminded me of *Trading Places* (1983) because it's set in a real world with real characters and it's played for comic effect and irony. It works on a political level and it's also a great chase. The story employs Jack Lemmon's comic timing abilities and Garner's sort of easygoing, quipster kind of approach—they're both masters." Producer Tracy Barone also praised the script for being "smart and insightful, just what we wanted. It pokes fun at everyone—the Democrats, the Republicans—it's an equal-opportunity comedy that takes on the entire political scene."

More noteworthy than its authenticity, however, is the script's jigsaw-like connectedness. Seemingly no detail is wasted. The scene on the train, for example, in which the two ex-presidents hear for the first time a blunt layman's view of themselves, works simultaneously as comedy and as character development. In another instance, a passing reference to Rita (Esther Rolle), the cook both Kramer and

CREDITS

Russell Kramer: Jack Lemmon
Matthew Douglas: James Garner
William Haney: Dan Aykroyd
Margaret Kramer: Lauren Bacall
Ted Matthews: John Heard
Joe Hollis: Wilford Brimley
Kaye Griffin: Sela Ward
Carl Witnaur: Brad Whitford
Col. Paul Tanner: Everett McGill

Origin: USA
Released: 1996
Production: Jon Peters, Tracy Barone, Craig Zadan, Jean Higgins, and Michael Ewing for Peters Entertainment and Storyline Entertainment; released by Warner Bros.
Direction: Peter Segal
Screenplay: E. Jack Kaplan, Richard Chapman, Peter Tolan
Cinematography: Julio Macat
Editing: William Kerr
Production design: James Bissel
Music: William Ross
MPAA rating: PG-13
Running Time: 102 minutes

Douglas cherished while in office, seems like only a moment of nostalgia until she later becomes the ex-presidents' accomplice for sneaking back into the White House. The compass is slipped slyly into the action as a practical way for Douglas and Kramer to trek to the presidential library in Ohio, but, like some of the props in Billy Wilder's comedies, it assumes symbolic meaning as the story develops. After Kramer and Douglas have realized again the difference between celebrity and substance, between holding office and serving the people, a final closeup of the compass when all the wrongdoers have been exposed visually underscores the larger meaning of finding direction in life. Benjamin Svetkey, in a recent article in *Entertainment Weekly* (October 4, 1996), asked, "Who Killed the Hollywood Screenplay?" The work of writers E. Jack Kaplan, Richard Chapman, and Peter Tolan in *My Fellow Americans* makes an exception to the trend of flat scripts that Svetkey deplores.

The crisp, careful editing of the film also contributes to the comedy. William Kerr, relatively new to feature films, has won eight Emmy Awards for his work editing television shows like "TV Nation." Kerr and director Peter Segal's use of reaction shots both quickens pace and injects humor. When Vice-president Matthews (John Heard) beans a black spectator with his tee shot at a golf match, his nervous attempt to make amends drips with racial condescension. A cutaway to eager reporters writing furiously and flipping pages in their notepads comically deflates Matthews even more. In the woods after the copter crash, Kramer tries to talk Douglas into going public rather than travelling in secret to Ohio. Douglas asks why people would believe them. "Because we're presidents!" Kramer naively replies. A closeup of Douglas's skeptical reaction ends that discussion. When the ex-presidents take over as guides of a White House tour during the film's climax, they excitedly command their civilian guests to hurry. A quick cutaway shows a gasping elderly woman on a staircase sneaking a gulp from her inhaler before she rushes to catch up with the tour.

The script and storyboards for the film suggest that some of these inserts may have been added during post-production. A scene at a fast-food restaurant, when Kramer, driving a rented Hyundai, smashes out of the parking lot and tries to escape federal agents, was scripted and storyboarded simply to map out the series of cuts needed for the escape. In the finished film, however, Segal and Kerr cut from the parking lot as Kramer starts the car to show the feet of Douglas in a men's room stall. He hums "The Macarena." The visual contrast between the frantic parking lot action and the static men's room adds some wit to the scene.

It should be said that these favorable remarks represent a minority view of the film. Except for the comments of Richard Schickel in *Time* magazine, almost all of the notices for the film were mixed. Most critics faulted the film for a premise that resembled too closely that of *Grumpy Old Men* (1993), and almost every writer except Schickel managed to work the phrase "Grumpy Old Presidents" into the review. Perhaps this similarity obscured some of the film's merits. *My Fellow Americans* is a light, well-made comedy that adds a touch of seriousness to the farce of two ex-presidents trying to stay ahead of the villains. The decades of scandals and party politics since Watergate provide the background for this point of two men who learn almost too late that the real prize in politics is serving the people rather than basking in the limelight.

—*Glenn Hopp*

REVIEWS

Entertainment Weekly. December 6, 1996, p. 51.
Hollywood Reporter. December 10, 1996, p. 14.
New York Times. December 20, 1996, p. B2.
Time. December 30, 1996, p. 160.
USA Today. December 19, 1996, p. 6D.
USA Today. December 20, 1996, p. 13D.
Variety. December 9, 1996, p. 103.
Wall Street Journal. December 20, 1996, p. A14.

My Life and Times with Antonin Artaud; En Compagnie d'Antonin Artaud

Box Office: $10,972

My Life and Times with Antonin Artaud is about the relationship between aspiring poet, Jacques Prevel (Marc Barbe), and the inventor of "The Theater of Cruelty." The point of view is Prevel's. He wrote to Artaud (1896-1948) during the latter's stay in a mental asylum outside Paris. Artaud's generation saw him as the suffering, alienated poet, director, and actor—perhaps most widely known for his appearance in Carl Dreyer's *The Passion of Joan of Arc* (1928), in which he played a handsome young priest drawn to her martyrdom.

In the film, Prevel is all nerves anticipating the release of his aesthetic god and his return to Paris. Will Prevel speak to his hero? He is uncertain. But he must see him. In the event, Prevel introduces himself to the master, who seems aloof and disdainful, saying that judging from Prevel's poems he had expected an older and fatter man. Is Artaud provoking Prevel? It is difficult to say because Artaud is so wrapped up in himself and expects the world to revolve around him. When people carry on without him, he considers their actions a drain on his own vitality—as if they are somehow crowding out his imaginative possession of the world. Indeed existence is one vast conspiracy against his creative freedom. He says to Prevel's pregnant wife: "Every time a man and woman have sex, it deprives me." A fly, he tells Prevel, is "an evil thought from someone far away."

Prevel comes seeking Artaud's approval, for the great one has written an encouraging letter to the young poet. But Artaud denies Prevel the use of the letter, which Prevel would like to use as a preface to the publication of his poems. Undaunted, Prevel becomes Artaud's toady, supplying him with laudanum and other drugs that Artaud says he needs in order to function. Prevel becomes Artaud's alter ego. Artaud speaks of dying; Prevel later falls to the floor in what looks like a death agony, unable to stop a coughing fit. His eyes become hollowed out, and he looks skeletal. Catering to Artaud's demands transforms Prevel into a kind of ghoul, so that he has little, if anything, to give to others.

The presentation of Prevel is far more realistic than that of Artaud. As one reviewer points out, Artaud had lost all his teeth and was suffering from cancer—facts absent from the film which romanticizes him. He looks entirely too robust when he denounces bourgeois society and says sickness is a strength. He seems merely a good-looking man in middle age prone to too much posturing.

It is hard to see what an audience unfamiliar with Artaud's work would make of this film. Sami Frey is stunning as Artaud; he is fascinating to watch: dark featured, brooding, intense, and vampiric—everything that could be expected of Artaud on-screen. But as the writer who attracted Prevel, the Artaud character is a failure. The one extended scene of Artaud at work shows him haranguing an actress, cruelly driving her to the point of exhaustion, making her feeling (presumably) the anguish that prompts Artaud to scream the lines and to scream at her. A similar scene has Artaud and Prevel screaming at each other.

To Prevel's long-suffering wife, her husband's obsession with Artaud is incomprehensible and disgusting. As she rightly points out, Prevel has ceased to be a husband. He simply comes and goes and uses her as a convenience, even writing while she screams at him. Prevel has better luck with his mistress, a dopey blonde who takes everything Prevel says on faith.

The film's only theme is the isolation of artistic genius. As Prevel and Artaud draw closer, everyone else drops out of their consciousness. And since what they accomplish is never shown, it is hard to care about them. One reviewer notes that Artaud was far more productive in his last years than the film suggests. Indeed, on the evidence of the film alone Artaud seems merely mad and a burnt out case, with flashes of sensitivity and sympathy for the suffering of others.

CREDITS

Antonin Artaud: Sami Frey
Jacques Prevel: Marc Barbe
Jany: Julie Jezequel
Rolande: Valerie Jeannet

Origin: France
Released: 1994; 1996
Production: Denis Freyd for an Archipal 33/Laura Prods./La Septe-Arte/France 2 production; released by Leisure Time Features
Direction: Gerard Mordillat
Screenplay: Gerard Mordillat and Jerome Prieur; based on the diaries of Jacques Prevel
Cinematography: Francois Catonne
Editing: Sophie Rouffio
Music: Jean-Claude Petit
Art direction: Jean-Pierre Clech
Sound: Pierre Lorrain, Dominique Dalmasso
MPAA rating: Unrated
Running Time: 93 minutes

More successful is the film's stark black-and-white photography that captures the aura of Paris right after the war. People look incredibly gaunt and have little to spend in cafes. The emaciated Prevel (coughing like a consumptive) orders a bowl of broth for two to go with the wine he and his mistress Jany (Julie Jezequel) are drinking. Such scenes are refreshing because they do not gloss over the gnawing poverty and worries over money.

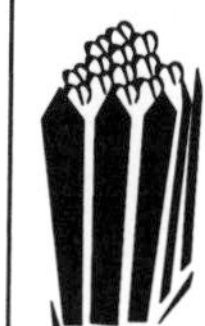

"He looks like my father just before he died."—Prevel on first meeting Artaud

If the film is trying to make a connection between artistic freedom and madness, and if Prevel's cruelty to his wife (he is with his mistress when his wife gives birth) is supposed to be the price he pays for pursuing art, then *My Life and Times with Antonin Artaud* is a failure. Artists may feel they need to reject society in order to create, but the film does not show why that is necessary. And clearly not all artists have to be Van Goghs or Artauds in order to create great work.

Debating points about what makes for great art are surely lost in the interminable love scenes between Prevel and his mistress Jany. They lead a slovenly, undisciplined life. It is a little surprising that when they visit Artaud and he casually wipes off his plates on his coat and throws slices of meat on the plates, Jany is repulsed. Surely Artaud is no dirtier than she is, and when has she last seen so much food set before her?

Does Prevel have any talent that would justify the mess he is making of his life? Publishers reject his work. Artaud is cagey. He tells Prevel that he did not actually say he liked his work. Nothing that Prevel reads aloud sounds good. There is the distinct possibility that he is deluding himself, and that Artaud just uses him as a convenience. Yet there are so many scenes of the two men together, sharing confidences, that it is hard to tell. Perhaps it was so for Prevel, and perhaps it is always so when artists treat others both as confidants and as lackeys.

One reviewer may have it right by suggesting that the Artaud/Prevel relationship is rather like the one between Johnson and Boswell. After all, the film is a fictionalized treatment of Prevel's memoir of Artaud's last two years. Like Boswell, Prevel had great ambition but no sense of accomplishment when he met the great man who was to dominate his life. And the film's title clearly focuses on the relationship between the two men.

Finally, then, what the film seems about is Artaud's demand for complete self-sacrifice to him as the incarnation of the artist. When Artaud shouts his actress into a state of hysteria, he is robbing her of any resistance to his direction. He humiliates her in order to get her to surrender her will. Everything must be given to the art, to the role, to the theater. This is the lesson, evidently, that Prevel must learn: jettison anything that gets in the way of his service to Artaud, who becomes the embodiment of an abstraction, of art itself. If everything Artaud says is viewed through his sense of himself as "the artist," then, yes, the world does get in his way, and he requires his art slaves.

It is a delusion, of course for any man to think so grandly of himself. Artaud was, after all, mad. But after the surrealism of the 1920s that presaged the theater of the absurd and the existentialism of the post World War II years, Artaud's career has a kind of allegorical finish to it. He rejected realism and bourgeois values and craved greater authenticity—a word that Sartre and his followers would make central to their code of militant individualism. As a transitional figure, he hovers between genuineness and fraudulence. His statements are so extravagant that they seem fashioned only to provoke. But in the 1950s, often called the age of conformism, it was Artaud's outrageousness that proved attractive. For he was asking the artist to put himself first. In the 1960s and early 1970s Artaud's program for artistic renewal was tried out, especially in New York, where off Broadway and off off Broadway flourished under the auspices of such groups as "The Living Theater" and critic Susan Sontag's call for a rededication to the idea of art and to the quest for aesthetic form.

But that period is over and Sontag and others have gone on to emphasize art's relationship to society, and especially to history—in other words, art in greater context than Artaud himself acknowledged. It is this shift away from the manic definitions of art that makes *My Life and Times with Antonin Artaud* seem, in some respects, a trifle boring and even silly.

—Carl Rollyson

REVIEWS

Los Angeles Times. January 26, 1996, p. F14.
New York Times. July 19, 1995.
Sight and Sound. June, 1996, p. 48.
Variety. October 6, 1994, p. 85.
Village Voice. July 25, 1996, p. 58.
Washington Post. October 13, 1995, p. F6.

Mystery Science Theater 3000: The Movie

Every year Hollywood makes hundreds of movies. This is one of them.—Movie tagline

"Sidesplittingly funny! I still hurt from laughing!"—Jeffrey Lyons, *Sneak Previews*

"The funniest movie of the year! The jokes fly at you like hailstones."—Michael Atkinson, *Spin Magazine*

"One of the best reasons to be alive in the '90's."—Richard Corliss, *Time*

Box Office: $1,007,306

Perhaps it should have occurred to someone at Gramercy Films that there is an inherent problem in making a motion picture out of a television series that is based on making fun of motion pictures. It is rather like throwing stones into one's own glass house. And sadly, *Mystery Science Theater 3000: The Movie* breaks a few of its own fine windows.

Mystery Science Theater 3000: The Movie is apparently the spoonful of sugar offered to fans of the series to help the medicine of its cancellation go down a little smoother. Alas, the frequent reruns on cable's Comedy Central channel, the release of the first three of twenty plus episodes on Rhino Video, and Bantam Books' new *Mystery Science Theater 3000 Amazing Colossal Episode Guide* would probably have done the job just as well and without watering down the original premise behind the addictively clever program.

The eight year old cult phenomenon sprang forth from the fevered minds of Trace Beaulieu and Joel Hodgson, in Minneapolis, Minnesota in 1988. Twenty two episodes played locally before HBO's Comedy Channel, which later merged with Viacom, gave it a national home. "Mystery Science Theater 3000" can now boast a 67,000 member fan club as well as a Peabody Award and nominations for both Emmys and Cable Ace awards.

The film opens with Dr. Clayton Forrester (Trace Beaulieu) maniacally explaining the concept to first time viewers (a task performed better, quicker, funnier and more musically in the series' opening credit sequence). The mad and nasty scientist has sent a mild mannered, sweet, regular guy named Mike (Mike Nelson) into space in order to "break his will" by forcing him to view the worst films in motion picture history. How this plan is supposed to accomplish Forrester's desired effect is unclear. It failed to work on Mike's predecessor, Joel (Joel Hodgson, series creator who departed in 1993), who before escaping the evil doctor's clutches, created three robotic friends out of spare parts found about the spaceship, Crow T. Robot (voice supplied by Trace Beaulieu), Gypsy (voice supplied by Jim Mallon) and Tom Servo (voice supplied by Kevin Murphy). Joel and his three goofy friends sit in the front row of an shipboard screening room, silhouetted against the backlit screen, and do what most people do in the privacy of their own homes—talk back to the screen.

Sometimes bad films can be better than good films, if one is willing to contribute to the experience. Mike and his cohorts show no mercy in exposing the facades of tough-guy leading men, anti-feminist leading ladies in cone shaped brassieres, sets that wobble when the actors bump into them, scores that sound more like sound effects than the sound effects, and even credit sequences that run longer than the film they credit. Not since Woody Allen's dubbed comic snub, *What's Up, Tiger Lily?* (1966) have audiences enjoyed such a professional manifestation of what would be considered rude and worthy of eviction from the theater coming from an actual filmgoer.

Crow T. Robot can be found among other motion picture icons at restaurant/museum Planet Hollywood.

CREDITS

Dr. Clayton Forrester: Trace Beaulieu
Mike Nelson: Michael J. Nelson
Gypsy: Jim Mallon (voice)
Tom Servo: Kevin Murphy (voice)
Crow T. Robot: Trace Beaulieu (voice)

Origin: USA
Released: 1996
Production: Jim Mallon for a Best Brains production; released by Gramercy Pictures
Direction: Jim Mallon
Screenplay: Michael J. Nelson, Trace Beaulieu, Jim Mallon, Kevin Murphy, Mary Jo Pehl, Paul Chaplin, and Bridget Jones; based on the televisions series created by Joel Hodgson
Cinematography: Jeff Stonehouse
Editing: Bill Johnson
Music: Billy Barber
Production design: Jef Maynard
Sound: Tom Naunas
MPAA rating: PG-13
Running Time: 74 minutes

The filmmakers have made a large mistake, though. The film they have chosen to satirize, utopian science fiction near-classic *This Island Earth* (1955) is too good. It certainly does not measure up to current outer space motion picture standards such as *Alien* (1979) and its sequels, but it is in a league with *The Day the Earth Stood Still* (1951), *When Worlds Collide* (1951) and other science fiction classics of its time.

Another mistake is that in their excitement at being free of the censorial limitations of network and even cable television, the latitude taken in language and innuendo lean not as much toward the sexual or in any way sophisticated, as much as to the sophomoric. If undergarments worn on the heads of human performers are distasteful and boring, they are redundantly so worn on the heads of puppets.

In case viewers new to the milieu forget what is going on, or television fans cannot sit still for the whole film, there are built in intermissions to simulate the ones caused by commercial interruptions. Even these, though designed to stay close to the formula that has worked so well on the small screen, only jar the viewer out of the lull induced by the rhythm of the bantering stars and the not so awful film they are bantering about. The good news is that *Mystery Science Theater 3000: The Movie* runs a speedy seventy-three minutes, making it thirteen minutes shorter than *This Island Earth* was in its original release.

—*Eleah Horwitz*

REVIEWS

Boxoffice. May, 1996, p. 71.
Entertainment Weekly. April 19, 1996, p. 58.
Los Angeles Times. April 19, 1996, p. F1.
New York Times. April 19, 1996. p. C8.
USA Today. April 19, 1996, p. 4D.
Variety. April 22, 1996. p. 90.

Nelly & Mr. Arnaud; Nelly et Monsieur Arnaud

"A masterpiece! A film of uncommon intelligence, depth and beauty."—Jim Svedja, KNX

"Exquisite and emotional! A film about hope, longing and loss."—Kenneth Turan, *Los Angeles Times*

"Delicious and succulent."—Andrew Sarris, *New York Observer*

"Two thumbs up!"—*Siskel & Ebert*

"A perfection-piece! Emmanuelle Beart and Michel Serrault give performances of astonishing delicacy in this tale of unexpected love."—John Powers, *Vogue*

"A brilliant, moving film!"-Mike Caccioppoli, *WABC Radio*

"A winning romance! Exceptionally touching and astonishing. Recommended with heartfelt enthusiasm."—Gary Arnold, *Washington Times*

"My candidate as best foreign film of the year!"-Casper Citron, *WOR Radio*

Box Office: $949,853

At 25, the unhappily married Nelly is barely making ends meet supporting herself and her unemployed husband. Emmanuelle Beart, whom Sautet similarly employed in his successful *Un Coeur en Hiver* (*A Heart in Winter* [1993]), creates a reserved Nelly who meets an older gentleman, Arnaud, at lunch, through their mutual friend Jacqueline (Claire Nadeau). When Jacqueline excuses herself for a moment, Nelly and Arnaud instantly connect, with the elderly Arnaud recounting every detail of their first meeting a few years previous. The film, in fact, clearly emphasizes the keen acuity of Arnaud—a character who misses nothing, but also reveals nothing, not unlike the protagonist Stephane (played by Daniel Auteuil) in Sautet's *Heart.* Arnaud, however, does embody more spirit than the emotionally retarded Stephane, who is incapable of emotion, while we sense that Arnaud merely conceals his.

Nelly mentions her financial plight to Arnaud, causing him to casually offer a check, free of strings, to clear her debts. Nelly declines and returns home to recount the story of Arnaud's generous gift to her husband but intriguingly tells him she accepted the offer as a test to see if he protests. When this reaction fails to occur, Nelly unceremoniously leaves him and installs herself on a friend's couch while apartment hunting. Within a very short time after meeting Arnaud, Nelly's life has profoundly changed. She has left her husband, her home, and will soon find other employment, as well.

Newly free, Nelly accepts an offer from Arnaud to type his memoirs at his elegant home. Nelly diligently transcribes his words as he restlessly dictates stories about his days as a colonial judge, gleaning insight into the man in the prime of his life. Arnaud chides her for being prudish when she offers minor changes in the story, and she, in turn, attempts to spice up his straightforward style in a series of conversations that say much while revealing little of either's obviously growing attachment. Arnaud especially conceals his feelings because of his great pride, bordering on arrogance, which prevents him from seeming an old fool—even in love.

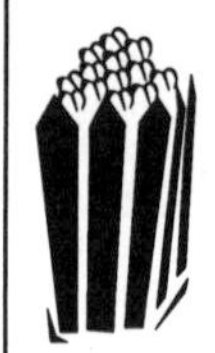

"Could your puritanical rigor in fact border on intolerance?"—Nelly to Monsieur Arnaud

Nelly is soon courted by Arnaud's publisher, Vincent (Jean Hugues-Anglade), who is young, handsome and very attracted to Arnaud's cool and beautiful assistant. Arnaud is visibly agitated by their relationship and eventually asks her for intimate details. Here, again, Nelly performs a test on Arnaud, just as she did with her husband, with the untrue response that they had been intimate. She acts this way toward men partly because of her rebellious nature and partly because she is concealing her vulnerability.

Arnaud takes Nelly out that night to an elegant restaurant and the couple proceed to cause somewhat of a stir with their age difference and Nelly's striking beauty. Both are aware of the impression they make but enjoy the mild scandal and seem nonchalant. While this act of secret conspiracy draws them even closer, they are still too afraid of such unconventional appearances to succumb completely to their emotions. Nelly is further intrigued by her elderly employer, who grows even more complex, when she witnesses a visit by the mysterious Dollabella (Michael Lonsdale), who seems to drop by regularly to conduct some sort of private business with Arnaud. She later finds out from him, that, among other things, Arnaud was a very successful and ruthless businessman and Dollabella is, in fact, blackmailing him. Needlessly blackmailed, it should be noted, as the very wealthy Arnaud is actually keeping Dollabella afloat and the scam is more of a game that both enjoy playing. The lonely Arnaud is secretly glad to have an old friend drop in.

Even while her non-affair is proceeding with Arnaud, Nelly is able to go from her dinner with Arnaud to the bedroom of Vincent and Nelly's former confession to Arnaud about their degree of intimacy is no longer a lie. In this way, Sautet displays a very modern Nelly, who wishes to have both the close companionship of Arnaud and the virility of Vincent. She is perfectly happy with this arrangement—however, both Arnaud and Vincent eventually want more than either is getting from their relationship with her.

When Nelly learns that her soon to be ex-husband is in the hospital, she assumes he has tried to commit suicide and rushes to his side, perhaps feeling guilty for leaving him so abruptly. There she learns he did not attempt suicide, but has found a job and a new girlfriend who makes an appearance. Nelly is somewhat disturbed that she no longer has control over her former love. A short time later, in another restaurant scene, Vincent asks Nelly to move in with him. Since Nelly doesn't want to give up her relationship with Arnaud and devote herself only to Vincent, she rejects his desires for a more serious relationship. Vincent cold-heartedly orders her out of the restaurant and the distraught Nelly withdraws to Arnaud's to seek comfort and winds up spending the night in a guest bedroom.

As Arnaud enters the sleeping girl's room, he almost takes action on his desire as he silently starts to caress her bare back. She awakens, questioning him, and he respects her wishes as he calmly retreats. She has now driven away all other contestants for her love and although she still cannot submit to her feelings for the disappointed Arnaud, the scene is set for their eventual coupling. In an unforeseen turn of events, Arnaud's long-divorced wife shows up with news

CREDITS

Nelly: Emmanuelle Beart
Pierre Arnaud: Michel Serrault
Vincent Grandec: Jean-Hugues Anglade
Jerome: Charles Berling
Jacqueline: Claire Nadeau
Lucie: Francoise Brion
Dollabella: Michael Lonsdale

Origin: France
Released: 1995; 1996
Production: Alain Sarde for a TF1 Films, Cecchi Gori Cinematografica, and Prokino production; released by Artificial Eye Film Company Inc.
Direction: Claude Sautet
Screenplay: Claude Sautet, Jacques Fieschi
Cinematography: Jean-Francois Robin
Editing: Jacqueline Thiedot
Music: Philippe Sarde
Art direction: Carlos Conti
Costume design: Catherine Bouchard, Corinne Jorry
Sound: Pierre Lenoir
Casting: Gerard Moulevrier
MPAA rating: Unrated
Running Time: 105 minutes

AWARDS AND NOMINATIONS

Cesar Awards 1996: Best Director (Sautet), Best Actor (Serrault) *Nominations*: Best Film, Best Actress (Beart), Best Supporting Actor (Lonsdale), Best Supporting Actress (Nadeau), Best Screenplay (Sautet/Fieschi), Best Score (Sarde), Best Editing, Best Sound

that her second husband has died and she and Arnaud plan a trip to take care of family matters. This is the pivotal moment for Arnaud, who realizes he will not stay and take his chances with Nelly, but has regained a part of his former joie de vivre from his time spent with her. He's regained enough to make him believe in a second chance with his ex-wife and he tells Nelly they will be gone quite a long time together. Nelly realizes that her hesitation and ambivalence may have cost her more than she realized.

Much of the power of the film is based on the ability of Beart and Serrault to convey an extreme depth of emotion that never surfaces. The action is sublimated, which usually makes a convincing character portrayal, not to mention an interesting film, very difficult to execute. What shapes a character or plot if not action? Both actors manage wonderful performances despite the extreme limitations the story requires. Serrault is especially capable of playing a highly complex character who, at the outset, seems playful yet world-weary. Sautet allows the camera to dissect both lead actors completely—telling the story beautifully.

—*Hilary Weber*

REVIEWS

Los Angeles Times. May 2, 1996, p. F1, 6.
New York Times. April 12, 1996, p. C12.
New Yorker. April 22, 1996, p. 91.
Sight and Sound. April, 1996, p. 50.
Variety. September 18, 1995, p. 95.
Village Voice. April 16, 1996, p. 84.

Nico-Icon

Goddess. Popstar. Junkie. Icon.—Movie tagline

"Sensational. The diva of the damned. Her story is shocking and often morbidly funny. Not to be missed."—Dennis Dermody, *Paper*

"*Nico Icon* is more than investigation of a doomed celebrity: It's also a mirror reflecting her friends, her audience and pop culture."—Edward Guthmann, *San Francisco Chronicle*

Box Office: $306,691

It is perhaps not too much of a stretch to say that what Marilyn Monroe was to the 1950s and early 1960s, Nico was to the late 1960s and 1970s. (The two actually met late in the 1950s at the Actors Studio, where they were in a class together.) Both women achieved fame early owing to extraordinary beauty, and both grew to loathe the long shadows their gorgeous facades cast over the rest of their lives. While the physical appeal of each was manifest, their abilities were—and still are—hotly debated. Monroe is both adored and derided for her acting; similarly, while some of the interviewees in the new documentary *Nico Icon* mock Nico's singing and song writing, John Cale goes so far as to call her music a major contribution to the western European canon.

> "She had beauty, she had intelligence. That's what makes it so sad."—Edith Boulogne

Monroe hated the fact that she was not taken seriously as an actor or as a person. In an interview given towards the end of her life, Nico expressed almost the same sentiment when she said her only regret was not having been born a man. Both icons were in fact illegitimate children raised by surrogate parents (although director Susanne Ofteringer repeats the story that Nico's father was a soldier possibly executed by the Wehrmacht, this lineage is apparently apocryphal). Both adopted pseudonyms once they achieved fame. And both were drug addicts who seemed to see death as the only means of escaping the burdens of that fame.

Nico was born Christa Paffgen in 1938 in Cologne, Germany. Her statuesque figure and blond, high cheekboned visage made her the embodiment of the Aryan ideal, and in her teens she embarked on a modelling career, first in Germany and then elsewhere in Europe. She regarded modelling as a frivolous career and sought work as an actor and singer. In the early 1960s, she did appear in a few mediocre French films and even landed a cameo role in Fellini's *La Dolce Vita*. She recorded a hit single in London. Her breakthrough, however, came in 1965, when she joined Andy Warhol's Factory.

Warhol made active use of Nico, featuring her as one of his "superstars" in the film *Chelsea Girls* and promoting her as the singer fronting the avant-garde band, the Velvet Underground. With her silence, her seeming ennui, and her monotonous, tuneless singing style, she epitomized the alienated affectedness that was the hallmark of the Factory and the dark side of the radical rebellion we now refer to collectively as the Sixties.

As the Sixties came to an end, Nico put herself through another metamorphosis, exchanging her blond hair and white clothing for dark henna and an all-black wardrobe. Throughout her life, she had drifted from one famous man to another, having a child with actor Alain Delon (who refused to acknowledge paternity), but finding a soulmate only in the flamboyantly self-destructive Jim Morrison. Now, she took up with the minor French film director Philippe Garrel and began a long-term involvement with heroin.

Edith Boulogne, Alain Delon's mother, was disowned by her son when she took in grandson Ari and raised him.

The remainder of Nico's life consisted of a perverse, defiant quest for oblivion—what the suicidal poet Anne Sexton called "the awful rowing toward god." Drugged out but still producing music, Nico managed to scrape by as a solo performer. One of her band members from this period describes her pride in her gray hair, her rotten teeth, her bad skin, her track marks. She was approaching some kind of depraved apotheosis, and she almost took her son with her.

Nico had been separated from Ari Boulogne, who was raised by his paternal grandmother, from the time he was a child. After he was grown, Ari and Nico reunited, and Nico initiated him into her world by introducing him to heroin. The eeriest part of this disturbing but fascinating film occurs during an interview with the lost and beautiful son who describes how, when he was hospitalized during a drug-induced coma, his mother visited him so that she could record the sound of his life support system for use on some future album.

Nico finally died in 1988 at the age of forty-nine, of a brain hemorrhage occasioned by a bicycle accident. The lovelorn Ari blames her demise on overexposure to the sun, rather than on drug abuse. After watching seventy-five minutes of images of and interviews about Nico, however, viewers are more likely to agree with another observer whose most profound impression of her was that she simply found life a bore. Warhol superstar Viva claims in *Nico Icon* that Nico had "no interest in anything," but the film makes it clear that—at least in the second half of her existence—Nico cultivated a profound interest in death.

—Lisa Paddock

CREDITS

Jonas Mekas: Jonas Mekas
John Cale: John Cale
Paul Morrisey: Paul Morrisey
Jackson Brown: Jackson Brown
Viva: Viva

Origin: Germany
Released: 1995
Production: Thomas Mertens, Annette Pisacane for a CIAK-Filmproduktion GmbH production; released by Roxie Releasing
Direction: Susanne Ofteringer
Screenplay: Susanne Ofteringer
Cinematography: Judith Kaufmann, Katarzyna Remin
Editing: Elfe Brandenburger, Guido Krajewski
Sound: Jens Tuklendorf, Charles Blackwell
MPAA rating: Unrated
Running Time: 72 minutes

REVIEWS

Boxoffice. February, 1996, p. R-12.
Entertainment Weekly. February 2, 1996,p. 41.
Los Angeles Times. January 12, 1996, p. F8.
New York Times. January 3, 1996, p. C9.
Sight and Sound. November, 1996, p. 56.
Village Voice. January 16, 1996, p. 41.

Nobody Loves Me; Keiner Liebt Mich

"An anarchic urban comedy . . . get caught up in the swirl!"-Stephen Holden, *New York Times*

"You will not only leave the theater laughing, you'll leave the theater singing."—Barbara & Scott Siegel, *Siegel Entertainment Syndicate*

Box Office: $230,044

A quirky but touching romantic comedy, *Nobody Loves Me* is the story of Fanny Fink (Maria Schrader), a single woman confronting her biological clock on the cusp of her thirtieth birthday. The film follows her on her desperate odyssey to find a mate, but, on a much deeper level, *Nobody Loves Me* is about finding the meaning of real love.

Fanny is a shy, self-absorbed young woman who works as a security officer at the Cologne airport. Ironically, because of her work, she is physically intimate with strangers everyday, yet has no intimacy in her private life. At home Fanny is perennially alone, reading late into the night or listening to self-help tapes, as she mindlessly mouths affirmations to keep her spirit afloat through long comfortless nights in singledom.

Her life outside of work is a social vacuum, and her only human contact is through a class she is taking on "conscious dying," where Fanny indulges her morbid fascination with death. With wonderful comedic insight, the film's director Doris Dorrie explores the irony of people, who don't know how to live, trying to learn how to die. In one of the funniest moments in the film, the earnest students sit with plastic bags over their heads as the leader of the class promises them happiness in death. The curriculum includes learning the most effective means of suicide, and designing and building their own coffins and tombstones. In one scene Fanny, hands folded over her chest, is lowered into a grave in her plexiglass coffin, as the teacher instructs the students to start shoveling. Fanny's wide-eyed deadpan face gazes up through the glass, a little startled yet passively accepting it all.

"Is your biological clock digital? Don't you hear it ticking?"—Fanny's mother to her 30-year-old daughter

The main setting for *Nobody Loves Me* is an old graffiti blemished high-rise, where Fanny lives. It is an unlikely place for her to find the man of her dreams, but when she meets Orfeo (Pierre Sanoussi-Bliss), her luck changes and so does her life.

Alone on the elevator with a strange man dressed in a fur coat and full body paint, an uncomfortable Fanny waits for her floor. When the elevator suddenly stops between floors, he leaps into a manic tribal dance, shouting and slamming the walls of the car, and the elevator miraculously starts up. Fanny is amazed, even more so when he hands her his card, introducing him as Orfeo de Altmar, Psychic and Card Reader.

Orfeo, whose real name is Walter Rattinger, was born in East Germany to a German mother and an African father. He is the ultimate poseur, dressing in flamboyant African clothes and painting his body like a voodoo sorcerer during the day and dressing as famous torch singers at a gay bar at night.

Orfeo may be an eccentric, but he is also very much alive. Whether he is dancing to wild African rhythms on his boom box or fawning over a large statue of what looks like some primitive fertility god, Orfeo overflows with a passion for life. That is not to say that he hasn't any problems. He is a black man living in white Germany, is months behind in his rent, has a tenuous relationship with his boyfriend, is suffering from some unknown disease, and really isn't very good at female impersonations, which appears to be his bread and butter.

In contrast Fanny, who has a good job and her own flat, lays in her cocoon of an apartment reading and sighing the evenings away. During one too many lonely nights as she listens to Orfeo's music pulsating through her walls, Fanny succumbs to temptation and asks him to tell her fortune.

Upon entering Orfeo's apartment, Fanny finds herself in an exotic world full of primitive artifacts, where a mass of candles drips down a TV that is always on, and the psychic Orfeo lies sprawled out on a unmade bed, smoking cigarettes while pensively considering Fanny's future.

He tells her that she will meet a man with long blond hair and a black car. This, of course, is no mystery. Orfeo has already met the building's new manager, Lothar (Michael Von Au), a blond man with a black car, who has been going door to door introducing himself.

Finally when Lothar comes to Fanny's door, she's convinced that it is Orfeo's prophecy coming true. Unfortunately, the womanizing manager doesn't feel the bond, but Fanny takes the initiative and intentionally rams his car in the parking lot. But the ploy doesn't work, and Fanny returns to Orfeo to learn what she can do to make the manager fall in love with her. He has her get a photo of him, a lock of his hair, and a piece of his clothing, promising her that the manager will be hers forever.

Meanwhile, the manager has a disappointing liaison with the girl of the hour. When she leaves, he decides to try his luck with the smitten Fanny. They make love, and while he sleeps, Fanny cuts off his long blond ponytail and steals his Armani suit. But Fanny's happiness is short-lived, and the manager quickly and predictably breaks her heart.

While Fanny is going through the ups and downs of her romance, Orfeo's boyfriend dumps him for another, and he is evicted from his apartment. Fanny finds Orfeo collapsed in the hallway in front of her door, and, when she runs to his side, he asks her weakly for some "champagne—any champagne."

She takes him in, and in the days that follow, while Fanny nurses him, they comfort one another. Orfeo, sick and sorrowful, needs Fanny as much as she needs him, and a caring and giving friendship is forged.

But Fanny's nursing has little effect on Orfeo, who gets weaker and weaker everyday. She pressures him to let her call a doctor, but he refuses. Finally Orfeo reveals to Fanny that in his youth, he was abducted by aliens and taken to the star Arcturus. He tells her that the aliens removed all his unhappiness and he was content. But after a time he longed to experience love just once more, so they brought him back to Earth. Now that he has lost his lover, Orfeo is certain they will return for him and take him home. In his weakened state, Fanny humors him, preparing him for his journey, but really expecting him to die.

One day, he tells her that his time has come. She dresses him in the manager's Armani suit, and gives him a small gold bar for him to give "them" as a gift. He has told her that when they come, the air will fill with the sound of thousands of aircraft, so Fanny has made a tape of planes landing and taking off at the airport. By now Orfeo is even too weak to walk, so Fanny carries him to her coffin and puts on the tape at top volume. While she waits outside the apartment door, the roar of the aircraft resounds through the high-rise and her neighbors rush into the hall in alarm.

When all is once more calm, Fanny enters her apartment, expecting to find Orfeo's dead body dashed against the sidewalk below, but in fact finds that he has disappeared, and she finally believes him.

Fanny is now a changed person; her friendship with Orfeo has produced an unintended result. By opening up to one person, Fanny has opened up to life. One day while in the elevator with a group of her oddball neighbors, the elevator stalls between floors. Fanny does Orfeo's wild dance and, of course, the elevator responds. She invites everyone in the elevator back to her apartment for coffee, and there she meets a man who most surely will turn out to be her soul mate.

Maria Schrader's performance in *Nobody Loves Me* is deliciously understated, especially in the opening scene, where she is recording a video for a dating service. She's a woman who has been through the dating scene so much that she has it down pat. "It starts with a cup of coffee," she tells the camera. "You go out, eat, talk, sleep together. Then you're smoking again, buying new lingerie, going to the health club, and stocking beer in the fridge."

Schrader plays the Everywoman with a dry comic charm and waifish vulnerability that is disarming. In one poignant moment in the film, Fanny reveals that all she really wants is to have someone she can say "Don't forget your keys" to, or "Isn't it a beautiful day?"

Pierre Sanoussi-Bliss is captivating as Orfeo and almost steals the show, leaping from manic to depressive in a single bound. He plays Orfeo with such sympathy, that even when he's conning Fanny, it's hard to dislike him.

Filmmaker Doris Dorrie, known for her films *Men* (1985) and *Straight Through the Heart* (1983), found her inspiration for *Nobody Loves Me* in the characters from Dorrie's own short story "Orfeo." She says *Nobody Loves Me* ". . . is about how two worlds collide," but Fanny and Orfeo's worlds also merge through their friendship. By showing the ultimate irrelevance of their differences, Dorrie has successfully and gracefully imbued her romantic comedy with a social conscience.

Although the message that women are "unfinished" without a mate grates on the nerves like fingernails on a blackboard, *Nobody Loves Me* successfully captures the isolation of modern life, where a hundred people live in the same building, yet never touch one another. In this milieu, the bond of Fanny and Orfeo's friendship becomes as miraculous as Orfeo's travels to Arcturus. *Nobody Loves Me* is a

CREDITS

Fanny Fink: Maria Schrader
Orfeo de Altamar: Pierre Sanoussi-Bliss
Lothar Sticker: Michael von Au
Madeleine: Elisabeth Trissenaar

Origin: Germany
Released: 1994
Production: Gerd Huber and Renate Seefeldt for a Cobra Film production; released by CFP Distribution
Direction: Doris Dorrie
Screenplay: Doris Dorrie
Cinematography: Helge Weindler
Editing: Inez Regnier
Music: Niki Reiser
Production design: Claus Kottmann
Costumes: Siegbert Kammerer
Sound: Wolfgang Wirtz
Makeup: Evelyn Dohring
MPAA rating: Unrated
Running Time: 104 minutes

warmly optimistic film that promises that if we open ourselves to the diversity and unique charm of the people around us, then the miracles will happen.

—*Diane Hatch-Avis*

REVIEWS

Boxoffice. April, 1996, p. 120.
Los Angeles Times. February 23, 1996, p. F16.
New York Times. November 3, 1995, p. C3.
Variety. January 3, 1995, p. 16.
Village Voice. November 7, 1995, p. 74.

Normal Life

Love was their addiction. Crime was their drug.—Movie tagline

"Judd hasn't had this juicy a role since her 1993 debut, *Ruby in Paradise.* Her energy blasts through . . . "—Peter Travers, *Rolling Stone*

"Two thumbs up."—*Siskel & Ebert*

Box Office: $11,800

Movies about crazy, criminal couples have evolved from the brilliant, pioneering *Bonnie and Clyde* (1967) and the brutal, elegiac *Badlands* (1973), to the overwrought *Wild at Heart* (1990) and the hysteric *Natural Born Killers* (1995). But few in the genre have made their protagonists so achingly real as *Normal Life,* an overlooked little gem that resists the obvious impulse to sensationalize an already sensational story.

Pam (Ashley Judd) and Chris Anderson (Luke Perry) aren't out to be famous or fearsome, they're just doomed to fail at trying to make their life together work. If their impulses are exaggerated and their behaviors extreme, their desperation is fearfully familiar. That's the noteworthy achievement of director John McNaughton and his two young stars: they make Pam and Chris go terribly off-kilter while keeping them within the strained bounds of normality. They are disturbingly like people we know, and that makes *Normal Life* different from the other cult killer-couple films that revel in the bizarreness of their characters.

This true story was also the basis for the 1997 TV movie *In the Line of Duty: Blaze of Glory.*

With the blank, unyielding pavement of suburbia as his canvas, McNaughton sketches a portrait of emotional desperation lurking just beneath the surface of what passes for normality in modern America. Pam and Chris aren't untamed spirits streaking across the wild, unfinished frontier of the American heartland; they are thwarted, boxed-in basket cases trying to find their way through an unresponsive world.

Pam is all messed up. Mortally wounded in her self-esteem by a childhood abandonment whose exact nature is not clear, Pam has grown dependent on men for love, while also hating that dependence and the men who provide it. She's addicted to booze, pot and sex, but none of it can break through her armor and really satisfy her. An amateur astronomer fascinated by the black holes of outer space, she keeps hoping to be swallowed up.

Her suicidal nature is made clear early on in the film as the script by Peg Haller and Bob Schneider indulges a bit too obviously in Pam's cosmological musings to symbolize her psychic distress. Pam confesses she finds the idea of "dark matter" thrilling because, "it makes you seem as if nothing you do matters." As she seduces him, her own scientific speculation obviously getting her hot, Pam tells Chris: "I wish we could fall into a black hole. I'd like to die that way ... so that a billion years later an alien starship could pass by and see me still falling."

Chris, who's a cop, thinks often about death too. It's a blankness, "the end of the tape, white light" that might swallow him any time he pulls over someone on a routine traffic stop. To fend off that intolerable uncertainty, he puts his faith in his guns. "To me, shooting is precision control," he tells Pam as he takes her to target practice on their first date.

While Pam is constantly unraveling, Chris is tightly wound. What they share is emotional desperation. Chris, mesmerized by Pam's beauty and wild abandon, begs her to return his love. He promises to take care of her, seeing her need as confirmation of his still unrealized manhood. Pam, desperate to maintain control and horrified of intimacy, plunges in way over her head.

In a marvelously understated way, McNaughton is keenly observant. The wedding of Pam and Chris is a masterful scene. They are seated in front of a justice of the peace. Chris's father is coughing. Pam's face is puffy. After the vows, she runs to a bathroom and vomits.

The next scene, a visit from Chris's parents to the newlywed's apartment, is just as vividly realized. As her father-in-law breaks down at dinner into a spasm of coughing, Pam retreats to the bathroom, puts on her headset, and deadens the intolerable demands of normal life with rock and roll. After they leave, she ravages Chris; her sexual aggressiveness is the only way she knows how to connect.

Based on a true story about suburban Chicago bank robbers Jeffrey and Jill Erickson, *Normal Life* errs in revealing too much, too soon about where the couple are heading. The opening scene has the pair getting caught by the FBI as their crime spree ends, and most of the rest of the film is a long flashback starting from two years earlier. It would be better for audiences not to know where Pam and Chris are heading, but perhaps the filmmakers thought that would make the first half of the film too dull. As it is, the film does unwind as a slow-paced character study of a relationship that is loaded with bad chemistry. McNaughton's exposition is so stark it is perversely compelling, and the couple's domestic fight scenes are more frighteningly honest than anything since the boozy battles of *Who's Afraid of Virginia Woolf?* (1966).

The tensions, the suicidal impulses, the break ups and the make ups escalate as giddily as do Pam's substance abuse and mental problems. Chris has problems of his own: he's so arrogant on the job that he alienates his co-workers and eventually is fired from the force. As Pam is placed on probation by her employer and ordered to go into rehab, the once straight-arrow Chris unravels and turns into a robot-like criminal.

Chris robs banks, and his modus operandi strains credibility. Carrying a huge duffel bag and wearing dark glasses, he steals cars in open daylight from shopping center parking lots. Don't any of these places have security systems? Then, he dons a fake beard and holds up banks, also in broad daylight, calmly drives the stolen cars to their original location, removes his beard, climbs into his van and fades back into normality. Why cops aren't staking out the locations the cars were stolen from is incomprehensible. The absurdity is underlined by a scene in which Pam accidently discovers Chris's gig by spotting him skulking in a parking lot. Isn't anybody else watching?

The film's nice twist on the American dream is that Chris has become the rescuing provider, leading the couple out of debt and into a dream house, a new motorcycle, and a legitimate business; a bookstore. Chris's crime spree was merely a crafty means to his desired end of living a normal suburban married life. But, predictably, Pam is fascinated by the thrill of being a criminal once she discovers what her man has been doing. She doesn't want to be a mad housewife, she wants to go out in a blaze of glory.

One of the few uncharacteristically sensational scenes is one in which Pam makes love to one of Chris's guns to demonstrate her erotic attraction to violence. It's unnecessary and tawdry. Except for that, however, McNaughton sticks to an almost documentary, chilly style, depending on Judd and Perry to provide the fireworks. And they do.

It's this lack of histrionics and faith in his two lead actors' abilities to make their characters compelling which distinguishes McNaughton from the David Lynches and Oliver Stones of the genre. Perry and Judd reward their director's faith. The minor characters in the film, including Dawn Maxey as Pam's lesbian co-worker, are very minor; this is basically a two-person stage play, and Ashley and Judd are both brilliant.

Judd takes plenty of risks in letting her character go to obsessive extremes of self-indulgence. But she's got the character of a smart, addicted, mentally unstable woman perfectly tuned. She is just as good at appearing to have her act together as she is at falling apart. And it's this continual promise of possible normality, this incredible unrealized potential, that helps keep Chris mesmerized past the point when most men would give up. It's not just Pam's eroticism that entraps him, it's her emotional depth. Judd unerringly captures this irritating inconstancy that is the hallmark of the addictive personality.

Perry also succeeds in portraying the hint of desperate emotional need behind the facade of a man trying to be a

CREDITS

Pam Anderson: Ashley Judd
Chris Anderson: Luke Perry
Agent Parker: Bruce Young
Officer Hank Chilton: Scott Cummins
Mike Anderson: Jim True

Origin: USA
Released: 1996
Production: Richard Maynard for a Spelling Films International production; released by Fine Line Features
Direction: John McNaughton
Screenplay: Peg Haller, Bob Schneider
Cinematography: Jean DeSegonzac
Editing: Elena Maganini
Music: Robert McNaughton, Ken Hale
Costume design: Jacqueline Saint Ann
Production design: Rick Paul
MPAA rating: R
Running Time: 101

savior. Chris needs to be needed; he must be essential to Pam in order to find a meaning in life. Why does he put up with her? Because without her, he's a lost little boy. Perry's portrayal is so realistic that he acts just like countless men you've seen and known; he's chafing to fill that traditional male role and always falling short.

The performances of Perry and Judd are a large part of what makes *Normal Life* special. And McNaughton, heretofore best known for the cult hit, *Henry: Portrait of a Serial Killer* (1990) and the box-office bust *Mad Dog and Glory* (1993), shows remarkable maturity and laudable restraint. In the best tradition of filmmakers like John Cassavetes, *Normal Life* is a fantastic expose of what passes for normal life and a chilling depiction of the madness that coils behind the neatly trimmed shrubs and featureless streetscapes of suburban Anywhere, USA. It deserved a better fate than its (almost) straight to video journey, but it took that path because McNaughton refused to compromise his vision with a sensationalist veneer.

"It's not a lot of fun to see this film," McNaughton admitted to one reporter. And maybe that's OK. Maybe crime sprees by deranged couples shouldn't be fun. But a film can still be compelling without being outrageous, and *Normal Life* definitely is compelling.

—*Michael Betzold*

REVIEWS

Chicago Tribune. April 1, 1996, p. 2.
New York Times. December 1, 1996, p. C8.
Rolling Stone. November 14, 1996, p. 126.
Sight and Sound. March, 1997, p. 57.
Variety. February 12, 1996, p. 82.

The Nutty Professor

"Absolutely hysterical."—Mose Persico, *CFCF*
"A hilarious hit."—Katie Warner, *Popcorn Channel*
"Hilarious. Great fun! Eddie Murphy is brilliant."—Jim Ferguson, *Prevue Channel*
"A ton of laughs."—Gina Sirico, *WSVN*

Box Office: $128,814,019

The Nutty Professor stars Eddie Murphy in a remake of the classic 1963 hit by Jerry Lewis. In the original, Lewis, director and co-writer of the script, spins the "Jekyll and Hyde" formula for comic results. He plays a gawky, shy scientist named Julius Kelp who develops and drinks a secret formula that transforms him into a cocky swinger named Buddy Love. The astonishing effects are temporary, however, resulting in many farcical misunderstandings when the formula wears off at unexpected moments. Cigarette permanently in hand, Buddy modeled after Lewis' ex-partner, Dean Martin, woos the lovely heroine played by Stella Stevens. The film's success demonstrated Lewis didn't need Martin and could play both comic and straight roles.

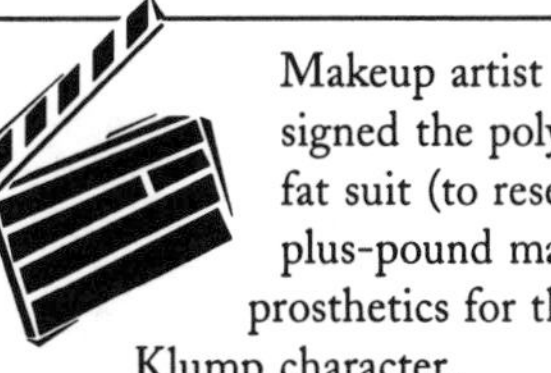

Makeup artist Rick Baker designed the polyurethane foam fat suit (to resemble a 400-plus-pound man) and facial prosthetics for the Sherman Klump character.

Eddie Murphy's *The Nutty Professor* follows the same story framework, but makes some startling and exuberant changes which adds to the film's general hilarity. Murphy's character, now called Sherman Klump, is also a shy, sweet-natured chemistry professor, but with a vast difference. He is now grossly overweight, tipping the scales at well over four hundred pounds. The film opens with Professor Klump waddling to work. Cut to the campus, filled with terrified students, professors and guests overwhelmed by over five thousand furry hamsters, escapees from Sherman's laboratory where he has been conducting experiments on fat reduction. Klump's research looks very promising, and he and his lab assistant, Jason (John Ales), believe they may make a genetic breakthrough to radically eliminate obesity.

Into Sherman's life steps Carla Purty (Jada Pinkett), a new, pretty graduate assistant. She teaches an introductory chemistry course and admires the professor's research. The love-starved Sherman is much taken by his new colleague, but is too shy and self-conscious about his appearance to ask her out. On top of that, he is having a serious problem at work with his boss, Dean Richmond (Larry Miller), who views Klump with contempt, but needs the professor's research to entice heavy funding from financial backers.

Sherman Klump (Eddie Murphy) is as brilliant as he is plump in the hysterical remake of *The Nutty Professor.*

Sherman lives alone and is unhappy with his eating habits. He often watches a "Richard Simmons wannabe" white fitness guru named Lance Perkins (Eddie Murphy) exhort his television listeners to exercise and eat right, disciplines the affable Sherman cannot master because of his junk food addiction.

Klump's idea of a good time is to visit his home and dine with members of his family, all of whom are as large as he. In a hilarious dinner sequence, with Murphy playing all the adult roles, we are introduced to the other members of the Klump family: Papa Klump who "breaks wind" at the slightest provocation; Mama Klump, sweet and kindhearted; Grandma Klump, a feisty, foulmouthed matriarch; and Ernie Klump, Sherman's ill-mannered brother. It's a tour de force performance by Murphy that generates much amusement.

Following one such dinner, Sherman goes to Carla's apartment and finds the courage to ask her on a date. She accepts willingly. They agree to go to a popular student hangout called The Scream. An amusing montage follows with Sherman attempting to lose weight and ends with a "Rocky" run up the campus steps, arms flung triumphantly in the air. Unfortunately, the much anticipated evening ends up a disaster. Both Sherman and Carla hit it off and the dinner proceeds smoothly, but Reggie Warrington (Dave Chappelle), an obnoxious stand-up comic, spots them. He spews forth an insulting string of invectives about Sherman's obesity that deeply embarrasses the hapless couple. Needless to say, Sherman and Carla go home totally humiliated. Sherman returns to his old ways of eating. He experiences a "Walter Mitty" daydream where he keeps growing fatter and fatter and roams the city like some gigantic monster with terrified people fleeing from him. The amusing sequence spoofs both *Godzilla* and *King Kong,* concluding with a "gassy bang."

Determined to fight back, Sherman goes to his laboratory, radically increases the DNA level of his experimental solution, then takes the formula. It works. In his place emerges Buddy Love (Eddie Murphy), a svelte, cocky, randy, lady-killer. Buddy meets Carla and invites her to The Scream. While there, Buddy proceeds to engage comic Reggie in an insult-hurling contest and totally destroys him at his own game. Inadvertently, the formula begins wearing off, forcing Buddy to make a hasty departure from the club.

Sherman decides to win Carla on his own. He invites her to his family's place for dinner. Big mistake. The irasci-

AWARDS AND NOMINATIONS

Academy Awards 1996: Best Makeup
Golden Globe Award 1997 Nominations: Best Actor-Musical/Comedy (Murphy)
National Society of Film Critics 1996: Actor (Murphy)

CREDITS

Sherman Klump/Buddy Love/Lance Perkins/ Papa Klump/Mama Klump/Grandma Klump/ Ernie Klump: Eddie Murphy
Carla Purty: Jada Pinkett
Harlan Hartley: James Coburn
Dean Richmond: Larry Miller
Reggie Warrington: Dave Chapelle
Jason: John Ales

Origin: USA
Released: 1996
Production: Brian Grazer, Russell Simmons for an Imagine Entertainment production; released by Universal Pictures
Direction: Tom Shadyac
Screenplay: David Sheffield, Barry W. Blaustein, Tom Shadyac, and Steve Oedekerk; based on the motion picture written by Jerry Lewis and Bill Richmond
Cinematography: Julio Macat
Editing: Don Zimmerman
Music: David Newman
Production design: William Elliott
Art direction: Greg Papalia
Costume design: Ha Nguyen
Sound: Jose Antonio Garcia
Visual effects: Jon Farhat
Special makeup effects: Rick Baker
Casting: Aleta Chappelle
MPAA rating: PG-13
Running Time: 95 minutes

ble and very earthy Klump-clan embarrass both Carla and Sherman. In the meantime, Dean Richmond orders Sherman to show up at the Ritz Hotel to sell his research project to rich alumni, Harlan Hartley (James Coburn), or lose his job. Somehow, Buddy shows up instead with Carla, piques Hartley's interest in the project, rudely chases Carla away, and leaves with three women to party at Sherman's place.

Sherman realizes his experiment has gotten way out of hand and decides to destroy Buddy by getting rid of the solution. Unknown to Sherman, Buddy has hidden some in a diet drink, enabling him to emerge again. Only this time, Buddy is going to remain forever by "killing" off Sherman. The film comes to a climax at the annual alumni ball attended by hundreds of people. Buddy and Sherman (in a wonderfully realized performance by Murphy oscillating between both characters) fight within themselves to see which will be victorious. Sherman wins in the end, abjectly apologizes to all present for not being true to himself, wins the ten-million dollar grant proposal from Hartley to save his job, and gains the hand and heart of Carla who loves Sherman for himself.

Eddie Murphy hasn't had a hit in years. *The Nutty Professor* may just be the right vehicle. In the 1980's Murphy was a superstar. Following a successful career in television on "Saturday Night Live," he teamed with Nick Nolte in *48 Hrs.* (1982) and a new star was born. He then enhanced his reputation with the creation of Axel Foley (a role written specifically for Sylvester Stallone) in *Beverly Hills Cop* (1984) that cemented his wildly hip screen persona. By 1990, Murphy reached his peak by being named the first ever NATO/Sho West Star of the Decade. It's been downhill ever since. Murphy sabotaged his own career with poor film choices and an obsessive desire to produce, write, direct, as well as, star in his own work. His last picture, *Vampire in Brooklyn* (1995), dropped quickly out of sight and many people believed his film career finished.

The Nutty Professor should change that perception. Murphy reveals himself, as he has in the past, to be a first-rate comedian and actor whose considerable talent is focused on the screen rather than behind the camera. His multi-range portrayal of seven uniquely funny characters reveals why many critics consider him the most talented of the early "Saturday Night Live" ensemble. Whether playing the "windbreaking" Papa Klump or the frenetically charged, frizzy-haired Lance Perkins (actually a hold over role from SNL's "Little Richard Simmons" satire), Murphy individualizes each role with compelling characteristics. Murphy's take on the hapless hero, Sherman Klump, however, is the best realized, projecting a character full of compassion, empathy, and pathos worthy of Chaplin. More important, Murphy, like Jerry Lewis before him who attempted to break away from the continuing Dean Martin identification, willingly deconstructs his "Axel Foley/Buddy Love" persona by showing the character is not so much witty, brave, and romantic, but shallow, reckless, and lecherous. Some film critics believe Murphy has closed the door forever on his hip, arrogant attitude. Time will tell.

Acting credit should also be extended to actress Jada Pinkett who is fast emerging as another of the screen's versatile talents in a performance radically different from previous efforts. Larry Miller and Dave Chappelle offer up strong comic support that plays off well against Murphy and adds to the film's fun. James Coburn, one time star who now is more comfortable making brief screen appearances, offers up the same solid presence he performed in the current *Eraser.* Perhaps the film's biggest star apart from Murphy, however, is makeup artist Rick Baker who not only skillfully and successfully transforms the slim Murphy into a four-hundred-plus pound blimp, but also metamorphosizes the comic into six other, completely different, roles.

The Nutty Professor, be advised, is not without its drawbacks—nor for the squeamish. The film's humor is often juvenile and sophomoric, laced with bathroom jokes and sexual innuendo, and the too frequent flatulent jokes make *Blazing Saddles* seem like an English tea party. Also, the film's basic message of tolerance for other people and being true to oneself gets lost. Having said that, however, the film is fun to watch, and, for Eddie Murphy fans, a positive welcome back and a happy reminder that he is still one of the screen's funniest and most talented comics.

—Terry Theodore

REVIEWS

Boxoffice Online. June 28, 1996.
Detroit News. June 28, 1996, p. 1D.
Entertainment Weekly. June 28, 1996, p. 82.
New York Times. June 28, 1996, p. C5.
People. July 1, 1996, p. 20.
Variety Online. June 27, 1996.
Village Voice. July 9, 196, p. 41.

Of Love and Shadows

Two lovers with a dangerous secret will risk everything they have for a chance at freedom.—Movie tagline

"Antonio Banderas gives the finest performance of his career! One of the year's most passionate and powerful films."—Jim Svejda, *CBS Radio*

Box Office: $100,000

The books of Chilean writer Isabel Allende—now California resident—have reaped international acclaim. Yet the motion pictures that have been adapted from her first two novels, *The House of the Spirits* (1993), and now *Of Love and Shadows,* hardly add luster to her name.

Yet Allende is certainly not to blame, especially for *Of Love and Shadows,* a disappointing reach at epic filmmaking that is curiously stillborn despite—or perhaps because of—the sincerity of its intentions.

In an opening voice-over, the beautiful and idealistic Irene (Jennifer Connelly) sets the scene. It is post-1973 Chile, and a military junta has taken over the country. Irene is a journalist at a magazine, and has been engaged to Captain Gustavo Morante (Camillo Callardo) since early adolescence. Despite the curtailing of democracy, her life has been minimally affected by the army takeover. Her family's house has became a retirement home to generate needed income, and the range of stories she can get past the censors has narrowed. But she is free and happy until one day, as she puts it, she begins to "wake up."

The catalyst for Irene's awakening is Francisco (Antonio Banderas), although he is hardly a firebrand revolutionary. Yet, in his quiet way, he is working against the oppression of the junta, as he admits to one woman who witnessed her husband's torture and is now testifying to the human rights organization to which Francisco belongs. In essence, as he explains to the woman, he operates "in the shadows."

Once a psychotherapist, Francisco now works as a photographer, and meets with Irene to land shooting assignments. Over lunch, the attraction is clear. The following day, the pair travel on Francisco's moped to a village in the countryside. A young woman called Angelina is reputed to be a miracle worker there, and this is the kind of story Irene feels she can publish. As Angelina writhes on her bed before a crowd of local people, the army arrives and disrupts proceedings. Aroused, the miracle worker hurls the commander across the yard and the army personnel withdraws, but not before Francisco's film has been confiscated.

Back in the city, Gustavo meets his new rival Francisco along with Mario (Patricio Contreras), a gay makeup artist unhappily trapped into working for the junta. Gustavo refuses to shake the hand of Mario. Later, Francisco visits Mario and the two make a toast. "To illusion," offers the makeup artist. "To reality," replies the intense Francisco.

Irene is taken to meet Francisco's large and loving family, headed by a father who dreams of returning to his homeland, Spain. At once, Francisco's mother is urging her handsome son to marry this well-bred woman at their dinner table. That, of course, seems to be out of the question given Irene's engagement to Gustavo.

Francisco and Irene return to the village only to learn that Angelina has disappeared. When Irene makes a decision to trace her, her life irrevocably changes.

Death and turbulence now encroach into the couple's fortunes. Francisco's brother—bereft of job and spirits—hangs himself. Irene questions the police about Angelina, and it takes a secretly taped interview with a Sergeant Faustino for it to be confirmed that Angelina has been murdered.

Angelina's brother is hiding in the mountains, and when he has been tracked down, he tells Irene and Francisco that his sister's body lies in an abandoned mine near their village. Inside the mine, Francisco finds the corpses of many victims.

CREDITS

Francisco: Antonio Banderas
Irene: Jennifer Connelly
Beatriz: Stefania Sandrelli
Gustavo: Camillo Gallardo
Mario: Patricio Contreras

Origin: USA
Released: 1994; 1996
Production: Richard Goodwin, Betty Kaplan, Paul F. Mayersohn for a Alephi Producciones S.A., Tesauro S.A. Producciones Cinematograficas, and Pandora Cinema production; released by Miramax Films
Direction: Betty Kaplan
Screenplay: Donald Freed; based on the novel by Isabel Allende
Cinematography: Felix Monti
Editing: Kathryn Himoff
Music: Jose Nieto
Production design: Abel Faccello
Costume design: Beatiz De Benedetto
MPAA rating: R
Running Time: 109 minutes

As they comfort each other following their horrible discoveries, caresses turn passionate, and the couple makes love.

Francisco's brother, Father Leal, who is also working for human rights in Chile, appeals to his Cardinal for help. Meanwhile, the mine story breaks on TV, but the murders are blamed on "terrorists." Realizing she is in love with Francisco, Irene tells a cool but furious Gustavo that she cannot marry him, and formally breaks off their engagement. Growing as a revolutionary and an individual, she meets again with the police sergeant and is given notebooks documenting the atrocity in which Angelina perished. The police officer is then run down as he crosses the street, and Irene is shot twice in the city.

After emergency surgery, and a flat-lining of her vital signs, Irene rallies at last. Gustavo confronts Francisco in the hospital corridor, but later is seen to shake his hand, telling the photographer that only he, Francisco, can protect her now.

Although soldiers are posted in the hospital, a plan is hatched and carried out in which Irene is walked out of the building in disguise. Both she and Francisco have been made-up by Mario. At a safe house, Francisco, Mario and Father Leal discuss an escape route out of the country. The Cardinal, meanwhile, has promised to publicize the mine massacre when the couple have left Chile.

A still weakened Irene recuperates with Francisco at a spa before they tackle the border crossing. They get away just in time after being pinpointed by the army. A stoic-looking Gustavo is seen watching the now infamous mine being blown up, and later he is seated around a table with colleagues discussing the murders until being surprised by armed gunmen. He is shortly executed.

As Francisco and Irene make their way over the mountains on horseback, Irene's voice-over spells out Gustavo's heroics. Convinced by Francisco of the brutality of his military superiors, he was trying to counter the junta with like-minded officers when he was betrayed.

Irene reports that she and Francisco lived in Spain for fifteen years until democracy is restored in 1989. They return to Chile and lay flowers on Gustavo's grave.

Of Love and Shadows has most of the right elements to be an involving and significant film, yet it is often awkward. Screenwriter Donald Freed plots the story in a straightforward manner, but his work is marred by self-conscious dialogue such as: "It's a risk I must take," and "My God, you love her, don't you?"

More significantly, perhaps, Connelly and Banderas are forced to struggle with their slender characterizations as written. Although they play heroic figures, they are often smaller than life. Connelly is an attractive actress and brims with emotion, but she is given few character nuances with which to work. Banderas brings sincerity and calm to his role, but there is little depth. More ire in performance might have helped illuminate the humanistic desires driving them both to make the sacrifices and take the risks they do as the story progresses.

Variety was one of the few publications to give a positive notice to the film. Karen Regelman called it "intriguing," and she praised Connelly's "evolution from a frivolous young woman to one willing to take risks." Kevin Thomas of the *Los Angeles Times* was more representative of reviewers when he declared that the film had a "deadly synthetic quality" because of the cast's "ill-matched accents," and Thomas stated flatly that it was "way beyond the abilities of . . . director Betty Kaplan . . . to make this . . . production come alive."

The story told is slighter than it promises to be. Set against a society at war with itself, the scope is more often intimate than grand, and some of the film's more successful scenes are the familial ones, especially those involving Francisco's family. The societal figures of Chile's structures of power are never more than figurines.

Technically, the film is shot and edited competently, and Jose Nieto's music features lyrical Spanish guitar and lush string arrangements for the more impassioned moments.

As a testament of history, *Of Love and Shadows* is a worthy tribute to the sacrifices made by ordinary people in extraordinary times, but it fails to grip and move as a movie. No doubt the stilted dialogue and the accents of the cast contribute to a feeling of artifice. Director Betty Kaplan's work is neither remarkable nor lamentable; instead, she directs carefully but without flair.

It is a shame that the courage of the individuals represented by Irene, Father Leal, Mario, Gustavo and Francisco ultimately remain "in the shadows" as the credits roll.

—Paul B. Cohen

REVIEWS

Boxoffice. June, 1996, p. 59.
Hollywood Reporter. May 7, 1996, p. 10.
Los Angeles Times. May 10, 1996, p. F10.
Variety. October 24-30, 1994, p. 69.

Once Upon a Time . . . When We Were Colored

"Powerful! One of the most important films I've seen this year!"—Roger Ebert, Chicago Sun-Times

"This is a fine, fine film."—Joel Siegel, *Good Morning America*

"An unabashed nostalgic portrait . . . "—Stephen Holden, *New York Times*

"Two thumbs up!"—*Siskel & Ebert*

Box Office: $2,200,000

Few mainstream films and filmmakers have been able to portray the lives of African-Americans in ways that are at once positive, historically accurate, and thematically resonant. *Sounder* (1972) and *The Learning Tree* (1969) are two exceptions from the recent past, and, of course, the films of Spike Lee have been at the vanguard of films made about African-American contemporary life. So it is a rarity when a film comes along that has resonance for African-American audiences while also having interest for other audiences simply because it is a good movie. Wouldn't it be nice if eventually it made no difference which segment of the American population was represented in a film, but that audiences would recognize the film's relation to their own lives simply because it is a fine portrayal of the human condition?

"Put a call in to Jesus, his line is never busy."—Preacher Hurn

Once Upon a Time . . . When We Were Colored, directed and produced by Tim Reid (most famous for his role on TV's "WKRP in Cincinnati"), is a touching film which is universal in its portrayal of family and community life. It is an historically accurate view of 20th-century African-American life, filled with sorrow and sadness and joy and love. *Once Upon a Time* is a film for which all its participants should be proud.

Based on an autobiography by Clifton L. Taulbert, it tells the story of Cliff (played at different ages by different actors: Deiyonos Llerena, Charles Earl Taylor Jr., Willie Norwood Jr., and Damon Hines, plus narrator Phill Lewis), and his extended family in the rural south. The film shows the terrible effects of entrenched American and (especially) Southern racism, and how people's lives were affected by Jim Crow laws and implicit barriers against blacks. Reid and scriptwriter Paul W. Cooper accomplish the task of recreating the racism of the era through various plot points and dialogue. Perhaps the most profound and disturbing of these comes when young Cliff's first words taught by his grandpa (the wonderful Al Freeman, Jr.) are "whites" and "coloreds," so that Cliff will not get himself into trouble by using the wrong water fountain, etc. Another powerful moment includes a Ku Klux Klan parade in which the stoic grandpa crushes the vanilla ice cream cone in his hand to channel his rage at the incendiary words and images of the Klan.

For the most part, however, this film is not filled with political and sociological rhetoric. It doesn't need to be. The lives of the characters are richly interwoven with the racism of the period, and Reid and company do not hammer the point home. In fact, *Once Upon a Time* shows the resilience, warmth, and strength of community of the population of Glen Allan, Mississippi. Sometimes lapsing into some extra sentimentality, this film is more a warm, fuzzy memoir than anything else.

The rich, detailed, and earthy photography of John Simmons beautifully complements Reid's (and writer Cooper's) earnest storytelling. Cliff's growth into young manhood is

CREDITS

Poppa: Al Freeman, Jr.
Ma Pearl: Paula Kelly
Ma Ponk: Phylicia Rashad
Miss Maybry: Polly Bergen
Cleve: Richard Roundtree
Cliff at 5: Charles Earl (Spud) Taylor Jr.

Origin: USA
Released: 1996
Production: Michael Bennett and Tim Reid for a United Image Entertainment production; released by Republic Pictures
Direction: Tim Reid
Screenplay: Paul W. Cooper; based on the book by Clifton L. Taulbert
Cinematography: John Simmons
Editing: David Pincus
Production design: Michael Clausen
Art direction: Geoffrey S. Grimsman
Costume design: Winnie D. Brown
Sound: Michael A. Patillo
Music: Steve Tyrell
Casting: Jaki Brown-Karman
MPAA rating: PG
Running Time: 112 minutes

told in essentially three episodes. The first details his birth and his mother's handing Cliff over to his grandparents (Freeman and Paula Kelly). It is during this time that Cliff learns, at the hands of his gentle grandpa, about the differences between blacks and whites. The second section is dominated by Cliff's pre-adolescence and his relationship to an older liberal white woman (played with charm by Polly Bergen), who challenges prevailing tradition and law by checking out countless books for Cliff at the "white's only" public library. Finally, Cliff witnesses the growing pains of emerging African-American unity, as the local ice man (Richard Roundtree) fights to save his business from a new, white-owned competitor.

Directorial debut of Tim Reid.

Numerous familiar faces dot the earthy landscape of this film, from Roundtree's sensitive ice man to Phylicia Rashad's Aunt Ponk. Performances are uniformly excellent, as is Tim Reid's poignant direction. The episodic nature of the film may be what keeps it a good film instead of a great one. The narrative seems to get lost a bit each time there is a new actor playing Cliff. The plot also meanders a bit into territory that is interesting, but keeps the film from feeling as if it is a story with a beginning, middle, and end. Then again, life meanders from one story to the next, and if the aim of *Once Upon a Time . . . When We Were Colored* is to show a slice of life, then it succeeds beautifully.

—*Kirby Tepper*

REVIEWS

Boxoffice. February, 1996, p. R-11.
Chicago Tribune. January 26, 1996, p. 5.
Los Angeles Times. January 26, 1996, p. F1.
New York Times. January 26, 1996, p. C17.
USA Today. March 1, 1996, p. 6D.
Variety. January 8, 1996, p. 73.
Village Voice. January 16, 1996, p. 41.

One Fine Day

She was having a perfectly bad day . . . Then he came along and spoiled it.—Movie tagline

"*One Fine Day* is one sweet bubbly beaker of star chemistry."—Jay Carr, *Boston Globe*

"Pfeiffer and Clooney cook up the just right chemistry that sizzles the screen and pumps the pulse."—Bonnie Churchill, *National News Syndicate*

"As a romantic team, these two click like a contemporary Hepburn and Tracy. *One Fine Day* is one fine movie."—Leah Rozen, *People*

"A charmer that lifts off on the winning chemistry between Pfeiffer and Clooney."—Peter Travers, *Rolling Stone*

Box Office: $22,722,971

"ER" heartthrob George Clooney moves beyond television to establish himself as a filmic romantic lead in the well-intentioned, but contrived comedy, *One Fine Day*. The film attempts to recapture the tone of the screwball comedies that Katherine Hepburn and Spencer Tracy made famous in the '40s and while Clooney and co-star Michelle Pfeiffer have undeniable chemistry, the film suffers from a predictable script that fails to generate the kind of heat this duo promises. Throw in two of the most precocious children to ever be captured on celluloid and the result is a film only a working mother could love. And even then, it is hard to imagine that this scenario is anyone's idea of escapist entertainment.

One Fine Day is, as the title tells us, one hellish, hectic day (one critic called it *From Dawn Till Dusk*) that turns out great for Jack Taylor (Clooney), the kind of muckraking Daily News columnist who gets his picture plastered on the sides of buses all over New York, and an ambitious architect, Melanie Parker (Michelle Pfeiffer). Both are single parents, although Melanie is the only primary custodian. The two meet when Jack's laid-back approach to child care causes his visiting five-year-old daughter, Maggie (Mae Whitman), and her kindergarten classmate, Sammy (Alex D. Linz), Melanie's mop-top boy with a penchant for sticking things up his nose, to literally miss the boat when they arrive too late for the class trip on a ferry boat cruise. Jack and Melanie take an instantaneous dislike to one another. She thinks he is an arrogant, egocentric, irresponsible Peter Pan, while he professes to abhor her kind of control-freak feminist who refuses to accept the smallest gesture of kindness, let alone admit that she might need help. But this kind of exaggerated antagonism, with its accompanying bitter bantering back and forth, fools no one, particularly the two children—and certainly not the audience.

Stuck with the children all day—along with the inadvertently swapped matching oh-so-'90s cellular phones—Jack and Melanie must reluctantly join forces in order to jump through every parental hurdle imaginable as they make their way through crucial appointments and critical career crises. Call it a marriage of inconvenience. On their way to love and what we can only presume will be happily-ever-after, this photogenic couple must each begrudgingly admit their respective prejudices and preconceived notions about the other, while also acknowledging their own weaknesses. Jack learns a bit about responsibility and the pressures of being a primary custodian, while Melanie learns to lighten up a bit and let someone else do some of the work.

> Movie title comes from the '63 Gerry Goffin-Carole King song recorded by The Chiffons.

It is actress Michelle Pfeiffer who comes up with the short end of the stick in *One Fine Day*. Not only is her character pretty humorless and hard-edged, she carries the burden of some of the film's most blatantly obvious screenwriting shorthand, not the least of which is the verbal tic of barking out directions to every taxicab driver she encounters—a trait immortalized by Holly Hunter in *Broadcast News* as the personification of control freak. The writers have really stacked the deck against poor Melanie. Even her on-screen child is more challenging than Clooney's; Maggie just wanders off, which is never much of a problem until Melanie is in charge, while Sammy wrecks his mother's big presentation model. Melanie teeters on the brink of martyrdom when she tries to explain that even though she does not like the way she responds, it is necessary in order to take care of her child and to keep her job. It is Ms. Pfeiffer's most touching moment in the film, displaying her ability to find the vulnerability beneath the self-discipline that begs for compassion.

One of Michelle Pfeiffer's strengths as an actress is the contradictory nature she projects. She is strikingly beautiful, luminous on film, while her emotional streak tends to be dark; she is intelligent and wary, yet at the same time, begrudgingly vulnerable. Arguably, some of her most compelling work includes Jonathan Demme's *Married to the Mob* (1988), *The Fabulous Baker Boys* (1989), and her sultry, whip-snapping interpretation of Catwoman in *Batman Returns* (1992). But Ms. Pfeiffer's most recent efforts have been less successful from an artistic standpoint: *Dangerous Minds* (1996), *To Gillian on Her 37th Birthday* (1996) and *Up Close and Personal* (reviewed in this volume), in which she plays a fictionalized version of newscaster Jessica Savitch opposite Robert Redford.

George Clooney gained critical notice for his work in the Robert Rodriguez/Quentin Tarantino bloodfest, *From Dusk Till Dawn* (1996), though the film failed to attract anything other than a cult audience. Still, Clooney's work was impressive and he demonstrated an unwavering ability to capture the screen, while effectively delivering some pretty bad B-movie dialogue. His roguish star presence did not go unnoticed; soon Clooney seemed to be in demand by many of Hollywood's top filmmakers, including Steven Spielberg. He even managed to grab the Caped Crusader mantle in the fourth installment in the highly successful superhero series, *Batman and Robin*, following in the footsteps of actors Michael Keaton and Val Kilmer.

Director Michael Hoffman, who also made the daytime soap opera spoof, *Soapdish* (1991), seems to equate frantic with funny—though both of these films fall short of their

AWARDS AND NOMINATIONS

Academy Awards 1996 Nominations: Best Song ("For the First Time")
Golden Globe Award 1997 Nominations: Best Original Song ("For the First Time")

CREDITS

Melanie Parker: Michelle Pfeiffer
Jack Taylor: George Clooney
Maggie Taylor: Mae Whitman
Sammy Parker: Alex D. Linz
Lew: Charles Durning
Elaine Lieberman: Ellen Greene

Origin: USA
Released: 1996
Production: Lynda Obst for a Fox 2000 Pictures and Via Rosa production; released by 20th Century Fox
Direction: Michael Hoffman
Screenplay: Terrel Seltzer and Ellen Simon
Cinematography: Oliver Stapleton
Editing: Garth Craven
Music: James Newton Howard
Production design: David Gropman
Art direction: John Warnke
Costume design: Susie DeSanto
Sound: Peter Hliddal
Casting: Lora Kennedy
MPAA rating: PG
Running Time: 108 minutes

humorous potential. While he is adept at maintaining a non-stop pace, Hoffman fails to appreciate the power of the quieter moments. *One Fine Day,* co-written by the divergent pair of frequent Wayne Wang collaborator, Terrel Seltzer, and Ellen Simon (daughter of playwright Neil Simon), has a predictable and almost mechanical feel. There are no surprises, neither in the main characters nor in the plotline, while some of the more amusing secondary characters disappear far too quickly. Droll comedian Robert Klein has only one brief, but hilarious scene as Jack's therapist and Ellen Greene shines as the scorned woman who saves Jack's story by going on the record before the newspaper prints a retraction.

Reviews for *One Fine Day* were decidedly mixed, with many critics expressing their desire to have liked the film more than they did. The filmmakers felt so confident about *One Fine Day* that it was moved ahead from its original spring release to the powerhouse Christmas time slot. But box office receipts were weak, which might be explained in part by the stiff competition provided by the surprising Tom Cruise romantic comedy, *Jerry Maguire* (reviewed in this volume). While romantic comedies tend to fall into that infamous "Chick Flick" category, *Jerry Maguire* managed to pull in the male audience by extending its story beyond that of just finding love and romance. It is a film more about integrity and how to maintain it in one's life when everything seems to be pulling in the other direction. And while that film also has a child in it—the adorable Jonathan Lipnicki—his character is never used as a plot device, as in *One Fine Day,* but rather feels more like an honest, fully-developed character.

There appears to be a fine line between adhering to the conventions of a genre and playing it by the numbers when it comes to filmmaking. In horror films, it is a given that one of the comely young women is going to venture into some dark, creepy place that the entire world but her knows she should not go. With big, budget disaster films, like those produced by Irwin Allen in the '70s, certain characters are doomed by their earlier actions, even if they are repentive later. By their very nature, romantic comedies are a tricky lot. While love stories demand that we be drawn in and feel the emotions of the characters we are watching, comedies require that we step back in order to view the hilarity in the moment—something that is extremely difficult to do while one is in the midst of the emotion. Viewed in this manner, it is easier to understand the delicate balance involved in writing romantic comedies and perhaps why some succeed, while others fail. Sometimes even the death of a spouse can help to create immediate empathy for a main character—even though death itself is not very funny—as witnessed in *Sleepless in Seattle* (1993), a film that struck an emotional chord with audiences in part by relying heavily on the evocation of a classic tearjerker, *An Affair to Remember* (1957), as a plot device.

One Fine Day benefits from the on-screen pairing of Michelle Pfeiffer (who executive-produced the project with her partner, Kate Guinzberg, from an idea by producer Lynda Obst), but ultimately, the film is undermined by cliched contrivances and uninspired writing. What is most disappointing, however, is the lack of lyricism and big-screen romance; the film is restrained, the mood too dour. Like its two tiresome child actors, the cuteness of *One Fine Day* wears thin long before the camera's last drowsy pull-away.

—Patricia Kowal

REVIEWS

Boxoffice. February, 1997, p. 64.
Chicago Tribune. December 20, 1996, p. 4.
Entertainment Weekly. December 20, 1996, p. 53.
Los Angeles Times. December 20, 1996, p. F1.
People. December 23, 1996, p. 18.
Sight and Sound. March, 1997, p. 57.
USA Today. December 20, 1996, p. 13D.
Variety Online. December 2, 1996.
Village Voice. December 31, 1996, p. 70.

101 Dalmatians

So many dogs. So little time.—Movie tagline

"Magical!"—Bill Diehl, *ABC Radio Network*

"Disney magic has done it again!!"—Ron Brewington, *American Urban Radio Network*

"Unforgettable!"—Bobbie Wygant, *KXAS-TV*

"Brilliant! Outstanding entertainment for the entire family."—Paul Wunder, *WBAI Radio*

Box Office: $109,686,111

Disney's live action version of their animated classic *101 Dalmatians* creates the perfect Cruella DeVil in Glenn Close.

Walt Disney Studios continues its series of Christmas time box-office hits with the live action remake of *101 Dalmatians*. The original animated version was made in 1961, and this updated, live version is certain to become as lovable a film to a new generation of filmgoers as the original animated version was to the baby-boomers. Oddly enough, many critics did not receive it well, taking the filmmakers to task for several aspects of the production, most notably the choice to keep the animals from talking as they do in the animated version. But anyone who sees this delightful film would have to be a dyed-in-the-wool Scrooge not to enjoy it.

"Darling, red is not your color."—Cruella to a raccoon wearing her hat

Roger (Jeff Daniels) and Anita (Joely Richardson) meet quite by chance when his male Dalmatian (named Pongo) spots Anita's beautiful female Dalmatian (named Perdita, or "Perdy"). Pongo leads Roger on a wild chase through Hyde Park just to get another glimpse of Perdy, and love immediately blooms between both canines and the humans. After the couples get married (in a hilarious double ceremony, complete with an array of canine guests sitting outside the church), Perdy and Pongo have a litter of fifteen puppies. All of this happens under the evil eye of uber-villainess Cruella DeVil (Glenn Close), a wealthy fashion designer who happens to be Anita's boss. Cruella, a fanatic about animal fur, becomes fascinated with Dalmatian fur when Anita innocently suggests that spots might look good on a new stole she is designing. From then on, Cruella is obsessed with nabbing the litter of Dalmatians for herself, with the intention of sending them to a taxidermist named Skinner (John Shrapnel), who (as if his name didn't already give it away) will present the puppies' hides to the nefarious DeVil. She enlists the aid of two bumbling thieves, Horace (Mark Williams) and Jasper (Hugh Laurie), who kidnap Anita and Roger's fifteen puppies, and botch their attempt to deliver a total of ninety-nine of the spotted pups. An elaborate network of canine heroes, led by an Airedale named Kipper and an Old English Sheepdog named Fogey, as well as horses, rabbits, skunks, birds, mice, raccoons, sheep, and others all help to save the puppies from the clutches of Cruella DeVil.

Director Stephen Herek more than meets the task of shifting the animated film to a live-action movie. Mixing real dogs with a number of computer-generated ones, Herek fills the screen with a lot of cuteness—but it works. Somehow he and writer John Hughes bring a note of irreverence which undercuts the cuteness. Of course, they do fall prey now and again to the slapstick style Hughes employed in *Home Alone* (1990). For example, when the two bumbling criminals are electrocuted on a wire fence after already suffering several indignities, the film skirts perilously close to being childish instead of childlike.

Joely Richardson and Jeff Daniels make a charming pair of lovers as the worried parents of Pongo and Perdita.

AWARDS AND NOMINATIONS

Golden Globe Award Nominations: Best Actress-Musical/Comedy (Close)

Richardson, the daughter of Vanessa Redgrave and director Tony Richardson, is a graceful beauty whose British elegance is reminiscent of Lady Di. Daniels, whose incredible range has made him one of the busiest leading men in Hollywood, is as engaging as ever. His first scene, the extended chase through Hyde Park while Pongo tries to find Perdita, could lapse into cheesy scene-chewing in the hands of a lesser actor, but Daniels underplays the reaction shots as Pongo pulls him through the park. (Herek should be credited for filming the intricate chase scene as well.) Though Daniels' and Richardson's roles are thankless, they seem aware that they are there to look worried and to appear perfect, and they do it beautifully.

220 puppies from 50 breeders in the United Kingdom were used on the London film set.

Glenn Close should have been nominated for an Academy Award for her performance. Perhaps in a film that is ultimately inconsequential, a comic performance isn't usually noticed at awards time. But Close is splendid, managing to give one of the most outrageous performances ever without seeming to mug or to pass "ridiculous" into "irritating." Even when the film falls into its slapstick mode and Close is covered in mud she stays in character and seems to be having a marvelous time. Her costumes (by Anthony Powell with Rosemary Burrows) are each a campy but lavish joke relating to DeVil's love of fur; these costumes are a highlight of the film.

Director Stephen Herek and writer/producer John Hughes have struck gold with this re-working of the old film (which in itself was a film version of a novel by Dodie Smith.) There is something for everyone to love in *101 Dalmatians*, from the adorable puppies to the extraordinary look of the film, to the tour-de-force performance by Glenn Close.

—*Kirby Tepper*

CREDITS

Cruella DeVil: Glenn Close
Roger: Jeff Daniels
Anita: Joely Richardson
Nanny: Joan Plowright
Jasper: Hugh Laurie
Horace: Mark Williams

Origin: USA
Released: 1996
Production: John Hughes, Ricardo Mestres for a Walt Disney Pictures and Great Oaks production; released by Buena Vista
Direction: Stephen Herek
Screenplay: John Hughes; based on the book *The One Hundred and One Dalmatians* by Dodie Smith
Cinematography: Adrian Biddle
Editing: Trudy Ship
Music: Michael Kamen
Production design: Assheton Gorton
Art direction: John Ralph
Costumes: Anthony Powell
Sound: Clive Winter
Visual effects supervisor: Michael Owens
Head animal trainer: Gary Gero
Stunt coordinator: Simon Crane
MPAA rating: G
Running Time: 103 minutes

REVIEWS

American Cinematographer. November, 1996, p. 75.
Chicago Tribune. November 27, 1996, p. 1.
Detroit News. November 27, 1996, p. F1.
Entertainment Weekly. November 29, 1996, p. 69.
Los Angeles Times. November 27, 1996, p. F1.
New York Times. November 27, 1996, p. C9.
New Yorker. December 9, 1996, p. 119.
Newsweek. December 2, 1996, p. 82.
People. December 2, 1996, p. 19.
Variety. November 25, 1996, p. 71.
Village Voice. December 3, 1996, p. 64.

Original Gangstas

It's time for some respect.—Movie tagline

"It's fun, exciting, nostalgic and the best time I've had at the movies this year."—Bill Hoffman, *New York Post*

". . . they are fiercer than the Magnificent Seven and the Seven Samurai put together."—Carrie Rickey, *Philadelphia Inquirer*

Box Office: $3,300,000

Original Gangstas is a film rich in nostalgia. A narrator begins to describe how a once prosperous neighborhood in Gary, Indiana with steel mines and plenty of jobs created a sense of peace in the community. However, when the steel mills closed and jobs were lost, the chaos began. This could be said of many inner cities, which also makes *Original Gangstas* a topical film. The chaos takes the shape of rampant violence by ruthless gang members who gun down an innocent teenager just for a prank. Not only does the subject matter of this film suggest days gone by, but the starring cast is made up of veterans of B grade exploitation films from the '70s. This film stars Fred Williamson, who also produced it, Jim Brown, and Pam Grier, with supporting roles from Richard Roundtree and Ron O'Neal.

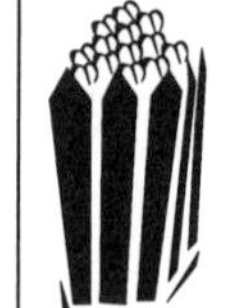

"You're a *dead man.*"—Trevor to gang leader Spyro

The murder of the teenager sets the stage for John Bookman (Fred Williamson) to go face-to-face with gun toting thugs and win back the streets. *Original Gangstas* is a revenge tale that is timely, but very misguided.

Yes, a lot has changed in Gary, Indiana since the '60s and this movie keeps reminding one of that. Gangs are running the neighborhood, and violence isn't as petty as it used to be. The old-school gangs created in the days of penny candy used fists and bottles to end disputes, now the only way to resolve a fight is through spraying bullets. A teenager destined for college basketball greatness is brutally murdered in front of a neighborhood store by the Rebels gang. The store owner witnesses the shooting and notifies the police. When the elderly store owner goes against the neighborhood norm and identifies the gang, the gang members retaliate by attacking and shooting the man.

Little do these cold-blooded thugs realize that this is no ordinary store owner, but the father of football legend John Bookman, who returns to his hometown and gets the shock of his life.

On his return, he bumps into many of his old neighborhood friends who always seem to ask the same question, "Why did you leave, man?" Well, since John Bookman became a famous football hero and successful NFL coach, this question becomes idiotic. He left because of opportunity. The question is too often followed with this statement, "Man, things aren't the same around here."

Bookman visits his father in the hospital and tries to convince his parents to move out of Gary and come live with him in L.A. Without much success, John takes it upon himself to change things, again.

Bookman initially appeals to the politicians who seem unable to bring peace to the neighborhood and curb the gang violence. The Mayor (Charles Napier) and his deputy Michael Casey (Wings Hauser) seem helpless, and turn the tables on John by blaming him for creating the Rebels in the first place. The only suggestion the politicians have is to meet with the local gang mediator, Rev. Marshall Dorsey (Paul Winfield).

Bookman, his mother, and Laurie Thompson (Pam Grier), grieving mother of the murdered teen, attend the meeting

CREDITS

John Bookman: Fred Williamson
Jake Trevor: Jim Brown
Laurie Thompson: Pam Grier
Rev. Marshall Dorsey: Paul Winfield
Slick: Richard Roundtree
Bubba: Ron O'Neal

Origin: USA
Released: 1996
Production: Fred Williamson for a Po' Boy production; released by Orion
Direction: Larry Cohen
Screenplay: Aubrey Rattan
Cinematography: Carlos Gonzalez
Editing: David Kern and Peter B. Ellis
Music: Vladimir Horunzhy
Production design: Elayne Barbara Ceder
Set decoration: Aaron Holden
Costume design: Lisa Moffie
Sound: J. Byron Smith
Casting: Craig Campobasso
MPAA rating: R
Running Time: 98 minutes

and request from the gang that they name the member who shot both Thompson's son and Bookman's father. The strong-willed gang members reveal nothing, the meeting ends, and Rev. Dorsey proclaims, "World War III has just been declared."

Sensing that serious retaliation will ensue, John Bookman seeks support and backup from the neighborhood inhabitants who are victims of the Rebels' violent rampage. Bookman's team consists of Laurie, Jake Trevor (Jim Brown), Slick (Richard Roundtree), and Bubba (Ron O'Neal). The inevitable showdown between Bookman's crew and the Rebels does happen, and it certainly doesn't take a genius to predict the outcome of a battle between a gang of scrawny teenagers against *Black Caesar* (1973), *Foxy Brown* (1974), *Shaft* (1971), and *Superfly* (1972).

As *Original Gangstas* reduces itself to a death wish plotline, it becomes a throwback to the old blaxploitation films of the early '70s that had all but revenge rummaging through their plots. Other than the saying that the steel mills have dried up, and the children don't have enough playgrounds or other creative outlets, the history behind the individual gang members, including the leader Spyro (Christopher B. Ducan), is practically non-existent. There's no depth, just a group of youngsters who spew out obscenities as much as they do bullets. This picture truly lacks the conviction of such black films as *Boyz N the Hood* (1991) and *New Jack City* (1991) and seems only to ride on their coattails.

Gangstas tries to be a message film, but the execution of the film seems more like a vanity project for its star, Fred Williamson. As producer and star (directed by Larry Cohen, who directed Williamson in the blaxploitation classic *Black Caesar*), Williamson is given full reign to strut his stuff, even if it's wider and silver around the edges. It reminds you of that scene in *I'm Gonna Git You Sucka* (1988), a movie that successfully parodied blaxploitation films, when Bernie Casey is walking down the street with a live band behind him when Keenan Ivory Wayans questions this odd pairing. Casey replies, "Every superhero's got to have his own theme music." But wait, *Original Gangstas* is not a parody. To further prove that Williamson's light must not be outshined, Ron O'Neal's and Richard Roundtree's presence are little more than cameos and their tough personas are overshadowed with their characters' cowardice when first approached about confronting the Rebels.

Pam Grier as a grieving mother is a far departure from the roles she became famous for during the early '70s, but she does bring more than a one-dimensional approach to her character, and does seem the most believable of them all as a member of a community that is surrounded by youths who "just don't care."

What comes around seems to go around in *Original Gangstas*. The initial gang that Bookman and crew created has mutated into a violent enclave that has taken over this small Gary, Indiana community. The film's most important message is not about inner city violence, but how the past is connected to the present and future. Without the blaxploitation films of the '70s, there probably would not have been a "New Black Cinema" in the early '90s. The success of the blaxploitation films rested not on their cinematic genius, but on their comic book, hyper reality that gave its audiences a perverse pleasure. The old school also reveled in violence. *Original Gangstas* is not a good film and is cheaply made, but it's the nostalgia that holds any interest. But if Williamson and crew want to beat the message out of films with gunplay, then maybe the old school methods should remain in our memories and not on the big screen.

—Michelle Banks

REVIEWS

Boxoffice Magazine Online. May 14, 1996.
Los Angeles Times. May 11, 1996. Section F, p. 8.
The New York Times. May 11, 1996. p. 14.
Sight and Sound. October, 1996. pp. 49-50.
USA Today. May 9, 1996. Section D, p. 4.
Variety Online. May 10, 1996.

The Pallbearer

A comedy about lifelong crushes, mistaken identity, and one really bad eulogy.—Movie tagline

"A relentlessly funny movie!"—Anne Marie O'Connor, *Mademoiselle*

"It's drop dead hilarious!"—Sara Edwards, *NBC-TV*

"One of the best films of the year! Wildly entertaining! David Schwimmer is a brilliant new movie star!"—James Grant, *Scene Magazine*

Box Office: $5,500,000

David Schwimmer, one of those geeky, twenty-something "Friends," the NBC hit television show, makes his feature film debut in *The Pallbearer,* co-written and directed by first timer, Matt Reeves, borrows heavily from the 1967 Mike Nichols film, *The Graduate,* which helped make Dustin Hoffman a star. Schwimmer seems unable to shed his persona of Ross, the self-deprecating paleontologist on the situation comedy, playing the lead character as a depressed, spineless slacker unable to make the transition to adulthood.

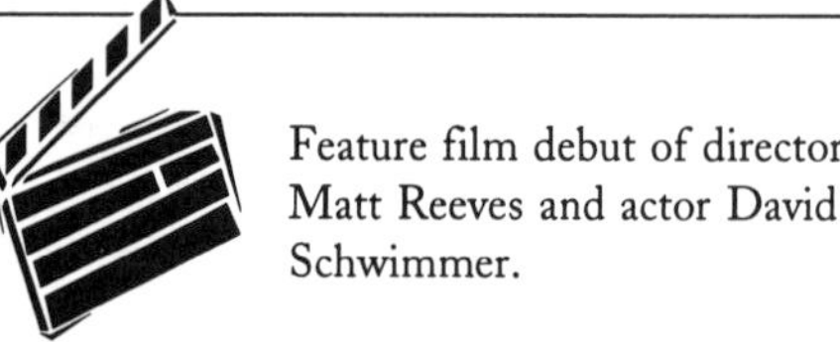

Feature film debut of director Matt Reeves and actor David Schwimmer.

Tom Thompson (David Schwimmer) is stuck in limbo. He graduated college a year ago, but seems unsure of how exactly to overcome those post-adolescent blues. Jobless and still living at home in Brooklyn, Tom sleeps in his childhood bunkbeds and locks his door to keep out his eccentric mother (Carol Kane). His best friends are the same ones he went to high school with, Brad (Michael Rapaport) and Scott (Michael Vartan) and their respective girlfriends (the incessantly shrill Bitty Schram and Toni Collette). Tom even longs for the same girl he used to share a music stand with in band, Julie DeMarco (the fetching Gwyneth Paltrow), when she makes a sudden reappearance back in town.

Tom's aimlessness is interrupted when he receives a phone call from the comely widow Ruth Abernathy (Barbara Hershey with platinum blonde hair) requesting that he be a pallbearer at the funeral of her son who just committed suicide. Tom is deeply moved by her grief—but the problem is he has nary a clue who Bill Abernathy is. The man's death triggers feelings of morality for Tom and for whatever reason, he agrees. Things get out of hand, however, when Mrs. Abernathy asks Tom to give the eulogy. Rather than admit the truth, Tom obliges her and the results are more than a bit embarrassing. Before long, Tom finds himself sexually involved with Ruth, while pining away for Julie, who refuses to allow herself to become involved with Tom because she intends to move away again. When Mrs. Abernathy finds out about Tom's feelings for Julie, she acts in true scorned fashion and Tom must finally grapple with the issue of his own integrity.

Viewers under the age of thirty are unlikely to be hampered by *The Pallbearer*'s obvious comparisons to *The Graduate.* Apart from the blatant similarities in the two scripts, director Matt Reeves goes as far as to stage several shots that seem direct recreations from the earlier film. While no film is sacred and certainly this is not the first time that writers have tried to mine the creative fields of successful projects that have gone before, the makers of *The Pallbearer* deserve some amount of reprimand for not trying to transcend its predecessor. As seems indicative of most of the films about the Generation X, the angst that comes out of *The Pallbearer* is more like a generalized ennui rather than any kind of heightened anxiety. The humor is not scathing and the filmmakers fail to follow through on the darkness of the premise. Rather than crafting a piece of social commentary, Reeves and co-writer Ja-

CREDITS

Tom Thompson: David Schwimmer
Julie DeMarco: Gwyneth Paltrow
Ruth Abernathy : Barbara Hershey
Brad Schorr: Michael Rapaport
Cynthia Edelman: Toni Collette
Scott Edelman: Michael Vartan
Tom's Mother: Carol Kane

Origin: USA
Released: 1996
Production: Jeffrey Abrams, Paul Wester; released by Miramax Films
Direction: Matt Reeves
Screenplay: Jason Katims, Matt Reeves
Cinematography: Robert Elswit
Editing: Stan Salfas
Production design: Robin Standefer
Art direction: Stephen Alesch
Costume design: Donna Zakowska
Music: Stewart Copeland
MPAA rating: PG-13
Running Time: 94 minutes

son Katims (television's "My So-Called Life") succeed more on the level of a lightweight romantic comedy.

David Schwimmer fails to ignite the big screen, although he is not particularly offensive, either. He merely stays within the confines of the character that he has constructed on television and seems reluctant to explore new territory, to take chances in his acting. His pleading puppy dog eyes reveal his obvious desire to be liked and Schwimmer, who often seems to be doing a Dustin Hoffman impersonation with his line readings, falls into an annoying whine that adds to his character's pathetic neediness and inertia. Gwyneth Paltrow is warm and conveys a great deal of conflicted longing, but her character is sadly underwritten. Julie is someone we would like to know more about and her indecision is far less frustrating than Tom's because she is willing to take chances, even if it means being hurt in the process. Ms. Paltrow has a charismatic and unpretentious film presence, an openness and emotional depth that has yet to be fully exploited in her screen appearances to date.

Critics were divided in their reviews of *The Pallbearer,* although most conceded that the film failed to pursue the black comedy that is suggested by the funeral set-up. The filmmakers have borrowed far too liberally from *The Graduate* without placing their story within any socio-cultural framework and the film is never able to transcend its small-screen look and feel. As a result, the story plays far too simplistically, a trivial attempt to find some interest in an otherwise uninteresting man. As an aside, several critics made mention of David Lipsky's novelization of *The Pallbearer* as having more depth, dark humor and lyricism than the film itself.

—*Patricia Kowal*

REVIEWS

Chicago Tribune. May 3, 1996, p. 5.
Detroit News. May 3, 1996, p. 4D.
Entertainment Weekly. May 17, 1996, p. 40.
Los Angeles Times. May 3, 1996, p. F8.
New York Times. May 3, 1996, p. C18.
Rolling Stone. May 2, 1996, p. 62.
Variety. April 29, 1996.

Palookaville

One foot in the door. The other one in the gutter.—Movie tagline

"A witty portrait of affable losers."—Bruce Williamson, *Playboy*

Box Office: $331,180

A wry, pungent look at working-class America, *Palookaville* neither denigrates nor romanticizes its three bumbling protagonists. Like millions of unsuccessful, left-behind Americans—a group rarely the subject of cultural attention—the three are young men on the cusp of desperation, unable to gain entrance to the middle class. *Palookaville,* which is wonderfully free from moralizing, doesn't attempt to blame society or the men for their plight. It merely observes their ineptitude and their attempts to rise out of their muddle with a bemused yet sympathetic detachment.

> "Boys don't always grow up. They age, they put on weight, they lose hair, they grow lumps and warts, they have regrets, lose their tempers and they blame women, but they do not automatically grow up and become men."—June

Written by David Epstein and directed by Alan Taylor, *Palookaville* takes its title from a term Marlon Brando uses in *On the Waterfront* (1954) to refer to a kind of working man's wasteland. The title is the closest the film comes to degrading its characters; its connotations are inapt. "Palookaville" is a Jersey City which looks more like a small town in the 1950s, the kind of place where a young woman working alone in a second-hand clothing store hands a cup of tea to a stranger waiting in the rain.

The hard edge of life on the fringe of 1990s America has been softened enough to give the film a universal, timeless feel without sacrificing too much authenticity. *Palookaville* has European inspirations. It was producer Uberto Pasolini's idea to transpose three Italo Calvino stories of postwar life in Italy to an American setting. The film also genuflects to Mario Monicelli's 1958 film *Big Deal On Madonna Street,* another movie about a gang of incompetent thieves.

Yet *Palookaville* has thoroughly American sensibilities. It never succumbs to the smaltzy romanticism that plagues some of its European cousins that explore the Everyman genre. Its tone is well illustrated by a scene in which the gang's nervous, motormouth leader Russ (Vincent Gallo) quiets the moral objections of Jerry (Adam Trese) by calling their robbery plots "a momentary shift in lifestyle." Russ compares it to driving the prevailing speed on a highway where everyone's cruising at 80 miles an hour. This is America, Russ and the gang's third member, Sid (William Forsythe) believe, and we're supposed to be on the road to success by whatever means necessary.

Dedicated to Italo Calvino and based on three of his short stories.

The problem, as Jerry keeps reminding the others, is that these three guys were not cut out to be crooks. They not only lack the necessary nerve and brains, they have trouble staying focused. In a hilarious hold-up scene, after their carefully laid plan goes awry and they bump their car into the back of an armored truck, the three get out of the car, momentarily forget they are wearing ski masks and brandishing fake guns, and argue about damage to the car's grille. The armored-car driver has to ask them what they're up to before they snap back to attention and Russ yells: "We're going to rob you, asshole!"

The film's deft opening scene is taken wholesale from *Madonna Street.* The three use sledgehammers to break through a brick wall behind a jewelry store, but they end up in the bakery next door. While Russ lifts chump change from the cash register, Jerry dreamily downs and pockets pastries. When the cops arrive, he's still munching and grabbing, and the cops prove just as dazed as Jerry at the paradise of free donuts. All the men, as one character reminds us in an unusually blunt mid-film speech, are nothing but overgrown boys. The clever capper to the scene has a cop praising a brownie and reaching for another as he leaves; Jerry, who's crouching behind a cart, grabs one from the back of the tray at the same time.

There's not much plot from there to the armored-car holdup, but that's hardly necessary. *Palookaville* is loaded with wonderful little scenes and splendidly on-target characters. After their doughy heist, Sid, a nerdish type who keeps pictures of his wife at his bedside ten years after she left him, snuggles up with his two pet dogs, who dominate his life. Russ, who's as cheesy a ladies' man as he is a criminal mastermind, stops at the house of June (Frances McDormand), a neighborhood whore who dispenses more comfort and wisdom than sex. Another client shows up: one of the cops the gang eluded at the bakery! When Russ asks the cop to give him a ride home, there's a delightful frisson of confusion that's cleared up with the revelation that the cop, Ed (Garth Williams), is Russ's brother-in-law.

Jerry stumbles home, jelly-mouthed and covered with powdered sugar, to his sleeping wife Betty (Lisa Gay Hamilton). He insists she open his shirt and see his pastry collection, which gets her laughing. They initiate lovemaking, interrupted by the coughing of their sick infant son—a remarkably anti-Hollywood moment that will ring true with many parents.

Epstein has created a recognizable world of real people, and Taylor deftly serves as a tour guide, never insulting his characters no matter how ridiculously they act. The three guys aren't the world's brainiest or most likeable bunch, but they aren't evil. They don't do drugs, other than the legal kind; they're constantly dragging on cigarettes during their criminal plotting sessions, the more to look like crooks. And they don't degrade women. In fact, the women in the film are much smarter, more ambitious and more interesting than the guys, and the men are in thrall to them despite their pathetic efforts to be hardened crooks.

Their world and their puny attempts to better their situation in it are portrayed with bemused, slightly affectionate indifference. The film's tone is perfect. The fact that Jerry and Betty have an interracial marriage (she's black) passes without notice, a delightful example of the way the film downplays everything.

Betty's got the only job in their circle, its income providing the trio's only car. She's fired after Jerry finds her boss pawing at her and slugs him. Jerry's reluctance to be a crook is overcome by desperation. Russ's motivation for crime is an intense desire to escape from his intolerable home life, where he's an overgrown adolescent under the thumb of his mother, his sister and Ed, a swaggering dolt who wears his

CREDITS

Sid: William Forsythe
Russ: Vincent Gallo
Jerry: Adam Trese
Betty: Linda Gay Hamilton
June: Frances McDormand
Enid: Bridget Ryan

Origin: USA
Released: 1996
Production: Uberto Pasolini for a Playhouse International Pictures and Redwave Films production; released by Samuel Goldwyn Co.
Direction: Alan Taylor
Screenplay: David Epstein; based on the short stories of Italo Calvino
Cinematography: John Thomas
Editing: David Leonard
Music: Rachel Portman
Production design: Anne Stuhler
Costumes: Katherine Jane Bryant
MPAA rating: R
Running Time: 92 minutes

T-shirt and gun holsters around the house. Russ's only relief is a back-alley romance with a teenage neighbor, Laurie (Kim Dickens, who lights up the screen in a small role). She signals by flickering her room lights when she's about to do a schoolgirl striptease for him. They execute their trysts by climbing in and out bedroom windows.

Sid, who's about to be evicted from his apartment, mooches off his pals, often showing up for dinner at Russ's house. There, he chows down spaghetti as family members erupt in mutual insults and skulk off to watch separate TV shows in separate rooms—a particularly compelling slice of Americana. The purported brains of the bunch, Sid thinks up a legal moneymaking scheme, a ride service for senior citizens. But the paltry plan is foiled by the riders' distaste for Sid's smelly dogs and the local taxi drivers' wrath.

Stranded in the rain a long way from home, Sid pretends to be blind in order to board a bus with his dogs, but the driver sees through his act and orders him off. That's when Enid (Bridgit Ryan), who works at a resale clothing store, invites him in for tea and genteelly puts the make on him. She's the film's only slightly unbelievable character, but a spark of mischief in Ryan's eye salvages the part, explaining Enid as a curious adventurer. The best little moment in a film full of great little moments is when Enid finds Sid asleep under a fur in a back room; Taylor follows with a shot of the storefront as the lights are turned off. It's sweet and telling and illustrates Taylor's marvelous economy of style.

Palookaville is quietly, disarmingly brilliant. Most compelling is a kitchen fight between Betty and Jerry which ends with her ordering him to go back to the store, apologize to the boss that harassed her, and beg for her job back. It's the sharpest depiction of economic desperation in the film. The rest of the time, Taylor paints a picture of everyday life on the brink of poverty with subtle, pinpoint detail, such as Russ's tirade when Sid tries to escape a diner without paying his share of the bill.

The three guys who botch things in *Palookaville* are people disturbingly like the rest of us—not clowns, but people whose plans always go awry. They have a screw or two loose, but not all their screws, and they have a familiarity which keeps *Palookaville* funny, sharp and forgiving. The film's performances are as deft as its directing, especially Gallo as the braggart whose tough-guy facade keeps slipping; Forsythe as a horn-rimmed, lost little puppy who looks like he escaped from a '50s TV show; Hamilton as a no-nonsense breadwinner with a sense of priorities, and Dickens as an awakening woman with a thwarted yen for adventure.

—Michael Betzold

REVIEWS

Boxoffice. April, 1996, p. 112.
Film Threat. January, 1997, p. 55.
Los Angeles Times. November 1, 1996, p. F12.
New York Times. October 25, 1996, p. C14.
Variety. September 18, 1995, p. 100.
Village Voice. October 29, 1996, p. 45.

Paradise Lost–The Child Murders at Robin Hood Hills

Witchcraft or witch hunt? In some places, dressing in black can get you arrested.—Movie tagline

"Stunning . . . a twisting, serpentine tale of intriguing ambiguity and paradoxes."—*Los Angeles Times*

"Mesmerizing . . . the fascination of detective fiction . . . true crime reporting at its most bitterly revealing."—*The New York Times*

"Daring . . . provocative . . . a real life *River's Edge*."—*San Francisco Chronicle*

Box Office: $272,750

Joe Berlinger and Bruce Sinofsky's *Paradise Lost—The Child Murders at Robin Hood Hills* takes a long, stinging look at the American criminal justice system at its worst. On May 5, 1993, three 8-year-old boys were found murdered in a watery creek bed alongside Interstate 40 in West Memphis, Arkansas. Two of the boys, Steven Branch and Michael Moore, were bludgeoned and drowned; a third, Christopher Byers, was bound and sexually mutilated.

The case creates an enormous uproar in the deeply conservative, Bible Belt community of West Memphis. Enraged citizens demand a scapegoat, and state prosecutors are eager to comply. Feeling enormous pressure to produce a suspect, local authorities zero in on Jessie Misskelley, Jr., Damien Echols and Jason Baldwin—three renowned misfits with records for minor juvenile offenses and a reputation for offbeat behavior. The teenagers are quickly rounded up and charged with murdering the children as part of a grotesque "Satanic" ritual.

The arrests are motivated by the supposed "confession" of Jessie Misskelley, Jr., 17, a developmentally-challenged runt of a boy with an I.Q. of 72. This confession is the result of an extremely prolonged police interrogation which takes place without the presence of Misskelley's lawyer. Confused by an endless barrage of highly manipulative questions, Misskelley implicates Echols and Baldwin. From the outset, local authorities strive to create the impression that the accused killers have formed an unholy alliance in order to commit a bloodthirsty murder, but in reality, the three teenagers barely know one another: They are little more than schoolyard acquaintances.

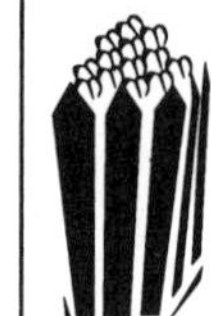

"Johnny Cash wears black, doesn't he?"—Damien's father defending his son's clothing choices

The defendants are at a loss from the very beginning. Despite many inconsistencies in his statements to the police and numerous procedural errors on the part of the prosecution, Misskelley is brought to trial and convicted. He receives a "reduced" sentence of forty years in prison in return for implicating Echols and Baldwin, who are tried in a second, separate proceeding.

The prosecution proceeds unimpeded despite a startling lack of physical evidence: No murder weapon is ever found, and the crime scene is remarkably "clean"—that is, free of spilled blood—suggesting that the murders may have been committed elsewhere and the bodies dumped in the ravine at Robin Hood Hills. Local police and prosecutors point to the defendants' shared interest in black clothes and heavy metal music and their (very minimal) knowledge of Satanism as evidence of their guilt. Despite what is said about them, it is hard to picture Misskelley, Echols and Baldwin as hardened social deviants with a shared thirst for murder and mayhem. The three teenagers are at first bewildered and then oddly amused by all the attention that is suddenly thrust upon them. They do not seem to be aware that they are facing charges which could wreck their lives.

Outrageously simple-minded symbolic meaning is attached to the murders themselves as well as every detail of the defendants' daily lives. Rumors abound concerning Satanic ceremonies, blood sacrifices and homosexual orgies which are believed to have taken place at the murder scene. Reporters seize upon the victims' families, eager to pose questions which are as heartless as they are inane. (One such reporter insists upon asking Pam Hobbs, the mother of Steven Branch, "what it's like to be alone on Mother's Day.")

The nail that sticks out gets hammered down. Echols is the eldest and most outrageously flamboyant of the three defendants, and is therefore singled out as the ring-leader and alleged mastermind of the Satanic "plot" to murder the young boys. (It doesn't help that he bears the same name as the villainous child lead in *The Omen* [1976].) He becomes a prime suspect by virtue of his punkish look and weirdly affected manners, which are already the stuff of legend in West Memphis. His outlandish clothes, his tastes in music and his pseudo-intellectual airs—he reads books by Stephen King and Anton LaVey—are enough to ensure his conviction. To his own detriment, Echols also displays a rudimentary understanding of the difference between "Satanism" and white witchcraft, or Wicca. This distinction, which counts for very much in the eyes of Echols and his immediate family —"Even Johnny Cash wears black," says his bewildered father—is lost on the local citizenry, most of whom are grossly uneducated and permanently quagmired in Old Testament religious values.

The atmosphere surrounding both trials becomes so bizarre and sensationalistic that the attorneys for Echols and Baldwin are compelled to secure a change of venue for their clients. This tactic makes no difference: Echols and Baldwin are quickly convicted and sentenced to death by lethal injection and life imprisonment, respectively, for their role in the "Satanic" ritual murder.

By the film's end, two lurid and lengthy trials have transpired, and dozens of lives have been ruined. The outcome satisfies no one (except perhaps the ambitious prosecutors), and the sentences of Misskelley, Echols and Baldwin are immediately placed under appeal. The community contents itself with the belief that the real killers have been found. But an air of skepticism remains, and the viewer is left with the distinct impression that justice has been badly served. The filmmakers' main objective is to draw attention to this element of doubt.

Paradise Lost benefits from Berlinger and Sinofsky's extraordinary ability to establish conversational intimacy with key figures on both sides of the case. In the course of an arduous, nine-month shoot, their camera travels everywhere—

CREDITS

Origin: USA
Released: 1996
Production: Joe Berlinger and Bruce Sinofsky for a Hand-To-Mouth Productions; released by Home Box Office
Direction: Joe Berlinger and Bruce Sinofsky
Cinematography: Robert Richman
Editing: Joe Berlinger and Bruce Sinofsky
Music: Metallica
Sound: Michael Karas
MPAA rating: Unrated
Running Time: 150 minutes

in and out of the courtroom, through sensitive strategy sessions involving the prosecution as well as the defense, and perhaps most importantly, into the beleaguered daily lives of the families involved. This makes the film extremely compelling. It is less an investigation of a grisly murder than a portrait of a tragically backward community awash in ignorance and superstition.

West Memphis itself is already in deep trouble by the time the murders take place. As captured by the filmmakers, it is little more than a benighted cultural backwater on the shores of the Mississippi. Although it is geographically close to Memphis, the legendary home of Elvis and the birthplace of bluegrass music, the big city is a world away: Memphis might as well be on the dark side of the moon.

Berlinger and Sinofsky said the idea for the film came from a *New York Times* story on the murders.

Berlinger and Sinofsky do an expert job of communicating the degraded position of this small but typical Bible Belt town. They do this by simply observing the small details of local life—the stubbornly omnipresent Confederate flags, the dilapidated trailer parks, and the startling proliferation of Southern Baptist churches—without putting too much of a spin on the material. In the face of such conditions, it is easy to understand how the citizens of West Memphis could be whipped into a state of hysteria.

It is hard to feel entirely sympathetic toward members of the victims' families, some of whom display malignant, anti-social attitudes of their own. This is especially true of John Mark Byers, the stepfather of one of the victims. Byers makes repeated visits to the murder scene, where he assuages his grief by delivering drunken, idiotic religious homilies for the benefit of the filmmakers and anyone else who will listen. He is then shown leading his church congregation in a round of song, and taking Polaroid snapshots of his son's grave site. In one very disturbing scene, Byers and Todd Moore, the father of another victim, vent their anger by blasting pumpkins with a .38-caliber service revolver: The pumpkins are assigned the defendants' names.

The crazed, witch-hunt atmosphere surrounding both trials makes it practically impossible for the defense to question the methods, motives and thought processes of the prosecution. The attorneys for Echols and Baldwin are confronted by a community which is already hostile toward "outsiders" and outmaneuvered by prosecutors who play to the prejudices of the local citizenry. It is impossible to present an argument in the defendants' favor without being tarred as a devil worshipper or potential child molester, or both.

Events in the second trial take a turn toward the surreal when John Mark Byers presents the filmmakers with a serrated hunting knife which, forensic evidence suggests, may have served as the murder weapon. Berlinger and Sinofsky are suddenly faced with the peculiar dilemma of holding evidence which may influence the outcome of the trial. They respond by turning this potentially crucial item over to the state.

For a brief time, suspicion is leveled at Byers, who is now known to have possessed a possible murder weapon as well as an unusual degree of familiarity with the murder scene. He seems to be a plausible suspect, but this development occurs too late to make any difference: The prosecutors and most of the citizens of West Memphis are already satisfied that they have found the perpetrators of the crime. The fact that the prosecution scores a resounding victory despite such a incredible paucity of physical evidence underscores the filmmakers' deeper objective, which is to illuminate the many ways in which the "trial" is little more than a witch-hunt in the first place.

Berlinger and Sinofsky have previously demonstrated a remarkable flair for capturing the oddities of life in small-town America as well as the stunning depravity of the American criminal justice system. They are well-known in independent filmmaking circles for producing and distributing the highly successful documentary *Brother's Keeper* (1992). That film centers upon the lives of Delbert Ward and his three very eccentric brothers, who live together on a decrepit farm in upstate New York. (The brothers share everything, including a bed.) Enormous havoc ensues in the small town of Munnsville when Delbert Ward is implicated in the mysterious "death by asphyxiation" of one of his ailing siblings.

Local police and prosecutors quickly set their sights on Delbert, who is generally too befuddled to understand their accusations. The attempt to cast blame is punctuated by shocking tales of the brothers' supposedly incestuous homosexual escapades, but this line of attack backfires completely. The local townspeople, who are not nearly as impressionable as the prosecutors wish to believe, rally to Delbert's defense, and the case against him falls to pieces.

Paradise Lost concerns a much more ambiguous situation, unfolding in a considerably more troubling social atmosphere. The film is reminiscent of other recent documentaries which pertain to gross miscarriages of justice. The most notable of these is Errol Morris's *The Thin Blue Line* (1988), which dealt with the subject of police corruption in Texas and the unjust imprisonment of a black defendant. *Paradise Lost* differs from Morris's film in that Berlinger and Sinofsky examine the details of a crime without attempting to advance an opinion concerning the defendants' actual guilt or innocence. This approach is wise, as the evidence presented in the West Memphis case is either too sparse or too ambiguous to be truly conclusive. It is never entirely certain whether the defendants are guilty as charged, but it is undeniably clear that an unfair trial has occurred.

Something is deeply wrong in the city of West Memphis, something which has nothing to do with satanic worship, rock 'n' roll music or local teenagers' taste in clothes. *Paradise Lost—The Child Murders at Robin Hood Hills* is unsettling because it presents a real-life community, one in which Satan and his minions play a central role in everyone's imagination. It is hard to conceive how such a place could be described as a paradise, except by those who wish to believe that ignorance is bliss.

—*Karl Michalak*

REVIEWS

The Boston Globe. September 10, 1996.
The Boston Globe. September 22, 1996.
The Boston Phoenix. September 6, 1996.
Details. October, 1996.
Filmmaker. Fall, 1996.
The Hollywood Reporter. January 24, 1996.
The Hollywood Reporter. January 25, 1996.
The Los Angeles Times. June 10, 1996.
The New Jersey Star-Ledger. December 29, 1995.
The New Jersey Star-Ledger. September 20, 1996.
The New York Daily News. September 20, 1996.
New York Newsday. January 31, 1996.
New York Newsday. September 20, 1996.
The New York Post. September 20, 1996.
The New York Press. September 25, 1996.
The New York Times. March 26, 1996.
Spin. November, 1996.
Variety (Daily). August 5, 1996.
Variety (Weekly). February 12-18, 1996.

The People vs. Larry Flynt

You may not like what he does, but are you prepared to give up his right to do it?—Movie tagline

"A great, liberating movie! An exultant comedy of American repression and revolt."—*Entertainment Weekly*

"A blazing triumph! Smart, funny and shamelessly entertaining!"—*New York Times*

"A stunning achievement! Brave and unexpectedly stirring."—*Newsweek*

"The best movie of the year!"—*Rolling Stone*

"Enormously entertaining and surprisingly touching."—*Washington Post*

Box Office: $13,017,419

In the early 1970s, the sexual revolution that had begun in the mid '60s was approaching its zenith. Larry Flynt, a grade-school dropout from the backwoods of Kentucky, sensing the sexual repression in the quiet suburbs in his neighboring state of Ohio, was operating a modest chain of strip joints all called "The Hustler Club." After receiving positive feedback with his complimentary risque newsletter, Flynt took a major financial gamble by putting his nightclubs up for collateral and sinking it all into a new men's magazine titled simply *Hustler.*

Publisher Hugh Hefner had thrown the country into culture shock some 25 years earlier by publishing *Playboy.* Hefner tempered the resistance to *Playboy* by including fresh-faced, girl-next-door types, posing scantily clad in the most tasteful way he knew how while still allowing the sensational, forbidden nature of erotic photography to bleed through. In addition, he commissioned world renowned writers in an effort to deliver the magazine some "redeeming social value" and literary cachet that would bestow an air of "respectability," thus making it safe for mass consumption. Larry Flynt had no intention whatsoever of ever making *Hustler* respectable.

While Hefner featured essays by the likes of John Updike and Norman Mailer, coupled with the artwork of LeRoy Neiman and Antonio Vargas, Flynt matched the frank, often crude, almost clinical nature of *Hustler*'s photos with equally disturbing sexually-drenched articles and "comical" drawings of pedophiles.

In *The People vs. Larry Flynt,* Alan Isaacman (played by Edward Norton), Flynt's longtime attorney states emphatically, "I don't like what Larry Flynt does, but I like living in a country that allows him the right to do it." This one line captures the essence of Milos Forman's brash, bold, thoroughly engaging film chronicling Flynt's life.

The feigned, indifferent reaction to the first edition of *Hustler* practically bankrupt Flynt. His financial salvation soon arrived in the form of an anonymous phone caller, looking to sell pictures of Jacqueline Kennedy Onassis in the buff. The legendary "Jackie O" issue was released and cata-

Hustler magazine creator Larry Flynt (Woody Harrelson) has his court battles chronicled in Milos Forman's acclaimed, *The People vs. Larry Flynt.*

pulted Flynt into fiscal solvency. It also ushered in the first of his many legal altercations that, besides costing him millions of dollars, exacted a heavy personal and spiritual toll.

Cincinnati civic leader Charles Keating was the first of Flynt's many moral adversaries when he brought Flynt up on obscenity charges. During the trial, Flynt displayed a flippant disregard for Keating (James Cromwell) and the justice system in general (Forman adds a brilliant ironic twist by casting the real-life Larry Flynt as the unflappable, unwavering judge in the case). Despite his utter contempt for authority figures, Flynt was, above all, a very honest, forthcoming man. He made no pretense about who he was or what his publication stood for. He referred to himself as "The Pervert" and declared that "all I'm guilty of is bad taste." He advises prosecuting attorney Simon Leis (given expert treatment by political strategist-turned-actor James Carville) that if he doesn't like *Hustler,* he shouldn't buy it. That's a choice given to all Americans by the constitution. Judging what is or is not offensive is completely subjective and everyone should make that decision for themselves. Flynt's arguments fell on deaf ears and he was convicted of distributing pornography and sentenced to 25 years.

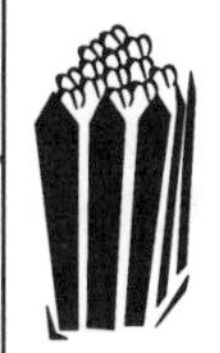

"I'm your dream client! I'm the most fun, I'm rich and I'm always in trouble."—Flynt to his lawyer

After posting a rather hefty bail while awaiting his appeal, Flynt organized a rally in Cincinnati ballyhooing his free-speech issue before a friendly, handpicked crowd of supporters. In one of the films' many (often disturbing) high points, Flynt faces the crowd, standing before a silver screen that practically dwarfs him. This visual recalls the opening scene in *Patton* (1970), where George C. Scott stands on a stage in front of an American flag, providing tough-love inspiration to his troops. Flynt begins speaking to the crowd while slides appear on the screen. Flynt questions society's perception of sexuality and violence. Why is he being persecuted for showing off God's own beautifully designed human body while others receive medals and public adulation for traipsing off to war? Provocative photographs are punishable while pictures of terrified, napalm-burned, naked children running through the streets of Vietnam win the Pulitzer prize. Making love is bad. Making war is good. This particular passage of the movie carries the indelible fingerprints of two time Oscar-winning director Oliver Stone (*Platoon* [1986] and *Born On the Fourth of July* [1989]), one of the films' three producers. Stone's complete lack of fear or self doubt, when it comes to being a controversial figure, seems to mirror that of Flynt.

Flynt's next legal altercation took place at the Gwinnett County Courthouse in Lawrenceville, Georgia. While leaving the courthouse during yet another obscenity trial, both Flynt and Isaacson are shot by an assassin. While Isaacson recovered fully from his wounds, Flynt lost the use of both legs and to this day, remains in a wheelchair (Flynt's solid gold wheelchair was loaned to the picture during filming). During the credits at the end of the movie, a caveat states that Flynt's assailant has "never been brought to justice." While this is technically true, Flynt's shooter has been in jail for the last ten years (on another charge) and has admitted to committing the crime. For one reason or another, he has not been formally charged in the shooting. While recovering from his injuries Flynt was prescribed heavy medication to make his convalescence easier, eventually overcoming his need for the painkillers through surgery. The same cannot be said for his wife Althea. In what could have been a symbolic gesture on Althea's part, she begins using Larry's drugs and becomes a junkie. She never shook her addiction and eventually died in 1985 of AIDS.

The trial that really put Flynt on the legal map involved part-time political activist and full-time preacher Jerry Fal-

AWARDS AND NOMINATIONS

Academy Award 1996 Nominations: Best Actor (Harrelson), Best Director (Forman)
Golden Globe Awards 1997: Best Director (Forman), Best Screenplay (Alexander, Karaszewski)
Nominations: Best Film-Drama, Best Actress-Drama (Love), Best Actor-Drama (Harrelson)
Los Angeles Film Critics Association 1996: Supporting Actor (Norton)
National Board of Review 1996: Best Supporting Actor (Norton)
New York Film Critics Circle 1996: Best Supporting Actress (Love)
Screen Actors Guild 1996: Actor (Harrelson)

well. After *Hustler* published a mock ad that lampooned his sexual initiation, Falwell sued Flynt for liable and emotional distress. Falwell sought close to $40 million in punitive damages. Isaacson brilliantly deflected the charges by likening the ad to political cartoons. It was Isaacson's contention that, because he was a public figure, Falwell was fair game and is just as subject to satire as any other public figure. The decision handed down by the jury turned out to be a minuscule victory for Falwell and a huge one for Flynt. While it was determined that Falwell suffered emotional distress and was awarded a token cash settlement, Flynt was cleared of libel charges. The entire affair would have been put to rest had it not been for a televised broadcast Falwell later made, which Flynt saw, where the clergyman lambasted and vilified AIDS victims. Because of the recent loss of his wife to the disease, an incensed Flynt ordered Isaacson to appeal the Falwell case, which led to the unanimous Supreme Court decision in Flynt's favor. (It has been reported that Norton's dialogue in this scene was taken directly from Court transcripts.) Jerry Falwell received nothing and Flynt's place in jurisprudence history was secured.

> Controversial film drew strong reaction, including Gloria Steinem's castigating op-ed piece in the January 7, 1997 edition of *The New York Times.*

While Oliver Stone obviously saw something of a kindred spirit in Flynt, director Forman certainly did not. Initially at least. Forman has also won two Academy Awards for Best Director (*One Flew Over the Cuckoo's Nest* [1975] and *Amadeus* [1984]). In an interview prior to the film's release, Forman was quoted as saying that he "associated Flynt with pornography, sleaze and exploitation" and had to pass on the project. Only after reading the completed script did Foreman recognize, not only the obvious cinematic appeal such a richly textured character could provide, but the stunning personal and professional parallels Flynt's story presented. In addition to the two previously mentioned films, other Forman projects (including *Ragtime* [1981] and *Valmont* [1989]) focused on one central character who found resistance, resentment and recrimination in all that surrounded them. Forman's native Czech homeland, where first the Nazis, then the Communists became the country's self-appointed thought police, suffered and struggled for artistic expression.

The casting in a project of this magnitude is pivotal to the films' success and believability. Forman has turned unknowns into stars before and it seems as though that trend will continue. In addition to the aforementioned Carville, Forman struck gold by including actor Richard Paul to play the part of Falwell. Paul's doughboy likeness to the preacher is uncanny and is actually the second time he has played Falwell in a film (the first being a made-for-television movie, "Fall From Grace"). As Keating, James Cromwell too, possesses a striking resemblance to the man who not only chased Flynt, but went after Hugh Hefner some 20 years earlier on a similar witch-hunt. Keating himself felt the wrath of the American judicial system in the late '80s when he was convicted of playing a major role in the country's huge scandal involving a number of Savings & Loan institutions that went belly-up, subsequently costing the taxpayers over $2 billion.

While Flynt clearly had found enemies in Falwell and Keating, he discovered an unlikely ally in the person of Ruth Carter Stapleton (played by New York television reporter Donna Hanover, who also happens to be the wife of current Mayor Rudolph Giuliani). Stapleton, sister of then president Jimmy Carter, succeeded in convincing Flynt to (very temporarily) embrace religion and was even responsible for his old-time, country-style baptism.

In the role of Alan Isaacman, Edward Norton turns in what many pundits believe to be his second Oscar caliber performance of the year. His portrayal of an accused, psychopathic killer in *Primal Fear* (reviewed in this issue), was one of that film's few highlights. With the outstanding rendering of Flynt's stalwart attorney, Norton's future in the film industry appears secure. Long before the film even

CREDITS

Larry Flynt: Woody Harrelson
Althea Leasure: Courtney Love
Alan Isaacman: Edward Norton
Charles Keating: James Cromwell
Jimmy Flynt: Brett Harrelson
Simon Leis: James Carville
Ruth Carter Stapleton: Donna Hanover
Jerry Falwell: Richard Paul
Arlo: Crispin Glover

Origin: USA
Released: 1996
Production: Oliver Stone, Janet Yang, and Michael Hausman for a Phoenix Pictures and Ixtlan production; released by Columbia Pictures
Direction: Milos Forman
Screenplay: Scott Alexander and Larry Karaszewski
Cinematography: Philippe Rousselot
Editing: Christopher Tellefsen
Music: Thomas Newman
Production design: Patrizia von Brandenstein
Art direction: James Nezda, Shawn Hausman
Costume design: Theodor Pistek, Arianne Phillips
Sound: Chris Newman
Casting: Francine Maisler
MPAA rating: R
Running Time: 127 minutes

opened, critics were hailing the performance of rock singer Courtney Love in the role of Flynt's tragic wife Althea. Love has been given a handful of generic supporting roles recently but this is her first venture as a leading lady. Her performance, as good as it is—and it is superb—doesn't seem to be much of a stretch from her real-life persona. A long history of drug abuse, unusually erratic behavior and the fallout that resulted from the high profile suicide of her musician husband, Kurt Cobain, made her a natural for this role. However, playing one's self in a film, while being believable, doesn't necessarily equate to great acting.

The film's most important role, that of Flynt himself, was given to Woody Harrelson. It is the type of character most actors only dream of getting and one he seems to have been born to play. Besides the striking physical similarities he has to the younger Flynt, Harrelson becomes more impressive as the movie progresses. His performance is nothing less than outstanding. Who would have thought that out of all the former cast members from the landmark television show "Cheers," that the man who played cute-but-dim bartender Woody would find the most (some might say the only substantial) success in the movies. Harrelson's rural Texas and Ohio upbringing isn't that far removed from Flynt's and, like Flynt, he's proven that hard work and being in the right place at the right time can snare you that elusive piece of the American dream. This is not the prototypical American success story, but it is a slice of Americana that every citizen of this country should witness.

—*J.M. Clark*

REVIEWS

Boxoffice. February, 1997, p. 60.
Chicago Tribune. December 27, 1996, p. 4.
Entertainment Weekly. January 10, 1997, p. 34.
Entertainment Weekly. January 31, 1997, p. 16.
Los Angeles Times. December 25, 1996, p. F1.
New York Times. October 12, 1996, p. 13.
New Yorker. January 13, 1997, p. 80.
Newsweek. December 23, 1996, p. 62.
People. January 20, 1997, p. 18.
Rolling Stone. December 26, 1996, p. 204.
Sight and Sound. March, 1997, p. 58.
Time Online. January 27, 1997.
Vanity Fair. November, 1996, p. 154.
Variety. October 14, 1996, p. 77.
Village Voice. December 31, 1996, p. 59.

A Perfect Candidate

Oliver North for Senate? You don't know the half of it . . . —Movie tagline

"Revealing. A chilling portrait."—Janet Maslin, *The New York Times*

"Absolutely fascinating."—Gene Siskel, *Siskel & Ebert*

Box Office: $134,485

A seemingly straightforward documentary about the 1994 Virginia U.S. Senate race, *A Perfect Candidate* is an embarrassingly revealing examination of the sideshow that passes for electoral politics in modern America. Avoiding partisan preachiness and editorializing, this shoestring-budget film by R.J. Cutler and David Van Taylor effectively uses offhand comments and offstage moments to illuminate the dark corners of the campaigns of ex-Marine Oliver North and his Democratic opponent, Charles Robb.

"Do you want mumps or the flu?" is how one unusually perceptive undecided voter characterizes the choice Virginia voters face. The unsavory options are North, the ex-convict who deceived Congress about his extra-constitutional gun-running in the Iran-contra affair, and Robb, a clueless dolt who has squandered his once-bright political career by bedding bimbos and attending cocaine parties.

> ". . . the daily sideshow of getting people elected has a lot to do with dividing, which is the opposite of what it takes to govern."—North political strategist Mark Goodin

It would be easy to poke fun at this pair, but the filmmakers do something more effective: They follow around the candidates and their handlers with a camera and microphone. In hilarious scenes, the personality-challenged Robb stalks shoppers down supermarket aisles to spring handshakes on them. At a factory-gate press opportunity, Robb proves incapable of answering a journalist's straightforward question about his stand on striker replacement laws. Playing the martyr-hero, North takes a pulpit to compare his political torture to the sufferings of Jesus Christ, shoots clay pigeons as part of a rural campaign appearance, and blithely lies to student interviewers at a high school.

Cutler and Taylor open the film with clips of North admitting at the Iran-contra hearings that "I misled Congress" while defending his arms-for-hostages swap as "a neat idea." At the high school, seven years later, he baldly contends "I never lied to Congress." His pimply-faced questioner responds: "Thanks for clarifying that." A more cogent depiction of how history can be reinvented could not be imagined.

But *A Perfect Candidate* doesn't settle for simply skewering its ridiculous combatants. North and Robb are revealed as rather unremarkable people rather than larger-than-life villains. Without a trace of grandstanding, but simply by piling up revealing moments, *Candidate* rises above its subject matter and becomes an honest, unbiased look at the sad condition of American politics.

Gradually, two unlikely figures steal the film from the candidates. One is Mark Goodin, North's chief political operative, a beer-guzzling, chain-smoking, cagey and surprisingly sympathetic architect of mudslinging campaign strategy. The other is Washington Post reporter Don Baker, a sly, cynical but unexpectedly good-natured journalist with a Santa-like twinkle in his eye, who serves as the film's window to the world outside.

Surprisingly, Baker overcomes his initial knee-jerk liberal-media antipathy and finds himself impressed by the adulation of North's devotees and by the candidate's folksy, winning style. The real story, he believes, is how North has captured the affection of working-class folks in the heartland. Baker even professes that a victory for North might be good for the nation because America could use a real debate over ideology rather than the two-party system's endless shadow play.

Even more amazingly, the steely-eyed Goodin provides the film's most effective homily on the misplaced priorities of political campaigns. It's all a sideshow, he admits in a moment of candor, a game to feed the media every day so the media doesn't feed on the candidates. The way to get elected is to divide people, he says, but governing requires building consensus. He tells the camera: "We're obsessed with getting people elected. We're obsessed with the show, and so are you, or you wouldn't be here." It's a jarring sequence.

With surprises like this, *A Perfect Candidate* manages to become an indictment not just of the candidates but of a system that has turned politics into entertainment. Yet it is not a heartless polemic; far from it. Cutler and Taylor aren't snide in their depictions of North's followers or handlers. They don't go overboard on showing Robb as a buffoon or in lionizing Baker. They show Goodin, who easily could have been depicted as a scoundrel, writing a sensitive conciliatory acceptance speech for North, who uses it instead as a concession speech. And in a chilling conclusion, Goodin blames himself for North's defeat because he didn't keep the campaign negative enough. "I won't make that mistake again," he says, ominously. "Next time around, I cut the guy's balls off."

A Perfect Candidate isn't always clearly focused and at points would have benefited from more background exposition. Those expecting nothing more than a caustic salvo against Ollie North will be disappointed. Those looking for any hint of solutions to our political quagmire should look elsewhere. But because it takes risky rather than safe paths through the electoral wilderness, *A Perfect Candidate* becomes the most engaging and perceptive political documentary of the 1990s. It's an honest, unsparing, surprisingly uplifting and eminently watchable saga of the mess that America has made of its electoral system. It's a small voice resounding with justifiable alarm.

—Michael Betzold

CREDITS

Origin: USA
Released: 1996
Production: R.J. Cutler and David Van Taylor for an Arpie Films production; released by Seventh Art
Direction: R.J. Cutler and David Van Taylor
Cinematography: Nicholas Doob
Editing: Mona Davis
MPAA rating: Unrated
Running Time: 105 minutes

REVIEWS

Los Angeles Times. September 27, 1996, p. F8.

The Phantom

The Ghost Who Walks. The Man Who Cannot Die.—Movie tagline

"Energetic summer movie fun."—Michael Medved, *New York Post*

"Leaps off the screen!"—Jim Ferguson, *Prevue Channel*

"A great family picture! Thumbs up! I really loved this movie."—Roger Ebert, *Siskel & Ebert*

"Thrilling! If you have any kid in your heart and adventure in your soul, this is the ticket."—Gene Shalit, *Today,* NBC-TV

Box Office: $17,323,216

The Phantom is based on the venerable King Features comic strip which began syndication in 1936. The masked hero created by Lee Falk therefore antedated the much-better-known Superman and Batman by several years, although he never achieved anything like the popularity of such formidable rivals. Whereas Superman and Batman often appear to be bursting right out of the page, the artwork in "The Phantom" is inhibited and uninspired.

The creators of "Superman" and "Batman" had the inspiration to give their heroes dual identities as Clark Kent and Bruce Wayne, respectively. This was an effective way—at least in the comic strip world—of making their heroes three-dimensional. The Phantom never had much of a personality. He did not relate well to human beings; his best friends were Devil the wolf and Hero the white stallion.

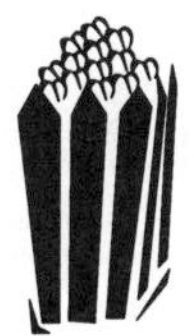

"*The Phantom* comics always had a kind of good old-fashioned adventure.... It was action-adventure with a twinkle in the eye."—Director Simon Wincer

"The Phantom" comic strip was further hampered by its conception. According to the cover story (partially recapitulated in the film), a British trading vessel was attacked by pirates in the sixteenth-century and the crew was slaughtered except for the captain's son. Kit was washed ashore on an island off the coast of Africa where he was adopted by a tribe of pygmies. He grew up to become the Phantom. He took an oath to devote his life "to the destruction of all forms of piracy, greed and cruelty." For succeeding centuries the role of the Phantom has been passed on from father to eldest son. The comic strip stories are generally confined to Third World settings and the plots resemble those of *Tarzan, the Ape Man* (1932) and its many sequels. The Phantom was unlikely to encounter such bizarre villains as the Joker or the Penguin—and a super-hero without super-villains to test his mettle never shows to his best advantage.

Love interest is supplied in the new film by spoiled heiress Diana Palmer (Kristy Swanson). Most of the Phantom's problems revolve around saving Diana, who gets into trouble again almost immediately. She begins as a self-sufficient, globetrotting adventuress, not unlike Sue Charlton (Linda Kozlowski) in *Crocodile Dundee* (1986), and, like Sue, she undergoes a process of feminization as a result of finding herself hopelessly dependent on a strong man for her safety and chastity. This may not set well with feminists, but the makers of *The Phantom* would contend that theirs is a 1930s not a 1990s story. Diana does manage, after all, to assert herself by delivering any number of right crosses and knees to groins. She is just not as powerful as The Ghost Who Walks—but who is? Is it possible that recent films could be reflecting a backlash or counter-trend in American society? In another recent release, *The Arrival* (1996), the heroine is a stockbroker but seems ready to give up her lucrative career for lace curtains and bassinets.

Although the Phantom and Diana are in love, the physical expression of their emotions is limited to one chaste kiss. There is very little flesh showing in this PG-rated production. The Phantom himself, of course, even has his head covered by a hood. Women's clothes of the period were often very attractive. Fashion designers used generous amounts of beautifully cut natural fabrics—wool, cotton, and silk. Kristy Swanson manages to look feminine in what used to be called "man-tailored suits." Her pretty face never gets smudged. Her hair never gets mussed in spite of jumping out of planes, fleeing through jungle foliage, and engaging in fistfights with both men and women. She would seem the ideal mate for the Phantom, and that possibility is strongly suggested at the end.

No doubt producers Robert Evans and Alan Ladd Jr. were preparing the way for a possible *Phantom 2* if there was sufficient interest in the original. They have invested fairly heavily in the prototype, including shooting much beautiful footage in Australia and Thailand. They are likely to be disappointed. *Variety,* reflecting that "box office has plummeted for period-set films based on pulp heroes of yore," reported a first-weekend gross of only $5.1 million, which was ominous in view of the approaching release of such lavishly publicized summer competitors as *Eraser, The Hunchback of Norte Dame,* and *Independence Day.*

The Phantom is full of much-too-familiar sights, including a hoary climax in which an island is torn apart by dynamite and volcanic eruptions while the yowling villains are buried alive. The escape of the Phantom and Diana in a submarine recalls the climax of *20,000 Leagues Under the Sea* (1954). Kenneth Turan, writing for the *Los Angeles Times,* calls *The Phantom* "pleasantly old-fashioned," but viewers may find it old-fashioned in the wrong sense. The hero in his plum-colored jumpsuit looks too much like the heroes of Saturday matinee serials that went on for fifteen weeks with the hero getting into one impossible situation after another only to get out, plausibly or implausibly, by the following weekend. The new film has the flavor of the old Columbia Pictures serial *The Phantom* (1943).

Lee Falk created the Phantom comic strip in 1936 and still writes every story.

The creators of the new film version of the strip have chosen to retain its quaintness. The new Phantom (Billy Zane) is still dealing with African explorers and air pirates. They are all working for power-mad Xander Drax (Treat Williams), who wants to obtain possession of the three lost Skulls of Touganda. The three jewel-eyed statuettes united can, like the lost Ark of the Covenant in *Raiders of the Lost Ark* (1981), generate a power far greater than any number of hydrogen bombs. Drax is already fabulously wealthy but wants nothing less than to rule the earth. At least one of the lost skulls belongs to the Phantom, which is how The Ghost Who Walks gets embroiled in Drax's skullduggery.

Drax already owns one of the skulls. Another is on exhibit in a Manhattan museum. The Phantom and Diana go there to take possession before Drax's emissaries can steal it. But they are minutes too late. The bandits shoot up the museum, pulverizing the huge glass showcase with total disregard for human life or the laws of civilized society.

The filmmakers have recreated a part of 1930's Manhattan in order to provide welcome contrast to all the jungle footage. Some of the charming old New York buildings are still in existence. The rest is represented on backdrops. Outdoor scenes are animated with hundreds of strolling extras and an endless parade of 1930's cars and taxis. Interiors are furnished in the ostentatious style of the period, with enormous desks and deep armchairs nearly the size of baby-grand pianos, all suggesting, like the superfluous material in the men's and women's clothes, the wasteful spirit of early-modern America.

For this visit to New York the Phantom has to shed his familiar costume and appear in mufti as Kit Walker, the handsome and very well-tailored cosmopolitan who went to college with Diana some years before. For reasons of his own he does not reveal his alter-identity as The Ghost Who Walks, nor does he try to explain what he has been doing since graduation or why he never phoned for a date. The headstrong Diana gets Kit involved in just as much trouble as she did the Phantom in the jungle. But their shared adventures have a bonding effect which the dialogue promises will eventually become sanctified by marriage. When Diana taxis off in a seaplane just before the credits roll, indications are that she is only ordering her trousseau and will soon return to Bengalla.

Like the old-fashioned Saturday matinee serials, *The Phantom* is heavily action-oriented. The hero uses acrobatics and martial arts techniques to cope with hordes of villains. These include the dreaded Brotherhood of Sengh pirates who were responsible for sinking the British trading vessel in the sixteenth century and more recently murdered the current Phantom's own father. A supernatural element is added by appearances of the dead father (Patrick McGoohan) who, like Hamlet's ghost, can only be seen and heard by his son.

In spite of the Phantom's efforts, Drax eventually obtains possession of the long-coveted Skulls of Touganda. Clasping them together, he unleashes the violet ray which, like a super-laser beam, has more destructive power than fractured atoms. The filmmakers have managed to obtain a PG rating for the production by soft-pedaling violence in a variety of clever ways. The villains are heavily armed, but most of the damage is inflicted on personal property. One man actually gets hit in the stomach by a cannon ball, but

CREDITS

Phantom/Kit Walker: Billy Zane
Diana Palmer: Kristy Swanson
Xander Drax: Treat Williams
Sala: Catherine Zeta Jones
Quill: James Remar
Kabai Sengh: Cary-Hiroyuki Tagawa

Origin: USA
Released: 1996
Production: Robert Evans, Alan Ladd, Jr. for a Village Roadshow production; released by Paramount Pictures
Direction: Simon Wincer
Screenplay: Jeffrey Boam; based on comic strip characters created by Lee Falk
Cinematography: David Burr
Editing: O. Nicholas Brown
Music: David Newman
Production design: Paul Peters
Art direction: Lisette Thomas
Costume design: Marlene Stewart
Sound: Ben Osmo
Casting: Deborah Aquila, Jane Shannon
MPAA rating: PG
Running Time: 100 minutes

instead of being eviscerated he is carried off camera by the impact. The death ray emitted by the combined three skulls causes no bloodshed or mutilations because it simply disintegrates the people it touches, turning them into computer-simulated stardust.

Nobody in the audience seriously believes that the Phantom is going to get bested by such a one-dimensional character as Xander Drax. At the darkest moment, with the Skulls of Touganda directing their death ray at him, the Phantom turns the tables on Drax and saves the world from a tyrant more powerful and more implacable than Adolf Hitler.

The children in the audience will no doubt be excited by the unusually rich feast of action and adventure, while their parents may enjoy the visual spectacle which includes aerial shots of unspoiled beaches and unravaged tropical forests. The film received unenthusiastic reviews and promises to have only modest success because it lacked the mammoth advertising and promotional budgets that helped to make blockbusters out of *Superman: The Movie* (1978), *Batman* (1989) and their highly lucrative sequels.

—Bill Delaney

REVIEWS

Boxoffice. July, 1996, p. 89.
Detroit Free Press. June 9, 1996, p. 6H.
Los Angeles Times. June 7, 1996, pp. F1, F11.
The New York Times. June 7, 1996, p. C5.
Rolling Stone. June 27, 1996, p. 62.
San Francisco Chronicle. June 7, 1996, p. D3.
USA Today. June 7, 1996, p. 6D.
Variety. June 10, 1996, p. 40.

Phat Beach

Ain't Nothin' but a G-string . . . —Movie tagline

Box Office: $1,383,553

This comedic tale of two African-American high schoolers on summer break looking for fun in the sun on the bikini-clad beaches of L.A. holds one distinction—it doesn't involve gunplay or drug use. *Phat Beach* is an innocent, but mostly raucous exercise from first-time writer/director Doug Ellin that will easily slip from the annals of art, but should be noted for its individuality in a genre that usually consists of urban war and decay.

"It's all attitude."—Durrell on his sexual success

Bennie (Jermaine "Huggy" Hopkins) is an overweight teen with some heavyweight problems with girls. The virginal Bennie is the symbol of romanticism and would rather write poetry to girls than readily bed them. He spends a great deal of time either eating, or fantasizing about sultry women who in reality would not give him the time of day. On the other hand, his slim sidekick Durrel (Brian Hooks), wayward and clueless more than cool, goes through women like they were tissues. They make an unlikely pair, but they are best buds because Durrel often times offers the much needed confidence that naive Bennie needs to get through his female woes.

Summer has come to the quiet suburb of Bakersfield, and Bennie has been sentenced to hard labor in a burger joint by his father. Bennie would much rather spend his summer in a poetry class, but his father is stern in teaching his son about work ethics and responsibility. "After all, hard work earned me this Mercedes," Bennie's father proudly tells his son. Durrel has no ambition, and plans his summer hanging out, listening to tunes, and sleeping. Durrel senses his friend's unhappiness at The House of Burgers and convinces Bennie to quit his menial job and help him sell sunglasses at Venice Beach in L.A. Bennie is resistant at first, but once Durrel assures him of the high number of scantly clad women at the beach, Bennie is game. With his parents gone for a week on vacation, Bennie can afford to rebel.

From a suggestion that started out with just selling sunglasses at the beach, the deal turns out to be more than Bennie ever bargained for. Following Durrel's simple request, Bennie has now withdrawn all his savings of $300 from the bank and is driving his dad's prized Mercedes to the beach. As with all teen romps, nothing goes as planned.

With a collection of speeding tickets and an abrupt visit to a topless bar, the two chums are now penniless. They could make their money back if they sell the sunglasses, but entrepreneur Durrel's attention always seem to be diverted when someone of the opposite sex passes him by.

Soon, the two are stuck with no sunglasses to sell, no money to spend, and an impounded Mercedes. If the situation could get any worse for them, it does when Bennie's parents show up at the same motel where he and Durrel are staying. This coincidence leads to the crux of this feeble story that has Bennie confronting his father about playing in a $10,000 volleyball tournament on the beach. It seems Bennie possesses a killer serve and has a great chance of winning the money. Bennie defiantly ignores his father's request to leave. Bennie, for the first time in his life, has a chance to win at something.

Rapper Coolio has a cameo.

The story line and acting is a level or two above an "ABC Afterschool Special," with the supporting cast acting as if they are reading their lines from cue cards. Yet the lightheartedness of the film has its charm, and its hip-hopness surely satisfies its target audience which is similar to that of the *House Party* trilogy (1990, 1991, 1994). Director Ellin's best asset in this film are his two leads, Hopkins and Hooks. Hopkins is perfectly cast as the awkward and fat Bennie, and Hooks' Durrel may be a sexist pig and unapologetic opportunist, but it becomes difficult to dislike him. Durrel may be a bad influence for Bennie, but he accepts Bennie for what he is, although it often seems that Durrel's psychology only works to his advantage and Bennie is left holding the short end of the stick. Eventually you hope things work out for the both of them, but you will also wish the clock would speed up on the anticipated resolution.

Phat Beach employs a catchy rap soundtrack that gives Ellin the opportunity to film sequences in an MTV style. This technique can only be Ellin's confession that his film is rather bland and needs some energy injected into it. Even rap star Coolio plays an emcee at the bikini contest. Advertisements for the film suggested Coolio is a cast member, but his appearance is no more than a cameo.

Saturated with beautiful women in bikinis and misogynistic overtones, this movie wears very thin on the level of taste. Its crassness is proven when Durrel is slapped in the face by a woman using her large breast as the weapon, and by its raunchy scenes of casual sex in the back seats of cars. Even when Bennie does find his true love and Durrel receives his comeuppance in the end, Ellin flippantly places the messenger of the moral—that woman should not be treated like objects—in his main character Bennie, who is constantly beaten down and hardly noticed. The females that are given enough screen time to be called a role, such as Bennie's fantasy girl, Candace (Claudia Kaleem), are nothing more than money-grubbing airheads.

Phat Beach is weak in plot, loaded with profanity, and laden with hip-hop music. Fun for its target audience of hormonally-charged teens who are more forgiving, unimaginative to others. In some regards, this movie could be deemed a coming-of-age story, but judging from the subject matter, it is director/writer Ellin who needs to grow up.

—*Michelle Banks*

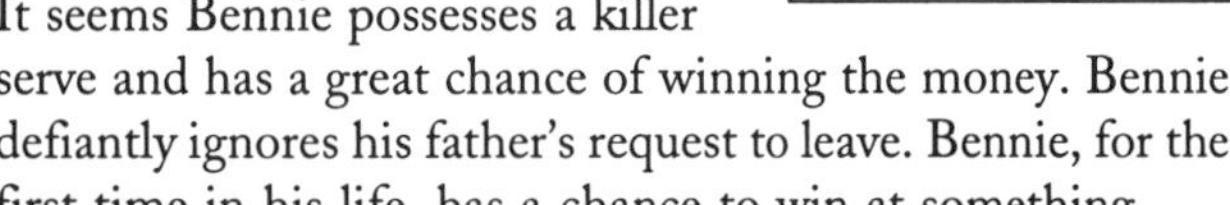

CREDITS

Bennie King: Jermaine (Huggy) Hopkins
Durrel Jackson: Brian Hooks
Mickey Z: Gregg Vance
Candace Williams: Claudia Kaleem
Carl King: Erick Fleeks
Janet King: Alma Collins

Origin: USA
Released: 1996
Production: Cleveland O'Neal for a Live Entertainment and Connection III Entertainment production; released by Orion
Direction: Doug Ellin
Screenplay: Doug Ellin, Brian E. O'Neal and Ben Morris
Cinematography: Jim Lebovitz and Jurgen Baum
Editing: Richard Nord and Jeremy Craig Kasten
Production design: Terri Schaetzle, Colleen Devine
Art direction: Le'Ce Edwards-Bonilla, Suzan A. Muszynski
Costume design: Mona Thalheimer
Sound: Paul Ratajczak
Music: Paul Stewart
MPAA rating: R
Running Time: 84 minutes

REVIEWS

The Detroit Free Press. August 4, 1996. Section F, p. 6.
Los Angeles Times. August 3, 1996. Section F, p. 22.
The New York Times. August 3, 1996. p. 14.
Variety Magazine Online. August 5, 1996.

Phenomenon

Some things in life just can't be explained.—Movie tagline

"The must see movie of the year!"—Bonnie Churchill, *National News Syndicate*

"Travolta gives the performance of his life."—Rex Reed, *The New York Observer*

"One of the finest films you will see this year!"—Paul Wunder, *WBAI Radio*

"This summer's sleeper hit!"—Pat Collins, *WWOR-TV*

Box Office: **$104,464,977**

Everyone knows and likes George Malley (John Travolta). He leads a simple life, running the town's auto garage, tending his garden, and lusting after the town's beautiful newcomer Lace Pennamin (Kyra Sedgwick) who has two children, makes willow chairs, and is quite cold to George's small overtures.

"You know what that light was? A mistake, that's what it was."—George

But George has other friends, especially local farmer Nate Pope (Forest Whitaker) whose hobby is operating a ham radio and who has a crush of his own . . . on Diana Ross, and the town's doctor (Robert Duvall) who sees George as the son he never had.

Then something happens to shake up George's uncomplicated world. On the night of his 37th birthday party, George wanders out from the bar only to be knocked flat by an unusual and inexplicable flash of light. With this bolt from the blue, George is transformed. He suddenly begins winning chess games, speaking fluent Spanish, reading several books a day, and resolving problems both simple (how did that rabbit get into his fenced garden) and complex (creating a 90 m.p.g. methane fuel). The only problem George can't seem to solve is how and why this all happened to him. (Popular consensus seems to think the light belonged to aliens.)

The Eric Clapton song "Change the World," from the film's soundtrack, hit No. 5 on Billboard's Hot 100 Singles chart.

Although George is changing intellectually, he's still the same sweet George and his new "gifts" just become incorporated into George's desire to benefit his neighbors. He uses his new empathic powers to find a very sick lost boy and then uses his telekinetic abilities to reveal his hiding place. He calls Berkeley in the hope of showing them how he can predict earthquakes. He develops a fertilizer to help Nate grow crops on his barren south forty. George never even contemplates using his abilities to get rich. That's just not George. But if there were just one thing he'd like to do for himself with his new skills, it would be to win Lace's heart. This, however, he accomplishes not with brains but with wildflower bouquets and his winning charm. (The culminating shave and haircut may be the most romantic ever captured on celluloid.)

At the same time he's winning Lace, though, he's also losing his neighbors. Although basically the same, George's new mental abilities take his old friends from discomfort to fear to suspicion. Except for Lace, Doc and Nate, George is becoming isolated in his brilliance.

But where the locals may be shying away from George, his talents soon attract a few outsiders: first the scientists show up wanting answers to his abilities, then the newshounds arrive wanting exploitable tales of UFOs, and then the government steps in because George just plain scares them. Now the smart George must wise-up the sweet George in order to maintain any semblance of the simple life he so loves.

Since Quentin Tarantino's hit *Pulp Fiction* revived John Travolta's career yet again, he is proving to be one of Hollywood's most accomplished actors. He is also proving to be more versatile than many would have suspected. In director John Woo's *Broken Arrow* Travolta adroitly plays a sinister, cartoonish villain. In *Get Shorty* he plays a deliciously laid-back mobster. In *Phenomenon* he plays an innocent, good-natured, and gentle man so proficiently that one leaves the theater wishing he were more than fiction. To be able to subtly portray the average George and the extraordinary George as being different and yet the same is a feat worthy of note. They are different people, but underneath, they are not. Travolta eloquently shows that. Needless to say, if Travolta's George were not endearing or if he had hit a wrong note in his characterization, our belief in the film would have been shattered. Luckily, it is not. And considering that it was launched the same week as the blockbuster *Independence Day, Phenomenon* is doing very well in the summer box office sweepstakes, finding a receptive and steady audience in those who want a break from all the special effects and explosions.

Hollywood may have a hard time believing it, but there are people out there who will spend the price of admission on a film that gives them a small story, memorable characters, and an uplifting message . . . if it's done well. Luckily, director Jon Turteltaub (*While You Were Sleeping*) has done a solid job with Gerald DiPego's story of what happens to ordinary people when given an extraordinary gift. Comparisons will obviously be made between *Phenomenon* and Cliff Robertson's 1968 *Charley*, but that should not diminish this film's power to please. There will also be those who find the story too condescending, purposefully pushing all the right buttons to get us to smile or to pull out our handkerchiefs, but they are as cynical (but maybe less self-serving) as those who condemn Hollywood for not portraying strong "family values."

Yes, *Phenomenon* is sentimental and manipulative—but what good story isn't? We just don't want to notice the strings. Yes, *Phenomenon* has a message. In fact, it has several messages. It is a study in the meaning of friendship and acceptance and of America's anti-intellectual bias, in being suspicious of what we don't understand or can't explain, and in being distrustful of those who delight in knowledge and discovery. "I'm what everybody can be," says George at one point in the film, "I'm the possibility." George's intellect has a heart, but it still won't stop some from suspecting it.

Considering how many films Hollywood has been putting out lately touting how wonderful it is to be stupid (from *Dumb and Dumber* to *Forest Gump*), here's one that says although it is a mixed blessing to be special and different, it's marvelous to be intelligent. It's a message America can't hear often enough, and to be couched in such a well-crafted film is a plus.

—*Beverley Bare Buehrer*

CREDITS

George Malley: John Travolta
Lace Pennamin: Kyra Sedgwick
Nate Pope: Forest Whitaker
Doc: Robert Duvall
Professor Ringold: Jeffrey DeMunn
Dr. Wellin: Richard Kiley
Niedorf: Brent Spiner

Origin: USA
Released: 1996
Production: Barbara Boyle, Michael Taylor for a Touchstone Pictures production; released by Buena Vista
Direction: Jon Turteltaub
Screenplay: Gerald DiPego
Cinematography: Phedon Papamichael
Editing: Bruce Green
Music: Thomas Newman
Production design: Gareth Stover
Art direction: Bruce Alan Miller
Set design: Richard Fernandez, Lori Rowbotham
Costume design: Betsy Cox
Sound: Ronald Judkins
Casting: Renee Rousselot
MPAA rating: PG
Running Time: 124 minutes

REVIEWS

Chicago Tribune. July 3, 1996, p. 1.
Entertainment Weekly. July 12, 1996, p. 40.
New York Times. July 3, 1996, p. C9.
Newsweek. July 8, 1996, p. 64.
People. July 15, 1996, p. 23.
Variety Online. June 19, 1996.

Pie in the Sky

The only thing that stands in the way of fate and true love is a little traffic.—Movie tagline

"Hilarious! *Pie in the Sky* is a winner!"—Carol Cling, *Las Vegas Review*

"A wonderfully fresh and endearing comedy about first love."—Rene Rodriguez, *The Miami Herald*

Writer/director Bryan Gordon (*Career Opportunities* [1991]) shows he is ably talented to present his second feature *Pie in the Sky,* a lightweight, offbeat romantic comedy, to the Generation-X audience it most likely appeals to. The characters' quirky aspirations and the actors' portrayals provide much of the appeal within this predictable narrative of a classic odd couple, Charlie (Josh Charles) and Amy (Ann Heche), who face the problem of trying to overcome their personal differences in order to stay together. Amy is a free-spirited dancer while Charlie is more traditional and responsible. However, there is another side to Charlie, one which makes him a bit more complex: Charlie has an unusually intense relationship with traffic.

The opening scene attempts to explain the origin of Charlie's unusual interest. In an unmoving traffic jam, Charlie's mom and dad (Christine Ebersole and Peter Riegert) go about the business of what will eventually result in Charlie's arrival nine months later. A teenaged Charlie seems to be rebelling against his strict and humorless father who appears to hate driving altogether . Charlie begins to study traffic every chance he gets and becomes inexplicably enchanted with its poetry. Charlie shares his strange hobby with his true love, a cute, blond, neighbor girl. The budding romance is thwarted when Amy and her parents move away from northern California, breaking young Charlie's heart.

Fast-forward to Charlie's young adulthood where he is about to enter college. This sets up one of the films major themes: conformity and compromise vs. individuality and happiness. Charlie's room is an extension of that individuality—the ceiling depicts a giant, lighted, road map tracking traffic and the radio blares brilliant traffic insights from Charlie's hero and traffic maven, Alan Davenport (John Goodman). This is Charlie's oasis in the otherwise oppressive household where his parents spout the most traditional, uncreative rhetoric and middle-class morality. Charlie, through years of this conditioning, seems to be slowly falling into the same trap, just as he unexpectedly finds Amy returning once again to his life. She happens to be visiting relatives who live next door and the two renew their childhood attraction. Amy is invited to dinner at Charlie's house, and as they make small talk, Amy manages to represent all that the Dunlaps despise—independence, danger, nonconformity, and unconventionality. Despite his parents tacit disapproval, Charlie and Amy manage to consummate their short-lived relationship just before both must leave for college. Heche's performance is subtle and believable as Charles' is sweetly appealing, and they do exhibit a certain chemistry in their love scenes. Ebersole and Riegert, however, have little to do as the wonderfully oppressive and completely one-dimensional parents.

Director Gordon does exhibit a sense of humor, proving he can make fun of avant-garde types as well as traditional family-values types. As Charlie dines with Amy's freakish family, it is obvious that they are just as stereotypical, but as hippie, New Agers who swing just as much to the left as Charlie's folks do to the right, and are just as annoying. Gordon's goal seems to be to place two rounded characters (Charlie and Amy) within the confines of almost cartoonish surroundings. The duo represent the fleshed-out, more balanced versions of their progenitors, which gives one an idea about the audience Gordon is seeking. However, the two cannot withstand the pressures of college, parents, and their own differences and after an argument following dinner at Amy's house, they break it off.

CREDITS

Charlie Dunlap: Josh Charles
Amy: Anne Heche
Alan Davenport: John Goodman
Dad Dunlap: Peter Riegert
Mom Dunlap: Christine Ebersole
Jack: Wil Wheaton
Ruby: Christine Lahti
Paul Entamen: Bob Balaban

Origin: USA
Released: 1996
Production: Denise Shaw, Allan Mindel; released by New Line Cinema
Direction: Bryan Gordon
Screenplay: Bryan Gordon
Cinematography: Bernd Heinl
Editing: Colleen Halsey
Production designer: Linda Pearl
Music: Michael Convertino
Art direction: Michael Atwell
Costume design: Louise Frogley
Sound: Walt Martin
Casting: Rick Pagano, Debbie Manwiller
MPAA rating: R
Running Time: 95 minutes

On the verge of insurance salesmanship with his father, Charlie's dreams are finally realized. He receives a letter requesting an interview with his hero Davenport in Los Angeles. This sets up the film's other theme: going the extra mile. Rejected by an unenthusiastic Davenport lackey, who has none of Charlie's dubious passion for traffic, Charlie refuses to give up. The rest of the film also brings us to the conclusion that most life changing events occur in unexpected places—like bathrooms. Gordon seems to share Quentin Tarantino's fascination with the lavatory, beginning with Charlie's career changing encounter with Davenport, whom Charlie, a fellow "grid-lock guy," flatters with his in-depth knowledge of Davenport's historic traffic-career milestones. This lands him a meager job at the radio station working for Davenport.

Bryan Gordon won an Academy Award for his short film *Ray's Heterosexual Male Dance Hall.*

Upon his arrival in gridlock city, Charlie finds a squalid apartment with a freeway view and a kooky Latin music-loving landlady, Ruby (Christine Lahti), with whom he must share a bathroom. When Lahti shows up, adding depth to her quirky character that could have been one-dimensional, it is refreshing. Charlie begins a relationship with Ruby in yet another bathroom liaison. As unlikely a couple as they are, you almost begin to wish they would end up together. From her, Charlie learns to loosen up and she teaches him rhythm. She brings him home unexpectedly to meet her elderly parents, which rounds out the "dinner-with-parents theme." Later, a funeral Charlie and Ruby attend puts perspective on both their lives, and with her encouragement, Charlie resumes his quest for his dreams of both a satisfying traffic career and Amy.

Lahti is outstanding in her role, and Goodman's performance as the egotistical traffic expert is typically energetic and consistently strong in a film that loses speed about halfway through. The main characters' single-mindedness, especially Amy's, seems strained and gives the actors little to work with. However, for a genre crowded with mindless, formulaic eye-candy, this one still manages to stand out for its fresh twists.

—*Hilary Weber*

REVIEWS

Boxoffice. November, 1995, p. 97.

The Pompatus of Love

Women are a mystery. Love is a tragedy. Naturally, it's a comedy.—Movie tagline

"Deftly explores each character's approach to life, love, and the pursuit of chicks."—*Buzz Magazine*

"A better guy-talk comedy than *The Brothers McMullen* . . . a fast, funny relationship comedy"—*The Chicago Tribune*

"I enjoyed *The Pompatus of Love,* showing bright, literate, articulate guys who are completely baffled by women."—Roger Ebert, *Chicago Sun-Times*

"Well acted, smartly written, deeply felt . . . an independent movie that's finally about people rather than style."—Barbara and Scott Siegel, *Siegel Entertainment Syndicate*

You never really do find out what a "pompatus" is, in this New York buddy film about four longtime friends, alleged grownups, who are baffled by life, love, and women. (As usual, all the significant women characters are smarter than any of the men around them.) Yes, the title is from the Steve Miller song "The Joker:" "Some people call me the space cowboy./Yeah! Some call me the gangster of love./Some people call me Maurice,/Cause I speak of the Pompatus of love." The guys, who seem to spend a lot of their time hanging out, drinking, hear the song in a bar and first try to figure out what the word is: pom-poms?, prophetess?, impetus? They also talk—a lot.

Therapist Mark's (Jon Cryer) written a self-help book (which quickly wound up in the remainder bin) and tries to follow his own advice. He's an annoyingly "sensitive" guy, who succeeds in driving his edgy designer girlfriend, Tasha (Kristen Wilson), crazy by his constant "understanding" of her feelings. What she's feeling is trapped in a needy relationship that makes them both unhappy, although neither is willing to admit to it. You can see the writing on the wall when the twosome decide to cohabitate and can't agree on an apartment, so Mark impulsively puts a down payment on a brand new house (without Tasha's input).

Scruffy motormouth Runyon (Tim Guinee) is also wallowing in the romantic abyss. Living in personal chaos in a dingy apartment, he has managed to get a California TV producer interested in the one play he's written and is about to take off for a meeting in Los Angeles. He's also desperate to see his former girlfriend Kathryn (Dana Wheeler-Nicholson), constantly phoning her to say he's going to be in town. She ignores all his calls and the trip turns out to be a disaster. The "meeting" goes badly—the would-be producer isn't actually interested in Runyon's play but wants the writer to pitch him an idea for his ghastly-but-successful TV show. Runyon goes back to his hotel, gets drunk, and decides to pay Kathryn a visit, breaking into her bedroom where's she's asleep with her new boyfriend. After getting him out of the house, she tells him in no uncertain terms to take his obsessions and get lost.

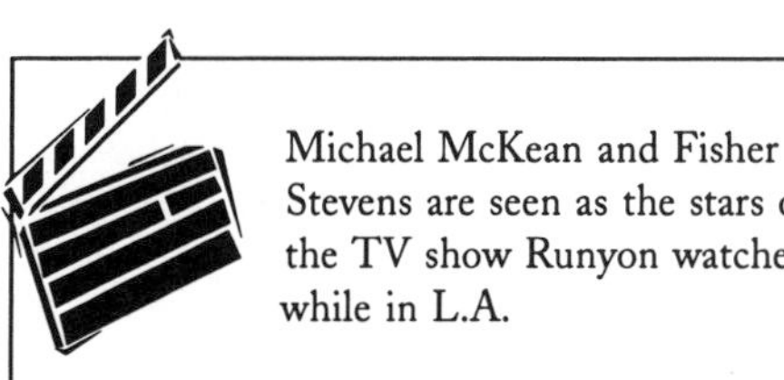

Michael McKean and Fisher Stevens are seen as the stars of the TV show Runyon watches while in L.A.

CREDITS

Mark: Jon Cryer
Runyon: Tim Guinee
Phil: Adam Oliensis
Josh: Adrian Pasdar
Lori: Arabella Field
Cynthia: Mia Sara
Gina: Paige Turco
Caroline: Kristen Scott Thomas
Kathryn: Dana Wheeler-Nicholson
Tasha: Kristen Wilson
Ting: Liana Pai
Tarzaan: Jennifer Tilly

Origin: USA
Released: 1996
Production: D.J. Paul, Jon Resnik for a Why Not, Monte Cristo, and Counterproductions project; released by BMG Independents
Direction: Richard Schenkman
Screenplay: Jon Cryer, Adam Oliensis, Richard Schenkman
Cinematography: Russell Fine
Editing: Don Rosen
Music: John Hill
Production design: Michael Krantz
Art direction: Bill Perkins
Costumes: Carolyn Grifel
Sound: Bill Kozy
MPAA rating: R
Running Time: 99 minutes

Josh (Adrian Pasdar) is charming and a compulsive womanizer. He picks up hatcheck girl Ting (Liana Pai) for some noncommittal sex (that's almost derailed by her objection to his lambskin condom since she's a vegetarian. Fortunately, Ting also came prepared.) And "meets cute" with the beautiful Cynthia (Mia Sara), who's also willing to take a chance with a handsome stranger. However, Josh is really hung up on buddy Phil's (Adam Oliensis) married sister, Gina (Paige Turco), who's been teasing him since high school. When Gina's abusive husband hits her once too often, she begs shelter from Josh (and later winds up sleeping with him). But Josh is devastated to learn that he's only a temporary refuge and Gina's not interested in becoming his true love.

Average schmoe Phil is the one guy who seems to have a normal life, he's married to the sensible Lori (Arabella Field), who tolerates his nights out with the boys, has a couple of kids, and runs a plumbing supply store. But even Phil is tempted by the charms of English interior designer Caroline (Kristen Scott Thomas), although it turns out he's misconstrued her natural flirtiness for something more.

Situations come to a head when Tasha breaks up with Mark and he decides to take a sledgehammer to their under-construction home. The guys build a bonfire with some of the pieces, pass around the alcohol, and keep talking about love and the differences between men and women. Oh yeah, the "pompatus" argument comes up again and it's decided that what it is is that inexplicable, undefinable feeling that's the mystery of love itself (or maybe it just sounded cool).

Well-acted by a quartet of appealing actors, this film is nonetheless maddening (at least to a woman) because, with the possible exception of Phil, these guys are unwilling to become adults. They don't really want the responsibilities associated with making a commitment, they're alternately compulsive about one woman or keeping their options open for someone better to come along, and they're more interested in their own neuroses than anything else. The buddy relationship of this foursome is the strongest bond any of them have.

—*Christine Tomassini*

REVIEWS

Boxoffice. July, 1996, p. 88.
The Hollywood Reporter. July 25, 1996, p. 6.
Los Angeles Times. July 26, 1996, p. F8.
New York Times. July 26, 1996, p. C25.

The Portrait of a Lady

"Sexy, edgy and sublimely satisfying."—Graham Fuller, *Interview*

"Darkly gorgeous, fascinating and undeniably audacious."—David Ansen, *Newsweek*

"A truly mesmerizing *Portrait*. The 1881 Henry James novel has been superbly rendered by director Jane Campion. Nicole Kidman's startling intensity holds you in thrall and Barbara Hershey has the role of her career."—Peter Travers, *Rolling Stone*

Box Office: $2,007,646

Director Jane Campion takes the title of Henry James' novel quite literally, making the focus of *The Portrait of a Lady* the visual portrayal of the problem of femininity, where gender and image share equal weight. While James "portrait" was metaphoric, and his "lady" the perfect occasion to consider the difference between American and British social and psychological nuances, Campion has managed to shift the focus in the direction of contemporary interests without deviating too far from the original narrative. Though this film does not command the power, originality, and subtlety of her previous films, *Sweetie* (1989), *An Angel at My Table* (1989), and *The Piano* (1993), there is still much to be admired.

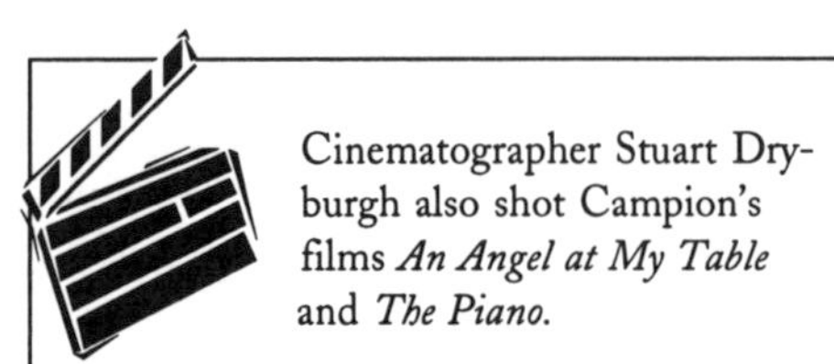

Cinematographer Stuart Dryburgh also shot Campion's films *An Angel at My Table* and *The Piano.*

Campion's focus and dominating theme is introduced immediately by a slow camera pan across the faces and bodies of an assortment of contemporary women at rest within a natural landscape. These images are beautiful and silent and draw attention to the camera and the act of seeing. From this opening it is evident that Campion wants us to "see" and to "look" at women, and in this gaze to find a universality that ties the 19th century and its seemingly archaic problems to the present. Abruptly these images break away to the past, where a scene is already transpiring, giving the effect of entering a film already in progress. The strong-willed Isabel Archer (Nicole Kidman), an American visiting relatives in Britain, has just refused the proposal of the wealthy Lord Warburton (Richard E. Grant). He chases her into the bushes where she has apparently run to hide her tears. Isabel's emotional conflict as she struggles between two competing and irreconcilable desires—the desire to satisfy social expectations and achieve the comforts that come along with it, and the desire to pursue freedom and adventure and achieve power and autonomy—is the theme that is developed in this interpretation, understood not so much in historical or geographic terms, but as the problem of women in patriarchal cultures. There have been a number of Hollywood interpretations of 19th century novels, but the focus in these interpretations has been more generally the anguish of the upper classes as they fight their true sensual desires and passions in favor of strict, conservative, conventions. This dichotomy is expressed in terms of society versus nature, or reason versus emotion. In Campion's film the ambiguity is richer. Sexual gratification is the lure which threatens to imprison Isabel in a conventional marriage, so she must repress her eroticism in order to become an autonomous woman.

Isabel's suffering is only augmented by the appearance of several other equally desirable suitors, the American businessman Caspar Goodwood (Viggo Mortensen) who has followed her to Europe if only to see her for a moment, and the handsome, consumptive cousin Ralph Touchett (Martin Donovan) who is the only one who recognizes and appreciates her determination to be free. Isabel finds inspiration in Madame Merle (Barbara Hershey), an intelligent and independent woman who appears to have passed through youth without committing herself to either motherhood or marriage. Isabel's wish to travel the world alone seems an impossibility, socially and economically, until she suddenly inherits a fortune from her deceased uncle. The inheritance has been arranged by her cousin Ralph, so that he may spend his final days of life watching what an intelligent woman will do with the freedom afforded by money, but Isabel imagines Madame Merle to have been the cause of her fortune, and looks to her as a mentor. When Madame Merle introduces her to Gilbert Osmond (John Malkovich), a somber and arrogant aesthete and failed artist with no financial prospects, Isabel abandons her plans for travel, falls madly in love, and

AWARDS AND NOMINATIONS

Academy Award 1996 Nominations: Best Supporting Actress (Hershey), Best Costume Design
Golden Globe Award 1997 Nominations: Best Supporting Actress (Hershey)
Los Angeles Film Critics Association 1996: Supporting Actress (Hershey)
National Society of Film Critics 1996: Supporting Actor (Donovan), Supporting Actress (Hershey)

quickly marries him, much to the disappointment of her cousin.

Osmond gradually reveals himself to be neither the somber, lone genius she imagined, nor the adoring lover. Rather he is an opportunistic, cruel, arrogant, dilettante concerned only with his good taste and the prospects of his young daughter Pansey (Valentina Cervi), who he has hidden away in a nunnery for most of her life. In his rare visits with his devoted daughter Osmond has sought to instill in her an unquestioning obedience to the authority of the father—an obedience enforced by fear and cruelty. The film depicts three generations of women, Madame Merle, Isabella, and Pansy, caught in the web of male dominance and the society that enforces it, and unable to offer any help either to themselves or to one another. When Pansy falls in love with a young man who does not meet her father's exaggerated expectations, she is forbidden to marry or to see him, and she obeys. A visit from Lord Warburton sparks the hopes of the opportunistic Osmond, who bullies Isabel into serving as middleman in the desired proposal for his daughter's hand. When Warburton leaves town without proposing, Isabel is viciously accused, both by Osmond and Madame Merle, of having thwarted their plans out of jealousy.

"I think I have to begin by getting a general impression of life, do you see? And there's a light that has to dawn. I can't explain it, but I know it's there. I know I can't give up. I'm not afraid."—Isabel Archer

Desperately unhappy, Isabel plans an escape by suggesting to her cousin Ralph who is leaving for America, that if he should become quite ill and call for her, she would come. When she receives the message from Ralph, Osmond refuses to permit her to leave. Only now does she learn from Osmond's frivolous sister, Countess Gemini (Shelley Duvall), that Madame Merle has been Osmond's longtime lover and that Pansy is their illegitimate daughter. The realization that she has been used for her wealth by a calculating, opportunistic duo gives her the strength to leave and join her cousin for his final days. Realizing now that it was Ralph who gave her the opportunity for freedom and loved her unconditionally, she showers him with gratitude and appreciation before his death. At his funeral her old American suitor Casper Goodwood appears and in the final scene she is shown outdoors in nature, struggling against the frozen discomfort of a winter landscape and the desire and demands of Goodwood. She gives in to a kiss at one point and then flees desperately for the lighted windows of a bourgeois interior, stopping at the door and turning back indecisively.

There are perhaps too many obvious visual and verbal metaphors in this film, such as a gate casting its shadow across Isabel like prison bars, and Madame Merle reprimanding Osmond for mishandling a delicate and very valuable piece of China. But Campion spices up what could be simply another pretty period piece by taking some cinematic risks, such as unconventional framing and camera angles, fantasy scenes, changes in film speed, and visual exaggeration. These forays into avant-garde film techniques are at times wonderfully successful and at other moments ridiculous. This is a film that draws one's attention to formal elements repeatedly and purposively, and as such is a pleasure to watch. The result though is a distancing from the character identification that sustains such romantic period pieces. John Malkovich is cast in a role he has played repeatedly over the past few years, and though he has become accomplished as the complicated and cruel villain, it is threatening to lose its force to stereotype. Nicole Kidman is surprisingly convincing in the 19th century, especially in the light of her excellent performance as the murderous media professional in Gus Van Sant's *To Die For* (1995). Her portrayal of Isabel is complex and thoughtful, but ultimately too indecisive, timid, and weak to measure up to the novel's and the screenplay's depiction of Isabel's unusual strength, determination, and intelligence. The screenplay by Laura

CREDITS

Isabel Archer: Nicole Kidman
Gilbert Osmond: John Malkovich
Madame Serena Merle: Barbara Hershey
Ralph Touchett: Martin Donovan
Henrietta Stackpole: Mary-Louise Parker
Lord Warburton: Richard E. Grant
Mr. Touchett: John Gielgud
Mrs. Touchett: Shelley Winters
Caspar Goodwood: Viggo Mortensen
Edward Rosier: Christian Bale
Pansy Osmond: Valentina Cervi

Origin: Great Britain and USA
Released: 1996
Production: Monty Montgomery and Steve Golin for a Propaganda Films and Polygram Filmed Entertainment production; released by Gramercy
Direction: Jane Campion
Screenplay: Laura Jones; based on the book by Henry James
Cinematography: Stuart Dryburgh
Editing: Veronika Jenet
Music: Wojiech Kilar
Production design: Janet Patterson
Costume design: Janet Patterson
Art direction: Mark Raggett
Sound: Peter Glossop
MPAA rating: PG-13
Running Time: 144 minutes

Jones, who was responsible for the excellent screenplay in Campion's *An Angel at My Table,* has toned down the verbal wit and acerbity of the characters in James' novel for a contemporary audience, forfeiting the psychological force of human interaction in a constrained social class and climate.

Despite its faults this is a film that has been made with considerable effort, care and risk. It is not Jane Campion's best work, but it is an adequate follow-up to the success of *The Piano.* By reinterpreting the 19th century from a feminist viewpoint she has run the risk of absurdity and incongruence, as was the case with Demi Moore's rendition of Nathaniel Hawthorne's Hester Pryne as a feminist in *The Scarlet Letter* (1995). Campion avoids this absurdity by remaining sincere and intelligent in her project, rather than merely riding the wave of a fashionable identity politics commingled with the Hollywood success of 19th century period pieces. Instead she seems determined to address the larger problem of freedom, pointing out that there are certain social structures and hierarchies that generate a loss of freedom which even unlimited wealth cannot overcome. And that these structures define the frame within which a portrait of femininity must be set.

—*Reni Celeste*

REVIEWS

American Cinematographer. January, 1997, p. 50.
Boxoffice. November, 1996, p. 130.
Chicago Tribune. January 17, 1997, p. 4.
Entertainment Weekly. January 17, 1997, p. 42.
Los Angeles Times. December 24, 1996, p. F1.
New York Times. December 27, 1996, p. C3.
Newsweek. December 23, 1996, p. 68.
People. January 27, 1997, p. 21.
Rolling Stone. January 23, 1997, p. 72.
Sight and Sound. March, 1997, p. 60.
Variety Online. September 13, 1996.
Village Voice. December 31, 1996, p. 66.

The Preacher's Wife

They needed help. What they got was a miracle.—Movie tagline

"Whitney Houston and Denzel Washington are a sheer delight!"—David Sheehan, *CBS-TV*

"Denzel Washington and Whitney Houston light up the screen."—Joel Siegel, *Good Morning America*

"An inspirational comedy. Whitney Houston and Denzel Washington look wonderful together."—Janet Maslin, *New York Times*

"Two thumbs up!"—*Siskel & Ebert*

Box Office: $30,783,747

The Preacher's Wife is a updated remake of the familiar holiday film *The Bishop's Wife* (1947) with Cary Grant, David Niven, and Loretta Young. Director Penny Marshall and screenwriters Nat Mauldin and Allan Scott have set their version in a small city on the East Coast and changed the principal characters to a Baptist preacher of an African-American congregation and his wife, the director of the church choir.

The opening scenes focus on the preacher and his problems. Henry Biggs (Courtney B. Vance) is beset with a number of difficulties. His wife tries to juice up his sermons by directing the choir to join it at times and echo Henry. The men counting the proceeds from the morning's offering come up with only "$96 and a button," not enough for the church to pay its bills. Moreover, the church youth center is endangered, and at home Henry's little boy Jeremiah (Justin Pierre Edmund) is about to lose his best friend to a foster care program. Even worse, one of the teenagers Henry knows from the youth center has been falsely accused of robbing a neighborhood market. When Henry prays at the beginning of the film ("Lord, I'm a little tired. I sure could use some help"), he cannot imagine the type of answer he will get.

An angel named Dudley (Denzel Washington) tumbles out of the sky to land in a snow mound next to Jeremiah as the boy makes a snow angel. After two unsuccessful attempts to convince Henry of his heavenly credentials (such as his "angel handbook"), Dudley finally works his way into Henry's life by telling his secretary Beverly (Loretta Devine) that he has been sent to help Henry as his assistant. Both Henry's widowed mother-in-law Marguerite (Jenifer Lewis) and his wife Julia (Whitney Houston) take to Dudley, but more complications arise before even Dudley is able to set things right. The boiler of the church explodes one night during choir practice, and a self-made real-estate magnate Joe Hamilton (Gregory Hines) pressures Henry to abandon the neighborhood. Pitching a lucrative plan to Henry and the church council, Hamilton asks them to move to a bigger sanctuary so that he can take over the present church property to build a mall and some tennis courts. Henry resists, but he is weakening.

Yet another complication involves Julia, who is clearly neglected and who struggles at times to support her husband. Henry is too busy even to take Julia dancing. Dudley unexpectedly must fill in for Henry by accompanying Julia to Jazzie's, a local nightclub where before she was married Julia used to sing and where Henry proposed to her. Britsloe (Lionel Richie), the owner of the club, talks Julia into singing again, and Dudley is mesmerized by the beauty and talent Julia displays. When Christmas shopping necessitates that Dudley take Julia out again and they pause for some ice skating at a local pond, the beginnings of a love triangle develop.

Lionel Ritchie makes his acting debut as the owner of a local nightclub.

The filmmakers have added new material to the original story (the music, the plotlines of saving the area youth from the foster home and from jail), and one of their best changes is the addition of the character of Marguerite. She is a no-nonsense widow who works as much as Dudley to bring a happy ending to the film. Jenifer Lewis's comic performance is also one of the acting highlights. "It gave me an opportunity to have a lot of fun with the character and present attitude," Lewis said. "There's a lot of heart and soul in Marguerite. She was a preacher's wife herself, and now that her husband has died, she feels she has the freedom to act up and act out. Yet, she is still the overly concerned mother, telling her daughter to support her husband, be a good wife, and be careful of the pitfalls. Marguerite is a very whole, full, and spiritual character." Many of the film's thematic points about hope and support find an effective embodiment in Marguerite.

"Lord, I'm a little tired. I sure could use some help."—Rev. Henry Biggs who gets his prayer answered

Another addition to the original is the music. In spite of the holiday favorite on which *The Preacher's Wife* is based, the real focus of the new version falls as much on the music as on the drama of Henry and his crisis. Stories about the production of the film emphasized the music sessions that ran on past the director's call to cut. "I just kept the cameras rolling," Penny Marshall said. "We loaded magazine after magazine of the film, as if we were shooting a documentary. It was dizzying." Whitney Houston also described the recording of the songs: "At that point, we had all been working so hard for so long that these scenes were a release. It was a spiritual time. I truly believe the Holy Spirit came down and took over, because I saw people on the set—people you never dreamed would be touched—crying and sobbing. It made me think of the saying 'Weeping may endure for the night, but joy comes in the morning.'"

Dudley's angel handbook is another clever addition to the original script by Robert E. Sherwood and Leonardo Bercovici. This device reveals character by showing Dudley's charming unfamiliarity with earthly customs. It also suggests the authority Dudley represents, and he consults his handbook with complete confidence: perhaps rightly so, since in one scene he even finds the Windows 95 logo pictured among other icons in its pages. The handbook also facilitates the final conflict between Henry and Dudley. When Dudley fussily consults the book once too often, a jealous and angry Henry tosses it into the fireplace. Dudley's shock ("Now you've done it.") registers on the audience as a sign of how badly Henry's faith has become endangered. With the angel handbook the scriptwriters make economical use of a seemingly slight prop.

On the other hand, the film's movement lumbers a bit under the added weight of all the songs and the subplots. The scene in which the boiler explodes, for example, is protracted so as to include more singing by Houston and the choir, but the cutaway shots to the overworked boiler merely belabor the point of the church's impending financial crisis. The repeated early meetings between Dudley and Henry before Dudley shows up as Henry's assistant also risk overworking the idea of Henry's having to be convinced that angels exist. The point of Henry's exasperation and Dudley's smiling patience has been conveyed long before these scenes conclude. At times like these, director Penny Marshall could have streamlined the action somewhat and sharpened the sense of drama by cutting some extraneous passages.

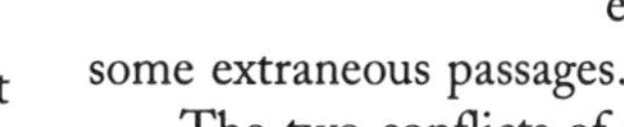

The two conflicts of the love triangle and the need to save the church are resolved separately. First, Julia and Dudley meet in a room adjoining the auditorium of the church as the children perform their Christmas musical. He tells her that he must go, and her sorrow at his departure is suddenly interrupted by a crisis onstage. The child singing the part of the Virgin Mary has run off, and Julia must step in

AWARDS AND NOMINATIONS

Academy Awards 1996 Nominations: Best Original Score (Zimmer)

at the last moment to sing her song. Dudley watches offstage with mixed emotions. Some reviewers faulted the film for a lack of chemistry between the stars, and this scene's failure to find a satisfying climax may be an example. In the second conflict, Dudley himself visits Joe Hamilton to persuade him not to continue with the destruction of the church. He tries to penetrate Hamilton's heart hardened by his wealth and success to remind him that St. Matthew's will serve the community better than a mall and some tennis courts.

One of the best aspects of the film is the idea that these concluding scenes bring out, that a church like St. Matthew's is the glue that holds a neighborhood together. With regard to Joe Hamilton, this idea questions whether anyone, regardless of success, can really leave his roots. Hamilton arrives at church the next morning for the Christmas service. Henry's sermon is cued up on the TelePrompTer, and cameras are in place to televise his words to the community as Hamilton has intended. After Dudley's visit of the night before, however, Joe is receptive to the music and the sermon that Henry improvises after rejecting the carefully scripted text. "When we love someone, we are really loving God," Henry says. He talks about forgiveness and reconciliation to the warm responses of the congregation. The combination of the preaching and the music have done their work. On the way out of church, Joe greets Henry and assures him that he will influence the town council to save the church. Dudley stands by smiling in satisfaction, but though Henry and Julia see him, they fail, as Dudley had told them they would, even to recognize him now that his work is done.

—Glenn Hopp

CREDITS

Henry Biggs: Courtney B. Vance
Julia Biggs: Whitney Houston
Dudley: Denzel Washington
Marguerite Coleman: Jenifer Lewis
Joe Hamilton: Gregory Hines
Britsloe: Lionel Richie
Beverly: Loretta Devine
Jeremiah: Justin Pierre Edmund

Origin: USA
Released: 1996
Production: Samuel Goldwyn, Jr. for the Samuel Goldwyn Company and Parkway Productions and Mundy Lane Entertainment; released by Touchstone Pictures
Direction: Penny Marshall
Screenplay: Nat Mauldin and Allan Scott; based on the screenplay *The Bishop's Wife* by Robert E. Sherwood and Leonardo Bercovici
Cinematography: Miroslav Ondricek
Editing: Stephen A. Rotter and George Bowers
Art direction: Dennis Bradford
Set decorator: George DeTitta
Music: Hans Zimmer
Song: David Wolfert (music), Sandy Linzer (lyrics), "I Believe in You and Me"
MPAA rating: PG
Running Time: 125 minutes

REVIEWS

Entertainment Weekly. December 20, 1996, p. 53.
New York Times. December 13, 1996, p. B16.
Newsweek. December 23, 1996, p. 68.
People. December 23, 1996, p. 105.
Sight and Sound. March, 1997, p. 61.
Time. December 16, 1996, p. 73.
USA Today. December 13, 1996, p. 4D.
Variety. December 9, 1996, p. 102.
Wall Street Journal. December 13, 1996, p. A12.

Primal Fear

Sooner or later a man who wears two faces forgets which one is real.—Movie tagline

"A first-rate thriller! Spellbinding, heart-stopping suspense!"—Ron Brewington, *American Urban Radio*

"Prepare for a primal jolt. I'll do you a favor and not even hint at the genuinely shocking twist."—Guy Flatley, *Cosmopolitan*

"A riveting, smart thriller that keeps you guessing. Richard Gere is superb."—Veronica Mixon, *Philadelphia Inquirer*

"A tense thriller."—Bruce Williamson, *Playboy*

"A classic sit-on-the-edge-of-your-seat suspense film with a brilliant double-twist ending."—Paul Wunder, *WBAI-TV*

Attorney Martin Vail (Richard Gere) takes on the controversial murder trial of Aaron Stamplers (Ed Norton) in the suspenseful *Primal Fear.*

Box Office: $56,116,183

Director Gregory Hoblit is no stranger to the world of cops and lawyers. He won four Emmys for producing "Hill Street Blues," another for producing the made-for-television film "Roe vs. Wade," another for producing "L.A. Law" and still two more for directing the two-hour pilot for the same show. His ninth and most recent Emmy came for producing "NYPD Blue." So, it's no surprise then that when he turns his talents to the big screen for the first time, he would take on author William Diehl's best-selling novel, the first in a trilogy featuring the character of Chicago lawyer Martin Vail. It also shouldn't surprise then that the director's TV style shows through. But so too does his expertise with the genre.

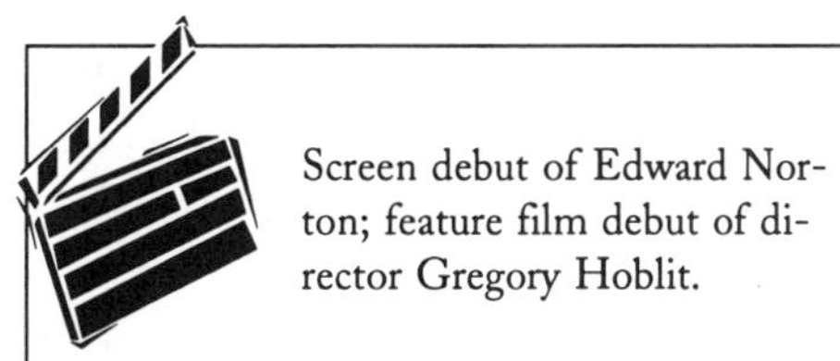

Screen debut of Edward Norton; feature film debut of director Gregory Hoblit.

Martin Vail (Richard Gere) is a limelight loving-lawyer. Where some attorneys gain a reputation for chasing ambulances, Vail chases magazine covers. At one time he used to work for the District Attorney's office, but now he's out on his own as a defense attorney defending some of the most famous (and scummy) criminals. When asked why he does this, Vail replies, "The money's nice. It's very, very nice." But early on, we learn it's more than just the money. Vail likes to see his name in headlines; he loves the publicity of controversial cases; he thrives in the spotlight of media questions.

That's why when Vail sees a live TV news broadcast about the gruesomely violent murder of Chicago's archbishop his self-promotion instincts immediately kick in. When one adds that media helicopters are watching as the police chase a blood-covered suspect, then one knows Vail will chase the suspect himself in order to defend him. If the suspect can get on TV, then so can Marty.

But what a surprise awaits Vail. The suspect turns out to be a shy, stuttering southern boy, Aaron Stampler (Edward Norton), who is so self-effacing that even Vail, despite all the evidence to the contrary, becomes convinced that there is more to his story than is being told. What is known is that Aaron was begging on Chicago's lower Wacker Drive when he was "rescued" by the Archbishop who took him to Savior House where he also sings in the choir. Aaron thinks of the Archbishop as a father figure, for heaven's sake, how could he possibly have murdered him? As for Aaron's explanation as to why he was covered in the Archbishop's blood, all he can say is that he is prone to blackouts ("I lose time," according to Aaron) that started when he was twelve back in Kentucky. Surely there was someone else in the

AWARDS AND NOMINATIONS

Academy Award 1996 Nominations: Best Supporting Actor (Norton)
Golden Globe Awards 1997: Best Supporting Actor (Norton)
Los Angeles Film Critics Association 1996: Supporting Actor (Norton)
National Board of Review 1996: Best Supporting Actor (Norton)

room. Now Marty sets out to find out who that someone might be, or at least to find out what really happened.

Championing the prosecution's side of this confrontation is Janet Venable (Laura Linney) of the District Attorney's office. But this is more than just another assignment for Janet. Martin and Janet had, in her words, "a one night stand that lasted 6 months," but their relation frayed when Marty left his government job in favor of finding his own fame and fortune while Janet stayed on. Now she feels she has something to prove and can and do so by defeating Vail in this trial.

Also treading in the background of Martin's life are his former (and Janet's current) boss, John Shaughnessy (John Mahoney), who seems to revel in his power and also seems to be involved in a shady land development deal which the Archbishop squashed; a shadowy underworld figure named Joey Pinero (Steven Bauer) whom Vail is also defending and who tips him off to the problems of an hispanic alderman caught up in the land deal; the trial's judge, Miriam Shoat (Alfre Woodard), who has no love for Vail's showboating ways; and Vail's two assistants, Tommy Goodman (Andre Braugher) and Maura Tierney (Naomi Chance).

"I don't have to believe you. I don't care, I'm your attorney."—Martin Vail to Aaron.

CREDITS

Martin Vail: Richard Gere
Janet Venable: Laura Linney
Aaron Stampler: Edward Norton
Shoat: Alfre Woodard
Shaughnessy: John Mahoney
Molly: Frances McDormand
Yancy: Terry O'Quinn
Goodman: Andre Braugher
Pinero: Steven Bauer
Stenner: Joe Spano

Origin: USA
Released: 1996
Production: Gary Lucchesi for a Rysher Entertainment production; released by Paramount
Direction: Gregory Hoblit
Screenplay: Steve Shagan, Ann Biderman; based on the novel by William Diehl
Cinematography: Michael Chapman
Editing: David Rosenbloom
Music: James Newton Howard
Production design: Jeannine Oppewall
Art direction: William Arnold
Costume design: Betsy Cox
Sound: Steve Cantamessa
MPAA rating: R
Running Time: 129 minutes

But most important of all is Dr. Molly Arrington (Frances McDormand), a psychiatrist who spends hours interviewing Aaron in the hopes of unlocking the mystery of who really killed the Archbishop. As to what she discovers, all that should be told is that the revelation is not really a surprise—which can make a viewer feel as if there's not much to the plot. After all, with the assumed murderer behind bars early in the film, there's not much suspense going on here. However, there is a punch at the end that even the most mystery-solving viewer may not have seen coming.

What makes *Primal Fear* more than just another crime-and-trial movie is one actor . . . and it's not Richard Gere. Yes, Gere does his usual yeoman job of portraying a slick and devious character, but we've seen him play this before. If anything is against type in this film for Gere it's the way Vail seeks out publicity while Gere avoids it as much as possible. Nor is it the acting of Laura Linney, last seen in *Congo.* Her character could have been played by dozens of actresses, and the fact that Janet and Martin were once at item is almost an annoying subplot rather than something integral to the story. Nor is it the numerous well-known secondary characters. Mahoney, Woodard, McDormand, Bauer, et al bring authenticity to their roles, but they're not the reason to go see *Primal Fear.*

What everyone is talking about in *Primal Fear* is the feature film debut of Edward Norton as Aaron Stampler. Chosen after an extensive casting search in the U.S., Canada and Great Britain, this 1991 graduate of Yale University (with a degree in history) beat out all contenders. It is safe to say that if Vail and the audience had never bought Norton's Stampler, if they never believed for one instant that he wasn't the innocent choirboy, then they probably would have begrudged buying their tickets to the film. But Norton offers us such a convincing portrayal of the guileless soul caught in a web beyond his control that we, like Vail, are sure he's innocent. It is this believability that makes the film's ending all the more powerful. It is a debut not to be missed.

—Beverley Bare Buehrer

REVIEWS

Boxoffice. May, 1996, p. 71.
Chicago Tribune. April 3, 1996, p. 1.
Entertainment Weekly. April 12, 1996, p. 44.
Los Angeles Times. April 3, 1996, p. F1.
New York Times. April 3, 1996.
Rolling Stone. April 18, 1996, p. 78.
Time. April 15, 1996, p. 100.
USA Today. April 3, 1996, p. 7D.
Variety. April 1, 1996, p. 54.

The Proprietor

"A haunting, mesmerizing masterpiece and one of the year's best and most powerful pictures."—Susan Granger, *CRN International*

"Witty, warm and wise, a profoundly touching comedy. Beautifully played by a wonderful ensemble. The great Jeanne Moreau deserves to be remembered at Oscar time."—Joanna Langfield, *The Movie Minute*

"One of the finest films of the year. A moving, provocative, and highly entertaining masterpiece. Don't miss it."—Paul Wunder, *WBAI Radio*

Box Office: $111,636

In *The Proprietor,* a renowned French novelist, Adrienne Mark (Jeanne Moreau) has settled in New York City after World War II. She is Jewish, and her mother (Charlotte De Turchheim), a celebrated Parisian couturier lost her life when she was betrayed to the Nazis. When her mother's old apartment is put up for sale in Paris, Mark decides to return after an absence of thirty years. It is not an easy decision. She has made a successful life in America and memories of her European past are painful. She has never quite understood her mother's feelings during the war, or why her mother's lover turned her over to the Nazis. But America has also changed, and Mark feels less secure in the country which was once so welcoming to immigrants and refugees. On balance, then, she will try to come to terms with the Holocaust, and take possession of her rightful inheritance. It is in this sense, perhaps, that Mark is "the proprietor" referred to in the film's title.

The Paris apartment used for Adrienne's home is that of acclaimed interior designer, the late Madeleine Castaing.

Screenwriters Jean-Marie Besset (a French playwright) and American dramatist George Trow complicate Mark's story with several subplots that are not very well integrated into the action and which suffer from gross sentimentality. First, there is the story of the bond between Mark and her housekeeper, Millie Jackson (Nell Carter). Carter is a competent actress and attacks her role with enthusiasm. But there is not much for her to do except to be critical when Moreau is being obstinate or obtuse, or sympathetic when Moreau is suffering. And it is rather embarrassing to watch the mistress-maid dialogues. Millie is such a cliche—the salt-of-the-earth black woman who has striven and suffered too. The worse moment comes when Carter sings an a capella version of the stage act Millie once performed. It is really just a poor excuse to take advantage of her singing talents.

Then there is the subplot of the American remake of the French film based on Mark's famous novel *Je m'appelle France.* Virginia Kelly (Sean Young), a vulgar American producer does not have the slightest sensitivity. She has never seen the French film she wants to remake. Instead, she has seen the tawdry American version. So she is producing a remake of a remake. Mark is brought in to talk sense to Virginia. She is seconded by Patrice Legendre (Marc Tissot), the son of an old friend who was also the director of the original French film adaptation of Mark's novel. Patrice is appalled at Virginia's ignorance and lack of taste. He fears she will trash his father's original film. Gradually, Mark helps Patrice to see that Virginia is malleable and that she can learn to do the right thing. Patrice falls in love with Virginia when he realizes that for all her faults she has a good heart. The cliches tumble over each other in one unconvincing episode after another. For one thing, the scene from the original French film—the one that is supposed to be a tasteful rendition of Mark's novel—is ludicrous in its pretentious and portentous atmosphere.

Sean Young's one-note acting makes it nearly inconceivable that Patrice should fall in love with her. When he takes her to his ailing father's bedside, the father pronounces that Young is "adorable"—this in spite of the fact that she looks overweight and wears dresses that do not become her awkward looking figure. Perhaps the stroke that Patrice's father has suffered has impaired his eyesight. The only reason Virginia and Patrice fall in love is because the plot says they have to.

Jeanne Moreau has an elegance and grace that still make most of *The Proprietor* watchable. Her raspy voice and wry remarks give the film a color and texture it otherwise lacks. But nothing in script presents a convincing portrayal of a writer. We believe that Adrienne Mark is an institution because Jeanne Moreau is an institution. This is lazy and perhaps even cynical moviemaking.

The only outstanding performance comes from Sam Waterston as a voracious dealer eager to scoop up all the possessions in Mark's New York apartment and auction them off. He is like a Dickensian character, powerfully motivated by his drive to acquire. The few truly amusing moments in the film come from his bravura turn.

The serious story that is supposed to undergird *The Proprietor* is clumsily presented. Mark sees a doorman and his appearance reminds her of a Nazi in uniform. How strange. The woman has been living in New York for thirty years and suddenly doormen begin to look like Nazis?

The scenes of Moreau entering Paris are more provocative. Talking with a taxi driver, she realizes the racism that killed her mother is still alive. Now it is the Arabs who are hated, and who the taxi driver would like to run over. When the taxi driver gets involved in an altercation with Arabs, Moreau gets out of the car in disgust. Later she becomes a controversial figure because she speaks out against such bigotry. On French television, a right-winger makes reference to her Jewishness, calling her Markowsky (her mother's Jewish name).

> There is a very circular aspect to this story, in that memories continue to relive themselves until they are resolved, and in the process, they shape our present and our future."—Ismail Merchant

Such scenes are handled well but they add nothing new to the story of contemporary France or of the country's role in the Holocaust. Indeed, Moreau's ill-defined quest to deal with her tragic past trivializes the subject. This aspect of the film is never allowed to develop. Instead, the plot is diverted once again when Mark's young American admirer, William O'Hara (Josh Hamilton), turns up. Why he finds Mark interesting, and why she tolerates his puppy-like advances, are hard to fathom. Moreau seems so self-contained that she hardly needs this kind of fan-like adoration. And O'Hara, though he is impressed with Mark's fame and writing, has no special reason for looking her up. This subplot, like the others, simply defuses the film's dramatic impact.

The Proprietor is a shocking lapse for the Merchant-Ivory team, justly lauded for films such as *The Remains of the Day* (1993) and *Howard's End* (1992). Ismail Merchant is usually the producer and Ivory the director. This time Merchant as director displays a startling lack of control. A clever director might have made up for some of the woeful script deficiencies by stimulating good performances. But for the most part, the actors seem lost in the maze of competing stories. It is as if each subplot is offered as a substitute for the last one in a desperate effort to rescue a muddled script.

Several reviewers have suggested that *The Proprietor* will only appeal to an art house crowd. But it is difficult to see how even on those terms the film can be accepted. Audiences familiar with the history of foreign cinema will surely be disappointed by this mishmash. After all, they have seen Moreau in classics such as *Jules and Jim* (1962), *Diary of a Chambermaid* (1964), and *The Victors*. If *The Proprietor* were simply a minor film, it might escape the critical censure it has already earned. But instead it explores its portentous subjects ineptly.

It is of not that a good movie might not have been made out of this material. *The Proprietor* is, after all, asking serious questions about the nature of human commitment, about where we belong, and how a sense of place establishes identity. Mark wants somehow to honor and to understand her mother, and to relate that quest to her life's work as an artist. Moreau might almost have been able to rescue this film singlehandedly if she had somehow seemed more vulnerable and less in charge of every scene. Her supreme self-confidence is a joy to watch, but in this case it also deadens the drama. If she realized just how terrible the script was, she may have opted for a serene demeanor that at least knit together certain scenes and reduced the film's virtually hysterical search for a convincing, unifying theme.

It is, of course, presumptuous to speculate on what Moreau thought she was doing in this film. But the results are so flawed that critics are forced to ponder what went wrong. Supposedly Adrienne Mark is coming out of a long dry spell. She is writing again because she has found a theme that takes her back to Paris and presumably back to the origins of whatever made her a writer. It is unfortunate that *The Proprietor* cannot portray that theme which remains only a figment of Mark's imagination.

—Carl Rollyson

CREDITS

Adrienne Mark: Jeanne Moreau
Harry Bancroft: Sam Waterston
Millie Jackson: Nell Carter
Virginia Kelly: Sean Young
Eliott Spencer: Christopher Cazenove
Franz Legendre: Jean-Pierre Aumont
Willy Kunst: Austin Pendleton
William O'Hara: Josh Hamilton

Origin: USA
Released: 1996
Production: Humbert Balsan, Donald Rosenfeld for a Merchant Ivory production; released by Warner Bros.
Direction: Ismail Merchant
Screenplay: Jean-Marie Besset, George Trow
Cinematography: Larry Pizer
Editing: William Webb
Music: Richard Robbins
Production design: Bruno Santini, Kevin Thompson
Costumes: Anne de Laugardiere
Art direction: Bernadette Saint-Loubert
Sound: Larry Loewinger, Didier Sain
Casting: Frederique Moidon
MPAA rating: R
Running Time: 113 minutes

REVIEWS

Boxoffice Online. October 8, 1996.
Chicago Tribune. October 18, 1996, p. 5.
Los Angeles Times. October 9, 1996, p. F4.
New York Times. October 9, 1996, p. C17.
Variety. October 10, 1996.
Village Voice. October 22, 1996, p. 78.

Purple Noon; Plein Soleil

Passion at Ten. Envy at Eleven. Murder at Noon.—Movie tagline

"Highly entertaining . . . suspenseful!"—*CBS Radio, Los Angeles*

"First-rate thriller!"—*Chicago Tribune*

"An edge-of-your-seat movie."—*Philadelphia Daily News*

"Hypnotic!"—*San Francisco Examiner*

Box Office: $640,945

Rene Clement's *Purple Noon/Plein Soleil* is a worthy re-release of a stylish thriller little known in this country. Restored under the supervision of Martin Scorsese and Robert and Raymond Hakim, and seen in its original format for the first time since 1960, *Purple Noon* proves to be a technically proficient thriller worthy of Hitchcock, with homoerotic undercurrents reminiscent of the master's *Strangers on a Train* (1951). Not surprisingly, both are based on novels by Patricia Highsmith.

Purple Noon also provided a career-making role for Alain Delon as Highsmith's "amazing Mr. Ripley." Delon is by turns deferential, sycophantic, calculating, and seductive, and *Purple Noon* made him a star in Franee. Also excellent are Maurice Ronet, best known for his role as the suicide in Louis Malle's *The Fire Within* (*Le Feu Follet*) (1962), and French pop singer Marie Laforet, in her film debut.

Hewing closely to Highsmith's *The Talented Mr. Ripley, Purple Noon* opens on lazy American playboy Philippe Greenleaf (Ronet) sucking up drinks and atmosphere in Rome's teeming cafes. Philippe's protege, Tom Ripley (Delon), tags along. Ripley has, supposedly, been sent by Philippe's father in San Francisco to bring his errant son home for a bounty of $5000. Tom watches as the charismatic Philippe picks up women, hustles for money, and treats with cavalier indifference his long-suffering French girlfriend, Marge (Laforet), an art-history student writing her thesis on Fra Angelico.

Ripley appears to be very much in Philippe's shadow, but soon reveals to the audience that he has bolder plans to steal not only his friend's girl, but also his identity. When Philippe and Tom return to the town of Mongibello after a five-day bender to see Marge, Tom tries out Philippe's clothes and even imitates his voice in front of a mirror while Philippe and Marge have sex off-screen. Ever the transient playboy, Philippe suggests the three of them take his boat to the Sicilian coastal town of Taormina, where he has an apartment.

On board Philippe's sailboat, Tom relates to Marge how he worshiped Philippe as a teenager, and how Philippe's father hated him. Funny, then, remarks Marge, that his father sent you to find him. Marge is also perturbed by Tom's and Philippe's closeness, even as Philippe barks orders to Tom in an escalating game of dominance and submission. When Marge remarks to Philippe that he treats Tom terribly, he responds that he is merely testing Tom to see how far he can be pushed. Philippe promises Marge that they'll get rid of Tom, and that they will be able to spend time alone.

The next morning, Tom—supposedly inadvertently—allows himself to be cut adrift in the sailboat's emergency skiff while Philippe and Marge have sex. By the time Philippe and Marge rescue him, Tom is semi-conscious with a bad case of sunstroke. "What kind of game is this?" Marge wants to know. Philippe answers that all the stories Tom has told about their childhood are made up. Marge tells Tom they will have to part ways once they reach Taormina.

Tom sneaks around the boat and snoops on Philippe and Marge as they engage in non-stop lovemaking, pretending not to see. When Philippe discovers that Tom has stolen his bank statements and confronts him, Tom admits to the theft and tells Philippe frankly that he may kill him. Philippe simply takes this as a further escalation of the game, and hides any sign of discord from Marge.

When Marge tries to read her thesis to Philippe, however, Philippe grows irritated and says he doesn't want to hear about it, whereupon Marge produces the earrings from the girl he picked up in Rome, which Tom has cleverly planted among Philippe's things. Philippe takes Marge's only copy of the thesis and tosses it overboard. Enraged, Marge gets off at the next port and leaves. Philippe says he must return to Mongibello to find her.

Once again at sea, Tom reveals to Philippe his plan: he will kill him, sign a letter of credit, and take on his identity. Philippe, still amused, asks Tom to do his imitation of him, even to imitate his signature. Philippe tries to buy Tom off with $12,500 for the watch given to him by Philippe's father. Suddenly, in a bravura action sequence, Tom stabs a genuinely surprised Philippe in the chest with a fish knife, then wraps the body in a tarpaulin and dumps it over the side of the boat.

Sailing back to Mongibello, Tom finds Marge and tells her that Philippe refuses to see her—thus beginning his seduction. She wants Philippe back, she says, but is glad Tom has come in his place. Because Marge assumes everything—that Philippe is back in Rome living the high life, that he has sent Tom to break up with her—Tom does not even have to make up a story for her benefit. And, giving Tom a perfect window of opportunity, Marge tells him she feels lost. As Tom removes Marge's things from the boat, Marge remarks that she must talk to Philippe about the remaining debt on the boat, and also how typical it is of him to have taken the typewriter and not his pajamas.

It is Tom, however, who has taken the typewriter. Tom sells the boat as Philippe Greenleaf and pockets the advance on it while the boat remains in escrow in Taormina, then checks into the Hotel Excelsior in Rome under Philippe's name. Tom carefully doctors Philippe's passport, and imitates Philippe on the phone with Marge, telling her to write him at American Express. Pleased that, in order to make Philippe jealous, Marge has lied that she has cheated on him with Tom, Tom-as-Philippe forbids Marge to come to Rome, or to return to Paris. Tom also types a letter to her from Philippe, and delivers it to her by hand in Mongibello. "It's so flat, insipid," says Marge. "He might as well be dead."

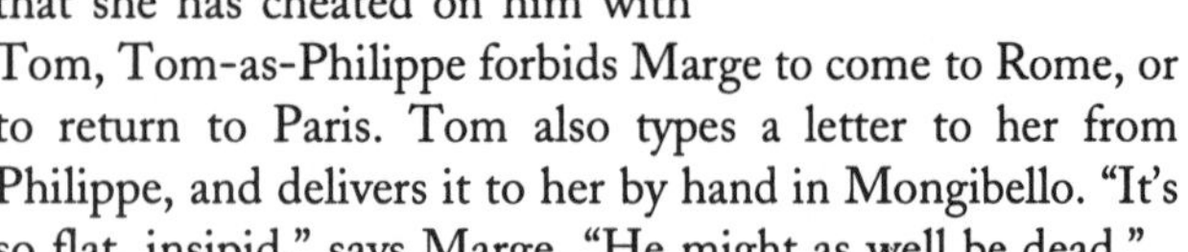

Film was renamed *Lust for Evil* when it made its U.S. TV debut.

Tom begins to revel in his deception, but when an old friend of Philippe's, Freddy Miles (Billy Kearns), comes by the hotel, he realizes that Tom has been posing as Philippe. Tom kills Freddy, and, in a perverse scene, cold-bloodedly cooks and eats a chicken dinner with the body still on the floor. The scene is one of Clement's best: Decae's disorienting camera work shows Tom's senses heightened by fear. Tom puts a cigarette in Freddy's mouth and walks the body downstairs as if Freddy is drunk, then leaves the body in a car.

The police arrive, but Tom escapes with his suitcase by rooftop. After withdrawing 10 million lire from Philippe's account, Tom calls the hotel room as Tom, and gets the inspector on the case, Riccardi (Erno Crisa), to bring him in for questioning. Tom dismisses the inspector's theory that Philippe killed Freddy, but Riccardi tells him Philippe was seen leaving the hotel with the victim.

His plan seemingly complete, Tom tells Marge that Philippe has had to flee, and he sends a suicide note to Philippe's mother, leaving all his worldly goods to Marge. Marge, in mourning, goes into seclusion in Taormina. Although Riccardi remains suspicious of Tom, Tom breaks through Marge's isolation, seducing her and telling her that Philippe never loved her.

Tom obliviously lies out on the beach, basking in the success of his seduction, as Marge, some distance away and out of earshot, pulls Philippe's boat into dry dock and discovers Philippe's body hanging off the propeller. The audience hears Marge's scream off-screen. In the final moments, Riccardi asks a maid to tell Mr. Ripley, still sunbathing, that he has a phone call.

Purple Noon benefits from a tightly wound adaptation of Highsmith's novel by Clement and Paul Gegauff, as well as atmospheric location shooting. The film was shot in Rome and on the Italian coast in Eastmancolor by legendary New Wave cinematographer Henri Decae, whose credits include Jean-Pierre Melville's *Bob le Flambeaur/Bob the Gambler* (1955), Malle's *Ascenseur pour l'Echafaud/Elevator to the Gallows* (1957), and Francois Truffaut's *Les Quatre Cent Coups/The Four Hundred Blows* (1959), all black-and-white films. Here, Decae proves himself a master of color as well. *Purple Noon*'s images often have the richness of travel posters of the period, and the film's visual lushness provides an appropriate backdrop for this tale of effete playboys, sailing, and murder.

Also extraordinary are the editing and sound, particularly in the shipboard murder sequence. Intercutting between Delon, Ronet, the waves, the spray, the rocking boat, and the creaking rigging, Clement creates a scene of suspense that ranks with any of Hitchcock's, Scorsese's or Spielberg's. (The scene seems a likely influence on the climactic scene of Scorsese's remake of *Cape Fear* [1992].)

With the exception of his *Jeux Interdits/Forbidden Games* (1952), Clement's work remains little-known in the United States. Poised on the cusp between the French films de qualite tradition of the immediate post-War era and the innovations of the New Wave-Cahiers crowd of Truffaut, Godard, and Chabrol, Clement was for the most part overlooked in this country, and derided in France for undertaking big-budget international projects such as *Paris Brule-T-Il?/Is Paris Burning?* (1966). The efforts of Scorsese and the Hakim brothers do much to rectify this neglect. With its technical prowess and perverse undertones, *Purple Noon* proves to be worthy of rank with Hitchcock's best films of the 1950's.

—*Paul Mittelbach*

CREDITS

Tom Ripley: Alain Delon
Philippe Greenleaf: Maurice Ronet
Marge: Marie Laforet
Mme. Popova: Elvire Popesco
Inspector Riccordi: Erno Crisa
Freddy: Bill Kearns

Origin: France
Released: 1960
Production: Raymond Hakim, Robert Hakim for a Paris/Panitalia/Titanus film; released by Miramax Films
Direction: Rene Clement
Screenplay: Rene Clement, Paul Gegauff; based on the novel *The Talented Mr. Ripley* by Patricia Highsmith
Cinematography: Henri Decae
Editing: Francoise Javet
Art direction: Paul Bertrand
Music: Nino Rota
MPAA rating: PG13
Running Time: 118 minutes

The Quest

A lost city. A man of destiny. A test of honor. Go the distance.—Movie tagline

Box Office: $21,685,669

The Quest a turning point for action-hero Jean-Claude Van Damme, since it marks his debut picture as director. Now, that takes real courage. One might argue that if Clint Eastwood can direct his own films, why not Jean-Claude Van Damme? The answer is obvious: Eastwood is older and far more experienced, and he has far greater range as an actor. Besides Westerns, Dirty Harry police thrillers, and the odd chimp movie, Eastwood has directed features dealing with jazz (*Bird,* 1988), Hollywood celebrities (*White Hunter, Black Heart,* 1990), and adultery (*The Bridges of Madison County,* 1995). By contrast, Van Damme is one-dimensional. His image is that of a kickboxer, and his genre is the martial-arts movie.

At least the first film he directed is solidly in the genre he knows best, and in fact he does a reasonably good job of directing the fight scenes. He needed to in order to protect his image. The reviews were mixed, of course, since any self-respecting reviewer would think twice before proclaiming "the Muscles from Brussels" a talented auteur. Those who favor the sort of pictures he makes seemed almost willing to call *The Quest* the *Citizen Kane* of martial-arts movies; but most reviewers could simply not tolerate the absurdities of the plot as it meanders from the United States to Thailand and then to the "Lost City" of Tibet, where everyone seems perfectly fluent in English (or at least as fluent as Jean-Claude Van Damme), so that something resembling the Olympic Games of martial arts can be announced in a language understood by American audiences.

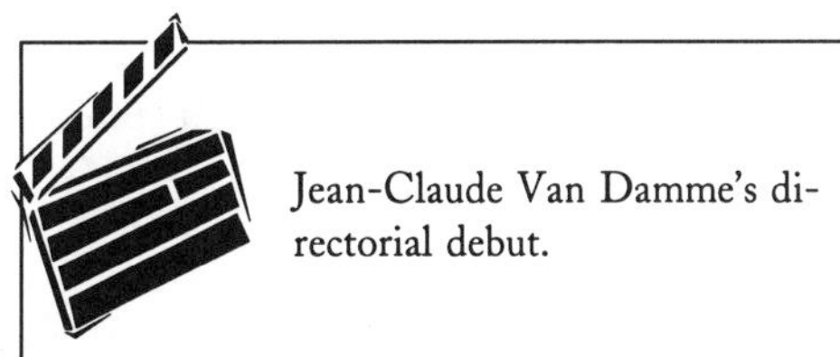

Jean-Claude Van Damme's directorial debut.

The film begins with Van Damme heavily made up as an old man who goes into a New York bar for a drink. In this clean, well-lighted place he finds a friendly bartender who offers to spike his coffee with a little whiskey. While he is waiting at a table, three thugs come in to cause trouble. "You don't want to do that," he quietly tells one of them, who attacks him and is immediately disabled and dispatched. After he then dismantles a second thug, the third leaves voluntarily. "How did you learn to fight like that?" the bartender asks, and Chris Dubois (Van Damme) proceeds to tell his life story in flashback.

The story begins in New York City in 1925. The young Dubois is seen made up as a pantomime performer on stilts who is a sort of Fagin to a group of thieving street urchins, giving the plot an "Oliver" twist. One of his wards steals a satchel filled with money belonging to the mob. Before long the police are in pursuit, and so are the mobsters, seeking revenge. Dubois eludes them on the docks by jumping on to a load of cargo being crane-loaded on a freighter. Exhausted, he falls asleep and awakens to find himself at sea, a stowaway. It turns out that the ship is loaded with rifles bound for Southeast Asia. Dubois is forced into slave labor but is eventually rescued by a band of pirates, led by a renegade Royal Navy officer, Edgar Dobbs (Roger Moore), who turns out to be too shifty to be trusted. Dobbs and his sidekick Harry Smith (Jack McGee) sell Dubois to a fight trainer named Khao (Aki Aleong), who coaches him in the art of Muay Thai (Thai kickboxing), for which Dubois has a natural talent.

After a period of indentured training, Dubois later catches up with Dobbs in Bangkok and confronts him about the way he was double-crossed. But the ever-charming Dobbs has a scheme, since he has got wind of a fabled Ghan-gheng competition scheduled to take place in the mysterious Lost City of Tibet, high in the Himalayas. The prize of this winner-take-all competition is a dragon cast entirely of gold. Only the best fighters in the world are invited to compete, however, and Dobbs cannot find the "Lost City" without a map. Fortunately, he meets Maxie Devine (James Remar), the American heavyweight champion, who has both an invitation and a map. They are also joined by Carrie Newton (Janet Gunn), an American reporter who wants to cover the competition. She is the film's token woman and adds absolutely nothing to the plot, other than the fact that she later writes a book called *The Quest.* There is no romantic subplot developed here, though Carrie flirts and flutters a bit.

So off they go, by truck, elephant, and, finally, on horseback, searching for the Lost City. Before they find it Maxie gets wise to the fact that the others are using him and challenges Dubois to a fight. After he gets kicked around, he quickly concedes his title to Dubois and gives him permission to fight in his stead. It's a little surprising to see that the heavyweight champ is such a chump, but the character is likable enough, as engagingly played by Remar. He does better with this role than Roger Moore does with the campy and devious Dobbs.

The final third of the film features the spectacle of the competition at the Lost City, the city of champions, each of whom has developed his own distinctive style of fighting, which adds exotic variety to the spectacle. The styles are eclectic: Muay Thai (Siam), Sumo (Japan), Shotokan Karate (Okinawa), Shaolin King-Fu (China), Boxing (England's "manly art of defense"), Savate (French kickboxing), Capoeire (Brazilian acrobatic kickboxing), Greco-Roman Wrestling, and Tae Kwon Do (Korea).

These basic styles are further embellished by national and ethnic characteristics. The Spanish fighter (Albanian-born Peter Malota), for example, choreographs his movements like a Flamenco danger. The fighter from Scotland wears kilts. Most of the combatants have in fact studied the martial arts. Peter Wong, the Chinese fighter, for example, won the All-China Wu Shu (martial arts) Championship in 1990 and 1991. Abdel Qissi (Khan, the Mongolian champion in the film) held the Belgian Amateur Boxing title from 1978 to 1980 and the Amateur Moroccan Boxing title from 1980 to 1983.

Khan, the mean Mongolian, defeats the Muay Thai champ (Jen Sung Outerbridge) and Kitao, the Sumo champ. It soon becomes apparent that the final championship bout will pit Dubois against the brutal Khan, a larger and more powerful man. By the time the final round takes place the stakes are high. While Dubois has been fighting his way to the top, Dobbs and Smith have attempted and failed to steal the fabled golden dragon. If Dubois wins, he will also save their lives.

CREDITS

Christopher Dubois: Jean-Claude Van Damme
Lord Edgar Dobbs: Roger Moore
Maxie Devine: James Remar
Carrie Newton: Janet Gunn
Harry Smith: Jack McGee
Riggi: Louis Mandylor
Khao: Aki Aleong
Khan: Abdel Qissi

Origin: USA
Released: 1996
Production: Moshe Diamant for an MDP Worldwide production; released by Universal Pictures
Direction: Jean-Claude Van Damme
Screenplay: Steven Klein, Paul Mones
Cinematography: David Gribble
Editing: John F. Link
Music: Randy Edelman
Production design: Steve Spence
Art direction: Chaiyan (Lek) Chunsuttiwat
Set direction: Kuladee (Gai) Suchatanont
Costume design: Joseph Porro
Sound: David Stephenson
Special effects supervisor: David Watkins
Casting: James A. Tarzia
MPAA rating: PG-13
Running Time: 95 minutes

The screenplay for this exotic spectacle, written by the relatively inexperienced Paul Mones as his second feature film, is spectacularly goofy. Janet Maslin of *The New York Times* accurately described it as "far-fetched" and "far-flung." Steven Rea of *The Philadelphia Inquirer* scoffed at the "Zen Madison Square Garden" in the Lost City, "populated by saffron-robed monks who seem to have a thing for guys with muscles," but as Stephen Hunter pointed out in the *Baltimore Sun,* "you don't go to a Van Damme movie for logic, you go for the fights, and the fights are pretty good."

For Kevin McManus of *The Washington Post The Quest* was "a recruitment film" for the martial-arts genre. Of course, the film is "mindless"—the final third is all action, hardly interrupted by dialogue—but it is also "pure fantasy and fun." There is no message here. The screenplay is uncontaminated by serious meditation. Its violent spectacle is staged as entertainingly as possible, at times balletic, at times operatic. Anyone who listens carefully to Randy Edelman's music will hear melodic echoes of *Les Miserables,* amusingly ripped-off.

In directing this kind of movie Van Damme knows exactly what he is doing. Richard Harrington of *The Washington Post* considered Van Damme "much smarter than his previous directors, constructing a set of encounters that are consistently fast, furious, and entertaining." Harrington believed that there were no surprises in *The Quest* "beyond the solid achievement of Van Damme's direction."

The film is carefully tailored to Van Damme's strengths. The story for example is mainly a variant on Van Damme's first film, *Bloodsport* (1988), directed by Newt Arnold for Cannon International, said to be based on the true story of Frank Dux, an American who travels to Hong Kong to enter an underground martial-arts competition; *The Quest* replicates this story, even including the reporter, but shifts the time frame back to the 1920s. Even so, it is not surprising that Van Damme makes his mark as an action auteur, since he had choreographed his fight scenes in films directed by others. If one looks for the contours of his auteur "signature," one will surely find the solid imprint of his chop.

—James M. Welsh

REVIEWS

The Baltimore Sun. April 26, 1996, E3.
Entertainment Weekly. May 10, 1996, p.56.
The New York Times. April 26, 1996, C8.
The Philadelphia Inquirer Weekend. April 26, 1996, p. 8.
Rolling Stone. May 16, 1996, p.72.
Variety. April 29-May 5, 1996, p. 132.
The Washington Post. April 26, 1996, B7.
Washington Post Weekend. April 26, 1996, pp.45-46.
The Washington Times Metropolitan Times. May 3, 1996, C16.

Race the Sun

From 0 to 60 . . . eventually.—Movie tagline

A dream can make all the difference under the sun.—Movie tagline

"*Race the Sun* is a definite must-see! A first-rate adventure, where human spirits soar to new heights!"—Ron Brewington, *American Urban Radio Network*

"It's hard not to feel inspired."—Doug Hamilton, *Atlanta Journal Constitution*

"An entertaining and inspiring come-from-behind fight-to-the-finish!"—Jeanne Wolf, *Jeanne Wolf's Hollywood*

"A lively and appealing variation on *The Karate Kid* formula."—Gary Arnold, *Washington Times*

Box Office: $1,945,552

Instead of exploiting the unique aspects of solar car racing, *Race the Sun* settles quickly into a pat rehashing of the formula used in *The Bad News Bears* (1976), *The Mighty Ducks* (1992), et. al. Start with a diverse group of kids who are losers—not because they're bad kids, but just because no one has inspired them or recognized their hidden talents. Bring in an adult who believes in them—in this case, Halle Berry as teacher Sandra Beecher. Toss in another adult to serve as skeptic, here James Belushi as Frank Machi. Create some snotty, rich competitors; add a conniving corporate type, make the odds as long as possible—and the rest is predictable.

The script, by Barry Morrow, plays like it was written by rote. The directing, by Charles Kanganis, is also strictly a paint-by-numbers affair. Berry and Belushi are both badly miscast, but Belushi at least develops a low-key schtick; Berry, however, is annoying. What saves the film is, as usual in these uninspired affairs, the cast of youngsters, who try their best to burst out of the stereotypical roles assigned them.

The roster of underachieving students includes four boys and four girls. The boys are Daniel Webster (Casey Affleck), a daydreaming designer who serves as the team's idea man; Eduardo Broz (Anthony Ruiviar), Daniel's menacing rival for team leadership, the muscle guy; Marco Quito (Dion Basco), the class clown; Gilbert Tutu (J. Moki Cho), the much-ridiculed fat kid who (guess what?) is a sensitive computer genius. The girls, whose roles are all underwritten, include Cindy Johnson (Eliza Dushku), the loose girl who is Daniel's stepsister; two friends named Uni and Oni, and Eduardo's girlfriend, whose part is almost non-existent.

Dushku, who vamps in sleazy black outfits, turns in the strongest performance as a bored teen who's tempted by booze and boys; the rest of the group talks in mild profanity but is squeaky-clean. Ruiviar strains mightily to break out of his swaggering, quick-tempered character. Affleck slurs his lines and seems far too dreamy to be effective as the team captain. Cho is wooden but oddly loveable, and the rest of the youngsters are serviceable.

That's more than can be said for Berry, who turns in an excruciating performance. Berry's uneven career includes strong, earthy portrayals in films such as *Losing Isaiah* (1995); here she is insufferably upbeat and vacuous. Her Ms. Beecher is supposed to be a woman escaping a failed marriage and starting over far from home, but it's a character devoid of depth and emotion. As a teacher who's going to whip her misbehaving students into line, Berry is utterly unconvincing; she's much too perky.

The film's worst scene is the one in which the students try to convince Beecher to accept their solar car project. Berry actually says: "I don't know. I'd have to fill out all these forms and apply for grants." Then she shrugs and agrees to do it. It's terrible dialogue and even worse acting. Once past that scene, Berry becomes little more than a cheerleader for the rest of the film, providing absolutely no insight or leadership to the students. When a problem arises, she throws up her hands and begs ignorance. It's a lightweight role and a lighter-than-air performance.

Belushi, as the shop teacher coaxed by Beecher into going along for the ride, comes to life occasionally. His surly, cynical characterization is a jarring foil for Berry's unbearable perkiness. In mid-film he suddenly becomes more Belushi-like. When asked by Berry to chaperone the kids' Australian trip, he deadpans: "Did you know that Australia has more poisonous snakes than anywhere on Earth?" But despite his efforts, there is absolutely no chemistry between Machi and Beecher, though the script wants there to be a gradual turning of distrust into friendship and a hint of romance.

The filmmakers fail to make solar-car racing the least bit interesting. The scientific or technical aspects get short shrift; Morrow clearly doesn't want to challenge his audience in any way. Daniel's first design fails, but we don't know why. He gets his inspiration for a new design from a cockroach alighting near his bed, so the successful car is called Cockroach. Why is this a clever design? We aren't told, because the filmmakers don't know.

The underdogs win the all-Hawaiian race because Daniel is also a crack weather forecaster who can tell from gazing at the sun that it will cloud up later in the day. He adds a battery to the car, making it slower but giving it more reserve power. When Marco drives the car to the finish, the battery cables fly off and he has to hold the battery connection with his hand, but most young viewers won't understand what he's doing.

During the Australian race, there's a promise of exotic dangers along the 2,000-mile highway from Darwin to Adelaide, but the only perils that materialize are a dust storm, unexplained physical effects of the heat and a near-collision with side-by-side oncoming trucks. Near the end, Uni (or is it Oni?) chirpily suggests using a technical change in a gear ratio; again, the film provides no explanation for why this is a great idea.

Of course, there are down-to-the-wire finishes in both races. To concoct worthy enemies to defeat, Kanganis's script plays heavily on racial sentiment. The Cockroach crew is mostly of Asian/Pacific extraction, except for Daniel and Cindy, who are "haoles" (the islanders' term for "whites"). Though haoles, Daniel and Cindy are accepted by the others because they are "lolos"—a term that is never defined clearly. At first it seems to mean "locals" (Daniel and Cindy were born and raised on the Big Island), but later it's defined as a self-derogatory term meaning "stupid" or "losers" or "quitters."

The enemies in the Hawaii race are a group of privileged white kids. If the film had bothered to provide a little more background or insight into the class divisions on the islands, the showdown would be more compelling. As it is, the enemies are supposed to be evil just because they are rich and white, just as their corporate sponsor is automatically demonized just because he represents a corporation.

For the Australian race, it's the kids against the world. The rival singled out to be derided and beaten is a cocky European champion named Hans, a stereotyped German near-Nazi. The ending pits the overweight Gilbert against Hans in a battle of the physically handicapped, non-white underclass versus the technician overlords. *Cool Runnings* (1994) had basically the same battle lines, but it deflated the class conflict with humor; *Race the Sun* is way too serious, creating cardboard enemies.

To fill in the film, Kanganis's script relies on a series of soap-opera conflicts that come and go willy-nilly. Daniel and Cindy are at odds over her drinking; Daniel and Eduardo are rivals for leadership; Uni bosses Oni; Oni and Gilbert fall in love; and Frank Machi reveals that Gilbert's father died saving Frank in a Navy submarine accident, making Gilbert his surrogate son. None of these threads is realized enough to constitute even a subplot; they just seem to be thrown into the film to fill time.

Despite the flat and uncreative tone of *Race the Sun,* the settings and the cars themselves remain intriguing. Too bad the filmmakers didn't have enough confidence in their audience to delve more deeply into the design methods and racing tactics of this growing sport. A film about solar cars still begs to be done; *Race the Sun* is only about playing it cute and safe.

—Michael Betzold

CREDITS

Sandra Beecher: Halle Berry
Frank Machi: James Belushi
Daniel Webster: Casey Affleck
Cindy Johnson: Eliza Dushku
Jack Fryman: Kevin Tighe
Eduardo Broz: Anthony Ruiviar

Origin: USA
Released: 1996
Production: Richard Heus, Barry Morrow for a TriStar Pictures production; released by Sony Pictures
Direction: Charles T. Kanganis
Screenplay: Barry Morrow
Cinematography: David Burr
Editing: Wendy Greene Bricmont
Music: Graeme Revell
Production design: Owen Paterson
Art direction: Richard Hobbs, Michelle McGahey
Solar car coordination: Michael Hendrum, Tapio Piituloinen
Costume design: Margot Wilson
Sound: David Lee
Casting: Sharon Bialy
MPAA rating: PG
Running Time: 99 minutes

REVIEWS

Boxoffice. May, 1996, p. 72.
Chicago Tribune. March 22, 1996, p. 2.
Entertainment Weekly. April 5, 1996, p. 62.
Los Angeles Times. March 22, 1996, p. F10.
New York Times. March 22, 1996, p. C12.
People. April 9, 1998, p. 19.
Variety. March 25, 1996, p. 67.

Ransom

Someone is going to pay.—Movie tagline

"A real stunner!"—Bill Diehl, *ABC Radio Network*

"White-knuckle filmmaking!"—Joel Siegel, *Good Morning America*

"A slam-bang thriller!"—Leah Rozen, *People Magazine*

"A tension-packed thriller that will shake your head and rattle your brain!"—Peter Travers, *Rolling Stone*

"Incredibly intense!"—Jeff Craig, *Sixty Second Preview*

"The most exciting thriller of the year!"—Paul Wunder, *WBAI Radio*

"A heart-pounding, nail-biting thriller!"—Pat Collins, *WWOR-TV*

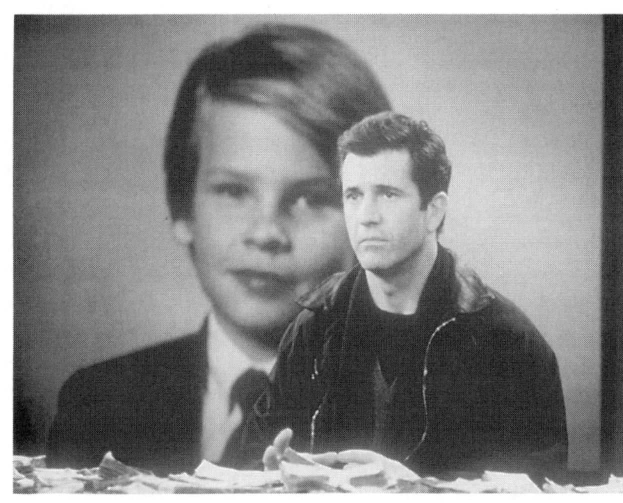

Grieving dad (Mel Gibson) turns a ransom into a reward against the kidnappers of his son in the thriller *Ransom*.

Box Office: $125,810,051

Who can think rationally when their only child is kidnapped? Who can suppress their emotions long enough to design the best plan of action? Who can see through the fog of fear and anger with enough clarity to take charge of the situation instead of being its passive victim. Who? Tom Mullen (Mel Gibson), Vietnam fighter pilot, self-made millionaire, and owner of Endeavor Airlines, that's who.

Mullen has it all: a New York city penthouse apartment overlooking Central Park, a thriving business, a beautiful wife (Rene Russo), and an adoring son (Brawley Nolte). But one day it is all threatened when kidnappers stealthily steal his son Sean from Central Park. When the gut-wrenching e-mail arrives with digital photos of a bound Sean and demands for $2 million in ransom, Tom has no choice but to call in the FBI who have, unfortunately for Tom, spent the last three years trying to bury him for bribery. They suspect Tom of giving money to Jackie Brown (Dan Hedaya) to suppress a machinists' strike at his airline. Jackie is now in jail and becomes suspect number one in the kidnapping. But he did not do it.

Loosely based on the 1956 film of the same name, which starred Glenn Ford and Donna Reed.

The real kidnappers are an odd group. Maris Connor (Lili Taylor) has been in the Mullen household as a catering/bartending temp during their parties. She is cold and calculating and seems to be in charge. She is assisted by two brothers, Clark (Liev Schreiber) and the younger Cubby (Donnie Wahlberg) Barnes, small-time crooks whose youngest member is also a bit dimwitted. But to keep them all safe from modern high-tech crime fighting tools is the alcoholic Miles (Evan Handler) a computer hacker who wreaks havoc on all the FBI's attempts to track, trace and entrap the kidnappers. But leading them all, the real brains and the force behind the troop, is a rogue cop who has been emersed in the cesspool of human malfeasance for so long that he is now a part of it, Jimmy Shaker (Gary Sinise).

Upon Tom's first fevered attempt to pay the Ransom, he follows Shaker's orders to the letter. It is a labyrinthine road that leads through swimming pools and stolen cars and ends in a quarry where, via two-way radio, Shaker tells Tom that when he hands over the money, he will be given the address where Sean can be found. When Tom comes face to face with Cubby, the kidnapper demands the money but is totally puzzled by Tom's insistence on an address. Now Tom realizes the kidnappers have no intention of returning Sean. The boy is dead if his father pays; he's dead if he doesn't.

Now Tom becomes the take-charge kind of guy that made him a millionaire in the first place. He goes on tele-

Golden Globe Award Nominations: Best Actor-Drama (Gibson)

vision, surrounded by the $2 million, and turns the tables on Shaker. "This is as close as you'll ever come to the ransom," Tom taunts them. Tom will not pay it to the kidnappers on the hope that Sean will be released, but instead offers it as a reward to anyone who turns in the kidnappers. And if Sean is not returned, he will double it so the kidnappers will be looking over their shoulders for the rest of their lives.

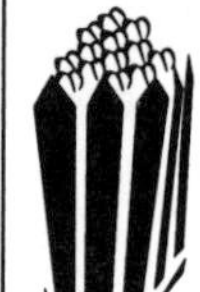

"Because you buy your way out of trouble. You're a payer. You did it once, and now you're gonna do it again."—Shaker to Mullen on why his child was kidnapped.

It is a daring and risky gambit, but despite his wife's misgivings and FBI agent Lonnie Hawkins' (Delroy Lindo) warning that he must rescind the offer, Tom believes Sean is dead no matter what by the two options (pay or not pay) offered by the kidnappers and the FBI. This third option he has invented at least seems to offer hope.

Now *Ransom* becomes a game of chicken played by two macho men who both demand to be in control, to have all the power. It devolves into a war of threats where emotions run high and so do the stakes. As to which, if either, of these men will be the first to pull his strategy to the side of a road that twists and turns where neither they nor the audience expects it to, is not something to be disclosed before seeing the film. To do so would defuse the excitement and suspense which will grip the viewer during the film's final and best section.

It is in this closing segment that *Ransom* rises above just being another action-drama. And this, in large part, is due to the skills of scriptwriter Richard Price (*The Color of Money* [1986], *Clockers* [1995]). *Ransom* owes a bit of its storyline to a 1956 film by the same name which starred Glenn Ford, Donna Reed, and Leslie Nielson and which, itself, was based on earlier television shows. (It also owes its visual theme—the Mullen's lofty penthouse and the kidnappers basement apartment—to Japanese director Kurosawa's *High and Low* (1962), another gripping kidnapping film.) Price did a two week rewrite of an updated script by Alexander Ignon which eventually turned into two more years of work, four rewrites, and on-set tune ups—not to mention an on-screen cameo.

But also helping *Ransom* rise above standard fare is an unusually adept and eclectic cast. From the world of the paradigm Hollywood release are such big-budget stars as Mel Gibson who here was allegedly paid $20 million for three months work. And while he may not have subverted production by doing typical mega-star antics which aren't his style, he did hinder it slightly when he had to undergo an emergency appendectomy and claim two Oscars for *Braveheart* (1995), both while shooting was underway. (This may explain why the film's shooting schedule fell so far behind that Buena Vista moved the film from its original August summer release date to November.) Gibson does an excellent job of making his character appear to be a paradoxical good guy. We're rooting for him, but we see the hints of ethical darkness at his edges. (Mad Max gets a penthouse?)

Ransom also mines the indie film actors list with such people as Lili Taylor (*Short Cuts* [1993], *I Shot Andy Warhol* [1996]) who delivers a chillingly callous portrayal of someone who is devoid of all compassion and morals. But perhaps the biggest surprise in *Ransom* is the actor who bridges these two sources, Gary Sinise. Seen in both small films (*Of Mice and Men* [1992] which he also directed) and large (*Apollo 13* [1995], *Forrest Gump* [1994]), Sinise, who usually plays a good guy, here plays a royal creep with ease and energy. An actor of versatility and intelligence, Sinise turns his contemplative demeanor toward evil instead of good. To listen as he compares Tom's penthouse life high above the dregs of humanity to that of the elite Eloi in H.G. Wells' *The Time Machine,* is positively riveting. He is a terrific counterpart to Gibson's Tom because they are both so similar and yet so different.

CREDITS

Tom Mullen: Mel Gibson
Kate Mullen: Rene Russo
Sean Mullen: Brawley Nolte
Jimmy Shaker: Gary Sinise
Agent Lonnie Hawkins: Delroy Lindo
Maris Connor: Lili Taylor
Clark Barnes: Liev Schreiber
Cubby Barnes: Donnie Wahlberg
Miles Roberts: Evan Handler
Agent Kimba Welch: Nancy Ticotin
Agent Jack Sickler: Michael Gaston
Agent Rhodes: Kevin Neil McCready
Wallace: Paul Guilfoyle
Jackie Brown: Dan Hedaya

Origin: USA
Released: 1996
Production: Brian Grazer and Scott Rudin for Touchstone Pictures; released by Buena Vista Pictures
Direction: Ron Howard
Screenplay: Richard Price and Alexander Ignon; from a story by Cyril Hume and Richard Maibaum
Cinematography: Piotr Sobocinski
Editing: Dan Hanley and Mike Hill
Music: James Horner
Production design: Michael Corenblith
Art direction: John Kasarda
Costume design: Rita Ryack
Set decoration: Susan Bode
MPAA rating: R
Running Time: 121 minutes

The other actors, like Rene Russo, who worked with Gibson in 1992's *Lethal Weapon 3,* Delroy Lindo (*Get Shorty* [1995], *Broken Arrow* [1995]), former New Kid on the Block singer Donnie Wahlberg, and especially 10-year-old Brawley Nolte (son of Nick) provide a realistic atmosphere in which Gibson and Sinise play their power game.

Holding it all together, however, is the constantly growing talent of one-time actor and now director Ron Howard. Howard started his directing career with sweet family films like *Parenthood* (1989), *Splash* (1984), and *Cocoon* (1985). As he developed he took on larger ensemble casts and added the dynamic of more tension in his story. Sometimes the tension was milder (*The Paper* [1994]) and sometimes it was harder hitting (*Backdraft* [1991]). With his Academy Award nominated *Apollo 13,* Howard gained the filmmaking respect he so richly deserved. (Oddly enough, when *Apollo 13* ran for its Oscar, one of its major competitors—and the eventual winner—was Mel Gibson's *Braveheart.*)

With *Ransom,* Howard's 12th feature film, he truly shows that he is one of Hollywood's premier directors. He seems to have found the secret to making films that are not only popular, but also good. His work is never trite and manages to capture the best of Hollywood filmmaking. Unlike other mainstream directors, Howard never assumes his audience is dumb nor does he use action as a substitute for an intelligent story. He puts before us a well-crafted film in which scenery, actors, script and camera work create a whole that is much greater than the sum of its parts.

The result is a film that is masterfully filled with cross-cutting camera work that keeps the tension high and keeps the film from becoming static, with actors who breathe life and believability into their characters, a story that keeps us guessing right until the end, sets that frame the "high" life of the rich against the "low" life of the criminals, and a director who knows how to pull it all together in the best Hollywood tradition.

—Beverley Bare Buehrer

REVIEWS

The Boston Globe. November 7, 1996.
Boxoffice Online. November 12, 1996.
Chicago Sun Times. November 8, 1996.
Chicago Tribune. November 8, 1996, p. 4.
Detroit Free Press. November 8, 1996.
Detroit News. November 8, 1996, p. 1D.
Entertainment Weekly. November 8, 1996, p. 47.
The Hollywood Reporter. November 4, 1996, p. 5.
New York Times. November 8, 1996, p. C1.
The New Yorker. November 11, 1996, p. 124.
Newsweek. November 11, 1996, p. 74.
People. November 18, 1996, p. 20.
Rolling Stone. November 28, 1996, p. 141.
Time Magazine. November 11, 1996.
USA Today. November 8, 1996, p. 1D.
Variety. November 4, 1996, p. 81.

Rendezvous in Paris; Les Rendez-vous de Paris

"Achieves a richness of the highest order!"—William Kelly, *Cover Magazine*

"Makes you want to go to Paris and fall in love."—Donald Lyons, *Film Comment*

"Wonderful!"—Graham Fuller, *Interview*

Box Office: $843,617

Eric Rohmer's films often involve characters moving from point A to point A1. The beauty is in the logic of the journey there. For Rohmer, the mystery, the very essence of life, is contained in the minute emotional tremors his characters undergo in their relationships with others—tremors which Rohmer records in precise detail. The tremors always add up to a detectable seismological change in character, in point-of-view, in outlook on life.

Rohmer has been tagged as a philosophically conservative filmmaker, and in the strictest sense, this is true: Rohmer's movies are a testament to a belief in evolutionary, not revolutionary, emotional change. (Rohmer's long-time affiliation with the French political center-right, an anomaly among French New Wave directors, is invisible in his films; rarely has a cinematic body of work comparable to Rohmer's been so studiously apolitical.) A Rohmer film is almost inevitably "about" a young man or woman vaguely, if not deeply, dissatisfied with his or her lot in life, yet uncertain how to change it, perhaps unaware that change is even an option. When the means of change does make itself manifest to the character in the form of an epiphany, the beauty of the change for the character is modulated by the irony of Rohmer's having laid out the inevitability of the change as the logical result of a buried need.

Rohmer's recent films—*Pauline at the Beach/Pauline a la Plage* (1982), *Summer/Le Rayon Vert* (1986), *Boyfriends and Girlfriends/L'Ami de Mon Amie* (1987)—all deal with young protagonists, usually in their twenties or younger, who possess a vague unease about their situation, but fail to see the root of it. Rohmer's technique is to gradually expose the characters to new options and revelations, usually romantic, until they are able to see and accept what they really need.

"Maybe one shouldn't reveal one's feelings, but that's so sad."—Esther

The three vignettes that make up *Rendezvous in Paris* are the distilled essence of the 76-year-old master's method. Each vignette is a variation on the theme of the follies and treacheries of love; each is shot in natural light, with the editing and camerawork kept as simple as possible. Yet the epiphany at the end of each episode is stunning, all the more so for its being absolutely logical.

In the first, "The Seven O'Clock Rendez-Vous," a young law student, Esther (Clara Bellar), suspects her lover, Horace (Antoine Basler), is cheating on her. She dismisses as jealousy the story told by her fellow student, Felix (Malcolm Conrath) that he has seen Horace at a cafe with another woman. But a talk with her friend Hermione (Cecile Pares) convinces her something is amiss. Hermione tells her to make Horace jealous. "Whenever I'm myself," advises Hermione, "it backfires."

At an open-air market, a flirt desperately tries to pick Esther up; at first she is not interested. On second thought, however, she tells the suitor to meet her at the same cafe, Dame Tartine, where Felix has told her Horace meets another girl. When she arrives home, Esther discovers that her boldness has cost her her wallet, which she assumes the flirt has stolen from her.

Aricie (Judith Chancel), another attractive young woman, arrives at the door later that afternoon with the wallet, which Aricie says she found in the open-air market. The two women make conversation and discover they have quite a bit in common—including that Aricie, too, has a rendezvous at Dame Tartine. They go there together, and Aricie tells her that the man she's meeting calls her four or five times a day, but she doesn't entirely trust him. Of course, when they arrive there, Aricie turns out to be the woman Horace meets regularly at the cafe. Esther sits down with them, and not only makes Horace jealous, but also breaks up with him. Horace runs out after her in vain, a chastened Aricie leaves Horace, and the flirt takes Aricie's place at the table and waits in vain for Esther. The vignette is essentially a series of coincidences, but through them, Esther discovers that her instinct, to mistrust Horace, is the right one. Her mistrust, and her yearning for someone she can trust, have simply been displaced for an afternoon onto the flirt.

The second episode, "The Benches of Paris," is the best and most perfect of the three; it is also Rohmer stripped down to the bare essentials. Through a series of walks in different parts of Paris over several seasons, two lovers reveal the adulterous nature of their relationship, make plans for the future, and ultimately break apart. The magic of Rohmer's touch is such that the break-up of the lovers never seems inevitable except in retrospect. Under Rohmer's direction, a real relationship actually seems to be unfolding before our eyes.

Each scene in the episode takes place in a different part of Paris. The first, in the Luxembourg Gardens, begins with the unnamed man (Serge Renko) telling the unnamed woman (Aurore Rauscher) that in suburban Bobigny he has twice the space of a comparable Paris apartment for half the cost. But the woman resists his pleas to break off with her boyfriend and move in with him. "Why leave my brilliant boyfriend with the great future for a teacher whose only ambition is to live in Paris when he retires?" she retorts teasingly. The woman also scolds him for trying to touch her in public, although he points out that she has let him do it before on the quays of the Seine. It turns out that the woman's fear is of being seen with him in *this* neighborhood: being spotted here by her boyfriend, she says, would be a "double betrayal. I wouldn't want him to see us in the same places where we did things. It means I have no imagination." Imagination turns out to be the fragile foundation on which the relationship is based.

Subtly, Rohmer reveals that this relationship is in fact a kind of negative, phantom image of the woman's primary relationship, taking place in the parts of Paris where the main relationship does not. (Significantly, the never-seen boyfriend, Benoit, is the most concrete character of the piece, and the only one with a name.) The would-be lovers—who have not yet consummated their union—smooch on park benches around the city; the woman, however, refuses even to set foot in the man's apartment. For the woman, who keeps stressing the importance of the imagination, this imaginary relationship allows her to distance herself from her boyfriend without having to commit to anyone else.

Finally, the woman sets up an assignation for them at a hotel during a weekend when her boyfriend will be out of town. When they arrive at the hotel, however, the woman sees her boyfriend going in with another woman. The man is delighted. But the woman, instead of running to her new lover, accuses him of trying to take advantage of her in a humiliating moment and abruptly leaves him. "You're the mirror image of Benoit," she tells him. "Without him you're nothing." The uncertain future of the man and the woman has been totally dependent on the uncertainty of the woman's relationship with Benoit. Once Benoit is removed from the equation, the rest of the relationship, in all its delicious ambiguity, dissolves. The would-be lovers' illusion of a shared future turns out to have been the only cement holding them together.

The third vignette, "Mother and Child 1907," takes its name from a painting at the Picasso Museum in Paris. A young painter (Michael Kraft) finishes a painting in his studio as a young Swedish interior decorating student (Veronika Johansson), new to Paris, arrives. A mutual friend, Anita, has set them up. The student is nice and extremely attractive, but the painter seems deadset on finding reason they're not compatible. She's a decorator; he's a painter. She finds his paintings sad; he says they're not. She finds his neighborhood sad and lacking in white; he says pastels aren't what Paris is about. She points out a gray tone she likes; he says it's not a "Paris gray."

They plan to visit the Picasso Museum, but the painter abruptly says that Picasso would upset him now that he's in a creative period. He suggests they meet that evening at La Coupole, the famous cafe, where she can give him her impressions.

Leaving her at the door of the museum, however, the painter is struck by another woman who passes him in the street. Lovestruck, he follows her into the museum. While she sits down and begins to sketch "Mother and Son" from 1907, the painter runs into his Swedish friend. He lies and tells her that he became obsessed by this Picasso and couldn't work until he got it out of his mind. The Swedish student says she prefers a later Picasso in another room because it has so much color. The painter, to impress the other woman, launches into a disquisition about the grotesqueness of the painting the Swedish student likes, and says that, by contrast, "Mother and Son" is the most significant Picasso canvas of the pre-Cubist period.

Leaving the Swedish student to her own devices, the painter strikes up a conversation with the other woman. It turns out she is a newlywed whose husband is a well-known publisher of art books; she leaves for Geneva with him in just a few minutes. In fact, she is not convinced of the historical significance of the painting; her husband is using it in an art book on the theme of mother and child. She tells the painter she is disappointed in him—that she thought he would turn out to be a professor, not a pick-up artist. Besides, she says, he and the blonde would make a good couple. He responds that he thinks they would make a better one.

The woman consents to see his paintings. He tries to explain to her his working methods, his desire to capture a certain type of light. The woman, however, is more curious about his distancing himself from the blonde. "She intimidates you," she tells him. The painter admits that as a student he went out with too many American and Swedish blondes and didn't like them, so now he puts up emotional barriers when he meets them. The woman surmises that his friend, Anita, who keeps setting him up, must be in love with him. The painter responds that this is probably true, but she knows he doesn't love her. Besides, he has made a vow to pursue only women to whom he is totally attracted. "But since fate isn't on your side," she says, "don't give up the blonde." He makes a pitch for her, but she tells him she loves painting too much to ever go out with a painter. "To make me happy," she tells him, "kiss the blonde again. Invite her to a party." The woman leaves to meet her husband, and steps out of the painter's life—having momentarily and unexpectedly helped the painter play out a mother-son dynamic in his life.

Having second thoughts about the Swedish student, the painter calls a friend and asks whether he can bring her to a party. But when he waits for her later that evening at La Coupole, she never shows up. Chastened, the painter realizes he has given up the real possibility of love for an ideal. He returns to his painting, saying, "Well, at least the day wasn't a total loss." Perhaps he can find in his painting the intangible ideal that eludes him in real life.

As in his previous films, Rohmer's technique is deceptively simple. His natural lighting, unfancy editing, and lack of background music allows his actors to play scenes in the most natural way possible. Rohmer also prefers to shoot his films in sequence, a technique which allows his actors to explore their characters in a relaxed manner. Rohmer also encourages improvisation and collaboration with his actors, much in the manner of Mike Leigh.

Rohmer's sole adornment in *Rendezvous in Paris* is the use of a Parisian musette-singer duo in the interstices of the film, between vignettes. Playing French *caf'conc'* classics and wearing traditional garb in the streets of modern Paris, the

CREDITS

Esther: Clara Bellar
Horace: Antoine Basler
The Woman: Aurore Rauscher
The Man: Serge Renko
The Painter: Michael Kraft
The Young Woman: Benedicte Loyen

Origin: France
Released: 1995
Production: Francoise Etchegaray for a Compagnie Eric Rohmer production; released by Artifical Eye Film Company
Direction: Eric Rohmer
Screenplay: Eric Rohmer
Cinematography: Diane Baratier
Editing: Mary Stephen
Music: Sebastien Erms
Sound: Pascal Ribier
Running Time: 100 minutes

duo ironically accentuates the timelessness of Rohmer's seemingly modern tales. Rohmer's intertitles for each vignette, using old-fashioned graphics, heighten this sense. At 76, Rohmer seems to be saying, yet, I've seen all these stories before—aren't the ways in which people experience them anew wonderful?

—Paul Mittelbach

REVIEWS

Detroit News. November 8, 1996, p. 3D.
New York Times. August 9, 1996, p. C8.
Sight and Sound. February, 1996, p. 52.
Variety. April 3, 1995.
Village Voice. August 13, 1996, p. 57.

The Rich Man's Wife

The price of wealth just went up.—Movie tagline

Box Office: $8,543,587

The Rich Man's Wife is a thoroughly pedestrian thriller overall. Now, as harsh a statement as that may be, it doesn't mean that the film is all bad. Writer/director Amy Holden Jones shows fine technical control over the proceedings, and, working with veteran cinematographer Haskell Wexler, the film has a thoroughly top-notch look to it. If Jones' script was as taut as the technical credits, perhaps the film would have risen above its unfortunately cliched roots.

The story concerns Josie Potenza (Halle Berry), who, at the film's outset, is shown making a statement to police detectives in a homicide. (The film flashes back as she tells her story.) Josie is a beautiful young woman married to an older wealthy man named Tony (Christopher MacDonald). Tony, a workaholic television executive, is also an alcoholic and a philanderer. Josie has been having an affair with a suave restaurateur named Jake Golden (Clive Owen). (Note: the corny name "Jake Golden" should be a tip-off that this is not going to be a groundbreaking suspense thriller.)

Josie decides to break off her affair with Jake and give it another go with Tony; she convinces him to take a trip to a remote cabin and try to rekindle their marital spark. Once there, Tony is called back to L.A. on business. Josie stays, and meets a slimy character named Cole (Peter Greene) at the local bar. He coerces her to acknowledge that sometimes she wishes her husband were dead. Cole offers to help her; she gets afraid of him; he forces himself on her; she gets rid of him.

Writer/director Amy Holden Jones got the idea for her story when her car broke down on a dark country road and she wondered what would happen if a stranger came along to help.

But a character with a scar on his face and only one name cannot be gotten rid of for long. Some months go by, and Tony and Josie have happily reconciled. But, Cole shows up in L.A., brutally murders Tony (this scene is gruesome, in keeping with America's penchant for gratuitous violence), and blames it on Josie. He blackmails her, saying he would tell the police that she asked him to do it back in that rural mountain bar. The rest of the film has to do with Josie's struggle against the evil Cole, resulting in the kind of person-in-distress thriller that audiences have seen in *Play Misty for Me* (1971), *The Hand that Rocks the Cradle* (1994), and countless others. Amy Holden Jones seems to go for a film noir effect at times, trying to evoke the feel of *Double Indemnity* (1944) or other stories where an innocent person was either duped into murder, or framed for a murder they didn't commit.

Perhaps the director/writer unconsciously allowed her film to be derivative of much that has come before it. And there is no harm in that. But *The Rich Man's Wife* is not quite entertaining enough to have its audience wish they were watching the films from which it is derived. An additional criticism made of the film by some critics is that it did not adequately deal with the inherent problem of murder within an interracial marriage. But in this day and age, perhaps writer/director Jones wished only to make a thriller and not a social polemic; and she shouldn't be faulted for wanting to make a potboiler that doesn't have a lot of social value.

Halle Berry is credible and strong as Josie, making her character believable with moments of vulnerability and of strength. Christopher MacDonald gives a thoughtful portrayal of a character who in other hands might be one-note. And speaking of one-note—Clea Lewis makes a hilarious one-note romp out of the character of Nora, Jake's ex-wife.

CREDITS

Josie Potenza: Halle Berry
Tony Potenza: Christopher McDonald
Jake Golden: Clive Owen
Cole: Peter Greene
Dan Fredricks: Charles Hallahan
Ron Lewis: Frankie Faison
Nora Golden: Clea Lewis

Origin: USA
Released: 1996
Production: Roger Birnbaum, Julie Bergman Sender for a Caravan Pictures and Hollywood Pictures production; released by Buena Vista
Direction: Amy Holden Jones
Screenplay: Amy Holden Jones
Cinematography: Haskell Wexler
Editing: Wendy Greene Bricmont
Music: John Frizzell
Production design: Jeannine Oppewall
Art direction: William Arnold
Costume design: Colleen Kelsall
Sound: Ed Novick
Casting: Nancy Klopper
MPAA rating: R
Running Time: 94 minutes

She plays it like a character in a "Saturday Night Live" sketch, and as different as hers is from the rest of the performances, Lewis provides the only completely fresh moments in this film.

As a director, Amy Holden Jones finds interesting cinematic pictures, such as the rainy playground in which Cole murders Tony. As a writer, she provides a vivid and surprising ending that belies the script's inherent cliches. If the story were different, and the film had been directed and acted with the same freshness brought by Clea Lewis and by Jones own surprise ending, this film would most definitely have been considered a winner. Clearly, this director/writer has the talent, and audiences can have hope that her next film will live up to her potential.

—*Kirby Tepper*

REVIEWS

Detroit Free Press. September 13, 1996.
Entertainment Weekly. September 27, 1996, p. 58.
Los Angeles Times. September 13, 1996, p. F6.
New York Times. September 13, 1996, p. C20.
People. September 30, 1996, p. 18.
USA Today. September 13, 1996, p. 4D.
Variety. September 16, 1996.

Ridicule

Wit is the ultimate weapon.—Movie tagline

"Full of heart, wit, originality, juicy performances and contemporary relevance."—Jay Carr, *Boston Globe*

"Fiercely entertaining!"—Andrew Sarris, *New York Observer*

"An elegant, scathing satire!"—Janet Maslin, *New York Times*

"A wicked, worldly spectacle!"—Bruce Williamson, *Playboy*

Box Office: $1,540,241

Ridicule is set in the cynical world of Louis XVI six years before the French Revolution. At this royal court in 1783 "vices are without consequence but wit can kill." Writer Remi Waterhouse and director Patrice Leconte's excellent film explores the refined style and moral shallowness of social climbing as a reformer tries to rise in favor at Versailles to accomplish some social good.

A pre-credit sequence acquaints the audience with the revenge that smolders below the tailored surface of the royal court. A dying marquis who can no longer speak sits confined to a chair before slightly open shutters, the only source of light in his room. (Leconte told his cameraman that he wanted "the strip of light to be so intense that it would seem like a laser beam. . . . It gave a threatening effect." In fact, nearly all of the interiors are shot in high-contrast lighting.) A recently exiled courtier slips into the shrouded room. "Where is your fine wit now?" he asks, quoting to the old man an insult he has never forgotten. Calmly, he begins to urinate on him. The cripple tries to cry out, but the courtier slips away again and tells the attendant that the marquis in his excitement has "forgot himself."

The film concerns the efforts of an engineer, Gregoire Ponceludon de Malavoy (Charles Berling) to obtain a grant enabling him to drain the mosquito-infested swamps of le

Dombes and thereby end the epidemics and fevers that ravage the peasant populations. To gain approval for such a project, however, Ponceludon must have the ear of Louis XVI (Urbain Cancelier), which means he must ascend the slippery ladder of courtiers and their favors. At the court of Louis XVI, wit is the needed currency to make such transactions and advancements. Ponceludon is even asked to document his family tree before he may gain entrance to Versailles. His early failures result in part from the scathing insensitivity of the elite, who remark indifferently that the mosquitoes feed on the peasants just as the aristocrats themselves do. Not only are the poor dying, but "they're boring," one wit sniffs in contempt.

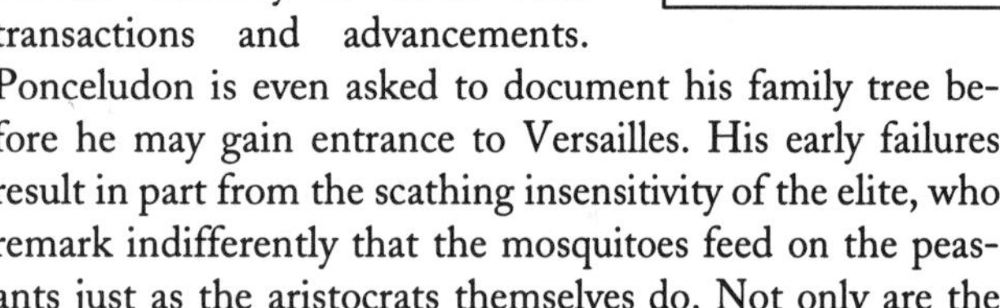

"... be witty, sharp and malicious and you'll succeed."—Bellegarde's advice to Malavoy

The Marquis de Bellegarde (Jean Rochefort), a kindhearted doctor, takes sympathy on the young engineer and offers him advice on how to win the favor of the jaded aristocrats. The doctor is a master at reading the code of the unwritten rules of court behavior, and a number of effective scenes show Bellegarde, who actually keeps an index of witticisms, schooling Ponceludon in proper manner. It is coarse to laugh with the mouth open, the doctor advises, but it is worse to laugh at your own joke. As they practice quips, Ponceludon wonders if he should be seeking "fruit from a rotten tree."

Bellegarde and his daughter Mathilde (Judith Godreche) humanize the film and provide a context of sincerity to set off the ruthless scheming of Versailles. The doctor lacks the malice of the courtiers, and his witty analogies come at no one's expense: when he bleeds a patient, he promises to read the blood the way a connoisseur would determine the vintage of a good wine; when he touches a current to a frog's muscle in a galvanic experiment, he likens wit to the crackle of electricity. Bellegarde exercises himself with memory games to keep his aging mind nimble and to postpone the dreaded day when he will no longer be fit to take part in the repartee. Mathilde also has a scientific mind and is even willing to marry an aged courtier so that she will have the money to continue her study of underwater life. A pre-contract is agreed upon in which her future husband Monsieur de Montalieri (Bernard Bheran) stipulates that twice a month he may enter her bed and that to protect her innocence she may never attend the court. On her father's estate, Mathilde shows Ponceludon a crude diving suit in which she places a rabbit to see if it can survive at the bottom of a well. She and Ponceludon gradually fall in love, but her engagement and his social climbing keep them apart.

The development of the film is driven by these two concerns of Ponceludon's efforts to gain the King's ear and his growing attraction both to Mathilde and to Madame de Blayac (Fanny Ardant), a powerful widow who can assist his advancement. The organization focuses on the push-pull Ponceludon feels between court and country, wit and sincerity, dissembling and candor. Mathilde eventually accuses him of enjoying the refined games and of wanting to become one of the elite himself. He gains cachet when he recognizes that the current lover of Madame de Blayac uses notes concealed in her fan as a cheat during an impromptu game of rhyming epigrams. When Ponceludon exposes this false wit with some cleverly improvised rhyming couplets of his own, he moves closer to an audience with the king.

In a film in which words are often intended to mask feelings, subtext must be carefully presented, and Leconte's direction relies on a number of important closeups to convey thought and feeling. Social gatherings gain drama from the shots of the expectant faces of the onlookers and the nervous faces of those about to speak. A shot of Ponceludon's clenched fist during a tender moment with Mathilde reveals his hesitant attraction to her. The widow de Blayac's seduction of Ponceludon includes some well-chosen closeups as well, such as her sardonic look as she advises him, "Learn to hide your insincerity so that I can yield without dishonor." When she later wishes to toy with him a bit and frustrate his success, closeups reveal her amorously probing foot under the dinner table distracting him during a tournament of wit and making him misquote Voltaire to his embarrassment. Ponceludon eventually gains his preferment, only to learn that Mathilde has broken her engagement with Montalieri. The later scenes show the costs inherent in reaching the elite as Ponceludon struggles to maintain his tarnished honor and reunite with Mathilde. He discovers what a two-edged sword wit can be.

Few films feature such a large number of truly absorbing scenes. In one, a group of mutes is brought before the king and his courtiers to perform their newly learned sign language. Their exhibition receives only the sarcasm and laughter of the onlookers, but one of them, a former servant on Bellegarde's estate, wins the sympathy of Mathilde and Ponceludon. In a scene in which would-be courtiers wait in hopes of being called to advance to the inner circle, the king observes their eagerness through a peephole. When names are read of those who may enter the king's presence, one wag tosses a sleeping courtier's shoe into the fireplace, keep-

AWARDS AND NOMINATIONS

Academy Awards 1996 Nominations: Best Foreign Language Film
Cesar Awards 1997: Best Film, Best Director (Leconte)
Nominations: Best Actor (Berling)
Golden Globe Award 1997 Nominations: Best Foreign Language Film

ing him from receiving his advancement. A later shot shows that this shoeless wit has hanged himself after missing the moment of a lifetime. Another scene pictures the widow de Blayac standing naked before her servants who blow powder on her before she slips into her gown. And in another an American Sioux Indian is brought before the courtiers for their assessment: "Half naked and with the name of Stinking Bear, and he almost makes us look ridiculous," one of them replies.

The unwritten rules are always the most binding. Whether the social circle is a high school clique, a prestige dinner party, a power committee, or simply a workplace, gaining passage to the inner ring usually involves an ability to read and act on the subtle signs that delineate desired behavior. Ignorance of the unwritten rules usually leads to outsider status if not actual ostracism. *Ridicule* sets its story in pre-revolution France, but its impact is as fresh and forceful as any contemporary narrative.

—*Glenn Hopp*

CREDITS

Gregoire Ponceludon de Malavoy: Charles Berling
Marquis de Bellegarde: Jean Rochefort
Madame de Blayac: Fanny Ardant
Mathilde de Bellegarde: Judith Godreche
Abbot de Vilecourt: Barbard Giraudeau
Monsieur de Montalieri: Bernard Bheran
King Louis XVI: Urbain Cancelier

Origin: France
Released: 1996
Production: Giles Legrand, Frederic Brillion, and Philippe Carcassonne for Epithete/Cinea/France 3 Cinema and Le Canal Plus; released by Miramax Films
Direction: Patrice Leconte
Screenplay: Remi Waterhouse
Cinematography: Thierry Arbogast
Editing: Joelle Hache
Production design: Ivan Maussion
Music: Antoine Duhamel
MPAA rating: R
Running Time: 102 minutes

REVIEWS

American Cinematographer. December, 1996, p. 103.
Boxoffice. August, 1996, p. 55.
Chicago Tribune. December 6, 1996, p. 5.
Entertainment Weekly. December 6, 1996, p. 44.
New York. December 9, 1996, p. 74.
New York Times. November 27, 1996, p. C20.
People Weekly. December 9, 1996, p. 25.
Variety. May 5, 1996, p. 68.
Village Voice. December 3, 1996, p. 64.
Vogue. December, 1996, p. 168.
Wall Street Journal. November 29, 1996, p. A5.

The Rock

Alcatraz. Only one man has ever broken out. Now five million lives depend on two men breaking in.—Movie tagline

"A slam-bang action thriller!"—Roger Ebert, *Chicago Sun-Times*

"A rock-solid adrenaline rush!"—Joanna Langfield, *The Movie Minute*

"Hang on for dear life!"—Bonnie Churchill, *National News Syndicate*

"One of the best films ever!"—Jeff Craig, *Sixty Second Preview*

"The drop-dead thrill ride of the year!"—Patrick Stoner, *WHYY-TV*

Box Office: **$134,069,511**

British spy John Patrick Mason (Sean Connery) and chemical weapons expert Stanley Goodspeed overcome the obstacles of their dubious partnership in *The Rock.*

Is it impossible to top *Mission Impossible* and *Twister? Entertainment Weekly* wanted to know in mid-June. The question is absurd, since these two films marked only the beginning of a blockbuster summer. *The Rock,* which is better than both of them combined, should obviously eclipse the earliest hits of summer, if only because of the talent involved, Sean Connery linked with Nicolas Cage, among the best actors of two generations. *Mission Impossible* only had Tom Cruise to serve up, and *Twister* had no talent at all to speak of, only special effects.

The Rock also had Ed Harris as a villain who is a study in contrasts, a decorated war hero, an honorable Marine who served with valor in Vietnam and the Persian Gulf. His character, Brigadier General Francis Xavier Hummel, is fighting a holy mission (as his Christian names suggest) for truth and justice. He demands that the Government pay restitution to the families of soldiers who died on secret missions. These men died honorably, in the service of their country, and he wants that fact to be recognized. The only problem is that he opts to use terrorist tactics to make his point.

The final collaboration between producers Don Simpson (who died of a drug overdose in January, 1996) and Jerry Bruckheimer.

The film begins with a credit sequence that is so engaging that one forgets to read the credits as Hummel and his ex-Marines break into a military complex and steal fifteen V.X. poison gas missiles. The mission is accomplished with far more efficiency than the one that opened *Mission Impossible.* The next mission is to secure Alcatraz Island as an operations base, taking eighty civilian tourists as hostages. Hummel threatens to launch the chemical missiles across the Bay towards San Francisco if his demands are not met, a million dollars to each of his men and a million dollars to the families of all the soldiers who died on covert missions. Otherwise, the whole city will be wiped out.

The FBI is in charge of this crisis, working with the military. A Navy SEAL team is assigned to infiltrate Alcatraz and take out the terrorists. But they need directions in order to get in, and they are forced to request the aid of John Patrick Mason (Sean Connery), the only man who ever managed to escape from Alcatraz prison. Mason's identity has been erased. A British national, he was an agent in Her Majesty's Secret Service who got caught at the Canadian border after managing to steal J. Edgar Hoover's secret files, which would clear up such mysteries as the Roswell aliens and the Kennedy assassination.

This is sensitive, classified stuff. It's interesting how the plot exploits the concerns of "The X-Files" and its cult television audience. Moreover, distrust for big Government and its agencies, such as the FBI, also links the film to the madness of the Montana militia, whose standoff with the FBI dominated the news at the time of the picture's release.

Mason had been left to rot in prison without a trial for thirty years, a man without a country and with no legal rights. FBI director Womack (Fred Salvallon) thinks Mason is about as dangerous as Hannibal Lecter and does not want him released. But, as Mason, brought out of his cell looking like Methuselah, tells them in the script's best line, the FBI "is between a Rock and a hard case." Womack offers Mason his freedom for his cooperation, but he clearly intends to double-cross him after the mission is accomplished. But, as is soon apparent, Mason is not to be underestimated.

If Mason has the unlikely assignment of breaking into Alcatraz, another expert is needed to disarm the chemical rockets. That dicey assignment goes to a nerdy goof named Stanley Goodspeed (Nicolas Cage), an educated chemist and weapons expert who works for the FBI. He was about to marry Carla Pestalozzi (Vanessa Marcil), his pregnant girlfriend, who follows him to San Francisco. Mason has a daughter, Jade Angelou (Claire Forlani), who lives in San Francisco. So both Mason and Goodspeed have personal reasons for saving the city. This is a necessary plot detail, for otherwise Mason would surely be tempted to escape from San Francisco and the mission altogether.

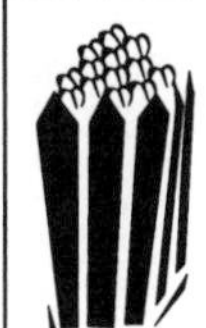

"Losers always whine about their best. Winners go home and f*** the prom queen."—Mason to Stanley

Once the plot lunges into motion, it's nonstop action-adventure. Before he agrees to cooperate, Mason demands a hotel suite, a haircut, and a proper change of clothes. Once he looks presentable, he manages to escape from the Fairmont hotel, with the FBI and Goodspeed at top speed in pursuit for the film's obligatory chase sequence. Where does it lead? To an artificial father-daughter reunion that attempts to humanize Mason as he tells his daughter "I'm not an evil man." But, good as this sequence is as action-adventure, it cannot match the razzmatazz of Alcatraz.

After getting into the complex with Mason's help, the SEAL team gets into a Mexican standoff with the terrorists and is utterly wiped out, but Mason and Goodspeed escape this shoot-out, then, one by one, they undertake to disarm the missiles. When it appears that Hummel's bluff has been called by the FBI, he displays a conscience, but his men consider themselves mercenaries, no longer Marines, and Hummel is faced with mutiny. The resolutions of these conflicts come hot and heavy in the film's final minutes.

For Owen Gleiberman of *Entertainment Weekly* the prototype for this kind of summer blockbuster was *Die Hard* (1988), which seemed excessive at the time of its release, but in comparison to *The Rock* now seems "a model of classical restraint." The trick is to make each action sequence "meaner, louder, smashier than any such sequence before it." Hence *The Rock* outdoes *Die Hard* and pushes the envelope for senseless violent action so far that it is not likely to be outdone by any other summer hit.

The brutality and vulgarity of the dialogue is likewise artificially pumped-up, as when Cage asks Connery after they have been captured, "How, in the name of Zeus' butt-hole did you get out of your cell?" or when a black mercenary says to Cage, whom he has taken prisoner, "I'll take great pleasure in gutting you, boy." These are not words to live by, and they are intended to shock. Gleiberman rightly praised Connery, however, for "expressing his wit less through dialogue," as is usually his strength, "than through his quicker-than-eye reflexes." Problem is, this finely nuanced performance is in the service of a film that "invites you to feel thrilled at feeling nothing at all."

Washington Post critic Desson Howe dismissed Michael Bay as a "hack-director," and his colleague Hal Hinson wrote that the film was "directed like a music-video Gotterdammerung," but Janet Maslin of the *New York Times* was more on target, praising the director who graduated to feature films after making several prize-winning commercials. She noted that *The Rock* "is shot and edited with flagrant salesmanship, from the film's blue backlighting to its sheets of rain, masses of flowers and other decorative touches," right down to the lethal green strands of poison gas Goodspeed is forced to handle. Indeed, the film's opening, with Hummel in his dress blues visiting Arlington National Cemetery, looks like a commercial for the Marine Corps.

The Rock was put together by the production team of Jerry Bruckheimer and the late Don Simpson, purveyors of such action hits as *Beverly Hills Cop* (1984), *Top Gun* (1986), and last year's *Crimson Tide* (1995). The film is dedicated "in loving memory to Don Simpson." In fact, this film belongs more to the producers than to the director, who had only one feature film, *Bad Boys* (1995) to his credit.

Writer John Gregory Dunne described Don Simpson as Hollywood's "icon of excess" as well as success in his *New Yorker* obituary (Feb. 5, 1996): "Don invented the high concept formula for the eighties," Dunne quotes producer Lynda Obst as saying. "Announce the big idea in the first act and resolve it in the next two acts, often with a contest." And that is exactly the formula of *The Rock.* What one remembers about the Simpson-Bruckheimer movies, Dunne adds, "is the momentum and the beat, the music as much as the story; the pictures they made were essentially MTV videos of feature-film length." That is no doubt why they chose Michael Bay to direct, and that is why *The*

AWARDS AND NOMINATIONS

Academy Awards 1996 Nominations: Best Sound

Rock is like a geode, glittering on the inside, but essentially hollow.

The producers summarize the story in the following promotional slogan that pretty well describes the film: "Alcatraz. Only one man has ever broken out. Now five million lives depend on two men breaking in." Janet Maslin noted the "slogan-caliber simplicity" of the plot as a "Simpson-Bruckheimer hallmark," as is the film's commercial slickness "and an unwavering faith in the superiority of appearance over sense."

For what it is, however, this is an excellent movie, dazzling in its special effects and unrelenting pace. Sean Connery, Nicolas Cage, and Ed Harris all have enough starpower to take any film to box-office profits. Working together, they form an unbeatable team. There were surely far better films available when *The Rock* was released, notably Bernardo Bertolucci's *Stealing Beauty,* which opened the same weekend, but for summer entertainment, *The Rock* was hard to beat, even if viewers felt crushed by its loud and vulgar weight.

—James M. Welsh

CREDITS

John Patrick Mason: Sean Connery
Stanley Goodspeed: Nicolas Cage
Gen. Francis X. Hummel: Ed Harris
Charles Anderson: Michael Biehn
Eddie Paxton: William Forsythe
Major Tom Baxter: David Morse

Origin: USA
Released: 1996
Production: Don Simpson, Jerry Bruckheimer for a Hollywood Pictures production; released by Buena Vista
Direction: Michael Bay
Screenplay: David Weisberg, Douglas S. Cook, and Mark Rosner
Cinematography: John Schwartzman
Editing: Richard Francis-Bruce
Music: Nick Glennie-Smith, Hans Zimmer
Production design: Michael White
Art direction: Ed McAvoy
Stunt coordinator: Kenny Bates
Costume design: Bobbie Read
Sound: Keith A. Wester
Casting: Heidi Levitt, Billy Hopkins
MPAA rating: R
Running Time: 136 minutes

REVIEWS

Entertainment Weekly. June 14, 1996, p. 41.
New York Times. June 7, 1996, p. C1.
New Yorker. June 17, 1996, p. 101.
News Journal (Wilmington, Delaware). June 7-9, 1996, p. H6.
Newsweek. June 10, 1996, p. 31.
Rolling Stone. June 27, 1996, p. 61.
Time. June 10, 1996, p. 85.
Variety. June 3, 1996, p. 49.
Washington Post. June 7, 1996, p. D1.
Washington Post Weekend. June 7, 1996, p. 37.
Washington Times Metropolitan Times. June 7, 1996, p. C16.

Rumble in the Bronx

No fear. No stuntman. No equal.—Movie tagline

Box Office: **$32,380,143**

Rumble in the Bronx stars Hong Kong martial arts phenomenon Jackie Chan, arguably the world's most popular film performer. The versatile star, director, producer, screenwriter, kung fu fighter and stunt director has amassed an impressive list of movie credits. He has worked in almost fifty films over the past two decades.

Chan's international popularity, however, rests on more than his dynamic screen presence and versatility. He brings to film an unusual kind of martial arts champion differing completely from the stolid personas of such celebrities as Jean-Claude Van Damme, Chuck Norris, or Steven Seagal. Chan's approach to action/adventure is more closely akin to the silent screen comics—a kind of Bruce Lee meets Buster Keaton. He is a warrior clown. Chan is the master of, and popularizer of, comedy kung-fooey, a zany action mix of blazingly fast hand and footwork, balletic daredevil stunts, improvisational thrills, all surrounded by a sweetly naive and lovably good-natured personality. It's a heady combination that has worked surprisingly well for the Hong Kong star. Let's face it, would Norris, Seagal or Van Damme run away from their opponents? Yet Chan, when faced with danger, routinely uses his legs for running, as well as, kicking.

Chan is currently riding the latest wave of interest in Asian cinema, particularly the Hong Kong variety. Today, a number of Oriental artists such as performers Jet Li, Gong Li, Chow Yun-Fat and directors Wong Kar-Wei, Tsui Hark, John Woo, and Ringo Lam are becoming increasingly familiar to American audiences. It's an interest shared by Hollywood as well, eager to showcase the foreign talent as part of its own global entertainment. Recently, controversial filmmaker Quentin Tarantino released Wong's *Chungking Express* for his first release under the Miramax-affiliated, Rolling Thunder imprint.

During the filming Jackie Chan broke his ankle making a leap from a high bridge piling to a hovercraft. The jump and its aftermath are shown in the outtakes.

None of the current hot Asian stars, however, come even close to Chan's enormous worldwide appeal. He has even won an MTV Lifetime Achievement Award. Chan, despite his success, has never realized one important dream—to become a big star in the United States. Despite appearances in such American films as *Battle Creek Brawl* (1980), *Cannonball Run* (1981), *Cannonball Run 2* (1984), and *The Protector* (1985), his screen success here has been negligible. *Rumble in the Bronx* may just change all that.

Rumble in the Bronx opens with the hero, Keung (Jackie Chan), a Hong Kong cop and kung fu champion, arriving in New York City to attend his uncle's wedding planned for the following day. He is met at the airport by Uncle Bill (Bill Tung) who takes him to his supermarket, located in the Bronx. Uncle Bill is not only getting married, but is also in the process of selling his store and retiring. The new owner is Elaine (Anita Mui, a popular Hong Kong actress and singer), a somewhat naive individual. There is a nice comic sequence at the beginning when Keung poses in front of a one-way mirror unaware that Elaine is watching him closely from the other side.

That night, Keung is startled awake by the sound of motorcycles. Stepping out onto the fire escape, he sees a large gang of bikers planning some serious mischief on all the cars parked below. Thinking only of his uncle's limousine, Keung jumps down and disrupts the racing carnage, thereby earning the enmity of the gang members, particularly the leader, Tony (Marc Akerstream) and his lieutenant, Angelo (Garvin Cross).

At the wedding, Keung meets a lot of people, including Danny (Morgan Lam), a crippled boy whom he befriends. Elaine persuades Keung to help her at the store for one week while Uncle Bill is on his honeymoon. It is a decision that will bring regret to both parties. Keung's first day on the job is a difficult one. The same bikers come in and begin stealing and destroying property. A frightened Elaine wants them to leave with their loot, but when they begin threatening her, Keung steps in and pummels the hoodlums into submission. Keung is a highly imaginative and inventive fighter who uses objects and food at hand to disarm his opponents.

Later that day, his attempt at being a Good Samaritan almost undoes him. Rushing to the aid of a "kidnapped" woman, Keung runs into an ambush and is immediately assaulted by the biker gang. He manages to fend them off and run away only to become trapped in a blind alley. The bikers throw liquor bottles at the hero until he collapses from the barrage of glass into unconsciousness. He is left to die in a pool of blood and alcohol.

Somehow, Keung manages to drag himself home and get help from Danny and his older sister Nancy (Franchise Yip) who turns out to be Tony's girlfriend and "the woman" who betrayed him hours before. Eventually, Nancy will come to see Keung as a positive influence in her life, become romantically interested in the hero, and move quickly away from Tony and the gang. Tony, however, not pleased with Keung's presence and Nancy's growing alienation, has his gang chase the hapless hero to the top floor of a parking building. Trapped, Keung makes a death-defying leap to another building and safety. (All the super spectacular stunts are shot using three cameras filming in slow motion and shown consecutively.)

"Why spend all of your time beating people up and robbing them? Don't you know you are the scum of the earth?"—Keung to the bad guys

Keung's problems escalate rapidly when crime lord White Tiger (Kris Lord) steps into the picture as the chief villain. The mobster is after a large bundle of recently stolen diamonds. Somehow, Angelo gets his hands on them and hides the diamonds in one of Danny's wheelchair cushions. White Tiger comes after the bikers and they in turn, completely trash Elaine's supermarket because Keung works for her and, at the moment, is romancing Nancy.

A now furious Keung confronts Tony and his gang in their hideout and a battle royale ensues with the hero more than a match for his opponents. Utilizing everything at hand, including billiard balls and cue sticks, large appliances, shopping carts, skis, and dozens of other items, Keung completely overpowers the bikers and admonishes them to clean up their act and unite against White Tiger. But the mobster remains one step ahead. He kidnaps Tony, Nancy, and Angelo forcing Keung to locate and return the missing diamonds. Later, with the diamonds in hand, Keung and Elaine become trapped on the second floor of her supermarket. While she is settled on the toilet, White Tiger cunningly choreographs the total destruction of her building. It is a hilarious sequence and eerily reminiscent of Danny Glover trapped on an explosive toilet seat in *Lethal Weapon 2*.

Keung finally notifies the cops. They send him back to White Tiger for the final confrontation—a full twenty minutes of organized and inspired mayhem which involves a running shootout in a boat marina, a stolen hovercraft, another spectacular leap by Keung, police boats, and lots of action in and on the water, the beach, the streets, and a golf course. Needless to say, the film ends on a happy note with Keung triumphant, the hostages released, White Tiger humiliatingly subdued, and the stolen jewelry returned.

One should forget the plot, however, on a Jackie Chan film. The real joy is in watching him perform his balletic maneuvers through the air and outrageously displaying his own special brand of chop socky foolishness. Chan wants us to sit back, relax, and enjoy the fun as he takes us on a roller coaster ride of nonstop action thrills.

The weaknesses in *Rumble in the Bronx* are glaringly evident as is the apparent lack of reality. The film is supposedly set in the South Bronx, but there is never any real sense of its unique urban life. And since when did that famous borough suddenly acquire large snow-covered mountains (film actually shot in Vancouver, British Columbia)? Also, the film is badly dubbed, like many cheap video imports, setting up a number of unintentional laughs.

Somehow, director Stanley Tong makes it all work as he wisely concentrates on his star's amazing physical abilities and legendary rapport with the camera. Make sure you stay for the credits (easily the most interesting part of the film) which features a Chan tradition—out-takes of the Chan stunts that didn't work. The hapless star is shown being brutally battered time and again during the making of the film.

Rumble in the Bronx should bring Chan the large American audience and approval that he has been seeking. The film showcases his unique style of action comedy, displays his amazingly fast aerial kicks and brutal chops, his adroit physical grace, his resourceful use of available props and scenery to disarm his adversaries, his incredible ability to out kick and out punch all his opponents, and all underscored by a goofy, good-natured, infectious grin.

—*Terry Theodore*

CREDITS

Keung: Jackie Chan
Elaine: Anita Mui
Nancy: Francoise Yip
Uncle Bill: Bill Tung
Tony: Marc Akerstream
Angelo: Garvin Cross
Danny: Morgan Lam
White Tiger: Kris Lord

Origin: Hong Kong
Released: 1996
Production: Barbie Tung for a Golden Harvest production; released by New Line Cinema
Direction: Stanley Tong
Screenplay: Edward Tang, Fibe Ma
Cinematography: Jingle Ma
Editing: Michael Duthie, Peter Cheung
Music: J. Peter Robinson
Production design: Oliver Wong
MPAA rating: R
Running Time: 100 minutes

REVIEWS

Detroit News. February 24, 1996, p. C1.
Los Angeles Times. February 23, 1996, p. F1.
New York Times. February 23, 1996, p. C6.
People Weekly. February 26, 1996, p. 17.
USA Today. February 23, 1996, p. 1D.
Village Voice. February 27, 1996, p. 72.

Scream

Someone has taken their love of scary movies one step too far. Solving this mystery is going to be murder.—Movie tagline

"The scariest movie of the year!"—Anne Marie O'Connor, *Mademoiselle*

"*Scream* is a delicious blend of fun and fright that's smashingly scary!"—Peter Travers, *Rolling Stone*

"The most enjoyable thriller of the year!"—Bob Healy, *Satellite News Network*

"Clever, hip and scary!"—Paul Wunder, *WBAI*

Box Office: $24,464,954

Wes Craven's tongue-in-cheek, but seriously scary film *Scream* is a highly creative and entertaining addition to the horror genre. *Scream* combines heart-thumping terror with self-conscious humor to create an unnerving cinematic experience. The neophyte cast, along with veterans Courteney Cox, David Arquette and Drew Barrymore, are an interesting mix adding lots of youthful appeal to an already well-written script and exciting storyline. The Agatha Christie whodunit element keeps things interesting until the very end. Craven's unusual creativity and imagination, which have been developed in previous films (*A Nightmare on Elm Street* [1984] and *Wes Craven's New Nightmare* [1994]), seem to peak in this more subtle, yet just as gory thriller.

Casey Becker (Drew Barrymore) has the opening segment which easily captures the picture's most frightening moments. Casey is alone in her home, making popcorn and waiting for her football player boyfriend to come over to watch a horror video together. As expected, yet still very disturbing, the phone starts to ring and a deep voice at the other end starts a friendly chat after seemingly dialing the wrong number. Casey goes along cheerily, even flirting a little with the mysterious caller until he reveals he is actually watching her through a window in her house. She abruptly hangs up but the phone begins to ring over and over, the caller getting increasingly agitated. When she threatens the caller with the wrath of her soon-to-be arriving boyfriend, the caller instructs her to turn on an outside light, which illuminates her boyfriend, bound and gagged out back. Casey is then forced to play along in a horror movie trivia game with the caller in order to save both their lives in a scene that finds Craven paying homage to fellow horror master, *Halloween* (1978) director John Carpenter. Barrymore puts a lot of energy into her brief performance where she struggles bravely against becoming the typical teen victim found in many slasher films. In fact, none of Craven's "victims" simply fall helpless prey to their attackers and all put up valiant resistance. There are no gratuitous victims to illustrate the killer's power.

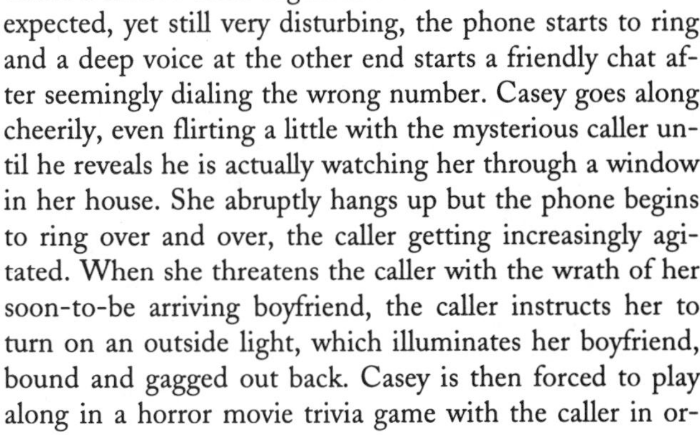

Craven was set to film at a San Francisco-area high school when the Santa Rosa School Board banned the project because of the script's violence.

After the initial murders of the teens, their circle of friends in the local high school brainstorm on possible suspects within their ranks, ranging from the nerdy video store clerk Randy (Jamie Kennedy) to Casey's wacky ex-boyfriend Stuart (Matthew Lillard), now dating a perky new blond. This circle of teens includes the film's main character, Sidney Prescott (Neve Campbell), a shy and serious brunette with an enviably good-looking and sensitive boyfriend Billy Loomis (Skeet Ulrich). Sidney lives alone with her father after having lost her mother to a murderer, who is currently in jail. Since the tragedy, Sidney's mental distress has prevented her from becoming intimate with her long-term boyfriend, who has patiently put up with lengthy make-out sessions while waiting to deflower his true love.

Sidney's arch-nemesis appears as Gale Weathers (Courteney Cox), the tenacious reporter and author of a book about Sidney's mother's murder, which argues that the man who was convicted of the crime is actually innocent. Gale shows up at the school to cover the murders and when she approaches Sidney for some comments on the case and mentions her book in the process, Sidney strikes the reporter, giving her a black eye. Gale subsequently encounters Deputy Dewey Riley (David Arquette), older brother of Sidney's close friend Tatum Riley (Rose McGowan) and resident bumbling, rookie policeman with a chip on his shoulder. Dewey does not share Sidney's negative feelings for the perky reporter and Gale easily charms him into giving her vital information on the case.

As the hysteria mounts over the murders, Sidney's father leaves town on business, leaving Sidney to become the next victim of the killer-on-the-loose. She receives the first of several ominous phone calls made worse by the fact that the caller admits to her mother's murder, as well as those of two of her friends. Sidney prepares to stay with a friend that night but a short nap turns into two hours and she is awoken by the shrill ringing of the phone. That begins the next attack of the killer, who wears a currently popular Halloween mask and cape. The killer apparently uses a cell phone to terrorize his victims from nearby watch points. Sidney manages to call the police before the killer is able to make her his next victim. As the killer flees, her boyfriend appears in her room through the window and accidentally drops a cell phone in the process. Now doubting that the man who is in prison for her mother's murder is the real killer after all, Sidney turns Billy in to the police as a suspect.

The only problem is that, as guilty as he seems, other murders and phone calls are going on while Billy is in police custody. He is subsequently released, and later completely forgiven by Sidney, although she still harbors some doubts. When the killer's next victim is school principal Himbry, played in a delicious deadpan by Henry Winkler, everyone is given the day off. Sidney's boisterously happy friends decide to throw a party to celebrate.

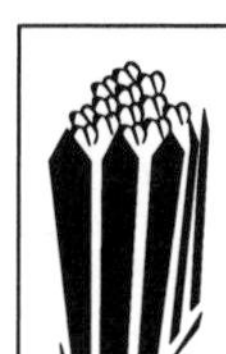

"The flicks just make psychos more creative."—the killer on slasher films

Scream's humor, while definitely dark, aims right at the types of films Craven makes and is perfectly illustrated in the "movie buff" video clerk character, Randy, at the party. The teens are all watching *Halloween,* the movie that made Jamie Lee Curtis a famous scream queen, as Stuart begins to recite the golden "rules" of how to survive a horror film (rules which do not always apply to *Scream,* but come close)—rules anyone who has ever watched a horror movie are well acquainted with, such as, don't ever say you'll be right back. Saying that ensures death, as does drinking alcohol and making love and all the other clichés found in most slasher films. The many cliched devices that are used in this film are done so on purpose, and both the filmmaker and the viewer are playfully aware of them.

Craven's movie-within-a-movie technique comes into play with an interesting twist when Gale, trying to catch a killer, plants a mini, hidden camera at the teen's party, the results being monitored by a cameraman outside in the news van, while she mingles inside. The problem is that there is a slight delay between the events of the party and the transmission to the van. This slight time difference causes serious consequences for those relying on the transmission as an accurate picture of the events taking place. The self-conscious illustration shows that an audience isn't always getting the whole picture either. After some very unusual action resulting in multiple murders, the film's ending is surprising, strangely funny, and fresh.

Technically, the movie is well-shot with the gruesome action pitted against the picturesque northern California scenery. The gore is not over-the-top, wisely relying more on imminent terror and actually very creative death scenes to evoke response. The film is also well-lit, avoiding the frustrating darkness and resulting confusion that too often pervades other horror pictures. Structurally, the murder/mystery aspect is the most satisfying aspect of the film. Everyone is a suspect: some blatantly stated and some merely hinted at, with a handful of dark horse contenders as well. It is most relieving when half-way through the film you don't already know who the killer is and have to watch as the rest of the film plays out.

Craven's characters manage to have more dimension than is usually allowed in these types of films. He has written interesting characters with actual personalities. This aids the actors' efforts, all of which are notable. Campbell has the most difficult job, playing a character who is depressed and confused while being stalked throughout the film. She manages it with sincerity in her actions and a certain heroic vulnerability. Most of the remaining parts are lively and seem to be more fun to play. Newcomer Lillard is hilarious in his role. Ulrich, though not particularly talented, gives off a certain intensity, making him watchable. Most notably, Arquette displays considerable ability in taking his Barney Fife-esque character and making him charming and attractive. In a most interesting plot twist, Cox's character, who is ini-

CREDITS

Sidney Prescott: Neve Campbell
Deputy Dewey Riley: David Arquette
Gale Weathers: Courteney Cox
Stuart: Matthew Lillard
Billy Loomis: Skeet Ulrich
Casey Becker: Drew Barrymore
Tatum Riley: Rose McGowan
Principal Himbry: Henry Winkler
Cotton Weary: Liev Schreiber

Origin: USA
Released: 1996
Production: Cary Woods and Cathy Konrad for a Woods Entertainment production; released by Dimension Films
Direction: Wes Craven
Screenplay: Kevin Williamson
Cinematography: Mark Irwin
Editing: Patrick Lussier
Music: Marco Beltrami
Production design: Bruca Alan Miller
Art direction: David Lubin
Special makeup effects: Robert Kurtzman, Greg Nicotero, Howard Berger
Sound: Richard Goodman
Casting: Lisa Beach
MPAA rating: R
Running Time: 110 minutes

tially seen as taking the poor policeman for a ride, eventually partners with him and becomes genuinely smitten by his sincerity and good-hearted nature. It is precisely these interesting plot twists, lively dialogue, and humor in unexpected places that work together in a must-see, modern slasher.

—Hilary Weber

REVIEWS

Boxoffice. February, 1997, p. 66.
Entertainment Weekly. January 10, 1997, p. 39.
Film Threat. February, 1997, p. 52.
Los Angeles Times. December 20, 1996, p. F14.
Newsweek. December 23, 1996, p. 96.
Rolling Stone. December 26, 1996, p. 206.
Variety. December 16, 1996, p. 79.
Washington Post Weekend. December 20, 1996, p. 44.

Screamers

The last scream you hear will be your own.—Movie tagline

"Smart, sexy, sci-fi fun!"—Terry Lawson, *Detroit Free Press*

"The sci-fi action thriller of the year!"—Howard Benjamin, *Interview Factory Entertainment Network*

"Shrieking good fun!"—Scott Siegel, *Siegel Entertainment Syndicate*

"A dark satisfying futuristic thriller."—Stephan Talty, *Time-Out New York*

"A first rate thriller."—Mark Ladlaw, *Wired Magazine*

Box Office: $5,711,695

Screamers could have become a sleeper hit. Although it lacked the big special effects sci-fi budget of *12 Monkeys* and the star power, it should have been able to compete effectively with Terry Gilliam's expanded remake of Chris Marker's classic *La Jetee* (1962), for reasons summarized by the following *New York Times* headline: "Existential Questions Plus Androids. Cool." The film could still assume cult significance because its an adaptation of Philip K. Dick's short story "The Second Variety."

Screamers should satisfy sci-fi purists. The story is set well into the 21st century on an alien planet, colonized by human beings sent there to mine a powerful radioactive mineral. But mining excavations released a deadly radioactive gas that eventually ruined a beautiful planet fit for human habitation and brought about a conflict between business and government interests, a conflict that escalated into nuclear war, conveniently confined to the planet Sirius 6B.

In Philip K. Dick's original 1952 story, "The Second Variety," the interplanetary civil war was between the U.S. and the USSR.

The goverment Alliance forces developed robotic weapons called "screamers," described as automated swords, killing machines designed to move rapidly just beneath the soil and to chop, slice and dice the enemy. The prototypes are all hardware, but these androids, run by computer intelligence, have evolved and have learned how to breed, duplicate, change, and repair themselves. They have also learned how to clone themselves to appear human.

Alliance Commander Col. Hendricksson (Peter Weller of *Robocop* fame) gets word that his enemies, the New Economic Bloc, have called for a truce. He decides to risk crossing the radiated Wasteland, patrolled by the screamers, to see if the truce offer is genuine. He wants nothing more than to end the war and return to Earth. He gets computer instructions to pursue the truce, but these instructions are contrary to what he learns from a young survivor of an Alliance space shuttle that crashes near his compound. His story is that, far from being near a truce, the war has been extended to other colonized planets.

Clearly, something is wrong, and Hendricksson is obliged to check out the situation. He literally does not know his enemy. He does not understand that the screamers have modified themselves to destroy all forms of human life. To infiltrate human fortifications, the screamers have developed now models that appear to be human children but can kill just as effectively as their underground cousins. Hendricksson later discovers that the screamers have developed even more sophisticated human models that will even shed blood and replicate other human functions. Menace, therefore, is everywhere.

Another reason *Screamers* should succeed is its association with visionary Philip K. Dick, who also wrote *Do Androids Dream of Electric Sheep?,* the novel that was the basis for the 1982 film *Blade Runner,* which was not a runaway success when it was released but has since developed a strong cult following. By 1993 *Blade Runner* was judged important enough to be added to the Library of Congress National Film Registry, an elite listing of films targeted for preservation because of "cultural, historic, or aesthetic significance."

> "You're coming up in the world. You know how to kill each other now."—Hendricksson observing two Screamers fighting each other

Screenwriter Dan O'Bannon, who also worked on *Alien* (1979) and *Total Recall* (1990, based on another Philip K. Dick story), explained that *Screamers* has some of the same thematic concerns that distinguished *Blade Runner* and persuaded viewers to take it seriously: "His primary moral concern," O'Bannon told *The New York Times,* "is the nature of what it is to be human." One of the androids in *Screamers* takes on such a strong human identity that her allegiance shifts away from her own kind. At the end she clearly wants to be human and fights to protect the man she loves. The film constantly questions what O'Bannon calls "the unreliability of reality."

The understated elegance of *Screamers* arises from a thoughtful and questioning screenplay. The landscape is appropriately bleak and stark. Special effects are relatively modest but sufficient. The acting is more than adequate, despite a cast of generally unknown actors.

CREDITS

Hendricksson: Peter Weller
Becker: Roy Dupuis
Jessica: Jennifer Rubin
Ace: Andy Lauer
Ross: Charles Powell
Elbarak: Ron White

Origin: USA
Released: 1996
Production: Tom Berry and Franco Battista for an Allegro Films, Fuji Eight Co and Fries Film company production; released by Triumph Films
Direction: Christian Duguay
Screenplay: Dan O'Bannon and Miguel Tejada-Flores; based on the short story "Second Variety" by Philip K. Dick
Cinematography: Rodney Gibbons
Editing: Yves Langlois
Production design: Perri Gorrara
Music: Normand Corbeil
Digital effects supervision: Richard Ostiguy
Visual effects supervision: Ernest Farino
Stunt coordination: Michael Scherer
Costume design: Trixi Rittenhouse
MPAA rating: R
Running Time: 107 minutes

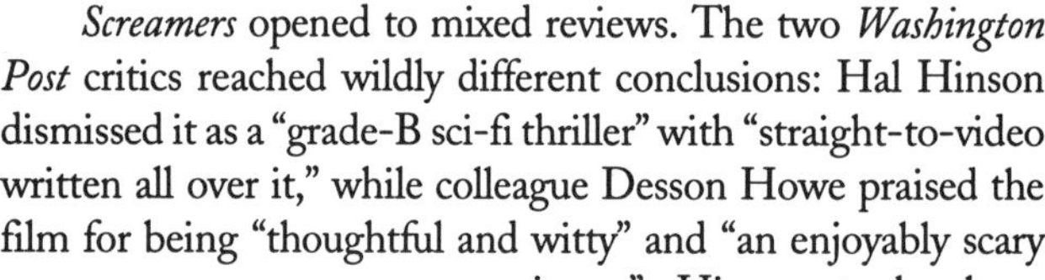

Screamers opened to mixed reviews. The two *Washington Post* critics reached wildly different conclusions: Hal Hinson dismissed it as a "grade-B sci-fi thriller" with "straight-to-video written all over it," while colleague Desson Howe praised the film for being "thoughtful and witty" and "an enjoyably scary experience." Hinson took cheap shots at Peter Weller (claiming he "seemed more expressive with his face half-covered in the *Robocop* films than he does here") and Jennifer Rubin ("the queen of the modern B-girls, the diva of the after-midnight cable movie"). At least Stephen Hunter of the *Baltimore Sun,* who found *Screamers* "preposterous," noticed that Weller was "quite good."

Ken Tucker of *Entertainment Weekly* praised Weller for giving Hendricksson "both a steely sense of humor and despair," adding that *Screamers* gave Jennifer Rubin "the break she deserves." At the end she is at odds with herself. The way this character is divided against herself recalls the two Marias in Fritz Lang's classic *Metropolis* (1926).

Stephen Hunter objected, however, to the film's conclusion, which he found "truly incoherent, with one phony climax piling atop another." Stephen Holden of *The New York Times* thought that the cautionary "fable of technology run amok" did "an efficient job of generating a stomach-knotting tension" before succumbing "to one cliche too many" and degenerating into a "formulaic thriller." He would seem to agree with Desson Howe of *The Washington Post* that Christian Duguay is effective as "an atmospheric, suspense-savvy filmmaker" capable of creating "an authentically inhospitable world."

It's worth remembering that *Blade Runner* originally had its detractors, too. Even though *Screamers* is not in the same league, it's close. All this film lacked was an extravagant budget and high-profile actors; but it succeeded in the inventive use of available resources such as a sandpit and cement quarry near Montreal and Montreal's Olympic stadium. *Screamers* is more a buzz than a bore, really, and what it suggests about humanity possibly mucking up the whole universe is a point worth considering.

—James M. Welsh

REVIEWS

Baltimore Sun. January 26, 1996, p. El.
Chicago Tribune. January 26, 1996, p. 5.
Entertainment Weekly. February 9, 1996, p. 38.
Los Angeles Times. January 26, 1996, p. F6.
The New York Times. January 26, 1996, p. C23.
USA Today. January 26, 1996, p. 7D.
Village Voice. January 30, 1996, p. 41.
The Washington Post. January 26, 1996, F6.
Washington Post Weekend. January 26, 1996, p.37.

Secrets and Lies

Roxanne drives her mother crazy. Maurice never speaks to his niece. Cynthia has a shock for her family. Monica can't talk to her husband. Hortense has never met her mother.—Movie tagline

"Remarkable! Truthful and emotional. Exquisitely balances humor and pain without ever tipping over."—Kenneth Turan, *Los Angeles Times*

"A beautifully acted exploration of guilt, sorrow and redemptive love."—Janet Maslin, *New York Times*

"Transcendent & moving! Blisteringly funny! *Secrets & Lies* is something very special indeed!"—Peter Travers, *Rolling Stone*

Box Office: $6,400,000

Adopted daughter Hortense (Marianne Jean-Bapiste) searches for her birth mother Cynthia (Brenda Blethyn) in *Secrets & Lies.*

To say that director Mike Leigh's latest film, *Secrets and Lies,* is about an adopted woman meeting her birth mother is like saying that Shakespeare's *King Lear* is about an old man who gets caught in a rainstorm. It is true that the central event of Leigh's film is the meeting between Hortense (Marianne Jean-Baptiste), a twenty-seven-year-old black professional, and her working class white mother, Cynthia (Brenda Blethyn), but as Leigh's filming of the encounter makes clear, there is far more to this story than first impressions. The meaning of what happens in the scene lies somewhere in the secrets and lies that form the subtext of the confrontation. As usual, Leigh has chosen a trite expression as his film title (others include *High Hopes* [1989] and *Life Is Sweet* [1991]), and as usual, that title implies far more than filmgoers presume it to mean.

Leigh's unconventional method of filmmaking is by now well-known. He has been directing television and stage productions, as well as films, in England for over thirty years, and with the success of recent efforts such as *Naked,* which won Leigh the Best Director Award at Cannes in 1993 and now *Secrets and Lies,* which won this year's Palme d'Or at the same film festival, he has achieved the recognition his originality merits. Leigh is no traditional auteur, instead approaching a project by assembling a group of actors who create the film with him. While Leigh may have some preliminary idea of a plot before beginning a project, he does not share it with the actors, who are instead directed to find some character from their past and become it. Several weeks of improvisation ensue, and during this period, the actors are obliged to remain strictly in character during rehearsal. Janine Duvitsky tells the story of how, during rehearsals for *Abigail's Party* (1977), Leigh followed her to a grocery store, where he observed her buying a can of food for her dog. Leigh interrupted her right in the pet food aisle, hissing, "Your character doesn't have a dog!"

> "Why do the people I love most in the world hate each other's guts?"—Maurice about his wife and sister

Such extreme measures are meant to insure the reality that eventually comes across on screen. The actors are forbidden to discuss their characters outside rehearsals, and Leigh goes to great lengths to prevent his players from knowing things that their respective characters cannot know. Reportedly, in *Secrets and Lies,* Leigh did not even introduce Jean-Baptiste and Blethyn before filming the reunion between Hortense and Cynthia. And in filming the scene, he simply let the camera role, recording the pivotal moment in real time. What he got during the seven-minute take were bravura performances from both actors. Blethyn, who won the best actress award at Cannes this year, is overwhelmingly good, placing not a foot wrong in her portrayal of a woman who is at once stunned, hysterical, embarrassed, and overjoyed to be meeting a daughter she has practically forgotten—and more importantly, someone who actually wants to be near her.

Leigh did not arrive at this scene until well on into the rehearsal process for *Secrets and Lies.* Jean-Baptiste had by that point already been performing eye tests for several months in order to portray Hortense, an optometrist whose father has died, when the director decided to kill off her mother as well. This decision in turn triggered an adopted Hortense's search for her birth mother. When mother and daughter finally meet, the least surprising element of the encounter is their racial difference (Hortense has already learned from her files, given her by a social worker, that her birth mother is white). Instead, the focus is on Cynthia, with her tragic-comic agitation and her concern that Hortense will not approve of her. Indeed, after a short time Cynthia seems not to notice the color of her daughter's skin, instead begging for Hortense's understanding and forgiveness. "I'm sorry," she wails, "I must be a bit of a disappointment to you. You'd be better off without me." Hortense, who with her neat appearance and refined accent presents a vivid contrast with the disorganized, rambling older woman, at first reacts to Cynthia as we do: a little put off by Cynthia's conspicuous neediness, she stands apart from her. Appearances aside, however, Cynthia is appealing, and both we and Hortense are won over by her genuineness and her desire to connect.

Cynthia, who at first denies any possibility that she can be Hortense's mother, gradually reveals a secret so old and so closely-guarded that she seems herself to have forgotten it: when she was fifteen, she had had a brief encounter with an African medical student. She never saw the child that resulted from this liaison, as it was taken from her and put up for adoption immediately after it was born. Since then, Cynthia's life has been swamped with other troubles, the most prominent of which is another daughter born out of wedlock. Roxanne (Claire Rushbrook) is white, twenty-one, and mad at the world. The focus of her agitation is Cynthia, with whom she lives and with whom she is perpetually fighting. Unlike Hortense, Roxanne has not made a success of herself. Roxanne works as a street sweeper, and she gives every evidence of repeating her mother's pattern, ending up in a dismal urban flat which she leaves only to go to her dead-end job in order to support an unwanted, ungrateful child. "Sweetheart! Darling!" Cynthia cries, as she perpetually hounds Roxanne about birth control. Not surprisingly, Roxanne reacts to Cynthia obsessive concern by running in the opposite direction.

Cynthia, it turns out, spent her youth taking care of her father and her younger brother, Maurice (Timothy Spall). Maurice is a successful portrait photographer married to Monica (Phyllis Logan), an interior decorator. Maurice and Monica live in considerably posher surroundings than Cynthia does, and since his marriage, Maurice has hardly spoken to his sister. Maurice is a big, agreeable man who seems not to harbor ill will towards anyone, but Monica looks down on her sister-in-law, regarding her as a slattern. But Monica and Maurice have problems of their own, and one day, after watching Monica furiously vacuuming her house, we learn what they are: Monica is barren. Her inability to have a child creates tensions not only within her own household, but throughout the family. Because of her infertility, she resents Cynthia's fecundity, while at the same time cherishing her role as Roxanne's aunt. Monica's jealousy has forced Maurice and his sister apart and now, Cynthia fears, threatens to drive a wedge between her and Roxanne.

Cynthia, however, has finally found someone to love, and she is eager to introduce Hortense to the rest of the family. When Maurice and Monica propose to host a birthday barbeque for Roxanne, Cynthia asks if she can bring along a friend from work. But when Hortense arrives at the party, it quickly becomes apparent that she does not work side by side with Cynthia at the box factory. Cynthia then announces the truth about Hortense, and the revelation not only disrupts the gathering, but forces Monica to admit her own sense of failure and guilt about her inability to conceive a child. A truce somehow ensues, and in the last scene of the film, we see Cynthia together with her two illegitimate daughters in the chaotic patch of garden in back of her flat. Basking in the sunshine as she puts her feet up, Cynthia rhetorically remarks, "This is the life, ain't it?"

Well, yes and no. Presumably, owing to the fact that their most closely guarded secrets and lies are out in the open, Cynthia and her family will now be closer, and Cynthia will have the love she needs. But will she? The economic and social factors that caused the disruptions in her life remain unchanged, as the setting of this final scene makes clear. And will Roxanne and Hortense be able to maintain the level of equanimity towards one another that they seem to have found? Leigh, to his credit, ends the story with a question mark.

Secrets and Lies is a wonderful film, but credit belongs just as much to the actors as to the director. The film is filled with bravura performances, a term which can be applied to the principals, but also to the actors playing minor roles. Lesley Manville, who appears as the social worker who counsels Hortense at the outset of her search for her birth family, is especially notable for the light touch she brings in combining professional apathy and impersonal amiability. Even those who make brief screen appearances

AWARDS AND NOMINATIONS

Academy Awards 1996 Nominations: Best Picture, Best Actress (Blethyn), Best Supporting Actress (Jean-Baptiste), Best Director (Leigh), Best Original Screenplay (Leigh)
Cannes Film Festival 1997: Palme d'Or, Best Actress (Blethyn)
Cesar Award 1997 Nominations: Best Foreign Film
Directors Guild of America 1996 Nomination: Best Director (Leigh)
Golden Globe Awards 1997: Best Actress-Drama (Blethyn)
*Nominations:*Best Film-Drama, Best Supporting Actress (Jean-Baptiste)
Los Angeles Film Critics Association 1996: Best Film, Best Director (Leigh), Best Actress (Blethyn)
Screen Actors Guild 1996 Nominations: Actress (Blethyn)
Writers Guild of America 1996 Nominations: Original Screenplay (Leigh)

as the subjects of Maurice's studio portraits manage to convey—in a matter of seconds—a great deal of individuality. The quick cut montage of Maurice's work is a small but telling commentary on the film's larger action, and in it, as in the long take of Hortense and Cynthia meeting for the first time, Leigh lets us know that few secrets can escape the camera.

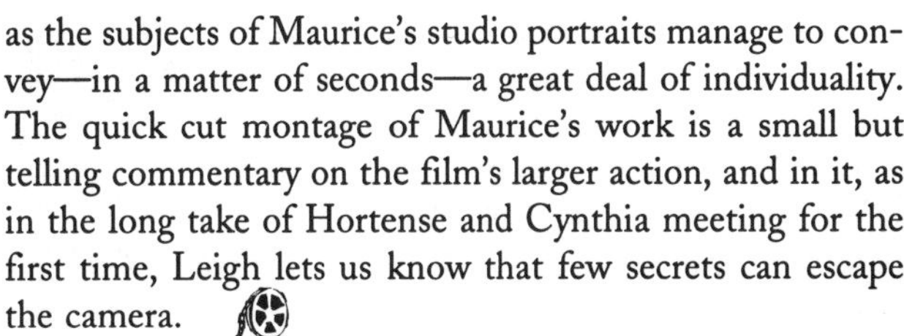

—*Lisa Paddock*

CREDITS

Cynthia: Brenda Blethyn
Hortense: Marianne Jean-Baptiste
Maurice: Timothy Spall
Monica: Phyllis Logan
Roxanne: Claire Rushbrook
Stuart: Ron Cook

Origin: Great Britain
Released: 1995
Production: Simon Channing-Williams for a Channel Four Films, Ciby 2000, and Thin Man production; released by October Films
Direction: Mike Leigh
Screenplay: Mike Leigh
Cinematography: Dick Pope
Editing: Jon Gregory
Music: Andrew Dickson
Production design: Alison Chitty
Art direction: Eve Stewart
Sound: George Richards, Peter Maxwell, Mick Boggis
MPAA rating: Unrated
Running Time: 142 minutes

REVIEWS

Boxoffice. July, 1996, p. 82.
Detroit News. October 11, 1996, p. 3C.
Entertainment Weekly. October 18, 1996, p. 58.
Los Angeles Times. October 4, 1996, p. F1.
New York Times. September 27, 1996, p. C1.
Newsweek. September 30, 1996, p. 74.
Rolling Stone. October 17, 1996, p. 143.
Sight and Sound. June, 1996, p. 51.
USA Today. September 27, 1996, p. 4D.
Variety Online. May 16, 1996.
Village Voice. October 1, 1996, p. 64.

Sgt. Bilko

"A jeepful of laughs."—Patrick Stoner, *PBS Flicks*
"One of the funnies comedies of the year."—Jim Ferguson, *Prevue Channel*
"Absolutely hilarious!"—Jeffrey Lyons, *Sneak Previews*
"The funniest film since *Stripes*."—Kyle Osborne, *WDCA*

Box Office: $30,356,589

In his prime, few comedians could outshine that wild and crazy guy, Steve Martin. With his banjo and an arrow through his head, Martin treated his audiences to an unpredictable rapid-fire onslaught of some of the best comedy to combine intelligence and culture with sheer zaniness. Over the years, however, Steve Martin appears to have lost his edge and the comedian has sunk into a conservative complacency, abandoning his comic tour de force from such films as *The Man with Two Brains* (1983) and *All of Me* (1984) for such maudlin dribble as *Parenthood* (1989) and worst of all, *Father of the Bride* (1991) and its 1995 sequel. Like his female counterpart Bette Midler, Martin has chosen the middle road on the way to the box office and middle America's acceptance while turning their backs on the bold and audacious comedy routines that made them famous.

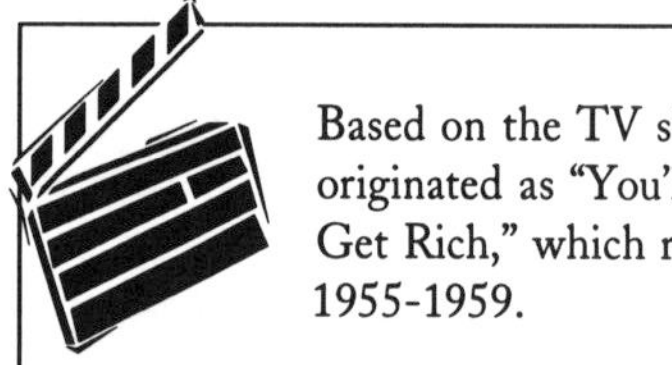

Based on the TV show that originated as "You'll Never Get Rich," which ran from 1955-1959.

In the late 1950s, Phil Silvers struck gold with a television series bearing his name and succeeded in crafting an American comic legend in Master Sergeant Ernie Bilko, a military con artist at Fort Baxter's motor pool. Created by Nat Hiken, Silvers' Bilko was basically a likable guy who, despite his false sincerity and non-stop attempts at swindling any one who came near this fast-talking gambler, was decent at his core. It was no coincidence that "The Phil Silvers Show" carried the by-line, "You'll Never Get Rich." His schemes often failed, but Bilko never ceased to dazzle with his verbal footwork. Thankfully, the filmmakers of this new film version of *Sgt. Bilko* have chosen to leave the original motormouth intact, having sculpted instead their own version of the unscrupulous scam artist. As played by Steve Martin, a true comic genius himself, this new Bilko is less verbal and more physical. The trouble is this updated Bilko comes across more like a self-centered, money-hungry con man who wins mostly at the expense of the lowly enlisted men. Martin succeeds in imbuing his Bilko a degree of charm and actually has moments of his old comedic spark.

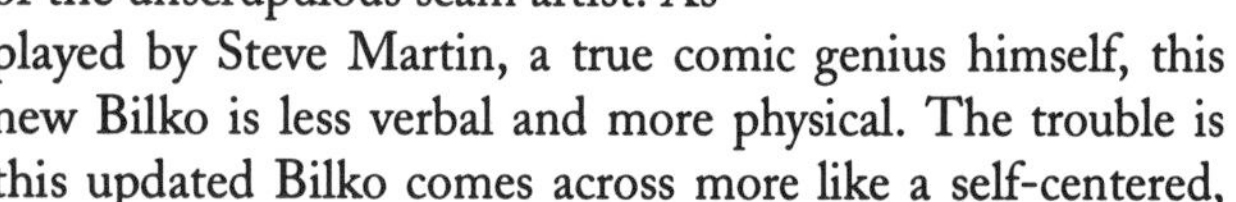

"Sir, all I ever wanted was an honest week's pay for an honest day's work."—Sgt. Bilko

At Fort Baxter's motor pool, it is business as usual for Sgt. Bilko (Steve Martin) and his merry band of swindlers. When straight-arrow Wally Holbrook (Daryl Mitchell of television's "The John Larroquette Show") arrives, he is appalled at the extensive gambling conducted by this Sergeant who can literally smell money on his potential victims. But it does not take long before Holbrook, the first bona fide mechanic to ever be assigned to Bilko's motor pool, succumbs to the Sergeant's charm. When Bilko's arch enemy, Major Thorn, shows up to try to shut down the base by exposing corruption, the gang must rally together, including Wally. Bilko, of course, foils Thorn by transforming the white elephant secret weapon Hover Tank into a resounding success that saves the base and brings honor to the chubby and ineffectual Colonel Hall (a wasted Dan Aykroyd). Not really, for this too is just another of Bilko's shams.

The storyline of *Sgt. Bilko* is thin, at best, and in order to stretch it to its feature length, writer Andy Breckman has added the subplot of Bilko's longtime fiancee, Rita Robbins (Glenne Headly), finally giving the Sergeant thirty days to marry her, or else. Seems Bilko has jilted her several times at the altar and this is supposed to be funny. Her character is by far the most offensive. Rita is very much a throwback to the Fifties, with her tiny little voice and white ankle socks, enduring all sorts of humiliation because only she can see the true Ernie Bilko. Along the way to finally trapping her man, Rita allows herself to be romanced by the scheming Major Thorn, but only for Ernie's own good.

One cannot help but question the Industry's decision to remake a 1950's television show about the military at a time when Generation X-ers are so removed from anything outside their limited sphere of experience. World War II was a source of great pride for Americans and the country rallied around its returning soldiers. They were treated as conquering heroes. Since that time, however, the United States has been severely divided over the role of the military. The Vietnam War nearly crushed the nation and subsequent involvement in Desert Storm caused further dissention. It is curious that the film-

CREDITS

Master Sgt. Ernie Bilko: Steve Martin
Colonel Hall: Dan Aykroyd
Major Thorn: Phil Hartman
Rita Robbins: Glenne Headly
Wally Holbrook: Daryl Mitchell
Dino Paparelli: Max Casella
Duane Doberman: Eric Edwards
Tony Morales: Dan Ferro
Sam Fender: Brian Leckner
Luis Clemente: Brian Ortiz
Sgt. Raquel Barbella: Pamela Segall

Origin: USA
Released: 1996
Production: A Brian Grazer Production for Imagine Entertainment; released by Universal.
Direction: Jonathan Lynn
Screenplay: Andy Breckman; based on the television series created by Nat Hiken
Cinematography: Peter Sova
Editing: Tony Lombardo
Production design: Lawrence G. Paull
Art direction: Bruce Crone
Costume design: Susan Becker
Music: Alan Silvestri
MPAA rating: PG
Running Time: 92 minutes

makers of *Sgt. Bilko* chose to update their project to the 1990's rather than keep it in period. Times have changed dramatically and the moral fiber of the country seems to have eroded far past the point that we can embrace yet another freeloading, larcenous schemer as funny. If *Sgt. Bilko* had been played out with any degree of irony or satire, such as Robert Altman's *M.A.S.H.* (1970), the film may have enjoyed some success. But director Jonathan Lynn (*My Cousin Vinny* [1992]) failed to commit to a strong creative vision and as a result, ended up with a very mediocre film.

Not without its laughs, *Sgt. Bilko* fails to capitalize on the verbal ferocity of the original television series, choosing instead to update the premise by removing the moral goodness of the Master Sergeant. With a few exceptions, the film was generally panned by the critics.

—Patricia Kowal

REVIEWS

Chicago Tribune. March 29, 1996, p. 4.
Detroit News. March 29, 1996, p. 2D.
Entertainment Weekly. April 12, 1996, p. 49.
Los Angeles Times. March 29, 1996, p. F1.
The New Yorker. April 8, 1996, pp. 106-107.
New York Times. March 29, 1996, p. C14.
Orlando Sentinel. March 29, 1996.
USA Today. March 29, 1996, p. 4D.
Variety. April 1, 1996, p. 55.

Set It Off

The only breaks you get are the ones you take.—Movie tagline

It's about crime. It's about payback. It's about survival.—Movie tagline

"Intensely dramatic, pulse pounding action!"—Lee Thomas, *ABC-TV*

"Fresh, engaging and powerful."—Lisa Schwarzbaum, *Entertainment Weekly*

"Extravagantly action packed . . . "—Stephen Holden, *New York Times*

"They're not *Waiting to Exhale,* they're breathing fire."—Susan Wloszczyna, *USA Today*

Box Office: $34,325,720

Critics immediately began comparing *Set It Off* with *Boys N the Hood* (1991). Some compared it with the trend-setting buddy-road-heist film *Thelma & Louise* (1991), which portrayed reckless young women doing the kinds of things that had been done in previous films only by reckless young men. *Set It Off* is a better film than *Boys N the Hood* because, for one thing, it had a much bigger budget; it has the feeling of a major studio production, whereas *Boys* had the diamond-in-the-rough feeling of a low-budget independent project. *Set It Off* is better than *Thelma & Louise* in some respects because the black adventurers are more credibly motivated. Their hostility is not fueled by white middle-class ennui or inchoate feminism but by black rage.

Frankie (Vivica A. Fox), an upwardly mobile young African American bank teller, is very unjustly fired because she happens to know one of the young bandits who come to make a violent unauthorized withdrawal. She finds herself wearing a janitor's uniform along with three other embittered black women who all dream of escaping from the ghetto and minimum-wage slavery. It is Frankie's banking experience that tempts them into a life of crime. They believe she can show them when and where to find the most money and how to avoid getting caught.

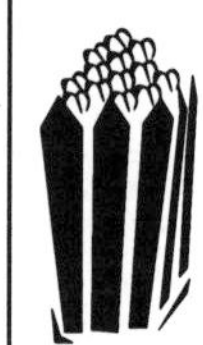

"Where will I go? I belong in this hood."—Cleo to Stony who wants to get out of the projects.

The beautiful Stony (Jada Pinkett) is trying to push her younger brother into UCLA while working hard to support him. She becomes totally disillusioned when he is mistaken for a robber by racist, trigger-happy cops and shot dead. Tisean (Kimberly Elise) wants to regain custody of the little boy who was taken from her by an insensitive social worker. Tisean does not want to live on welfare but cannot earn enough to pay for child care while she is away at work—a familiar Catch-22 situation in the black ghetto.

Cleo (Queen Latifah), is indispensable to the gang of four as well as its greatest liability. This rowdy lesbian wants lots of money and all that money can buy, including drugs. Her conspicuous consumption of her share of the loot is one of the things that help the police identify the foursome. She can steal a locked car in under one minute and she is a demon when she gets behind the wheel. It takes little provocation to start her firing her Uzi. She knows what the others either failed to realize or refused to think about: that if you start waving guns around you might have to use them.

While most of the audience is reveling in the shooting, car chases, explosions, mountains of stolen cash, and anti-establishment obscenities, a few low-profile viewers may be wondering what kind of message all this is sending. Do films like *Set It Off* encourage violence or do they defuse aggressive impulses by providing vicarious gratification? Do they plant suggestions in impressionable minds? Will there be copycats holding up banks across the country because they think they have learned how it is done? Will the film encourage young black women to get more involved in hard-core crime? Will the story persuade young viewers that crime pays or that crime does not pay?

Even though three of the four sisters in crime end up on slabs in the morgue, Stony, the principal viewpoint character, escapes from the ghetto to a tropical paradise with a big bag of money. Like both the 1972 and 1993 versions of *The Getaway, Set It Off* seems to be saying that crime does pay—at least some of the time. The film even justifies violent criminal behavior on the basis of racial discrimination, gender discrimination, and the evils of "the system." When the gentle Tisean naively asks if it might not be a little bit wrong to hold up banks, she is quickly reminded that there is no other way to beat the system. Furthermore, the loss will be reimbursed by "the insurance company," which adjusts premiums to offset such casualties while still reaping fat profits. Although *Set It Off* is state-of-the-art in technique, the philosophy behind it is reminiscent of apologist films like *Dead End* (1937) and *Angels with Dirty Faces* (1938), which partially exonerated criminals by implicitly blaming capitalism.

Set It Off follows a plot pattern similar to that of the classic *Bonnie and Clyde* (1967). What begins as an adventure for high-spirited but woefully ignorant malcontents escalates into tragedy as reality takes the place of illusion. The bank heists are well staged with many cowering tellers and customers, plus the occasional misguided guard or plainclothes cop who pulls a gun and starts a shoot-out in which innocent people are mowed down. The viewer often has the feeling of being one of the bystanders caught in the melee. The robbers' pistols and submachine guns are pointed directly at the camera, making the audience feel like ducking behind seats.

CREDITS

Stony: Jada Pinkett
Cleo: Queen Latifah
Frankie: Vivica A. Fox
Tisean: Kimberly Elise
Keith: Blair Underwood
Detective Strode: John C. McGinley

Origin: USA
Released: 1996
Production: Dale Pollock and Oren Koules for a Peak production; released by New Line Cinema
Direction: F. Gary Gray
Screenplay: Kate Lanier and Takashi Bufford
Cinematography: Marc Reshovsky
Editing: John Carter
Music: Christopher Young
Production design: Robb Wilson King
Set decoration: Lance Lombardo
Costume design: Sylvia Vega Vasquez
Sound: Richard Lightstone
Casting: Robi Reed-Humes
MPAA rating: R
Running Time: 120 minutes

AWARDS AND NOMINATIONS

Independent Spirit Awards 1997 Nominations:
Supporting Actress (Queen Latifah)

Young director F. Gary Gray is innovative and professional. What is especially impressive is the way he keeps the viewer emotionally off balance with contrasting scenes and shifting camera angles. At times the viewer is sympathetically in league with the female bandits, sharing in their emotions as they divide their loot, plan their next caper, or try to escape in a hail of bullets. At other times the viewer is on the side of the law as Detective Strode (John C. McGinley) and his army of white and black, male and female assistants patiently work to identify the perpetrators, unravel their past histories, and track them down. At still other times the viewer—in mortal danger from bullets, flying glass, and airborne automobiles—is only concerned about self-preservation.

During their second robbery the four rebels come up against the same sort of unforeseen contretemps that foiled the carefully laid plans of would-be bank robber Sonny (Al Pacino) in *Dog Day Afternoon* (1975). Two uniformed cops try to arrest a schizoid derelict right out in front of the bank. They call for back-up. Pretty soon there is a bank robber's nightmare of patrol cars, motorcycles and blue uniforms blocking escape. The four frantic amateurs manage to crash out of the building in a stolen car—but it is becoming obvious they have gotten in over their heads. Their adventure has involved them in murder as well as robbery. The police will stop at nothing to track them down. They have all been photographed many times over by monitor cameras. Their dark glasses and wigs have not disguised them very well, and the fact that they are women makes it impossible for them to blend in with the male majority in the mug files.

During one of the rare interludes of non-violence, Stony meets handsome, Harvard-educated Keith in what Stephen Holden of *The New York Times* calls "a preposterous romantic subplot." Keith just happens to be an executive with the bank that Stony just happens to be casing. She enjoys a Cinderella adventure with this yuppie Prince Charming. The camera lavishes considerable attention on their naked love-making. Even though Stony is obviously from the wrong side of the tracks, it would appear that Keith is sufficiently in love to propose marriage. This dream evaporates when Stony's three confederates insist on robbing the very bank where Keith is carving out his career. All Stony can do is lure him away from work with a last-minute phone call so he will be sitting safely in a restaurant waiting for a rendezvous she will never keep.

In the grand finale the four women barge into one of the biggest banks in Los Angeles, waving guns, jumping over counters, and scooping piles of currency into trash bags. They know the police have identified them. They want to make this their last big score and then retire. Before they are out the door, however, they have become the objects of what looks like the biggest manhunt in L.A.P.D. history. They are pursued on freeways, boulevards and back streets by squad cars with screaming sirens and omniscient helicopters with blinding searchlights. They crash through one police barricade after another. Only Cleo's suicidal driving keeps them from being brought to bay.

As ultra-butch-lesbian Cleo, the popular rap star Queen Latifah steals the show. She is like a black, female James Cagney who will die rather than surrender to the hated pigs. The audience feels sympathy for this desperate woman because of her rugged individualism and loyalty. When escape is impossible and Tisean is already dead of bullet wounds, Cleo makes the ultimate sacrifice. She orders her two friends to flee on foot in the opposite direction while she plows straight into a police barricade and is killed in a visually poetic, slow-motion shootout.

Cleo's suicidal behavior is one of the similarities that reminded critics of *Thelma & Louise.* Such endings have been the only feasible resolutions for gangster films since the genre was invented. They gratify the viewer's antisocial impulses while at the same time offering some assurance that society is still protected by law. Humphrey Bogart died that way in *High Sierra* (1941) and James Cagney did the same in *White Heat* (1949). Al Pacino died that way more recently in *Scarface* (1983). Now with the triumph of feminism it is the ladies' turn to go down in defiance. As Alphonse Karr said 150 years ago, "The more things change, the more they remain the same."

—Bill Delaney

REVIEWS

Boxoffice Online. November 12, 1996.
Chicago Tribune. November 6, 1996, p. 1.
Detroit Free Press. November 6, 1996.
Entertainment Weekly. November 8, 1996, p. 48.
Los Angeles Times. November 6, 1996, p. F1.
The New York Times. November 6, 1996, p. B3.
People. November 11, 1996, p. 21.
Rolling Stone. November 28, 1996, p. 143.
Sight and Sound. March, 1997, p. 62.
USA Today. November 6, 1996, p. 8D.
Variety. November 4, 1996, p. 82.

She's the One

A romantic comedy about two brothers . . . and the one thing that came between them.—Movie tagline

"A sexy comedy! Ripples and roars with surprise."—Guy Flatly, *Cosmopolitan*

"A knock out! It will charm your socks off."—Joel Siegel, *Good Morning America*

"Marvelously sly . . . irresistible."—Richard Schickel, *Time*

"For laughter and romance, this film's the one."—Michele Shapiro, *Time-Out New York*

"Incredibly funny!"—Paul Wunder, *WBAI Radio*

Box Office: $9,538,948

Writer-director-actor Edward Burns made an impressive debut in 1995 with *The Brothers McMullen,* a low-budget comedy he shot in his spare time while working as a production assistant for "Entertainment Tonight." Burns' depiction of the typical American male's bewilderment over women, Irish-American families, and life on Long Island and in New York City was praised by many reviewers as the introduction of a potentially important new voice in American film and earned him comparisons with Woody Allen, among others. Those delighted by *The Brothers McMullen* looked forward to Burns' second film to see what he could accomplish with more money and time at his disposal. *She's the One,* however, is disappointing since the filmmaker does not do anything new or better than in his first effort.

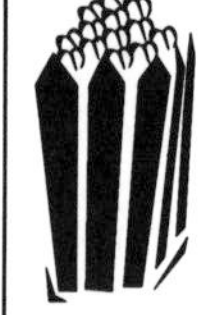

Mickey: "Look at you. You make a pile of dough and you're miserable." Francis: "Hey, and I'm not miserable, okay. I'm dissatisfied. That's what makes me a success."

The Brothers McMullen shows how three brothers are confused about what their wives, girlfriends, and mistresses want and about what they want from women themselves. *She's the One* does much the same, although with two brothers and a father. Mickey Fitzpatrick (Burns) is a young New York City cab driver with little ambition, typical of his generation, drifting through life until something develops. This something begins developing when he starts talking with Hope (Maxine Bahns), an attractive young woman he is driving to an airport. She is on her way to a friend's wedding in New Orleans and impulsively asks Mickey to drive her there in his cab. He agrees, and they even more impulsively marry on the way. Back in New York, Mickey is still content to drift while Hope works as a waitress, but she wants more and plans to go to Paris to study for a Ph.D. Their dilemma, recalling a similar situation in Allen's *Manhattan* (1979), becomes whether he will go with her.

Mickey's brother Francis (Mike McGlone) is his opposite: a successful Wall Street executive with a chauffeur-driven limousine. (What exactly Francis does on Wall Street is never made clear.) Francis is married to Rene (Jennifer Aniston), but they have not had sex in some time. His problem is his affair with Heather Davis (Cameron Diaz), another Wall Streeter. Francis' adultery is complicated by his inability to decide to break with Rene and commit himself to Heather, Heather's continuing relationship with an older man, and the fact that she is Mickey's former fiancee. (The older brother in *The Brothers McMullen* has an affair with a woman dating the character played by Burns.)

The third Fitzpatrick male is their Brooklyn father (John Mahoney). Something of a cliche of a misogynistic Irish-American, Mr. Fitzpatrick takes his wife for granted, cares only for going out on his boat, named, appropriately, "The Fighting Fitzpatricks," taunts his sons by calling them "girls" whenever their behavior is not up to his standards, and is suspicious of Hope's dark complexion. "Is she from one of the islands?" he constantly asks. To which Mickey responds, "Yeah. Rhode Island." The head of the family thinks his wife, because of her worries about their sons, spends hours consulting with the local priest (Tom Tammi). Fitzpatrick learns she has been having an affair with a neighbor, Mr. De Lucca (Robert Weil), only after she has left him for a man who thinks she is wonderful. (Like Heather's other lover, Mrs. Fitzpatrick remains unseen with Burns providing only a glimpse of her car as she drives away in despair, ironically, upon learning that Francis has left Rene.) His wife was of relatively little importance when she was around, but now that she has gone, Fitzpatrick is at a loss.

As in *The Brothers McMullen,* only two of the plotlines carry any weight. In both of Burns' films, the relationships between the characters played by Burns and Bahns (his real-life girlfriend) have little substance or humor. Neither Mickey nor Hope seems even remotely romantic, making their quick courtship less than credible. Connie (Leslie Mann), who works at the same bar, tells Hope to ignore her husband's qualms and go to Paris, and Connie challenges Mickey by announcing she is sexually attracted to Hope. Connie gives a slight edge to the Hope-Mickey story but not enough.

Bahns has improved considerably since her awkward, amateurish performance in *The Brothers McMullen* but is not given enough to do to display much acting skill. She is at her best, is more natural, when Hope tries to have a heart-to-heart with her father-in-law. Burns is a likable performer with some presence but does not play off his fellow actors the way a veteran such as Mahoney can.

The Francis-Rene relationship has plenty of edge since he is indecisive about their marriage at a time she is desperate for affection. Aniston is a much more skilled comic performer here than she shows on "Friends," her inexplicably popular television situation comedy. Rene's despair over not having sex with Francis, a predicament she is willing to share with everyone, including her parents (Anita Gillette and Frank Vincent), is delightful, especially since it makes the despicable Francis squirm.

Francis is meant to represent the kind of creep who is successful in the business world because of his lack of concern for anyone but himself, and Burns relishes tormenting him. Rene is reminiscent of the slightly tawdry middle-class world from which Francis has raised himself, and the beautiful, seductive Heather represents the rewards to which he feels entitled. She is made even more attractive by taunting him with her continuing affair with her older lover. Francis is a hypocrite who preaches one set of values while practicing another. A walking sore of selfishness, Francis is enraged that he cannot have everything his way, and he is punished by losing both his wife and his mistress.

CREDITS

Mickey Fitzpatrick: Edward Burns
Francis Fitzpatrick: Mike McGlone
Heather Davis: Cameron Diaz
Rene Fitzpatrick: Jennifer Aniston
Hope Fitzpatrick: Maxine Bahns
Mr. Fitzpatrick: John Mahoney
Connie: Leslie Mann
Tom: Malachy McCourt
Ron: Frank Vincent
Carol: Anita Gillette
Molly: Amanda Peet
Mr. De Lucca: Robert Weil
Father John: Tom Tammi

Origin: USA
Released: 1996
Production: Ted Hope, James Schamus, and Edward Burns for Good Machine/Marlboro Road Gang Productions in association with South Fork Pictures; released by Fox Searchlight Pictures
Direction: Edward Burns
Screenplay: Edward Burns
Cinematography: Frank Prinzi
Editing: Susan Graef
Production design: William Barclay
Art direction: Caty Maxey
Set design: Harriet Zucker
Costume design: Susan Lyall
Music: Tom Petty
Sound: T. J. O'Mara
Casting: Laura Rosenthal
MPAA rating: R
Running Time: 95 minutes

McGlone gives by far the best performance in *The Brothers McMullen* and by far the worst in *She's the One.* He is too busy, twitching nervously in every scene. It is as if the actor is too uncomfortable with this nasty character and never truly connects with him. Burns might have helped by softening Francis in some way so that he is not entirely repellant.

She's the One is mean spirited in other ways. Heather has worked her way through college as a prostitute, and Mickey tastelessly reminds her of her past in a jarringly uncomfortable scene. As with the other women, Heather is underdeveloped. Is she having an affair with Francis just to get revenge on his brother, or is she really attracted to him? If the latter, what can she possibly see in this slug? That Diaz emerges unscathed from this somewhat ridiculous role is noteworthy. She subtly invests Heather with a sense of mystery and dignity missing from the screenplay.

Mahoney has a challenging role since the head of the Fitzpatrick family, almost as clueless as his sons, is full of prejudices. Because Francis is not having sex with Rene, the father worries that his son may be homosexual, ignoring that he has questioned his sons' manliness all their lives. Like Aniston, Mahoney is undervalued on "Frasier," his popular situation comedy, but he makes the most of this part, showing how Fitzpatrick, unlike Francis, is more foolish than detestable. Fitzpatrick is the most well-rounded character because he is allowed to have flaws and remain likable since he cares about his family but does not know how to show affection. Without condescending to or sentimentalizing the character, Mahoney makes him believably human. The screen brightens whenever he appears.

Both Burns' films are stylistically conservative, but Tom Petty's songs give *She's the One* some needed energy. The instrumental portion of his soundtrack, however, sounds like something that might be heard on an earnest low-budget film. But even with all these defects, *She's the One* is not a bad film. It has many wonderful moments, as when Rene discusses her problems with her parents and sister (Amanda Peet) or when Francis talks with his elderly, philosophical driver, Tom (Malachy McCourt). *The Brothers McMullen,* even though it too is flawed, simply creates expectations higher than Burns delivers here.

—*Michael Adams*

REVIEWS

Boston Globe. August 23, 1996, p. F1.
Chicago Tribune. August 23, 1996, p. C7.
Entertainment Weekly. September 6, 1996, p. 53.
Los Angeles Times. August 23, 1996, p. F4.
The New York Times. August 23, 1996, p. C3.
The New Yorker. September 9, 1996, p. 93.
San Francisco Chronicle. August 23, 1996, p. D3.
USA Today. August 23, 1996, p. D8.
Village Voice. August 27, 1996, p. 50.
Washington Post. August 23, 1996, p. D1.

Shine

"Films hitting the 'triumph of the human spirit' note of uplift rarely play it as powerfully or as tenderly as *Shine.*"—Janet Maslin, *New York Times*

"*Shine* is an utterly extraordinary true story . . . It's scrappy, sexy, touching and fun. Rank it with the very best movies of the year."—Peter Travers, *Rolling Stone*

"Two thumbs up!"—*Siskel & Ebert*

"*Shine:* Once seen, forever remembered!"—Gene Shalit, *Today, NBC-TV*

"A glorious film."—Joe Morgenstern, *Wall Street Journal*

Box Office: $10,680,840

Brilliant concert pianist David Helfgott (Geoffrey Rush) receives the will to return to the stage from his wife Gillian (Lynn Redgrave) in *Shine.*

When Australian film director Scott Hicks read in 1986 a brief newspaper notice about David Helfgott, an eccentric pianist who was then performing in a Perth restaurant, he found the idea that ten years later led to *Shine.* Hicks went to hear David perform in a concert, and with the help of screenwriter Jan Sardi and producer Jane Scott, he eventually brought to the screen the story of David's struggle to overcome a mental breakdown that kept him from performing for years. Making the independent film budgeted at only $4.5 million proved difficult. "I persevered" explained Hicks, "because I was so inspired by David. I couldn't get over the fact that he had endured such a tortuous and chaotic life and come out the other side in this remarkable relationship, an eccentric but still brilliant performer. I knew he was a wonderful story."

"The piano is a monster. Tame it or it will swallow you whole."—Music professor Parkes to Helfgott

The opening scene shows David (Geoffrey Rush) in the pouring rain tapping on the door of a wine bar called Moby's in Perth, Australia. The owner Sylvia (Sonia Todd) invites him in even though the restaurant is closed. David speaks in a high-speed, nonstop hodgepodge of words: "Live, Sylvie, live—live and let live—that's very important, isn't it? Molto, molto. But then again it's a lifelong struggle, isn't it Sylvia—Tony, to live, to survive, to survive undamaged and not destroy any living breathing creature. The point is, if you do something wrong you can be punished for the rest of your life, so I think it's a lifelong struggle; is it a lifelong struggle? Whatever you do it's a struggle, a struggle to keep your head above water and not get it chopped off. I'm not disappointing you am I Sylvia-Tony-Moby-Sam, yay Sam!" Sylvia and her friends eventually return David to his home and his attendant. The structure of the film effectively flashes from present to past and back again to show how David came to such a state.

As a boy (Alex Rafalowicz), David is taken by his father Peter (Armin Mueller-Stahl) to a piano competition. David does not win but he does impress one of the judges Ben Rosen (Nicholas Bell), who offers him lessons. Peter rebuffs Rosen and speaks to David of both his love for him and of the absolute necessity of winning. Peter's strictness stifles David's early years. The father interrupts his son's tentative conversations with girls, and when David forms a friendship with writer Katharine Susannah Prichard (Googie Withers), he naturally looks to the older woman as a mentor. As an adolescent (played by Noah Taylor), David has a success that leads to an offer to study in the United States, but on the night he receives a letter from the American family he is to reside with, his father angrily throws the letter in the fire. Later, he wins a scholarship to the Royal College of Music in London, and upon this opportunity he finally defies his father's pummeling words and fists: "David, if you go you will never come back to this house. You will never be anybody's son. The girls will lose their brother. Is that what you want? You want to destroy the family? . . . David, if you love me you will stop this nonsense."

The character who dominates the early scenes is David's father Peter, and the film is really less about music than about healing the scars of childhood. His ancestors having died in the Holocaust, Peter holds his own family together in a suffocating bind. At times he wears his suffering like a badge, and he even dismisses Ben Rosen as a potential teacher for David because Rosen has not suffered enough. Peter's own father, in an often-repeated story to David, had smashed the violin Peter had saved for when he was a boy. He endlessly reminds David what a "lucky boy" he is to be able to make music. Part of Peter's fixation on music for David and in particular on the emotionally demanding Rachmaninoff third piano concerto grows out of his own frustrated childhood experiences. Armin Mueller-Stahl does an excellent job of bringing out the destructive strength of Peter's love for David.

The real-life Helfgott dubbed almost all the piano playing heard in the film.

Once in London, David shows signs of erratic behavior. He coils on his dorm floor in the fetal position. He sleeps on the stone lions in Trafalgar Square. He collects his mail wearing only a pullover sweater. David also comes under the instruction of Professor Cecil Parkes (John Gielgud). Gielgud, who celebrated his 91st birthday during the shooting of the film, brings dignity and passion to this small part. "Don't you just love those big fat chords?" he shouts above David's playing. Though Parkes's advice to David indulges in a few cliches ("play as if there were no tomorrow; once you've done it, there is no one can take it away from you"), he nonetheless initiates him in the daunting "Rach 3" for his concert piece. An effective montage sequence includes shots of Parkes's hand movements accompanying David's performance, Peter listening tearfully back in Australia to a tape of David playing the piece, and canted angles of David's own fingering during the concert. Following this success, David collapses and returns to Australia for psychiatric treatment.

Throughout the film director Hicks and screenwriter Sardi use water as a unifying device. While the title suggests the eventual outcome of David's talent shining forth, the film shows the dark, rainy struggle that precedes this success. David's first words in the film refer to "a struggle to keep your head above water," and Geoffrey Rush, who plays David as an adult, remarked in observing the real David Helfgott: "David babbles like a brook, but I found when I went over transcripts of his wonderful monologues, the rhythms and syntax were like poetry." Visual images of water also appear. A number of scenes are played in or against a backdrop of rainstorms. Both as a young boy and later in the institution, David sits unmoving in tubs of water, once with only his nose and eyes above water, as if he longs for whatever womb-like security he can find. As David gets to know the woman he will later marry, he takes her to the beach where he splashes happily in the waves. Preparing

AWARDS AND NOMINATIONS

Academy Awards 1996: Best Actor (Rush)
Nominations: Best Picture, Best Supporting Actor (Mueller-Stahl), Best Director (Hicks), Best Original Screenplay (Sardi/Hicks), Best Film Editing, Best Original Score (Hirschfelder)
Australian Film Institute Awards 1996: Best Film, Best Actor (Rush), Best Supporting Actor (Mueller-Stahl), Best Director (Hicks), Best Screenplay (Sardi), Best Cinematography (Simpson), Best Music (Hirschfelder), Best Editing, Best Sound
Directors Guild of America 1996 Nomination: Best Director (Hicks)
Golden Globe Awards 1997: Best Actor-Drama (Rush)
Nominations: Best Film-Drama, Best Director (Hicks), Best Screenplay (Sardi), Best Original Score (Hirschfelder)
Los Angeles Film Critics Association 1996: Best Actor (Rush)
National Board of Review 1996: Best Film
New York Film Critics Circle 1996: Best Actor (Rush)
Screen Actors Guild 1996: Actor (Rush), Supporting Actor (Taylor), Cast
Writers Guild of America 1996 Nominations: Original Screenplay (Sardi/Hicks)

CREDITS

David Helfgott: Geoffrey Rush
David (as a child): Alex Rafalowicz
David (as a young man): Noah Taylor
Peter Helfgott: Armin Mueller-Stahl
Gillian: Lynn Redgrave
Cecil Parkes: John Gielgud
Katharine Susannah Prichard: Googie Withers
Sylvia: Sonia Todd
Ben Rosen: Nicholas Bell
Beryl: Beverly Dunn

Origin: Australia
Released: 1996
Production: Jane Scott for Momentum Films; released by Fine Line Features
Direction: Scott Hicks
Screenplay: Jan Sardi; based on an original story by Scott Hicks
Cinematography: Geoffrey Simpson
Editing: Pip Karmel
Art direction: Tony Cronin
Production design: Vicki Niehus
Costumes: Louise Wakefield
Music: David Hirschfelder
MPAA rating: PG-13
Running Time: 105 minutes

for a return to the concert hall, David litters a pool with pages of a Ravel score, as if swimming with the music will intensify his bond with it. The filmmakers use the motif of water as an effective way to reflect David's many moods.

Lisa Schwarzbaum, writing in *Entertainment Weekly,* made the observant point that director Scott Hicks "has constructed this elegant piece ... into a concerto form (there are 'movements,' changes of tempo, etc)." The equal emphasis on the three stages of David's life and the excellent casting of Rafalowicz, Taylor, and Rush to mark each of these parts furnish some additional examples for her comment. The first section of the film depicts David in childhood at his most repressed time, while in the second he seems to experience emotions most keenly. This adolescence is the part of his life in which he feels the grief of Katharine's death, the exhilaration of playing the Rachmaninoff in a concert, and the pain of his collapse. The third section chronicles his steady movement as an adult back to a life of performing.

This final section is the only aspect of the film that has been consistently faulted by some critics. More linear in its development than the effective flashbacks and -forwards of the first two sections, this recovery phase focuses primarily on the three women whose kindness and acceptance of David eventually creates a type of anti-father atmosphere. The first of these nurturing friends is Sylvia, into whose wine bar David staggers on the rainy night that opens the film. The next is Beryl (Beverly Dunn), a woman he meets at the mental institution who recognizes his name from his early years as a prodigy. The third is Gillian (Lynn Redgrave), who meets David when she arrives for an extended visit with her friend Sylvia. Gillian takes the time to converse with David about his fears, and when her visit concludes, he abruptly proposes to her. Some critics pointed out correctly that Gillian's character is too hastily introduced and too thinly developed to offset the strong negative impression left by the domineering presence of David's father. However, it is really the combined work of the three women whose support helps to return David to the concert hall.

The biographical subject matter and the extreme breakdown that David experiences (the real David Helfgott's mental condition has never been clearly diagnosed) limit the identification the audience experiences with this film. Rather than being pulled into the characters, the audience watches them from the outside, absorbed by Hicks and Sardi's effective structure and by the fine performances. *Shine* effectively documents the painful fall and rise of David Helfgott.

—Glenn Hopp

REVIEWS

Cosmopolitan. December, 1996, p. 21.
Entertainment Weekly. November 29, 1996, p. 73.
The Nation. December 2, 1996, p. 36.
New Republic. November 18, 1996, p. 26.
New York. December 2, 1996, p. 115.
New York Times. November 22, 1996, p. B4.
The New Yorker. December 2, 1996, p. 116.
Newsweek. November 25, 1996, p. 78.
People Weekly. December 9, 1996, p. 25.
Rolling Stone. November, 1996, p. 92.
St. Louis Post-Dispatch. December 25, 1996, p. 3E.
Time. November 25, 1996, p. 108.
USA Today. November 22, 1996, p. 5D.
USA Today. December 20, 1996, p. 1D.
Variety. December 16, 1996, p. 22.
Vogue. December, 1996, p. 168.
Wall St. Journal. November 22, 1996, p. A14.

The Shot

Box Office: $2,970

Think of a much less clever, garage-band version of Robert Altman's *The Player* (1992), and you'll have a rough fix on *The Shot,* Dan Bell's ultra-low-budget riff on the cruelties of the Hollywood star system. Filmed in two weeks for $40,000 in between the cast and crew's other small-time jobs, *The Shot* is a comic exorcism of the frustrations of the small fish at the bottom of the Los Angeles food chain. Los Angelinos and struggling actors will most appreciate it; the rest of us are more likely to yawn, laugh occasionally and wonder what all the fuss is about.

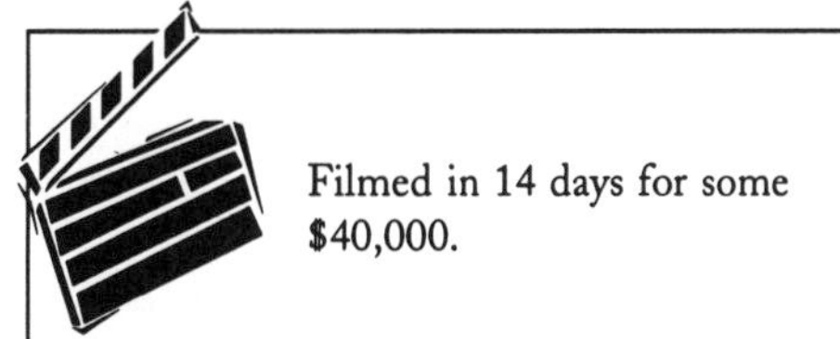

Filmed in 14 days for some $40,000.

Writer-director Dan Bell based the film on a 1989 play he wrote. He cast himself in the lead as Dern Reel, a shaggy-haired type who wants so much to be a serious actor that he is heartbroken when auditions for a fourth-rate theater's revival of *Cat on a Hot Tin Roof* are closed. His roommate Patrick St. Patrick (Michael Rivkin) is also a down-and-out actor. St. Patrick is obsessed with his looks (even though he doesn't have any) and with getting aboard the gravy train.

The two actors are so broke they borrow money from kids in their apartment complex and skip out on restaurant bills. They both are insanely jealous of Tinseltown's current hot director, David Egoman, and its hunk acting flavor of the month, Bob Mann (Michael DeLuise). St. Patrick, who took acting classes with Mann, is apoplectic when he learns Mann has the lead in Egoman's latest bloated release, "Burnt Sienna Sunset." While slicing golf balls off a garage roof overlooking L.A. (one of the film's best location shots), St. Patrick proposes to Reel that they steal the film from Egoman's house.

They pull off the heist, but find one or more other intruders also present. Egoman has been stabbed, shot and bludgeoned to the brink of death. A dictatorial studio boss, Sheila Ricks (Mo Gaffney), takes over his film, revamping it to give the female star a larger role. The two cops investigating the death are a bitter law-and-order type who loves gory, graphic talk and his milquetoast partner. Also involved in the overwrought plot are Reel's neglected girlfriend (Jude Horowitz), a maniacal writer who claims Egoman has stolen his script (Vincent Ward), a transvestite landlord (Paul Provenza), and several assorted street lunatics.

The film careens merrily from one improbable scene to another. Some are entertaining, few memorable. The production values are scant, and outdoor scenes especially look ghastly. It's clearly a labor of madcap love for all involved, who donated time between other stints during the dizzying 14-day shoot. Some multi-actor scenes are patched together from solo scenes separately performed because the necessary ensemble couldn't be assembled at the right time.

The Shot has the look, feel and humor of a sophomoric prank. The purpose seems to be for down-in-their-luck actors to vent some steam at their exclusion from bigger roles. Fortunately, Bell and the gang also poke fun at themselves, saving *The Shot* from pretentiousness. But there's so much inside stuff going on here, so many jokes only those in the industry will get, that a middle American audience would be mostly befuddled. Not to worry: Few people saw the film in theaters, since the only distribution was what the cast and crew could beg on their own. Even prospects for video release remained iffy a year after the film was made.

As a look at the underbelly of Hollywood, the refuse bin in the back of the movie industry, *The Shot* is of some interest. It's intermittently clever, but not enough to rescue it from its overworked theme, its preposterous and inconsistent plot, its scrap heap production values and its uneven

CREDITS

Dern Reel: Dan Bell
Patrick St. Patrick: Michael Rivkin
Anna: Jude Horowitz
Sheila Ricks: Mo Gaffney
Bob Mann: Michael DeLuise
Detective Markinson: Jack Kehler
Detective Corelli: Ted Raimi
Smith: Vincent Ward

Origin: USA
Released: 1995
Production: Jude Horowitz and Sherrie Ross for Bread & Water Productions
Direction: Dan Bell
Screenplay: Dan Bell; based on his play
Cinematography: Alan Claudillo
Editing: Kevin Greutert
Production design: Diamond Jim Braverman
Music: Kevin Sonis
Sound: Ben Patrick
MPAA rating: Unrated
Running Time: 84 minutes

acting. Rivkin turns in a shrill, supremely annoying performance that by itself would ruin any film. Jack Kehler and Ted Raimi as the hapless cop duo provide most of the laughs. The most recognizable face in the no-star cast is Dana Carvey, who does a cameo.

The Shot is little more than a curio. Bell's iconoclastic view and his wacky humor might be better put to use in a film with a bigger budget and a more accessible story line. *The Shot,* however, is unlikely to give him the ticket to fame that this film's characters so desperately want. No matter. It sure looks like this gang had a lot of fun being so amateurish in between their more professional, more boring acting jobs in that star system they love to hate.

—*Michael Betzold*

REVIEWS

Boxoffice. February, 1996, p. R-11.
Variety. February 5, 1996, p. 60.

Sleepers

Four friends have made a mistake that will change their lives forever.—Movie tagline

"A powerful, riveting thriller! Astonishing. Smashingly successful!"—Susan Granger, *CRN International*

"Barry Levinson's skilled direction is the stuff of Oscars."—Raj Bahadur, *NBC Radio Network*

"One of this year's best films. A big winner with a dream cast."—Jim Ferguson, *Prevue Channel*

"A stunning, unforgettable, moving and unique motion picture."—Paul Wunder, *WBAI Radio*

Box Office: $52,528,577

Director-screenwriter Barry Levinson is that rare filmmaker who can create highly effective small-scale films such as *Diner* (1982) and *Tin Men* (1987) as well as enormously entertaining crowd pleasers like *The Natural* (1984) and *Rain Man* (1988). He can also make personal films that fail to work as effectively, such as *Avalon* (1990) and the underrated *Jimmy Hollywood* (1994), embarrassing failures like *Toys* (1992), badly made but popular sentimentality, as with *Good Morning, Vietnam* (1987), extremely well-made but emotionally uninvolving dramas such as *Bugsy* (1991), and coldly efficient hack work like *Disclosure* (1994). While *Sleepers* has some of the virtues of Levinson's best efforts, particularly his skill at directing actors, its good elements fail to add up to much.

Based on Lorenzo Carcaterra's controversial book, *Sleepers* is a sordid tale of revenge. Four boys growing up in the late 1960's in the Irish-Italian-Puerto Rican neighborhood known as Hell's Kitchen on the west side of Manhattan see their lives come undone because of a prank. After Shakes (Joe Perrino), Michael (Brad Renfro), John (Geoff Wigdor), and Tommy (Jonathan Tucker) steal a hot-dog vendor's cart, it topples down a subway entrance and almost kills a man. They are sentenced to a juvenile facility in upstate New York that prides itself on its superficial resemblance to a prep school.

For the four, it turns out to be closer to hell than their old neighborhood because four sadistic guards led by Sean Nokes (Kevin Bacon) torment and sodomize them. With Michael's encouragement, they try to pay back the guards by defeating them at a football game only to receive brutal beatings when they win. The inmates' best player, Rizzo (Eugene Byrd) dies as a result of his punishment.

A dozen years later, Shakes (Jason Patric) is a journalist, and Michael (Brad Pitt) is a prosecuting attorney, while John (Ron Eldard) and Tommy (Billy Crudup) are career criminals. When John and Tommy spot Nokes dining in one of their neighborhood bars, they promptly gun him down in front of witnesses. Michael and Shakes then launch an elaborate plot to save their friends while meting out further revenge on the remaining guards. Michael arranges to prosecute the case himself, keeping his connection to the defendants secret, while finding a defense lawyer, the alcoholic, drug-addicted Danny Snyder (Dustin Hoffman), so desperate he will conduct the case as Michael dictates. The final piece of the puzzle is having Shakes convince Father Bobby (Robert De Niro), the priest they have known most of their lives, to provide an alibi for John and Tommy.

> Father Bobby: "You're asking me to swear to God and then lie?" Shakes: "I'm asking you to save two of your boys."

Tommy (Jason Patric) and Father Bobby (Robert De Niro) play pivotal roles in the controversial film *Sleepers.*

It all sounds more than a bit far-fetched but hardly in a league with Watergate, the O.J. Simpson case, or many other causes celebre of recent years. The veracity of Carcaterra's 1995 book has been strongly debated, particularly in the New York media, with attorneys, police, reporters, and others claiming no such case has ever occurred. The writer (called Shakes in *Sleepers*) has vehemently defended himself, saying he has simply altered real events slightly to protect those involved. The Catholic Church has also condemned the book and the film for their depiction of a duplicitous priest.

Whether these people really existed and these events transpired as Carcaterra claims is finally irrelevant. Levinson's goal as a filmmaker is to make it all dramatically effective. He does an excellent job in the first half hour of establishing a sense of community in Hell's Kitchen with the kids seeking the refuge of the streets and the rooftops because of troubled home lives, especially as a result of fathers beating mothers. Shakes, ignoring Father Bobby's warnings, becomes a protégé of King Benny (Vittorio Gassman), the neighborhood godfather, and convinces Benny to hire his friends as well. The boys are entranced by the romance and adventure of crime just as later, in the institution, they fall for the romance and adventure of escape and revenge as depicted in Alexandre Dumas' 1844 novel, *The Count of Monte Cristo.*

While the domestic violence side of the neighborhood is unpleasant, the later molestation theme is even more so, particularly in what is offered as a star-driven mass-market entertainment. Except for Nokes' forcing the boys, after a dining-hall brawl, to eat food off the floor, Levinson thankfully refrains from showing the rapes and beatings, but he strongly suggests their brutality and keeps returning to the four's memories of this humiliation. They must be given motivation for their revenge, but these scenes are difficult to watch.

The latter would not be a justifiable complaint if Levin-

AWARDS AND NOMINATIONS

Academy Awards 1996 Nominations: Best Original Dramatic Score (Williams)

CREDITS

Father Bobby: Robert De Niro
Danny Snyder: Dustin Hoffman
Michael: Brad Pitt
Shakes: Jason Patric
John: Ron Eldard
Tommy: Billy Crudup
Carol Martinez: Minnie Driver
King Benny: Vittorio Gassman
Fat Mancho: Frank Medrano
Sean Nokes: Kevin Bacon
Ferguson: Terry Kinney
Young Michael: Brad Renfro
Young Shakes: Joe Perrino
Young John: Geoff Wigdor
Young Tommy: Jonathan Tucker
Shakes' father: Bruno Kirby
Rizzo: Eugene Byrd
Little Caesar: Wendell Pierce
Mrs. Salinas: Aida Turturro
Judge Weisman: Ben Hammer
Jerry: Patrick Tull
Addison: Jeffrey Donavan
Styler: Lennie Loftin

Origin: USA
Released: 1996
Production: Steve Golin and Barry Levinson for Propaganda Films, Polygram Filmed Entertainment, and Baltimore Pictures; released by Warner Brothers
Direction: Barry Levinson
Screenplay: Barry Levinson; based on the book by Lorenzo Carcaterra
Cinematography: Michael Ballhaus
Editing: Stu Linder
Production design: Kristi Zea
Art direction: Tim Galvin
Set design: Beth Rubino
Costume design: Gloria Gresham
Music: John Williams
Sound: Tod Maitland
MPAA rating: R
Running Time: 105 minutes

son intended an expose of the treatment of juvenile offenders, but as with *Bugsy* (1991) and *Disclosure* (1994), he seems to have no reason for telling this tale. He apparently was intrigued by the chance to venture into Martin Scorsese territory, and *Sleepers* bears a superficial resemblance to Scorsese's *Mean Streets* (1973) and shares one of its stars, De Niro. Not only does Levinson use Scorsese's cinematic alter ego but Michael Ballhaus, cinematographer of five Scorsese films, including *Goodfellas* (1990), as well. While Ballhaus, one of the masters of dark, brooding lighting, helps set an appropriately ominous tone, Phil Joanou's *State of Grace* (1990) creates a much stronger sense of the violence of criminal life in Hell's Kitchen.

Lorenzo Carcaterra's book was published as a non-fiction memoir though the author has admitted changing names, dates, and other details, which has sparked controversy about its veracity.

Scorsese's films can often make up for narrative deficiencies with style, energy, and audacity while Levinson, despite occasional bursts of inspiration, is primarily a craftsman with strong storytelling skills. Ironically, the latter often proves evasive in *Sleepers.* Why do the boys never even think of complaining about their treatment? The shame that keeps Shakes from telling Father Bobby is not enough. Would John and Tommy, professional killers, simply wait for Nokes to fall under their guns? (Michael has been plotting revenge but has not yet had an opportunity to initiate it.) Why do John and Tommy, who are not in on the prosecutor's plot, show no sign of recognition of Michael in court? Is Father Bobby the only one who could provide an alibi?

An even worse flaw is the lack of tension in the courtroom scenes which seem as mechanical as a "Perry Mason" episode from the 1950's. Snyder's easily reducing Nokes' fellow pedophile Ferguson (Terry Kinney) to a tearful confession is not dramatically credible. Snyder's more systematic destruction of the testimony of an eyewitness (Aida Turturro) is the only lively moment in the entire proceedings. *Sleepers* is generally less emotionally engaging and visually interesting than an episode of "Homicide," the gritty television series Levinson created and executive produces.

Some of the actors in *Sleepers* keep it from being a total loss. As he has shown numerous times, De Niro can give great over-the-top performances, as with *Mean Streets* and *Cape Fear* (1991), as well as comparatively quiet, subtle ones, as with *The Godfather Part II* (1974). He does perhaps his best work as the guilt-ridden priest in the underrated *True Confessions* (1981), and Father Bobby is a variation on that somewhat corrupt monsignor. While the priests played in the 1930's by the likes of Pat O'Brien and Spencer Tracy are never quite convincing as bad boys grown into saintly men, De Niro's Father Bobby, a neighborhood hoodlum turned world-weary man, realizes that no moral decision by either him or those seeking his guidance is clear-cut. For all the effortless strength of his performance, however, De Niro can be faulted for letting the priest's perjury appear to come too readily.

Hoffman is another great actor sometimes given to overkill. Although his seedy lawyer resembles a better-dressed version of his Ratso Rizzo from *Midnight Cowboy* (1969), Hoffman does not indulge in as many neurotic tics as might be expected with such a substance-abusing failure. Hoffman can mumble with Marlon Brando at his most unintelligible, but here such a technique seems fitting as a courtroom device for keeping witnesses off guard. His interplay with Turturro as he moves slowly from friendliness to aggression to outrage is masterful.

Good performances also come from some of the supporting players. Minnie Driver appears as Carol Martinez, a social worker from the neighborhood who has loved three of the four protagonists at different times. The part is not particularly well written, especially compared to Driver's roles in *Circle of Friends* (1995) and *Big Night* (1996), but she makes the most of it through her considerable presence. The seventy-five-year-old Gassman, who has never had a particularly memorable role in an English-language film, is arresting as the calm gangster. The most colorful performance is given by Frank Medrano as Fat Mancho, the profanely philosophical neighborhood storekeeper who watches the boys grow up. Much more than comic relief, Medrano dominates each of his scenes with style as well as his considerable bulk.

As for the boys, Patric is surprisingly adequate, a great improvement over his deadly work in such films as *After Dark, My Sweet* (1990) and *Geronimo: An American Legend* (1993). Pitt has shown in *12 Monkeys* (1995) that he is capable of more than sub-James Dean posturing, but here he returns to too-sensitive-to-live gazing. The younger versions of the protagonists, especially Perrino and Wigdor, are more interesting than their adult selves.

—*Michael Adams*

REVIEWS

Entertainment Weekly. November 1, 1996, p. 40.
The New York Times. October 18, 1996, p. C3.
Newsweek. October 28, 1996, p. 74.
People Weekly. October 28, 1996, p. 23.
USA Today. October 18, 1996, p. D1.
The Village Voice. October 29, 1996, p. 45.

Sling Blade

Sometimes a hero comes from the most unlikely place.—Movie tagline

"*Sling Blade* is virtuoso writing, acting and directing."—Roger Ebert, *Chicago Sun-Times*

"*Sling Blade* announces a vital and daring new talent!"—Patrick McGavin, *Chicago Tribune*

"First rate . . . A mesmerizing story! Writer/director Billy Bob Thornton delivers an astonishing performance."—Guy Flatley, *Cosmopolitan*

"Utterly original! This is the best storytelling to come out of the South since William Faulkner and Flannery O'Connor."—Steve Oldfield, *FOX-TV*

"Billy Bob Thornton gives an arresting performance. As writer/director, he elicits strong, solid work from his other actors."—Janet Maslin, *New York Times*

Box Office: **$198,450**

"Sometimes a hero comes from the most unlikely place." This is the tag line seen on the poster advertising *Sling Blade.* It's ambiguous and generic. Not what you'd call a "grabber." It could have been used for any one of a thousand other films. But after viewing, what is arguably, one of the finest and most original films ever made, the simple line speaks volumes. Karl Childers, the lead character, is the hero. He's also a convicted multiple murderer.

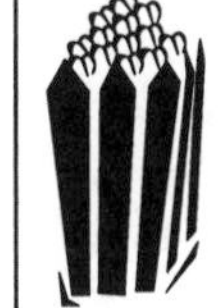

"I killed some folks."—Karl to Frank on why he was in a mental hospital

Above that same tag line is a gushing quote from critic Roger Ebert that reads "*Sling Blade* is virtuoso writing, acting and directing." Despite the cachet that a quote from Ebert can lend a film, it too sounds like it's been heard too many times before. Until you consider the fact that Ebert is talking about just one person who is virtually unknown to moviegoers. Simultaneously wearing the three most important movie hats on a film is usually reserved for well established, heavyweight Hollywood mega-stars with time-proven track records: Clint Eastwood, Sir Laurence Olivier, Orson Welles, Warren Beatty, Woody Allen and, most recently, Kenneth Branagh.

Until now, Billy Bob Thornton's major claim to fame was co-writing (with collaborator Tom Epperson) the screenplay and starring in the magnificent but largely ignored crime thriller, *One False Move* (1992). Earlier in 1996 Thornton (again with Epperson) co-wrote (but did not appear in) the superb *A Family Thing* (reviewed in this issue). He made frequent appearances on "Evening Shade" and was a regular cast member for three seasons on "Hearts Afire," both on CBS television. What all of the above projects have in common (besides Thornton's participation), is their Arkansas setting. As a native Arkansan, Thornton has captured the offbeat, quirky, poetic charm of the South without turning his characters into caricatures. He is to Arkansas what Woody Allen is to New York.

As the film begins, Karl (Thornton) has all but finished serving a 25 year sentence in, what he calls, the "nervous" hospital for the brutal murders of his mother and her lover. He discovered them having sex and hacked them to death with what he describes as a kaiser knife, which is also known as a sling blade. A local high school student wants to interview Karl before his release but is told by a hospital administrator that she may not ask him any questions. "How can I interview him if I can't ask him any questions," she says, understandably perplexed. Karl is brought into a dimly lit room, and somehow knowing what the student would have asked, begins to explain his entire life. He was the first born child of abusive, fundamentalist, religious zealots, who interpreted their child's retardation to be a punishment from God. For the duration of the movie, Karl's voice barely rises above a whisper. He is completely devoid of emotion and shows no signs of remorse. In other words, he's the textbook example of a cold-blooded, unrepentant killer. Yet we never fear him.

In spite of his stoic air and obvious ignorance of the modern world, he must vacate the hospital where he has spent his entire adult life. But he doesn't want to leave. Who could blame him? As was the case with the James Whitmore and Morgan Freeman characters in *The Shawshank Redemption* (1994), Karl is a man who has been "institution-

AWARDS AND NOMINATIONS

Academy Awards 1996: Best Adapted Screenplay (Thornton)
Nominations: Best Actor (Thornton)
Independent Spirit Awards 1997: First Feature (Thornton)
Screen Actors Guild 1996 Nominations: Actor (Thornton), Cast
Writers Guild of America 1996: Adapted Screenplay (Thornton)

alized" to such a degree, he prefers confinement over freedom. Karl gets out and starts walking the streets of Millsburg, his hometown, carrying all of his worldly possessions, a stack of books. Among the few vocational texts are copies of Dickens' *A Christmas Carol* and the Bible, which took him four years to read.

After viewing Thornton in other roles, it's hard to believe that this same actor is playing Karl. The transformation is not done with makeup or electronic trickery. Thornton's slouched hunchback and slow deliberate walk, matched with a fixed gaze and frozen, tight-lipped grimace give Karl a body language that can't be taught in acting class. The ponytail from *One False Move* is gone and in its stead is a bowl-style crew cut. At first glance, audiences are going to think, this is Forrest Gump with a criminal record. Or possibly Dustin Hoffman's Raymond. Or even Cliff Robertson's Charly. As good as Tom Hanks performance was in *Forrest Gump* (1994), the tremendous amounts of only-in-the-movies dumb luck that preceded his every move made the character unrealistic. In *Rain Man* (1988), Hoffman's idiot savant also suffered from a similar synthetic quality. His often sudden bursts of hysterical emotion were unsettling and left many viewers ill at ease. In *Charly* (1968), the chemically imbibed transformation of Robertson's character from retard to genius and back again looked more like improbable science-fiction than the intended social commentary it was meant to be. While all these actors turned in tremendous, almost otherworldly performances, they lacked just the slightest amount of real-life identifiability. Thornton's Karl is completely unaffected and utterly believable. It is acting at its most sublime. If Hanks, Hoffman and Robertson could all win the Academy Award for their roles, giving Thornton the 1996 Best Actor Oscar should be a no-brainer.

Within what seems like mere minutes back in town, Karl meets Frank (Lucas Black), a 12-year-old boy who is doing the laundry for his widowed mother. Black garnered the praises of many during the short-lived, highly underrated, Southern-flavored television series, "American Gothic," where he played a young, mystical clairvoyant. Having committed his crime at the same age and having his emotional growth arrested because of it, Karl establishes an inseparable bond with Frank, which is quickly reciprocated. They both like the way the other one talks. Karl finds a non-judgmental friend while Frank sees a comrade and possible father figure. His mothers' current boyfriend, Doyle (Dwight Yoakam), is sorely lacking in anything resembling suitable parental skills.

Grammy-winning country singer Dwight Yoakam, who showed immense promise as a menacing stalker in the direct-to-video film, *A Little Death* (1995), has hit full stride with his chilling portrayal of Doyle. Embodying the idiosyncratic redneck archetype, Yoakam shows just how dangerous small minds can be. Doyle is a construction worker, whose typical evening relaxation consists of pounding down boilermakers, playing loud guitar in a very bad garage band, and insulting everyone who surrounds him. We never see Doyle with a firearm or any other dangerous weapon; Thornton's carefully chosen, scornful words are Doyle's rod and staff. Frank's mother Linda (Natalie Canerday) is fully aware of Doyle's volatile tendencies, but doesn't dare consider kicking him out. Doyle regularly threatens to kill her if she does. Frank has become conditioned to Doyle's insults and basically ignores him. After meeting Karl, Linda seems to share Frank's opinion that he is safe and together they offer him a cot in their garage. Not the Ritz by any means, but a marked improvement from the quarters at the machine shop where Karl has gotten a job fixing small engines.

Besides Frank, Doyle seems to get special glee when directing his vicious barbs at Vaughan (John Ritter), Linda's homosexual boss. Ritter's association with Thornton dates back to their "Hearts Afire" days together, and his work on the landmark show "Three's Company," as a man pretending to be gay, made him a natural choice for the role. Vaughan moved to Millsburg from St. Louis where he left behind a family completely intolerant of his alternative lifestyle. Vaughan's attempts to protect Frank and Linda from Doyle always fall short, but certainly not from any lack of valiant effort. He recognizes immediately that Karl will likely become the next target for Doyle's merciless tirades and councils him on what to expect. Vaughan doesn't realize that Karl has already surmised the situation completely,

CREDITS

Karl Childers: Billy Bob Thornton
Frank Wheatley: Lucas Black
Daryl Hargraves: Dwight Yoakam
Linda Wheatley: Natalie Canerday
Vaughan Cunningham: John Ritter
Charles Bushman: J.T. Walsh
Jerry Woolridge: James Hampton
Karl's Father: Robert Duvall

Origin: USA
Released: 1996
Production: Brandon Rosser, David L. Bushell for a Shooting Gallery production; released by Miramax Films
Direction: Billy Bob Thornton
Screenplay: Billy Bob Thornton
Cinematography: Barry Markowitz
Editing: Hughes Winborne
Music: Daniel Lanois
Production design: Clark Hunter
Costume design: Douglas Hall
Sound: Paul Ledford
Casting: Sarah Tackett
MPAA rating: R
Running Time: 133 minutes

and will, in turn, attempt to rectify it in his own circumspect, methodical manner.

Karl recognizes the parallels between his new, adopted family and the fractured biological one from which he came. Knowing he will likely be rebuffed, Karl attempts to reconcile with his only living relative, who disowned him long ago. In what could be the briefest appearance of his long, distinguished career, Robert Duvall plays the part of Karl's father. Living in a dilapidated hovel, wallowing in self-pity, Duvall's character confirms Karl's fears. Acknowledging defeat, Karl unearths another equally tragic family secret then leaves his father to fester in his own self-made world of piety and hate.

The films' shrewdly realized final act, resulting from Thornton's long set-up of entangled bits of Gothic American squalor, is bare-bones filmmaking at its finest and is nothing less than Shakespearean in its depth and scope. Karl's last scene with Frank is as moving and heart-wrenching as anything ever committed to film. The movie has no loose ends, but does leave the audience its own set of moral conundrums to contemplate long after the credits have finished rolling. Thornton has laid out a small cross section of Americana for us to examine and draw our own, often conflicting conclusions. It's hard to recall any director who has achieved such high levels of perfection in every area with their first film, or meshed life so seamlessly with art. Thornton has nakedly exposed us to the belly of the beast and delivered one of the greatest motion pictures of all time.

—J.M. Clark

REVIEWS

Boxoffice Online. November, 1996.
Chicago Tribune. November 27, 1996, p. 1.
Detroit News. February 14, 1997, p. 3D.
Entertainment Weekly. December 6, 1996, p. 48.
Los Angeles Times. November 27, 1996, p. F6.
New York Times. September 30, 1996, p. C15.
Newsweek. November 25, 1996.
People. November 25, 1996, p. 19.
Variety Online. September 4, 1996.

Small Faces

"*Small Faces* is a Scotch treat!. Best taken straight, no chaser! A period piece-de-resistance!"—Andrew Berg, *Detour Magazine*

"A piece of bravura filmmaking!"—Oren Moverman, *Interview Magazine*

"Electrifying! Wonderfully brash, lacerating, intense & riveting!"—Daphne Davis, *Movies and Videos*

"Pure visual brilliance!"—William Arnold, *Seattle Post-Intelligencer*

Box Office: $155,239

The opening credits of *Small Faces* roll over a comic-strip tableau drawn by the film's 13-year-old protagonist, the confused Lex MacLean (Iain Robertson). The comic tells the story that will unfold, in crude caricatures. As the cartoon images rush by, the viewer struggles to make sense of them.

When this rowdy drama of a perilous adolescence in working-class 1968 Glasgow fills out the lines and characters suggested by the comic, the viewer's struggle to make sense continues. One longs for a translator. For an American viewer, the thick Scottish brogue employed by all the film's characters is a formidable obstacle to comprehension, but it's not the only one.

Lex, the youngest of three brothers who live in a cramped flat with their mother, is caught between a rough-edged childish pranksterism and the real violence of local gangs. It takes Lex awhile to sort out what's play and what's deadly serious, and by the time he's done so, it's too late to save his oldest brother, the emotionally troubled and mentally challenged Bobby, who's become a pawn in the gang warfare.

Small Faces is truly a tragic comic-of-age movie. Not even a veneer of sentimentality mars its determinedly authentic depiction of the price of maturity. Wounds that adolescents experience emotionally in other stories take on physical form in *Small Faces.* It is antithetical to the perspective embodied in Truffaut, Techine and other Continental directors, for whom adolescence is a psychosexual battleground. Lex doesn't have the luxury of resolving inexplicable urges and peer pres-

Director Gilles MacKinnon has said the character of Alex is based on himself and the character of Lex on his brother and co-scripter, Billy.

sures in his mind; he must sink or swim, fight or flee on the mean streets.

Director Gillies MacKinnon, working from a script he co-authored with his brother Billy, veers anarchically from one scene to the next, often landing in media res. Suddenly Lex is on a rooftop with a gang of older boys, being lowered by a rope through a ceiling opening. Suddenly he is scooped up into a car and threatened by gang leaders. Suddenly he is wielding an air gun and shooting it at a group of rugby players. Realistically, the film depicts male adolescence as life lived impulsively. But this tone makes for a story that's difficult to follow. Who's who and what's happening are often unclear.

Lex is used to a life full of grotesque images. Bobby (J.S. Duffy) has terrifying nightmares and does inexplicable things, such as killing Lex's fish with too much food. The middle brother, Alan (Joseph McFadden), is a sensitive, talented artist whose huge, unnerving works cover the walls of the brothers' shared bedroom. Playing with surrealism, the film's first half-hour promises variations on Bunuel and Fellini. The toilet bowl fills the screen as the dead fish is flushed down it. At a carnival, a row of fiendish-looking wooden clown heads spin eerily. Lex watches the older boys plotting evil deeds, then spies a circus elephant emerging from the dark.

If MacKinnon had sustained this feverish, walking-nightmare quality throughout the film, *Small Faces* would have been quite an accomplishment. Unfortunately, the confusing gang activity soon comes to dominate the film. Lex's impulsive shot at the rugby match hits the forehead of Malky Johnson (Kevin McKidd), the leader of the Tongs, a ghetto gang from the high-rise projects across town. A rival gang leader, the foppish Charlie Sloan (Gary Sweeney), hears of the incident and adopts Lex, treating him sometimes as a lieutenant, sometimes as a plaything. In the film's best scene, after Lex leads the way through the roof into an art museum, Sloan poses among the gang members as Lex, working by flashlight, adds Sloan's face to a group portrait of famous men hanging on the gallery wall.

Adding a little luster to the boys' world is Laura Fraser (Joanne MacGowan), who, like most of the film's other characters, pops out of nowhere to court the shy Alan. It turns out Laura is also Malky's girl, and it's unclear whether she's doing some double-dealing and for what reasons.

Lex is actually a smart kid who plays it close to the chest. He's no angel, and MacKinnon resists even the temptation to make him even slightly lovable. Like many 13-year-olds, he's always trying to test his limits. As his mother, an American uncle and some family friends celebrate New Year's Eve, Lex keeps sneaking out into the kitchen to swig liquor.

Lex is the one in the family who's usually ignored, and when he disappears his mother, shockingly, says she's so angry at him she doesn't care that he's gone. Bobby attracts attention with his torments and Alan is the star of the family, destined for art school. Lex, whose artistic talents are the equal of Alan's, hides his work from the family and shows it only to another artist.

All the acting is terrific, but Robertson carries the film. He wears a look of perpetual befuddlement mingled with mischievousness. His performance is gritty and compelling. He makes you feel Lex's mental anguish as he searches for moral guideposts in a strange, hostile environment. As Lex moves through his family and neighborhood, he doesn't seem to belong anywhere. It's a familiar adolescent feeling; *Small Faces* makes that anomie painfully palpable.

The other players also are remarkable. As Bobby, Duffy places an appealing, puppy-dog face over a disagreeably twisted mind; he somehow is maliciousness, pathetic and lovable all at once. McFadden is quietly intense as the born-to-succeed middle brother; he is the only adolescent in the film who isn't discomfiting. The gang leaders are suitably bizarre and malevolent, with Sweeney as Sloan sporting double-breasted zoot suits and a genuinely twisted look. As the three boys' beleaguered, rock-solid mother, Clare Higgins provides the only respite from the film's bleak, frightening environment. MacGowan is fetching but surprisingly unaffecting as the girl in the middle of the gangs.

Small Faces is a pungent slice-of-life that never glosses over the desperation of Lex's plight. But neither does it romanticize brutality. MacKinnon never abandons his frank, unsentimental admiration of Lex's ingenuity and his ceaseless efforts to make his way in a chaotic world. Unlike its contemporary Scottish arthouse hit, *Trainspotting,* it does-

CREDITS

Lex MacLean: Iain Robertson
Alan MacLean: Joseph McFadden
Bobby MacLean: J.S. Duffy
Lorna MacLean: Clare Higgins
Joanne MacGowan: Laura Fraser
Charlie Sloan: Garry Weeney
Malky Johnson: Kevin McKidd

Origin: Great Britain
Released: 1995
Production: Billy MacKinnon, Steve Clark-Hall for a Skyline Films production; released by October Films
Direction: Gillies MacKinnon
Screenplay: Gillies MacKinnon, Billy MacKinnon
Cinematography: John De Borman
Editing: Scott Thomas
Music: John Zeane
Production design: Zoe MacLeod
Costumes: Kate Carin
MPAA rating: R
Running Time: 108 minutes

n't indulge in cynicism, either. But MacKinnon fails to provide the coherence necessary to drive home the film's challenging observations.

In the end, it's Lex's ability to make the story of his life into a bizarre comic strip that saves him—and us—from being overwhelmed by the tragedy his impulsiveness has brought upon his world. His art functions as a way of facing the truth by putting a perspective between events and personality. Gaining that perspective is how Lex reaches a genuine, well-deserved maturity, not the Hollywood kind.

—Michael Betzold

REVIEWS

Boxoffice Online. August 19, 1996.
The Hollywood Reporter. August 20, 1996, p. 5.
Los Angeles Times. August 23, 1996, p. F12.
New York Times. August 14, 1996, p. C11.
Sight and Sound. April, 1996, p. 96.
Variety. August 28, 1996, p. 67.
Village Voice. August 20, 1996, p. 45.
Wall Street Journal. August 23, 1996, p. A8.

Small Wonders

When funding for the arts was cut, these kids and one great teacher decided to pull their own strings.—Movie tagline

"It's music for the heart! It's hard not to fall in love with these children and their mentor."—Lea Russo, *Boxoffice*

"Essential viewing for bureaucrats who think of arts programs as frills!"—Matt Zoeller Zeitz, *New York Press*

"She could inspire even the most tone deaf to discover the music in their souls!"—Justine Elias, *Village Voice*

Box Office: $20,819

Small Wonders, an Oscar-nominated documentary, presents the stirring story of violin teacher, Roberta Guaspari-Tzavaras. She teaches in three East Harlem schools, developing a program that has resulted in student concerts at Carnegie Hall and playing the national anthem at a New York Knicks game. Her proteges are visited by world renowned violinists such as Isaac Stern and Itzhak Perlman, who not only teach the students but also perform joyfully with them. An honest movie, *Small Wonders* is also superb propaganda for the arts, emphasizing that developing the esthetic sense is not a frill or an extra but a core human activity. If teaching the arts is eliminated from the school curriculum, children are deprived of the nourishment and discipline essential to their maturation as complete human beings. As one school administrator puts it, a school without the arts had done some damage to the very students it seeks to benefit. In fact, arts classes have been eliminated in many school systems, and Guaspari-Tzavaras herself confronted a period when funding was cut off for her program. She responded by establishing a nonprofit organization. But work like hers is as exhausting as it is rewarding, and the effort to secure outside funding must, in some cases, fail for lack of time and energy.

Indeed, Guaspari-Tzavaras is shown in scene after scene climbing flights of stairs, looking for parking places close to schools (she gets many parking tickets), and lugging several instruments. She looks sturdy and undeterred, but even this dedicated teacher is shown sometimes losing her temper with students who fail to practice or to bring their violins to class. But when she is upset with students, she explains why she needs their whole attention and commitment to the work.

This is not a sentimental view of the arts or of those who practice it. Guaspari-Tzavaras is very demanding. When a young girl shows up pleading to be excused because of a sporting event, the teacher issues an ultimatum to child and parent: either it is going to be sports or the violin class. Guaspari-Tzavaras is firm, though not abrasive. She explains that there are many students who want to be in her class, and she simply has no time for those who cannot meet her

AWARDS AND NOMINATIONS

Academy Award 1995 Nominations: Best Feature Documentary

requirements. Many of her students are thrilled by her intense focus on them. She is constantly guiding them, showing them how to hold a violin, to draw the bow, and how to stand. She has older students teaching the younger ones. When class is noisy, she shouts that she does not want to shout, that the students are making the class difficult for her. They pipe down. They want her approval; they crave her attention.

Film was originally released under the title *Fiddlefest.*

At the same time, it is clear that the violin program is not for everyone. When a group of young students learn that they have been accepted (by lottery) into her program, one of them begins crying. Why is he upset? The child moans that the work will be too much. But he chose to be in the lottery, the teacher points out. The truth seems to be that when the little boy is chosen, he is overwhelmed with the commitment he knows he has to make. It is an extraordinary scene because one would not expect a child so young to be so keenly aware of the consequences of his choice. This incident alone demonstrates how deeply the significance of the violin program has penetrated these youthful minds.

Like all great teachers, Guaspari-Tzavaras has a wonderful sense of process; that is, she knows how to convey to students not only what they are going to learn but also how they will feel when they have learned their lessons. She exuberantly explains how the audience will be thrilled by the music, and how good she knows her student musicians will become. In effect, she is offering them recognition and fostering a sense of ambition and pride in their work.

Small Wonders shows not only the violin classes and Guaspari-Tzavaras's hectic schedule, it also forages into the students' lives, revealing the support they get from their families and how they struggle to practice each day. A small boy, Jose, pins up a note chart on the wall. His mother watches him play his instrument, encouraging him to repeat his exercises. Soon she learns the routine and is surprised to find that her son is improvising on his instrument when the lesson is done. He is beginning to advance from rote learning to creativity and independence.

CREDITS

Origin: USA
Released: 1995
Production: Susan Kaplan for a Four Oaks Foundation production; released by Miramax Films
Direction: Allan Miller
Cinematography: Kramer Morgenthau
Editing: Allan Miller
MPAA rating: G
Running Time: 120 minutes

Jose's development becomes one of the plot threads of *Small Wonders.* He is shown in his first class, learning how to take possession of his instrument. In subsequent classes, his ability to concentrate on the music increases as Guaspari-Tzavaras corrects and encourages him. One of his high moments comes when he dresses up for a concert. The handsome boy in a suit is his mother's pride, and she tells him how well he looks and shows him off to his sister. The boy, obviously pleased, maintains a fairly sober mien. All those violin classes, the discipline he has practiced, pay off in his graceful way of taking a compliment. The cliche that the arts make for better students and citizens is re-vivified in Jose's story.

But Guaspari-Tzavaras's first loyalty is to music. Playing the violin is an end in itself; loving music is enough of a justification for what she does. Her classes do not depend on the argument that studying music will translate into other areas of life. Music is her life and the life of her students. They become fine musicians because they believe in their music. The purity of their feelings is a cleansing antidote to the pragmatic, cynical messages that assault these people every day.

Guaspari-Tzavaras teaches 150 students ranging in age from five to fifteen. She is often operating at several different age levels at once. Not only does this demanding schedule make her a better teacher, it has considerable impact on students of different ages who are learning from each other. As their teacher points out, she cannot give every student equal time. But as she demonstrates technique for one student, the others intently watch and imitate her instructions. The sense of a collective enterprise makes each individual concentrate even harder. And the pride of being in a large successful group is apparent in the concerts given for parents and the school community. Parents rush up after the concert to thank the teacher and to beam at their children.

What the parents feel is shared by the great musicians who perform with the students. At Carnegie Hall Isaac Stern gazes raptly at the student musicians beside him, clearly invigorated by their strength and concentration. They seem far less aware of the occasion than he is and just what a wonder it is for them to be assembled together. This is the same Stern who in class is critical and encouraging, engaging in a dialogue with Guaspari-Tzavaras about teaching that surely impresses students with the importance of their efforts.

Ultimately, *Small Wonders* is about more than music; it is about wonders, or miracles. As one reviewer notes, the film reminds us of teachers who have made a difference. Perhaps for most people there has been only one like Guaspari-Tzavaras, who has made artists and scholars out of students who never dreamed of such achievements.

As a documentary, the film is well put together—straightforward and without gimmicks or eye-catching techniques. Its veracity is enhanced by its simplicity. It is, as another reviewer comments, "gritty urban sociology," directed by Alan Miller, winner of Academy Awards for *From Mao to Mozart: Isaac Stern in China* and *The Bolero,* with Zubin Mehta and the Los Angeles Philharmonic. Miller has also directed well received documentaries on Eubie Blake (*Memories of Eubie*) and *High Fidelity: The Adventures of the Guarneri String Quartet.*

Although the focus is rightly on the violin program, enough is shown of Guaspari-Tzavaras's life to make the point that her students' struggles are matched by her own experience. She learned the violin as a child in a school program in Rome. Two of her grown-up children are also musicians, and when they visit her, there is music making at home.

A comparable process is at work in her students lives. Parents and siblings, regardless of how much or little musical training they have—become involved in music at home. For some at least, the violin program becomes another way of grounding their lives and giving them a sense of common purpose. Small wonders, indeed.

—*Carl Rollyson*

REVIEWS

Boxoffice. October, 1996, p. 44.
Los Angeles Times. October 9, 1996, p. F5.
New York Times. October 4, 1996, p. C4.
Village Voice. October 8, 1996, p. 72.

Solo

Part man. Part machine. Total weapon.—Movie tagline

"A pure escapist action fare."—Louis B. Hobson, *Ottawa Sun*

"Van Peebles gives a winning if not witty physical performance."—Susan Wloszczyzna, *USA Today*

Box Office: $5,107,600

A derivative, low-budget *Terminator* (1985) and *Robocop* (1987) knock-off, *Solo* nonetheless proves a mildly amusing action diversion for early-adolescent male audiences. As U.S. military robot Solo, Mario Van Peebles demonstrates an aptitude for both action stunts and comic scenes in which the Mr. Spock-like robot betrays a sense of deadpan humor. Action veterans Barry Corbin, the general of *Wargames* (1983), and William Sadler, the villain of *Die Hard 2: Die Harder* (1990), round out a surprisingly good cast.

"If your brain is in your chest, then where's your heart?"—Agela to android Solo

Solo is a $2 billion U.S.-Army-developed cyborg programmed to perform in combat situations. In addition to his expertise with weapons and explosives, Solo can also distinguish between combatants and non-combatants, giving him a measure of moral decision-making skill.

The opening of the film finds Solo accompanying U.S. soldiers on a mission to neutralize a Central American airstrip where drug lords force indigenous Indians to harvest their illegal crop. When Solo perceives the presence of innocent non-combatants, however, he overrides the mission's objectives and detonates explosives which blow off half a mountainside—much to the chagrin of the mission's supervising officers, General Haynes (Corbin) and Colonel Madden (Sadler). At headquarters, Haynes orders Solo's inventor, Bill Stewart (Adrien Brody), to get the bugs out of Solo so that this type of accident won't happen again. The bloodthirsty Madden favors destroying Solo, but Haynes hangs tough.

Since Solo's primary programmed objective is "preserve self," however, when he sees that Operation Solo is being suspended, meaning his mothballing or dismantling, Solo flees in a helicopter, which he promptly crashes in the middle of the Central American jungle. General Haynes tells Madden to bring Solo back alive. Madden, however, plans to destroy the robot.

Solo finds refuge in a cave, his circuitry clearly damaged. Communicating with Solo electronically, Bill tells him that he can only recharge twice. Solo's self-recharging causes him to undergo the electronic equivalent of an acid trip, in which he sees a combination of X-rays, explosions, colorful test patterns, and "memories" of his creation. (The scene is reminiscent of the bear's hallucinogenic experience in Jean-Jacques Annaud's *The Bear* [1988].)

As Solo comes to, a boy, Miguel (Abraham Verduzco), enters the cave. Solo kills a poisonous snake that threatens Miguel (Solo's brain can also translate Spanish into English), and Miguel soon reappears with villagers holding torches to show them his new friend. Since Solo's body is cold, the villagers think he is dead and give him a funeral. When indigenous rebel troops in league with the drug lords disrupt the ceremony, Solo awakens and fends off the soldiers. An old village woman pronounces him a yagallo, an eater of human flesh that does not die.

Having recharged, Solo shows the villagers how to get better reception for their television set, but frightens them when he exposes his wires. Solo proposes a "mutually beneficial" exchange, in which they provide him with electricity, and he shows them how to defend themselves.

Solo helps the villagers construct better bows and arrows and a kind of swinging battering ram constructed from a giant log. When the ram's rope breaks, however, and Miguel saves his little brother from its path, Solo learns about the "illogical" ties of blood, love, and family devotion. Solo also learns about bluffing through watching the village children play basketball, and about laughing from the men who play cards and smoke cigars. Solo's laughter causes flocks of birds to fly from their perches.

Back at headquarters, however, Madden busily rounds up a group of mercenaries armed with explosives and high-powered weapons in order to bring Solo down.

In the jungle, Miguel's sister, the beautiful Agela (Seidi Lopez), shows Solo the lost tunnels of the villagers' ancestors which run under the village's great tomb. She tells him that the tunnels terminate in the "Chamber of Warriors," but have fallen into disuse because the villagers no longer have any warriors. Agela asks Solo where his heart is. "I have no heart," responds Solo. "Hearts are for living creatures." "But you're alive," insists Agela. "No," says Solo. "I exist."

Under Solo's guidance, the villagers fend off the druglord's commandos with the battering ram and flaming spears. But the battle tips off the U.S. military to Solo's whereabouts, and Madden heads into the jungle with his search-and-destroy force, in spite of Haynes's request that Solo be brought back alive. Madden and his men burn a village and broadcast a transmission with fake witnesses testifying that Solo has gone haywire and must be destroyed; Madden also kills one of his own men whose honesty appears to be a threat to the mission. At Madden's request, Haynes sends Bill into the jungle to find Solo, but Madden in fact plans to kill Bill as well.

In the village, the farmers argue that Solo must leave, that he is making them a target. Although Miguel's father and Agela argue that they need Solo for protection, Solo, in a *Shane*-like sequence, walks into the jungle, leaving the admiring Miguel behind. Madden uses Bill as bait to attract Solo into a firefight, which severely wounds Bill. To Bill's amazement, Solo rescues him amid a hail of bullets, in direct violation of directive 712, to "save your own ass first." Before he dies, Bill tells Solo he is the only one who can stop Madden.

The Americans and the rebel troops hustle the villagers out of town and into a large hut, but Miguel escapes via the tunnels and finds Solo in the Chamber of Warriors, where he has just buried Bill. Solo recharges, then overrides the directive to preserve himself. Led by Miguel, the villagers escape into the tunnels below the hut just as Madden blows it up. Madden then has his men kill the rebel troops. Solo, however, kills Madden's mercenaries, and gravely wounds Madden.

Just as all seems well, however, a Madden cyborg arrives by chopper. The Madden robot finishes off the real Madden, then goes after Solo on Haynes's orders. Solo saves Miguel by telling him to run away, and the Madden cyborg is puzzled that Solo has used his last bit of power to save the boy instead of himself. "You are a malfunction," says the Madden robot. "You must be deleted!" "Delete this!" responds Solo, having learned to bluff from humans. Miguel flees as Solo destroys the other robot and the temple collapses, much in the manner of the collapse of the burning windmill at the end of the James Whale *Frankenstein* (1931). Haynes expresses dismay at the destruction of both robots, but the sight of a flock of birds tells the audience that Solo still lives, and that a sequel is probably in the offing.

CREDITS

Solo: Mario Van Peebles
Gen. Clyde Haynes: Barry Corbin
Col. Frank Madden: Bill Sadler
Bill Stewart: Adrien Brody
Agela: Seidy Lopez
Lorenzo: Jaime Gomez

Origin: USA
Released: 1996
Production: Joseph Newton Cohen, John Flock for a Triumph Films production in association with Van Peebles Films; released by Sony Pictures Entertainment
Direction: Norberto Barba
Screenplay: David Corley; based on the novel *Weapon* by Robert Mason
Cinematography: Chris Walling
Editing: Scott Conrad
Music: Christopher Franke
Production design: Markus Canter
Art direction: Jose Luis Aguilar
Set decoration: Jorge Lara Sanchez
Costume design: Maria Estela Fernandez
Sound: Salvador de la Fuente
Weapons specialist: William Ungerman
MPAA rating: PG-13
Running Time: 94 minutes

David Corley's script for *Solo,* based on the novel *Weapon* by Robert Mason, owes much to the James Whale-Boris Karloff *Frankenstein,* particularly in the scenes in which the villagers carry torches, and in its final scenes reminiscent of Karloff's being buried in the windmill. Solo's emerging humanoid conscience and his befriending a young boy also owe much to the first two Whale Frankenstein films.

Director Norberto Barba moves the action along efficiently, and weaves a surprising amount of humor into the proceedings. The film's special effects, if not spectacular, are well-executed, particularly in the sequences involving Solo's electronic flashbacks.

Van Peebles plays Solo as a cyborg version of Mr. Spock, and gives amusing inflection to lines like, "I am chilling, Bill." Corbin does his familiar turn as a gruff general with a Southern drawl, and Harden gives his by-now standard performance as a psychotic rogue officer with no apparent motive for his actions other than world domination. The film's stock sentimentalized Central American villagers are a major weakness, however; the actors playing the villagers look too well-fed to resemble long-suffering Central American peasants.

Much of *Solo* has this too familiar ring about it. But, like a chain-restaurant franchise, *Solo* provides better-than-average standard fare at an affordable price. Given the foreign market for action films and *Solo*'s limited budget relative to other high-priced, star-driven action vehicles, a sequel seems probable.

—Paul Mittelbach

REVIEWS

Detroit News. August 23, 1996, p. 7D.
Los Angeles Times. August 24, 1996, p. F12.
New York Times. August 24, 1996, p. 20.
Variety. August 26, 1996, p. 60.

Some Mother's Son

"Great acting, a gripping drama."—Marshall Fine, *Gannett Newspapers*

"Magnificent . . . compelling . . . utterly believable. Nothing in recent film captures with more devastating force the perilous atmosphere of life during wartime."—Stephen Holden, *New York Times*

"Mirren and Flanagan give wonderful performances - George does a remarkable job - Powerful stuff."—Jack Mathews, *Newsday*

Box Office: $441,631

Some Mother's Son recounts the events that took place in Northern Ireland in 1981. A hunger strike, staged by close to 300 men, grabbed headlines the world over. Most of these Irishmen were captured and jailed as a result of their terrorist actions against the state, with their venom being directed at the British monarchy. The basic crux of their battle, and the centerpiece of this film, was how they were viewed by the British government and how they perceived themselves. The government regarded these men as common criminals, and treated them as such. The prisoners, always abundantly zealous and fervent with their actions and soap box political grandstanding, regarded themselves as prisoners of war.

"You had a choice in what you did. But you left us no choice."—Kathleen to son Gerard

Bobby Sands, the first of ten men to die during the strike, became the martyr and (literally) the poster boy for the cause and has the name that is most closely associated with the event. Although the Sands character appears in the film, he doesn't show up until way past the halfway mark and the role itself is incidental. The story centers around two other men, Frank Higgins (Aidan Gillen) and Gerard Quigley (David O'Hara), and their mothers. After borrowing his mother's car under false pretences, Quigley, along with Higgins, destroy an armed forces vehicle, killing a British soldier in the process (the British army had been setting up roadblocks on the major thoroughfares connecting Ireland and Northern Ireland).

The two escape capture until a few days later when, on Christmas Eve, government police, joining forces with the army militia, corner the two men at the home of Higgins' mother, Annie (Fionnula Flanagan). The working class Higgins family seems to have expected the raid; the family has already lost one son to the long-running holy wars. The same cannot be said for the Quigleys. Led by mother Kathleen (Helen Mirren), the Quigleys don't seem as involved with the country's social disorder to the same degree as their counterparts. Kathleen teaches at a nearby girls school (the young Higgins daughter is one of her students) that is so close to the terrorist bombing, the walls shake. Kathleen is stunned to learn of Gerard's participation in the crime. The two families are near each other in the courtroom during the subsequent trial, but it is apparent that they have little in common.

Director Terry George was himself a prisoner in Belfast's Maze (Long Kesh) Prison in the mid-70s.

The government sees to it that the trial goes quickly and without incident. The fact that the men refuse council only makes that job easier. Being prisoners of war as they claim, they don't even recognize the court's decision: Higgins gets life in prison, Quigley receives 12 years; both without the possibility of parole. As part of their processing when entering the jail, Higgins and Quigley are given prison uniforms, which they refuse to wear. Citing insubordinate behavior, their handlers put them with other prisoners of like mind. Showing the men wrapped in blankets, barefoot, disheveled, and unshaven with long hair, Irish-born director Terry George paints his infirmed characters as modern-day messiahs, sent down to save Ireland from the demonic British. George furthers this same technique in a later scene with Sands (John Lynch) and others on their deathbeds. Gaunt, their bodies virtual skeletons, their eyes look to the heavens with George's carefully chosen lighting giving the men the appearance (surely intended) of Christ dying on the cross.

The British government, led by prime minister Margaret Thatcher (who shows up in older newsreels), preached compromise, but in reality were dead set on clamping down on the IRA by any means at their disposal. They were looking for a reason, any reason, to break the back of the resistance. In a move that was obviously implemented without a second of forethought, the jailers refuse the men toilet privileges. The men counter by spreading their feces on the walls of their cells. To even the most untrained eye, it's apparent that something has got to give soon. During a carefully monitored visit with Kathleen, Gerard passes her a note to be delivered to Danny Boyle (Ciaran Hinds), the then leader of the well entrenched, radical political faction, Sinn Fein. Collectively, the prisoners, under Sands' direction, decide to start the hunger strike.

Up until this point, Annie and Kathleen have existed in a very uncomfortable forced alliance, their only bond being their imprisoned sons. The performances of Flanagan and Mirren (who also serves as one of the executive producers) are the film's driving force. Being the one who has a little more knowledge of the goings-on in the IRA, Annie seems to have more of an emotional investment in her son's predicament. Her blue-collar manner and brash defiance of British authoritarian figures initially rubs Kathleen the wrong way. Kathleen, being the more genteel and patrician of the two, partially blames Annie for her son's predicament. After some tough confrontations, the two realize that taking a power-in-numbers approach to their problem is the best way to expend their energies. At one point, Kathleen drives her car to the beach, in a comical attempt to give Annie driving lessons.

After meeting with Boyle in a very dangerous, ghetto-ridden area, a town meeting of sorts is set up with Annie, Kathleen, Boyle, and a member of the British parliament who represents the district. His impassioned dedication to getting the prisoners their rights is genuine (he also has one eye on the upcoming election and is aware that the group will play a major role in re-electing him). Just when it appears that the situation will be resolved quickly, this same said member of parliament dies. With their options quickly dwindling, Annie drafts prisoner Sands as a candidate to run for the now-vacant seat. When the mother superior of her school catches wind of Kathleen's participation in the election, she is fired.

CREDITS

Kathleen Quigley: Helen Mirren
Annie Higgins: Fionnula Flanagan
Gerard Quigley: Aidan Gillen
Frank Higgins: David O'Hara
Bobby Sands: John Lynch
Harrington: Tim Woodward
Danny Boyle: Ciaran Hinds

Origin: Ireland
Released: 1996
Production: Jim Sheridan, Arthur Lappin, Edward Burke for a Hell's Kitchen and Castle Rock Entertainment production; released by Columbia Pictures
Direction: Terry George
Screenplay: Terry George, Jim Sheridan
Cinematography: Geoffrey Simpson
Editing: Craig McKay
Music: Bill Whelan
Production design: David Wilson
Art direction: Conor Devlin
Costume design: Joan Bergin
Sound: Brian Simmons
Casting: Nuala Moiselle
MPAA rating: R
Running Time: 112 minutes

With absolutely nothing to lose at this point, Annie and Kathleen hit the campaign trail with a vengeance. As Sands begins deteriorating in the prison hospital, much of the local population, and more importantly, the local and national press, hear their rallying cry and ardently back Sands. To the rest of the world, America in particular, fighting over wardrobe and bathroom privileges may seem trivial, but it was enough for over 30,000 Northern Ireland residents to get out and vote and subsequently elect Sands (by the narrowest of margins) to the parliament. Sands died on the 66th day of his hunger strike, never having the chance to assume his post where truly significant changes could have been implemented. After nine more men died, the government, under enormous public and international pressure, gave in and granted all of the prisoners' demands.

For all intents and purposes, this film could be called "Michael Collins, Part 2." Having been released on the heels of that film (also reviewed in this issue), it showcases the dogged strength and iron will of a small band of people who wanted desperately to break free from the age-old shackles of the British Empire and were willing to die in the process. Collins himself was instrumental in organizing the IRA in the 1920s, when his guerilla warfare tactics were used as a last resort to get the Brits' attention. When Collins bargained the armistice agreement with the British, he was chastised and ridiculed by his alleged "followers" for not getting everything they wanted, i.e., the entire island. His negotiated settlement delivered Ireland its sovereignty, and as thanks for his efforts, he was promptly assassinated. In a land where people have been fighting for over 700 years over basically the same issues, distant onlookers might be (understandably) outraged over the tactics used first by Collins and then, to an even greater extent, by the minions who followed in his footsteps. But a certain amount of acknowledgment should be given to people so dedicated to their ideals and dogmatic in their pursuits.

Some Mother's Son was co-scripted by director Terry George and Jim Sheridan, who not so coincidentally were the two who wrote *In the Name of the Father* (1993), another gut-wrenching Irish epic. Sheridan directed that project and placed his trust in George to helm the second unit. With his first solo outing, George shows remarkable maturity and a brilliant ability to treat the facts with just enough dramatic license. For his part, Sheridan further reinforces his already strong position as Ireland's strongest voice (with the possible exception of Neil Jordan) in the motion picture industry.

—J.M. Clark

REVIEWS

Boxoffice. August, 1996, p. 52.
Chicago Tribune. January 27, 1996, p. 5.
Detroit News. January 31, 1997, p. 3D.
Entertainment Weekly. January 17, 1997, p. 44
Hollywood Reporter. May 14, 1996, p. 13.
Los Angeles Times. December 25, 1996, p. F2.
New York Times. December 26, 1996, p. C11.
New Yorker. January 27, 1997, p. 83.
People. January 20, 1997, p. 18.
Variety. May 20, 1996, p. 38.

Someone Else's America

Two friends. Two worlds. One dream.—Movie tagline

"Tom Conti and Miki Manojlovic are delightfully charming!"—*Interview Magazine*

Box office: $170,607

"We are simple and crazy," explains Bayo (Miki Manojlovic), a Balkan immigrant, to Alonso (Tom Conti), his Italian immigrant friend, about an half-hour into *Someone Else's America.* The line was written by a Yugoslav expatriate (Gordan Mihic) in a film directed by another Yugoslav expatriate (Goran Paskaljevic). Yet it seems as if the goal of this turgid seriocomic film is to justify stricter immigration laws. For Bayo and especially Alonso, the film's forlorn anti-heroes, do act ridiculously simple and crazy, for no apparent reason.

"This is USA of America. This is the place where if you work hard, and you worry, you can be anything you want."—Alonso

The title suggests a film about the cruel deception of the American promised land, the injustice of a nation that beckons with Lady Liberty's torch yet fails to provide those who answer with a fair chance to make a living. But *Someone Else's America* is not a story of what's wrong with America's economy or culture. In fact, Bayo and Alonso suffer a notable lack of prejudice. Not once is either immigrant denied an opportunity. Not once is either one the target of an ethnic slur or slight. Bayo and Alonso don't make it big in America not from any discernible flaw in the American dream, but because they are stubborn and weak, short-tempered and shortsighted. With such qualities, they wouldn't make it big anywhere.

For some reason, they have been thrown together in a seedy, melting-pot section of Brooklyn. The ragtag script provides few insights into how they got there and reveals next to nothing about its lead characters' backgrounds or motivations. Why Bayo left his family behind in the former Yugoslavia is never sufficiently explained. No clue is given how Alonso got stuck owning a desultory restaurant-bar and living with his blind, aged mother who longs to return to her old country village. How Bayo took up cleaning Alonso's place in exchange for room and board is also given short shrift.

The logical conventions of a story line appear to have eluded screenwriter Mihic. The concept of a dramatic buildup of tension also seems foreign to director Paskaljevic. The few significant events of the film occur in the middle, in tight sequences that are gripping in contrast with the rest of the film's lackluster pacing. The film begins and ends with slice-of-life scenes. It starts nowhere and ends nowhere, which is exactly where Bayo and Alonso have been and where they are going.

Paskaljevic promises an irony on which he never delivers by opening with the Statue of Liberty as backdrop for a crew of illegal aliens, including Bayo, spraying for vermin as part of a developer's on-the-cheap environmental cleanup. Immediately, Andrew Dickson's annoying faux-gypsy musical score starts crying out for attention. Right from the start, the film seems to be begging viewers to adopt it and its characters as a sort of cinematic homeless puppy. How cute and how quaint these immigrants are! Members of the hard-hat crew are apt to break out into ethnic song and dance on a coffee break.

To a fellow worker, Bayo displays photos of his children and offers his sad story of a wife who left him for his best friend. A quick cut back to the Old Country shows Bayo's daughter Savko so lovesick for her father that she cannot sleep. She spends her days and nights awake in a bed on their home's front yard watching for him. The doctor says the only cure is for her to hear from her father. It's an overwrought sequence, the cinematic equivalent of a child's temper tantrum to gain attention.

Back in Brooklyn, Bayo is inexplicably preoccupied with doing the bidding of the pitiful Alonso. His duties include acting as go-between for Alonso and a lady he longs for. Bayo gets beaten by the woman's family for making an overture on behalf of Alonso, who hides in his truck. Explaining his courageous stand, Bayo says his heritage dictates "No surrender." He is impossibly, stupidly stubborn and homespun. He always wears plaid shirts and a proud, stolid peasant's blank stare. He's such a rube that he keeps a pet rooster who pecks his feet each morning to awaken him. Bayo is impulsive, thin-skinned, compulsively honest, absurdly naive and strangely subservient to Alonso—all qualities which seem to keep him from getting ahead in his new country.

Manojlovic tries to lend authenticity to this silly character. Solely because of Manojlovic's unblinking, unpolished performance, Bayo could pass as an accurate if slightly absurd depiction of a working-class Montenegran immigrant. It's possible to extend toward Bayo the sympathy the film constantly begs to receive. But Conti's Alonso is another matter: He is an insufferable stereotype. With droopy eyelids constantly at half-mast, a hang dog expression, and a penchant for singing and playing mournful guitar, this is one puppy dog that won't hunt in the empathy chase. Conti, born in Scotland, makes the Italians that Frederico Fellini loves to lampoon look dignified and gracious by comparison with Alonso. His performance is cloying in the extreme.

At moments, the filmmakers try for an absurdist approach. Alonso's blind mother (Maria Casares) demands to go home to her village and her beloved well, so Alonso and Bayo strap her to a chair, play a tape of jet noise, then "land" her beside a well Bayo dutifully has dug in the back alley. She immediately dies of happiness, though Casares clearly takes a breath in an unfortunate close-up after her character supposedly has expired. It's the most glaring example of the general sloppiness of the film.

Other useless absurdities include Alonso's truck, which for no good reason has a steer with a checkered bib and blinking eyes mounted on its roof. There's a fanciful ending in which the buddies are lifted above the New York skyline in their fake airline seats. Rather than playing as a whimsical delight, this climax seems like a desperate attempt to cover up the lack of an ending to the story, whose threads lead nowhere.

CREDITS

Bayo: Miki Manojlovic
Alonso: Tom Conti
Alonso's mother: Maria Casares
Luka: Sergej Trifunovic
Bayo's mother: Zorka Manojlovic

Origin: France; Germany; Great Britain
Released: 1995
Production: Antoine De Clermont-Tonnerre, David Rose, and Helga Bahr for MACT Productions, Intrinsica Films, Lichtblick Filmproducktion and Stefi 2; released by October Films
Direction: Goran Paskaljevic
Screenplay: Gordan Mihic
Cinematography: Yorgos Arvanitis
Editing: William Diver
Art direction: Wolf Seesselberg
Production design: Miljen Kljakovic
Music: Andrew Dickson
Costumes: Charlotte Holdich
MPAA rating: R
Running Time: 96 minutes

The film is strongest in the middle sequences where the theme is the crossing of boundaries. Paskaljevic deftly switches back and forth between Alonso's mother's death and Bayo's family's attempts to reach America by sailing to Mexico and then crossing the Rio Grande. But even the central tragedy of the film—the disappearance of Pepo, Bayo's son—plays as shamelessly maudlin: Pepo is swept away from his family by the river current after he chases his beloved accordion.

It's not clear until much too late in the film why Bayo's family has to come to America to regain contact with him. The explanation has to do with the conniving of Bayo's eldest son, Luka (Sergej Trifunovic), a manipulative, ambitious young man who takes to America—and to revitalizing Alonso's moribund business—like a fish to water. The conflict between Bayo and Luka is both trite and forced, shifting the focus of the last half of the film to a tiresome showdown between Old World and New World sensibilities. At one point, Luka berates his father for clinging to the past and accuses him of being unable to string three English words together—a nonsensical charge, since Bayo's English is quite serviceable.

Though the sequences of Bayo searching for his lost child along the Rio Grande are haunting, they too, like most everything in the film, are overplayed. Paskaljevic seems to think repetition of scenes drives them home, when in fact it makes them lose their impact. The main problem with *Someone Else's America* is this constant dissipation of its energies and characters, with themes and threads that blossom and fade. It doesn't add up.

As a buddy picture, *Someone Else's America* lacks the adventures that might test a starring duo, and Manoljovic and Conti lack the chemistry for memorable comedy. As a dissection of the immigrant experience in America, the film lacks any discernible social context: Bayo and Alonso could be two lovable losers anywhere in the world. As social commentary, *Someone Else's America* never takes off. As entertainment, it's very spotty. Only viewers who fall for sad puppy dogs will want to adopt this film.

—Michael Betzold

REVIEWS

Boxoffice. July, 1996, p. 92.
Detroit Free Press. August 11, 1996, p. 3F.
New York Times. May 10, 1996, p. C12.

Space Jam

Get ready to jam.—Movie tagline

"Michael makes it a winner. He scores!"—Joel Siegel, *Good Morning America*

"An ingenious blend of live-action comedy and cutting edge animation."—Amy Dawes, *Los Angeles Daily News*

"A hilarious, happening film. The funniest thing in the galaxy."—Sara Edwards, *NBC News Channel*

"Energetic. Innovative. A high tech, hip-hopping thing of the future."—Janet Maslin, *The New York Times*

"A jammin' hit!"—Mike Clark, *USA Today*

Box Office: $83,038,821

Live action and animation are partnered along with basketball superstar Michael Jordan and Bugs Bunny in *Space Jam.*

It was a marketing match made in heaven which, despite doubts, became a Hollywood match that provided heavenly delight to audiences young and old. Michael Jordan and Bugs Bunny, a combination that was born from Nike and McDonald's commercials has made a successful leap onto the big screen.

In *Space Jam*, a mix of live-action and animation, Air Jordan and Hare Jordan, along with his other Looney Tunes pals, have to win a basketball game against a group of aliens. Although it's no *Who Framed Roger Rabbit?* (1988) or *Toy Story* (1995), *Space Jam* has just enough charm to individualize itself and place film studio Warner Brothers on the map for animation, an area that Disney has monopolized for quite some time.

Daffy: "How's . . . the Ducks?" Bugs: "What kind of Mickey Mouse organization would name their team the Ducks?"—on trying to pick a team name

On a far away planet called Moron Mountain, there's a theme park that is on the decline. The chief resident and owner of the park, Swackhammer (voice of Danny DeVito), needs new attractions to rejuvenate his asset. His puny underlings, called Nerdlucks, suggest Swackhammer needs some "looney" attractions. He spots the Looney Tunes characters on his television and orders his army of Nerdlucks to forcibly bring these characters to Moron Mountain.

As the Nerdlucks arrive to another far away planet called Looney Tunes, they are spotted by its leader, Bugs Bunny. The Nerdlucks are outwitted by the ever quick-witted Bugs, but the Nerdlucks have one advantage; heavy space-age firepower. A meeting of the Looney Tunes characters convenes with the Nerdlucks stating their intentions to kidnap the characters and bring them to their planet as entertainment slaves. This audience, packed with the likes of Taz, Daffy, Elmer, Sylvester, and Foghorn, laugh uncontrollably at the aliens, but the Nerdlucks bring out their firepower and the Looney Tunes make their first mistake of underestimating their opponents. As a last ditch effort, Bugs concocts a loophole for his cohorts to avoid slavery by challenging the Nerdlucks to a game of basketball. The Looney Tunes are convinced that they have the Nerdlucks at an extreme advantage since the diminutive aliens aren't familiar with any sports.

Aware of their athletic ignorance, the Nerdlucks take a field expedition to a basketball game and are introduced to the sport of pro basketball. With a magical basketball, the Nerdlucks begin sapping the basketball skills of such talents as Charles Barkley, Patrick Ewing, Muggsy Bogues, Larry Johnson, and Shawn Bradley. After their talents are mysteriously erased from them, these basketball stars are reduced to useless mounds of jelly in sneakers that can't even catch a basketball.

The Looney Tunes haven't touched a basketball in a while, but they definitely have a height advantage over the Nerdlucks, until the Nerdlucks bring out their throbbing, glowing basketball and touch it. The basketball has turned the small, basketball-impaired Nerdlucks into gigantic, slam-dunking monsters called the Monstars. Bugs can't help his crew this time, unless he brings in someone as cunning and skillful as he.

Meanwhile, on earth, Michael Jordan has escaped the fate of his fellow playmates like Barkley and Ewing since he has retired from basketball and has set his sights on baseball. But even as a failing baseball player, he is treated like royalty. He is assigned a rotund and clumsy assistant named Stan Podolak (Wayne Knight). Jordan seems content with his career change and the availability of more spare time for golf with buddies Bill Murray and Larry "Bird" Johnson.

NBA players include Charles Barkley, Patrick Ewing, Larry Johnson, Shawn Bradley, and Muggsy Bogues.

It is on a golf course that Bugs kidnaps Jordan and the plot then plays itself out like the domino effect. It may come as a surprise, but it took four screenwriters to come up with the whimsical plotline that is as transparent as color gels. In what proves to be a more spunky breed of Looney Tunes players, Jordan convinces Bugs that he is no longer a basketball player but a baseball player. Bugs in turn replies that Jordan is no more a baseball player than he is a Shakespearean actor. It's a crude rip, based on Jordan's real-life baseball record, but it's all in fun. After a confrontation with the obnoxious Monstars, Jordan finally agrees to help out the Looney Tunes.

With two such icons on one screen, it can be difficult to decide which of the two warrants or needs the most screen time. Credit commercial director Joe Pytka for mixing the right ingredients and dishing up a nice visual and audio cocktail. Even if the opening credits do resemble a saintly tribute to Jordan, after seeing it, you can understand how and why a 36-year-old famed basketball player is paired with a 50+-year-old institution. After all, Jordan, like Bugs and the Looney Tunes characters, have more than just fans, they have legions. The sequence is compiled of actual footage of Jordan in action on the court backed with firework brightness and hip-hop music.

The appearance and voice of Bugs Bunny has changed (since the death of Mel Blanc, Billy West provides the voice to Bunny and other characters), but the spunk that has endured decades is still resident in the land of Looney Tunes. Even in the presence of two massive figures, Pytka squeezes in a new Looney Tune character named Lola Bunny. And as her name suggests, she is one sizzling female version of Bugs and has some queen-size skills on the basketball court.

The budget for *Space Jam* is no laughing matter. Made on schedule, the tab for this 88 minute film totals $125 million. With such commercialism at stake, half, if not more of that budget would have to go to marketing such a highly anticipated film. Jordan and Bugs may brighten up a TV commercial, but the duo's presence could not insure a box office coup without a little push on the marketing side. Similar to the onslaught of Disney merchandise that precedes their animated films, Warner Brothers pulled no stops either. In toy stores and in McDonald's, Warner Brother characters were everywhere. It would have been very easy to just compile a mishmash of animation and live action and just let Jordan and Bugs do their thing and call it a film. But, fortunately, *Space Jam* is more than that, it is a marketing concept with thought, detail, and wit.

The money is well spent on-screen with its eye-popping, colorful animation. The meticulousness of the animation is evident in one scene where Bugs and Daffy are rummaging around Michael Jordan's house for his sneakers and lucky shorts. They enter the bedroom of Jordan's youngest daughter. Initially she is sleeping, but hears the voices at her doorway and turns around to see Bugs' and Daffy's shadows on the wall. It is a charming sequence. This scene is sure to make any child wonder if they could ever receive a visit from Bugs and pals.

With commercialism top priority on *Space Jam*'s list, it uses it to its advantage to create a few good laughs. Jordan's assistant, Stan, manages to combine four commercials in one sentence which includes Wheaties, Nike, McDonald's, and Hanes. While they see their likenesses on mugs and toys in the little girl's bedroom, Bugs asks Daffy if he's seen any money from such merchandise. Daffy's answer leads to his

CREDITS

Michael Jordan: Michael Jordan
Stan Podolak: Wayne Knight
Juanita: Theresa Randle
Bugs Bunny: Billy West (voice)
Elmer Fudd: Billy West (voice)
Daffy Duck: Billy West (voice)
Tazmanian Devil: Billy West (voice)
Bull: Dee Bradley Baker (voice)
Swackhammer: Danny DeVito (voice)

Origin: USA
Released: 1996
Production: Ivan Reitman, Joe Medjuck and Daniel Goldberg; released by Warner Brothers
Direction: Joe Pytka
Screenplay: Leo Benvenuti, Steve Rudnick, Timothy Harris, and Herschel Weingrod
Cinematography: Michael Chapman
Editing: Sheldon Kahn
Music: James Newton Howard
Production design: Geoffrey Kirkland
Art direction: David Klassen
Set design: Marco Rubeo
Special visual effects and animation: Cinesite
Live-action-animation visual effects: Ed Jones
Sound: James Larue, Gene Cantamessa
MPAA rating: PG
Running Time: 87 minutes

comment on the need for new agents since, "we're getting screwed." Daffy is even seen kissing his own butt which has the Warner Brothers logo on it. Bugs and Warner Brothers both take on the mighty Mouse of Disney by outright cutting it down to size. As Daffy and Bugs ascend to their native soil, they ponder on the name of their newly formed basketball team. Daffy suggests the name "Ducks." Bugs retorts, "What kind of Mickey Mouse operation would name their team the Ducks?" A definite cinematic slam-dunk for Warner Brothers over Disney.

It is evident that the animated cast provide their share of laughs and the live action does its part too. Since Michael Jordan is playing himself, it seems that he's not acting at all, which is just fine. Jordan is smooth on the basketball court and he proves his coolness and sleekness on-screen also. In shooting this film, Jordan had to do many scenes with himself talking on a green sound stage or with people in green suits. This sort of acting for a basketball player could be strenuous and frustrating, but for Jordan, he pulls off the illusion with just enough patience and grace to make his interactions with the Looney Tunes crew seem credible.

Wayne Knight, famous for his character, Newman, on the hit TV show "Seinfeld," offers lighthearted comic relief as the out-of-place assistant whose out-of-shape visage provides some amusement when met with the animation world. Also along for the ride is the ever confidently funny Bill Murray who casually calls Lola, "the girl bunny."

Surprisingly, some of the film's funnier moments are with the NBA stars who have lost their talents. They are shipped from hospitals to shrinks to mediums for an explanation and cure. Charles Barkley is seen in church praying to God that he will be a good guy on the court if his talent is returned. *Space Jam* takes on a lot to get a laugh, and sometimes it may not be sidesplitting hilarity, but it does amuse.

Space Jam is definitely a tribute to many things; basketball, Michael Jordan, Bugs Bunny and his Looney Tunes friends. It is also a fun, innovative, and hip (with a soundtrack that includes songs by R&B artists R. Kelly and Barry White) contribution to animation. Michael Jordan confesses to Stan that Bugs and the rest of his Looney Tunes menagerie are his friends. In that case, we hope this friendship can endure a repeat.

—Michelle Banks

REVIEWS

Boxoffice Magazine Online. November 18, 1996.
The Detroit News. Section C, pp. 1-2. November 15, 1996.
Entertainment Weekly. November 22, 1996. p. 107.
The Hollywood Reporter. November 12, 1996. pp. 10-14.
New York Times. November 11, 1996. Section C, p.18.
Newsweek. November 11, 1996. p. 77.
People Magazine. November 25, 1996. p. 20.
Time Magazine Online. November 25, 1996.
USA Today. November 15, 1996. Section D, p.1.
Variety Magazine Online. November 12, 1996.

The Spitfire Grill

To a town with no future, comes a girl with a past.—Movie tagline

"A wonderful film - uplifting and inspiring. A beautifully woven tale of friendship, redemption and trust. Go see it and bring boxes of Kleenex."—Joel Siegel, *Good Morning America*

"The tears you cry are for the film's perfection as much as its drama."—Steve Persall, *St. Petersburg Times*

"Perfect! Filled with Oscar-caliber performances."—Jeff Craig, *Sixty Second Preview*

"One of the year's most beautiful and touching films."—Michael Medved, *Sneak Previews*

"Alison Elliott is unforgettable! A film that should not be missed!"—Paul Wunder, *WBAI-FM*

Box Office: $12,658,486

The financing of *The Spitfire Grill* makes an altogether more inspirational and interesting story than the one told in this highly contrived film. Originally called *Care of the Spitfire Grill,* the film was financed, produced, and marketed by the Gregory Corporation, a company owned by the Priests of the Sacred Heart, a Roman Catholic order. Gregory is the for-profit arm of a Mississippi-based, non-profit group owned by the order called the Sacred Heart League, which publishes religious books and videos. Gregory's mission, as told to the *New York Times,* is to "promote Judeo-Christian values" and to "increase the outreach of the ministry through movies." Proceeds from the film go to the Sacred Heart League's charitable works, which include AIDS counseling and health care for children.

> "Until I forget my name or start drooling at the mouth, I'll thank you to let me make my own decisions."—Hannah

The Spitfire Grill was the result of a lengthy search by Roger Courts, the executive director of Gregory and director of the Sacred Heart League, for an appropriately inspirational script. Lee David Zlotoff, the creator of the television show "MacGyver," submitted the entry that came closest to meeting Gregory's criteria. Zlotoff was also hired to direct. (Gregory has pointed out with some pride that although the film was backed financially by a Catholic order, it portrays Protestant characters and was created by a Jewish writer-director, and as such promotes no particular denomination.)

Care of the Spitfire Grill went on to win the Audience Award at the 1996 Sundance Film Festival, where Castle Rock Entertainment reportedly paid $10 million for the distribution rights to the film—a record among deals made for films premiering at the Sundance Festival. Castle Rock slightly modified the film's title between its premiere at Sundance and its release later in 1996.

In spite of the order's good intentions and the film's reception at Sundance, *The Spitfire Grill* remains a cloyingly predictable film. Zlotoff's heavy-handed "inspirational" plot, as well as his overt and obvious use of symbolism, never transcends its mechanical contrivances. In hammering home at almost every turn the film's message of forgiveness, love, and redemption, Zlotoff never lets the characters in *Grill* breathe or come to life as people. Only Alison Elliott, in a lovely, nuanced performance in the film's central role, and Marcia Gay Harden, as a woman who befriends her, manage to overcome the banalities of Zlotoff's script to create winning characters. Will Patton, as an all-but-mustache-twirling villain, and the usually redoubtable Ellen Burstyn, in a virtual parody of Katharine Hepburn, are particularly grating.

The Spitfire Grill begins cleverly with the too-symbolically-named Perchance Talbott (Elliott), known as Percy, adeptly fielding phone calls for the Maine Tourist Board with a thick Southern accent. A pullback reveals that the operators are in fact inmates at the state prison, where Percy is serving a five-year sentence for manslaughter.

Upon her release, Percy picks the—again, all-too-symbolically named—town of Gilead, Maine, in which to settle and serve her parole. Percy arrives in the midst of a winter storm, and is taken in by Hannah Ferguson (Burstyn), a self-described "sour old apple" who runs the Spitfire Grill, a local diner and institution. Reluctantly, Hannah hires Percy as a waitress and gives her room and board. Percy, unbeknownst to all, will become the "balm in Gilead" the town so sorely needs.

Gilead, however, does not welcome outsiders or iconoclasts, and when Percy, angered by belittling comments from patrons of the Grill, announces that she is a convicted felon on parole, word spreads quickly that she is a stranger to be watched carefully. Hannah's nephew, Nahum Goddard (Patton), in particular suspects Percy of having designs on the

Sundance Film Festival 1996: Audience Award

ailing Hannah's cash and property. Nahum, a real estate agent, also fears that any stain on Gilead's reputation will ruin the chances for the reopening of Gilead's granite quarry.

Percy, however, has won over the ornery Hannah. When Hannah has an accident and can no longer run the Grill—really the true heart of Gilead, Percy takes over along with Shelby (Harden), Nahum's wife. Shelby, a woman cowed into submission by her husband, is originally sent to spy on Percy, but the two women end up becoming friends, much to Nahum's chagrin. Scenes of the developing closeness between Percy, Shelby, and Hannah play out much in the manner of *Fried Green Tomatoes* (1990). Shelby, however, tells Percy that there is a reason the heart of Gilead is broken: Hannah's son, the star athlete and golden boy of the town, went to Vietnam and never came back. Hannah no longer speaks of him. For Shelby, it was with Hannah's son's disappearance that a light seemed to go out in Gilead.

The paradise of this trio of new friends, however, cannot last. Hannah has long been looking to sell the Spitfire Grill, but has never been able to find the right person to take care of it. Percy comes up with the idea of having a nationwide contest in which contestants would submit a $100 fee and an essay explaining why they would like to take over the Spitfire Grill. The three women begin placing ads in newspapers and magazines around the country; to the disbelief of the townspeople and the consternation of Nahum, applications and checks begin pouring in.

With change imminent and threatening Nahum's and the quarry's interests, at least three mysteries haunt Gilead and Percy: Who is the mysterious stranger for whom Hannah leaves out food every night and who disappears into the forest at dawn? Why did Percy go to jail for manslaughter? And what are the intentions of Nahum's alliance with the quarry owners?

The answers to each of these riddles are telegraphed well in advance of their resolution on-screen. In the end, Percy redeems the best part of Gilead and heals the wounds of Shelby's and Nahum's marriage, of the loss of Hannah's son, and of the threat to the forest from the granite quarry—at the cost of her life.

The mechanics of Zlotoff's script grind obviously and none too quickly. The film's main "secret"—the identity of the mysterious stranger—is obvious literally from the moment it is introduced. The juxtapositions of good and evil in the film—the dappled sunlight in which the women peel potatoes, for example, versus the darkness in which Nahum belittles his wife and tries to ruin Percy, are painfully simplistic. Little audience empathy with the characters is possible because each character in the film is lashed to the film's "message" of forgiveness and redemption. Zlotoff's characters simply seem to be stick figures acting out a foreordained plot.

In spite of the film's predictability, however, Elliott and Harden shine through. Elliott, previously seen in the femme fatale role in Steven Soderbergh's *The Underneath* (1994), manages to downplay the most laughable of Zlotoff's lines to create a character of spunk, humor, courage, and previously untapped resilience. If in Zlotoff's script Percy is a saint of sorts, Elliott makes her vulnerable and heartbreakingly unaware of her spiritual effect on others. If Harden's, like most of the cast's, Way Down East accent is a bit too broad, Harden also manages to give Shelby a quiet dignity, even as she delivers some groaner lines of exposition in explaining the disappearance of Hannah's son.

In the end, *The Spitfire Grill*'s undeniable sincerity is done in by the heavy-handedness of the plotting and symbolism. Although the film's—and the production company's—goals and aspirations are laudable, its laborious contrivances make for plodding art and extremely difficult viewing.

—Paul Mittelbach

CREDITS

Perry Talbott: Alison Elliott
Hannah Ferguson: Ellen Burstyn
Shelby Goddard: Marcia Gay Harden
Nahum Goddard: Will Patton
Joe Sperling: Kieran Mulroney
Sheriff Gary Walsh: Gailard Sartain
Effy Katshaw: Louise De Cormier
Johnny B.: John Jackson

Origin: USA
Released: 1996
Production: Forrest Murray for a Mendocino Corporation and Gregory production; released by Castle Rock Entertainment
Direction: Lee David Zlotoff
Screenplay: Lee David Zlotoff
Cinematography: Rob Draper
Editing: Margie Goodspeed
Music: James Horner
Production design: Howard Cummings
Art direction: Peter Borck
Costume design: Louise Mingenbach
Sound: Stuart Pearce
Casting: Marci Liroff
MPAA rating: PG-13
Running Time: 116 minutes

REVIEWS

Entertainment Weekly. August 23, 1996.
San Francisco Chronicle. August 23, 1996, p. D3.
San Francisco Examiner. August 23, 1996, p. D3.

Spy Hard

All the action. All the women. Half the intelligence.—Movie tagline

"Utterly hilarious! Nielsen is simply marvelous!"—Ron Brewington, *American Urban Radio Networks*

"You'll laugh your socks off!"—Bob Polunsky, *KENS-TV*

"A truly entertaining and very funny film."—Sam Rubin, *KTLA Morning News*

Box Office: $26,960,191

At one time, Leslie Nielsen was probably best known as the skipper of the spacecraft sent to rescue Anne Francis and her father from the *Forbidden Planet* (1956). But in 1980, the innovative comic team of Jim Abrahams and the Zucker Brothers cast him as a dotty doctor in *Airplane!* their spoof of the ubiquitous airliner crash films. Since then, Nielsen has probably made a fortune playing the stiff and officious idiot. He successfully brought the inept Detective Frank Drebin from the cult television series "Police Squad" to the big screen in a trio of hit *Naked Gun* films, but even Nielsen's dependable persona of hero as bumbling simpleton who never quite gets the joke, is not enough to carry *Spy Hard.* Surely, (I know, "Don't call me Shirley") as the executive producer, even Nielsen has to realize that he needs funny "stuff" to say and do for a film to be successful. The ZAZ guys could do it, the Friedbergs, director and writer, father and son, can't.

"Bullies have very bad self-esteem."—Dr. Joyce Brothers

Normally, plots don't count for much in parodies, and *Spy Hard* is no different. What plot there is revolves around the evil villain General Rancor (Andy Griffith) who was responsible for the death of Dick Steele's first love and partner, Barbara Dahl (Stephanie Romanov) and who, in return, was caught in an explosion which tore his arms off. Once thought dead, Rancor is back with replacement arms, designs on ruling the world, and a grudge against Steele. So, he takes Barbara's daughter Victoria (also Romanov) as hostage in order to lure Steele into his trap.

Includes cameos by Fabio, Dr. Joyce Brothers, Ray Charles, Robert Culp, Mr. T, and Pat Morita.

Steele is supposed to be retired, but he is recalled into service by the director of the Secret Service (Charles Durning) who, for some reason, is a "master of disguises" in his own office. However, Steele's reactivation is objected to by lead agent Norman Coleman (Barry Bostwick with an unaccountable thick Kennedy accent), but the Director is convinced only Steele can save the day.

Along the way to rescuing Victoria and the world, Steele takes on a few partners: a sidekick/love interest, Veronique Ukrinsky (Nicollette Sheridan) who is looking for her father (Elya Baskin) the inventor of the computer chip Rancor needs to gain complete power, and there is also his driver, Kabul (John Ales), who seems to find a variety of vehicles and mismatched maxims to try and keep the film and Steele moving.

Since the plot is not important in this type of film, it should be no surprise that Steele will accomplish his mission. Unfortunately, the filmmakers don't accomplish theirs. This comedy is not funny. It desperately wants to be another entry in the quick witted, oblique punchlined, and gag-a-minute films like those created by the Zuckers and Abrahams. And *Spy Hard*'s filmmakers try every ZAZ trick in the book to try and recreate their magic. They bring in celebrity cameos such as Ray Charles "driving" a bus, but they don't work as well as *Airplane!*'s use of Ethel Merman. They try to sneak in the trademark ZAZ phoney credits such as listing after "Rigging Key Grip," "Kung Fu Grip . . . G.I. Joe," but we've seen this trick before, and they do nothing new with it.

The problem here is that director Rick Friedberg is no Zucker or Abrahams. His primary claims to comedy fame are the Dollar Rent-A-Car commercials he did with Nielsen along with the actor's two golf videos, *Leslie Nielsen's Bad Golf Made Easier* and *Bad Golf My Way.* To make matters worse, he based his film on a story written by his son and his son's college roommate. Jason Friedberg and Aaron Seltzer are graduates of the University of California, and *Spy Hard* has the feel of a fraternity skit hastily written while they were drunk and everything seemed funny. Jason and Seltzer have no previous work to their credit, and after this, they might find it hard to get more.

So, in one last attempt to recreate the ZAZ magic, Friedberg Sr. tries his hand at reworking his son's script and brings in someone with a ZAZ connection. Abrahams and the Zuckers began their careers in Milwaukee where they

CREDITS

Dick Steele "Agent WD-40": Leslie Nielsen
Veronique Ukrinsky "Agent 3.14": Nicolette Sheridan
The Director: Charles Durning
Miss Cheevus: Marcia Gay Harden
Norman Coleman: Barry Bostwick
Kabul: John Ales
General Rancor: Andy Griffith
Professor Ukrinsky: Elya Baskin
McCluckey: Mason Gamble
Slice: Carlos Laúchu
Victoria/Barbara Dahl: Stephanie Romanov
Steele's Tag Team Member: Dr. Joyce Brothers
Bus Driver: Ray Charles
Agent Clinton: Roger Clinton
Businessman: Robert Culp
Fabio: Fabio
Agent Steve Bishop: Robert Guillaume
Steele's Tag Team Member: Hulk Hogan
Brian The Waiter: Pat Morita
Woman in Murphy Bed: Alexandra Paul
Agency Helicopter Pilot: Mr. T
Agency Tape Recorder Voice Over: Alex Trebek

Origin: USA
Released: 1996
Production: Rick Friedberg, Doug Fraizin and Jeffrey Konvitz for Hollywood Pictures; released by Buena Vista
Direction: Rick Friedberg
Screenplay: Rick Friedberg & Dick Chudnow and Jason Friedberg & Aaron Seltzer
Cinematography: John R. Leonetti
Editing: Eric Sears
Production design: William Creber
Art direction: William J. Durrell, Jr.
Set decoration: Ernie Bishop
Costume design: Tom Bronson
Music: Bill Conti
Opening Title Sequence: "Weird Al" Yankovic
MPAA rating: PG-13
Running Time: 81 minutes

created the Kentucky Fried Theater along with Dick Chudlow. It is to Chudlow that Friedberg turns for a little script doctoring, but his credits are not as a writer. He is the founder/owner of ComedySportz live theater and teaches improvisation at the University of Wisconsin, Milwaukee. He may be good at running comedy clubs and improv, but he seems to come up short when it comes to bringing silliness to the screen.

Although Nielsen tries his best with the poor material at hand, the resulting film is stale and superficial. It has nothing to offer on its own, it can only steal from others. Which is why, in the end, its greatest claim to fame (and the substance of most of its trailer) is its take-offs of other movies. You know it's bad when the only slightly entertaining thing about the film is recognizing and counting the other films which are parodied. Here there are no less than a dozen, including *Speed* (1994), *Sister Act* (1992), *In the Line of Fire* (1993), *Pulp Fiction* (1994), *True Lies* (1994), and one which may escape younger viewers, *Butch Cassidy and the Sundance Kid* (1969).

Spy Hard breaks no new ground, never reaches for the better gag or the more unexpected punchline. It never even tries to offer amusing background teases to keep us on our toes. In fact, it's so tired it just doesn't try at all.

This film will only make money this summer if the theaters showing *Twister* and *Mission Impossible* are full and the overflow crowd would rather see a movie, ANY movie, than go home.

So if it's a very funny spoof you want, rent *Airplane!*. If it's a parody of a James Bond spy film you crave, rent *Casino Royale* (1967).

—Beverley Bare Buehrer

REVIEWS

Boxoffice. July, 1996, p. 90.
Chicago Tribune. May 24, 1996, section Friday, p. C.
Detroit News. May 24, 1996, p. 3D.
Entertainment Weekly. May 31, 1996, p. 40.
New York Times. May 24, 1996, p. C3.
Variety. May 27, 1996, p. 66.

The Star Maker; L'uomo Delle Stelle

Everyone dreams of becoming a star. One man can make those dreams come true.—Movie tagline

"A great movie!"—*The Boston Globe*

"Entertaining!"—*San Francisco Examiner*

Box Office: $371,674

The Star Maker is another homage to the movies by director Giuseppe Tornatore, whose *Cinema Paradiso* won an Oscar in 1989 as best foreign language film. It concentrated on a young Sicilian boy's love affair with the screen. This time the setting is again Sicily, still recovering from the Second World War in the early 1950s. Joe Morelli (Sergio Castellitto) is a con man billing himself as "Dr. Morelli." He travels in a truck to villages announcing that he is the representative of a major film production company. He is offering people screen tests and the opportunity to become movie stars. His booming voice issuing out of the truck's speakers galvanizes the young and the old who come to audition for the cameras.

"I like love stories where everybody kisses and are happy ever after."—Beata

Morelli, of course, is only interested in bilking people of their 1500 lire, the fee he charges for the screen tests. He makes no promises, he says, but he builds up peoples' hopes by praising the way they deliver their lines or their facial structures which photograph so well. He scorns the ignorance of the villagers and is contemptuous of a land that seems so backward to him.

The human pageant that parades before the cameras is amusing and affecting. A group of old men sit together rehearsing the lines from *Gone With the Wind* which Morelli has distributed for the screen tests. Soon they are improvising hilariously, turning the Southern epic into a Sicilian story reflecting their hopes and sorrows. A silent villager, traumatized by the war, breaks years of silence to passionately evoke the terror of war. A young woman outcast takes the screen test in order to denounce her neighbors who suspect her of prostituting herself for American soldiers. She can't wait to get out of this "shithole," she tells the camera. A policeman recites poetry, showing an esthetic side carefully concealed from his community.

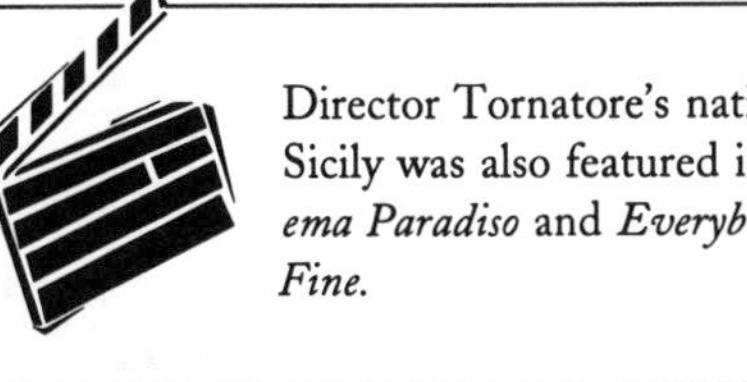

Director Tornatore's native Sicily was also featured in *Cinema Paradiso* and *Everybody's Fine.*

Thus the camera stimulates people to focus on their lives. Beata (Tiziana Lodato), a young girl brought up in a convent, longs for escape and recognition. She is still a virgin but earns extra money by showing her statuesque body to people—as long as they do not touch her. Morelli is tempted by her luscious body, but she is so needy and persistent that he keeps rebuffing her efforts to join him on the road—which she believes leads to Rome and to stardom.

As people pour out their hearts to Morelli, he becomes even more cynical and greedy. Then he is stopped by a band of Sicilian bandits. It would seem that his number is finally up. They demand everything. Morelli stops trying to placate them and suddenly looks at their faces. Exploding in enthusiasm he mentions vast sums of money. At first, the band's leader refuses to understand, but Morelli persists, saying they have just the looks and the bloodcurdling stories that would make a good movie. Soon they are bragging about their exploits and posing for the camera. Afterwards, they again demand Morelli's money. He shakes his head, saying they have misunderstood. They should pay him for the screen test to cover his expenses. They are aghast, but eventually settle up with their promoter.

Morelli's con works so well that he is invited to film the casket of a distinguished local citizen. Later he is invited to a card game in which he fleeces the table. On the way out of the village he looks at his loot and laughs. Dr. Morelli obviously thinks he can outsmart anyone.

On the road again Morelli's old truck breaks down. A beautiful woman in a chauffeured car asks him if she can be of assistance. She takes him to a ruined place where she says her husband, a local nobleman, stays once a month to visit his people. Attracted to the woman, who implies her husband, a burnt out case, no longer interests her, Morelli lingers. It seems the perfect set up for him. The husband sits atop a little ruin and explains to Morelli how his plans for rebuilding have gone awry. He does indeed seem pitiful. The next morning Morelli awakes to find that the couple has departed with his cash box.

His truck's breakdown has presaged his own swift descent. He is arrested by the police officer who posed for his camera. The officer has done a check on Morelli and finds that he has a criminal record. The villagers who had him film their beloved mayor in a casket catch up with Morelli and break his legs. He spends two years in prison. Through both his ascent and descent he has been followed by Beata, whom he has deflowered. Yet she retains an innocence that refuses to be corrupted by the world. When she loses Morelli to prison, she turns to prostitution. But rather than turning her cynical, it drives her mad.

Out of prison Morelli searches for her. She is in an asylum. She tells him that Morelli is dead, and he tells her that he is Morelli's friend who has promised to take care of her. Beata is all that Morelli has left; she represents the only possibility that he can recover his humanity.

Tiziana Lodato turns in a remarkable performance as Beata. Her innocence is believable, as is her inability to become a corrupt person even when she does corrupt things. She is the exact opposite of Morelli, who can appear to be compassionate and supportive when people give their halting speeches before the camera but who is not moved in the slightest by their efforts. As the police officer tells him, people offered him their hearts and hopes—real treasures that he rejected in favor of money.

A bald description of *The Star Maker*'s plot makes it sound trite, but the performances are so good that they revive a sense of the magic that movies represent. Joe Morelli does not work for Universalia Pictures, as he claims. And yet he is doing the work of the movies, a universal work that has opened human faces and lives to the whole world. Morelli, it is revealed late in the film, has been in America, and his experience there has undoubtedly brought conviction to his line "Success awaits you!" When he is conning people, he is merely perpetuating the promise that the villagers already know, reciting the line from *Gone With the Wind:* "Tomorrow is another day." This is what he is selling, of course, endless possibility. Before the movies another day meant for millions of people no more than that one day would be like another. But after *Gone With the Wind* it meant another chance, the rebuilding of lives, the rebuilding of Italy after the war just as that other group of Southerners in the United States had to rebuild their world. The link between movies and dreams is so axiomatic that *The Star Maker* does not have to link Sicily and the South. The people in the movie, the people watching the movie, make the connection effortlessly.

Some reviewers have objected to the sentimental ending and to lines that seem too scripted. But surely screenwriters Tornatore and Fabio Rinaudo are suggesting that their characters have learned to speak from the movies. They are not merely expressing life in Sicily but the life that has been infected by the worldwide influence of film. These are people grasping for their fifteen minutes of fame long before artist Andy Warhol coined the expression.

As critic Kenneth Turan points out, *The Star Maker* is *Cinema Paradiso* with a twist. Whereas the earlier film deals with the fulfillment of dreams, *The Star Maker* concerns what happens when dreams are dishonored. This is why Morelli has to be punished and why his redemption has to follow a Hollywood plotline. It seems pointless to criticize the screenplay for being unrealistic. It is a fable about film and the human imagination. That is why Lodato's performance is crucial. She embodies the screenplay's contradictions. Like Marilyn Monroe, she is sexually charged and guileless. The world will defile her and yet she will remain untouched. She frustrates Morelli because she refuses to learn from experience and to become as cynical as he is. Yet that is what, in the end, draws him back to her. She will not forsake the dream he represents, no matter how poor a representative of that dream he actually is. So it is with movies, *The Star Maker* suggests. They make suckers of everyone, and yet people keep watching, craving the world of make-believe.

—Carl Rollyson

CREDITS

Joe Morelli: Sergio Castellitto
Beata: Tuzuaba Lodato
Nastropaolo: Franco Scaldati
Bordonaro: Tano Cimarosa

Origin: Italy
Released: 1995
Production: Vittorio Cecchi Gori, Rita Cecchi Gori for a Sciarlo production; released by Miramax Films
Direction: Giuseppe Tornatore
Screenplay: Giuseppe Tornatore, Fabio Rinaudo
Cinematography: Dante Spinotti
Editing: Massimo Quaglia
Music: Ennio Morricone
Production design: Francesco Bronzi
Costume design: Beatrice Bordone
Casting: Marco Guidone
Sound: Massimo Loffredi
MPAA rating: R
Running Time: 113 minutes

REVIEWS

Boxoffice. May, 1996, p. 74.
Detroit News. March 22, 1996, p. D3.
The Hollywood Reporter. March 5, 1996, p. 13.
Los Angeles Times. March 8, 1996, p. F6.
New York Times. March 8, 1996, p. C4.
Variety. September 11, 1995, p. 108.

Star Trek: First Contact

Planet: Earth. Year: 2063. Population: 9 Billion. None human. Resistance is futile.—Movie tagline

"One of the 10 best films of the year! You'll love this film."—Steve Oldfield, *FOX-TV*

"Pure adrenaline and full-blast entertainment!"—Dan Graney, *KPNT-FM*

"The special effects are absolutely astounding. It has all the suspense of *Aliens* wrapped up in a nice *Star Trek* package. You don't have to be a Trekker to enjoy."—Jerry Peterson, *Orbit Magazine*

"*First Contact* has it all - adventure and a sense of humor. One of the best."—Jim Ferguson, *Prevue Channel*

"*First Contact* stands proud and apart. Glides along with purpose and style."—Richard Corliss, *Time*

Captain Picard (Patrick Stewart) must resist the advances of the Borg Queen (Alice Krige) in order to save his Enterprise and Earth from a Borg invasion in *Star Trek: First Contact.*

Box Office: $86,249,815

The phenomenon known as *Star Trek*—in all of its myriad incarnations—celebrated its 30th anniversary in 1996. Along with the *Star Wars* (1977, 1980, 1983) series of films—which it predates by a decade—*Star Trek* has become a modern popular-culture equivalent to the myths, legends, and epic poems of ancient cultures. There is something universally appealing about the series, which offers variations of many of the exploits of such ancient heroes as the Babylonian god-king Gilgamesh and his savage companion Enkidu battling demons and deities while seeking out the secrets of life; the eternally wandering—and abundantly resourceful—Odysseus and his encounters with strange, god-like entities in fabulous locales; and the adventurous Jason and his crew of Argonauts in search of the Golden Fleece.

"You can't begin to imagine the life you denied yourself."—Borg Queen to Picard

Like its ancient predecessors, *Star Trek* offers its legion of followers a way of looking at life's challenges as an adventure fraught with danger, excitement, tragedy, and triumph, when human courage and ingenuity are the best resources one can display when dealing with any and all elements of the universe.

The eighth film in the motion picture series, *Star Trek: First Contact* is the first to feature exclusively the cast of the "Star Trek: Next Generation" television series. The previous film, *Star Trek: Generations* (1994) suffered from its inability to mesh the cast members from the first two television series into a coherent and effective story line. Its problems mirrored those of the first film in the series, *Star Trek: The Motion Picture* (1979), which suffered from a too reverential approach to the characters as well as an overemphasis on big-budget special effects in an attempt to distinguish it from the television series.

Like the second film in the series, *Star Trek:The Wrath of Khan* (1982), the latest film finds the right balance between its television roots and its cinematic incarnation by using a memorable villain from the television show as the focus for the story line. The result is a film that is not only one of the best in the series but a standout in the science fiction film genre.

The opening scene is, literally, an eye-opener, one of the longest and most elaborate dolly tracking shots used in film. It begins in the eye of Capt. Jean-Luc Picard (Patrick Stewart), with the camera slowly pulling back out of his eye to reveal his face, emotionless, half of it encased in black wires. With the camera continuing to pull back, Picard is shown as part of a huge, black machine-like structure surrounded by other humans also covered in black wires. Pulling back further, Picard's form disappears, an insignificant cog in a monstrous, asteroid-sized space ship, part of a fleet of ships belonging to a collective entity called the Borg.

Picard suddenly jars awake on board his space ship, the Enterprise E, having dreamed about his experience with the

Borg. However, those familiar with the television series know that Picard's dream was more of a nightmarish remembrance. In one of the most effective and memorable two-part episodes from the series, Picard was abducted by the Borg and became one of them—half-human, half-machine—part of a collective consciousness devoid of individuality and emotions.

The Borg's ultimate goal is to assimilate every living entity in the entire universe to its collective thinking, a thinking that robs all life forms of their capacity to function as unique entities, an ultimate goal considered by the Borg as the ultimate in perfection. What makes the Borg such an effectively monstrous nemesis is that, along with assimilating life forms to its machine-like collective thinking, it can also assimilate all forms of weaponry, adapting to the destructive force of any weapon after having experienced it.

Picard's dream becomes reality when he learns that the Borg is attacking Earth. Wanting to help curtail the attack, Picard readies his crew for battle. However, he is disappointed to learn from his superiors that the Enterprise must remain out of the fight. Picard knows this decision is based on his experiences with the Borg; his superiors are afraid Picard will act irrationally during the battle, his personal hatred for the Borg clouding his judgement.

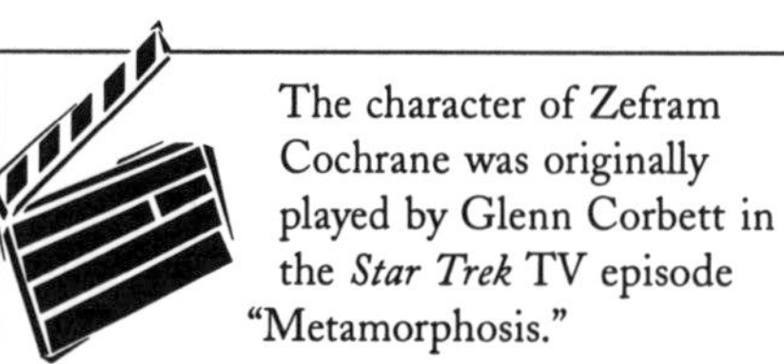

The character of Zefram Cochrane was originally played by Glenn Corbett in the *Star Trek* TV episode "Metamorphosis."

Picard finally ignores his command when Federation starships are crippled by the Borg's onslaught. He arrives in time to curtail the attack, then follows a Borg ship as it attacks Earth. Caught unexpectedly in a time warp along with the Borg ship, the Enterprise travels from the 24th century to the 21st, just prior to a momentous occasion in Earth history: first contact with aliens from another planet. This historical meeting, however, did not occur between humans and the Borg. Picard realizes that the Borg have traveled back in time to the year 2063 to prevent this event from happening, thus changing history so that Earth will never become part of the Federation; instead, it will become part of the Borg collective.

Before the Borg ship has time to attack Earth, the Enterprise destroys it. Wanting to make sure Earth has not been affected by the event, Picard orders an away team to investigate. The team encounters a band of survivors from a devastating world war. Among this band is Zefram Cochrane (James Cromwell), an eccentric yet brilliant scientist, who is destined to invent the warp drive and revolutionize space travel. Cromwell is working on a nuclear warhead which he has converted into a crude but effective space ship and which he plans to launch the following day with help from his assistant Lily Sloane (Alfre Woodard).

Cromwell acts like an aging, alcoholic Hippie. In order to win his confidence, Counselor Deanna Troi (Marina Sirtis) joins him in several drinks and promptly becomes drunk, much to the amusement of Commander Will Riker (Jonathan Frakes). Meanwhile, Lily guards the rocket ship from the rest of the away team whom she mistakes as hostile invaders. In an unexpected confrontation with human-like android Data (Brent Spiner), Lily passes out from fright. Dr. Beverly Crusher (Gates McFadden) and Data beam back to the Enterprise, taking Lily with them for treatment.

While Lily is being treated, Picard and the rest of the Enterprise make a horrifying discovery: just prior to the destruction of the Borg ship, the Borg beamed on board the Enterprise and are methodically taking over the entire ship, assimilating crew members as they progress toward the ship's bridge. Refusing to abandon ship, Picard decides to confront the Borg.

Entering into the assimilated areas, Picard and his back-up team enter into a futuristic chamber of horrors peopled by the zombie-like Borg. After many violent confrontations, the Borg assimilate the force of the Enterprise weaponry. Retreating from the Borg, Data is captured and Picard is cut off from the rest of the crew.

Data is ushered into the presence of the Borg Queen (Alice Krige). She first appears as a disembodied head attached to a spinal column dangling from the ceiling who then descends into a lower body cavity. Although she is hideously inhuman, she has a slinky, reptilian seductiveness about her. She and her Borg drones attempt to assimilate Data but cannot break his computer code. Learning that Data desires to become more human, something the Queen pronounces as a loathful, imperfect goal, she decides to control Data by granting his fondest wish. She grafts human skin onto him so that he can experience the feel of human flesh. Then she seduces him.

Meanwhile, Picard struggles through the bowels of the Enterprise attempting to escape from the Borg. He encounters Lily who has escaped from the hospital ward. Bewildered, angry, and frightened, Lily threatens to shoot Picard with a phaser she has found. Picard, realizing she is frightened out of her wits in this strange and hostile futuristic environment, calms her down. They continue to escape from the Borg, at one point entering the ship's holodeck which Picard programs to simulate a 1920s gangster nightclub. The contrast between the hologram gangsters with Picard and

AWARDS AND NOMINATIONS

Academy Awards 1996 Nominations: Best Makeup

Lily dressed to fit the era, and the zombiesque Borgs wandering around like wind-up robots in this setting makes for a surrealistically lighthearted, visually effective moment.

Back on Earth, Riker and the other away team members break the news to Zefram Cochrane that he is destined to become one of Earth's greatest historical figures, a modern savior of mankind, celebrated as the man who first made contact with aliens and who ushered in the age of space exploration with his invention of the warp drive. Cochrane responds by getting drunk and running away, not able to accept the responsibility nor the idea of becoming a reverential figure. However, he ultimately decides to go through with the launch. With Riker and Geordie LaForge (Levar Burton) on board, he blasts off to the tune of raunchy rock and roll.

The launch is witnessed by the Enterprise crew. Picard, who has finally managed to outmaneuver the Borg and make it back to the bridge, finally orders the remaining crew members to abandon ship. He, however, refuses to leave the Enterprise, wanting to personally confront the Borg Queen.

When Picard enters the Borg Queen's lair, he finds Data by her side, appearing as if he has become one of her drones. At her orders, Data launches weapons that will destroy Cochrane's rocket before it reaches warp drive. Data, however, has set the weapons to miss Cochrane's rocket. In the ensuing chaos, Data sets off a deadly gas that eats away the flesh and wiring of the Borg Queen and her cohorts. Picard is saved when he climbs above the cloud of gas, dangling by a wire as the Queen clutches at him in vain.

In the film's final moments, Cochrane, surrounded by Enterprise crew members and a motley band of Earth survivalists, stands in awe as a space ship lands in their midst, the ship having been attracted by Cochrane's warp drive-powered rocket. It is a crew of pointy-eared Vulcans. Cochrane steps forward to welcome them.

Star Trek: First Contact has many stellar attributes, although three stand out. The first is the script by Brannon Braga and Ronald D. Moore, who also co-wrote the previous film. Although containing elements from such classic science fiction films as *Invasion of the Body Snatchers* (1956), and *The Terminator* (1984), Braga and Moore's script is still highly unique, juggling three separate yet interwoven plot lines—one involving Cochrane and the away team; one involving Picard and Lily and their struggles with the Borg; and one involving Data and the Borg Queen.

Each subplot has its own mood. Cochrane's is mostly humorous; Data and the Borg Queen's is a psychological game of seduction; and Picard and Lily's is one of survival, scheming, and revenge. Only rarely does the shifting between these three plot focuses become jarring, for example, in a scene when Picard and his crew have an intensely violent confrontation with the Borg which is followed by the comical scene of a drunk Deanna Troi weaving around Cochrane's makeshift camp.

However, Braga and Moore's script manages to smooth over some of the less effective segments by maintaining an underlying theme in each of the three subplots: the theme of individuals sacrificing their own personal desires for the sake of a greater good. In Picard's case, he is as Lily describes him in an effectively played scene—an intergalactic Captain Ahab, nearly blinded by his desire for vengeance against the Borg for scarring him forever with their previous attempts to change his personality. In Cochrane's case, he cannot stand the idea of becoming a hero, only wanting to make money off of his new invention so he can live out the rest of his days as a debauched millionaire. In Data's case, his desire to become more human makes him vulnerable to the wiles of the Borg Queen. In the end, however, each of these characters sacrifices personal desires in order to serve humanity.

This well-developed theme is also contrasted with the Borg mentality which views individuality as anathema, that perfection can be achieved only when personal desires and feelings have been meshed into an inhuman collective consciousness. Obviously, Braga and Moore are commenting on the dark side mass-thinking, of blindly following a concept or philosophy without questioning its principals.

By making the Borg followers half-human and half-machine, Braga and Moore might have also had the Internet in mind, the idea of individuals throughout the world linked together and communicating en masse via

CREDITS

Capt. Jean-Luc Picard: Patrick Stewart
Cmdr. William Riker: Jonathan Frakes
Lt. Cmdr. Data: Brent Spiner
Lt. Cmdr. Geordie La Forge: LeVar Burton
Lt. Cmdr. Worf: Michael Dorn
Dr. Beverly Crusher: Gates McFadden
Counselor Deanna Troi: Marina Sirtis
Lily Sloane: Alfre Woodard
Zefram Cochrane: James Cromwell
Borg Queen: Alice Krige

Origin: USA
Released: 1996
Production: Rick Berman for Paramount Pictures
Direction: Jonathan Frakes
Screenplay: Brannon Braga and Ronald D. Moore
Cinematography: Matthew F. Leonetti
Editing: John Wheeler
Music: Jerry Goldsmith
Production design: Herman Zimmerman
Set decoration: John M. Dwyer
Costume design: Deborah Everton
Make up: Michael Westmore
MPAA rating: PG-13
Running Time: 111 minutes

a computer system, a system developed by modern technological wizards who have taken on god-like status in contemporary culture. In this respect, Braga and Moore have achieved something for which the original "Star Trek" series was highly commended—using the science fiction genre to comment upon contemporary, controversial topics in a highly entertaining and thought-provoking manner.

The second stellar attribute is the fine acting by the entire cast which works well as an ensemble, an attribute that has distinguished all of the most effective films in the series. Again, the script must be credited for paying close attention to character nuances amid the big-budget science fiction gadgetry and pyrotechnics. But, credit is also due to first-time film director Jonathan Frakes who, because of his close association with the cast—having been a part of it since its television inception—obviously contributed to the close-knit feel generated by the television cast veterans.

This well integrated, emotive emphasis on character also includes the three principal non-crew cast members. James Cromwell is comically effective as the loopy scientist Zefram Cochrane. Alfre Woodard gives dramatic punch to her character, endowing her confrontations with Picard with an edgy, forceful verve, making her challenges to his vengeful decisions believable and sensible. And Alice Krige does the near-impossible with her extremely intelligent and riveting portrayal as the Borg Queen: although covered in a slimy, cream-like make-up with black tubes jutting out of her head, she emerges as one of the sexiest and most seductive villains in the science fiction film genre.

The film's third outstanding attribute is Patrick Stewart. As fine as the other cast members are, Stewart as Picard is the film's central focus and does an outstanding job of riveting the audience's attention to his every move, every command, every look. Stewart, an actor of incredible talent, with his booming, mesmerizing, kingly-Shakespearian voice, makes the viewer believe the story, makes Picard's internal wounds and vengeful motives seem like every man's deeply etched scars and volatile anger. Having replaced William Shatner's supremely popular Captain Kirk as captain of the most famous starship in the science fiction film genre, Stewart is more than qualified to lead the series into realms where no film audience has gone before.

Star Trek: First Contact proves beyond a doubt that the *Star Trek* phenomenon will endure on the big screen. With such talented and resourceful filmmakers guiding its success, it might even endure into the century in which it takes place.

—*Jim Kline*

REVIEWS

Boxoffice Online. December 9, 1996.
Chicago Tribune. November 22, 1996, p. 4.
Detroit Free Press. November 22, 1996.
Detroit News. November 22, 1996, p. 4E.
Entertainment Weekly. November 29, 1996, p. 72.
Los Angeles Times. November 22, 1996, p. F1.
New York Times. November 22, 1996, p. C3.
New Yorker. November 9, 1996, p. 121.
People. December 2, 1996, p. 19.
Sci-Fi Universe. February, 1997, p. 49.
Time. November 25, 1996, p. 106.
TV Guide. November 23, 1996, p. 39.
USA Today. November 22, 1996, p. 5D.
Variety. November 18, 1996, p. 59.
Village Voice. December 3, 1996, p. 68.

Stealing Beauty

The most beautiful place to be is in love.—Movie tagline

"Provocative and dreamy! It's like spending a soothing day in the Italian countryside."—Marshall Fine, *Gannett Newspapers*

"Glorious! The perfect midsummer night's dream."—Juliann Garey, *Glamour Magazine*

"Seductive and intoxicating! Dizzyingly beautiful . . . another sensation."—Janet Maslin, *New York Times*

"Ravishing!"—Anthony Lane, *New Yorker*

"No thoughtful romantic will want to miss it."—Bruce Williamson, *Playboy*

Box Office: $4,722,310

Renowned Academy Award-winning director, Bernardo Bertolucci, has returned to Italy after fifteen years. During those fifteen years, he was busy making films of great spectacle such as *The Last Emperor* (1987), *The Sheltering Sky* (1990) and *Little Buddha* (1994). In 1973, Bertolucci shocked filmgoers with the depiction of raw sexual obsession in *The Last Tango in Paris.* Marlon Brando gave one of his most honest and remarkable performances in this extremely controversial film about a middle-aged man and a young girl. Once again, Bertolucci, at 56 years of age, deals with sexuality in his latest film, *Stealing Beauty,* starring Jeremy Irons and newcomer, Liv Tyler. It explores a 19-year-old girl's journey back to Italy where she was conceived (in an olive grove) to find out the identity of her real father. She also hopes to explore her own personal sexuality by consummating her relationship with a boy that she fell in love with four years earlier.

"I think it would be great, you know, to just sit around all day and express yourself."—visiting lawyer Richard Reed

This "exquisite, erotic adventure," as it was called by Guy Flatley of *Cosmopolitan,* was written by novelist Susan Minot (*Monkeys, Lust and Other Stories*). The setting for this coming-of-age tale, takes place in a farmhouse in Tuscany, owned by a retired art dealer, Monsieur Guillaume (Jean Marais). It seems that the property has become somewhat of a haven for several creative "bohemian" types. There is the sculptor, Ian Grayson (Donald McCann), who is going to do a portrait of young, virginal Lucy (Liv Tyler); Alex (Jeremy Irons), a dying playwright; Diana (Sinead Cusack), Ian's wife; Miranda (Rachel Weisz), their spoiled daughter; and Richard (D.W. Moffett), the chronically horny entertainment lawyer, who is either talking on his cellular phone or having sex. Lucy's deceased mother, who was a poet, was once a member of this eclectic avant-garde little colony. When she arrives for her visit, everyone is napping. It appears that life is gentle and quite lethargic in this pastoral Italian commune until the young and quite beautiful Lucy arrives. It is as if she herself is awakening in them all sorts of dormant emotions. When they learn of Lucy's "virginal" status, they all enthusiastically express their opinions on the subject. No one more so than Alex, whose own poor body is being ravaged by leukemia. He becomes a combination father/teacher/confidante to the young beauty, as they sit outside smoking pot. He hazily advises her, "You're in need of a good ravisher." (This line will certainly not fly with the feminists in the audience.) Eventually, Lucy finally meets up with her former boyfriend, Niccolo (Roberto Zibette), but discovers that he is more about hormones than heart. His roving eye for the girls turns her away from the young Lothario. All the while, Ian is intensely and feverishly working on Lucy's portrait, as life is unfolding in front of her large and very beautiful eyes. In the end, the question of her birth father is resolved, as is her entry into womanhood.

The sculptures shown in the film are the work of artist Matthew Spender, who also served as artistic advisor.

Stealing Beauty was greatly anticipated by critics, considering the scope of the filmmaker's previous body of work. Also, the fact that Bertolucci's other film dealing with sexual mores (*Last Tango*) received so much attention (24 years earlier) added to the interest. In reality, *Stealing Beauty* is sexually very mild in comparison. Anthony Lane of *The New Yorker* said, "The trouble with *Stealing Beauty* is not that it's dirty—it's not quite dirty enough to be honest." It is a beautiful movie to look at thanks to cinematographer Darius Khondki (*Seven* [1995]), but the slow pace and listless atmosphere dampen the film's impact. It lacks a momentum that makes the plot seem arbitrary to the visual images. The countryside is beautiful, Liv is beautiful, Italy is beautiful . . . but now what? There needs to be more substance than just stunning visuals. The relationship that warrants the most interest is certainly between Alex (the dying playwright) and Lucy. The character of Alex seems to be somewhat of an alter-ego for Bertolucci himself. Certainly, the most insightful dialogue is written for him and it is the most analytical. Also, his terminal illness is such a marked contrast to the vibrancy of a 19-year-old that it creates a reflective urgency to everything that he says to her. The ever-evolving cycle of life and death always commands attention and gives the film some weight and substance. The focus on Lucy offering her virgin body to someone, however, is not a life or death issue. The seriousness of the conversations that Alex has with Lucy about it make it seem as if they're talking about a cure for cancer. This seems like a disproportionate amount of attention to this personal decision. Lucy's other agenda of uncovering the identity of her real father seems like a far more important issue than having sex. There needed to have been more focus on that aspect of her life, which would have given better balance to the film. It may also have made it more relevant to the audience, making it seem less trivial.

In this era where many films are so jam-packed with action, violence and special effects, *Beauty* is a refreshing departure. There is no doubt that Bernardo Bertolucci is extraordinary at creating beauty and magnificence. All of his proficiency at aesthetic filmmaking is quite evident in this project. It is very much like taking a brief vacation abroad—relaxing and filled with scenic wonderment. All of the players are professional and skilled in their craft. Liv Tyler, although not required to stretch too far from her own personality, is lovely and captures the necessary child/woman sensuality of her character. There is a dreamy quality to the film, which captures the romance of the countryside. However, this should set the mood for something exciting to happen. In *Stealing Beauty,* nothing ever does. Even the actual "ravishing" scene is anti-climatic and seems too choreographed. The story simply meanders to a finish, with yet another shot of the director's beloved Italy.

Scenery and mood should be a setting for the plot to unfold, not a goal unto itself. Audiences soon tire of pretty pictures and need to have glimpses of the strength and inner spirit within human nature. One without the other limits the creative process, turning it into a one-dimensional experience. As the old adage says, "Beauty is only skin deep."

—Rob Chicatelli

CREDITS

Lucy Harmon: Liv Tyler
Alex Parrish: Jeremy Irons
Diana Grayson: Sinead Cusack
Ian Grayson: Donald McCann
Miranda Fox: Rachel Weisz
Monsieur Guillaume: Jean Marais
Richard Reed: D.W. Moffett
Noemi: Stefania Sandrellia

Origin: France, Great Britain, and Italy
Released: 1996
Production: Jeremy Thomas for a Fiction, Recorded Pictures Co., and UGC Images production; released by Fox Searchlight Pictures.
Direction: Bernardo Bertolucci
Screenplay: Bernardo Bertolucci, Susan Minot
Cinematography: Darius Khondji
Editing: Pietro Scalia
Music: Richard Hartley
Production design: Gianni Silvestri
Art direction: Domenico Sica
Costume design: Louise Stjernasward, Giorgio Armani
Sound: Ivan Sharrock
Casting: Howard Feuer, Celestia Fox
MPAA rating: R
Running Time: 118 minutes

REVIEWS

Entertainment Weekly. June 14, 1996.
The New Yorker. June 10, 1996.
San Francisco Chronicle. June 21, 1996.
Time Magazine. June 17, 1996.

Stephen King's Thinner

Let the curse fit the crime.—Movie tagline
"A ghoulish romp!"—Mike Floyd, *Detroit Free Press*
"Creepy! Spooky!"—Bill Hoffman, *New York Post*
"Wicked humor!"—Arthur Salm, *San Diego Union-Tribune*
"A thriller!"—Mick LaSalle, *San Francisco Chronicle*

Box Office: $14,860,808

Thinner is the second film to be adapted from a novel written by Stephen King under the pseudonym of Richard Bachman. The previous film, *Running Man* (1987), was a big-budget, futuristic action film starring Arnold Schwarzenegger which used only the basic premise of King's book to fashion its ultra-energized, special effects-laden story line. The result was an exciting, entertaining, and financially successful film.

Thinner is a much more modest, low-budget effort. It is also much more faithful to the original story, and even features an effective cameo appearance by King himself. However, because so many of King's books have been adapted into films—some successfully, some dreadfully, some faithful to the original, some bearing only the slightest resemblance to the original—it has become quite obvious that a film based on King's work, or, for that matter, any film based on material from another medium, must be judged by its own merits. Although King himself has had much to say about the films adapted from his works—both damning and praising the cinematic efforts—even he realizes that a film is quite different from a novel, and that a faithful adaptation, no matter if the original material is by Shakespeare or Sidney Sheldon, does not guarantee the success of a film.

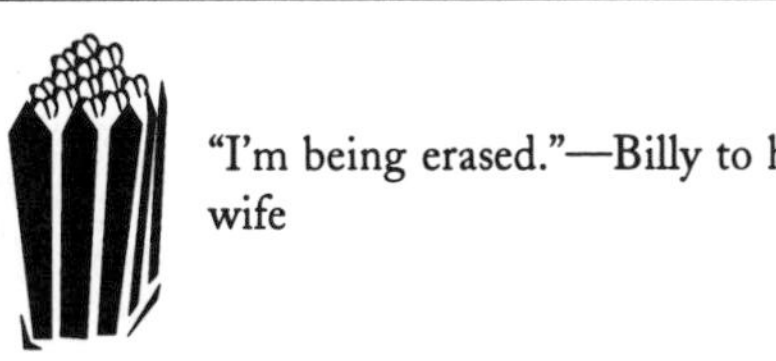
"I'm being erased."—Billy to his wife

Although *Thinner* closely follows the book's original story line, it leaves out the one crucial ingredient that has made King the phenomenal success that he is: empathy for his protagonists. King's specialty is horror, the supernatural, the bizarre, the grotesque, the nightmarish. Yet, all of his scenes of gratuitous mayhem, of people possessed by demons and inflicting the most atrocious acts of slaughter on fellow humans, are made compelling by King's ability to make his audience empathize with the madness experienced by his main characters. This is the crucial ingredient missing from *Thinner,* something it desperately needs but is sadly lacking in every scene, every character, every plot twist.

The film follows the tragic fate of Billy Halleck (Robert John Burke), a successful attorney based in a small town in upstate Maine. Billy lives comfortably in an elegant home with his beautiful wife Heidi (Lucinda Jenny) and teen-age daughter Linda (Joy Lentz). He has many friends, most of whom are the lawyers, judges, and law enforcement officers with whom he works. Billy's only problem is that he is grossly overweight. But, he is dieting and exercising and is confident that he will lose weight.

One night, driving back from a party, his wife becomes sexually frisky in the car and decides to fellate Billy while he drives. Distracted by this activity, Billy fails to see an old woman crossing the street and runs her down, killing her instantly. The old woman turns out to be a Gypsy, part of a troupe that had set up a carnival in town but had been expelled by the local judge repulsed by their sinister, heathen customs.

During the inquest that follows the car accident, Billy is completely exonerated from blame by the Gypsy-hating judge—a close friend of Billy's—and by a policeman friend who investigated the accident. However, while leaving the courthouse, Billy encounters Tadzu Lempke (Michael Constantine), the old leader of the Gypsy troupe and the father of the woman killed. Tadzu touches Billy and whispers, "Thinner."

After this encounter with the Gypsy man, Billy rapidly begins to lose weight. He tries to compensate at first by compulsively eating. But he continues to shed pounds at an alarming rate. Billy also discovers that his Gypsy-hating judge friend and the policeman who helped prove his innocence in the car accident inquest also had encounters with the Gypsy man. After their encounters, the judge began developing animalistic, inhuman characteristics, and the policeman's flesh began to fall off. Convinced that he and his friends have been cursed by the Gypsy, Billy decides to track down the old man and demand that he remove the curse.

With help from law enforcement friends, Billy is able to locate the whereabouts of the Gypsy troupe. He confronts the old Gypsy man, demanding that he remove the curse. When Tadzu refuses, Billy pleads with him to show compassion. The Gypsy reminds Billy that he showed no compassion for the old man's daughter, making sure, with help from cronies, that he was proven completely guilt-free of the death. Enraged, Bill curses the man himself, saying that he puts the curse of "The White Man from Town" on him.

Billy then calls a former client of his, Richie (Joe Mantegna), a Mafia member whom Billy was able to prove innocent in a recent trial. He asks Richie to help him force the Gypsy man to lift the curse. Richie agrees to help. By this time, Billy is so emaciated that he can hardly stand. He also knows that his judge friend and policeman friend have already succumbed to their own curses. However, after Richie shows up and kills several members of the Gypsy troupe, one of whom is Tadzu's grandson, Richie finally forces the old man to lift his curse.

When Billy meets with Tadzu, the Gypsy hands him a pie and tells him that whoever eats the pie will then be infected with Billy's curse. Billy immediately knows who he wants to infect with his curse: his wife Heidi, whom he blames for causing the car accident, and whom he suspects is having an affair with the local doctor.

By the time Billy returns home, he has gained much of his weight back. He is greeted with love and affection by Heidi, then returns her affection by handing her a piece of the cursed pie. When he wakes up the next morning with her in bed, she is an emaciated corpse. Chuckling at the gruesome sight, Billy walks downstairs into the kitchen and finds his daughter eating the pie. Realizing that soon she too will suffer the same fate as his wife, Billy decides to have a piece himself. However, just as he is about to bite into the pie, the doorbell rings. It is the doctor who is having an affair with Heidi. Billy smiles, welcomes the doctor inside and invites him to sample a piece of the pie. As the front door closes, the film ends.

Because Billy is such an unforgiving, insensitive character who shows not one shred of remorse for his actions, it is impossible for the audience to identify with his vengeful plans against the people whom he blames for his predicament. In fact, every principal character displays this same venal attitude. The film actually revels in this one-dimensional, unsympathetic attitude toward its characters, even managing to present characters who deserve audience sympathy—the wife of the infected judge, for example—with an hysterical, vicious nastiness.

Billy's character—egotistic, obnoxious and gross, whether fat or emaciated—never allows the audience a chance to perceive him as someone undeserving of his punishment. This could have been a plus if Billy, in the end, had taken a big bite of the poisonous pie. But, even in the last moments of the film, his vengeful, egotistic nastiness goes unpunished.

This caricaturish and misogynistic approach to the characters could have been slightly redeemed if the filmmakers had pushed the misogyny to the maximum and made the film an over-the-top, grand guignol experience, the approach that Stanley Kubrick took with his flamboyantly depraved adaptation of Anthony Burgess' novel, *A Clockwork Orange* (1971). In fact, this is certainly the approach the filmmakers must have had in mind. However, even Kubrick had his ultra-violent, depraved protagonist show remorse when he became cursed with an inability to enjoy his inhumanity.

Thinner, therefore, is a failure on all counts. With its total absence of empathy, it alienates its audience. And with its overemphasis on being nasty rather than scarily horrific, it provides no reason for having been made other than the obvious: released only one week prior to Halloween with no advanced screening for film critics, and prominently bearing the name in its title of the modern master of the horror genre, the makers of this low-budget film obviously hoped to take advantage of the timing of its release rather than rely on the merits of its contents, which are thin to the point of nonexistence.

—Jim Kline

CREDITS

Billy Halleck: Robert John Burke
Richie Ginelli: Joe Mantegna
Tadzu Lempke: Michael Constantine
Gina Lempke: Kari Wuhrer
Heidi Halleck: Lucinda Jenney
Dr. Mike Houston: Sam Freed

Origin: USA
Released: 1996
Production: Richard P. Rubenstein and Mitchell Galin for a Spelling Films production; released by Paramount
Direction: Tom Holland
Screenplay: Michael McDowell and Tom Holland; based on a novel by Stephen King
Cinematography: Kees Van Oostrum
Editing: Marc Laub
Music: Daniel Licht
Production design: Laurence Bennett
Art direction: Chuck Parker
Costume design: Ha Nguyen
Special makeup effects: Greg Cannom
Sound: Jay Meagher
Casting: Leonard Finger
MPAA rating: R
Running Time: 93 minutes

REVIEWS

Chicago Tribune. October 28, 1996, p. 3.
Entertainment Weekly. November 8, 1996, p. 49.
Los Angeles Times. October 28, 1996, p. F3.
New York Times. October 26, 1996, p. 21.
Rolling Stone. November 28, 1996, p. 143.
Variety. October 28, 1996, p. 66.

Stonewall

The fight for the right to love.—Movie tagline

"A fabulous fantasy . . . dressed up in movie magic."—Amy Taubin, *Village Voice*

Box Office: $692,400

The defining event of the modern American gay rights movement happened on June 28, 1969 at a drag bar called the Stonewall, in New York City. From Martin Duberman's book, *Stonewall*, comes a fictionalized film also called *Stonewall* that puts a human face on that momentous event. "There are as many Stonewall stories as there are drag queens in New York," says LaMiranda (Guillermo Diaz), a fiery drag queen whose story is the heart of this film. "I'm a drag queen," says LaMiranda, "And we don't always deal in reality; we deal in dreams." This disclaimer allows writer Rikki Beadle Blair and director Nigel Finch to take liberties with their subject matter, focusing on the emotional climate surrounding the events leading up to Stonewall instead of presenting a dry chronology.

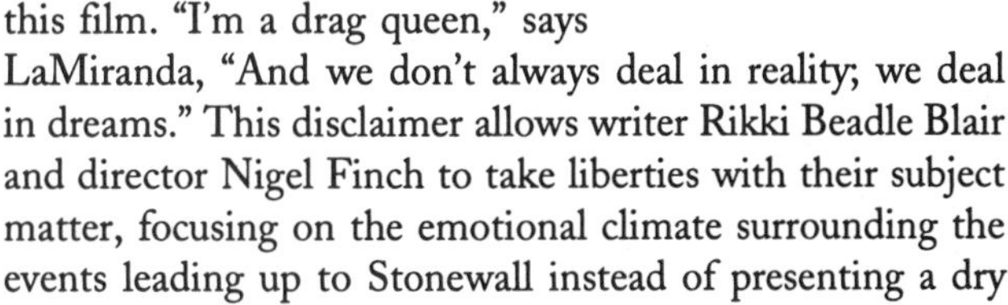

"I'm a drag queen. And we don't always deal in reality. We deal in dreams. We're as American as apple pie."—LaMiranda

Perhaps Duberman's sprawling book might have been better served by a documentary, and perhaps one day it will. But for now, this film, together with a proliferation of gay-themed films, describe the struggle for civil rights among gays and lesbians.

The story concerns Matty Dean (Frederick Weller), a country bumpkin who comes to New York to participate in a peaceful civil rights march led by the Mattachine Society. (The Mattachine Society was a real organization which was a conservative precursor to the numerous gay political organizations of today.) Fresh off the bus and flush with the excitement of being "out" in New York, Matty follows the cute drag queen LaMiranda into the Stonewall bar. After a raid on the bar by the police which leaves Matty in jail and LaMiranda physically beaten by the police, Matty ends up staying with LaMiranda and beginning a love affair. "I don't do tears; I don't do love," LaMiranda tells Matty, but s/he falls in love anyway. Meanwhile, Matty, whose political antennae have begun to rise, attends the Mattachine Society meetings in earnest, and meets a second beau, the handsome but starchy Ethan (Brenda Corballis).

The film's problems have more to do with Matty's dilemma about being torn between two lovers who are polar opposites than being specifically about the events leading to Stonewall. And yet, writer Blair and director Finch pack their rather pedestrian story with a lot of history. For example, the scenes in the Stonewall bar when the police arrive are as enlightening as they are upsetting—the police, long on the take from the Mafiosi owners of the bars, would come in and rough up the drag queens, dunking their heads in water to "wash off" their makeup, and severely beating them. The crafty way in which the occupants of the bar try to outsmart the police are reminiscent of the backroom bars that proliferated during Prohibition—everyone scampers like roaches when a bell goes off signalling the police arrival.

One historically interesting aspect involves the Mattachine Society's inept attempts to change societal attitudes about gays "from within." For example, a well-meaning Mattachine Society member (Peter Ratray) takes a journalist around to a bunch of bars in order to show how no one will serve a known homosexual; the results are hilarious. "We're four homosexuals, and we'd like a beer," says Ratray's character, receiving no negative reaction from any bartender or waitress, and pointing up the silliness of overly polite political protest.

CREDITS

Matty Dean: Fred Weller
LaMiranda: Guillermo Diaz
Ethan: Brendan Corbalis
Bustonia: Bruce MacVittie
Vinnie: Duane Boutte

Origin: Great Britain and USA
Released: 1995
Production: Christine Vachon for a BBC Films and Arena NY production; released by Strand Releasing
Direction: Nigel Finch
Screenplay: Rikki Beadle Blair; based on the book *Stonewall* by Martin Duberman
Cinematography: Chris Seager
Editing: John Richards
Music: Michael Kamen
Production design: Therese DePrez
Costume design: Michael Clancy
Sound: Coll Anderson
Casting: Kerry Barden, Suzanne Smith, Billy Hopkins
MPAA rating: Unrated
Running Time: 99 minutes

The struggle between civil disobedience versus passionate unrest doesn't get a full cinematic discussion in this film, granted, but the issues are raised, and the filmmakers are to be commended for that. The depiction of the Stonewall riots themselves, though, is weak, and ultimately dilutes the impact that the climactic moments should have. Impactful climactic moments are left to two fine actors who share a subplot: Vinnie (Bruce MacVittie), the Stonewall's closeted owner, and drag queen Bustonia (Duane Boutte) are a couple caught in a struggle to live "normally" versus the reality of their homosexuality. Boutte and MacVittie are both excellent actors whose dilemma is handled with grace and a real sense of tragedy. The outcome of this subplot is far more resonant than the depiction of the riots.

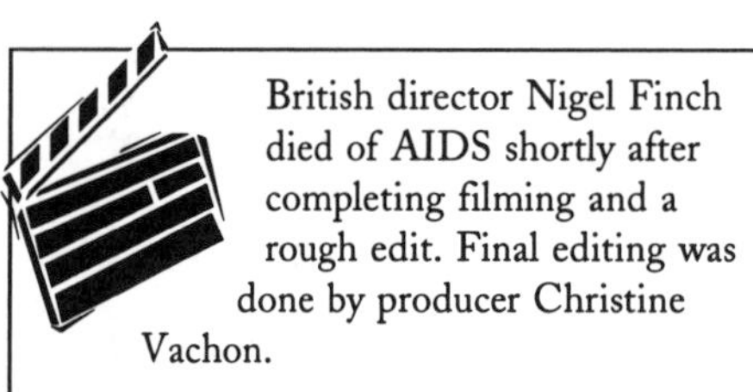

British director Nigel Finch died of AIDS shortly after completing filming and a rough edit. Final editing was done by producer Christine Vachon.

The other actors handle their roles with varying skill: one of the best actors is Guillermo Diaz, who is a dynamic, streetwise, yet vulnerable LaMiranda. In general, the acting reflects the uneven nature of Rikki Beadle Blair's script. But the fact that Blair's script is at times rudimentary should not take away from the value of her ability to make history interesting and personal for those who may not have been there.

—*Kirby Tepper*

REVIEWS

Boxoffice. August, 1996, p. 58.
Los Angeles Times. July 26, 1996, p. F12.
New York Times. July 26, 1996, p. C8.
Washington Post. August 2, 1996, p. 31.

Striptease

Some people get into trouble no matter what they wear.—Movie tagline

"Demi Moore is hot! hot! hot!"—Don Stotter, *Entertainment Time-Out*

"Tremendously enjoyable."—Rene Rodriguez, *Miami Herald*

"Fresh and witty. A giddily goofy confection."—Marshall Fine, *Westchester Gannett Newspapers*

Box Office: $33,190,858

Erin Grant (Demi Moore) seems to have more than her share of problems. Her ex-husband Darrell (Robert Patrick) is a not-too-bright, drug-addicted thief who has cost her her job as a secretary for the FBI. Since she's unemployed, she has lost custody of her daughter Angela (Rumer Willis) to Darrell whose only "job" is an informer for the Dade County vice squad (with the extra-curricular job of stealing wheelchairs from hospitals with Angela's help) and whose only qualifications for being awarded Angela was that the judge thinks he was a heck of a football tailback in high school.

"It's honest work. You have nothing to be ashamed of."—A fellow stripper to Erin

But Erin doesn't give up easily. Her goal now is to earn $15,000 for a custody appeal. Unfortunately, the only way she can earn that kind of money is by stripping at the Eager Beaver club. While this may not be the kind of job the judge will respect when he reconsiders the case, the money is good and Erin makes fast friends with her fellow strippers and especially with the club's tough bouncer, Shad (Ving Rhames), who is very protective of the dancers.

That's a good thing, since Erin not only needs protection from her mean-streaked husband, but also from an obsessed club patron, Jerry Killian (William Hill), and from a besotted Congressman, David Dilbeck (Burt Reynolds), who professes the right-wing Christian line while living anything but. Then, one night, when a soon-to-be groom at an overly enthusiastic bachelor party takes his excitement onstage to talk to Erin, Congressman Dilbeck jumps to defend his angel. However, only Jerry seems to realize who Erin's knight in drunken armor is, but it's enough for him to hope he can use this knowledge to gain custody of Angela for Erin and win points with his beloved.

Jerry, however, soon shows up dead, floating in Lake Okeechobee, right in front of Miami homicide police officer Al Garcia's (Armand Assante) vacation cottage. Now the custody battle becomes a murder investigation involving incriminating photos, political corruption, upcoming elections, sugar refineries, get-rich-quick schemes featuring wolves and cockroaches, and unusual uses for Vaseline and dryer lint.

So the question is, is this a comedy or a drama? Good question. Wish the filmmakers had made up their minds before they released the film. The original book written by Carl Hiaasen on which the film is based is a humorous thriller, but somewhere along the way the story's comedy was compromised. Even the film's fluffy ending is contrived and unconvincing.

Striptease obviously could have used a few rewrites. Not only are there genre problems, but much of the dialogue is flat and unfunny. This, however, is not the film's only difficulty. The biggest obstacle is the lead character.

It seems as if the only thing one is not allowed to make fun of in *Striptease* is the main teaser, Erin Grant. Erin just takes herself too seriously, and that stops the comedy in its tracks. Considering director Andrew Bergman's credits (*It Could Happen to You, Honeymoon in Vegas, The Freshman*), he certainly seems to be able to capture peculiar characters and off-center plots on-screen, but for some reason, he just can't make Demi laugh at her character. What with her custody troubles, her angelic daughter, her fawning admirers, why this woman must be a saint. And to think that she is so intelligent and talented that she was an FBI secretary one minute and an admired dancer the next. Furthermore, it's absolutely incredible how many men feel protective and/or lustful towards her. What a woman!

Demi Moore's daughter, Rumer, plays her character's daughter, Angela, in the film.

There's no doubt about it, *Striptease* is a Demi Moore vehicle. And she may be the main reason why the film seems to have such a split personality. On the one hand Moore's Erin hates her job so much she becomes nauseous before she goes onstage, but then she seems to delight in prancing around semi-naked in her apartment to rehearse a new routine. Similarly, the message to the audience is not to take the stripping too seriously—it's just a job, after all—but then the camera's voyeuristic tendencies belie that point.

With her record-breaking $12.5 million for starring in *Striptease,* it would appear that the filmmakers were counting on Moore's penchant for exhibitionistic behavior (helping David Letterman with his Top Ten burlesque list, offering Barbara Walters instruction on how to shimmy, and posing naked on the cover of *Vanity Fair* magazine not once, but twice) to bring in the box office dollars. Add to this her sleazy character in *Disclosure,* her bath in *The Scarlet Letter,* and a few earlier "exposures" in other films, then it would seem that Moore is even giving Madonna a run for her overexposed money.

One might be able to understand Moore's delight in displaying her finely tuned body—the best that surgery, personal trainers and leisure time can buy—and that studio accountants would see dollar signs at offering a peep show look at it, but all that vanity has taken precedent over having a coherent film. And, to some extent the accountants were right. The hype of seeing Moore in the buff brought the film a $12.3 million opening weekend which was better than many expected.

However, in the end, not only does Moore's narcissism override the film's comedy, it's not even sexy. And when it comes right down to it, *Striptease* will probably die a quiet death at the box office only to be reborn to a vigorous video rental life. There it won't cost so much to watch her dances which are rather awkward, mechanical, slick and more like a well-choreographed bodybuilder's routine, and not very revealing. (If you want sexy dancing, rent *Flashdance.*) Moore's numbers don't ooze sexiness or even delight in the dance, they're just played like they're hard work; they're just part of the job.

CREDITS

Erin Grant: Demi Moore
Al Garcia: Armand Assante
Shad: Ving Rhames
Darrell Grant: Robert Patrick
David Dilbeck: Burt Reynolds
Malcolm Moldovsky: Paul Guilfoyle
Angela: Rumer Willis

Origin: USA
Released: 1996
Production: Mike Lobell for a Columbia Pictures and Castle Rock Entertainment production; released by Sony Pictures Entertainment
Direction: Andrew Bergman
Screenplay: Andrew Bergman; based on the novel *Strip Tease* by Carl Hiaasen
Cinematography: Stephen Goldblatt
Editing: Anne V. Coates
Music: Howard Shore
Production design: Mel Bourne
Art direction: Elizabeth Lapp
Costume design: Albert Wolsky
Sound: James J. Sabat
Choreography: Marguerite Pomerhn Derricks
Casting: John Lyons
MPAA rating: R
Running Time: 115 minutes

And that's the way the other strippers play it too. Oh sure, they have cute names (Urbana Sprawl, Tiffany Glass), all have the proverbial hearts of gold, and are a little goofy and dense, but when it comes to stripping, it's just a job. The emphasis here is on the grind, not the bump. And there are no messages in this movie about performing it. (Even though after the debacle of *Showgirls* one would think the genre would be ripe for parody.)

Another actor who can't seem to lift this film out of the morass is Burt Reynolds attempting a cinematic comeback without much success. His drunken, leering, corrupt and hypocritical Dilbeck is not funny, he's disgusting and pathetic. Dilbeck is a one-note character played with plenty of mugging and virtually no funny lines.

Even the usually solid Armand Assante is given little to do except feel protective of Moore's Erin—but who really knows why? Is it Moore's unavoidable attractiveness? (And is it a pro or a con for the talented Frances Fisher's career that her role as Assante's wife is all but nonexistent?)

If there are two winners in this film, they are Robert Patrick as Erin's wacky husband Darrell and Ving Rhames as the bouncer Shad. Patrick who is most well-known to audiences as T-1000, Arnold Schwarzenegger's menacing amorphous rival in *Terminator 2: Judgment Day*, here shows a real flare for comedy. But the most entertaining character is undoubtedly Rhames' Shad. Big, black, bald, surly, and witty, he is given the funniest role and the funniest lines. Winning recognition as the dreaded Marsellus Wallace in *Pulp Fiction*, he here, like Patrick, does a nice comic turn with his deadpan delivery of lines one doesn't expect: His furor over the fact that *Free Willy* is not available at the video store, his explanation of how he got tendinitis from auditioning strippers, his recalling of how Meryl Streep once stripped under the name Chesty La France. Rhames has taken what could have been yet another one-note character and breathed life into it. And aren't we all thankful.

—*Beverley Bare Buehrer*

REVIEWS

Boxoffice Magazine Online. July 8, 1996.
Chicago Tribune. June 28, 1996.
Detroit News. June 28, 1996, p. D1.
Entertainment Weekly. July 12, 1996, p. 38.
Los Angeles Times. May 22, 1996, p. F1.
New York Times. June 28, 1996, p. C1.
Newsweek. July 8, 1996, p. 67.
People. July 8, 1996, p. 19.
Sight and Sound. October, 1996, p. 51.
Time. July 8, 1996, p. 66.
Variety Online. June 24, 1996.

The Stupids

They came. They saw. They didn't get it. *The Stupids* . . . America's dumbest family.—Movie tagline

Box Office: $2,424,603

If there was ever a motion picture that best lived up to its title, that motion picture is *The Stupids*. Yet, the film delivers exactly what it promises, and admittedly does it with some humor. Directed by John Landis (*National Lampoon's Animal House* [1978], *Blues Brothers* [1980], *Trading Places* [1983]) and starring Tom Arnold (*True Lies* [1994], *Carpool* [1996]), *The Stupids* is based on a series of children's books by James Marshall and Harry Allard. The film, written by Brent Forrester, also stars Jessica Lundy, Bug Hall, Alex McKenna, Mark Metcalf, Matt Keeslar, Christopher Lee, and Bob Keeshan (television's Captain Kangaroo).

The story begins with the aptly named Stanley Stupid (Arnold) determined to discover who is stealing his trash when he leaves it by the curb. The trail leads to the dump, where he stumbles upon what he believes to be the crime of the century, proclaiming that there must be thousands of people's garbage here. This is just the beginning of the Stupids' adventures. Stanley inadvertently stumbles onto a plot by an army colonel (Metcalf) to sell arms to international terrorists. He has now unwittingly become targeted by the colonel, but narrowly escapes death attempts by mere milliseconds, simply because he happens to move out of the way. During this time, he is also the object of a search by his equally dimwitted wife, Joan (Lundy) and his kids, Buster (Hall) and Petunia (McKenna). At one point in the film, Joan explains to the children that their father is a former government courier (in reality a mailman) who was fired upon presenting to his superiors mail that had been marked "return to sender," suggesting that this Mr. Sender was plotting something evil. This touches off another family search: for the evil Sender (Chistopher Lee).

What makes the Stupids so stupid is simply that they take everything so literally, as in the scene at a gas station, where Stanley is asked if he knows he has a hole in his gas tank. Stanley's daft response is that actually, that's how to get the gas in.

There is one intelligent moment in the film when Stanley is jolted by a car battery and has a streak of logical thought.

In another scene, the insipid Stupids find themselves at the planetarium. Here, under the display of the stars, Stanley and Petunia think they have met the Lord, but are corrected when they meet the Lloyd (Frankie Faison), a planetarium worker Stanley and Petunia believe is their maker.

CREDITS

Stanley Stupid: Tom Arnold
Joan Stupid: Jessica Lundy
Buster Stupid: Bug Hall
Petunia Stupid: Alex McKenna
Colonel: Mark Metcalf
Lieutenant: Matt Keesler

Origin: USA
Released: 1996
Production: Leslie Belzberg for a Rank Film Distributors, Savoy Pictures and Imagine Entertainment production; released by New Line Cinema
Direction: John Landis
Screenplay: Brent Forrester; based on the characters created by James Marshall and Harry Allard
Cinematography: Manfred Guthe
Editing: Dale Beldin
Music: Christopher Stone
Production design: Phil Dagort
Art direction: Rocco Matteo
Costume design: Deborah Nadoolman
Sound: Owen Langevin
Stunt coordination: Rick Avery
Casting: Amy Lippens
MPAA rating: PG
Running Time: 93 minutes

Meanwhile, upon taking an elevator ride that ends up at the dinosaur exhibit, Joan and Buster conclude they have been transported back in time.

In the world of the Stupids, Phil Dagort's production design draws heavily on clean comic book primary colors. Once in the real world, Stanley's blue suit and 1960s straw boater hat do not, of course, fit in. Deborah Nadoolman's costumes fit quite well with the image of the Stupids, making the characters look as out of place in the real world as the Bradys did in *The Brady Bunch Movie* (1995).

In *The Stupids* the audience gets exactly what it expects from the film, keeping in mind the title. Yes, the film is stupid. It is supposed to be. Admittedly, there are moments of stupidity that actually elicit laughs, as when Stanley wants to start the car by administering mouth-to-mouth to the battery; and when the children are in a restaurant, deciding how they can find their parents, when the waiter asks them if he can recommend the cashew chicken. They respond by saying, "you'll get your cash when we get our parents. And don't call us chicken." The humor in *The Stupids* is reminiscent of *National Lampoon's Vacation* (1983), *The Brady Bunch Movie* and *Airplane!* (1980).

The Stupids is, in fact, well-cast. Tom Arnold creates a believable, yet not unlikable Stanley Stupid. Jessica Lundy plays exceptionally well opposite Arnold, as his dimwitted wife Joan, and Hall's and McKenna's performances as the children are equally on par with the adults.

Unnecessarily thrown into the mix, however, are confusing characters in the form of the Stupid's pets, an animated cat and animated dog and space aliens who come to earth. These characters are simply out of place and take the film to a level past mere innocence of the main characters.

The film contains cameos by talk show hostess Rolonda Watts, director Norman Jewison, Robert Wise, Costa-Gavras, and Gillo Pontecorvo.

—*Debbi Hoffman*

REVIEWS

Los Angeles Times. September 2, 1996, p. F4.
The New York Times. August 31, 1996, p. 16.
Sight and Sound. October, 1996, p. 52.
Variety. August 26, 1996, p. 60.

The Substance of Fire

The substance of fire. The substance of memory. The substance of hope.—Movie tagline

"Powerful! One of the autumn's treasures. Ron Rifkin delivers a towering performance. He is titanic, larger than life."—Jay Carr, *Boston Globe*

"Ron Rifkin is transcendent! He gives a career-defining performance."—John Anderson, *Los Angeles Times*

"Provocative and extremely poignant!"—Jeffrey Lyons, *NBC-TV*

Box Office: $24,583

When a man, a once successful publisher of quality books on serious topics, the father of three accomplished children, and a child survivor of the Holocaust, embarks on a wilful journey of self-destruction because of his unbending principles, how much of his behavior can be blamed on the trauma of living through one of the 20th century's darkest hours?

This is the implicit question raised in *The Substance of Fire.* It teases the viewer's consciousness as one watches Isaac Geldhart (Ron Rifkin) crumble. Unfortunately, beyond the clinical fact of Isaac's mental fragmentation, the man arouses little sympathy. And ultimately the Holocaust—although it drives Geldhart's morbid fascination with the period—is marginal in this contemporary story.

Playwright Jon Robin Baitz has adapted his acclaimed play of the same name for colleague Daniel Sullivan to direct in the latter's first feature. The text's theatrical roots are always distinct, even in the expanded second half of the story. This is not all bad, however, as Baitz is capable of writing vigorous scenes of conflict; and conflict could be Isaac Geldhart's middle name.

Baitz chooses to have Aaron Geldhart (Tony Goldwyn) open the film with a voice-over, and intermittently allows him to speak directly to the audience in this manner. The device is at once self-conscious and a distraction to the unfolding of events. Still, one learns from Aaron that his father Isaac spent a portion of his childhood during the war hidden in a attic full of books. Even as his family was deported to their deaths—Isaac's exact losses are not specified—the young boy was able to lose himself in the joys of narrative.

In modern day New York, Isaac publishes expensive books with titles such as *The Architecture of the Holocaust.* Determined always to have his way, Isaac shows his printers how he wants that book produced, and declares his own example "perfecto." This was his wife's favorite word; but she, clearly a stabilizing influence, is dead now.

In denial over the perilous finances of his firm, Isaac refuses to listen to Aaron's pleas for the house to widen its list, and to include a potentially hot, hip novel being offered to them. The writer is a young man called Val (Gil Bellows), whom we discover to also be Aaron's lover. Isaac condescends to read the manuscript, but he is scorching about its literary quality, uninterested in any commercial value it may possess. And when confronted by Aaron about the company's plight, Isaac announces that a project that has taken decades to be written—a four volume work on genocide—will clear up all their monetary problems, Aaron is shocked. The caring entreaties of Miss Barzakian (Elizabeth Franz), his father's long-suffering aide/secretary/bookkeeper, are of little help.

In crisis, Aaron calls together his siblings: Sarah (Sarah Jessica Parker), a presenter on a children's television show, and the environmental college professor Martin (Timothy Hutton). The meeting between the children and the ever-more rigid Isaac soon turns nasty, and after Martin offers his shares to Aaron, which would make the latter the majority stockholder, Isaac nakedly declares war on his family. This draws out a comment from Sarah: "You don't know how to love," a charge which increasingly will be seen to be true. But why is that?

Headstrong, Isaac sets up his own company, and forces Aaron to remove the Geldhart name from the firm he built up. Obsessed with publishing the book on genocide, Isaac cuts off contact with his children by refusing to receive them or to answer their calls. His demands as to the quality of his

CREDITS

Isaac Geldhart: Ron Rifkin
Aaron Geldhart: Tony Goldwyn
Martin Geldhart: Timothy Hutton
Sarah Geldhart: Sarah Jessica Parker

Origin: USA
Released: 1996
Production: Jon Robin Baitz, Randy Finch and Ron Kastner; released by Miramax Films
Direction: Daniel Sullivan
Screenplay: Jon Robin Baitz; based on his play
Cinematography: Robert Yeoman
Editing: Pamela Martin
Music: Joseph Vitarelli
Production design: John Lee Beatty
MPAA rating: R
Running Time: 100 minutes

new product are punitive. Once the genocide book is completed, it does not match his ideal. He orders it destroyed, even taking a knife to the pristine pages of a copy. All his staff are appalled.

No longer merely wilful and eccentric, Isaac's world crumbles as he rages, Lear-like, against it. His once immaculate apartment becomes a mess, and his bookshelves are humbled by recent sales of once prized volumes. Summoning Sarah into his new offices—apparently to give her a copy of Mark Twain's *Huck Finn* (her childhood favorite)—he peremptorily has a security guard throw her out.

Ron Rifkin originated the role of Isaac in the 1991 Off-Broadway production.

Once *The Science of Genocide* is completed to Isaac's specifications, he and its cantankerous author take to hawking it at bookstores. One buyer admires its superlative quality, but says that it is simply too expensive. Isaac seems to accept the decision, and walks stiffly past a garish display of Val's novel which is "soon to be a film by Mike Nichols."

The downwards spiral is merciless. Mrs. Barzakian resigns, yet Isaac barely notices, lost in his world of memorabilia, poring over a Hitler postcard he has acquired. His company folds, and Aaron and Sarah bail their father out of a prison cell after he has hounded a man in a restaurant in an attempt to purchase his shoes. A scuffle between father and son ensues on a rain-scudded street outside the police station.

Martin elects to look after Isaac, moves in, and employs a housekeeper to clean. Isaac is furious about this, and refuses to take all his medications, even tossing some out of the window. Ironically, it is Martin who needs medicine most. A fleeting reference earlier to a childhood illness is recalled when he collapses during an unpleasant visit by a social worker to assess Isaac's mental competency. A quiescent Isaac watches over the stricken Martin in the hospital, but it is too late. Martin's funeral follows.

Following the burial, Isaac drifts into Martin's room and burns the Hitler postcard. Is this meant to symbolize his move towards connecting with humanity, and a move away from a veneration of his Holocaust collection? The final tableau of Isaac and his two remaining children sitting in a park Martin loved leaves this question unanswered.

In contrast to its reception in New York and Los Angeles as a play, this story has not met with many favorable notices from film critics. J. Hoberman in the *Village Voice* identified the strength of the family business meeting scene—a confrontation that constituted the first act of the play—only to charge that the film "turns terminally episodic and increasingly maudlin." In the *Los Angeles Times,* John Anderson complained of the story's "outbursts and tantrums that are disconcertingly overblown and incongruous."

In a dissenting view, Stephen Holden in *The New York Times* praises the levelheaded treatment of the movie's difficult themes. "The film, to its credit, never tries to pluck your heartstrings." Some would find the film's antiseptic, unemotional tone a problem, but not Holden. "The Geldharts . . . are figures in a meditative dialogue on human values that reaches no easy conclusions." Or, perhaps, no conclusions at all.

Almost all critics have pointed to Ron Rifkin's brilliant work. Playing a character with whom empathy is almost forbidden, Rifkin inhabits Isaac Geldhart with a fiery core and yet a reverence for the possibilities of civilization despite the atrocities of the modern age. Fine clothes, good manners, and most of all, great and important books published in the best possible bindings and on the best possible paper are his principal, unswerving demands. But as a father, Isaac veers from the coolly indifferent to the imperious. Whether his mental illness is the full story one cannot tell, despite Rifkin's modulated performance; and Isaac's disintegration is unfortunate but not moving—or particularly involving.

As a consequence of Isaac's cruelty, one should have sympathy for his suffering children. But in this cold film, our feelings are hardly provoked. Sarah Jessica Parker and Timothy Hutton turn in professional performances, and Ronny Graham provides twinges of comic relief as the screeching, dedicated author of the genocide book. It is Tony Goldwyn who manages to wring from the viewer an emotional response. He battles against his father to do the right thing, but is doomed from the start. As Aaron, Goldwyn is impassioned and finally hardened; this is good work.

The look of the picture, with interiors and exteriors almost totally to be found in New York, is classy, thanks to the efforts of director of photography Robert Yeoman and John Lee Beaty's production design. Joseph Vitarelli's music is used somewhat sparingly but provides a mellow accompaniment.

Director Daniel Sullivan has modest aims for what ends up being a modest film—at best. *The Substance of Fire* is a true collaboration between Sullivan and Jon Robin Baitz, but it is a disappointing chamber work of a film, promising much, but delivering less than it should, despite Rifkin's resounding performance.

—Paul B. Cohen

REVIEWS

Boxoffice. November, 1996, p. 137.
Los Angeles Times. December 6, 1996, F10.
New York Times. December 12, 1996, C10.
People. December 16, 1996, p. 25.
Village Voice. December 10, 1996, p. 75.

The Substitute

The most dangerous thing about school used to be the students.—Movie tagline

"A+"—Tom Brown, *KDNL-TV*

"Riveting"—Nancy Jay, *KTVT-TV*

"Powerful"—Jim Ferguson, *Prevue Channel*

"Explosive, exciting and energetic."—Maria Salas, *Telemundo Network*

Box Office: $14,818,176

The Substitute sounds preposterous, because it is. The film features an unemployed soldier of fortune who uncovers a principal running a huge drug ring out of a high-school basement. But the premise of the film is even more ridiculous than the plot. Audiences are asked to believe that Tom Berenger's steely mercenary, Shale, is a paragon of morality, more virtuous and noble than most of the people who run and attend a typical inner-city high school.

"Power perceived is power achieved."—Principal Claude Rolle's motto

Making a sensitive hero out of a hired gun is no mean feat, and though Berenger gives it a go, he fails miserably. It's not all his fault. The concept of the film is so exploitive, so miserably out of whack, that even Oscar-worthy acting couldn't have earned *The Substitute* a passing grade.

The film is ill-conceived, way too long and much too preachy. Yet it has a certain cockeyed charm. Director Robert Mandel gives it a fitful zippiness and the trio of screenwriters (Roy Frumkes, Rocco Simonelli, Alan Ormsby) infuses occasional wit and bluster. If it went further over the top and crossed into campiness, it might have been a very funny film. But *The Substitute* takes its bizarre plot seriously, and so it veers dangerously close to self-parody.

Berenger's mercenary, who lacks a first name, is conceived as a stereotypical action hero. He's slack-jawed, cynical, endlessly resourceful and overbearingly righteous. Unfortunately, he's also quite drab. Berenger plays the part listlessly, and no wonder: Here's a fine actor doomed to re-playing steely military types ever since his Oscar-nominated performance as a satanic sergeant in *Platoon* (1986). Berenger has said he prefers to act in "guy" films, and *The Substitute* certainly qualifies. He doesn't need to stretch his talents much, merely raise his eyebrows occasionally.

Shale (the name itself has a rocky glint) is seeking work for his motley gang of mercenaries after a botched Cuban raid. He is so bored that he spends his days throwing star nails at a wall map of the world. *The Substitute* doesn't shy from such hackneyed shots.

Shale is hanging with his sometime lover, teacher Jane Hetzko (Diane Verona), when she is kneecapped by a gang member. Jane has enraged the school's gang leader, Juan Lucas (Marc Anthony), by asking the principal to get him transferred after Juan threatens her in the schoolyard. Juan's gang, the Kings of Destruction or KOD, runs the school, or so it seems.

With the feisty Jane out of commission with a broken knee, Shale sees his chance to exact revenge on Juan. He arranges for a fake resume and shows up at school as James Smith, Jane's substitute teacher.

Shale has scruples. We know this because he turns down a gig to help protect drug shipments for Wolfson (Cliff DeYoung), an attorney who interviews mercenary candidates as if they were applying to be junior partners in his law firm. One applicant for Wolfson's services is John Janus, a slick mercenary who has his own video ad. Shale is so old-fashioned that he has no video and no patience for Wolfson's mission. "You don't want soldiers, you want killers," Shale tells Wolfson. When Wolfson doesn't get the difference, Shale grabs him by the throat, then tells him: "The difference is that you're still breathing."

The only further explanation of this delicate ethical distinction comes when Shale tells a partner that he hates the dictionary definition of a mercenary as someone who works merely for money. "It's not the money that bothers me, it's the 'merely,'" Shale complains. So what else does Shale stand for besides money? Transformed into Mr. Smith, he makes the answer crystal clear: Order. Discipline. No drugs. And the American way.

Critic Stephen Holden said the high school in *The Substitute* "makes *The Blackboard Jungle* look like Sunnybrook Farm." The ghetto school milieu is way overdone. Students carry ice picks in class, play cards and dance to rap music all day and hurl profane insults and pop cans at their teachers. Any teacher who questions the rule of the mob is accused of harassing students.

When Shale/Smith challenges the order, he is fired by the oily principal, Claude Rolle (Ernie Hudson), an ex-cop who is running for City Council. Smith gets to hang on only when he cites a union rule requiring two weeks' notice. It's not clear whether the filmmakers see this as ironic, since unionism presumably is part of the internal enemy Shale is attacking.

Aside from Jane, the school's other teachers are all scripted as gutless or stupid. Afrocentric teacher Darryl Sherman (Glenn Plummer) tells Shale: "You can't just come in here as the Great White Hope," but that's exactly Shale's stance. Shale is the hero who straightens out the incredible mess that people of color have made out of the high school. The non-whites in the film are portrayed as incredibly ignorant (almost all the students), venal (almost all the students and the principal) or dupes (Sherman and the students). There are even racial insults hurled at a Seminole goon who is part of the drug gang. Native Americans, Hispanics and blacks are all portrayed as part of a moral decay that has progressed so far that only a white male anti-Communist vigilante has the solution.

Shale's a snarling incarnation of anti-political-correctness rage. "Who discovered America?" he taunts the class, trying to polish the tarnished image of Columbus. He instructs them on the Vietnam conflict, explaining simply: "We were fighting Communism." It's no accident that the KOD is only one letter distinct from the KBD. In Shale's cosmology, the Red Menace must still be working behind the scenes, infusing these kids with traitorous anti-Americanism.

The Substitute shamelessly posits that even a mercenary's values are superior to those of people of color, unless they're on his side. It's a nonsensical conceit even on the movie's own terms. Shale's gang does include some non-whites, who seem to have "passed" into righteousness merely because they're in Shale's gang.

In the end the film degenerates into a war between the good gang and the bad gang, which is led by the principal and rival mercenary Janus. That's how Shale portrays the Vietnam conflict to the students, as a gang war. When he lectures the students on why they shouldn't belong to a gang, not one of them asks why it would be better to grow up and have an honorable career as a mercenary.

Preposterous as the film is, it's at times enjoyable to watch. Berenger has some fun with his role, throwing students out the library window in one confrontation. The villains are comic-book types, with Lucas wearing a tattoo around his neck that reads "DEATH BEFORE DISHONOR."

The most intriguing character is Venora's Jane Hetzko. Portrayed against Hollywood leading-woman type, she is a female version of Shale, macho and cool. Rarely has a lead female role looked less glamorous. Jane spends most of the film hobbling about in a leg cast and wearing scruffy T-shirts, jeans and sweats. With close-cropped hair and little makeup, Verona looks like Demi Moore after a bad night's sleep. Yet she's got a very appealing feline fire and almost melts the screen with her growls in the snippet of a foreplay scene the film allows Jane and Shale. Unfortunately, Shale seems like the kind of guy who believes sex would sap his energy for warfare, so he and Jane mostly pal around. Too bad the film doesn't do more with Verona.

Both Berenger and Verona deserve better than *The Substitute.* And so do audiences who expect their intelligence not to be insulted. As teacher-as-savior films go, the best that can be said is that this is a clear contrast to *Mr. Holland's Opus* (1995).

—Michael Betzold

CREDITS

Shale: Tom Berenger
Claude Rolle: Ernie Hudson
Jane Hetzko: Diane Venora
Juan Lacas: Marc Anthony
Darryl Sherman: Glenn Plummer
Wolfson: Cliff DeYoung
Hollan: William Forsythe
Joey Six: Raymond Cruz
Wellman: Richard Brooks
Johnny Glades: Rodney A. Grant
Rem: Luis Guzman

Origin: USA
Released: 1996
Production: Morrie Eisenman, Jim Steele for a Live Entertainment and Dinamo/H2 production; released by Orion Pictures
Direction: Robert Mandel
Screenplay: Roy Frumkes, Rocco Simonelli, Alan Ormsby
Cinematography: Bruce Surtees
Editing: Alex Mackie
Music: Gary Chang
Production design: Ron Foreman
Art direction: Richard Fojo
Set decoration: Barbara Peterson
Costume design: Patricia Field
Sound: Joe Foglia
Casting: Mary Colquhoun, Carol Lewis
MPAA rating: R
Running Time: 114 minutes

REVIEWS

Chicago Sun-Times. April 19, 1996.
Detroit Free Press. April 19, 1996, p. 6D.
Entertainment Weekly. May 3, 1996, p. 89.
Los Angeles Times. April 19, 1996, p. F8.
The New York Times. April 19, 1996, p. C18.
Variety. April 22, 1996, p. 89.
Village Voice. April 30, 1996, p. 62.

Sunchaser

It began as a kidnapping. It became a journey of hope.—Movie tagline

"The director's best film since *The Deer Hunter.* Harrelson does some of his best work in his career. Jon Seda is riveting."—Bob Thomas, *Associated Press*

"Superb, uplifting, first class entertainment."—Paul Wunder, WBAI Radio

Box Office: $21,508

Director Michael Cimino's first film, *Thunderbolt & Lightfoot* (1974), brought in good reviews and profits, allowing him to make his next film, which would prove to be an astounding success—and the beginning of his downfall. *The Deer Hunter* (1978) not only brought him a Best Director and a Best Picture Oscar that year, but also afforded him the leverage to make one of the biggest financially disastrous films in Hollywood's history. His 1981 film *Heaven's Gate* almost single-handedly ruined its financier, United Artists, and black-marked Cimino as a director. The story of a Wyoming cattle war in the 1880's, the movie was declared plotless and melodramatic by some, and a modern classic by others. Nevertheless, Cimino has yet to regain the stature or artistic respect he held in the late 1970's. Since then, his projects have received fairly bland reviews, lacking both the greatness of *The Deer Hunter* and the overindulgence of *Heaven's Gate.*

In *Sunchaser,* Woody Harrelson stars as Dr. Michael Reynolds, a well-off Los Angeles physician who, while wrestling with the idea of purchasing a two million dollar house for himself and his new family, suddenly gets stuck with a new patient; a 16-year-old convicted murderer with incurable cancer. Jon Seda (*I Like It Like That* [1994]) plays Brandon "Blue" Monroe, a half Cherokee "gang banger" who, despite his condition, has a habit of beating up his pediatricians and immediately resents his new privileged white doctor. Already, stereotypes abound, and you get the feeling things aren't going to improve much. Blue talks how most young hoods talk in movies, using the "f" word in every possible fashion and punctuating his sentences with the threat to "peel yer cap," i.e. kill you. Harrelson's Dr. Reynolds is just as paper-thin; a doctor who puts on his bedside manner like a mask when he isn't spending his money or sucking up for his promotion.

Learning he has just two months to live, Blue, in one of the film's first implausibilities, gets his hands on a gun—ala *The Godfather*—on an unsupervised trip to the bathroom. While being transported in broad daylight to a treatment center, Dr. Reynolds in tow, Blue makes his move, leaving his police escort tied in the backseat of the car kicking and screaming for help, and taking Reynolds as a hostage at gunpoint. Hours later, when Michael doesn't show up for an important meeting with his boss (the man who sent him out with the cop and prisoner), he only speculates sarcastically that Reynolds might have forgotten to come. Following the film's nonsensical motif, nothing is mentioned regarding the cop hogtied in the backseat of his police car.

By now, Blue has made his motive clear and he and his hostage have switched cars, made a scene at a convenience store, and are on their way to a sacred mountain in an Arizona Indian reservation, where, according to Blue, it's rumored a magic lake exists, capable of healing him of his cancer. This only increases the schism between the two, as Dr. Reynolds' tries to persuade Blue to turn himself in for traditional treatment. The pair's relationship up to this point is volatile to say the least, with Blue incessantly threatening Reynolds' life and proving how dangerous he is by forcing his hostage to drive erratically through traffic. The film is loaded with silly dialogue, made especially awkward when conversations are obviously dubbed-over during sequences of the car speeding through town or driving wildly across

CREDITS

Dr. Michael Reynolds: Woody Harrelson
Brandon Monroe: Jon Seda
Dr. Renata Baumbauer: Anne Bancroft
Victoria Reynolds: Alexandra Tydings

Origin: USA
Released: 1996
Production: Arnon Milchan, Michael Cimino, Larry Spiegel, Judy Goldstein, and Joseph M. Vecchio for a Regency Enterprises production; released by Warner Bros.
Direction: Michael Cimino
Screenplay: Charles Leavitt
Cinematography: Doug Milsome
Editing: Joe D'Augustine
Music: Maurice Jarre
Production design: Victoria Paul
Art direction: Lee Mayman, Edward L. Rubin
Sound: Douglas Axtell
Casting: Terry Liebling
MPAA rating: R
Running Time: 122 minutes

the desert. After one such incident, Harrelson's character resorts to exclaiming, "You're crazy, man." Clearly.

For the next hour of the film Dr. Reynolds and Blue work their way towards the magic lake, meeting bikers, new age philosophers, and rattlesnakes along the way. In an apparent attempt by the filmmakers to make a point, the pair come to gain begrudging respect for each other's circumstances and position in life. Although what this whole thing has to do with Harrelson's character is never really addressed—wouldn't it have been easier for an escaped convict to escape without a hostage? Especially considering that, until the film's climax, no real effort is made by anyone to find them, aside from the occasional reference to Reynold's worried wife and daughter and a scene in which a police chief alludes to the possibility that the two men are in cahoots. And, are we supposed to feel sorry for this kid who does nothing but threaten people for two hours? Apparently his disease and his Native American roots are supposed to draw sympathy from the audience; but nobody in the movie is likeable, or even believable. Questions about character motivation seem pointless. Personalities change from scene to scene and everyone involved seems to know where this thing is headed early on, giving up on any effort to make a watchable film.

Sunchaser is a ridiculous and puzzling venture for a director like Cimino, who has the ability to make truly classic films, and an embarrassment for actors Harrelson and Seda, who have also demonstrated genuine talent in previous efforts.

—Jeff Hermann

REVIEWS

Boxoffice. August, 1996, p. 54.
Entertainment Weekly. November 11, 1996, p. 50.
Los Angeles Times. October 25, 1996, p. F14.
New York Times. October 25, 1996, p. C31.
Variety. May 27, 1996, p. 68.
Village Voice. November 5, 1996, p. 71.

Sunset Park

You gotta represent.—Movie tagline

Box Office: $10,163,782

Sunset Park is a low-key, lackluster, badly cast movie about an inner-city high school basketball team. Its only redeeming quality, besides its notable lack of histrionics, is its realistic game sequences.

The idea of casting second-banana comedienne Rhea Perlman in this film's central dramatic role was an odd one. It probably had something to do with her husband, Danny DeVito, being one of the producers. Perlman doesn't have the screen presence or emotional power necessary to sustain interest in her character, Phyllis Saroka, a Jewish high school teacher who takes the job of coaching the inept boy's basketball team because she needs the extra money.

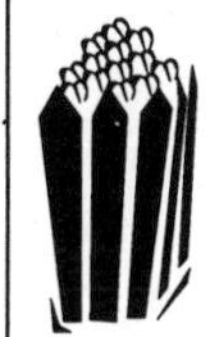

"I have three words for you: 'Condom. I'm serious.'"—Coach Saroka

Inexplicably, Phyllis's dream is to open a restaurant on St. Croix. Like much of the film's script, that ambition doesn't make much sense. And at the end, when Phyllis gives up the idea, she shrugs and says: "I don't like to cook anyway."

Phyllis is desperate to be "great," and at middle age she isn't satisfied with her achievements. Her latest man has left her high and dry, as many other men had done. She doesn't seem to have any real passion for teaching. In the coaching job, she's just a mercenary putting in time—at first.

Of course, you know right from the start that the players on the team are going to make Phyllis stop pouting and start caring about doing whatever is necessary to be a success. And Phyllis is going to awaken ambition in them by giving them the spark of confidence they need to get out of the ghetto victim role and on the road to a better life. But first, both coach and players must earn each other's respect and trust. In short, it's the usual sports-film pablum.

The players lack ambition for anything other than bedding girls and scoring drugs. Director Steve Gomez, working from a script by Kathleen McGhee Anderson and Seth Zvi Rosenfeld, is determined to make the kids gratingly authentic, but he goes overboard. Spouting obscenities, dissing constantly, and breaking into rap improvisations at a moment's notice, the young characters come off as unsympathetic stereotypes, crudely drawn and underwritten.

Most sports films create teams with a variety of easily identifiable and conflicting personalities, but most of the Sunset Park squad is dimly painted with the film's condescending broad brush. The only identifiable personalities are Butter (James Harris), the team's womanizing star; Busy-Bee (De'Aundre Bonds), a hyperkinetic goofball; Spaceman (Terrence Dashon Howard), a drug-addled and mentally challenged victim; and Shorty (Fredro Starr), the smart, sensitive and troubled one.

Fredro Starr, from the rap group Onyx, debuts as "Shorty."

The plot shies away from complexity. The film focuses almost entirely on the rocky relationship between Phyllis and Shorty. Along the way, Busy-Bee is hospitalized after being shot on the street, so the film can have the obligatory coach-at-the-bedside inspirational moment. In another throwaway scene, Phyllis stops Spaceman from assaulting another teacher with a butcher knife; it's a clumsy and contrived sequence. As for Butter, Phyllis stops his showboating for the ladies by pointing out that he's got a great butt and will score off court no matter how many points he totes up on court. It's one of the film's many embarrassing moments.

Both Phyllis and Shorty, quite obviously, are smart folks who've sold themselves short. But it's positively preposterous that director Gomer tries to suggest there is some sexual tension between them. The bedraggled Perlman is definitely not up to that assignment.

The film takes matters one slow step at a time. First Shorty takes the lead in helping Phyllis understand basketball, serving as a sort of assistant coach for her. Phyllis repays him by befriending him. They have a falling out when Shorty finds out about Phyllis's restaurant plans; he feels betrayed she's not sticking around for another season. Then, suddenly, Shorty lands in jail, accused of shooting another kid. Phyllis gets a lawyer friend to spring him, and even is willing to perjure herself to give him an alibi. But Shorty still is not mollified.

Why he feels so betrayed by Phyllis's plans to abandon the team is never sufficiently explained. The suggestion is that he is torn between the allure of life on the street and the promise of a straighter road to success that Phyllis's counsel represents. But this is very thin gruel indeed.

Starr is truly the star of the film, his wide range of emotions registering subtly on his revealing face. Asked to play a complex, conflicted character—the only character in the film that's not simplistic—Starr pulls it off without a hint of self-contradiction. The script makes Shorty jump through nearly impossible hoops in terms of character development, and he makes it intact.

Unfortunately, Perlman can't match Starr. She seems utterly lost, in over her head in a role which demands a strength and vitality that Perlman can't muster. The film makes little use of her considerable comic talents, and that's a shame. She's so low-key she almost disappears.

The players eventually hail her coaching "genius," but in fact the film never shows her developing any understanding of basketball. She at times is a stern disciplinarian, but during games she seems little more than a cheerleader.

Fortunately, *Sunset Park* has some wonderful action sequences. Most are poorly shot, from a camera that seems to be placed far behind the grandstands on one side. But even that works to make the basketball realistic; it's just the kind of second-rate camera angle you see in telecasts of a high-school basketball game. The game sequences perfectly capture the gritty flavor of inner-city high-school basketball, down to the echoing sounds of squeaky shoes in a partially-filled old gym, and the off-beat chants of the cheerleaders.

At these times, and in the raunchy locker-room conversations, *Sunset Park* seems to be striving for a documentary feel. But that sense is undermined by the contrivances of the barely serviceable plot. To its credit, *Sunset Park* ends

CREDITS

Phyllis Saroka: Rhea Perlman
Shorty: Fredro Starr
Mona: Carol Kane
Spaceman: Terrence Dashon Howard
Barbara: Camille Saviola
Busy-Bee: De'Aundre Bonds
Butter: James Harris

Origin: USA
Released: 1996
Production: Danny DeVito, Michael Shamberg, Daniel L. Paulson for a Jersey Films production; released by TriStar Pictures
Direction: Steve Gomer
Screenplay: Seth Zvi Rosenfeld, Kathleen McGhee-Anderson
Cinematography: Robbie Greenberg
Editing: Arthur Coburn
Music: Miles Goodman, Kay Gee
Production design: Victoria Paul
Art direction: Lee Mayman
Costume design: Carol Ramsey
Sound: Felipo Borrero
Basketball consultant: David Ian Benezra
MPAA rating: R
Running Time: 99 minutes

not in the expected ultimate triumph, but in a near-miss. But that creates the scary possibility that someone is planning a sequel. What audience there might be for such a film is hard to imagine.

—*Michael Betzold*

REVIEWS

Boxoffice. July, 1996, p. 94.
Chicago Tribune. April 26, 1996, p. 5.
Detroit News. April 26, 1996, p. 3D.
New York Times. April 26, 1996, p. C18.
Variety. April 29, 1996, p. 133.

Surviving Picasso

Only his passion for women could rival his passion for painting.—Movie tagline

"Picture perfect!"—Bill Diehl, *ABC Radio Network*

"Anthony Hopkins plays Picasso in one of his most vivid performances."—David Sterritt, *The Christian Science Monitor*

"A spellbinding film."—Rex Reed, *The New York Observer*

"Dazzling. Daring. Vigorously inventive."—Janet Maslin, *New York Times*

"A masterwork! Hopkins continues to amaze, an Oscar caliber performance."—Mike Caccioppoli, *WABC Radio*

"Gloriously entertaining. The finest performance of Hopkins' career."—Jules Peimer, *WKDM-AM*

Box Office: $2,015,612

The films directed by James Ivory, written by Ruth Prawer Jhabvala, and produced by Ismail Merchant have a somewhat underserved reputation for dainty dilettantism. For many, their films evoke images of elaborately costumed figures, usually the aristocratic English, drinking tea amid scrupulously manicured gardens. Such scenes do occur in their most popular—and best—films: *A Room with a View* (1986), *Howard's End* (1991), and *The Remains of the Day* (1993). While *A Room with a View* is relatively light and frothy, though with a subtext about the ease with which people pass up opportunities and waste their lives, the other two films have harder edges. *Howard's End* shows the destructiveness of the upper crust while straining to maintain its slippy spot in the world, and *The Remains of the Day,* the filmmakers' darkest effort, is an often painful examination of repressed emotion (a common Ivory-Jhabvala-Merchant theme), misplaced loyalty, and political naivete.

"I really like intelligent women - sometimes. Of course, I like stupid ones, too."—Picasso to Francoise Gilot

Surviving Picasso also attempts to explore serious themes but fails, like *Jefferson in Paris* (1995), the trio's previous film, to explore them fully. The best work of Ivory, Jhabvala, and Merchant is based on novels. Even though Jhabvala is herself a highly regarded novelist—*The Householder* (1962) and *Heat and Dust* (1983) are based on her fiction—the filmmakers seem unfocused when their work is not based on a solid narrative foundation. *Jefferson in Paris* asks how could Thomas Jefferson, a revolutionary leader and intellectual, be both a symbol of political liberty and an owner of slaves. *Surviving Picasso* asks how Pablo Picasso could be the artistic giant of the twentieth century and treat everyone in his life, especially women, so shabbily. The answer, in both cases, is a shrug. Despite this failure, both films are engrossing because of the stature of their subjects and the attention to period detail. Of the two, *Surviving Picasso* is the more interesting because of yet another of Anthony Hopkins' towering performances.

The focus of the film is not really Picasso (Hopkins) himself but the great Spanish-born painter and sculptor as seen through the eyes of Francoise (Natascha McElhone), the young French painter who was his mistress from 1944 to 1954 and bore him two children. (The film never mentions Francoise's last name, Gilot.) The film's title refers to Francoise's not being psychologically damaged by Picasso as the other women in his life have been. According to the film, she is admirable for leaving him on her own terms when she is finally fed up with his behavior, specifically his affair with Jacqueline Roque (Diane Venora). *Surviving Picasso* presents flashbacks to Picasso's relationships with his wife, Olga (Jane Lapotaire), Dora Maar (Julianne Moore), and Marie-Therese Walter (Susannah

Harker), and Francoise encounters the mental instabilities of each during her tenure.

Ivory and his collaborators fail to elucidate what draws Francoise and Picasso together in the first place. She is interested in him because he is, well, Picasso, but there is no sense of passion. She may intend for him to help her advance her career as a painter, but it becomes obvious early on that he cannot take any serious competition. Why he selects her, from all the attractive young women he could have, is never made clear. If a biographical film is to be more than a pageant of names and events, it must elaborate upon whatever influences the characters' behavior.

The filmmakers could not get permission from Picasso's estate to show the artist's actual works on-screen.

A particular motivational concern is why Francoise wants to be the mistress of a man forty years older, regardless of who he is, because of her relationship with her cold, jealous, possessive father (Bob Peck). The exceedingly unpleasant scene in which the father beats Francoise is nearly the most unsettling in any Ivory film. (The most shocking occurs when Picasso forces Francoise to watch an owl swoop down and carry off a cat.) They do not see each other again until years later when she is summoned to Paris because of the illness of her beloved grandmother (Joan Plowright), and he casually takes charge of the grandchildren he has never seen as if being with them and his daughter is not unusual.

Francoise wrote of her affair in *Life with Picasso* (1964), co-written with Carlton Lake, but the filmmakers were unable to acquire rights to this book. Instead, the film is based on Arianna Stassinopoulos Huffington's *Picasso: Creator and Destroyer,* a 1988 biography dismissed by many as a hatchet job. Like Huffington's book, *Surviving Picasso* is a soap opera giving little sense of its subject as an artist. Without creating some idea of Picasso's importance, he is simply a stocky old man who neglects his women before tossing them aside, a cruel master who takes advantage of all those closest to him, making Sabartes (Peter Eyre), his secretary of many years, pay his own train fare when called to the Riviera from Paris, and abruptly firing his longtime driver (Peter Gerety). (He also gives Francoise no money, not even for housekeeping.)

Francoise Gilot originally planned to cooperate on the project but withdrew, as Ivory and Merchant explained to television interviewer Charlie Rose, because her son, Claude, apparently wanted to make a documentary about the same subject. More damaging is the estate's refusal to allow even copies of Picasso's art to appear in the film. Instead, the great man is represented by imitations of his paintings, drawings, and sculptures meant to suggest his style but which could not, for legal reasons, resemble any specific work too closely. William Rubin, a Picasso scholar and director emeritus of the department of painting and sculpture at the Museum of Modern Art, told *The New York Times* that while the drawings are "passable" the paintings are "laughably bad." Without the art, nothing is left but a boor.

It is ironic that the art fails in a film in which the period details sparkle. The work of production designer Luciana Arrighi, whose impressive credits include *Women in Love* (1970), *My Brilliant Career* (1979), *Howard's End,* and *Sense and Sensibility* (1995), creates both a dark Paris studio and a sunny, expansive country house that look as lived in and disorderly as the bright, expensive home of Henri Matisse (Joss Ackland). Picasso's places suggest the rowdiness of their owner, Matisse's fragile order. Yet the Spaniard can create order out of chaos as when he scavenges Arrighi's immense junkyard to find materials for his sculptures. Picasso's obscenely big, bright blue Buick Roadmaster convertible implies some of the contradictions within this hedonistic communist.

Cinematographer Tony Pierce-Roberts captures this paradox by alternating brightly lit scenes with gloomy ones

CREDITS

Pablo Picasso: Anthony Hopkins
Francoise: Natascha McElhone
Jacqueline Roque: Diane Venora
Dora Maar: Julianne Moore
Marie-Therese Walter: Susannah Harker
Olga Picasso: Jane Lapotaire
Henri Matisse: Joss Ackland
Sabartes: Peter Eyre
Francoise's grandmother: Joan Plowright
Francoise's father: Bob Peck
Kahnweiler: Joseph Maher
American art dealer: Dennis Boutsikaris
Paulo Picasso: Dominic West
Picasso's driver: Peter Gerety

Origin: USA
Released: 1996
Production: Ismail Merchant and David L. Wolper; released by Warner Brothers
Direction: James Ivory
Screenplay: Ruth Prawer Jhabvala; based on the book *Picasso: Creator and Destroyer* by Arianna Stassinopoulos Huffington
Cinematography: Tony Pierce-Roberts
Editing: Andrew Marcus
Production design: Luciana Arrighi
Costume design: Carol Ramsey
Music: Richard Robbins
MPAA rating: R
Running Time: 125 minutes

since Picasso's world is full both of life and despair. Costume designer Carol Ramsey contributes to the film's visual style with the very 1950's capri slacks in which Francoise glides into the meeting with Matisse and the black velvet gown with enormous white lace collar Francoise wears to her first visit to Picasso. Her disrobing to seduce him is made more dramatic by what she takes off.

Picasso's women are presented with a variety of appearances and acting styles. Lapotaire offers Olga as an anachronistically dressed harridan like something out of Jean Giraudoux's *The Madwoman of Chaillot* (1945). Lapotaire's excesses can be justified since Olga is always pouring out her Russian soul. Harker's Marie-Therese is at the other extreme as the symbol, except for one scene, of tranquil domesticity. Marie-Therese calmly accepts being Picasso's woman only on Sunday, when she cuts his hair and nails, the only one he can trust to do so. Harker seems to have gained weight to convey better the character's earth-mother image. Moore's usually irritatingly mannered, attention-getting style is fitting since Dora is constantly calling attention to her dismay and seems always on the verge of violence.

Venora, who continues to get roles that do not demand enough of her, is confident and luminous in all her early scenes as Jacqueline. After she has moved in with Picasso, Pierce-Roberts lights Venora so that she looks haggard and years older. This neurotic, tentative Jacqueline is virtually a merging of the other Picasso victims. McElhone, discovered by Ivory and Merchant while performing Shakespeare in a London park, is arresting as Francoise because of her height and large eyes. She has presence but is given little opportunity to create a true identity for Francoise who exists only to respond to her master. McElhone is good at small gestures, as when Picasso tells Francoise she should be his woman and have his child and she shakes her head as if it is useless to resist.

As Picasso, Hopkins continues his run as the dominant film actor of the decade. He told *Vanity Fair* that he embraced the role "because I've been playing half-dead men for years." While he compresses his body into repressed balls as the butler in *The Remains of the Day* and the beleaguered anti-hero of *Nixon* (1995), Hopkins lets his intense eyes dominate as Picasso. The artist stares at everyone he encounters as if he is sucking in their essence like a vampire. Hopkins indulges in large gestures, as with the childish mugging while Francoise and Marie-Therese strain to have a civil conversation, and he can also be subtle. When Dora and Marie-Therese find themselves in Picasso's studio at the same time at the beginning of his affair with Dora and launch into a cat fight while the painter looms godlike over them on a scaffold, Hopkins smiles in delight like a spoiled little boy given a second ice cream cone only to turn his back on the combatants and assume a more contemplative gaze as he returns to his painting and the more worthy world of art.

Only in a few scattered moments like this does Ivory display his talent and breathe life into *Surviving Picasso*. The film had the misfortune of appearing shortly after the release of Julian Schnabel's *Basquiat* (1996), a flawed but much livelier interpretation of a painter's life. Henri-Georges Clouzot's documentary *Le Mystere Picasso* (1956) demonstrates the artist's stature and temperament much more economically than does *Surviving Picasso*. Another short film, Martin Scorsese's "Life Lessons" (from the 1989 trilogy *New York Stories*) is a more affecting portrait of a painter at war with his libido. *Surviving Picasso* disappoints so much because of the talents involved and the wonderful opportunities their subject should have given them.

—*Michael Adams*

REVIEWS

Boston Globe. September 7, 1996, p. C1.
Boxoffice Online. September 20, 1996.
Chicago Tribune. October 4, 1996, p. 5.
Entertainment Weekly. September 27, 1996, p. 54.
Los Angeles Times. September 20, 1996, p. F1.
The New York Times. September 20, 1996, p. C5.
People. October 7, 1996, p. 20.
Rolling Stone. October 3, 1996, p. 77.
USA Today. September 23, 1996, p. 4D.
Variety. September 10, 1996.
Village Voice. October 1, 1996, p. 66.

Sweet Nothing

A story about saving your dreams from going up in smoke.—Movie tagline

"Beautifully acted. Mira Sorvino's touching vulnerability makes it clear that Oscar-wining talents are only a small part of her range."—Janet Maslin, *New York Times*

"An intelligent study. Lovingly done. Michael Imperioli and Mira Sorvino strike just the right balance."—*New Yorker*

"Two thumbs up, way up! Insightful and powerful, with strong performances - Michael Imperioli is wonderful!"—*Siskel & Ebert*

Box Office: $102,350

A comparatively quiet flip side of the more prominent *Trainspotting*'s stylish horror and hype, *Sweet Nothing* is the tale of a young family man's descent into the drug world in spite of his seemingly promising existence. Compounding the tragedy is the story's origin: director Gary Winick and writer Lee Drysdale reportedly based the film on actual diaries, found in a Bronx apartment, that detail the author's struggle to balance his family responsibilities with his addiction. While ultimately the tale is fiction, the desperation and sadness with which it is told is disturbingly real.

"Life is to live and there's nothing wrong with taking short cuts to get ahead as long as no one gets hurt."—Angel justifying his drug dealing

Character actor Michael Imperioli plays Angel Gazetta, a mid-level Wall Street worker who lives modestly with his wife Monika (a pre-Oscar Mira Sorvino) and their young children. After the birth of his daughter, Angel meets up with Raymond (Paul Calderon), an old friend from the Marines, who offers him a celebratory hit off a crack pipe as well as a chance to make extra cash by getting in on some drug deals. In a narrative voice-over that drives the entire film, Angel justifies both activities: the profits from a few months of dealing would be a nice boost for him and his family, and as for the crack smoking, it is only for kicks. Monika, a doting mom and devoted wife, reluctantly agrees to his plan: get in, make a killing, get out.

Flash-forward three years. The Gazettas' apartment is lavishly furnished, and Monika wears designer dresses to her hair and nail appointments. But their new prosperity is as fake as the blond streaks in Monika's naturally brown hair. Angel is smoking more than ever, often disappearing to the bathroom to get high, and despite his wife's accusations and nagging, he has no intentions of quitting the life. Even as Monika lets Angel fasten the new pearl choker he has bought for her, she begins to question her trust in Angel and the price of their lifestyle on their marriage and family life. Angel has become increasingly cocky, untrustworthy, and, after a fallout with Raymond cuts off his piece of the action, desperate. From this point, his descent is quick and painful. Angel is paranoid and detached, concerned only with his next score, and his actions are increasingly dangerous and demeaning. He measures his "clean" stretches in hours. At the same time, Monika, out of desperation of her own, has become increasingly intolerant and independent; after watching her possessions and her marriage whittle away, she gets a job and, in a jarringly simple scene that ends with Angel curled up on the mat outside their door, throws Angel out of their home. In a last-ditch attempt for cash involving Monika's choker and a confrontation with Raymond, Angel ends up nearly busted and severely beaten, as his narrative reflects on the depths to which he has sunk. The film closes on Angel alone on a train, fresh from rehab, contemplating the skeleton of a life to which he's returning.

CREDITS

Angel Gazetta: Michael Imperioli
Monika Gazetta: Mira Sorvino
Raymond: Paul Calderon
Rio: Billie Neal
Dee Dee: Brian Tarantina

Origin: USA
Released: 1996
Production: Rick Bowman, Gary Winick for a Concrete Films production; released by Warner Bros.
Direction: Gary Winick
Screenplay: Lee Drysdale
Cinematography: Makato Watanabe
Editing: Niels Mueller
Music: Steven M. Stern
Production design: Amy Tapper
Costume design: Franne Lee
Sound: Steve Rogers
Casting: Brett Goldstein
MPAA rating: R
Running Time: 90 minutes

Sweet Nothing largely avoids melodramatic trappings; there are no episodes of wrenching withdrawal or explosive marital confrontation, for example, and there are few surprises in the largely predictable plot. What gives the film weight are the riveting performances of Imperioli and Sorvino. Imperioli is balanced and focused portraying a character who is neither; his average-Joe looks and twitchy demeanor lend credibility to Angel's demise. Sorvino is unsentimental as the put-upon wife who gains her sense of self only under desperate circumstances; one wishes the film had given her story equal time.

Debut feature for producer/director Gary Winick.

Equally compelling is the brutal honesty of Angel's diary-style narrative. He describes his first crack high as "a long lost-friend I never met before," and from there poignantly reveals the weapons he uses to justify his drug use and eventually battle addiction: bravado, denial, despair, and acceptance. A stylishly shot action scene in which Angel confronts Raymond and a slew of unsavory characters is out of place with the rest of the film's street-level plainness, and, in what some critics contend is its biggest flaw, the film all but ignores the whys of Angel's predisposition. It can be argued, however, that the lack of subtext gives the Gazettas' story an everyman quality. As for the real-life addict upon whom the story is based, the filmmakers reportedly sponsored his participation in several rehab attempts until one finally stuck. Overall, *Sweet Nothing* remains an intimate, unjudgmental look at the damage a dabble into drugs can do.

—*Terri Schell*

Chicago Tribune. September 20, 1996, p. 5
Los Angeles Times. September 6, 1996, p. F10
New York Times. March 27, 1996, p. C15

Swingers

Cocktails first. Questions later.—Movie tagline

"Fresh, funny and right on target!"—Jay Carr, *Boston Globe*

"A terrific comedy! A rare, honest expose of the modern mating dance."—Owen Gleiberman, *Entertainment Weekly*

"Confident, funny, and hip!"—Kenneth Turan, *Los Angeles Times*

"Hugely original! Laugh-out-loud funny!"—Michael Medved, *New York Post*

"Irresistible . . . Buoyantly entertaining!"—Janet Maslin, *New York Times*

Box Office: $4,400,000

Hipsters Mike (Jon Favreau) and Trent (Vince Vaughn) are on the prowl in Vegas in the hilarious comedy *Swingers*.

Hip, sweet and hilarious, *Swingers* is a low-budget comedy about five young guys on the make in Los Angeles. Set against the backdrop of the '90s "cocktail nation" of swing dancing, martinis, cigars, and Sinatra, these retro-twentysomethings look for career breaks and beautiful "babies" while hanging out in Hollywood clubs like the Dresden and the Derby.

Screenwriter and co-producer Jon Favreau stars as Mike, a struggling actor-comedian who's relocated from New York and is having a tough time getting over his ex-girlfriend back East. His Rat-Packer buddies, all aspiring show-biz wannabes, try to get him back in the game with their nightly rounds of parties and nightclubs, but it's to no avail.

Deciding that a change of scenery would do him good, Mike's slick, good-looking friend, Trent (Vince Vaughn), drags him off to Las Vegas. Their vision of Vegas—that some casino boss will think they are "money" (cool, hip) and offer to put them up in the "Rain Man suite" differs radically from what they experience. Instead of picking a glitzy casino, they choose one populated by senior citizens smoking cigarettes and playing the slot machines. The film makes its comedic mark as both guys end up at the loser's table. Janet Maslin of the *New York Times* comments: "Las Vegas, traditionally a movie mecca for cheesy hipsters, has never looked as comically woe-begone as this."

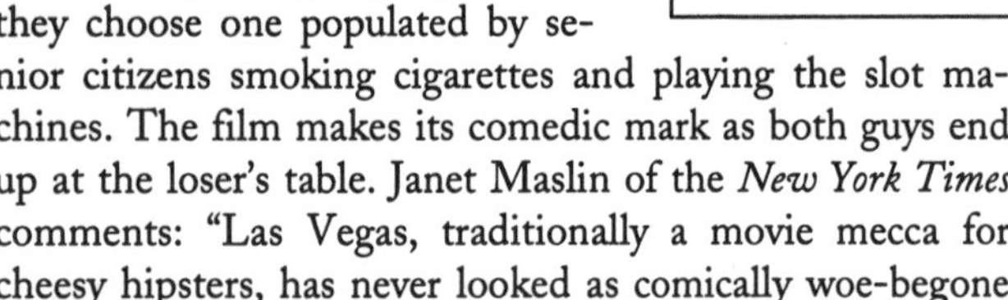

"All I do is stare at their mouths and wrinkle my eyebrows, and somehow I turn out to be a big sweetie."—Trent on his luck with women

It finally all comes together one night for Mike when he meets a pretty, unattached woman (Heather Graham) with whom the chemistry is right. When they eventually take to the dance floor at the Derby, you just know that everything is going to turn out alright for our nice-guy hero.

The smooth-talking yet insincere Trent is the one who gives the film its catchy slang with his ultracool hepcat lingo. "You're money" he tells Mike. "You're so money and you don't even know it." Most of those lines were based on conversations that Favreau had with his real-life unemployed-actor friends (they also star as his friends in *Swingers*). In *USA Today,* Vaughn says "When I moved to L.A. (from Illinois), I heard people say things like 'Daddy-O,' and I thought, 'Are these guys for real?' But it's like a bad song on the radio; you hear it enough and it starts to stick."

Although *Swingers* doesn't have much of a plot, the clever camera work by first-time director Doug Liman keeps this film moving. Liman's models for the film were reportedly action films like *The French Connection* (1971), *Raiders of the Lost Ark,* (1981) and *Lethal Weapon* (1987). Liman also drops in sneaky movie references—paying homage to Martin Scorsese's *Goodfella's* (1990) and Quentin Tarantino's *Reservoir Dogs* (1992). In *Entertainment Weekly,* Owen Gleiberman states, "He [Liman] captures something hilarious and touching—a new attitude of wistful modesty on the part of young macho cruisers, a recognition that what works today is raw testosterone in a velvet glove."

Despite a budget of only $250,000, Liman's goal was to make a movie that looked like a million. He achieved this by focusing on the actors and shooting guerilla-style, without permits, in natural light. Amazingly, *Swingers* was shot in 21 days with a hand-held Aaton 35 camera packing ultra high-speed stock. When that film ran out, the producers scrambled around Hollywood gathering "ends"—the unused portions of reels shot for other movies, to complete the production.

Swingers is enhanced by a well-chosen score which includes the excellent live band (Big Bad Voodoo Daddy), a lounge act (Marty and Elayne), and swanky recordings by Dean Martin, Bobby Darin, Louis Jordan, George Jones, and Roger Miller. Ironically, Frank Sinatra is never actually heard, although he's definitely here in spirit.

Favreau's witty and engaging script was actually nothing more than an unemployed actor's attempt to make his friends laugh and to submit something to his agent. His fellow actor friends did laugh and pushed the idea of making and appearing in the film. The script generated buzz, but no studio would produce the film with a cast of unknown actors. Favreau rejected all offers and insisted that his friends be cast in the film. His persistence finally paid off when he hooked up with Liman.

Winning the raves of several critics, the success of *Swingers* has opened up many doors in the industry for both cast and crew. Favreau has just finished a script for Universal called *Leatherheads* and he's been hired to write and direct *The Bachelor's Secret Handbook* for Touchstone. First up though, he's planning to direct his script *The Marshall of Revelation* about a Hasidic gunfighter in the Old West. As for his buddy Vaughn, he's really hit the big time. Besides co-starring in *The Marshall of Revelation,* Vaughn has a co-starring role in Steven Spielberg's upcoming *Jurassic Park* sequel. Director Liman and producers Victor Simpkins and

CREDITS

Mike: Jon Favreau
Trent: Vince Vaughn
Rob: Ron Livingston
Sue: Patrick Van Horn
Charles: Alex Desert
Christy: Deena Martin
Lisa: Katherine Kendall
Nikki: Brooke Langton

Origin: USA
Released: 1996
Production: Victor Simpkins for an Independent Pictures production; released by Miramax Films
Direction: Doug Liman
Screenplay: Jon Favreau
Cinematography: Doug Liman
Editing: Stephen Mirrione
Music: Justin Reinhardt
Production design: Brad Halvorson
Costume design: Genevieve Tyrrell
Sound: Alan B. Samuels
MPAA rating: R
Running Time: 97 minutes

Nicole Shay Laloggia are all fielding offers and associate producer Avram Ludwig is already at work on the independent project *River Red* for *That Thing You Do!* star Tom Everett Scott. It's all pretty incredible for a little film that isn't about much more than a group of lounge-lizards looking for some action.

As one of the best small independent films of the year, *Swingers* scored not only with the industry, but with audiences as well. Blessed with a funny script, great cast and good direction, it couldn't miss. In the words of hipster Trent, this film is "money, baby, money!"

—*Beth Fhaner*

REVIEWS

American Cinematographer. November, 1996, p. 16-17.
Boxoffice. November, 1996, p. 133.
Detroit Free Press. October 27, 1996, p. 1F, 8F.
Detroit News. November 1, 1996, p. 1E.
Entertainment Weekly. November 1, 1996, p. 44.
Film Threat. January, 1997, p. 58.
Los Angeles Times. Sunday Calendar Section, October 13, 1996.
New York Times. October 18, 1996., p. C3.
Rolling Stone. October 31, 1996, p. 78.
Time Magazine. October 21, 1996.
USA Today. October 25, 1996, p. 1-2D.
Variety. September 4, 1996.

Tales from the Crypt Presents Bordello of Blood

"A bloody romp. Dennis Miller has never been funnier."—Jack Mathews, *Newsday*

"Out of control horror!"—Joe B. Mauceri, *World of Fandom*

Box Office: $5,771,721

After a modest success with *Tales from the Crypt Presents Demon Knight* (1995), the creators responsible for that, and the successful HBO series, decided that vampires and prostitution (the oldest profession, second only to vampirism) would make a good combination for a bit of fun. However, the execution of such a premise fails miserably to arouse much fright, or laughs. Beginning with *Interview with the Vampire* (1994) and ending with Abel Ferrara's *The Addiction* (1995) and Quentin Tarantino's *From Dusk Till Dawn* (1996), vampires had become those creatures of the dark side that piqued moviegoers interests, and their success proved a hunger for such material. They brought new blood to the vampire lore. But *Bordello* adds nothing new or original to the whole mysticism.

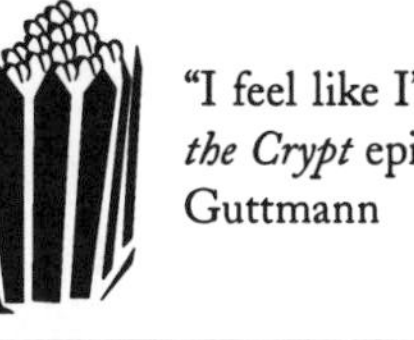

"I feel like I'm in a bad *Tales from the Crypt* episode."—PI Rafe Guttmann

Despite their outright campiness, the *Tales from the Crypt* films attract substantial talent in Hollywood. *Demon Knight* was directed by Spike Lee's cinematographer Ernest Dickerson, and starred Billy Zane and the up-and-coming Jada Pinkett. The series has seen the likes of Tom Hanks, Michael J. Fox, Arnold Schwarzenegger, and Demi Moore. It seems that working on these projects shows how loose these actors are; "Hey, look at me in this schlock horror movie." It may be all fun and games around the sets, but in *Bordello*'s case, it isn't much fun to watch.

With its comic book pacing, *Bordello* starts off with an archeological dig in Terra del Fuego for a hidden treasure, which turns out to be the ancient vampire named Lilith (Angie Everhart). The dwarf leader tells his cronies (and audience) about the legend of Lilith before she awakens and rips out their hearts and eats them. The dwarf remains and suppresses the vampire's killer instinct with a religious locket that is the same deterrent of evil used in *Demon Knight*. With this key, Lilith is forced into submission and opens a brothel to feed her hunger and the bloody slaughters begin. The first victim, Caleb Verdoux (Corey Feldman), is a leather clad, body-pierced rebel hanging with his four buddies at the local bar. They are propositioned by a catatonic biker who suggests they seek further damnation at the local funeral parlor that doubles as a whorehouse. Only Caleb, the lost soul, and his flunky sidekick follow up on the biker's advice. The boys are hoisted away to the haven of fanged hookers and are never seen again. The disappearance of her brother leads Katherine Verdoux (Erika Eleniak) to hire fledgling private investigator Rafe Guttman (Dennis Miller) to find her brother. With only one business card and a million sarcastic remarks, Rafe Guttman takes the case which leads him to the deadly brothel. Coincidentally, Katherine is the press secretary for flamboyant televangelist Jimmy Current (Chris Sarandon), otherwise known as J.C. among his entourage.

The business of the bordello turns out to be the master plan of preacher Current, who is the keeper of the holy locket, which is the only thing that keeps Lilith in line. He has brought Lilith back to rid the world of all the sinners, via the brothel, and sell their belongings (cars, trucks, and jewelry) to further his Christian mission.

J.C.'s plan backfires when the biggest sin, greed, enters his congregation. His dwarf assistant, who originally retrieved Lilith from her ancient slumber, wants more green as Lilith wants more red, and decides to oust the Reverend. As Rafe and Katherine work together, an attraction develops which leads to a brief competition between Lilith and Katherine. Even though Rafe may look like your average Joe, he has something special: a rare blood type that Lilith hasn't seen, in her words "since 'Ivan the Terrible.'" In a unique twist of the old Dracula legend, Rafe becomes Lilith's Lucy. And when Katherine is kidnapped by Lilith, Rafe and Current do an O.K. Corral-type demolition as they gun down vampire hookers with the help of Uzi water pistols filled with holy water. This technique was derived from *From Dusk Till Dawn* (1996), indicating the minute imaginations these filmmakers possess. The water gun blasts cause these vampires to explode and the end result is a room full of strewn, bloody body parts, a metaphor of how messy the task has become to deliver a coherent and feasible plot.

It's comforting that *Bordello* doesn't take itself too seriously. The choices in casting reiterate this notion, beginning with Angie Everhart as chief villain/vampire. Based on appearance, Everhart makes the perfect head mistress vampire with her voluptuous, sculptured looks and fiery auburn-colored hair. But unlike sexy bad boy Billy Zane in *Demon Knight*, Everhart is nothing more than a pretty face reciting cheap lines in order to obtain cheap laughs. The dialogue reduces her to a porn queen instead of a powerful, evil deity.

The presence of Chris Sarandon as the shady televangelist Jimmy Current does two things. It makes you wonder if they could have gotten someone other than a dark-haired, European featured man to speak in a Southern tongue. Second, Sarandon reminds you of a much more entertaining vampire film he starred in ten years ago. In *Fright Night* (1985) Sarandon played the sensual vampire Jerry Dandrige, and his performance in that movie was similar to Zane's in *Demon Knight*, it was the perfect mixture of menace and sexy bravado that transgressed to killer charm on-screen. Another cast member with vampire ties is Corey Feldman, who starred in the cult favorite *Lost Boys* (1987), but his disobedient character Caleb cannot be considered a stretch since his off-screen life has taken many turns into the dark side with his well-publicized instances of drug abuse. Erika Eleniak, thought to have great promise after her debut as Steven Segal's spunky but unwilling assistant in *Under Siege* (1992), seems lost. Here, she is not given much, and reflections on her recent career choices may be the reason for her wooden and stiff performance as the symbol of innocence. She seems truly out of place, which leaves Miller's character Rafe Guttman to carry the film and pick up most of the laughs.

His entrance into the film is a little bit odious. Rafe just happens to be sitting on a bench in the police station when Katherine reports her brother to be missing. From then on, Miller's comedy routine/film performance begins. He does offer some comedy relief as the average private dick who stumbles into something as far-fetched as a brothel of vampire hookers, but his constant barrage of sarcastic one-liners gets a bit tired and loses it bite. Many of his comebacks include references to movies and television shows (similar to his comedy routine that covers the gamut of pop culture) that become distracting. When Rafe first suggests to Katherine that vampires may be the culprit in her brother's undoing, he opens his theory with "I'm going to advance a weird Duchovnian riff," referring to the actor from the popular strange phenomenon show, "The X-Files." After Rafe brings a deputy to check out the mortuary/bordello for evidence of prostitution, the evidence is suddenly disguised by the twisted mortician McCutcheon (Aubrey Morris). The deputy is not convinced of evil doings and is ready to haul Rafe to jail. Rafe interjects with, "Hey, they're Gaslighting me, man." Finally, as he and Katherine wander through a cave, Rafe mentions how he feels like he's in a "bad 'Tales from the Crypt' episode." *Interview*

CREDITS

Rafe Guttman: Dennis Miller
Katherine Verdoux: Erika Eleniak
Lilith: Angie Everhart
Reverend Current: Chris Sarandon
Caleb Verdoux: Corey Feldman
McCutcheon: Aubrey Morris
Crypt Keeper: John Kassir (voice)

Origin: USA
Released: 1996
Production: Gilbert Adler; released by Universal
Direction: Gilbert Adler
Screenplay: A.L. Katz and Gilbert Adler
Cinematography: Tom Priestly
Editing: Stephen Lovejoy
Music: Chris Boardman
Production design: Gregory Melton
Art direction: Sheila Haley
Costume design: Trish Keating
Sound: Paul Rodriguez
Visual effects design: John T. Van Vliet
Special effects: Tim Storvick
MPAA rating: R
Running Time: 87 minutes

with the Vampire and *Fright Night* suspended belief, but at the same time made one wonder about the possibilities of the existence of vampires and perhaps encountering one. These films further fueled the mythology of the vampire legend and its power. It's never explained if Rafe is a movie buff or horror film fanatic (something that provided innocent charm in the teenager from *Fright Night*), so Miller reminds us that we are watching a movie, and not a very good one, either.

Campiness has become a trademark of the "Tales from the Crypt" brand of entertainment and it is not lost in *Bordello of Blood.* It still has its quota of blood, disembowelments, and gore to stand alongside the series which has become a cult favorite, probably for those same reasons. But, *Bordello* does go overboard with the bare-breasted hookers, hinting at exploitation and misogyny. One other reason for its popularity has been the CryptKeeper. With its deadpan humor and morbid puns, the CryptKeeper opens and ends each segment on the series and the films without exception. In his latest film, the CryptKeeper shows signs of a worn-out welcome. *Bordello of Blood*'s short running time could have been saved five minutes if a useless encounter between the CryptKeeper and a mummified creature (a cameo by William Sadler from *Demon Knight*) were edited out and the CryptKeeper would just introduce the story.

Unlike *Demon Knight,* where the creatures looked similar to what could be seen in the comic books, the special effects in *Bordello* are rather bland to say the least. Lilith's final beastly change into the evil vampire temptress is very lackluster, and for the main creature's grand finale to be so-so says a lot about the quality of a movie intended to scare viewers. *Demon Knight* provided some of the most unusual looking flesh-eating demons and proved the filmmakers did want to create some fright for its viewers. The demons were so impressive that their creepy walk induced both laughs and chills.

Watching *Bordello of Blood* may in fact be worse than watching a bad "Tales from the Crypt" episode on television. At least you're only dealing with a half-hour of bad cheesiness . . . for free.

—*Michelle Banks*

REVIEWS

Los Angeles Times. August 16, 1996, p. F10.
New York Times. August 16, 1996, p. C14.
People. September 9, 1996, p. 18.
USA Today. August 16, 1996, p. 4D.

Target

"Powerful and intelligent."—*Vancouver Sun*
"A showdown with the flavorful tang of a spaghetti western."—*Variety*

If a filmic narrative from a distant film culture can be seen to take on the guise of a myth, then its impact on us would depend on how far we are prepared to shed our conditioning to contemporary filmic realism.

From its international production setup, Sandip Ray's *Target,* based on a screenplay by his father, the renowned Satyajit Ray, would appear to have one eye cleverly poised on the film festival cognoscenti. More's the surprise then that the film, like its protagonist, emerges as too forthright and honest to allow conventions of realism to dilute its elemental wallop.

Bharosa (Om Puri), the film's mythic hero, his name literally signifying trust, serves as the epitome of the guileless, open-faced simpleton, emblematic of those masses of the subcontinent who have trusted their fate to one wave of invaders after another.

The film's time and setting are kept appropriately vague. We are somewhere in the hinterland of India, where the legacy of British rule has left behind a system of landlordism dominating an illiterate peasantry, for whom government reforms exist somewhere on paper rather than in actual practice.

Singh (Mohan Agashe), his name literally signifying lion, is one such landlord, a timeless father figure, holding the power of life and death over those in his district, with the concomitant corruption slowly devouring his insides like a rot. He is addressed never by name, but as Sarkar, a term signifying ruler. Singh's anachronistic plight is brought home in the opening scene, in which a cross section of village notables have assembled to watch a display of his marksmanship. To their shock, and Singh's dismay, the event turns into a demonstration of his middle-aged debility as bullet after bullet misses the target.

Choubey (Anjan Srivastava), one of Singh's lackeys, then introduces Bharosa, a professional shikari, or hunter of big game, now reduced to much tamer sport, owing to the government ban.

"I am now the government," Singh counters, inviting Bharosa to show his prowess.

As Bharosa's aim hits the bull's-eye, it becomes clear that Singh will use the hunter's skills as an extension of his own, as if Bharosa were nothing more than an implement to be bought with money. Bharosa, true to his name, shows his trust in the benevolence of the aristocracy by openly admitting to being an Untouchable, the lowliest order of traditional Hindu society, a division long outlawed by the country's secular constitution, but which survives to this day in the form of prejudice.

Though repelled by Bharosa's lowly origins, Singh nevertheless employs the servile hunter to lead his expeditions, and orders that quarters be found for him in the segregated village of Untouchables. The stage is thus set for the enmity between the socio-historical forces symbolized by Bharosa and Singh respectively that, with mythic predictability, will result in an inversion of power.

Change is already brewing in the village of Untouchables, where an elder is urging an assembly to break free from Singh's economic clutches, in favor of more secure employment offered by the government. Bharosa is thus seen as an outsider, an agent of the villainous Singh. Even Bijri (Champa Islam), the attractive village maiden, once married but now abandoned, who is assigned the task of cooking for Bharosa, seems initially prone to keep her distance. The two, however, find they share a tragic past that has left them outside the customary folds of domesticity: Bijri has no family in the village, while Bharosa has lost his mother and sister to the drought.

We can thus see why Bharosa's job consumes him with a renewed sense of self-worth as a hunter of wild and dangerous game, while his trusting nature blinds him to his real status. On the roof of Singh's decaying mansion, he stands proud and tall, as a tailor takes his measurement for a hunting outfit, careful not to let the tape touch Bharosa's person.

Singh's power over the abject lot of the Untouchables in the nearby village comes to the fore when his lust is aroused at the sight of Bijri exerting herself while threshing grain. All the decadent hypocrisy of the Hindu caste system is laid bare as Singh seeks the help of the hight caste Choubey in a plan to procure Bijri. When Choubey hesitates, Singh threatens to expose his Untouchable mistress. For Singh, Bijri becomes a displacement for the target he has been unable to hit. "I've lost one sport," he admits to Choubey, "but not the other."

On the morning of the hunt, Singh, atop a ceremoniously decorated elephant, allows Bharosa to lead the party on foot. The festive air, however, cannot shake Singh out of a sense of his own lack. Safe in his tree perch, he drinks to drown his sorrow. Then, as the callers draw a leopard to the site, Singh, in his stupor, raises his rifle, but has to be stopped from scaring the animal away. It is Bharosa, at the foot of the tree, who shoots the leopard with surefire ease.

At the camp site, however, as Bharosa is about to pose for a photograph as the triumphant hunter, Singh becomes enraged, spitting out venomous abuse, and banishes Bharosa from the scene. Singh then poses by himself, with the leopard at his feet.

The incident serves as an epiphany for Bharosa, who suddenly seems to realize the toll in basic self-respect that working for Singh entails. That night, against the darkness of the hut that appears to take on a timeless quality, Bijri, in close-up, tries to console Bharosa. "That is our lot," she explains. "Such is our fate." Bharosa though remains adamant, as if all the humiliation that has been heaped on him and his community now demands that he retaliate.

The occasion presents itself when he foils an attempt by Choubey's servant to abduct Bijri. When Singh learns of Bharosa's interference, his rage boils over. Soon Bharosa himself becomes the victim of an assault by Choubey's henchmen. No doubt to cover his own tracks, Singh pays for Bharosa to be treated in the nearby town. When Bharosa wakes up in a hospital bed, a doctor informs him that he will have to forgo the use of his right arm.

Stripped thus of the only means of his sustenance, Bharosa, though seemingly unaware of it, is also freed from any institutional loyalty. At first he admits to sharing Bijri's sense of resignation. "We are like vermin in this society," he muses. "The poor man's skill has no value." Then it dawns on him that even in his emasculated state, his rifle is his only friend. With slow diligence, Bharosa attempts target practice, awkwardly using his left arm to rest the butt of his rifle on his shoulder. His aim however keeps going wayward. In despair, he throws the rifle to the ground.

Then, a change seems to overcome him as the voices of a crowd appear to emanate from the rifle, as if urging him, in true mythic fashion, to take it up again. In a montage of extreme close-ups, we see the tip of the barrel, then the finger on the trigger, followed by the result: a magical bull's-eye.

CREDITS

Bharosa: Om Puri
Singh: Mohan Agashe
Bijri: Champa Islam
Choubey: Anjan Srivastava

Origin: India
Released: 1995
Production: A.J. Vincent, A.J. Francis, Zachary Y. Lovas and Jason L. Lovas; released by Filmopolis Pictures
Direction: Sandip Ray
Screenplay: Satyajit Ray; based on the novel *Manusher Juddha* by Prafulla Roy
Cinematography: Barun Raha
Editing: Dulal Dutt
MPAA rating: Unrated
Running Time: 122 minutes

Bharosa is thus ready for his final confrontation with Singh, who has decided to end his ongoing labor dispute with the Untouchables by setting their village on fire. In the pitch dark night, Singh on horseback, armed with his rifle, leads a phalanx of flaming torches towards the village.

The helpless Untouchables have only Bharosa to lead them. With one arm in a sling and the other holding his rifle, Bharosa looks deceptively pathetic as he strides up alone to confront Singh. Confident of his own superiority, Singh decides to shoot first, but before he can take aim, it is Bharosa's bullet that finds the ultimate target. As Singh slumps dead, those behind him scatter. In the midst of the melee, Bharosa proposes to Bijri, and the two begin a new life.

Critical take on the film has ranged from interpreting it as a personal confession on the part of the elder Ray to seeing it as a political fable-cum-samurai drama. Georgia Brown, in *The Village Voice* sees the film as an "oedipal struggle between an aging tyrant who can no longer realize his dreams and the man he hires to front for him. If the older man is furious at the loss of power, the younger knows he can never receive the glory."

Dave Kehr, in *The New York Daily News* finds the elder Ray's screenplay "a model of interlocking dramatic construction" displaying "the logic and elegance of a mathematical proof." Kehr notes that while this film "brings the career of Satyajit Ray to an end; it may mark a beginning for his son."

Target is Sandip Ray's fourth feature, but only his second to be seen here. His previous film, *The Broken Journey*, also based on a screenplay by his father, had a limited release last year.

—*Vivek Adarkar*

REVIEWS

The Hindu. May 5, 1995.
The New York Daily News. February 28, 1996.
The New York Post. February 28, 1996.
The New York Times. February 28, 1996, p. C18.
News India-Times. March 8, 1996.
Newsday. February 28, 1996.
The Village Voice. March 5, 1996, p. 44.

That Thing You Do!

In every life there comes a time when that dream you dream becomes that thing you do.—Movie tagline

"Will put a smile on your face and keep it there."—David Sheehan, *CBS-TV*

"Just do it. You'll feel great after seeing this film."—Bill Zwecker, *NBC-TV*

"A bright, bubbly shoe-tapper of a tale."—David Ansen, *Newsweek*

"A brightly entertaining blend of humor and heartbreak."—Peter Travers, *Rolling Stone*

Box Office: $25,513,987

No one expected entertainment lightning to strike in Erie Pennsylvania in the summer of 1964, but strike it did. Guy Patterson (Tom Everett Scott) works in his father's appliance store, but after-hours, when the front door is locked, he retreats to the basement where he drums along with records by jazz great Del Paxton. His secret life, however, is about to be brought into the light by that bolt from the blue.

Meanwhile, a small garage band called the One-ders (pronounced wonders) has a gig at a local college talent show, but just before the performance, their drummer, Chad (Giovanni Ribisi) breaks his arm while jumping parking meters. Desperate to find a replacement, the band's leader, Jimmy (Johnathon Schaech), approaches Guy who accepts—if he buys two phonograph needles and a clock radio. At practice, everything seems to be OK, but that night at the contest, Guy purposely gives the band's one song, a ballad called "That Thing You Do," an upbeat tempo. The other members, Lenny (Steve Zahn) and the bass player (Ethan Embry) keep up, but Jimmy is a bit reluctant to speed up the song he originally wrote. But as the college kids go wild, a rock hit is born.

The winning of the college talent show is followed by a job at an Italian restaurant where the band attracts quite a following . . . and the attention of a manager whose office is a camper trailer. He promises to get the band playtime on a local radio station and succeeds. (The sheer exuberance of this scene is a pleasure to watch as the song goes from tinny radio earphones to the full stereo effect of one of Patterson appliance's largest radios.) Their new manager also gets them an appearance at a rock stage show in Pittsburgh which leads them to a promoter from Play-Tone records, Mr. White (Tom Hanks).

Sensing that the One-ders have a hit on their hands, White changes their name to the Wonders (because the original spelling was constantly being pronounced "Oh-need-ers") and books them on a tour of state fairs. As their song racks up air time, it climbs the *Billboard* top 100 chart going from 93 to 71, then to 49 and 21 until finally it reaches number 7. That's when White decides it's time for them to abandon the fairs and head for Hollywood.

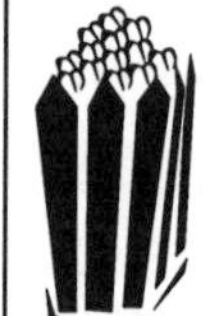

"Jimmy, I've wasted thousands and thousands of kisses on you."—Faye to boyfriend Jimmy when they break up

So, with Jimmy's long-time girlfriend Faye (Liv Tyler) in tow, the gang proceeds westward where they appear, dressed in sailor suits, in a major motion picture, *Weekend at Party Pier* (directed by director/producer Jonathan Demme in a cameo). Jimmy finds the experience demeaning and his attitude becomes one of the first cracks in the band. By the time they're supposed to appear on "Hollywood Television Show Case" their bass player is AWOL in Disneyland with a couple of marines and Lenny has eloped to Las Vegas. The lightning strike is over.

There's one problem with watching a film set in 1964 when viewers have a 1990's mentality. One is always looking for the bad guy. Will it be the cast-off drummer out for revenge? Will it be the authoritarian father who will force his son to choose between his "career" or his family? Will it be the manager who runs off with their money? Will it be the big-time promoter who will eat them up and spit them out? Will it be racists who beat up the bass player for dating a black singer? Or will it involve fisticuffs between the two rivals in a love triangle? The answer? None of the above.

This is not a time when jaded fans throw themselves into mosh pits and give themselves whiplash keeping time with the music. It is a time which actor Tom Hanks, in his writing and directing debut, wants to paint as innocent and lighthearted. No villains, no four letter words. This film is as nice as everyone always says Tom Hanks is. We should have expected it.

With back-to-back Oscars for *Philadelphia* (1993) and *Forrest Gump* (1994) and six hits in a row, the last being *Apollo 13* (1995), Hanks, with the help of Jonathan Demme's production house Clinica Estetico and $26 million from Twentieth Century Fox managed to catch the opportunity not only to direct his first feature, but also to realize it from a script he wrote. But his involvement in the film doesn't end there. He also takes a starring turn as Mr. White, personally selected the cast, and even helped compose at least four of the film's songs.

So it should be no surprise that this gentle and entertaining tale about the perils of fame is as pleasant and sincere as its auteur. It should also be no surprise that lead actor Tom Everett Scott acts as Hanks' alter ego. They not only share the same first name, look alike and have similar smiles, they both also come across as "good guys."

Hanks has purposely cast relative unknowns in his film. (Although there are some great cameos like that of Jonathan Demme. There's Hanks' old "Bosom Buddies" partner Peter Scolari as the TV show host, there's singer Chris Isaak

AWARDS AND NOMINATIONS

Academy Award 1996 Nominations: Best Song ("That Thing You Do!")
Golden Globe Award 1997 Nominations: Best Original Song ("That Thing You Do!")

CREDITS

Guy Patterson: Tom Everett Scott
Faye Dolan: Liv Tyler
Jimmy: Johnathon Schaech
Lenny: Steve Zahn
The Bass Player: Ethan Embry
Mr. White: Tom Hanks
Tina: Charlize Theron
Lamarr: Obba Babatunde
Chad: Chris Ellis
Horace: Chris Ellis
Sol Siler: Alex Rocco
Del Paxton: Bill Cobbs
Troy Chesterfield: Peter Scolari
Marguerite: Rita Wilson
Uncle Bob: Chris Isaak
Boss Vic Koss: Kevin Pollak

Origin: USA
Released: 1996
Production: Gary Goetzman and Edward Saxon for Clinica Estetico in association with Clavius Base; released by Twentieth Century Fox
Direction: Tom Hanks
Screenplay: Tom Hanks
Cinematography: Tak Fujimoto
Editing: Richard Chew
Production design: Victor Kempster
Art direction: Dan Webster
Set decoration: Merideth Boswell
Costume design: Colleen Atwood
Music: Howard Shore
MPAA rating: PG
Running Time: 110 minutes

as Uncle Bob who records their first song, Kevin Pollak plays the Pittsburgh show MC, and Hanks' own wife Rita Wilson appears as a jazz club waitress.) Tom Everett Scott, probably best known as Brett Butler's missing son on TV's "Grace Under Fire" is nicely cast. Handsome in an offbeat kind of way, funny and likeable, he makes a charming romantic lead. Johnathon Schaech (most recently seen in *How to Make an American Quilt* [1995]) persuasively evokes the temperamentalness of talent while Steve Zahn's Lenny is engagingly funny. Only poor Ethan Embry (*White Squall* [1996]) as the nameless bass player is relegated to the land of little dialogue, but he still manages to incorporate innocence and fun into his character.

Tom Everett Scott nearly didn't get cast because Tom Hanks felt the young actor looked too much like himself in *Big*. But when wife Rita Wilson saw Scott's audition tape, she convinced Hanks to reconsider.

Also supplying a solid character is Liv Tyler as the girlfriend. Most recently seen in *Stealing Beauty* (1996), it is interesting to note that she is the daughter of Aerosmith singer Steven Tyler and rock groupie Bebe Buell. Great credentials for a rock and roll picture, even if it is set several decades before she was born.

Besides some good acting by relative unknowns, *That Thing You Do!* also benefits from its wonderfully authentic look. With Orange, California substituting for Erie, the town's fifties look and plethora of antique stores provided a convincing backdrop and a profusion of props appropriate for the time. Production designer Victor Kempster (*JFK* [1991]) and art director Dan Webster should be proud of their work.

And as if the authentic look weren't enough, even the music has that pseudo-Beatle's sound and simplicity so indicative of the time. It also helps that like the actors, the music is also unknown but perfect for the situation. Hanks and his producer Gary Goetzman actually put out a general call to virtually anyone for the title song. They ended up with more than 300 entries. (The winner was 28-year-old Adam Schlesinger, an independent songwriter from New York's West Village.) Besides Schlesinger's song, Hanks and Goetzman themselves also composed parts of the soundtrack. And, they even managed to convincingly capture different styles true to the period. ("Voyage Around the Moon" sounds as if it belongs on a Ventures soundtrack while "Mr. Downtown" could easily have played under a TV detective show's opening credits.)

In the end, it is the look, the feel, the innocence, the enthusiasm, and the entertainment that carries *That Thing You Do!* There's no great conflict, no hidden agenda, and no profound meaning here. There's also nothing offensive. Politicians who have been decrying the lack of good family movies should love Hanks' first directing effort.

But before this kind of recommendation can turn off viewers who fear walking into a movie so sweet they might get diabetes, it should also be noted that although the film is disarmingly cheerful, it never crosses the line to become treacly or sappy. The innocence Hanks' gives us is one that comes deep from within his own sense of integrity and he imbues it with energy, good humor and guilelessness.

Sure, *That Thing You Do!* never reaches the dramatic qualities of *Backbeat* (1994) or *The Commitments* (1991), to which it will surely be compared, but that was never its goal. To provide an entertaining and nostalgic experience, that's what Hank's was after. And this he has done well.

—Beverley Bare Buehrer

REVIEWS

Chicago Tribune. October 4, 1996.
Detroit News. October 4, 1996, p. G1.
Entertainment Weekly. October 4, 1996, p. 40.
Los Angeles Times. October 4, 1996.
New York Times. October 4, 1996, p. C4.
Newsweek. October 7, 1996, p. 76
People. October 7, 1996, p. 19.
Rolling Stone. October 17, 1996, p. 142.
USA Today. October 4, 1996, p. 4D.
Variety. September 23, 1996, p. 125.

Thieves; Les Voleurs

"An especially dense web of intimate relationships and insights . . . It encompasses different philosophies, generations and sexual orientations with discreet finesse."—Janet Maslin, *New York Times*

"Deneuve and Auteuil are astonishing! The film comes together with great passion and power!"—Dennis Dermody, *Paper Magazine*

Box Office: $439,937

To know 'who-dun-it' holds no comfort, Andre Techine's *Thieves* seems to say, when 'what-dun-it' is still at large. Taking its narrative drive from the occupation and sensibility of its central character, Alex (Daniel Auteuil), a hyperalert police detective in his forties, in a small city in Northern France, this thinking man's film noir manages to convey a broader, even philosophical perspective on crime than most crime and police dramas bent on bringing the criminal to justice.

In the process, it highlights yet another direction by which contemporary filmic realism can avoid a sterility of narrative form. The film records, and thereby reveals, as if it were Alex, treating all narrative moments, whether directly related to the crime, or tangential to it, as the same, caring not which account is true or false, which mere pretense and which genuinely tragic, all just so much testimony to be filed away into metal drawers. One can almost sense a digital chronometer, just out of frame, subjugating each narrative peak, each emotional crisis, to the passage of time.

"You never knew how to enjoy life. Careful, you're not young anymore."—Ivan to his brother Alex

"You prefer classifying to identifying," Alex is told, "but people aren't files." Eventually, neither Alex, nor the film, nor we, can evade that charge.

A prologue and epilogue frame the film's nodal event: the killing of Alex's criminal brother, Ivan (Didier Bezace), during a car heist. The caper gone awry, the staple of many a crime thriller, here functions as only a narrative linchpin for the mosaic of flashbacks narrated by the film's three main characters.

In the prologue, we are introduced to Alex's death through the precocious gaze and viewpoint of his ten-year-old son, Justin, who is merely told that his father has had an accident. As his mother, Mireille (Fabienne Babe), clutches him, it is clear that he is more comforting than comforted.

The first segment, narrated by Alex, then shunts us to a year before the heist. We see the slick Ivan posing as a respectable nightclub owner, and responsible family man. "Kids are what life is about," he tells the long-divorced, now single Alex. This extended flashback also introduces us to the film's most enigmatic character, Juliette (Laurence Cote), a recalcitrant, boyish 'generation-x' student-cum-shoplifter, first let off the hook by Alex, then encountered as part of Ivan's circle. As a club crawler, Juliette is sexually forthright towards the repressed Alex, inciting him into a burst of raw machismo, thereby lending the film a sudden jolt of sexual frankness. Herself unfazed by the way she is manhandled, Juliette can only remark, "It'd be fun to try it in a four-star hotel once." Through Alex, we also see Marie (a mature fifty-ish Catherine Deneuve) revelling with Juliette in Ivan's club. As Juliette's philosophy professor, Marie also functions as the film's conscience.

Alex's exclusion from the world of female bonding becomes evident in the next two segments. As he drops Juliette off outside Marie's building, the film switches gears once again. We are now led into Marie's story, starting from that very night. As Juliette steps into her apartment, Marie wants to greet her with a kiss on the lips, but Juliette draws away. For the erudite Marie, Juliette represents the throbbing center of street life, a timely mutation of the feminine sensibility that she would like to absorb into her work. She even has a book in progress built around Juliette's experiences. For Juliette, Marie is clearly a refuge from the devouring jungle life that individualizes her in Marie's eyes.

Their relationship, which deserves a film to itself, remains *Thieves'* most troubling aspect. It is as if the filmmaker had stumbled upon more depth than he had planned for, and found his bearings by resorting to Alex's functional viewpoint.

Like Alex, we too remain on the outside, despite our being let into the lesbian couple's most intimate moments. We watch without understanding as Juliette, within the secure warmth of Marie's kitchen, suddenly breaks a glass and tries to swallow the pieces. Also, like Alex, we are kept in the dark about just how much Juliette has told Marie about herself.

AWARDS AND NOMINATIONS

Cesar Award 1997 Nominations: Best Film, Best Actress (Deneuve), Best Director (Techine)

In the following segment, entitled "Juliette six months before Ivan's death," we come to know that the relationship between the two women extends beyond the merely physical. As they share a bathtub, they make intelligent talk. In the world of schlock TV and celebrity best-sellers, Juliette is quite aware of the lucre that can be mined out of her lurid past. As she prepares to assume the role of a painter's model, Marie reminds her how much more difficult writing can be. "You don't paint with others' words," Marie says. Juliette's concerns, however, remain sophomoric. When Marie confides, "I've never been so happy," Juliette asks, "Happier than with a man?"

Catherine Deneuve and Daniel Auteuil also co-starred in Andre Techine's *Ma Saisson Preferee,* in which they played a sister and brother.

Soon, through Juliette, we are led back to the ostensible focus of the film's narrative: the events leading to Ivan's death. Ivan's use of Juliette appears relatively simpleminded compared to what she has been through with Marie. He merely wants her as an insurance against Alex. As a human resource planner, Ivan realizes the value of family ties. Having Juliette's brother, Jimmy (Benoit Magimel), in on the heist isn't enough. He wants Juliette to be actively involved as well.

A curious aspect of the impending heist is its international flavor. Not only is one youth, Nabil (Naguime Bendidi), clearly of Middle Eastern origin, but the cars themselves are meant for the distant shores of the third world. This inspires the film's composer, Philip Sarde, to use a contemporary blend of 'world music': untranslated Arabic-sounding singing against synthesized western instrumentation. This recurrent exotic musical motif serves as an extension of Ivan's machinations, which seek to not only assimilate the foreign, as part of a shifting world order, but to exploit it as well.

Despite Ivan's seemingly expert planning, the heist is bungled by the most rudimentary of lapses. The gang, it seems, had not counted on the presence of two watchmen. This results in an unexpected shootout, during which one watchman is killed, and Ivan is shot in the forehead and dies instantly. While the other watchman goes off to get help, Juliette saves the gang by agreeing to drive them away in a stolen Mercedes.

Juliette's consequent need to go into hiding creates a vacuum in the lives of both Alex and Marie. Yet it also brings them closer. In the segment entitled "Alex ten days after Ivan's cremation," the two strike a deal. Each will share with the other any information about Juliette's whereabouts. Alex thus tells Marie that Ivan's gang will go unpunished, since the only one spotted was Juliette, but because of her attire, the police are looking for a man with Juliette's face. Two months later, Marie tells Alex that Juliette is in Marseilles, where she's found a job in a bookstore. They both seem to agree that Juliette is better off without them. Only later do we learn of the loss that Marie has been harboring.

That night, we see them at the Opera, where Marie is visibly moved by the love suicide from *The Magic Flute.* Two days later, Alex learns that Marie herself has leapt to her death from her window. Dutifully, he collects what has been bequeathed to him: the completed manuscript of the book about Juliette, as well as the audiocassettes of Juliette's recollections. The accompanying note is intended to explain it all: "We never renounce, only replace. I don't want to replace Juliette."

Alex, who has always doubted the depths of Marie's passion, now appears struck by guilt. Driven by his conscience, he tracks down Juliette in Marseilles, wanting to rid himself of Marie's work, but becomes transfixed when he sees how she has changed. She now looks like a responsible working woman, suitably dressed and coiffed. Rather than burden her with the past, Alex decides to withdraw, without even greeting her. Back in his apartment, alone one night, he has an epiphany: if Marie wanted Juliette to know, she would have mailed everything to her. Clearly, the manuscript and the tapes are meant for just him, as an assault on his cynicism.

The epilogue then establishes the film's leitmotif: the agony and sadness accompanying the transition from one phase of youth to another. Little Justin learns the truth about his father's death from his grandfather, Victor (Ivan Desny),

CREDITS

Alex Noel: Daniel Auteuil
Marie Leblanc: Catherine Deneuve
Juliette Fontana: Laurence Cote
Jimmy Fontana: Benoit Magimel
Justin: Julien Riviere
Ivan: Didier Bezace
Victor: Ivan Desny
Mireille: Fabienne Babe

Origin: France
Released: 1995
Production: Alain Sarde for a TF1 Films, Rhone-Alpes Cinema, and D.A. Films production; released by Sony Pictures Classics
Direction: Andre Techine
Screenplay: Andre Techine, Gilles Taurand, Michel Alexandre
Cinematography: Jeanne Lapoirie
Editing: Martine Giodano
Music: Philippe Sarde
Art direction: Ze Branco
Costume design: Elisabeth Tavernier
Sound: Jean-Pierre Laforce
MPAA rating: Unrated
Running Time: 118 minutes

whom we discover has been behind the heist all along. Once in the know, Justin's sense of loss gives way to reconciliation, as he accepts the unrepentant Jimmy, who is now courting his mother, as a kind of elder brother-cum-stepfather.

While critics have taken note of the film's complexity, their response to its ambitious form has been mixed. Janet Maslin, in *The New York Times*, finds the film's narrative akin to a crystal, whose "cold, hard facets (are studied) with a somber, penetrating wisdom that is the film's main reward." But even she finds the film's dramatic center, the sudden death of Ivan, as lacking the tragic impact required to hold the "many-layered film" together. Similarly, while John Anderson, in *Newsday*, praises the "revelations and questions (in) each concentric circle of the story," James Verniere in *The Boston Herald* finds the flopping "back and forth in time switching narrators . . . (shedding) little light and sometimes (muting) the rumbling face-offs between two lovers or siblings." In a similar vein, Barbara Schulgasser in *The San Francisco Examiner* finds Juliette's transformation towards the end "unexplained and utterly noncredible."

All said, the most lavish praise garnered by the film must surely be from Edward Guthmann in the *San Francisco Chronicle*, who believes that Andre Techine "is filling the void left by the deaths of Truffaut and Louis Malle, and ought to be considered his country's finest humanist filmmaker."

Thieves, Techine's thirteenth feature, was selected to be the Centerpiece of the 1996 New York Film Festival.

—*Vivek Adarkar*

REVIEWS

The Boston Herald. January 17, 1997.
Boxoffice. July, 1996, p. 87.
Chicago Tribune. January 27, 1997, p. 5.
Entertainment Weekly. February 7, 1997, p. 52.
Los Angeles Times. December 27, 1996, p. F2.
The New York Times. October 5, 1996, p. 13.
Newsday. December 27, 1996.
San Francisco Chronicle. January 17, 1997.
The San Francisco Examiner. January 17, 1997.
Variety. May 27, 1996, p. 67.
Village Voice. December 31, 1996, p. 70.

A Thin Line Between Love and Hate

She's had it with bad boys. Now it's time to get even.—Movie tagline

" . . . an African-American *Fatal Attraction* with the twist that it's harder on the man than on his dangerously scorned woman."—Roger Ebert, *Chicago Sun-Times*

"It's hilarious! It's exciting! It's wonderful!"—Sylvia Flanagan, *Jet Magazine*

"You'll laugh your head off while your hair stands on end."—Bonnie Churchill, *National News Syndicate*

"Funny, frightening, and fantastic!"—Bill Brogoli, *Westwood One*

Box Office: **$34,767,836**

A *Thin Line Between Love and Hate* is a self-proclaimed remake of *Fatal Attraction* (1987), with director Martin Lawrence casting himself as the star chauvinist. As smooth-talking Darnell, a ladies man par excellence, he exudes a crude charm. He is the kind of man who keeps coming on to a woman even after she rejects him, and his persistence pays off. At least some women succumb—not out of love but because they seem to need the flattery or the attention. Darnell is a heartbreaker, but he is not violent or abusive in a physical sense. Rather, his smart-aleck demeanor makes the audience yearn for his comeuppance, and when it arrives, it is greeted with claps and laughs at a richly anticipated reckoning.

Darnell is ambitious. He wants every good looking woman who interests him. He wants to be a partner-owner of Chocolate City, the club for which he works. He seduces women, giving them VIP cards for special privileges at the club. But he is also caught in a self-contradiction—worrying about what other men might attempt with his little sister and anxious about what Mia (Regina King), his childhood sweetheart, thinks of him. Evidently, Darnell has some decent instincts, but it is just too easy for him to get by conning women.

Then Darnell sees Brandi (Lynn Whitfield) step out of her limousine. This beautiful, elegant, woman is his idea of class, and his appetite is only stimulated when she scornfully rejects his advances. Darnell does everything to get this ice-lady's attention. He shows up at her real estate firm with flowers and is thrown out before he gets a chance to romance her. Then he sets up an appointment with her to show him a mansion he cannot possibly afford. Like other women, Brandi sees through him, but little by little she is taken with his persistence. The guy won't quit—even riding a horse (for the first time) that nearly gets him severely injured.

Movie title is taken from a 1971 R&B song sung by the Persuaders and remade in 1984 by the Pretenders.

Darnell's talent is to get women to think he really wants them, and it is almost irresistible—the idea that this man will do just about anything to win her heart. Once she melts, she becomes like the Glenn Close character in *Fatal Attraction*, obsessed with her man. The trouble is that there is little tension in the plot or in Darnell's character. The best Lawrence can do with his character is indicate that Brandi is too much for Darnell and that he yearns for the simpler but more sensible Mia.

Even when Darnell realizes that Brandi won't let go, he is macho enough to suppose he can "handle it." He finally admits defeat in the funniest scene of the film, when he discovers that Brandi has removed all four wheels from his prized sports car. He sits at the wheel in frustration saying this woman has stripped him right down to his tires.

A desperate Darnell drops his engagement to Mia, but it is a gesture that comes too late and it does not pacify Brandi. It would be unwise to rehearse the film's final frames or to explain the price Darnell has to pay for his duplicity. What little suspense and action the film has is contained here. Besides, the film's opening scene pretty much shows what happens to Darnell. The only question is whether or not he will survive—or like the narrator in *Sunset Boulevard* (1950) is actually telling his story after his murder.

Lynn Whitfield is sensational as Brandi. There is nothing new in the writing of her role—indeed a lesser actress would have exposed the shallowness of her character. Lawrence's acting is too much on one note and his newfound moral complexity is not very convincing. He is a hustler who supposedly learns his lesson. This is rather tame, hackneyed stuff. One of the better moments comes when Brandi drives by Darnell's house and she has it out not only with Darnell but with his feisty mother, played with gumption by Della Reese. Reese's spot-on performance is every bit as good as Irma P. Hall's in *A Family Thing* (1996). What is it about older black women? They speak with an authority that is electrifying. They have become the soothsayers and truthtellers of contemporary cinema—no longer sentimentalized, but strong, dignified, no-nonsense conveyers of folk wisdom and experience.

—*Carl Rollyson*

CREDITS

Darnell: Martin Lawrence
Brandi: Lynn Whitfield
Mia: Regina King
Tee: Bobby Brown
Ma Wright: Della Reese
Smitty: Roger E. Mosley

Origin: USA
Released: 1996
Production: Doug McHenry, George Jackson for a You Go Boy! Productions and Savoy Pictures production; released by New Line Cinema
Direction: Martin Lawrence
Screenplay: Martin Lawrence, Bentley Kyle Evans, Kenny Buford, and Kim Bass
Cinematography: Francis Kenny
Editing: John Carter
Music: Roger Troutman
Production design: Simon Dobbin
Art direction: David Lazan
Set decoration: Tessa Posnansky
Costume design: Eduardo Castro
Sound: David Barr Yaffe, Robert Allan Wald
Casting: Mary Gail Artz, Barbara Cohen
MPAA rating: R
Running Time: 108 minutes

REVIEWS

Chicago Tribune. April 8, 1996, p. 1.
Entertainment Weekly. April 12, 1996, p. 49.
USA Today. April 3, 1996, p. 7D.
Variety. April 1, 1996, p. 55.
Village Voice. April 16, 1996, p. 82.

Three Lives and Only One Death; Trois Vies et Une Seule Mort

"A brilliant comedy . . . sexy . . . elegantly surreal . . . Marcello Mastroianni in one of the richest performances of his career."—Stephen Holden, *New York Times*

"Exhilarating! In my book, Best Actor goes to Mastroianni for his foxy performance . . . If you're lucky, the film becomes your life to live."—Georgia Brown, *Village Voice*

Box Office: $110,838

Like a set of Chinese boxes, one hiding within the other, Raul Ruiz' latest film fable introduces us to three levels of filmic reality.

Inside the largest box, we find a storyteller (Pierre Bellemare), within a state-of-the-art recording studio, reading aloud a tale set in the year 1999. Then, the box within opens to reveal Paris, and the story's supporting characters leading their humdrum lives. But there is an even smaller box, which lets us into the film's secret sanctum: the three fantastic 'lives' led by the protagonist of the story being read.

In the first 'life,' Mateo Strano (Marcello Mastroianni), a travelling salesman, accosts Andre Parisi (Feodor Atkine) on the most ordinary Sunday morning of his life. After waking up with a hangover, Andre steps out to get his cigarettes, while promising his wife, Maria (Marisa Paredes), to bring back some bread and tomatoes. As he steps into the sunlight, he seems to wince. Not knowing why, he finds himself looking up at an apartment with a rental sign in the window. Then, as he is waiting in line before a counter in a bar, the man in front of him, none other than Mateo, turns round and starts a conversation. Despite Andre's taciturn civility, the kindly gray Mateo orders a bottle of champagne and insists that Andre help him celebrate his winnings at the race track. Claiming to be starved for company, Mateo, it seems, wants nothing more than a listener. He is even prepared to pay a thousand francs an hour, and promptly inserts the bills into the front pockets of Andre's overalls. The deal struck, if only for an hour, Mateo gradually reveals himself to be no stranger at all, but Maria's first husband, whom Andre had presumed dead, and who has now returned after an absence of twenty years.

Like Andre, we become transfixed as the film gradually lures us away from the mundane, and towards the uncanny. As he speaks, Mateo's bizarre memories of his time with Maria now begin to come alive. "You fell out of love?" Andre asks. Mateo denies it, adding, "I love her more than ever."

Then, as the even smaller Chinese box opens, Mateo recounts how he stepped out of the apartment he was sharing with Maria one ordinary morning, twenty years ago, and became drawn to a rental sign in a window. Upon finding the large two-story apartment going for a song, Mateo promptly snapped it up. Then before he could even tell Maria, its unfurnished space began to seem a 'twilight zone.' As Mateo claims he once did, we see its walls shifting, expanding, restructuring the interior design. Mateo then found that in the neighborhood bar, those whom he had known for years ignored his presence. This led Mateo to cling to his solitude, and move into the apartment by himself.

As Mateo recounts it, that very night, he became privy to the world of the tiny, mean fairies. Their voices woke him from his sleep. Their miniature Paris could be glimpsed through the floor, and between corners. Mateo could even see himself stepping out to buy cigarettes. This filmic rendition of the otherworldly must surely rank as one of the most insightful uses of digital technology.

Waking up the next morning, Mateo found that twenty years of his life had gone by. "Tell me again," Andre says, by now twelve thousand francs richer. "You say you spent twenty years in a fairy house?"

"Just one night!" Mateo insists.

Hesitantly, Andre agrees to visit the surreal world of Mateo's apartment. However, when Mateo points to fairies, Andre sees only chirping chicks, but says nothing. It soon becomes clear that what Mateo has been after all along is an exchange of pasts. He wants Andre to live in his apartment, so that he can return home to Maria. Andre's response is to laugh out loud, then return the money. But then, when he tries to leave, Mateo takes a hammer and creeps up from behind. Andre then reappears, bleeding, with the hammer sticking out of his bald pate, yet oblivious of it, as though some spell cast over him has neutralized the pain. Instead of writhing in agony, Andre casually sits down and opens a leftist newspaper.

It should be pointed out that such idiosyncratic departures from verisimilitude, common to Ruiz' other films, are here confined to just this scene. Even so, this instance of the outright nonsensical is enough to detract from the ambiguity the film has skillfully established. While we may choose not to believe Mateo's story, or his flights of fancy, the actions of the dying Andre, howsoever symbolic the filmmaker's intent, can only appear a 'black hole' within an otherwise engrossing film narrative.

As it happens, it is only when Andre sees himself in the mirror that he collapses, and presumably dies. We then see his lifeless body lying amongst the chicks, before Mateo finds a place for it under the stones of his front yard.

The film now leaps back to the larger Chinese box of everyday life in Paris. The next morning, Mateo sets out to reclaim Maria, who welcomes him back into her life, without asking any questions. Though Andre has been away for only a day, she is certain he will not return. She then shows Mateo the baby girl she has adopted. As the two look down at the sleeping infant, the film returns to the largest of the Chinese boxes: the storyteller in the recording studio, who adds the final touch, "And so, Mateo Strano returned home and lived there quietly till the day he died."

To describe the film's narrative largely in terms of the first 'life' in its title may seem disproportionate, but the other two lives pall in comparison. They are revealed in the same manner, and even follow similar paths of disavowal of institutional status by the central character, but without resulting in any innovations of filmic form. Nor does the fact that they crisscross with each other make up for their relative lack of originality in the dramatic motifs they espouse. The first of the film's promised "Three Lives" thus remains a hard act to follow.

In the 'life' of Professor George Vickers, a 69-year-old bachelor, living with his ailing mother in a stately apartment, the fantastic takes the form of a "strange force" from within. On an ordinary morning, while climbing the marble steps of the Sorbonne, on his way to deliver a lecture in the arcane subject of 'negative anthropology,' he decides to cast off the institutional yoke of both the university and the family. Taking up the life of a tramp, he becomes friends with a prostitute, Tania (Anna Galiena, a Kirstie Alley look-alike), who is enamored by the writings of Carlos Castaneda, whom George decries as a fraud. Tania later turns out to be a corporate president driven to prostitution by a perverted husband (Jacques Pieiller). Despite sharing six months of passion, George and Tania's relationship ends in a friendly parting.

The film's third 'life' belongs to 70-year-old Luc Allamand (Mastroianni), a successful businessman who, posing as a secret benefactor, bestows upon a struggling young couple, Martin and Cecile (Melvil Poupaud and Chiara Mastroianni, the star's daughter) the gift of a huge mansion and money. In return, all Luc seems to want is the privilege of serving them as a butler. As this 'life' begins to unfold, we learn that the couple are being spied upon by George as the tramp. This explains Martin, as a house painter, being hired by Maria, who uses him to fill the lonely hours while Mateo's business keeps him away. Similarly, Cecile is interviewed for the position of Tania's secretary, upon the recommendation of George the tramp. Luc's generosity eventually sees the young couple into a mansion, where he awaits them as Bell, the butler. However, when he starts entertaining the beggar friends cultivated by George the tramp, and when Cecile, now pregnant, overhears the beggars planning to do away with them, she and Martin flee the palatial estate. Eventually, they come to know that it is their infant baby daughter that their benefactor is really after. In return for an assured monthly stipend, they hand over the baby to Luc, who then proceeds to leave it in front of Maria's door, thereby linking the third 'life' with the first.

Luc's own 'life,' however, starts to fall apart when he stumbles upon his sixth wife, the ravishing young Helene (Ariel Dombasle), an opera singer, in the arms of her accompanist (Jean Badin). To make matters worse, the various deceptions Luc has been practicing in his past 'lives' now threaten to undo him, owing to the villainy of Tania's jealous husband, who has been spying on him all along, and attempts to expose him through anonymous letters.

This so disorients Luc that he finds himself flitting from one 'life' to the other. We see him with Maria as Mateo, then with Tania as George, then with Cecile as Bell, before he returns to Helene as Luc. Then, even these divisions give way as his condition worsens. When he is with Tania as George, the mere sound of a bell is enough to make him start behaving like Bell, the butler. In a surreal twist, he even meets up with little Carlos (Bastien Vincent), who is meant to evoke Luc as a child.

The film juggles these 'lives' to form an amusing lattice of subplots, including one involving a business associate (Jean-Yves Gautier), who attempts to cure Luc with the help of a radical psychoanalyst (Smain). A resolution is at-

CREDITS

Mateo Strano/Georges Vickers/Butler/Luc Allamand: Marcello Mastroianni
Tania: Anna Galiena
Maia: Marisa Paredes
Martin: Melvil Poupaud
Cecile: Chiara Mastroianni
Helene: Arielle Dombasle
Andre: Feodor Atkine

Origin: France
Released: 1995
Production: Paulo Branco for a Madragoa Filmes, Gemini Films, and La Sept Cinema production; released by New Yorker Films
Direction: Raoul Ruiz
Screenplay: Raoul Ruiz, Pascal Bontizer
Cinematography: Laurent Machuel
Editing: Rodolfo Wedeless
Music: Jorge Arriagada
Production design: Luc Chalon
Sound: Lauren Poirier, Gerard Rousseau
MPAA rating: Unrated
Running Time: 123 minutes

tempted when everyone is brought together at the climactic rendezvous during which Cecile is revealed as Luc's daughter. But this is no denouement, since in front of her, he changes into George the tramp. Maria, Tania and Helene, also called to the same place, then find a desperate Luc shooting at them, but ensure a safe getaway.

The film then ends with Luc strolling with little Carlos beside the Seine in the evening light. The storyteller's voice-over informs us that Mateo, George, Bell, Luc and little Carlos all died on the same day, August 30, 1999, "in the same place, at the same time, for they all inhabited the same body."

Critics by and large have found *Three Lives* witty and entertaining, but have refrained from making sense of it as a visionary statement. Instead, the death of its star seems to have taken precedence. Peter Stack, in the *San Francisco Chronicle*, notes the irony in the film opening in that city the day after Mastroianni's death, since the film "deals with death as both pretense and reality."

—*Vivek Adarkar*

REVIEWS

The Boston Herald. November 27, 1996.
Boxoffice. March, 1997, p. 38.
The New York Times. October 9, 1996, p. C15.
San Francisco Chronicle. December 20, 1996.
Variety. May 27, 1996, p. 69.
The Village Voice. October 15, 1996.

A Time to Kill

"A lawyer and his assistant fighting to save a father on trial for murder. A time to question what they believe. A time to doubt what they trust. And no time for mistakes. Experience a time you'll never forget.—Movie tagline

"A searing, enthralling 10. The best Grisham yet."—Susan Granger, *CRN International*

"A must-see! Another brilliant film by Joel Schumacher. Riveting!"—Jim Ferguson, *Prevue Channel*

"Stirring, compelling, entertaining."—Peter Travers, *Rolling Stone*

"One of the year's most powerful films! Superbly acted and extremely compelling."—Jeffrey Lyons, *Sneak Previews*

"The best movie of the season."—Jules Peimer, *WKDM-AM*

"Gripping, passionate, electrifying! Bullock, Jackson, McConaughey and Spacey are brilliant. The best Grisham yet!"—Kathryn Kinney, *WPIX-TV*

"An emotional firestorm!"—Pat Collins, *WWOR-TV*

Box Office: **$108,766,007**

As Joel Siegel rightly pointed out on *Good Morning America* (July 28), *A Time to Kill* was the first Oscar-worthy film of the 1996 Summer season. As adapted from John Grisham's first novel published in 1989 (and written well before *The Firm*) by director Joel Schumacher and screenwriter Akiva Goldsman, it tells a story of racial justice in the Deep South, a story tied to what would seem to be a justification for vigilantism and homicide.

In his Introduction to the movie-tie-in edition of his novel, Grisham explains how, as a young lawyer, he "stumbled upon a horrible trial in which a young girl testified against a man who brutally raped her." Grisham wondered what he would do if she were his daughter: "As I watched her suffer before the jury, I wanted personally to shoot the rapist." Grisham decided to explore "what an all-white jury would do to a black father who did what every juror would want to do" under similar circumstances. In the process, he builds a morally suspect case for justifiable homicide.

Obsessed with the idea of a father's retribution, Grisham, who describes himself as a "street lawyer" who "represented people, never banks or insurance companies or big corporations," began to write the novel in his spare time. The novel was partly autobiographical in that Jake Brigance (Matthew McConaughey) is exactly the sort of lawyer Grisham considered himself to be. Because of this personal link, Schumacher had to persuade Grisham to turn over the movie rights for the book, but he was finally persuaded that Schumacher would treat the source respectfully. Grisham later testified on national television that this was the best film version of any of his novels. Grisham cannot be entirely objective, however, since he is listed as one of the film's producers.

The story begins with cracker rednecks on a drunken rampage in a pick-up truck in rural Mississippi. The driver, Billy Ray Cobb, had served time on a drug charge (in the novel) at Parchman Farm, the state penitentiary. They kidnap a ten-year-old black child, Tonya Hailey, whom they brutalize, then

A Time to Kill examines vigilante justice when young attorneys Jake Brigance (Matthew McConaughey) and Ellen Roark (Sandra Bullock) take on the case of a black man accused of killing two white men.

rape. After they have finished with her, they throw her off a bridge, leaving her for dead, but she survives and is hospitalized. Enraged, her father, Carl Lee Hailey (Samuel L. Jackson), takes the law into his own hands and murders the two rapists at City Hall, when they are being taken to court.

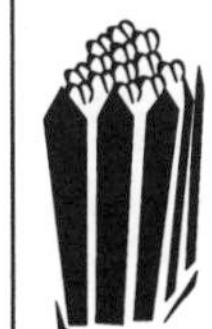

"Until we can see each other as equals, justice is never going to be even-handed."—Jake Brigance

Jake Brigance agrees to become his defense council in the politically-charged trial that follows. District Attorney Rufus Buckley (Kevin Spacey) has ambitions of running for governor, and the trial becomes a means of showcasing his brilliance. Ford County, as described in the novel and film, was seventy-five percent white, unlike surrounding counties that were predominantly black and where Carl Lee would be more likely to face a jury of his peers; but the judge refuses Jake's request for a change of venue. Sleazy Judge Omar Noose (Patrick McGoohan) and Rufus Buckley are clearly in cahoots to make Jake look like a fool, since he insists on pleading temporary insanity for his client, whom they promise to send to the gas chamber if he does not plead guilty.

Meanwhile, the community turns on Jake and his family, branding them "nigger-lovers," and then the Klan is called in by Billy Ray Cobb's brother Freddie (Kiefer Sutherland). First crosses are burned, then, during an angry confrontation, the Grand Dragon himself is ignited by a firebomb. Jake's house is burnt down, but, fortunately, by that time Jake had sent his wife Carla (Ashley Judd) and their daughter out of town to stay with her parents. The Klan does capture Jake's hotshot researcher Ellen Roark (Sandra Bullock) and beats her up, but she is rescued mysteriously. A possible romance between Jake and Ellen is suggested, but nothing comes of that.

The rest of the film takes the form of a racially charged extended courtroom drama. The NAACP wants to take over the defense with a team of northern lawyers identified as the "death squad," but Carl Lee chooses to stay with Jake and forces a local minister who has raised funds for Carl Lee's defense (and his own glory) to turn over the money to Carl Lee's family so that they can survive and so that Jake's expenses can be paid. The question is whether or not Jake can successfully defend his client against a prejudiced, redneck jury. The foreman clearly wants an early "guilty" judgment. The District Attorney wants to use the trial to further his political ambitions.

The odds are against Jake, assisted by his divorce-lawyer friend Harry Rex Vonner (Oliver Platt), his drunken mentor Lucien Wilbanks (Donald Sutherland) and Ellen Roark (Bullock), a Boston-born law student from "Ole Miss," who volunteers to help. By himself, Jake seems to be outclassed, but the verdict is never seriously in doubt. It is also doubtful that family-man Jake would have an affair with Ellen while his wife is out of town. Her flirting with him is merely a tease to keep the audience interested.

The story waves its civil-rights banner energetically. The film seems to be set in the present, though the atmosphere depicted seems to be outdated by at least thirty years. The film was shot in Canton, Mississippi, a town of just over 10,000 people, some fifteen miles north of Jackson, the state capital. With its imposing antebellum courthouse and square, it doubles easily for the town of Clanton Grisham invented for the novel. The film seems to enter a time warp, both older and deeper than the current South.

The problem with this film is in the motivation that drives the characters. At first Jake shuns Ellen's offer to provide free help, even though she is obviously razor-sharp. She is an idealist who hates the death penalty, but she later discovers Jake does not share her idealism at all. Sandra Bullock agreed to take this secondary role, a good career move, since she emerges after Jackson as the film's strongest screen presence,

AWARDS AND NOMINATIONS

Golden Globe Award Nominations: Best Supporting Actor (Jackson)

managing to steal scenes with her own spirited charm against newcomer McConaughey, who barely manages to hold his own with her. Terrence Rafferty skewered the actor in *The New Yorker* as having been "untimely ripped from his obscurity, delivered before his talents have come to term."

Ashley Judd as Jake's worried wife Carla criticizes him for grandstanding and appears to be a little bitchy when she makes the perfectly sensible decision to leave Clanton when the situation heats up. Later, she comes back to stand by her man and espouses an apologetic line, claiming she now understands that Jake was simply trying to do the right thing.

Before selling his first novel to the screen, John Grisham made certain he had co-casting approval (along with the director) on the lead role of Jake Brigance.

Carl Lee chooses Jake as his defense lawyer simply because Jake, apparently a novice, once represented his cousin. Later on, Carl Lee tells Jake that he wanted him to represent him because he considered Jake one of "them," since he believes all white men are racists at heart: "We're not friends," he explains to Jake. "We're on different sides of the line. Our daughters are never gonna play together." At the end of the film Jake proves him wrong by bringing his daughter to a picnic at the Hailey house.

Samuel L. Jackson asserted his own star power by requesting that screenwriter Akiva Goldsman give Carl Lee more "wisdom and warmth" than the character had in the novel, according to *Entertainment Weekly.* In the film, for example, "it is Carl Lee, not Jake, who leads the fight against a greedy minister" and representatives of the NAACP who want to take over the defense. Jackson also wanted Carl Lee to be less chauvinistic in the film: "I grew up in a house full of women," Jackson told *Entertainment Weekly*, "and they were the dominant people."

Matthew McConaughey, said to resemble a young Paul Newman (though Hal Hinson also saw a resemblance to a "young Brando," who is not exactly Newman's twin), is well cast as Jake as an awkward boy who means well, and Samuel L. Jackson is brilliant as Carl Lee. Sandra Bullock is smart and perky. Though her role is not as big as one might have wished, she could earn an Academy Award nomination for Best Supporting Actress. Kevin Spacey is also excellent as the District Attorney; he is perhaps the most underrated actor of his generation, but his reputation is growing. Patrick McGoohan is equally excellent as the Judge, but it would be good to see more of him. The Sutherlands, Donald and Kiefer, come and go flamboyantly from time to time. Kiefer Sutherland's Klansman is a pretty transparent villain. Charles S. Dutton leaves a strong imprint as black Sheriff Ozzie Walls, as does Anthony Heald as a sleazy psychiatrist who has, Jake discovers, never in several trials found the insanity defense justifiable. Heald is recognizable as Dr. Frederick Chilton from *The Silence of the Lambs* (1991), the "friend" Dr. Hannibal Lecter is having for dinner at the end.

The film succeeds on the basis of its strong cast and the emotive direction of Joel Schumacher, who has a talent for displaying characters living on the edge under extreme emotional duress. Schumacher was drawn to another character who was driven to extreme violence in *Falling Down* (1993), but there was never any question that D-FENS, the central character of that film played by Michael Douglas, was insane. The man was a walking bomb, known only by his license plate, an unemployed defense worker maladjusted to contemporary life and waiting to explode. When D-FENS reacts defensively like a vigilante, the audience is expected to understand, if not to cheer. Carl Lee gets a very similar treatment in *A Time to Kill*, but Carl Lee is not crazy.

The film opened to mixed reviews. Stephen Hunter of the *Baltimore Sun* ridiculed the film as "high-grade, solid gold hokum" that left "no stone and no cliché . . . unturned in its quest for utter mediocrity and lowest-common-denominator crowd-pleasing." Gary Arnold of *The Washington Times* objected to the film's "near-epic ineptitude and self-righteousness." Although Carl Lee is "clearly a murderer," he "is never seriously threatened with conviction." Arnold found the murder trial "a cut-and-dried preamble to moral vindication" and sneers that Jake ultimately

CREDITS

Jake Brigance: Matthew McConaughey
Carl Lee Hailey: Samuel L. Jackson
Ellen Roark: Sandra Bullock
Rufus Buckley: Kevin Spacey
Ethel Twitty: Brenda Fricker
Lucien Wilbanks: Donald Sutherland
Carla Brigance: Ashley Judd
Harry Rex Vonner: Oliver Platt
Judge Omar Noose: Patrick McGoohan

Origin: USA
Released: 1996
Production: Arnon Milchan, Michael Nathanson, Hunt Lowry, and John Grisham for a Regency Enterprises production; released by Warner Bros.
Direction: Joel Schumacher
Screenplay: Akiva Goldsman; based on the novel by John Grisham
Cinematography: Peter Menzies, Jr.
Editing: William Steinkamp
Music: Elliot Goldenthal
Production design: Larry Fulton
Art direction: Richard Toyon
Set design: Keith P. Cunningham, Maya Shimoguchi
Costume design: Ingrid Ferrin
Sound: Petur Hliddal
Casting: Mali Finn
MPAA rating: R
Running Time: 150 minutes

"clinches the case by making himself cry during his own summation."

With reason, viewers might be troubled by the film's scrambled moral framework. The film defends an act of murder. Ellen is against the death penalty, but Carl Lee has taken the law into his own hands and served as executioner for those who molested and hurt his daughter. In a moral universe, should such a man be found "not guilty" after he has taken two lives? The killings were clearly premeditated, by Carl Lee's own admission.

The film is timely in the way it recalls the legacy of O.J. Simpson. The plot demonstrates how the law can be beat and manipulated in favor of a black man who, at least in the film, literally gets away with murder. When the "not guilty" verdict is taken out to the streets by a young black girl, one recalls the exuberance that followed the Simpson verdict in black America.

As Terrence Rafferty concluded in *The New Yorker*, although the film "never questions the novel's most dubious argument—Grisham's defense of vigilante justice—it nonetheless presumes to set the audience on the true path of racial understanding." If vigilante justice is the issue here, then a better director than Joel Schumacher could not have been found.

—*James M. Welsh*

REVIEWS

Baltimore Sun. July 24, 1996, p. El.
Entertainment Weekly. August 2, 1996, p. 40.
Movieline. September, 1996, p. 36.
New York Times. July 24, 1996, p. C9.
New Yorker. July 29, 1996, p. 75.
Newsweek. July 29, 1996, p. 68.
Premiere. August, 1996, p. 74.
Time. July 29, 1996, p. 76.
Variety. July 15, 1996, p. 37.
Washington Post. July 24, 1996, p. B1.
Washington Post Weekend. July 26, 1996, p. 31.
Washington Times Metropolitan Times. July 24, 1996, p. C11.

Tin Cup

Golf pro. Love amateur.—Movie tagline

"A hole in one from the heart."—Bill Diehl, *ABC Radio Network*

"Enormously enjoyable."—David Sheehan, *CBS-TV*

"Rousing! Thrilling!"—Owen Gleiberman, *Entertainment Weekly*

"A wonderful new romantic comedy."—Peter Rainer, *Los Angeles Magazine*

"A solid gold romantic comedy. Costner and Russo are sensational together."—Bill Zwecker, *NBC-TV*

"Touching and funny. Costner and Russo work together beautifully."—Terrence Rafferty, *The New Yorker*

Box Office: $53,888,896

After venturing into the darker side of sports with *Cobb* (1994), a warts-only portrait of baseball legend Ty Cobb that was loved by some reviewers, hated by as many more, and ignored by audiences, writer-director Ron Shelton returns to sports comedy with *Tin Cup*. Shelton is the acknowledged master of this genre with such films as *Bull Durham* (1988) and *White Men Can't Jump* (1992), and *Tin Cup* is his most accomplished film since *Bull Durham* as well as star Kevin Costner's best performance since that baseball comedy.

Costner plays Roy "Tin Cup" McAvoy, owner and operator—after a fashion—of a seedy West Texas driving range. Roy has plenty of golf talent but has never accomplished much because of insufficient ambition and discipline. One of the highly entertaining film's many virtues is that it never tries to explain its protagonist. The film not only accepts Roy's eccentricities and limitations but relishes them. In Shelton's highly—some might say excessively—masculine world, men such as Roy do not have "problems"; they have character.

Roy's life changes dramatically when Dr. Molly Griswold (Rene Russo) arrives for golf lessons. (How such a psychologist finds herself at the Salome Wellness Center is also never explained.) Roy is immediately smitten and is not deterred by her obvious superiority nor by her being the lover of David Simms (Don Johnson), a successful professional golfer and Roy's longtime antagonist. Roy even accepts the humiliation of being David's caddy at a local tournament before being fired for failing to resist the chance to show that he can make a shot that Mr. Professional Golf Association cannot.

Impulsiveness and stubbornness are central to Roy's nature. He decides to try to impress Molly by qualifying for the U.S. Open. Playing a qualifying round, he disagrees with Romeo Posar (Cheech Marin), his best friend and caddy, over club selection, and when Romeo breaks the club Roy wants to use, the golfer, to prove he is his own man, breaks all but one of the remaining clubs to make his task even more difficult. This scene and showing up David set up the climactic scene in the well-structured screenplay by Shelton and John Norville. When Roy finally makes it to the big tournament and shocks everyone—particularly the CBS crew televising the event—by leading going into the last round, he faces a moment of truth in which he can take safe shots, like David and all the other golfers who strive to make professional golf predictable and colorless, or he can be the reckless Roy he has always been. Guess which route he chooses.

"This is without a doubt, the most stupidest, silliest, most idiotic grotesquery masquerading as a game that has ever been invented."—Molly about golf

"Waggle it and let the big dog eat."—Roy's golf advice

Only Michael Ritchie, whose films include *Downhill Racer* (1969), *The Bad News Bears* (1976), and *Semi-Tough* (1977), approaches Shelton's skill at delineating the American fascination with sports. While Ritchie's films debunk sports, Shelton's glory in their quirkiness. In *Tin Cup*, he must strip golf of some of its country-club patina to reveal this quality. He does so by setting much of the film at Roy's scruffy driving range and by inhabiting the range with an even scruffier melange of hangers-on. It is difficult to determine which ones are employees and which are merely lazing about since none ever seem to do anything. The contrast with David's slick, pastel world is jolting. If, however, *Tin Cup* fails to attain the same lofty level as *Bull Durham*, it is because golf is not as visually interesting as baseball and because it also lacks the latter sport's mythic overtones.

Shelton also underscores the differences between Roy's and David's milieus with a soundtrack of country and blues songs by such artists as Buddy Guy, Los Lobos, and Mary Chapin Carpenter. This is definitely not country-club music. Unfortunately, the traditional score by William Ross conflicts with these songs. His overly dramatic music for the U.S. Open scenes resembles Miklos Rozsa or John Williams at their most grandiloquent.

Shelton shows how difficult and unpredictable golf is, as when Roy suddenly loses and just as quickly regains his stroke, but as with *Bull Durham*, *Tin Cup* is less a sports movie than a romantic comedy in the great tradition of such films as *Midnight* (1939) and *The Lady Eve* (1941): bringing together, after several ups and downs, two people who, despite seemingly clashing differences of background and temperament, are made for each other. He makes it easy for Molly and Roy to fall in love both by having them attracted by their differences and by slowly revealing that Molly, despite a slightly severe surface, is as confused and contrary as Roy is. Initially bemused by his outlandish behavior, she ends up encouraging it.

Shelton also copies the classic screwball comedy structure of the 1930's and 1940's by having a secondary romance develop between supporting comic characters: Romeo and Doreen (Linda Hart), Roy's former girlfriend who buys the

AWARDS AND NOMINATIONS

Golden Globe Award Nominations: Best Actor-Musical/Comedy (Costner)

CREDITS

Roy "Tin Cup" McAvoy: Kevin Costner
Dr. Molly Griswold: Rene Russo
David Simms: Don Johnson
Romeo Posar: Cheech Marin
Doreen: Linda Hart
Earl: Dennis Burkley
Clint: Lou Myers
Dewey: Rex Linn
Curt: Richard Lineback
Turk: Mickey Jones
Boone: Michael Milhoan
CBS golf analyst: Gary McCord
CBS producer: Frank Chirkinian
CBS announcer: Jim Nantz
ESPN reporter: Jimmy Roberts

Origin: USA
Production: Gary Foster and David Lester for a Regency Enterprises production; released by Warner Brothers
Direction: Ron Shelton
Screenplay: Ron Shelton and John Norville
Cinematography: Russell Boyd
Editing: Paul Seydor and Kimberly Ray
Production design: James Bissell
Art direction: Gae Buckley, Chris Burian-Mohr
Set design: Ric McElvin
Costume design: Carol Oditz
Music: William Ross
Sound: Kirk Francis
Casting: Victoria Thomas, Ed Johnston
MPAA rating: R
Running Time: 105 minutes

driving range to help him finance his quest for Molly. While such a relationship between the goofy caddy and the tough-taking stripper could have been too cutesy, Shelton handles it economically with brief exchanges between the two and a quick glimpse of a tango which signals the beginning of a romance.

Some 23 PGA touring pros are featured in the film including Craig Stadler, Fred Couples, Peter Jacobsen, Corey Pavin, and Phil Mickelson.

As Marin has shown in his work on the "Nash Bridges" television series, he can be a delightful comic performer with impeccable timing. When David sneers at the child's wading pool outside Roy's trailer and asks if it is a Jacuzzi, Romeo, after a pause, proclaims it a spa and proudly raises his head with a smug smirk, easily deflating the golfer's meanness. Johnson, an underrated actor who has never fared particularly well on the big screen, coats David's vicious selfishness with a veneer of charm. It is easy to see why Molly fell for such a superficial cad. Hart ably tries to elevate Doreen above the stripper-with-a-heart-of-gold cliche Shelton has given her to play.

Also noteworthy among the supporting cast are the real-life golfers and broadcasters making cameo appearances. Such sports personalities are usually stiff at pretending to be themselves, but Shelton gives a few the opportunity to create believable characters, especially Gary McCord's zany golfer/golf analyst, who provides satirical commentary when Roy attempts a trick shot from inside a country-club bar, and veteran CBS Sports producer Frank Chirkinian who becomes comically outraged at the audacity of the unknown Roy's upstaging his conservative telecast. Chirkinian and McCord are to be commended for risking letting themselves appear ridiculous.

Tin Cup succeeds most of all because of the perfect performances of Costner and Russo. Costner has chosen too many roles that present him as stiff, as with *The Untouchables* (1987), sentimentally cuddly, as with *Dances with Wolves* (1990), angry, as with *JFK* (1991) and *Wyatt Earp* (1994), or glum, as with *Waterworld* (1995). Except for the complex escaped convict he created for Clint Eastwood's *A Perfect World* (1993), Costner is most effective as a comic performer. Roy recalls Costner's Crash Davis in *Bull Durham* but is less insightful and more rambunctious, a perpetual American adolescent who does whatever feels right at the time. Such a character could easily have been unsympathetic, but Costner injects Roy with considerable aw-shucks, James Stewartesque charm. Costner is at his best when Roy goes to Molly's office ostensibly for therapy but actually to profess his love. Roy knows what he wants to say but not how he is going to say it, and as he stumbles for the right words, Costner peels back the man's cockiness to expose, with slightly embarrassed head down, the sentimental romantic fool lurking within.

Russo plays off Costner well throughout but particularly in this scene. Molly is somewhat uncomfortable with having him in her office to begin with, begins to relax when he identifies his problem as wanting to tell a woman of his feelings, and, after encouraging him to do so, becomes all flustered by discovering she is the object of his affection. The range of emotions Russo displays—she is especially good at shocked amazement—is fitting since Molly is the most well-rounded character she has had the opportunity to portray. The best model-turned-actor since Lauren Bacall, Russo has grown steadily with particularly good work in *Lethal Weapon II* (1992), *In the Line of Fire* (1993), and *Get Shorty* (1995). Her Molly is a walking contradiction: sophisticated yet silly, confident yet uncertain, restrained yet passionate. Russo must make Molly credible for Roy and the entire film to be believable, and she succeeds marvelously. Just as Roy and Molly are made for each other, Russo is perfect for this wonderful role.

—*Michael Adams*

REVIEWS

Christian Science Monitor. August 16, 1996, p. 12.
Entertainment Weekly. August 16, 1996, p. 44.
New York. August 26, 1996, p. 117.
The New York Times. August 16, 1996, p. C1.
The New Yorker. August 12, 1996, p. 78.
Newsweek. August 19, 1996, p. 66.
Time. August 19, 1996, p. 68.
USA Today. August 16, 1996, p. D1.
Village Voice. August 20, 1996, p. 45.
The Wall Street Journal. August 16, 1996, p. A8.

To Gillian on Her 37th Birthday

Some love lasts a lifetime. Real love lasts forever.—Movie tagline

"Irresistibly romantic, one of the year's best."—Dennis Cunningham, *CBS-TV*

"If you believed in *Ghost,* you're going to love this movie!"—Susan Granger, *CRN International*

"A great romantic comedy in the truest sense. It will make you laugh and cry and hug the one you love. Michelle Pfeiffer is luminous."—John Corcoran, *KCAL-TV*

Box Office: $4,188,713

The tragedy of untimely death is as poignant a theme today as it was when Poe wrote "The Raven." But unlike Poe, *To Gillian on Her 37th Birthday* avoids the darker side of grief, provoking our tears but never really capturing our hearts.

To Gillian on Her 37th Birthday is about David Lewis (Peter Gallagher), who lost his beautiful wife Gillian (Michelle Pfeiffer) on Labor Day two years before, when she fell from the mainmast of a sailboat during a daredevil prank. Her death is made more horrible in that her teenage daughter, Rachel (Claire Danes) and her husband were witness to the fatal fall.

The main thrust of the film is that David is unable to accept her death, and two years after, he not only communes with her spirit but he also swims, dances, and frolics with Gillian on the beach each night.

In an effort to keep his beautiful illusion alive, David has made their summer home on Nantucket, where Gillian died, their permanent residence. His behavior verges on madness, and as he runs and laughs with his ghost, his daughter Rachel watches him unseen from the dunes, as she mourns the loss of her only remaining parent. But David is determined to remain in his blissful illusory world, too self-absorbed to see the plight of his sixteen-year-old daughter who is coming of age alone and unguided.

As they did in the past, David has invited Gillian's sister Esther (Kathy Baker) and her husband Paul (Bruce Altman) to visit over Labor Day weekend, ostensibly for the holiday, but really to celebrate what would have been Gillian's 37th birthday, which is also the date of her death.

"What's wrong with marrying for life?"—David

His in-laws arrive on the island with an attractive woman named Kevin Danford (Wendy Crewson), who they hope will seduce David out of his delusions. But their timing is more than bad, it's in bad taste. On the second anniversary of Gillian's death, David has planned the weekend as a sort of posthumous re-creation of past birthdays, replete with their traditional black-tie dinner, a little karaoke, and the annual sand castle competition.

This morbid re-creation of past celebrations thwarts Esther's attempts to bring David back to his senses. Finally, she accuses David of neglecting his daughter in lieu of keeping his fantasy alive and tells him that she has begun proceedings to get custody of Rachel.

Esther and Paul provide the comic relief of the film, with their clever sparring and playful sniping. But their passionless relationship stands in stark relief against the backdrop of David's fantasy love affair, and they are forced to take a good look at their

CREDITS

David Lewis: Peter Gallagher
Gillian Lewis: Michelle Pfeiffer
Rachel Lewis: Claire Danes
Esther Wheeler: Kathy Baker
Paul Wheeler: Bruce Altman
Kevin: Wendy Crewson
Cindy: Laurie Fortier
Joey: Freddie Prinze, Jr.

Origin: USA
Released: 1996
Production: Marykay Powell and David E. Kelley for a RaStar production; released by Triumph Films
Direction: Michael Pressman
Screenplay: David E. Kelley; based on the play by Michael Brady
Cinematography: Tim Suhrstedt
Editing: William Scharf
Music: James Horner
Production design: Linda Pearl
Art direction: Michael Atwell
Set design: Andrew Menzies, Tim Eckel
Costume design: Deborah L. Scott
Sound: David Kirschner
Casting: Lynn Stalmaster
MPAA rating: PG-13
Running Time: 92 minutes

marriage. But like every other denouement in the film, it falls flat. They simply shake their heads and accept their relationship.

Although the film sanitizes the widower's grief into a pop psychology formula, where denial must be dealt with and overcome, the film does succeed in portraying a man whose love for his wife and his need to keep her alive is so real that reality becomes the fantasy world. It is more than a longing for the lost loved one, it is a fulfillment of that longing. The love affair is so perfect that even the viewer is loath to relinquish it for the more practical reality of work and responsibilities.

Michelle Pfeiffer, who plays Gillian, is the wife of producer/screenwriter David E. Kelley.

David's fantasy is more than denial. It is a sort of madness. But this madness, like everything else in the film, is benign. Although David drives his car almost out of control, nothing bad happens, and it is portrayed as amusing. Although his daughter gets drunk for the first time with a boy she hardly knows, Rachel is just a cute drunk. Although Paul makes lecherous advances to Rachel's teenage girlfriend, he never crosses the line, even when invited. Although David interacts nightly on the beach with his dead wife, he never slips over the edge into insanity. If there is any true denial in this film, it is in the denial of the darkness inherent in the plot, where David's hallucinatory behavior is seen as acceptable eccentricity. All the events in the film are diminished into the pale shadows of what they would be in the real world, and even the summoned ghost of Gillian is levelheaded and understanding about her dismissal. The agony is left to the audience, wrenched by a half hour of tearjerking manipulation that would reduce Ivan the Terrible to tears.

If you're up for a good cry, a couple laughs, and some lovely cinematography, *To Gillian* is the answer. But if you want an honest romantic drama that deepens your understanding of what it is to experience a grief that is both passionate and profound, re-read "The Raven". 

—Diane Hatch-Avis

REVIEWS

Boxoffice. October, 1996, p. 44.
Entertainment Today. October 18, 1996.
Entertainment Weekly. October 25, 1996, p. 94.
Hollywood Drama-Logue. October 24-30, 1996, p. 28.
Hollywood Reporter. October 14, 1996, p. 5.
L.A. Weekly. October 18, 1996.
Los Angeles Times. October 18, 1996.
The New York Times. October 18, 1996, p. C22.
People. October 28, 1996, p. 24.
Rolling Stone. October 31, 1996, p. 78.
USA Today. October 18, 1996, p. 5D.
Variety. October 14, 1996, p. 58.
The Village Voice. October 22, 1996, p. 84.
Vogue. November, 1996, p. 158.

Trainspotting

Choose life. Choose a job. Choose a starter home. Choose dental insurance, leisure wear and matching luggage. Choose your future. But why would anyone want to do a thing like that?—Movie tagline

"Massively entertaining."—Graham Fuller, *Interview*

"A terrifically energetic film. A brash comedy . . . all style and attitude with a hip soundtrack."—Kenneth Turan, *Los Angeles Times*

"Hip . . . clever . . . tauntingly decadent and willfully outrageous."—Janet Maslin, *New York Times*

"Electrifying and hilarious."—Peter Travers, *Rolling Stone*

Drugs, crime, and techno music are served up in the Scottish black comedy hit *Trainspotting*.

Box Office: $16,491,080

There are no trains in *Trainspotting*, unless one counts the locomotives printed upon the wallpaper in Mark Renton's bedroom. But in this much hyped film, there are scenes of drug use, drug paroxysms and overdose, sex and graphic nudity, defecation, drinking in pubs ad nauseam, smoking, burglary, violence, and sordid death. And yet, most remarkably of all perhaps, *Trainspotting* boasts a firm foundation of humor, even a vitality belied by so much of the nihilistic activities on-screen.

The film has been a sensation in Britain, and reached the United States with a reputation for its explicit drug content. In a frenetic opening, Renton (Ewan McGregor) and two of his fellow heroin users and pals, Spud (Ewen Bremner) and Sick Boy (Jonny Lee Miller) sprint down Edinburgh's main street. In a voice-over, Renton delivers what will become a trademark of the film: his cynically intelligent commentary on his life and those of his friends. As the gang run from the police, Renton proclaims the values of the middle class, and even why one should adopt those values. Then he asks, "Who needs reasons when you've got heroin?" Heroin, prima facie, is its own reason.

The gang inhabit a squat, and seem to live primarily for their drug use. As they inject themselves with heroin, pleasure is the key note, a point made by the looks on their faces, and in Renton's voice-over. And what pleasure: "Take the best orgasm you ever had, multiply it by a thousand and still you're nowhere near it."

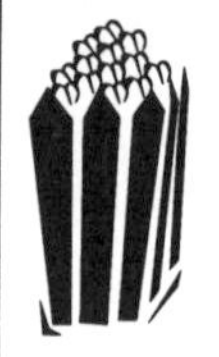

"I hate being Scottish. Some people hate the English, but I don't. They're just wankers. We, on the other hand, are colonized by wankers. We can't even pick a decent culture to be colonized by."—Renton

Yet Renton knows what the drug does to their bodies and their lives, and declares his intention to get off heroin. He makes preparations to go cold turkey by loading a tabletop with cans of food and drink, and he nails his door shut with planks of wood to ensure he will stay inside, away from temptation, during the process. A succeeding shot reveals the broken planks and the open door; Renton cannot quit yet.

The wit and energies displayed in the opening sequences ensnare the viewer. The drug life is not so much celebrated as laid open for inspection, and soon the darker side of addiction is unmistakable.

One of the side effects of heroin use is sudden diarrhea, and Renton, walking the streets, is struck by it. He is forced to use a most appalling bathroom, titled cheekily as the 'filthiest toilet in Scotland.' The sound effects tell us everything we need to know as Renton relieves himself. But what he has forgotten are the opium suppositories he has recently inserted. In a scene that will forever remain in the memory of everyone who sees the film, a desperate Renton reaches into the foul, non-flushable bowl to retrieve them. He plunges his head in, then his body, and he gracefully slides into the bowl, disappears, and is swimming in clear ocean waters. His suppositories are lying with sea pebbles. Joyously he picks them up and swims back to the surface to emerge from the bowl.

Renton now introduces his clean-living friend Tommy (Kevin McKidd), and episode upon episode continues to build the comically renegade nature of the film. With pleasure as the driving force in Renton and his group's lives, scenes in the pub and a nightclub illustrate the grasping for kicks. We meet Begbie (Robert Carlyle) and witness his taste for violence. We see Renton slyly switching a soccer videotape from Tommy's collection with the latter's home video of sex with his girlfriend, and Renton making a play for an attractive young girl as she leaves a nightclub. The girl, Diane (Kelly Macdonald) outwits our hero, but nevertheless allows him to come home with her. A kaleidoscope of sex scenes ensues, with Tommy and his partner searching for their home movie while undressing, with Spud passing out in bed even with a girl ready for him, and with Diane throwing a condom on the bed and beckoning to Renton.

On the morning after, a meek Renton sits down hungrily to breakfast with a man and a woman he assumes are Diane's roommates. In fact, they are her parents, and she is still a schoolgirl in uniform! As for Spud, his bowels have betrayed him, and in his sleep he has covered the bed sheets with his defecation. In a marvelously tasteless scene over the breakfast table, a battle of the sheets with his conquest's mother ends with excretion flying liberally over everyone.

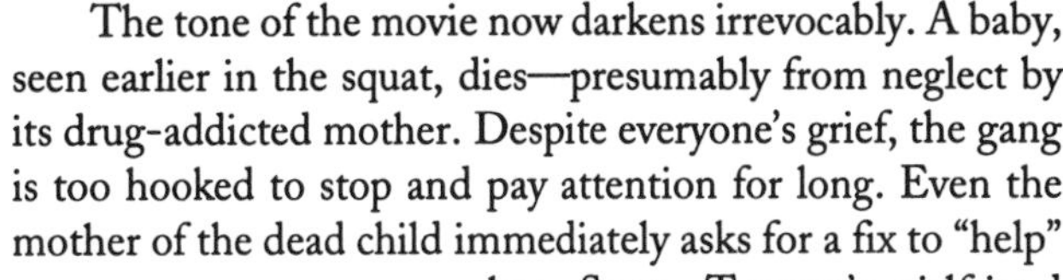
The director, producer, writer, production designer, editor, and cinematographer all previously worked together on the 1994 film *Shallow Grave.*

The tone of the movie now darkens irrevocably. A baby, seen earlier in the squat, dies—presumably from neglect by its drug-addicted mother. Despite everyone's grief, the gang is too hooked to stop and pay attention for long. Even the mother of the dead child immediately asks for a fix to "help" her. Soon, Tommy's girlfriend leaves him, and this precipitates Tommy's decline. Robbery provides some income for drugs until Renton and Spud are caught by the authorities. Spud gets six months in prison, but a contrite Renton is allowed to remain out of jail by enrolling in a methadone program to reduce his addiction. It is not enough to satisfy his craving, and when he caves in and gets a fix, he overdoses. His supplier roughly drags him into a taxi cab, and Renton is delivered to the E.R. to be rescued.

At this point Renton's parents take over and lock him in his room so that he can detox. A series of hallucinations provides a vivid sense of the process of withdrawal. At last, a thin Renton makes it through, and is clean—for now. He visits a sick Tommy, who has tested positive for HIV; Renton has not. In a misguided touch of sympathy, Renton gives his one time drug-free friend some money for a fix.

In an attempt to create a new life for himself, Renton moves to London and gets into the real estate business. He succeeds for a while, but his past soon catches up with him. The increasingly borderline Begbie moves in, followed by Sick Boy, and Renton's life begins to disintegrate. The trio returns to Scotland for Tommy's funeral; he has died prematurely of toxoplasmosis, an AIDS-related death. The evening following the ceremony, the group discusses a drug deal that could make them some nice cash, and Renton agrees to get involved. He even tries some of the smack to test its quality; it is good. Will he become addicted again?

Back in London, the deal is concluded, and the quartet gains four thousand pounds each. A celebration in a pub turns very ugly when Begbie explodes. During the vicious melee, in which Spud is injured, Renton asks Sick Boy if he wants to run off together with the bag of cash; Sick Boy refuses. That night, while his friends sleep, Renton takes off with the loot, ultimately leaving two thousand for Spud in

CREDITS

Mark Renton: Ewan McGregor
Spud: Ewen Bremner
Sick Boy: Jonny Lee Miller
Tommy: Kevin McKidd
Begbie: Robert Carlyle
Diane: Kelly Macdonald

Origin: Great Britain
Released: 1995; 1996
Production: Andrew Macdonald for a Channel 4 Films, Figment Film, and Noel Gay Motion Picture Co. production; released by Miramax/Polygram Filmed Entertainment
Direction: Danny Boyle
Screenplay: John Hodge; based on the novel by Irvine Welsh
Cinematography: Brian Trufano
Editing: Masahiro Hirakubo
Production design: Kave Quinn
Art direction: Tracey Gallacher
Costume design: Rachel Fleming
Sound: Colin Nicolson, Brian Saunders, Ray Merrin, Mark Taylor
Casting: Gail Stevens, Andy Pryor
MPAA rating: R
Running Time: 94 minutes

AWARDS AND NOMINATIONS

Academy Award 1996 Nominations: Best Adapted Screenplay (Hodge)
British Academy Awards 1995: Best Adapted Screenplay (Hodge)
Independent Spirit Awards 1997 Nominations: Foreign Film
Writers Guild of America 1996 Nominations: Adapted Screenplay (Hodge)

a safety deposit box, and a final shot shows him crossing one of London's bridges over the Thames River, looking forward to a new life.

A tidal wave of rave reviews and heated controversy about the film's messages concerning drugs brought *Trainspotting* to these shores. American critics have found much to recommend in the film, stopping short, however, of hailing the motion picture as a masterpiece. And they were amused by the fact that some of the broadly accented Scottish dialogue was re-dubbed for easier comprehension by U.S. audiences.

Newsweek called the film a "romance that is seductive yet repellent, terrifying but hilarious, depressing and exhilarating . . . a lousy piece of propaganda..a masterful waltz on the wild side." *The Los Angeles Times* gave high praise to actor Ewan McGregor, the "marvellous words" of John Hodge's screenplay, adapted from Irvine Welsh's best-selling novel of the same name, and declared that "this is a film that creates smiles out of things that can in no way be described as funny."

Despite the fact that the film's situations and characters are rooted in the grittiest of reality in dead-end Edinburgh, *Trainspotting* revels in its non-realistic sequences. The above mentioned toilet scene and Renton's withdrawal are two of the most notable surreal episodes. Another scene that lodges in the mind is Renton's overdose. He feels himself—and we see him—sinking into the ground to be transported like a coffin to the hospital. The soundtrack, with gleeful irony, plays Lou Reed's "Perfect Day."

Danny Boyle's direction is kinetic and often playful. John Hodge's screenplay is sharp, and there are knowing, committed, appealing and also shocking performances throughout, all contributing to *Trainspotting*'s undeniable appeal. In the main role, McGregor is haunted, vulnerable, and empathetic, even when he is driven by the demons of addiction, lust or greed. Bremner, Miller and McKidd deliver skilled support, and Kelly Macdonald is a welcome feminine presence in this very male film. Robert Carlyle, the most familiar actor to British audiences (before the movie catapulted McGregor into the limelight), gives a horrifying picture of character destruction without the use of drugs.

It should be recognized that the energy of the film does not—perhaps could not—sustain itself for the entire length of the proceedings. The madcap humor and adventures early on transition into a depiction of addiction and recovery, including Renton's vivid detoxification. The final section of the film is rather conventional, settling into a less inspiring question of whether or not "the boys" can pull off the drug deal. As such, the conclusion of the film takes something away from the twisted invention of what precedes. But the residue of *Trainspotting*'s visual inventiveness, its acrid social commentary, its black wit and unflinching look at the deathly joyride of heroin is a clear affirmation, and ultimately a condemnation, of the needle and the damage done.

—*Paul B. Cohen*

REVIEWS

Boxoffice Magazine. July, 1996, p. 86.
Chicago Tribune. July 26, 1996, p. 5.
Detroit Free Press. July 21, 1996, P. H1.
Detroit News. July 26, 1996, p. D1.
Entertainment Weekly. July 19, 1996, p. 56.
Los Angeles Times. July 19, 1996, p. F1.
New York Times. July 19, 1996, p. C3.
The New Yorker. July 22, 1996, p. 78.
Newsweek. July 15, 1996, p. 52.
People. July 29, 1996, p. 17.
Rolling Stone. August 8, 1996, p. 67.
Sight and Sound. March, 1996, p. 52.
USA Today. July 19, 1996, p. D1.
Variety. February 12, 1996, p. 79.
Village Voice. July 23, 1996, p. 66.

Trees Lounge

A story about one man's search . . . for who knows what.—Movie tagline

"Sharp . . . memorable . . . the most kinetic cast since *Pulp Fiction.*"—Thelma Adams, *New York Post*

"Steve Buscemi . . . makes a striking directorial feature-film debut."—Stephen Holden, *New York Times*

"Steve Buscemi's directorial debut is a smashing success . . . Excellent."—Jim Ferguson, *Prevue Channel*

Box Office: $698,988

Steve Buscemi founds his directorial career with a self-described "speculative autobiography" that captures the downward spiral in the life of an aging Gen-Xer living in a small, working-class Long Island suburb. Buscemi's ample knowledge of the subject matter and substantial acting experience in numerous and successful indies (*Mystery Train* [1989], *In the Soup* [1992], *Reservoir Dogs* [1992]) has aided him in creating an honest and accurately told story of failure in a small town. The reality and subtle, dark humor which Buscemi injects into the characters, situations, and emotions is the film's greatest strength, and is matched by the performances of the diverse cast.

The Assembly Bar in Queens substitutes for the original Trees Lounge, which had been converted into a sports bar.

Tommy (Buscemi) is an unemployed mechanic who lives above and frequents the titular Trees Lounge, a local watering hole filled with a colorless assortment of locals and losers. The initial scene has Connie (Carol Kane), the establishment's sympathetic bartender, kicking Tommy awake from the booth he's napping in so that she may close up. She seems to be the only person who still tolerates Tommy's ways, and it is her he turns to for support. Further scenes serve to reinforce the fact that Tommy's life is quickly going nowhere. A vengeful Tommy stalks the garage where his brother Raymond works (Michael Buscemi) and where he also used to be employed, making his unwelcome presence known to the garage's owner Rob (Anthony LaPaglia), his former best friend who stole his girlfriend and fired him. He searches for a new job, but cannot even fix his own car and is turned away everywhere he looks. One night the drunken Tommy hits on an attractive lounge patron, a heavily intoxicated Crystal (Debi Mazar), only to find her passed out in a booth on his return from trying, unsuccessfully, to score some cocaine in the men's room. The humor found in the rest of the film is patterned after the humor found in these early scenes: all jokes are at Tommy's expense and punctuate the fact that Tommy has nothing going for him.

A scruffy looking bar regular, Mike (Mark Boone Jr.), befriends Tommy, and while driving around one night Tommy confides in Mike and tells him about the tragedy of losing his now pregnant, former girlfriend Theresa (Elizabeth Bracco) to his best friend, and not knowing who the father actually is. When Mike inquires about the name of his former friend, Boone utters one of the film's funniest lines: "Rob? He steals your girlfriend and that's his name?" Mike soon changes his tune, however, when Tommy also

AWARDS AND NOMINATIONS

Independent Spirit Awards 1997 Nominations: First Feature (Buscemi), First Screenplay (Buscemi)

CREDITS

Tommy: Steve Buscemi
Debbie: Chloe Sevigny
Theresa: Elizabeth Bracco
Rob: Anthony LaPaglia
Jerry: Daniel Baldwin
Mike: Mark Boone, Jr.
Raymond: Michael Buscemi

Origin: USA
Released: 1996
Production: Brad Wyman and Chris Hanley for a Seneca Falls Productions and Live Entertainment production; released by Orion Pictures
Direction: Steve Buscemi
Screenplay: Steve Buscemi
Cinematography: Lisa Rinzler
Editing: Kate Williams
Music: Evan Lurie
Production design: Steve Rosenzweig
Art direction: Jenifer Alex
Sound: Coll Anderson
Casting: Sheila Jaffe, Georgianne Walken
MPAA rating: R
Running Time: 94 minutes

reveals that the reason he was fired was for "borrowing" $1500 from the garage and blowing it in Atlantic City. Even while it appears that bar-mates Mike and Tommy are equally shiftless, Mike makes it clear that he believes Tommy's actions are despicable. Later it is revealed that despite Mike's slovenly looks, he is actually a modestly successful business man, and his time at the lounge appears to be a fleeting one. Even the seemingly lowest denizens of the bar all have more success in life than Tommy.

Raymond comes by the bar to inform Tommy that his Uncle Al (Seymour Cassel), who drives an ice cream truck, has died. The amusing funeral sequence shows Tommy's relationship with his family is strained. Some relatives he clearly does not even recognize, and those he does recognize chastise him for always being in need. Not only does Tommy accept a paltry handout from his father, but falls asleep while paying his respects at the coffin of Uncle Al, and then later joins his brother and cousin upstairs to indulge in some cocaine. Uncle Al's grieving son Matthew (Kevin Corrigan) admits, emotionally, that he doubted his father's love. Here Tommy displays his impressive insight and empathy, giving an eloquent monologue on the nature of people, and reassures Matt that he just misunderstood his father, who indeed loved him. When Tommy is finished talking, Matt appears to tear up, and leans over with his hands up to his face in what actually turns out to be a move to snort more drugs, in an ironically humorous gesture. By the end of the funeral, however, Tommy is offered the chance to take over his uncle's ice-cream route, which he reluctantly takes as a last resort.

This seems to be the last stop for Tommy, whose life, nonetheless, manages to get increasingly worse. He is terrible at his new job, to the great disappointment of one pathetic child who is never able to get Tommy to stop the truck. Hilariously, this is the same child who, while waiting on the curb with his money ready, witnessed Uncle Al's heart attack as he drove at slow speeds into his neighbor's car. Tommy then corrupts his friend's under-age daughter Debbie, played by Chloe Sevigny (*Kids* [1995]), who is also cousin to his ex-girlfriend. Even so, Tommy manages to remain a sympathetic character. He is not a bad person without morals; he merely lacks ambition, and succumbs to his laziness and to his wish to remain a carefree youth. Buscemi also ensures that Tommy does have his good points. He is always nicely dressed, clothes pressed and hair neat. He even comments in one scene about wanting to go home and change his t-shirt for an interview. He is good at impersonations, funny, and refuses to treat Debbie like a child. Theresa even seems to still have a soft spot for Tommy, and in one touching scene, replays a home movie of a family gathering when she and Tommy were together. Tommy himself realizes he is making a mess of his life, and in a desperate act, asks Teresa to come back to him. The film ends as ambiguously as Tommy's life seems.

A solid, well-made first directorial outing for Buscemi also displays one of his richest characterizations. Buscemi, without being sappy, likens Tommy to both the child who never gets the ice-cream, but continues to try, and an ornery, alcoholic old man. Situations and dialogue are genuine, partly due to the amount of improvisation that was successfully incorporated into the film. There is none of the quirkiness of some of his past characters and movies, just an on-the-level representation of suburban angst.

—Hilary Weber

REVIEWS

Boxoffice. October, 1996, p. 46.
Entertainment Weekly. October 11, 1996, p. 69.
New York Times. October 11, 1996, p. C26.
People. October 14, 1996, p. 28.
Variety. May 20, 1996, p. 31.

The Trigger Effect

When nothing works, anything goes.—Movie tagline

"Powerful filmmaking. A thriller full of surprises."—Ron Brewington, *American Urban Radio Network*

"Real suspense! Brilliant."—Stephen Farber, *Movieline*

"Riveting entertainment! A stunner. Written with passion and power."—Barbara & Scott Siegel, *Siegel Entertainment Syndicate*

"One of the most realistically frightening movies you'll ever see."—Jeff Craig, *Sixty Second Preview*

Box Office: $3,622,979

It seems writer-director David Koepp is hooked into society's collective unconscious. In the past few years he has written or collaborated on *Jurassic Park* (1993) and *Mission Impossible* (1996), both of which tapped into areas of the American cultural psyche, taking the country by storm during their initial releases.

Debut feature for director/ writer David Koepp.

In his directorial debut, Koepp has proven to have his finger on the pulse of America once again: the film is about a complete blackout and the effects of the lack of technology on a technologically dependent world. Koepp was prophetic: just a month prior to the release of *Trigger Effect*, a massive blackout affected nine Western states, creating widespread concern about America's dependence on electricity. In *The Trigger Effect*, Koepp makes the point that without the infrastructure provided by computers, street lights, radios, phone lines, et al, human behavior is reduced to primitive, reactive responses.

It is an interesting premise, and an interesting movie—to a point. For some reason, Koepp's script seems a bit contrived and its message heavy-handed. The story begins with a four-minute steadicam shot of several different people at a movie theater. Matt (Kyle MacLachlan) and Annie (Elisabeth Shue) are a suburban couple out for an evening whose night is made more irritating by Raymond (Richard T. Jones), who in turn is offended by a woman at the candy counter. All of the characters seem to boil under the surface over petty indignities and annoyances. Matt and Annie return home to discover their child needs medication. A blackout during the night sets in motion an increasingly tragic chain of events, beginning with Matt's decision to steal the baby's medication from a pharmacist unwilling to fill the prescription because the computer is down.

After the blackout Matt and Annie are visited by Joe (Dermot Mulroney), a construction-foreman friend whose earthy sexuality entices Annie and sets off tension between the two men. As the blackout extends longer than anticipated, the characters feel a palpable sense of danger, as looters come into their safe suburban world and neighbors become enemies. As tension mounts, Matt and Joe buy a rifle to protect themselves which leads to the murder of a prowler and the decision to leave town. Here is where the film becomes almost preposterous, and it is a shame. With their infant child, the couple go off on a trip to Annie's parent's home, five hundred miles away. They do not have enough gas, and they have no money. They do not know how far the blackout extends; in fact, they know nothing about what is outside their town because they don't seem to make much effort toward asking. They simply react. Koepp's point—that people in such a situation would become irrational—may be salient, but Matt and Annie seem a bit too intelli-

CREDITS

Matt: Kyle MacLachlan
Annie: Elisabeth Shue
Joe: Dermot Mulroney
Raymond: Richard T. Jones
Gary: Michael Rooker

Origin: USA
Released: 1996
Production: Michael Grillo for an Amblin Entertainment production; released by Gramercy
Direction: David Koepp
Screenplay: David Koepp
Cinematography: Newton Thomas Sigel
Editing: Jill Savitt
Music: James Newton Howard
Production design: Howard Cummings
Art direction: Jeff Knipp
Costume design: Dana Allyson
Sound: John Pritchett
Casting: Nancy Nayor
MPAA rating: R
Running Time: 98 minutes

gent to subject their child to a dangerous situation such as driving across a desert without the certainty of getting enough gas to reach their destination. What about food? What about the baby's needs? This small point makes the rest of the film hard to swallow.

From there, things get really out of hand when, out in the middle of the desert (filmed near the abandoned Rancho Seco nuclear power plant in California for maximum doomsday effect), they come across Raymond once more (the man who irritated them in the movie theater.) Neither Raymond nor Matt remembers each other in a (well-played) climactic scene where they hold guns on each other. The fact that they would encounter each other again seems a bit far-fetched.

Now, the fact that this is all ridiculous doesn't stop the film from making some interesting points. For example, Raymond is black, and by the end of the film he is in a position to help the white Matt—reminiscent of the recent *White Man's Burden* (1995). It is a fine piece of social commentary, well filmed as Raymond looks through a doorway at the frantic Matt, unsure he can trust this man. Koepp's thematic material is interesting, particularly his theme that our technological world keeps us from feeling the passion inherent in our humanity.

Elisabeth Shue, fresh off her Academy Award-nominated performance in *Leaving Las Vegas* (1995), and Kyle MacLachlan are fine as young people baffled as to what forces have taken the passion out of their lives. Dermot Mulroney delivers a sexy, intelligent performance, breathing life into a possibly stereotypical character.

Koepp should be commended for his attempt to make an allegorical piece, commenting on important social themes. *The Trigger Effect* seems absurd sometimes, and may not be wholly successful, but Koepp is, at least, trying.

—Kirby Tepper

REVIEWS

New York Times. August 30, 1996, p. C1.
People. September 9, 1996, p. 17.
Variety. June 10, 1996, p. 41.
Village Voice. September 3, 1996, p. 53.

The Truth About Cats & Dogs

Brian's about to discover the woman he loves isn't the woman he loves.—Movie tagline

"Truthfully, one of the best romantic comedies to hit the silver screen!"—Mose Persico, *CFCF-12*

"A quick-witted romantic comedy directed with steady laughs and disarming comic finesse."—Janet Maslin, *New York Times*

"Two thumbs up!"—*Siskel & Ebert*

"The one-two punch of Thurman and Garofalo is irresistible."—Jeff Craig, *Sixty Second Preview*

"Warmhearted and hilarious. It's hard to imagine that we'll see a more pleasing romantic comedy this year."—Michael Medved, *Sneak Previews*

Box Office: $34,848,673

In yet another modern-day version of *Cyrano de Bergerac*, screenwriter Audrey Wells reverses the gender and updates the tale into the fresh, romantic comedy *The Truth About Cats & Dogs*. The title refers to the popular radio talk show hosted by Abby Barnes (Janeane Garofalo), a smart, funny veterinarian who dispenses useful advice to L.A. pet owners.

In one of the film's best moments, Abby talks a British photographer named Brian (Ben Chaplin) through a real crisis involving a Great Dane on roller skates. After that unusual photo shoot experience, Brian decides to keep the dog and names him Hank.

Intrigued by Abby's charm, Brian calls back and tells her that he wants to thank her for her advice in person. Abby agrees to a meeting, but when asked what she looks like, Abby describes her tall blonde neighbor, Noelle (Uma Thurman), who is a gorgeous, but dim-witted model. Abby asks Noelle to assume her identity and together they attempt to pull off the ruse, which becomes even more complicated when both women develop feelings for the shy Englishman.

Throughout their extended ploy, Abby and Noelle develop an unlikely friendship that really carries the rest of the film. They are complete opposites: The petite, cynical, brunette Abby, who is intelligent, plays the violin and likes classical music—and Noelle, the attractive, scatterbrained blonde, who wants to be a serious newscaster and is saddled with a loser boyfriend. One thing they do share, however, is that they both suffer from low self-esteem—Noelle from an excessive amount of attention and Abby from the lack of it.

As with most mixed-identity comedies, *The Truth* requires a certain suspension of disbelief. It seems like Brian has to play dumb for an unusually long period of time before he figures out the deception. Newcomer Ben Chaplin, an English actor making his U.S. film debut, plays the befuddled Brian with just the right amount of self-effacing charm. His sensitivity and puppy-dog appeal work nicely in this role. Thurman also gives a good performance as the beautiful but confused model. Even Hank, the four-legged performer who was rescued from a pound, steals a scene with his roller-skating stunt work.

"Did you ever look into a mirror so long that your face didn't make sense anymore?"—Noelle to Abby

However, the real star of the show is Garofalo. In a standout performance, Garofalo makes it impossible not to fall in love with her character as she gives Abby a real sweetness to go along with her acid-tongued sarcasm. As David Ansen of *Newsweek* comments: "It's a tricky challenge playing a woman who must be both unglamorous and irresistible, but Garofalo, with her unforced comic timing, makes it look easy." Best known as the acerbic talent booker in the award-winning cable series "The Larry Sanders Show," Garofalo also appeared in *Reality Bites* (1994) and *Bye Bye, Love* (1994). *The Truth About Cats & Dogs* is her first starring feature role and she is a most welcome new presence on the film scene.

Two girlfriends trade identities to impress a man, only to learn a basic lesson in love in the romantic comedy *The Truth About Cats & Dogs.*

Screenwriter and executive producer Wells drew upon her own experiences as a disc jockey to come up with the premise of the story. Wells was particularly interested in the way women are perceived—and how they deal with these perceptions. Her very human characters, their relationships, and the situations they get themselves into require the audience to reflect on the nature of true beauty and all of the endless possibilities offered by love and friendship.

In the press kit for the film, Wells explains the inspiration for her thought-provoking theme, which can be traced back to Edmond Rostand's *Cyrano de Bergerac.* "Cyrano was poetic, witty, brilliant and brave, yet people could look no further than his giant nose. His situation reminds me, frankly, of what women go through every day. In our beauty obsessed society, in which a woman's looks are considered to be the measure of her worth, a woman doesn't need to have a grotesque feature like Cyrano's nose in order to be judged romantically unfit. The slightest deviation from the Madison Avenue ideal and she finds herself right in Cyrano's shoes."

CREDITS

Noelle: Uma Thurman
Abby: Janeane Garofalo
Brian: Ben Chaplin
Ed: Jamie Foxx
Roy: James McCaffrey
Eric: Richard Coca

Origin: USA
Released: 1996
Production: Cari-Esta Albert for a Noon Attack production; released by 20th Century Fox
Direction: Michael Lehmann
Screenplay: Audrey Wells
Cinematography: Robert Brinkmann
Editing: Stephen Semel
Production design: Sharon Seymour
Costume design: Bridget Kelly
Art direction: Jeff Knipp
Sound mixing: Douglas Axtell
Make-up: Deborah LaMia Denaver
Music: Howard Shore
Casting: Debra Zane
MPAA rating: PG-13
Running Time: 97 minutes

Director Lehmann was drawn to the script's universal themes and also to the story's depiction of the unconventional friendship between Abby and Noelle. In the press kit, he states: "Their bond is partially based on an incompatibility between them. They find things about the other one that they don't recognize within themselves. So, they really complement each other and grow from their relationship, and bring out sides of themselves of which they previously weren't aware."

American film debut of Ben Chaplin.

Lehmann previously directed the black comedy *Heathers* (1989), the Bruce Willis flop *Hudson Hawk* (1991) and the 1994 rocker *Airheads.* For his first foray into romantic comedy, he avoids making the movie sentimental while keeping the characters real and the story's humor intact. Although the film contains several hilarious romantic escapades, it never evolves into the screwball farce it might have been. Nevertheless, Lehmann keeps this breezy pic afloat with a nice balance of tenderness and comic finesse.

Shot entirely in Los Angeles, the film makes the most of its Santa Monica locales—giving the movie a romantic and magical feel. (It's nice to see L.A. portrayed in a positive manner for a change.) With a witty, offbeat script and Garofalo's engaging performance, this charming romantic comedy is a real treat.

—Beth Fhaner

REVIEWS

Chicago Tribune. April 26, 1996, p. 5.
Detroit News. April 26, 1996, p. D2.
Entertainment Weekly. April 26, 1996, p. 34-35.
New York Times. April 26, 1996, p. C8.
Newsweek. April 29, 1996, p. 82.
Rolling Stone. May 16, 1996, p. 74.
Variety. April 8, 1996, p. 59.
Village Voice. April 30, 1996, p. 51.

Twelfth Night

Before Priscilla crossed the desert, Wong Foo met Julie Newmar, and the Birdcage was unlocked, there was . . . *Twelfth Night.*—Movie tagline

"Flawlessly acted and breathtakingly beautiful."—Jim Svedja, *CBS Radio*

"This film has it all - laughs, tears, action, beautiful women and dashing men. It's fast-paced and great fun!"—David Poole, *Cover Magazine*

"A gleeful, cross-dressing romp."—Stephen Holden, *New York Times*

"This rollicking classic is definitely something to see! Trevor Nunn's direction is crisp, funny and great fun!"—Bruce Williamson, *Playboy*

Box Office: $551,545

While there are many memorable film adaptations of the plays of William Shakespeare, most of the best ones, such as those directed by Laurence Olivier, Orson Welles, and Kenneth Branagh, are drawn from his tragedies and histories. Shakespeare's comedies have been mostly neglected by filmmakers with the most noteworthy efforts being the 1935 version of *A Midsummer Night's Dream* directed by Max Reinhardt and William Dieterle, one of the most beautiful black-and-white films ever, and Branagh's energetic *Much Ado About Nothing* (1993), though both suffer from weak casting. Trevor Nunn's *Twelfth Night* is another mostly satisfying cinematic attempt at Shakespearean comedy, generally well cast, visually splendid, and thoroughly charming.

Twins Viola (Imogen Stubbs) and Sebastian (Steven MacKintosh) are separated when they are washed overboard during a storm at sea, each thinking the other has drowned. Making her way to the coast of Illyria with a handful of other survivors, Viola assumes male attire and becomes Cesario, an aide to Orsino (Toby Stephens), the Duke of Illyria. Orsino is in love with Olivia (Helena Bonham Carter), who will not receive him because she is mourning the death of her brother. When the Duke sends Cesario as his emissary, Olivia slowly becomes attracted to the youth.

Comic relief is offered by the exploits of Olivia's drunken uncle, Sir Toby Belch (Mel Smith), and his friends who include Sir Andrew Aguecheek (Richard E. Grant), a foolish fop who longs for Olivia's hand; Feste (Ben Kingsley), Olivia's philosophical clown—by far the most intelligent character; and Maria (Imelda Staunton), Olivia's maid with whom Sir Toby has a flirtatious relationship. All are aligned against Malvolio (Nigel Hawthorne), the household's humorless butler. While Sir Toby and company are engaged in singing and various high jinks, Malvolio sits in his room trying to read, looking annoyed at all the commotion.

"If music be the food of love, play on."—Duke Orsino

A plot against Malvolio develops, involving convincing him that Olivia is romantically inclined toward him and that she wants him to wear ridiculous stockings of yellow, a color she actually abhors. When the butler professes his love for his mistress, she has him locked up as a madman. Just as Olivia realizes she is in love with Cesario and Orsino finds himself strangely drawn to the same young man, Sebastian turns up to be mistaken for Cesario. All, of course, ends happily for the lovers once the confusion over identities is sorted out.

CREDITS

Viola: Imogen Stubbs
Olivia: Helena Bonham Carter
Malvolio: Nigel Hawthorne
Feste: Ben Kingsley
Sir Andrew Aguecheek: Richard E. Grant
Sir Toby Belch: Mel Smith
Orsino: Toby Stephens
Sebastian: Steven MacKintosh
Maria: Imelda Staunton
Antonio: Nicholas Farrell
Valentine: Alan Mitchell
Fabian: Peter Gunn

Origin: Great Britain
Released: 1996
Production: Stephen Evans and David Parfitt for Renaissance Films; released by Fine Line Features
Direction: Trevor Nunn
Screenplay: Trevor Nunn; based on the play by William Shakespeare
Cinematography: Clive Tickner
Editing: Peter Boyle
Production design: Sophie Becher
Art direction: Ricky Eyres
Costume design: John Bright
Sound: David Crozier
Music: Shaun Davey
Make-up: Christine Beveridge
MPAA rating: PG
Running Time: 105 minutes

Nunn is well-known for his many years as a director of Royal Shakespeare Company productions, including *The Life and Times of Nicholas Nickelby* (1980) and for staging commercial West End and Broadway kitsch such as *Cats* (1981), *Les Miserables* (1985) and *Sunset Boulevard* (1993). His film career before *Twelfth Night,* however, consists of the uninspired costume drama *Lady Jane* (1986), also starring Bonham Carter. *Twelfth Night* represents a major leap for Nunn as a filmmaker, partly because it is visually resplendent thanks to the beautiful setting—the film was shot in Cornwall—and the sensual cinematography of Clive Tickner, who usually works on grittier projects like *Ploughman's Lunch* (1983) and *Hidden Agenda* (1990). Rather than making Illyria a mystical isle, Tickner and Nunn imagine it as a mixture of the romantic and the realistic: sunny at times, gloomy at others, with lots of shadows underscoring the characters' uncertainties about themselves and their relations with the others.

In addition to expertly condensing and rearranging the play's action, Nunn makes two departures from traditional interpretations of *Twelfth Night.* First, he shows the violent storm that sets the plot in motion, including a haunting shot of Sebastian fruitlessly trying to rescue Viola underwater, their fingers barely eluding each other as the sister, in a ghostly image, drifts away to her apparent death. The other is to change the setting to the late nineteenth century, seemingly to make the events less remote for audiences impatient with Renaissance trappings. Sebastian is shown consulting "Baedeker's Illyria," but this witty inclusion of the omnipresent Victorian guidebook is the only such period detail other than the costumes. Nunn can be faulted for not doing more with this aspect of his adaptation. *Twelfth Night* has a reputation for being unusually demanding for audiences among Shakespeare's comedies because of the relative subtlety and its plot and characters and because of the sophistication of the language—even more the play's essence than is usual with Shakespeare. This factor, and the lack of major stars, may explain why the film, despite the adaptor's efforts to make it more contemporary, did mediocre business in the United States.

Nunn achieves an excellent balance between the stories of the couples and the comic relief since the latter threatens to overwhelm the play in some stage productions. Keeping the lovers and would-be lovers in focus is essential since a main reason for attempting a film of *Twelfth Night* at this time is its topicality since sexual identity in general and cross-dressing in particular are hot topics on the big screen in the 1990's in numerous films ranging from the sublime—*The Crying Game* (1992)—to the ridiculous—*The Birdcage* (1996).

Stephens, the son of Maggie Smith and Robert Stephens, making his film debut, presents Orsino almost like an exhausted playboy out of a Noel Coward play. His Orsino sends Cesario to do his bidding almost as if he cannot summon the energy to do it himself. He would seemingly rather lounge about with his aide than anything else. Stephens' soft, slightly high-pitched voice is appropriate for Nunn's conception of the blurring of sexual identities.

Even though Trevor Nunn was for many years the director of the Royal Shakespeare Company and directed many of its productions, he never directed *Twelfth Night* on the stage.

Stubbs, the director's wife, has a tomboyish quality, best seen in "Anna Lee," her private detective series seen on the Arts and Entertainment Network, but she does little to hide her femininity within Cesario. When Orsino has his aide bathe him, Stubbs' response combines fear of exposure, discomfort at the presence of a naked man, and sexual excitement. Viola sees Cesario as a reincarnation of Sebastian, and Stubbs has him walk in a good imitation of MacKintosh's rolling gait.

MacKintosh is well cast for his physical resemblance to Stubbs and for his athleticism in the swordfight with the jealous but cowardly Sir Andrew, which Nunn directs as a good blend of slapstick and actual danger. The director also exploits the similarity between the performers by having Sebastian and Viola do a musical drag act aboard ship in which they pretend to be sisters. This comic bit also helps set up what is to occur thematically for the rest of the film. Nunn's touch is less certain with Sebastian's friend Antonio (Nicholas Farrell), whose attachment of the younger man is homoerotic with no necessary payoff.

Bonham Carter makes for a luminous Olivia. It is easy to see why almost every man she encounters becomes besotted with her even with her black mourning clothes. Bonham Carter specializes in effortlessly portraying moral innocence, and this quality is especially helpful in conveying Olivia's confusion as Cesario awakens emotions she thinks she has effectively repressed.

One gnawing flaw in Nunn's adaptation is the lack of balance between Malvolio's humiliation and the happiness of the young couples. In Shakespeare's play, Malvolio is punished for refusing to yield to the festive spirit of the lunacies of Sir Toby and his friends. He must be expelled from this joyful world to prevent his upsetting the equilibrium of the happy lovers. Nunn's Malvolio, however, is merely a pompous prig who deserves to have his nose tweaked but hardly merits the treatment Feste and company mete out. His punishment unbalances the happy ending with his swearing revenge taking much of the glitter off the nuptials. Hawthorne, to his credit, has Malvolio, in the final shot of the character, depart more embarrassed than angry, softening the negative effect a bit.

Hawthorne's performance is also notable for making Malvolio more sympathetic than Nunn may have intended. His Malvolio is totally in control when carrying out his duties as butler but more uncertain and inept when doing anything else. In creating this pompous yet pathetic character, Hawthorne makes him a combination of two of his best-known television roles, the autocratic Sir Humphrey Appleby in the "Yes, Minister" and "Yes, Prime Minister" situation comedies of the 1980's and the easily flustered Georgie Pilson in "Mapp Lucia" (1986).

The other comic performers are equally able. Staunton's Maria is less comic than most interpretations because, as she told *The Times* of London, Nunn suggested she imagine the character as being like Sonia in Anton Chekhov's *Uncle Vanya* (1899). The sadness underlying the character provides some poignancy to her relationship with the more foolish Sir Toby. Smith, an excellent farceur, indulges in flamboyance, particularly when Sir Toby is drunk, but stops just short of making him annoyingly buffoonish. Smith offers some balance to the character when Sir Toby and Maria depart and his expression shows he realizes he may have overstepped himself with the treatment of Malvolio. Another performer given to overacting, Grant can be inventively excessive, as in *Withnail and I* (1987), or too camp, as in *Hudson Hawk* (1991) and *Ready to Wear* (1994). As Sir Andrew, he is more subtly silly than usual, especially when he learns Olivia detests yellow, a color he fancies, and during the swordfight he justly fears.

Nunn's greatest achievement is in balancing the light and dark elements of *Twelfth Night,* and this balance is exemplified by Kingsley's Feste, a fool in name only. Feste can throw himself into Sir Toby's exploits and can just as easily stand back from the action to act as the play's moral center. Kingsley has both a gleam in his eye and a melancholy expression when he first spies Viola on the beach, as if he knows what will transpire and that it will not be easy on any of them. Feste's commentary often takes the form of songs, and Kingsley excels here as well. His assured performance unifies the film's often conflicting elements.

—Michael Adams

REVIEWS

Boxoffice. November, 1996, p. 132.
Chicago Tribune. November 8, 1996, p. 5.
Entertainment Weekly. November 15, 1996, p. 49.
Los Angeles Times. October 25, 1996, p. F28.
The New York Times. October 25, 1996, p. C3.
Newsweek. November 4, 1996, p. 74.
Rolling Stone. November 14, 1996, p. 124.
Sight and Sound. VI, November, 1996, p. 60.
USA Today. October 25, 1996, p. 5D.
Variety. September 16, 1996, p. 71.
The Village Voice. October 29, 1996, p. 52.

Twister

Don't breathe. Don't look back.—Movie tagline

"Amazing . . . thrilling . . . hair-raising."—Bill Diehl, *ABC Radio Network*

"An eye-popping, nail-biting, edge-of-your-seat roller coaster ride."—Neil Rosen, *NY1 News*

"Director Jan De Bont has created a special effects blockbuster masterpiece."—Jules Peimer, *WKDM Radio*

"Truly amazing! You have never seen anything like it before!"—Pat Collins, *WWOR-TV*

Box office: $241,721,524

There are two very elementary co-plots to this first big entry into the 1996 race for summer boxoffice dollars. The first is a typical love triangle. It deals with an estranged husband named Bill Harding (Bill Paxton) and his estranged wife, Jo (Helen Hunt), who were once fellow members on a storm chasing team and are now on the verge of finalizing their divorce. Bill plans on quitting the tornado hunts, settling down as a television weatherman, and marrying his fertility therapist fiancee, Melissa (Jami Gertz). However, everyone knows that giving up the thrill of following threatening weather is not that easy, nor is giving up a spouse one may really love.

The second plot deals with the standard good guys vs. bad guys conflict. Here the good guys are a ragtag bunch of university storm chasers who rely on instinct, minimal funding, personal vehicles, and secondhand instruments. The good guys are in this dangerous game for the science and for the betterment of humanity. The bad guys, headed by Dr. Jonas Miller (Cary Elwes) obviously rely on expensive technology which means heavy corporate investment, top-of-the-line equipment and sleek, sinister black chase vehicles. They're in it for the profit, and they don't care what they have to do to win.

Both plots are so predictable that early on we know which two sides of the triangle will get together, and that the bad guys not only can't win, they must lose in a most appropriate manner. So, if you're looking for a well-written script, a compelling story line, and fully-created characters, *Twister* is not the movie for you. That being the case, it must also be said . . . it doesn't matter! The plot of this movie is just the slightest of wires on which to suspend what is really the star of the film, the special effects. In fact, the only characters on the screen who really rivet one's attention are the tornadoes themselves.

The objective for both Jo's good team and Miller's bad team is to get into the path of a tornado where they hope their newly developed scientific instruments, drums filled with sensor balls, will be sucked into the tornado's vortex where they will send back scientific data. The problem is, they have to watch out that they don't get sucked in themselves. (It should be no surprise that Miller has ripped off Bill's idea for the sensors, and that in an expected tribute to

AWARDS AND NOMINATIONS

Academy Awards 1996 Nominations: Best Sound, Best Visual Effects

CREDITS

Jo Harding: Helen Hunt
Bill Harding: Bill Paxton
Dr. Jonas Miller: Cary Elwes
Melissa: Jami Gertz
Aunt Meg: Lois Smith
Rabbit: Alan Ruck
Dusty: Philip Seymour Hoffman
Laurence: Jeremy Davies
Beltzer: Todd Field
Eddie: Zach Grenier
Kubrick: Nicholas Sadler
Bubba: Abraham Benrubi

Origin: USA
Released: 1996
Production: Kathleen Kennedy, Ian Bryce and Michael Crichton for Amblin Entertainment; released by Warner Bros. and Universal Pictures
Direction: Jan De Bont
Screenplay: Michael Crichton and Anne-Marie Martin
Cinematography: Jack N. Green
Editing: Michael Kahn
Production design: Joseph Nemec III
Art direction: Dan Olexiewicz
Set design: Patrick Sullivan
Costume design: Ellen Mirojnick
Music: Mark Mancina
Sound: Geoffrey Patterson
Special Visual Effects and Animation: Industrial Light & Magic
Stunt Coordinator: Mike Runyard
MPAA rating: PG-13
Running Time: 117 minutes

The Wizard of Oz, Bill's drum is called Dorothy while Miller's drum is called D.O.T.) So, for about twenty-four hours both teams roam the flat Oklahoma countryside looking for twisters to tempt. And do they find them. These crews are bigger tornado magnets than a trailer park.

"You people are all crazy, do you know that?"—Melissa to Dusty

And believe it or not, there is more than one kind of tornado. Technically they are rated according to what is called the Fujita Scale, which, as one character explains, rates tornadoes by how much they eat. An F4, for example, can efficiently relocate your house, while an F5 is ominously described as the finger of God. Of the good guy's crew, only one of them has been in an F5, Jo herself, and it defines the rest of her life. As a child, Jo watched as her father was sucked out of a storm cellar by a tornado. It is the film's opening sequence and it starts the adrenaline as well as the *Oz* tribute since Jo's dog is a Cairn terrier, just like Toto, only her's is named Toby.

In doing their research, the filmmakers met with meteorological experts from the National Severe Storms Laboratory in Norman, Oklahoma, and went on the road with storm chasers from their government-funded program.

Director Jan De Bont, (best known for his directing debut, *Speed*) keeps the tornadoes coming, the energy high, and the action fast. (That way maybe we won't notice the predictable plots and characters.) Through hail (really milk-colored ice chips), and rain, and jet-engine created wind and tons of debris that includes a drive-through house, we experience one tornado after another. A cow flies by, a tanker truck explodes in front of us, a drive-in theater is demolished along with an entire town, farm implements drop on us, and finally we live through a direct hit while tied to well pipes (although Jo manages to keep her radio headset on the whole time—Ah, the capriciousness of twisters).

Besides De Bont's frenetic direction and the superior special effects of Industrial Light & Magic, *Twister* also owes a lot to editor Michael Kahn, who deservedly won Oscars for *Raiders of the Lost Ark* and *Schindler's List*, and the great outdoor cinematographer Jack N. Green, who won an Oscar for Clint Eastwood's *Unforgiven*. Both help to heighten the "experience" of the film. But as mentioned before the "experience" is about all there is to it.

It also sounds as if it might have been quite an experience filming *Twister*. There have been reports that De Bont's directing style so alienated people that the original cinematographer, Don Burgess, and more than twenty other crewmen walked off the picture. As if that weren't enough, Helen Hunt ended up with burned cornea's from too-bright lighting, both Hunt and Paxton were bruised from doing their own stunts in debris-laden winds, and they both also required emergency hepatitis shots after filming in an irrigation ditch in which they found animal waste. Perhaps the "making of *Twister*" would make a more plot-driven film than what was eventually delivered to theaters.

As for the plot, it was written by Michael Crichton, best known for writing techno-thriller novels like *The Andromeda Strain*, *Rising Sun*, and *Jurassic Park* which all became hit films. Here, however, he forgoes the literary step and wrote *Twister* (along with his wife Anne-Marie Martin) directly for the screen. (There were also uncredited writing touch-ups done by Steven Zaillian (*Schindler's List*) and Joss Whedon (*Speed* script doctor).

Tornadoes are a very visual villain, which may be why Crichton wrote it as a screenplay, but what plot and characters he has provided, don't really add much to the film. Hunt's Jo and Paxton's Bill have a lot of "stuff" to do in the chase, but not much to say. We don't even know why they are getting divorced. And all the secondary characters have very specific and predictable purposes. Miller gives us someone to hate, and Melissa's primary purpose is, along with Dusty (Philip Seymour Hoffman), to provide the film's humor. She's uptight, he's laid-back, eventually they will end up in a car together. Aunt Meg (Lois Smith) is there so we can sympathize with the tornado's victims, but it is hollow sympathy. Rarely does De Bont ask us to experience the terror of tornadoes. He's more interested in exhilaration. After all, this is an adventure not a horror film. *Twister*'s victims, for the most part, are faceless and nameless. The destroyed homes and devastated lives left in the tornado's wake are not of interest to De Bont, only the excitement of this destructive and fascinating phenomenon.

Twister was not meant to be high drama, nor was it meant to be a weather documentary. It was meant to be entertainment. This isn't a Shakespeare festival, it's Disneyland. It is also undeniably the first boxoffice smash of the summer of '96—just what the filmmakers wanted it to be.

—Beverley Bare Buehrer

REVIEWS

Boxoffice Magazine. July, 1996, p. 92.
Chicago Tribune. May 10, 1996, p. 4.
Detroit Free Press. May 10, 1996, p. D1.
Entertainment Weekly. May 17, 1996, p. 70.
New York Times. May 10, 1996, p. C1.
Newsweek. May 20, 1996, p. 70.
Time. May 20, 1996, p. 62.
USA Today. May 10, 1996, p. 1D.
Variety Online. May 10, 1996.

2 Days in the Valley

You have one minute to decide the rest of your life.—Movie tagline

"Violent, sexy, romantic, hilarious, and always intriguing - 2 of the best hours you can spend in the theatre!"—John Corcoran, *KCAL-TV*

"A 5-star cast, in a 5-star movie! It out-pulps *Pulp Fiction.*"—Bob Polunsky, *KENS-TV*

"The funniest, sexiest, most dangerous movie in a long time!"—Barry Krutchik, *Premiere Radio Networks*

Box Office: $10,900,000

Bryan Singer. Gary Fleder. John Herzfeld. These are not household names. All three men are in the movie business, but you would be hard pressed to find a handful of regular movie patrons who could identify them. This is largely due to the fact that they all work exclusively behind the camera. There are so few unseen Hollywood celebrities. Ask anyone in the general public to pick Martin Scorsese or Francis Ford Coppola out of a lineup. Most would fail. Only Steven Spielberg, just by the sheer behemoth box-office numbers he leaves in his wake, could be recognized walking down the street. This presents an interesting dichotomy.

"I know we're Valley detectives so we're not all that bright, but how stupid does he think we are?"—Detective Creighton

The person who is most responsible for the success or failure of a film is the one who (generally) receives the least recognition in the eyes of the public. If the movie fails, this is a good thing. The director's talent lies in his or her ability to take the writer's vision and channel it to the performers, while hoping everyone involved has the same artistic interpretation. Having to do this with a huge, multi-talented, ensemble cast while still allowing all of them to make their own unforgettable mark is no mean feat.

With *2 Days in the Valley,* John Herzfeld put together a powerful list of A-grade talent. He did so based on the sheer power and strength of the script (which he wrote himself) and every major star involved in the production showed their own personal dedication to the project by working for scale. Not having to compete with aliens, explosions, natural disasters or computer generated special effects allowed each of the cast to practice their handiwork while working with peers who share their vision.

2 Days in the Valley is a nontraditional, nonlinear crime story. Its own television trailers claim that it "out pulps *Pulp Fiction,*" a very daring statement to make. Whether you love him or hate him (and there are vast numbers of people on both sides of the fence with very few undecided), Quentin Tarantino christened a brand new genre of American movies with *Pulp Fiction* (1994). Two subsequent films, *The Usual Suspects* and *Things to Do in Denver When You're Dead,* both from 1995, took their cue from Tarantino. Bryan Singer and Gary Fleder, both young, first-time directors of those films saw the appeal of taking a complex script and mixing it with brutal, graphic violence and sarcastic, tongue-in-cheek black humor. With *2 Days,* Herzfeld has made his first feature (although he has enjoyed acclaim for his made-for-television productions, "The Preppie Murder," "Stoned" and "The Ryan White Story") and delivered a film that continues that trend and is at once, immensely cerebral and mainstream audience friendly.

Herzfeld's film also owes a great deal to Robert Altman's *Short Cuts* (1993). Based on a collection of short stories by Raymond Carver, Altman profiled small groups of characters, separate to themselves, but eventually intersecting each other during a small, two day period in Los Angeles. *2 Days in the Valley* also takes place in California, this time in the comfortable and very suburban San Fernando Valley. Altman's picture had a wider, more panoramic scope, where Herzfeld's concentrates on the ripple effects of just one mob-style murder.

Without any opening credits, save for the title, the film opens with two hit men parked on a hill, eavesdropping via radio, on a couple in bed at a nearby home. One man, Lee Woods (James Spader) is impeccably groomed. Whenever he speaks, it's done in an exacting and curt manner; he never minces his words and feels that dealing with people at all is a tedious and arduous chore. Many times throughout the film, Lee employs the use of his omnipresent stopwatch. His fascination with what can happen in a mere minute's time coupled with the grandiose speeches he delivers are a perfect accompaniment to his manipulative, reptilian charm. Spader's frosty, detached portrayal of Lee is near perfect and recalls his previous roles in *sex, lies and videotape* (1989) and *Wolf* (1994).

Sitting next to Lee in the car is Dosmo Pizzo (Danny Aiello). Dosmo is a rumpled, frumpy, somewhat washed-up mob assassin from New Jersey with a predilection for profanity and an innate fear of canines. Dosmo believes he's been brought in by Lee to take out Roy Foxx (Peter Horton) because of an outstanding gambling debt. In actuality, Lee is setting Dosmo up as a patsy. He wants to make it look like Dosmo killed Roy and then met his own fate during the commission of a drug deal gone terribly awry.

Roy is the man in the aforementioned bedroom who is trying desperately to have sex with his ex-wife Becky (Terri Hatcher). Becky is a three-time Olympic skier who has placed fourth each time. Although not addressed directly, it's apparent that Becky divorced Roy because of his fairly blatant dalliances that broke Becky's concentration, causing her to finish out of medal contention. She rebuffs his advances, citing disinterest and the two finally fall asleep. Lee and Dosmo then break into the home, inject Becky with sedatives and confront the startled Roy. Lee begins to question Roy about his most recent liaison with what he describes as some North Korean operative. He shows Roy a picture of a naked and bloodied female corpse and tells Roy he's got exactly one minute to decide the rest of his life. Dosmo begins to wonder what he's got himself into. He wasn't prepared for this kind of political imbroglio. Once Roy begrudgingly confesses his involvement, Lee finishes

CREDITS

Dosmo Pizzo: Danny Aiello
Alvin Strayer: Jeff Daniels
Lee Woods: James Spader
Wes Taylor: Eric Stoltz
Allan Hopper: Greg Cruttwell
Becky Foxx: Teri Hatcher
Helga Svelgen: Charlize Theron
Susan Parish: Glenne Headly
Teddy Peppers: Paul Mazursky
Audrey Hopper: Marsha Mason
Roy Foxx: Peter Horton

Origin: USA
Released: 1996
Production: Jeff Wald, Herb Nanas for a Rysher Entertainment and Redemption production; released by MGM-UA
Direction: John Herzfeld
Screenplay: John Herzfeld
Cinematography: Oliver Wood
Editing: Jim Miller, Wayne Wahrman
Music: Anthony Marinelli
Production design: Catherine Hardwicke
Art direction: Kevin Constant
Set design: Gary Sawaya
Costume design: Betsy Heimann
Sound: Kim H. Ornitz
Casting: Mindy Marin, John Papsidera
MPAA rating: R
Running Time: 107 minutes

him off and Dosmo unwittingly leaves behind evidence that could implicate his involvement in the crime.

With a quick and abrupt switch, the character of Teddy Peppers (Paul Mazursky) is introduced. As we meet Teddy, he is taking care of some last minute chores before committing suicide. At one time, he was an important Hollywood director, but no more. He leaves his apartment, gun in hand, with his dog Bogey, but still can't bring himself to take his own life. The next day, he visits his wife's grave (perhaps the source for his disconsolate attitude). Just before another go-around with the gun, he spots Audrey, who's dressed like an off-duty nurse (Marsha Mason), visiting another grave site. Convinced he can finally carry out his desperate act, he asks Audrey to look after Bogey. She initially turns him down, but quickly senses his despondency and agrees to find the dog a home, but wisely insists that he meet the new owner, thereby getting him out of the cemetery and into a better state of mind.

Audrey takes Teddy and Bogey to the home of her art dealer brother Allan (Greg Cruttwell). Due to a recent illness, Allan is ailing and makes it his mission to let everyone within earshot feel his pain. He's a spoiled, demanding brat who treats his dog like a lover and his longtime personal assistant, Susan (Glenne Headly), like a dog. Allan's house is painstakingly appointed with objects that only truly gifted avant-garde minds could appreciate. Audrey and Teddy walk into a pre-existing hostage situation and diffuse the situation slightly, preventing the predicament from getting completely out of hand.

The next scene in the film (that chronologically takes place earlier) finds a dazed and blood-crusted Becky screaming for help and running into vice detectives Alvin Strayer (Jeff Daniels) and Wes Taylor (Eric Stoltz). Strayer is a bitter and wrathful man who feels slighted (the reasons are explained later) by everyone. He's been a cop a little too long and his priorities and personal convictions seem askew. Taylor feels his talents are being wasted in vice and wants desperately to work in homicide. Becky grants his wish and directly delivers his professional salvation.

Charlize Theron, the least known of all the principal players, plays a very pivotal role and is the only character that interacts with the entire cast. Arriving on the scene as the statuesque Nordic Helga, her character goes from being a trophy-like ornament to scrappy street fighter and by the time film is over, she elicits a great deal of audience sympathy. Ironically enough, Theron had a smaller, much less significant role in Tom Hanks' *That Thing You Do!* that opened the same weekend as *2 Days in the Valley.*

With his airtight script and remarkably fluid, assured direction, Herzfeld has crafted a film with an amalgamation of different directing styles that is still uniquely his own. He is the true star of this project. *2 Days* walks an emotional tightrope and his characters share desires, fears, phobias and everyday quirks not normally found in movie characters; it seems to be anchored in a true, very sincere, non-Hollywood reality. At times, it is hysterically funny and at other times, devastatingly poignant. It is one of the richest, most refreshing films of 1996.

—*J.M. Clark*

REVIEWS

Boxoffice Online. October, 1996.
Detroit News. September 27, 1996, p. 3D.
Los Angeles Times. September 27, 1996, p. F14.
New York Times. September 27, 1996, p. C10.
Sight and Sound. November, 1996, p. 61.
USA Today. September 27, 1996, p. 4D.
Variety Online. September 16, 1996.

Two If By Sea

A new comedy about love, laughter and larceny.—Movie tagline

"The best comedy, caper, date film of the year. Romantic and delicious."—Norman Mark, *WMAQ-TV*

Box Office: $9,800,000

Not even Sandra Bullock can save *Two If By Sea* from sinking. With a winning streak in such films as *Speed* (1994), *Sleepless in Seattle* (1993), and *The Net* (1995), Bullock can chalk up a big minus for this disaster. This film casts her as Roz, an unhappy, tag-along, working class girlfriend to an equally uninteresting petty thief, Frank (Denis Leary). After seven years of a nowhere relationship, Roz wants out, but can't make the break. Instead she tags along on what is supposedly his last job, to steal a painting and deliver it to a buyer. Unbeknownst to them they have stolen a Matisse, valued at $4 million, and are in over their heads.

The couple bickers and the relationship unravels while they nonchalantly head off a squadron of police cars, and move from car, to train, to boat, ruggedly carting along their painting wrapped in a garbage bag. The script has them personifying every class, race, and gender stereotype imaginable. She is a simple cashier, a Jewish girl from New York with a heavy accent and dyed hair who reads fashion magazines and dreams of settling down, having kids, and one day taking a trip to Italy. He is an unwashed, dimwitted, homophobic, part-time plasterer, who wears a leather jacket, doesn't shave, and just wants a beer in front of the TV. To try to mend their fraying union Frank decided to pull the job off early and make the trip into a weekend getaway, leaving three days between the robbery and the Sunday drop off, but by the time they make their destination, they've run out of money. They break into an enormous New England home whose owners are on vacation, and get a taste of the good life. Evan (Stephen Dillane), a sophisticated bachelor next door, believing that they are friends of his neighbor's children, invites the couple to his party and takes an interest in Roz. Surrounded by a privilege and sophistication beyond their reach, the rift between Frank and Roz widens throughout the weekend as they both cope with their class status in different ways. Frank takes a cynical, belligerent and complacent attitude, but Roz tries to play along, takes up painting and goes horse riding and boating with Evan, imagin-

CREDITS

Frank O'Brien: Denis Leary
Roz: Sandra Bullock
Evan Marsh: Stephen Dillane
O'Malley: Yaphet Kotto
Beano: Wayne Robson
Todd: Jonathan Tucker

Origin: USA
Released: 1996
Production: James G. Robinson for a Morgan Creek production; released by Warner Brothers
Direction: Bill Bennett
Screenplay: Denis Leary and Mike Armstrong
Cinematography: Andrew Lesnie
Editing: Bruce Green
Production design: David Chapman
Art direction: Mark Hack
Costume design: Olga Dimitrov
Sound: Glen Gauthier
Music: Nick Glennie-Smith
Casting: Todd Thaler
MPAA rating: R
Running Time: 96 minutes

ing that an opportunity is opening up to her through the interest of the wealthy man.

The plot is brought to its rather flat climax by the development of two very sketchy subplots. Frank's boss Beano (Wayne Robson), after learning on TV of the painting's value, sets out with his three thugs to intervene before the painting is handed over. These cigar smoking, polyester-clad, hoods are followed by Detective O'Malley (Yaphet Kotto), a man devoted to capturing a legendary art thief, who everyone but him believes to be dead. Frank, meanwhile has learned from an art book that the paintings in Evan's home are stolen goods of immense value. On Sunday afternoon the three parties converge at the drop off point. The buyer escapes unseen, and Frank, Roz and Beano are busted. Frank decides to tell the truth and admit everything if Roz will be freed. He leads the detective to Evan's home and the real bad guy is revealed.

> Evan: "I think you're the sexiest woman I ever met."
> Roz: "You don't get out much, do you?"

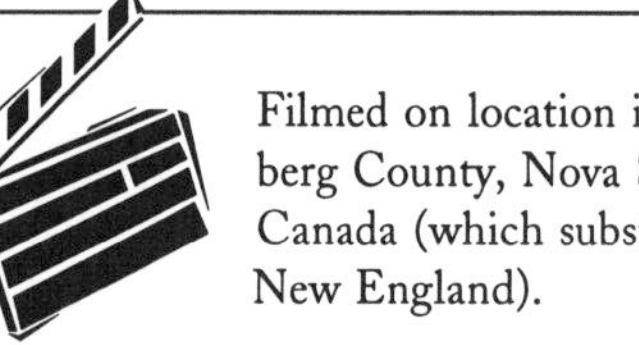

> Filmed on location in Lunenberg County, Nova Scotia, Canada (which substitutes for New England).

When it appears that there is no way out of this for Evan, and even his lawyer can't help, Roz comes to her senses and gives him a piece of her mind. Frank, she insists, is a petty thief, but at least he doesn't pretend to be something else. With disgust and hatred she slugs Evan and knocks him to the ground. The class antagonism expressed by this film is now given its full weight as a morality tale. The wealthy only seem to be respectable, but they are in fact even more lowly than common thieves, who at least are what they appear to be. Detective O'Malley commends Frank for his good detective work, drops all charges and nearly offers him a respectable job. Frank and Roz reconcile after Frank promises once again to give up the criminal life and settle down. While this is supposed to be a happy Hollywood ending, there is absolutely no reason to feel good about this couple recommitting themselves to their lousy relationship. For a film billed as a romantic comedy, it fails to offer any moments that would qualify as either romantic or funny. The script, co-written by Denis Leary, seems determined to subvert every opportunity to develop tension or suspense, and the undistinguishable performances by both Bullock and O'Brien do nothing to overcome the predictable directing by Bill Bennett.

—Reni Celeste

REVIEWS

Boxoffice. March, 1996, p. R-27.
Detroit Free Press. January 14, 1996, p. 3F.
Detroit News. January 13, 1996, p. C1.
Entertainment Weekly. January 26, 1996, p.40.
Hollywood Reporter. January 16, 1996, p. 11.
Los Angeles Times. January 15, 1996, p. F3.
New York Times. January 13, 1996, p. 21.
Rolling Stone. February 8, 1996, p. 45.
USA Today. January 15, 1996, p. 4D.
Variety. January 15, 1996, p. 126.
Washington Post. January 13, 1996, p. D1.

Two Much

A comedy about two sisters who thought they had nothing in common.—Movie tagline
"Light and beguiling!"—*Drama-Logue*
"Frantic!"—*The Hollywood Reporter*

Box Office: $1,141,556

The term "hot" applied to Hollywood stars these days seems to suggest that they will be cast in as many films as possible before the onset of the "cool-down period." This appears to be the case with the smoldering Spanish star of *Mambo Kings* (1992), Antonio Banderas. There is one thing for certain; Mr. Banderas has been busy! Recently, he has appeared in *Assassins* (1995) with Sylvester Stallone, *Desperado* (1995) directed by Robert Rodriguez, and *Never Talk to Strangers* (1995) opposite Rebecca DeMornay. *Two Much,* starring Melanie Griffith and Daryl Hannah was released in March while he was in Brazil shooting *Evita* with Madonna. This prolific amount of work gives new meaning to the word overexposed.

"God, you are so gorgeous, you know that? You're gonna look so good with me up at the altar."—Betty to boyfriend Art

As most film fans are probably aware, Banderas and Griffith fell in love while shooting *Two Much.* This fact not only caused a stir in the United States but also abroad as well. It became a mega-event in the Spanish press and propelled *Two Much* into becoming the country's highest-grossing national production in its history, bringing in an estimated 10 million dollars. Unfortunately, this "romance factor" failed to attract American audiences, in spite of some decent reviews in the trades.

Two Much, described as a "would-be modern screwball comedy" by *Chicago Tribune* critic, Michael Wilmington, is based on a novel by Donald E. Westlake. This Touchstone Pictures release was co-written and directed by Fernando Trueba, who won the 1992 Foreign Language Oscar for his work in *Belle Epoque.* Along with Pedro Almodovar, he is considered to be one of Spain's leading contemporary comic filmmakers and *Two Much* appeared to be a good English language project for Trueba to helm. This zany, screwball comedy also happens to fit nicely into the light comedies of the '30s and Trueba has been reported to be infatuated with Billy Wilder, Preston Sturges and Ernest Lubitsch. It is interesting to note that Paul Diamond (son of longtime Wilder collaborator, I.A.L. Diamond) was associate producer and rewrite man on this project.

Antonio Banderas plays Art Dodge, an art dealer who cons recent widows into buying his paintings. He surveys the obituary columns and shows up at the widow's doorstep carrying one of his expensive paintings, claiming their recently departed husband ordered it right before his untimely and tragic death. On one of these outings, he happens to show up at a mobster's funeral and encounters a very skeptical Danny Aiello (Gene), who proceeds to tell him, "When they get through with you, your face is going to look like a Picasso." Obviously not welcome, Art manages to escape and hides in the back seat of a sexy blonde's convertible as she leaves the services. She just happens to be the mobster's ex-wife, Betty (Melanie Griffith), who lovingly flips off her ex-husband as she peels out of the driveway. Surprisingly, the two are attracted to one another and end up in bed. It's not long before Betty decides that this sexy painter is for her and starts the wedding plans. She exclaims, "God, you are so gorgeous, you know that? You're gonna look so good with me at the altar." Thank you, Betty Boop. During these prenuptial proceedings, Art lays eyes on Betty's sister, Liz

CREDITS

Betty Kerner: Melanie Griffith
Art/Bart Dodge: Antonio Banderas
Liz Kerner: Daryl Hannah
Gene Paletto: Danny Aiello
Gloria: Joan Cusack
Sheldon: Eli Wallach

Origin: Spain and USA
Released: 1996
Production: Cristina Huete for an Interscope Communications, Polygram Filmed Entertainment, Sogetel, and Lola Films production; released by Touchstone Pictures
Direction: Fernando Treuba
Screenplay: Fernando Treuba, David Treuba; based on the novel by Donald Westlake
Cinematography: Jose Luis Alcaine
Editing: Nena Bernard
Music: Michel Camilo
Production design: Juan Botella
Costume design: Lala Huete
Sound: Pierre Gamet
Casting: Johanna Ray, Elaine J. Huzzar
MPAA rating: PG-13
Running Time: 115 minutes

(Daryl Hannah), who is a vision of loveliness lounging around the pool on their estate. Suddenly, panic sets in and Art is thrust into a complicated love triangle. Betty is sweet, but Liz is supreme. He ingeniously decides to disguise himself as his own twin brother, Bart, in order to woo them simultaneously. He manages to convince these two lovelies of this by pulling the ponytail out of his rubber band, donning gloves, and presto, he's Bart. The plight of this double identity is what catapults the overtaxed hero into all sorts of farcical and intricate dilemmas.

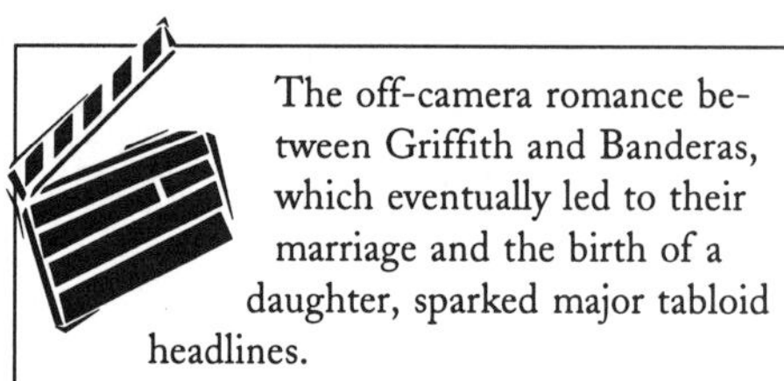

The off-camera romance between Griffith and Banderas, which eventually led to their marriage and the birth of a daughter, sparked major tabloid headlines.

As stated earlier, Banderas has been working a lot these days and working hard. It's apparent that no matter what the vehicle or the character, the actor gives it his best. He is always working diligently and tirelessly and this is evident in *Two Much.* Although he does not have the physical comedic talents of Robin Williams (*Mrs. Doubtfire*) or Jim Carrey (*The Mask,* etc.), he certainly is no embarrassment. There is one scene, in particular, where he is hopping from one bed to another and ends up falling into the swimming pool. It showcases not only the actor's comedic timing, but physical agility as well. In spite of this earnest attempt, Banderas cannot resuscitate the nonsensical script written by Fernando Trueba and his brother, David.

There has been some attempt to turn Melanie Griffith into a modern-day Judy Holliday, the delicious comedic actress of the '40s and '50s. In fact, the remake of *Born Yesterday,* one of Holliday's most well-known performances starred Griffith and her then-husband, Don Johnson. It was not received well by the audience or the critics. However, the comparisons continue to be drawn—"Griffith stands out in the moments when she does a Judy Holliday, *Born Yesterday*-ish assault on her mobster ex-husband." (*Hollywood Reporter*). There are those moments during *Two Much* when the actress does hit the target and gets some laughs. However, mostly she just overplays the stereotypical "dumb blonde" with little variation. After awhile, her Betty Boop voice seems shrill rather than sexy. When ex-mobster husband, Gene, (played competently by Danny Aiello) kisses Art on the cheek, she whines, "What are you giving him, the kiss of death?" This same line could be used about her one-note, lackadaisical performance.

Daryl Hannah, who plays Liz Kerner (Betty's sister) looks lovely and glamorous. She doesn't really have much to do other than look surprised and amused and offer a "classy contrast" to her flashy "airhead" sister. There is a certain vague blandness about her performance and at times she seems to dwarf Banderas with her gangly physicality. Somehow, it diminishes Banderas's "sex symbol stature" and he suddenly appears to be very short and diminutive in his scenes with Hannah.

Yet another problematic aspect of this film was the casting of Eli Wallach as Banderas' father, Sheldon Dodge. Mr. Wallach is a fine actor and was actually quite funny in this film, although he had to cope with some lame and unwitty dialogue. When trying to escape from the mob in one scene, he has difficulty driving a stick shift. "It's just like a woman, put it in slow and then floor it," advises one of his cronies. Is this vulgar line really necessary in any context? The problem with Mr. Wallach playing Art's father, Sheldon Dodge, is that one speaks with a Spanish accent (Art) and dear old Dad doesn't. None of this makes much sense.

Joan Cusack as Art's assistant provides some welcome comic relief from the silly shenanigans going on around her. The actress's inherent offbeat quality serves her well here, and her deadpan reactions are quite funny. As she continually covers for her boss, she laments, "I can't believe this is how I'm using my degree in architecture." Although her character is thinly written, her one-liners consistently get laughs.

Upon watching *Two Much,* it becomes evident how demanding romantic farce is and how difficult it is to execute well. Fernando Trueba combined some promising elements that could have made this vehicle sparkle. He had three attractive leads; he had Spain's finest cinematographer, Jose Luis Alcaine, as director of photography; he had great music by Michel Camilo, and nice pizazz added by costumer Lala Huete. Unfortunately, these elements did not come together to make this a good film. In order for an impossible premise like the one in *Two Much* to work, the film must make an audience suspend a certain amount of disbelief to work as a romantic, somewhat magical farce. This can only be achieved by skillful and specific writing, directing and acting, not to mention precise timing. The humor needs to be grounded in the relationships between the central characters and enhanced by the physical pranks. Otherwise, it is like watching a "Tom and Jerry" cartoon. Trueba tries to rely too heavily on the overexerted pratfall comedy that ultimately doesn't pay off. After awhile, these wacky vignettes become tedious and tiresome and make the audience forget about the people. They simply become acrobatic and hold no meaning.

The lesson here is that comedy must be taken seriously by those creating it. If human interaction is overlooked and mugging replaces responding, then it all becomes too one-dimensional for the audience to care. A lot of effort appears to have gone into the making of *Two Much,* but ultimately, it misses the mark.

—*Rob Chicatelli*

REVIEWS

Boxoffice Magazine. May, 1996, p. 74.
Chicago Tribune. March 15, 1996, p. 5.
Los Angeles Times. March 15, 1996, p. F18.
New York Times. March 15, 1996, p. C21.
Variety. February 26, 1996, p. 66.
Village Voice. March 26, 1996, p. 58.

Under the Donim Tree; Etz Hadomin Tafus

Box Office: $53,532

Under the Domim Tree *is a poignant look at orphans of the Holocaust living at Oudim State Boarding School in 1953 Israel. The film, directed by Eli Cohen, is shown in Hebrew, with English subtitles. It is based on Gila Almagor's autobiographical novel of the same name, the sequel to *The Summer of Aviya,* the subject of Cohen's 1989 film.

Under the Domim Tree follows the children, now teenagers, dealing with inner conflicts as a result of the war, and normal interpersonal relationships—having lived less than a normal childhood.

The film tells the stories of four youths at the village: Aviya (Kaipo Cohen), who is searching for information about her dead father; Yola (Orli Perl), who learns her father is alive in Warsaw; Yurek (Ohad Knoller), who struggles with his feelings for Aviya and his need to take care of a young boy in the village; and Mira (Riki Blich), whose story is at the heart of the film.

The film opens as the entire school searches for a boy who has run away. It is nighttime when they find his body in a swamp. While there is no explanation for what happened to him or why he ran away, the children accept as much responsibility for his accident as he had, as someone is heard saying they should have taken care of him. Their past, clearly, will always be a part of them.

The film is led by a competent cast of mostly unknowns, and the simple cinematography by David Gurfinkel draws you in quickly. There are some haunting images in the film, such as the white sheets blowing in the nighttime wind; eerily remindful of the ghosts that hang over the children.

The author, Almagor, portrays her own mother in the film, with Kaipo Cohen portraying her daughter, Aviya, the young Almagor, seeking answers about her father. While Aviya is not technically an orphan and was not in the Holocaust, she is at Oudim because she is declared a ward of the state, without a father and whose delusional mother lives in a mental hospital. Almagor depicts a grim character, the mother living in an institution, inscribing numbers on her arm like those used in the concentration camps; although she, herself, was not in the war. A determined Aviya eventually discovers a photograph of her father, leading her to find out that her father was killed before she was born. A trip to his grave site finally gives the teenager closure.

In the more eerie moments of the film, Yurek (Knoller) dashes through the school grounds late at night carrying on piggyback the young boy, Ze'evik (Jeniya Catzan), while Ze'evik emits shrieking animal cries. Thinking the boy might be mentally impaired, he is sent to another school, separated from Yurek. Zev runs away and the children at Oudim spend a morbidly familiar night searching for their friend. When Zev turns up at Oudim, Yurek takes measures to insure the boys are never again separated.

The most touching stories are that of Yola (Perl) and Mira (Blich), paradoxically, the story of one girl looking forward to reuniting with her father, and the other one refusing parents who want their daughter back.

As Yola prepares for the trip to Poland and the reunion with her father, the girls ceremoniously shower her with letters to take to their homeland, dreaming it will one day be them making this journey. Sadly, she never makes the trip; her father, she finds out, has indeed, perished in the war.

Mira, new to Oudim, refuses to assimilate with the other students. When a couple arrives at the school claiming to be her parents, she rejects them and demands a hearing with a judge to prove they are not her relatives. Ironically, the youth from the school, whom she had snubbed, become her strongest supporters. In the emotional climax, a vindicated Mira realizes she is, after all, one of them.

Throughout the film, the children each escape their bitter past by finding solace under the title Domim tree, the only tree on the dry hillside near the school. There is

CREDITS

Aviya: Kaipo Cohen
Yurek: Ohad Knoller
Ariel: Julino Mer
Mother: Gila Almagor
Yola: Orli Peri
Mira: Riki Blich

Origin: Israel
Released: 1995
Production: Gila Almagor and Eitan Evan for a HSA Ltd. production; released by Strand
Direction: Eli Cohen
Screenplay: Eyal Sher, Gila Almagor; based on the novel by Almagor
Cinematography: David Gurfinkel
Editing: Danny Shik
Music: Benny Nagari
Production design: Eitan Levy
Costumes: Rona Doron
MPAA rating: Unrated
Running Time: 102 minutes

a sweet underlying bit of humor in the form of a Dutch émigré who envisions a field of tulips surrounding this arid hillside, and his perseverance at achieving his dream. In the charming end of the film a new hope for life springs up in the form of hundreds of tulips sprouting up around the tree.

—*Debbi Hoffman*

REVIEWS

Boxoffice. March, 1996, p. R-24.
The Hollywood Reporter. December 4, 1995, p.16.
The Los Angeles Times. May 15, 1996, p. F3.
The New Republic. May 13, 1996, p. 29.
The New York Times. May 5, 1996, p. H23.
Variety. June 5, 1995, p. 40.

Unforgettable

He loved her. He lost her. He won't let her memory die . . . until it tells him who killed her.—Movie tagline

"A gripping and spellbinding piece of work."—Michael Medved, *New York Post*

"Dahl's visual imagination is in fine form."—Janet Maslin, *New York Times*

"A well-paced, stylish thriller."—Kevin McManus, *The Washington Post*

Box Office: $2,500,000

Ray Liotta is suspected of killing his wife in *Unforgettable.*

John Dahl has had one of the most unusual careers of any American film director. His first three films had varying degrees of difficulty finding exposure in theaters, but he has developed a strong cult following for his stylish low-budget films noir primarily through their exposure on Home Box Office, Cinemax, and videocassette. *Unforgettable* is finally his chance to work with a larger budget ($20 million, eight times that of his previous film) and to have his film advertised and distributed as it should be, but the result, though well made and engrossing, is primarily a busier but less interesting treatment of Dahl's previous themes.

Dr. David Krane (Ray Liotta), a Seattle medical examiner, is suspected of murdering his wife, Cara (Caroline Elliott), but the charges are dropped because a rookie policeman mishandles some incriminating evidence. David is equally obsessed by the loss of his wife, for which he blames the alcoholism he has since overcome, and by proving his innocence. Investigating a drugstore shooting, he discovers a clue that links these murders with his wife's, and then an unexpected way of finding the killer comes his way when he hears a lecture by a university researcher, Dr. Martha Briggs (Linda Fiorentino), who has experimented with memory transference by injecting laboratory rats with a serum combined with the cerebral spinal fluid of other rats.

Nat King Cole's ballad, *Unforgettable,* is heard over the closing credits.

Martha has not even considered a human experiment because of her drug's side effects which have caused thirty percent of her rats to die of heart attacks. David breaks into her laboratory, steals her serum, and then takes his wife's spinal fluid from a police evidence room. Injecting himself, he experiences her murder but does clearly see the killer, so he takes fluid from one of the drugstore shooting victims and, after experiencing her death, creates a sketch of the killer, Eddie Dutton (Kim Coates). He tracks down Dutton and corners him in a church only for Dutton, while holding a child hostage, to be shot by Don Bresler (Peter Coyote), a police detective sympathetic to David. The desperate David then steals fluid from Dutton's corpse and finds that some unknown person finished off his wife after Dutton strangled her. He continues his relentless pursuit, ignoring even a heart attack, until he finds the real killer.

Unforgettable is far-fetched, though less for the science-fiction aspects of memory transference than for the headlong twists and turns and coincidences of Bill Geddie's screenplay, but Geddie and Dahl never give the viewer much time to think about how ridiculous it all is. The plot's biggest flaw is that it is clear from the first scene that the villain is one of two characters. Since one of these potential villains is too obvious (because he seems to hate David), it must be the other. The mystery at the center of the film is rendered anticlimactic.

"I think you've been watching too many episodes of 'Quincy,' Doc."—detective to Krane

There are problems with the memory transference device since when David has one of these experiences he is both inside the person whose memory he is sharing and outside observing what is happening to this person. The film's title is also misleading since David's obsession with his dead wife is less important than his need to find her murderer—especially after he discovers she had been having an affair. Having her sister (Kim Cattrall) identify Cara's lover as a policeman is a red herring of sorts since the viewer assumes he is one of the detectives who have already appeared in the film, but he turns out, after several minutes of wrong assumptions, to be an entirely new character, though one essential to the plot's resolution. It is as if Geddie and Dahl have painted themselves into a corner only to knock down a wall to get out.

Unforgettable has the traditional film noir element of the slightly corrupt innocent caught up in a potentially fatal conflict with evil, but its film noir side is secondary to its thriller side. While the film, although entertaining, is not that significant in itself, it is interesting to consider in light of Dahl's earlier, much better films. In both *Kill Me Again* (1989) and *Red Rock West* (1992), the hero innocently wanders into life-threatening situations only to survive (rather than triumph) through a combination of perseverance, luck, and the incompetence of the villains. Dahl reverses this approach with *The Last Seduction* (1994) since the villain is the protagonist, taking advantage of both her corrupt husband and an innocent bumpkin who falls into her trap.

The hero of *Unforgettable* is much smarter, more resourceful, and more determined that Dahl's earlier innocents, and David has the too-good-to-be-true Martha to help him as well. The latter is a major departure for Dahl since women are extremely treacherous in his previous films. What is good about Dahl's earlier work is his wit and visual style. His first three films are increasingly comic with *The Last Seduction* a classic black comedy, but *Unforgettable* is too concerned with getting from one plot point to the next to have a sense of humor. Dahl usually likes a slow pace with long scenes enlivened by camera movement that helps create a sense of menace.

Unforgettable has considerably more camera movement than usual with left-right, right-left, top-bottom, and diagonal pans and tracks, but Dahl never has a chance to create his usual hypnotic mood because the violent flashback nature of the film demands hyperkinetic editing. Cara's murder is shown so many times in much the same way that it grows monotonous if not sadistic. What tone Dahl is able to sustain is aided by Christopher Young's music which heightens the drama without overpowering it, recalling occasionally Bernard Herrmann's great scores for such Alfred Hitchcock masterpieces as *Vertigo* (1958), which *Unforgettable* superficially resembles.

After an impressive debut as the sadistic psycho in *Something Wild* (1986), Liotta has declined into a bland leading man, being the weakest link in such films as *Goodfellas* (1990) and *No Escape* (1994). He is suitable, however, for such a character as David since he is too pleasant for the audience to be too concerned over the sanity of David's obsession, and his passivity is strangely appropriate for David's

CREDITS

Dr. David Krane: Ray Liotta
Dr. Martha Briggs: Linda Fiorentino
Don Besler: Peter Coyote
Stewart Gleick: Christopher McDonald
Dr. Curtis Avery: David Paymer
Eddie Dutton: Kim Coates
Kelly: Kim Cattrall
Cara Krane: Caroline Elliott
Michael Stratton: Duncan Fraser
Joseph Hodner: Garwin Sanford

Origin: USA
Released: 1996
Production: Dino De Laurentiis and Martha De Laurentiis; released by Metro Goldwyn Mayer
Direction: John Dahl
Screenplay: Bill Geddie
Cinematography: Jeffrey Jur
Editing: Eric L. Beason and Scott Chestnut
Production design: Rob Pearson
Art direction: Doug Byggdin
Costume design: Terry Dresbach, Glenne Campbell
Sound: Eric J. Batut
Music: Christopher Young
Casting: Carol Lewis
MPAA rating: R
Running Time: 111 minutes

essential function as an observer of others' memories. Liotta spends much of the film lying on his back responding to violent acts only David—and the audience—can see.

After years of mostly unmemorable performances in even less memorable films—with the notable exception of Martin Scorsese's underrated *After Hours* (1985)—Fiorentino was discovered by critics and discerning viewers with her delightful portrayal of the wonderfully ruthless manipulator in *The Last Seduction.* She may have taken this less demanding role out of a sense of debt to Dahl or to avoid being typecast. That her almost mousy scientist is the complete opposite of that temptress allows Fiorentino to show her considerable range. In conveying Martha's concern for David so effectively, she creates a sane center necessary to counterbalance his excesses.

The ultimate irony of *Unforgettable* in terms of Dahl's career is that it was much less enthusiastically embraced by reviewers and, despite heavy television advertising, made an unusually quick exit from theaters. Unfortunately, it is also less likely, unlike Dahl's previous work, to be rediscovered or reevaluated later on.

—Michael Adams

REVIEWS

Interview. February, 1996, p. 60.
Los Angeles Times. February 23, 1996, p. F4.
Mademoiselle. February, 1996, p. 92.
New York Times. February 23, 1996, p. C6.
Playboy. March, 1996, p. 20.
USA Today. February 23, 1996, p. 4D.
Variety. February 26, 1996, p. 64.
Village Voice. March 3, 1996, p. 41.
The Wall Street Journal. February 23, 1996, p. A11.

Unhook the Stars

When prim & proper meets wild & crazy, get ready to . . . *Unhook the Stars.*—Movie tagline

"A warm, fresh joy of a film! Gena Rowland's performance reminds us just why she's one of the glories of American acting. This is Marisa Tomei's best role ever."—Jay Carr, *Boston Globe*

"A knockout! A funny, perceptive slice-of-life movie! Gena Rowland's performance is perfection!"—Ed Kelleher, *Film Journal*

"A joy to watch! Gena Rowlands and Marisa Tomei are in top form!"—Kevin Thomas, *Los Angeles Times*

"Gena Rowlands delivers a wonderfully detailed portrait! She effuses a tenderness, humor and joy that are utterly winning!"—Stephen Holden, *New York Times*

"A marvelous film! Gena Rowlands is spectacular!"—John Anderson, *Newsday*

Box Office: $123,774

"Mothers are the architects of society but they're too often abandoned once their apparent maternal function is complete." This quote by Nick Cassavetes (son of Gena Rowlands and the late John Cassavetes) was printed in the January issue of *Film Threat.* Actually, it is a very insightful statement made by Cassavetes and is the basic premise for *Unhook the Stars,* starring Mom Rowlands and Academy Award winner, Marisa Tomei. (Tomei won the Oscar for 1992's *My Cousin Vinny.*) This subject matter raises a myriad of questions concerning society's view of a matriarchal family unit. In addition, it opens up the issue of aging women's roles in a youth-centered culture. It is most definitely a formidable challenge for a young director to tackle for his directorial debut.

It certainly was a wise choice for Cassavetes to put his mother, the incomparable Gena Rowlands, in the starring role—a very wise decision. When asked how it felt to be directed by her son, Ms. Rowlands responded, "We're just totally separate. I have no problems taking orders from Nick, none whatsoever. He just has to go to bed without dinner sometimes." The actress is used to working with her loved ones. It is well known that this superlative actress has primarily worked in projects with her late husband, the controversial, and often brilliant, actor/director, John Cassavetes. Films such as *Faces* (1968), *Husbands* (1970), *Minnie and Moskowitz* (1971), *A Woman Under the Influence* (1974), and *The Killing of a Chinese Bookie* (1976) are still considered to be cinema-verite classics. The attention and praise are well-deserved, since Cassavetes was not only a free spirit, but an innovative and imaginative filmmaker, as well. Inevitably, comparisons will be made between father and son when people go to see *Unhook the Stars.* The question everyone will ask is, "Has the banner been passed to the next generation?" Yet, another formidable challenge!

Stars is a story about a financially independent widow named Mildred (Gena Rowlands). She happens to live with her angry, rebellious daughter, Ann Mary Margaret (Moira Kelly). Ann Mary greets her mother at breakfast with comments such as, "You're a nightmare." Exactly why she feels this way is never carefully defined in this somewhat vague script—she just doesn't get along with Mom and decides to move out. Monica (Marisa Tomei), a crude party girl, lives next door to Mildred with her abusive husband, Frankie. He is a tattooed Lothario, who appears to be a distant relative of Stanley Kowalski. They also have a six-year-old son named J.J., played innocently by Jake Lloyd. It appears that they are a modern-day version of "white trash living in the burbs." Exactly how they afford this apparently affluent neighborhood is another point that is never fully explained. Monica's charming husband walks out on her, leaving her without any visible means of support. She finds herself a job, but is faced with another problem—who will baby-sit J.J.? It was not established (once again) if Monica had any prior relationship with Mildred, but she practically drops off the little tyke on her doorstep. Seemingly nonplussed, Mildred gladly accepts the responsibility and proceeds to become J.J.'s surrogate mother. Her relationship with the child rapidly grows into a strong, loving bond, which is depicted in a series of holiday vignettes. Lisa Katzman in the *Village Voice* wrote, "Did Hallmark finance this film?" Who knows, maybe they did! In addition to her idyllic maternal duties, Mildred becomes close friends with Monica—an unlikely match. Mildred doesn't seem to mind (or even notice) when Monica swears like a trooper over Thanksgiving dinner. The expression "love is blind" certainly applies here. One night on the town, Monica takes Mildred to a local pub, where she meets a sexy Canadian trucker named Big Tommy (played with subtle charm by Gerard Depardieu). He becomes somewhat smitten with this attractive, mature woman, which opens up untapped emotions in the still beauteous Ms. Rowlands. The scenes between these two fine actors possess an innocence and sweetness to them. It is more refreshing than lurid thanks to the delicacy with which it was handled.

"Right here in this life, you get reincarnated. You change."—Mildred

Unfortunately, for Mildred, the situation takes a radical turn when Monica's prodigal husband returns and takes over his neglected parental duties. Mildred is no longer needed and it is a crushing blow to her. In many ways, it is her day of reckoning—what now? Which direction will she take, now that she has become disposable? Fortunately, she does have options, which is not always the case with many widows. Due to the circumstances, her plight is more of a dilemma, rather than a crisis. This situation evokes curiosity, rather than concern, from the viewer. The stakes do not appear to be that high, which somewhat dilutes the audience's involvement.

Throughout the film, the one element that the young director has learned from his father is the importance of characterization. Each member of the cast fleshes out their roles into fully realized, three-dimensional people, in spite of a weakly written script. Perhaps Cassavetes, who wrote the script along with Helen Caldwell, took on too much for a first-timer. The final project seems to indicate that he is a better director than screenwriter. The strength of the piece can be attributed to a fine ensemble of actors, which is certainly a credit to casting director Matthew Barry. Excellent ensemble acting happens to be a Cassavetes trademark.

Gena Rowlands could be one of America's most interesting and unique actresses. She is consistently excellent and always fascinating to watch. There is a "luminosity" (for want of a better word) that she brings to the screen and a truthfulness to all her performances. Many critics feel that she has not received the acclaim that she deserves due to her

CREDITS

Mildred: Gena Rowlands
Monica: Marisa Tomei
Big Tommy: Gerard Depardieu
J.J.: Jake Lloyd
Ann Mary Margaret: Moira Kelly
Ethan: David Kelly

Origin: USA
Released: 1996
Production: Rene Cleitman for a Hachette Premiere production; released by Miramax Films
Direction: Nick Cassavetes
Screenplay: Nick Cassavetes, Helen Caldwell
Cinematography: Phedon Papamichael
Editing: Petra von Gelffen
Production design: Phedon Papamichael, Sr.
Costumes: Tessa Stephensen
Music: Steven Hufsteter
MPAA rating: R
Running Time: 105 minutes

AWARDS AND NOMINATIONS

Screen Actors Guild 1996 Nominations: Actress (Rowlands), Supporting Actress (Tomei)

lack of involvement in mainstream Hollywood projects. Whatever the reasons for this opinion, she still remains a great talent in films today.

Unhook the Stars should be viewed on its own merit. The film may not have the "grittiness" of a John Cassavetes film, or the feeling of spontaneity and improvisation, but it does have its own unique quality. It works hard on imagery, relationships and real people. It benefits greatly from the presence of Rowlands and a strong performance from Marisa Tomei. However, it doesn't dig deep enough into the issues and backgrounds of its characters. The viewer needs more information and the holes in the script leave too many unanswered questions for it to be completely satisfying. Stephen Holden of *The New York Times* called it a "sentimental contrivance constructed around its star." This statement does have some element of truth to it, albeit slightly harsh. It needed to delve deeper, to examine the lives of the characters more closely. It needn't have had the raw cutting edge of the director's Dad, but neither should it have been a Disney movie of the week.

—*Rob Chicatelli*

REVIEWS

Boxoffice Online. November, 1996.
Chicago Tribune. February 14, 1997, p. 5.
Entertainment Weekly. February 21, 1997, p. 107.
Film Threat. January, 1997, p. 59.
Los Angeles Times. November 1, 1996, p. F6.
New York Times. November 1, 1996, p. C20.
Rolling Stone. November 28, 1996, p. 143.
USA Today. November 1, 1996, p. 4D.
Variety Online. September 3, 1996.
Village Voice. November 5, 1996, p. 78.

Up Close and Personal

The attraction was unmistakable. The passion was undeniable. Their love was unconditional.—Movie tagline

"Redford and Pfeiffer turn up the heat!"—*Newsweek*

"Sensational."—Gene Shalit, Today, *NBC-TV*

Box Office: $51,088,705

Up Close and Personal joins the growing list of films centered around the world of television news journalism. Such distinguished films as *Network* (1976), *The China Syndrome* (1979), and *Broadcast News* (1987) have effectively captured the environment of broadcast news journalism in all of its neurotic intensity, zeroing in on the schizophrenic relationship this form of journalism has with objective reporting and glitzy, exploitative entertainment.

Therefore, it is surprising that *Up Close and Personal* takes such a basic, timid approach to its subject environment, as if it were the first film to stage a drama in a newsroom and were introducing its audience to this style of journalism. It takes this approach by recycling one of the oldest of plot lines, one which served as the basis for *What Price Hollywood?* (1932), and its three remakes, all titled *A Star is Born* (1937, 1954, 1976). This is the story line which details the life of an innocent, ambitious and talented woman who fulfills her career dreams with help and guidance from a lover/mentor as his own stellar accomplishments in the same line of business are eventually overshadowed by his protege.

Michelle Pfeiffer's sister Dedee also plays her character's sister in the film.

Told in flashback, the film begins with Tally Atwater (Michelle Pfeiffer), a successful broadcast journalist, preparing for a documentary based on her life. Insisting that she knew from a young age the type of career she wanted to pursue, Tally begins by relating her first attempts to establish herself in the broadcast journalism field. As a young woman—whose first name is actually Sally—she prepares a demo tape, filming news events around her home town of Reno, Nevada, and supplying journalistic commentary. She sends the tape to a multitude of television news stations around the country, and receives only one response, from an independent television station in Miami, Florida.

Flying out to Miami for an interview, she meets the news director, Warren Justice (Robert Redford). Upon meeting Sally for the first time, Warren calls her "Sweetheart" and ridicules her demo tape. He then makes her the station's "go-fer," responsible for making coffee and running meager errands. Eager to please, Sally performs her undistinguished duties and begins making changes in her appearance after Warren criticizes her make-up, wardrobe, and hairstyle. She also continually pesters Warren to give her a chance to report the news.

Sally gets her first break when the station director decides to take a comical approach to the way the weather is reported and makes her the new "wacky" weather girl. When she makes her debut, dressed in rain gear, Warren tells the anchorman to introduce her as Tally, which stuns Sally to the point of speechlessness while she is on camera. Although her first appearance is a disaster, Warren is impressed with her on-camera presence, saying, "She eats the lens."

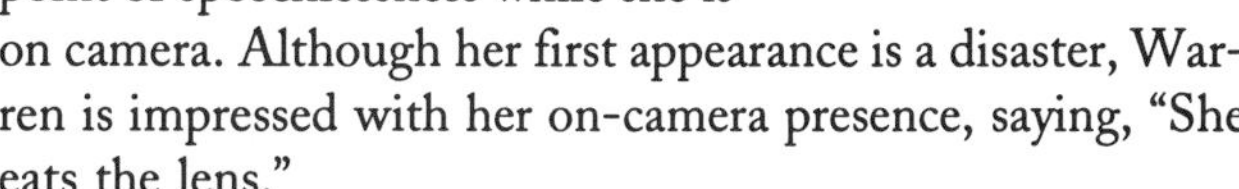

"Every day we have is one more than we deserve."—Warren Justice

Sally—now Tally—goes on to prove herself as a competent weather caster to the point where she is given lifestyle and human interest stories to report. Tally finally gets a full-fledged news assignment when a news van breaks down on its way to an ocean drowning story and Tally rushes to the sight where she meets Warren who coaxes her, off-camera, to a stunning commentary on the tragedy. After this event, Tally continually proves herself as Warren continually offers her guidance. Soon, their work relationship becomes a romantic one.

When their personal and professional relationships becomes more substantial, Tally begins delving into Warren's past and finds that he was once one of the top news reporters in the nation, having interviewed several United States Presidents, and covered international events including the Vietnam War. He was undone, however, by his insistence on finding out the truth of an event regardless if the reporting made a high-profile person appear hypocritical or an event appear to undermine the establishment. Thus, the reason for his working as a news director for a small Miami television station.

Warren still has influential contacts in the television news business, one of whom is Bucky Terranova (Joe Mantegna). When Warren introduces Bucky to Tally, Bucky ends up offering her a position in a station he owns based in Philadelphia, one of the top television markets in the nation. Warren encourages her to accept the offer, even though it will mean the end of their romantic relationship. Tally decides to accept the job offer.

She soon regrets her decision when the anchorwoman at the Philadelphia station, Marcia McGrath (Stockard Channing), treats her as if she were a brainless blonde. Tally responds by changing her hair color to brunette to match Marcia's. When this fails to earn her any respect, she calls Warren who flies out and reviews her earlier taped assignments. Warren tells her to remain true to her character, to give the public the real Tally Atwater. Tally takes his advice, and soon she has replaced Marcia as news anchorwoman.

Back in Miami, Warren repeatedly objects to the station director's insistence on the news becoming more entertainment-oriented. After Warren's objections become ultimatums, he is fired. Tally finds out about the firing and asks Bucky to give Warren a position at the Philadelphia station working with her covering election news. He agrees. Soon, the two have re-established their romantic relationship to the point where they agree to get married.

Warren, however, feels demeaned in his new position and decides to accept an offer to cover a developing story in Panama. Before he leaves, Tally covers a story inside a prison and becomes a hostage in a prison riot. Warren, directing her from a news van outside the prison, gives her emotional support, resulting in a stellar series of live newscasts during the riot.

Tragedy results when Warren leaves for Panama and is gunned down while reporting a skirmish between rebels and government troops. The film ends with Tally's documentary airing during a tribute dinner given in her honor as anchorwoman for the most prestigious news company in the nation.

Based loosely on the book, *Golden Girl* by Alanna Nash, which detailed the rise and tragic fall of national television news reporter Jessica Savitch, *Up Close and Personal* fails as both a film about the broadcast news business and as a love story.

The film's major failing is the script, a factor that is both surprising and not surprising since it is credited to two highly-respected non-fiction writers and former journalists—husband and wife John Gregory Dunne and Joan Didion—who also shared screenwriting credits for the third—and least compelling—remake of *A Star is Born*. *Up Close and Personal* uses the same story line as *Star*. However, it has none of the dark, obsessional nuances of the original story, something it could have easily incorporated into the drama had it been more faithful to the emotionally-charged life of Jessica Savitch. The result is a film with an overly-familiar story line peopled with attractive but bland and unconvincing characters.

Adding to the film's lack of emotional appeal is its lack of integrity, exemplified by the Warren Justice character. Justice is supposedly someone who values truth in reporting first and foremost, someone who abhors news reporting as

AWARDS AND NOMINATIONS

Academy Awards 1996 Nominations: Best Song ("Because You Loved Me")
Golden Globe Award 1997 Nominations: Best Original Song ("Because You Loved Me")

a form of entertainment. Yet, his attacks on Tally's physical appearance, his comments about her having a personality that "Eats the camera," and his faith in her as an honest reporter after she admits at one point that she faked most of the news events on her demo tape, all paint him as a person more interested tabloid glitz and on-screen glamour rather than truth in news reporting. Again, this is a reflection on the script which plays more like another remake of *A Star is Born* rather than a film in the tradition of *Broadcast News* and *Network*.

Director Jon Avnet was obviously hampered by the lackluster script. One of his recent previous efforts, *Fried Green Tomatoes* (1991) proved he has the ability to direct a film told in the flashback format and peopled with compelling, quirky characters full of dark as well as angelic nuances. Given the talent involved in *Up Close and Personal,* the film should have been a much more highly-charged drama with darkly incisive insights into the broadcast journalism field. Instead, it ends up as merely another uninspired remake of an old Hollywood standard.

—Jim Kline

CREDITS

Warren Justice: Robert Redford
Tally Atwater: Michelle Pfeiffer
Marcia McGrath: Stockard Channing
Bucky Terranova: Joe Mantegna
Joanna Kennelly: Kate Nelligan
Ned Jackson: Glenn Plummer

Origin: USA
Released: 1996
Production: Jon Avnet, David Nicksay and Jordan Kerner for a Touchstone Pictures and Cinergi Pictures; released by Buena Vista
Direction: Jon Avnet
Screenplay: Joan Didion and John Gregory Dunne; suggested by the book *Golden Girl* by Alanna Nash
Cinematography: Karl Walter Lindenlaub
Editing: Debra Neil-Fisher
Production design: Jeremy Conway
Art direction: Mark Mansbridge, Bruce Alan Miller
Costume design: Albert Wolsky
Sound: Charles Wilborn
Casting: David Rubin
Music: Thomas Newman
MPAA rating: PG-13
Running Time: 124 minutes

REVIEWS

Entertainment Weekly. March 15, 1996, p.46.
Los Angeles Times. March 1, 1996, p. F1.
New York Times. March 1, 1996, p. C1.
New Yorker. March 11, 1996, p. 107.
Newsweek. March 4, 1996, p. 70.
Rolling Stone. March 21, 1996, p. 103.
USA Today. March 1, 1996, p. 1D.
Variety. March 4, 1996, p. 72.
Village Voice. March 5, 1996, p. 44.

Vertigo

"Mesmerizing."—Richard Jameson, *Cinemania Online*

"Magnificent."—Larry Worth, *New York Post*

"The revival event of the season. Fascinating . . . the deepest, darkest masterpiece of Hitchcock's career."—Janet Maslin, *New York Times*

Box Office: $1,760,342

Jimmy Stewart and Kim Novak in Alfred Hitchcock's classic story of fear and obsessive love in the restored version of *Vertigo.*

Dizzy old Hitchcock—that's what *Vertigo* is—but when the fully restored 70mm. version in DTS stereo premiered at the New York Film Festival on October 4, it took the industry by surprise, proving once again that there is a market for restored cinematic masterpieces. The New York premiere was followed by an exclusive run at the Ziegfeld Theatre in New York. By early November the film had extended its run to other major cities, playing such venues as the Senator Theatre, a wonderfully restored picture palace in Baltimore. By the end of November *Vertigo* was "clocking the highest per-theater average ($22,407) in the country," according to *Entertainment Weekly.* The problem was that the restored version was in 70mm. VistaVision, a format that could not play just anywhere, and that there were fewer than a dozen prints circulating nationwide.

Vertigo is "classic" Hitchcock, made in 1958 when the "master of suspense" was in his prime, sandwiched in between *Rear Window* (1954), which also starred Jimmy Stewart, and *North by Northwest* (1959). *Psycho* was still to come in 1960. For many viewers *Vertigo* was worth a trip to the city to see in its original format. This film is simply too big for video. Universal Studios was fortunate to convince Marilyn Pauline Novak to help publicize the re-release of Hitchcock's "strangest and sexiest thriller," in the words of Tom Shales, who wrote an impressive cover story on Kim Novak's film career for *The Washington Post,* pointing out that this Ice Queen was dubbed Miss Deep Freeze in a hometown beauty contest before being recruited by Harry Cohn of Columbia Pictures as a twenty-year-old starlet in 1954.

It's interesting to watch the restored *Vertigo* nearly 40 years after it was made, to see if this reputed "masterpiece" will stand up over time. In some respects it may in fact seem flawed and dated and artificial. The studio shots, though not so obvious and distracting as those of *Marnie* (1964), for example, are more apparent today than they might have been when the film was first released, but the plot is as fascinating and bizarre as ever. The film was adapted from the French novel *D'Entre les Morts* (1954, translated into English under the title *The Living Dead*), by Thomas Narcejac and Pierre Boileau, whose first novel, *Celle Qui N'Etair Plus* (1952), became the film classic *Les Diaboliques* (1955), directed by Henri-Georges Clouzot. The plot of *Vertigo* derives from Poe's "The Fall of the House of Usher," as does the name of the character Madeleine, according to Dennis R. Perry's study of "The Poe/Hitchcock Connection" in *Literature/Film Quarterly.* Perry also notices that the way Madeleine is linked to the dead Spanish beauty Carlotta, also recalls Poe's "Legia," and concludes that *Vertigo* is Hitchcock's "most effective study of the irrational."

"Do you believe that someone dead, someone out of the past, can take possession of a living being?"—Gavin Elster to Scottie Ferguson

The film begins with John "Scottie" Ferguson (James Stewart) and another policeman chasing a gunman over the rooftops of San Francisco. Scottie slips when jumping from one rooftop to another and is left desperately clinging to a loosened gutter. When his partner attempts to help him, the man falls to his death. Hitchcock literally leaves his protagonist hanging and does not bother to explain how Scottie got out of his dilemma. Scottie later reappears, bruised and recuperating, his career as a policeman ended because of his fear of heights. He blames himself for the death of his partner, as he will later blame himself for the death of the woman he loves.

The film involves some rather obvious psychological trickery and begins with abstract whirling spirals behind the credits that now seem a bit peculiar. The acting, especially Kim Novak's portrayal of Madeleine Elster and her doppelganger Judy Barton, is excellent. As the more common Judy, hired by Madeleine's husband Gavin (Tom Helmore) to participate in an elaborate murder scheme, Novak has to represent a woman far different from the elegant Madeleine, with whom Scottie falls in love. Novak plays both roles convincingly.

Scottie has been hired by his erstwhile schoolmate Gavin Elster to look after Madeleine because she is said to be suicidal. An additional crazy detail is the suggestion that Madeleine is supernaturally linked to a dead Spanish beauty named Carlotta, whose grave she visits. Madeleine, in a sort of trance, leaps into the bay one day when Scottie is following her. When Scottie saves her from drowning, that begins a mysterious romantic attachment, but the twist in this film involves not the wrong man (a familiar Hitchcock theme), but the wrong woman. Gavin plots Madeleine's

CREDITS

John "Scottie" Ferguson: James Stewart
Madeleine Elster/Judy Barton: Kim Novak
Midge: Barbara Bel Geddes
Gavin Elster: Tom Helmore
Coroner: Henry Jones
Doctor: Raymond Bailey
Manageress: Ellen Corby

Origin: USA
Released: 1958
Production: Alfred Hitchcock; released by Paramount Pictures
Direction: Alfred Hitchcock
Screenplay: Alex Coppel, Samuel Taylor; based on the novel *D'Entre les Morts* by Pierre Boileau, Thomas Narcejac
Cinematography: Robert Burks
Editing: George Tomasini
Music: Bernard Herrmann
Costumes: Edith Head
Art direction: Hal Pereira, Henry Bumstead
Special effects: John Fulton
Makeup: Wally Westmore
MPAA rating: PG
Running Time: 127 minutes

death as a fall from a tower at the mission of St. John the Baptist. Scottie chases Judy posing as Madeleine up the tower stairs, but his fear of heights keeps him from getting to the top. Gavin is waiting up there with the real Madeleine's body, ready to throw her off while Judy screams. The trick works, and somehow Gavin and Judy are able to escape from the tower undetected after Madeleine's apparent suicide.

Blaming himself for Madeleine's apparently suicidal plunge from the tower, Scottie becomes severely depressed until he meets Judy by accident, now no longer a blonde, and attempts to remake her into Madeleine. Judy is not another man's wife, as Madeleine was, and she clearly loves Scottie, but she is tarnished because she was an accomplice to murder. Scottie is clearly obsessed by his fantasy of Madeleine, not the real Madeleine, but the one Judy created. Scottie never knew the real Madeleine, though he might have seen her from afar in the tradition of courtly love. Judy is artificially made over to be her double and can be resurrected to appear as her ghostly counterpart, but the irony is that she is not the ghostly counterpart of a living person, but a dead one. That is the ghost that haunts Scottie. The situation is pretty morbid.

"The thing I loved about Alfred Hitchcock," Novak told Tom Shales, "is that he left a lot of open ends there, a lot of clues that didn't really add up the way you think they would, and sometimes, not at all." The plot of *Vertigo,* as scripted by Alex Coppel and Samuel Taylor, has holes that are still apparent, but the acting and direction save the day, and the irrational development could be turned into an advantage. According to Terrence Rafferty, for example, the Cuban critic Guillermo Cabrera Infante praised *Vertigo* as "the first great surrealist film."

The fuss over *Vertigo* seems to be part of a larger Hitchcock revival. Christopher Hampton completed *Joseph Conrad's The Secret Agent* in 1996, which redoes the source of Hitchcock's *Sabotage* (1936), updated from Conrad's story into a World War II setting. Robert Towne will write and direct an updated version of *The 39 Steps* (1935) for Warner Bros., according to *Entertainment Weekly,* and producer Mark Gordon was to retool *To Catch a Thief* (1955) for Paramount. Walter Mirisch and Sid Scheinberg were working on a new *Spellbound* (1945) for Universal. Arnold Kopelson, the hamfisted, in-your-face producer of the repulsive *Seven* (1995) had two Hitchcock remakes under development: *Dial M for Murder* (1954) and the classic *Strangers On a Train* (1951). Whether any of these projects can begin to approach the achievements of the Master of Suspense remains to be seen, but Robert Harris surely had the best idea—to restore a proven classic and let the original speak for itself, and for Hitchcock, who is probably inimitable, after all.

The *Vertigo* restoration is not so impressive as the hype surrounding it suggested it might be. Though it is generally quite good, from time to time one notices murky footage where the lighting seems inferior. Overall, the sound is better than the image, but it is disappointing to think that this is the best print of the film currently available. With these reservations in mind, does the restored *Vertigo* justify the hype? Given the level of commercial junk that was playing in the movie hinterlands when *Vertigo* was re-released, it surely does, since few contemporary pictures can hope to measure up to Hitchcock. Why anyone would want to see a remake of a Hitchcock classic, without Jimmy Stewart, or Kim Novak, or Cary Grant, or Grace Kelly, and without the Master's touch is hard to understand.

One hopes, therefore, that the restoration campaign may continue while other Hitchcock titles are being recycled by lesser talents. Anyone who respects the achievements of the cinema owes a debt of gratitude to Robert A. Harris, who worked with Jim Katz, former head of the Universal Classics Division, on the restoration of *Vertigo*. Harris worked earlier with Francis Ford Coppola and Kevin Brownlow on the American re-release of Abel Gance's classic *Napoleon* (1927, the American version was a half-hour shorter than the five-hour Brownlow reconstruction presented in London and Paris, but the presentation at the Radio City Music Hall with a full orchestra was quite remarkable), followed by reconstructions of *Lawrence of Arabia* (1962), *Spartacus* (1960), and *My Fair Lady* (1964). The *Napoleon* revival proved that there was an audience for older classics, and the success of *Vertigo* confirms that conclusion. More work remains to be done.

—*James M. Welsh*

REVIEWS

Detroit Free Press. November 21, 1996.
Entertainment Weekly. December 6, 1996, p. 8.
Films in Review. September-October, 1996, p. 40.
Literature/Film Quarterly. Vol. 24, No.4 (1996), p. 393.
New York Times. October 4, 1996, p. C12.
New Yorker. November 18, 1996, p. p. D1.
Rolling Stone. October 17, 1996.
Washington Post Weekend. October 11, 1996, p. 44.
Washington Times Metropolitan Times. October 11, 1996, p. C12.

A Very Brady Sequel

Nothing could possibly come between the Bradys . . . except her first husband!—Movie tagline

"A genuine movie rarity - a sequel better than the original!"—Gene Siskel, *Chicago Tribune*

"A very Brady breakthrough; funnier than the first."—Jim Wilson, *FOX-TV*

"Laughs for everyone! Outshines the original."—Jim Ferguson, *Prevue Channel*

Box Office: $21,443,204

A Very Brady Sequel, the follow-up to *The Brady Bunch Movie,* features the main cast from the original motion picture successfully reprising their roles. Shelley Long returns as Carol, the mother everyone wanted growing up. Gary Cole re-creates his role as Mike Brady, the patriarch and problem-solver of the bunch, always ready with an irrelevant lecture about anything that comes to mind. And the children are portrayed by Christine Taylor, bearing an uncanny resemblance to the original Marcia Brady, played on television by Maureen McCormick and Christopher Daniel Barnes as Greg, the "grooviest" guy around—at least in his mind. Jennifer Elise Cox is the pathetic Jan, still overshadowed by older sister Marcia and Paul Sutera returns as pre-pubescent Peter. Jesse Lee portrays the inquisitive Bobby and Olivia Hack is the lisping Cindy. Henriette Mantel once again reprises the role of Alice, the Brady's live-in housekeeper. Mantel is very successful in re-creating the mannerisms that Ann B. Davis brought to the television character of Alice; however, the Alice on television was a good cook. There are only a few surprise guest appearances in this film, but not from any of the original cast members, which added to the amusement of the first Brady Bunch installment.

As in the first film, the resemblances to the original actors in the television series are remarkable. The directing, however, in the sequel is lackluster. In her feature film debut, Arlene Sanford's directing is awkward, and not as smooth as that of Betty Thomas, the director of the original Brady motion picture. The close-ups of the cast, most notably in the beginning of the film of Marcia (Christine Taylor) and of Carol (Shelley Long), are too close and very uncomfortable. The audio appears to be looped and unsynchronized.

"The Brady Bunch" television series aired from 1968 to 1974. It has enough of a following today, some twenty years after the television series was canceled, that a new generation is enjoying the escapades of the bunch in syndication on television. It has spawned a stage production that each week recreates episodes from the series and has generated two feature films and countless trivia books, one written by Barry Williams, the original Greg Brady. And the fans stay tuned! "The Brady Bunch" has become somewhat of an icon today, but it is not necessary to be a fan to appreciate *A Very Brady Sequel.*

Richard Belzer, from TV's "Homicide," has a cameo as a police detective.

Tim Matheson is once again typecast as the bad guy in good guy's clothing (*Fletch* [1985]); although the only people to whom it is apparent he is not a good guy is everybody—except, of course, the Bradys. In the film, Roy Martin (Tim Matheson) shows up at the Brady house claiming to be Carol's first husband, presumably lost at sea. He is unrecognizable due to elaborate plastic surgery he underwent after having an elephant step on his head. The surgery also rendered him taller and with a deeper voice. His long absence is also due to a lengthy bout of amnesia. His soul, however, is unchanged, according to Carol, and he is offered room and board at the house of Brady. Here creates the underlying dilemma: Carol is torn between her love for Mike, her current husband, and being faithful to her first husband, Roy. After all, a Brady is always true to his—or her—word. But, Roy, of course, is really there to filch a priceless statue of a horse, now in the possession of the Bradys; although how the Bradys acquired it is unclear. The Bradys, not realizing its value, sell it in a charity auction. In his attempts to retrieve the horse, Roy, along with the Bradys, eventually ends up in Hawaii, where Roy is to collect on the bounty for the horse.

As in the first film, *A Very Brady Sequel* is a humorous look at what if. What if the Bradys lived unchanged in today's world? How would the wholesome bunch survive in today's difficult times? With a song, of course! Or two, including a rousing chorus on the plane to Hawaii. And they sound eerily like the original Brady Bunch singers.

There are several humorous moments in the film. One of the more memorable and creative is a sequence where Roy, posing as Carol's long-lost first husband, having been invited to stay with the family, joins them for dinner. However, Alice's meal, a concoction of cabbages and lard, looks less than appetizing, so he politely declines. The next day, while cleaning Roy's bedroom, Alice discovers mushrooms among Roy's belongings. That night at dinner, Alice is proud to present to Roy spaghetti with sauce made from his "special" mushrooms, hoping this will entice him to eat. Upon discovering he has eaten a whole pot of spaghetti, laced with hallucinogenic mushrooms, a bewildered Roy proclaims he is "tripping with the Bradys!" At that point he enters into a drug-induced, amusing, animated trip through the '70s with the Bradys; one of the more clever segments of the film.

"As an architect, I've learned that a house isn't just made of fake-wood paneling, shag carpeting and Formica."—Mike Brady lecturing the bunch

The sequence with Carol at the beauty salon for a beauty make-over to clear her mind of the predicament she is in, at first appears to be one of the smarter sequences in the film. The audience is eager with anticipation at the chance to see what Carol Brady would look like today in the '90s, however, the audience is equally disappointed with the result.

One of the more comical trivialities pondered by fans of "The Brady Bunch" series, about the exploits of a widowed father of three boys having married a widowed mother of three girls, has always been the fact that, since the children are not really blood siblings, why have they never thought of dating each other? This leads to the question most fans of the series have asked these twenty some-odd years after the series ended, that, being teenagers, why haven't Greg and Marcia realized that? A daring aspect of *A Very Brady Sequel* happens when the film actually addresses this subject. There are laughable results, however, a bit on the risque side, possibly making the film a bit too sexy for younger audiences.

The humorous contrasts of the 1970s Bradys living in the 1990s, so successful in the first film, are present, yet less blatant in the sequel. There was more comparison with current styles (clothing and hair) in this sequel, than with the ways of life, as in the original. The excellent interaction between the Bradys and the kids they encounter today are nonexistent in this film; yet, they played so well in the first. Most of the interaction between the decades occurs between the Bradys and Roy.

There were several references to the television series that would make any Brady buff regale with nostalgia, including such plots as settling an argument over a house of cards, potato-sack races, Jan's imaginary boyfriend, George Glass, who, in the film, turns out to be a mannequin, which is more remindful of an episode of "I Love Lucy" than of "The Brady Bunch," and the fight over which sibling gets the attic for their bedroom. It is interesting to see how these situations are dealt with in the film, and even amusing to imagine producer (of both motion pictures and the television series) Sherwood Schwartz having fun with the preposterousness of the plots of his television series and laughing at how the show actually stayed on the air for so long with these faltering story lines.

Sanford's directing does shine in a clever comparison to television of the 1970s and television of the 1990s. The

CREDITS

Carol Brady: Shelley Long
Mike Brady: Gary Cole
Roy Martin/Trevor Thomas: Tim Matheson
Greg Brady: Christopher Daniel Barnes
Marcia Brady: Christine Taylor
Peter Brady: Paul Sutera
Jan Brady: Jennifer Elise Cox
Bobby Brady: Jesse Lee
Cindy Brady: Olivia Hack
Alice: Henriette Mantel

Origin: USA
Released: 1996
Production: Sherwood Schwartz , Lloyd J. Schwartz and Alan Ladd Jr. for a Ladd Co. production; released by Paramount
Direction: Arlene Sanford
Screenplay: Harry Elfont, Deborah Kaplan, James Berg and Stan Zimmerman; based on the characters created by Sherwood Schwartz
Cinematography: Mac Ahlberg
Editing: Anita Brandt-Burgoyne
Music: Guy Moore
Production design: Cynthia Charette
Art direction: Troy Sizemore
Costume design: Rosanna Norton
Sound: Jim Tanenbaum
Casting: Deborah Aquila, Jane Shannon Smith
MPAA rating: PG-13
Running Time: 89 minutes

Bradys are put into a segment of a reality style television police drama, with Richard Belzer. The contrasts of the clean-cut, colorful, properly primped Bradys play well against the gritty, shaky-camera, real-life style of the cop show.

A Very Brady Sequel is a fun film, yet less entertaining and slower than the original. However, it is a very good effort for a sequel film. While it's supposed to be on the implausible side, there are inconsistencies and uneven segments. For instance, the reference to "Gilligan's Island" didn't fit. Yes, both "The Brady Bunch" and "Gilligan's Island" television series were created by Sherwood Schwartz, but the reference doesn't fit here. Also, the last segment of the film was confusing. The character who appears in the end—not a Sherwood Schwartz character—seemed out of place, except maybe so the audience can anticipate this television character from the '60s also making her big-screen debut in the future.

Fans will enjoy *Sequel* for the nostalgia. Motion picture fans will enjoy the laughs. This film is not meant to be taken seriously as a neatly tied-up mystery with a beginning, a middle and an end. Rather, as exactly what it is—a look at a cult television show brought into today's society—nothing more, nothing less.

—Debbi Hoffman

REVIEWS

Entertainment Weekly. September 6, 1996, p. 55.
Los Angeles Times. August 23, 1996, p. F1.
New York Times. August 23, 1996, p. C5.
People. September 2, 1996, p. 19.
Variety. August 19, 1996, p. 48.

Walking and Talking

A comedy for everyone who wants to get married and stay single at the same time.—Movie tagline

"Filled with fresh and disarming humor!"—Janet Maslin, *New York Times*

"Finally, a movie about friends that gets it right!"—Dennis Dermody, *Paper Magazine*

"Two thumbs up!"—*Siskel & Ebert*

Box Office: $1,300,000

If cinema is always taking place in the present tense, then the time within it need not reflect our humdrum preoccupation with the past and the future, but can become uniquely its own. As the maestro of film, Federico Fellini is supposed to have said he would like to believe his characters are walking around somewhere, presumably independent of him, as well as his films.

Within their perpetual present, the principals in *Walking and Talking,* Nicole Holofcener's sprightly debut feature, clearly don't want anything to change, and as we watch them, neither do we. The debilities of advancing age, the inexorable progression of incurable diseases in our midst, costly medical treatments that serve no purpose, are all relegated to the film's sidelines. Nothing is allowed to rip the cocoon of living in the present that these attractive, economically privileged, thirtyish New Yorkers seemed to have earned for themselves as a kind of inalienable birthright. With no real predicament to resolve, their concerns remain intimate, but situated within a social milieu in which everyone seems to know pretty much everything about everyone else. As her characters put up a semblance of defending their private worlds, the writer/director seems to merely observe their earnestness, allowing the magnification built into the film medium to generate the comedy.

A snappy prologue introduces Amelia and Laura as giggling preteens, bonding in their revulsion at the explicit illustrations in *The Joy of Sex.* As if it were the next day, the film cuts to their present reincarnations as sex-wise urbane Manhattanites. Amelia (Catherine Keener), with darkly attractive good looks, works filing classifieds, while Laura (Anne Heche), waifish and blond, is in training as a therapist. Through snippets of scenes, we come to know that while Amelia's ostensible concern is that her overfed cat is dying, what threatens to change everything is Laura's impending marriage to Frank (Todd Field), her live-in boyfriend. The security that Laura seems to have found at the mere prospect of tying the knot throws Amelia into a private tizzy, made more distressing by the fact that she herself has no one in whom to confide her woes at being desperately single. Even Laura has most of her time swallowed up by either Frank or her patients. As an assertion of her self-worth, Amelia thus decides to embark on a love life of her own, even if it means dating the freakish, self-absorbed Bill (Kevin Corrigan), a video store clerk taken up with horror film memorabilia while working on a play about the life of Colette.

Around this basic situation revolve everyday scenes of social blundering, flashes of repressed fantasy, and confidences only momentarily exchanged. For all their seeming willingness to embrace change, the new, for both Amelia and Laura, only seems to point to the need for that lost bond they once shared against a world driven mad by sex. For Amelia, Bill proves an inarticulate but willing partner in bed, despite his allergy to her cat. Then he overhears Laura's voice on Amelia's answering machine referring to that "ugly guy" Amelia has been seeing. Bill promptly erases the message, gathers together bits of his wounded pride and, without taking his leave, exits sneezing. Amelia, ignorant of what has happened, can only interpret his gesture as a reflection of her own inadequacy. Laura meanwhile, despite the romantic trappings of engagement rings and wedding gown tryouts, grows weary with the bedroom routine that has become part and parcel of her sexual commitment. One night, just as Frank begins his advances, she punctures his urge by voicing her boredom, itemizing each bit of foreplay he is about to perform. We then begin to see how the spirit of introspective therapy suffusing their lifestyles will not allow either Amelia or Laura to let sleeping dogs lie.

Amelia corners Andrew (Liev Schrieber), a kindly exboyfriend. "What went wrong with us?" she demands to know. "Did I do something horrendous to turn you off?" After much hesitation, Andrew confesses, "You made me feel too important . . . like I was everything," implying thereby that Amelia became too dependent on him. For her, that still doesn't explain what could have alienated Bill. Similarly, Laura pounces on Frank when he calls a waitress by her name, interpreting it as a sign that he wants everyone to like him. This time, however, Frank shows he can be as analytical of her. "Why do you have to be so controlling?" he probes. It soon becomes clear that nothing is going to make Amelia and Laura accept their sexual lot in life.

AWARDS AND NOMINATIONS

Independent Spirit Awards 1997 Nominations: Actress (Keener), Supporting Actor (Corrigan)

Unable to contain her restlessness, Amelia begins stalking Bill. She first spies on him from outside the window of the video store. Then, posing as a customer, she rings to query in a false voice. She even follows him after work, ducking behind a garbage can just as he turns round. Thinking he has seen her, she calls after him, but he keeps on walking, no doubt equally embarrassed. She is finally driven to a face to face confrontation. When her turn comes up in the checkout line, Bill at first feigns casualness: "Where've you been? You haven't rented lately." Pretending he has forgotten her phone number, he is dutifully taking it down, when Amelia explodes: "Rented lately? Are you crazy? I had sex with you two weeks ago!"

When she storms out, Bill chases after her. "I know you think I'm ugly," he starts to explain, then tells her about the message he erased on her machine. Even so, his frankness only drives the wedge in deeper.

Laura too, quite independently, finds breathing room behind Frank's back by putting out feelers for Peter (Randall Batinkoff), an actor/waiter who takes her to an Off-Off-Broadway play he is in. Outside the stage door, however, on the threshold of her fling, Laura develops cold feet and heads back to Frank. Yet, despite her loyalty, Laura and Frank soon break up over, of all things, a mole on Frank's chest. When Frank moves out, Amelia is unable to sympathize. Laura then retorts, "I knew you wouldn't understand. You think getting married is the be-all and end-all to life and it is not."

The film then attempts a change of tone by allowing Amelia and Laura to be by themselves at Amelia's family house in the Pennsylvania countryside. Yet even here, all it takes is an obscene phone call for Amelia to sense the danger of living in a remote place. She calls Andrew, begging him to join them. The true friend that he is, Andrew takes the next train out. When the caller rings again, Andrew is there to answer him. The country house, along with its garden and the nearby lake, serves to realign the three old friends, as friends. Now Laura feels the lonely outsider as Amelia and Andrew get drunk and go swimming in the middle of the night. This rustic interlude also allows the film to attempt a fresh start, not that that is ever a distinct possibility for either Amelia or Laura.

Amelia returns home and soon decides to try Bill once again. In one of the film's many moments of incidental hilarity, Bill, who claims to have returned to his old girlfriend, speaks of his new passion for the spectator sport of dwarf bowling: "People pick up dwarfs and use them as bowling balls. It's great. The dwarfs like it." Laura does manage to get back with Frank, but not before an equally bizarre twist. Across a restaurant table, after both have admitted to missing each other, Frank presents a small jewelry box as a customary gesture of reconciliation. Laura opens it to find the mole of contention mounted as a souvenir.

Apart from the subplot having to do with Andrew's Father (Lawrence Holofcener) and his battle with Alzheimer's, it would appear that everything is as it once was, at least between Amelia and Laura. A rift threatens to open when Amelia accuses Laura of not needing her anymore, now that she has Frank. "I do need you," Laura attempts to console her. Then Amelia blurts out the real reason for her unease: "You're so wrapped up in what's happening to you that you don't know what I'm going through!" Having cleared the air, Amelia is quick to apologize, and the two embrace, reassuring each other of their love. As if to cement their closeness, Amelia confesses to having slept with Andrew, which allows both to convulse laughing. On the eve of Laura's wedding at Amelia's country house, we catch a glimpse of the two friends in the fading twilight, amidst the tranquil water of the lake. Laura is floating, calm and carefree, while Amelia provides her the support of her arms. Both seem content to cherish the moment as a moment, and nothing more.

The final scene shows Amelia about to lead Laura to the ceremony, arm in arm. We still don't know just where her relationship with Andrew is headed, but like her, we feel no uncertainty, since Amelia herself is not sure she wants it to go anywhere.

It would appear natural for critical opinion to read either too little or too much into the filmmaker's unassuming stance. The film though seems to have fared well at the hands of the women who have reviewed it. Karen Schoemer in *Newsweek* points out how the Hollywood formula for girl bonding "was safe and stressless: beaming faces, lots of hugs and pointed gripes about men." For her, *Walking and Talking* shows "girl bonding as the messy, complex experience it really is." She goes on to note the filmmaker's "wonderful, breezy touch (which) hides life issues in such

CREDITS

Amelia: Catherine Keener
Laura: Anne Heche
Frank: Todd Field
Bill: Kevin Corrigan
Andrew: Liev Schreiber

Origin: USA
Released: 1996
Production: Ted Hope, James Schamus; released by Miramax Films
Direction: Nicole Holofcener
Screenplay: Nicole Holofcener
Cinematography: Michael Spiller
Editing: Alisa Lepselter
Music: Billy Bragg
Production design: Anne Stuhle
Costume design: Edi Giguere
Casting: Avy Kaufman
MPAA rating: R
Running Time: 90 minutes

sweet moments, you barely notice them as they go down." Janet Maslin in *The New York Times* calls the film "a date movie so enjoyably prickly it will seem funniest if you don't have a date." She notes the film's "revealing little intimacies and nicely neurotic wit," as well as its "brisk style and clean good looks, thanks in large part to exceptionally attractive cinematography by Michael Spiller." She describes the film as moving "confidently toward a warm affirmation of its heroines' lifelong bond (while) it appreciates every bump in the road along the way."

Walking and Talking premiered at the 1996 Sundance Film Festival, and was featured the same year in the Museum of Modern Art's New Directors/New Films showcase.

—Vivek Adarkar

REVIEWS

Entertainment Weekly. July 26, 1996, p. 36.
The Hollywood Reporter. July 22, 1996, p. 10.
Los Angeles Times. July 17, 1996, p. F4.
The New York Daily News. July 17, 1996.
The New York Times. March 29, 1996.
The New York Times. July 17, 1996.
Newsweek. August 5, 1996. p. 73.
People. July 22, 1996, p. 19.
USA Today. July 26, 1996, p. 4D.
The Village Voice. July 23, 1996.

Welcome to the Dollhouse

Not all girls want to play with dolls.—Movie tagline

"A piercing black comedy about growing up geeky."—Dave Kehr, *Daily News*

"A highly original take, both funny and poignant."—Kenneth Turan, *Los Angeles Times*

"A sly, hilarious black comedy."—Janet Maslin, *New York Times*

"A smart film with an uncompromisingly dark vision."—Harlan Jacobson, *The Toronto Star*

Box Office: $4,565,364

Just when seventh grade had been safely forgotten, along comes the vicious black comedy *Welcome to the Dollhouse* to revive every horrible detail. Winner of the Grand Prize at the Sundance Film Festival, this low budget film, directed, written, and produced by Todd Solondz, is cunning, perfectly executed, well cast, and fearless in the face of remembrance. Though the setting is a junior high school in suburbia, and the central cast is under the age of 18, this is not a film made to entertain a young audience. The film is best appreciated as a shocking remembrance, a glance from adulthood into a long forgotten reality. For an audience accustomed to the coming-of-age genre, usually defined by a sentimental, mature, male voice fondly recollecting the bittersweet mischief and lost innocence of youth, as in the hit television series "The Wonder Years" or *Stand By Me* (1986), this film offers a stark reminder of how emotionally trying and strange pre-adolescence actually was.

Dawn Weiner (Heather Matarazzo) becomes the poster child for adolescent angst in Todd Solondz's acclaimed *Welcome to the Dollhouse.*

As the middle child in an unremarkable suburban New Jersey family, eleven-year-old Dawn Wiener (Heather

Matarazzo) looks longingly in each direction. She envies her computer nerd brother Mark (Matthew Faber) for having escaped grade school, and she loathes her adorable little sister Missy (Daria Kalinina) for her grace and perfection and her monopoly on the adoration of her parents. Missy dances about the house and yard in a tutu, wears pink, and plays with dolls, and Mark busies himself making horrible noises in the garage with his band the Quadratics. The parents, Harv (Bill Buell) and Marj (Angela Pietropinto), demonstrate a ghastly preference for their youngest daughter and only annoyance for the awkward Dawn. But home life is only one of Dawn's many problems. Each school day is an excursion through a burlesque world of cruelty and alienation. Her locker awaits her scrawled with every derision in the grade school vocabulary and her life seems to merely serve the purpose of being an outlet for the rage and cruelty of her schoolmates. Known by her peers as Wiener Dog, Dawn has heavy eyeglasses, bad clothes, no talent, and a dopey body, and is so vastly unpopular and unpleasing that even her parents and teachers don't like her. She is the kind of nerd who alerts the teacher when she catches her schoolmate cheating, but rather than winning the much coveted approval of the adult world, Dawn is punished and despised. Her only friend is a much younger boy who lives down the block and is the sole member of Dawn's special people clubhouse, a rickety shack in her backyard where Dawn lives out her exile from the world.

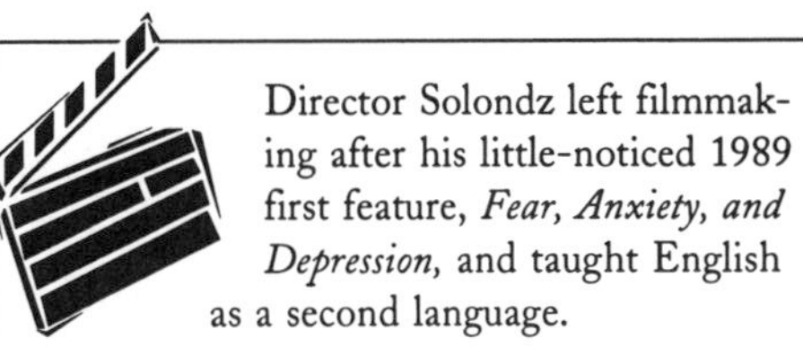

Director Solondz left filmmaking after his little-noticed 1989 first feature, *Fear, Anxiety, and Depression,* and taught English as a second language.

Just when life seems its bleakest Dawn falls in love and things only get harder. The object of her desire is the new vocalist in her brother's band, Steve Rodgers (Eric Mabius), who miraculously transforms the band from a travesty to something quite provocative. Steve is the epitome of hip, with long hair, unbuttoned shirt, shapely muscles, and big plans to drop out of high school and flee the suburbs for New York City to become the next Jim Morrison. Stunned by his beauty she follows him about with jaw open. At night she builds a shrine with candles surrounding his school I.D. card and dreams of salvation in his arms. Meanwhile at school Dawn develops a strange relationship with her most vicious tormentor, Brandon McCarthy (Brendan Sexton). Brandon pursues her relentlessly and exists always in the peripheral of her vision mouthing swear words at her, making lewd gestures, and refusing to avert his gaze. He threatens her continuously with rape, in the kind of harsh direct manner that only a seventh grade bully can achieve. He even sets a date and time when he will rape her and demands that she be there, and strangely enough, she appears at the appointed time. Instead of raping her, he kisses her, and makes her swear to secrecy. He then admits to having a retarded brother at home. Their relationship is as complicated and confusing as preadolescence itself, and truly one of the highlights of the film. When they are both not invited to a popular classmate's birthday party they spend the night listening to sugary pop songs and staring at the moon in Dawn's clubhouse. Hesitantly, Dawn tells Brandon that she cannot be his girlfriend because she is in love with someone else and he leaves in a rage.

Dawn decides to make her move for Steve at her parent's anniversary party, where he is being paid to perform. She dresses herself up in heels and funky clothes and hunts him down after his performance. When she finds him necking with a girl and he annoyingly asks her what she wants, she blurts out that she would like him to be an honorary member of her special people club. Confused and disgusted, he informs her that special people means retarded people. Late that night Dawn takes the home video recording of the day's events out to the asphalt and hammers it to smithereens.

Family crisis brings all the injustices and humiliations of Dawn's life into even greater clarity. Sweet little Missy never returns from ballet class one day and a manhunt commences. Dawn is partly responsible for the misfortune because she vindictively forgot to tell Missy that their mother would not be able to pick her up after class and that she should drive home with a neighbor. In the absence of Missy, the family gradually falls apart from despair. Dawn leaves home silently and heads to New York City to search for Missy. Despite being away from the home overnight, no one notices Dawn's absence. She phones home and learns from Mark that Missy has been found and that Dawn's mother is too busy rejoicing and telling the story to reporters to come to the phone. Dawn returns home and submits to the torments of her life. She is last seen heading out with a busload of schoolmates on a field trip to Disney World. The kids are all singing their school song in happy unison, and Dawn moves her lips reluctantly and out of synch with the others.

This is a bleak but incredibly amusing and painfully accurate depiction of childhood suffering. Solondz has managed to both critique and broaden the genre of coming-of-age films by setting a black comic tone, a form which seems ideally suited to both remembrance and childhood.

AWARDS AND NOMINATIONS

Independent Spirit Awards 1997: Debut Performance (Matarazzo)
Sundance Film Festival 1996: Grand Jury Prize
Nominations: Feature, Director (Solondz), Supporting Actor (Faber), Debut Performance (Sexton Jr.)

Rather than having the characters grow and develop, reaching new levels of maturity and wisdom, Solondz chooses to depict a state of entropy and helplessness that mirrors the feeling in childhood that things will never change and that life is moving at a begrudging pace. When Dawn asks her brother if things get better in high school he replies honestly and with a cold weariness that the kids still hate you but they are not as much in your face about it anymore. Maturity in this interpretation is not an emergence into a greater communion with the world, but merely the ability to don masks and pretend at tolerance. The children of the suburbs do not become less cruel but merely move forward into the realm of good manners and professionalism. Solondz also breaks from the genre by making the central character female. Unable to achieve the ideal of feminine grace and cuteness represented by Missy, Dawn is free to relish in her anger, sawing the heads off her sister's Barbie dolls, and fantasizing about smashing in Missy's head with the hammer she uses to destroy the family video. As an unattractive and unpopular girl, Dawn suffers a double dose of alienation.

"They call you names, but not as much to your face."—Mark's reply when Dawn asks if getting older makes life easier

Solondz first feature, *Fear, Anxiety and Depression* (1989), was virtually ignored, but after a long hiatus from filmmaking he has reemerged with a film to be reckoned with. *Welcome to the Dollhouse* demonstrates some first-rate performances by the young actors, with a particularly strong performance by Heather Matarazzo as Dawn. The casting of the film could not have been better, and each character manages to flesh out and enrich a particular childhood prototype, without ever becoming merely stereotypical. While the humor of the film depends to a certain extent on presenting easily recognized types from childhood, the film is so rich in forgotten detail, that it never lapses into the predictable. The soundtrack is right on, with the title track appearing as Steve's garage band solo that Dawn swoons over—a sultry angst-ridden song of suburban loneliness. This is a film well deserving of the critical praise and awards it has received.

—Reni Celeste

CREDITS

Dawn Wiener: Heather Matarazzo
Steve Rodgers: Eric Mabius
Brandon McCarthy: Brendan Sexton, Jr.
Missy: Darla Kalinina
Mrs. Wiener: Angela Pietropinto
Mark Wiener: Matthew Faber

Origin: USA
Released: 1996
Production: Ted Skillman and Todd Solondz; released by Sony Pictures Classics
Direction: Todd Solondz
Screenplay: Todd Solondz
Cinematography: Randy Drummond
Editing: Alan Oxman
Production design: Susan Block
Music: Jill Wisoff
Costume design: Melissa Toth
MPAA rating: not listed
Running Time: 87 minutes

REVIEWS

Boxoffice. April, 1996, p. 107.
Chicago Tribune. June 9, 1996.
Entertainment Weekly. May 31, 1996.
New York Times. March 22, 1996, p. C1.
Premiere. April, 1996.

The White Balloon; Badkonake Sefid

"A nearly perfect gem! Dazzling!"—Geoff Pevere, *Globe & Mail*

"A miracle of minimalism! It has no equivalent in western cinema."—Dave Kehr, *New York Daily News*

"Perfect simplicity! Charming. Directed with lovely precision."—Janet Maslin, *New York Times*

Box Office: $924,940

For the most part, most films foreign to the United States are imports from Europe; their cultures and values are only slightly different than those here in the U.S. But every now and then a foreign film comes along whose success provides Americans with an interesting perspective on a non-Western culture. The wonderful films by Zhang Yimou, for example, such as *To Live* (1994), have provided a virtual education on Chinese culture and history. And now from director Jafar Panahi comes *The White Balloon,* a simple but unusual story which sheds light on life in contemporary Iran.

Few Americans have experienced contemporary Iranian society firsthand. Since the Iranian revolution in the late 1970's and early 1980's, the political and sociological landscape of Iran has vastly changed, bringing with it a longstanding and stubborn ideological wall between the United States and the government of Iran. With the release of *The White Balloon,* Americans can have one of their best recent chances to see Iranian society from the perspective of an insider. For such audiences, the film will be of great interest and will no doubt be entertaining. As wonderfully made as it is, though, it must be understood within the context of its culture to fully appreciate and understand it. On the surface, this is a sweet little film which boasts a remarkable performance by a child actress (Aida Mohammadkhani). But audiences familiar with Iranian culture and society will see themes, allusions, and ideas the meaning of which the rest of us can only guess. In addition, its cinematic style is far different from the action-packed, visual style of western films, which may make the film difficult for westerners to fully appreciate.

Panahi's debut feature was made for Iranian TV station IRIB.

The White Balloon is produced and directed by Jafar Panahi and written (in the original Farsi) by Abbas Kiarostami, from a story by Panahi. It is an allegorical fable about a little girl named Razieh (Aida Mohammadkhani) in contemporary Teheran who wishes to buy a special goldfish for her New Year's celebration. (Goldfish play an important symbolic role in Iranian New Year's celebrations.) Seeing her family's goldfish, she says that she would prefer one of the chubby ones being sold at a nearby market. Her brother Ali (Mohsen Kalifi) wonders aloud why she would want to spend 100 tomans on a goldfish when "you can watch two films for that money." But the determined 7-year-old pushes her gentle mother into giving the last of her money so that Razieh can get the goldfish. Accompanied by her brother, Razieh's attempt to buy the goldfish turns into quite an adventure: her money is nearly taken by some snake charmers; she does not have enough for the fish; the money is lost; she and Ali go to great lengths to find the money. The film takes place in real time; there are one-and-a-half hours to go before the New Year. In a neo-realist style reminiscent of DeSica's *The Bicycle Thief* (1947), Razieh's journey several blocks from her home becomes an odyssey filled with dangerous obstacles, strange characters, and life lessons.

Screenwriter Abbas Kiarostami is Iran's preeminent film director, and the director of this film, Jafar Panahi, is his protegee. Kiarostami has chosen the simplest of stories: very little happens beyond Razieh's attempt to buy the goldfish and then find the money she loses. But given the proscriptions against filming anything with a political, violent, sexual, feminist, or anti-government thematic content, it is easy to see why Kiarostami and Panahi chose this simple style. Without doubt, they are able to make thematic and ideological statements which would have been subversive had this film been about adults. For example, Razieh's stubborn insistence on getting what she wants, and her strong-willed behavior relative to the males she encounters, would have been anathema had she been a grown woman. There are other moments of nascent feminism which are palatable because she is a child. For example, Razieh encounters a soldier who seems to want more from her than she is willing to give: though his behavior is not overtly sexual, their interaction has the flavor of a possible child molester with a potential victim. Razieh verbally spars with this man who is 15 to 20 years older than she is. When he insists that he is not a stranger, she says, "how could you not know me and not be a stranger?" Viewing this interaction as allegory rather than a scene of an older man flirting with a young child, the scene could be about the constant threat of sexual exploitation facing young women.

Without a vast knowledge of Iranian culture, it would be impossible to assume the meaning of many of the images and events. But as stated before, knowledge of Iran's prohibitions against sex and politics in film make it seem as if Panahi and Kiarostami have made a far more political film than appears on the surface. Is there significance in Razieh's stubborn insistence that a group of traditional snake charmers return money they have swindled? Perhaps that could be a symbol for a new generation insisting that the old generation change its ways, or that women are not to be treated as second-class citizens by men. Is Razieh and Ali's treatment of a young Afghan boy a piece of political symbolism? Their exploitation of the boy's kindness may be a symbol for the way in which minorities are treated within the culture of present-day Teheran. Analysis of the political symbolism in these events and images should probably be left to students of contem-

AWARDS AND NOMINATIONS

New York Film Critics Circle 1996: Best Foreign-language Film

porary Iranian culture, but other audiences can probably understand and relate to the film on a purely human and artistic level.

Panahi's style is both realistic and static. It is not an exciting film; the audience won't be waiting on the edge of its collective seats to see the outcome. This is certainly a function of the simplicity with which Panahi tells his tale. The fact that the film feels slowly paced may merely be the reflection of a western view that something always has to be happening on screen in order for the film to be interesting. But even the most benevolent critic is challenged by Panahi's inclusion of a scene which seems to last some 30 minutes and has only one camera angle. This long scene (in which Razieh sits on a curb above a grate into which the money has fallen) diminishes the momentum of the early part of the film. It is a shame, because the early sequences, involving various shopkeepers and other characters, are quite interesting. The scene is emblematic, however, of Panahi's ability to precisely capture the most specific and mundane of human emotions with his camera.

"I want the one that's white as a bride."—Young Razieh explaining which goldfish she intends to buy.

In Aida Mohammadkhani, Panahi has found as charismatic an actress to film as any director could ever hope to find. Panahi seems well aware that her extraordinary ability to be completely natural in front of the camera is this film's main attraction. This little girl is truly amazing: her expressive face is simply made for long close-ups. Unlike virtually all of the child stars we see in American film, she has not a trace of self-consciousness, nor does she try to make her audience love her. In fact, she seems completely unaware that there is a camera recording every movement. In interviews, Panahi has described his clever techniques to keep Mohammadkhani fresh before the camera. For example, he refused to tell her the next part of the story before shooting, so that the little girl was just as uncertain about her fate as the character she played. Another technique involved causing her to cry during the early days of shooting—and then reminding her of it each time he needed her to cry. To remind her, Panahi has said that, standing behind the camera, he would cry too and that they would "cry together." Imagine Steven Spielberg and, say, the young Drew Barrymore involved in the same kind of artistic endeavor, and the difference between Iranian and American cinema becomes ever clearer.

For a little film, *The White Balloon* has caused quite a furor. It won the Camera d'Or and the International Critics prizes at the 1995 Cannes Film Festival. It was also the official Iranian entry to the foreign language category of the Academy Awards. After Speaker of the House Newt Gingrich pushed for a $20 million covert action program against Iran, the film was withdrawn for Academy consideration by Iranian officials. The Academy refused to withdraw it, however, and the film received ever-greater publicity.

The bottom line is this: this film could be deadly dull for a lot of people. *The White Balloon* is for true aficionados of cinema and for intellectuals armed with some knowledge of contemporary Iranian culture.

—Kirby Tepper

CREDITS

Razieh: Aida Mohammadkhani
Ali: Mohsen Kalifi
Mother: Fereshteh Sadr Orfani
Old woman: Ann Bourkowska
Soldier: Mohammad Shahani
Tailor: Mohammad Bahktiari

Origin: Iran
Released: 1995
Production: Kurosh Mazkouri for a Ferdos Films production; released by October Films
Direction: Jafar Panahi
Screenplay: Abbas Kiarostami
Cinematography: Farzad Jowdat
Editing: Jafar Panahi
Production design: Jafar Panahi
Sound: Majtaba Mortazavi, Said Ahmadi, Mehdi Dejbodi
MPAA rating: Unrated
Running Time: 85 minutes

REVIEWS

Boxoffice. November, 1995, p. 100.
Los Angeles Times. January 31, 1996, P. F2.
New York Times. September 29, 1995, p. C28.
Premiere. February, 1996, p. 20.
Sight and Sound. January, 1996, p. 57.
Village Voice. January 30, 1996, p. 46.

White Squall

The strongest force in nature is the will to survive.—Movie tagline

"Jeff Bridges is fabulous!"—Bill Diehl, *ABC Radio Network*

"An unforgettable experience!"—Ron Brewington, *American Urban Radio Network*

"Powerful!"—Jack Kroll, *Newsweek*

"Riveting!"—Peter Travers, *Rolling Stone*

"A thrilling adventure!"—Jeffrey Lyons, *Sneak Previews*

Box Office: $10,292,300

From its fine lead performances (by Jeff Bridges and Scott Wolf), to its extraordinary direction (by Ridley Scott) and photography (by Hugh Johnson), to its stirring main title song ("Valparaiso" by Sting), *White Squall* is an "A" film from start to finish. Some critics complained that its screenplay, by Todd Robinson (and based on a true story), was a little too simple. But the adventure, the fine performances, and excellent production values are undeniable. If *White Squall* is occasionally overly glossy, it more than makes up for it with the aforementioned fine creative elements.

Jeff Bridges stars as Christopher Sheldon, skipper of the Albatross, a two-masted sailing vessel which is also a prep school for wealthy young high school boys. The film is the story of a horrible tragedy that befell the vessel in the fall of 1960. While in the Caribbean, the vessel became victim to what is known as a "white squall;" a brief but ferocious storm at sea which causes huge and dangerous waves. During that squall, six people (students and crew of the Albatross) lost their lives, and the ship was destroyed. *White Squall* portrays the events leading up to the tragedy, and follows the Coast Guard tribunal which investigated the incident.

The real-life 90-second sinking takes up 16 minutes of screen time.

Screenwriter Todd Robinson and director Ridley Scott go beyond telling a simple seafaring yarn: told through the eyes of one of the students, Chuck Gieg (Scott Wolf), *White Squall* is also a coming-of-age film, a sort of cross between *Captains Courageous* (1937) and *Dead Poets Society* (1989).

Robinson has done a fine job of creating identifiable and likable characters in several of the thirteen students. Gieg becomes the narrator of the story, providing a voiceover that personalizes the tale even while it makes it sound like one of those stories that grizzled old sailors tell. Besides Gieg, there is Tod Johnston (Balthazar Getty), a veteran of the Albatross; Frank Beaumont (Jeremy Sisto), a spoiled, self-destructive and disruptive presence aboard ship; Tracy Lapchick (Ethan Embry), a naive young man who still mourns the death of his beloved older brother; and Dean Preston (Eric Michael Cole), a rebellious bully who hides massive insecurities. The large ensemble is rounded out by Caroline Goodall, who plays Skipper Sheldon's wife, and John Savage, playing the theatrical English teacher.

One of the pitfalls of such a film is that the boys could blend into one another, without creating idiosyncratic characters. When audiences look back on *Dead Poets Society* and other such ensemble films, the actors might be remembered as interchangeable: they were all nice-looking and intense. In *White Squall* they are more than that: Scott and company should be proud that they have assembled a cast that works cohesively as an ensemble even while each character is thoroughly individual and interesting.

In particular, the role of Chuck Gieg is capably and compassionately played by Scott Wolf (best known as the star of television's "Party of Five"). Wolf is earnest and believable as a young man who doesn't "want to be what I was when I left: anonymous." Wolf does a fine job developing Gieg's growing admiration of Captain Sheldon, which seems to fuel his own growth into manhood. His final scene, in which he delivers an emotional monologue to the skipper, beseeching him to allow the boys to share in the blame for the tragedy, is intense and touching.

Similarly, the other characters are well-drawn and well-acted, with Jeremy Sisto a standout for his surly character, and Ethan Embry for his sweet and sad characterization of a boy who seems lost without his older brother.

Of course, none of this might be half as acceptable with an actor of less stature than Jeff Bridges. Paying homage to the memory of his father Lloyd Bridges' indelible character from the 1960s television series "Sea Hunt," Bridges is gruff, grizzled, a little intimidating, and a little vulnerable. There is no question about it: he looks like a man of the sea. His imposing presence invites the fear and admiration of the young men. Perhaps without Bridges' strength, the film could have lapsed into a more standard Hollywood treatment of a real-life event. The essential ingredients needed in skipper Sheldon's character are all present in Bridges. His first scenes, where he surveys the new crew of boys, is notable because he establishes a specific relationship with each young man he meets. When he tells them, "don't test me; not even a little," he means it. He is intimidating and lovable in the cinematic tradition of teachers from John Houseman in *The Paper Chase* (1973) to Sidney Poitier in *To Sir, With Love* (1967).

Since the real-life white squall only lasted ninety seconds, Scott has embellished the truth a bit for exciting theatrical effect, making the storm the centerpiece of the film. They have extended the length of the squall to something like 15 minutes, and the film is better for it. It is an extraordinary sequence; terrifying and realistic, and filled with a stirring mixture of action and drama. The squall was actually filmed in Malta, in a giant tank where tons of water came crashing down on the actors, many of whom did not have stunt doubles so that the camera could better catch the terror in their faces as the waves hit. (A footnote: the same giant tank was used in the colossal disaster *Cutthroat Island* [1995], directed by Renny Harlin and starring his wife, Geena Davis.)

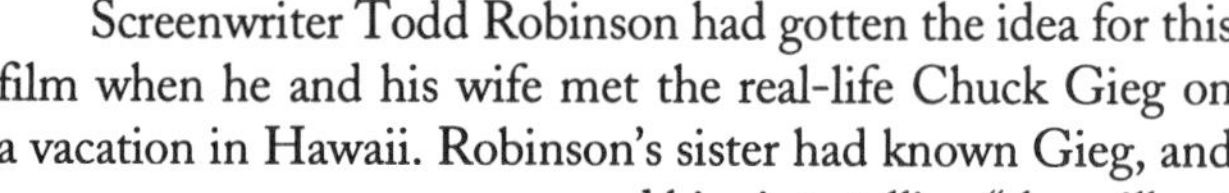

"If we don't have order, we have nothing. Where we go one, we go all."—Captain Sheldon

Scott and writer Robinson wisely choose to start the squall out small, as if it were just another storm. The tension builds as the boys laugh at the first waves; it is the same kind of tension Scott brought to the hair-raising scene in *Alien* (1979) where the monster first jumps out of John Hurt's body. Scott is a master at creating the calm before the storm, lulling the audience into a false sense of security and then allowing the action to take their breath away. This sequence is notable as well for Scott's attention to the actors and the story: the deaths of some important characters have been foreshadowed beautifully, making the already tragic circumstances even worse. This sequence leaves audiences stunned.

CREDITS

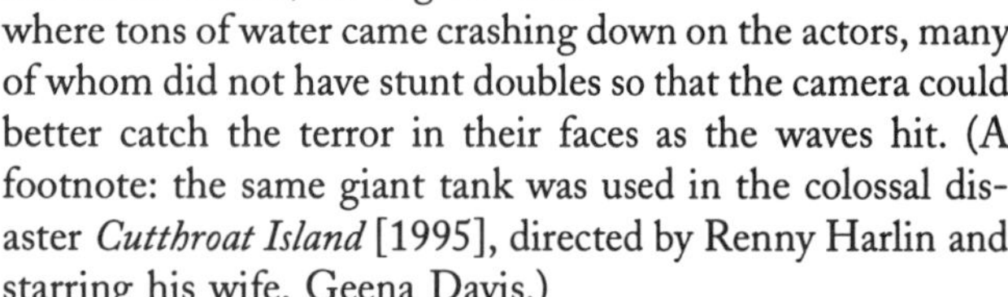

"Skipper" Sheldon: Jeff Bridges
Dr. Alice Sheldon: Caroline Goodall
McCrea: John Savage
Chuck Gieg: Scott Wolf
Frank Beaumont: Jeremy Sisto
Gil Martin: Ryan Phillippe

Origin: USA
Released: 1996
Production: Mimi Polk Gitlin and Rocky Lang for a Hollywood Pictures, Largo Entertainment and Scott Free production; released by Buena Vista Pictures
Direction: Ridley Scott
Screenplay: Todd Robinson
Cinematography: Hugh Johnson
Editing: Gerry Hambling
Production design: Peter J. Hampton, Leslie Tomkins
Art direction: Joseph P. Lucky
Costume design: Judianna Makovsky
Sound: Ken Weston
Special effects: Joss Williams
Casting: Louis Di Giaimo
MPAA rating: PG-13
Running Time: 127 minutes

Screenwriter Todd Robinson had gotten the idea for this film when he and his wife met the real-life Chuck Gieg on a vacation in Hawaii. Robinson's sister had known Gieg, and coaxed him into telling "the sailboat story" to Robinson, who decided to write a screenplay. Eventually, he and producer Rocky Lang brought the film to Ridley Scott, and the film was made with the help of Gieg and the real-life skipper, Sheldon, who had not seen each other in twenty years. Their advice and expertise prove invaluable: not only does the story flow believably and poignantly, but the sailing sequences are far above the usual Hollywood fare. In recent years, actors have trained for films which required vast technical knowledge—*Platoon* (1989) is an example—and it pays off. The boys look as if they know just what they're doing on a sailboat; the sequences showing them working on the vessel are clearly borne out of the expertise of the film's advisors, the director's attention to detail, and the actor's dedication to more than an appearance of realism.

Director of photography Hugh Johnson is responsible for the lush, colorful pictures of the sailboat set against a gorgeous horizon. Johnson also manages to fill the squall scene with depth and its own eerie beauty. In fact, one of the most beautiful images is of a flare shooting out from the lifeboat after the tragedy. Johnson had some beautiful scenery to photograph, from the tiny island of Grenada, where most of the Caribbean sequences were filmed, to Cape Town, South Africa, whose waters provided a beautiful backdrop for the rough seas sections.

This is a film that could stand the test of time: it has high adventure, good performances, and beautiful photography. The only thing going against it is that the film runs the risk of not being taken seriously simply because its young stars are just a little too good looking, which made some audiences think this was just another "Hollywood-ized" version of a true story. But it is much more than that. Ridley Scott, Todd Robinson, Jeff Bridges, and the rest have created a film that is as entertaining and as dangerous as a ride on the high seas, not to mention that it has a few things to say about the nature of male camaraderie.

—*Kirby Tepper*

REVIEWS

Boxoffice. April, 1996, p. 118.
Chicago Tribune. February 2, 1996, p. 5.
Entertainment Weekly. February 2, 1996, p. 40.
New York Times. February 2, 1996, p. C16.
New Yorker. February 5, 1996, p. 75.
Newsweek. February 5, 1996, p. 65.
Rolling Stone. February 22, 1996, p. 69.
Variety. January 29, 1996, p. 60.
Village Voice. February 6, 1996, p. 48.

The Wife

Box Office: $46,830

After an auspicious first film, *What Happened Was . . .* , (1994) an incisive portrait of an awkward first date, director/writer/actor Tom Noonan doubles his cast to four to dissect two dysfunctional marriages over dinner in his latest movie. Like *What Happened, Wife* is also based on a Noonan scripted play (*Wifey*) and both are completely character-driven vehicles with virtually nonexistent plotlines. Free to take off in a multitude of directions, the picture frequently does. While some of these, often painful, explorations shed some light on the inner workings of the emotionally damaged group of characters, equally many paths do not serve much of a purpose.

The evening begins simply enough in the chic New York home of New Age therapist Jack (Noonan) and his wife Rita (Julie Hagerty), also a therapist. It is clear the couple have a plethora of marital issues to deal with. Hagerty does a wonderful job of setting up her complex character who craves love and attention from a distant spouse who seems particularly adept at avoiding intimacy. In their out-of-the-way abode where Jack listens to assonant mood music and Rita flutters about, neurotically preparing dinner, they have created a secluded hideaway where they take refuge from their work and, unintentionally, each other.

Suddenly, one of Jack's patients, Cosmo (Wallace Shawn), comes crashing into their serenely divided world when he and his somewhat overbearing wife, Arlie (Karen Young), get stranded in front of the couple's home while out for a drive. The snivelling Cosmo seems to have an ulterior motive for the coincidence, being in desperate need of counseling. Soon, the two are inside and, after a private debate between Jack and Rita, invited to stay for dinner against Rita's protests that it is unprofessional to socialize and analyze at the same time. Jack and Rita's obvious personal and professional schisms are even further illustrated by the arriving couple, who themselves are quite a peculiar pair. The two men venture outside to walk the grounds and discuss Cosmo's current psychological crisis while the women prepare dinner. The visual differences between the uninhibited Arlie—a dancer who struts around in six inch platform shoes and a mini dress—and the completely self-contained Rita—tastefully dressed in a loose fitting sari-like getup—are as humorously vast as their conversation.

Over dinner, the deep-rooted problems of the concerned parties come out in various ways: openly discussed where Cosmo is concerned, as he talks nonstop about himself in great detail; subtly revealed in the case of Rita, whose plentiful supply of downers are discovered by Arlie; or overtly manifested in Jack, with his heavy drinking, manipulation, and roving eye. Young's Arlie, troubled as she is, seems to be the only character who has a clue. Her character's monologue is especially truthful and revealing. No nice, neat solutions, however, are offered to anyone by the end of dinner, and everyone is left with pretty much the same problems they had at the film's start, except, perhaps, with a few walls temporarily knocked down by the evening's events.

The characters are very interestingly written and universally well acted. The dialogue occasionally reveals Noonan's dry and somewhat skewed sense of humor in an otherwise very heavy and dark film. Noonan mocks the characters he's written: Jack with his pretentious therapist-speak; Cosmo with his nonstop whining and cloying neediness; and the tight-lipped Rita, who analyzes everything to within an inch of its life. Noonan also seems to question the validity of therapy, with Jack portrayed as a man with a serious dark side, a sadist who simply enjoys stirring the emotional pot and then sitting back passively to see what happens. It is clear Rita needs to help herself before she can come close to healing anyone else. Together, they are the ultimate hypocritical advice givers, trapped in their own failing marriage. Only Arlie is exempt from the writer's contempt. In their intellectual, over-analytical nightmare, she represents a little of the "authenticity" of which Jack so of-

CREDITS

Rita: Julie Hagerty
Jack: Tom Noonan
Cosmo: Wallace Shawn
Arlie: Karen Young

Origin: USA
Released: 1995
Production: Scott Macaulay and Robin O'Hara for a Genre Film and Ciby 2000 production; released by Artistic License Films
Direction: Tom Noonan
Screenplay: Tom Noonan; based on his play *Wifey*
Cinematography: Joe DeSalvo
Editing: Richmond Arrley
Music: Ludovico Sorret
Production design: Dan Oulette
Art direction: Sarah Lavery
Costume design: Kathryn Nixon
Sound: Juan Carlos Martinez
MPAA rating: Unrated
Running Time: 100 minutes

ten refers to. She, unlike the "therapists," recognizes the nature of her relationships and sees the twisted co-dependency she and Cosmo have with one another for exactly what it is.

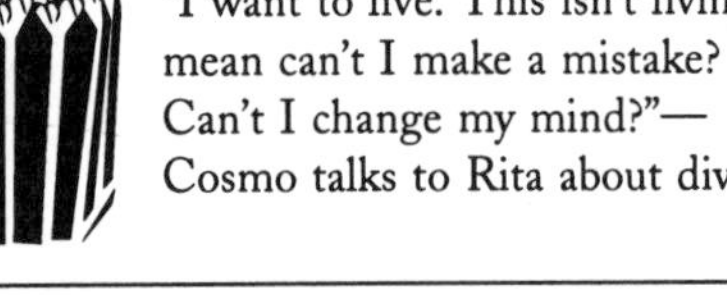

"I want to live. This isn't living - I mean can't I make a mistake? Can't I change my mind?"—Cosmo talks to Rita about divorce

An uncomfortable, claustrophobic feeling comes from watching the film, partly because of its theatrical origins and partly because it reinforces the themes and tone of the film. Compensating for the fact that only two locations were used are the camera techniques, which are numerous and inventive. Wonderful use of reflections abound. Images are seen at various times through pane glass, mirrors, wine glasses, and the lake where Jack goes to meditate, all of which aid in the production value of the picture.

The emotions this movie evokes are not pleasant. Garnering comparisons to *Who's Afraid of Virginia Woolf?* (1966) because of subject matter and theatricality, *The Wife* does not make use of the former's feel of underlying promise amidst big, scary confrontations, but rather utilizes small, desperate revelations that foretell little measure of hope. It is a tense, emotional film that probes uncomfortable issues that are often not particularly entertaining. Stark and bleak, it is a picture of a grim sort of reality where some truth may be discovered.

—*Hilary Weber*

REVIEWS

Hollywood Reporter. January 26, 1995, p. 14.
Los Angeles Times. September 13, 1996, p. F10.
New York Times. August 16, 1996, p. C5.
Variety. January 25, 1995, p. 12.
Village Voice. August 20, 1996, p. 48.

William Shakespeare's Romeo & Juliet

My only love sprung from my only hate. The greatest love story of all time is happening in our time.—Movie tagline

"A potent vision."—David Ansen, *Newsweek*

"Shakespeare has never been this sexy on-screen."—Peter Travers, *Rolling Stone*

"A *Rebel Without a Cause* for the '90s."—Richard Corliss, *Time Magazine*

Box Office: **$44,020,123**

Hot young actors Leonardo DiCaprio (Romeo) and Claire Danes (Juliet) star in Baz Luhrmann's *William Shakespeare's Romeo and Juliet.*

Never let it be said that there is nothing new under the sun. But if it is said, be sure that Baz Luhrmann is far removed from earshot. Writer/director Luhrmann's 1993 rookie effort, *Strictly Ballroom,* took a cliche-riddled format (musical) and turned it on its ear. It was immensely engaging and won the raves of many film fans who detest movie musicals. He was the perfect choice to head the unconventional, attack-on-the-senses update of *William Shakespeare's Romeo & Juliet.*

Considered classics even at the time they were written, Shakespeare's three dozen plus plays have been told and retold for over four hundred years. Once Hollywood discovered that the motion picture business wasn't just a passing fad, it was only natural that they would make their own lives easier by wisely choosing material that was tried and true. The recent resurfacing of the silent feature *Richard III* (1912) lends the necessary credence to this theory.

In addition to his directorial duties, Luhrmann is co-writer and co-producer of the project which follows a recent trend that finds modern filmmakers again returning to the drawing board and giving the Bard-of-Avon vibrant new life. For the seventh time in the last 12 months, producers have enlisted Shakespeare as a source for scripts. *Othello* (1995) was performed in its original chronological time frame without any structural variations. Despite winning critical raves, the public's response was lukewarm. *Twelfth Night* has been reset in the mid- 1870s. The rather tepid, restrained direction by Trevor Nunn hindered the production far more than the negligible time change. *Looking for Richard* and *A Midwinter's Tale* are not technically considered Shakespeare at all. The former, from first time director Al Pacino, was years in the making and the finished product looks and feels like a home movie about the meaning and social relevance of Richard III and Shakespeare in general. While being off-the-cuff and informal, it is never less than reverential in its homage to Shakespeare. The latter is a black and white comical send-up by director/Shakespeare enthusiast Kenneth Branagh about a less than perfect interpretation of Hamlet by a band of dedicated, albeit moderately talented actors. It was more or less a warm-up for Branagh's own very faithful, very serious, very splashy, very long version of *Hamlet.* Sir Ian McKellen stirred up the dirt and irritated droves of staunch Shakespearean purists with his *Richard III* (1995). McKellen set the play in a fictional 1930s England and portrayed Richard as a leather-clad fascist. In doing so, he attracted a new (not huge, but definitely new) audience that was curious to see Shakespeare done in a more modern, identifiable context.

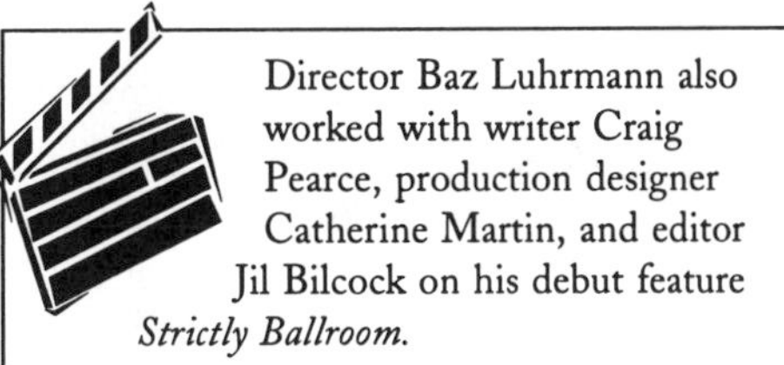

Director Baz Luhrmann also worked with writer Craig Pearce, production designer Catherine Martin, and editor Jil Bilcock on his debut feature *Strictly Ballroom.*

Luhrmann's film picks up right where McKellen's left off. The story's prologue and epilogue are delivered by a talking head newscaster. Many scenes are shot from news helicopters that swoop down on Verona Beach, a congested, bustling city that resembles Miami (the film was actually shot in Mexico). Skyscraper-sized religious statues appear between two gargantuan office buildings. The sign atop one reads "Montague," the other "Capulet." Apart from the original 1600 era performances, Luhrmann is the first person to film Shakespeare in a current, modern day setting. He is definitely trying to attract the MTV generation with this project. Some may think of it as selling out, but Luhrmann is actually making a brave, bold move.

In keeping with current social behavior, Luhrmann displays the rival factions of the Capulet and Montague families as urban street gangs battling for turf. Think of it as the Crips and the Bloods with refined speech patterns mixed with the ballet-like jousting movements of the Jets and the Sharks from *West Side Story* (1961), itself being a thinly veiled reworking of *Romeo & Juliet.* Souped-up cars with blaring rap music carry the buzz-cut punks with shocking pink hairdos and loud Hawaiian beach shirts. In this Verona beach, unconcealed firearms are an accepted, if not required, fashion accessory. Not only does everybody carry their own 9 millimeter hand cannon, they are all personally tailored to their owner—pearl handles decorated with ornate images of the Virgin Mary. Instead of coat check rooms, there are gun check rooms that have signs reading "No Ticket, No Gun." Despite the omnipresence of the firearms, these characters don't shoot indiscriminately. Strangely akin to the fencing battles of Shakespearean times, the guns serve as surrogate sabres in a strategic, gentlemanly form of chicken. The opening standoff, set in a downtown gas station ends without bloodshed, but instead leaves bruised egos and horrific petrol explosions in its wake.

Filmed and edited in such a blazing and dizzying manner, it makes MTV's incoherent music videos seem New Age and sedate by comparison. Later in the film, Luhrmann even pays slight, tongue-in-cheek homage to the age of MTV by bringing the worlds of new and old together with the inclusion of Prince's "When Doves Cry." Delivered innocent and straight-faced by a boys choir, the lyrics of the song are a perfect compliment to Shakespeare's own paradoxical questions of delight and despair, family allegiances, confusion and bewilderment and the harrowing Bermuda Triangle of romance, sex, and love. The pivotal, but often overlooked role of Romeo's confidant Mercutio is brilliantly played by Harold Perrineau (*Smoke* [1995] whose crossing-dressing dance numbers and rebel-with-a-pout posturing eerily recall a younger, pre-symbol monikered, Prince.

Romeo makes his entrance during a scene with his cousin Benvolio (Dash Mihok), one of the participants of the earlier service station clash. It takes place at a beachside pavilion, that appears to have been ravaged by revelers the previous evening. In casting his Romeo, Luhrmann could not have made a better choice than Leonardo DiCaprio. Barely out of his teens, DiCaprio has already been anointed as the premier thespian of his generation. He pumps vital new life into this Romeo. Complete with a slight, moping swagger and wrought romantic brooding, he is sure to invite favorable comparisons to the late James Dean. His face simultaneously projects the look of an experienced man-child and innocent, wide-eyed cherub. DiCaprio makes it clear, early on, that Romeo has strong, unwavering convictions about life and love and would die to protect them.

AWARDS AND NOMINATIONS

Academy Awards 1996 Nominations: Best Art Direction

Day turns to night and the scene shifts to the Capulet mansion, which is in frantic disarray preparing for an elaborate masquerade ball. Juliet herself will wear angel's wings. The party itself is being used merely as elaborate window dressing for Juliet's parents who intend to arrange the coupling of their daughter with Paris (Paul Rudd), a handsome, slightly vacant suitor with many social and political connections. Juliet's father Fulgencio Capulet (Paul Sorvino) is a boorish, neglectful patriarch who views his daughter as a mere pawn to be used in his strategic battle to further advance his own political and business agendas.

What is true of DiCaprio can also be said for Claire Danes, who plays Juliet. Even younger than DiCaprio,

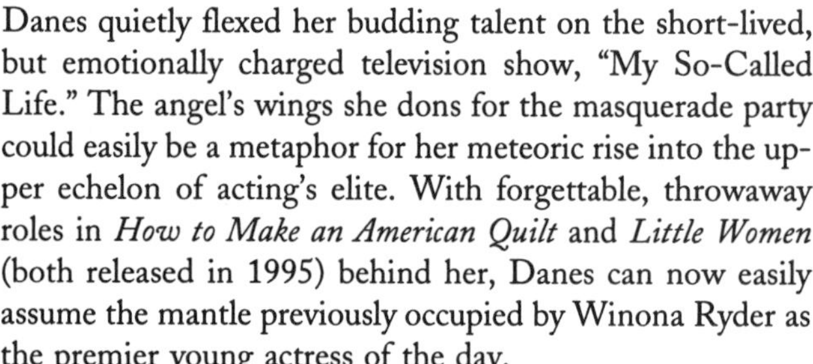

Danes quietly flexed her budding talent on the short-lived, but emotionally charged television show, "My So-Called Life." The angel's wings she dons for the masquerade party could easily be a metaphor for her meteoric rise into the upper echelon of acting's elite. With forgettable, throwaway roles in *How to Make an American Quilt* and *Little Women* (both released in 1995) behind her, Danes can now easily assume the mantle previously occupied by Winona Ryder as the premier young actress of the day.

With this version, *Romeo & Juliet* has been filmed four times. The most notable of the previous three being Franco Zeffirelli's version from 1968. Zeffirelli succeeded on many levels, not the least of which was the spectacular costume and set designs. As Luhrmann paints his young lovers with the current societal garb, Zeffirelli tried to dress-up his version with the then prevalent "summer-of-love" motif. In doing so, he cast two actors (Leonard Whiting and Olivia Hussey) in the title roles who, while being glowingly attractive, lacked the pluck and fervor needed to convincingly display the required passion, drive, and angst that gives the characters their very necessary believability. To make up for his actors' obvious lack of thespian wherewithal, Zeffirelli trimmed the dialogue down to the bare minimum. In spite of his artistic compromising, Zeffirelli's film did tremendous box office, but ultimately suffered from a "style over substance" mentality. Luhrmann garnered two of the most (arguably) talented young actors in the business. He didn't shorten or alter the dialogue one bit and his leads' chemistry together and effortless rendering of the verse is what throws this production into the "greatness" category. He successfully blends style and substance. Luhrmann's brazen approach is a welcomed, if slightly uncomfortable, jolt to an often complacent, business-as-usual filmmaking establishment. He has taken one of the most famous, universal pieces of literature and proven that it is indeed "timeless."

—J.M. Clark

CREDITS

Romeo: Leonardo DiCaprio
Juliet: Claire Danes
Tybalt: John Leguizamo
Father Lawrence: Pete Postlethwaite
Mercutio: Harold Perrineau
Ted Montague: Brian Dennehy
Fulgencio Capulet: Paul Sorvino
The Nurse: Miriam Margoyles
Dave Paris: Paul Rudd
Gloria Capulet: Diane Venora
Caroline Montague: Christina Pickles
Balthazar: Jesse Bradford
Captain Prince: Vondie Curtis-Hall

Origin: USA
Released: 1996
Production: Gabriella Marinelli and Baz Luhrmann for a Bazmark production; released by Twentieth Century Fox
Direction: Baz Luhrmann
Screenplay: Craig Pearce and Baz Luhrmann; based on the play by William Shakespeare
Cinematography: Donald M. McAlpine
Editing: Jill Bilcock
Music: Nellee Hooper
Production design: Catherine Martin
Art direction: Doug Hardwick
Set design: Catherine Doherty
Costume design: Kym Barrett
Sound: Rob Young
Choreographer: John O'Connell
Visual effects supervisor: Rebecca Marie
Casting: David Rubin
MPAA rating: PG-13
Running Time: 120 minutes

REVIEWS

Chicago Tribune. November 1, 1996, p. 4.
Entertainment Weekly. November 8, 1996, p. 46.
Film Threat. January, 1997, p. 60.
Los Angeles Times. November 1, 1996, p. F1.
New York Times. November 1, 1996, p. C1.
Newsweek. November 4, 1996, p. 73.
People. November 11, 1996, p. 21.
Rolling Stone. November 14, 1996, p. 123.
Time Online. October 29, 1996.
USA Today. November 1, 1996, p. 1D.
Variety. October 28, 1996, p. 65.
Washington Post. November 1, 1996, p. D1.

Without Evidence

Without Evidence is a gripping mystery that will sweep you up into a maelstrom of intrigue and conjecture. But it is also much, much more. It is the true story of a murder, a murder that the filmmakers believe is still unsolved.

Michael Francke, head of Oregon's corrections department and a man some considered a future gubernatorial candidate, was stabbed in front of his office on January 17, 1989. Despite evidence uncovered by the press and by Michael's brother Kevin that pointed toward a conspiracy, the police insisted that the murder was the result of a bungled car robbery and Frank Gable, a police informer, was convicted of the crime.

Ever since his brother's death, Kevin Francke has been on a mission to find the man who hired the killers of his brother. Along the way, he has also inspired others. The people who made *Without Evidence* were people who had either known and admired Michael Francke, or were people who were inspired by Kevin's unfaltering search for justice. These filmmakers are angry, angry about a justice system that they feel is protecting the real perpetrators, angry that a good man has been murdered because he was courageous enough to fight corruption, and angry that an innocent man is doing life in prison for a crime he did not commit.

These people are serious about their search for the real murderers, so serious in fact that they have posted a reward in the film of $1 million for "voluntary testimony leading to the apprehension, arrest, conviction and sentencing of the person or persons responsible for the murder of Michael Francke."

In an effort to offer its audience a true account of the actual murder, the filmmakers shot the film on the original locations, sometimes even shooting in secret. The audience is given the clues that Kevin uncovered, and, because it is real life, there are more than a few red herrings among them. But real life isn't as simple as a dime store novel, and the true solution to this mystery is left for the audience to decide.

The credits offer a $1 million reward for testimony leading to the apprehension, arrest, conviction, and sentencing of the killer(s).

The film opens in Florida, where Michael Francke (Ernnie Garrett) is visiting his brother, Kevin (Scott Plank). Michael confides in his brother that things at his work aren't going well. He says that he has to clean up his department, and he has stepped on a few toes in the process.

When Michael Francke is stabbed to death in front of his office in Salem, Oregon, Kevin is notified. From the beginning, Kevin is told conflicting stories. First they tell him that Michael has been shot and, later, that he was stabbed. The time of the murder appears to be around 7 or 8 p.m., but they tell Kevin that he was found after a search, five hours later. This seems strange, since he was found on the portico of the office building where he worked.

After the funeral, Kevin returned to Michael's home to find shotgun shells strewn all over the deck and two guns by Michael's bed. But when Kevin tells the police about this and other inconsistencies in the case, they warn him to stay out of it.

Kevin, now suspicious, demands an autopsy report. When he finally receives it, pages are missing, and most of the text is blackened out. This confirms Kevin's opinion that his brother was a victim of a conspiracy.

Kevin Francke is now a man obsessed. He gives up his construction business, his home in Florida, and even his marriage to find out the truth of his brother's murder. Taking only a suitcase, Kevin drives to Oregon in search of justice.

Once in Oregon, he is befriended by John Nelson (Andrew Prine), a TV reporter who has been following the murder from the outset. Nelson has already uncovered a composite drawing the police had made from descriptions of a strange man in the dome building after it was closed. The drawing is never released to the public and the man is not a suspect. Kevin and Nelson can only speculate why not.

In another case entirely, a woman, Liz Godlove (Ann Gunn), is accused of shooting her boyfriend, but a jury acquits her, calling it self-defense. But when Nelson runs the police composite on the news, Godlove recognizes the drawing as the man she killed, Tim Natividad, a local drug-dealer. She contacts Nelson and he puts her on the news. She says that around the time that Francke was murdered, Natividad came home with a wound on his leg and his head. But the police feel they have the man who did the murder in custody and won't consider Natividad as a suspect.

Meanwhile Kevin has become romantically involved with Liz and moves in with her and her six-year old son. While he is there, the police come to Liz's apartment and try to get her to change the statements she made on TV. Their intimidation and their constant tailing of Kevin convince him that they should move out of town and into the country. They move into a trailer of a friend, and Kevin, while setting up a new life with Liz and her son, continues his quest.

When the case goes to court, the judge doesn't permit witnesses to even mention Natividad's name in front of the jury. This omission nullifies all the evidence Kevin and Nelson have gathered, since Natividad is the cornerstone to their conspiracy theory. Frank Gable (Jason Tomlins) is convicted of Michael Francke's murder and sentenced to life in prison.

Even before the trial, Nelson has been interviewing a possible witness to the crime. After the trial Jodie (Angelina Jolie), a young, strung-out junkie, meets with Kevin and, in a cryptic but engrossing scene, she reveals bits and pieces of the murder. All her information points to a conspiracy, but Jodie refuses to tell Kevin who was behind it. She says that if he knew who really did the murder, they would kill him.

Soon after, Kevin is out for a drive one night and notices that he is being followed by a police car. Every intersection brings another police car, and they all quietly follow him to his home outside of town. When he pulls into his driveway, they surround him, and Kevin gets out of his car, half expecting to be shot at any moment.

They handcuff him and throw him into the back of a police car. After they check his gun, they tell him that they were just following a lead about an individual who had been threatening someone with a pistol. Then they return his gun and take off the handcuffs, but before they let him go, one of the policemen asks, "What did you learn from Jodie?" "That I'm not done here," is his answer. The cops leave, but by now it is obvious that Kevin is close to the truth, and we also know that he will not give up his search.

Gill Dennis, director and co-writer of *Without Evidence,* has gone beyond the typical TV docu-drama format to create a mesmerizing drama that leaves an indelible question mark in the mind of the viewer. Filmed in 16mm under more than trying circumstances, *Without Evidence* is sometimes distractingly grainy and its opening scenes tend to drag, but by the middle of the film the plot becomes so intriguing that technical issues become irrelevant. The second half of the film is captivating, unfolding in ways that only real life can. A battered girlfriend who murders her abuser, a young but wasted junkie who can't let go of her sense of justice, and a man whose love for his brother outweighs even his own life, these are the unique personalities of real life, where warts and virtues are scrambled together into human form.

Although *Without Evidence* leaves a lot of questions unanswered and the story has more than a few holes, the impact of the film isn't diminished by these flaws. The really important questions are left for the audience to answer. Was Francke's death the result of a conspiracy, or is the conspiracy theory the result of our very human need to find a reason for a great man's death beyond the senselessness of random violence?

Sometimes the making of a film turns out to be even more dramatic than the film itself. This film is a testament to the life of the man who was murdered, but it is also a testament to the people who made this film, people who honor justice and refuse to settle for a scapegoat. But justice doesn't come without sacrifice.

Kevin Francke lost his business, his marriage, and, if he is right about the conspiracy, he could have lost his own life in his journey to find the murderer of his brother.

Phil Stanford, a staff reporter with *The Oregonian,* was fired from the paper after relentlessly following the story. He later co-wrote the screenplay for *Without Evidence* with director Gill Dennis.

Producer Eric Epperson, also a lawyer, became involved in the film when he became convinced that "our criminal justice system is broken," and he decided to do something about it.

Alan James, the film's executive producer, knew and admired Michael Francke. He was so affected by his death that he put up more than a million dollars to make the film and contributed heavily to the reward. Spurred by what he called "the arrogance of the public officials," James was driven to seek out the truth through the public forum of cinema. When asked his motivation for making the film, he posed, "Did you ever get a cause you couldn't let go of?"

Perhaps we will never know the truth about Michael Francke's death, but we do know something of his life. Mark Twain once wrote, "Let us endeavor to live so that when we die even the undertaker will be sorry." Obviously, that is how Michael Francke lived.

—Diane Hatch-Avis

CREDITS

Kevin Francke: Scott Plank
Liz Godlove: Anna Gunn
John Nelson: Andrew Prine
Jodie Swearingen: Angelina Jolie
Michael Francke: Ernnie Garrett
Sgt. Unsoeld: Paul Perri
Dale Pen: Alan Nause

Origin: USA
Released: 1996
Production: Eric R. Epperson for an MFD Ltd. production
Direction: Gill Dennis
Screenplay: Gill Dennis, Phil Stanford
Cinematography: Victor Nunez
Editing: Erik Whitmyre, Jay Miracle
Music: Franco Piersanti
Production design: Robert Garner
Art direction: Debbie DeVilla
Costumes: Marilyn Wall-Asse
Sound: Pete Winter
Casting: Judy Courtney
MPAA rating: Unrated
Running Time: 132 minutes

REVIEWS

Hollywood Reporter. December 12, 1995, p. 4.
Hollywood Reporter. March 14, 1996, p. 6.
Variety. April 1, 1996, p. 57.

World and Time Enough

"A memorable new addition to the world of gay cinema."—B.J. Callaghan, *Bay Windows*

"An engaging romantic comedy."—Kevin Thomas, *Los Angeles Times*

Box Office: $91,879

A number of good films have been released in the past year or two which deal directly and honestly with gay relationships. Gay cinema, commercially speaking, is still in its early stages. Due quite often to budgetary constraints (which affect the quality of everything from script to production values to casting), the quality of the films has been uneven. Sometimes the films are brilliant; sometimes they are just plain bad.

Sometimes these films find audiences, and even a bit of acclaim, in spite of their weaknesses. Such a film is *World and Time Enough.* It received some uneven reviews (mostly from "mainstream" press) and excellent reviews from some small gay publications, while receiving some positive response from usually more discerning film festival audiences. Unfortunately, it is a substandard film in most respects. It would deserve praise for tackling some of its subject matter—most notably the relationship of the Catholic church and homosexuality—if other films, such as *Priest* (1995), had not done so with considerably more intelligence and style.

Contemporary gay cinema has grown up, for the most part, in the last couple of years. In particular, *Jeffrey* (1995) brought out into the open as never before the concept that a relationship between two men can be fraught with the same kinds of ups and downs as a heterosexual one. Prior to that, it was up to far darker films such as *Making Love* (1982) to bring gay relationships out of the closet. The cultural context in which that film was made required that its characters be quite sad and gloomy most of the time. But in recent years, gay romantic comedies have begun to find audiences. This past year, *Go Fish* (1994), *The Incredibly True Adventures of Two Girls in Love* (1995), and *Bar Girls* (1995) treated lesbian relationships with a matter-of-fact style which made room for the normalcy of gay relationships. These films all told their stories with good humor and grace, showing that gay people can have just as many problems with love as straight people. *Lie Down with Dogs* (1995) dealt with a gay man's quest to find love in the '90s, with a good amount of wit and a moderate amount of success.

In addition to these films about love and dating, there have also been some notable films which dealt with the difficulties of being HIV positive, not to mention having AIDS. *The Living End* (1993), Gregg Araki's controversial independent film about two HIV positive men on the run, and *Postcards from America* (1995) met varying critical response in their portrayals of fringe characters dealing with HIV. The more mainstream *Longtime Companion* (1990) and the huge hit *Philadelphia* (1993), which won an Oscar for Tom Hanks, dealt head-on with AIDS, to great critical acclaim.

World and Time Enough deals with all of the issues found in these aforementioned films. It is the story of Mark (Matt Guidry), his life-partner Joey (Gregory G. Giles), and their struggles to make their lives work as a couple in contemporary Minneapolis. The Catholic church, coming out, dating, love, the vicissitudes of life as an HIV positive man—these issues are all thrown into the pot in *World and Time Enough.* The pot doesn't seem big enough, and (to overextend a metaphor) the ingredients don't mix well.

Now, it is certainly appropriate to include all of these problems in the film. After all, these are the issues that might face any gay male in contemporary society. But somehow writer director Eric Mueller stuffs an awful lot of themes and issues into his slim story. It appears that he sees this film as encompassing a lot of big themes, perhaps in a manner similar to Broadway's brilliant, sprawling, *Angels in America.* The fact that Mueller doesn't succeed may be due to the exigencies of filmmaking and due to the fact that this is his debut film. Good or bad, it does get people thinking once again about some of those big themes, right. But the inclusion of all of these themes are not enough to make the audience ignore the clumsy symbolism, the simplistic plot and dialogue, and the rudimentary acting skills of most of its actors.

The story is told by a narrator, David (Kraig Swartz), as if it were an incredible story that begs to be told. It isn't. And if it must be told, director Mueller could not have chosen a more irritating person to tell it than the actor portraying David. Sucking a lollipop, making inane jokes, digressing into his own lackluster love life, all with a nasal whine, Swartz begins to grate on one's nerves rather quickly. He appears to be doing a sort of impression of what Woody Allen would be if he were a crudely stereotypical gay person, but it doesn't work. Mercifully, Mueller seems to have recognized this problem, and David's interruptions diminish in length and number as the film proceeds.

Luckily, the film's lead, Mark, is not half bad. Mark is an HIV positive man who stops working as an office temp in order to go around the city creating works of guerrilla art which are intended to raise awareness about AIDS. Putting signs on storefronts and painting fences everywhere, Mark is the model of a committed HIV survivor who channels his anger into his politics and his art. His commitment is commendable, and Guidry makes Mark rather believable and moderately likable. Without showing a vast range of emotion, Guidry manages to bring his character a measure of passion and dignity, even through some ridiculous moments.

For example: Having lost his mother (many years earlier) to a giant falling crucifix, Mark decides to erect a makeshift cathedral in an open field and commit suicide by jumping off the top. He builds the structure out of iron scaffolding, and when he decides to jump, it is only a couple of stories high. Director Mueller seems to want the audience to think that Mark's life is truly in danger, but instead, Mark seems only to be an eccentric attempting to find resolution about his mother's horrible death. All of this foolishness could have ruined Guidry's credibility with the audience, but somehow the actor manages to emerge with the audience's good will.

Mark's lover, Joey, is another eccentric. Joey seems a bit slow-witted but has a heart of gold, and is sweetly if simplistically performed by Gregory Giles. Joey, who is HIV negative, is perfectly content with his job picking up trash for the city. He brings home countless strange figurines and pieces of junk which he finds in the course of his job. Joey's simple and happy world is shattered, though, when he tries to come out to his adoptive parents and instead is thrown out of the house. The problem here is that Joey comes out rather crudely: He tells his parents he is bringing home his girlfriend for Thanksgiving, and then shows up at the door with Mark. Though his parents' reactions are nasty and mean, it is hard to forget that Joey was dumb enough to come out in this way. Like Guidry, Giles does his best to overcome the silliness of his character and infuse him with some humanity. The overly-adorable quirkiness of the character might only serve to destroy any relationship between him and the audience, but Giles seems to be a likable fellow. He would probably do better with a well-written character.

Perhaps it is unfair to pick on some of Mueller's story and character choices, but much of the film invites sarcasm. There is something simply (and unintentionally) hilarious about the character of Mark's father, for example. Having lost his wife to a falling crucifix, Mark's father has apparently spent the rest of his life building model cathedrals (there is probably some symbolism here, but the significance of it is elusive). Tragically, the father dies while building a model cathedral, dropping face first onto the table. Mark finds him several days later, and though the scene should be touching, it seems nothing more than ludicrous to see the actor playing the father slumped over in his chair, his head buried in cut-out cathedrals.

By the time Mark finds him, though, there have been numerous quick-cutting sequences of churches accompanied by ghastly, loud liturgical music. Up until the revelation about the mother's death (and the father's subsequent death), it is never clear why Mueller has included these sequences. It seems as if they are about something important, but, instead of being intriguing, these images are merely annoying. And unfortunately, that sums up the film.

—Kirby Tepper

CREDITS

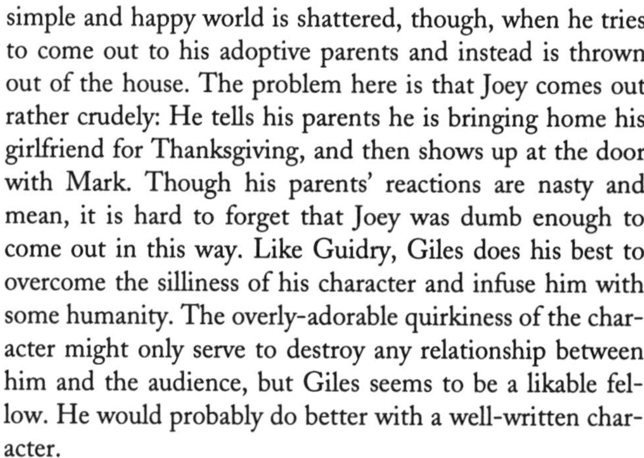

Mark: Matt Guidry
Joey: Gregory G. Giles
David: Kraig Swartz
Mike: Peter Macon
Marie: Bernadette Sullivan

Origin: USA
Released: 1995
Production: Julie Hartley, Andrew Peterson for a 1 in 10 Films production; released by Strand Releasing
Direction: Eric Mueller
Screenplay: Eric Mueller
Cinematography: Kyle Bergersen
Editing: Laura Stokes
Music: Eugene Huddleston
Production design: Heather McElhatton
Casting: Lynn Blumenthal
MPAA rating: Unrated
Running Time: 90 minutes

REVIEWS

New York Times. September 1, 1995, p. C8.

The Young Poisoner's Handbook

Meet Graham. He's not your ordinary teenager.—Movie tagline

He gave his life to his research. So did his family.—Movie tagline

"A ghoulish, expertly made black comedy loaded with macabre glee."—Janet Maslin, *New York Times*

"A wonderfully nasty concoction!"—Maitland McDonaugh, *The Paper*

"Deliciously dark and fiendishly funny."—Dominic Griffin, *Sassy*

"Completely spellbinding. At once breathtakingly funny and terrifying."—Jeff Craig, *Sixty Second Preview*

Box Office: **$536,825**

Director Benjamin Ross' first feature film, *The Young Poisoner's Handbook,* takes on one of the most intriguing of social figures, the psychopath. Sidetracking the usual treatment of this theme by refusing to take a moral stand or stake out ground for terror, and only lightly touching the format of the black comedy, this film turns out to be invigorating and astonishingly unique. Based on the true story of Graham Young (Hugh O'Conor), documented primarily in the British tabloids of the 1970s, the film tells the story of an alienated young perfectionist who takes his science experiments to lethal conclusions by slowly poisoning his family. After being committed to an insane asylum, he is released several years later only to continue his hobby on his fellow employees.

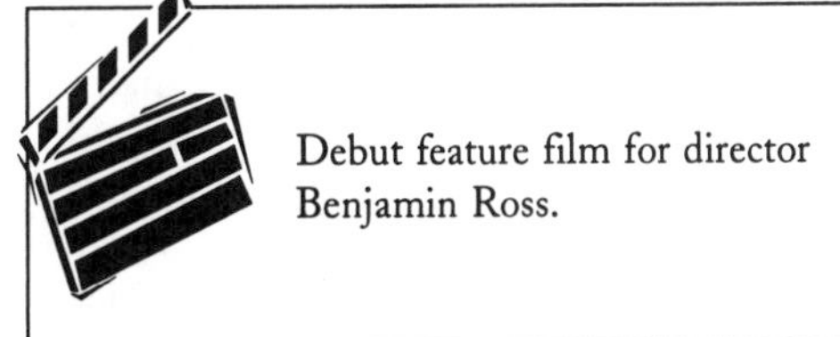

Debut feature film for director Benjamin Ross.

The film travels through three different periods of time, early adolescence, life in the mental institution, and young adulthood in the workforce. Each segment documents not only the changes in the young Graham, but also in the world around him, as music, home decor and fashions transform. Always removed from these changes in popular culture, Graham emerges as a social anomaly, a boy dedicated to a private project rather than following the current of the larger culture. Actor Hugh O'Conor, who first exhibited his talents as the young Christy Brown in *My Left Foot* (1989), is perfectly suited to this role and plays the nonchalant killer to perfection. Much of the cast is comprised of British stage actors, giving the film a slightly exaggerated and bizarre edge which is well suited to the offbeat, decadent style of the work.

The story is told from the point-of-view of the young Graham, often with deadpan voice-overs that reveal his emotional estrangement and general boredom in the face of his crimes. The 14-year-old Graham is strange and studious, engaging in careful research projects and frequenting the local drugstore for chemicals. Annoyed by the nuances of his family life, his docile father, nagging stepmother (Ruth Sheen), and frivolous older sister, he sinks deeply into his work. After being humiliated by his stepmother who accuses him of hiding dirty magazines, and after his prize experiment ends in an explosion, Graham sets out on a revenge track. First he poisons his stepmother's chocolates with antimony, and spikes his sister's eyedrops, blinding her in one eye. Then, taking his inspiration from comic books, he moves on to Thallium, a more treacherous poison, which he administers to his stepmother in lieu of the medicine the doctor prescribed for her stomach pains. He proceeds keeping careful records of the doses and reactions until she is bedridden, loses all her hair, and becomes catatonic. Convinced that she is dying, and unaware of the cause, his stepmother reaches out to Graham in a rare gesture of affection and gives him her coveted diamond ring as a keepsake. Graham enjoys the irony of the situation but he gradually realizes that in order to be the very best poisoner, he must eventually get caught. Before her death Graham lets his mother discover the hideous handbook which charts her decline, but unable to speak and growing further removed from reality, she is helpless in the face of her horrible knowledge. After her funeral, Graham begins to poison his father, but having left enough traces, he is soon captured and sent to an insane asylum.

In the asylum Graham attracts the attention of a Dr. Zeigler (Anthony Sher), a man devoted to proving that psychopaths can recover and be reintegrated into society. Dr. Zeigler begins to work with Graham and looks to his dream life for signs of a hidden conscience. Having no recollection of his dreams, Graham resorts to stealing the nightmares of the boy in the neighboring bed, Berridge, who honestly is tortured by having butchered his parents. By pulling the nightmares from the exhausted Berridge each evening, Graham pushes the poor boy over the edge and drives him to suicide. Without the aid of Berridge's nightmares, it becomes obvious that Graham has been lying, and Dr. Ziegler abandons him. In desperation Graham makes one last attempt at freedom by confiding in the doctor that he has been tormented by images of diamond patterns ever since the failure of his adolescent chemistry experiment. The doctor develops an interpretation whereby the diamonds signify Graham's original intention to create beauty with his chemicals. This ambition according to the doctor was thwarted by the failure of the experiment and misdirected into destructive behavior. Graham makes a model recovery once his interests are redirected into constructive behavior, and the review board votes in favor of his release.

"Do you think there's a virus going 'round?"—Graham to his coworkers (whom he's poisoning)

Though shunned by his remaining family, Graham finds a job and a new life in a community that has no knowledge of his past. He reintegrates into his new community quite smoothly, but before long his coworkers begin to selectively exhibit signs of illness. Guided by detailed drawings of each of their coffee mugs, Graham is able to keep careful records in his handbook and to selectively control the degrees of illness of each person. On the day when Graham intends to deliver the fatal portions he discovers that all the individualized mugs in the cabinet have been replaced by a slew of identical mugs. In desperation he tries to memorize who should receive which mug by their position on his serving tray, but he loses track. He becomes frantic in the face of his lost control, inadvertently revealing his secret to his stunned coworkers. In order to allay their suspicions he takes a gulp of one of the random mugs himself. He becomes violently ill and returns to his room where he is overcome by hallucinations of his mother's balding head reaching up to devour him from the toilet bowl.

Graham is sent back to an insane asylum where he lives until his death in 1990. Though the actual Graham Young died of unknown causes, this film proposes an interesting scenario for his final day. Graham is shown alone in his room meticulously scraping his stepmother's diamond ring into a fine powder. He then ingests the powder and lies down to die.

Though critics have complained that this film suffers from refusing to follow the rules of black comedy, the film succeeds due to its originality and cleverness as well as its skillful directing and editing. Creating a moribund mood similar to the likes of the cult-classic *Harold and Maude* (1971), but without the optimistic ending, this film relies on a deadpan presentation and a morose objectivity that suits the content quite well. Despite the potentially moral subject matter there is little motivation to either condemn or sympathize with Graham. The viewer's position is not unlike Graham's relationship to his handbook of carefully collected data, keenly interested but emotionally removed. This attitude gives the film a sinister and delightful ambience not often found in films that take notorious real-life crimes as their subject matter.

The film's structure in three parts holds together quite well, though the first two segments are noticeably stronger and tighter than the final segment. The soundtrack of popular songs spanning three decades, and the sets revealing gaudy fashions and dated interiors, make the film's movement in time both comical and bizarre, but always consistent. Graham Young's life somehow seems less strange in such a strange world. With this film, Benjamin Ross has proven himself to be a director to watch closely.

—Reni Celeste

CREDITS

Graham: Hugh O'Conor
Dr. Zeigler: Anthony Sher
Molly: Ruth Sheen
Fred: Roger Lloyd Pack
Winnie: Charlotte Coleman
Dennis: Paul Stacey
Sue: Samantha Edmonds

Origin: Great Britain
Released: 1994; 1996
Production: Sam Taylor for a Mass Productions, Kinowelt, and Haut et Court Film production; released by Cinepix Film Properties
Direction: Benjamin Ross
Screenplay: Benjamin Ross, Jeff Rawle
Cinematography: Hubert Taczanowski
Editing: Anne Sopol
Music: Robert Lane, Frank Strobel
Production design: Maria Djurkovic
Art direction: Mark Stevenson, Matthias Kammermeier
Costume design: Stewart Meacham
Sound: Eckhard Kuchenbecker
Casting: Michelle Guish
MPAA rating: R
Running Time: 99 minutes

REVIEWS

Chicago Tribune. April 19, 1996.
Detroit Free Press. May 12, 1996, p. 8F.
Los Angeles Times. March 1, 1996, p. F10.
New York Times. February 22, 1996, p. C3.
Sight and Sound. September, 1995, p. 64.
Variety. January 25, 1995, p. 12.
Village Voice. February 27, 1996, p. 61.

Zero Degrees Kelvin; Kjaerlighetens Kjotere

"A Norse version of *The Good, the Bad and the Ugly*. Savagely awesome beauty."—Jami Bernard, *Daily News*

"Raw-boned polar adventure."—Stephen Holden, *New York Times*

"Stunningly beautiful."—Elliot Stein, *Village Voice*

Box Office: $10,493

The production notes for *Zero Degrees Kelvin* contain the following observation: "the film production team [was] obviously concerned about life imitating art during the two-month shoot in close quarters." To say the least, this is an understatement. The conditions under which the film was shot on one of the nearly uninhabited Svalbard Islands, halfway between Oslo and the North Pole, were more than trying. The crew, nearly all made seasick by the voyage there, traveled by leased missionary boat to a location where they then had to arm themselves at all times to ward off threats from polar bears and endure endless delays occasioned by fog and ice. One shoot even resulted in members of the crew becoming stranded on a glacier until the weather improved enough for them to be helicoptered out.

The product of these extraordinary measures is a stunning, original motion picture in which, in the best sense, art imitates life, a film that *Variety* calls "a Nordic existential Western." The plot of *Zero Degrees Kelvin,* taken from Peter Tutein's novel, *Larsen,* revolves around Henrik Larsen (Garb B. Eidsvold), a poet in 1925 Oslo. When Larsen's girlfriend, Gertrude (Camilla Martens), declines to become engaged to him, Larsen suspects that her refusal might reflect an attraction to some other type of man. While the two stroll through a parade ground, Larsen suspiciously eyes a mustachioed military swordsman in whom Gertrude might be taking an interest—obviously a man of action, and possibly a rival. But Gertrude's refusal of Larsen's proposal may have more to do with the fact that, in an effort to gain experience as well as background information for a book, he has signed on for a year's tour of duty in Greenland with a fur trading company.

Film won a special mention at the 1995 San Sebastian Film Festival for the performance of its three lead actors.

When Larsen arrives at the company's desolate trapping outpost, he is at first enamored of the gorgeous scenery sculpted by the wind and ice. The station chief, Randbaek (Stellan Skarsgard), in contrast, is far from happy to see Larsen: the company has doubled the station's quota of furs while providing only an intellectual by way of reinforcements. Randbaek is an angry, uncivilized man who, unlike Larsen, has not come to this godforsaken place in order to broaden his horizons. As played by Skarsgard (whom American moviegoers saw earlier in 1996 in *Breaking the Waves*), Randbaek is a hulking, greasy-haired misanthropist who quickly proves also to be a sadist.

The contrast between Larsen and Randbaek could hardly be more vivid—or so it initially seems. Their interaction is complicated by the presence of a third party, Holm (Bjorn Sundquist), a scientist who has been stationed with Randbaek for a number of years. Unlike Randbaek, towards whom he feels tremendous loyalty, Holm adopts a neutral attitude towards the interloper, Larsen. His scientist's rationality helps him understand that in this hostile environment, the three men are dependent on one another for their very survival. Holm, who exhibits elements of Larsen's observer status as well as Randbaek's rough survival skills, initially acts as a sort of buffer between the other two men.

The antipathy between Larsen and Randbaek is at first almost entirely psychological, revolving around the issue of women. Randbaek, who seems incapable of love, speaks only vulgarly and demeaningly of his experiences with the opposite sex—indeed, one suspects that such experiences have contributed to the animosity that seems his most pronounced characteristic. He steals Larsen's diary, using its contents as ammunition to demean the younger man, and when he discovers that Larsen has lied about Gertrude, telling the others that she is his fiancee, Randbaek clearly feels he has vanquished a potential adversary.

Larsen, for his part, is a stronger, more resourceful individual than Randbaek—or indeed, Larsen himself—knows. Initially, Larsen is cowed by Randbaek's extreme demonstrations of bellicoseness, linking him mentally to the parading officer he had seen in Oslo with Gertrude. But *Zero Kelvin* is far from a simplistic drama about an intellectual weakling who is bullied by a seasoned strongman. Larsen proves an able hunter, far exceeding his daily quota and besting Randbaek at his own game. And Larsen also proves his mental toughness. Against Randbaek's express wishes, he has befriended a female sled dog, who becomes his only real ally. In order to teach Larsen a lesson—and also, clearly, in order to destroy him emotionally—Randbaek injures the dog. Then, full of contrition, he stages a sentimental Christmas celebration for the others. Larsen at first participates in the festivities, then lashes out at Randbaek once he is softened up and vulnerable. The apparent interaction of the feud between these two finally breaks Holm, who deserts. When the stricken Randbaek implores him to stay, telling him he will never survive a solo attempt to reach the nearest settlement, Holm states that he will take his chances. In the end, it seems, Holm lacks Larsen's passionate intensity and would prefer to wrestle with nature than with another man.

Larsen and Randbaek are thus left to face off alone. The question then becomes which, if either, of them will survive, and whether the hostile environment outside or that inside will do them in. After an accidental fire destroys their hut, the two enemies are obliged to combine forces and set off for help. But even after they discover the remains of Holm, undone by the environment, the enmity between them proves stronger than the survival instinct. Through nearly unbelievable conditions, Larsen and Randbaek battle one another as they pass through the beautiful but eerie arctic wasteland. In the end, Larsen proves the victor, but only after paying a terrible price. Before Larsen shoots him, Randbaek tells him that no woman will ever love him after he has killed a man.

And indeed, although Larsen makes it back to Oslo, where he is cleared after an inquest into Randbaek's death, he is unable to resume his former life. Gertrude, who has been waiting for him, is now ready to marry him, but Larsen is no longer a fit object for her love. In killing Randbaek, it seems that Larsen has changed places with his enemy. Although he may be the only person to understand his own transformation, as *Zero Degrees Kelvin* ends, it is clear that Larsen is now at war with himself every bit as much as the tortured, uncivilized man he thought he had exterminated.

This rough sketch of the plot of *Zero Degrees Kelvin* hardly does the movie justice. The interplay between Larsen and Randbaek, often carried out in ostentatiously brutal gestures, is nonetheless fraught with psychological nuance. And this drama of existential archetypes is played out against a backdrop at once breathtakingly beautiful and deeply menacing. What could have been a conventional action picture is thus rendered extraordinary. Skarsgard, who delivered such an understated performance as the husband in *Breaking the Waves,* here gives one of sometimes shocking unpredictability. Randbaek, whose discourse with the world consists largely of shouted obscenities, is also capable of dressing up in a red silk Mandarin costume to celebrate Christmas and of breaking down in tears when Holm declares he no longer wishes to be his friend. And Eidsvold brings just the right element of wide-eyed innocence to Larsen; when Larsen's empathy shifts to enmity, the transformation is just as unexpected as the changes in Randbaek's persona. In the end, Larsen seems as nonplussed by his own metamorphosis as we are.

Larsen's tragedy is finally greater than Randbaek's, if for no other reason than his acute self-awareness. When we last see Randbaek, his upright carcass is floating magisterially out to sea on an ice sheet; Larsen, it seems, has paid his worthy enemy a final homage by giving him a quirky kind of Viking burial. Larsen, for his part, is left to struggle with survivor's guilt and the knowledge that he has lost his innocence forever.

Far from being a conventional action picture, *Zero Degrees Kelvin* is more of an arctic *No Exit,* in which hell is not the environment so much as it is other people. It is wonderful to see what a range of emotions and experiences director Hans Petter Moland is able to wrest from three characters in a tiny cabin at the end of the world. Such situations typically produce dramas concerned with social interaction; here, the action amounts to an inquiry into the heart of darkness.

—Lisa Paddock

CREDITS

Larsen: Garb B. Eidsvold
Randbaek: Stellan Skarsgard
Holm: Bjorn Sundquist
Gertrude: Camilla Martens

Origin: Norway
Released: 1995
Production: Bent Ronglien for a Norsk Film AS and Sandrew Film AB production; released by Kino
Direction: Hans Petter Moland
Screenplay: Hans Petter Moland and Lars Bill Lundheim; based on the novel *Larsen* by Peter Tutein
Cinematography: Philip Ogaard
Editing: Einar Egeland
Music: Terje Rypdal
Art direction: Janusz Sosnowski
Costumes: Bente Winther-Larsen
Sound: Sturla Einarson
MPAA rating: Unrated
Running Time: 113 minutes

REVIEWS

Boxoffice. October, 1996, p. 40.
Hollywood Reporter. December 23, 1996, p. 10.
Variety. October 2, 1995, p. 41.
Village Voice. December 3, 1996, p. 61.

List of Awards

Academy Awards

Best Picture: *The English Patient*

Direction: Anthony Minghella (*The English Patient*)

Actor: Geoffrey Rush (*Shine*)

Actress: Frances McDormand (*Fargo*)

Supporting Actor: Cuba Gooding Jr. (*Jerry Maguire*)

Supporting Actress: Juliette Binoche (*The English Patient*)

Original Screenplay: Ethan Coen and Joel Coen (*Fargo*)

Adapted Screenplay: Billy Bob Thornton (*Sling Blade*)

Cinematography: John Seale (*The English Patient*)

Editing: Walter Murch (*The English Patient*)

Art Direction: Stuart Craig (*The English Patient*)

Visual Effects: Volker Engel, Douglas Smith, Clay Pinney and Joseph Viskocil (*Independence Day*)

Sound Effects Editing: Bruce Stambler (*The Ghost and the Darkness*)

Sound: Walter Murch, Mark Berger, David Parker and Chris Newman (*The English Patient*)

Makeup: Rick Baker and David Leroy Anderson (*The Nutty Professor*)

Costume design: Ann Roth (*The English Patient*)

Original Musical or Comedy Score: Rachel Portmann (*Emma*)

Original Dramatic Score: Gabriel Yared (*The English Patient*)

Original Song: "You Must Love Me" (*Evita:* music by Andrew Lloyd Webber, lyrics by Tim Rice)

Foreign-language Film: *Kolya* (Czech Republic)

Short Film, Animated: Tyron Montgomery and Thomas Stellmach (*Quest*)

Short Film, Live Action: David Frankel and Barry Jossen (*Dear Diary*)

Documentary, Feature: Leon Gast and David Sonenberg (*When We Were Kings*)

Documentry, Short Subject: Jessica Yu (*Breathing Lessons, The Life and Work of Mark O'Brien*)

Directors Guild of America Award

Director: Anthony Minghella (*The English Patient*)

Writers Guild Awards

Original Screenplay: Joel Coen and Ethan Coen (*Fargo*)

Adapted Screenplay: Billy Bob Thornton (*Sling Blade*)

New York Film Critics Awards

Best Picture: *Fargo*

Direction: Lars von Trier (*Breaking the Waves*)

Actor: Geoffrey Rush (*Shine*)

Actress: Emily Watson (*Breaking the Waves*)

Supporting Actor: Harry Belafonte (*Kansas City*)

Supporting Actress: Courtney Love (*The People vs. Larry Flynt*)

Los Angeles Film Critics Awards

Best Picture: *Secrets & Lies*

Direction: Mike Leigh (*Secrets & Lies*)

Actor: Geoffrey Rush (*Shine*)

Actress: Brenda Blethyn (*Secrets & Lies*)

Supporting Actor: Edward Norton (*Primal Fear, Everyone Says I Love You, The People vs. Larry Flynt*)

Supporting Actress: Barbara Hershey (*The Portrait of a Lady*)

Screenplay: Joel Coen and Ethan Coen (*Fargo*)

Cinematography: Chris Menges (*Michael Collins*); John Seale (*The English Patient*)

Foreign Film: *La Ceremonie*

Outstanding Documentary: Leon Gast and David Sonenberg (*When We Were Kings*)

National Society of Film Critics Awards

Best Picture: *Breaking the Waves*

Direction: Lars von Trier (*Breaking the Waves*)

Actor: Eddie Murphy (*The Nutty Professor*)

Actress: Emily Watson (*Breaking the Waves*)

Supporting Actor: Martin Donovan (*The Portrait of a Lady*); Tony Shalhoub (*Big Night*)

Supporting Actress: Barbara Hershey (*The Portrait of a Lady*)

Screenplay: Albert Brooks and Monica Johnson (*Mother*)
Cinematography: Robby Muller (*Breaking the Waves, Dead Man*)
Documentary: Leon Gast and David Sonenberg (*When We Were Kings*)
Foreign Language Film: *La Ceremonie*

National Board of Review Awards
Best English-Language Film: *Shine*
Direction: Joel Coen (*Fargo*)
Actor: Tom Cruise (*Jerry Maguire*)
Actress: Frances McDormand (*Fargo*)
Supporting Actor: Edward Norton (*Primal Fear, Everyone Says I Love You, The People vs. Larry Flynt*)
Supporting Actress: Juliette Binoche and Kristin Scott Thomas (*The English Patient*)
Documentary: Joe Berlinger and Bruce Sinofsky (*Paradise Lost: The Child Murders at Robin Hood Hills*)

Golden Globe Awards
Best Picture, Drama: *The English Patient*
Best Picture, Comedy or Musical: *Evita*
Direction: Milos Forman (*The People vs. Larry Flynt*)
Actor, Drama: Geoffrey Rush (*Shine*)
Actress, Drama: Brenda Blethyn (*Secrets & Lies*)
Actor, Comedy or Musical: Tom Cruise (*Jerry Maguire*)
Actress, Comedy or Musical: Madonna (*Evita*)
Supporting Actor: Edward Norton (*Primal Fear*)
Supporting Actress: Lauren Bacall (*The Mirror Has Two Faces*)
Screenplay: Scott Alexander and Larry Karazewski (*The People vs. Larry Flynt*)
Original Score: Gabriel Yared (*The English Patient*)
Original Song: "You Must Love Me" (*Evita:* music by Andrew Lloyd Webber, lyrics by Tim Rice)
Foreign-Language Film: *Kolya* (Czech Republic)

Life Achievement Award

Martin Scorsese

The American Film Institute's twenty-fifth annual Life Achievement Award was awarded to Martin Scorsese, widely considered the most talented director of his generation. Scorsese's sixteen feature-length films have won him the respect of his peers for their artistry much more than for their box-office grosses. Scorsese makes original, personal films rather than big-budget crowd pleasers, refusing to compromise his vision for fear of critical and commercial failure.

Scorsese, the second of two sons, was born November 17, 1942, in Flushing, New York. His parents, Charles and Catherine Cappa Scorsese, worked in Manhattan's garment district and, when Martin was eight, moved from Queens back to Elizabeth Street in Little Italy, where they had grown up. The Lower East Side of Manhattan, heavily populated by Italian, Irish, and other immigrant groups, as well as by major and minor criminals, made a profound impression on young Scorsese.

An even more significant effect was films. Scorsese suffered from chronic asthma and was unable to take part in games or sports. A lonely child as a result—his brother was six years older—he sought refuge in theaters, where his father took him to see worlds totally different from that of Little Italy. Scorsese also frequently had to stay home from school because of his illness and in the 1950's saw thousands of films on television, often watching the same ones over and over. In love with the medium but unable to afford a camera, Scorsese created elaborate drawings of both the films he had seen and those he imagined.

Another major influence was religion. Other than the gangsters in his neighborhood, the people given the most respect were priests, and Scorsese spent years considering becoming a priest. At thirteen, he entered Cathedral College, the seminary for the Archdiocese of New York, but felt confined and restless and was expelled. He graduated with honors from Cardinal Hayes High School in the Bronx in 1960, still with hopes of the priesthood, but failed to gain admission to Columbia University's divinity program. Scorsese summarized the powerful influences of his upbringing to Mary Pat Kelly in *Martin Scorsese: A Journey* (1996): "I was raised with them, the gangsters and the priests. That's it. Nothing in between. I wanted to be a cleric. I guess the passion I had for religion wound up mixed with film, and now, as an artist, in a way, I'm both gangster and priest."

Scorsese studied film at New York University, receiving a bachelor's degree in 1964 and a master's in 1966. He also taught filmmaking there while a graduate student and for brief periods thereafter. His students included Oliver Stone and Spike Lee. While at New York University, Scorsese wrote and directed three short films: *What's A Nice Girl Like You Doing In A Place Like This?* (1963), *It's Not Just You, Murray* (1964), and *The Big Shave* (1967). The latter, in which a young man slices his face, won Le Prixe de l'Age d'Or at the Brussels Film Festival.

The most significant of these student films is *It's Not Just You, Murray* since its protagonist, a minor gangster, is the prototype of later Scorsese characters. JR, the hero of Scorsese's first feature, *Who's That Knocking At My Door?* (1969), grew out of this character. This film, dealing with a young Italian-American's confused courtship of a better-educated woman, was shown at the 1967 Chicago Film Festival but was unable to find a distributor until Scorsese added a nude scene requested by Joseph Brenner, a sexploitation producer. The film is significant for recreating the rhythms of Little Italy, its cinema-verite style, and the performance of Harvey Keitel in his first film role.

While waiting for another chance to make a feature film, Scorsese made *Street Scenes* (1970), a documentary about anti-war demonstrators in New York and their encounter with an angry mob of construction workers, and worked as assistant director and supervising editor on *Woodstock* (1970), the documentary of the famous rock festival made by Michael Wadleigh, the cinematographer of *Who's That Knocking At My Door?* Legendary B-movie director/producer Roger Corman then hired Scorsese to direct *Boxcar Bertha* (1972), a low-budget Depression-era crime melodrama.

Jonathan Taplin, road manager for the rock group The Band, helped raise the money to finance *Mean Streets* (1973), which graphically announced Scorsese's presence as a major filmmaker. This story of a godfather's nephew torn between his attraction to a life of crime, his spiritual values, and his loyalty to his friends from the neighborhood showed the director in full command of his art. *Mean Streets* refines the themes of *Who's That Knocking At My Door?* with an increased dose of violence because of the affection of Charlie, the protagonist, for Johnny Boy, his uncontrollable cousin, a small-time hoodlum.

Pauline Kael, whose enthusiasm for *Mean Streets* in *The New Yorker*, helped create a small but eager audience for the film, calls it "a true original for our period, a triumph of personal filmmaking." *Mean Streets* has, writes Kael, "a thicker-textured rot and violence than we have ever had in an American movie, and a riper sense of evil." The level of graphic violence in most of Scorsese's films is a key element in his style, appearing as an inseparable part of the complex moral world the director has created. *Mean Streets* is also significant for joining Scorsese with Robert De Niro, as Johnny Boy, his on-screen alter ego in half of the director's films.

Mean Streets got Scorsese's foot in Hollywood's door, and *Alice Doesn't Live Here Anymore* (1974) proved that he could work within the studio system. Scorsese, a student of film genres, invigorates this tale of a single mother who longs to be a nightclub singer with flourishes inspired by Douglas Sirk's Technicolor soap operas of the 1950's.

Taxi Driver (1976) returns Scorsese to the gritty, bloody Manhattan streets as Travis Bickle, a lonely soul with barely a breath of personality, journeys from taxi driver to potential assassin of a political candidate to vigilante who murders the pimp and a customer of a teenaged prostitute, becoming an ironic hero. With the stylized neo-neon lighting and gliding camera work of Michael Chapman, the haunting jazz score by Bernard Herrmann—the great composer's last—and the frightening portrayal of a nonentity by De Niro, *Taxi Driver* perfectly captures the paranoia of its time. Along with Francis Ford Coppola's *The Conversation* (1974), it is the definitive cinematic statement about its era.

Scorsese followed this triumph with his biggest failure, the bloated musical *New York, New York* (1977), a poorly received melange of cinematic styles borrowed from 1950's musicals, soap operas, and melodramas. Devastated by this experience, Scorsese recovered his confidence with *The Last Waltz* (1978), a vibrant documentary about the final concert by the original members of The Band.

Raging Bull (1980), based on the life of boxer Jake LaMotta, solidified Scorsese's stature. With powerful performances from De Niro, Joe Pesci, and Cathy Moriarty, beautiful black-and-white cinematography by Chapman, the most realistic boxing scenes ever filmed, and wonderful use of classical music in counterpoint to the graphic violence of the fights and LaMotta's tormented domestic life, *Raging Bull* is one of those films, like *Citizen Kane* (1941), whose reputation has increased steadily since its release. Named the best film of the 1980's in a critics' poll, the film has come to be considered Scorsese's masterpiece.

The King of Comedy (1983) takes on another sordid aspect of American life, the morbid fascination with celebrity. *After Hours* (1985) takes a comic look at a type of paranoia worlds away from that of *Taxi Driver. The Color of Money* (1986) is the story of a man who must come to terms with himself, a major Scorsese theme. *The Last Temptation of Christ* (1988), a film the director struggled for years to realize, explores Scorsese's spiritual concerns more overtly than elsewhere in his films. It is his most controversial film because of condemnations from religious groups, most of whom had not seen it. It has been criticized by others for artistic failings, such as weak dialogue and casting.

Scorsese followed his biblical epic with perhaps his most perfect film, the forty-four-minute *Life Lessons*, part of the *New York Stories* trilogy. This portrait of a painter who retreats to art from the chaos of his personal life—in this case the loss of his disillusioned protege/lover—conveys better than any other film how an artist's deficiencies as a human being are irrelevant to the art he creates. In the painter's engrossment with his huge abstract canvas, Scorsese, cinematographer Nestor Almendros, and editor Thelma Schoonmaker do a superb job of conveying how art is created.

Goodfellas (1990) returns Scorsese to the idealized but gruesome gangster world of New York in the 1950's, 1960's, and 1970's and was praised by many as a continuation of the themes of *Mean Streets. Cape Fear* (1991), the director's only true commercial hit, is ostensibly a remake of a 1962 potboiler about a psychopath, but with Scorsese's even more primal concerns, it develops into a powerful elemental struggle between good and evil of almost mythic proportions. *The Age of Innocence* (1993), from the Edith Wharton novel, examines Scorsese's concerns with ritual and repressed emotions. It is his most visually resplendent film. *Casino* (1995), dealing with the Mafia in Las Vegas, received the most critical reviews of any of Scorsese's films since *New York, New York*.

Like any true artist, Scorsese has been both overpraised and undervalued. *Raging Bull* and *Goodfellas* are perhaps not quite the achievements some have claimed, while *After Hours*, *The Color of Money*, *Cape Fear*, and, particularly, *The Age of Innocence* are better than the critical consensus has indicated. Whatever the final view of Scorsese, he has created an extraordinary body of work in part because of his ability to select and work with unusually adept collaborators: actors Keitel, De Niro, and Pesci; screenwriters Mardik Martin, Paul Schrader, Richard Price, and Nicholas Pileggi; editor Schoonmaker; cinematographers Chapman and Michael Ballhaus; and producer Irwin Winkler. In the spirit of collaboration, Scorsese has also produced films such as Stephen Frears' *The Grifter* (1990), and acted not only in his films but those of other directors, most notably Robert Redford's *Quiz Show* (1994). Scorsese cast his late parents in several films, and they both appear prominently in his short film *Italianamerican*, which features dinner and conversation with them in their Little Italy apartment. His mother also worked with other directors.

Scorsese's sensitivity to actors is apparent in the honors received by performers in his films. Thirteen Scorsese performances have been nominated for Academy Awards, and four have won: Ellen Burstyn for *Alice Doesn't Live Here Anymore*, Robert De Niro for *Raging Bull*, Paul Newman for *The Color of Money*, and Joe Pesci for *Goodfellas*. Scorsese has been named best director by the National Society of Films Critics for *Taxi Driver*, *Raging Bull*, and *Goodfellas*, and his work in the latter also earned honors from the New York Film Critics Circle, the Los Angeles Film Critics Association, and the British Academy Awards. While he has been nominated for *Raging Bull*, *The Last Temptation of Christ*, and *Goodfellas*, Scorsese, who does not make the kind of uplifting films the Academy loves, has never won an Oscar.

Like the painter in *Life Lessons*, Scorsese has not been as successful in his private life as in his art. He has three children by four wives: fellow New York University student Larraine Brennan, screenwriter Julia Cameron, actress Isabella Rossellini, and producer Barbara De Fina. For several years, he has been romantically involved with actress-director Illeana Douglas, granddaughter of Melvyn Douglas and Helen Gahagan.

Scorsese's films easily betray that their creator is obsessed with the medium. His work displays the cinema-verite realism of Roberto Rossellini and John Cassavetes; the nouvelle vague freedom and energy of Francois Truffaut; the operatic grandeur of Luchino Visconti; the baroque excesses of Sam Fuller, Michael Powell, Douglas Sirk, and King Vidor; the craftsmanship and awareness of the conventions of genre of John Ford and Howard Hawks; the distinctive genius and love of filmmaking of Federico Fellini, Alfred Hitchcock, and Orson Welles. His love of film has inspired him to lead the fight for preserving and restoring the films of the past, including the restorations of David Lean's *Lawrence of Arabia* (1962) and Anthony Mann's *El Cid* (1961). He has summarized the history and styles of the medium in the British television documentary "A Century of Cinema" (1995), and his enthusiasm for the work of others has helped revitalize the reputations of other directors, most notably Michael Powell. Scorsese's life and work are consumed by his passion for films.

—Michael Adams

Obituaries

John Abbott (May 12, 1906–May 24, 1996). Abbott was a British actor who worked extensively on stage, television, and film from the 1930s through the 1960s. His film credits include *Mademoiselle Docteur* (1937), *Anna and the King of Siam* (1946), *Humoresque* (1946), *The Merry Widow* (1952), *Gigi* (1958), and *The Greatest Story Ever Told* (1965).

John Alton (October 5, 1901–June 2, 1996). Born in Hungary, Alton was a cinematographer who worked on nearly one hundred films in his career. After working in Europe and Latin America in the 1920s and 1930s, Alton hit his stride in Hollywood in the 1940s. Often working with director Anthony Mann at RKO and Republic studios, he became known for his effective use of contrast in noir films such as *Atlantic City* (1944) and *T-Men* (1947). He later graduated to films with bigger budgets, and earned an Academy Award (with Alfred Gilks) for his work on *An American in Paris* (1951). His additional screen credits include *The Courageous Dr. Christian* (1940), *He Walked by Night* (1949), *Father of the Bride* (1950), *The Teahouse of the August Moon* (1956), *The Brothers Karamazov* (1958), and *Elmer Gantry* (1960).

Morey Amsterdam (December 14, 1912–October 27, 1996). Amsterdam was a comic writer and actor who was best known as Dick Van Dyke's wisecracking co-worker Buddy Sorrell on "The Dick Van Dyke Show," a popular television series which ran from 1961-1966. He was once credited with co-authorship of the hit song "Rum and Coca Cola," but the courts ruled that the real author was Trinidad calypso singer Lord Invader. Amsterdam's film acting credits include *Murder Inc.* (1960) and *Muscle Beach Party* (1964).

Annabella (July 14, 1909–September 18, 1996). Born Suzanne Charpentier, Annabella was a French actress who made her film debut in Abel Gance's *Napoleon* (1927). Films such as *Le Million* (1931) and *Quatorze Juillet* (1933) made her France's most popular actress. She subsequently made films in both England and the United States. She worked with Tyrone Power in *Suez* (1938), and married Power a year later; they were divorced in 1948. Her additional film credits include *Flight Into Darkness* (1935), *Escape From Yesterday* (1935), *Wings of the Morning* (1937), *Dinner at the Ritz* (1937), *Hotel du Nord* (1938), *Bridal Suite* (1939), *Bomber's Moon* (1943), *13 Rue Madeleine* (1947), and *Don Juan* (1950).

Lew Ayres (December 28, 1908–December 30, 1996). Ayres was an actor best known for his portrayal of the title character in the numerous Dr. Kildare films, including *Young Dr. Kildare* (1938) and *Calling Dr. Kildare* (1939). Originally a musician, he was signed to an acting contract in 1928 and within a year was featured opposite Greta Garbo in *The Kiss* (1929). His best role was probably that of a sensitive young German soldier in *All Quiet on the Western Front* (1930). Ironically, Ayres engendered some controversy when his pacifistic beliefs led him to refuse to fight in World War II, although he did volunteer for medical service and served with distinction in the war effort. After the war, he appeared in films only sporadically, although he was nominated for an Academy Award for his work in *Johnny Belinda* (1948). He directed one film, *Hearts in Bondage* (1936), and was married to actresses Lola Lane (1931-1933) and Ginger Rogers (1934-1941). His additional acting credits include *The Spirit of Notre Dame* (1931), *State Fair* (1933), *Holiday* (1938), *The Secret of Dr. Kildare* (1939), *Dr. Kildare's Wedding Day* (1941), *The Dark Mirror* (1946), *Donovan's Brain* (1953), *Advise and Consent* (1962), *The Carpetbaggers* (1964), *Battle for the Planet of the Apes* (1973), and *Battlestar Galactica* (1978).

Lew Ayres

Martin Balsam (November 4, 1919–February 13, 1996). Balsam was a veteran character actor who had a long career in film, on stage, and in television. His first film was *On the Waterfront* (1954), and he played the unlucky detective in Alfred Hitchcock's *Psycho* (1960). Balsam won an Academy Award for his supporting role in *A Thousand Clowns* (1965).

Martin Balsam

On Broadway, he won a Tony Award for his work in *You Know I Can't Hear You When the Water's Running.* On television, he appeared in the "Archie Bunker's Place" series from 1979-1981. Balsam's additional screen credits include *12 Angry Men* (1957), *Marjorie Morningstar* (1958), *Breakfast at Tiffany's* (1961), *Seven Days in May* (1964), *Hombre* (1967), *All the President's Men* (1976), and *Cape Fear* (1991).

Saul Bass (May 8, 1920–April 25, 1996). Bass was an animator and graphic designer who introduced animation to screen credits, replacing the customary list of typed names. He also directed short subjects, and won an Academy Award for his documentary short *Why Man Creates* (1968). His additional screen credits include *The Seven Year Itch* (1955), *Around the World in 80 Days* (1956), *Psycho* (1960), *West Side Story* (1961), *Broadcast News* (1987), and *Cape Fear* (1991).

Saul Bass

Les Baxter (1922–January 15, 1996). Baxter was a composer and bandleader who recorded extensively from the 1940s into the 1960s. His "exotica" style of lounge music has recently enjoyed a resurgence in popularity. He scored numerous films, including many youth exploitation films of the late 1950s and early 1960s. His screen credits include *Untamed Youth* (1957), *The Pit and the Pendulum* (1961), *Black Sunday* (1961), *Beach Party* (1963), *Beach Blanket Bingo* (1965), *How to Stuff a Wild Bikini* (1965), and *Dr. Goldfoot and the Bikini Machine* (1965).

Pandro S. Berman

Pandro S. Berman (March 28, 1905–July 13, 1996). Berman was a producer who was associated with many Fred Astaire-Ginger Rogers films, including *Top Hat* (1935) and *Swing Time* (1936). He worked for RKO in the 1930s, and moved to MGM in 1940. He was awarded the Irving G. Thalberg Memorial Award at the Academy Award ceremonies in 1977. His additional film credits include *The Gay Divorcee* (1934), *Follow the Fleet* (1936), *Gunga Din* (1939), *The Story of Vernon and Irene Castle* (1939), *National Velvet* (1944), *Father of the Bride* (1950), *The Blackboard Jungle* (1955), *Butterfield 8* (1960), *A Patch of Blue* (1965), and *Move* (1970).

Whit Bissell (1919–March 5, 1996). Bissell was a character actor who appeared in over two hundred films in a career that spanned four decades, often playing fussbudgets or priggish bureaucrats. His film credits include *Holy Matrimony* (1943), *Riot in Cell Block 11* (1954), *The Creature from the Black Lagoon* (1954), *Invasion of the Body Snatchers* (1956), *The Defiant Ones* (1958), *The Manchurian Candidate* (1962), *Hud* (1963), *Airport* (1970), *Pete 'n' Tillie* (1972), and *Casey's Shadow* (1978).

Priscilla Bonner (1899–February 21, 1996). Bonner was a leading lady of the Silent Era, appearing in some twenty-six films before the advent of sound. She was featured opposite Will Rogers in *Honest Hutch* (1920), and appeared with Clara Bow in the famous *It* (1927). Her additional screen credits include *Homer Comes Home* (1920), *April Showers* (1923), *Red Kimono* (1926), *Long Pants* (1927), and *Girls Who Dare* (1929).

Roger Bowen (1933–February 16, 1996). Bowen was an actor who was best known for his portrayal of Colonel Blake in Robert Altman's classic *M*A*S*H* (1970). Bowen also wrote novels and television scripts. His additional film acting credits include *Petulia* (1968), *Heaven Can Wait* (1978), *The Main Event* (1979), and *What About Bob?* (1991).

Albert Broccoli (April 5, 1909–June 27, 1996). Broccoli was a producer who specialized in action and adventure films. He was best known for co-producing, with Harry Saltzman, the James Bond films. He was awarded the Irving G. Thalberg Award at the 1982 Academy Award ceremonies. His production credits include *Hell Below Zero* (1954), *Safari* (1956), *Killers of Kilimanjaro* (1959), *Dr. No* (1962), *From Russia With Love* (1963), *Goldfinger* (1964), *Thunderball* (1965), *You Only Live Twice* (1967), *Chitty Chitty Bang Bang* (1968), *Diamonds Are Forever* (1971), *The Spy Who Loved Me* (1977), *Octopussy* (1983), and *License to Kill* (1989).

George Burns (January 20, 1896–March 9, 1996). Born Nathan Birnbaum, Burns was an actor and comedian who starred in a variety of entertainment media from vaudeville and radio to television and film. He and his wife, Gracie Allen, had a popular network radio show, which they took to television as "The George Burns and Gracie Allen Show" from 1950-1958. Burns wrote the pair's material, playing the straight man to his wife's caricature of a scatterbrained woman. Burns and Allen were featured in several films in the 1930s, including *The Big Broadcast* (1932), *Many Happy Returns* (1934), and *Here Comes Cookie* (1935). Though dev-

George Burns

astated by his wife's death in 1964, Burns continued to work regularly in television. A decade later, he was given a part opposite Walter Matthau in *The Sunshine Boys* (1975), ironically taking the role that had been assigned to his friend Jack Benny after Benny died unexpectedly. His performance earned an Academy Award as Best Supporting Actor, and his film career was reborn. By this time Burns had become a show business icon, writing best-selling books and appearing regularly onstage in Las Vegas and Atlantic City. Burns made good on his boast that he'd live to be one hundred, although he had been in ill health for the last two years of his life. His additional screen credits include *College Humor* (1933), *The Big Broadcast of 1936* (1935), *A Damsel in Distress* (1937), *College Swing* (1938), *Oh God!* (1977), *Movie Movie* (1978), *Just You and Me Kid* (1979), *Oh God! Book II* (1980), *Oh God! You Devil* (1984), and *18 Again!* (1988).

Donald Cammell (1942–April 23, 1996). Cammell was a writer and director who was best known as the co-director, with Nicolas Roeg, of the cult classic *Performance* (1970), which featured rock star Mick Jagger and which has been cited as an influence on the rock video style of filmmaking. Cammell seemed to be dogged by misfortune throughout his career, and often left projects unfinished. He died a suicide, apparently distraught over the handling of one of his films. He co-wrote the Brooke Shields comedy *Tilt* (1979), and directed the thrillers *Demon Seed* (1977) and *White of the Eye* (1988).

Marcel Carne (August 18, 1909–October 31, 1996). Carne was a French director who came to exemplify the poetic realism movement of the late 1930s and early 1940s. He is best known for his collaborations with poet-screenwriter Jacques Prevert, including *Bizarre Bizarre* (1937), *Port of Shadows* (1938), and *Children of Paradise* (1945). He continued to work extensively after World War II, but fell out of favor with New Wave filmmakers and critics. His additional film credits include *Jenny* (1936), *Daybreak* (1939), *The Devil's Envoys* (1942), *Gates of the Night* (1946), *The Adultress* (1953), *The Cheaters* (1958), *The Young Wolves* (1968), and *La Bible* (1976).

Marcel Carne

Maria Casares (November 21, 1922–November 22, 1996). Born Maria Casares Quiroga in Spain, Casares was a French actress best known for her role as Death in Jean Cocteau's *Orpheus* (1950). Her additional screen credits include *Children of Paradise* (1945), *The Wench* (1948), *Ombre et Lumiere* (1951), *Testament of Orpheus* (1960), and *La Reine Verte* (1964).

Virginia Cherrill (April 12, 1908–November 14, 1996). Cherrill was an actress who was discovered by Charlie Chaplin and chosen, despite no previous acting experience, to appear opposite him as the blind flower girl in *City Lights* (1931). She appeared in several films over the next two years, and then gave up acting to marry Cary Grant. When she and Grant were divorced two years later, she resumed her acting career briefly, only to retire again upon remarrying. Her additional acting credits include *The Brat* (1931), *Fast Workers* (1933), *Charlie Chan's Greatest Case* (1933), *White Heat* (1934), and *Troubled Waters* (1936).

Virginia Christine (March 5, 1920–July 24, 1996). Born Virginia Kraft, Christine was an actress who appeared in many film and television roles, although she was probably best known for her Folger's Coffee television commercials, in which she played Mrs. Olson. Her film acting credits include *Edge of Darkness* (1943), *Mummy's Curse* (1944), *High Noon* (1952), *Invasion of the Body Snatchers* (1956), *Judgment at Nuremberg* (1961), *Guess Who's Coming to Dinner* (1967), and *Hail, Hero!* (1969).

Rene Clement (March 18, 1913–March 17, 1996). Clement was a prominent French director, who won two Best Foreign Language Film Academy Awards, for *The Walls of Malapaga* (1949) and *Forbidden Games* (1952). He began his career making documentaries, and he brought some of that sensibility to his feature films. He is regarded as one of the major French filmmakers of the early postwar period. His additional film credits include *L'Arabie interdite* (1937), *La Bataille du Rail* (1946), *Le Chateau de Verre* (1950), *Purple Noon* (1959), *Is Paris Burning* (1966), *Rider on the Rain* (1970), and *And Hope to Die* (1972).

Claudette Colbert (September 13, 1905–July 30, 1996). Born Claudette Lily Chauchoin in France, Colbert was an actress who was best known as a leading lady of screwball comedy. She moved with her family to the United States at the age of six, and began acting as a teenager. After some Broadway roles and one silent film, she won a contract with Paramount Pictures in 1929. She was cast in a wide variety of roles, attracting attention for her milk bath scene in Cecil B. DeMille's *The Sign of the Cross* (1932). Paramount loaned her to Columbia to appear opposite Clark Gable in what was expected to be a minor comedy, in a role that had been turned down by several more prominent actresses. The

Claudette Colbert

film, Frank Capra's *It Happened One Night* (1934), swept the Academy Awards that year, and Colbert won the Award for Best Actress. She became one of Hollywood's top stars, specializing in sophisticated comedy. She earned two more Academy Award nominations for her work in *Private Worlds* (1935) and *Since You Went Away* (1944). She continued to appear in films into the early 1960s, and also worked on stage after the death of her second husband in 1968. Colbert's additional screen credits include *For the Love of Mike* (1927), *The Lady Lies* (1929), *The Smiling Lieutenant* (1931), *I Cover the Waterfront* (1933), *Imitation of Life* (1934), *She Married Her Boss* (1935), *Bluebeard's Eight Wife* (1938), *Boom Town* (1940), *The Palm Beach Story* (1942), *The Egg and I* (1947), *Bride for Sale* (1949), *Let's Make It Legal* (1951), and *Parrish* (1961).

Jordan Cronenweth (1935–November 29, 1996). Cronenweth was a cinematographer best known for his work on *Blade Runner* (1982), which earned him a British Academy Award. His additional film credits include *Brewster McCloud* (1970), *The Front Page* (1974), *Altered States* (1980), *Peggy Sue Got Married* (1986), and *U2: Rattle and Hum* (1988).

Irving Cummings, Jr. (1923–March 26, 1996). Cummings was a writer, director, and producer of films and television series; he produced the popular children's television series "Fury" in the 1950s. His father, Irving Cummings, Sr., was an actor and director who directed some of Shirley Temple's most famous films in the 1930s. The younger Cummings wrote *Yesterday's Heroes* (1940) and *Deadline for Murder* (1946); he produced *The Sign of the Ram* (1948) and *Where Danger Lives* (1950); and he produced and directed *Double Dynamite* (1951).

Pasqualino De Santis (1928–June 23, 1996). De Santis was an Italian cinematographer who had worked extensively with prominent Italian filmmakers since the 1960s. He was a cameraman on Federico Fellini's *8 1/2* (1963) and *Juliet of the Spirits* (1965), and director of photography on *Fellini: A Director's Notebook* (1969). He won an Academy Award for his work on Franco Zeffirelli's *Romeo and Juliet* (1968).

Joanne Dru (January 31, 1923–September 10, 1996). Born Joanne LaCock, Dru was a leading lady in Hollywood films of the late 1940s and early 1950s. She is best remembered for her performances in classic Westerns such as *Red River* (1948) and *She Wore a Yellow Ribbon* (1949). She was married for a time to actors Dick Haymes and John Ireland. Her additional screen credits include *Abie's Irish Rose* (1946), *All the King's Men* (1949), *Wagonmaster* (1950), *The Pride of St. Louis* (1952), *The Siege at Red River* (1954), *The Light in the Forest* (1958), *The Wild and the Innocent* (1959), and *Sylvia* (1965).

Joanne Dru

Vince Edwards (July 9, 1928–March 11, 1996). Born Vincent Edward Zoimo, Edwards was an actor best remembered for his starring role in the early television medical drama "Ben Casey" (1961-1966). His film credits include *Mr. Universe* (1951), *Cell 2455 Death Row* (1955), *The Three Faces of Eve* (1957), *Too Late Blues* (1962), *The Devil's Brigade* (1968), *The Seduction* (1982), and *The Gumshoe Kid* (1989).

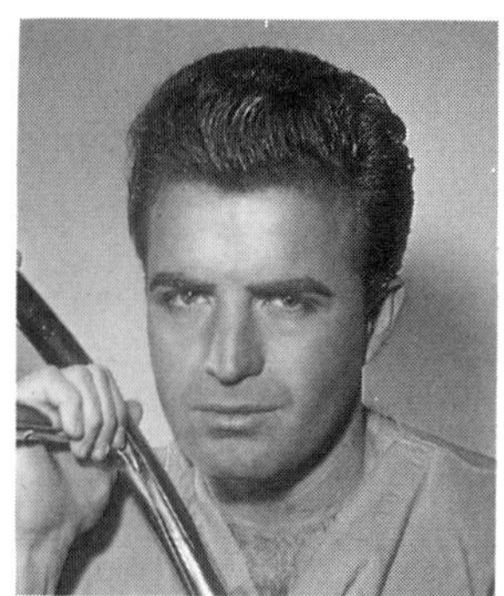
Vince Edwards

Lonne Elder III (1927–June 11, 1996). Elder was an African-American playwright and screenwriter. He is best known for his screenplay for *Sounder* (1972), which earned him an Academy Award nomination. His additional screenwriting credits include *Melinda* (1972) and *Bustin' Loose* (1981).

Louise Fitch (1915–September 11, 1996). Fitch was an actress who worked extensively in film and television. Her career was disrupted in the 1950s when she was identified as a communist and blacklisted for a time. Her screen credits include *I Was a Teenage Werewolf* (1957), *Blood of Dracula* (1957), *I Want to Live!* (1958), *They Shoot Horses, Don't They?* (1969), and *Opening Night* (1977).

Greer Garson (September 29, 1908–April 6, 1996). Born in Ireland, Garson was an actress whose role as a brave British housewife during the Blitz in *Mrs. Miniver* (1942) made her the symbol of womanly courage during World War II. She received six Academy Award nominations, including one for her first role, in *Goodbye Mr. Chips* (1939). Garson became a big star for MGM in the 1940s, though

Greer Garson

she often came to be typecast as a gallant housewife, to the ultimate detriment of her career. In 1949, she married and soon retired from films, although she acted in films sporadically thereafter. Her additional screen credits include *Pride and Prejudice* (1940), *Madame Curie* (1943), *Julia Misbehaves* (1948), *That Forsyte Woman* (1949), *The Miniver Story* (1950), *Sunrise at Campobello* (1960), *The Singing Nun* (1966), and *The Happiest Millionaire* (1967).

Tomas Gutierrez Alea (December 11, 1928–April 16, 1996). Gutierrez Alea was a Cuban director who was a leading figure in Latin American cinema. He directed a feature-length documentary on Castro's Cuba, *Stories of the Revolution* (1960). His *Memories of Underdevelopment* (1968), combining newsreel footage with fiction, won several international prizes. *Strawberry and Chocolate* (1993) was nominated for an Academy Award as Best Foreign Language Film. His additional film credits include *The Twelve Chairs* (1962), *Death of a Bureaucrat* (1966), *The Last Supper* (1976), and *Up to a Certain Point* (1984).

Margaux Hemingway (1955–July 1, 1996). Hemingway was a model and actress. The granddaughter of author Ernest Hemingway, Hemingway was tall and attractive, and her career got off to a promising start with *Lipstick* (1976), but a flamboyant lifestyle led to alcoholism and increasingly limited roles. Her sister, Mariel Hemingway, is also an actress. Hemingway's screen credits include *Killer Fish* (1979), *They Call Me Bruce?* (1982), *Over the Brooklyn Bridge* (1984), and *Killing Machine* (1986).

Margaux Hemingway

Brigitte Helm (March 17, 1906–June 12, 1996). Born Brigitte Schittenhelm, Helm was a German actress whose first film, Fritz Lang's *Metropolis* (1927), made her a star. Often cast as a femme fatale, Helm did not prosper with the advent of sound, and her outspoken criticism of Germany's Nazi leaders hurt her career. Her acting credits include *At the Edge of the World* (1927), *Unholy Love* (1928), *The Wonderful Lies of Nina Petrovna* (1929), *The Blue Danube* (1932), *Gold* (1934), and *Ein idealer Gatte* (1935).

Camilla Horn (April 25, 1906–August 14, 1996). Horn was a German actress who was an international star in the late Silent Era and into the 1930s. Discovered by director F.W. Murnau, she became a star in his *Faust* (1926). She moved to Hollywood where she made three films before returning to Europe, where she worked in German and British films, in which she was usually cast as a femme fatale. Her screen credits include *Tempest* (1928), *Eternal Love* (1929), *The Royal Box* (1929), *The Return of Raffles* (1932), *Matinee Idol* (1933), *Red Orchids* (1938), *Die letzte Runde* (1939), *Vatti macht Dummheiten* (1953), and *Schloss Koenigsberg* (1988).

Ross Hunter (May 6, 1916–March 10, 1996). Born Martin Fuss, Hunter was an actor who became a producer, specializing in glossy melodramas and light comedies. He broke into acting in the mid-1940s, and was featured in lead roles in a variety of mostly B pictures, including *Louisiana Hayride* (1944), *A Guy a Girl and a Pal* (1945), and *Sweetheart of Sigma Chi* (1946). Illness forced him out of acting, and he entered production, working his way up at Universal. He made a series of lucrative soap operas, including *Magnificent Obsession* (1954) and *Imitation of Life* (1959). He also produced comedies, most notably films featuring Doris Day, who earned an Academy Award nomination for her work in Hunter's *Pillow Talk* (1959). His biggest commercial success was *Airport* (1970), the prototype for the all-star cast disaster movies which were popular in the 1970s. His follow-up, a musical version of *Lost Horizon* (1973), was a commercial failure, and he thereafter limited his work to television. Hunter's additional screen credits include *Tammy and the Bachelor* (1957), *Portrait in Black* (1960), *Flower Drum Song* (1961), *The Thrill of It All* (1963), *The Chalk Garden* (1964), *The Pad* (1966), and *Thoroughly Modern Millie* (1967).

Ben Johnson (June 13, 1918–April 8, 1996). Johnson was an actor who specialized in Westerns and action films. He was a rodeo star who broke into Hollywood as a horse wrangler. Director John Ford put him in front of the camera, ultimately giving him the lead role in *The Wagonmaster* (1950). He is best remembered for his supporting roles, and won an Academy Award as Best Supporting Actor in *The Last Picture Show* (1971). His additional screen credits include *She Wore a Yellow Ribbon* (1949), *The Mighty Joe Young* (1949), *Rio Grande* (1950), *Shane* (1953), *One-Eyed Jacks* (1961), *The Wild Bunch*

Ben Johnson

(1969), *The Getaway* (1972), *Dillinger* (1973), *The Sugarland Express* (1974), *Tex* (1982), and *My Heroes Have Always Been Cowboys* (1991).

Gene Kelly (August 23, 1912–February 2, 1996). Kelly was an actor, dancer, choreographer, and director. By the 1950s, he had succeeded Fred Astaire as cinema's most prominent male dancer. He started out in show business as a dancer and choreographer on Broadway, and made his screen debut opposite Judy Garland in the musical *For Me and My Gal* (1942). His dancing style was far more physical than that of Astaire, whose art was to make the difficult look easy. Kelly brought his athletic style to such films as *Cover Girl* (1944) and *Anchors Aweigh* (1945), choreographing both films and earning an Academy Award nomination as best actor for the latter, in which he danced a duet with Jerry, the cartoon mouse. His lengthy collaboration with choreographer-director Stanley Donen reached its zenith in the three films with which Kelly is most often associated. *On the Town* (1949), co-starring Frank Sinatra, was the story of sailors on a one day leave in New York City. *An American in Paris* (1951) was set to a George Gershwin score and featured a twenty minute balletic climax. And *Singin' in the Rain* (1952), set in a Hollywood making the transition from silents to sound, has been cited as a candidate for the title of the greatest musical ever made. In 1951, Kelly was given a Special Academy Award in appreciation of his unique contributions as an actor, singer, director, dancer, and choreographer. Kelly continued his varied contributions to film for nearly three more decades, sometimes acting, sometimes directing, sometimes singing and dancing, and sometimes combining all those activities in the same film. His work was introduced to a new generation with the MGM compilation series *That's Entertainment* (1974) and *That's Entertainment Part II* (1976), in which he appeared as on-screen narrator. His additional film credits include *Living in a Big Way* (1947), *The Pirate* (1948), *Take Me Out to the Ball Game* (1949), *Brigadoon* (1954), *It's Always Fair Weather*, (1955) *Invitation to the Dance* (1956), *Les Girls* (1957), *Marjorie Morningstar* (1958), *Tunnel of Love* (1958, as director only), *Inherit the Wind* (1960), *Gigot* (1962, as director only), *Hello Dolly!* (1969, director only), and *Xanadu* (1980).

Gene Kelly

Krzysztof Kieslowski (June 27, 1941–March 13, 1996). Kieslowski was a Polish director whose satire on film censorship, *Camera Buff* (1979), was banned in his native land, earning him international recognition for the first time. Two of his films, *A Short Film About Killing* (1988) and *A Short Film About Love* (1988) were part of a ten-film series about life in Poland; based on the Ten Commandments, they were the centerpiece of the Venice Film Festival in 1989. Another multi-film series, "Three Colors," included *Red* (1995), which earned him an Academy Award nomination as Best Director. His additional film credits include *Picture* (1969), *Politics* (1976), *Seen by the Night Porter* (1978), *Talking Heads* (1980), *Blue* (1993), and *White* (1994).

Krzysztof Kieslowski

Paul Donaldson King (1927–July 10, 1996). King was a writer and producer best known for his work on popular Western television series of the 1950s and 1960s, including "Bat Masterson," "Bonanza," "Rawhide," and "Wagon Train." His contribution to film includes the screenplay to *Operation Petticoat* (1959), which earned him an Academy Award nomination along with co-writer Joseph Stone.

Masaki Kobayashi (February 14, 1916–October 5, 1996). Kobayashi was a Japanese director who served as an assistant to filmmaker Keisuke Kinoshita in the years after World War II. He began directing his own films with *My Son's Youth* (1952), and became internationally famous for his film trilogy *The Human Condition* (1959-61), which demonstrated the brutalities of war in a graphic fashion. His additional screen credits include *Black River* (1957), *Harakiri* (1962), *Kwaidan* (1964), *Inn of Evil* (1971), *Glowing Autumn* (1979), and *The Empty Table* (1985).

Dorothy Lamour (December 10, 1914–September 21, 1996). Born Mary Leta Dorothy Kaumeyer, Lamour was an actress who was often cast as a South Seas temptress. She won fame as the exotic, sarong-clad sidekick of Bob Hope and Bing Crosby in their famous "Road" comedies of the 1940s. Her screen credits include *The Jungle Princess* (1936), *Her Jungle Love* (1938), *Road to Singapore* (1940), *Road to Zanzibar* (1941), *Road to Morocco* (1942), *Star Spangled Rhythm* (1943), *Duffy's Tavern* (1945), *Road to Utopia* (1946), *My Favorite Brunette* (1947),

Dorothy Lamour

Road to Rio (1947), *The Road to Bali* (1953), *The Road to Hong Kong* (1962), and *Donovan's Reef* (1963).

Lash LaRue (June 15, 1917–May 24, 1996). Born Al LaRue, the actor won the nickname "Lash" because of his trademark bullwhip, which he used to subdue villains in over twenty low budget Westerns released between 1946 and 1952. Early in his career, he played a character known as Cheyenne Davis in films such as *Cheyenne Takes Over* (1947) and *Stage to Mesa City* (1947), but often his protagonist was simply known as Lash LaRue. With the advent of television and the subsequent decline in the market for B Westerns, LaRue starred briefly in the 1952-53 television series "Lash of the West," which was put together from clips of his old films. His additional film credits include *The Caravan Trail* (1936), *Law of the Lash* (1947), *Mark of the Lash* (1948), *King of the Bullwhip* (1950), and *The Black Lash* (1952).

Guy Madison (January 19, 1922–February 6, 1996). Born Robert Moseley, Madison was an actor who became a leading man in television and film on the strength of his looks. Usually cast as an action hero, his early films included *Massacre River* (1949) and *The Charge at Feather River* (1953). From 1951-1958, he starred in the title role of the television series "Wild Bill Hickock." He became so identified with this role that he found trouble finding suitable film roles in America, and spent most of the latter part of his career in Europe, making costume dramas and spaghetti Westerns. His additional screen credits include *Till the End of Time* (1946), *Texas Brooklyn and Heaven* (1948), *Five Against the House* (1955), *Bullwhip* (1958), *Sword of the Conqueror* (1961), *Gunmen of the Rio Grande* (1965), *This Man Can't Die* (1970), and *Won Ton Ton: The Dog Who Saved Hollywood* (1976).

Marcello Mastroianni (September 28, 1923–December 19, 1996). Mastroianni was an Italian actor who came to symbolize the urbane European male in films made in Europe and the United States. He began acting after World War II, and after his first film, *I Miserabili* (1947), joined director Luchino Visconti's stock company. By the release of Visconti's *White Nights* (1957) a decade later, he had established himself as an important leading man in Italian cinema. His work with director Federico Fellini, especially in *La Dolce Vita* (1960) and *8 1/2* (1963), made him an international star. Mastroianni was equally adept at comedy and dramatic roles, and was nominated for Academy Awards for his work in *Divorce Italian Style* (1961), *Special Day* (1977), and *Dark Eyes* (1987); he won numerous European honors as well. His additional film credits include *Domenica d'Agosto* (1950), *Cronache di Poveri Amanti* (1954), *The Big Deal on Madonna Street* (1958), *Il Bell'Antonio* (1960), *La Notte* (1961), *Yesterday Today and Tomorrow* (1963), *Marriage Italian Style* (1964), *Casanova '70* (1965), *The Tenth Victim* (1965), *The Pizza Triangle* (1970), *We All Loved Each Other So Much* (1975), *A Special Day* (1977), *Wifemistress* (1977), *City of Women* (1980), *The Skin* (1981), *Ginger and Fred* (1985), *Miss Arizona* (1988), *Used People* (1992), *The Bee Keeper* (1993), and *Ready to Wear* (1994).

Marcello Mastroianni

Ruggero Mastroianni (1929–September 9, 1996). Mastroianni was an Italian film editor who worked with many prominent directors. Like his brother Marcello Mastroianni, he worked frequently with Federico Fellini, including on *Fellini Satyricon* (1970) and *Fellini's Casanova* (1976). His additional film credits include *Vento del Sud* (1960), *Juliet of the Spirits* (1965), *Death in Venice* (1971), *Amarcord* (1974), and *And the Ship Sails On* (1984).

Audrey Meadows (February 8, 1924–February 3, 1996). Born Audrey Cotter, Meadows was an actress best known for her role of Alice Kramden, opposite Jackie Gleason on the 1950s television series "The Honeymooners." She worked extensively in television, but her film credits include *That Touch of Mink* (1962), *Take Her, She's Mine* (1963), and *Rosie* (1967).

Richard Morris (1923–April 28, 1996). Morris was a screenwriter whose greatest film success was the musical comedy *The Thoroughly Modern Millie* (1967). He also wrote the script for the Broadway musical "The Unsinkable Molly Brown" in 1960, and worked extensively in television. His additional film credits include *Finders Keepers* (1951) and *Ma and Pa Kettle at the Fair* (1952).

Jean Muir (February 13, 1911–July 23, 1996). Born Jean Muir Fullarton, Muir was an actress who was featured in over thirty films for Warner Bros. in the 1930s and 1940s. Her last film was *The Constant Nymph* (1943), but she continued to act on stage until she ran afoul of the House Un-American Activities Committee and was identified as a Communist sympathizer. After a decade of personal turmoil, she returned to acting on Broadway and in television. Her additional screen credits include *Son of a Sailor* (1933), *As the Earth Turns* (1934), *Oil for the Lamps of China* (1935), *A Midsummer Night's Dream* (1935), *White Fang* (1936), *The Outcasts of Poker Flat* (1937), and *And One Was Beautiful* (1940).

Haing S. Ngor (1950–February 25, 1996). Ngor was a Cambodian actor who was trained as a doctor in his native land

Haing S. Ngor

until he was imprisoned by the Khmer Rouge. He escaped and made his way to the United States, where he was cast as Cambodian journalist Dith Pran in *The Killing Fields* (1984), for which he won an Academy Award as Best Supporting Actor. Ngor continued to appear in films, and was also involved in work with Cambodian refugees. He was murdered in an unsolved killing that some attributed to political forces in Cambodia. Ngor's additional screen credits include *The Iron Triangle* (1989), *Ambition* (1991), and *Heaven and Earth* (1993).

Liam O'Brien (1914–March 24, 1996). O'Brien was a screenwriter and television producer. Among his contributions to film, he his best remembered for the screenplay of the Frank Capra film *Here Comes the Groom* (1951), for which he was nominated for an Academy Award. He was the brother of actor Edmund O'Brien. His additional screenwriting credits include *Chain Lightning* (1950), *Young at Heart* (1954), *Elephant Walk* (1954), *Trapeze* (1956), *The Great Imposter* (1960), and *The Devil at 4 O'Clock* (1961).

Luana Patten (1938–May 1, 1996). Patten was an actress who made her screen debut as a child star of the Walt Disney feature *Song of the South* (1946), which combined live action with animation. As she matured, she was featured in ingenue roles in such films as *Rock Pretty Baby* (1956) and *Johnny Tremaine* (1957). Her additional film credits include *Melody Time* (1948), *So Dear To My Heart* (1948), *Joe Dakota* (1957), *The Restless Years* (1958), *Home from the Hill* (1960), *Go Naked in the World* (1961), and *Follow Me Boys* (1966).

Joan Perry (1911–September 15, 1996). Born Betty Miller, Perry was an actress who wound up marrying Columbia Pictures co-founder Harry Cohn. She appeared in several films for Columbia, and then moved to Warner Bros., for whom she worked until she retired from acting in 1941. Her screen acting credits include *Shakedown* (1936), *Counterfeit Lady* (1937), *Blind Alley* (1939), *Nine Lives Are Not Enough* (1941), and *International Squadron* (1941).

William Prince (January 13, 1913–October 8, 1996). Prince was an actor who worked extensively on stage, in films, and on television, playing a variety of lead and character roles. His screen acting credits include *Destination Tokyo* (1944), *Objective Burma* (1941), *Cinderella Jones* (1946), *Cyrano de Bergerac* (1950), *The Vagabond King* (1956), *The Heartbreak Kid* (1972), *The Stepford Wives* (1975), *Bronco Billy* (1980), *Spies Like Us* (1985), and *The Taking of Beverly Hills* (1991).

Juliet Prowse (September 25, 1936–September 14, 1996). Born in India and raised in South Africa, Prowse was an actress and dancer who created a stir when Soviet Premier Nikita Khrushchev denounced her performance in the musical *Can Can* (1960) as immoral. She was featured opposite Elvis Presley in *G.I. Blues* (1960), and was linked romantically to both Presley and Frank Sinatra, to whom she was briefly engaged. She also starred in the television series "Mona McCluskey," which ran for one season in 1965-1966. Her additional film credits include *Gentlemen Marry Brunettes* (1955), *The Second Time Around* (1961), *Run for Your Wife* (1966), and *Spree* (1967).

Juliet Prowse

Tommy Rettig (December 10, 1941–February 15, 1996). Rettig was a child actor who was best known for his role as Jeff Wilson, the boy who owned "Lassie" from 1954-1957 in the television series about the famous collie dog. As he grew older, he was unable to attract more mature roles, and gave up acting. His screen acting credits include *Panic in the Streets* (1950), *Weekend with Father* (1951), *The 5,000 Fingers of Dr. T* (1953), *So Big* (1953), *River of No Return* (1954), *The Cobweb* (1955), and *The Last Wagon* (1956).

Adam Roarke (1937–April 27, 1996). Roarke was an actor who was featured in nine films in the "biker" genre in the late 1960s and early 1970s. He appeared with Jack Nicholson in *Hell's Angels on Wheels* (1967) and *Psych-Out* (1968), and was reported to have turned down a role in the most critically acclaimed example of the genre, *Easy Rider* (1969). His additional film acting credits include *The Savage Seven* (1968), *Play It as It Lays* (1972), *Dirty Mary, Crazy Larry* (1974), and *The Stunt Man* (1980).

Howard E. Rollins, Jr. (October 17, 1950–December 8, 1996). Rollins was an African American actor who was nominated for an Academy Award as Best Supporting Actor for his work in *Ragtime* (1981). Rollins also had a starring role in the television series "In the Heat of the Night," which ran from 1988-1994, but he was forced out of the series because of a persistent substance abuse problem. Rollins' additional film credits include *The House*

Howard E. Rollins, Jr.

of God (1979), *A Soldier's Story* (1984), *On the Block* (1989), and *Drunks* (1996).

Tupac Shakur (June 16, 1971–September 13, 1996). Shakur was an African American actor and rap star. He had been a best-selling recording artist since 1991, and was regarded as a promising young actor, based on his performances in *Juice* (1991) and *Poetic Justice* (1993). Seemingly intent on living out the gangster images in his music, Shakur was frequently in trouble with the law. He was murdered in what police believe was a gang-related shooting. His additional film credits include *Above the Rim* (1994) and *Gridlock'd* (1997).

Tupac Shakur

Stirling Silliphant (January 16, 1918–April 26, 1996). Silliphant was a screenwriter and producer in film and television. He wrote the screenplays for some hugely popular films in the 1970s, including *The Poseidon Adventure* (1972) and *The Towering Inferno* (1974). He won an Academy Award for his work on *In the Heat of the Night* (1967). His additional film credits include *Five Against the House* (1957), *The Lineup* (1958), *Village of the Damned* (1960), *Charly* (1968), *Marlowe* (1969), *The New Centurions* (1972), *Shaft in Africa* (1973), *The Enforcer* (1976), *When Time Ran Out* (1980), and *Catch the Heat* (1987).

Don Simpson (October 25, 1945–January 19, 1996). Simpson began his career as a marketing executive, but wound up as a successful producer at Paramount and Disney studios before succumbing to personal problems, including drug addiction, that led to the breakup of his partnership with Jerry Bruckheimer a few weeks before his death. Simpson and Bruckheimer collaborated on such blockbusters as *Flashdance* (1983), *Beverly Hills Cop* (1984), *Top Gun* (1986), *Beverly Hills Cop II* (1987), *Bad Boys* (1995), *Crimson Tide* (1995), and *The Rock* (1996).

Don Simpson

Lyle Talbot (February 8, 1902–March 3, 1996). Born Lysle Hollywood Henderson, Talbot was an actor who began his film career in the early days of the sound era, winning both lead and supporting roles in a wide variety of films. While often cast as a villain in films, he had a lengthy career in television situation comedies as well, appearing as the genial neighbor in "Ozzie and Harriet" from 1956-1966. Talbot's screen credits include *Love Is a Racket* (1932), *20,000 Years in Sing Sing* (1933), *Oil for the Lamps of China* (1935), *Go West Young Man* (1936), *Torture Ship* (1939), *Batman and Robin* (1949), *Atom Man Vs. Superman* (1950), *Purple Heart Diary* (1951), *There's No Business Like Show Business* (1954), *The Great Man* (1957), and *Sunrise at Campobello* (1960).

Steve Tesich (September 29, 1942–July 1, 1996). Born Stoyan Tesich in Yugoslavia, Tesich was a screenwriter who moved to America as a teenager. He became a playwright and then tried his hand a screenwriting. His first film, *Breaking Away* (1979), reflected his passion for bicycling, and earned him an Academy Award. He wrote several more screenplays during the 1980s before returning to the theater. His additional screen credits include *Eyewitness* (1981), *Four Friends* (1981), *The World According to Garp* (1982), *American Flyers* (1985), and *Eleni* (1985).

Jamie Uys (1921–January 29, 1996). Uys was a South African screenwriter, director, and producer who is best known to American audiences for his comedy *The Gods Must Be Crazy* (1981), about a Bushman's encounter with civilization. He also won a Golden Globe Award for Best Documentary for *Animals Are Beautiful People* (1974), a study of African desert animals. His additional film credits include *Dingaka* (1965), *After You, Comerade* (1967), and *The Gods Must Be Crazy II* (1989).

Jo Van Fleet (December 30, 1919–June 10, 1996). Van Fleet was an actress who worked extensively on stage and in film. A successful Broadway career, including a Tony Award for her work in *The Trip to Bountiful* in 1954, led her to Hollywood. In her first film, she played James Dean's fallen mother in *East of Eden* (1955), a performance which earned her an Academy Award as Best Supporting Actress. Her additional screen credits include *The Rose Tattoo* (1955), *I'll Cry Tomorrow* (1955), *Gunfight at the O.K. Corral* (1957), *Cool Hand Luke* (1967), *I Love You Alice B. Toklas!* (1968), *The Gang That Couldn't Shoot Straight* (1971), and *The Tenant* (1976).

Jo Van Fleet

Jack Weston (1925–May 3, 1996). Born Jack Weinstein, Weston was an actor who specialized in character parts, playing comic or dramatic roles with equal facility. He also

Jack Weston

worked extensively on stage and in television. His film credits include *Stage Struck* (1958), *Please Don't Eat the Daisies* (1960), *The Honeymoon Machine* (1961), *The Cincinnati Kid* (1965), *Wait Until Dark* (1967), *The Thomas Crown Affair* (1968), *Cactus Flower* (1969), *Fuzz* (1972), *Cuba* (1979), *The Four Seasons* (1981), *Dirty Dancing* (1987), and *Ishtar* (1987).

Faron Young (1932–December 10, 1996). Young was a country music star who made several movies at various stages of his career. In the 1950s, he was featured in several Republic Westerns, including *Hidden Guns* (1956), *Daniel Boone, Trailblazer* (1957), and *Raiders of Old California* (1957). He also appeared in three films aimed at country music fans—*Country Music Holiday* (1958), *Nashville Rebel* (1966), and *Road to Nashville* (1967).

—*Robert Mitchell*

Selected Film Books of 1996

Abel, Richard, editor. *Silent Film.*
New Brunswick, New Jersey: Rutgers University Press, 1996.

Abel collects thirteen scholarly essays on a wide variety of topics relating to international cinema of the Silent Era.

Anderson, Joseph D. *The Reality of Illusion.*
Carbondale, Illinois: Southern Illinois University Press, 1996.

Anderson ties various cognitive sciences, including social and developmental psychology and anthropology, to film theory in this scholarly work.

Andrews, Nigel. *True Myths: The Life and Times of Arnold Schwarzenegger.*
Secaucus, New Jersey: Birch Lane Press, 1996.

In this popular biography, Andrews notes how the actor has consistently been able to turn his liabilities into assets throughout the course of his career.

Antonioni, Michelangelo. *The Architecture of Vision.*
New York: Marsilio, 1996.

This is a collection of the writings of and interviews with the great Italian filmmaker, ranging over the entirety of his career.

Bacher, Lutz. *Max Ophuls in the Hollywood Studios.*
New Brunswick, New Jersey: Rutgers University Press, 1996.

Bacher argues that, despite certain difficulties, Ophuls' lightly regarded work in Hollywood during the 1940s remains an important part of his canon.

Bakari, Imruh, and Mbye B. Cham, editors. *African Experiences of Cinema.*
London: British Film Institute, 1996.

This collection of twenty-five scholarly essays on African cinema is accompanied by a collection of manifestos and other official resolutions by African filmmakers.

Ball, Lucille. *Love, Lucy.*
New York: G.P. Putnam's Sons, 1996.

This posthumous memoir from the late film and television comedienne breaks little new ground, but it does offer her insights into her life and career.

Berenstein, Rhona J. *Attack of the Leading Ladies: Gender, Sexuality, and Spectatorship in Classic Horror Cinema.*
New York: Columbia University Press, 1996.

Berenstein offers a scholarly analysis of the gender dynamics of the classic horror films of the 1930s.

Bergan, Ronald. *Katherine Hepburn: An Independent Woman.*
New York: Arcade, 1996.

This lavishly illustrated review of Hepburn's career highlights her screen image as a strong, independent woman.

Bernstein, Walter. *Inside Out: A Memoir of the Blacklist.*
New York: Alfred A. Knopf, 1996.

Bernstein was a Hollywood screenwriter whose leftist politics resulted in his being prevented from working under his own name in the early 1950s. This is his own account of that era.

Biggs, Melissa E. *French Films, 1945-1993.*
Jefferson, North Carolina: McFarland, 1996.

This reference work is a critical filmography of 400 important postwar French films. Entries include information on cast and credits, plus a short analysis of the film.

Bradley, Edwin M. *The First Hollywood Musicals.*
Jefferson, North Carolina: McFarland, 1996.

This is a filmography of 171 feature-length musicals produced in the first five years of the Sound Era. Entries include information on cast and credits, as well as brief commentaries on the films and their music.

Brantley, Will, editor. *Conversations with Pauline Kael.*
Jackson, Mississippi: University Press of Mississippi, 1996.

This is a collection of interviews with influential critic Pauline Kael, conducted by various interviewers between 1966 and 1994.

Cameron, Ian, and Douglas Pye. *The Book of Westerns.*
New York: Continuum, 1996.

This book contains 29 essays on the Western genre since 1939. Some essays focus on specific films, while others deal with actors or themes.

Carroll, Noel. *Theorizing the Moving Image.*
Cambridge, England: Cambridge University Press, 1996.

In this collection of essays, critic/scholar Carroll attempts to reinstate aesthetics to a prominent place in film theory.

Cartmell, Deborah, I.Q. Hunter, Heidi Kaye, and Imelda Whelehan. *Pulping Fictions: Consuming Culture Across the Literature/Media Divide.*
London: Pluto Press, 1996.

This is a collection of twelve scholarly essays, which examine issues relating to bringing literature to the screen.

Cary, Diana Serra. *Whatever Happened to Baby Peggy.*
New York: St. Martin's Press, 1996.

Cary was Baby Peggy, star of dozens of Silent Era short subjects at the age of two. This is her autobiography.

Cavell, Stanley. *Contesting Tears: The Hollywood Melodrama of the Unknown Woman.*
Chicago: University of Chicago Press, 1996.

Cavell examines the subgenre of melodrama, which focuses a woman's search for her own identity in this close study of four films from Hollywood's golden age.

Couvares, Francis G. *Movie Censorship and American Culture.*
Washington, D.C.: Smithsonian Institution Press, 1996.

Couvares collects a dozen scholarly essays, which examine the issue of film censorship in America, covering topics such as sex, politics, and ethnicity.

Curry, Ramona. *Too Much of a Good Thing: Mae West as Cultural Icon.*
Minneapolis, Minnesota: University of Minnesota Press, 1996.

This scholarly work examines the widespread image of actress Mae West in a cultural context, and also analyzes her role in the development of film censorship in the 1930s.

Dalle Vacche, Angela. *Cinema and Painting: How Art Is Used in Film.*
Austin, Texas: University of Texas Press, 1996.

Dalle Vacche examines eight films in detail, noting how each makes use of painting to further its themes.

Davis, Darrell William. *Picturing Japaneseness: Monumental Style, National Identity, Japanese Film.*
New York: Columbia University Press, 1996.

Davis offers a scholarly examination of the subject of Japanese identity in its national film industry, focusing on the years leading up to World War II.

Denvir, John, editor. *Legal Reelisms: Movies as Legal Texts.*
Urbana, Illinois: University of Illinois Press, 1996.

This is a collection of fourteen scholarly essays by academic philosophers and legal scholars, discussing the portrayal of legal issues in cinema.

Dewey, Donald. *James Stewart: A Biography.*
Atlanta, Georgia: Turner Publishing, 1996.

This popular biography of one of golden age Hollywood's most prominent leading men notes the work which Stewart put into creating his image as a "nice guy."

Dmytryk, Edward. *Odd Man Out: A Memoir of the Hollywood Ten.*
Carbondale, Illinois: Southern Illinois University Press, 1996.

Dmytryk was a director who was caught up in the Hollywood Red Scare of the late 1940s, and later recanted his conversion to communism. This is his second autobiography.

Dougan, Andy. *Untouchable: A Biography of Robert De Niro.*
New York: Thunder's Mouth Press, 1996.

Dougan offers a survey of De Niro's career and a look at this private life in this popular biography.

Edelman, Rob, and Audrey F. Kupferberg. *Angela Lansbury: A Life on Stage and Screen.*
New York: Birch Lane Press, 1996.

This is a popular biography of the actress who starred on Broadway, in films, and in television's long-running series *Murder, She Wrote.*

Fischer, Lucy. *Cinematernity: Film, Motherhood, Genre.*
Princeton, New Jersey: Princeton University Press, 1996.

This is a scholarly analysis of the portrayal of motherhood in a variety of film genres, from the silent melodrama to horror films.

Fox, Julian. *Woody: Movies from Manhattan.*
Woodstock, New York: Overlook Press, 1996.

Fox examines Woody Allen's career from its origins in stand-up comedy through the films of the early 1990s, noting especially the inspiration which the filmmaker seems to derive from his beloved Manhattan.

Fuller, Kathryn H. *At the Picture Show.*
Washington, D.C.: Smithsonian Institution Press, 1996.

Fuller examines the small town movie audience and the creation of the fan culture in the early days of the motion picture.

Galbraith, Stuart, IV. *The Japanese Filmography.*
Jefferson, North Carolina: McFarland, 1996.

This useful reference work provides information on cast, credits, and American release (if any) for over 1,250 Japanese films released between 1900 and 1994; as well as biographical information on over 200 major figures in Japanese cinema.

Genini, Ronald. *Theda Bara.*
Jefferson, North Carolina: McFarland, 1996.

Genini offers a biography and filmography of the legendary vamp of the Silent Era, Hollywood's first sex goddess.

Ginsberg, Terri, and Kirsten Moana Thompson, editors. *Perspectives on German Cinema.*
New York: G.K. Hall, 1996.

This is a collection of 42 scholarly essays on German film, some of which are reprinted and some of which were commissioned for this volume.

Greene, Eric. *Planet of the Apes as American Myth.*
Jefferson, North Carolina: McFarland, 1996.

Greene examines the popular film and television series as a metaphor for race relations and other political concerns of late twentieth century America.

Griffin, Nancy, and Kim Masters. *Hit and Run: How Jon Peters and Peter Guber Took Sony for a Ride in Hollywood.*
New York: Simon & Schuster, 1966.

Griffin and Masters portray producers Peters and Guber as self-promoting hustlers whose miscalculations cost Columbia Pictures both prestige and billions of dollars.

Hadleigh, Boze. *Bette Davis Speaks.*
New York: Barricade Books, 1996.

Beginning in the mid-1970s, Hadleigh conducted a series of frank interviews with the late Hollywood leading lady, which are compiled in this volume.

Hanna, Bill, with Tom Ito. *A Cast of Friends.*
Dallas, Texas: Taylor, 1996.

With his partner Joe Barbera, Hanna was a prolific animator who created such television series as "The Flintstones" and "Yogi Bear." He also worked on the "Tom and Jerry" cartoons for MGM. This is his autobiography.

Harmetz, Aljean. *On the Road to Tara: The Making of Gone With the Wind.*
New York: Harry N. Abrams, 1996.

Using material from the personal archives of David O. Selznick, and other private collections of memorabilia, Harmetz produces a handsome coffee-table account of the making of *Gone With the Wind.*

Harris, Erich Leon. *African-American Screenwriters Now.*
Los Angeles: Silman-James Press, 1996.

Thirteen African-American film and television writers analyze the opportunities and obstacles they've encountered in this collection of interviews.

Higgins, Lynn A. *New Novel, New Wave, New Politics.*
Lincoln, Nebraska: University of Nebraska Press, 1996.

This is a scholarly study of the representation of history, in film and the novel, in France, from 1959 to the present.

Hofstede, David. *James Dean: A Bio-Bibliography.*
Westport, Connecticut: Greenwood Press, 1996.

Hofstede provides a brief biography of the famous actor, as well as a filmography (including radio and television appearances) and bibliography of critical works on Dean's career.

James, David E., and Rick Berg, editors. *The Hidden Foundation: Cinema and the Question of Class.*
Minneapolis, Minnesota: University of Minnesota Press, 1996.

This collection of twelve scholarly essays analyzes the role, both overt and indirect, of class in film, focusing primarily on English language examples.

Jancovich, Mark. *Rational Fears: American Horror in the 1950s.*
Manchester, England: Manchester University Press, 1996.

Jancovich notes that American horror films and fiction of the 1950s mark the transition from earlier gothic trappings towards issues relating to the contemporary world.

Johnson, Tom, and Deborah Del Vecchio. *Hammer Films: An Exhaustive Filmography.*
Jefferson, North Carolina: McFarland, 1996.

Hammer was a British studio best known for its gothic horror films of the 1950s, '60s, and '70s. This volume provides information on cast and credits, a plot synopsis, and a brief analysis of each of the studio's productions.

Jones, Chuck. *Chuck Reducks: Drawings From the Fun Side of Life.*
New York: Warner Books, 1996.

Jones was chief among the artists responsible for the classic Warner Bros. animated cartoons of the 1940s and 1950s. He offers thoughts on animation techniques, illustrated by drawings and photographs from his personal archives.

Jones, D.B. *The Best Butler in the Business: Tom Daly of the National Film Board of Canada.*
Toronto: University of Toronto Press, 1996.

This is a biography of Tom Daly, a major figure in Canadian cinema history through his work as producer for the National Film Board.

Jowett, Garth S., Ian C. Jarvie, and Kathryn H. Fuller. *Children and the Movies.*
New York: Cambridge University Press, 1996.

This is a scholarly examination of the Payne Fund controversy, in which a series of books in the mid-1930s linked movie attendance with juvenile delinquency.

Klepper, Robert K. *Silent Films on Video.*
Jefferson, North Carolina: McFarland, 1996.

Those wishing to view films from the Silent Era are often frustrated by the relative lack of availability of these films. This work lists over 700 such films, both feature length and short subjects, which are available on video; as well as sources for obtaining the tapes.

Knapp, Laurence F. *Directed by Clint Eastwood.*
Jefferson, North Carolina: McFarland, 1996.

Most books about Eastwood focus on his acting. Knapp analyzes the eighteen films which Eastwood has directed since 1971.

Kreimeier, Klaus. *The Ufa Story.*
New York: Hill and Wang, 1996.

Ufa, Universal Film AG, was the premier film studio in Germany from 1918-1945. Kreimeier tells of its rise and fall.

Lally, Kevin. *Wilder Times: The Life of Billy Wilder.*
New York: Henry Holt, 1996.

Although this is not an "authorized biography," Lally did succeed in winning the cooperation of Wilder for his analysis of the filmmaker's life and career.

Lentz, Harris M., III. *Western and Frontier Film and Television Credits, 1903-1995.*
Jefferson, North Carolina: McFarland, 1996.

This two volume reference work provides information on the cast and credits for thousands of films and television series in the Western genre from the Silent Era to the present day.

Levy, Shawn. *King of Comedy: The Life and Art of Jerry Lewis.*
New York: St. Martin's Press, 1996.

Levy offers a well researched popular biography of the comic actor, from his vaudeville days with Dean Martin through his film career.

List, Christine. *Chicano Images: Refiguring Ethnicity in Mainstream Film.*
New York: Garland, 1996.

List examines the work of Mexican-American filmmakers in Hollywood over the past two decades, as they have altered the image of the Hispanic on screen.

MacCabe, Colin, and Duncan Petrie, editors. *New Scholarship from BFI Research.*
London: British Film Institute, 1996.

This volume collects eight scholarly essays on topics as varied as race and gender in Hollywood melodrama to a study of film histories of Pompeii.

Mackey-Kallis, Susan. *Oliver Stone's America.*
Boulder, Colorado: Westview Press, 1996.

Mackey-Kallis examines the work of the leftist director, placing his films in the context of political filmmaking in Hollywood.

McBride, Joseph. *Orson Welles.*
New York: Da Capo, 1996.

McBride published one of the first monographs on Welles in 1972; this volume is a revised and significantly expanded version of that study of the seminal American filmmaker.

McFarlane, Brian. *Novel To Film: An Introduction to the Theory of Adaptation.*
Oxford: Clarendon Press, 1996.

McFarlane argues that critics should abandon the issue of fidelity and focus on the methods which filmmakers use to convey their sense of the novel being adapted to film.

McGee, Mark Thomas. *Faster and Furioser.*
Jefferson, North Carolina: McFarland, 1996.

This is a major revision of McGee's history of American International Pictures, the studio famous for its campy low-budget horror films; a filmography is included.

Maxfield, James F. *The Fatal Woman: Sources of Male Anxiety in American Film Noir, 1941-1991.*
Madison, New Jersey: Fairleigh Dickinson University Press, 1996.

Maxfield examines a half century of American film noir, focusing particularly on the convention of the woman who has a destructive effect on the male protagonist.

Miles, Margaret R. *Seeing and Believing: Religion and Values in the Movies.*
Boston: Beacon Press, 1996.

Miles examines the role of religion in recent popular film, concluding that the frequent mockery of religion derives from the public's nervousness about the topic.

Milton, Joyce. *Tramp: The Life of Charlie Chaplin.*
New York: HarperCollins, 1996.

Milton offers a well researched and evenhanded biography of the first international film star.

Noriega, Chon A., and Ana M. Lopez, editors. *The Ethnic Eye: Latino Media Arts.*
Minneapolis, Minnesota: University of Minnesota Press, 1996.

This is a collection of fifteen scholarly essays on the state of contemporary Hispanic-American cinema, television, and video art.

Nowell-Smith, Geoffrey, editor. *The Oxford History of World Cinema.*
New York: Oxford University Press, 1996.

This massive one-volume text has chapters on various genres, important filmmakers, and major national cinemas, in a definitive survey of the history of world film.

Obst, Lynda. *Hello, He Lied — and Other Truths from the Hollywood Trenches.*
Boston: Little, Brown, 1996.

Obst is a producer; she offers this humorous look at the perils and pleasures of being a woman filmmaker in Hollywood.

Oldham, Gabriella. *Keaton's Silent Shorts: Beyond the Laughter.*
Carbondale, Illinois: Southern Illinois University Press, 1996.

Oldham traces the genesis of Buster Keaton's on-screen persona and his filmmaking style in the nineteen two-reel silent short subjects he made from 1920 to 1923.

Pierson, John, with Kevin Smith. *Spike, Mike, Slackers & Dykes.*
New York: Hyperion, 1996.

Pierson has been a longtime supporter and financial backer of independent filmmakers; this is the story of a decade's worth of involvement with these films.

Pointer, Michael. *Charles Dickens on the Screen.*
Lanham, Maryland: Scarecrow Press, 1996.

This analysis of the film, video, and television productions of the works of Dickens includes a filmography.

Powers, Stephen, David J. Rothman, and Stanley Rothman. *Hollywood's America: Social and Political Themes in Motion Pictures.*
Boulder, Colorado: Westview Press, 1996.

The authors compare social and political themes in films released from 1946-1965 with those of films released between 1966-1990 in this scholarly study.

Prideaux, James. *Knowing Hepburn and Other Curious Experiences.*
Boston: Faber and Faber, 1996.

Prideaux is a playwright and screenwriter who knows Katherine Hepburn professionally and personally. He offers this behind the scenes account of her life.

Rainey, Buck. *The Reel Cowboy.*
Jefferson, North Carolina: McFarland, 1996.

Rainey offers essays on the image of the cowboy in American films, and how that image diverges from reality; and on the works of Zane Grey and other classic writers in the Western genre, and how their stories were adapted to film.

Rhines, Jesse Algeron. *Black Film/White Money.*
New Brunswick, New Jersey: Rutgers University Press, 1996.

Rhines examines the ways in which the economics of the Hollywood film industry has affected films made by and for African-Americans from the Silent Era onwards.

Robertson, Pamela. *Guilty Pleasures: Feminist Camp from Mae West to Madonna.*
Durham, North Carolina: Duke University Press, 1996.

This is a scholarly study of actresses who have engaged in gender parody, including Mae West, the Busby Berkeley dancers, Joan Crawford, and Madonna.

Robinson, David. *From Peep Show to Palace: The Birth of American Film.*
New York: Columbia University Press, 1996.

Robinson examines the evolution of American film from its roots in Edison's Kinetoscope in 1893 to the construction of the first movie theatre in 1913.

Rogin, Michael. *Blackface, White Noise: Jewish Immigrants in the Hollywood Melting Pot.*
Berkeley, California: University of California Press, 1996.

Rogin examines the influence of blackface minstrelsy on the films of the early sound era, arguing that these films played an important role in Americanizing European immigrants.

Ross, Karen. *Black and White Media.*
Cambridge, England: Polity Press, 1996.

Focusing on contemporary works, Ross examines the image of Black people in American and British film and television.

Rumble, Patrick. *Allegories of Contamination: Pier Paolo Pasolini's Trilogy of Life.*
Toronto: University of Toronto Press, 1996.

Rumble offers a scholarly study of *Decameron*, *Canterbury Tales*, and *Arabian Nights*, the final films Pasolini released during his lifetime.

Sanello, Frank. *Spielberg: The Man, the Movies, the Mythology.*
Dallas, Texas: Taylor Publishing, 1996.

Sanello bases this popular survey of the filmmaker's career on a wide variety of interviews, including interviews with Spielberg himself.

Schickel, Richard. *Clint Eastwood: A Biography.*
New York: Alfred A. Knopf, 1996.

Film critic Schickel offers this appreciation of the famous American actor/director, revealing the man behind the "icon."

Seger, Linda. *When Women Call the Shots.*
New York: Henry Holt, 1996.

Seger discusses the increasing influence of women in the film and television industries, as directors, producers, and studio executives.

Sherzer, Dina, editor. *Cinema, Colonialism, Postcolonialism.*
Austin, Texas: University of Texas Press, 1996.

Sherzer offers eleven essays on the issue of colonialism in French language cinema, in France as well as former French colonies in Africa and Southeast Asia.

Silverman, Stephen M. *Dancing on the Ceiling: Stanley Donen and His Movies.*
New York: Alfred A. Knopf, 1996.

This is a biography of filmmaker Stanley Donen, best known for his 1950s musicals and other sophisticated films.

Singular, Stephen. *Power to Burn: Michael Ovitz and the New Business of Show Business.*
Secaucus, New Jersey: Birch Lane Press, 1996.

Singular explores the business of making films in contemporary Hollywood via the persona of studio executive Ovitz. The book culminates with the beginning of Ovitz's brief career with Disney.

Skal, David J. *V Is for Vampire.*
New York: Plume, 1996.

Skal offers an encyclopedic survey of films, filmmakers, and other figures associated with Dracula and other screen vampires.

Smith, Dave. *Disney A to Z.*
New York: Hyperion, 1996.

Subtitled "The Official Encyclopedia," this reference work contains over 6,500 entries on people, characters, and films associated with the Disney Studio through 1995.

Sobchack, Vivian, editor. *The Persistence of History: Cinema, Television, and the Modern Event.*
New York: Routledge, 1996.

Scholars grapple with issues surrounding the representation of history in film and television in this collection of eleven essays.

Spoto, Donald. *Rebel: The Life and Legend of James Dean.*
New York: HarperCollins, 1996.

Veteran star biographer Spoto tackles the James Dean mystique, from his Indiana roots to his complex love life as a Hollywood star.

Stephens, Michael L. *Gangster Films.*
Jefferson, North Carolina: McFarland, 1996.

This reference work is an alphabetical list of people, films, and terms associated with the Gangster genre, from the Silent Era through contemporary films.

Stoliar, Steve. *Raised Eyebrows: My Years Inside Groucho's House.*
Los Angeles: General Publishing Group, 1996.

Stoliar was Marx's personal secretary and archivist during the last years of the comic's life, and provides insights into the legal battles that followed his death.

Studlar, Gaylyn. *This Mad Masquerade: Stardom and Masculinity in the Jazz Age.*
New York: Columbia University Press, 1996.

Studlar analyzes the appeal of Douglas Fairbanks, John Barrymore, Rudolph Valentino, and Lon Chaney, four stars of the late Silent Era, in this scholarly work.

Suid, Lawrence. *Sailing on the Silver Screen: Hollywood and the U.S. Navy.*
Annapolis, Maryland: Naval Institute Press, 1996.

Suid examines the portrayal of the Navy in American films, focusing on how this particular branch of the military has used Hollywood to burnish its image, even in the aftermath of Vietnam.

Toplin, Robert Brent. *History by Hollywood: The Use and Abuse of the American Past.*
Urbana, Illinois: University of Illinois Press, 1996.

Toplin examines the phenomenon of film as the interpreter of history in this scholarly study of eight, mostly recent, American films.

Vitti, Antonio. *Giuseppe De Santis and Postwar Italian Cinema.*
Toronto: University of Toronto Press, 1996.

This is a scholarly study of the work of the Italian filmmaker best known for *Bitter Rice*, who is less well known to American audiences than other major Italian directors.

Vorderer, Peter, Hans J. Wulff, and Mike Friedrichsen, editors. *Suspense: Conceptualizations, Theoretical Analyses, and*

Empirical Explorations.
Mahwah, New Jersey: Lawrence Erlbaum, 1996.

This is a collection of sixteen scholarly essays on the subject of suspense in cinema, seeking to identify the elements of a film which are perceived as suspenseful by its audience.

Waldman, Harry. *Hollywood and the Foreign Touch.*
Lanham, Maryland: Scarecrow Press, 1996.

Many foreign filmmakers have worked in the United States. This reference work provides information on the American portion of the career of such filmmakers, including actors and writers.

Walsh, Frank. *Sin and Censorship: The Catholic Church and the Motion Picture Industry.*
New Haven, Connecticut: Yale University Press, 1996.

This is a scholarly study of the influence of the Catholic church on American cinema, covering the rise and fall of the Legion of Decency.

Warren, Charles, editor. *Beyond Document: Essays on Nonfiction Film.*
Hanover, New Hampshire: Wesleyan University Press, 1996.

Warren collects twelve scholarly essays on the nonfiction film and docudrama, from the Silent Era to modern works.

Weaver, James B. III, and Ron Tamborini, editors. *Horror Films: Current Research on Audience Preferences and Reactions.*
Mahwah, New Jersey: Lawrence Erlbaum Associates, 1996.

The editors collect eleven essays on various aspects of audience response to horror films, from the sociological to the psychological.

Williams, Christopher, editor. *Cinema: The Beginnings and the Future.*
London: University of Northminster Press, 1996.

Williams collects sixteen scholarly essays on the early days of cinema, and seven more on the present and future of the medium.

Williams, Tony. *Hearths of Darkness: The Family in the American Horror Film.*
Madison, New Jersey: Fairleigh Dickinson University Press, 1996.

Williams analyzes the modern American horror film's convention of disrupting the ideological norms of the traditional nuclear family in this scholarly study.

Winokur, Mark. *American Laughter: Immigrants, Ethnicity, and 1930s Hollywood Film Comedy.*
New York: St. Martin's Press, 1996.

Winokur analyzes the influence of European immigrants on Depression-era comedy, focusing on such major figures as Charlie Chaplin and the Marx Brothers.

Witney, William. *In a Door, Into a Fight, Out a Door, Into a Chase.*
Jefferson, North Carolina: McFarland, 1996.

Witney directed action serials for Republic Pictures in the 1930s and 1940s. He reminisces about his career in this work.

Zaniello, Tom. *Working Stiff, Union Maids, Reds, and Riffraff.*
Ithaca, New York: Cornell University Press, 1996.

Zaniello's compilation of labor-related films includes information about cast and credits, as well as a brief analysis of each film and suggestions for further reading.

—Robert Mitchell

Magill's Cinema Annual 1997
Indexes

Directors

Screenwriters

Cinematographers

Editors

Art Directors

Music Directors

Performers

Performers

Subjects

Title Index

This cumulative index is an alphabetical list of all films covered in the sixteen volumes of the *Magill's Cinema Annual.* Film titles are indexed on a word-by-word basis, including articles and prepositions. English and foreign leading articles are ignored. Films reviewed in this volume are cited in bold with an arabic number indicating the page number on which the review begins; films reviewed in past volumes are cited with the year in which the film was originally released. Film sequels are indicated with a Roman numeral following the film title. Original and alternate titles are cross-referenced to the American release title. Titles of retrospective films, as well as those cited in the Life Achievement Award section, are followed by the year, in brackets, of their original release.